ELEANOR MARX

ELEANOR MARX

YVONNE KAPP

VERSO

London · New York

This edition published by Verso 2018
First published in two volumes as *Eleanor Marx: Family Life
(1855–1883)* and *Eleanor Marx: The Crowded Years (1884–1898)*,
Lawrence and Wishart, 1972 and 1976 respectively
Yvonne Kapp © 1972/76, 2003, 2018
Preface © Sally Alexander, 2003, 2013

All illustrations are reproduced courtesy of Betty Lewis, unless otherwise indicated

1 3 5 7 9 10 8 6 4 2

Verso
UK: 6 Meard Street, London W1F 0EG
US: 20 Jay Street, Suite 1010, Brooklyn, NY 11201

versobooks.com

Verso is the imprint of New Left Books

ISBN-13: 978-1-85984-515-8
ISBN-13: 978-1-78663-595-2 (US EBK)
ISBN-13: 978-1-78663-594-5 (UK EBK)

British Library Cataloguing in Publication Data
A catalogue record for this book is available from the British Library

Library of Congress Cataloging-in-Publication Data
A catalog record for this book is available from the Library of Congress

Typeset in Garamond Three by YHT Ltd, London
Printed and bound by CPI Group (UK) Ltd, Croydon, CR0 YY

· CONTENTS ·

· PREFACE ·

"TUSSY IS ME":
ELEANOR MARX'S LEGACY

Sally Alexander

Eleanor Marx, third living daughter of Karl Marx and Jenny von Westphalen, was "dramatic to the depths of her being", wilful and unusually brilliant.[1] She yearned for love and freedom and wanted to be an actress, but instead devoted herself to another sort of vaga-bondage – political agitation. An excellent linguist, she earned her living as a translator, lecturer and writer, and worked tirelessly for "the cause" of socialism among the late nineteenth century new lifers, anarchists, radicals and feminists of London's socialist sects and the Second International.

Little was known of Eleanor Marx's life until the 1970s, when this book was first published, as two volumes. Yvonne Kapp, a writer and a communist, had twenty years earlier been translating the Frederick Engels/Laura and Paul Lafargue correspondence in which Eleanor kept appearing; the seeds of the biography lay in "curiosity, aroused by tantalising glimpses of Eleanor as she flitted in and out of other peo-ple's letters". Kapp was sixty-three before space, time and a small legacy from her mother afforded the opportunity of completing the work.[2] Hailed on publication as a masterpiece of political biography, Kapp's description, in volume one, of the Marx household adrift in London among exiles in the 1850s, the sympathetic portrait of Marx as a father and Eleanor's childhood, cast unexpected light on the domestic life of a philosopher. Eleanor's work among the unemployed, unskilled and Jews of London's East End, described in the second volume, along with her experiments in living and translations of her father's work, introduced a vibrant new voice and character to the moral theatre of international socialism and the British labour movement at the end of the nineteenth century. Eleanor's life, in Kapp's account, is as much about the history of socialism in the second half of the nineteenth century as it is about the life of its heroine – as Kapp herself put it, the movement kept "breaking in".[3]

Eleanor's life was much more than a heroic exemplar of socialist struggle and marxist principles, however. She was a woman of her time. Raised to be a "lady" she earned her living as a "literary hack". Wanting to be an actress she succumbed to filial duty and financial need. "Devilling" for others in the reading room of the British Library, teaching Shakespeare and literature – to private pupils, schools and classes in adult education – and translating only just held at bay the spectre of "governessing", that low-paid, servile employment which her older sister Jenny was forced to do for three miserable years and which haunted impoverished independent women throughout the nineteenth century. Eleanor was always working – "Indeed, I really work from about 9 in the morning till late at night and often till early into the next day", she wrote to her sister Laura in 1884.[4] Always short of money ("I am very poor"), she longed for children, the artistic life and love. "O how my whole nature craves for love", she wrote to Olive Schreiner, the South African novelist and close friend.[5]

From 1884 until her death fourteen years later Eleanor lived in a "free union" with Edward Aveling, freethinker, socialist, minor playwright and scoundrel. Aveling, according to Bernard Shaw, "would have gone to the stake for Socialism or atheism, but (had) absolutely no conscience in his private life. He seduced every woman he met, and borrowed from every man."[6] His infidelities, financial scandals and betrayals drove Eleanor, at the age of forty-three, to suicide. His final betrayal was astonishing. Ten months earlier he had married an actress twenty years his junior. This love affair and death are the stuff of melodrama, Kapp observes, and does her best to subject its events – and Eleanor's own nature – to reason. But melodrama shadowed women's sexual lives and loves throughout the nineteenth century.[7]

Aveling's betrayal alone might not have precipitated Eleanor's death. In the last months of her life, Eleanor was also faced with Engels' deathbed revelation that Freddy Demuth, the illegitimate son of Helen Demuth (the Marx family's servant and friend), was in fact not Engels' child, as everyone had supposed, but Marx's. Freddy, Eleanor's close friend, was Eleanor's half brother.[8] Eleanor revered her father. Family guilt and disillusion compounded her despair. In Eleanor the tensions between the wish for the artistic life and poverty, between the craving for love and the cruelty of betrayal, caused her severe mental pain which the political promise of a new world and the revision of all human relations in the future could not assuage. Ardent, clever and ultimately tragic, Kapp's biography dramatises the life of a late Victorian new woman.

Eleanor was born in January 1855 in Westminster. The household – parents, three small children (four including Eleanor) and Helen Demuth – lived in two small rooms in Dean Street, Soho, nearly opposite the Royalty Theatre.[9] The baby's arrival did not augur well.

Two children, a son and a daughter, had died before Eleanor's birth, and the beloved Mouche, eight years old, died a few months afterward. Anticipated as a "catastrophe" by her father, Marx pronounced Eleanor's birth a disappointment to his friend Frederick Engels, because of her sex. A sickly infant, she was sent to a wet-nurse because she screamed and her mother could not feed her. Yet, by nine months, according to her nine-year-old sister, Eleanor was jumping and crawling, captivating her family, in spite of the delicate health which pursued her throughout her life. The first years of exile in London for the Marx household were years of "horrible poverty, of bitter suffering".[10] With her mother ill and her father writing volume one of *Capital* – that "accursed book" as Engels called it[11] – Eleanor became Helen Demuth's child. Helen, nicknamed Lenchen or Nim, a "feudal gift" from Jenny's mother to her daughter shortly after her marriage, was the "soul" of the household, Eleanor wrote after Helen Demuth's death, and a life-long friend.[12] Because her own child, born in 1851, had been fostered, Demuth's "sturdy peasant soul" was freely given to the youngest child.[13]

Several fortuitous legacies from German relatives enabled the household, with the addition of a second maid, to move into the first of several houses in Kentish Town. Kentish Town was, in the 1850s, a new suburb of London, "a barbarous region" carved out of clay mud and woodland, without pavements or lighting (one of the delights of this book is the descriptions of London). Eleanor followed her sisters, Jenny and Laura, to South Hampstead School, where they learned the piano, drawing, French and callisthenics, but received no preparation for an independent life, no training for a profession – the reader sniffs Kapp's disapproval. Indeed Marx was mortified at the suggestion. Keeping up appearances mattered at least as much to him as to his wife (whom Kapp likens to Mrs. Bennett in *Pride and Prejudice*). The Marxes hid their poverty from neighbours, doctors (the family were constantly ill with everything from carbuncles to smallpox), future sons-in-law, even their own daughters. "It would be all the same to me if I went to the knackers' yard", Marx wrote gloomily to Engels (whose unbroken generosity largely kept the family afloat) in 1866, as long as there was some money for the family.[14]

Marx himself, or his "towering genius", threatens – as it did in real life – to take centre-stage in Eleanor's biography. Marx, or Mohr, as he was known to the children, and his work, dominated the household. But he was an adoring, loving and playful father. Coaxed out of his study, he made up stories – he spun one unending tale of Hans Rockle, a magician who kept a toyshop but was never able to meet his obligations, until against his will, he was forced to sell his toys – and read aloud to the children the whole of Homer, and Shakespeare, "who was the bible in our house", as well as Grimm's fairy tales. He carried them on his back around the garden, led them on picnics to Greenwich and Hampstead Heath. Irascible, quarrelsome and rude to friends and fellow revolutionaries who crossed him, the company of children, Wilhelm Liebknecht observed, was a "social necessity".[15] Children teach their parents, Marx believed. When he told Eleanor the story of the Passion – as a story of "the carpenter whom the rich men killed" – he added that Christianity could be forgiven much because it taught adoration of the child. In his sixties, ill and indifferent to how he might be "launched into eternity", he wrote to his daughter Jenny that he wanted "absolute peace and quiet", by which he meant, he explained, family life and "the microscopic world of children's noises".[16] This is Marx at his most endearing. He could also be a tyrant.

Eleanor's voice – "eager, warm, alive, and ... true as a bell"[17] – takes the lead in the book from the age of nine. Her childhood letters evinced a lordly confidence in herself and her capacities: "I am getting on very well with my chess", she wrote to a great uncle in Holland, "I nearly always win and when I do Papa is *so* cross".[18] She was "something of a romp, and what was called a tomboy", Kapp tells us, fearless in her play with the "bigger, wild urchins".[19] At one point she wanted to run away to sea, to join a man of war, which won her father's admiration for the intelligent "little fellow". And like so many spirited daughters she sought her father's attention: her letters to him list her achievements, especially her reading (Fennimore Cooper, Captain Marryat as well as Shakespeare and the brothers Grimm), stamp collecting, and the progress of the nursery of dolls, and she signed herself your "UNdutiful daughter".[20]

Aged seventeen, Eleanor took her first step towards independence, when in defiance of her father she became secretly engaged to Hyppolite-Prosper-Olivier Lissagaray, an exiled communard sixteen years her senior. She fled to Brighton to earn her living, and completely broke down. Mohr's disapproval of and political antipathy towards her chosen lover did not extend to his history of the Paris Commune, which Eleanor translated ten years later, and which he, Marx, supervised with meticulous care through the press. Eleanor, in fragile emotional health because of the conflict between love and duty, needed Lissagaray's tender concern. "I want to know dear Mohr, when I may see L. again", she wrote pleadingly, "It is so *very* hard *never* to see him". Kapp admires Eleanor's "spirit so touching in its candour and affectionate obedience".[21] That spirit of obedience, devotion even, was exacted from his daughter by an overbearing love which was not removed by death; his will governed her thoughts and actions all through her life. Jenny was his favourite, Eleanor recalled after Marx's death, but, he had once remarked, "Tussy [Eleanor's family nick-name] is me".[22]

Eleanor grew up a revolutionary who wanted to act – the two dispositions in close proximity within her. Her imaginary world hosted a whole cast of characters acquired from reading and life, whose voices amplified her own. Garibaldi was her hero. An advocate for the North in the American Civil war, she wrote to Abraham Lincoln to offer her services; her passionate identification with the Poles won her the nickname "poor neglected nation"; a visit to Manchester and Lizzie Burns (Engels' companion and Irish nationalist) turned her into a "staunch Irishman".

Theatre, like politics, was a family passion. Shakespeare was Eleanor's favourite poet (as he was of the young Tom Mann who led the 1889 dockers' strike[23]) and by the age of four she knew long passages by heart, one of her favourites being the scene between Hamlet and his mother which Henry Irving made the turning point in his radical re-reading of Hamlet in 1874.[24] The family played charades, held play-readings, made pilgrimages on foot to Rosebery Avenue to watch Irving's and Samuel Phelps' productions of Shakespeare. The Dogberry Club, which read Shakespeare and attended Irving's performances, often met in the Marx home, and Eleanor joined the New Shakespeare Society (founded in 1873 by Edward Furnivall), gave readings and recitations herself, and received a few paid commissions from her theatrical and literary friends. In 1881 she "made a brilliant appearance at the Dilettante Club theatre in two one-act plays", very much in the style of Ellen Terry, Engels informed Marx, and after her mother's death at the end of that year she resolved, in spite of the expense, to take acting lessons with a retired American actress, Mrs. Vezin. She was twenty-seven: "I feel I've wasted quite enough of my life, and its high time I did something", she confided in Jenny. "You know my dear, I am not a bit vain", wrote Eleanor. "I have seen too often – and with such different people that I can *move* an audience . . . the chance of independence is very sweet".[25] Jenny, whose bedroom as a child had been a shrine to Shakespeare, endorsed her decision: "I congratulate you with all my heart, and rejoice to think that one of us at least will not pass her life in watching over a *pot au feu*", she wrote, " . . . the artistic life is the only free life a woman can live".[26]

Eleanor's theatrical ambitions – easily quashed by a combination of unfavourable reviews, economic reality and self-doubt – were soon redirected into supporting Aveling's theatrical career as a playwright, actor and poet. They met early in the 1880s, and Eleanor, at least, fell instantly in love. Unable to marry because Aveling's first wife would not release him, they publicly announced their "union" to friends, fearing – wrongly – ostracism. Olive Schreiner and Havelock Ellis visited them on their "honeymoon". Only later did Aveling's behaviour lose Eleanor several close women friends, and the trust of many others. The Avelings were enthusiasts for Ibsen, whose hatred of conventions – the pillars of society – insistence on individual truth and on the force of personality amounted to a "revolution in the mind", which supplemented marxism's condemnation of capitalism and bourgeois society.[27] George Bernard Shaw, in the early 1880s a young critic and Fabian who had encouraged Eleanor to become an actress, appeared with them in one of the first readings of "The Doll's House" in London, in 1889.[28] Ibsen, Shaw thought, brought the whole of the nineteenth century to an end.[29] Women, according to Ibsen, exemplified the "new spirit" alive in the world, but first they had to give up self-sacrifice and pursue self-realisation. Ibsen "sees our lop-sided modern society suffering from too much man", Aveling wrote clumsily, "and he has been born the women's poet".[30]

Actors live – for the moment – other people's lives. And Eleanor's capacity for empathy – "you know I have the power very strongly developed to see things from the 'other side'", she wrote to Dollie Radford, her dearest friend, announcing her union with Aveling[31] –

enabled her to identify with a character or a cause and ultimately threatened her own self-belief. Self-doubt had been one motivating force behind her wish to act: she "knew", she told her sister Jenny, that "I'm not clever enough to live a purely *intellectual* life nor am I dull enough to be content to . . . do nothing".[32] The insistence with which Eleanor's empathy steers her thoughts back to death makes unsettling reading. An identification with suffering runs through her letters and speeches, from her snatched observations of the London poor in the 1870s, through the systematic explorations of the city's East End undertaken with the novelist Margaret Harkness in the mid-1880s, to the claim "I am a Jew", in 1889. This "preoccupation with personal suffering" became, in Eleanor's own words, "a nightmare to me. I can't get rid of it . . . Sometimes I am inclined to wonder how one *can* go on living with all this suffering around one".[33]

From the moment she "threw in her lot" with Aveling, Kapp declares, Eleanor's life gained purpose and fulfilment. But Eleanor's letters, even those sent from her honeymoon, give intimations of disillusionment, excruciating loneliness, and despair, states of mind with which she was to become familiar over the next fourteen years. Eleanor's serious work for socialism began, however, with her relationship with Aveling. The "marxists" were a tiny band of writers and artists in the early 1880s, whose task, as Eleanor saw it, was to transform socialism from a literary into a mass political movement. Radicals and socialists had to be wrenched away from spiritism and other "fooleries" of the inner life, while workmen, about whose lives Eleanor knew nothing, needed education and experience in class struggle. The Avelings left the Socialist Democratic Federation in 1883, to form the Socialist League with William Morris, in order to "make socialists". Eleanor spoke at open-air meetings all over Britain, gave her first political lectures in 1883, and contributed notes on the international movement to various socialist newspapers. The Avelings provided almost single-handedly the international wing to the British socialist movement schooled by Carlyle, Ruskin, Thoreau and John Stuart Mill. Eleanor translated her father's writings as well as Lissagaray, Ibsen, Flaubert; with Aveling she wrote pamphlets on Shelley's socialism, the Factory Acts and the "Woman Question".

Under the direction of Frederick Engels, the Avelings reinforced marxism's evolutionary determinism.[34] Engels, Marx's intimate friend and collaborator, known as "Staff" or "the General" to the Marx daughters, regarded Eleanor as the practical and living realisation of Marxist principles on the ground. Eleanor formed a women's branch of the new Gasworkers' Union, sat on the union's executive committee from 1889 to 1894, and attended inexhaustibly to the detail of fund-raising and organising between strikes. Had she lived, declared Will Thorne, leader of the Gasworkers' Union, she would have made the best women's trade union organiser of her generation.

Eleanor's socialism was a hybrid. It incorporated the constitutional principles and apocalyptic vision of the revolutionary exiles of 1848, the inflammatory nationalism of the Irish Fenians, Poles and Italians, and the spirit of the "workers' uprising" of the Paris Commune of 1870. In the 1880s, the American New Labour Party, the French Workers Party and German Social Democratic parties were models for the advance of socialism and workers' consciousness, and Eleanor believed that the demands of new unionism – organisation of the unskilled, in the eight-hour day, the Universal Strike, Will Thorne's practical reforms – sig-nalled the imminence of socialist revolution. But Eleanor's conscious-ness of grief, with its motifs of suffering and martyrdom, mirrored the political emotions of many feminists. Josephine Butler, for example, whose affinity with her "clandestines" was prompted by the wish to find a suffering keener than her own after the sudden death of her beloved only daughter; or Maria Sharpe, member of the Men and Women's Club in the 1880s, who "reluctantly" voted against Eleanor's membership of the Club, and who spoke of the "enquiring fear" young women felt towards prostitution, the subject of her own research; or the young Beatrice Potter (later Webb), another daughter of an educated man who devoted her life and work to socialism, who shared Eleanor's sense of guilt and her hysterical symptoms – chronic sleeplessness, anorexia, compulsive over-work, and unflinching self-criticism. Beatrice, like Eleanor, used work to stamp out personal ambition, sexual love, even the desire for happiness.[35]

Eleanor's yearning for love and work, the conflict within her between self-sacrifice and self-realisation, mark her as a feminist. But Kapp plays down her feminism in the name of Eleanor's modest good sense: "she went her way without fuss, feminism or false constraint and, having no illusions about her own intellectual range, simply did not see herself as in competition with more powerful minds, objectively alive to the social injustice that shackled women's freedom, sub-jectively free".[36] Discussion of Eleanor's marxism and the feminist movement between the 1870s and 1890s is confined to the footnotes. Yet, canvassing for schoolboards, advocating on behalf of the "white slaves", building friendships with Olive Schreiner, Dollie Radford, Clementina Black and Amy Levy (among others), doing her literary "hack-work" or pursuing her "free union", brought her closer to the "higher minds" of those "earnest" and "thoughtful" women the Avelings' "Woman Question" pamphlet (1887) mildly patronised. Eleanor's analysis of the position of women in capitalist societies condemned domestic drudgery, prostitution and the double standard, the sexual frustration of spinsters and their incarceration in madhouses and Poor Law Institutions. It combined a critique of marriage as a commercial transaction with Engels' and August Bebel's anthropology of the family and the origins of private property: "Women are the creatures of an organised tyranny of men, as the workers are the creatures of an organised tyranny of idlers" – a formulation which still shocks.[37] The relations between feminist and international socialist politics then and throughout the twentieth century were always tense, but what strikes the reader today is not their incompatibilities, as Kapp supposes, but their affinities. The two movements belonged in the same world, and breathed the same air. Both feminism and marxism were in thrall to evolutionism and materialism; both con-demned poverty and individual oppression; both demanded education and economic emancipation for the mass of the people. Both were pre-democratic, pre-communist philosophies and movements which believed, with a religiosity as yet uninhibited by either universal suffrage or Soviet communism, in their respective "cause".

Kapp does not want us to read Eleanor's life as a preparation for death. Her commitment to Eleanor's secure childhood of unconditional love (which, as Alison Light has recently pointed out, was in part the childhood she herself never had[38]), to a cast of characters deserving of a Balzac novel, and to Marx's philosophy of history, which Kapp herself never relinquished, retrieves Eleanor from tragedy until the end. Eleanor's death is the final image of the biography. She staged her own death. She sent her maid to the chemist, put on a white dress, wrote a short note to Aveling affirming love, and died. Neither the inquest nor rumour ever made clear who had signed for the poison, or what Aveling had been doing that day. Like Emma Bovary, Eleanor was "unable to work through her passions and so they consumed her"; she was driven to madness and suicide by "disappointed love", a euphemism for unsatisfied sexual instincts.[39] Aveling was unanimously condemned by those who paid tribute to Eleanor at her cremation and memorial. He died himself three months later. Eleanor had loved him – with an "obstinate" love, as one exasperated admirer put it. Eleanor's explanation was that he made her feel feminine: "I was irresistibly drawn to him ... Our tastes were much the same ... We agreed on Socialism. We both loved the theatre ... We could work together effectively."[40]

After publication, Kapp, who had interviewed everyone she could find who had known Eleanor and her family, was surprised by the numbers of people who contacted her to claim that they had been at Eleanor's side when she died. Eleanor knew about ghosts and generational haunting. Henry Hyndman, the leader of the Social Democratic Federation, remembered an "inspired speech" given at the anniversary of the Paris Commune and her father's death, in which she spoke of the eternal life gained by those who fought and fell in the great cause of the uplifting of humanity.[41] When these volumes were published in the 1970s they sparked fascination and debate among a generation of feminists for whom "the personal was political", and socialists well versed in the histories of socialism and the labour movement discovered a brilliant – if troubled – daughter of marxism.[42] Now a generation of readers who have grown up in a post-Cold War world, under Thatcherism, New Labour and a "war on terror", with no memory of these histories and lives, will encounter them for the first time and give them fresh meanings.

NOTES

(1) Margaret Comyn, "My Recollections of Karl Marx", *The Nineteenth Century*, XIX–XX, vol. xci, Jan–June, 1922, p. 166.

(2) Allen Hutt, the communist historian, was already at work on a biography, so, for a while, they collaborated. Yvonne went on alone after Hutt's death (he bequeathed her his notes) with the help of Elizabeth Whitman, her "brilliant" research assistant and typist. Volume one (*Family Life*) appeared in 1972, and volume two (*The Crowded Years*) – delayed by an irksome accident, assisted by

two small Arts Council Grants – in 1976. Chushichi Tsuzuki's *The Life of Eleanor Marx 1855–1898: a socialist tragedy*, Clarendon Press, Oxford, appeared in 1967.

(3) This volume, p. 261.

(4) Ibid., p. 282.

(5) Ibid., p. 277.

(6) E.P. Thompson, *William Morris, Romantic to Revolutionary*, Merlin Press, 1977 edn., p. 367; also this volume, p. 214.

(7) Judith R. Walkowitz, *City of Dreadful Delight, Narratives of Sexual Danger in Late-Victorian London*, Virago, 1992.

(8) Engels' death-bed revelation has been questioned by T. Carver, *Friedrich Engels, His Life and Thought*, London, 1989. See also Gareth Stedman Jones, "Friedrich Engels", *Dictionary of National Biography*, 2003/4 edn. forthcoming.

(9) This volume, p. 334.

(10) Eleanor Marx Aveling, ed., "Note", in Karl Marx, *Revolution and Counter-Revolution*, Union Books, London, 1896, p. vi.

(11) This volume, p. 52.

(12) Marx, *Revolution and Counter-Revolution*, p. v; Wilhelm Liebknecht, *Karl Marx, Biographical Memoirs* (1896), Journeymen's Press, 1975 edn., pp. 122–3.

(13) This volume, p. 9.

(14) Ibid., p. 42.

(15) Liebknecht, *Karl Marx, Biographical Memoirs*, p. 113.

(16) This volume, p. 185.

(17) Ibid., p. 215.

(18) Ibid., p. 31.

(19) Ibid., p. 13.

(20) Ibid., p. 52.

(21) Ibid., p. 114.

(22) Ibid., p. 178.

(23) Dona Torr, *Tom Mann and his Times*, Lawrence and Wishart, 1956, pp. 130, 179. Torr's book was an inspiration for E.P. Thompson: see Preface, *William Morris, Romantic to Revolutionary*, p. xi.

(24) Laurence Irving, *Henry Irving, The Actor and His World*, Faber and Faber, London, ch. XIX.

(25) This volume, p. 177.

(26) Ibid., p. 183.

(27) Havelock Ellis, *The New Spirit*, London, 1890, p. 154.

(28) John Stokes, ed., *Eleanor Marx, Life, Work, Contact*, Ashgate, 2000, includes several essays on Eleanor and theatre.

(29) George Bernard Shaw, *The Quintessence of Ibsenism*, Walter Scott, London, 1891.

(30) Tsuzuki, *The Life of Eleanor Marx* p. 161.

(31) This volume, p. 268.

(32) Ibid., p. 177.

(33) Ibid., p. 460.

(34) Gareth Stedman Jones, "Engels' Contribution to Marxism", in E.J. Hobsbawm, ed., *History of Marxism*, vol. 1, Brighton, 1981.

(35) Josephine E. Butler, *An Autobiographical Memoir*, eds, George W. and Lucy A. Johnson, Bristol and London, 1909, p. 58; Maria Sharpe, "Autobiographical Notes", July 1885, p. 16, Sharpe Papers, University College London Library; *Glitter Around and Darkness Within: The Diary of Beatrice Webb, Volume One, 1873–1892*, eds, Norman and Jeanne MacKenzie, Virago, 1982, pp. 50, 193 and

passim. Karl Marx, in common with medical opinion of the time, attributed Eleanor's breakdowns to virginal abstinence, described as a problem of spinsters in the Avelings' pamphlet "The Woman Question" (1887), p. 9: "How is it that our sisters bear upon their brows this stamp of lost instincts, stifled affections, a nature in part murdered?" Elizabeth Garrett Anderson was Eleanor's doctor at this time, See Sheila Rowbotham, "Shadowed Intimacies: The Letters of Marx's Daughters", in *Threads of Time, writings on history and autobiography*, Penguin, 1999, pp. 238–259, for further discussion of love and suffering.

(36) This volume, p. 325.

(37) Eleanor Marx and Edward Aveling, "The Woman Question", London, 1887, p. 8.

(38) Alison Light, "Preface", in Yvonne Kapp, *Time Will Tell: Memoirs*, Verso, London and New York, 2003.

(39) Translator's Preface in Gustave Flaubert, *Madame Bovary*, 1886 edn., translated by Eleanor Marx, p. xix. Eleanor attempted suicide at least once before 1898; and she talked of suicide when her ambition was disappointed, if her friend Marian Comyn is to be believed: *Recollections of Karl Marx*, p. 167. Amy Levy, novelist and friend of Eleanor, committed suicide, and Kapp's footnotes mention the suicides of several other contemporary artists and actresses.

(40) This volume, p. 418.

(41) Ibid., p. 288.

(42) Sally Alexander, "Interview with Yvonne Kapp", in *Becoming A Woman, and Other Essays in 19th and 20th Feminist History*, Virago, London, 1994, pp. 183–200.

· VOLUME I ·

FAMILY LIFE
(1855–1883)

Dedicated to

Bianca Margaret Mynatt

· AUTHOR'S NOTE ·

This book covers the first 28 years of Eleanor Marx's life, up to and throughout the year of her father's death in 1883. It has a section devoted to her common law husband, Edward Aveling, whom she had met before the end of this period.

The research done and material gathered since 1966 cover also Eleanor Marx's last 15 years, when, emerging from her international background, here described, she entered the British working class movement in which she played a significant part, to be dealt with in the second volume. Thus my acknowledgments refer to more matter than appears in the present book.

This applies also to a number of memoirs and autobiographies mainly if not entirely concerned with later events. It may be said in passing that, by and large, such secondary sources have not proved of paramount value. Though written by contemporaries with personal knowledge of the people and affairs involved, they were more often than not set down in old age when faulty memory and hindsight can play strange tricks. Many of these beguiling reminiscences are contradicted on matters of fact by the testimony of private letters and public prints of the day, by official records, trade union archives, school and university registers and verifiable information from surviving kin, as also by pilgrimages to the houses, streets and neighbourhoods where Eleanor Marx lived. So if any reader feels disappointed that some of the more familiar legends about the Marx family are not included here, it means merely that no reliable evidence could be found to bear them out.

My staple source material has been the German edition of the works of Marx and Engels (*Marx Engels Werke*. Dietz Verlag, Berlin 1956– 1968), in particular the correspondence which appears as Volumes 27– 39. At the risk of distressing the academic historian, no separate references to this pervasive source are given, save where the first appearance of a publication, or where the writer, recipient or date of a letter is enlightening. When the holograph was written in a language other than German – for the photostat of which I am indebted to the

Moscow Institute of Marxism-Leninism and the Berlin Institute of Marxism-Leninism – acknowledgment is made.

For the translation of quotations from the *Marx Engels Werke*, as of those from other foreign sources, I am responsible unless otherwise stated. Here a slight difficulty arises. Marx and Engels frequently interspersed letters written in another language with English expressions, phrases and whole passages. Where these are used naturally they are left unchanged. Thus there are instances where my rendering of a mainly German – or French – text is combined with its original English interpolations: always clear and forceful but sometimes rather odd. The erratic punctuation in extracts from Eleanor Marx's and her sisters' original letters, where not an obstacle to sense, has been retained.

Other material to which attribution is not always made, since much has been traced and is acknowledged to its primary source, comes from the collected pieces by divers hands known in English as *Reminiscences of Marx and Engels* (Foreign Languages Publishing House, Moscow, n.d. probably 1956) and, in German, with slight variations of text, as *Mohr und General* (Dietz Verlag, Berlin, 1964).

All certificates of births, marriages, deaths and all copies of wills registered in England were obtained from Somerset House. A few foreign birth and death certificates were traced to the appropriate Registries abroad. Census returns were examined at the Public Record Office, contemporary local Directories at the Guildhall Library. Information on weather conditions was supplied by the Meteorological Office or found in *The Times* newspaper of that date. Changes of street names and house numbers since the 19th century were obtained from the Greater London Council. Ratebooks, by permission of the Borough Treasurer, were investigated under conditions of extreme cold, dirt, peril and difficulty in the basements of St. Pancras Town Hall.*

All other source material is numbered and the references will be found at the end of each section. This has the disadvantage advantage of spangling the text with numerals of no possible interest to the general reader who may, however, like to feel assured that the book is

---

* Now Camden Town Hall. I understand that the Ratebooks – dusted, repaired and accessibly ranged according to date and Ward – have been removed to another place since January 1967.

properly documented.* Abbreviations for the most frequently used sources are given at the head of each series of Notes.

These references are not furnished with the full scholarly apparatus of page numbers in published works or piece numbers of unpublished documents. The reason is not that it would have been too much trouble to put them in: indeed, having served their purpose for work in progress, they have been deliberately set aside because I have often felt depressed by such elaborate annotations to otherwise unpretentious books: mountainous appendages to mouselike products. This is not a doctoral thesis, inadvertently published, nor yet a textbook. Further, I believe that the reader who may be unfamiliar with some of the magnificent published sources will find it more rewarding if his attention is directed, not to a page – or to learn whether an extract has been faithfully quoted – but to those works as a whole.

To avoid deadening each page with references, footnotes are reserved for additional matter thought pertinent but not essential to the text (except in the few Appendices where references are given in footnotes).

While the Reference Notes provide a fairly representative sample of the chief works consulted, a Select Bibliography is given on pp. 233–238 in conformity with custom and good practice.

But the acknowledgments are another matter altogether.

No writer venturing into a fresh and specialised field can have met with more cordial goodwill at every step from scholars and historians, from archivists, librarians and from friends both old and new in many countries. Nor could any writer feel more sensible of this generosity.

Among the names appended below, in alphabetical order, my sole fear is that, by oversight, some may have been omitted, so widespread has been the help extended. The shortcomings of the book are all mine.

First and foremost my thanks are owed to the Director and Staff of the Institute of Marxism-Leninism in Moscow, but for whose interest and encouragement the long period of research could not have been sustained. To my regret I was unable to avail myself of invitations to examine the archives in Moscow but, to compensate, the Institute sent me photostats of much important material from those archives,

---

* I have allowed myself to use one qualifying word – "battered" – for which there is no documentary evidence whatsoever.

including letters, documents and answers to questions relevant to my subject.

Equally great is my indebtedness to the Institute of Marxism-Leninism in Berlin, where I spent much profitable time studying documents, newspaper articles and conference reports. The Berlin Institute also gave me photographs from their valuable collection and, by courtesy of the Moscow IML, photostats of original material.* I wish to place on record the friendly co-operation of all the members of the Berlin IML staff in whose sections I worked and, above all, the extreme kindness of Professor Dr. Heinrich Gemkow and Mrs. Rosie Rudich of the Marx-Engels Department.

Dr. Emile Bottigelli of the University of Paris (Nanterre), the fruits of whose ripe erudition have been offered me again and again, not only allowed me access to those Marx family letters – formerly the property of the Longuet heirs – of which he is the custodian, but provided every facility, including the privilege of working in a room set aside for me in his own house. My warmest thanks are extended for this and other hospitality from Dr. and Madame Bottigelli at a time when they were under the considerable pressure attendant upon the Happenings of Paris May Week 1968.

With all efficiency the International Institute of Social History in Amsterdam produced from the wealth of their archives all the material I asked to see and, by an exceptional act of courtesy, gave me permission to reproduce certain items in this biography.

Some other names are not included in the appended list because they represent such rare experiences that it will not be thought invidious I hope if, like those already mentioned, they are singled out.

I wish to pay a special tribute of appreciation and respect to Mrs. Gwendoline Redhead and her younger sister Mrs. Aileen Reynish, nieces of Edward Aveling and the daughters of the Rev. Frederick Wilkins Aveling (1851–1937), the brother closest in age to Edward with whom he shared his schooldays and remained in touch until the end. These ladies, who received me on separate occasions in the summer of 1967, subsequently keeping up an informative correspondence, gave me not only some enjoyable hours of their company, answering my questions with the greatest patience and civility, but also the use of

_____

* Where these are used, the Moscow Institute is acknowledged as the source.

unique family documents, photographs and anecdotes for the purposes of this book.

With similar friendliness Mrs. Muriel Radford, the daughter-in-law of Caroline ("Dollie") Maitland and Ernest Radford who, both before and after their marriage, were among Eleanor Marx's closest friends, allowed me to visit her and to draw upon family papers, photographs and her own recollections.

To Miss Blanche Ward, the niece and close companion in the last days of Edith ("Biddy") Lanchester (1874–1966), I owe the pleasure of a memorable occasion in February 1967 when she submitted with grace to a recorded interview, again both preceded and followed by correspondence and material compiled from her aunt's reminiscences.

Throughout the writing of this book I have enjoyed the constructive criticism of Mrs. Noreen Branson of the Labour Research Department and the privilege of drawing freely, not to say importunately, upon the immense scholarship of Mr. Andrew Rothstein of the Marx Memorial Library and upon the wisdom of Mr. Bob Stewart.

It is common form to acknowledge research assistance, but in Mrs. Elisabeth Whitman I have had a matchless collaborator, without whose aid in Paris and Amsterdam and, since 1969, continuous team-work and independent research, the book could not have been written.

I am also greatly obliged to Mrs. Ann Kirkman and Mrs. Janet Rubidge for their conscientious typing of the final manuscript.

I now express my liveliest sense of gratitude to these outstanding benefactors, to all those whose help is acknowledged in the body of the book and to: Mr. Bert Andréas of the Graduate Institute of International Studies in Geneva; Mr. Robin Page Arnot; Professor Shlomo Avineri of the Hebrew University of Jerusalem; Dr. Theodore Barker, M.A., Ph.D., of Keynes College, Kent University; Miss P. H. Bodington, former Headmistress of South Hampstead High School for Girls; Dr. J. P. Bodmer of the Manuscript Department of the Zentralbibliothek, Zurich; Mr. Michael Brook, Reference Librarian of the Minnesota Historical Society; Mrs. Peggy Burkel; Miss Betty England of the Labour Research Department; Professor Philip Foner of Lincoln University, Pennsylvania; Mr. Edmund Frow; Mr. Henry Grant for his new and the brilliant reproduction of old photographs used in this book; Mr. H.-P. Harstick and Miss Marie Hunink of the International Institute of Social History, Amsterdam; Mr. Malcolm Holmes and Mr.

E. Jeffcott, former Librarians of the Chester Road Library, Highgate which, until 1969, had the custody of the most valuable St. Pancras archives, including the local newspapers of the 19th century; Mr. Walter Holmes for the use of the late Dona Torr's unpublished papers; Mr. Bernard Honess, Manager and Librarian, and his assistant, Mr. Derek Leask, of the Memorial Hall; Mr. G. Allen Hutt; Mr. Frank Jackson, formerly Librarian of the Communist Party of Great Britain; Mr. Alfred Jenkin; Mr. Mick Jenkins; Mr. James Klugmann for his sage advice; the London County Council – (now Greater London Council) – research staff at County Hall and, in particular, Mr. V. R. Belcher and Mr. J. F. C. Phillips, the former and present curators of the Map and Prints Collection, Miss J. Coburn and Mr. M. Pearce of the Record Room, Miss Anne Riches of the Historic Buildings Department and Dr. J. O. Springhall, Historical Research Assistant; Professor Henry Mayer of the University of Sydney; M. Paul Meier of the University of Paris (Nanterre); Mr. B. Y. Michaly, Manager of the Archive and Museum of the Jewish Labour Movement, Tel-Aviv; Mr. A. L. Morton; Mr. Alastair Pettigrew, Administrative Assistant to the Registry of King's College, London; Mr. G. Radice, Research Officer of the General & Municipal Workers' Union; Mr. Boris Rudyak, Mrs. Irma Sinelnikova and Mrs. Olga Vorobyova of the Institute of Marxism-Leninism, Moscow; Miss Pauline Seear of the History Research Library, Lewisham; Professor Dr. Johannes Siebert of Dresden; the late Mrs. Dorothy Thornycroft, the daughter of Eleanor Marx's friend, Edward Rose; the late Sir Stanley Unwin for permission to read the letterbooks of Swan Sonnenschein & Co.; Mrs. Hertha Walcher, formerly secretary to Clara Zetkin; Mr. H. E. Wells-Furby, M.A., Headmaster of Christ's College, Blackheath; Mr. Edward Weber, Curator of the Labadie Collection at the Library of the University of Michigan; Miss Bernadette Wilson (now Mrs. Harris), formerly of the Long Room in the Public Record Office; and the Public Relations Officers of the British Museum, the Ministry of Agriculture and Messrs. Philips Electrical Ltd.

Y.K.
London, June 1971.

· PART I ·

THREE SISTERS

Jenny Julia Eleanor – all Karl Marx's female children were named Jenny after their mother – was born at 28 Dean Street, Soho, in the borough of Westminster, between six and seven o'clock on the cold grey snowy morning of Tuesday, 16 January 1855. Her father was nearly 37, her mother 41, and she was the sixth child – the fourth daughter – of their twelve years of marriage; the only one to be born, to grow up, to live, to work, to cast her lot with an Englishman and to die in England.

A few days before her birth Marx wrote of his wife "approaching the catastrophe with firm steps". He announced to Frederick Engels* the arrival of "a *bona fide* traveller" – meaning one who, by law, cannot be refused sustenance and lodging – "unfortunately of the *sexe par excellence*", adding "had it been a male the matter would be more acceptable". It does not sound a particularly warm welcome.

But circumstances were hardly such as to occasion great rejoicing. Already one boy, Henry Edward Guy, known as Guido or Föxchen, after Guy Fawkes,† and one girl, Jenny Eveline Frances, known as Franziska,‡ had died in London, while the surviving son Charles Louis Henri Edgar, the beloved Mouche,§ had for a year past shown grave and progressive symptoms of the mesenteric disease, possibly of tubercular origin, from which he died, aged eight, three months after Eleanor's birth.

Wilhelm Liebknecht has left an account of the infant Eleanor as "a merry little thing, round as a ball, all cream and roses". Less obligingly, her nephew Edgar Longuet – writing from distant hearsay, since he was not born until his aunt was 24 – described her as "so puny that she was daily expected to die". The only certain facts, since they were recorded at the time and with some vexation, were that she screamed a great deal, "grew every day worse", disturbed the whole household and had to have a

---

* On 15 November 1850 Engels had re-entered his father's Manchester textile business, Ermen & Engels. At the time of Eleanor's birth he was contributing to the Chartist journals *Notes to the People* and the *People's Paper* and also writing articles for the *New York Daily Tribune*.

† b. 5 November 1849 at 4 Anderson Street, Chelsea; d. of meningitis 19 November 1850 at 64 Dean Street, Soho.

‡ b. 28 March 1851 at 28 Dean Street; d. of broncho-pneumonia 14 April 1852 at the same address.

§ b. 5 February 1847 at 42 rue d'Orléans, Brussels; d. 6 April (Good Friday) 1855 at 28 Dean Street. See Michael Knieriem, *Protokoll des Internationalen Kollogurums der Marx-Engels-Stiftung e.V. am 28 November 198 in Wuppertal Elberfeld. Dokument Nr. 4 p. 81.*

change of wet-nurse. So much, then, is clear: whether a sicklier or merely a hungrier and lustier than normal baby, she was breast-fed, but not by her mother, and managed to get on everybody's nerves.

However, once the "hospital atmosphere" created by a sick wife, a dying child and a yelling baby was dispelled, Eleanor grew more popular. She earned herself a pet-name, Tussy,* the forerunner of many but the one that was to stick. A sympathetic account of her at nine months was recorded by her sister Jenny, aged eleven, who wrote in her far from perfect English† to tell her father on a visit to Manchester that "Tusschen" was very lively, jumping and crawling. "She is quite in raptures when the little crucked (*sic*) greengrocer calls. I think this little man is her first amour."³ She was, indeed, much cossetted by the whole family who transferred to her the protective concern inspired by the loss of Edgar and the great love they had borne him.

Conditions in the Dean Street lodgings to which the Marxes had moved five years earlier in December 1850, only a few weeks after Guido's death were so cramped that the other infant born there, Franziska, had been put out to nurse since it was found impossible to cope with her and three other small children.‡ The census returns of 30 March 1851 show that at the time there were eight people – four adults including a midwife and four children – living in the Marxes' two furnished rooms, while at no stage in the years that followed were they ever fewer than six.

The Marxes rented these rooms for £22 a year as sub-tenants of Morgan Kavanagh,⁵ an Irishman who penned a number of controvertible works on the origins of myth and language, while his daughter Julia gained

---

* Virginia Bateman (Mrs. Edward Compton, 1853–1940) recalled in 1935 meeting Tussy half a century before and that the parents pronounced their daughter's name to rhyme with pussy and not fussy.¹ Unreliable in other respects – she believed she had called upon the Marxes in St. John's Wood where they never lived – her memory is here corroborated by others, such as Mrs. Muriel Radford, the daughter-in-law of Eleanor's two close friends Dollie Maitland and Ernest Radford, who often spoke of "Toossy" in her hearing.² There was a great fondness for nicknames in the Marx family and everyone had several. Marx himself, however, was generally known as Mohr – the Moor – and her children called Mrs. Marx Möhme or Möhmchen: a Teutonised form of Mummy.

† Jenny's first language was French. In the last years of her life, married and back in France, her English became rather peculiar again. She complained of a servant railing at her "like a fishmonger".⁴

‡ The circumstances of the family before Eleanor was born are movingly described in her introduction to the series of articles she edited in 1896 under the title *Revolution and Counter-Revolution*, believing them to have been written by Marx in the years 1851–1852. As is now known, they were in fact mainly the work of Engels. Eleanor drew upon her mother's unfinished autobiographical notes, set down in the mid-'60s but not published for nearly a century, when an incomplete version appeared (in Russian, English and the original German): *Kurze Umrisse eines bewegten Lebens* (*Short Sketches of an Eventful Life*).

unlasting fame as a novelist.* But it is to his landlady that Marx refers in his letters, and with no more cordial feeling than is usual in that relationship, writing to Engels in September 1852 to say that the thing most to be desired was that she should throw him out, which would at least save the rent, but she was unlikely to prove so obliging.

In that one Dean Street house† – still standing and now, since August 1967, bearing a commemorative plaque to Marx's residence – there were in all 13 people. That this was not conspicuous overcrowding for that time and place is made clear by the Report on the 1851 census which shows that the 1,354 inhabited buildings in the Soho parish of St. Anne housed a population of 17,335: an average of 14 persons to each house and 327 to the acre.‡

This was the period, and even briefly the scene, of Edwin Chadwick's labours to establish elementary sanitary conditions and domestic drainage for London's 300,000 houses, since the Metropolitan Commission of Sewers in Greek Street, Soho, was for a few years his base of operations. This obstinate, arrogant but dedicated little public servant – Dickens' "indefatigable Mr. Chadwick" – who was honoured by neither friend nor foe, fought tirelessly against opposition, ignorance and apathy to introduce a primitive Public Health Act§ in the belief that "the sullen resentment of the neglected workers might organise itself behind the Trade Union leaders and the Six Points men" and that "if a Chartist millennium were to be averted, the governing classes must free the governed from the sharp spur of their misery by improving the physical conditions of their lives".[7]

In the year of Eleanor's birth England's population was almost 18

---

* A quotation from one of her mawkish works[6] has a certain relevance: " 'What has the world done for me that I should love it? ... Why did I see my children die from hunger, when others had more wealth than they could spend? I once said ... that it seemed to my poor judgment the world would be better arranged if all human creatures shared in its wealth alike ...' 'Well, but what is to be done?' 'I know not ... how should I? But there are wise men in the land paid to find out everything. Let them find out that ...' " The authoress might have learnt from the lodger more about this subject, including the fact that such men were not exactly paid and that their own children also hungered and died. She is said by the *Dictionary of National Biography* to have devoted herself to the care of an "aged and infirm" mother who, however, outlived her by many years. Neither of these ladies was at 28 Dean Street on the night of the 1851 census. They lived much abroad.

† Built *c.* 1735 under a 65-year lease granted by the Portland family to John Nolloth, carpenter.

‡ Compared with 42.1 to the acre in the Soho Ward covered by the 1961 Census, a figure which does not greatly differ from the average for the London Administrative County as a whole.

§ Passed in 1848.

million* and of the 425,703 deaths registered in that year, 97,503, or almost 24 per cent, were infants under one year of age.†

In that year, too, Louis Pasteur, then a young professor of chemistry and Dean of the Faculty of Sciences at Lille University, examined microscopically fermentation processes which led him to the germ theory and laid the foundations of modern biochemistry and bacteriology, revolutionising medical practice.

It was a time when an engineering fitter in London – among the highest paid of skilled workers – earned 34s for a 58-hour week. It was also a moment of great technological inventions, of which the Bessemer steel process was possibly the most important. But in fact Eleanor's life of little over 40 years witnessed the expansion of the railways by the opening to traffic of over 12,000 track miles,‡ saw the introduction of the telegraph as a world-wide means of communication, the mechanisation of manufacture in a score of industries, the introduction of the modern sewing-machine, the typewriter, the telephone, the bicycle, the gramophone, electric generators and lighting, the turbo, the gas, the Diesel and the petrol engine, though she barely lived to know the motor car, since it was not a commercial proposition in Britain until after the repeal of the Red Flag Act of 1897. However, a power-driven model plane took off and landed safely in 1857, while the first two street letterboxes appeared in London, the Colt revolver, the Gatling machine-gun and the system of competitive examination for entrance to the Civil Service came into the world almost at the same time as she did, when the Crimean War was in full swing and Lord Aberdeen's Tory and Peelite government was about to fall on a vote of censure concerning "the condition of the army before Sebastopol", making way for Palmerston's Liberal administration. In that same year too, and in the street where she was born, St. Anne's churchyard, where some tens of thousands of bodies had been interred in its three-quarters of an acre, was finally closed and the new burial ground, the London Necropolis, where Eleanor herself was cremated, was bought at Woking.

---

* Roughly 20 million in England and Wales. The population of London had just passed the 2 million mark.
† Compared with 3.2% for England and Wales exactly a century later.
‡ 13½ thousand track miles – rather more than were opened between 1855 and 1897 – were closed between 1963 and 1969.

In this world Eleanor grew up as one of three sisters, though Jenny* and Laura† were so much her seniors that she enjoyed to some extent the status of an only child while sharing precociously in the interests of her elders. But there was one circumstance of the utmost importance to her early development.

In April 1845 Mrs. Marx, then pregnant with Laura, received from her mother, the widowed Baroness von Westphalen, "the best present she could send her: dear faithful Lenchen". This feudal gift consisted of Helene Demuth, a young person then in her 25th year, who had been born at St. Wendel in the Palatinate where her father, of peasant stock, was a baker. Eleanor believed, and stated, that her birth date was 1 January.[7a] However her death certificate of November 1890 gives her age as 67, in accordance with which her gravestone bore the words: "Born January 1st 1823". Thanks to the researches of Dr. Heinz Monz of Trier it is now known that she was born at, precisely, 1 a.m. on 31 December 1820.[7b] At the age of eleven or twelve the child left home for Trier, some 30 miles away, to go into domestic service, bettering herself three years later, after some harsh experiences, by entering the Westphalen household. Jenny von Westphalen, her mother's only surviving daughter, was then 21 and already secretly betrothed to the 17-year-old Karl Marx, though the engagement was not formally – or easily – recognised for another two years nor the marriage celebrated until 1843, by which time her father, Baron Ludwig von Westphalen, had been dead for a year and Jenny was 29. Thus, when bundled off to Brussels to rejoin her young mistress, Lenchen had been but briefly separated from her.

This abrupt transfer from her homeland and from the placid round of waiting upon the petty nobility in a sleepy provincial town to the hugger-mugger family life of a revolutionary, hounded from one European capital to another, certainly tested Lenchen's stoicism but failed to daunt her. She shared the distresses of cheap hotels and squalid lodgings, of expulsions and evictions, flitting from country to country with the hard-pressed Marxes, whose children were born and whose children died, while Lenchen's wages were seldom paid and her clothes more often than not in pawn. If she had time off it was as porter of the laden picnic basket on family outings, or else she played chess with Marx when not running his errands and beating off his creditors. Yet in that heyday of overworked

---

* Jenny Caroline. b. 1 May 1844 at 28 rue Vanneau, Paris. d. 11 January 1883 at 11 boulevard Thiers, Argenteuil, Val d'Oise. Her death certificate states that she was born 4 May; but since Eleanor told Liebknecht that Jenny was born in 1845 and Eleanor's own birth date was incorrectly carved upon the present Marx monument in Highgate Cemetery, too much attention should not be paid to these little slips of the pen and chisel.

† Jenny Laura. b. 26 September 1845 at 5 rue de l'Alliance, Brussels. d. 26 November 1911 at Draveil, Seine-et-Oise.

and underpaid slaveys who were also despised, Helene Demuth was never looked upon by any of the Marxes as less than a most valued friend.

It was not, however, until 1856, after twelve restless years, that she came into her own. There was still no money, but in the haven of a small suburban house with a settled family whose numbers were not again to vary – save for the advent of a last-born child who lived but a few hours – Lenchen ordered and sustained the whole establishment where bread was baked, clothes were made and patched, boots were mended, linen was washed and beer was brewed. Her own son, born in 1851, had early been put out to foster-parents* and on Eleanor she lavished all her motherliness.

It was during the years of Eleanor's childhood that some of Marx's most significant work was done. She was six weeks old when the inaugural meeting of an international committee, foreshadowing great things, was held under the chairmanship of Ernest Jones, with Marx in attendance, at St. Martin's Hall, Long Acre. In 1855 and early 1856 Marx wrote his famous articles on the conduct of the Crimean War and the fall of Kars,[8] in 1857 those on the Indian Mutiny.[9] In June 1859 his *Critique of Political Economy* appeared; in December 1860, *Herr Vogt*; in September 1864 the International Working Men's Association, the First International, was founded, Marx's *Inaugural Address* and *Provisional Rules* being published that November. In June 1865 he gave the address to the General Council of the IWMA known to later generations as *Value, Price and Profit*, while September 1867 saw the first edition of Volume I of *Capital* on which Marx had worked for ten years, plagued throughout by ill-health and debt.

Mrs. Marx, who was also often unwell, spent a good deal of her time running to the pawnbroker to pledge the linen and plate, her own and her family's personal belongings, clothing and all such household objects as were not immovable. Occasionally, when impending guests made the denuded home an embarrassment positively more acute than the need for ready cash, she ran to redeem a few of these articles. When not so engaged she was copying out by hand the successive drafts of Marx's manuscripts. Doting mother though she was, dwelling on her daughters' beauty, brains, prizes and attainments in letters to her friends, she had scarcely more time than Marx himself – an extremely loving father – to devote to the small Eleanor. Nor is there evidence that, apart from the true affection that bound all members of the family, her big sisters, who were either at school or busy mastering the ladylike accomplishments so unsuited to their actual – and future – circumstances, paid overmuch attention to the child.

---

* See Appendix I.

So she was Helene Demuth's baby, nurtured by that warm and sturdy peasant soul. Something of its down-to-earth simplicity, its *Demut*,* its kindliness and unselfish devotion were reflected in Eleanor all her days.

Unlike the other members of the family Eleanor cannot be regarded as a Soho character. She spent her first seven months there during some part of which her parents were in Manchester and her mother, when in London, was frequently laid up. She was then taken to Camberwell – a suburb so pastoral compared to the environs of Leicester Square that the Marxes referred to it quite simply as "the country" – to live in a cottage lent by Peter Imandt, a German exile. There she spent the summer, returning to Dean Street, a few days after the fall of Sebastopol, to remain until the following May when she went with her mother and sisters to Trier until September to stay for the first and last time with her maternal grandmother who died during the visit in July, shortly after her 81st birthday.

For this expedition and on the strength of a little over £100 which came to her on the death of a 90-year-old uncle,† Mrs. Marx paid off some of the most pressing debts, redeemed certain items from the pawnbroker and made the journey to her old home with her children "newly attired".

Now, on her return, she could look to another legacy, enough to make the break from Dean Street and, indeed, within a month she was househunting. It turned out, however, that her half-brother, as is usual in such circumstances, was holding up her inheritance, that endless debts, large and small, had again accumulated and that everything was back in pawn.

The househunting went on blithely nonetheless and, with Engels' help, the family moved into No. 9 Grafton Terrace, Kentish Town, in the borough of St. Pancras,‡ on 29 September 1856. Eleanor was nearly 21 months old.

---

* The word means modesty, humility.

† Heinrich Georg von Westphalen. Six years later Mrs. Marx wrote to Mrs. Bertha Markheim, a lady who had made the acquaintance of the Marx family in 1854, stating that she had inherited £150 to £200 in 1856 from a Scottish relative, using the occasion to mention her Campbell and "Argyle" (*sic*) connections.[10] Later still, in her reminiscences, she referred to this as "a small English inheritance". There is no reference in the correspondence of the time to any legacy from such a source and no means of tracing the will, since the testator, whether Scottish or English, is never named.

‡ Now, since 1965, Camden.

Grafton Terrace, where Eleanor lived until she was nine, was in what we should now call a development area. It had been built in the late forties on a parcel of land sold as two Lots of just under half an acre each at the auction in August 1840 of a portion of freehold ground rents on Lord Southampton's Haverstock Hill and Kentish Town estate.* The presumed building value of the combined plots at the time of the sale was £140 a year.

This short terrace of 14 paired and three singlefronted brick cottages – or "third-class houses" as they were designated by the District Surveyors of the short-lived Metropolitan Building Office (1844–1855)[11] – was built in a slightly whimsical style, with balconies and stone coping, quoins, balustrade and window surrounds. It was as yet an island in a morass of churned London clay and building operations, the street unlit and unpaved. It represented a fairly typical example of small builder's enterprise, spurred by the exodus of Londoners from the centre to the outskirts which, thanks to the railways, was one of the distinguishing features of London life in the second half of the 19th century.† The speed of the suburban spread to the northwest may be judged by the fact that in 1843 a duel was fought at Chalk Farm as one of the "least frequented parts". At the end of that decade it had become a favourite out-of-town Sunday resort for costermongers because it had "plenty of life",[12] yet within two years of the Marxes' move, that is, by 1858, the fields surrounding Grafton Terrace had been completely built over, prefiguring the neighbourhood where Eleanor was to spend the best part of the next 27 years.

To Mrs. Marx this mean little house in Kentish Town,‡ covering an area of 16 ft. (frontage) by 20 ft. with its eight small rooms on four floors,

---

* The St. Pancras almshouses begun in 1850 on a site facing the length of Grafton Terrace, and the public house opposite – The Lord Southampton, frequented by Marx – which forms the corner of Grafton Terrace and what is left of Southampton Road, are still extant.

† The population of St. Pancras increased by an average of 3,723 and the number of houses by 397 in each year of the decade 1841–1851. Over the 20 years 1841 to 1861 the population rose from 48 to 74 persons to the acre.

‡ The house is still standing, though threatened with demolition at one stage in the 1960s. Its rateable value is £134 p.a. and it is occupied by several families. It is now listed by the Borough of Camden as of 'special architectural and historical interest' – the only house in the terrace owing to its association with Marx.

including a basement, seemed in truth "a princely abode compared with our former holes".[13] She had inherited something like £120 from her mother. She now proceeded to take her household goods out of pawn again, to pay off some of the Soho tradesmen* and to spend £40 on furniture, mostly "second-hand rubbish" as she described it.[13] This, supplemented by some rickety chairs and a tea-table cast off by Peter Imandt when he left Camberwell to settle in Dundee, more than met her needs: she pronounced the living room (15 ft. by 12) positively magnificent, sold a few old dresses and shoes to buy ornaments, and the money was gone; in fact they were short of £15 for the move. It then struck Marx that if he did not pay at least his first quarter's rent punctually he would be "utterly discredited".

Marx considered the place a bargain at £36 a year, attributing the low price to its "unfinished surroundings". In fact, its rateable value at the time and for most of the years he remained there was £24 a year and the gross estimated rental – which in those days bore an intelligible relation to rateable value – was £27, with rates of £25s. 10d., some part of which covered the lighting and paving which were not there. The truth is that throughout his seven-and-a-half years' tenancy of No. 9† Grafton Terrace, Marx was never able to pay for the upkeep of this princely abode. "We were permanently hard up," Mrs. Marx recalled, "our debts mounted from day to day" and when Engels undertook in January 1857 to provide £5 a month – which was rapidly stepped up as one crisis followed upon another – it was in response to Marx's dismayed recognition that the hand-to-mouth existence of Dean Street was no longer feasible for a householder and ratepayer with three daughters to bring up.

There were other disadvantages for the parents. Though exile was nothing new to the Marxes who had known little else since their repeated expulsions from France, Prussia and Belgium, this was a new version.

The England where they had landed seven years before had been no more than their last country of immigration,‡ the London to which they came was but another foreign city that turned out to be home for the rest of their lives. Apart from the first few months in Chelsea, their stamping ground had been Soho – the German Hotel at No. 1 Leicester Square, then 64 Dean Street for half a year and 28 Dean Street for close on six years: a Soho flooded with the 1848 refugees from Poland, Hungary,

---

* Though not all: three years later the Dean Street milkman and baker were still owed the substantial sum of £9.

† Now, and since October 1888, No. 46. For some years, from 1872, with the extension of the street, the renaming of adjacent terraces and the renumbering of the first houses, it became No. 36.[14]

‡ Following Marx's refusal to accept banishment by the authorities from Paris to Vannes: at that time a swamp in Morbihan (Brittany).

Russia, Italy, France and Germany – a tide that was not to recede for nearly a decade – and the Marxes had been among the "incongruous elements" described by Herzen as "caught up from the Continent and deposited ... by those ebbs and flows of revolution ... in the alleys ... of Leicester Square and the adjoining back streets ... a wretched population wearing hats such as no one wears, and hair where none should be, a miserable, poverty-stricken, harassed population ..."[15] whose "dissolute habits" shocked the easygoing Engels.[16] But the Marxes' Dean Street lodgings had been a homing point for new arrivals and the natural meeting place for socialist friends already in London, few of whom had any means of support and most of whom fell prey to the internecine strife, mutual recrimination and spy-mania endemic to political émigré circles.

Now many of the old friends had departed while to those still left Kentish Town seemed wildly inaccessible. The Marxes missed the social life of the Clubs and pubs they had used to frequent in the West End. Nor did they relish going out at night to encounter the hazards of darkness, refuse, mud and rubble of this "barbarous region",* preferring the comfort of their own hearth. In any case, Marx felt, his time was too valuable to spend on the futile plottings and petty squabbles of refugee politics and he retreated more and more into his study, or repaired to the British Museum where in 1857 the rotunda Reading Room was opened.

For the children it was an unqualified change for the better. Jenny and Laura had been to a little school in Soho but now their education made strides. They were coached for a brief period by Wilhelm ("Fridolin") Pieper who had formerly been Marx's secretary. Marx did not think much of him as a tutor and he was extremely tiresome into the bargain. So the girls were sent to the rather high-sounding South Hampstead College for Ladies at Clarence House, 18 Haverstock Hill, run by the Misses Boynell and Rentsch. Here they constantly won prizes, came out top in everything though the youngest in the form, and cost their father a good deal of money, for the fees were £8 a term to which were added extra lessons in languages and drawing. "And now I have to engage a music fellow", Marx wrote ruefully to Engels in April 1857, which step was followed by the hire of an inferior piano.

Eleanor, not to be outdone by so much brilliance and something of a wag, announced that she had two brains – one for each of her years presumably – and exercised them both to good purpose with incessant chatter. She later recalled that when she had whooping cough, which

---

* The rubbish from building, railway cutting and sewer works was tipped into the fields behind Haverstock Hill abutting Grafton Terrace at the rate of some 37,000 loads a year (1 load = 1 cubic yard) in the period when Hampstead, added to the metropolis in 1846, was being developed.

lasted the best part of the year 1858, she "took advantage of the fact to insist upon open house being kept for every street child in the neighbourhood". As there were no fewer than 50 young children living on their side of Grafton Terrace alone* – and it may be remarked that some of the little maids-of-all-work were barely in their 'teens – social life at No. 9 must have lacked a certain restraint. It was perhaps fortunate that for some part of that time Marx himself was stopping with Engels in Manchester. But then, as Eleanor wrote, she had made "bond slaves" of the family and "as is usual in slavery, there was general demoralisation".[17] Three years later she went down with jaundice. Adept at turning her afflictions to good account and perceiving that she was yellow, she decided that she had become Chinese and that her rather frizzy hair should be made into a little pigtail. Her renown as a hostess, by no means dependent upon her indispositions, was so widespread that the Marx family was known in the neighbourhood to children and grown-ups alike as "the Tussies"; and such was her conviviality that, as Lenchen recalled in after-years, Tussy could not be induced to come to table in summertime but sat on the doorstep with a mug of milk and then, snatching a slice of bread, was off to join her companions at their street games. She was something of a romp and what was called a tomboy; fearless in play with the bigger, wild urchins.[18]

All Eleanor's recollections are of an unclouded childhood. One of the earliest is of careering over fields and round the long narrow garden of Grafton Terrace on her father's shoulders at the age of three with convolvulus flowers in her hair. She remembered the unending tale which Marx spun for her, month after month, concerning one Hans Röckle, a magician who kept a toyshop but was "never able to meet his obligations either to the devil or the butcher and was therefore, much against the grain, constantly obliged to sell his toys ...". She listened entranced to the fairy stories of the Brothers Grimm until she not only had them by heart but had picked up fluent German in this way.†

Then Marx began to read aloud, as to her sisters before her, "the whole of Homer, the whole *Niebelungenlied, Gudrun, Don Quixote*, the *Arabian Nights*" and Shakespeare, who was "the bible of our house, seldom out of our hands or mouths". By the time she was four she knew long passages by heart and, at six, "recited whole scenes", one of her favourites being that between Hamlet and his mother. As Mrs. Marx occasionally played

---

* There was, for example, the family of John Withers, master-baker, who lived at No. 1 at the end of the street with three small daughters. The Marxes' neighbour at No. 10 was Samuel Sawyer, a builder, also with three daughters and a son under seven. In later years both these families played some part in Marx's affairs.

† She never learnt to write German correctly.

the Queen, Eleanor "fancied that the line: 'Mother, you have my father much offended' must have been the attraction".[19]

She did not learn her letters at some prodigiously early age. Indeed, her mother claimed that she could not read to herself with ease until she was eight.[20] Eleanor's own memories blur or belie this, for she relates that on her sixth birthday she was given *Peter Simple* and then went on to the rest of Marryat and to Fenimore Cooper, Marx also reading these books so that he could discuss each one in detail with her. When, fired by Marryat's tales, she "declared she would become a 'Post-Captain' (whatever that may be)* and consulted her father as to whether it would not be possible for her to 'dress up as a boy' and 'run away to join a man-of-war', he assured her he thought it might very well be done, only they must say nothing about it to anyone until all plans were well matured".[21] It was at this period too that Eleanor, convinced that Abraham Lincoln could not do without her advice on the conduct of the American Civil War, wrote – or possibly dictated – long letters to the President for Marx to read and post. These letters so amused him that he kept them, though they have not come down to us, and many years later showed them to her.

"Children should educate their parents", said Marx and lived up to the dictum by keeping in step with the reading, entering the fantasy life, encouraging the confidences and adjusting his views to meet the religious scruples of his engaging Tussy. He told her the story of the Passion – "the carpenter whom the rich men killed" – adding that much could be forgiven Christianity because it had taught the adoration of the child.

Mrs. Marx, who admitted that her sporadic efforts to teach her elder daughters German were vain, for they "had no mind to obey", while her authority, like their respect for her, "left much to be desired",[13] was also quite good at learning. She derived instruction from Tussy's facility in making up stories, in which she rivalled her father, and her more than facile gymnastic ability. To the child herself it seemed in after-years that there had never been a more "merry pair" than these two whom she helped to educate.

It is hard to realise that the laughing, loving parents of Eleanor's childhood memories were racked by the most sordid misery and distress; that her father was brought to the point of desperation and her mother to the verge of a mental breakdown in those same years. It is a tribute of a kind rarely paid to Karl Marx that what Eleanor knew – unlike Maisie – was untainted.

Almost from the time they moved to Grafton Terrace, Mrs. Marx, who

---

* It is curious that Eleanor, writing as an adult, should have been puzzled by what she had known as a child, for "Post Captains" do not occur only in Marryat but also in Jane Austen. They were naval officers with the substantive rank of Captain, having "taken post".

immediately became pregnant with her seventh child which did not survive, was ailing and also exceedingly ill-humoured, "for which at heart I can't really blame her under present auspices", Marx wrote, "though it annoys me".

This was the year (1857) of world economic crisis, starting in November in America, with the result that the *New York Daily Tribune* reduced Marx's contributions, thus halving this source of income.* It was now that he began his first draft of *Capital*, but before the year was out he was threatened with the broker's men for failure to pay his rent while hordes of "hungry wolves", the angry shopkeepers, also suffering hard times, were at the door.

A cold snap in January 1858 found the family without coal or money in the house and, feeling that the position was fast becoming insupportable, unable to work, Marx spent his time trying to raise loans and borrowing from one tradesman to fend off another. These shifts were not calculated to produce a lasting solution to any of the problems and but for Engels' help the family could barely have survived. By the summer Dr. Allen of Soho Square, with a surgery in Dean Street, who still attended them† – and was himself owed £10 in fees – insisted that Mrs. Marx must have a change of air, which was the last straw. Marx sent Engels a detailed account of his current debts, amounting to £113, of which £30 was owed to the pawnbroker and over £32 to the local butcher, baker, grocer, milkman, greengrocer and newsagent, the last not having been paid for a twelvemonth. "Even if I were to reduce my expenses to the utmost", Marx wrote, "by, for example, removing the children from school, going to live in a strictly working-class dwelling, dismissing the servants and living on potatoes", the sale of the furniture would not realise enough to satisfy his creditors, while such drastic steps could have dangerous consequences for his wife in her nervous state and were hardly suitable for his growing girls.

Although at this point Engels, having poked some gentleman in the eye with his umbrella for insulting the "bloody foreigner", was being sued for £200 damages,‡ he still came to the rescue of the Marxes, as he did again and again, not only with cash but also with crates of wine – regarded on all sides as the sovereign remedy for every bodily ill – yet when winter came round the household was "more dreary and desolate than ever", an atmosphere of gloom prevailed and Mrs. Marx, unable to

---

* He had at first received £1 an article, then £2 for each one published. Later the editor (Dana) agreed to pay for every article sent, whether printed or not.
† Doing so until 1868 when he suffered a paralytic stroke and was unable to make his rounds.
‡ In the event he got off with £30 damages and £20 costs, though Marx had thought the only course open was for Engels to flee the country.

provide any Christmas cheer for the children, tore herself free of the rabid creditors to celebrate the festive season by paying yet another visit to the pawnbroker and copying out the MS. of the *Critique of Political Economy*. "Never, I think, was money written about under such a shortage of it", said Marx.

The year 1859 saw no change in this state of affairs; rather was it aggravated by Marx's recurrent liver complaint and toothaches. Indeed, this whole wretched string of years, with all its incongruities, could be summed up in the scene presented by the family that Christmas when, with a County Court summons pending, the instalments to the tallyman for Marx's very trousers sorely in arrears, most of the others' clothing at the pawnshop and everyone ailing in one way or another, they gathered round the notional *Weihnachtsbaum* to drink the champagne Engels had sent.

It is among other inconsistent features of this poverty-stricken household that letters in which Marx recounts the most seamy efforts to raise money, while being sued for debt and about to have the water and the gas supply cut off, were written to the accompaniment of Laura and Jenny singing delightful duets at the piano, having made good progress with their music lessons.

These girls, now aged 15 and 16, left school in 1860 but they continued to take the "single class in any subject" offered by the South Hampstead College to learn French, Italian, drawing and singing, while there were now two servants to wait upon the family, Helene Demuth having been joined by Marianne Kreuz as housemaid.

For three months of that year Marx was continuously ill, while money troubles swarmed ever more ominously about him, but in the late summer he managed to send the family to Hastings for a fortnight, where it rained all the time. In November, though twice vaccinated, Mrs. Marx contracted smallpox. The nature of her illness had to be kept a great secret for some reason, though not, it must be thought, an anti-social one, for immediate steps were taken to isolate the invalid and the children were sent to stay with the Liebknechts nearby. Marx remained in the house and, with Lenchen's help, tended his wife who was fed on sips of claret. Though not allowed to come near the members of the contagious household – and, indeed, Jenny had to post a letter from just round the corner "as the thoroughfare to 9 Grafton Terrace is closed"[22] – Eleanor, viewing her father in the street from Liebknecht's windows, cried in true hunting style "Halloo, old boy!". There was some scheme for sending the girls temporarily to a little boarding school which they scotched by objecting to the "religious rites" they would have to perform. In any case Mrs. Marx was sufficiently recovered for them all to return home by

Christmas, to everyone's relief, for Marx had been obliged to pay for the upkeep of two separate establishments in their absence, Liebknecht being in no position to provide for three additional hungry young persons.

The homecoming was festive, but almost at once in the New Year Marx, worn out by nursing his wife who was still far from well, inclined to be crotchety and extremely demanding, went down with an attack of his chronic liver trouble which now became acute. For fear of incurring fresh medical expenses he doctored himself for some weeks with such lamentable results that, suffering a severe relapse, he had to call in Dr. Allen, who came every three days and prescribed horse riding and a change of air. "I'm as plagued as Job, if less godfearing", wrote Marx to Engels as, sardonically reporting the doctor's advice, he remarked that he was being sued for rates and school fees while grocer and butcher were refusing both further credit and supplies. But Dr. Allen must not be told the truth or "where the shoe pinches". Once more Marx set about exploring the possibilities of a Loan Society, but his guarantees were not sound enough.

With the usual timely £10 from Engels he settled the gas bill and the rates, beat off the bailiffs once again and prepared to go to Holland. He was there from March till May 1861. Eleven years earlier, desperate at the prospect of the fifth child then on the way, Mrs. Marx had gone to Holland to beg her husband's uncle Lion Philips for help, which was refused. Marx had little taste for courting a similar rebuff and had set his face against an expedient long urged by Engels. But there was no alternative. His income from the *New York Daily Tribune* had dwindled to nothing and was about to cease; that from the *New American Cyclopaedia*, to which he had contributed since July 1857, had completely dried up in the autumn of 1860.

Lion Philips, a successful businessman in Zaltbommel, near Nijmegen, married to Marx's aunt Sophie, managed the affairs of his sister-in-law, Marx's mother, herself of Dutch origin.* Marx hoped to borrow an advance on his expectations from the old lady, widowed for the past twenty-three years and now aged 74. Apart from occasional loans against IOUs, grandmother Marx had not been generous, usually answering her son's appeals with prolonged silence and holding the view that he would be better employed accumulating capital than writing about it. His

---

* "My grandmother", wrote Eleanor, "... belonged by descent to an old Hungarian Jewish family driven by persecution to Holland ... [they] became known by the name of Presburg (*sic*), really the town from which they came. These Presburgs, of course, intermarried, and my grandmother's family name was afterwards Phillips (*sic*) ... To the day of her death ... I believe ... [she] spoke very bad German."[23] Pressburg is now Bratislava. The Philips family founded the firm of Philips Lamps Ltd. in Eindhoven in 1891.

mission was moderately successful. He established excellent relations with his Dutch cousins and eventually came back to London with £160; but not before he had used the opportunity to go, without papers, into Prussia* where he tried but failed to reclaim citizenship and to travel widely in Germany and the Low Countries, while laying the groundwork for contributing regular articles to the Vienna *Presse.* He also involved himself in highly complicated manoeuvres to arrange a long-term loan on the Continent. Though he claimed to have been bored to death in Berlin, where he was lionised, this brief interlude was something of a respite for him.

During his absence it was Lenchen's turn to fall ill and she was out of commission for several weeks. Mrs. Marx was obliged to turn to Engels for money, at which juncture her husband was trying to raise his return fare.†

He arrived home to be confronted by the familiar mountain of debt, swallowing up every penny he had brought back – and small wonder, since £40 went on school and doctor's fees alone – so that by June he was again unable to meet an inexorable rate demand.

---

* While there he obtained a passport valid until May 1862. An amnesty for political refugees had been granted on the accession of Wilhelm I in January 1861. It did not, however, apply to Marx who – like most other Prussian revolutionaries – had lived abroad for over ten years and thus became "a foreigner".

† From Carl Siebel (28 March 1861), in order to travel back *via* Elberfeld, Cologne, Trier, Aachen, Zaltbommel again, Amsterdam and Rotterdam.

With an inflammation of the eyes that prevented him from reading or writing, a variety of summonses and a law-suit hanging over his head – not for the first time – but without the means to employ a solicitor, Marx had now to take stock of the fact that his wife could no longer withstand the stresses of their situation. Her loyalty to his interests, which she shared, was unfaltering, her determination that he should "pursue his purpose through thick and thin, not allowing bourgeois society to turn him into a money-making machine"[24] was as steadfast as his own – she always looked back on the days spent in his tiny study "copying out his scrawled articles" as the happiest of her life – but the struggle had been too nasty, brutish and long.

Mrs. Marx was not an hysteric but nor was she cast in the heroic mould. The truth is that, while she met uncommonly trying circumstances with more than common fortitude, her origins were against her. Though much has been made of her high birth, she came of no ancient or exalted aristocracy.

Her paternal grandfather, Christian Heinrich Philip Westphalen (1724–1792) had been an able administrator who rose to become the Duke of Brunswick's general factotum and acting Chief of Staff, or Quartermaster General, in the Seven Years' War. Having refused military honours both from Brunswick and the British Government, he accepted the German title of Baron on his alliance with Jean Wishart (1746–1811) the daughter of an Edinburgh minister and a kinswoman of the third Duke of Argyll. On her mother's side, Mrs. Marx was descended from a minor Prussian functionary called Heubel. She was born at Salzwedel in the Mark.

There was more in her make-up of the good provincial *bourgeoise* – except in the matter of thrift – than of the great lady who gives not a snap of the fingers for anyone. Her indignities and deprivations were so much the harder to bear. She cared very much what others thought, was intensely house-proud and entertained meek worldly ambitions for her daughters. Her courage is thus the more to be admired as she stood perpetually on the brink of the relentless tide of debt that rose to disaster level every few weeks, threatening to engulf the whole family. It never quite swamped her but it damped her spirits. Nevertheless, there was an unquenchable optimism in her nature and more than a touch of Mrs. Bennet.

Something of her attitude to the upbringing of children can be discerned from letters written many years later and is wholly sympathetic. Describing a meal at the house of a widower she wrote: "... the children are constantly watched and called to order: they must eat correctly, they must speak correctly; the only thing that is not done according to rule is drinking; to my great astonishment there was neither beer nor wine on the table. ... The children have never yet tasted spirits ...".[25] "... The little boy, a friendly though ugly child, was in a fearful state over an unmanageable duck's leg. He very much wanted to get the little bit of meat off it, but as he did not dare lay a finger on the bone (the governess's eye never leaves the children) the piece of leg slid off the plate. You should have seen the poor boy and, indeed, the whole to-do at the table, the tittering of his sisters, the threatening glare of the governess, the flurry of domestic servants and, on top of it all, G.'s grave sermonising on good table manners...".[26]*

Since Mrs. Marx found this behaviour so absurd it is clear that her own children were never drilled and corrected in a like manner; but as the years advanced she grew more querulous, showing signs of nervous depression until there were times when Marx thought she was taking leave of her senses. Looking back at the age of 58 over her troubled life she wrote to Wilhelm Liebknecht: "In all these struggles, the harder because the pettier part falls to us women. While the men are invigorated by the fight in the world outside, strengthened by coming face to face with the enemy, be its number legion, we sit at home and darn stockings. It does not banish care and the little day-to-day worries slowly but surely sap one's vitality. ... I can truly say that I did not easily allow my spirits to flag. Now I am too old to hope for much any more ...".[28] But then, in 1861, she still hoped, and reacted, with passion, so that the mere mention of the interminable negotiations for a loan – at high interest – which figured so largely in Marx's correspondence, provoked outbursts of a most disquieting nature.

Whether undermined by the combination of her husband's absence abroad, the lack of friendships with women of her own kind, Lenchen's indisposition, Tussy's jaundice, her aversion from the scheme to resume Prussian nationality and the after-effects of smallpox, which had prema-

---

* Mrs. Marx also expressed horror at the cruelties inflicted upon children in the name of medical science. "Poor little H. is in an advanced stage of dropsy. He has a dreadful abdomen and is otherwise like a skeleton ... The cure is appalling. Just imagine, the child is given nothing whatever to drink, not a drop of water, no tea, no coffee, but on the other hand every four days a few glasses of wine. Neither is he allowed a morsel to eat except quite stale bread, dry rusks and nothing else, nothing. At night he is wrapped in wet towels and swaddled in long bandages of linen, flannel, etc., and so put to bed; then dry bread again, without water. And this is supposed to cure dropsy! It is frightful to see...".[27]

turely ravaged her looks, or whether by her time of life – she was 47 –
Mrs. Marx's fortitude collapsed.

Even Dr. Allen was alarmed by her condition whose etiology he
guessed – diagnosing before his time a psychosomatic illness – but had
the delicacy not to name. "This dog's life isn't worth living", wrote Marx:
now that Jenny was old enough to realise the situation, its vileness and
horror were telling on her health; daily Mrs. Marx bemoaned the fact that
she and her children were not in the grave. All this was going on, and felt,
and said. Yet it was impossible to admit to the family doctor or allow him
to mention their hopeless straits.

This keeping up of appearances is not to be mocked. To be sure, a
century later it strikes one as grotesque that a man of such powerful
intellect, a woman of such proper spirit as Karl Marx and his wife should
have deigned to hide their circumstances; should have persisted in
employing two domestic servants and encouraged their almost full-grown
daughters to draw and sing and thump upon the piano with indifferent
talent while the household fell about their ears.

What has to be seen is that, at the time, the gulf between the
respectability of the professional class to which the Marxes belonged and
its alternative, a proletarian way of life, was vast and unbridgeable.* It was
not a question of doing without certain fribbles or cutting down on
luxuries, as they would now be regarded; the Marxes did without and cut
down on sheer necessities. There was often neither food nor fuel in the
house. Rather it was a matter of social and historical realities pressing no
less on Marx than on his contemporaries. The interesting thing about him
is not that he was subject to these pressures, but that it was he who
evolved an entirely new concept of both society and history. "Men's social
being determines their consciousness" he wrote and nowhere claimed
exemption from the rule.

In 1861 nearly a quarter of the male and over one-third of the female
population of England and Wales were illiterate, while the professional
classes represented under 3 per cent: considerably less than the proportion
of paupers. In every trade nine-tenths of the workers were unskilled with
an earning capacity that rarely reached 20s. a week; the Scottish miner
(with a family of above the average of six children to support) earned 24s,
the Manchester carpenter 28s. and the craftsman in the London building
trade 32s. Their living conditions were atrocious and had not greatly
changed since Engels wrote his *Condition of the Working Class in England in*

---

* It is of interest to note that in the Debates on the abortive Reform Bill in 1859 it was
recognised that no working man could afford to pay £10 a year for a house. When the 1867 Bill
finally went through the franchise included householders paying £7 p.a. at which date Marx's
rent was some ten times that amount.

1844. Indeed, he was able to say in the new preface he wrote to the English edition of that work in 1892: "... the most crying abuses described ... have either disappeared or have been made less conspicuous. ... But what of that? Whole districts which in 1844 I could describe as almost idyllic, have now, with the growth of the towns, fallen into the same state of dilapidation, discomfort and misery. Only the pigs and the heaps of refuse are no longer tolerated. The bourgeoisie have made further progress in the art of hiding the distress of the working class. ... Police regulations have been as plentiful as blackberries; but they can only hedge in the distress of the workers, they cannot remove it."

By the 1860s the arts of hiding and hedging were not yet widely cultivated. As late as 1875 "the average age at death of the Manchester upper middle class was 38 years, while the average age of the labouring class was 17; while at Liverpool those figures were represented as 35 against 15. It thus appeared that the well-to-do classes had a lease of life which was more than double the value of that which fell to the lot of the less-favoured citizens."[29]

Keeping up appearances meant most to Marx where his daughters were concerned. He might rail against his wife's mild pretensions as false and pernicious, as "roasting him over a slow fire", yet he shared her aspirations for the girls and took offence at any suggestion that they should attempt to earn their living, for which, in however restricted a field, their polite studies might be thought to have equipped them.

He lamented that they could not join in the amusements of their young friends whose visits to the house they dreaded; he pitied them because they were not presentable enough to attend either their classes or the 1862 International Industrial Exhibition,* for which he himself obtained a permanent press ticket in August as correspondent of the Vienna *Presse*, though it is not known that he ever took his daughters with him. But that they might become self-supporting he looked upon as a mortification outweighing any to which they were daily and hourly exposed. Marx treated as impertinence Lassalle's well-intentioned proposal that they should go to Berlin as companions to the Countess Hatzfeldt; and when he expounded to Engels his plan to declare himself bankrupt, let the landlord sell his furniture, find another situation for Lenchen and move with Mrs. Marx and Tussy into a Model Lodging-House at 3s a week,

---

* Open from 1 May until 1 November 1862 in South Kensington (hence Exhibition Road). Its success was slightly marred by the death from typhoid of the Prince Consort on 14 December 1861. The domes and other distinctive features of the buildings (known as the "Brompton Boilers"), designed by Captain Francis Fowke, R.E. – who was also partly responsible for designing the Albert Hall – were used in the construction of Alexandra Palace, completed in 1873, where, two years later, to commemorate the 21st anniversary of the charge of the Light Brigade, a banquet was given for the 195 survivors.

quite the cruellest aspect of the whole design was that Laura and Jenny —
then 18 and 19 — should take posts as governesses.

Even training for a profession was unthinkable. When Jenny approached Mrs. Charles Young* with a view to studying for the stage, she did
so without her parents' knowledge and naturally nothing came of this
reprehensible step, even though her mother told Mrs. Bertha Markheim in
January 1863 that, were Jenny's health not so delicate, nothing would be
done to discourage her from such a career.

Mrs. Marx might be driven to try to sell her husband's books when all
else had been sacrificed; she might suffer another paroxysm at the renewed
threat of the broker's men and make scenes that caused Marx to go more
frequently to the British Museum than he required for his reading; but it
never struck her that her girls might with greater dignity pursue an
independent life.

With his children's and his servants' footwear in pawn, so that none of
them could leave the house on which a whole year's rent was owing, the
plight of Marx's family appears as great as that of the most miserably paid
worker. In some ways it was worse, for preoccupation with these base
problems effectively stopped Marx working for weeks on end, contributing to and aggravating his ill-health to complete the vicious circle.
But, however their situation compares with that of the proletariat in the
England of the 1860s, one matter is beyond dispute: a middle-aged,
middle-class, Middle-European Doctor of Philosophy simply could not
have been assimilated into it. He had either to struggle on against all odds
— as a few of his kind, but not many, did — to emigrate again or to go into
commerce. In August 1862, conceding that it was a little late in the day
to entertain the thought, he wrote to Engels: "If I but knew how to start a
business"; and, a month later, in a throwaway postscript, he announced
that he might be going to work in the office of an English railway
company in the New Year. Luckily or unluckily, he was not sure which,
his application was turned down on the grounds of his bad handwriting,†
and nothing more was heard of these fantasies.

---

* Jane Elizabeth Thomson (1827–1902), an American actress who made her first appearance in
England in 1857. Previously the wife of an American actor, Charles Young, whose name she
used at this period, she married Hermann Vezin (1829–1910) in 1863 and became well known
under her second husband's name.
† It was indeed appalling and special training was needed to decipher it. Such training Engels
gave to Eduard Bernstein and Karl Kautsky in the late '80s when his eyesight troubled him, so
that others might be able, if he failed, to complete the work of preparing for publication the
"hieroglyphic script" of Marx's literary remains. It was a not inconsiderable factor in the
confusions that arose over the Marx-Engels *Nachlässe*. It proved almost impossible to assign
correctly the authorship of individual manuscripts: Engels had frequently written out *en clair*
his friend's work.[30]

The fact was that at this period Marx was not only writing articles on the American Civil War[31] but, despite the strain of trying to make ends meet, his "brainbox", rather to his surprise, was positively working better than for years past and he produced the whole first draft of Volume I of *Capital*.

For three weeks in the late summer of 1862 Mrs. Marx took the children to Ramsgate. (No distinction was ever made between the two grown girls and their little sister: they were always *"die Kinder"*.) Tussy was still slightly "Chinese" and Jenny, who had been asthmatic since childhood, now had a persistent cough and was rapidly losing weight, a source of uneasiness – and doctor's bills – for many months. During their absence, his negotiations for a loan having proved fruitless, Marx again visited his uncle in Zaltbommel and his mother in Trier. Reunited in September the family found that progress had been made: everyone was in a better state of health and Marx had set in train new and even more hopeful and elaborate transactions to raise a loan. Nevertheless, the butcher was owed £6, the tide of debt was rising irresistibly again and there was no money in the house. Engels' rescue operations temporarily stemmed the inundation while Mrs. Bertha Markheim now sent Mrs. Marx three separate money orders from Germany in as many months at the end of 1862 and the beginning of 1863, one at least of which was known to be for £6.[32]

That winter, when Tussy was nearing her eighth birthday, her parents' misfortunes reached their high-water mark. As though all the malign forces, from the merely mischievous to the near-tragic, had awaited this moment to conspire, the Marxes were buffeted by wave upon cruel wave.

For a year past the second servant, Marianne Kreuz, had been on the list of Dr. Allen's patients. She suffered from a heart complaint that caused him serious misgivings in mid-December 1862, at which juncture Mrs. Marx had just left for France.

Prone to minor accidents, Mrs. Marx had but to step out on a frosty morning to fall and sprain her hand*, or to bite upon something hard to lose two of her front teeth, whereas should she go to the dentist in frightful pain an unoffending tooth that had not caused a single pang was bound to be drawn; but what befell her on this journey defies the laws of probability.

She intended to see Monsieur Arbabanel, a banker who had befriended her and Marx in their Paris days. Her purpose goes without saying. On crossing to Boulogne the Channel packet ran into a high storm and while it did not positively founder, as did a sister-vessel, it tossed about horridly

---

* In extenuation it should be noted that, where they existed, the pavements in Kentish Town until late in the 19th century were of slate, notoriously treacherous in wet or icy weather.

so that the passengers were much alarmed. Monsieur Arbabanel lived
outside Paris. To reach his house Mrs. Marx took a train whose locomotive
broke down, necessitating a halt of two hours for repairs, during which
interval M. Arbabanel had a stroke, lying paralysed and at death's door
when she arrived.* On her return to the city after this hapless errand, she
boarded an omnibus which was at once involved in a collision. Shaken but
uninjured she made her way back to London where, not feeling at her
best, she allowed herself the luxury of a fly whose wheels became somehow
interlocked with those of another. In consequence she had to get out and
walk, two small boys carrying her trunks. She arrived at Grafton Terrace
to be met by the news of Marianne's death which had occurred during the
hour when she was plodding her homeward way. It was 23 December and
the funeral had to be postponed until Christmas was over. Marianne was
buried on 27 December.†

Still the tide of troubles did not ebb. At the culminating crisis of
Marx's money difficulties and in the oppressive atmosphere of a house in
mourning, with the bailiffs at the door, came the news that on the night
of 6 to 7 January 1863 Mary Burns, with whom Engels had lived for
twenty years, had died very suddenly at the age of 40 "of natural causes",
as the coroner's inquest established.

Marx's first response to this event, a dismissive phrase of condolence
followed by a lengthy and precise account of his own troubles, came near
to wrecking a friendship of the utmost importance to both men.

Owing largely to his exceptional qualities, and also a little to Marx's
isolated life, Engels was at this stage of history the only person in the
world who recognised Marx's towering genius and the true importance of
his work. Without Engels' support, intellectual and moral no less than
financial, *Capital* could not have been written. Whether Marx's letters
dealt with the most far-reaching and profound questions of economic,
political and philosophical theory or with his own practical and domestic
difficulties, Engels responded unstintingly with advice, encouragement,

---

* He did not in fact die for another month.
† Mrs. Marx in her reminiscences said that Marianne had been with the family for five years
before her death. This would have meant that she had come to them in 1858 and certainly in
the summer of that year Marx referred to his domestic servants in the plural. Eleanor, on the
other hand, in the passage she wrote for incorporation in Liebknecht's memories of Marx, speaks
of Marianne joining the household "after your time", that is, August 1862 when Liebknecht
went back to Germany. Here Eleanor is mistaken, for Marianne appears in the 7 April 1861
census returns at 9 Grafton Terrace, aged 25. It is curious nonetheless that in his intimate
picture of the Marx household as he knew it Liebknecht never mentioned her existence.
Although she is entered in the census returns under the surname Kreuz, as her death certificate
confirms, she is said to have been Lenchen's half-sister, having been born on 27 June 1835 of
unknown paternity to her widowed mother by whose maiden-name, Kreuz, for no clear reason,
she was known.

the fruits of his own knowledge and with money. Now, for the first and only time, it was he who had a need – the need for sympathy – and Marx failed him.

This stark insensibility, which Engels chose to interpret as great fortitude of mind, cut him to the quick. There were delays in writing and then there were gaps in what had been a continuous, at times a daily – even twice daily – correspondence.*

Engels' reply, a modified version of his first draft, expressed his bitterness, but briefly and with all restraint, and he turned immediately to Marx's concerns, promising £25 and suggesting the name of a life insurance society for a loan. With his innate charity of mind he snatched wholeheartedly at Marx's half-hearted apology; for it was this moment that Marx chose to unfold his desperate scheme to declare himself bankrupt with all it entailed, thus aggravating while professing to repent of his initial lack of grace. Upon this Engels sent £100, borrowed at some risk to himself, to stave off the extreme measures threatened. Thanking for this "great and unexpected help", Marx threw the blame for the rift on Mrs. Marx's shoulders – with musings upon the irrational nature of women – and so it was healed. For a short moment the calamity of losing this friendship loomed darker for both men than any part of their separate anguish. They averted it, but narrowly. Perhaps Engels never quite forgot the injury, for when his sister, Marie Blank, died of scarlet fever in 1869, he wrote to her husband: "No condolences can help in such cases ... and I do not write to condole but simply because I know it does one good to be shown the sympathy of those from whom one can allow oneself to expect it."

For the next many weeks Engels felt his loneliness unbearably. He tried to learn Slavonic which proved small consolation and turned to less exacting diversions. He also took to sending Tussy stamps for her collection. She could not be dissuaded from acknowledging these in person and there must have been a brisk exchange of letters for, in May 1863, not having heard from Marx for some time, Engels wrote to ask whether he was ill, deep in economics or had he perhaps appointed Tussy as his secretary to deal with his correspondence. Though Marx had done nothing quite so reckless, he had now enlisted Laura as an assistant and she accompanied him to the British Museum, for which she held a Reader's ticket.[33]†

---

* There were twelve postal deliveries on weekdays in Kentish Town at this time and one on Sundays. The gaps in the correspondence of this period cannot be attributed to the known destruction of letters by Engels after Marx's death and by Laura and Eleanor after Engels'. Those that have survived are not only clearly in sequence but there are references to the absence of communication.

† The lower age limit for the Reading Room was raised from 18 (in 1842) to 21 in 1863. Laura's ticket, issued on 18 May 1863, was granted on the recommendation of Mr. A. Deutsch

Marx was in fact still anxious about Jenny's continued loss of weight and exasperated by Mrs. Marx's latest symptom, which took the form of partial deafness, so it was with relief that, on the strength of a further remittance from Mrs. Markheim, he packed off the family to Hastings attended by Mr. Henry Banner, the girls' music teacher, from 14 August to 1 September. That autumn of 1863, by which time his long established habit of working far into and sometimes throughout the night had taken its toll, Marx underwent the first operation for the abscesses and carbuncles that were to plague him from now on.‡ This condition was not at the time always dealt with by surgery and the recommended treatment was more usually large doses of opium. Marx, however, was prescribed four times his usual intake of food, four glasses of port and half a bottle of claret daily. This regimen failed to cure him and he could not sleep, so one-and-a-half quarts of the strongest London stout were added to his diet. Still he did not recover; and he was in considerable pain when, at 4 p.m. on 30 November – the hour and the date of her marriage fifty years before – his mother died. A week later, borrowing the fare from Engels, he set out for Trier, then travelled to Frankfurt to see his aunts, Esther Kosel and Babette Blum, and finally to Zaltbommel to settle the formalities of his mother's will with Lion Philips, her executor. The strain told on him: fresh boils and carbuncles broke out and he was obliged to stay in Holland for nearly two months, by which time he received his inheritance of some £750.[35] Part if not all of the money he received in 1,000 Dutch gulden notes which he changed on his return journey *via* Rotterdam in February 1864.[36]

It looked as though the direful years were over. Eleanor was nine and can safely be left to speak for herself.

---

who was employed at the Museum. Regrettably, for she was not 18 until the following September, Laura signed a declaration that she was over 21.
‡ Marx's liver disorder and his carbuncles could well have been connected, both conditions arising from a generalised staphylococcal infection, which could not have been diagnosed as such until the late 1880s. Both ailments were liable to be aggravated by alcohol.[34]

Not that she had been exactly silent, for Eleanor was a great talker, a passionate partisan of the North in the American Civil War, with a sneer at *The Times* leader which expressed admiration for Lee's strategy – "It considers this very canny, I daresay" – and in general pronouncing her views upon international affairs in and out of season. That she was well informed on worldly matters and never excluded from their discussion in the family is illustrated by her comment upon Ferdinand Lassalle who, at the end of August 1864, was killed at the age of 39 in a senseless duel fought over Helene von Dönneges whom he had wished to marry. According to Laura, Lassalle had always made clear to each lady in her turn that he was constitutionally unable to love her for more than six weeks. Tussy, on the *nil nisi bonum* principle, remarked kindly that at least he could be relied upon – she used the grand word "warranted" – for that length of time.

She also emerges in another sense, for now one can see what she looked like. Perhaps the best-known photograph of her – it has so often been reproduced – is also the earliest to have survived. There she is, the centre of a group composed of her father, Engels and her two large sisters who, with their hats like ornamented pancakes and voluminous skirts sweeping the ground, look about 45 though they were not yet 20. Smug and neat in her little sporting topper, Eleanor, apparently perched on her sisters' crinolines, her thin legs and elastic-sided boots dangling, looks away from the camera with dark, amused eyes. She is not so much a pretty as an attractive child, anxious to please, one feels, and confident of succeeding; a little girl who would have had some difficulty in keeping still and even more in keeping quiet for the photograph to be taken. But the wide, firm, good-humoured mouth and resolute chin are unmistakably those of Abraham Lincoln's adviser.

During these years, as may be imagined, her schooling had been irregular and her treats rare. These, when they occurred, were sedate and free of charge. At five or six she was taken to a Roman Catholic Church – arousing qualms in so confirmed an atheist – to listen to the music; at eight she went twice to hear a secular preacher make Voltairean quips at the Bible. She never resented this lack of lighter entertainment, though in after years she did complain that little had been spent on her education. At the time it troubled her not at all. She was far too busy with her letter-writing, her chess, her stamp collection, her political interests and the dressing of dolls. Thanks to Engels she was also a wine connoisseur from the most tender age.

She kept up a correspondence on and off all her life with Wilhelm Liebknecht, about whom a word must be said if for no other reason than that Eleanor sent almost her last, as she wrote her very first letter to him. This is not the place to record his career as a revolutionary socialist, a member of the Reichstag and a most frequent inmate of German gaols. Born in Giessen, Hesse, on the east bank of the Lahn near Marburg in 1826, he took part in the Paris street fighting of 1848 and the Baden insurrection of 1848–49 after which he was "forcibly transported through France from gaol" to Switzerland. In 1850 or 51 – the date is somewhat uncertain – he came to London where he stayed for a time in a Model Lodging-House in Old Compton Street and then, for some years, at 14 Church Street,* Soho. He was a daily visitor to the Marxes in Dean Street. Shortly after they moved to Kentish Town he followed them, living at 3 Roxburgh Terrace until he went back to Germany in August 1862. He maintained a continuous correspondence with both Marx and Engels and many of their letters to him – as to each other about him – are peppered with irate not to say furious criticism: he was slapdash, a donkey, a dunderhead, almost invariably did the wrong thing at the wrong time, a wretched, even catastrophic, tactician, he muffed his chances and his inefficiency was unspeakable. He so exasperated them that the letters would scarcely lead one to believe that they held him in deep affection. Yet such was the case and during his many terms of imprisonment Engels never failed to send words of comfort and material help to his wife. It is the only case in his published letters in which Engels did not mince his words – Marx was never a mincer – and is to be explained by the fact that he expected more and better things of one he loved and unreservedly trusted.†

Liebknecht's importance to the biographer of Eleanor – as also to other biographers – lies not only in the correspondence but also in the publication of his reminiscences of Marx[37] incorporating a long passage he had asked Eleanor to write.‡ Liebknecht came to England in the early

---

* Renamed Romilly Street in 1937. The French socialist émigrés of 1848 founded their London club in this street in 1850.
† Engels later described him as "an optimist by nature who sees everything through rose-coloured glasses. This keeps him cheerful and is one of the main reasons for his popularity, but it also has its drawbacks". (May 1883.)
‡ While of the greatest interest, his sympathetic account is not a completely reliable guide. Wrong dates are given for the births and deaths of the Marx children, some of the misinformation being supplied by Eleanor who seems to have been rather hazy on these points, while a letter she wrote to Liebknecht correcting her first version of Helene Demuth's early life

summer of 1896 to stop with Eleanor and together they made a pilgrimage to the old haunts he had known: to Dean Street and to Grafton Terrace, noting the familiar landmarks that remained and the bewildering changes that had taken place.

Her earliest letter to him – written at the age of six when he was 35 years old – is a note of small consequence, as one would expect between close neighbours. It is in a less rounded hand, more in the German style, than her efforts of a year or two later – as though it had been taken down by someone else at her dictation and painstakingly copied – addressed to "Dear Library", as the family called him,* and signed, mysteriously, "*Niemand*".†[38] Later, when the Liebknechts had left London, she also kept up a correspondence with Alice Liebknecht, two years her junior, to whom she was always inclined to show off, boasting first of her stamp collection and then of her "measels", while affectionately regretting that her little friend, now in Berlin, was no longer there to play with the cats and go for long walks on Hampstead Heath.

While her father was staying with the Philips family in the winter of 1863 Eleanor started a genial correspondence with her great-uncle Lion.

> "My dear Uncle", she wrote, "Although I have never seen you I have heard so much about you that I almost fancy I know you, and as there is no chance of my seeing you I just write these lines to ask you how you are. Are you enjoying yourself? I am, and always do at Christmas time which I think is the jolliest in the year. I wish you a very happy new year, and dare say you are as glad to get rid of the old one as I am. I hear from papa that you are a great politician so we are sure to agree. How do you think the Poles are getting on? I always hold up a finger for the Poles those brave little fellows.‡ Do you like A.B.?§ He is a good friend of mine.

---

was never used in this little volume of 1896 which, perpetuating the errors of fact, has remained a source-book for students ever since.

* Although Liebknecht himself never understood how he derived this nickname, it seems fairly obvious that in England the natives found his name altogether too difficult and pronounced it in a garbled manner that suggested to the Marx children the first syllable of the familiar word "library".

† "Nobody".

‡ From early in 1863 there had been a general insurrection in Poland, put down by the Russians with great violence, including the execution of prisoners. At the time of Eleanor's letter the final defeat of the uprising was not yet assured. On 12 November 1863, at the Bell Inn, Old Bailey, George Odger, secretary of the London Trades Council, read out the text of an appeal to the governments of England and France calling for a united effort in support of Poland's freedom, "to prevent ... the devil's tragedy" being "played over again ... making that fair land once more a huge slaughterhouse to the everlasting shame and disgrace of the civilised world". The Inaugural Address of the IWMA, written by Marx in October 1864, included the words: "The shameless approval, mock sympathy, or idiotic indifference, with which the upper classes of Europe have witnessed heroic Poland being assassinated by Russia ..." Marx's own writings of this period on the subject were found amongst his unfinished MSS. after his death and not published until nearly a century later.[39]

§ (Louis) Auguste Blanqui.

But I must say goodbye now, but dare say you will hear from me again.
Give my love to cousin Nettchen* and to Dada.
Goodbye, dear Uncle.
                    I am
                         your affectionate
                              Eleanor Marx."[40]

It speaks volumes that Christmas, a season which had heralded with
awful regularity the climax of her parents' tribulations, was for Tussy the
"jolliest in the year". Here is Mrs. Marx on the same subject: "Our last
two Christmases"– she is speaking of 1862 and 1863 – "were inexpres-
sibly sad. Two years ago we were all lamenting our poor little Marianne
who had just relinquished her sweet young life. ... Last year my husband
was recuperating from a dangerous and painful illness...."[41]

To Eleanor's great satisfaction Philips sent her a doll for which she
thanked him in a letter with an enclosure purporting to be written in
Chinese characters. Her Chinese leanings† were, indeed, so marked at this
period that her father called her the "Chinese Successor"; but that may
have been because occasionally Jenny was known as the Emperor, and
sometimes the Empress, of China and had evidently abdicated.

A bitterly cold wet March confined Tussy to bed with a cough, interrupting the correspondence with her great-uncle to whom she continued to
send greetings and communicate her opinions on the political scene. "In
regards to the Danish question", her father wrote to Philips on 29 March, "she
begs me to tell you that 'she don't care for such stuff' and that 'she considers
one of the parties to the quarrel as bad as the other and perhaps worse'."‡

To cement the bonds with her relations in Holland she learnt to read
Dutch and to get by heart some Dutch children's songs. The next letter to
her great-uncle, written in June that year, provides a thumbnail self-
portrait of Tussy at nine.

"My dear Uncle,
    It was very kind of you to send me your Carte de Visite.§ I am getting on very well
with my chess. I nearly always win and when I do Papa is *so* cross.

---

* Annette Philips.
† In case these should be thought a trifle bizarre, it may be recalled that between 1853 and
1860 Marx wrote a series of articles on China for the *New York Daily Tribune*.[42] China and the
"Opium Wars" of 1856 and 1859, the capture of Pekin and destruction of the Summer Palace
in 1860, and Gordon's campaigns in 1863 and 1864 must have been matters of common table-
talk in Grafton Terrace.
‡ This refers to the dispute between the Danes and the Prussians over Schleswig and Holstein.
Lord Palmerston cannot have known about Tussy when he said that only three people had ever
understood the Schleswig-Holstein question: the Prince Consort, who was dead, a German
professor who was mad, and Palmerston himself, who had forgotten all about it.
§ A small photograph, 3½" by 2½", mounted on a card.

What do you think of affairs in America? I think the Federals are safe, and though the Confederates drive them back every now and then, I am sure they will win in the end. Were you not delighted about the Alabama?* Of course you know all about it; at all events a Politician like you ought to. As for poor Poland I am afraid there is no help for it. But I have had enough of Politics.

I hope to see you soon in Holland and till then goodbye. Don't forget to give my love to Nettchen.

I am, dear Uncle,
Your affectionate friend,
Eleanor Marx.

They tell me this is the longest day but to me it seems as short as any other – perhaps shorter. Can you make that out?"[43]

Meanwhile, of course, she kept up with Engels who was the main source of supply both for her stamp collection and her dolls' wardrobe. He sent her pieces of cotton whose quality, she asked Marx to convey to him that summer, had "somewhat improved". She also wrote frequently to "lupus", Wilhelm Wolff, who enjoyed her letters during his last illness in the spring of 1864. He was thought – though there was some disagreement among the doctors – to have meningitis but, whatever the cause, he died on 9 May at the age of 55. Marx was the main beneficiary under his will.†

Legacies, like misfortunes, seem never to have come singly to the Marxes. Now the double inheritances from Wolff and Marx's mother – assessed in all at some £1,500 – as those from Mrs. Marx's relatives eight years before, floated them to a new house. Without an instant's delay, Marx having got back from Holland only on 19 February, they moved

---

* *Alabama*, a steam vessel built by Laird's at Birkenhead for the Confederate service, was launched on 15 May 1862 under the name *Eurica* and ostensibly on trials. Once in the open sea, she made for Holyhead, dropped the name – and the passengers who had acted as neutral cover for her warlike purpose – and picked up her armament at the Azores. After doing considerable damage to Federal mercantile shipping as a privateer, she was destroyed on 19 June 1864 off Cherbourg by the Federal ironclad *Kearsage*. The government litigation and claim for damages dragged on for years. When, in 1872 an international court settled that the British government should pay over £3 million in compensation, it was a moment of such prosperity and large revenues that the nation was said to "have drunk itself out of the *Alabama* difficulty". Extra concessions, wrung from the British in the course of the lengthy negotiations, were attributed by Marx to the anti-British pressure of the Irish in America. Incidentally, the engagement between *Kearsage* and *Alabama* was the subject of Manet's first seascape.
† Born on 21 June 1809 in Tarnau, the son of a Silesian farmer, Johann Frederick Wilhelm Wolff was imprisoned in Prussia for four years in the 1830s for his part in the revolutionary students' movement. He emigrated to Brussels where he first met and worked with Marx in 1845, from which time they remained on the closest terms. After a stay in Switzerland, Wolff came to England in 1851. He died at 29 Carter Street, Chorlton upon Medlock. His will provided that if Marx predeceased him, the legacy should be divided among the Marx girls at the age of 21 or on marriage. Marx dedicated Volume I of *Capital* to Wilhelm Wolff: "My unforgettable friend; intrepid, faithful, noble protagonist of the proletariat."

before the end of March 1864 into No. I Modena Villas* where they were to stay for the next eleven years.

This house, one of two dwellings of the better sort built near to Haverstock Congregational Chapel, was in Maitland Park, "a pleasing and elevated locality on which new buildings of a neat and commodious character have within a few years been erected", according to the first (1862) St. Pancras Directory.† It was barely a stone's throw from Grafton Terrace but in every way more elevated and commodious than anything the family had known, Marx working in a large airy study on the first floor overlooking the park, not yet then entirely built over, while each girl had a room of her own.

Marx took a three-year lease from the landlord, Mr. Sawyer,‡ at £65 a year, with rates of £4 8s. 0d., an increase of over 80 per cent on the expenses at Grafton Terrace.§ Naturally before they left the old home the debts and duns had to be paid off. Mrs. Marx then spent £500 on the move and, subscribing to the view that "it is a sad thing to pass through the quagmire of parsimony to the gulf of ruin", let herself go with rollicking improvidence. Early in July Marx recorded that she was attending auction sales. Later that month she wrote to the first Mrs. Liebknecht (Ernestine), referred to the inheritance from her mother-in-law and went on to say that, after redeeming their belongings from pawn: "the first thing we did with the rest of the money ... was to move to our present new house. You have no idea how hateful to me the old house had

---

* Also spelt 'Medina' on contemporary maps and in Directories, justifying Engels' pretty pun that Marx's home was "the Medina of the emigration". It is now demolished, so that the size and character of the house can be deduced only from descriptions and the Ratebooks. But when Engels planned to live in London he stipulated his need for two living rooms, a study and four or five bedrooms, adding: "it does not have to be as big as your house and smaller rooms would do for me".

† In 1842 Ebenezer Maitland bought 13 acres of a property known as "Morgan's land", adjoining the former Southampton Estates, where he financed the building of new premises for an Orphan Working School of which he was the president. This non-sectarian institution, for children of both sexes between the ages of seven and eleven, had been founded in Hoxton in 1758, moved to the City Road in 1773 and to Maitland Park in 1847. It was incorporated by Act of Parliament in 1848. In 1860 the orphanage was enlarged to house some 400 children, at which time the whole of Maitland Park was developed as a residential area. Damaged by bombing in the Second World War, the old houses were pulled down to make way for the site of the present Maitland Park Estate of Council flats the first block of which was opened in 1948.

‡ This was Samuel Sawyer, a builder, who had occupied the next-door house in Grafton Terrace. He appears in the 1861 census as "Sanger", but that need not worry anyone, for his neighbour is entered as "Karl Mara" under which surname even Helene (Demuth) appears. The 1862 Directory, more reliable in its spelling, gives the occupant of No. 10 as Sawyer.

§ The rateable value of No. 1 Modena Villas when Marx first occupied it was £64 and the gross estimated rent £75, so this time, unlike the last, Marx was getting a bargain. There was also a "House Duty", imposed instead of window tax in 1851, on all dwellings rented at over £20 a year for domestic as distinct from farm or trade purposes.

become since the death of our little Marianne and how happy we all feel in
the cheerful new rooms. ... If only I could show you into our drawing-
room or, better still, into the charming conservatory, decked out with
flowers and climbing plants which flourish under Jennychen's excellent
care. But before I take you into the holy of holies, let me acquaint you
with the setting of the palace. Do you remember the small chapel at the
entrance to the Park? Close by two pretty, elegant houses have been built.
The first of these – not next to the church but the first as you enter the
Park – is our present domicile. Elegant wide steps lead through a small
flower garden into the house whose spacious pleasing entrance-hall strikes
everyone. We bought the so-called fixtures from the previous tenant* and
instead of being obliged to furnish as before in the most sparing fashion,
this time we set aside something more for the furniture and decorations,
so that we can receive anyone without embarrassment. I thought it better
to put the money to this use rather than to fritter it away piecemeal on
trifles. Both girls have arranged their charming bedrooms for themselves
and Jennychen's is a sort of Shakespeare museum. ... But the best thing
about the house is its open healthy situation, standing, so to speak,
entirely on its own, without neighbours or anyone opposite and at the
same time with a large well laid-out garden. Tussy has shot up and
engages in a host of unprofitable pursuits. She is a first-rate chess-player
and Mr. Wilhelm Pieper came off so badly against his young opponent
that he lost his temper.

"I cannot tell you how deeply pained we were by the death of our dear
good lupus . . .".[44]

Flown with pleasure in her new house, Mrs. Marx quite forgot to
mention the legacy from dear good lupus. Probate had now been granted
and Marx had received some £230 in early June, using part of it to
speculate in American funds, on which he made a killing of £400:
"squeezing a bit out of the enemy", as he called it. A further £350 from
the Wolff estate came in early July, a week or so before Mrs. Marx penned
her euphoric letter.

The year 1864 certainly went with a swing. After the excitements of
the move the glorious spending spree was kept up. In the summer Jenny
accompanied her father to Ramsgate for three weeks' convalescence. There
they were joined by Laura and Tussy and, for a few days a little later, by
Lenchen. Upon their return Mrs. Marx took a fortnight's holiday by
herself as a "parlour boarder" with a family in Brighton. There was also a
plan for Marx to take the girls to Zaltbommel in September, frustrated at

---

* A Mr. Henry John Watkins in whose day, curiously enough, and up to the year before the
Marxes occupied the house, the rateable value and gross estimated rent were considerably
higher.

the last moment by an outbreak of smallpox in the Philips household, though not before "the children" had been finely rigged out for the visit.

Tussy now went punctually to school. Another innovation was that the family dined at 5 p.m. – it is uncertain when and if they had dined in former days – while the girls embarked on a course of calisthenics to strengthen their physique.

It was indeed a year of beginnings, great and small, for on 28 September the First International was inaugurated at a meeting in St. Martin's Hall, Long Acre,* and now Tussy gave her first real party, though admittedly a makeshift.

"It has become possible to provide the girls with a pleasant and respectable setting, so appointed that now and again they can receive their English friends without fear or shame", wrote Mrs. Marx to Ernestine Liebknecht. "We had placed them in a false position and the young are still thin-skinned and sensitive."[45] They had been asked out so often and unable to return hospitality that they had reached the point of declining all invitations. Now they themselves could entertain. Accordingly on 12 October they gave a ball for 50 young people who kept up the revelry until four in the morning. It was a lavish affair with so many good things left over that on the next day an impromptu children's party was arranged for Tussy.

This whirl of pleasure, with no thought of the morrow, continued into the next year. The Marxes began to behave like people who enjoy a tolerably good and perfectly assured income. In February 1865 Tussy wrote to "My dear Frederick," (Engels) to say that she and her sisters were organising a little party "in honour of Mama's birthday"† and "should be very much indeed obliged if you would send us a few bottles of hock and claret". As they were giving the party without the help of their elders they wanted it "to go off very grandly". This gift was to be in the nature of a Valentine, but "to be sent as early as you can, please".[46] Engels was prompt and efficient as always and received a warm acknowledgment from his "affectionate friend Eleanor Marx".[47]

House guests were entertained too. In March Marx's brother-in-law Jan

---

* Where on 27 February 1855 the inaugural meeting of an International Committee had been held (see p. 8). The Hall was built by subscription in 1847 and presented to John Pyke Hullah, a Worcester-born composer who enjoyed great renown in his day. It was inaugurated in 1850 as a concert hall and burnt down ten years later. It was in the rebuilt hall, dating from 1861, that the foundation meeting of the IWMA took place. This was demolished in 1867. In the years 1865–1866 the headquarters of the General Council was at 18 Greek Street. (In 1961, at the same address, a night club known as The Establishment was opened and flourished briefly as a satirical cabaret.) From January 1866 to June 1867 the General Council met at 18 Bouverie Street.

† On 12 February.

Juta, a Dutch merchant, bookseller and publisher who had settled in the Cape, came to stay for a week bringing with him Caroline Schmalhausen, the daughter of Marx's elder sister, Sophie, from Maastricht.

At this point Eleanor, now ten, wrote her "Confession", a popular pastime of the day.[48]

Your favourite virtue		Truth
" " " in man		Courage
" " " in woman		(left blank)
" chief characteristic		Curiosity
" idea of happiness		Champagne
" " " misery		Toothache
The vice you excuse most		Playing the Truant
" " " detest "		Eves Examiner*
Your aversion		Cold mutton
Your favourite occupation		Gymnastics
" " poet		Shakespeare
" " prose writer		Captain Marryat
" " hero		Garibaldi
Your favourite heroine		Lady Jane Grey
" " flower		All flowers
" " colour		White
" " names		Percy, Henry, Charles, Edward
" " maxim and motto		"Go a head"

Eleanor's favourite hero, Garibaldi, had visited London the year before, when the largest procession of workers that London had ever seen, trade union banners flying, took six hours to escort him from Nine Elms Station to Stafford House† in Stable Yard, St. James's Palace.

This little document was filled in on 20 March 1865, the day after

---

* The detestable vice referred to was *The School Examiner* by Charles Eves, a volume published in 1852 containing some 4,000 exercises on Sacred History, Geography, English Grammar, Arithmetic and the like.

† This sumptuous mansion was originally built on borrowed money at the instigation of the Duchess of Rutland by Benjamin Dean Wyatt in 1825–26 for George IV's brother, the Duke of York, thus finally ruining his shaky finances. He died before it was completed and it was taken over by the then Marquess of Stafford who became the first Duke of Sutherland. The Crown lease was sold to the second duke in 1841 when the building was completed by Charles Barry and Robert Smirke. It was here that the third duke accorded Garibaldi the scant hospitality of one room. Herzen commented: "One could easily without inconveniencing the owners have lodged in [Stafford House] all the peasant families turned homeless into the world by the duke's father."[15] Renamed Lancaster House in 1912, when it was bought by Sir William Lever, a Lancashire man better known as Lord Leverhulme, who presented it to the nation, it housed the London Museum from 1914 until after the Second World War. A relief bust of Garibaldi remained to commemorate the brief visit of 1864.

Marx had left for Holland, where he stayed for three weeks with the Philipses.

Although it was only now that the Wolff estate was finally wound up* the money had vanished into thin air. It was not a year since he had received his handsome legacies, yet Marx could not find the fare to escort his niece Caroline back to Maastricht. During his absence Mrs. Marx had to appeal to Engels for £3 in order to be able to carry on. The tide of debts flowed back. Back came the familiar round of borrowing, pawning and raising loans. The old pattern of life was re-established.

Engrossed in *Capital*, which had been going well, and his work for the International Working Men's Association† Marx was not earning a penny. Now the well-appointed house – on the furnishing of which he had tried to keep an account, for he was truly amazed that the money had melted away – and the way of life it had inaugurated became a gross and unbearable burden. But how to retrench?

The facts had to be faced: it was not as if he and his wife were on their own; they had three girls of whom two had reached marriageable age – it would have been a different matter had they been boys – and there were still three more chapters of the theoretical section of *Capital* to be written. A new standard of living had been set, the girls were no longer placed in a "false position" but in one of apparent ease and *bienséance*, occupying an altogether more desirable station in life and one likely to improve their prospects. Already there was a young French medical student, Paul Lafargue, who had first met Marx in February 1865, made a good impression and, on his return to London in the autumn, was brought to the house where it became clear that his admiration was not confined to the father. On the occasion of Jenny's 21st birthday on 1 May 1865, celebrated in a subdued manner, most of the principal guests being leading members of the IWMA‡ and of her father's generation, Laura received a proposal of marriage from a younger man, Charles Manning, for whom she "didn't care a pin". But it was evident that suitors would appear, whether acceptable or not and, in the interests of the Misses Marx, it was imperative to maintain at least an air of solvency.

---

* Probate was granted on an estate of £1,348 17s. 0d. on 1 June 1864 but the final winding up of the accounts did not reach Marx until 11 March 1865. Bequests, lawyer's fees, funeral expenses, death duties and a small outstanding debt left a residue of £842 14s. 9d. and some £50 worth of books and other personal effects for Marx.

† Including his answer to propositions on wages put to the General Council on 2 April by John Weston, an old Owenite, and defended by him in *The Bee-Hive*.[49] The answer, given as an Address to the General Council on 20 and 27 June, was found among Marx's papers after his death and, edited by Eleanor, was published in 1898 after her own death under the title *Value, Price and Profit*.[50]

‡ Ernest Jones, George Odger, William Cremer, Hermann Jung and Peter Fox.

It is worth enquiring at this point how much it really cost the Marxes to live. The Board of Trade did not officially record retail prices of consumer goods until 1893; but, taking the first (1904) Cost of Living Index "weights", which assigned between one-sixth and one-seventh of total minimum family income to rent (including rates and water charges), it appears that life in Modena Villas could not have been sustained on less than £430 a year.[51] In 1868 Marx himself wrote to Dr. Ludwig Kugelmann, a gynaecologist in Hanover, that it cost him between £400 and £500. This of course would not include balls and parties or, indeed, any form of entertaining and now, towards the end of May, Edgar von Westphalen came to stay for six months.

This broken man, aged 46, was Mrs. Marx's only brother, after whom she had named her first-born son. She had not seen him for 16 years. In early life he had briefly played a small part in politics and then, when he was 26, he had emigrated to America where he hoped to make his fortune in Texas, leaving behind a fiancée, Lina Schoeler, whom, in the event, he never married and who came to England in the year of Eleanor's birth to seek employment as a teacher, a position she took up in the autumn of 1856. Defeated and ill, Edgar returned to Europe in 1849, only to go back to Texas two years later. Still he did not prosper and, from 1862 onwards, he fought for the South in the Civil War, losing all he had, including his health. As Marx put it: "It is a most remarkable irony of fate that this Edgar, who never exploited anyone except himself and was a workman in the strictest sense of the word, should have fought for the slaveholders in a war of and with starvation."

Mrs. Marx loved him dearly and although his arrival was neither anticipated nor timely, for Marx was suffering from abscesses, toothache and debts, she gave a warm welcome to her "poor, sick, helpless brother".

Marx, while not antagonistic to Edgar, whom he pronounced a "rum customer", "as egoistic as a cat or a benevolent dog", had scant sympathy with this idle, vain, greedy, sexless, selfcentred valetudinarian, described on a rising note of exasperation in letters to Engels. Edgar's major crime, as the months passed, was that he showed no sign of leaving. Admittedly Marx was not the ideal host. He had been driven almost insane by Lassalle who, on his visit to London three years before, had assumed that, since Marx had no job and was engaged on purely theoretical work, he had nothing better to do than to devote his time to the coxcomb.*

Edgar had lived so long as a recluse that he was hardly fit for human

---

* In his rage Marx repeatedly referred to Lassalle as the "Jewish nigger", the "parvenu", the "tuft-hunter" and so forth; but at his death Marx paid him a sober tribute: "after all, he was one of the old guard, and his enemies were our enemies", regretting that their relations had been clouded in the last years.

intercourse, in Marx's view. His cold in the nose, his vegetable existence and pitiable preoccupation with clothes and food – "even his interest in sex has been transferred to his belly" – not to mention the expenses of his keep, became a sore trial.

There was a serious outbreak of cattle-plague that summer.* "Food prices went up so much", Mrs. Marx wrote to Ernestine Liebknecht, "that an extra person with a particularly healthy appetite was noticeable in the exorbitantly higher bills from the ... greengrocer, etc. Meat rose to 1/4 or 1/6 and milk is still today 5d. a quart with proportionate increases for everything else."[52]

The girls took a gentler view of their uncle, Laura with mild irony calling him "an exceedingly bright fellah", while Jenny allowed that he and his deserted fiancée might congratulate themselves on having "safely got rid of each other". Tussy frankly liked him "because he's *so funny*".

There was no question of a seaside holiday and a letter from Marx to Eleanor in that summer was written on the inter. com. system. His address is given in an execrable pun as "Maidena Towers" – over which she probably split her sides – and the date is 3 July 1865:

"Dear Miss Lilliput,

You must excuse the 'belated' character of my answer. I belong to that sort of people who always look twice at things before they decide one way or the other. Thus I was rather startled at receiving an invitation on the part of a female minx quite unknown to me. However, having ascertained your respectability, and the high tone of your transactions with your tradespeople, I shall feel happy to seize this rather strange opportunity of getting at your eatables and drinkables. But, pray, don't neglect the latter, as spinsters usually have the bad taste of doing. Suffering somewhat under an attack of rheumatism, I hope you keep your reception room clear of anything like drafts. As to the ventilation required, I shall provide for it myself. Being somewhat deaf on the right ear, please put a dull fellow, of whom, I dare say, your company will not be in want of, at my right side. For the left I hope you will reserve your female beauty. I mean the best looking female amongst your guests.

I am somewhat given to tobacco chewing; so have the stuff ready. Having from former intercourse with Yankees taken to the habitude of spitting, I hope spittoons will not be missing. Being rather easy in my manners, and disgusted at this hot and close English atmosphere, you must prepare for seeing me in a dress rather Adamitic. I hope your female guests are somewhat in the same line.

---

* The rinderpest, or steppe murrain, originating among the cattle herds of the Russian steppes, spread to Europe and was brought to London in 1865. Several weeks elapsed before the disease was recognised by which time it had been carried to all parts of the country by animals bought at the Caledonian Market, known then as Copenhagen Fields, which had replaced Smithfield for livestock in 1855. It was calculated to have caused a loss of between £5 million and £8 million. On 21 February 1866 an Act of Parliament authorised the slaughter of the infected animals and provided for compensation. The next serious outbreak occurred in 1872. Unlike foot-and-mouth disease, it was eradicated in Britain in 1877.

> Adio, my dear unknown little minx.
>> Yours for ever
>>> Dr. Cranky.
> No *British* wines, I hope!"[53]

It is evident that the Yankee did not curtail the family's social life nor yet Marx's political activities; for it was during his stay that *The Workman's Advocate*, the official journal of the IWMA,* was launched with an authorised capital of £1,000. Marx took five £1 shares: the only subscriber to do so. The others were Friedrich Lessner, tailor; William Cremer, joiner; Edwin Coulson, bricklayer; Robert Applegarth, joiner; George Eccarius, tailor; William Morgan, shoemaker; Hermann Jung, watchmaker; Thomas Grant Facey, painter; William Stainsby, tailor; and John Weston, handrail manufacturer, accounting in all for £23.[54]

When "with a heavy heart" poor Edgar† at last took his leave in November, matters hardly improved at all. Mrs. Marx felt desolate and her husband dared not tell her that the landlord was threatening to withdraw the lease on the house, so badly was the rent in arrears. However, she could not be spared from knowing that Laura was unwell and losing weight, that Tussy had a severe bout of measles, that Jenny had diphtheria and that there was no coal. Engels sent £15, port, sherry and claret. There seemed to be a ray of light when one of Marx's Frankfurt aunts, Esther Kosel, died intestate. (She had refused to draw up a will for fear that it might cause her death.) Her estate in the event was divided between 20 of the next of kin with equal claims upon it and Marx's share turned out to be £13. He decided that, once his book was finished, he would go abroad, possibly to Switzerland, to live more cheaply. He was ill with worry and by no means cheered when Lina Schoeler, who had tactfully kept clear of the house during Edgar's visit but was owed money she had lent to her hosts during a previous stay, came for the month of December.

The New Year was ushered in for Marx, as usual, with blazing carbuncles and mounting debts. There were also serious difficulties with the French branch of the IWMA, founded in London during the previous autumn. The disagreements were over the Polish question and both Charles Longuet, the editor of the anti-Bonapartist paper *La Rive Gauche*, and Paul Lafargue, one of its contributors, were involved.

---

* This weekly journal under the editorship of Eccarius lasted barely six months in its original form. In February 1866 it was reorganised to appear as *The Commonwealth*.

† He was not altogether hypochondriac. On his return to Germany he was medically examined and found to have heart disease. Mrs. Marx believed this to be merely a convenient diagnosis for any condition the doctors did not understand and personally thought that his lungs and brain were affected. However, he lived to the age of 72.

For Tussy, also as usual, the season brought good cheer. Using Laura's writing paper and desk, she left a letter there addressed on the outside in elaborate script "To Miss L. Marx from E. Marx", with many smudges and illegibilities within, to thank for "a darling dolly", "a regular angel", whose christening was her most pressing problem. She already had a Laura, a Beatrice, a Rose Blanch (*sic*), a Jenny, an Athalie, an Edith and an Alice. The stock of female names appeared to have run out until she recalled her Dutch cousin Annette.[55] The cares of so large a family on her eleventh birthday did not prevent her from assisting at the first of the "Sunday Evenings for the People", held at St. Martin's Hall on 28 January in defiance of the Lord's Day Observance Acts, to hear music by Handel, Mozart, Beethoven, Mendelssohn and Gounod. The event proved so popular that over 2,000 people had to be turned away from the hall. As Mrs. Marx wrote: "Until then they had not been allowed to do anything but bawl 'Jesus, Jesus, meek and mild' " – Mrs. Marx was a little weak on her Charles Wesley – "or frequent gin palaces."

Marx's health reached a critical pass that winter and spring of 1866. He suffered abominably and wrote that "it would be all the same to me if I went to the knacker's yard, that is to say, kicked the bucket today or tomorrow", if only there were enough money for the family – "something above minus zero" – and his work were finished. In fact it was, but the "damned book" had been completed in December 1865 only by dint of reading all day at the British Museum and writing all night. However, it was not quite true that he would as soon have died, for he was distinctly enjoying himself. He had begun copying out his manuscript and revising the style. "Naturally", he wrote, "it gives me pleasure to lick the child clean after so many birth pangs."

He had now embarked on a course of arsenic, taking one grain daily as prescribed at long range and second hand *via* Engels by Dr. Gumpert.* Marx did not relish this treatment but Engels assured him that in any case it could do no harm even if it did his carbuncles no good. On these, without anybody's advice at all, he performed a surgical operation, using one of the old razors inherited with Wilhelm Wolff's other effects. What he needed, Gumpert now advised, was sea air. He was willing to go away, but postponed his departure from day to day: first there was a meeting held at his house with the foreign "Corresponding Secretaries" of the International, including Paul Lafargue (for Spain) and Charles Longuet (for Belgium). Then, following a crisis in February, the shareholders of *The Workman's Advocate*, now re-issued as *The Commonwealth*, had to meet; and finally he attended and spoke at the General Council of the IWMA. Thus it was not until mid-March that he went to Margate where he spent the first night at the King's Arms, disliked it and looked for lodgings the next morning. These he found at 5 Lansell's Place: a large sitting-room and a bedroom facing the sea for which he paid 10s. a week to Mrs. Grach the landlady, who was as deaf as a post but considerate.

Undeterred by his ailing condition he at once took a warm sea-bath and went for a five-hour walk. A couple of days later, a Sunday, after

---

* Edward Gumpert, (1843–1893) M.D., Wurzburg 1855, established at 102 Bloomsbury, Manchester. He was a friend of Engels' and a member of the Manchester IWA in 1864. Marx – who said he was the only doctor he trusted – frequently sought his advice, both for himself and his family, either when Dr. Allen's bills were too long unpaid or because the forms of treatment he prescribed entailed rest or other interruptions of work to which Marx would not submit.

promenading the piers for two health-giving hours, he walked the 17 miles to Canterbury – "an old, ugly, medieval sort of town" – in under four hours, but was "happily" too tired and too late to visit the Cathedral. He came back by train to spend a sleepless night as a result of these exertions.

"Ellie", as she temporarily called herself, wrote to her "dear dada" at this point to recall him to his paternal duties. Although he was to have stayed away for an unbroken month the girls were having a party on 22 March which he had promised to attend. "Now, Dr. Karl Marx of bad philosophy", wrote Eleanor, "I hope you will keep your promise and come on Thursday",[56] as of course he did.

This spring festivity was in place of the Christmas party they had planned to give on receiving £5 from uncle Lion Philips. The gift had been instantly expropriated for "general purposes" and was only now restored. The least Marx could do was to be present at the tardy event. As soon as it was over he went back to Margate where he was shortly joined by Jenny and Tussy for ten days, Mrs. Grach letting them have a room without extra charge. Though no letters from Tussy at this period have been traced, she never forgot her Margate holiday, referring to it more than 30 years later, three weeks before her death, when she found herself again in Margate in very different circumstances.[57]

While the family was away Mrs. Marx wrote at some length to Ernestine expressing her views on the evil consequences of an atheistic upbringing. There were all manner of things she could tell Mrs. Lieb-knecht about her girls' little doings and acquaintances, but such relationships were often of so delicate a nature that she did not care to commit an account of them to paper. Laura and Jenny were of very different character, but for both of them "the peculiar bent of their education is bound to bring them into painful conflict with their friends. They have been brought up with ideas and views that form a complete barrier to the society in which they move, and at the same time they are not materially independent." They could not expect their views, running so sharply counter to accepted opinion, to prevail. Had they been young persons of means, they might have managed without "baptism, church and reli-gion"; as things were, they would both have to face bitter struggles. "I often think", wrote Mrs. Marx, "that if one cannot offer one's children riches nor complete independence of others, it is hardly the right thing to bring them up in harsh disagreement with society. They will always find themselves in a false position and these matters weigh heavily upon me." She then confessed that she often seemed cross-grained and peevish to her daughters; this was merely a reflection of her awareness that they would never be able to claim from life the degree of happiness to which their outer and inward endowments entitled them. Both of them, she felt she could truthfully say without the besotted delusions of a mother, were of radiant beauty "but perhaps for this very reason, all the more *out of place* and *out of time*". Naturally, this was strictly in confidence: "girls brought up in England and who have always lived under English conditions, do not much care for outpourings of this kind …".[58]

The "outpouring" appears to have been tapped by the news that Alice Liebknecht, at nine years of age, might have to be baptised, for which, in Mrs. Marx's view, her mother should be thankful, such rituals being less harmful than their omission. Tussy had been proposed as Alice's godmother and was vastly amused by the notion. While on the subject of Tussy, her mother reported her equally irreverent attitude to her father's toothache. Since this affliction, according to her Confession, was her "idea of misery" it might have been expected to excite her sympathy but merely elicited the jeer that her father was frightened of the dentist's forceps. This had the desired effect and Marx went off bravely to have two teeth drawn (in keeping with his own Confession that his "favourite virtue in man" was Strength).

There is an undoubted connection between Mrs. Marx's pessimistic reflections in April and the fact that, at long last in the May of 1866, Jenny and Laura ceased their lessons, the younger giving up her music altogether, the elder, now 22, confining herself to one session a week. There could be no point in their pursuit of social accomplishments if their heathen upbringing foredoomed them to ostracism. This precipitated a fresh crisis, for it is impossible to take final leave of a school without paying the bill and three full terms, amounting to £25, were owing. Engels, who had sent £50 in February and various minor sums throughout the spring, now promised another £50 in July and sent £10 in the meantime.

Toothache and bills were not Marx's only discomforts. The arsenic cure, though he was temporarily free of carbuncles, now appeared to be affecting his liver adversely; he was unable to work and turned again to Dr. Allen but did not follow his prescriptions. The vexatious problems of *The Commonwealth* also came to a head. Always in difficulties and never fulfilling the early hopes that, as a London workers' organ, it would win enough support to become independent, the paper had accepted subsidies to keep it afloat from a Bradford manufacturer named Kell. Marx found this situation ludicrous: he recognised that with such backing and control the character of the journal must inevitably change and, thoroughly sick of the whole affair, he proposed selling out the bankrupt enterprise to Kell and his friends.

As soon as he was well enough, he attended the IWMA meetings where, in June, he heard Paul Lafargue address the General Council, though unfortunately in French of which language nine-tenths of his audience did not understand a word.

This young man, despite political differences with Marx – for he was an adherent of Proudhon* and held the view, according to Marx that, "all Europe must and will sit quietly on its backside until the gentlemen in France abolish 'poverty and ignorance' " – was playing an increasing part in the Marxes' family life. The only son of a successful planter, born on 15 January 1842 in Santiago de Cuba, Paul Lafargue, the last of his line, was of extremely mixed descent. His paternal grandfather, a Frenchman who had emigrated to the Antilles, married a mulatto from St. Domingo, herself a refugee in Cuba from the French Revolution, and it was in St. Domingo that her husband was killed in a revolutionary uprising. Paul's mother's maiden name was Armagnac and she was the daughter of a Frenchman, assumed to be Jewish because he was called Abraham, who had married a Caribbean Indian. In 1851 Paul's parents left Cuba for Bordeaux where M. Lafargue went into the wine trade and Paul to school, later attending the *lycée* at Toulouse until he entered the Medical Faculty of the University of Paris. There he contributed to *La Rive gauche*, edited by Charles Longuet, a fellow-student three years his senior. In 1865, when he was 23, Lafargue was sent to London to report on the French working-class movement to the General Council of the IWMA, where naturally he met Marx. Later in the same year he helped to organise the first Students' International Congress, held in Liège, with the result that he and other delegates, including Longuet, were expelled from the university, a decision that provoked violent student riots. Paul hoped to take his finals in Strasbourg but in the meantime he returned to London where, without much urgency, he continued to study higher mathematics, physics and chemistry under Dr. Carrère, himself a refugee, at Bart's.

As if to confound Mrs. Marx's gloomy forebodings and undaunted by Laura's profanity, Paul now proposed to marry her and by the beginning of August they were "half-engaged". Engels, informed of this curious

---

* Pierre Joseph Proudhon (1803–1865) had propagated and left a legacy of petty bourgeois socialism, attractive both to students and to workers employed in the more sophisticated trades of the metropolis but without much appeal to the peasants or industrial workers of France as a whole. Marx's *Poverty of Philosophy*, an answer to Proudhon's *Philosophy of Poverty*, had ended their friendship as far back as 1847. Proudhonism, however, persisted as an active principle in French politics because, as Marx had put it long before: "Proudhon has the merit of being the scientific interpreter of the French petty bourgeoisie – a genuine merit, because the petty bourgeoisie form an integral part of all impending social revolutions. ... Indeed, he does what all good bourgeois do. They all tell you that in principle ... competition, monopoly, etc., are the only basis of life, but that in practice they leave much to be desired. They all want competition without its tragic effects. They all want the impossible, namely, the conditions of bourgeois existence without the necessary consequences of those conditions."[59]

arrangement, was at a loss whether to offer his half, his whole or no congratulations. He did, however, send a further £50, for since 1864 he had been a partner in the firm of Ermen & Engels and he now guaranteed Marx £200 a year, with apologies that it could not be more.

Apart from young Lafargue's Proudhonism, there were other things about him not entirely to Marx's liking. He applied for references from Lafargue's former professor in Paris, Dr. Jules-Antoine Moilin;* he withheld a direct reply to a civil communication from Lafargue *père* asking him to accept Paul as a son-in-law and finally he sat down and wrote a letter to the *demifiancé*, prompted by regard for Laura's welfare, bidding the young man mend his torrid manners if he wished to consort with her, but couched in such needlessly stern language as to exhibit the Victorian father at his least endearing.†

At the same time he was not only revising his completed draft of Volume I of *Capital* but he had just received and was incorporating the findings of the latest (5th) *Report of the Children's Employment Commission* and the (8th) *Board of Health Report*, an enquiry into the housing of the poor. On the Commission's reports he commented: "Bourgeois complacency since 1850 could receive no more fearful blow than these five Blue Books."

He was also following with close interest the agitation over Gladstone's Reform Bill, now taken up by the London Trades Council‡ through the newly formed London Working Men's Association whose leadership was inspired by the IWMA. When the Bill was rejected, in terms so insulting that the class nature of the opposition was exposed in the crudest way, there was an outcry. Demonstrations took place all over the country and vast meetings were held in Trafalgar Square, where, on 2 July, Benjamin Lucraft, a member both of the Executive Committee of the Reform League and of the General Council of the International, was the main speaker. "The workers' demonstrations in London, which are marvellous compared with anything we have seen in England since 1849", wrote Marx, "are purely the work of the International. ... This shows the difference between *working* behind the scenes while not appearing in public and the Democrats' way§ of being self-important in public while doing nothing."

On 23 July a huge protest demonstration in Hyde Park was called, to

---

* 1832–1871. In 1870 Dr. Moilin was condemned to five years' imprisonment but was liberated on the Proclamation of the Republic, only to be shot in the Luxembourg Gardens by the Versaillais for his part in the Commune.
† See Appendix 2.
‡ Formed in 1860.
§ Under Bright, Cobden having died in 1865.

forestall which Sir Richard Mayne, the Commissioner of Police, declared the meeting illegal and the Cabinet ordered the park gates to be closed.* The angry demonstrators in their thousands stormed the park in the Bayswater Road. Despite the massive presence of police and troops they tore up a hundred yards of the iron railings up to Marble Arch and then, under the provocation of police brutality, proceeded to tear up the rest as far as Hyde Park Corner. "It was touch and go", wrote Marx. "If the railings had been used offensively and defensively against the police and some 20 of them had been struck dead, the military would have had to 'intervene' instead of merely parading. And then there would have been some fun. . . ."

While this great movement was shaking the British working class into furious activity the first Congress of the International was held in Geneva at the start of September. Sixty delegates – English, French, German and Swiss – attended, and Paul Lafargue worked manfully, though not well, at translating the "Instructions to Delegates". With disarming honesty Marx admitted that he could not help liking the young man nor feeling a slight jealousy of him.

Still Laura's fate hung in the balance and, at the end of August, she took Tussy to Hastings where they boarded at a school run by a Miss Davies. One of the drawbacks to this arrangement, Laura wrote to her mother, was "the regular recurrence of meals . . . like the march of destiny . . . they haunt me like ghouls – the four monsters – breakfast, dinner, tea and supper; they cast shadows before them and behind. . . ."[60] Not foreseeing the four monsters Laura, who feared that Tussy might starve, had laid in a stock of biscuits. It rained a great deal and they were often obliged to stay indoors where the windows were hermetically sealed and a piano was played from morning till night. But, conceded Laura, it was not the fault of Hastings, "a divine place", that Miss Davies' school should contain compulsive pianists, unaired rooms, a white dog and an elderly maiden-lady called Miss Case. Firmly Laura announced that Tussy and she would neither go to church on Sunday nor undertake to be home by nine in the evening. Having asserted their spiritual and temporal independence the sisters enjoyed themselves to the top of their bent, using up the £5 Marx had sent them on bathing tickets and cab-rides and then asking him for a further £3. Jenny now joined them, while Mrs. Marx took a week's holiday by herself at the Rose and Crown in Dover and a further week at another resort.

---

* The demonstration was called in part to assert the right of assembly, challenged when the police had put down the mass meeting held on Primrose Hill in 1864 by the Working Men's Garibaldi Committee to protest against the abrupt curtailment, on political grounds, of their hero's too popular visit to England.

Whatever doubts and reservations Marx still harboured, Laura's engagement was formally announced on 26 September 1866, her 21st birthday. She had insisted on also having Engels' consent, which was readily given since he was a great believer in personal happiness. Mrs. Marx was jubilant. In glowing terms she described her son-in-law to Ernestine Liebknecht. Even his "dark olive complexion and extraordinary eyes", which proclaimed him a Creole on sight, did not detract from her enthusiasm. His parents, she wrote, who owned considerable estates in Cuba, had established a prosperous wine-merchant's business in Bordeaux. Paul had acquitted himself brilliantly at the university, taking his BM degree with honours after four years' study. "Fortunately", Mrs. Marx exulted, "he will not be dependent on his practice, always so precarious at the start. His parents are very well-off, owning plantations and house property in Santiago and Bordeaux and, as Paul is their only child, naturally all this will pass on to him. They have behaved capitally towards Laura, welcoming her as their daughter with open arms and have promised the young couple a gift of 100,000 frs. on their wedding-day.* So you see, Frau Liebknecht, in respect of externals, there is nothing left to be desired; but what is even more important is the young man's fine character, his kindheartedness, his generosity and his devotion to Laura. What I consider a quite remarkable piece of luck is that he has the same principles, in particular where religion is concerned; thus Laura will be spared the inevitable conflicts and sufferings to which any girl with her opinions is exposed in society. For how rare it is nowadays to find a man who shares such views and at the same time has culture and a social position. ... I always thought Laura would be a lucky girl!..."[61]

Poor Mrs. Marx, who had not thought so at all barely six months before. And poor Mr. Marx. For Paul Lafargue "in respect of externals" did not come up to scratch nor do what his father-in-law preached but rather what he practised, and for most of his married life, without a vestige of justification – since he was no genius and had no children to feed – Lafargue sponged shamelessly on Engels whose ears and purse were never closed to any of Marx's kin.

Tussy jubilated too and wrote to tell Alice of the engagement "at which you will be as surprised as we were"[62] – her powers of observation and her celebrated curiosity must have failed her here – and that Paul had given her "a *delicious* swing" on which, according to her mother, she performed marvels of daring the livelong day and forgot to go to school.

As though these excitements were not enough, the daughter of an "eminent and aristocratic family of their acquaintance", the Cunning-

---

* Roughly £4,000.

hams, did Jenny and Laura the honour of inviting them to be the sole bridesmaids at her wedding. Mrs. Marx was so overcome by this mark of distinction that it was all she could do to collect her wits and what little money she could to buy the girls "bonnets, cloaks and heaven knows what else" for the occasion.

This incidental extravagance, though unwarranted, was as nothing to the expenses now incurred. Although Mrs. Marx did not approve of long engagements there could be no question of an immediate marriage and, for the time being, life would have gone on much as before but for the rub that "the real state of things" must be scrupulously hidden from the prospective son-in-law who, until he took himself off to see his parents in Bordeaux early in November, was always about the place. The rent was unpaid; Marx borrowed from Withers the baker to pay Sawyer the landlord who held a promissory note from Marx for the wrong amount; and he wrote to his pen-friend the gynaecologist Dr. Kugelmann begging him to try to arrange for a private two-year loan of 1,000 thaler* at 5 or 6 per cent, revealing that he had been paying 20 and even 50 per cent to small lenders. This move miscarried too, for, unable to do what was asked of him, Kugelmann proposed appealing to Engels on Marx's behalf, for which innocent but officious design Marx coldly snubbed him.

As he approached his annual nadir Marx declared that things were as bad as in his worst refugee days: he owed money everywhere; so many articles of clothing were in pawn that, given the season, his wife could hardly venture out of doors; he could not afford the new books he needed – not yet available in the British Museum nor at "Mudy"† – he was working at night and, though on arsenic again, horrifying carbuncles had appeared. To crown all, before 1866 was out, news came of the death not only of his old friend Joseph Weydemeyer in America, but also of his uncle Lion Philips, the last of his relatives to whom he could turn and a man he had grown to trust and admire.

There were just three flickers of light as the year went out: Engels sent another £50, some port and a case of claret; James Stephens, the leader of the Fenians in Ireland, recently escaped from Dublin's Richmond jail, joined the IWMA; and the first batch of Marx's manuscript had at last gone off to Otto Meissner, the Hamburg publisher.

---

* Roughly £175.
† Mudie's Lending Library was founded in 1842 and failed in 1937.

It was of course the publication of his book that mainly absorbed Marx in the year 1867, though not without many distractions.

In January the tiresome Sawyer sold No. I Modena Villas to a Mr. Burton of Torquay where he did not choose quietly to remain but came only too often to London and made devilish trouble about the rent.* He established from the start the character of their future relations by holding a pistol to Marx's head: he must make up his mind here and now whether, when the lease fell in on quarter-day, he wished to take a longer lease, a yearly tenancy, or clear out; the rent was disgracefully in arrears and more satisfactory tenants were not hard to find. It gave Marx insomnia. Engels settled the arrears of rent and, since no more was heard of this problem – though plenty more was heard of Mr. Burton – and the family stayed on for another seven years, it may be assumed that the lease was renewed.

Until the end of March Marx worked intensively on his book, not even pausing to write to Engels. Though his carbuncles, as in the past three winters, were excruciatingly painful, he dropped the arsenic because it made him feel "too stupid" and so long as he was capable of writing his head must be clear. Then the work was done and he planned to take the rest of the manuscript to Meissner in person. He emerged from his concentrated labours to take note that the family was penniless – in which state he could not leave them while he went abroad – and that he would require his watch and some clothes, presently at the pawnbroker, for his journey to Hamburg. Laura was languishing for no very clear reason but one that demanded a small bottle of champagne (costing £2), a course in gymnastics, to be paid in advance, and, as she regained her strength, claret of a quality better than her father could afford. Engels sent £35, but his mind, too, was on other things and: "Hurrah!" he wrote. "This exclamation was irrepressible as I read at last in black and white that Volume I

---

* This gentleman had been hard hit by the failure of Overend & Gurney in 1866, a bankruptcy which not only dealt a blow at joint stock discount houses, from which they were said never to have recovered, but became a national scandal and a *cause célèbre* when the directors were prosecuted in 1869, though acquitted. Mr. Burton, following the crash, prudently decided to put what capital remained to him in house property whereby he hoped to live comfortably on rent for the rest of his days. His misfortune in acquiring Marx as a sitting tenant so soon after the earlier experience might well have shaken his faith in the whole system of rent, interest and profit, but did not do so.

is finished and that you are going straight off to Hamburg with it." He also sent a chit to Meissner instructing him to pay Marx money owing on his own work.[63]

Marx left London on 10 April and was away for nearly six weeks. He took a liking to Meissner, remained at hand to correct the proofs of his book, which was to be printed in four or five weeks by Hugo Wigand in Leipzig, and stayed with Dr. Kugelmann in Hanover, where he was overwhelmed and more than a little bored by the whole family's gushing admiration for Engels and himself. Indeed, it came to him as a great surprise to find in what high esteem he was held among educated Germans.

During his stay he received a tragic letter from Liebknecht, whose wife Ernestine, Mrs. Marx's friend and *confidante*, was desperately ill. Her health had been undermined by the years of poverty in exile while the shock of her husband's expulsion from Prussia in the summer of 1865, followed by his arrest and three months' prison sentence in October 1866, at which time she was pregnant, had dealt a mortal blow. "It is frightful for me to watch her slowly dying", wrote Liebknecht.*

Marx reported this and other news in long and loving letters to his daughters who kept up a regular correspondence with him, including at least one letter from Tussy, written on 26 April:

"My dear Dada, Just as your letter came I was deciding that you never could stay away a whole fortnight without writing, and I never would forgive you but my rage began to evaporate amazingly quickly as soon as your letter was read and now I'm actually writing to you. ... Paul has been keeping me in books, he got me Cooper's *Deerslayer, Homeward Bound, The Effinghams*, and I am going to read the *Watermate* and *Two Admirals*. You see I'm quite 'going the hog'. ... On Good Friday I eat sixteen hot cross buns, Laura and Jenny eat eight. Louisa and Percy Freiligrath came here the other day. Percy jumped out of the window on the first landing, because I said he could not, and he wrote me he would jump out again if I ordered him to. ... Paul and Laura have had three riding lessons. ... The days after the lessons however both were rather stiff and I had to make Paul a cushion to rest his bruised behind upon. I was

---

* A month later, on 29 May 1867, Ernestine Liebknecht died in great agony, leaving two little daughters: Eleanor's friend Alice, now ten, and the infant Gertrud. The one married Bruno Geiser the other Wilhelm Swienty. In 1868 Liebknecht took a second wife, Natalie. She presented him with five sons of whom the second, Karl, born on 13 August 1871, became the leader of the German *Spartakus* movement and was murdered, together with Rosa Luxemburg, on 15 January 1919.

much surprised to receive a letter from Franziska.* Now dear Dady goodbye. Believe me, Your UNdutiful daughter Eleanor."[64]

There were also letters from Engels, who was providing for the family in Modena Villas, not forgetting Jenny's birthday, and who now, on 27 April, wrote to tell Marx that in all probability he and his partner, Godfrey Ermen, who did not hit it off, would separate at the end of their present contract in two years' time, if not earlier. In that case he would abandon altogether the filthy world of commerce, with its utterly demoralising waste of time. At all events, he wrote, his life as a businessman would cease in a few years. Of course this meant that the flow of income would be reduced to a trickle and, a matter always on his mind, what would he be able to do for Marx? But if things went as they now promised, that too could be arranged, even if the Revolution took place to put a stop to all financial schemes. Rejoicing at the prospects opening for Marx with the imminent publication of his book, Engels summed up the past unhappy years in a memorable passage: "It always seemed to me that this accursed book which you gestated for so long was at the root of all your troubles and that you neither would nor could ever emerge from them until you had shaken yourself free of it. This everlastingly unfinished thing exhausted you physically, mentally and financially, and I can very well conceive that, now you have rid yourself of this incubus, you will feel an altogether different fellow, more particularly since the world, when once you go into it again, does not look so dismal as it did before. . . ."

In reply, despite complaints about the printer who had been held up over the Easter holiday, thus making it impossible after all for him to see the proofs as they came off the press, Marx expressed great optimism. "I confidently hope and believe," he wrote, "that in a year's time I shall be able to make a fundamental change in my economic circumstances and stand on my own feet again at last. Without you I could never have finished the work and I can assure you it has always lain as a deadweight on my conscience that your splendid powers were left to waste and rust in commerce mainly for my sake and that, into the bargain, you had to share the experience of living through all my petty miseries. . . ."

Nevertheless, he dreaded his homecoming, where the "Manichaeans"† were waiting to pounce and the accumulation of debt was truly imposing. He also foresaw domestic wailings, clashes and hounding, whereas all he

---

* Franziska Kugelmann, aged 8, the daughter of the house where Marx was staying. A correspondence started, though they were not to meet for some years, and Dr. Kugelmann became a regular contributor to Eleanor's stamp collection from now on.
† His creditors.

wanted was to settle down, fresh and unhampered, to work. He had, however, hopes of raising £100 before he left for London.

He travelled from Hanover to Hamburg on 15 May and a day or two later crossed to England. His homeward journey was diverted, in both senses, by a young lady of military bearing whose imperious wish to travel straight on from London to Weston-super-Mare none but the British railway system could have gainsaid. It was a Sunday and as there were no porters on duty Marx gallantly took charge of operations, escorting her and her mighty baggage to the wrong railway station, then to the right one on the other side of London, only to find that the next train for Weston-super-Mare would not leave for another six hours. They spent the long afternoon in affable conversation, sauntering about Hyde Park and eating ices, quite charmed by each other. Long before he saw her off at 8 o'clock that evening the truth was out: he had been consorting with Fräulein Elisabeth von Puttkamer, Bismarck's niece,* she with the most abhorred of all the Reds in Europe. They parted on the best of terms at Paddington station.

Matters at home were much as he had anticipated and he speedily left again for Manchester to spend a fortnight with Engels. It was only after he had picked up life again in Maitland Park that the familiar torments started in earnest. "I hope that as long as it lasts the bourgeoisie will remember my carbuncles", he wrote on 22 June. He grumbled that the girls planned to give a dance on 2 July as they had done no entertaining at all that year and were afraid of losing caste. Even less enchanting was the prospect of a visit from Lina Schoeler to whom Mrs. Marx would again have to repay the money she had borrowed from her guest during the last stay. Having taken defensive action against the first assault of creditors, Marx did not know how this was to be done. He had heard nothing from the various people on the Continent who had promised to raise money for him.

Engels sent £100 before going abroad in early July. While he was away and Marx thereby cut off from the source of supplies, the three girls received an invitation from the Lafargues to spend a holiday in France at the seaside. They were to travel with Paul to his home in Bordeaux and he offered to pay for the journey, but this Marx could not allow. The return fares cost £30 and – concomitant with every excursion – there were watches and clothing to be taken out of pawn. Reflecting that the girls' health would benefit by this change – "the seaside" was, in medical as in lay opinion, a panacea second only to alcohol – Marx quite simply used the £45 he had set aside for the rent.

---

* Bismarck married Johanna von Puttkamer in 1847.

Unfortunately Eleanor has left no account that can be traced of this, her first conscious experience of foreign travel, though it is unlikely that in the seven weeks she spent with her sisters at Royan* she did not communicate her impressions of life abroad in the family of a prosperous wine merchant.

It was now, while the girls were away, that Marx received the forty-ninth and last sheet of his proofs and during the night of 16–17 August he wrote to Engels: "It is thanks to YOU alone that this has been possible. Without your self-sacrifices for me I could never possibly have done the enormous work for the three volumes. I embrace you, full of thanks!† ... I salute you, my dear, beloved friend! ..."

The second IWMA Congress, with 64 delegates, was held in Lausanne from 2 to 8 September. Paul Lafargue drew up the French version of the Report, edited by Marx, though neither of them attended. Paul brought the girls home and then planned to visit Engels in Manchester, hoping Marx would accompany him. Marx could think of no plausible excuse for refusing but he could not afford the fare and, naturally, Paul was not "in the secret" of his financial state. Engels sent £5 to cover up for him and enable Mrs. Marx to meet household expenses in his absence.

Thus it was that Marx was not at home but, perhaps where it was most proper that he should be, with Engels when at last, on 14 September 1867 the first edition of Volume I of Das Kapital was published.

It was for this that not only Marx's health but also that of his wife had been ruined; for this that Helene Demuth had slaved and skimped to keep the family going; for this that Jenny and Laura had forgone the little vanities and sweets of adolescence, each in her turn acting as a part-time secretary or devilling for Marx at the British Museum.

Only for Tussy, now twelve, was no other way of life conceivable. For ten years Marx had been working on the preparation of this book.[65] To write Capital was the most natural, indeed the only thing a father might reasonably be expected to do. Capital had, as it were, grown up with her – or she with it – and she was not conscious that this activity, whose end-product would change the world, had meant inordinate pain and sacrifice to all those she loved, or that hers had been in any way an unusual childhood.

---

* At the mouth of the Gironde estuary. They stayed from 21 July to 10 September.
† This phrase in English.

By chance Marx arrived in Manchester at a time of tumultuous excitement.*

Two Fenian officers, Thomas Kelly and Timothy Deasy, seconded for duty in Lancashire after evading the Irish police for their part in the abortive March rising of that year, had been arrested in dubious circumstances on 11 September 1867. Tracked down and denounced by a Crown spy, John Joseph Corydon, they were remanded in custody and lodged in the old Manchester city gaol. They were brought before the magistrates on 18 September and again remanded, when they were driven with convicted prisoners in a Black Maria from the Bridge Street court to Belle Vue prison in Gorton, then a separate small township surrounded by brickfields. As the police van, drawn by two horses and followed by a cabful of constables, passed under a railway viaduct on the Hyde Road it was ambushed by a posse of armed men. One horse was wounded and both were cut loose, the roof panel was hammered open with a stone, while a shot fired either at the lock of the door or into the ventilator grille immediately above it fatally wounded a 51-year old police sergeant, Charles Brett, standing just inside the van. In the general confusion Kelly and Deasy escaped, never to be recaptured, but a ferocious man-hunt began, ending in the arrest of over 30 Irishmen and the later identification of five who stood trial for the murder of Brett.

On Saturday, 21 September, Engels took Paul Lafargue to the scene of the attack on the van: the railway bridge which, until its rebuilding nearly a century later, was a brick structure that became known as Fenian Arch.

Though Marx and Paul had left Manchester before the trial opened in October, passions were aroused throughout the land, inflaming everyone from the highest to the lowest. Queen Victoria, howling and drunken hordes of whose English subjects were to spend the night a few weeks later under the prison walls below the gallows to witness the killing of three fellowmen, wrote to Sir Stafford Northcote on 2 October: "These Irish are really shocking, abominable people – not like any other civilised

---

* Another chance visitor in Manchester at the time was young Annie Wood, the future Mrs. Besant, staying with the family of the radical lawyer, W. P. Roberts, known as "the pitmen's advocate".

nation",[66] while monster demonstrations, petitions and questions in the House greeted the pronouncement on 1 November of the death sentence on all five prisoners. One of the men was subsequently pardoned, without redress for his wrongful conviction and sufferings, while another had his death sentence remitted to penal servitude for life but, as a citizen of the United States, was released after eleven years.

The remaining three men, William Philip Allen, Michael O'Brien and Michael Larkin, the "Manchester Martyrs", were publicly hanged on 23 November.*

Engels described the courageous demeanour of the three as they went to the gallows where the public hangman, Calcraft, bungled his work, despatching only one man by means of the rope and the "long-drop" method he had humanely devised.

While all the "Martyrs" protested their innocence to the end, none disclosed the name of their companion – Peter Rice – who had fired the mortal shot. On the day, a Sunday, following the executions and in defiance of rabid English feeling, every Catholic priest in Manchester – where with the influx of unemployed Irish the hierarchy had been restored in 1850 for the first time since the Reformation – denounced from their pulpits the "murder" of the hanged men. Masses were said throughout the country, processions marched through the streets playing the Dead March on black-draped instruments, while in Hyde Park a vast concourse of people gathered to kneel and pray. The Irish Question had become an English question and few were left untouched. "All the Fenians lacked was martyrs", wrote Engels. "These they have been presented with ... through the execution of these men, the liberation of Kelly and Deasy has been made an act of heroism which will now be sung over the cradle of every Irish child. ... Irishwomen will see to that."

From that time Jenny took to wearing black and the cross, given to her by Polish patriots on her 23rd birthday earlier that year, she hung on a green ribbon to honour the Irish Brotherhood, while Tussy became emotionally involved for the first time in a political issue whose interest for her was never to abate.

Marx was in something of a quandary: anxiously awaiting the first reception of *Capital* and fidgety because as yet there had been no word of comment, his views on the Fenian affair were being sought on all sides. He had promised Meissner Volume II of *Capital* by the late autumn, the third volume by the winter of 1867,† so there was no change either in his

---

* This gruesome gala was among the last public executions in England. Ten more were to take place before, by Act of Parliament, executions were carried out behind prison walls.
† Volume II appeared in 1885, Volume III in 1894, both posthumously, assembled and edited by Engels from the mass of papers Marx had left.

circumstances or occupation as a result of this first major publishing event. The IWMA General Council had sent a Memorial to the Secretary of State (Gathorne-Hardy) on 20 November declaring that the forthcoming executions bore the stamp "not of a judicial act, but of political revenge", and the Council debated the Fenian question on 26 November[67] but failed to reach agreement, the resolution proposed being described by Marx as "absurd and meaningless". He thought that a great deal of rubbish was being talked: that, on the one hand, the significance of Irish emancipation was imperfectly understood and that, on the other, some misguided Fenian tactics were unlikely to lead to a better understanding. In the circumstances he was not willing to "hurl revolutionary thunderbolts" on the Irish question and gratuitously present reviewers of his theoretical work with the means to dismiss him as a demagogue. He was incensed by the "melodramatic folly" of the Clerkenwell Explosion: an event which took place on 13 December, barely three weeks after the execution of the Manchester Martyrs, whereby, in an attempt to release two Fenians held in the House of Detention,* a 548-lb. barrel of gunpowder was ignited, blowing up the prison wall and wrecking a number of nearby working-class houses with dire consequences to their inhabitants.†

Marx justly concluded that this exploit would alienate the wide public sympathy displayed by the London workers at, among other demonstrations, a massive torchlit meeting held in defence of the Manchester Martyrs on nearby Clerkenwell Green so short a time before. As Marx commented, English workers could hardly be expected to regard being blown up by Fenian emissaries as an honour.

Stirring as were the events of that autumn, the family had nevertheless

---

* The gaol stood on the site of what later became the Hugh Myddleton school in Corporation Row, Finsbury.[68]

† According to *The Times* of 29 April 1868: "Six persons were killed outright, six more died from its effects according to the coroner's inquests; five in addition owed their deaths indirectly to this means; one young woman is in a madhouse, 40 mothers were prematurely confined, and 20 of their babes died from the effects of the explosion on the women; others of the children are dwarfed and unhealthy. One mother is now a raving maniac; 120 persons were wounded; 50 went into St. Bartholomew's Gray's Inn Lane, and King's College Hospitals; 15 are permanently injured, with loss of eyes, legs, arms, etc.; besides £20,000 worth of damage to persons and property." The melodramatic folly of this report, with its dwarfs and raving maniacs, is evident. More sober accounts of the outrage put the figures at twelve killed and 20 seriously injured, though it is not disputed that women and small children were among the victims. Moreover, the breach made in the prison wall would have killed those it was intended to deliver had they been, as their rescuers supposed, at exercise in the yard rather than in their cells. The hanging of Michael Barrett in May 1868 for his part in the outrage was the last public execution in England.

to cope with its own affairs, among which Laura's forthcoming marriage, arranged for the following April, presented a problem different for each of the bride's parents. To Marx it was a matter of finance. Paul was more or less living in the house – though officially lodged at 35 Kentish Town Road – and expenses soared, since he must not be allowed to feel nor even to detect the pinch. Now a trousseau was to be added to the burden. "After all, she can't be sent out into the world like a beggar." Marx's borrowings became frantic. At last, in December, with Engels as security, he applied to a life insurance society, submitted himself, reluctantly, to a medical examination for actuarial assessment and, rather to his surprise – for his body was scarred with the evidence of past and aflame with present carbuncles – came through with credit, in both senses, for his deep chest-barrel impressed the doctor and he obtained a loan forthwith.*

Mrs. Marx's preoccupations were of a more delicate but no less troubling nature: how to conceal the scandal of a civil marriage? She was in a great taking and Engels was asked to consult Ernest Jones, the old Chartist, on the necessary formalities. It is not quite clear why Jones was to be consulted, for, ten years earlier, both Marx and Engels had broken off relations with him on political grounds and the friendship had not been renewed until 1864, when it took on a socially pleasant but by no means intimate character.† However, Jones responded. He had recently emerged from graver considerations, having figured prominently not only in the activities of the Reform League but also in the defence of the Martyrs.‡

Engels passed on the vital information regarding civil marriage, adding: "Your wife can tell her Philistine neighbours that this course has been elected because Laura is a Protestant and Paul a Catholic." Whether Mrs. Marx was appeased by this advice is not known.

That year, 1867 – a year which, incidentally, saw the passing of the Second Reform Bill, the founding by John Stuart Mill of the London National Society for Women's Suffrage and the demolition of the old St.

---

* This was not strictly a life insurance policy, but a straight loan given against a bond, for a fixed term, to be cancelled in the event of death occurring before the term expired but otherwise to be repaid at enormous interest. "The worst and most expensive way of raising cash", as Marx said.

† It will be recalled that he was a guest at Jenny's 21st birthday party in 1865. On his death in January 1869, when a vast concourse followed his bier to the cemetery, Engels said of him: "He was the only educated Englishman who was at heart entirely on our side".

‡ After an initial outburst of justified but, in the circumstances, unhelpful indignation, he had thrown up his brief at the preliminary hearing. He objected not only to the presence of troops stationed inside the magistrates' court but, more vigorously, to his clients entering the dock handcuffed and, when the magistrates refused to unfetter the men, Jones declared he would not appear in a courtroom under police rules and swept out. At the Grand Jury trial, however, he was again briefed by W. P. Roberts to defend Allen and O'Brien, who were hanged, and the American, Condon, whose death sentence was remitted.

Martin's Hall of IWMA fame – ended, like most years for Mrs. Marx, with a dismal Christmas. It was not, however, without its heavy humour, for on Christmas Eve, while Marx, unable to lie on his back and groaning with pain, tossed from side to side and the females were busy making the Christmas pudding below stairs, there arrived a tremendous bust of Jupiter Tonans, which daunting gift, slightly chipped *en voyage*, had been sent by Dr. Kugelmann as a conspicuous token of his friendship.

Laura's marriage was solemnised on 2 April 1868 before Messrs. Matthews and Ivimey, the St. Pancras Registrars, in the presence of Marx and Engels. It was followed by a luncheon at Modena Villas* when, as Laura recalled 25 years later, Engels "cracked a lot of silly jokes at a very silly girl's expense and set her a-crying".[70] The young couple then spent a brief honeymoon in Paris, where her father sent Laura a letter rejoicing that "the spring and sun and air and Paris jollities conjure in your favour", followed by requests for catalogues and journals which, acknowledged as untimely, he excused by saying: "I am a machine, condemned to devour books and then throw them, in a changed form, on the dunghill of history."[71]†

Laura and Paul were back in London in time for Marx's fiftieth birthday (5 May), which he spent – "still a pauper" – tortured by carbuncles and distracted by debts, the most pressing of which appeared to be those for Tussy's school fees and her course of private gymnastic lessons with a Mr. Winterbottom.

Meanwhile, after spending a few extra days in London, Engels had gone back to Manchester to toast the bride and groom *in absentia* with such a will that even his pet hedgehog, referred to as "The Right Honourable", got fuddled and, as Engels informed Tussy, suffocated itself in a blanket. Tussy herself was soon to experience at first hand the joys and sorrows of Engels' home life, so different from her own, for at the end of May, advised to travel "by the new Midland line from King's Cross",‡ she accompanied her father to Manchester for a fortnight.

During their stay – Marx seems accidentally to have timed his visits to Manchester to coincide with significant happenings – a conference of 34 delegates took place at the Mechanics' Institute in David Street. This was the first Trades Union Congress, held in Whit Week from 2 to 6 June 1868. The invitation to attend had been issued on 21 February by the

---

* On 1 May 1868 it was renamed No. 1 Maitland Park Road.[69]
† Strangely enough, the other great man of that epoch, Charles Darwin, writing in 1876, described his function in almost the same terms: "My mind seems to have become a kind of machine for grinding general laws out of large collections of facts."[72]
‡ The new Midland line, "the picturesque and favourite route between London and Manchester via Matlock and the Peak of Derbyshire", started in fact from the terminus of St. Pancras, opened in 1868. The journey took roughly five hours. There were no corridors on the trains.

president and secretary of the Manchester and Salford Trades Council, the compositors Samuel Caldwell Nicholson and William Henry Wood, whose names do not appear in the index to the Webb's *History of Trade Unionism* where this first Congress is accorded two modest sentences in a footnote.

It was not in itself a world-shattering event: boycotted by many of the most powerful Associations and representing fewer than 120,000 organised workers, it was nevertheless a landmark in the peculiarly British development of the working-class movement and one which, in days to come, was to prove both a stepping-stone and a stumbling-block in Eleanor's path.

At the time she was oblivious to it, passionately engaged in the Irish cause with the example and encouragement of Lizzie (Lydia) Burns* who, added to the distinction of being Irish herself, had on more than one occasion given asylum to Fenians on the run. These dazzling exploits and the warmth of her partisanship fired the young Eleanor with such fanatical enthusiasm that, on her return home, she earned herself the nickname of "the Poor-Neglected-Nation", so constantly was this phrase on her lips and, transferring her allegiance from the much-wronged Emperor of China, she declared: "Formerly I clung to a man, now I cling to a nation." She took to buying *The Irishman*,† reporting back to Lizzie such items of news as that the Fenians had held a Congress lasting 19 hours. Splendid as a proof of stamina, it aroused in Eleanor the compassionate reflection that it must have left them very tired. She also sent Lizzie the words of a revised version of the National Anthem – "God Save Our Flag of Green" – and signed herself "Eleanor, F.S." (Fenian Sister).

Back in London, her panegyrics upon the delights of Manchester and her intention to return there as soon as might be, stirring up bad blood as Marx recorded, were temporarily halted by an attack of scarlet fever to which both she and Jenny succumbed in June.‡ Her case was more serious than her sister's but she had the good fortune to be attended by an Irish doctor named Korklow who, in addition to his meritorious nationality, was a close neighbour and a "scarlet fever man", recommended to the Marxes as physician to the South Hampstead College for Ladies. This was not the only thing Tussy owed to the school, for she had caught the infection from a fellow pupil: no less a person than the daughter of

---

* 1827–1878, with whom Engels had lived since shortly after the death of his early love, her elder sister Mary (1823–1863).

† The organ of the Irish Nationalists, published first in Belfast and then in Dublin from 1858 to 1885. In 1867 the editor, Richard Piggott (1828–1889) was imprisoned for his support of the Fenian cause.

‡ They were put on a diet of Liebig's beef-tea laced with port.

Professor Frankland,* as Marx was at pains to point out when Lizzie Burns reproached herself in the belief that the illness had been picked up in Manchester.

Marx now played two curiously conflicting roles: he was both a notability while remaining a notable debtor. He was invited to such functions as the annual conversazione of the Royal Society of Arts, an occasion to which Jenny accompanied him.† He and his family were looked upon as among the distinguished patrons of the Maitland Park Orphan Working School at a time when he was still borrowing from the baker to pay the cheesemonger and could not meet the rent or rates. This double life reached its final absurdity when he was simultaneously elected Constable by the vestry of St. Pancras and summoned by the same body to "show cause why his goods and chattels should not be distrained". The former mandate – "an honour much valued by the Philistines of St. Pancras", according to Dr. Korklow – he evaded by going to Manchester when he should have been taking his oath of office, with the remark: "They can kiss my arse". Engels was vastly amused by the whole medieval nonsense,‡ apostrophising him: "*Salut, ô connétable de Saint-Pancrace!*", suggesting that Paul, suitably accoutred, should act as Squire.

While the invalids made slow but satisfactory progress it was planned that they should go to the seaside in July: not only they, but Laura, now four months pregnant, Paul, his parents and also Mrs. Marx, who was anxious not to be parted from Laura in these last weeks before the young couple left to make their home in France.

From week to week, while Marx fumed over the delay, the holiday was

---

* Sir Edward Frankland, F.R.S. (1823–1899), Professor of Organic Chemistry at the Royal Institution, where he succeeded Faraday in 1863. With Sir Joseph Lockyer, the astronomer, he discovered helium in the sun's chromosphere in 1868, when he also became a member of the Royal Commission on the Pollution of Rivers and, as Superintendent of the Royal College of Chemistry, made monthly reports from 1865 onwards to the Registrar-General on the character of the London water supply.
† Jenny commented on the occasion: "... of the works of art (the Queen has sacked all the museums of the people, in order to carry off their treasures to this aristocratic and favourite resort of the 'belated lamented') it was next impossible to get a glimpse ... My impression of the Society of Arts is that it is a Society of Snobs ..."[73]. This is one of the rare, and not illuminating, references to the visual arts in the entire available correspondence of the Marx family. While literature and music played a formative part in their cultural environment, drawing, painting and sculpture – despite the art lessons enjoyed by Jenny and Laura – do not so much as figure among the tastes and preferences in the "Confessions" of Marx, Jenny, Laura or Eleanor. It comes as something of a shock to realise that, though Eleanor grew up in the England of Leighton, Holman Hunt and Alma-Tadema, her contemporaries included Manet, Degas, Cézanne, Monet, Gauguin, Renoir, Van Gogh and Seurat. Almost her only reference to painting occurs in 1881 when she likened one of her little nephews to a portrait "of" Murillo.[74]
‡ Instituted in the reign of Edward I, 1285. Parish Constables fell into desuetude by an Act of August 1872.

postponed. Paul, who had finally taken his MRCS degree and was now qualified "to kill men and beasts", had still to finish his term of duty as House Surgeon at the hospital and Mrs. Marx, though anxious to be off, was perturbed by the necessity of finding at least £20 for Laura's household linen at a time when Marx was already driven to distraction by the debts he had incurred in the past twelve months, now coming home – with interest – to roost.

At last, on 5 August, Mrs. Marx having forayed to find lodgings, the holiday party set out for Ramsgate with watches redeemed from pawn and clothing suitable and respectable enough for a seaside resort packed in the battered portmanteaux.

In the absence of the family, whose noise about the house he strangely missed, Marx wrote to Engels in despair: it had come to a matter of life and death; there had been no response to his bids for loans from abroad; everyone was away from home at this season so it was useless for him to go again to the Continent; his insurance society loan was falling due and, more immediately, unless he could raise the money the children could not stay by the sea. When Mrs. Marx came back after a fortnight she found her husband so ill with worry that she insisted upon his joining the others for a few days, which he did, returning with his daughters on 25 August.

A new note of panic had crept into Marx's appeals for money. Domestic rather than political economy obsessed him, despite his preoccupation with the IWMA Congress to be held in Brussels from 6 to 13 September.

On 15 October, by which time the money for the necessary equipment had been provided by Engels, the young Lafargues departed for Paris – to live in furnished rooms for a month before moving into a flat – where Paul found that his British degree was not recognised and that he would have to sit five further examinations to practise in France.* The news did little to cheer Marx who had counted upon his son-in-law, with student days behind him, assuming the responsibilities of a career and the support of a wife and family. This circumstance moved Jenny in the late autumn stealthily to seek a post as a daily governess to the children of a Scottish doctor named Monroe.† Her father, confronted by the *fait accompli*, did not oppose it, though, as if to confirm his opinion of such sorry undertakings, her employers failed to pay Jenny's salary for six months and then had to be dunned for it. But, as he explained in words that he admitted he would rather have spoken than written, he thought it no bad thing that

---

* He was in fact excused three of the examinations but intended, and promised his father, to take the other two at Strasbourg University.
† This arrangement, which entailed working five mornings a week, lasted for nearly three years until, in 1871, the Monroes made "the terrible discovery that I am the daughter of the petroleum chief who defended the iniquitous Communal movement".[75]

Jenny should have interests outside the home where Mrs. Marx's snappish temper had been for years a trial to the girls, no less vexatious for being both understandable and understandingly borne.

At the same point of time, at the end of November 1868, Engels began to take practical steps, long foreshadowed, to quit the firm of Ermen & Engels for good. His life as a businessman had never ceased to irk him while his relations with Godfrey Ermen, whose partner he had been since 1864, went from bad to worse. He now asked Marx to tell him how much he actually owed and, if he were able to make a clean start free of debt, whether he thought he could live on £350 a year – illness and other unforeseen contingencies apart – for this was the regular income Engels proposed to guarantee him for the next five or six years, to start in 1869.

Marx was overwhelmed. The outstanding bills – omitting Dr. Korklow's fees, not yet claimed – presented a total of over £275. The account was drawn up by Mrs. Marx who, with the futile cunning of the innocent, since it was bound to come out sooner or later causing embarrassment all round, knocked off £75. With "strict administration" Marx believed that they could manage on £350, though he could not claim that they had done so in the past few years.* This he attributed in part to their perennial insolvency, compelling them to spend more than they could afford on daily necessities since the credit and patience of the small shopkeepers had been exhausted.

Christmas 1868, then, was in every way a time of high optimism, though, as Eleanor wrote ruefully to Laura, the dinner was "neither goose nor turkey, but a hare", which "shameful treatment" was owed to the fact that they were to sup with friends† later in the day, when, *en travesti*, Eleanor scored a success in *Beauty and the Beast* and the evening was spent in much merriment.

On 1 January 1869 two events of great importance to the family occurred: Charles Etienne Lafargue was born at 47 rue du Cherche-Midi in Paris and the first quarterly instalment of a regular private income was deposited for Marx at the Union Bank of London.

The three sisters were now launched on their several ways: Jenny embarked upon contributing to her own keep; Laura, a wife and mother, moored in foreign parts; and the voyage of Eleanor's childhood, her formal schooling virtually at an end, was over.

---

* It is estimated that this would be equal to something over £1,750 in terms of 1968. This sheds some light on the magnitude of Engels' generosity, Marx's debts and the standards observed by his wife.
† A French family called Lormier.

REFERENCE NOTES

Abbreviations

Andréas   *Briefe und Dokumente der Familie Marx aus den Jahren* 1862–1873 by
                   Bert Andréas in *Archiv für Sozialgeschichte*, II. Band, 1962. Verlag für
                   Literatur und Zeitgeschehen, Hanover.
BIML   Institute of Marxism-Leninism, Berlin.
Bottigelli Archives Letters in the custody of Dr. Emile Bottigelli, Paris.
ELC   *Frederick Engels, Paul and Laura Lafargue: Correspondence* Volumes I–
                   III. Lawrence & Wishart, 1959–1963.
IISH   International Institute of Social History, Amsterdam.
IWMA   *Documents of the First International*, Volumes I–V. Lawrence &
                   Wishart, 1963–68.
Liebknecht   *Wilhelm Liebknecht Briefwechsel mit Karl Marx und Friedrich Engels*.
                   Edited by Georg Eckert. Mouton & Co., The Hague, 1963.
MEW   *Marx Engels Werke*. Dietz Verlag, Berlin, 1956–1968. Unless other-
                   wise stated Volumes 27–39.
MIML   Institute of Marxism-Leninism, Moscow.

(1)   Compton Mackenzie, *My Life and Times, Octave* 7 1931–1938, Chatto & Windus,
      1968.
(2)   Privately communicated.
(3)   IISH.
(4)   Jenny to Eleanor, 23 March 1882. IISH.
(5)   *The Parish of St. Anne, Soho, Survey of London*, Volumes 33 and 34, Athlone Press,
      1966. This provides the most splendid factual matter concerning the neighbour-
      hood. It is a pity that it should sink to the vulgarity of assessing Karl Marx's work in
      a particularly silly footnote.
(6)   *Madeleine*. 2nd edition. Bentley 1851.
(7)   Quoted in *Edwin Chadwick and the Public Health Movement* 1832–1838 by R. A.
      Lewis, Longman, Green & Co., 1952.
(7a) 12 March 1896. Liebknecht, p. 445.
(7b) *Helena Demuth aus St. Wendel Heimatsbuch des Landkreises St. Wendel II Ausgabe*, 1969/
      70.
(8)   Originally published in the *New York Daily Tribune* and later forming part of the
      volume known as *The Eastern Question*, edited by Eleanor and Edward Aveling, Swan
      Sonnenschein & Co., 1897.
(9)   Also written for the *New York Daily Tribune* and collected under the title *The First
      Indian War of Independence*, Lawrence & Wishart, 1960.
(10) Andréas.
(11) District Surveyors' Returns. Office of Metropolitan Buildings. G.L.C. Records. (See
      also "The Metropolitan Buildings Office: A missing chapter in the History of the
      Development of London" by Ida Darlington in *The Builder*, 12 October 1956.)
(12) Henry Mayhew, *London Labour and the London Poor*, Volume I. Chas. Griffin & Co.,
      n.d., probably 1861.
(13) Mrs. Marx to Luise Weydemeyer, 11 March 1861. MEW.
(14) Metropolitan Board of Works, G.L.C. maps 1280 and 4121.
(15) *My Past and Thoughts*, Volume 5, translated by Constance Garnett. Chatto &
      Windus, 1924–1927. Herzen himself came to London in August 1852.
(16) Gustav Mayer, *Friedrich Engels*. Chapman & Hall, 1936.

(17) To Kautsky, 19 June 1897. IISH.

(18) Eduard Bernstein, *Die Neue Zeit*, No. 30. 1898.

(19) To Kautsky, 1 January 1898. IISH.

(20) Mrs. Marx to Mrs. Markheim, 6 July 1863. Andréas.

(21) *Österreichischer Arbeiter-Kalender für das Jahr* 1895.

(22) Jenny to Marx, November/December 1860. IISH.

(23) To Frank Van der Goës, 31 October 1893. IISH.

(24) Marx to Weydemeyer, 1 February 1859. MEW.

(25) Mrs. Marx to Marx from Manchester, November 1877. MIML.

(26) Mrs. Marx to Marx from Manchester, 1877 (probably November). MIML.

(27) Mrs. Marx to Mrs. Liebknecht, April 1866. BIML.

(28) 26 May 1872. MEW.

(29) Quoted in Volume I of *Das Kapital* (3rd German edition 1883) from the opening address to the Sanitary Conference at Birmingham by Joseph Chamberlain, then mayor, on 15 January 1875.

(30) *Geschichte des sozialdemokratischen Parteiarchivs und das Schicksal des Marx-Engels-Nachlasses* by Paul Mayer in *Archiv für Sozialgeschichte*, VI./VII. Band 1966/7. Verlag für Literatur und Zeitgeschehen. Hanover.

(31) Published in book form, together with Engels' writings on the same subject, under the title *The Civil War in the United States*. Lawrence & Wishart. n.d.

(32) Andréas.

(33) Mrs. Marx to Mrs. Markheim, 6 July 1863. Andréas.

(34) For this and other medical diagnoses made on the basis of the symptoms described in contemporary letters, I am indebted to Dr. Edwin Clarke, Senior Lecturer in the History of Medicine at University College, London.

(35) This is according to Werner Blumenberg's calculation (*Karl Marx*, Rowohlt, Hamburg, 1966), which converts the thaler into marks, though the mark did not become German currency until 1875. (14,000 marks= 4,667 thaler. The thaler was worth 6.20 to the £ sterling in 1863–1864. *Exchanges on London*, Soetbeer 1886.)

(36) 100 gulden were worth about £9 at the time.

(37) *Karl Marx zum Gedächtnis*, Nuremberg, 1896. To be found in English in *Karl Marx, Biographical Memoirs*, translated by Ernest Untermann, Charles H. Kerr and Co. Co-operative, Chicago 1901 and *Karl Marx Selected Works*, Vol. I. Lawrence & Wishart, 1942.

(38) IISH.

(39) Karl Marx. *Manuskripte über die polnische Frage*, edited by Werner Conze and Dieter Hertz-Eicherade. Mouton, The Hague, 1961.

(40) Reproduced by kind permission of the IISH.

(41) To Ernestine Liebknecht, 10 December 1864. BIML.

(42) Collected and edited by Dona Torr under the title *Marx on China*. Lawrence & Wishart, 1951.

(43) Blumenberg. *International Review of Social History*, Volume I, Part I. Amsterdam 1956.

(44) 16 July 1864. MIML.

(45) 10 December 1864. BIML.

(46) 13 February 1865. IISH.

(47) 16 February 1865. IISH.

(48) MIML.

(49) *The Bee-Hive* was founded by George Potter in 1861. He was the sole proprietor

from 1868 until 1873. A weekly which appeared until 1876, it was adopted as the organ of the IWMA from November 1864, which connection it retained until 1870.

(50) George Allen & Unwin, 1899. It has also appeared in more recent editions as *Wages, Price and Profit.*

(51) A more elaborate though equally imprecise way of arriving at much the same result has been calculated on the basis of the cheapest retail commodities and services advertised in the *Camden & Kentish Towns Gazette* over the years 1866–1870 and in the local Directories 1862–1870; food prices given in the first edition (1861) of Mrs. Beeton's *Book of Household Management*; contemporary Ratebooks; the known rent, school fees, doctors' expenses and other items specifically mentioned in Marx's correspondence of the period and by examining the cost per head of certain basic items provided to the Orphan Working School for the years 1863–1867 whose accounts were kept in great detail. The calculation assumes that Helene Demuth's wages were paid, does not include travel abroad or seaside holidays, interest on loans, or drink, the last being relatively the cheapest single item in any budget of the period (the duty on French wines having been repealed in 1860) and, in the case of the Marxes, supplied by Engels. This leaves a large margin of guesswork. In 1969 prices the equivalent annual income would have been in the region of £2,250.

(52) Early 1866. Liebknecht.

(53) Original English MIML. A German version appears in *Familie Marx in Briefen* (Dietz Verlag, Berlin, 1966) and in Vol. 31 MEW.

(54) Reproduced by kind permission of the Public Record Office, crown copyright.

(55) Bottigelli Archives.

(56) March 1866. Bottigelli Archives.

(57) To Natalie Liebknecht, 1 March 1898. Liebknecht.

(58) Early April 1866. IISH.

(59) Marx to Annenkov, 28 December 1846. MEW.

(60) n.d. (August/September 1866). IISH.

(61) October 1866. This last sentence originally written in English. Liebknecht.

(62) 14 October 1866. IISH.

(63) *Die preussische Militärfrage und die deutsche Arbeiterpartei* (The Prussian Military Question and the German Workers' Party). Published anonymously in the *Berliner Reform* on 3 March 1865.

(64) Bottigelli Archives.

(65) Including the *Grundrisse der Kritik der Politischen Ökonomie (Rohentwurf)*, written in 1857 and 1858 but not published in full until 1953, and *Zur Kritik der Politischen Ökonomie*, written in 1858 and 1859, published in June 1859 by Franz Duncker, Berlin.

(66) Quoted by Anthony Glynn in *High Upon the Gallows Tree*. Anvil Books. Co. Kerry, 1967.

(67) IWMA, Vol. II.

(68) Post Office Records. HS No. 9A and F. Quinivan, *The History of the Hugh Myddleton School*, 1955.

(69) Metropolitan Board of Works G.L.C. map 742.

(70) Laura to Engels, 6 March 1893. ELC Vol. III.

(71) 11 April 1868. Original English. MIML.

(72) *Autobiography of Charles Darwin*, edited by Nora Barlow. Collins, 1958.

(73) Jenny to Engels, 2 July 1869. IISH.

(74) Letter to Natalie Liebknecht, 12 February 1881. Liebknecht.

(75) Jenny to Kugelmann, 21 December 1871. Andréas.

· PART II ·

SHADES OF THE PRISON HOUSE

Although well versed in politics and literature, subjects fostered in the home, Eleanor at 14 years of age had picked up only twittercrumbs of learning. She spoke German as a matter of course but wrote it poorly; her French was weak, her spelling of English eccentric and her scholastic attainments low. This is no reflection upon the Misses Boynell and Rentsch of the South Hampstead College: there was scant demand for anything more than they could supply.

As late as the '60s middle-class girls still went for the most part to the innumerable private establishments set up and staffed by amateur tutors of both sexes, who, harking back to the 18th century, directed their efforts towards turning out commodities for a marriage market where now even the rudiments of domestic – let alone of any other – science were not an essential stock-in-trade. There was no fixed curriculum nor qualified teaching. Isolated alternatives were of course in existence,* and in this year of 1869 the battle for women's higher education was marked by two signal victories: girls over 17 were permitted to sit for the equivalent of London matriculation and Hitchin College – the forerunner of Girton – was inaugurated. But the first Education Act had not yet been passed† and female secondary education was not generally available to the middle class until the Girls' Public Day School Company – the mother of the High Schools – was formed in 1872.

Eleanor, far from bracing herself to take some formal examination or qualify for future academic excellence, as her age group of a century later is condemned to do, spent her fourteenth year gadding about – to Paris, to Manchester, to Ireland – with never a textbook to hand. Not that her education ceased: in some senses it may be said to have started in earnest now; but it took an outlandish form, while in her unbounded leisure she confected little gifts of a tendentious nature: tatting a collar threaded with

---

* As far as London was concerned certificated teachers had been trained for the charity schools by the Home and Colonial Infant School Society since 1836 and by the National Society for Promoting the Education of the Poor in the Principles of the Church of England since 1842. Queen's College for Women in Harley Street, originally intended to improve the standards of professional governesses on principles devised by the Christian Socialist, the Rev. Frederick Denison Maurice, was opened in 1848 and Miss Frances Mary Buss established her North London Collegiate School for Ladies in Camden Town in 1850.

† It received the Royal Assent on 9 August 1870. Board School education was not compulsory until 1880 and fees not altogether abolished until 1918.

green ribbons to fasten with an Irish harp and a "steal" (*sic*) cross to hang upon a challenging green neckband.

In the early spring of 1869 Marx wished to go to Paris to discuss Charles Keller's French translation of his work* and to visit Laura, who had been unwell for many weeks before and ever since the birth of her baby. He announced his intention by letter to the Lafargues who were promptly called upon by a gentleman asking whether Monsieur Marx had yet arrived. Forewarned by this vigilance Marx thought better of the plan† and it was decided that Jenny and Eleanor should go instead. They set out on 26 March – Good Friday – to stay in the rue du Cherche-Midi. The streets in that quarter had not changed much since Laurence Sterne a century before had pronounced them so villainously narrow that "there was not room in all Paris to turn a wheelbarrow", and in summer they stank. Nevertheless it was to Haussmann's Paris that Eleanor came and at the moment of its progenitor's fall from grace.‡ This was a Paris of nearly two million inhabitants, with the straight avenues, wide boulevards, handsome streets and public parks that, together with 40,000 new houses, had been built between 1853 and 1865 at a cost equivalent to £35 million. The reconstruction of the city's centre had given rise not only to furious and corrupt speculation in land but also to such inflated rents that working-class families, spending a third of their wages to keep a roof over their heads, were driven to huddle in the slums still festering on the outskirts, generally, as in so many capitals, to the east. It was estimated that those employed on the reconstruction had to walk an average of three hours a day to reach and return from their work.[1] Twenty thousand houses had been demolished to make way for modern Paris, whose *arrondissements*

---

* Immediately upon the German publication of *Capital* in 1867 Elisée Reclus and Moses Hess attempted and then abandoned a French translation. Two years later a second, equally unsuccessful, start was made. In the event the work did not appear until 1872, translated by Joseph Roy and published by Lachâtre to appear in a revised edition in 1885.

† The *loi des suspects* passed in 1858 after Orsini's attempt on the Emperor's life gave Napoleon III and his government unlimited powers to banish, expel or imprison any person suspected of opinions hostile to the Empire. The interception of his letter, spelling out the risks he would run in France, made Marx toy with the idea of acquiring British citizenship. He did not pursue the matter for another five years but went to Paris in July 1869 under the name of "A. Williams", staying in the rue St. Placide, near to the Lafargues, for six days. He was unmolested.

‡ Georges Eugène Haussmann (1809–1891), whose family originated in Alsace, studied singing at the Conservatoire as a youth but abandoned this career for the law and politics. He became Prefect of the Gironde in 1851 and, as a result of the impressive demonstrations he organised in Bordeaux in the following year to honour the visit of the newly proclaimed Emperor, Napoleon III, he was called to Paris where he became Prefect of the Seine in 1853. The malpractices which flourished under cover of his ambitious town-planning were brought to light in 1868 and he was forced to submit the budgets to the Chamber of Deputies. As a result he was deprived of office in January 1870, whereupon he retired to Nice on a modest pension.

were increased from twelve to twenty, while the glory of the Place de l'Étoile, with its radiating avenues strategically designed for the containment of disaffected mobs, was Haussmann's answer to that half of the Paris population which, on his own admission, lived in a state of poverty bordering upon destitution.*

Jenny could not stay long in Paris. She had to return to her job on 14 April, but Eleanor was there for seven weeks. All that spring she went "bockomanning" the boulevards: a portmanteau term of Laura's invention[2] for sightseeing strolls punctuated by small glasses of beer. The Second Empire in this, its last, year of carnival, far from presenting itself to the young visitor as "gorgeous, meretricious and debased"[3], seemed a place of simple and continuous delights. She saw Sardou's *Séraphine* at the Gymnase, and went to what she called "the fair of the pain d'épis"; she watched the open-air puppet-shows and gazed at the marvels displayed by the novel great department shops, pleased and amused by everything, but, above all else, she doted on her tiny nephew, known as Fouchtra and later in his short life as Schnaps or Schnappy. She had "never seen such a lovely child": his nose, his noble forehead – as immense as his grandfather's – his wonderfully good temper and his astonishing precocity in teething wrung from her paeans of praise cut short only by the need to attend to him. Her letters home, forwarded to Engels, bubbled over with gaiety, aberrant spelling and a relish for the absurd, as when she described the gentleman who, on the stormy Channel crossing, had worn spectacles for the prevention of seasickness. "Did you ever hear of such a think?" she brilliantly asked.†[4]

In reply Marx, after promising that Lenchen would regularly send her *The Irishman*, gave her a full report upon the conduct of her pets: Blacky, who behaved "always like a gentleman, but a very dull one"; the misnamed Tommy who had just presented the world with a large litter again and "done everything in her power to prove the truth of the Malthus

---

* In the years 1855 to 1869 prices had risen by some 45 per cent. The average wage of a man working 11 hours was 5 frs. a day (approximately 4s.). "Real" wages, i.e. purchasing power, may be measured by the price of bread which was 50c. a kilo. Almost 60 per cent of wages was spent on food alone. Women, of whom some 17,000 were employed in the Paris of 1869, earned roughly half the male rate, while several thousand children were put to work at the age of eight at half the female rate. There had been no legislation governing children's working conditions since 1851: none, that is, under the Second Empire. Thus an entire family of four persons gainfully employed might earn less than 9 frs. a day. Contemporary economists estimated that such a family needed 1,700 frs. a year in order to subsist. This was not achieved by the average family, not all of whom could be wage-earners, since most trades had a high incidence of seasonal unemployment. In the case of building workers – among the best paid – it was not uncommon to be laid off for as long as from four to six months in the year.

† In the same letter Eleanor deemed that a former acquaintance (Sassonov) had remarkably improved in looks and was now "hansom".

theory"; the dog Whiskey, "a great and good personage" who repined in his mistress's absence, exhibiting the sufferings of a beautiful soul, unlike the bird Dicky who profited by the occasion to develop a fine voice, and so on.[5]

While Marx was regaling Tussy with news of her menagerie he was growing more and more uneasy about his son-in-law's position.

Paul Lafargue had finished a translation of *The Communist Manifesto* for Jenny to take back with her to London. Despite his promises, he appeared to have discarded all notion of finishing his medical studies and was deeply involved in French politics. Marx disapproved. He feared that Lafargue *père* "should suspect me to push his son to premature political action. ... As it is, he has not much reason to delight in his connexion with the Marx family".[6] He thought Paul ought to qualify in France; moreover he did not favour the political company Paul kept – "a pack of Blanquists" – which could only lead to trouble. Despite earlier quarrels and their fundamental differences, Marx was quite willing "to oblige" Blanqui,* as he wrote to Paul, by contributing to his projected journal *La Renaissance*,† but he was averse from Laura's husband courting unnecessary dangers in that well-organised police state, the Second Empire.

Nothing, however, could immunise Paul against the election fever that swept France in April with the dissolution of the Legislative Assembly. Over a month before Eleanor's arrival in Paris the Government had intensified its repressive measures to paralyse the Republican and working-class movement in anticipation of the elections. When these measures proved ineffective and riots – said to have been instigated by the police – broke out, wholesale and illegal arrests were made both in Paris and the provinces. Charles Louis Napoleon Bonaparte, the putative nephew and step-grandson of Napoleon I – none of whose titles to fame he seems to have inherited – had staged a *coup d'état* in 1851 and was proclaimed Emperor Napoleon III in December 1852 "after 20 years' vagabondage and a number of preposterous adventures".[9] These had included enrolment as an émigré in England among the 150,000 special constables

---

* Louis-Auguste Blanqui (1805–1881) though not a socialist was a genuine revolutionary firmly wedded to what Engels called "the fantasy of overthrowing an entire society through the action of a small conspiracy".[7] Politically active at a time before organised workers' parties had emerged, he never recognised that "the time for surprise attacks, of revolutions carried through by small conscious minorities at the head of unconscious masses, is past".[8] Blanqui had a passionate faith in insurrection and none in working-class organisation, nor was he much interested in the nature of the society that would succeed the overthrow of capitalism. He spent in all over 33 years of his life in gaol for his beliefs. Elected to the Executive Committee of the Commune while serving his last sentence, he was not released until towards the end of his life when, in April 1879, he was elected deputy for Bordeaux.
† It never appeared.

assigned to protect the banks and other seats of power against the Chartists' procession to Westminster on 10 April 1848. He had not changed his spots and though he was shortly to meet his Waterloo – its name was Sedan – his manoeuvres to retain what amounted to a personal dictatorship were supported by every reactionary section of the population whose luxurious greed his reign had encouraged. Paul was 27 years of age, with a record of student revolt behind him and married into the Marx family. It was too much to expect him to stand aside not merely from the increasing opposition to the régime but, more importantly, from the militant socialist wing within the Blanquist party now emerging under such people as Jules Guesde and Edouard Vaillant. Paul plunged into the campaign. Eleanor's unorthodox education progressed.

Her mother came to Paris for a fortnight and they left for home just before the elections took place.* No sooner had Eleanor reached London on 19 May than she learned that she was to set out on her travels again.

In her absence there had been a recurrence of the Marxist syndrome (carbuncles and liver trouble). Engels was sure that a change of air, combined with a brisk daily walk and treatment by Dr. Gumpert in person, would enable Marx to do in a week more work than now took him a month in his debilitated state. Marx was persuaded to go to Manchester; but, apart from urgent IWMA business, he was not willing to deprive Jenny of her pleasure in his undivided company while the rest of the family was abroad and he waited until Mrs. Marx's return, when he wrote proposing to bring Tussy with him. There was great rejoicing at this plan and Engels made it clear that there would be no getting out of it. Indeed, father and daughter would have started off at once had there not been certain obstacles to paying for the railway tickets. Marx had been giving and lending money to those in greater need than himself – a fresh and agreeable experience – but ancient debts had an uncomfortable way of catching up with him just when he had lavished his funds, on Lessner,† on Liebknecht and on Eugène Dupont, a member of the IWMA General Council, and on his family's jaunts to Paris. Naturally Engels sent the fares and on 25 May Eleanor and Marx left for Manchester, where he stayed for some three weeks and she for five months.

Only a short time before, in April that year, had Engels finally "cut the navel cord" with his life in the "gloomy city", giving up his rooms in

* The first ballot was held on 23 and 24 May, the second on 6 and 7 June. The Republican opposition polled three million votes – against 4,300,000 for the Government – and more than trebled its seats in the new Assembly which first met on 26 June 1869.

† Frederick Lessner (1825–1910) was a tailor by trade who, after a revolutionary career and imprisonment in Germany, emigrated to England in 1856. One of the closest friends of both Marx and Engels, he remained in touch with Eleanor to the end.

Dover Street and moving finally into 86 Mornington Street, Stockport Road, Ardwick, where his household consisted of Lizzie Burns, now 43 years of age, her nine-year old niece Mary Ellen, known as Pumps, and the servant Sarah Parker.

Eleanor's relations with Engels had always been close. She looked upon him as a second father: the giver of good things. From him had flowed wine and stamps and jolly letters all her childhood. She may not have been aware that to him she owed not only every holiday by the sea, all minuscule treats and luxuries, but the very food she ate: she knew that he was the soul of loyalty and generosity to her family and that his beneficence embraced herself.

Not every member of the family was on terms of equal intimacy with him. After 25 years of friendship, during the greater part of which she had lived at his expense, Mrs. Marx still addressed him as *lieber Herr Engels* in her far from effusive letters. Though invited to do so, Jenny had never once stayed with him in Manchester and there is no evidence that Laura went there either. Only once, in the spring of 1855, following the death of her son Edgar, did Mrs. Marx visit Engels with her husband. But to Eleanor he had been "My dear Frederick" from her earliest years. Their correspondence, referred to though not apparently preserved, had been at its liveliest when she was eight, but it never ceased and she was said to know by heart the six letters he wrote to her when she was ill in 1868. He had also impressed upon her early in life that not to answer letters was "unbusinesslike" and occasionally she had acknowledged his letters to her father. Thus it had come to her knowledge that he sometimes sent Marx five-pound notes (cut in two halves).

Engels was now 48 years of age. Well over six feet, this handsome, fair, strongly-built Westphalian was neatly characterised when addressed by Paul Lafargue as "my ever-laughing Engels".[10] An enthusiastic rider to hounds, a mighty walker and a deep drinker, Engels was a man of equable temper, with a tender and chivalrous regard for women, turning a blind eye to the imperfections of those who successively held the reins of his household. He took things in his stride and constantly found in people with whom he had otherwise nothing in common qualities that were "jovial" or "genial", detecting in them a kindred streak.* It was indeed the ease and grace of his style that gave harmony to his many-sided life as active revolutionary, astute businessman and a master of political, economic, scientific, historical and military theory. His erudition owed nothing to a university education. Though in his private correspondence he was capable of criticising with brutal frankness the stupidities and ineptitudes of others, he used the rapier rather than the bludgeon in his polemical writings and, large in all things, he never descended to petty malice. He suffered fools patiently provided their hearts were in the right place. His venial tolerance was sometimes interpreted as lack of judgment. He scorned to misuse his superior intellect to browbeat or discourage and he took infinite pains with the tiresome and the bungling, the jejune and the wrong-headed, so long as they did not positively harm the cause of revolution, though he had no illusions about their capacity to learn and shrewdly estimated those who were and those who were not fitted to interpret and disseminate Marx's theories correctly. If lack of judgment means that to attain a human end one must accept and work with such fallible human material as offers itself, then Engels was guilty; but he could be a stern teacher of tactics and few came up to his standards.

Life never gave him much opportunity to "take it aisy", in the words of his own favourite maxim, but like most people of imperturbable temperament who have too much work to do, he found time for everything and did it with zest, whether translating *Humpty-Dumpty* into Latin, *The Vicar of Bray* into German, annihilating the pretensions of others,†

---

* See Appendix 3, p. 300.
† A curious instrument called the rhigometer Engels demolished with the phrase that it served as "a measure not of temperatures either high or low but simply and solely of the ignorant arrogance of Herr Dühring".[11]

writing his outstanding works on science, philosophy and economics, his articles on current political and military matters, or, during the last twelve years of his life, devoting himself to the immense task of ordering the endless pages of manuscript which were to become the second and third volumes of *Capital* left unfinished when Marx died.

It was during Eleanor's stay with him in 1869 that Engels finally threw off the servitude to commerce he had voluntarily entered upon 19 years before in order to support and further Marx's work.

In 1837 Engels' father had become a partner of the three Ermen brothers – Peter, the founder of the cotton manufactory in Lancashire, Anthony and Godfrey – one mill operating in Engelskirchen near Cologne the other in Eccles near Manchester. In 1842, at 22 years of age, the young Engels had been sent to England to learn the business, arriving a few months after a general strike of the Lancashire cotton workers. He was employed at the Victoria Mills in what was then known as Pendlebury Without in the parish of Eccles[12] where he met and fell in love with Mary Burns, a mill-hand then aged 19, whose father, recently emigrated from Ireland, followed the trade of dyer. The product of Engels' two years' apprenticeship was *The Condition of the Working Class in England in 1844*, that earliest and still most telling social survey. Dedicating the 1st edition of 1845 to "The Working Classes of Britain", he wrote:

> "I have tried to lay before my German countrymen a faithful picture of your condition, of your sufferings and struggles, of your hopes and prospects. ... I have ... devoted my leisure hours almost exclusively to intercourse with plain working men; I am both glad and proud of having done so. ... Having, at the same time, ample opportunity to observe the middle-classes, your opponents, I came to the conclusion that you are right, perfectly right in expecting no support whatever from them. ... What have they done to prove their professed goodwill towards you? ... Have they even done as much as to compile from those rotting Blue Books a single readable book from which everybody might easily get some information on the condition of the great majority of 'freeborn Britons'? Not they. ... They have left it to a foreigner to inform the civilised world of the degrading situation in which you have to live. A foreigner to *them*, not to *you*, I hope. Though my English may not be pure, yet I hope you will find it *plain* English...."[13]

The Manchester experience, his introduction into the world of Mary Burns, had given Engels a new and poignant awareness of "the cause of contemporary class antagonisms" and of the economic factors that made capitalism a scourge to the majority of men and women. He left England a confirmed revolutionary, pledged to the abolition of private property and to the violent overthrow of the ruling class. He was ripe for the most important event of his life which now occurred.

On his way back to Germany in 1844 he stopped in Paris for ten days

(28 August to 6 September) and these he spent with Marx. The two men had met briefly in Cologne a couple of years earlier, but at a time when Engels was freshly caught up by the Young Hegelians and their club of "The Free" while Marx had outgrown that philosophy and was disenchanted with its adherents. The encounter had meant little to either Engels or Marx. Now, however, there was a fusion of interests, outlook and objectives. They began to work together on *The Holy Family* and so the basis was laid for that friendship and collaboration which were to determine Engels' entire future.

In the following year, 1845, he rejoined Marx in Brussels, where they collaborated on the writing of *The German Ideology* and spent the summer in England. Engels was able to initiate Marx into the workings of the most highly developed industrial country. On their return to the Continent Engels took Mary Burns back with him. He now threw himself into political and revolutionary activity, writing *The Communist Manifesto* with Marx, contributing articles on France and Germany to *The Northern Star* and, again with Marx, starting the publication of the *Neue Rheinische Zeitung* in Cologne.* In 1849 Engels took part in the armed uprising in defence of the German Constitution – voted but not put into effect – and directed the defences of Elberfeld. He fought in the campaigns in Baden and the Palatinate, crossing into Switzerland with the last of the defeated insurgent armies when the order for his arrest was out. After a short holiday in Italy he again rejoined Marx, now settled in London. There he stayed for a year, living at No. 6 Macclesfield Street,† within a stone's throw of the Marxes.

As the revolutionary wave of 1848 subsided it became clear to both men that the paramount need of the time was to broaden and deepen the theoretical principles of revolution, as a guide to future action, and that Marx was best fitted for this task. Thus, in November 1850, in deference and homage to Marx's gifts, Engels took the hard step of going back into the firm of Ermen & Engels in Manchester. As corresponding clerk and "general assistant" his salary was not large: £100 a year with 10 per cent of the firm's net profits, yet out of this he managed to provide for the Marx family. After ten years, following his father's death, he became the general representative of the Manchester branch and in 1864 a full partner. During all those years, despite long hours of hated work, he

---

* The organ of the Communist League, it appeared from June 1848 until May 1849 when proceedings were taken against it and Marx was expelled from Prussia. Thereafter six numbers, which published in 1850 Marx's *Class Struggles in France 1848 to 1850* and Engels' *The Peasant War in Germany*, were edited in London and printed in Hamburg.
† Macclesfield Street runs from Gerrard Street to what was then King Street, now Shaftesbury Avenue: the southern extension, as it were, of Dean Street. No. 6 was roughly in the centre of the west side.

produced pamphlets, pursued researches into linguistics and military history, kept abreast with the new developments in science and technology, wrote articles for the *New York Daily Tribune* when Marx's English was still too imperfect and maintained by almost daily correspondence that friendship which had become his *raison d'être*, his life's blood.

His own part he considered negligible save in so far as it enabled Marx to work: this was the sole justification for remaining in commerce, that most senseless misapplication of human effort in his view. When at last he was within sight of his freedom, he wrote to Frederick Lessner in gentle rebuke for compliments which were "the more embarrassing to me inasmuch as in the past 18 years I am afraid I have been able to do practically nothing *directly* for our cause and have had to devote all my time to bourgeois activity. Now, I hope, that will soon be otherwise ... and then I shall certainly do my part to deserve your compliments, for it will always be a joy to me to fight at the side of an old comrade like yourself on the same battle ground and against the same enemy."[14] He was resolved to dedicate the rest of his days to the revolutionary movement. "You have always known", he wrote to his mother with whom, until her death in 1873, he maintained a loving and frank relationship, "that I have never in any way changed the views I have held for nearly 30 years and it can come as no surprise to you that, when occasion demands, I should not only speak out but do my duty in other respects. You would need to feel ashamed of me if I did not. Were Marx not here, if he did not exist at all, it would not alter the situation by one jot."[15] Many years later, looking back, he corrected this assessment and said with dignified and reasonable modesty: "All my life I did what I was made for, that is, played second fiddle and I believe I acquitted myself tolerably well. And I was fortunate to have so excellent a first violin as Marx."[16]

Now, in the May of 1869, on Eleanor's arrival in Manchester, Engels was still tied to the firm. Since January he had been negotiating the legal and financial terms of his release which eventually took place on 1 July. Recalling that summer day twenty-one years later Eleanor wrote: "I was with Engels when he reached the end of this forced labour and I saw what he must have gone through all those years. I shall never forget the triumph with which he exclaimed 'For the last time!' as he put on his boots in the morning to go to his office. A few hours later we were standing at the gate waiting for him. We saw him coming over the little field opposite the house where we lived. He was swinging his stick in the air and singing, his face beaming. Then we set the table for a celebration and drank champagne and were happy...."[17]

"Then we ... were happy": Eleanor could have said this of her whole stay with Engels. Though there is little evidence for it, Marx was under the impression that her Paris life had been one of restraint. "Here," he wrote to Jenny from Mornington Street, "she feels quite at her ease, like a new-fledged bird"[6] and, a week later: "She looks quite blooming ... a little longer stay will do her good."[18] If a round of pleasure does one good – as Engels for one firmly believed – then Eleanor was much benefited. There were fireworks at Belle Vue, an excursion to Bolton Abbey – including a stay at the Devonshire Arms – a week-end house party with friends of Sam Moore*; there were picnics and shopping expeditions, an evening at the theatre and tea-parties of bread and treacle. There was even a glimpse of the Prince and Princess of Wales when they came, the guests of the Earl of Ellesmere, to visit the Royal Agricultural Show at Old Trafford, on which occasion Eleanor hoped the children would greet the royal pair by singing "The Prince of Wales in Belle Vue jail for robbing a man of a pint of ale".[19]

Running through it all, like the green ribbon of the collar Tussy had made for her, was Lizzie Burns with her Irish lore; not only the old folk tales which Mary Ellen, her niece, recited, but more stirring stuff, for Lizzie now took Eleanor to the market and showed her the very stall where Kelly – one of the Fenian prisoners rescued from the police van two years before – had once sold pots. She saw the house where he had lived and heard "a great many amusing things about Kelly and 'Daisy'† whom Mrs. B had known quite well having been to their house and seen them three or four times a week".[19]

That the "so-called liberty of English citizens is based on the oppression of the colonies",[20] of which Ireland was the first with a history of 700 years of disaffection under "the most abominable reign of terror and the most reprehensible corruption",[21] was an article of Lizzie's faith. Like Engels in his youth, now Eleanor saw with her own eyes the conditions of the immigrant Irish in Manchester. A quarter of a century earlier Engels had written:

---

* c. 1838–1911. An English lawyer, one of the firmest friends of Marx and Engels, the translator of The Communist Manifesto and co-translator of Volume I of Capital.
† Lizzie's way of referring to Deasy, the second rescued prisoner.

"The rapid extension of English industry could not have taken place if England had not possessed in the numerous and impoverished population a reserve to command. The Irish had nothing to lose at home, and much to gain in England. ... These Irishmen ... migrate for 4d. to England, on the deck of a steamship in which they are often packed like cattle. ... The worst dwellings are good enough for them; their clothing causes them little trouble ... shoes they know not; their food consists of potatoes and potatoes only; whatever they earn beyond their needs they spend on drink. What does such a race want with high wages?"[22]

Since then the number of immigrants, and their distress, had been balefully multiplied by famine and evictions. Between 1846 and 1851 nearly a million Irish emigrated and, though Manchester was by no means their main destination, it is recorded that in one week during November 1847 the city paid out relief to 5,000 Irish paupers,[23] while in the decade 1851–61 "one-sixth of [Hibernia's] toiling sons and daughters perished by famine and its consequent diseases, and a third of the remainder were evicted, ejected and expatriated by tormenting felonious usurpers".[24]

Lizzie Burns exercised a lasting influence on Eleanor. "She was quite illiterate ... but she was as true, as honest and in some ways as fine-souled a woman as you could meet. She was the staunchest of friends", Eleanor wrote many years after Lizzie's death and but two weeks before her own.[25] What Lizzie meant to Engels he himself recorded in a letter to August Bebel's wife: "She was of genuine Irish proletarian stock and her passionate, innate feeling for her class was of far greater value to me and stood me in better stead at moments of crisis than all the refinement and culture of your educated and aesthetic young ladies."[26]

There was also another side to Lizzie: a *laisser-aller* unknown in the Marx household and very stimulating to the young guest. As the summer advanced, the ladies, overcome by the heat "laid down on the floor the whole day, drinking beer, claret, etc.", which was how Engels found them in the evening when he came home: "Auntie, Sarah, me and Ellen ... all lying our full length on the floor with no stays, no boots and one petticoat and a cotton dress on and that was all."[27] Drink, indeed, played an overflowing part in the Engels environment. Carl Schorlemmer, the distinguished chemist,* was a frequent visitor and, according to Eleanor, on one occasion "got so 'screwed' that we had to make a bed for him and he slept there too, for he couldn't get home", while in the same letter Engels was reported as having returned from a party "as drunk as

---

* 1834–1892. Engels had known him for some years and wrote of him later to Bernstein (27 February 1883): "After Marx, Schorlemmer is undoubtedly the most eminent man in the European Socialist Party. When I got to know him ... he was already a Communist." In 1874 the Chair of Organic Chemistry was specially created for him at Owen's College, Manchester, and he became an F.R.S.

jelly".[27] Inebriated men – and women – did not trouble Eleanor in the least: she accepted the current view that they were screamingly funny.

However, life in Manchester was not all uncorseted bliss and alcohol. Engels relinquished to Eleanor the task of teaching Mary Ellen to play the piano and he also set her a stiff course of reading. Starting with the Young Edda,* she went on to 14th century Serbian folk ballads, translated by Goethe, and then graduated to Goethe himself – *Herrmann und Dorothea, Goetz von Berlichingen* and *Egmont* – and by midsummer she was engrossed in Firdousi† though Engels doubted that she would get through the enormous tome.

Eleanor at this age, having always been the baby of the family, was still in many ways a child. Engels and Lizzie insisted upon addressing her as "Miss Marx", to cure them of which teasing habit she dropped the formal "Mrs. Burns" and called the couple "Uncle" and "Auntie", making them repeat "Tussy, Tussy, Tussy" 24 times until they – and Sarah Parker – had mended their ways. But while Engels devised such playful mystifications as sending her a letter in a disguised hand, to be posted by Marx from some improbable place, he also went out for a walk with her each day and they enjoyed a true companionship. They were in fact temperamentally alike, sharing a lively humour, gaiety, consideration for others, good temper and commonsense.

The days and the weeks sped by so congenially that when, in August, Marx wrote to say that the Lafargues were coming to London he feared that Tussy would be on the horns of a great dilemma: if she were not told that her nephew was there she would have good cause to reproach Marx but would be torn between her longing to see the baby and the delights of Manchester. Engels was not one to make heavy weather of such a problem. "I have cut the Gordian knot over Schnaps", he wrote, "and simply informed Tussy of the fact." Whether it had caused her a tragic conflict he really could not say, but in any case she had other things on her mind at the moment being distracted by toothache.

Eleanor elected to stay on and bear Lizzie company while Engels went abroad for a fortnight in August. The day after his return the three of them went to Ireland for a week, visiting Dublin, the Wicklow mountains, Killarney and Cork. It was thirteen years since Engels had been to Ireland with Mary Burns‡ and great changes had taken place since 1856.

---

* In the text of Frantz Eduard Christoph Diotrich's *Altnordisches Lesebuch*, Leipzig 1864.

† Author of the 10th century Persian national epic *Shah-nameh* (The Book of Kings), consisting of 60,000 couplets of which selections had been translated into German by both Adolf von Schack and Friedrich Rückert at that period.

‡ On that occasion he had journeyed from Dublin to Galway and Limerick, then down the Shannon to Tarbert and on to Tralee and Killarney.

He would not have recognised Dublin harbour, he said; while at Queenstown, formerly the insignificant Cove of Cork, which had vastly expanded during the American Civil War, he heard every conceivable language spoken on the quayside.

It was Eleanor's first visit to Ireland and it coincided with a new upsurge of the national liberation movement. The immediate cause of this ferment in the summer and autumn of 1869 was the demand for the Fenian prisoners to be amnestied. There were monster demonstrations: 30,000 people turned out in Limerick, 200,000 in Dublin. The English government was flooded with petitions demanding the release of the prisoners whose treatment had long been a matter of public scandal. Two years earlier Parliament had been forced to appoint a commission of investigation whose report[28] drew from Marx the furious comment: "These filthy swine boast of their English humanity because they do not treat their political prisoners any *worse* than murderers, footpads, forgers and paederasts."[29] Now, as Engels, Lizzie and Eleanor travelled through this country whose ruinous depopulation was only too manifest,* they found troops swarming everywhere, and everywhere, in battle order, the Royal Irish Constabulary, armed with short-swords, truncheons and revolvers. A field battery clattered through the centre of Dublin. The whole of Ireland appeared to be on a war footing. Although Engels' interest in the subject had never ceased since his early encounter with that "most horrible spot" in Manchester known as Little Ireland, it was now that he decided to write a social history of Ireland which, in Marx's view, would be a pendant to his *Condition of the Working Class in England*.†

At last, on 12 October, Eleanor came back to London in time for a brief family reunion: the Lafargues were there for another six or seven days, having had to prolong their stay because the baby had been ill and Laura, pregnant again, was also far from well, while Marx and Jenny had returned only a day before from their stay with the Kugelmanns in Hanover. "Tussy has returned from Ireland a stauncher Irishman than ever", Jenny reported to the Kugelmanns[32], and when the petitions for the release of the Fenians had been rejected by Gladstone, Eleanor not only went but insisted upon her father, mother and Jenny going to Hyde Park, where on 22 October some 100,000 demonstrators protested. Jenny described the event to the Kugelmanns: the vast crowds, the red, green and white banners, the defiant placards – "Disobedience to Tyrants is a

---

* "Since 1841 the population has dropped by two and a half millions, and over three million Irishmen have emigrated. All this has been done for the profit of the large landowners of English descent, and on their instigation."[30]

† Engels collected material for this work for a period of two years but was unable to complete it.[31]

Duty to God", "Keep your Powder Dry" – the "profusion of red Jacobin caps" hoisted higher than the flags to the strains of the *Marseillaise*, were all impressive and profoundly stirring. Except to the press, which dismissed the whole affair as "an utter failure". It was Marx who pointed out its real significance: "The main feature of the demonstration had been ignored, it was that at least a part of the English working class had lost their prejudice against the Irish."[33] Eleanor had been excited by the crowds, and was perhaps why she turned out to mingle with them when Queen Victoria opened Blackfriars Bridge and Holborn Viaduct on 6 November.* This, she found, was a very different and a sullen crowd, "staring sourly at Madame". It was put about that handbills had been distributed in the East End calling upon the famished workers to present themselves *en masse* before their sovereign on this public occasion. It may have been a hoax, but the police were taking no chances and by sheer force of numbers crushed the breath out of the spectators, thus stifling their loyal cheers.

Fresh from her Manchester training Tussy tried to persuade Marx to take a daily walk with her. He neatly turned the tables by giving her the alternative exercise of putting his chaotic study to rights, which at least served the purpose of giving them much time together at a moment when, for the newly founded Land and Labour League and for the General Council of the IWMA, Marx was drafting material on the Irish situation. In the midst of this, on 25 November, Jeremiah O'Donovan Rossa,† one of the leading Fenians serving a life sentence in Chatham gaol, was elected M.P. for Tipperary. Eleanor was not the only one to go "mad with excitement" over the success of this convicted felon who, though ineligible to take his seat in the House of Commons, changed the whole nature of the campaign. "It forces the Fenians to abandon their conspiratorial tactics and the staging of minor *coups* in favour of practical activities which, though seemingly legal, are far more revolutionary than anything they have done since their unsuccessful insurrection", wrote Engels.[34] Even before the Tipperary results Marx had proposed a resolution to the General Council of the International which was passed on 2 December saying that Gladstone "had deliberately insulted the Irish nation; that he

---

* The 18th-century bridge, fast sinking, was demolished in 1864 and a temporary structure took its place. The new bridge, built at a cost of £400,000, was designed by Joseph Cubitt. Since the name is not unknown in modern times it is of interest to record that an earlier Cubitt – William, the father of Joseph – was the inventor of the prison treadmill. He also drew up plans to house the 1851 Great Exhibition in Hyde Park. His plans were never adopted but he was knighted for his pains.

† The business manager of *The Irish People*, a paper issued in Dublin from November 1863, he had been arrested together with the editors, Thomas Luby and John O'Leary, on 15 September 1865.

clogs political amnesty with conditions alike degrading to the victims of misgovernment and the people they belong to" and expressing "admiration of the spirited and high-souled manner in which the Irish people carry on their amnesty movement".[33] Before the year was out this resolution was communicated to all branches of the IWMA in Europe and America and was published in London, Leipzig, Geneva and Brussels.

Gradually and grudgingly, under the pressure of the swelling movement inspired now by the IWMA and O'Donovan Rossa's unprecedented situation, Gladstone granted a shabby conditional amnesty to the Irish patriots at the end of 1870.

Living at the heart and centre of the campaign, endlessly debating the subject with her two great masters and listening to discussions between those better informed than herself, Eleanor, too, shifted her slightly romantic Fenianism on to the basis of political realities. She began to understand the import of Marx's words to Kugelmann: "The English working class . . . can never do anything decisive here in England until it separates its policy towards Ireland in the most definite way from the policy of the ruling classes . . . not as a matter of sympathy with Ireland, but as a demand made in the interests of the English proletariat"[35], and his pronouncement that "any nation that oppresses another forges its own chains".[33]

"Here, at home, as you are fully aware, the Fenian sway is paramount. Tussy is one of their head centres. . . ." So wrote Marx to Laura and Paul early in March 1870.[36] Though Home Rule for Ireland was a question insular only in the literal sense, Eleanor in the next two years was to become personally involved in Continental politics and the Fenians, though never banished, yielded pride of place to the French. She and her sister Jenny were infatuated with what Mrs. Marx called "*la grrrrande nation*", adding that they would soon get over it. But they did not.

Engels had decided in February to move permanently to London by the autumn. He was influenced partly by Lizzie's wish to leave Manchester, where she was squabbling with her relatives, and partly, it may be, by an admission wrung from Mrs. Marx at the cost of two points of exclamation. "How often over the years, *lieber Herr Engels*, have I silently wished you were here!! Many things might have been different." She was referring to Marx's ill health, caused by the incessant overwork that she was powerless to restrain and to which, at the age of 51, he now added learning the Russian language. With more than goodwill Mrs. Marx set about househunting for Engels.

Tussy's visit to the Manchester *ménage* in 1870 was thus her last, nor was it a long stay, for she was supposed to be at school again and this must have been regarded as a mere fortnight's mid-term break. Engels for his part seemed to have thought it a fine joke to propose that the time had come for her to be gainfully employed. "I am *very* much obliged to you for sending that advertisement", she wrote to him. "The situation is one that will suit me very well, so I shall lose no time in applying for it. You will I am sure give me a reference."[37]

Shortly before she went to Manchester in May, a plebiscite was held in France to test the support for Napoleon III and his "liberalised" Constitution, the questions being so framed that to vote against the Bonapartists was in effect to dissent from any measure of democratic reform. The result was a foreseen victory for the Emperor in all the constituencies except Paris, where the opposition won a small majority of 45,000.* Laura reported that the excitement was intense: the smell of war was in the air.

The reality was not long delayed. Napoleon III declared war on the

---

* The total vote for the Bonapartists was 7½ million with 1½ million against, but there were close on 2 million abstentions.

Prussians on 15 July, the proclaration was delivered to Berlin on the 19th and on the 29th hostilities opened. Between these latter dates Marx had written the General Council's *First Address on the Franco-Prussian War*, including the words:

> "Whatever may be the incidents of Louis Bonaparte's" [Napoleon III] "war with Prussia, the death knell of the Second Empire has already sounded in Paris. . . . On the German side, the war is a war of defence, but who put Germany to the necessity of defending herself? Who enabled Louis Bonaparte to wage war upon her? *Prussia!* It was Bismarck who conspired with that very same Louis Bonaparte for the purpose of crushing popular opposition at home and annexing Germany to the Hohenzollern. . . .*
> If the German working class allow the present war to lose its strictly defensive character and to degenerate into a war against the French people, victory or defeat will prove alike disastrous."[38]

This penetrating analysis was reflected quite soon in British public opinion. The popular enthusiasm for the Prussians was dissipated as they crossed the frontiers, 200,000 troops advancing before August was out, systematically sacking, burning and plundering French villages and shooting all *francstireurs*. Among English crowds the singing of the *Wacht am Rhein* was drowned by that of the *Marseillaise*. "Of course", commented Marx in a letter to Kugelmann, "the English did exactly the same in India, Jamaica, etc., but the French are not Hindus, Chinese or Negroes nor are the Prussians heaven-born Englishmen . . . Whatever the outcome of the war", he went on, "it has trained the French proletarians in the use of weapons and that is the best guarantee for the future."[39]

On 2 September 1870 at Sedan, an unimportant little town in the Ardennes noted only for its manufacture of black cloth,† the decisive battle of the war was fought. It raged from dawn until dusk ending with the capture of Napoleon III, 39 of his generals, some 3,000 officers, 28,000 men, the destruction of MacMahon's army and the downfall of the Second Empire.

Two days later, on 4 September, the Third French Republic was proclaimed. Although it marked the end of nearly two decades of the imperial rule that had resulted in unprecedented riches for the rich and poverty for the poor, the new Republic was not in any sense a progressive administration being almost entirely in the hands of those who had shamefully betrayed the 1848 rising.

The *Second Address on the Franco-Prussian War* was written between 6 and 9 September, that is, in the days immediately following Sedan when,

---

* On 18 January 1871 Wilhelm I, the Hohenzollern King of Prussia since 1861, became the first Emperor of Germany.
† It was also the centre of the German armoured breakthrough on 14 May 1940.

in Engels' view, the war was over to all intents and purposes. It was again an accurate assessment of the situation, penned when the English newspaper reader had barely caught up with the events themselves. Indeed, the political journalist, or "commentator" as he is often called today, who devotes so much energy to stoking hatred of Communism could well take a lesson from its founders who were also masters of his meaner trade.

Though Marx wrote this document Engels had provided much material for it. Since the end of July he had been contributing regular articles to the *Pall Mall Gazette** under the title "Notes on the War", many of which were plundered, without acknowledgment, by the other London papers: perhaps as an honorary tribute to the leading military theorist of the time.

It was these articles, for which he received 2½ guineas apiece – half of which he declared he owed and therefore paid to Marx, while Eleanor, "the ferocious girl", and Jenny laid claim to the "first spoils of the war as brokerage" – that earned Engels the nickname of "General" by which he was known to his intimates for the rest of his days. Originally it had been "General Staff" and arose from "a comical mistake of *Le Figaro* which paper showed its gross ignorance by speaking of the General Staff as if it were an individual",[40] meaning General von Moltke.

Though he continued to write his articles until February of the following year Engels was now actively preparing his move to London. From Ramsgate, to which the Marxes and Lenchen travelled by sea to spend the last three weeks of August, Tussy wrote to him: "I suppose you know that last Tuesday Mohr and Jenny went to look for houses."[41]

They need not have done so: Mrs. Marx had not merely inspected and reported on a number of possible places long before but in July she had indeed found a house near Primrose Hill for £60 a year which she heartily recommended. Eleanor and Jenny gave it the stamp of their approval and Marx advised him to take it: London was beginning to swarm with French refugees, bringing their money to safety, and "gentlemen's residences" would be in great demand – the price of house property was already rising – so that, despite the risks of taking and furnishing a place on a three-and-a-half years' lease at this time of uncertainty, Engels would always be able to dispose of it.

Thereupon Mrs. Marx and Lenchen with a keen eye to economy set about supervising the alterations, renovations and decorations of the house, which they lauded for its pleasing and attractive situation: near enough to the shops for Lizzie's convenience yet, at the very front door, an open space and the sight of thousands of Londoners taking the air. It was a four-storeyed house† with a basement, though modest in comparison with

---

* Founded in 1865.
† Still extant, still near to small shops and still with an unimpeded view of Primrose Hill.

the Marxes' place. As the time for Engels' arrival drew near Mrs. Marx was suddenly abashed by this fact and wrote imploring him to stay at Maitland Park for a few nights until all was in order. There was plenty of room for his entire household: "After all, we live in a veritable palace and, to my mind, far too large and expensive a house."

Engels moved on 20 September 1870 and lived at 122 Regent's Park Road for the next 24 years.

This was not the only move that preoccupied the Marxes at that period. Laura's second baby, a daughter, had been born on the anniversary of the first but had survived only two months, dying at the end of February. She was pregnant again and now she, Paul and their little son were living at 7 Place de la Reine Hortense,* Levallois-Perret, one of the most vulnerable areas close to the fortifications and liable to be "among the first casualties of the war" as their small house was threatened with demolition should things take a turn for the worse. "They will not listen; let us hope that they will not feel", and, on the day Sedan was fought: "Those idiotic Lafargues' delay in beating a retreat to Bordeaux is inexcusable", Marx wrote in a passion. But in fact, as the family soon learnt, the idiotic Lafargues had left Paris just before and in mid-September it was known that Paul had brought out a journal, La Défense nationale, in an attempt "to stir up the drowsy inhabitants of Bordeaux".[40] His efforts were vain, however, and within a couple of months the paper expired.

At the same moment of time Paris was completely invested, Wilhelm I making his headquarters at the Rothschild's château near Lagny, 18 miles outside the city. Versailles surrendered and on 11 October the first three shells were fired on Paris. From 7 November no one was permitted to enter or leave and, after a siege lasting 135 days, starving Paris capitulated. The armistice was signed at midnight on 27 January 1871.

---

* On 5 January 1872 this was renamed Place Cormeille until the liberation of 1945 when it became Place Anatole France under a communist municipality. The succeeding social democratic local authority gave it its present name of Place du Général Leclerc in the 1950s.

The short-lived Paris Commune which lasted from 18 March to 28 May 1871 was to have far-reaching consequences, both public and private, for the entire Marx family and not least for Eleanor herself.

At the beginning of March, even before the Peace Treaty was signed, the Prussians staged a 48-hour token occupation of Paris, whereupon the National Guard – the proletarians trained in the use of weapons – seized and removed the cannon, bought with its own subscriptions, to the heights and outlying quarters of the city. An overwhelmingly reactionary National Assembly had been brought to power by an election rushed through on 8 February, before the war-weary and famished population had had time to rally. Headed by Thiers and installed at Versailles by grace of the Prussians on 18 March, the government sent troops to recapture the 400 guns now fortifying Montmartre. These were the opening moves in a Civil War and a second siege of Paris that was to claim 50,000 victims at the hands of their compatriots among the defenders of the Commune who died in street fighting, indiscriminate slaughter, in cellar prisons, on transportation in coffin ships, in New Caledonia, in exile, on long terms of imprisonment and deportation.*

By the end of April "the shells, the bombs, battered the casemates, the grapeshot paved the trenches with iron"[43] and the defenders of Paris, with the connivance of the Prussians but no foreign intervention, were being mown down, prisoners shot out of hand and civilians massacred in greater numbers and with more appalling savagery than in any fratricidal conflict then known to modern times.

The Marxes were deeply affected: their oldest and best friends were involved in the carnage and they learnt with horror of the hideous death of Gustave Flourens, "the bravest of the brave", as Mrs. Marx called him.[44] He had not fallen in battle, as was first reported, but had been murdered on the night of 3 April when, fighting under the command of the ineffectual Bergeret,† Flourens had continued the advance towards St. Ger-

---

* 70,000 others, the dependants of the killed and proscribed, who were deprived of their means of livelihood, fled the city, thus Paris lost 120,000 of its working population.[42]

† Jules Bergeret (1820–1905) was on the General Staff of the National Guard and in charge of military operations in Paris. Having failed to reconnoitre before leading his troops to disaster in the direct line of the enemy's batteries, he was relieved of his functions and imprisoned from 8 to 12 April.

main while the two other columns had been surprised by artillery fire and forced to retreat. At the end of a gruelling day, unarmed and resting near the bridge at Chatou, he was denounced and surrounded by mounted gendarmes, of whom one, named Desmarets, dragged him to the river bank and, rising in his stirrups, cleft his head with a sabre stroke.

Flourens, the son of a Professor of Physiology and himself a widely travelled ethnographer and scientist who, for a time, deputised for his father at the Collège de France, was a combination of scholar and man of action. A fervent revolutionary who "knew no division of mankind but of the oppressor and the oppressed",[45] he had fled to England in the spring of 1870, implicated in the alleged plot to assassinate Napoleon III. The French government demanded his extradition, which Gladstone refused. While in London he frequented the Marxes, beloved by them all and a particular favourite with Jenny.

Back in Paris when the Republic was proclaimed, Flourens stood as a candidate in the local government elections of 5 November 1870 and became vice mayor of the 20th *arrondissement* (Ménilmontant), which district again returned him as a deputy to the Commune on 26 March 1871.* On 30 March he was appointed to the Military Committee with the rank of colonel. He was aged 33 when he was killed.

At this juncture and weighed down by such tragic events, Eleanor went to France with Jenny, arriving in Bordeaux on 1 May. Why she went is not altogether clear, though the circumstances provide grounds for reasonable conjecture. Certainly Laura was in need of help. Her third baby, a boy, had been born early in February and, like the little daughter who had died, was far from strong. Paul had gone to Paris in April "to obtain from the Commune *des pleins pouvoirs* to organise the revolutionary army in Bordeaux"[46] and had written to say that he was on his way home, but he did not arrive and nothing further was heard from him. This was hardly surprising since, though postal communications within the capital and

---

* The Central Committee of the Federation of the National Guard had taken control on 18 March. A week later it stood down to make way for an elected body of local deputies: the Commune. The election was held on 26 March and the results were published in the *journal Officiel* of 27 March (though not officially announced until the next day). They showed the following returns for the 20th *arrondissement*:

Ranvier	14,127
Bergeret	14,003
Flourens	13,498
Blanqui (who was in gaol and elected *in absentia*)	13,338

The first three were appointed to the Military Committee and Ranvier (1828–1879), who was also a member of the Executive Committee of the Commune, became the heroic defender of Buttes-Chaumont (the 19th *arrondissement*) in the final assault. He was condemned to 20 years hard labour *in absentia* in 1871 and sentenced to death in 1873 for setting fire to public buildings. Returning from exile in 1879, he died a month later.

the telegraph service had been restored by the middle of April,[47] the Versailles government was determined to isolate Paris from the provinces, to which end not only had railways been cut off but newspapers and letters were regularly intercepted and confiscated.[48]* Despite these good reasons for Paul's silence and failure to return, Laura was apprehensive, lonely and also alarmed when the baby now fell dangerously ill. Jenny's impulse, on learning the news, was to join her sister at once and "I do not mind confessing that in case of opposition on the part of my parents, I resolved to go off on the sly", she wrote.[46] She was dissuaded, however, by the fact that she would not be able to enter France without a passport and accepted the advice of her father and "Staff", as she now called Engels, to wait for the slow route by steamer. Probably, though Eleanor at the age of 16 could not offer much protection, it was thought wiser that Jenny should not make the journey alone at such a time.

On their arrival they found Paul back in Bordeaux, but as the month advanced and the Commune entered the Bloody Week of its final defeat on 25 May, making its last stand in the Père Lachaise cemetery,† it became imperative for the Lafargues to move. Paul was a marked man and no active supporter of the Commune was safe from the "legal" executions, wholesale denunciations and indiscriminate arrests now in full swing. Accordingly the four of them, with Schnappy and the sick baby, went to Bagnères-de-Luchon in the Haute-Garonne, a small town of some 4,000 inhabitants, close to the central Pyrenean range at the confluence of the rivers One and Pique, developed in the 18th century, with hotels, lodging-houses and a small casino, as "a place of fashionable resort".

Here they lived in complete retirement, seeing no one except the doctor whose services were in daily demand for the infant. On 13 June Marx who was, as he emphasised, *"in possession of full information"* – being in close touch with the progress of events through a German businessman, probably N. Eilau, who travelled constantly between Paris and London – wrote a carefully worded letter to his children recommending them to move to a better climate on the Spanish side of the Pyrenees. Paul's health in particular "will deteriorate and may even incur great danger if he any longer hesitates to follow the advice of medical men who know everything about his constitution and have besides consulted his doctors at Bordeaux, etc." He added that in London "the cousins from the country", meaning

---

* All stamps were removed to Versailles from the Paris post offices so that letters were franked, as they had been a century earlier, with a stroke of the pen.

† It will be noted that the final and fiercest resistance to the government troops, who had entered Paris on 5 May, took place in precisely those eastern districts of the city which had become working-class strongholds as a result of Haussmann's enterprise. The National Guard, composed of male – and female – civilians in arms, was locally based and assigned to the defence of the *arrondissements* from which its units were drawn.

the Communard refugees, "are thronging its streets. You recognise them at once by their bewildered air. ..."[49] Despite this very clear warning, Paul remained at Luchon for another six weeks. The reason is not far to seek: on 26 July, at six months old, the baby died. Within a few days, having been informed that his arrest was imminent, Paul crossed the frontier into Spain by mule path from Luchon by the Port de Portillon to Bosost, an ancient and rather derelict town 25 miles away. On 6 August the three sisters and Laura's little son went to visit him there. They had intended to go only for the day, but Schnappy was now ill with dysentery and Laura had to stay behind. Jenny and Eleanor, however, went back to Luchon that same evening.

Eleanor now takes up the story: "Jenny and I on returning from Bosost ... were arrested on the French frontier and conducted by 24 gendarmes right across the Pyrenees from Fos to Luchon, where we were staying. Arrived there we were driven to the door of M. de Kératry's house,* kept waiting in front of it in an open carriage with two gendarmes opposite us, and goodness knows how many around us, for three quarters of an hour, and then taken to our own house. At our house we found the police who had in the morning searched the house from top to bottom, and had treated our poor landlady and our servant who were alone in the house very badly. Kératry had already cross-examined them, and we were informed that he would presently arrive to do the same for us. At last he came, for he wouldn't leave the *parc* till the band stopped playing. Our room was already full of gendarmes, *mouchards*, and agents of every description when the *Préfet* Kératry arrived accompanied by Delpech, *procureur général*, a *juge de paix*, a *juge d'instruction*, the *procureur de la République*, etc. I was sent with the Commissaire de Toulouse, and a Gendarme, into a side room and Jenny's examination began, it being then about 10 o'clock. They examined her over two hours but to no use for they heard nothing from her. Then came my turn. Kératry told me most shameful lies. He got one or two answers from me by pointing to Jenny's declaration, and telling me she had said such and such a thing. Fearing to contradict her I said 'Yes, it is so'. It was a dirty trick wasn't it. However he heard precious little with all that. The next day when they came again we refused to take the oath. Two days after Kératry came and said he should in the evening send orders for our liberation (we were guarded by the police). Instead of that we were taken off to a 'gendarmerie', and there we passed the night. The next day we were, however, let off. Though we could not really move a step without being watched, besides we couldn't

---

* Emile, Comte de Kératry (1832–1905) was the first Police President of Paris under the Third Republic from 4 September till 12 October 1870, and Prefect of the Department of the Haute-Garonne in 1871.

get back our English passports. At last we got everything, and arrived at last in London. Laura went through much the same adventures at Bosost, though not quite as bad as we, for she was in Spain. It appears that Kératry after the first evening did everything he could to get us free but Thiers wished us to be imprisoned. What was very amusing were the blunders Kératry and the police made – for instance they looked in the mattresses for bombs, and thought that the lamp in which we had warmed the milk for the poor little baby who died, was full of '*pétrole*'! And all that because Lafargue is Mohr's son-in-law...".[50]

Marx, as he himself declared, had "the honour at this moment to be the best calumniated and most menaced man of London",[51] being accused of having instigated and controlled the Commune.

Jenny gave an even fuller account of the Luchon incident in a letter to the editor of *Woodhull and Claftin's Weekly*, written in September and published on 21 October 1871. From this it appears that the same "dirty trick" as had been played on Eleanor – the very use of this term betrayed her ignorance of police methods, pardonable in one so young – was first tried on Jenny who had been informed that the Lafargues were under arrest. It also emerges that Eleanor's interrogation lasted until two in the morning: something of an ordeal, as Jenny commented, for "a young girl of 16, who had been up since five a.m., had travelled nine hours on an intensely hot day in August, and only taken food quite early in Bosost". They were refused permission to write to their parents and Kératry was reported to have said to Jenny: "As for your sister and yourself, there is much more against you than against M. Lafargue and in all likelihood you will be expelled from France." The two girls were taken into custody on the following day at 11 p.m. and remained in the gendarmerie barracks, locked in, until five the next afternoon when Jenny demanded to see Kératry who explained that he had done them a kindness by confining them in the police station as "the government would have sent you to the prison of St. Godins, near Toulouse". Their passports were not returned to them for ten days after this, though they had received a *laisser-passer* to cross into Spain on 10 August. They were accused in the Toulouse press of being "emissaries of the International on the French and Spanish frontiers, 'But ... the Prefect is taking energetic measures in order to reassure the inhabitants of the Haute Garonne'."

Laura remained tied at Bosost by her ailing child, and when the police broke into her bedroom at three in the morning Paul escaped by the back door, was guided by peasants over mountain routes and gained the Spanish interior, only to be arrested in Huesca. On the day they learnt this news their passports were returned to the girls who decided to go to Huesca to allay Laura's fearful anxiety. They reached St. Sebastian where they heard that Paul had been released on 21 August. They immediately set off for London.

Writing to Kugelmann on 31 October Jenny added several other details concerning the episode, including the fact that Laura's little boy had been so ill at the time that they had thought he was dying, and that a letter found on her by the police had been written to O'Donovan Rossa* and was "an answer to his *shameful* condemnation in *The Irishman* of the Communal movement. I expressed my surprise that *he, of all men*, should believe the infamous calumnies against the Communists, invented by the wretched police organs...."[52]

One point emerged only after Jenny's death. In an obituary article by Engels published on 18 January 1883 in *l'Egalité* he stated that, when arrested, Jenny was carrying in her pocket a letter from Gustave Flourens. Had it been found it would have been a sure passport to New Caledonia for both girls. Left alone in the police station for a moment, Jenny had swiftly inserted the letter between the leaves of a dusty old ledger left lying about. "Possibly it is still there", he added.

It is of some interest that on her arrest Jenny should have been carrying these two letters – one to the exiled Fenian, the other from the murdered Communard – for she herself was the link between them. Rossa recalled that "while in prison in England I was treated pretty harshly and publicity of my treatment was the only protection I had for my life. There was a French exile in London named Gustave Flourens. He became interested in my case – more interested than many Irishmen."[53] Jenny had interested Flourens, "who would have died for the cause of Fenianism", in this particular case and he translated the *Irishman*'s account of Rossa's treatment for the *Marseillaise*,† to which paper Jenny contributed articles on Ireland under the pseudonym "J. Williams". "I do not know Rossa," wrote Flourens in the *Marseillaise*, "but I love him for his simplicity, the calmness and firmness with which he relates his frightful tortures." It is small wonder that the Irishman's attacks on the Frenchman's cause should have angered Jenny, the more so since the one was safely on the other side of the Atlantic where, according to his own account, he had been received with "deputations, invitations, addresses and congratulations",[53] while the other's mutilated corpse had been thrown into a dustcart and gloatingly paraded through the streets to Versailles.

---

* O'Donovan Rossa had been released from prison on 5 January 1871 together with other Fenians but forbidden to return to his own country, went to America where he edited the *Irish World* and *United Ireland*.

† A daily paper, the organ of the Left Republicans, published in Paris from December 1869 to September 1870. It was suppressed by the Government between 18 May and 20 July 1870.

If the outer eddies of the defeated Commune had caught up with Eleanor in the Pyrenees, she found herself on her return to Maitland Park Road at the centre of its vortex. She had now read her father's *Civil War in France*, drafted during Bloody Week and presented to the General Council of the IWMA on 30 May: two days after the dislodgment of the last defenders of the Commune on the slopes of Belleville. This *Address* became at once both the target for the most vicious attacks upon its author and the magnet which drew the Communard refugees to his house. Marx's admiration for the first proletarians to seize power had been expressed much earlier in a letter to Kugelmann. "What flexibility, what historic initiative, what capacity for sacrifice!", he exclaimed. "After six months of being starved into submission and brought to ruin by internal treachery rather than by the external enemy, they rise. ... History has no like example of a like greatness." These people were "storming heaven" and it was "the most glorious deed of our Party",[54] even if it were to be crushed.

Crushed it was and, from the end of May, larger and ever larger numbers of those who had escaped massacre and deportation flocked to London, "without clothes on their back or a farthing in their hands".[52] Their needs were imperative and Marx and Engels turned themselves into an *ad hoc* relief committee, raising funds, writing to potential employers, pacifying landladies whose refugee tenants could not pay the rent and appealing to foreign sections of the International for help. "You have no idea what we have been through here in London since the downfall of the Commune", wrote Mrs. Marx. "All the nameless misery, the unending distress."[55]

"There are a great many members of the Commune here and the poor refugees suffer frightfully", wrote Eleanor to Liebknecht, "they have none of them any money and you can't think how difficult it is for them to get work. I wish they'd taken some of the millions they're accused of having stolen."[56] The fact was that, although on 16 April there had been a Hyde Park demonstration in support of the Commune, British public opinion had veered with the gales of atrocity stories blown up by the press* and

---

* "Up till now it has been thought that the growth of the Christian myths during the Roman Empire was possible only because printing was not yet invented. Precisely the contrary. The daily press and the telegraph, which in a moment spread inventions over the whole earth,

the defenders of Paris were looked upon with "unmitigated horror". It came to Marx's ears that the Home Office had been asked by the French government to arrest and extradite the refugees so that they could be prosecuted for civil crimes; if they took work in England under assumed names they were dismissed as soon as their identity was known; their sufferings were "beyond description ... they are literally starving in the streets of this great city" and, while they congregated in idleness and poverty in a bare club room at No. 40 Rupert Street in Soho, "for more than five months the International ... supported, that is to say, held between life and death the great mass of exiles".[57] Such was the prejudice against them nourished by the hostile newspapers that when the first anniversary of the Commune came round, they were refused the use of a meeting place and "not *allowed* to meet in *any hall* in London".[58]

Eleanor has left a graphic description of that occasion, written twenty-one years later:

"No doubt few of you remember ... the condition of perfectly frantic fury of the whole middle class against the Commune. To many of you it will seem strange when I remind you that it was proposed – quite seriously – that the Communards who had taken refuge in England should be handed over to the doctors and the hospitals for purposes of vivisection. Perhaps exceptionally brutal in form, this proposition nevertheless largely expressed the feelings of the whole of respectable society. Saddest of all is the fact that in England the workers also, with rare exceptions (just as there were some middle-class exceptions among the Comtists) were as bitterly hostile to the Commune as their exploiters. And so it was but a small knot of English men and women who on that first anniversary came to meet the 'foreigners' – most of them persons escaped from Paris – and to celebrate the memory of the Commune.† But that meeting never came off at all. When we got to the Hall we found it closed against us.‡ The landlord preferred to return the deposit and to pay a penalty for breach of contract to allowing such a set of 'ruffians' in his highly respectable Hall. Then the said ruffians ... adjourned to a modest inn,§ and sat down together to an improvised – and not luxurious – supper. And ... despite the tragic horrors of that terrible year; despite the fact that most of these men and women had passed through deadly peril, that they were miserably poor, exiled, not a few suffering from still unhealed wounds; that

---

fabricate more myths ... in one day than could have formerly been done in a century", wrote Marx to Kugelmann on 27 July 1871.
† Those present included Marx, Eleanor, John Hales, George Milner, Martin Boon and the Communards Vaillant, Frankel, Theisz, Serraillier, Longuet, Lissagaray, Vallès, Ranvier.
‡ This was St. George's Hall, Upper Regent Street, famous from 1905 as housing Maskelyne's Mysteries or "Home of Magic".
§ The Cercle d'Etudes, Francis Street, off Tottenham Court Road.

there was hardly one among us who had not lost some near and dear to us, or – worse still – who had not some dear friend, who had not father or mother, sister or brother or child rotting in the horrible pontoons or on the awful plain of Satory; despite all this we were a merry party. In the midst of so much suffering, immediately after this overwhelming defeat, these men and women were gay with the gaiety of perfect faith. ... Alas! to many the hour of triumph was never to come, never even some small sign that it was approaching. Of all that goodly company few are left now. Yet through the long years of waiting and of exile they did not lose heart. ... While all the world – in England even the working class world – was thus against the Commune, one great organisation stood by the revolutionists, holding aloft the red flag. That organisation was the International Working Men's Association. In Spain, in Italy, in Belgium, in Switzerland its members went to prison for expressing their sympathy with the Commune; in Germany not only were they sent to prison, but when Moltke made a triumphal entry in Berlin, the workers received him with cries of 'Long Live the Commune' and were charged and dispersed by cavalry. In England certainly many members withdrew from the Association, but some remained faithful, even after the General Council had issued its now world-famous pamphlet *The Civil War in France*. This pamphlet, like nearly all the publications of the International, was written by my father, and is unquestionably the most valuable contribution to the literature of the Commune. To the brilliancy of its style even the reactionary press bore witness, although they did call its author 'infamous' and many demanded a State prosecution. It was then that my father publicly acknowledged himself as the author, though it was, of course, signed by the 'Council'. If the reactionary press admitted the literary excellence of the work, the Communards declared it to be a clear expression of what the Commune really meant, and had put clearly even to themselves, what they had only felt vaguely. ... But while this pamphlet will tell you the true meaning of the revolution of 18th March, and will remind you of the unparalleled heroism of its defenders, there is one thing this pamphlet cannot tell you – for it was written in 1871. And that is the way these men and women lived – that, almost without exception, the after lives of these Communards were worthy of their cause. To fight heroically is much. ... But how many are there who can be heroic not for a day, an hour, but every hour, of every day, in the long weary years? Yet these people bore hunger and privation, disappointment and the agony of hope deferred without faltering or falling. All honour to their memory! ..."[59]

Those who have mingled with the political refugees produced by the scourges of the present century will understand that there is no real contradiction between Eleanor's tribute to the spirit of the Communards, written in the light of memory, and Engels' words, penned in September 1874: "All these people want to live without any real work, their heads full of alleged inventions that are supposed to make millions if someone will put them in the way to promote these inventions, for which only a few pounds are needed. But should anyone be obliging enough to comply, he is not merely done out of his money but decried as a bourgeois into the bargain. ... The disordered life during the war, the Commune and exile has hideously demoralised these people and only sheer hard necessity can bring a disorganised Frenchman to his senses. The great mass of anonymous French workers on the other hand has abandoned politics for the time being and found work here."

To the time-consuming activities on behalf of the refugees which left him no peace, day or night, Marx added a tremendous burden of work on the General Council, often attending its sittings till one in the morning, and was further distracted by the need to answer personal calumnies and defeat attempts to suppress the IWMA, accused of having instigated the murder of the Archbishop of Paris and setting fire to the French capital. While Engels had been forced to lay aside his researches into Irish history, Marx, far from continuing to write the next volume of *Capital*, was not even able to revise the first volume for its second German edition, now urgently demanded by Meissner. Eventually, in July, a sub-committee of the General Council was set up to issue appeals and collecting sheets and to give aid to the refugees, drawing in such middle-class Comtists, to whom Eleanor refers, as Edward Beesly, Frederic Harrison and Thomas Allsop. Marx and Engels served on the committee until early September when, coincident with Eleanor's homecoming, foreign delegates began to arrive for the London Conference of the International,* some of whom were given hospitality by Marx and by Engels.

Eight of the leading members of the Commune had been elected to the General Council of the International in August, including Charles Longuet,† Albert Theisz,‡ August Serraillier§ and Edouard Vaillant,‖ who became close friends of the family, while a new London-based section, *Section française de 1871*, was formed in the autumn, to be almost at once torn by internal strife, its 24 members indulging in bitter recriminations and the mutual denunciation of agents and police spies, not altogether

---

* Held from 17 to 23 September 1871.
† Had previously served on the General Council from 1866 to 1867 and now remained a member from 1871 to 72.
‡ A member and the Treasurer from 1871 to 1872.
§ A member from 1869 to 1872.
‖ A member from 1871 to 1872.

without foundation, but nonetheless suicidal. Thus Eleanor's return from abroad in September 1871 was a time of turbulence both within the home and outside.

In all these years there have been but few glimpses of Eleanor's personal friends. She played in the street with the neighbours' children, she gave a small party, she romped with the young Freiligraths and caught infections from her school-fellows but, since there was no occasion for correspondence with any but the little Alice Liebknecht of long ago, almost nothing can be known now of her relations with people of her own age. Was she as popular with them as with the grown-ups who visited her father? Several of these went out of their way to send her their greetings when they wrote. Henri Perret, a Swiss engraver and member of the IWMA in Geneva, spoke of Marx's two charming daughters – Jenny and Eleanor – as "true international women who could serve as a model for many of our women".[60] This was written when Eleanor was not yet 16. Anselmo Lorenzo, the founder of the Spanish section of the IWMA, wrote that he retained "the most pleasant memory" of Tussy and laughed when he talked of "the conversation he had with her on the way to the post".[61] In his book *El Proletariado Militante*[62] Lorenzo described this occasion: "When I expressed my wish to send a telegram to Valencia to report my safe arrival in London, Marx's youngest daughter was sent with me to show me the way. I was most surprised by the alacrity with which the young lady helped a foreigner whom she did not know, this being contrary to the customs of the Spanish bourgeoisie. This young lady, or rather girl, as beautiful, merry and smiling as the very personification of youth and happiness, did not know Spanish. She could speak German and English well but was not very proficient in French, in which language I could make myself understood. Every time one of us made a blunder we both laughed as heartily as if we had been friends all our life."

It is thus enlightening to find a letter, undated, but from internal evidence written sometime in the summer or autumn of 1871, to "My dearest Eleanor" from a certain "Aggie", then aged 19.[63] The letter reveals a long-standing friendship and one intimate enough to allow of confiding family troubles. The writer, it emerges, is a Miss Agnes Frances C. The surname is not given, but it is just conceivable that she was a Cunningham: a younger member of that family which, eight years before, had offered to find posts for Jenny and Laura as governesses and, in 1866, had asked them to be bridesmaids at their daughter's wedding.* Miss C. has a bullying father, most of the time in India, a spying mother, almost

---

* The father in that case was quite possibly Dr. Cunningham, Sanitary Commissioner to the Government of India, who is known to have been home on leave in 1870. (See *Florence Nightingale* by Cecil Woodham-Smith.)

always at home, and innumerable "Reverend uncles" including "old Bishop T.". From this unpromising background the daring girl hopes to escape. She is dying to fight on the barricades; both she and Annie, her sister aged 15 who writes a postscript to this letter, are passionate revolutionaries and have read with attention the International's statement on the Civil War[64] which, by virtue of its force and clarity, Aggie attributes to Eleanor's father. She is, however, critical of the Geneva Programme of the International,[65] which she does not believe he can have written – as, indeed, he had not – arguing that it was foolish to propose abolishing God if He did not exist and that the equality of women could not be achieved by decree but must depend upon their being entitled to work like men. With such ideas and interests it is small wonder that Miss C. finds the "abominable home tyranny" irksome; this very letter has had to be smuggled out by a housemaid, given a diamond as a bribe, and she is under the necessity of "contriving means" by which she can continue to correspond with Eleanor. Her plans to run away, for which she steals £10 from her mother's desk, are foiled by a treacherous brother, Willy, who turns up from Brighton at the very moment of the theft of which, naturally, a servant is accused so that Aggie has to confess, whereafter an even closer watch is kept upon her. Horrid schemes are afoot to marry her off, but what she really cares about is the political situation – particularly that in France – and both sisters are authors, the elder having completed a work called *Rich and Poor* and being now engaged for the past year upon a long story, while Annie has written an excellent tale called *Home Rule* ("not Mr. Butt's!" Aggie exclaims).

The interest of this communication, which is signed "Yours for ever", lies not so much in the fact that Eleanor should be on close terms with young people of so totally different a social environment as that, leaving aside the farces and melodramas of that *milieu*, revolutionary politics should be the basis of this friendship in which Eleanor was clearly the dominant partner. While at this age she still, in letters to and from her adult correspondents – whether Marx, Engels, Liebknecht or others – seems young for her years, "Aggie" redresses the balance and shows that, among her equals and those slightly older, Eleanor was regarded as a fount and source of political wisdom.

Returning to the letter written on the 22nd anniversary of the Commune, when Eleanor used the phrase "many members withdrew from the Association" she was indicating the seeds of dissolution within the First International which, following the Hague Congress of 1872, was transferred to New York where it suffered a lingering death, to be formally buried in 1876. "The fall of the Commune placed the International in an impossible position", wrote Eleanor in an obituary article on her father.[66]

Much later she spelt this out in a letter to Kautsky saying that, to put it shortly, "there had been internal disintegration going on ... almost from the end of the Commune"; that the quarrels among the French refugees had created difficulties enough, but that the defection of such people as Howell, Odger and Lucraft – the last two refusing to sign the General Council Address on *The Civil War in France* and resigning over this issue – had rendered the situation untenable. In face of opposition, Marx, she said, had remained firm on the matter of transferring the International to New York. "He said [its] *real* work is *done*, we must not outlive ourselves and fall ignobly to pieces; the end must be voluntary and decent." Though he had admitted it only to his intimates, Marx had known full well that it was the finish. Eleanor went on to say that she had been aware of all that was going on at the time and that for some two or three years her father had kept the "discordant elements" together by sheer strength of will. "He was far too keen-sighted not to know that such a keeping together was no longer possible."[67]

Eleanor's perfectly truthful account is not, of course, nor did she claim that it was the whole story. In particular it omits the role of the anarchists who, under Bakunin, had from as early as 1867 tried by every means to "conquer the leadership of the International"[68] and in 1871 captured the demoralised sections of the French political exiles in both London and Geneva. Engels put the matter in clear perspective when, with the demise of the International in New York in 1874, he wrote to Sorge to say that it was well that it should be at an end: "It belonged to the period of the Second Empire. ... It was the moment when the common, cosmopolitan interests of the proletariat could be put in the foreground. ... Actually in 1864* the theoretical character of the movement was still very confused everywhere in Europe, that is among the masses. German Communism did not yet exist as a workers' party, Proudhonism was too weak to be able to insist upon its special fads,† Bakunin's new stuff-and-nonsense had not so much as entered his own head yet, even the leaders of the English trade unions believed that the programme ... gave them a basis for coming into the movement. The first great success was bound to burst asunder this naive combination of all fractions. This success was the Commune, unquestionably the intellectual child of the International, although the International did not lift a finger to bring it about. ... For ten years the International dominated one side of European history – the side on which the future lies – and can look back on its work with pride...".[69]

Combined with the wider issues at stake was also the fact that Marx's

---

* The year when the IWMA was founded.
† Although the Proudhonists had formed the majority, the Blanquists the minority, on the Central Committee of the Commune.

own position was fast becoming "untenable". "As long as he remains on the General Council", wrote Jenny to Kugelmann, "it will be impossible for him to write the second volume of *Das Kapital*",[70] adding that he had made up his mind to give up the secretaryship after the Hague Congress. His involvement with the refugees had been deep and personal, for he never forgot what it was to be a political exile, and when their disruptive activities bedevilled the General Council it was with bitterness that he wrote to Sorge: "This is my thanks for losing almost five months in work for the refugees and for saving their honour by the Address on the Civil War!"[71] On the same day, in a letter to Nikolai Danielson in St. Petersburg, he said: "Certainly, I shall one fine morning put a stop to all this, but there are circumstances where you are in duty bound to occupy yourselves with things much less attractive than theoretical study and research."*

Marx bowed to circumstances until the situation within the International and external political events combined to justify calling a halt. "How much better and happier it would have been for him had he quietly gone on with his work", wrote Mrs. Marx to Liebknecht. "And as for our private life, what ruin, what torture! Just at a time when our girls needed help."[73]

---

* One of these much less attractive things was a vituperative exchange of letters with Charles Bradlaugh who had given a lecture for the benefit of the French refugees and used the occasion to misrepresent passages of the *Civil War in France* and to attack "the Communists". Over £7 was collected at the meeting, but the refugees returned it as dishonourable to accept aid from "a man who had traduced and insulted them". While Marx told Bradlaugh that he had nothing to do with this incident and, on the contrary, thought the money should have been accepted in order not to offend the English workers who had given it, he was angry about the attacks which were "either stupid or malicious" and he had decided they were the latter.[72]

The reason why the girls needed help, or at least that some notice should be taken of them at this juncture, was that in March 1872 Jenny became engaged to Charles Félix César Longuet, Lafargue's former fellow-student, born at Caen, Calvados, in 1839. Under the Commune he had been a member of its Labour Committee and the editor of its official *Journal* until he applied for his release to take up military service.* At the same time Leo Frankel – a Hungarian socialist whose election to the Central Committee of the Commune as deputy for the 13th *arrondissement* (Gobelins), the head of the Labour and Trade Committee and a member of the Finance Committee, had demonstrated that there was no narrow nationalism among the defenders of Paris – was much drawn to Eleanor.†

"There is great rejoicing now in your family over the Longuet business", wrote Engels to Laura who was in Madrid where she and Schnappy had rejoined Paul in February. "Tussy, too, is very pleased about it and looks as if she should not mind to follow suit."[74] She did not merely look, she acted; but not in response to Frankel's marked attentions. Instead she became engaged to Lissagaray, a dashing character and one of the Commune's boldest fighters who was not, however, favoured by the Marxes as a son-in-law.

Jenny's engagement on the other hand elicited not only general approval but also one of Mrs. Marx's flights of eulogy and optimism. Longuet was "a very gifted and a very good, fine, proper man", she wrote to Liebknecht and, since the young people held the same views and convictions, "their future happiness is guaranteed". In the same letter she reported, with emphasis, that Tussy was *lively and well* and a politician from top to toe".[75] There was not a word of her attachment to Lissagaray. It was simply ignored. Indeed, although her engagement, entered upon secretly at first, lasted for nine years, there is only one recorded instance of her mother openly announcing it,[76] while her father refused to recognise

---

* In July 1866 he had been arrested in France while staying in Bagnères-de-Bigorre in the Pyrenees and imprisoned for eight months. He translated into French Marx's *Inaugural Address* to the IWMA and his *Civil War in France*.

† Frankel (1844–1896) shortly transferred his affections to the Russian exile Elisaveta Tomanovskaya, known as Dmitriyeva, who had taken an active part in the Commune, and whose marriage to Ivan Davidovsky – either before or after the birth of her child – in 1874 came as a blow to Frankel.

it altogether. Possibly Lissagaray's nationality was against him, for Mrs. Marx, despite her bliss, expressed some anxiety about the Longuet alliance on that score: "I had sincerely hoped that Jenny's choice (for a change) would have fallen on an Englishman, or a German, rather than a Frenchman, who, combined with the national qualities of charm, is naturally not without their weakness and irresponsibility."[75] She also complained bitterly to Becker about French chauvinism: "if one does not choose to believe their pack of lies and French fiddlededee, which I find impossible to do, one is considered a 'Prussian'."[77] Also, it must be borne in mind, Frenchmen – quite apart from carrying off two of his girls – had been a terrible nuisance to Marx in the recent past. Again, Lissagaray was seventeen years older than Eleanor: exactly twice her age at that date. But, above all, it was his flamboyance – the very quality that attracted Eleanor – which made him ineligible. Marx did not trust him. "I ask nothing of L.", he wrote to Engels, "but proof, not phrases, that he is better than his reputation and that one has some justification for relying upon him."

While preparations were in train for the Hague Congress, which Marx regarded as "a matter of life and death" for the International, another matter of life and death touched the family even more nearly as Laura's little son, her only surviving child, lay slowly dying in Spain. For a time Schnaps rallied, but by June all hope was relinquished and the end came early in July. Jenny's wedding, planned for that month, was postponed and the Lafargues travelled *via* Portugal to Holland where Marx and his wife met them on 1 September.* The Hague hotel registered and the police recorded the presence of "Karl Marx and wife with their daughter Laura and her husband Paul Lafargue".[78]

While her parents – and Engels – were abroad, Eleanor at home received a long scrawl from "yours lovingly, Maggie"[79] which throws out many dark hints concerning Eleanor's apparently tangled love life and sheds little light. "You may be sure he is under some restraint, perhaps some promise", wrote Maggie. This would account for "a change of tactic" that was admittedly puzzling but might be all for the best in the long run, though presently making Eleanor miserable. If she saw "*him*" she would do all Eleanor asked and lose no opportunity to put in a good word. "I hear Frankel is very attentive to you", she went on, "well after all he has always been so, if he did not show it always because he was afraid of

---

* The Hague Congress was held from 2 to 8 September 1872. Paul Lafargue was the official delegate for Spain and Portugal.

being strangled by J.J."* The letter makes it clear that the families of the two girls were on terms of friendship and that the purport of this correspondence must be kept secret from the parents on both sides, though it is a little hard to say what they could have made of it. It does, however, suggest that Maggie was keen to smooth the course of true love for some contestant who had been warned off the field, and that can have been no one but Lissagaray.

Jenny was married at the St. Pancras Register Office on 9 October 1872 in the presence of Engels and Albert Theisz, she being then 28. Longuet, though not more than 33 or 34, appears on the marriage certificate as 38 years of age. More reliably this document states that he was a journalist residing at 132 Malden Road and that his father was a deceased hosier. The wedded pair then moved to "orthodox, snobbish Oxford", where Longuet hoped to establish a connection as a teacher of French but gave up after six fruitless weeks which had not produced a single pupil.[80] It was to Jenny in Oxford that Eleanor wrote early in November complaining of the offensive manner in which the Lafargues – recently arrived in London – behaved towards Lissagaray. They had "treated him to a very cold bow" when introduced at her parents' house, but Eleanor had attributed this to "a certain *gêne* at a first meeting". On taking their leave, however, they were equally distant while, on a second occasion, they shook hands with everyone else present and pointedly omitted Lissagaray. Eleanor was nettled: "Either Lissagaray is the perfect gentleman Paul's letter and his own behaviour proclaim him to be and then he should be treated as such, or else he is no gentleman, and then ought not to be received by us – one or the other – but this really unladylike behaviour on Laura's part is very disagreeable. I only wonder Lissa comes at all. He told me, too, that he would come one day this, or early next week to read me some extracts from the second edition of his book which is shortly to appear."[81]

By the spring of 1873 the whole situation had become "very disagreeable" indeed and reached a climax. Towards the third week of March Eleanor went to Brighton with her father. In reply to a cheerful letter, Mrs. Marx wrote to her there on the 25th, giving news of Jenny, then three months pregnant, and an account of various meetings at one of which, badly chaired by Maltman Barry, Alfred Milner had spoken, a number of difficult Frenchmen had threatened to walk out because the

---

* The unknown strangler, evidently another of Eleanor's admirers, cannot be identified but may have been Jules Johannard (1842–1888), a Communard member of the General Council of the IWMA, who had reached London in November 1871. Another possible candidate is Jules Joffrin (1846–1890), a metalworker who was also a Communard refugee in London at the time, but he nowhere figures in the Marx circle.

documents under discussion and the resolution proposed were not translated, while Lissagaray had insulted Ranvier, and Roullier* had made an uncouth joke at Marx's expense.[82] The tone and content of this letter assume that Eleanor would wish to be kept in touch with all that went on during a brief absence and, indeed, it expresses the hope that this "'dead' fortnight" will do her good.

But on 1 April Marx came home alone leaving Eleanor in Brighton where she was determined to stay and earn her own living. That this decision was neither premeditated nor planned is clear.

Two days after Marx's return to London her mother is writing to Eleanor to say that she will send on "a little outfit" as soon as possible, that for the first week – the length of time it might take her to find a post – she had enough to wear and could always buy herself a few pairs of stockings in Brighton. "Be *brave*, be *courageous*", wrote Mrs. Marx. "Do not let this fearful crisis overwhelm you. Believe me, despite appearances to the contrary, nobody understands your position, your conflict, your embitterment better than I do. Let your young heart triumph and remember that where the *guilt* lies there also lies the heaviest suffering. ... Forgive me if at times you have felt that I hurt you. ...." There is much in this letter to suggest that Laura had played some part in the "fearful crisis", for the mother emphasises that whereas a sister may "cease to be and to feel as a sister", the child always remains the child, even if at fault and in the wrong. "The more at fault, the greater the compassion and sympathy", said Mrs. Marx and Eleanor's burden was the lighter in that she had nothing, or barely anything, with which to reproach herself.[83] But where the guilt lay, who was to blame, and for what, are not disclosed.

Eleanor had friends in Brighton – in particular a French socialist pastor named Pascal and his wife – through whom she hoped to get pupils. She also applied to an agency. "You see, I'm 'going in' for it with a vengeance", she wrote to Marx.[84]

Neither of her parents opposed this step, unforeseen though it was and taken at an age when her sisters had been regarded as children whose smallest attempt to stand on their own feet had been frowned upon. Mrs. Marx, though now approaching 60, had greatly modified her views on this subject, writing to Tussy that "I alone understand how dearly you long for work and independence, the only two things that can help one over the sorrows and cares of present-day society".[85] She sent off Eleanor's wardrobe without delay, hoping she would "recognise her old friends again" and promising other things to follow. There was a great deal more about

---

* A Proudhonist Communard who was said never to have read Proudhon.

clothing which, her mother was sure, would bore Eleanor to tears because: "I know how little store you set by such things and how lacking in vanity and a love of finery you are."[*][86]

Eleanor quickly found private pupils, who paid her 10s. a week, and throughout April she took all that came her way. She was also busy reading Polybius and asked her father for "some other of the old histories you promised me".[84]

But it was not until 5 May,[†] having turned down an offer from another school, that she started in regular employment with the Misses Hall who ran one of the 14 seminaries for young ladies (there were also three for young gentlemen) in Sussex Square. She was not, of course, engaged to give instruction on the fundamentals of socialism or current revolutionary affairs, though she had the good fortune to find at least one pupil who took "an immense interest" in these subjects and for whom she begged a copy of *The Civil War in France* from her mother.[88]

Eleanor did not live at the school, but in lodgings, first at 2 Manchester Street[‡] and then at 6 Vernon Terrace.[§] Mrs. Marx strongly approved her decision to stay with strangers rather than with friends who, like the Pascals, were involved in finding jobs for her, since if "business questions take on a sociable form ... independence and freedom are lost".[85] In any case, although Eleanor liked Pascal, she did not much care for his wife of whom he seemed "to stand rather in awe".[84] Her attendance at the school was part-time and she continued with her extra-mural teaching, for she found that prices in Brighton were almost double those in London.

Throughout this period Mrs. Marx wrote constantly to "Tussychen" and, indeed, at no other period of their lives was the correspondence between mother and daughter so frequent or more loving. At the outset Mrs. Marx had doubted the wisdom of Eleanor taking the post with the Misses Hall. "The one thing that troubles me is the thought that your health is not strong enough to recuperate on the treadmill of a boarding school with its strict routine and drudgery of business. Mohr and the others are very glad about your success and earnestly beg you not to overwork."[86] She also feared that the food would be too stodgy and too coarse for Eleanor's ticklish appetite and kept on sending potted meat, chocolates and bottles of mineral water with the incessant plea: "Tell me

---

[*] In this connection it is interesting to note that, although Eleanor is shown as rather "dressy" on posed photographs – no casual snapshots, these – later evidence is that "she didn't go in for floating things ... she wore severe, plain, simple clothes ... always very neat and tidy ... She wouldn't have looked good in frilly things".[87]

[†] i.e. The start of the summer term.

[‡] Now a motor tour office. Near the old Chain Pier, swept away by a storm in 1896, and replaced by the present Palace Pier.

[§] Now flats. Near the station.

what you would fancy"; "Let me know exactly what I should send you in the way of nourishment". The letters are equally concerned about clothes: "Next week I shall send you a light modern costume for church and promenade", also a new canary-yellow cotton frock, her old summer dresses being too shabby and washed out – "Shall I send you your black grenadine?" – "Shall I send you your black suit? As it is rather cheap and common, you could wear it out for everyday. The skirt is very trim" – while again and again she advises Tussy not to stay too long in the water, to worry her head about funds or to tire herself out by taking on more private pupils. Though there are few references to Marx or the Lafargues in these letters, there is much about Jenny whose late employer, Mrs. Monroe, had died in April and who, despite a difficult pregnancy, had become governess to the Manning family* and had placarded every window in Chalk Farm advertising lessons in singing, elocution "and the Lord knows what besides"[85] until, owing to her "dimensions" – so embarrassing to her that she would not go out until her mother had fashioned a polonaise† for her – she finally gave up in June and turned to making baby's clothes, as the "great catastrophe"‡ was expected – quite erroneously – at the end of July.[89] Mrs. Marx also reported on the little outings of the day: Lenchen was going to Astley's Circus; she herself had been to the theatre and once or twice to the "bonnefemme Redcap" for a drink with Lina Schoeler.

All these letters – homely, gossipy and solicitous albeit barely legible§ – show Mrs. Marx in a most kindly light, but also that she regarded the whole Brighton episode as a prolonged if misguided form of convalescence. There is a hovering anxiety about Eleanor's health: her chest is weak, her back aches, her appetite is wretched, she is sleeping badly but, though recommended to take chloral, is warned in the next letter not to do so without medical advice and, in general, she is addressed as a semi-invalid. None of this emerges from any of Eleanor's traceable letters.

---

* That of Laura's former suitor.

† *Shorter OED:* "A dress or over-dress consisting of a bodice, with a skirt open from the waist downwards." Mrs. Marx had earlier proposed making such a garment for Eleanor too.[86]

‡ It is now clear that "catastrophe", in its sense of dénouement rather than disaster, was used as an accepted euphemism for parturition, since it was applied not only to the forthcoming birth of children like Eleanor (see p. 3) who, by reason of hardships, might be seen as something of a calamity, but also to those joyfully awaited.

§ "I fear you will have trouble deciphering my letter", wrote Mrs. Marx at one point, "but at all events nothing is lost and it is good practice for you as a 'German teacher'."[86] The truth is that Mrs. Marx's old German script is legible only to people of high endowments. Although many of the originals were kindly put at my disposal by the archivists of Moscow, Amsterdam and Berlin, the extracts quoted here are taken from letters written in Latin script, in a mixture of German and English, decoded (i.e. transcribed in typescript) or else the result of the most arduous labour. I am still dumbfounded by the thought that Mrs. Marx was her husband's calligrapher.

While she promises not to overwork, she does not complain of her health nor appear to care about the advice and admonitions – or the garments – proffered. She enters little into her mother's chat concerning people and events in London but reports on the weather in Brighton, her pupils and acquaintances in a cheerful yet colourless tone.

On 22 May Marx went for twelve days to Manchester to consult Dr. Gumpert. No sooner had he left than Mrs. Marx visited Eleanor in Brighton.* There she learnt from one of the Misses Hall that Lissagaray had been calling on Tussy at the school, which was allowed "since she was engaged". This put Mrs. Marx in a dilemma but she extricated herself by voicing neither objection nor denial, merely saying that the "position" ruled out anything definite for the time being. "The question of 'position' is understood by every English person", she commented, adding that Marx would not be told of this but would be writing to Tussy who, she hoped, would have her mind set at rest by his letter and was not to worry until she had heard from him.⁹⁰

The parents were not wholly frank with each other about the situation. While Mrs. Marx could connive at Lissagaray's visits to Brighton, Marx was confiding only in Engels. He had been corresponding during these weeks with both Tussy and Lissagaray and, though neither his letters to them nor their replies have come to light, their content is indicated thanks to his absence from London and Engels' presence there at a critical moment.

The promised letter to Tussy was written from Manchester on 23 May, as he reported to Engels on the same day, concluding with the words: "for the moment Mr. L. will have to make the best of a bad job".† Unwisely Engels showed the letter to Mrs. Marx who pondered over this last sentence for a long time but said nothing. Engels hastened to tell Marx that no harm was done since she could have made little or nothing of it "and, should she ask me, I shall simply tell her that you expressed the assumption that L. was not to be relied upon implicitly and therefore, even before you went away, you had spoken of writing to Tussy to try to influence her".

A week later Marx received a reassuring letter from Tussy which he enclosed – together with one from Lissagaray – for Engels to read. He had told her there were no grounds for her accusation that he had been unjust to Lissagaray. "The damnable thing", he wrote on 31 May, "is that for the

---

* Mrs. Marx rarely, if ever, dated her letters. Where dates are assigned to them these are based upon the internal evidence of known events referred to as having occurred "yesterday", "last Monday" etc. and worked out on a Perpetual Calendar. This method, whose accuracy is infallible, sometimes produces results that conflict with the dates given for these and other letters from Mrs. Marx in the various archives by whose courtesy they were read.

† Marx used the French phrase *"bonne mine à mauvais jeu"*.

child's sake I have to tread very considerately and cautiously. I shall not reply until I have consulted you on my return. Keep the letter to yourself." With that return, on 3 June, the confidences are again verbal and the curtain comes down.

But while Eleanor and her father might try to sort things out by correspondence and otherwise conduct themselves as though nothing untoward – no "crisis" – had occurred; though she had written him a lively birthday letter for 5 May, quite as if their relations were not strained for the first time in their lives, the truth is that it made them both ill.

Since Eleanor was an 18-year-old, wildly in love and thwarted, it would be no overstatement to say that she was the greater sufferer. But it was Marx's illness that made news and, to his fury, Maltman Barry published in *The Standard* alarming reports on the state of his health which drew enquiries from all over Europe and made severe demands on Engels' powers of discretion, great strategist though he was. He assured Kugelmann that the rumours were grossly exaggerated, that Marx was merely suffering from the effects of overwork "attended by other unpleasantnesses". When Marx had decided to go to Manchester Engels had written a letter for him to take to Gumpert which, while giving every particular of his physical condition, deliberately left out any reference to the domestic upheaval that lay behind it. The Marxes were "very particular about family matters", as Engels wrote to Sorge when bidding him not to betray the great secret that Jenny was about to give birth.*

Despite her lack of formal qualifications as a teacher Eleanor was not only popular with the girls, as Mrs. Marx had observed on her visit, saying she had seldom met nicer children,[90] she also gave satisfaction to the Misses Hall who were outraged when, after scarcely a month, Mrs. Marx proposed that Eleanor should go abroad. Lenchen had received news that her sister was dying and she planned to leave at once for her native village. To Mrs. Marx, with her disdain for such paltry matters as the school term, nothing appeared more fitting than that Eleanor should accompany Lenchen to benefit by the steamer journey down the Rhine and the simple country fare of St. Wendel. The Misses Hall argued that unless she could find someone to replace her, Miss Marx must carry on the duties she had undertaken. This struck Miss Marx's mother as thoroughly unreasonable. She proposed coming to Brighton again "to talk to the old maids" but was dissuaded and a tart exchange between one of the "old maids" and the mother ensued.

"Dear Madam", wrote Miss Hall, "I am much surprised and annoyed at your daughter requesting to leave me ... without any notice whatever to

---

* This was written on 26 July 1873 at the end of which month, as is known, the child was confidently expected.

enable me to supply her place. She tells me it is your wish that she should do so, at which I must confess I am *much astonished*. ... With compliments, etc." To this Mrs. Marx retorted, at Jenny's dictation: "Dear Madam, I am much annoyed to hear you cannot spare my daughter ... It is the opinion of our medical adviser, Dr. Matheson, that she requires a change of air and scene. I greatly fear that in her delicate state of health her school duties will be too trying for her especially during the very warm weather. I know my daughter has made no arrangement with you or contract to stay a certain time; however she nevertheless considers it would not be right to leave without having given due notice, etc., etc."[91]

While everyone was annoyed with everyone else Eleanor herself had no intention of falling in with the plan. "Under present circumstances", she wrote to Mrs. Marx, "I do not think of going home. Of course", she went on, "I shall be only too glad to see some of you, but I think you had better come some other Saturday or Sunday."[88] In the event, Lenchen was seen off alone by Marx some time in mid-June, having had to postpone her departure owing to her own ill health, and Eleanor remained in Brighton until the end of the summer term. She was back at 1 Maitland Park Road when Charles Félicien Marx Longuet was born there on 2 September 1873.

Once in the family circle there was no dodging the issue over Lissagaray whom Eleanor was now forbidden to see. Precisely when and why this was enjoined is not known. That it caused no serious breach between her and Marx is told by the fact that, both being far from well, they set off together on 24 November to stay for three weeks in what Mrs. Marx called "aristocratic German Harrogate".[92] As a health resort this was a great improvement upon Brighton, for here, under Dr. Andrew Myrtle – a Scot, a Jacobite and the author of a work entitled "On Jaded Brains" – Eleanor took Kissingen waters, baths and was prescribed complete rest and early nights. Marx's cure differed from hers only in that it included much vigorous exercise. Of an evening they "took refuge" in chess.

There is much that remains obscure about this passage in Eleanor's life; and not surprisingly, for not only did it take place in the bosom of the family, but on two separate occasions – once after Marx's death and again after that of Engels – letters of a private nature are known to have been destroyed, while the long Odyssey of the Marx and Engels literary remains has still not been told in full.[93] But some things are abundantly clear: this family row, this break, this bid for independence on Eleanor's part when she stayed in Brighton – her first experience of self-reliance – was in no way a "rebellion". As for running away with Lissagaray, the thought seems never to have entered her head; and, though Franziska Kugelmann claimed in her reminiscences[94] that he addressed Eleanor in letters as "*ma chère petite femme*", there is no evidence to suggest that she had or was prepared to set the conventions – or her parents – at defiance. On the contrary, the only direct evidence of her attitude points quite the other way and is contained in a troubled, sweet letter written to her father on 23 March 1874. Letters from girls in love to unrelenting fathers are not rare; they seldom plead their cause with a spirit so touching in its candour and affectionate obedience.

"My dearest Mohr,*

I am going to ask you something, but first I want you to promise me that you will not be very angry. I want to know, dear Mohr, when I may see L. again. It is so *very* hard *never* to see him. I have been doing my best to be patient, but it is so difficult and I don't feel as if I could be much longer. I do not expect you to say that he can come here. I should not even wish it, but could I not, now and then, go for a little walk with him? You let me go out with Outine,† with Frankel, why not with him? No one moreover will be astonished to see us together, as everybody knows we are engaged ...

When I was so very ill at Brighton (during a week I fainted two or three times a day), L. came to see me, and each time left me stronger and happier; and more able to bear the rather heavy load laid on my shoulders. It is *so* long since I saw him and I am beginning to feel so very miserable notwithstanding all my efforts to keep up, for I have tried hard to be merry and cheerful. I cannot much longer. Believe me, dear Mohr, if I could see him now and then, it would do me more good than all Mrs. Anderson's prescriptions put together‡ – I know that by experience.

At any rate, dearest Mohr, if I may not see him now, could you not say *when* I may. It would be something to look forward to, and if the time were not so indefinite it would be less wearisome to wait.

My dearest Mohr, please don't be angry with me for writing this, but forgive me for being selfish enough to worry you again.

Your

Tussy

This is quite 'entre nous' "95

---

* It has often been said that Marx's nickname – variously Mohr or Moor – was owed to his dark complexion. However, it is more likely that the family, steeped in German literature, derived it from Karl Moor, the hero of Schiller's *Die Räuber*.

† Nikolai Isaakovich Outine (or Utin) (1845–1883), a Russian revolutionary who had been a member of the student movement and of the underground organisation *Zemlya i Volya* (Land and Freedom). Emigrating at the age of 18 he remained in exile until the late '70s, when he returned to Russia. Marx referred to him as "one of my dearest friends". He married a fellow exile at the age of 35 when he was already suffering from the heart condition from which he died three years later.

‡ Elizabeth Garrett (1836–1917). Overcoming great difficulties she became the first woman to qualify as a doctor in England, her name appearing on the Medical Register in 1866. (Elizabeth Blackwell had been put on the Register in 1858, but, though English, she had qualified in America.) In 1869 Dr. Garrett was appointed to the staff of the North Eastern (Shadwell) Hospital for Children (later known as the Princess Elizabeth of York's Hospital, closed in 1963 and now demolished). Dickens visited and described the Hackney Road branch of this institution, "A Small Star in the East" (*The Uncommercial Traveller*) in 1868, the year it was opened. Dr. Garrett married James Anderson in 1871 and was admitted to the B.M.A. in 1873 where, for the next 19 years, she was the only woman. She became Eleanor's doctor some time in the early '70s.

Hyppolite-Prosper-Olivier Lissagaray, who never called himself nor was
ever known by any but his surname, was born into an old Basque family
on 24 November 1838 in Auch, the chief town of the department of
Gers.[96] Nothing is known of his childhood, but as a student he read
classics and graduated before he was 22 when he went briefly to America.
On his return to France at the end of 1860 he organised a series of
lectures, a kind of "popular university", which became celebrated as the
Lectures de la Rue de la Paix,* where progressive writers, journalists and
also professors who had been deprived of their Chairs attracted large
numbers of young people. Lissagaray was bent upon reviving freedom of
thought and speech in the repressive first decade of the Empire. "Youth",
he declared, "must be earnest and austere rather than light-hearted, for we
have no time left to be young." He also launched the first of his many
ephemeral journals, *La Revue des cours littéraire* and, in August 1868,
founded *L'Avenir* in Auch, where in December he was sentenced to a
month's imprisonment for incitement against the government and vio-
lation of the new press laws, passed in March of that year as one of the pre-
election measures to silence the anti-Bonapartists. This was merely the
first of a series of arrests, imprisonments and penalties – amounting in all
to over two years in gaol and fines of some £150 before, during and after
the 1869 elections – on charges of "provocation, outrage and violence",
"misdemeanour" and violations of the laws on public assembly. While
retaining the editorship of *L'Avenir* in Auch he started *La Réforme* in Paris
where he held public meetings attacking the régime which earned him a
year's sentence for "offences against the Emperor". During the first term
of this captivity in Ste. Pélagie prison he wrote a book called *Jacques
Bonhomme: Entretiens de politique primaire*, dedicated to the Democratic and
Social Republic, which traces the history, stage by stage, of Bonhomme,
the eternally defeated common man who makes revolutions – for others.
On his release Lissagaray added to his political offences by championing
the killer of a policeman, then issued a seditious appeal to soldiers to
mutiny and, this time, to escape inevitable arrest, fled the country,
remaining in Brussels until after the outbreak of the Franco-Prussian war

---

* Later renamed the rue Cadet in the 9th *arrondissement* (Opéra).

and the first French defeats. He then returned to Paris and was among the crowd storming the gates of the Palais Bourbon* on 9 August 1870. Lissagaray now joined the army at Tours and saw fighting under Gambetta to whom he proposed a scheme of training camps for *francstireurs* at Toulouse where, in November, he was appointed Quartermaster to the army of the south-west and, as such, was Gambetta's personal representative. His main self-imposed function as *commissaire de guerre* was to inspire the men, whom he proposed to accompany into battle, with patriotic fervour and a spirit of sacrifice. Impatient of his responsibilities for the clothing, equipping and provisioning of the troops, he remained at his post only until early January 1871 when he went off to fight with the 2nd army of the Loire under General Chanzy. There the armistice caught him unawares. He was demobilised before the rising of 18 March which found him back in Paris where in April he brought out a daily paper under the title *L'Action*, of which only six numbers appeared. This was followed in May by another of his short-lived journals, *Le Tribun du peuple*, which again lasted but a week. Then, abandoning these journalistic efforts, he joined in the street fighting, first in the 11th *arrondissement* (Popincourt) and later on the heights of Belleville where on Whit Sunday, 28 May, he defended single-handed for a quarter of an hour the last barricade to be manned (at the intersection of the rue de la Tourtille and the rue Ramponeau)†. When his ammunition was spent he walked away and disappeared. It is not known how he escaped from Paris, but when he reached London – as he thought, undetected – he found himself among those whose arrest and extradition were immediately demanded by the French ambassador. Two years later a military court sentenced him *in absentia* to deportation and confinement in a fortress.

From 1871 to 1880 he lived in exile. Thanks to letters intercepted, private papers searched and dossiers compiled by the Paris police,[97] it is known that Lissagaray's London address was 35 Fitzroy Street and that he was in regular correspondence with his former associates in France.

Aware that his letters were being tampered with he thought to outwit the spies by having the envelopes addressed to "Evelyn Herbert". Natu-

---

* The Chamber of Deputies, originally built in 1722 for the Dowager Duchess of Bourbon, was later enlarged at great expense for the Prince of Condé and declared national property in 1790. In 1814 it was restored to the Prince, but the Legislative Assembly, which had sat there, continued to use it, paying rent until the Government decided that it would be cheaper to buy it outright.

† "The last barricade of the days of May was in the Rue Ramponeau. For a quarter of an hour a single Federal defended it. Thrice he broke the staff of the Versaillese flag hoisted on the barricade of the Rue de Paris. As a reward for his courage, this last soldier of the Commune succeeded in escaping," wrote Lissagaray.[43] This anonymous marksman is always thought to have been Lissagaray himself since no other witness was present.

rally this failed of its aim, but the police, ever alert if a trifle confused, were now under the impression that Lissagaray was in correspondence with someone of that name, while Carl Hirsch* was reported to be in touch with a certain Herbert Velyan and also Herbert Evelin, residing in Fitzson Street, when not in Fitzroy Square. (Meanwhile Engels was thought to be living at 112 Regent's Park Road whose occupants must have been entranced to receive his well-thumbed mail.†)

But for all their insouciant ways with names and addresses, the police recorded most exactly the restaurants where their suspects lunched and the cafés they frequented (which proves that, given a congenial field of operations, police intelligence is of a high order and not to be misprized). Thus we know that on 29 May 1877 Monsieur N. Azane ("lunches every day at the Café de Madrid"‡) undertook to place Lissagaray's book in France and also that Herman Lopatin, one of the Russian translators of *Capital*, was an *habitué* of the Café Copenhagen in the rue d'Argenteuil where he made appointments to discuss subversive matters.

The postal department was splendid, too, if less constant in its vigilance than the café squad, so that there are some gaps in otherwise fascinating correspondence. Eleanor's letters, written in French, were faithfully transcribed[99] and on 12 May 1876 she expressed on Lissagaray's behalf the hope that both Hirsch and Naquet – who was planning to start a paper, *La Revolution française*, which finally appeared in October of that year – would come to London to discuss it: "Lissagaray writes to him of course but that is not the same thing as talking". In July Eleanor wrote two letters asking Hirsch to trace material needed for Lissagaray's book§ and on 20 October she announced that the *History* was due to come out at

---

* Carl Hirsch (1841–1900) had taken over the editorship of the *Volksstaat* on Liebknecht's imprisonment in the spring of 1873 until his own arrest. Released in 1874 he went to Paris, where he remained for four years, going to Brussels in 1878 to edit *La Lanterne* which was smuggled into Germany. In 1875, in 1879 and on various other occasions he was in London.
† Oddly enough Engels himself made precisely the same mistake in writing to a Russian emigrée in Paris (Minna Gorbunova) in August 1880.
‡ This café in the boulevard Montmartre had long been regarded by the authorities as a meeting place for undesirable if not dangerous characters. In an illustrated volume on the Commune, with text written "By an Englishman, Eye Witness of the Scenes and Events of that Year", the Madrid is described as "the resort of a certain class of Parisian Journalists, more famed for the manufacture and circulation among themselves of current *bons mots* and passing flights of fancy involving delicate (and indelicate) innuendos than for the more solid parts of their profession. It is the 'Exchange' of tales of the hour and the birthplace of much 'News' derived from 'authentic sources'. From the depths of 'bocks' consumed within its precincts, many a wild rumour startling Paris and echoing throughout Europe has been evolved".[98]
§ Lissagaray required the full deposition made by Commandant Papillon and details concerning Bayard's part in the surrender of the fort of Vincennes which were to be found in the June 1872 files of *Le Radical* and in *Le Droit*.

the end of November, in which month* she told him to expect a visit from its publisher, Kistemaecker, to arrange for the book's distribution in Paris.†

In 1877 Lissagaray wrote a whole series of letters to Hirsch about unspecified "socialist journals", which may well have included *L'Egalité*, since this weekly, edited by Guesde, appeared for the first time at the end of the year (November), and continued until the following July.‡

Lissagaray's correspondents also included Henri Oriol, an employee of Lachâtre§ and, in 1878, one of Marx's letters acquainted the police with the fact that Lissagaray was keeping him informed of events in France and of the attempts by Pyat's followers to rehabilitate posthumously "that buffoon" Thiers.‖

As early as the end of 1871 the *Petit Journal* offices in Brussels had published a small volume by Lissagaray under the title *Les huit journées de mai derrière les barricades* – the work from which he read extracts to Eleanor – in effect a preliminary sketch for his classic *Histoire de la Commune de 1871*. In 1873 he also brought out a pamphlet, *La Vision de Versailles*, which has never been translated into English but has been described as "a literary evocation of the nightmare of the Versailles judges present at the resurrection of their victims".[1] His great work, the *History*, which has made his name known and remembered, was first published in Brussels by Henri Kistemaecker in 1876 at a moment when a Paris Congress, from which the first rudimentary organisation of a French Workers' Party was to emerge, disgraced itself by condemning the Commune. Lissagaray's *History* came out in a German translation in 1878 and again in 1891 and 1894, while the English version, translated by Eleanor, appeared in 1886 and, in Lissagaray's definitive edition, in 1898. He is said to have worked on this book for 25 years, constantly making fresh researches, assembling new material and rewriting.

In the meantime, while taking part in the first London anniversary meeting of the Commune in 1872, described by Eleanor, Lissagaray was active in the campaign for the proscribed Communards to return to France. In July 1876 and again in June 1878 he visited Jersey and, as soon as an amnesty was granted in July 1880, he finally went back to Paris where, in May 1882, he started a daily paper, *La Bataille politique et sociale*. This paper had a longer life than its predecessors, lasting full five months,

---

* On 25 November 1876.
† She adds, unconscious of absurdity: "This visit should not be talked about in case the police get wind of it."
‡ 31 issues appeared. The paper was restarted in January 1880 as the organ of the French Workers' Party.
§ The publisher of the first French edition of Volume I of *Capital*.
‖ Died of apoplexy at St. Germain-en-Laye on 3 September 1877.

but by no means a tranquil one. At daggers drawn with Paul Lafargue – with whom he had quarrelled violently in the early days of his exile in London, thereby contributing to the crisis in Eleanor's affairs – and not in sympathy with the French Workers' Party (*Parti ouvrier français*) formed by Jules Guesde* and Lafargue in 1880, Lissagaray allowed his paper to be used by their opponents to foster private feuds. In October, with the connivance of the proprietor, Adigé, Lissagaray absorbed the Guesdist paper, *Le Citoyen*, of which he claimed sole editorship having first turned out Guesde, Lafargue and Deville. A monumental rumpus ensued and for several days each issue of the paper appeared under a new title. The differences were never composed and Lissagaray continued to edit this paper until the competition of Guesde's *Cri du peuple*, revived in October 1883, put *Le Citoyen* out of business, whereupon he re-started *La Bataille*, only to be manoeuvred out of its editorship: "The same trick has been played on M. Lissagaray as he played on us ... they are but following the glorious example he once gave them", wrote Paul Lafargue to Engels.[100]

In 1885, before he had been ousted from the paper, he used it to set up an aid committee for disabled Communards, many of whom had been mutilated in the fighting or were suffering the after effects of transportation. A great admirer of Victor Hugo, he organised a contingent of these veterans to attend the writer's funeral,† carrying a red flag.

Twice Lissagaray stood in the Paris municipal elections but was not returned, though on the second occasion, as a candidate for Montmartre in 1890, he polled a higher vote than one of his opponents, Charles Longuet.

For the next many years he devoted himself to the revision of his *History of the Commune* for the 1898 French edition and is not known to have played an active part in politics. On 25 January 1901, too weak to undergo the tracheotomy which alone could have saved his life, he died at 43 rue Richer, within a stone's throw of the scene of his earliest exploits in the rue Cadet. He was 62 years of age. Two thousand people came to his burial in the Père Lachaise cemetery, including both Vaillant and Longuet.

A hot-headed and undisciplined individualist of superb physical courage, a dead shot and an enthusiastic duellist,‡ Lissagaray was a colourful figure, with a flair for leadership and a supreme contempt for

---

* Mathieu Basile, known as Jules Guesde (1845–1922), had been imprisoned under the Second Empire and defended the Commune in his journal *Les Droits de l'Homme*, published in Montpellier and suppressed in June 1871. He took refuge in Switzerland and in 1877 founded *L'Egalité*. The programme of the French Workers' Party was drafted jointly by Guesde and Lafargue with the help of Marx and Engels. (See below, fn.*, p. 149.)

† On 1 June 1885.

‡ In one sword duel, fought with a kinsman, Paul de Cassagnac, in 1868, he was wounded in the chest. In another, fought with Rochefort in 1889, both duellists were severely injured.

authority, who is never known to have written for any paper which he did not himself edit. He was a man of few intimates, possessed of a gift almost amounting to genius for quarrelling with those he had, his friendships and love affairs – except in the case of Eleanor – generally ending "in a row and blue fire".[101]

As a frequent guest at Maitland Park Road in the '70s and under Marx's tutelage, his views on socialism – which had been of the Utopian variety – underwent a change, but he boggled at the corollary: the need for orga-nised workers' parties. Thus when he returned to his native land at the age of 42, to find a political climate very different from that engendered by the conspiratorial sects of the past, he was rejected by the revolutionaries who had begun to learn the more up-to-date lessons of discipline and organisation. Dedicated, fiery and self-willed he remained, but a self-appointed leader without a following, owing allegiance to none, his star had set by the '80s, though in his famous *History of the Commune* it still shines brilliantly.

In the Preface to the first English edition, translated by Eleanor, he wrote in November 1877: "No doubt it is an exile who speaks, but an exile who has been neither member, nor officer, nor functionary of the Commune; who for five years has sifted the evidence; who has not ven-tured upon a single assertion without accumulated proofs; who sees the victor on the look-out for the slightest inaccuracy to deny all the rest; who knows no better plea for the vanquished than the simple and sincere recital of their history. This history, besides, is due to their children, to all the working-men of the earth. The child has the right to know the reason of the paternal defeats, the Socialist party the campaign of its flag in all countries. . . ."[43]

The cure in Harrogate had helped to restore Eleanor but it had done little for Marx who was advised – not for the first time – to take the waters in Carlsbad. Accordingly he wrote to Dr. Kugelmann to say he hoped they might meet there in the summer and, towards the end of June, asked him definitely to arrange lodgings for Tussy and himself from mid-August.

Before that time was reached, on 20 July 1874, Jenny's little boy died – as he had been born – at his grandparents' home, of gastro-enteritis* at the age of eleven months. Eleanor had nursed him devotedly, earning Jenny's "deepest love and gratitude",[102] but she collapsed under the strain. Her parents were in Ryde on the Isle of Wight and Marx at once hastened to London on learning of Eleanor's condition, to be followed by his wife who arrived on the day the baby died.[103] The loss of this, the fourth grand-child, hit Marx hard and he confessed that, being so much cut off from the outside world, he felt the more emotionally involved in his family circle. For some three weeks Eleanor was dangerously ill and was attended daily by Dr. Garrett Anderson. Then she began to improve, her appetite growing "in geometric proportions", according to Marx who went on to say that one of the curious features of women's ailments "in which hysteria plays a part" was that you had to affect not to notice that the invalid lived on earthly sustenance, which also became unnecessary once recovery was complete. He regarded Eleanor's illness as a recurrence, in severe form, of her trouble in the previous year, as it certainly was; and, while attributing it to "hysteria" – what is now called stress – he was not so obtuse as to pooh-pooh it for that reason but, on the contrary, thought that she should be spared all exertion; the journey to Carlsbad to be made by easy stages, taking four days.

It was now that Marx, foreseeing trouble at the hands of the Austrian police, resolved, after exactly a quarter of a century's permanent residence in England, to apply for British nationality.

Though not of a naturally sanguine temperament where his personal affairs were concerned and deeply learned in the works and ways of the British governing class, Marx showed a quaint, an even deluded faith in its Civil Service. He assembled his sponsors before a Commissioner for Oaths who drew up his petition to the Home Office for naturalisation on

---

* Summer or "European" cholera sporadic.

1 August – a Saturday, of all days – two weeks before he was due to leave for Carlsbad. Incorrectly submitted, it was returned for amendment. Nevertheless he was confident that he would be a full-fledged British citizen in time for his departure and was perplexed when, after ten days, his status was unchanged. He need not have worried: the application was quite expeditiously turned down within the month.

(In parenthesis it may be said that, while Marx was on his way to Austria with Eleanor, Detective-Sergeant W. Reimers begged to report in his own inimitable Scotland Yard style that this was "the notorious German agitator, the head of the International Society, and an advocate of Communistic principles. The man has not been loyal to his own King and Country." Sergeant Reimers forbore to mention that the man had twice been expelled by that King and Country; but then, so did Marx whose memorial tactfully stated that he, a "natural-born subject of the Emperor of Germany, having emigrated by permission of the Prussian Government in the year 1846 ceased to be a subject of Prussia and has not since been naturalized by any country". Marx's referees,* whose names the sergeant graced with inverted commas, as if he detected *aliases*, were passed as "respectable householders" and their claim to have known the petitioner for a stated period of time was endorsed, signifying that for long years Marx's most innocuous acquaintances had been kept under observation. The document was then passed in the approved manner from one official to another, each making a comment – "Report *not* satisfactory" – "Refuse certificate" – "I think so?" – with an appended squiggle; the last word: "Refused" being initialled by the top squiggler on 26 August 1874. A heavily polite letter was sent by Mr. Robert Willis, Commissioner for Oaths of 18 St. Martin's Court, Leicester Square, asking whether the refusal was "on account of any and if so what defect in the form of application" and, if not, "esteeming it a favour" if he could be informed of the grounds for refusal "in order to enable me to renew the application at a future period if so desired by my client". This was tentatively minuted "?Decline to give reasons", the query being eliminated on 2 September,[104] by which time Marx had been abroad for almost three weeks.)

Carlsbad, "The Queen of Bohemian Watering Places", as it was called by an English enthusiast,[105] had a long history of royal patronage. Named, according to legend, after the 14th-century King of Bohemia and subsequently Holy Roman Emperor, Charles IV, it was visited by Frederick I of Prussia, Peter the Great – who took the health-giving

---

* R. W. Seton, who vouched for Marx's respectability and loyalty, was his agent and attorney; Farquhar Matheson of 11 Soho Square, his doctor; Julius Augustus Manning, Jenny's employer, a merchant, of 55 Fellows Road Hampstead; and William Frederick Adcock, gentleman, of 6 Southampton Road, Maitland Park.

waters by the pitcher – the Emperor Charles VI and Napoleon's Empress Maria Louisa. A different category of distinguished visitors included Leibniz, Bach, Goethe – who came no less than a dozen times between 1786 and 1806 for his kidney trouble – Schiller, Beethoven and Paganini, while Mozart's son (Franz Xaver, who died in 1844) lies buried in the churchyard (the gravestone calls him Wolfgang Amadeus, as his widowed mother had renamed him) and Turgenyev – Marx's exact contemporary (1818–1883) – had spent June 1874 there, a few weeks before Marx and Tussy came.

In earlier days the arrival of every guest was heralded by a fanfare from the castle turret and a serenade outside his place of residence. This pretty welcome fell into disuse when, in the early 1850s, a jarring note was sounded by the horn-blowers and serenaders who took to asking for tips. Indeed, a marked change came over Carlsbad at this time, making it less a pleasure-resort with therapeutic adjuncts than a serious, even earnest *Kurort*, though the number of visitors rose by leaps and bounds and ladies were still presented with nosegays on departure, for which, however, they surreptitiously paid. The whole place, with its population of 9,000 and its one unprofitable local industry of pin-making* was put on to a sound economic footing: there were charges for *séjour*, for listening to the band, for swallowing the waters, for wallowing in them and for every other boon offered by a spa that boasted no fewer than ten mineral springs.

For 40 years, until his retirement in this year 1874, Dr. Hlawacek had been the reigning physician who had laid down the regimen followed by the innumerable flourishing doctors and by their patients. Another leading doctor of long standing who had published works on the Carlsbad cure was Dr. Leopold Fleckles who practised there from 1839 until his death in 1879. His son, Dr. Ferdinand Fleckles, had joined him from Vienna in 1864.

The tax Marx had to pay into the town funds was doubled both for himself and Eleanor because he had registered as Charles Marx, "private gentleman" in the hope of evading suspicion.† Dr. Kugelmann, his wife Gertrud and their 17-year old daughter Franziska were already installed and had taken rooms for the Marxes at the Germania in the Schlossburg: a

---

* The population figure refers to 1873. For the *souvenirs* market of some 20,000 visitors in the season curious little objects of iron, steel, ceramic, tin and wood were produced. By the '90s, when the population had grown to 12,000 and the number of annual visitors to over 42,000, porcelain, stoneware and cutlery factories were established. Later it became one of the centres of the Czech glass-making industry.

† Professional men paid a reduced tax and, Marx's hope proving vain on this first visit – for he was immediately identified and denounced in ugly terms by "the Vienna scandal-sheet *Sprudel*" – he registered the following year as Doctor of Philosophy and was let off more lightly. The denunciation had been written – and later regretted – by Dr. Ferdinand Fleckles.

narrow lane debouching into the wider more fashionable street misnamed the Schlossplatz. Though a guest-house* rather than an hotel, it was in an expensive quarter and, while acknowledging that "respectable appearances" had their advantage in putting the police off the scent, Marx wished he could have been accommodated more cheaply.

Eleanor found Carlsbad delightful and every prospect pleasing: "indeed one must be very *difficile* not to be enchanted with such admirable scenery", she wrote to Jenny on 5 September.[108] Marx, too, declared that he could never tire of the wooded mountain walks. These they took each day as part of a strict routine of which he gave an hour-by-hour account to Engels. "We are very exact indeed in all our duties", wrote Eleanor. "Papa being ... at the Brunnen† by 6 o'clock, frequently still earlier."[108]

There was no lack of social life and Eleanor gave a lively description of their circle. There was Simon Deutsch, an Austrian bibliographer with whom Marx, a fellow exile, had quarrelled in the far-off Paris days, but who was now accepted as an old friend, "a most amusing fellow and has known and knows *everybody*". There was the painter Otto Knille, "a charming fellow", as well as "an awful Frenchman" – fortunately departed – "a perfect idiot ... the most unbearable example of the bourgeois species that it is possible to imagine". There was also Count Platen, "good fellow enough in his way", who was "a regular aristo and catholic, but good Pole and Russia-hater. He was described in the local paper here as *chef* of the Nihilists (you may suppose how horrified the old fellow was) and was announced as being here with the *chef* of the International."[108] "Half the local medical faculty gathered round me and daughter", Marx reported, adding that they made rather a lot of noise but were congenial enough in an environment where much laughter and little thought were prescribed.

Yet this Carlsbad sojourn, for all the salutary waters, delightful surroundings and pleasant company, was not an unqualified success for it was marred by Kugelmann's behaviour which came near to wrecking Marx's cure.

Five years earlier Jenny and her father had stayed with the family in Hanover; Kugelmann had also met Mrs. Marx and Laura when he attended the Hague Congress in 1872.‡ This was Eleanor's first meeting with them, but it was also to be the last occasion for any intercourse between the families.§

---

* Run by Herr Friedrich Stadler and his wife Marie. During World War II the Nazis turned the place into a military hospital and the grand-daughter of Marx's landlord was pressed into service as a nurse.[106] It is now known as the Spa Hotel Karl Marx[107] in Karlovy Vary.
† The equivalent of the English pump-room in a watering place.
‡ Where he had also met and was said by his daughter to have been unfavourably impressed by Lissagaray.[94]
§ Apart from a few letters exchanged by Eleanor and Mrs. Kugelmann.

This final rupture was dismissed in Franziska Kugelmann's reminiscences[94] as "a difference ... which was never smoothed out" owing to her father's over-zealous convictions which "Marx could not countenance in a man so much younger". It was rather differently described by Eleanor at the time.

Kugelmann, nicknamed Wenzel by the Marxes, was "such an impossible person that it was inevitable that he and Papa *could* not help quarrelling", she wrote. And, indeed, Marx, whose nerves were frayed by the man's "incessant, deep-voiced, earnest trumpetings", called him "insufferable": "an arch-pedant and small-minded bourgeois Philistine", a bully and a bore. But the nub of the matter was that he brow-beat his wife, "a charming little woman", according to Eleanor, and that the life he led her and their young daughter was abominable. "It's a hard thing", wrote Eleanor, "when a woman has no money of her own and her husband tells her every minute that she is ungrateful for his *Wohltaten** to her and the child. You cannot imagine how brutish Kugel. is and how shameless."[108] He made scenes, he sulked, he took offence on the slightest provocation but, embarrassing as this was, he might yet have concealed his unattractive character had not Marx, in whose presence he tried to preserve a certain dignity, occupied an adjoining room at the Germania separated from the Kugelmanns only by a door. He thus became an unwilling listener to the most odious rows. Eventually Marx removed himself to another room on an upper storey, but not before the distracted wife and daughter had poured out their hearts to him. Franziska had hoped for her mother and herself that Marx would restrain her father and procure "at least four weeks' peace" from the perpetual quarrels that had soured the girl's whole life. Marx and Eleanor sided with the unhappy creatures, causing further unpleasantness, and the parties ceased to be on speaking terms.

Thus ended the friendship of twelve years, begun by a correspondence that elicited from Marx some of his most illuminating letters on the political events and his own work in the period from 1862 to 1874.[109]

There was no question now of Marx and Eleanor accepting the invitation to stay with the Kugelmanns in Hanover on leaving Carlsbad. Instead – though they met, liked and remained on excellent terms with Mrs. Kugelmann's brother, Max Oppenheim of Prague, whom Eleanor characterised as "the kindest person" – they went to Dresden on 21 September and then to Leipzig to visit Liebknecht for three days. After a brief stay in Berlin they arrived in Hamburg on the 29th for Marx to discuss his affairs with Meissner. They embarked for England at the beginning of October.

---

* Benefactions.

Perhaps the most lasting result of Eleanor's travels in 1874 was the renewal of her old friendship with Liebknecht and his daughter Alice after twelve years and her meeting, for the first time, with his second wife, Natalie, and their young family.*

"When I was in Leipzig", she wrote on 13 October, "I could not find words to tell you how happy I was to see you all. It has been one of my dearest wishes to see you again, for you know, dear Library, I have grown up with the remembrance of many a happy day spent with you. ... The three days we passed together ... will always be a bright and joyous souvenir."[110]

From that time forth she was never again wholly out of touch with her "dear Library".† The start of this revived correspondence was for the most part concerned with arranging for an exchange of reports on the socialist movements in France and Germany,‡ for publication in Liebknecht's *Volksstaat* and Lissagaray's newly launched *Rouge et Noir*.§ Eleanor also gave the Liebknechts news of the situation in England, saying that during her stay in Germany she had "seen how much the police do to help our Cause" and could not "but regret that the Prussian regime is not possible in England. It would do more than all the Trade Unions and Workingmen's Societies put together to bring life into the movement here",[111] which was at a standstill. "A kind of internal movement (strikes etc.) never entirely ceases in England, but John Bull has been accustomed for so long a while to behave himself that he goes the way he should go to an alarming extent. Who would think that in quiet respectable happy England millions of people are on the verge of starvation! Not a day passes in which 'death from want' of some 'pauper' is not recorded. It passes all understanding how the thousands of men and women starving in the East

---

* Gertrud, the daughter of the first Mrs. Liebknecht, was then seven years old; Natalie's elder son, Theodor, was four and the younger, Karl, three. The three other boys – Otto, Wilhelm and Curt – were born later.
† In April 1878 he came to London for a fortnight and again for the last three weeks of September 1880.
‡ Though the French Workers' Party was not yet formed, the German Social-Democratic Party had been founded, on Marxist principles, at Eisenach in 1869 by Liebknecht and August Bebel.
§ Only three issues appeared. Lissagaray, whose letters were still being intercepted, advised Liebknecht to send his contributions addressed to Mr. A. Bourgoyne at 7 South Crescent, Bedford Square (i.e. Store Street).

End of London – and starving by the side of the greatest wealth and luxury – do not break forth into some wild struggle. Surely nothing could make their lot worse than it is now. ...."[112] She reported the opening of a Medical School for Women, with Professor Huxley and Dr. Garrett Anderson as "the chief promoters",* adding that this was of benefit only to middle-class women though, she conceded, this was "always something".† Her words suggest that the achievements of British bourgeois democracy were not much in her line. Any but the most draconic methods of enforcing reactionary legislation, any widening of opportunities for women, regardless of the human suffering caused by the one and the human advantages offered by the other, were to be deplored since neither of them directly incited the working class to "wild struggle". Eleanor was not, of course, speaking in terms of political realities. In these "Leftist" opinions, as we should call them now, she was merely expressing the pity and passion that social injustice aroused in her warm nature, conditioned as it was by the most impressive and the central experience of her time – the heroic Commune, a fight that had indeed been waged by a wretchedly poor and largely unorganised proletariat – and the sense of frustration felt by many ardent young people of her (and not only of her) day when faced with the apathy of the masses and the political nullity of the trade unions in her own country. Her reactions also reflected Lissagaray's influence and, indeed, the furtherance of his interests and activities was Eleanor's main preoccupation as she approached her 20th year. For his sake she undertook, with some misgivings, the translation into French of the speech Liebknecht had made in the Reichstag on 21 November.‡

By the end of 1874 the Lafargues had settled at 27 South Hill Park and the Longuets had moved to 58 Fleet Road, both in Hampstead.§ Jenny's husband had been appointed as Assistant Master in French at King's College in the University of London at a salary of £182 a year,‖[113] while

---

* The leading spirit was, in fact, Sophia Jex-Blake who founded the London School of Medicine for Women opened on 12 October 1874 at 30 Henrietta Street off Cavendish Square (now Henrietta Place).

† Eleanor sent Natalie an advertisement from *The Times* to illustrate the "horrible position of governesses" (presumably also middle-class women): "A young lady desires an engagement as governess. She can give good references and teaches German, French, music and drawing, learnt abroad. Terms six shillings a week."[111]

‡ In which he demanded the suspension of the sentences on the Social Democratic Deputies who were in prison while condemning the conduct of their trial and the verdicts.

§ From September 1875 to 1877 the Lafargues lived at 225 Camden Road. (Ellen Terry was two doors off at 221.) They then moved to 37 Tremlett Grove, Junction Road, Islington.

‖ He held the appointment officially from 1875 until 1881 but in fact resigned in November 1880. Fourteen years earlier Thomas Hardy, then aged 21, had attended the French lectures at King's College.

she herself began teaching German at St. Clement Danes Parochial School in Stanhope Street.*

The house occupied by the Marxes for the past eleven years was now too large for them. In March 1875 they moved to 41 Maitland Park Road,† a substantial terrace house, by present day standards more than adequate for four people but, rated at £44 a year, far cheaper than their former spacious dwelling.

It was from this address that Eleanor now began her correspondence, in French, with Carl Hirsch. It shows another aspect of Lissagaray's influence upon her, for not only was she extremely well-informed on the political situation in France, both that of the present and of the immediate past – the *History of the Commune* was now being written – but her facility in French had vastly improved, at the expense of her German which was so shaky that she "felt quite ashamed of herself" as she told the Liebknechts to whom she wrote in English.

One of her earliest letters to Hirsch, dated 25 October 1875, shortly after he had spent a few days in London, concerned an article on Henry Irving written by Mrs. Marx. Eleanor asked Hirsch to use his many connections with the foreign press to have this published in the *Frankfurter Zeitung*. She also hoped that a review on the same subject by a Russian lady of her acquaintance might be printed in *Le Journal des débats*, *Le Temps* or *Le Siècle*. Marx himself, she said, would have written something on Irving had he found the time. This fervent propaganda for an actor who was not unknown nor yet in his first youth – he was then 37 – was occasioned by the production in October 1874 of his Hamlet whose novelty had puzzled and even shocked audiences – "why could not Mr. Irving be original in old-world fashion?" asked *The Times* of 2 November 1874 – followed by his Macbeth in September 1875. These were Irving's initial Shakespearean ventures and both met with a mixed reception, the "peculiarities" of his Macbeth, in particular, forming "the chief topic of discourse in theatrical circles", according to *The Times* of 2 October 1875. The press as a whole had been loud in its praises, but Irving had his

---

* Founded in 1700, this was one of the oldest 'voluntary' (Church of England) schools in London. Stanhope Street itself was demolished for the building of Aldwych and Kingsway (1899–1905), though the school had been rehoused in 1881. It is now the Church Primary School in Drury Lane.

† Known until May 1868 as 9 Maitland Park Crescent. In 1935 the then LCC put up a plaque bearing the words "Heinrich Karl Marx (1818–1883) Socialist Philosopher Lived and Died Here". Early in 1936 this was destroyed by vandals, replaced and once more smashed on 1 May. The County Council was prepared to restore it yet again but the occupant of the house, unwilling to be the target of further violence, refused consent.[114] The house was demolished after severe bombing in the area during the Second World War, though it was still standing in 1958, completely derelict. (See above, fn.†, p. 33).

detractors and controversy raged. The Marxes did not know him personally but they were acquainted with the Batemans, under whose management Irving had originally appeared at the Lyceum. Their eldest daughter Kate had played opposite him as Lady Macbeth, but it was certainly disinterested enthusiasm for an artist of rare talent, allied to her lifelong devotion to Shakespeare, that inspired Mrs. Marx's first journalistic essay. She asked Eleanor to make clear to Hirsch that her name was not to appear in the *Frankfurter Zeitung* should the article be printed, though its authorship could be revealed "among friends".

The article was published* and a few months later Mrs. Marx herself sent a letter to Hirsch to say that as a result of this initial success she had been seized by a writing mania and had submitted a little report on the London Season which, to her astonishment, had appeared on 4 April 1876.†[115]

Eleanor's own interest in the theatre was probably stimulated by the founding in 1873 of Furnivall's New Shakespeare Society, which she joined.‡

Mrs. Edward Compton, then Virginia Bateman who, like her sisters, Kate, Ellen and Isabel, was on the stage, using the name Virginia Francis, recalled that when "in her 'teens" she had visited the Marxes' "horrid little house" – more often than her parents because Eleanor was much attached to her – her young friend was always "most anxious to make me take Shakespeare seriously, indeed, she used to drag me to Furnivall's

---

* On 21 November 1875.

† Mrs. Marx was referring, of course, to the theatrical rather than the social Season, of which she cannot but have held unprintable views. In her letter to Hirsch she mentions that her article appeared below an obituary notice from Paris on the Frankfurt-born Countess d'Agoult (1805–1876), who wrote under the pen-name Daniel Stern and was chiefly famous for having been Liszt's mistress and figuring as such in Balzac's *Béatrix*. She had been known to Mrs. Marx 33 years earlier in Paris, at which time she was "running after the young Herwegh and Heine was fleeing from her". The *Frankfurter Zeitung* published in all five articles by Mrs. Marx: "The London Theatre World", 21 November 1875; "The London Season", 4 April 1876; "Shakespearian Studies in England", 3 January 1877; "Shakespeare's *Richard III* at the Lyceum Theatre London", 8 February 1877 and "From the London Theatre", 25 May 1877.

‡ Frederick James Furnivall (1825–1910) was the secretary of the Philological Society in 1853 and responsible for organising the preliminary work on the *New* (Oxford) *English Dictionary*. In 1861 he became the editor but, realising the long years that must elapse before it could be completed, he conceived the notion of the *Concise* (Oxford) *Dictionary*. He founded the Early English Text Society in 1864, from which stemmed the Chaucer Society (1868), the New Shakespeare Society (1873), the Sunday Shakespeare Society (1874), the Browning Society (1881) and the Shelley Society (1886). An "agnostic" – he adopted Huxley's neologism – with strong socialist leanings, Furnivall's enthusiasms included boating – he formed a Ladies' Rowing Club for Harrods' shop girls – women's higher education and working men's colleges. For many years he held court every afternoon at an ABC teashop near the British Museum.[116] Marx described him as looking like a pilgrim on the way to the Holy Land to seek St. Anthony's beard.

Shakespeare Society meetings".*[117] This interest in the theatre was to play an increasing part in Eleanor's life, was never entirely abandoned and, at one point, threatened to become her chosen career. But for the time being it played a secondary part to her concern for Lissagaray's work.

From 15 August to 11 September in 1875 Marx went to Carlsbad alone – missing Tussy sadly but thankful for the absence of Kugelmann – while Mrs. Marx took a holiday in Lausanne until 21 September. Though there is no indication of where the Longuets had been nor yet whether Eleanor had gone away that summer at all, Jenny wrote to her sister on 1 September, announcing her return to London, and recalling that on the morrow her little son would have been two years old had he lived and that, on this sorrowful anniversary, she would be thinking, too, of Tussy's loving-kindness.[102]

No celebration to mark Eleanor's 21st birthday on 16 January 1876 has been recorded, unless the present of a packet of cigarettes, for which she thanked Hirsch on 30 December, may be counted as a salutation to her coming of age.† Jenny was pregnant again at the time and early that spring her husband suffered a fever. They had recently moved to 30 Leighton Grove in Kentish Town where, on 10 May 1876, Frédéric Jean Florent Longuet – always known as Jean or Johnny and sometimes Jack – was born: a weakly infant, according to Mrs. Marx, but one who developed into a sturdy little child.[118] Two days later Eleanor wrote a long letter to Hirsch without mentioning this event, entirely concerned with the moves afoot to get a Bill passed by the French Government to amnesty the proscribed Communards.‡ The impersonality of this political correspondence was modified when Hirsch sent her a pair of pince-nez which, although the lenses were no good, she found enchanting: they were so much lighter and more comfortable than those she habitually wore. Ten days later the police must have been relieved to learn that she had changed the lenses.

This was in July, when Lissagaray had gone to Jersey and she was preparing to accompany her father for the second time to Carlsbad. She sent Hirsch her address – the old Germania – before she and Marx set off.

Their journey was not favoured by fortune or planned with foresight. Reaching Cologne on Saturday, 13 August, their arrival in Nuremberg coincided with the opening of Wagner's Bayreuth *Festspielhaus* and the

---

* Mrs. Compton (1853–1940) wrote this account when she was over 80. Since she remembered that the Marxes' house was approached by a "high flight of steps to the front door", this must have been at 41 Maitland Park Road and, quite apart from her reference to the Shakespeare Society, it is evident that the period was not, as she thought, in the sixties, but after 1875 when – like Eleanor herself – she was no longer "in her 'teens".

† Only this sinister item of information in the letter was filed by the police.

‡ The Bill was defeated in the Chamber of Deputies.

first performance of the Nibelungen Ring, attracting an audience from the ends of the earth.*

In addition to this "Festival of Fools", as Marx called it, Nuremberg itself had chosen that weekend to stage a Bakers' and Millers' Congress which, if less renowned and well-attended, also had its *aficionados*. With these and the "Siegfrieds, Valkyries and Götterdämmerung heroes" streaming into the town[120] there was not a bed to be had. For a radius of 50 miles every lodging, from the most expensive hotel to the humblest inn and doss-house, was full and could have been filled twice over. Somehow the Marxes had not got wind of these revels and had allowed their trunks to be taken off the train and placed upon a barrow whose sweating owner lugged it round the town for hours only to trundle it back to the station. Here they took tickets for Weiden: the nearest junction for Carlsbad on a branch line from Neukirchen. But the guard was tipsy and incapable of speech when they arrived at Neukirchen, so they were carried on to Irrelohe where they waited a couple of hours for a train back to Weiden, which little place with its one hotel also happened to be the junction for Bayreuth thus offering not the smallest hope of accommodation. It was now midnight and until four in the morning they had to make the best of the wooden benches at the railway station.

Small wonder that they were exhausted when they fetched up at the Germania. The tribulations of the journey were recounted to Mrs. Marx who, unmindful of her own past misadventures, pronounced them rather quixotic.[120] A few days later Eleanor wrote again to say that they were fast recovering but she wished to remind her mother "how proverbially stupid one gets at Carlsbad, so don't be surprised if I seem rather incoherent". At all events it was a relief to be without the "grumbling and quarrelling of Kugelmann" and the place was full. "There are as many Jews as ever, and more anxious than ever to get as much water as possible."† However, they

---

* As Shaw wrote in *The Perfect Wagnerite*: "When the Bayreuth Festival Playhouse was at last completed and opened in 1876 for the first performance of The Ring ... the precautions taken to keep the seats out of the hands of the frivolous public ... had ended in their forestalling by ticket speculators and their sale to just the sort of idle globetrotting tourists against whom the temple was to have been strictly closed ... The money ... was begged ... from people who must have had the most grotesque misconceptions of the composer's aims – among others the Khedive of Egypt and the Sultan of Turkey."[119]

† This little gibe is as nothing to the scurrilous comments on Jews that run through the private correspondence between Marx and Engels, entirely in accord with Marx's early assessment: "Let us not seek the secret of the Jew in his religion, but let us seek the secret of the religion of the real Jew. What is the profane basis of Judaism? *Practical* need, *self-interest*. What is the worldly cult of the Jew? *Huckstering*. What is his worldly god? *Money*." This was written in 1843.[121]

One should also, however, read Engels' letter to an unknown correspondent written in April 1890 and published in the Vienna *Arbeiterzeitung* of 9 May in which he analyses and denounces anti-Semitism as serving only reactionary ends.[122]

were outdone by an American who managed to swallow 24 glassfuls in one day: "It's a wonder he didn't die of it", she wrote.[123] In later life Eleanor was distinctly proud of her own Jewish antecedents, proclaimed herself a Jewess and, just as she revised her views on drunkenness – no longer regarding it as a joke once she had seen to what degradation and misery it could reduce whole working-class families – so she ceased to treat the Jews as a butt when she worked among the immigrants in Whitechapel.

Marx met and mixed with former Carlsbad acquaintances and made many new ones – a few Poles but for the most part German university professors and doctors – as did Eleanor, who took a great liking to the younger Dr. Fleckles – "really very witty and a very good fellow"[123] – and became friendly with Professor Heinrich Graetz of Breslau to whom she later sent a copy of Lissagaray's book, when it transpired that he had guessed she was engaged to the author.* The main subject of conversation, Marx reported, was Wagner's love life,† though no doubt he also found other matter for discussion in the company he kept. Nevertheless, his letters to Engels show a decided taste for the sort of gossip prevalent at watering-places.

The cure was to come to an end on 10 September and Marx had accepted an invitation from Max Oppenheim – Mrs. Kugelmann's brother

---

It should be said that not until news of the peculiarly bestial Russian pogroms of 1888 filtered through did the rabid and unthinking anti-Semitism prevalent in Western Europe receive a momentary check, a fund for the relief of the surviving victims being publicly launched by the Lord Mayor of London in 1890. Very shortly before this, Miss Beatrice Potter had been making her study of the Jews in the East End, published in Volume I of Charles Booth's *Life and Labour of the People* in 1889. Here she described the attitudes and habits of mind induced by the appalling persecution of Polish and Russian Jews. The following is but a short extract from this magisterial passage: "The Russian Government deliberately encouraged mob-violence of a brutal and revolting character as a costless but efficient means of expulsion. Robbed, outraged, in fear of death and physical torture, the chosen people have swarmed across the Russian frontier, bearing with them, not borrowed 'jewels of silver, and jewels of gold, and raiment', but a capacity for the silent evasion of the law, a faculty for secretive and illicit dealing, and mingled feelings of contempt and fear for the Christians amongst whom they dwelt..."

* It will have been remarked that, in her letter pleading to be allowed to see Lissagaray, Eleanor had used the phrase "everyone knows we are engaged", by which she meant that certain indiscreet friends knew it and would have passed the word round. But there is no evidence that she herself ever concealed the betrothal nor any that her father ever acknowledged it. Professor Graetz wrote: "I think you were already secretly engaged in Carlsbad. Hence your happy mood. In which case may I congratulate you on such a fiancé. Mr. Lissagaray's book is well-written, it has style and feeling ... please convey to your betrothed the greetings of an admirer."[124]

† Cosima (1837–1930) – the youngest of Liszt's three illegitimate daughters by Mrs. Marx's old Paris acquaintance, the Countess d'Agoult – married Wagner in 1870 after her divorce from the Munich court musician and pianist Hans von Bülow.

– to visit him in Prague,* but on the Wednesday before they were due to leave Eleanor suddenly developed a fever. Dr. Fleckles by taking swift action "saved her from a long and dangerous illness", Marx wrote to Oppenheim. Nevertheless, some days of convalescence were advised and the journey to Prague was not made until 15 September.

They stayed only a few days and on the 21st were writing to Fleckles in Carlsbad from Liège, having on the homeward journey paid a flying visit to Kreuznach where Marx had been in 1843, before his marriage, and where, in fact, the wedding had taken place on 19 June. For that occasion the Baroness von Westphalen with her daughter and her son Edgar had travelled from Trier,† preferring that reactions to this unpopular event should not be manifested in their home town. No other member of either the bride's or the groom's family was present, the witnesses being four Kreuznach citizens: a doctor, a law student, a Jewish gentleman of private means and an innkeeper.[126]

Back in England on 23 September, while Eleanor resumed her correspondence with Hirsch, Marx took on an unexpected role.

It must be admitted that he had reason to feel tepid towards his sons-in-law. Lafargue, having finally turned his back on a medical career, struggling with more optimism than success to establish himself as a commercial photo-engraver for which he had invented a new process, was writing every few days to Engels not so much begging letters as peremptory demands for sums of money that even in his days of direst need would have made Marx blush. Longuet, though he held to his modest teaching post at King's College, had not only introduced an odious mother into the family on the occasion of Jenny's confinements – "*la mère, la mère*," moaned Mrs. Marx[115] – but had turned out to be of a nervous and irritable temper: "he fumes, shouts, and argues";[118] while Jenny, to make ends meet and despite her now persistent asthmatic cough, was burdened with her morning duties at St. Clement Danes School to add to the care of her house, a young baby and this difficult husband.

For neither Longuet nor Lafargue did Marx lift a finger. But for Lissagaray – Lissagaray the unacceptable, the aspirant son-in-law who was not to be trusted, relied upon or so much as countenanced – Marx went into action, all guns blazing.

No one could have championed Lissagaray's interests with greater force

---

* One branch of Oppenheim's chemical dye and mineral oil manufactory was in Dresden, the other in Prague, where he lived.[106]
† Arriving in time for the mother to witness the Marriage Contract between "Herr Karl Marx, Doctor of Philosophy, resident in Cologne, on the one hand, and Fraülein Johanna Bertha Julia Jenny von Westphalen, without occupation, resident in Kreuznach", signed on 12 June 1843.[125]

or more partisan zeal than Marx displayed in his negotiations for a German translation of the *Histoire de la Commune* to appear simultaneously, as he hoped, with the French edition, now in the press.

The fact was that, despite reservations, he held the highest opinion of this book. It was, he emphasised "the first *authentic*" account and had, in his view, the unique quality of a work, almost a personal memoir, by a man who had been an eye witness to and participant in the events described, drawing upon all published sources as well as material available to no one else. As such, it could not be matched by any other book on the subject and its translation must be impeccable. Thus when a certain Julius Grunzig in Berlin volunteered to bring out a German edition, Marx wrote to Wilhelm Bracke, the socialist publisher in Brunswick, demanding that the character and credentials of this Grunzig be thoroughly investigated. Marx was taking no chances: the translator of this book must be not only a "professional" but also a party man. Grunzig could not be considered as the publisher while his competence to translate would have to be established before he could be accepted in any capacity whatsoever. "I suggest that you take on the publication of this interesting work, so important for our party and for the whole German reading public", Marx wrote to Bracke. He went much further, transacting the practical details to safeguard Lissagaray's rights: the life of a Communard refugee in London was a hard one and he must have his share of any profits from a German edition. However, since Grunzig was the first applicant to come forward Marx allowed that he might be sent a few pages of the French proof sheets to translate and convince Marx of his ability to undertake "this far from easy task".

These were but the first shots fired in the campaign waged on Lissagaray's behalf. Throughout that autumn of 1876 and the whole of the following year Marx took upon himself – even though slightly against his will[127] – the entire burden of seeing justice done to the *History of the Commune*. Until January 1876 he had laboured for months on the French edition of *Capital*, but never had he taken more pains over any work other than his own to ensure that a translation should be treated with so much respect as he claimed for Lissagaray.* At the end of September he learnt that another book of the same title was being written by a German, Bernhard Becker. Marx went into the question from every angle, discussed it with Engels – "as we always exchange views on matters concerning party interests" – and came to the conclusion that this work, "at best written from the standpoint of a *German critic*", could not be seen as a rival

---

* It is true he had also worked on J. J. Most's English edition of *Capital and Labour* (published October 1877) but, as he later wrote to Sorge, the French version of *Capital* had cost him so much time that he would never again co-operate personally on any translation whatsoever.

to Lissagaray's, whose first French edition was due to come out in a matter of weeks while Becker's book would not be finished until the following May. The only conceivable link between them was that the German author would be unable to ignore so important a new source.*

Early in November Grunzig submitted his test piece and Marx, after comparing it closely with the French original, wrote to say that he must decline his services. With this the hope of simultaneous publication was abandoned. Marx wrote to Bracke that, while "revisions *here and there* would doubtless be necessary in any translation", the improvements to Grunzig's effort would "cost more time than if I did the translation myself from start to finish".[128] He suggested another possible candidate – Samuel Kokosky – but feared that he lacked the polish and felicity of style required for this particular book. He applied to others, too, while Engels proposed Wilhelm Blos of Hamburg, who consented but did so just at the time – only two days after – Marx had approved a specimen translation by a lady named Isolde Kurz who was then entrusted with the work.

Lissagaray himself, on Marx's advice, made a number of substantial changes between the first publication in November 1876 and the following February. All these, Marx insisted, must be incorporated by Miss Kurz. In April he was complaining of her howlers – she was sending in her work piecemeal for his scrutiny – and also that she was "damned slow", while in the following month, by which time the harassed lady had spent almost half a year on the job, he delivered his final verdict: "The translation as a whole, where not downright incorrect, is often clumsy, pedestrian and stilted."† Possibly, Marx went on, this might suit certain German tastes, but not his, and he appended – as he had done several times before – a detailed list of her mistakes with scathing comments upon them: indubitable if insulting evidence that he had studied the text far more thoroughly than Miss Kurz. By August he was contemptuously remarking that she seemed to be better at pressing for money than translating.

At last, in October 1877, Wilhelm Blos was asked to re-work the translation as edited by Marx who wrote on 10 November to say that he had long tried to shake off and had roared in vain at the "abominable Isolde". He was far ruder about this misinterpreter of Lissagaray's book than ever he had been about its author.

By a coincidence quite fortuitous – for he was no longer speaking of anything connected with his painstaking and anonymous work on the

---

* The book was published in Leipzig in 1879 under the title: *The History and Theory of the Paris Revolutionary Commune of the year 1871.*

† One wonders what he would have thought, of some of the translations of his own work that have girdled the earth in the present century.

History – Marx included in this same letter to Blos what could almost be called a declaration of integrity: neither Engels nor he gave a straw for popularity, he wrote: "A proof, for instance, is that, during the time of the International, in my aversion from any cult of the individual, I never allowed the numerous manoeuvres of recognition by which I was molested from various countries to receive publicity; I never even answered them, except now and again with a rebuke. When Engels and I first joined the clandestine Communist League we did so only on condition that anything tending to foster irrational beliefs in authority should be expunged from the Rules."

The German edition of the *History* appeared, published by Bracke, in 1878,* by which time Lissagaray had made further emendations, while he wrote nearly a hundred more pages especially for the English version which Eleanor was to produce. Her translation, though it did not appear until 1886, was done many years before. Indeed, Mrs. Marx told Sorge in January 1877 that Lissagaray's book was "being translated at the present time into English and German". As Eleanor explained in her Introduction, she had done the work "at the express wish of the author . . . from the *Histoire de la Commune* as prepared for a second French edition – an edition which the French Government would not allow to be published. This explanation is necessary", she went on, "in view of the differences between the translation and the first edition of Lissagaray's book." Though much had happened in the years between her original translation and its publication which made certain passages out of date, she was "loth to alter the work in any way. It had been entirely revised and corrected by my father. I want it to remain as he knew it."[43] This is perhaps the only public reference to Marx's stubborn toil in the interests of a man whom he disliked and rejected in the family circle but whose work he thought of importance.

---

* It was banned in Germany.[129]

A conjuncture of circumstances at this period of her life drove Eleanor back upon her own resources. The demise of the International in 1872, its final winding up in so far as it affected her family, in 1874, followed in the next year by the move to a smaller dwelling meant that the home was no longer the centre and resort for revolutionaries from every country, while the other members of the family had flown – if not far – away. Even "the French emigration has gone to pieces", wrote Engels in September 1874. "All have fallen out with each other and with everyone else on purely personal grounds – mostly over money matters – and we are almost entirely rid of them." Parallel to this attenuated social life ran Eleanor's lingering engagement to Lissagaray, with no promise of personal fulfilment in sight, though her interest in him and his affairs was undiminished. Not that things were bleak at 41 Maitland Park Road to which, particularly on Sundays when open house was kept, friends old and new found their way, including many now introduced by Eleanor herself. But the days of passionate political involvement – the endless meetings and discussions at the very heart of the international movement – were over. Marx with continuing ill health seldom forsook his study. He does not appear to have confided in Tussy his initial exertions in connection with the German edition of the *History of the Commune* for, towards the end of October 1876, Eleanor wrote to Hirsch – thanking him for the cigarettes he had sent to Carlsbad and for a second pair of delightful pince-nez – confidently announcing that the book would be published in both languages at more or less the same time in about a month when in point of fact the translation was not so much as under way.

That autumn she plunged into an entirely new activity: working for the London School Board elections in the interest of a Mrs. Westlake, the only woman standing for the Marylebone division.* Eleanor explained in a letter to Hirsch that these bodies were responsible for the control of the Board Schools and that Mrs. Westlake, though basically a middle-class lady – "like almost all Englishwomen", she oddly said – was at least a free-thinking one and certainly of greater worth than any of the male

---

* The School Boards, established under the 1870 Education Act, were elected for three years. Women were eligible to sit on the Boards, as were representatives of the working class. "The candidates were elected on a cumulative voting system under which each rate-payer had as many votes as there were places on the Board."[130]

candidates. The main issue was the defeat of the "Church Party" which "sought to abolish compulsory education altogether".

Mrs. Westlake had been the treasurer of the Dispensary and New Hospital for Women in the Marylebone Road. She declared that she would give up all such work if elected, but it was to this connection that she owed the support of Dr. Garrett Anderson* who, as Eleanor's doctor, may well have pressed her into the campaign. Another influential backer was Miss Buss of the North London Collegiate School and both these well-known personalities were on the platform at Mrs. Westlake's election meetings during the last two weeks of November, while "The Only Lady Candidate" was well publicised, her policy and her views regularly reported, by the local press.

From the Committee Rooms at 157 Camden Road Eleanor went canvassing from door to door. "You cannot imagine the curious things I see and hear", she wrote to Hirsch. "In one house they demand that 'above all religion should be taught',† in another I am told that 'schooling is the curse of the country, that education will ruin us', etc., etc. Still, it is amusing, though sometimes rather sad, as when one calls on a worker who says he wants to 'consult his boss' first."[131] The election was held on 2 December and Mrs. Westlake romped home at the head of the seven successful candidates with 20,231 votes.

Engels approved of this activity and of women's entry into public office, casting all his seven votes for Mrs. Westlake. Shortly after the Reichstag elections of January 1877 he wrote to a lady in Germany who, of course, was not franchised: "When we take power, not only will women vote, but they will be voted for and make speeches, which last has already come to pass on the School Boards. ... Moreover, the ladies on these School Boards distinguish themselves by talking very little and working very hard, each of them doing on an average as much as three men. Ought one to say 'new brooms sweep clean'? Though most of these 'brooms' are rather old."

---

* Who had stood for the same division in the first School Board elections of 30 November 1870 and polled the highest vote (47,848), her nearest runner-up being Professor Huxley (13,494). Dr. Garrett – as she then was – served only one term of office and did not stand again. The new Hospital for Women was opened by the Earl of Shaftesbury in 1872, replacing the St. Mary's Dispensary for Women that had existed in Seymour Place since 1866. The Hospital moved to the site of the Great Central Railway Hotel in the Marylebone Road in 1874 and in 1888 to 144 Euston Road, opposite St. Pancras Church. Since 1917 – the year she died – it has been known as the Elizabeth Garrett Anderson Hospital.

† In this, as in claiming Mrs. Westlake as "free-thinking", Eleanor was departing slightly from her candidate's declared policy. "Mrs. Westlake approves of the manner in which the religious question has been dealt with, as she could not support an education from which the Bible was excluded," The Camden & Kentish Towns, Hampstead, Highgate, Holloway and St. Pancras Gazette reported on 11 November 1876.

With the turn of the year Eleanor embarked upon a fresh enterprise, translating a paper by Professor Nikolaus Delius of Bonn University on "The Epic Element in Shakespeare's Dramas"* which was printed in the *Proceedings of the New Shakespeare Society* where it earned general praise and Professor Delius's salute to a fellow-worker.

It was her mother's hope that this first entry into literary circles would lead to her finding remunerative work less strenuous than that of teaching, for, since the Brighton days, it had been accepted that, unlike her sisters, Eleanor was not going to be either a dependant or her father's unpaid secretary. Mrs. Marx had found her "pale and emaciated" on her return from Carlsbad and continued to regard her as of a peculiarly delicate constitution, though it is doubtful whether so frail a creature as she was thought to be could have done the election canvassing, than which activity nothing demands more physical and moral resilience.

It was, in fact, the health of two quite other people that became a genuine cause for anxiety in 1877: that of Lizzie Burns and of Mrs. Marx herself.

A real if incongruous friendship between these two had ripened since Engels moved to London. Though he and Marx might wish to meet daily, to go for long walks together and spend each evening at one another's houses, there was no necessity for the ladies to strike up an intimacy. Yet they did. Despite Tussy's devotion to Lizzie Burns and her own sense of what was owing to Engels' companion – expressed with warmth in the first letter she had written to him on finding the house in Regent's Park Road – Mrs. Marx had no reason on earth to spend holidays with Lizzie unless she had chosen to do so and enjoyed her company. In 1873 she had proposed to stay with her at the seaside and two years later she went with her to Shanklin on the Isle of Wight, while in 1876, when Marx and Tussy were in Carlsbad, she elected to leave Hastings where she had gone for her health in order to join Lizzie and Engels in Ramsgate. Each morning he took the ladies to the railway station bar to fortify them with a small glass of port before leaving them to their own devices. They strolled together on the beach and rejoiced that they had nothing to do and no letters to write.†

But in all these years Lizzie had not been well: even when she first came to London in 1870 she had what she called "a gammy leg"[132] and then, as

---

* The original was published in the *Jahrbuch der Deutschen Shakespeare-Gesellschaft* 12 Jg. Weimar 1877.

† It is not clear why Lizzie, who could not write, should have found this so singular a blessing.

time went on, complained of "pains all over".[133] By 1876 Engels* had to admit that she was "always ailing in the spring", for which the only cure was sea air, while, as the years advanced, he took her away for long periods – to Scotland, Ramsgate, Brighton, Germany – in the hope that "it would see her through the winter".

In the autumn of 1875, the couple went to Heidelberg to place Lizzie's niece Pumps in a finishing school under a Fräulein Schupp. The girl, now 15 years of age, was to remain there for a couple of years to be licked into shape and, indeed, after a few months she wrote a long letter to Mrs. Marx and Tussy upon which Marx commented that: "if the spelling is a little uncertain here and there, in style and in facility of expression, which are far more important, she has made truly astounding progress". Engels, too, was struck – though rather less – by the improvement shown. Throughout Pumps' stay abroad the family of Philip Pauli – the owner of a chemical factory in Rheinau, near Mannheim, and a friend of Schorlemmer's – promised to keep an eye on the girl. This they did to such good purpose that Engels became a regular and cordial correspondent, writing in April 1876 that if in years to come Pumps were to remember her schooldays as the happiest time of her life it would be thanks to Pauli and his wife. In August 1876 Lizzie and Engels broke their seaside holiday to visit Pumps in Heidelberg, at which time the Paulis invited Marx and Tussy to stay with them in Rheinau when they left Carlsbad. Tussy's sudden fever and the engagement to go to Prague prevented their acceptance, but Pumps' fortunes had now involved the entire circle in friendly intercourse and some years later, in May 1881, Mrs. Pauli visited Engels in London.

The two years that the girl was to have been at school did not run their full course, for, though Lizzie had withstood the tests of winter – including the Christmas season, which represented all bibulous jollifications rolled into one – "in the last six weeks", Engels wrote to Mrs. Pauli on 14 February 1877, "we have had all manner of servant troubles and just now, when she should rest, she has to exert herself beyond her strength, working her fingers to the bone". He had reckoned with this possibility and informed the school that he might have to recall Pumps at any time. That point had now been reached and since he could not leave London to fetch her he would avail himself of offers made to escort Pumps

---

* At which time he began writing *Anti-Dühring*, published in an unsatisfactory way – as a "space-filler" – in *Vorwärts* from 3 January until 13 May 1877. Later, translated into French by Paul Lafargue with Laura's help, that part known as *Socialism, Utopian and Scientific*, appeared in the *Revue Socialiste* (Nos. 3, 4 and 5 of 1880). The English translation of this, by Edward Aveling, appeared in 1892. Engels finished the book in the spring of 1878, when he took up again the writing of *Dialectics of Nature*, begun in 1873, on which he continued to work until Marx's death in 1883, leaving it uncompleted.

back to England by the beginning or, at the latest, the middle of March.*
He himself was doing all he could – "if you had seen me making the bed
last night and lighting the kitchen stove this morning, you would have
laughed" – but the burden of housework absolutely must be taken off
Lizzie's shoulders. She went with him to Brighton for a fortnight while
awaiting Pumps' homecoming. It was not a success.

Pumps was – and remained – a thoroughly tiresome creature. Despite
her kindly upbringing and the Heidelberg veneer she was an ill-conditioned and a flighty girl. It could have been said of her that "with all her
sail she carried not an ounce of ballast" and it is wonderful that anyone
should have bothered to take her seriously. But however badly she
behaved she was Engels' protégée and was shown a degree of consideration
that, in her own right, she had not earned. Never was this more so than
when the wind was taken out of her sails, as it shortly was, for on her
return to London she quarrelled with Lizzie, thereby affronting Engels,
both of whom had been as parents to her and, turning her back on their
needs, she left for Manchester to live with her own people. Whatever the
cause of the break – and while Lizzie's health deteriorated so badly that
Engels had to take her away from home for weeks on end – Pumps' life in
Manchester proved a hard school that did nothing towards improving her
literary style. Her father, Thomas Burns, made it clear that he could not
afford to let her stay for any length of time, or to support her at all: she
worked in her brother's fish-shop all day and every day, while in the home
she had the care of three tiny children, including a new-born infant,
whose mother, Mrs. Renshaw, was still unable to leave her bed.[134] Pumps
was not, therefore, averse from returning to London but she refused to eat
humble pie or apologise to her aunt and "uncle". Engels, who had not
answered her one unrepentant letter, was disinclined to make the first
move and deadlock was reached.[135]

This did not, however, emerge for some months and then only because
Mrs. Marx, who went to Manchester that autumn, reported on the
unhappy state of affairs and took a deal of trouble to bring the girl round,
though she was reluctant to meddle, since she believed hardly anything
that either Pumps or Lizzie told her "and the only upshot would be
rows".[135] Mrs. Marx's visit to Manchester was not of course primarily on
Pumps' account: she was there to seek the ever dependable Dr. Gumpert's
advice on her health which had begun to trouble her afresh despite a
foreign cure.

Though Marx had not been made aware of it at the time, the Austrian
authorities had tried to expel him from the country when he had been in

---

* Lina Schoeler travelled with her.

Carlsbad with Tussy in 1876. Rather than make the long expensive journey only to meet with an expulsion order, and also on medical grounds, he decided that for his wife's sake as much as for his own they must take a cure elsewhere. They set off, with Tussy, in the first weeks of August for Neuenahr. This little resort in the Rhineland on the banks of the river Ahr, whose thermal springs had not been tapped until 1854 nor the main source discovered until almost a decade later, was barely more than a village, without so much as a market, its railway still under construction in 1877.* Nonetheless, it had attracted good doctors for the annual influx of some 3,000 health-seeking visitors – though the trade slump in the year of the Marxes' stay had reduced them to no more than 1,700 or 1,800 – and Marx trusted and liked Dr. Richard Schmitz, who had practised there since 1863 and gave Mrs. Marx to understand that she had come for treatment only just in time to avert a serious malady. Tussy's appetite improved – always the best sign in her case, according to her father – and they were advised to go to the Black Forest after the three weeks' cure which ended on 4 September.

About a month after her return to England Eleanor took to going to the British Museum† where she worked for Dr. Furnivall in the interests of the Philological, the Chaucer and the Shakespeare Societies. But that her interests were somewhat dispersed is shown by the fact that she was busily reading the great naturalist Alfred Russel Wallace's "foolery"‡ on spiritualism and John Nevil Maskelyne's exposure of spiritualistic frauds at the end of the year 1877. It is also more than likely – though no record of this can be traced – that she now embarked upon her translation of Lissagaray's *History*, for she cannot have started it earlier than November 1877, when the second (unpublished) French edition which she used had been completed, nor later than 1880, when Lissagaray left England for good and Marx was unable to consult him – or advise Tussy – on the detailed revisions and rewriting of the English version which he is known to have done. It was a daunting task for a relatively prentice hand. Anyone reading it today – when the cottage industry of translating has reached a degree of excellence undreamt of until such practitioners as C. K. Scott Moncrieff appeared upon the scene – may well ask how it ever passed Marx's rigorous standards since, for all its fidelity to the original, it is grating, awkward and heavy-handed in its literalness. Notwithstanding, it

---

* By the end of the century it had developed into a stylish little town, with the grandest of its many new hotels built in the "English Gothic" style, its own railway station and fine Assembly Rooms. However, the little Hotel Flora on the left bank, where the Marxes had stayed, was still on the map.

† Her signature for 22 October 1877, the day of her first application for a ticket to the Reading Room, survives.

‡ Engels' word.

remains a brave piece of work that has provided countless English readers with the earliest and the fullest first-hand account of embattled Paris in the days of the Commune.

It was while Eleanor was daily occupied at the Museum that Mrs. Marx, the Neuenahr doctor's optimism having proved unfounded, felt so seriously unwell that she made her trip to Manchester. "The head and feet are all right", she wrote to Tussy, "but the centre of the machine, where the brewing goes on, is not yet in working order."[136] She stayed with Sam Moore and was made warmly welcome by all the old Manchester friends – many of whom sent greetings to the young Tussy they had known in former years – while Gumpert himself called for her each day to dine at his house. Marx had previously observed that the doctor had become commonplace and twaddling as a result of indulging in too much "town chatter". Mrs. Marx now found that, ageing and widowed,* he had, by virtue of this constant intercourse with "dyed-in-the-wool Philistines", unconsciously allowed a "formal stiffness and English conventionality to creep into his manner".[135] But he could not have been more attentive to her, either professionally or socially and, while she described his ridiculous and pompous behaviour at table, she felt ashamed of mocking a man to whom she owed such endless kindness, consideration and, indeed, affection. He examined her with care, dispelled her fear that her condition might develop into dropsy – "it's more wind than water", she wrote[136] – and, so far as one may judge from the treatment he prescribed and the general state of medical knowledge at that time, he may well have diagnosed her carcinoma correctly. After a few days' freedom from pain, when she thought of returning home at once, she suffered a severe setback which caused him no surprise and he warned her that she must expect such "ups and downs", saying that much patience and medicine would be needed for some length of time, though the attacks might occur less often and at greater intervals. Whenever she felt well enough she was taken sightseeing and to the theatre, while Schorlemmer showed her round Owen's College and she planned to go to a Hallé concert† to hear the new Wagnerian music, but in the end settled for the warmth of Moore's fireside where every evening they drank and chatted together for an hour. "Never", she wrote, "have I been so pampered in my life."[134] But conversation at dinner parties of the Manchester *beau monde* to which she was invited was more than she could stand. The Turco-Russian war was then

---

* In 1863 Gumpert had married Louisa Eller, an English widow with four children who bore five more between 1864 and 1870. She died to his profound grief in 1873 [see Erhard Kiehbaum: *Anmerkungen zur Briefen von Louisa Gumpert an Engels. Beihäge zur Marx-Engels?*]

† Charles Hallé (1819–1895) founded his orchestra in Manchester in 1858. Born in Westphalia he came to England after the 1848 revolution from Paris, where he had given his first concerts.

nearing its end and to, her horror, even some of Marx's associates, in particular the geologist Dakyns, proved to be "out and out Russians".* Unaccustomed as she was to discussion with political dunces, she remarked that "one could be driven to imbecility in such a *milieu*".[136]

And then she saw Pumps. The girl, dispirited and coughing, sullenly declined to seek a reconciliation with Lizzie and Engels, though there was plainly no alternative but for her to go back to them. Sam Moore, who was present when she came to tea with Mrs. Marx, pressed the point and said she had only to write that she was sorry for what had happened and Engels would respond. "Her life in London must have been very hard", Mrs. Marx commented, "for it is far from a bed of roses here."[136] There was no question of running about or enjoying herself and although, through the Catholic connections of an amiable priest, a friend of the family, it was hoped that some suitable work might be found, her father was in no position to buy her new dresses and Mrs. Marx thought she was too unpresentable to apply for a post with any chance of success.[134] Several times a day Mrs. Marx called upon Mrs. Lydia Renshaw who was much concerned about Mary Ellen's wretched situation. But Mrs. Renshaw, closely related to Lizzie, had no intention of meddling either. With the husband, James Renshaw, Mrs. Marx went to the Roman Catholic Church to hear the admirable music. She gave Tussy an amusing account of the preacher – a boorish figure where she had expected a resplendent Prince of the Church – who puffed and wheezed, sweating as though he were already suffering the torments of hell-fire and ceaselessly wiped his bald pate with his handkerchief. "The worst part", said Mrs. Marx, "was the endless kneeling which lasted close on an hour-and-a-half. Since not a soul was seated and every soul knelt, I, old fool that I am, knelt too . . ."[136] However, the painful experience did not deter her from going again, taking Pumps with her, for the sake of the music. She recovered from this

---

* The "Christian humbug and hypocritical atrocity mongers" of the English press, which was overwhelmingly pro-Russian, disgusted Mrs. Marx.[118] In April 1876 a Bulgarian uprising against the Turks had been ferociously crushed in a matter of weeks. Russia declared war on Turkey in April 1877. Both Marx and Engels held the view that the Tsar's war was launched to strengthen Russian influence in the Balkans – where he had the backing of Serbia, Montenegro, Rumania and Bulgaria – combined with the need to divert attention from internal social problems. They were convinced that it would give fresh impetus to the Balkan national liberation movements to throw off the rule of the Crescent and lead to a revolution in St. Petersburg. Engels considered the strength and efficiency of the Turkish army – as against the disorganisation of the Tsar's forces – a sufficient guarantee of victory, in which prediction he was, for once, confounded, for the war ended with the military defeat of the Turks, freeing a large part of the Balkan peninsula from the Turkish yoke. The armistice was signed on 31 January 1878. Nevertheless, Marx believed that in Russia this futile war, followed by fresh impolicies, would bring about a revolution, and indeed a revolutionary situation did result.

pious exercise but came back to London with little hope of curing her disease.

Eventually, of course, Pumps was forced to swallow her pride – or resentment – and return to Regent's Park Road where Engels thought that the Manchester lesson had done her a power of good. By this time and during the whole spring and summer of 1878 Lizzie was confined to her bed. Meanwhile Mrs. Marx consulted an eminent specialist who pronounced her condition incurable: all that could be done was to alleviate her sufferings. In July, though Marx had supposed that "Her ex-Ladyship the ex-Baroness von Westphalen"* might possibly be allowed into Carlsbad as non-contraband, he was unwilling to take the risk. Instead, she went to Malvernbury in Worcestershire. From there she wrote to Tussy, facing the fact that she might never quite recover – her illness was too longstanding and obstinate – but "all I know is that, had I come here earlier, at least I should have found great relief".[137] Gumpert's "wholesale pills" of belladonna had not helped her much and she preferred the treatment she now received daily at the hands of a "quiet, unassuming, honest little doctor". She worried about the "Leighton Grove Institution" – the Longuets – for on 4 July 1878 Jenny had given birth to another son, Harry Michel, known as "Harra",† whose troubled little life lasted not five years, while Jean, now two, had been dangerously ill the summer before and was again far from well, so that when Marx went to Malvern on 4 September for ten days, Jenny, leaving the baby in Tussy's care, took Jean to join her mother, staying with her until Mrs. Marx's own return on 22 September.

Thus Marx, his wife and their eldest daughter were away when at half-past one on the morning of 12 September 1878 Lizzie Burns, after years of pain and indignity, died of a tumour of the bladder and exhaustion from haemorrhages. The evening before the Rev. W. B. Galloway, vicar of St. Mark's Church, a short step from 122 Regent's Park Road, came to the house to perform the marriage ceremony, by special licence, according to the rites of the Church of England in the presence of Charles Read and James and Lydia Renshaw, the last of whom, like the dying bride, being unable to write and entering her mark on the register. "To please her,

---

* In this, one of his rare references to his wife's origins and their potential snob value abroad, Marx was being realistic. It must be admitted that there was one droll occasion, in 1871, when he induced Mrs. Marx to write to the editor of *Public Opinion* with her card bearing the words "*née* Baroness von Westphalen", under the impression that this would make him quail, unaware that nothing impresses the English less than a minor foreign title, usually thought to be bogus anyway and more particularly so when it is a lady claiming to be a Baroness in her own right, than which there is no rarer bird in the whole flock of the true British peerage.

† Like Jean, this child was born at 30 Leighton Grove, Kentish Town.

Engels married her legally ... on her death-bed", Eleanor recalled a fortnight before her own life ended.[25]

Immediately, in the very hour of Lizzie's death during that night, Engels wrote to Lessner to tell him the news and, on the same date, to his brother Rudolf in Barmen to say that his wife, "who had legally married me the evening before, died peacefully after long sufferings". He also sent an announcement to *Vorwärts*: "I herewith notify my friends in Germany that my wife Lydia, née Burns, was torn from me by death during the past night."[138]

Thus he made the eleventh-hour marriage as widely known as possible, including to his family, and Lizzie lies buried in St. Mary's (Roman Catholic) cemetery in Kensal Green under a stone engraved with a delicate small Celtic cross enclosing the sacred monogram I.H.S., above the words:

> In memory of
> Lydia
> wife of Frederick Engels
> born August 6th 1827 died September 12th 1878
> R.I.P.

which tomb, now weather-worn, overgrown and hard to find, is also a monument to the man of feeling who honoured her wishes to the very last.

Eleanor and Mrs. Renshaw went to the funeral, as did Pumps, who was rigged out in mourning attire regardless of expense. This elicited from Marx the comment that her dress, added to the airs and graces she now assumed, only served to emphasise her ill-concealed glee. Considering the bad relations that had existed between the girl and her aunt before the end and Pumps' seedy life in Manchester, her behaviour seems excusable; the more so since she was immediately elevated to the head of Engels' household – "knighted", as Marx called it, with the title of "Pumpsia" – where she reigned with some ineptitude for several years, earning Engels' affection and ever-increasing admiration, not shared by the Marxes.

It was during these years that Eleanor began to spread her wings. In the Reading Room of the British Museum she made several new acquaintances, including the young Irishman, George Bernard Shaw, her junior by 18 months, who had come to England in 1876 and to whom she was to draw much closer in years to come, not only by reason of their shared – then amateur – interest in the theatre, but also because he later claimed to have been completely converted by reading Marx's *Capital* – "the turning point in my career"[139] – and prided himself on being the only one of Hyndman's disciples in the Democratic Federation* to have read it, which

---

* Founded in June 1881.

he did in Gabriel Deville's popularised French version* "then accessible only ... in the British Museum Reading Room, my daily resort".[141]

Another place where Eleanor found a congenial circle was at the meetings of the New Shakespeare Society, held in the Women's Reading Room of University College in Gower Street, out of which grew the "Dogberry", a little private Shakespeare Reading Club, whose members' subscriptions were devoted to buying tickets for Irving's First Nights, when he always let them have seats in the front row of the dress circle. One of its adherents, Mrs. Comyn,† has left a description[142] of these Club meetings which were most often held at the Marxes' house since Eleanor "was the leading spirit". Marx himself, "who had a guttural voice and a decided German accent", sat at the end of the long double drawing-room. "As an audience he was delightful, never criticising, always entering into the spirit of any fun that was going on, laughing when anything struck him as particularly comic, until the tears ran down his cheeks – the oldest in years, but in spirit as young as any of us. And his friend, the faithful Frederic Engels, was equally spontaneous. ... Near him {Marx} sat his wife – a lovable and charming woman. She was said to have been beautiful in her youth, but ill-health and perhaps turbulent times had taken their toll. Her skin had faded to a waxen pallor, there were purplish stains under her eyes." Mrs. Comyn remembers that the company included Edward Rose,‡ Mrs. Theodore Wright,§ "pretty Dollie Radford"‖ and Sir

---

* Deville's abridged translation, published in August 1883, had been approved by Marx in its earlier and by Engels in its later stages. As a matter of fact Shaw himself says that he read it in 1885 when "William Archer found me ... poring over" it.[140]

† Marian Skinner, as she was at the time, married Henry Ernest Fitzwilliam Comyn in 1884. Her husband became Assistant Solicitor to the Treasury.

‡ Edward Rose became a playwright and the Vice-President of the Playgoers' Club founded in 1884. In 1886 Shaw acted – for the second and last time – in one of Rose's plays (*Odd to Say the Least of It*). Another of Rose's plays, *Her Father*, written in collaboration with J. T. Douglas, was performed in a Double Bill with *Dregs* by Edward Aveling – under the pen-name Alec Nelson – at the Vaudeville Theatre on 16 May 1889. Rose adapted Weyman's popular novel *Under the Red Robe* for the stage in 1896.

§ Mrs. Theodore Wright was the former wife of Austin Holyoake, the editor of *Bradlaugh's National Reformer*. An amateur actress of talent though little known in the professional theatre, she played Mrs. Alving in the first production of *Ghosts* at the Royalty Theatre in 1891 and was hailed by Shaw as "the pluckiest of the lot" among those performing Ibsen[141] and, at the same time, he offered her the eponymous role in *Mrs. Warren's Profession* (eventually taken by Fanny Brough, though not until 1902).

‖ Both the Maitland sisters, Caroline, known as "Dollie", and Clara, attended the Dogberry meetings at 41 Maitland Park Road in 1880–1881. Dollie had been a friend of Furnivall's since her schooldays when he had taken her regularly to theatre matinées. She published some dozen volumes of verse between 1897 and 1910 under the name of Dollie Radford. Ernest Radford, whom she married in 1883 when they were both in their early twenties, was also a member of this little band of Shakespeare enthusiasts, though not mentioned by Mrs. Comyn. Marx wrote to Jenny in April 1881: "Tussy has discovered a new *Wunderkind* among the Dogberries, a

Henry Juta.* The house in Maitland Park Road "was a very ordinary suburban villa", but the atmosphere "I suppose ... was Bohemian in its open-handed hospitality, its gracious welcome to strangers within its gates. And the strangers were numerous and shared the classic charm of great variety. There was one point of resemblance between them – for the most part they were impecunious. Shabby as to clothes, furtive in movement, but interesting, always interesting ... Dr. Marx's manners to his family were altogether delightful."

One revealing passage in Mrs. Comyn's recollections† relates to Lenchen, who was so much taken for granted by the family as barely to have figured in all these years,‡ while no one either before or since ever described her relations with Eleanor from personal observation. "The nice-looking old German cook-housekeeper ... was an excellent cook", wrote Mrs. Comyn. "She was a fresh-complexioned old woman, who wore gold ear-rings, and a chenille net over her hair, and who reserved to herself the right of 'speaking her mind' even to the august doctor. Her mind was respectfully, even meekly, received by all the family, except Eleanor, who frequently changed it...."[142]

On Jenny's return from Malvernbury she found Harry "flourishing" and claimed that Eleanor had "*changed him* – he is not the same at all. You have given him excellent habits at night ...". But poor Jenny, who had continued her teaching during her pregnancy and the suckling of her new-born infant, was now so harassed that she wrote in desperation to Tussy on 23 September that it was "with great reluctance and regret that I send you these lines to ask you to replace me at Clement Danes tomorrow and Tuesday. I know you have already too much work on hand ... it pains me ... to burthen you with work of mine...."[143]

---

certain Radford; this youth is already a barrister-at-law ... he looks well, cross between Irving and Lassalle ... an intelligent and somewhat promising boy. ... Dolly Maitland pays fearful court to him."

* Henry Juta, the son of Marx's sister Louise, came to London from Cape Town. In 1877, when his nephew was 21, Marx tried to obtain help for him to complete his law studies at the University of London and to be admitted to the Inner Temple. Juta became Attorney-General of the Cape in 1894 and Speaker of the Cape House of Assembly from 1896 to 1898. He was knighted in 1897.

† Which she places "in the early 'eighties'" but which, though they certainly cover incidents up to and including 1883, and are much bolstered by hindsight, must in fact refer for the most part to the period before October 1881, from which time Mrs. Marx took to her bed.

‡ She appears in many reminiscences of the Marx household, in particular in Liebknecht's *Karl Marx zum Gedächtnis* where he recalls the young Lenchen as he first knew her, then "27 years of age and, while no beauty, she was nice-looking with rather pleasant and pleasing features. She had no lack of admirers and could have made a good match again and again."

Eleanor was indeed busy. She did not go away at all that summer and when Hirsch invited her to contribute to his journal in early June 1878 – at which time Lissagaray had again gone to Jersey – she had to refuse "because my whole day is taken up by my work at the Museum".

But however absorbed she might be in her literary activities, one burning issue affected the entire family: the amnesty for the Communards in banishment and exile. The fight lasted for nine years having been begun at the start of the proscriptions in 1871. The French Assembly threw out Bill after Bill until its dissolution in 1875, when the new government went no further than to grant a partial amnesty to those condemned after Bloody Week. François Grévy became President on 30 January 1879, by which time some of the Communards were beginning to return, though thousands remained in New Caledonia and hundreds who had fled were under sentence. A full amnesty was still withheld but now popular sentiment began to assert itself and the people were recalling their old representatives by voting for them at every opportunity. Blanqui's election for Bordeaux in April 1879 was annulled by the government which, however, was obliged to extend the "pardons". The agitation, greatly strengthened by the organised forces of the new French Workers' Party,* took public forms: on 18 March 1880 the anniversary of the Commune was openly celebrated in Paris; on 23 May, despite police obstruction, enormous crowds flocked to the Père Lachaise cemetery to lay wreaths at the foot of the *mur des Fédérés*† and in July 1880 the ban on the proscripts was lifted.

Of the members of the family circle – if such he may be called – Lissagaray was the first to avail himself of the amnesty, returning to Paris on 4 July 1880. He was followed that autumn by Longuet, whom Jenny rejoined in March 1881, while Paul Lafargue delayed his departure until April – and Laura until July – 1882.

---

* This "genuine workers' party", as Marx called it, had emerged from the decision taken at the 3rd Socialist Congress at Marseilles in October 1879 to form a Federation of Workers' Socialist Parties. A letter to the Congress supporting the motion was written by the London Communard exiles Longuet, Lissagaray, Johannard and Theisz. The Rules were adopted in July 1880 at a Paris Regional Congress attended by 24 Federations and nationally approved at the Havre Congress in November of that year.
† The wall against which 147 people had been shot by the Versailles troops.

REFERENCE NOTES

Abbreviations

Andréas   *Briefe und Dokumente der Familie Marx aus den Jahren* 1862–1873 by
                   Bert Andréas in *Archiv für Sozialgeschichte*, II. Band, 1962. Verlag für
                   Literatur und Zeitgeschehen, Hanover.
BIML   Institute of Marxism-Leninism, Berlin.
Bottigelli Archives Letters in the custody of Dr. Emile Bottigelli, Paris.
Bottigelli L & D   *Lettres et Documents de Karl Marx* 1856–1883. Previously unpublished
                   texts edited by Dr. Emile Bottigelli. Annali dell' Istituto Giangia-
                   como Feltrinelli, Anno Primo. Milan, 1958.
ELC   *Frederick Engels Paul and Laura Lafargue: Correspondence*, Volumes I–
                   III. Lawrence & Wishart, 1959–1963.
IISH   International Institute of Social History, Amsterdam.
IWMA   *Documents of the First International*, Volumes I–V. Lawrence &
                   Wishart, 1963–68.
Liebknecht   *Wilhelm Liebknecht Briefwechsel mit Karl Marx und Friedrich Engels.*
                   Edited by Georg Eckert. Mouton & Co., The Hague, 1963.
MEW   *Marx Engels Werke.* Dietz Verlag, Berlin, 1956–1968. Unless other-
                   wise stated Volumes 27–39.
MIML   Institute of Marxism-Leninism, Moscow.

(1)   *La Commune de 1871* under the general editorship of Jean Bruhat, Jean Dautry and
      Emile Tersen. 2nd edition. Editions Sociales, Paris 1970.
(2)   Laura to Eleanor, January 1870. Bottigelli Archives.
(3)   *The Civil War in France.*
(4)   To Mrs. Marx, 31 March 1869. Bottigelli Archives.
(5)   26 April 1869. MIML.
(6)   To Jenny, 2 June 1869. Bottigelli Archives and Bottigelli L & D.
(7)   Letter to Vera Zasulich, 23 April 1885. MEW.
(8)   Engels, *Introduction* to Marx's *Class Struggles in France* 1848 to 1850.
(9)   *The Eighteenth Brumaire of Louis Bonaparte*, 1895.
(10) 25 March 1868. ELC, Vol. I.
(11) First preface to *Anti-Dühring.* June 1878.
(12) John Smethurst. *Ermen & Engels. Marx House Bulletin* No. 41. January–March 1967.
(13) Published in English in the first German edition of 1845 and again in that of 1892,
      but not included in any English (or American) editions until 1958 with the pub-
      lication of a translation by W. O. Henderson and W. H. Chaloner, Macmillan, New
      York, and Blackwell, Oxford.
(14) 4 April 1869. MEW.
(15) 21 October 1870. MEW.
(16) To Johann Philip Becker, 15 October 1884. MEW.
(17) *Sozialdemokratische Monatsschrift* Nos. 10–11. 30 November 1890. (In English in
      Reminiscences of Marx and Engels.)
(18) 10 June 1869. Original English MIML.
(19) Eleanor to Jenny, 2 June 1869. Bottigelli Archives.
(20) Engels to Marx, 23 May 1856. MEW.
(21) Marx to Kugelmann, 29 November 1869. MEW.
(22) *The Condition of the Working Class in England in 1844.* Trans. Florence Kelley
      Wishnewetzky 1892. George Allen & Unwin, 1936.

(23) Cecil Woodham-Smith. *The Great Hunger*. Hamish Hamilton, 1962.

(24) 4 November 1869. Address of the Land and Labour League (founded in October 1869) to the Working Men and Women of Great Britain and Ireland.

(25) To Kautsky, 15 March 1898. IISH.

(26) 8 March 1892. MEW.

(27) Eleanor to Jenny, 19 (misdated 20) July 1869. Bottigelli Archives.

(28) *Report of the Commissioners on the Treatment of the Treason-felony Convicts in the English Convict Prisons*. It was known as the Knox-Pollock Report after the investigators, Alexander Knox, a former *Times* correspondent turned Police Commissioner, and George Pollock, an army surgeon.

(29) To Engels, 27 June 1867. MEW.

(30) Engels in an unpublished manuscript wrtitten *c.* 5 July 1870 for a preface to a collection of Irish songs. First published in Italy (No. 2 of *Movemento Operaio* 1955), and then in France (*La Pensée* 1957), it appeared in English, translated from the manuscript by Angela Clifford, in *Frederick Engels: History of Ireland*. Irish Communist Organisation, London 1965.

(31) First published in German and Russian in *Marx-Engels Archives*, Volume 10, 1948. (MEW, Volume 16). See Ref. (30) for English translation.

(32) 30 October 1869. Andréas.

(33) IWMA. Vol. III.

(34) To Marx, 29 November 1869. MEW.

(35) 29 November 1869. MEW.

(36) 5 March 1870. English Original MIML.

(37) Postscript to letter from Marx to Engels, 10 February 1870. MEW.

(38) IWMA Vol. IV.

(39) 13 December 1870. MEW.

(40) Jenny to Kugelmann, 19 November 1870. Andréas.

(41) 12 August 1870. English Original MIML.

(42) Frank Jellinek. *The Paris Commune of 1871*. Gollancz, 1937. Lissagaray estimated the victims of the Commune, apart from dependants, at 100,000 compared with 140,000 killed in the entire Franco-Prussian War.

(43) *History of the Commune of 1871*. Translated from the French of Lissagaray by Eleanor Marx Aveling. Reeves & Turner, London 1886.

(44) Mrs. Marx to Kugelmann, 12 May 1871. Andréas.

(45) Letter in *The Irishman* of 29 April 1871 over Jenny's pen-name "J. Williams", published, following the obituary notice on Flourens, to give a fuller account of his devoted championship of the Irish cause.

(46) Jenny to Kugelmann, 18 April 1971. Andréas.

(47) 15 April 1871. *Réimpression (in extenso) du Journal Offciel de la Commune*. Victor Bunel, Paris 1872.

(48) *Ibid.*

(49) Marx to Jenny, Laura and Eleanor, 13 June 1871. English Original MIML.

(50) Eleanor to Liebknecht, 29 December 1871. Liebknecht.

(51) Marx to Kugelmann, 18 June 1871. MEW.

(52) English Original BIML.

(53) Jeremiah O'Donovan Rossa. *My Years in English Jails*. Originally published by the American News Company, New York, in 1874. English edition edited by Sean Ua Cearnaigh, Anvil Books, Tralee, Co. Kerry 1967.

(54) 12 April 1871. MEW.

(55) Mrs. Marx to Liebknecht, 26 May 1872. Liebknecht.

(56) 29 December 1871. Liebknecht.

(57) Jenny to Kugelmann, 21 December 1871. Andréas.

(58) Engels to Sorge, 17 March 1872. MEW.

(59) Eleanor to the Aberdeen Socialist Society, 17 March 1893. The original letter was lent by William Diack, former secretary of the Aberdeen Socialist Society, to Mr. G. Allen Hutt in 1939 and was published in *Labour Monthly*, March 1940.

(60) Henri Perret to Marx from Geneva, 8 October 1870. Original French MIML.

(61) Paul Lafargue to Engels, 26 December 1871. ELC, Vol. III.

(62) Volume I, Barcelona 1923. (English in *Reminiscences of Marx and Engels*.)

(63) This letter was one of those sold at Sotheby's on 15 May 1967 to the Soviet Embassy which allowed me to read it before it went into the archives in Moscow.

(64) Marx's *Civil War in France* was published on 13 June 1871.

(65) *Programme and Rules of the International Alliance of Socialist Democracy.* November 1868.

(66) *Progress*, May 1883. A second article appeared in June. Curiously enough Eleanor misdated the climactic Hague Congress 1873.

(67) Eleanor to Kautsky, 3 December 1897. IISH.

(68) Engels to Philip Patten in New York, 18 April 1883. MEW.

(69) 12–17 September 1874. MEW.

(70) 27 June 1872. Andréas.

(71) 9 November 1871. MEW.

(72) *Eastern Post*, 16 and 23 December 1871.

(73) 26 May 1872. Liebknecht.

(74) 11 March 1872. ELC, Vol. I.

(75) 26 May 1872. Liebknecht.

(76) Mrs. Marx to Sorge, January 1877. MEW.

(77) 7 November 1872. MIML.

(78) Andréas.

(79) 10 September 1872 from 134 Harley Street. Bottigelli Archives.

(80) Jenny to Kugelmann, 23 December 1872. Andréas.

(81) 7 November 1872. Bottigelli Archives.

(82) Mrs. Marx to Eleanor, 25 March 1873. MIML.

(83) Mrs. Marx to Eleanor, 3 April 1873. MIML.

(84) Eleanor to Marx, 3 May 1873. Bottigelli Archives and IISH.

(85) Mrs. Marx to Eleanor, before 3 May 1873. MIML.

(86) Mrs. Marx to Eleanor, late April 1873. MIML.

(87) Privately communicated.

(88) Eleanor to Mrs. Marx, 31 May 1873. IISH.

(89) Mrs. Marx to Eleanor, n.d. probably June 1873. MIML.

(90) Mrs. Marx to Eleanor, *c.* 22 May 1873. MIML.

(91) Quoted by Mrs. Marx in letter to Eleanor, *c.* 31 May 1873. MIML and IISH.

(92) Mrs. Marx to Thomas Allsop. 12 September 1874. (See Ref. 63.)

(93) See Paul Mayer: *Die Geschichte des Sozialdemokratischen Parteiarchivs und das Schicksal des Marx-Engels Nachlasses. Archiv für Sozialgeschichte*, VI./VII. Band 1966/67. Verlag für Literatur and Zeitgeschehen, Hanover. Since this first account there appeared in *Neues Deutschland* a series of ten articles (February/March 1972) giving an altogether more complete history of *Das grosse Erbe* (*The Great Heritage*) by Heinz Stern and Dieter Wolf (reprinted as a paperback volume, Dietz Verlag, Berlin 1972).

(94) Written in 1928. English in *Reminiscences of Marx and Engels*.

(95) Bottigelli Archives and IISH.

(96) Some of the biographical details are given in *Notice sur Lissagaray* by Amédée Dunois in a preface to *L'Histoire de la Commune de* 1871, Librairie de Travail, Paris, 1929; others from Ref. (1).

(97) Dossier on Carl Hirsch in the archives of, and officially stamped by the Secretariat General of the Paris Prefecture of Police found by Professor Dr. Bruno Kaiser in Switzerland and presented to the Berlin Institute of Marxism-Leninism in November 1963.

(98) Bertall. *The Communists of Paris* 1871. Buckingham & Co., Paris, London and Dublin 1873.

(99) In addition to information extracted from intercepted correspondence, there are nine complete letters from Eleanor and one from Mrs. Marx to Hirsch, written between 1875 and 1878. These could have been confiscated with such other items as his address book when Hirsch's rooms were searched by the police who did not then enjoy photocopying facilities. Three of Eleanor's letters – dated 25 October 1875, 25 November 1876 and 8 June 1878 – are published in MEW, Volume 34; five, including the above three, in the possession of the Ohara Institute for the Study of Social Problems attached to Hosei University, Tokyo, were published in the original French by Dr. C. Tsuzuki in *Bulletin No.* 8 of the Society for the Study of Labour History, Spring 1964. The two additional letters from this source are dated 12 May and 18 July 1876. Three further letters from Eleanor of 16 and 27 July and 20 October 1876, and one from Mrs. Marx to Hirsch in early May 1876 have not been published hitherto. The originals, owned by Professor Dr. Sakasaki of Japan, were given in photostat to BIML, by whose courtesy I was permitted to use a copy. While Eleanor wrote to Hirsch in French, his letters to her were in German. MIML.

(100) 12 May 1885. ELC, Vol. I.

(101) Jenny to Marx, 24 February 1882. MIML.

(102) Jenny to Eleanor, 1 September 1875. IISH.

(103) Mrs. Marx to Thomas Allsop, 12 September 1874. (See Ref. (63).)

(104) This document, in the archives of the Public Record Office, had been mislaid when searches were made. A photocopy was found in the IISH.

(105) An article of that title by W. Fraser Rae appeared in *The Nineteenth Century*, Vol. XVI, July–December 1884.

(106) Egon Erwin Kisch. *Karl Marx in Karlsbad*. Aufbau Verlag, Berlin, 1953.

(107) *Marx House Bulletin*, No. 39. July–September 1966.

(108) Eleanor to Jenny, 5 September 1874. Bottigelli Archives.

(109) Published in English as *Letters to Kugelmann*. Lawrence & Wishart, 1936.

(110) Liebknecht.

(111) To Natalie Liebknecht, 23 October 1874. Liebknecht.

(112) To Natalie Liebknecht, 1 January 1875. Liebknecht.

(113) Jenny announced the appointment to an unknown French correspondent on 25 December 1874. BIML.

(114) Information supplied by the Historical Research Department of the Greater London Council Record Office.

(115) Mrs. Marx to Hirsch, n.d. From internal evidence late April or early May 1876. BIML.

(116) *Frederick James Furnivall. A Volume of Personal Record* edited by Henry Froude, O.U.P. 1911.

(117) Quoted by her son, Compton Mackenzie, in *My Life and Times. Octave* 7, 1931–1938, Chatto & Windus 1968.

(118) Mrs. Marx to Sorge, 20 or 21 January 1877. MEW.

(119) G. Bernard Shaw. *The Perfect Wagnerite*. Constable, 1898.

(120) Mrs. Marx to J. P. Becker, n.d. after 20 August 1867. MEW.

(121) Published in the *Deutsch-Französiche Jahrbücher*, Paris 1844. *On the Jewish Question* appears in English in *Karl Marx: Early Writings* translated and edited by T. B. Bottomore. C. A. Watts, 1963.

(122) *Karl Marx and Friedrich Engels. Correspondence 1846–1895*. Translated and edited by Dona Torr. Martin Lawrence, 1934.

(123) Eleanor to Mrs. Marx, 19 August 1876. Bottigelli Archives.

(124) 1 February 1877. IISH.

(125) MEGA I. 1.

(126) Luise Dornemann. *Jenny Marx*. Dietz Verlag, Berlin, 1968.

(127) Marx to Lavrov, 24 February 1877. MEW.

(128) 6 November 1876. MEW.

(129) Liebknecht to Engels, 20 October 1878. Liebknecht.

(130) Brian Simon. *Education and the Labour Movement 1870–1918*. Lawrence & Wishart, 1965.

(131) 25 November 1876 (misdated September in the *Bulletin* of the Society for the Study of Labour History, Spring 1964).

(132) 16 November 1889. ELC, Vol. II.

(133) 9 August 1887. ELC, Vol. II.

(134) Mrs. Marx to Eleanor, 20 November 1877. MIML.

(135) Mrs. Marx to Marx, 25 November 1877. MIML.

(136) Mrs. Marx to Eleanor, n.d. probably November 1877. MIML.

(137) August 1878 from Malvernbury. MIML.

(138) Published on 18 September 1878.

(139) Quoted in Hesketh Pearson's *Bernard Shaw, His Life and Personality*. Methuen, 1961.

(140) G. B. Shaw. *Sixteen Self-Sketches*. Constable & Co., 1949.

(141) To William Archer, 23 April 1891. G. B. Shaw. *Collected Letters 1874–1897*. Edited by Dan H. Laurence. Reinhardt, 1965.

(142) *The Nineteenth Century and After*. Vol. 91, No. 539 January 1922.

(143) IISH.

· PART III ·

BREAKING POINTS

Eleanor has been described by many of those who knew her in these or later years – by Will Thorne, the founder and General Secretary of the Gas Workers' and General Labourers' Union; by Henry Mayers Hyndman, who formed the Social-Democratic Federation; by William Collison, employers' spy and strikebreaker who called himself "the Apostle of Free Labour"; by Henry Havelock Ellis, the first Englishman to bring sex out of the private into the public sector and by Beatrice Potter,* to mention but a few of whom more will be heard – but there are two accounts, admittedly written in retrospect, that show her as she was in her mid-twenties before she had broken out of the shell of family life.

They are of especial interest if only because the impression she made upon these observers, whose vantage points could not have been more disparate, is strikingly in accord.

Marian Skinner, the young lady who frequented 41 Maitland Park Road as one of Eleanor's literary-minded friends to whom Marx played host when his arcane studies permitted, says that he "treated Eleanor with the indulgent affection one bestows on a beloved but wilful child. Wilful indeed she was, but she was also an unusually brilliant creature, with a clear, logical brain, a shrewd knowledge of men and a wonderful memory. ... She either passionately admired or desperately scorned, she loved fervently or she hated with vehemence. Middle courses never commended themselves to her. She had amazing vitality, extraordinary receptivity, and she was the gayest creature in the world – when she was not the most miserable. Her appearance was striking. She was not really beautiful, but she somehow gave the impression of beauty by reason of her sparkling eyes, her bright colouring, her dark locky mass of hair...."[1]

Eduard Bernstein† met Eleanor for the first time in 1880 when he came to London for a week in November. His was no ordinary social visit. As private secretary to and one of the German socialists grouped round the

---

* Mentioned earlier as one of the collaborators in Charles Booth's *Labour and Life of the People* (see fn., pp. 131–2), Miss Beatrice Potter (1858–1943), who became Mrs. Sidney Webb in 1892, is not to be confused with the even more widely read Miss Beatrix Potter (1866–1943), later Mrs. Heelis, of *Peter Rabbit* fame.

† (1850–1932). From 1881 to 1890 Bernstein edited the German Social Democratic Party's official organ, the *Sozialdemokrat*, issued in Zürich until 1888 and, from October of that year in London.

wealthy publisher Karl Höchberg* who had emigrated to Switzerland in 1878, Bernstein had come under heavy fire from Marx and Engels. With August Bebel† he at last decided to clear the position by bearding the lions in their den: "Going to Canossa", Bebel called it.[2]

To Bernstein, then, on his political mission, Eleanor was simply the daughter of the house of whom he left two separate descriptions. In the earlier one he referred to her at this first meeting as "a lively young girl of slender build with beautiful black hair and fine dark eyes. ... At that time she was already working hard at the British Museum, partly for her father,‡ partly 'devilling', that is, taking excerpts or doing research for a pittance to save well-to-do people who wanted to write books the trouble of looking things up for themselves."[3]

At a Benefit Concert for the widow of a Communard, Bernstein – startled to find that the list of subscribers was headed by Queen Victoria with a donation of £10 – heard Eleanor recite *The Pied Piper of Hamelin* and was much struck by her "tremendous verve and wonderful voice". The occasion, despite its regal patronage, was graced by the presence of Marx, Engels, Bebel, Carl Hirsch, Leo Hartmann and a pack of "other Reds".[3]

In his later reminiscences, written in 1915, he repeated his commendation of her striking appearance and "exceptionally musical voice", adding: "She was unusually vivacious and took part, in her sensitive and emotional manner, in our discussions of party matters. With much greater devotion than her two elder sisters, Tussy ... had dedicated herself to the socialist movement ... On my first visit this girl was ... the pet of the family."[5]

It was natural that Marian Skinner should see only the "brilliant creature", whose diverse talents were to include speaking at socialist meetings, while Bernstein regarded her first and foremost as the "perfervid socialist".

Yet socialism in England was almost non-existent at that time.

It was to Bernstein, before he had met him, that Engels wrote: "For years the English working-class movement has revolved hopelessly in a

---

* The pseudonym of Dr. Ludwig Richter.

† 1840–1913. One of the founders of the German Social Democratic Party at Eisenach in 1869, Bebel remained continuously the Chairman of its Central Committee.

‡ There is no contemporary evidence that Eleanor was working for Marx at this time, apart from dealing with some of his vast correspondence when he was unwell. She herself wrote to Jenny a few months later to say that she had been offered the job of précis writer for a scientific journal. "I suppose you know that in literary slang a précis writer is one who summarises articles, books, etc. It is a mere trick to do it but ... I have never tried it and don't know if I can do it ... if I can I shall earn £2 a week and not have much work – about a quarter of what I'm doing now..."[4]

narrow circle of strikes for higher wages and shorter hours, not as a makeshift* nor as a means of propaganda, but as an end in itself. The Trades Unions in fact exclude on principle and in their rules all political action and thereby debar the working class from taking part in any general activity as a class. ... So one can speak of a workers' movement here only inasmuch as there are strikes which, successful or not, advance the movement not one step. To inflate such strikes – which, moreover, during the recent bad trade years have quite often been deliberately engineered by the capitalists to furnish a pretext for closing their factories – strikes by which the working class makes no headway, into struggles of world importance ... can, in my opinion, only do harm. It should not be concealed that at present no real workers' movement, in the Continental sense, exists here...."[6]

The population of Great Britain had reached nearly 30 million in 1881, an increase of 28 per cent in 20 years. 12,731,000 were "occupied persons", of whom one-third were females, with nearly two million in domestic service – "useless persons, eating their heads off and producing nothing"[7] – while in 1880 a mere quarter of a million were estimated to be organised in 34 trade unions.† Thus, in disparaging the trade unionists' futile round of strikes, sometimes instigated by the factory owners themselves, Engels was referring to class conflicts which were not only without political significance but which left the mass of the workers untouched.

As for "real workers' movements in the Continental sense", they were genuine and formidable enough for the German Reichstag to have passed the Anti-Socialist Law,‡ under which Liebknecht was gaoled yet again for three months at the end of October 1878 and whose long arm extended to Germans abroad, so that Carl Hirsch was arrested in Paris on 16 August

---

* Engels uses the word *Nothehelf*, generally translated as "expedient" in this context, which does not precisely convey the meaning.
† The Webbs' *History of Trade Unionism* (1919 edition) states that "until the appointment, in 1886, of John Burnett as Labour Correspondent to the Board of Trade, no attempt was made to collect any statistics of the movement, and the old Unions seldom possess a complete series of their own archives. No total figure can be given with any confidence." The estimated number of trade unionists in 1880 showed a slight decline from that of 1875 – when it was nearer to 300,000 – reflecting the first wave of the economic crisis in the period 1873 to 1879. With intermittent years of recovery, notably 1880 to 1882 and 1887 to 1890, the great depression lasted until 1896.
‡ The Bill was put before the Reichstag on 8 September 1878, debated for six weeks and passed by 221 to 149 votes on 19 October. The Act came into force two days later, was constantly renewed and not finally repealed until October 1890.

1879,* while a fresh stream of socialist refugees flowed into England.

But, dangerous as the workers' party appeared to the German ruling class, Marx saw it as increasingly under the influence of doctors, students and what he called "professorial socialist riff-raff ... nonentities in theory and useless in practice" who were eroding the movement with a brand of socialism "concocted according to university recipes", palatable to the petty bourgeoisie. Marx and Engels jointly drafted a circular letter to the leaders of the German Social Democratic Party analysing its position, making their own attitude towards it clear. "For almost 40 years", they wrote, "we have stressed the class struggle between bourgeoisie and proletariat as the main lever of modern social revolution; it is therefore impossible for us to co-operate with people who seek to expunge this class struggle from the movement. When the International was founded we explicitly formulated the battle-cry: The emancipation of the working classes must be brought about by the working classes themselves. We cannot therefore associate ourselves with people who openly state that the workers are too uneducated to emancipate themselves and must be freed from above by philanthropic big bourgeois and petty bourgeois ... for which purpose the working class must place itself under the leadership of 'educated and propertied' bourgeois, who alone possess the 'time and opportunity' to acquaint themselves with what is good for the workers."

In contrast to this view, Hyndman in England expressed the opinion "that the emancipation of the workers must be brought about by the workers themselves is true in the sense that we cannot have Socialism without Socialists. ... But a slave cannot be freed by the slaves themselves. The leadership, the initiative, the teaching, the organisation must come from those who are born into a different position and are trained to use their faculties in early life."†[8]

For a period of a few months from the end of 1880, Henry Mayers Hyndman – introduced according to his own account[8] by Carl Hirsch but according to Engels' by Rudolph-Hermann Meyer‡ – enjoyed an

---

* He was picked up in the street, taken before the Police Commissioner and then left for two days in the Prefecture before being sentenced to a month's imprisonment for "unauthorised re-entry" to France, which he left forthwith, arriving in London on 23 August.

† The interesting point here – for no one would deny that both Marx and Engels were "born into a different position" from that of the average worker – is Hyndman's blurring of the distinction between theory and practice: to lead and to teach slaves who have no initiative or organisation of their own would seem to be not a means to socialism but a perfect waste of time. "Hyndman's bourgeois mentality made it impossible for him to estimate the worth of industrial organization correctly", wrote Tom Mann who nevertheless admired his ability to address working men on socialism and "to state the case comprehensively, logically and argumentatively".[9]

‡ A German émigré economist and journalist who frequented the Marxes, Engels and the Lafargues.

acquaintance with Marx. The families visited each other, Eleanor accompanying her father to dine with the Hyndmans at 10 Devonshire Street, Portland Place, when her mother was not well enough to go, while the Hyndmans called – sometimes uninvited – at the Marxes' "modest dwelling in Haverstock Hill".[8] Though Hyndman was never shaken in his conviction that at this period the regard was mutual and that he was indeed favoured by a special intimacy with Marx "accessible to very few outside the immediate family circle", attributing to Engels – upon whom he never set eyes but called "the Teutonic Grand Lama of the Regent's Park Road"[8] – a jealousy and arrogance that severed this beautiful friendship, his belief was false. Marx did not take to him, thought him smug and overweening, resented the way he forced himself upon him and stole "many of my evenings to pick my brains and thus to learn things by the easiest means". In a letter to his daughter Jenny in April 1881 he wrote of "an invasion" by the Hyndmans on which occasion they so outstayed their welcome that Mrs. Marx was completely exhausted and had to retire. "I quite like the wife for her blunt, unconventional and decided manner of thinking and speaking, but the admiring way she hangs on the lips of her self-satisfied, garrulous husband is comical", wrote Marx.

Although his talks with Marx undoubtedly fired Hyndman's resolve to establish "a really democratic party in opposition to the monstrous tyranny of Mr. Gladstone and his Whigs in Ireland and their equally abominable policy in Egypt,* with the object of bringing about democratic changes in England",[8] the wide political differences between the two men were thereby brought to light.

The inevitable breach between them – ascribed by Hyndman to Marx's

---

* This refers to the Coercion Act of 1881 whereby the leaders of the Irish Land League suspected of "seditious conspiracy" could be arrested. It followed upon the effects of the 1870 Land Act which gave no security from eviction for tenants who did not pay the rent laid down by the landlord. A Bill mitigating these conditions was thrown out by the Lords and, in 1880, Lord Ernle's steward, Captain Boycott, refused the fair – but not full – rent offered by his tenants and issued eviction notices, whereupon the entire tenantry, including his parish priest, shopkeepers, postmen, laundresses, blacksmiths, farm-hands and domestic staff refused to serve him. A new word was added to the English language, while Irish M.P.s, notably Parnell, were sent to prison.

Britain and France between them had succeeded in bringing Egypt to a state of bankruptcy by means of loans for the building of railways, bridges, canals and docks paid for by the peasants, who had least need of these improvements which were of vital importance to Britain in particular, both for the control of the Suez Canal (opened in 1869) as the route to India, and as the chief importer of Egyptian cotton vastly developed at the time of the American Civil War. In 1881 the nationalist movement under army command seized power, whereupon the British and French sent battleships to Alexandria and, in the following year, the British bombarded the city and landed an army which, by September 1882, imposed military control over the whole country.

resentment at his name having been omitted and Hyndman's debt to him unacknowledged in the little book *England for All** – has been finally and fully documented by Dr. Emile Bottigelli.[10] Marx's objections were not to the half-baked plagiarism of *Capital*; certainly not to the fact that he received no personal credit, for, as he wrote to Hyndman, "Party programmes ought to be kept free of any apparent dependence upon individual authors or books"; and not even to the foolish excuse – as applied to the friend of the Chartists and the leader of the International – that his name "was so much detested" and "Englishmen have a dread of being taught by a foreigner", but quite simply – apart from Hyndman's disingenuousness in approaching him only after the booklet was in the press – to the fact that borrowings, however distorted, from *Capital* had no place in a programme whose professed aims were wholly at variance with its theories.

The Democratic Federation, founded in June 1881,† was composed on Hyndman's own showing of Comtists, Tories, middle-class Radicals and M.P.s, with a sprinkling of ancient Chartists, none of whom could have agreed on any but the mildest of social reforms. "What can you expect", wrote Engels, "of a set of people who take in hand the task of instructing the world about matters of which they themselves are ignorant? There is not a single burning question which they know how to tackle; Hyndman combines internationalist phraseology with jingo aspirations."[11]

In fact Hyndman had not picked Marx's brains thoroughly enough to arrive at the fundamental concept of an independent workers' party. He had read the French edition of *Capital* before he met Marx but "did not at the time" – nor ever after – "fully grasp all the significance of his theories"[8] and to have used them – however rightly or wrongly presented – for the embellishment of a programme acceptable to "*the* Englishmen"[10] – without distinction of class – was something Marx could not condone. He wrote to Hyndman on 2 July 1881 from Eastbourne where he was staying with his wife, having given himself time to turn the matter over. "On Saturday", Mrs. Marx reported to Laura, "the pale-eyed Hyndman received his blow on the head. He is not likely to prop up the letter on his looking-glass, although, for all its pungency, it was so wittily worded that anger was barely perceptible. I think Mohr was rather happy in this opus."‡[12]

---

* Published June 1881. Hyndman claimed it to be the "first socialist work that appeared up to 1881 in English".[8]

† Subsequently the Social-Democratic Federation.

‡ Far from putting this letter on show, Hyndman did not even keep it. Thus, were it not for Mrs. Marx's (unpublished) letter to Laura,[12] there would be no trace of it and Hyndman's version[8] the only explanation of the breach until Dr. Bottigelli discovered the original draft of Marx's letter among the Longuet papers.[10]

From this letter it would appear that the "refined and highly intelligent woman" of Hyndman's reminiscences, whose "great charm of manner and conversation"[8] had fed the fantasy that he was the most welcome of guests at Maitland Park Road, did not reciprocate this high esteem.

Nevertheless, Hyndman's Federation, which Eleanor joined, was to play a major part in the revival of socialism and the development of the labour movement in Britain at a time when America, France and Germany had begun to break England's monopoly of world trade.* But for the hostility between Engels and Hyndman, born of the latter's irrational conceit that he was regarded as a rival who had threatened to supplant Engels in Marx's life, the whole course of British socialism, Eleanor's part in it and her personal fate might have taken a different turn in the years to come.

In the meantime she was not only participating in political discussions with Bernstein and Bebel at her parents' table and dining with the Hyndmans but she associated with Helen Taylor† and Joseph Cowen,‡ both of whom were among the founder members of the Democratic Federation, writing to tell Hirsch of her various dealings with them,[14] though it is not clear from the context whether this was in connection with Miss Taylor's keen interest in the Irish question or another crusade on which Eleanor was now embarked.

In November 1880 she sent out two letters to 38 London and provincial papers§ drawing public attention to the state of siege declared under the Anti-Socialist Law and the expulsion of citizens from Hamburg, Altona, Ottensen, Blankenese, Wedel and Lauenburg (which included some of Bismarck's own landed property). "Of course", she wrote to Liebknecht, "very few – if any – will take notice of it but at least I wish to *try* and do something. . . . I am also going to try with Hirsch to get up a committee here to collect funds for the families."[15] She was so far suc-

---

* It may also be said that the character of the British labour movement was determined by the fact that, following the challenge to its position as the leading capitalist country, England entered the stage of exporting capital to its expanding Empire. The effects of this trend, which were not – and perhaps could not be – analysed until several decades later, were to give certain sections of workers a privileged position, damping down their need and desire for any basic social changes. One writer rammed home the point in the phrase: "There is not a more contented community, nor one less likely to be influenced by Communistic or Socialistic ideas, on the face of the earth, than the British working class."[13] Since these skilled workers were also the most powerful and best organised sections, the unskilled and unorganised were in a peculiarly vulnerable position and it was they who displayed the militancy otherwise so markedly lacking during the late '80s and the '90s.

† J. S. Mill's stepdaughter.

‡ M.P. for Newcastle, where he had organised meetings for Garibaldi in 1864. An old Chartist, Engels characterised him as "half if not a whole Communist and a very good chap".

§ See Appendix 4, p. 301.

cessful that in October 1881 she sent Karl Kautsky, then in Zürich, 40 marks subscribed by Helen Taylor for the families of the persecuted socialists.[16]

At the beginning of February 1881 Michael Davitt, who had founded the Irish Land League in 1879, was arrested*: "an act of cowardly retaliation and petty spite". Knowing that he was to appear at Bow Street on 11 February, Eleanor went to the Police Court "and found a large – and angry – crowd assembled outside the station". The crowd was angry because, contrary to all precedent, the prisoner had been brought before the magistrate at 8 a.m. "The government feared to face the public", was Eleanor's comment. She asked a policeman whether Davitt was still in Court and was told in a strong Irish brogue " 'No, it's meself put him in the van' ", whereupon she " 'went for him' " and asked "if there weren't enough Englishmen to do such dirty work that an Irishman must help 'put in the van' a man who like Davitt had done so much for his country". As she turned away in disgust an Irishman standing in the crowd came up to her and said: "Allow me to shake hands with you and thank you."[17] In the same letter to Liebknecht she asked him to send her any information he had about working-class opposition to the Jew-baiting in Germany: "I might get something about it into the press."

It will be seen that at this stage of her life, whatever other interests she pursued, Eleanor was involved in every social issue at home and abroad and was, indeed, as her mother had earlier pronounced her, "political from head to toe".

---

* He had previously served a seven year sentence (1870 to 1877) as a Fenian convict.

One feature of Eleanor's personality, seldom if ever described by her contemporaries, was her intense love of children. Not the least of her tragedies was that she had none of her own. Everybody's babies interested her. She never wrote to young parents without making the closest enquiries about their off-spring, but her most passionate maternal feelings were centred on her nephews.

On 17 August 1879, with Lenchen in attendance at 6 Artillery Road, Ramsgate, Jenny had given birth to another son, Edgar Marcel, nick-named Wolf. When she left England in February 1881 to rejoin her husband in Paris she was in her eighth month of pregnancy with the fourth son, Marcel Charles, known as Par.*

In a letter to Natalie Liebknecht written at that time Eleanor described these little boys: "Harry . . . is a very backward and very delicate child . . . and requires much care and attention – so much in fact that it is difficult for him to get it as the next child (who is very forward) is only 13 months younger than he and Jenny expects another baby in March! This last expectation is not altogether a blessing . . . it is difficult to attend to three-one might almost say four babies, for of course Johnny is still only a baby . . . five next May . . . a dear little fellow . . . a very beautiful boy . . . The second boy – *my* boy – Harry is not pretty . . . but I love him best of all because I think his nature is by far the sweetest of the three, and he is one of those children who seem destined to suffer. . . ." The youngest, Edgar, was his mother's favourite: "not so handsome as Johnny" in Eleanor's view, but "strong and healthy, bright – and terribly spoilt".[18]

One of the reasons why Longuet had gone back to France ahead of his family – apart from the Marxes' strong desire to keep Jenny and the children with them for as long as possible – was that his mother had written to her daughter-in-law in March 1879 complaining of her soli-tude and repeating the rather individualist argument, expressed on her last visit to England, that if she longed for an amnesty it was not that she wished to deprive Charles or Jenny of their employment in London but to enable her son to come to France where his property was being seque-strated, running her into losses to the tune of millions of francs.[19]

---

* Including the first child who did not survive, Jenny bore in all six children – five boys and a girl – between September 1873 and September 1882.

Although Madame Longuet senior does not appear a very sympathetic character, she did at least show genuine concern for Mrs. Marx's health and was perturbed when no news came, while her interest in her grand-children, though not overpowering, was enough for Longuet to send her reports on their characters, teething troubles, and locks of Johnny's and Harry's hair (Edgar's he could not send because, owing to eczema, the poor child was bald at six months).[20]

There is no question but that Jenny loved her husband dearly, parti-cularly in his absence, when she wrote that she realised "how lonely my life would be without you" and found herself waiting impatiently for the postman's knock to announce a letter from him.[21] Her departure for France – where for the short time that remained to her she lived in a house at Argenteuil*, once a rich man's summer residence – caused the family great unhappiness. Mrs. Marx had been dreading it.

When the amnesty was granted in the summer of 1880, before setting out for a last seaside holiday with the Longuets and Lafargues to Rams-gate, she had been to Manchester to consult Gumpert once again, accompanied this time by Marx who, not satisfied, wrote at the end of September to Dr. Ferdinand Fleckles in Carlsbad appealing for advice. Never having seen or examined the patient, the doctor set out a list of questions for her to answer. Instead of replying to these in detail she sent him a letter – unread by Marx – giving a comprehensive account of her state of mind and health in which she said: "What has made my condition worse recently perhaps is a great anxiety which weighs heavily upon us 'old ones'. The French amnesty will in all probability be synonymous for us with the loss of our children and grandchildren. And my own removal to Paris in my present condition frightens me ... So I clutch at every straw. Dear good Doctor, I should so like to live a little longer. How strange it is that the nearer the whole thing draws to an end, the more one clings to this 'vale of tears'." The entire household was topsy-turvy with the imminence of his eldest daughter's leavetaking, Marx wrote. The grandchildren were "an inexhaustible source of joy to me and my wife in whose present circumstances this separation is most painful". They had dearly hoped that Harry, at least, would be left with them because, as Marx later wrote to Jenny, "he is a child who wants a whole family's attendance being singly, exclusively concentrated upon him. As it is, with so many other little ones requesting your care, he is rather an impedi-ment." Eleanor, who also missed her nephews sorely, wrote: "This is a sad blow for Papa and Mama, as they are so devoted to the children"[18] and,

---

* This, the cradle of impressionist painting, was later to be the constituency for which Gabriel Péri was the Deputy from 1932 until his arrest in May 1941, when he was handed over by the Vichy government to the Nazis who executed him on 15 December 1941.

indeed, a month after the young family had left Marx wrote to Jenny: "I often run to the window when I hear children's voices ... forgetting for the moment that the little fellows are across the Channel."

The parting, however, was not final for there were visits to Argenteuil while, to the end of Jenny's days, Eleanor kept up an intimate correspondence with her, showing a love that was heightened not only by separation but also perhaps because, for reasons that remain obscure, there was a great coldness between Eleanor and Laura in these years.* Indeed, as early as 1879, while the parents were in Ramsgate with Jenny after her confinement and the two sisters in London, Engels was hard put to it to contrive that they should not meet at his house for the usual Sunday dinner. He communicated his stratagems to Marx and it was clearly understood on both sides that they were necessary. The antagonism of the Lafargues to Lissagaray – manifested at their first meeting and exploding into a quarrel between him and Paul – does not account for the estrangement between the sisters since Paul never evinced any ill-feeling towards Eleanor.

As the months passed Mrs. Marx's health grew ominously worse. Yet her cry from the heart to Dr. Fleckles was the only sign she gave of her knowledge and fear that she was dying. In her last decade Mrs. Marx became the gracious and serene figure recalled in so many reminiscences as to leave no doubt that this was her abiding image to all who knew her at the close of her days. Having weathered the storms of middle life during Eleanor's childhood, she developed with advancing age and despite sufferings that failed to crush her "bright spirit and great heart",[23] a gentle irony and self-mockery, a capacity to make light of her troubles, which had been lacking in the early years of struggle when they would have stood her in good stead.

In February 1879 she had so severe an attack that it was thought she could not recover. Two years later, Marx wrote to Danielson† that his wife's condition was daily becoming more dangerous though he had called in the most renowned consultant in London. The new doctor in regular

---

* In the summer of 1882, when Eleanor rejoined Marx in Argenteuil and the Lafargues were living in Paris (see p. 185), he wrote to Engels: "Tussy and Laura have not yet seen each other and are hardly yearning to do so." For the sake of decency, he went on, they would have to meet at least once while he was there. In later years they corresponded in friendly terms on practical matters, and there was real warmth in the relationship towards the end, though Laura did not attend Eleanor's funeral. According to *Justice* she was too "prostrated by grief".[22]

† Nikolai Frantsevich Danielson (1844–1918), Russian writer and economist who had long been in correspondence with Marx and Engels. He translated the three volumes of *Capital*, the first volume in collaboration with Lopatin.

attendance, Horatio Bryan Donkin,* a relatively young man who had qualified in 1873, "pleased both her and Mohr extremely, though he is still very doubtful as to the real nature of Mama's illness" wrote Eleanor.[25] Engels confirmed to Jenny at the end of May that her mother was unaware of the nature of her illness and he was inclined to agree that the doctors were groping in the dark, but she was visibly growing thinner and weaker, while what she had called her "ups and downs" were more marked: there were times when she was active from morning till night – in the course of June she went to the play several times a week – then again she would be laid low by pain, obliged to spend days in bed.

Her dearest wish was to see her grandchildren again and Dr. Donkin encouraged, even insisted upon the visit to France, though Marx thought it out of the question. In July he took her to Eastbourne for three weeks from where she wrote to Laura, who had done everything to keep up her mother's spirits: "I know how you long for good news of your old Möhme. Alas, I have none to give. In spite of the propitious circumstances, I do not feel better and have therefore written to Donkin again. Just imagine, I have actually sunk to a Bathchair, a thing that I, the pedestrian *par excellence*, should have regarded as beneath my dignity a few months ago."[12] Tussy joined her parents for a few days at the end of their stay, but whether her mother could go abroad was still unsure. Immediately on her return to London Donkin examined the patient and, four days later, on 26 July 1881, she, with Marx and Lenchen, left for France to stay with the Longuets at 11 boulevard Thiers in Argenteuil. "I never knew how dear you are to me till now", wrote Jenny on hearing the news that "her dearest Mama" was definitely coming. "The whole night I could not close an eye dreading the announcement that you would not come, because the promised telegram did not arrive. ... I do not know how I shall manage to live till Tuesday. ... Longuet who is always frightened when his mother comes is almost as pleased as Johnny to have you here."[26]

The journey was trying enough for Mrs. Marx but, once settled, she was subject to attacks that deprived her of her greatest pleasure, the children's company, and caused Jenny's doctor, Gustave Dourlen, to administer the pain-killing drugs Donkin had held in reserve. Marx was under no illusions about the character of the illness and, though thankful for intermittent improvements, wrote to Engels: "they do not stop the natural progress of the disease but they deceive my wife and confirm Jenny – despite my objections – in her belief that the stay at Argenteuil should be as long as possible. I know better and thus have the greater fear."

Lenchen, whom the little Longuet boys called Nym, or Nimmy – a

---

* He was deeply devoted to Olive Schreiner, "long cherishing the hope that she would become his wife".[24]

nickname which, with variations, stuck to her for the rest of her days – was of the greatest comfort to Jenny. The more so when, upon receiving a letter from Dollie Maitland to say that Tussy was desperately ill, Marx left abruptly on the same day – 16 August – taking an express train for London and leaving his wife to follow. A couple of days later Mrs. Marx and Lenchen set out to travel, first class, by slow stages, staying overnight at Amiens and then resting for a day or two at Boulogne before crossing to Folkestone where, again, they halted until Mrs. Marx felt able to complete the journey to London. "Naturally", wrote Marx, "it is painful for me to separate from her, but her real support is Helen, my own presence was not absolutely necessary."

Early in October Eleanor wrote to Jenny: "dear Mama is very ill – the *worst* is we can do absolutely nothing. It is a beastly illness ... in all other respects Mama is, Dr. Donkin says, so strong. All her organs are perfectly healthy. Is it not monstrous that ... so terrible an illness should have come to her?"[27]

At this juncture Marx fell ill with pleurisy. Eleanor stopped Jenny from rushing to London. "You must not leave the children", she wrote. "It would be the merest madness and would cause Papa more anxiety than your being here could give him pleasure or do him good – much as we all wish you were here."[27]

For a time, while pneumonia threatened, Eleanor did not stir from her father's bedside until, upon Donkin's orders, Lenchen relieved her on duty and she took a night's rest. Meanwhile her friend Clementina Black and others sat with and read to Mrs. Marx who had now lain for weeks in the adjoining room, so wasted that, to "give her a *little* change Dr. Donkin says we are to lift her – in her sheets – from her bed to the chair-bed".[28] "Engels", wrote Eleanor, "is of a kindness and devotion that baffle description. Surely there is not another like him in the world – despite his little weaknesses."[29] She described her father as a "cranky patient" but, once he was out of danger at the end of the month, he was able to get up and see his wife, by now in such unendurable pain that Donkin was prepared to give her the morphine injections he had withheld for fear that when this stage was reached she should have developed a tolerance to the drug, making it ineffective. He suggested that Eleanor should administer the injection, but she was repelled by the idea and thought that a nurse would be needed.[28] "It was a terrible time", Eleanor recalled later. "Our mother lay in the large front room, Moor in the little room behind. And the two of them, who were so used to one another, so close to one another, could not even be together in the same room. Our good old Lenchen ... and I had to nurse them both ... Never shall I forget the morning when he felt strong enough to go into mother's room. When they were together they were young again – she a loving girl and he a loving youth, on the threshold of life, not an old man devastated by illness and an old dying woman parting from each other for life."[30]

During that last month, when Mrs. Marx "suffered all the terrible tortures that cancer brings with it ... her good humour, her inexhaustible wit ... never deserted her for an instant. She enquired as impatiently as a child for the results of the elections then being held in Germany. ... Up to her death she remained cheerful and tried to dispel our anxiety by joking. Yes, in spite of her fearful suffering she joked – she *laughed* – she laughed at the doctor and all of us because we were so serious. She remained fully conscious almost until the last moment, and when she could no longer speak ... she pressed our hands and tried to smile",[30] but "the last word she spoke was to Papa: 'Good'."[31]

During those weeks of agony her mother wrote to Jenny. She rejoiced that she had made the journey to Paris, reliving the happiness it had given her and "to the *very last* she thought of you and the children more than of anyone", Eleanor told Jenny.[31]

Mrs. Marx was just under 68 years of age when she died on Friday, 2 December 1881. Laura, who had been present, notified the death of her mother.* She was to be buried on the 5th and on the day before the funeral Eleanor wrote to Jenny: "I do dread it – but of course Papa cannot go. He must not yet leave the house and I am glad of this in every way. We have asked all the people Mama liked. ..."[31]

Her mother's resting-place, as Jenny had wished, was near to that of her first-born son Charles Longuet in Highgate cemetery. The funeral was conducted with all simplicity. A few days before her death Mrs. Marx had told her nurse that she wanted no pomp or ceremony: "We are no such *external* people", she had said. Engels made a short oration, recalling her life, her "noble heart", with admiration and respect. He ended with the words: "What she did is known only to those who lived with her ... There is no need for me to speak of her personal virtues. Her friends know those virtues and will never forget them. If ever there was a woman whose greatest happiness lay in making others happy, this was she."[32]

An obituary notice appeared on 7 December in Clemenceau's *La Justice* of which Longuet had been joint editor since his return to France. It contained a passage saying that there had been great prejudice against the marriage to Marx mainly on the score of his Jewish origin, which angered him beyond measure. He wrote to Jenny on the same day: "I suppose I am not mistaken in crediting Mr. Ch. Longuet's inventive genius with this

---

* The death certificate gives Mrs. Marx's forenames as Jenny Julia Joan Bertha, the cause of death as cancer of the liver.

literary embellishment ... Longuet would greatly oblige me in never mentioning my name in *his* writings."

Although Laura and Eleanor had prepared her for the inevitable, Jenny was stunned by the news and could not resign herself to the death of "one who could so intensely enjoy life when there are so many creatures living whose dreary existence is only a burden to them. ... Only last week I had a letter from Mama. ... though far away I was not forgotten. Poor Mama's heart was large enough for all of us...."[23]

Eleanor wrote to Jenny now – sending her a piece of her mother's "dear hair ... as soft and beautiful as a girl's" – to recall the "sweet expression as she saw and recognised us, which she did at the end",[31] while later she was to say: "My mother and I loved each other passionately ... One of the bitterest sorrows of my life is that my mother died, thinking, despite all our love, that I had been hard and cruel, and never guessing that to save her and father sorrow I had sacrificed the best, freshest years of my life."[33]

Exactly what had precipitated Eleanor's illness, causing Marx to dash back to England in mid-August 1881, cannot be known with any certainty, but that it was in some way connected with her mother's decline is beyond doubt. Looking back and claiming that Mrs. Marx had died thinking her "hard and cruel" – when she was neither – is but one clear indication of the guilt she felt. Another is the nature of her illness.

While alone in London that summer she wrote cheerfully to her parents, saying "I get on capitally",[34] and sent a "jolly letter" to Engels in Bridport, but in fact she was unable to sleep and had stopped eating altogether,* until she reached a state of near collapse so alarming that Dollie Maitland, whose help she rejected, felt it necessary to summon Marx.

Eleanor had declined to see a doctor, but her father immediately sent for Donkin in whose opinion there was nothing organically wrong with her except for "a perfect derangement of the action of her stomach" thanks to her obstinate fasting. Nor did he think she stood in any danger so long as she obeyed his strict injunctions to feed herself rationally. Marx reported to Engels and to Jenny that her "overwrought nervous system" manifested itself in trembling hands, a facial tic and convulsive spasms.

Yet only on 5 July – a bare three weeks before her parents had left for Paris – she had made a brilliant appearance at the Dilettante Club theatre in two one-act plays with friends, including Ernest Radford and Dollie Maitland – who, as Engels reported, showed great self-possession and looked adorable on the stage – while Tussy had been "very good in the passionate scenes, though it was rather obvious that she modelled herself on Ellen Terry, as Radford on Irving. However, that will soon wear off; if she intends to make an effect in public she must undoubtedly strike out a line of her own, as she certainly will."

Not only Dollie but also Ernest Radford, whom Eleanor deemed "a very nice fellow",[34] going with him to see Irving's Hamlet in July, had

---

* Psychopathology recognises this type of *anorexia nervosa*, the refusal to eat, as a form of self-inflicted punishment: in extreme cases, capital punishment by starving to death. It most often occurs in adolescent girls and is thought by some to be a symptom of undisclosed feelings of guilt or aggression in relation to the mother as the giver of food. A notable feature is that such patients may remain in high good spirits while they waste away.[35]

tried his best to help her in her depression.* Marx was reassured by her promise to change her way of life: "Once she gives her word, she keeps it", he said.

Sometime in the spring of 1881, before she went to Jersey,† Leo Hartmann‡ proposed to Tussy. She still considered herself affianced to Lissagaray, but this – unacceptable – offer may have jolted her into reviewing her situation, for it was in these years leading up to and immediately following her mother's death that Eleanor went through the second personal crisis in her life. But, unlike the earlier one when she had been a mere girl, childlike in many ways, and half in love with all Communards, she was now a young woman who, though to all appearances immensely occupied, was more and more dissatisfied with her life.

Objections to a relationship have a way of making it become objectionable. It is idle to speculate what might have happened had the Marxes approved of Lissagaray and Eleanor had married him. The defiant engagement had by now lasted for many "long miserable years",[33] casting a shadow between her and her father, until the romance was nothing but an oppressive weight.

For months after Lissagaray had left England in July 1880 she made no move. She was immersed in work and play and politics, and it was of these – when not of her nephews – that she wrote to Jenny when first she, too, went to France. In April 1881 her news was of the appalling situation in Ireland – "two men shot and many wounded, and now a girl of 20 shot and several women hurt" – of the "newest 'New Party'", the Democratic Federation, which she did not think would amount to much and of the *Labour Standard*, a penny weekly about to be launched under the

---

* She sent him some books inscribed on 6 August 1881: "Will you accept these volumes as a small mark of my gratitude for all your kindness during my illness? 'Beggar that I am, I am even poor in thanks – but I thank you'. Eleanor Marx."[36]

† Although it is known that Eleanor spent a holiday there with Marx in 1879, (a holiday cut short by the birth of Jenny's son in Ramsgate whither Marx immediately went), staying at the Hotel de l'Europe in St. Helier – after a few days at the Trafalgar Hotel in St. Aubin where the unvarying diet of lamb and mutton turned Marx into a vegetarian – there is no evidence of this later visit other than in a letter from Marx to Jenny dated 6 June 1881.

‡ Leo (or Lev) Nikolayevich Hartmann (1850–1908) was a Russian member of *Narodnaya Volya* (The People's Will) implicated in an attempt on the life of Alexander II in December 1879. Hartmann fled abroad, but was arrested in 1880 in Paris which caused an outcry, headed by Victor Hugo, leading to his release. Thereupon he went to England, where he worked at Siemens Woolwich factory for a few weeks. Immediately before going to America for six months early in June 1881, he wrote to Engels asking for Pumps' hand. This evoked Marx's indignation, for he was under the mistaken impression that Hartmann had formerly lived in "free marriage" with Sofia Perovskaya, one of the leaders of The People's Will who, following the assassination of the Tsar on 13 March 1881, was tried and, on 15 April, hanged. "From Perovskaya to Pumps is really a bit much", commented Marx.

editorship of George Shipton,* to which Engels contributed from 7 May until 6 August 1881.[25,37]

But by June, at which time Marx felt he must warn Jenny that her mother's illness was mortal,† Eleanor was writing in a different vein. She was resolved to take acting lessons from Mrs. Vezin‡ who had moved conveniently nearby to Highgate Road. "Even if, as I fancy will be the case – Mrs. Vezin finds that she has much overrated my powers the lessons will still be useful to me, and I can always make the recitation venture", she wrote to Jenny. She intended to start in July. "I feel sorry to cost Papa so much, but after all very small sums were expended on my education, compared at least to what is *now* demanded of girls – and I think if I do succeed it will have been a good investment. I shall try too, to get as much work as I can so that I may have a little money by the time I need it. . . . You see, dear, I've a goodly number of irons in the fire, but I feel I've wasted quite enough of my life, and that it is high time I did something. . . ."[4]

Her breakdown, for such it was, thus occurred at a time when she was plotting a new course to discover and develop such talents as she might have.

All these thoughts were pushed into the background by her parents' illness, culminating in her mother's death. That she stood the strains of nursing, albeit shared with Lenchen, showed her powers of self-command. It carried her through the worst period when, in addition to all else, she had to entertain her cousin Willa Juta§ who wanted to talk all the time. "I think our family is going quite mad", she wrote to Jenny, for it turned out that another cousin, Jettchen Conradi‖, suffered from the strange hallucination that she was the author of *Little Women* – published when that young lady had been three years old – and Eleanor had not only to correspond with Louisa Alcott, who modestly admitted authorship, but to get a written assurance that the 1868 edition of the work was in the British Museum. To Eleanor's dismay, the hallucinated girl and her mother arrived in London at this juncture. "Is it not a damned nuisance", she wrote.[27]

However she still managed to put in a few hours at the Museum, for

---

* Secretary of the London Trades Council 1871–1896.
† In a letter written on Bank Holiday Monday, 6 June. The day before, Parnell's great demonstration in Hyde Park had been ruined by hideously cold weather and heavy rain "one of the bad jokes the Heavenly Father always keeps in readiness for His plebeian London flock", said Marx, a sentiment echoed by countless drenched and freezing British working-class demonstrators ever since in the phrase: "God knows which side His bread's buttered."
‡ See above, fn.*, p. 23.
§ Daughter of Marx's sister Louise from Cape Town.
‖ Daughter of Marx's sister Emilie who had married Conradi, an engineer, in Trier.

she was desperately anxious not to lose the work she had undertaken for Dr. Murray.* "You don't know how many people – most far better qualified to do the work than I am – try to get what I've been doing – and if I once give it up I may whistle for something else."[29] Eleanor also put to rights citations from *Capital* which had been mistranslated in the first eulogy of Marx to appear in England.†

In all it was a period that would have tried the staunchest and, though it took its toll of Eleanor's physical strength, so recently undermined by her refusal to eat, her good sense – and her good humour – did not waver. But once the abnormal demands upon her were relaxed – the guests departed, her father out of danger and her mother's sufferings at an end – then the reaction set in.

On 29 December Marx, on his doctor's orders, went to Ventnor with Tussy. She proved a poor companion: morose, twitching with nerves and miserably self-absorbed. While Marx wrote to Laura and to Engels, mildly complaining of his unhelpful daughter, Eleanor confided her fear that she was on the verge of another breakdown to her friends Clementina Black and Ernest Radford, who immediately took steps. Radford went to Maitland Park Road to beg Lenchen to go to Ventnor and, when this proved impracticable since she was now in sole charge of the deserted house, Dollie Maitland sped to the Isle of Wight.

It was an ill-judged move though well meant. In the first place the Good Samaritan demanded unremitting attention – "Dollie positively *groans* when she is left five minutes unentertained",[38] wrote Eleanor as she hastily finished a letter to Jenny – and, secondly, Dollie's sudden advent told Marx all that Eleanor had striven to conceal from him, including that she had turned to outsiders for help rather than to him. It made him "angry and anxious", yet she had felt she could not bother her "darling Mohr", who was still far from well. She knew that he must think her "disagreeable and dissatisfied – but I can't explain to him".[38]

Into his ear Dollie now poured endless gossip: "she tells Papa that she believes me to be secretly married and a lot of other cock-and-bull stories, that do far more honour to her imagination than her veracity".[39] She also provided details of the frightening hysterical symptoms Eleanor manifested at night which Marx, not being witness to them, had to take on trust. In one way and another, dear little Dollie whom everyone loved – "it was *very* good of the child to come" – was really "worse than

---

useless",[38] in this situation, causing an amount of trouble quite disproportionate to the length of her stay. Neither father nor daughter regretted her departure, but it left them face to face with each other, both suffering the grief and shock of recent bereavement, each labouring under present difficulties that, fearing to hurt each other, they could not communicate.

To Jenny Eleanor poured out her heart, and it was an unquiet one. She diagnosed her own condition shrewdly enough: "What neither Papa nor the doctors nor anyone else will understand is that it is chiefly *mental worry* that affects me." She dreaded beyond all things consulting doctors who could not or would not see that this was "as much an illness as any physical ailment could be". She was unable to sleep at night and "for a long time ... tried various drugs ... and am loth to try them again. It is not much better, after all, than dram-drinking and is almost if not quite as injurious." Her father, puzzled and annoyed, scolded her "as if I 'indulged' in being ill at the expense of my family – or gets anxious and that worries me most of all".[38]

Her problem was twofold and acute. For some time now she had tried to end her engagement to Lissagaray, but could not bring herself to do it because there was nothing to warrant the break: he was "blameless" and had been "so very good and gentle and patient" with her.[39] At the same time she longed to make a career for herself on the stage, to win a true independence by this means, and realised that now, at 27 years of age, time was running out. "It drives me half mad to sit here when perhaps my *last* chance of doing something is going", she wrote to Jenny.[38]

It was this inner struggle – to behave well to the man to whom she had given her word, holding to it through years of general disapprobation, and yet to face her situation realistically – that had so worked upon her during the summer before. Once free of this now artificial tie she might still make something of her life before it was too late. "I am not young enough to lose more time in writing* – and if I cannot do this *soon* – it will be no use to try at all. But I've no money (I mean not enough to begin my lessons even) – and it *is* hard. ... I think I *could* do something. I cannot believe Mrs. Vezin would have spoken as she did, nor offered to bring me out had she not thought I had *some* chance of success. For she can have no object in bringing out a failure. You know, dear, I'm not a bit vain and that if I err it is not from over confidence but from distrust in myself. ... I have seen too often – and with such different people that I can *move* an audience – and that is the chief thing."[38] On the eve of her birthday she wrote again to Jenny: "much and hard as I have tried I could not crush out

---

* This referred to her hackwork at the British Museum.

my desire to *try something*. The chance of independence is very sweet. . . . You see I'm not clever enough to live a purely *intellectual* life nor am I dull enough to be content to . . . do nothing." She felt heartily ashamed of herself for worrying her father by her disagreeableness and egoism. "How I love him no one can know – and yet – we must each of us, after all, live our own life."[39] She turned the question round and round, arguing more with herself than with Jenny. At last she "'screwed her courage to the sticking place'" and broke off her engagement. She told Jenny that not only had the burden become too heavy but she had "other reasons" which she could not write, and she asked her sister as a great favour to see Lissagaray from time to time, to "treat him just as an old friend". She hoped that he and she, too, might remain on good and amicable terms, to which end "nothing will help so much as if you and Longuet continue to see him. . . . Oh! it has been a terrible struggle. I sometimes wonder how I have lived through it all. . . ."[39]

However sympathetically Jenny received Eleanor's confidences, she wrote to Laura, who was at this time alone in London "without any distractions and surrounded by the thousands of things" to remind her of her mother, to say that she was "very much alarmed by the news Tussy gives me from the Isle of Wight". It was Marx's situation that concerned her: "Tussy's health, it seems, is breaking down altogether, and I think with much grief of poor Papa, ill as he is, with an invalid." Something must be done to help them both and, in Jenny's view, Tussy's woes were such that "she would be better in London hard at work than doing nothing, a prey to her fancies. Poor Papa in his present state of health, after the troubles he has undergone, required a cheerful and even-tempered companion. It is a thousand pities you did not go with him instead of Tussy". She begged Laura to talk the matter over with "our good devoted Nim". She herself would have wished to fly to her father but was tied by the children.[40]

A few days later Tussy made a lightning dash to London to appear in some dramatic performance but had barely returned to Ventnor when, owing to the bitterly cold weather, Marx decided he must leave. On 16 January they returned to London together and plans were made for him to go south for his now chronic bronchial catarrh.

The most painful side-effect of this crisis in Eleanor's affairs was the tension it had created between her and Marx. As so often happens when two people are very close and try to spare each other's feelings by being less than frank, they succeeded only in wounding. After her father's death Eleanor wrote "our natures were so exactly alike. I remember his once saying a thing that at the time I did not understand and that even sounded rather paradoxical. But I know now what he meant. . . . Father was talking of my eldest sister and of me and said: 'Jenny is most like me, but Tussy (my dear old home name) *is* me.' It was true – except that I shall never be good and unselfish as he was."[33] At present they were finely aware, she of being preoccupied with self, he of not being taken into her confidence. By their very likeness each knew the nature of the other's injury, but was powerless to assuage it. Eleanor wrestled silently with her problems; Marx would not encroach upon her privacy and thus, while she penned her remorseful letters to Jenny, he wrote to Engels saying that, from observation alone, for Tussy was not open with him, he was convinced that no medicine, no change of scene or air could cure her sickness: "Madame Jung", as he called Mrs. Vezin,* was the only doctor who could help her, since she was burning with the desire to find an opening for herself and believed it to lie in an artistic career. Certainly in one respect she was right: at her age there was no more time to be lost and, of all things in the world, he would hate her to imagine that she was being sacrificed on the "altar of the family" to be nurse to an old man. He added that he could hazard a guess at the root cause of her emotional perturbation, but this was too delicate a matter to set down in black and white; from which it must be inferred that he attributed her disorder, rightly or wrongly, to her long-preserved virginity.

---

* Formerly Mrs. Young (see above, fn.*, p. 23).

Trying companion Eleanor might be and Marx quite resolved that she should not be his escort on his further travels – he had rather do without one – nevertheless, in the first week of February 1882, she accompanied him to Argenteuil. He stopped there for a week on the first leg of his journey to Algiers, setting sail from Marseilles on 18 February to remain there and in the South of France until June, alone.

Eleanor stayed on with Jenny for a few extra days. On her last morning Lissagaray called and arranged to see her off at the Gare St. Lazare that night. It was barely a month since she had broken off her engagement. He had expressed a wish to see Marx too, but Eleanor had prevented this and "in doing so, I think acted with good taste", Jenny wrote to her father, for such a meeting at such a time could not have been agreeable to him. Lissagaray and Tussy "behave to each other as old friends and Tussy's manner seemed very cool and distrait* to her quondam fiancé". Jenny was more than satisfied by the upshot – "the very best one that could have been expected ... and these present amicable relations are most fortunate". She considered that her sister had had "a narrow escape", and felt positively grateful and therefore well-disposed to Lissagaray for not having carried out his plan to marry her, for "French husbands are not worth much at the best of times – and at the worst – well, the less said the better."[41] She repeated these uncompromising sentiments to Eleanor herself: "I feel you have acted for the best – you were right to break off your engagement. Though I bear no ill will to L. I know you could never have been happy with him. These Frenchmen at the best of times make pitiable husbands!"[42]

Marx was relieved that Tussy had conducted herself so tactfully in this delicate situation. Without committing himself one way or another on the general proposition of Frenchmen as husbands, he had some powerful things to say to and about his French sons-in-law now that they were again active in the politics of their own country: "Longuet as the last Proudhonist and Lafargue as the last Bakuninist! The devil take them both!"[43]

Eleanor's return journey to "murky old London" was not sweetened by a lady reeking of alcohol who struck up an acquaintance by asking Eleanor

---

* In the holograph the word could possibly be read as "distant".

to lend her a corkscrew and when she could not oblige, persevered with a pair of scissors until she had opened a fresh bottle "and drank one *tumbler* after the other of brandy", after which, since the train did not stop between Rouen and Dieppe she "relieved herself" in the carriage, causing Eleanor to take a vow that nothing on earth would ever again induce her "to travel in a compartment for *dames seules*".[44] She missed Jenny and the children so badly that she felt almost sorry she had been to Paris. "I don't know what I shall do without you all", she wrote,[44] and, indeed, the feeling was mutual for, by her "just and kind behaviour" Tussy had become "such a favourite that the little men have had some difficulty to get over the parting",[41] Jenny wrote to Marx and, to Eleanor herself: "You have so delighted the children that I think they would go out of their wits with joy if you were suddenly to appear".[45] "As you know ... your most devoted friend at present is the Wolf,* who since your departure has not woke up one morning without asking Where is Aunt Tutty? ... Harry's feelings are I suppose too deep for words. Johnny is old enough to know he must put up with the inevitable. ..."[42] They talked of her constantly, Jenny reported, and: "You cannot imagine what a deep impression you have produced upon the little ones and how eagerly they long to have you again."[46]

No doubt during her stay in Argenteuil Eleanor disclosed the "other reasons" that had made necessary her break with Lissagaray. Whatever they were, they certainly did not include the forging of fresh bonds to chafe her. In April Jenny began to receive frequent visits from "the uncanny Mrs. Kaub", the sister of Carl Hirsch, the object of which "feverish activity" was to ask for Eleanor's hand. She had not seen Hirsch in Paris at all, sending him a postcard from London to say that she had been there purely to be with her sister and apologising for having refused his offer to take her sightseeing.[47] "Though I have done all I could to explain to the enamoured Hirsch that his aspirations are doomed to remain unfulfilled, he insists upon hearing his doom from your own lips", Jenny wrote. The "fool" had gone so far as to settle his affairs in Germany and make preparations for his future home, whether in England or in France, according to Eleanor's preference. With infinite tedium and despite her "unseemly interruptions" Jenny had to listen to detailed accounts of his financial position while he, impervious to hints or advice, pressed his suit. "He is after all a true and devoted friend of the family"; Jenny admitted, nor was it a crime to have a tender heart, so, in charity, Tussy must send him some sort of "*decent* answer" as soon as possible without offending or exasperating him.[48] Eleanor thereupon wrote a kind

---

* Edgar, now two-and-a-half.

and courteous refusal which, according to Jenny, was "really more than the silly Jew deserved. ... I hope it will preserve eternal rest to the perturbed spirit of your irrepressible admirer." Though she pitilessly mocked the "lovelorn" man, Jenny yet held him in some regard and could not understand why Tussy should feel so angry at the proposal: to her it appeared "simply in a comical light".[49] Indeed, Eleanor's fury seemed unreasonable on the face of it. She had never failed to treat Hirsch as a valued acquaintance, they had corresponded for seven years, during which period he had visited London many times, staying for some months both in 1878 and in the following year when he was often invited to dine at Maitland Park Road. Mrs. Marx had both received him in her house and written to him in the kindest manner. Marx had pronounced him "an absolutely reliable man of the utmost loyalty", his main weakness being that, a poor judge of character, he was easily duped, if not for long, by those who affected a devotion to the cause of socialism.[50] It is true that Marx thought he had behaved like an imbecile, inviting martyrdom, at the time of his arrest, but both he and Engels championed him hotly against the Höchberg crew in Zürich long after that episode and it was only as time went on that Marx found him increasingly tiresome and tried to avoid meeting him. Hirsch finally fell from grace when he was suspected of having collaborated with Franz Mehring* in writing a perfidious article on Marx in the *Sozialdemokrat* for which "the party will never forgive him". That, however, did not occur till many months after he had proposed to Tussy and may even have been occasioned by the antagonism her treatment of him aroused for, however gently she declined him, Jenny had made it abundantly clear that he was scorned.†

Far from contemplating marriage, Eleanor now threw herself into her lessons with Mrs. Vezin, and into work to pay for them. It was as though, whatever inner conflicts had brought about her nervous derangement had been finally resolved, leaving her, all neurotic traces eliminated, full of energy and hope. Not that she was happy at her father's absence: she missed him sadly and concern for his health was never far from her

---

* Franz Mehring (1846–1919) had defended Lassalle and Bakunin against Marx and Engels in his early days and did not join the German Social Democratic Party until 1890. In 1918 he published his biography of Marx, having some years earlier been invited by Laura Lafargue to edit and publish the correspondence between her father and Engels. He came under severe attack for "anti-Marxism", "a breach of confidence" and "the basest betrayal of Marx" from both Kautsky and Ryazanov, but his *Karl Marx*,[51] allowing for the relative sparsity of research material available in his day, remains one of the most rewarding sources, while his political courage in the years before and during the First World War refutes any "betrayal of Marx" or of Marxist principles.

† On 8 July 1882 Hirsch married a Miss Lina Haschert in Paris, an occasion of so mournful a nature that, according to an eye-witness, one of those present at the ceremony had exclaimed: "This is a top class funeral!"

thoughts. "We are very anxious and we are eagerly awaiting further details as to how you are", she wrote to him in Algiers on 23 March.[52] Marx had run into bad weather, was making no progress, and Eleanor asked Engels if she should not go to him, but was dissuaded. In point of fact, though he did not mention it to his family – "why frighten them?" – Marx had another attack of pleurisy while in North Africa, less severe though lasting longer than the first one, as he told Engels after it was over. Again and again Eleanor wrote "How I wish we had you here again",[52] "How I do *long* for a sight of your face".[53] Indeed the very strong family feeling – discounting Laura – seems to have been heightened by Mrs. Marx's death, all Jenny's letters, too, being full of regret that they were now so far apart from each other. In May she begged Eleanor to visit her again, but this was impossible though she had found time to knit red petticoats for her nephews which, surprisingly, enchanted the boys who strutted about in them "like little peacocks".[49]

Since her return from Paris Eleanor had been "grinding at Juliet with Mrs. Vezin", an exercise that permitted her to comment on Ellen Terry's rendering of the part in the current performance, which was "*the* event" of the day, that it was "the most disappointing feature" of "an exquisite production": she "gets weaker and weaker as the tragic element appears till in the poison scene she collapses altogether".*[54]

Now 55 and in retirement, Mrs. Vezin no longer had many connections with the living theatre but gave Eleanor every encouragement. "Despite my absolute ignorance of stage business she would like me to try it publicly ... she wants to give me a chance if it is possible. What I should prefer would be to go to some small provincial place and get some practical knowledge of the stage to begin with. But all these are dreams and ten to one ... nothing will come of it all."[54] Jenny was full of enthusiasm and advice. She saw no reason why her sister's "ambition to live an artistic life" should not succeed. "Some lucky chance (you know my fixed idea is an interview with Irving) may turn up", she wrote, "and at the very worst should you never tread the boards, the fact of acquiring perfectly the art of elocution ... will be a great gain to you through life and will repay any outlay your lessons now will cost you."[42] An introduction to Irving was, indeed, her "fixed idea": "It is nonsense to say he would ... treat you as he does the thousand stage-struck simpletons who no doubt come to him. The superior cultivation of your naturally gifted mind would have at once raised you in his eyes ... and last but not least there is always something in a name and yours is Marx – not Smith or

---

* An opinion not shared by the critic of *The Times* who wrote on 9 March "Miss Terry's Juliet is an unmixed success."

Brown. ...."*[49] Not only in Jenny's view should Eleanor solicit Irving's patronage but she should apply to Engels, who was so generous, for the money that was needed to further her ambitions. Eleanor followed neither of these courses, she simply persevered; but she was touched by Jenny's sincere joy in her "prospect of living the only free life a woman can live – the artistic one", thus realising that which for years and years had been Jenny's "own day-dream",[49] and enabled her to write at a time when she herself was in the depths of misery: "The only bit of good news that I have had these many days is ... of your literary enterprises. I congratulate you with all my heart and rejoice to think that one of us at least will not pass her life in watching over a *pot au feu*."[55]

"Literary enterprises": not theatrical ones. Eleanor's aspirations had foundered. Exactly when this happened, and how long the experiment lasted, is not clear but Marian Skinner recollected that "she was dramatic to the depths of her being and I think one of the sorest disappointments of her life was that she never became an actress. ... Mrs. Hermann Vezin ... reluctantly told her that she would never achieve real greatness on the boards – the glory would always fall short of the dream. ... She came to me on the day Mrs. Vezin had given her ultimatum – white, tragic, despairing. ... 'It's damnably hard not to be able to get the one thing in the world you want'. ..."[1] Olive Schreiner,† too, recalled this time and her protective feelings towards Eleanor.

These two friends may have done much to help her withstand this dashing of her hopes but, during that spring and summer, Eleanor's social life took on a new momentum and she fairly whirled. With nothing to keep her at home – even Lenchen had gone to Argenteuil – she discovered, almost overnight, that she was attractive to people outside her own circle and a success when she went among them. She was invited to picnics, parties and At Homes. During a single week in July she recited at a Browning Evening – "the place was crowded and as all sorts of 'literary' and other 'swells' were there, I felt ridiculously nervous – but got on capitally" – saw Modjeska‡ in *Odette* – "... liked her more than ever – but the piece is vile – simply idiotic, in fact, in this English version" –

---

* Jenny seemed to forget that it rather depends on what your first name is. If, for example, you had been called Adam or Ford Madox there is no earthly reason why you should not have been received by a Brodribb.

† She came to London at the end of March 1882 and lived at 11 Guilford Street, Bloomsbury.

‡ Helena Modjeska, née Opido, (1844–1909), a Polish actress who emigrated to America in the mid-seventies and, despite her poor command of English, was a soaring success. She toured England and the Continent, for the most part in plays by Feuillet and Sardou.

Ristori* in *Macbeth* – "which she acts for the first time in English" – went to Toole's† benefit concert, where Mrs. Kendal and Irving performed and Ellen Terry recited Thomas Hood's "Bridge of of Sighs" – "which I look upon as a personal injury, that being one of my stock pieces" – and was "asked ... to a 'crush' at Lady Wilde's ... the mother of that very limp and very nasty young man, Oscar Wilde, who has been making such a d – -d ass of himself in America. As the son has not yet returned and the mother is nice I may go."‡[56]

She went down the river with the Furnivalls and dined with the Lankesters, while Mrs. Sutherland Orr, the sister of Sir Frederick Leighton, then President of the Royal Academy, proposed taking her to meet Browning that she might recite his poems to their author.

Her social circle, though it still contained and she saw much of the Black and the Maitland sisters, Radford and other members of the little Dogberry group, expanded vastly, as did her openings for employment. She did not allow her "dissipated evenings", as she characterised them, to interfere with her working life: she took on an "advantageous pupil", went regularly to the British Museum, was entrusted with the task of compiling a glossary, which she could do at home and was, as she declared, "hard at it" and "pretty well out all day".

It is probable, it is almost certain – though no written evidence exists to prove it – that her animated existence in the spring and summer of 1882 was not unrelated to those "other reasons" for having broken off relations with Lissagaray. It could also account for her outburst of indignation at Hirsch's pretensions. The name does not appear among the host of people with whom she was associating at the time, but since she was undoubtedly partnered on her several outings and the character of her interests, the places she frequented, were so similar to those of Edward Aveling, a married man, it is reasonable to assume that he had entered upon the scene.

Her outer gaieties did nothing to still the anxiety about her father. He had left Algiers, where his cough had been aggravated rather than cured, to stay in Monte Carlo at the Hotel de Russie from the first week in May

---

* Adelaide Ristori (1822–1906), an Italian actress who went to Paris in 1855 where she became a serious rival to Rachel. Her performance as Lady Macbeth in London was highly praised, Mrs. Kendall acclaiming her as a better actress than Bernhardt. She retired from the stage in 1885.

† John Lawrence Toole (1830–1906), an actor chiefly famous for his playing of Dickens roles, was a close friend of Irving's. In 1879 he went into management at the Charing Cross Theatre and in 1882 gave it his own name. Toole's Theatre, in King William Street, was demolished in 1895 to make way for an extension of Charing Cross Hospital.

‡ Later, when he came up for trial, it was not Wilde whom Eleanor criticised but the howling hypocrisy of the press and public, and that of the theatre managers who continued the profitable run of his plays to full houses at the Haymarket and St. James's but deleted the author's name.[57]

until early June when he planned to go to Jenny's. While he reported in great detail on his state of health to Engels – whom he rather blamed for the unfortunate Algerian venture which had led to no improvement – it was clear that he took a pessimistic view of the outcome. "Naturally, at a certain age, it is altogether a matter of indifference how one is 'launched into eternity' ", he wrote from Cannes, rather comforted than otherwise by Garibaldi's death from bronchitis.* On 6 June he left for Argenteuil where he stayed for almost three months.

Lafargue, who had been living in Paris since April, went to see him and reported to Engels that he looked well but that the Longuet household was too boisterous for a man in his condition. This was not Marx's view. He had told Jenny before his arrival that she was not to announce it to either Paul or Hirsch, that what he needed was absolute peace and quiet, adding as a postscript that what he meant by this was family life and the "microscopic world of children's noises". It was to help Jenny during Marx's stay that Lenchen had gone to France at the end of June, but that summer both Laura and Eleanor travelled to Paris, though not together. Laura rejoined her husband, spending a week at 38 rue de Lille, a small hotel on the left bank until, early in August, they moved the furniture sent from London – including the armchair bequeathed by Lizzie Burns – into a flat of their own,† at Engels' cost. She had seen her father for but a few hours when she wrote to Engels "Papa seemed to be very well and ... very lively",[58] so that Eleanor, when she joined the Longuet household, was taken aback by his changed appearance.‡

Marx wrote to Hirsch asking him to take Lenchen sightseeing in Paris before she left. Now that she had gone, Jenny, in her eighth month of pregnancy, was only too grateful to Eleanor who won Marx's golden opinions for her kindness and helpfulness to the children and to "poor Jenny". The situation had brought out traits in Tussy that were dormant in London, he wrote to Engels. She was "an excellent disciplinarian" and he dearly hoped that she would take Johnny back with her to England for a few months: the boy was running wild and giving more trouble than the three smaller ones put together, but Longuet, who generally stayed in bed the whole morning and left for Paris at five each afternoon, opposed the plan, out of his "love" for him, though he did nothing about the child himself and seemed not to care whether Johnny were helped or Jenny's

---

* On 3 June 1882 at the age of 75.
† 66 boulevard du Port-Royal, where they lived until 1887.
‡ Not because, in April, his head and face had been shaved in Algiers owing to the heat – for they had grown luxuriantly since, as contemporary photographs show – but because he had not made the progress she had been led to expect from Laura's report and found him looking aged and ill.

burden lightened. Nevertheless, against the father's wishes, Marx prevailed and when Eleanor left for London on 21 August it was with Johnny, who was destined to remain with her – and to submit to an unaccustomed regimen of cold water from top to toe each day, regular schooling and early bed-times – for many a month to come.

Quite soon after his return to Argenteuil in June Marx had written to Laura, still in London, a letter marked "Private and Confidential" in which he confessed that he could not risk travelling alone again and that therefore, "It's more or less your duty to accompany the old man of the mountains" when he went to Switzerland at the end of August. This plan, too, was realised and, a few days after Tussy's departure, Marx and Laura set out for Vevey by way of Lausanne, returning to France on 28 September, by which time Jenny had given birth to her only daughter.*

Eleanor, with Lenchen's help at home, was happily caring for Johnny and sending regular reports to his mother. She had taken him to Yarmouth where Engels was staying with Pumps and her baby† and, back in London, he was doing excellently at school.‡

"I have just put my boy ... to bed", she wrote to Jenny on 2 October. He was "very anxious to hear about his little sister. Having got over the shock he is taking more interest in her now". What troubled his aunt most was his English: "the way he speaks is awful, but I suppose in time he will grow out of it. I've no doubt we spoke Helen's English some time. The worst is when I correct the boy Helen is either offended or laughs."[59] Helen – or Lenchen – or Nimmy – played her full part, of course, in looking after the six-year-old for, though Eleanor postponed working on her glossary until the evenings, after he had gone to bed, she still had to go by day to the Museum where she was accorded the exceptional privilege of being admitted during Closed Week: "when the Reading Room is shut and the books are dusted, re-arranged, etc." She owed this to the intervention of Richard Garnett,§ in whose room she was allowed to work, and to "some half dozen of the head men. ... It is an immense favour which I was told today had been extended to no one since some years ago

---

* Jenny, known as Mémé, born on 16 September 1882.

† Pumps had married Percy White Rosher, an accountant and, later, unsuccessful small businessman, on 8 September 1881 at the St. Pancras Register Office in the presence of Samuel Moore and Paul Lafargue. A daughter, Lilian, was born on 25 March 1882, whose conversation at six months, according to Marx, was more interesting than her mother's.

‡ He was enrolled on 11 September at a little dame-school opposite the Marxes' old house in Grafton Terrace.

§ An official at the Museum, later Keeper of Printed Books (1890–1899), whose son, Edward, married Eleanor's friend Constance Black, better known under her married name as the translator of the great Russian classics.

Gladstone was allowed to go and finish his pamphlet on 'Atrocities'*
there!"[59]

Marx, when he arrived back in London in the first week of October,
thoroughly approved of Eleanor's ways with Johnny who was cheerful and
happy, he wrote to Laura. The little boy talked a great deal of his mother
and Harry, whom he obviously missed, but his progress left nothing to be
desired. At the end of the month, warned not to remain in London during
the season of damp and fog, Marx set off for Ventnor again, where Eleanor
and Johnny visited him for a few days in November, leaving on the 20th.
Thereafter Eleanor kept in constant touch with him and he wrote on 9
January that he was grateful to "his dear good child" for writing so often
and at such length, which encroached upon the little free time she had.
The intention was that Marx should remain on the Isle of Wight until the
spring. But that was not to be.

---

* *Bulgarian Horrors and the Questions of the East*, published in 1876.

Eleanor had long realised that Jenny had reached breakingpoint. What she did not, could not know, for it was never mentioned, was that ever since April her sister had been in terrible pain with a disease of the bladder* which, then, she attributed to her three months' pregnancy.

After Eleanor had left Argenteuil in March Jenny, who apologised for having "been so dull" during her stay,[42] wrote to her on a note of mounting despair. Though she forebore to speak of her physical ailments, she felt exhausted by her family cares. As early as January, still bitterly mourning her mother's death, she had complained that "when night comes I feel quite giddy from the exertion of having looked after four babies, three of whom no longer sleep in the day",[60] while to Laura, at the same period, she wrote that "what with carrying, washing, feeding, driving three babies and looking after Master Johnny who is not the least troublesome one of the lot, I feel physically and mentally worn out. I am often too tired to get repose at night and feel like Don Quixote did when he had been well thrashed."[40] Mother-in-law and servant trouble loomed large in her letters to Eleanor but the bane of her life was Longuet: "The cruelest (sic) of it all is that though I drudge like a nigger [he] never does anything but scream at me and grumble every minute he is in the house."[48] His "present mode of life", she wrote to Eleanor again in May, "makes matters 50 times worse than they were when we lived in London". He perpetually nagged and was never satisfied with her, though "I assure you I do all in my power to do the work for house and children for weeks and weeks not permitting myself the luxury of taking up a newspaper, not to speak of a book."[60] Her husband's worst offence, however, was that he constantly postponed taking the children on holiday, a move so essential for Harry "whose condition *absolutely* requires change of air".[49] It was for the sake of this daily expected, daily deferred vacation – which did not finally materialise until September – that Johnny had been kept from school since February, to become "not only a torment to me but also to himself, all day at home in a nursery, where the noise of three other babies prevents him from learning his ABC",[61] while Harry – "the best and sweetest little creature under the sun"[46] who knew "nought of life but

---

* In all probability cancer.

pain and sorrow"[49] — was left to linger in a state that filled Jenny with foreboding.

Added to these trials was an acute shortage of money. Longuet's paper, *La Justice*, paid him less and less regularly, while Madame Longuet senior, convinced of the wilful parasitic idleness of her daughter-in-law, wrote eight-page letters to her almost daily exhorting her to resume her teaching to contribute to the family exchequer, depleted by the lady herself who had cut off the small allowance remitted to her son in England. To go out teaching, Jenny wrote to Eleanor, "would be madness, as such lessons would not pay the cost of a servant to watch over the children during my absences",[61] yet she was haunted by the unpaid debts which weighted upon her "like crimes, by day and night".[46] She blamed her insolvency for depriving "our dear Nim" of her projected trip to Germany and saw but one way out of it: "to get some children from London, Indian* or others", to bring up with her own. The house — where adult boarders would never stay with so many babies about — was "excellently adapted" for the purpose: the young paying guests would have the advantage of learning three languages and at the same time provide Johnny with the much needed society of his coevals to correct the "habits of indolence into which neglect and a naturally lazy disposition" had plunged him. "Pardon me, dear Tussy", she wrote "for troubling you. . . . I must somehow get out of this plight. Pray give me your advice. . . ."[61] It is almost incredible that Jenny, who felt so "overdone, so jaded and worn out by every sort of worry and fatigue", should have entertained the notion of adding to her problems in this way. She was five months pregnant — and ill — when she proposed it, but she felt she must find some means to earn money. She hated her "uncongenial life", felt more sick of it than she could say, cursed her poverty and was at her wits' end; "I am dead beaten", she wrote to Tussy.[61] Never wholly reconciled to the loss of the warm family life she had known throughout her youth — "I cannot get used to this separation — it is as if my heart were cleft", she wrote[60] — she took comfort from her father's long stay in the summer of 1882 — grievously changed though she found him — coupled as it was with the familiar presence of first Lenchen and then Tussy. Small wonder that Paul should write to Laura in June "Jenny is much better, mentally and physically".[62]

There was little indeed to prosper her in the months to come, though she wrote to Laura in Switzerland making the most of the fact that, at long last, Edgar and Harry had gone to St. Aubin in Calvados with their Papa and that she was "having a holiday", alone with little Par (Marcel).

---

* That is, English children sent home for their education by parents in India.

Unfortunately, her mother-in-law, who had promised to join the family at the sea to keep an eye on the children, "left them in the lurch, pretending important business in Caen",[63] her home-town some 18 kilometers away, exciting Jenny's pity for her husband, always nearest to her heart when he was furthest from her.

During Marx's brief return to Argenteuil at the end of September, when he met his only grand-daughter for the first and last time, Jenny was able to conceal from him her desperate condition, her confinement being so recent as to account for her debility. The birth of the child had not relieved but, on the contrary, exacerbated her illness, and she finally wrote to Tussy in Ventnor disclosing the full horror of her situation, with strict injunctions that the news should be withheld from Marx. "This inflammation of the bladder", she wrote, "is *not a dangerous*, but the most unbearable of all diseases. To no one in the world would I wish the tortures I have undergone now since eight months, they are indescribable and the nursing added thereto makes life a hell to me."[55] Though unable to leave her bedroom, she could not get the rest she needed, not only because of the children, but because Longuet was now also at home all day, making an effort to devote himself to the household, while in fact adding to "the work and confusion". His mother, too, was behaving in a sympathetic and generous manner, though remaining firmly in Caen. Jenny worried about her Johnny, for "illness makes one so nervous"[55]; and since her father would be staying on in Ventnor alone, she feared that the plan for Harry to go there would not be feasible. It says much for Jenny that this letter of 8 November 1882, written in agony, should begin with expressions of pleasure and interest in Tussy's work and the conviction that her talents would ensure success.

A week later Paul Lafargue was summoned to appear before the Montluçon magistrate's court to show reason why he should not stand trial for subversive speeches he, Guesde and others had made. His failure to comply was followed by his arrest in Paris on the evening of 12 December. Laura immediately wrote to Engels who forwarded the letter to Marx the next day adding his own comment: "Just received this 9.20 p.m. After appearing at Montluçon Paul will of course be released at once. In the meantime I shall send Laura the needful tomorrow..."[64]*

The news elicited from Marx some of the kindliest comments he had ever made on Paul, whose recent articles he went out of his way to praise when he wrote to Laura, adding that her husband's "gallant fight with the powers that be make the man sympathetic, to use this, a French penny-a-liner's phrase". He hoped that, when her duties permitted, Laura would

---

* In the event Paul was tried in April 1883 for incitement to murder and loot, fined and committed to Ste. Pélagie prison for six months from 21 May.

come and stay with him in Ventnor. Though suffering from tracheal catarrh he was free from pleurisy and bronchitis. "This is very encouraging", he wrote, "considering that most of my *contemporaries*, I mean fellows of the same age, just now kick the bucket in gratifying numbers. There are enough young asses to keep the old ones alive."

But Laura was not at liberty to go to Ventnor, for Jenny's circumstances roused her from what appears to have been a life of total selfishness – apart from her devotion to her husband's interests – maintained in France, as in England, entirely at Engels' expense, and on no mean scale.

On the day of Paul's arrest she managed to work into her letter to Engels the news that she had 5 francs in her pocket and later gave this as the reason for having been unable to make the journey across Paris from the boulevard Port-Royal to Argenteuil: "I hadn't got the wherewithal. . . . For out of the five francs I had in hand three had to go for coals and one for lamp oil."[65] Her letter went on to announce that they were to dine with friends who had received a *poularde truffée* from the country and: "I want to compare notes with you on the subject of some new wines with which I have just become acquainted. . ." However, despite these graver considerations, she had eventually bestirred herself to visit Jenny whom she found "in a very precarious condition. . . . The inflammation she suffers from was rather worse than better when I saw her and she is altogether out of spirits."[65]

Engels sent the letter on to Marx with kindly words of reassurance. But Marx was not reassured and wrote to Tussy that he feared the worst if Jenny's illness were neglected. Could she not take poor Harry off her hands? If need be she could bring the child with her to Ventnor: it was obviously impossible for anyone to give the necessary attention to their own health with all those babies. He also feared that if Johnny were to return home, as planned, he would be neglected unless another of the children made way for him. Throughout the end of December and into the New Year apprehension grew. On 6 January 1883 Paul wrote to Engels: "Jenny's condition saddened us greatly; we thought it hopeless." He and Laura had been to see her and "were astonished to find her laid up and in a very sorry state . . . she was sunk in a torpor broken by nightmares and fantastic dreams. Since her last confinement she has had constant haemorrhages whose cause . . . the doctors have not yet been able to discover; she insisted upon suckling the baby which, combined with a chronic lack of appetite, completely drained her strength." Longuet had gone away at this juncture and there was no one to look after her. She had been unable to eat and, though the haemorrhages stopped, she was plagued by diarrhoea. "We did not know of her desperate condition", Paul unashamedly confessed, "so you can imagine our shock when we found her

... delirious." Now Laura was going daily to Argenteuil: a journey, he complained, that took four hours by omnibus and train there and back. It does not seem to have occurred to either of the Lafargues that to spare herself the expense and inconvenience of her transport, Laura might have stayed with her dying sister in a household clamorous for help. Paul's letter ended in the usual way: "Can you send me £10, for I am devilishly hard up."[66]

Marx longed to be with Jenny but knew it would be folly to cumber her with an invalid. He had begun to suffer from spasmodic attacks, unable to breathe on getting out of bed, which he believed to be of nervous origin brought on by his terrible fears for Jenny. Eleanor, too, wished to go to her sister, but she had Johnny on her hands. "You had *much* better let him stay on for the present", she wrote to Jenny on 9 January. She described the little boy's pleasure in being taken to a party, complete with conjurer, given by a Mrs. Bircham, the headmistress of the school in Kensington where Eleanor was teaching. His hosts had been delighted by the child who was "*wonderfully* well and in the highest spirits". In this, her last letter to Jenny, Tussy wrote: "I think of you day and night, and only wish I could *do* something. Tell Charles he is to send me a p.c. for I am too anxious to go on waiting like this."[67]

It was suggested that Lenchen should go to Argenteuil and, while the matter was debated, letters flew to and from Paris and London, day by day. On 10 January Marx forwarded to Eleanor Paul's latest news from which – though he thought it might have been written out of kindness – it seemed that the danger was passed. He had been enchanted by the reports of Wolf (Edgar) and Par (Marcel) and, momentarily cheered, he allowed himself to hope.

At five o'clock on the following afternoon, 11 January 1883, Jenny died. She was not quite 39 years of age. Her death certificate was registered at the Argenteuil Town Hall by Paul Lafargue and Gustave Louis Dourlen, her doctor. Her funeral took place on 13 January attended by many of the former Communards and by representatives of all the socialist papers in France. Engels wrote an obituary notice for the *Sozialdemokrat*[68] in which he paid a tribute to her activities on behalf of the Fenians and recalled her ordeal at the time of her arrest at Luchon. Her sorrowing father, he ended, had at least the solace of knowing that hundreds of thousands of workers in Europe and America shared his grief.

Solace it may have been, but Eleanor recalled in later years that she felt she was bringing him his death sentence when she left at once for Ventnor. "On the long anxious journey I tortured my brain thinking how to impart the news to him ... my face betrayed it – Moor said at once 'Our Jenny is dead'. I have lived many a sad hour, but none so sad as that." No sooner had she arrived than Marx urged her to go to Argenteuil to help with the children and "would not suffer any contradiction", though she would have preferred to stay with him in his unutterable woe at the death of his "first-born, the daughter he loved most". Within half an hour she was on her way back to London and then set off for Paris. "I can only think with a shudder of that time," she wrote.[30]

Marx himself immediately returned to London, but he had come home to die. Eleanor was right in saying that Jenny's death was the last terrible blow. He now suffered a series of the spasmodic attacks which reminded him of how distressfully Jenny must always have suffered from her asthma, while laryngitis and bronchitis made his voice hoarse and he found it painful to swallow. In February he developed a tumour on the lung. When Eleanor returned from France she brought with her poor little sick Harra whom she placed under the care of the children's hospital in Shadwell,* for the child was beyond the help of this stricken household. On 14 March 1883 at two o'clock in the afternoon, having been nursed by "good old Lenchen ... as a mother nurses a child", Marx died suddenly and peacefully at the age of 65. Eleanor, who was present, notified the death. "Mankind is shorter by a head, and by the most remarkable head of our time", wrote Engels.[69]

He was buried on 17 March in the same grave as his wife. A week later, it was reopened to receive the remains of his grandson, Harry Longuet, who had died in hospital on 21 March at the age of four-and-a-half.

Marx's funeral was attended by a relatively small company, which included Engels, Eleanor, Longuet, Lafargue, Liebknecht, Lessner, Schorlemmer and Edwin Ray Lankester. Laura did not leave Paris. Eleanor, who had received, among condolences from a multitude of her own and her father's friends, a warm letter from Richard Garnett, invited him to the ceremony though he was unable to be present.

The Congress of the illegal German Social Democratic Party was to be held in Copenhagen from 29 March to 2 April. Bebel wrote to Engels on the day of the funeral saying that he proposed to move a resolution that a monument to Marx should be erected, not as a grandiose memorial, but as a token of the gratitude and solidarity of the workers of the world. To this Engels replied on 30 April: "I don't know what should be done about a memorial to Marx. The family is against it. The simple gravestone designed for his wife and now bearing his own and his little grandson's name, would be desecrated in their eyes if it were replaced by a monument." Eleanor echoed these sentiments in her later writings: "Marx did not want a 'memorial'. To have desired to put up any other memorial to

---

* See fn.‡, p. 114.

the creator of *The Communist Manifesto* and of *Capital* than that which he had built himself would have been an insult to the great dead. In the heads and hearts of millions of workers, who have 'united' at his call, he has not merely a memorial more lasting than bronze, but also the living soil in which what he taught and desired will become – and in part has already become – an act.''[30]

Before he was laid in earth many people were allowed to see him in his coffin: days of lying-in-state, as it were. Mrs. Comyn wrote: "The last time I saw Dr. Marx he lay in his coffin, his hands folded over his breast – a warrior who had fought valliantly until weapons were taken from him by a force greater than his own. The serenity of his face was wonderful, wrinkles were smoothed out, old age had retreated, all traces of suffering were swept away. A tranquil ... power remained." She was alone with Eleanor in the room and wished to express her sympathy, but "she stopped me imperiously. ... 'I want no condolences. If he had lingered during a long illness, and I had seen his mind and body decaying before my eyes, I should have stood in need of consolation. But it was not so. He died in harness, his intellect untouched ... He has earned his rest. Let us be grateful for so much'."*[1]

Another of those who claimed to have paid his last respects to the dead man in his coffin was Edward Aveling, who had met Marx but once, briefly, many years before. "I stood by the side of his corpse, hand in hand with my wife", he wrote.[70] It is quite on the cards that Edward Aveling never stood by the coffin at all, hand in hand with anybody; but if he did it was not with his wife. His readers were being given to understand that it was he who stood lovingly at Eleanor Marx's side in the solemnity of her father's death chamber. Though she lived openly with Aveling for the last fifteen years of her life, the conjuring up of this intimate scene of March 1883 is more in keeping with Aveling's propensity to falsify facts than with Eleanor's sense of fitness.

---

* It is, of course, quite possible that Mrs. Comyn recorded at the time and accurately quoted Eleanor *verbatim* some 39 years later. However, in Engels' letter to Sorge of 15 March the following passage occurs: "All events occurring of natural necessity bring their own consolation with them, however dreadful they may be. Medical skill might have been able to vouch him a few more years of vegetative existence, the life of a helpless being, dying – to the triumph of the physician's art – not suddenly, but inch by inch. Our Marx, however, would never have borne that ... To see this mighty genius lingering on as a physical wreck for the greater glory of medicine and the mockery of the Philistines whom he had so often reduced to dust in the prime of his strength – no, it is a thousand times better as it is, a thousand times better that we bear him, the day after tomorrow, to the grave where his wife lies at rest."[69]

REFERENCE NOTES

Abbreviations

BIML   Institute of Marxism-Leninism, Berlin.
Bottigelli Archives   Letters in the custody of Dr. Emile Bottigelli, Paris.
Bottigelli L & D   *Lettres et Documents de Karl Marx 1856–1883.* Previously unpublished
                        texts edited by Dr. Emile Bottigelli. Annali dell' Istituto Giangia-
                        como Feltrinelli, Anno Primo. Milan, 1958.
ELC   *Frederick Engels Paul and Laura Lafargue: Correspondence*, Volumes I–
                        III. Lawrence & Wishart, 1959–1963.
IISH   International Institute of Social History, Amsterdam.
Liebknecht   *Wilhelm Liebknecht Briefwechsel mit Karl Marx und Friedrich Engels.*
                        Edited by Georg Eckert. Mouton & Co., The Hague, 1963.
MEW   *Marx Engels Werke.* Dietz Verlag, Berlin. 1956–1968. Unless other-
                        wise stated Volumes 27–39.
MIML   Institute of Marxism-Leninism, Moscow.

(1)   Marian Comyn. "My Recollections of Karl Marx". *The Nineteenth Century and After.*
      Vol. 91, No. 539. January 1922.
(2)   *Aus Meinem Leben.* Stuttgart 1911.
(3)   An obituary article published in *Die Neue Zeit* No. 30 1897–98. BIML.
(4)   Eleanor to Jenny, 18 June 1881. Bottigelli Archives.
(5)   *My Years in Exile.* Trans. by B. Miall. Parsons, 1921.
(6)   17 June 1879. MEW.
(7)   H. M. Hyndman. "Something Better than Emigration: A Reply to Lord Brabazon".
      The Nineteenth Century. Vol. XVI. December 1884.
(8)   *Record of an Adventurous Life.* Macmillan 1911.
(9)   *Tom Mann's Memoirs.* The Labour Publishing Co. Ltd., 1923. New edition Mac-
      Gibbon and Kee, 1967.
(10) *La Rupture Marx-Hyndman.* Annali dell'Istituto Giangiacomo Feltrinelli. Anno
      Terzo. Feltrinelli. Milan 1960. (MEW Vol. 35).
(11) Engels to Laura, 16 February 1884. ELC, Vol. I.
(12) Mrs. Marx to Laura, n.d. (but obviously first week in July 1881) from 43 Terminus
      Road, Eastbourne. MIML.
(13) James G. Hutchinson. "Progress and Wages. A Workman's View". *The Nineteenth
      Century.* Vol. XVI. October 1884.
(14) Eleanor to Hirsch, 16 September 1880. IISH.
(15) November 1880. Liebknecht.
(16) 7 October 1881. IISH.
(17) Eleanor to Liebknecht, 12 February 1881. Liebknecht.
(18) 12 February 1881. Liebknecht.
(19) 4 March 1879. BIML.
(20) 1 January 1880. BIML.
(21) 1 October 1880. Original English MIML. (German MEW).
(22) *Justice.* 9 April 1898.
(23) Jenny to Marx, 3 December 1881. BIML.
(24) Havelock Ellis. *Adelphi.* New Series. Vol. 6. September 1935.
(25) To Jenny, 7 April 1881. Bottigelli Archives.
(26) Pre-26 July 1881. IISH.
(27) 7 October 1881. Bottigelli Archives.

(28) 18 October 1881. Bottigelli Archives.

(29) Eleanor to Jenny, 31 October 1881. Bottigelli Archives.

(30) Reminiscences of Liebknecht. *Karl Marx Selected Works*. Vol. I. Lawrence & Wishart, 1942.

(31) Eleanor to Jenny, 4 December 1881. Bottigelli Archives.

(32) Published in the *Sozialdemokrat* on 8 December and in *l'Egalité* on 11 December 1881. Though delivered in English, the original text of the speech has not been traced.

(33) Letter to Olive Schreiner, 16 June 1884. Quoted in Ref. (24).

(34) Eleanor to Marx, 7 August 1881. Bottigelli Archives.

(35) Information kindly provided by Dr. Felix Brown, M.A., F.R.C.P., F.R.C.M., Member Royal Medico Psychological Association.

(36) In the Radford family collection.

(37) Engels' articles have been reprinted in pamphlet form as *The British Labour Movement*. Martin Lawrence 1934.

(38) Eleanor to Jenny, 8 January 1882. Bottigelli Archives.

(39) Eleanor to Jenny, 15 January 1882. Bottigelli Archives.

(40) Jenny to Laura, 10 January 1882. BIML.

(41) Jenny to Marx, 24 February 1882. MIML.

(42) Jenny to Eleanor, 7 March 1882. IISH.

(43) Marx to Engels, 11 November 1882. MEW.

(44) Eleanor to Jenny, 21 February 1882. IISH.

(45) Jenny to Eleanor, 10 April 1882. IISH.

(46) Jenny to Eleanor, 17 May 1882. IISH.

(47) Eleanor to Carl Hirsch, 24 February 1882. IISH.

(48) To Eleanor, 10 April 1882. IISH.

(49) Jenny to Eleanor, 12–13 April 1882. IISH.

(50) Marx to Bracke, 18 August 1877. MEW.

(51) English edition trans. Edward Fitzgerald. John Lane 1936.

(52) Bottigelli Archives.

(53) 3 April 1882. Bottigelli Archives.

(54) Eleanor to Jenny, 25 March 1882. Bottigelli Archives.

(55) Jenny to Eleanor, 8 November 1882. IISH.

(56) Eleanor to Jenny, July (n.d.) 1882. Bottigelli Archives.

(57) "Letter from England" in *Russkoye Bogatstvo* (Russian Wealth), No. 5 1895. MIML. (Retranslated from the Russian by Mr. John Gibbons.)

(58) 2 August 1882. ELC. Vol. I.

(59) 2 October 1882. Bottigelli Archives.

(60) Jenny to Eleanor, 15 January 1882. IISH.

(61) 3 May 1882. IISH.

(62) 22 June 1882. BIML.

(63) Jenny to Laura, early September (n.d.) 1882. IISH.

(64) ELC, Vol. I.

(65) 21 December 1882. ELC, Vol. I.

(66) ELC, Vol. III.

(67) Eleanor to Jenny, 9 January 1883. Bottigelli Archives.

(68) No. 4 1883, published 18 January. Vol. 19, MEW.

(69) To Sorge, 15 March 1883. MEW.

(70) Edward Aveling. "Charles Darwin and Karl Marx". *New Century Review*. April 1897.

· PART IV ·

THE NONCONFORMIST

Edward Bibbins Aveling, born on 29 November 1849 at 6 Nelson Terrace, Stoke Newington in the borough of Hackney, was the fifth of the eight children – six sons and two daughters – of the Rev. Thomas William Baxter Aveling and his wife, Mary Ann.

Nelson Terrace, from which Aveling derived the pseudonym he later adopted legitimately as playwright and critic, fraudulently in contracting his second marriage, was in the heart of Kingsland of whose Independent (Congregational) Chapel in Robinson's Row, High Street, his father was the incumbent for close on half a century.

Compared to the raffish environment of Eleanor's birthplace, with its shifting and foreign population, Aveling's was one of solid British worth. While at the lower end of the short terrace the residents followed such occupations as stonemason, laundress, gardener and dressmaker, the social scale rose with the house numbers to the gallant note struck by a retired major on full pay. Even when allowance is made for some slight over-crowding among the manual workers, the number of persons to the house in Nelson Terrace was roughly six, an average that included a plethora of domestic servants – cooks, footmen, housemaids, nurses – in some cases heavily outnumbering their employers.

Such a household was No. 14 where an elderly gentlewoman lived with her three servants. She was called Elizabeth Bibbins and it is inconceivable that the Rev. Thomas Aveling should have saddled his fourth son with her surname simply because it caught his fancy. "All the family were called after people with money", one of his surviving granddaughters remarked.[1]

As a small boy Edward was occasionally sent to dine with Miss Bibbins. In later life he recalled that she would ask him "Will you take peas or potatoes?" to which he would reply, characteristically, "Both, please".[2]

The next and fifth son, Frederic (or Frederick) Wilkins Aveling was named after the Treasurer of Kingsland Chapel, Frederick Robert Wilkins, a bullion merchant who conducted his business from Winchester Street in the City. The Rev. Thomas Aveling, with his large brood, can hardly be censured for these baptismal ploys. Though he supplemented his income by journalistic work, including the editorship of *The Jewish Herald* from 1848 until 1853, the Kingsland living was worth no more than between £400 and £500 a year.* Nor were the pious man's hopes disappointed. Under Miss Bibbins' will, drawn up on 22 January 1859, he was appointed one of her two executors and when she died six weeks later at the age of 85, he and his family received a goodly portion of her estate valued at some £15,000.†

While Miss Bibbins remained in Nelson Terrace until her death, the Avelings had moved some years before to 13 Amhurst Road, Shacklewell, in Hackney, where the last child, a boy, was born when Edward was six years of age. This was a larger house, as, indeed, was required. The 1861 census shows that theirs was the most populous dwelling in the street, with twelve persons, though by then the eldest son, aged 20, had already left home. Their neighbours, boasting more servants and fewer children, showed an average of no more than eight members to a household.

Here Edward lived until 1863 when he was sent with his brother Frederick, 18 months his junior, to the West of England Dissenters' Proprietary School in Taunton.‡ Rough notes jotted down for his memoirs by the Rev. Frederick Aveling shortly before his death in 1937§ contain the following passage: "Edward, at school with me at Taunton. Bad egg. Had fever, recovered. So father made us both join the Church. We were far too young. I was only 12, Edward 13½."[4]

Whether too young or not, these two, in being sent to a boarding school, differed from their elder brothers whose education ended roughly at an age when theirs began, Thomas having set out to earn his living as a youth (despite Miss Bibbins' will), Charles‖ and William,¶ though still at

---

* If this should be thought adequate for the times, there is the abiding witness of Trollope's Mr. Quiverful, the Rector of Puddingdale, whose income at the same period was also £400.

† After various bequests to distant relatives, faithful servants and the religious and charitable Institutions recommended by her pastor, the Rev. Aveling, Miss Bibbins left him £500, the same amount to Mrs. Aveling and £500 on trust in 3% Consolidated Bank Annuities Stock for each of his eldest children: Thomas Goodall, then 18, and Mary Elizabeth who was 17. The two next sons, Charles Taylor and William Arthur, and the three younger children received nothing, but Edward Bibbins was left £300 of Stock on trust. The trust funds were to be disbursed for the education of the minors who would be paid the money on attaining the age of 21. Provision was made that in the case of any legatee dying before that age, the money should revert to the father, who also received £100 as executor, all the old lady's books and book-cases and an equal share with his co-executor of the residue of her personal estate and effects.

‡ Founded in 1847. In 1868 the name of the school was changed to the Independent College, to which the Rev. Frederick Wilkins Aveling, M.A., B.Sc., returned as headmaster at the early age of 29, to remain for 14 years (1880–1894). It is now known as Taunton School.[3]

§ He and his wife lie buried, like the Marxes, in Highgate cemetery.

‖ 1844–1902. Later in life Charles qualified in medicine and became a highly successful general practitioner.

¶ b. 1846. Emigrated to Canada where he died in his thirties. He was the father of Dr. Francis Arthur Powell Aveling, M.C., Ph.D., D.Sc., sometime Professor of Psychology at King's College, London, after leaving the Roman Catholic priesthood.[1,5]

home, being employed as clerks while in their early 'teens: one in a grocery shop, or "Italian warehouse", the other by a shipping agent.

In the same year – 1863 – as the two boys entered Taunton, their elder sister, Mary, then 21, married Francis Robert Wilkins, the son of the bullion merchant whose glittering trade he followed. From that time forth the Rev. Thomas Aveling was relieved of his responsibility for this daughter whom he specifically referred to in his will as being "through her marriage well provided for". There can be little doubt that this circumstance also accounted for her younger brothers' superior education.

Frederick stayed at Taunton for four years, but Edward left after two, whereafter he was privately educated, for some part of the time in Jersey – by a tutor he hated[6] – until he entered University College, London, as a medical student in 1867. When he was 20 he transferred from the medical to the science faculty, obtaining a £40 Exhibition to study botany and zoology. He took his B.Sc. Honours degree in zoology in 1870, doing so brilliantly that he qualified for an annual £50 scholarship for a further three years. Thus by the time he had reached his majority he had proved himself a young man of outstanding ability.* In passing it may be said that his brother Frederick was such another. Though he won a scholarship to Oxford he refused to put his father to the expense it would entail[1] and entered New College, the School of Divinity in the University of London, then at Swiss Cottage (now at 527 Finchley Road) in 1870, was awarded two scholarships and an Essay Prize, to leave in 1874 with the degrees of M.A. and B.Sc.[7]

For a short period Edward worked as assistant to the eminent physiologist Sir Michael Foster in Cambridge,† returning to London in 1872 when he became a teacher of elementary physics and botany on the staff of Miss Buss's North London Collegiate School for Ladies in Camden Road. This was one of the many establishments which enjoyed his father's patronage and his influence may well have helped Edward to an appointment which, on a part-time basis, he kept until his resignation at

---

* One anecdote illustrating his gifts, attested to by both his surviving nieces in almost identical terms, was obviously handed down in family lore by the brother concerned. "Edward was so brilliant", writes Mrs. Gwendoline Redhead, "that when he wanted to take Logic for some exam. and had never touched the subject, he came to my father two days before the exam. My father said 'you can't cram up for it in two days'. Edward said he could and the two of them went ahead and worked till 2 a.m. and then slept for four hours, and grandfather called them at 6 a.m. and they carried on all day. The next day Edward took the exam. and passed it. He said to my father 'That's all right. I'll forget it all in a couple of days.'"[1]

† At that period there was no Physiology Department at Cambridge. Sir Michael Foster, who had been called to that University in 1870, had previously taught at University College, London, and the likelihood is that he employed this most promising of his former students privately since there is no record of Aveling's admission in any capacity to Cambridge University.[8]

the end of 1876.* Another institution in which the Rev. Thomas Aveling took a special interest was the Orphan Working School in Maitland Park, at whose 110th Anniversary dinner he was the guest of honour.[10] Again this could be the reason why it came about that, back in London and lodging near to both Miss Buss's school and the Orphanage, at 30 Bartholomew Road in Kentish Town, Edward examined the orphan boys in physiology during June 1872[11] and in the October of either that or the following year† was invited to give one of the lectures in his repertoire – "Insects and Flowers" – at the annual prize-giving fête before an audience of patrons and local notabilities. It was on this occasion that he was introduced to Dr. Karl Marx, his wife and their young daughter, Eleanor.[12] He never met either of the parents again.

By this time Edward was a married man. On 30 July 1872 his wedding to Isabel Campbell Frank was solemnised at the Union Chapel, Compton Terrace, Islington,‡ the ceremony being conducted by the Rev. Thomas Aveling according to the rites of the Congregationalists.

Isabel Frank, known as Bell, was one of the five children of a Leadenhall poulterer, John Frank who, dying in August 1868 at the age of 54, left an estate of £25,000. For many years the Franks had lived, though more opulently, in the same street as the Avelings, and it is probable that Edward and Bell, members of the same congregation and much of an age – she was but a few months younger than he – had known each other in Amhurst Road since childhood. At the time of her marriage Bell lived with her widowed mother at 178 Highbury Park Road in Islington. The Aveling family thought Bell a thoroughly nice young woman and her photograph, taken at about the time of the marriage, when she was 22, shows her to have been a plump and decorative one.

Edward's own account has it that he and Bell parted two years later "by mutual agreement". Engels, on the other hand, was given to understand that she had run off with a clergyman. Either way it will be seen that Edward was blameless in the matter. In later years he put it about that the whole Bell episode was foredoomed to failure: that in his green youth he had been caught by a spoilt and bigoted Miss who refused him a divorce even though she would not live with a man of his atheistic and socialist beliefs, neither of which in fact had manifested themselves as early as he claimed to have separated from Bell. Small discrepancies of this kind did not trouble Aveling and his story passed muster in various circles where it was also believed, several years after Bell's death, that his wife was still living and he not free to remarry. His brother Frederick, who knew better,

---

* Reported to the Governors in January 1877.[9]
† Whether 1872 or 1873 is uncertain.
‡ Founded in 1799, it was rebuilt in 1876 and is still extant.

told Eleanor Marx "long before Bell died, that at Bell's death Edward would not marry her".[4] He noted: "He married Bell Frank for her money (300 a year). She could only get half. He soon made her do that. When not able to get any more out of her, he left her."[4] And the Rev. Frederick Aveling's daughter writes: "Eleanor Marx said to father when Bell died 'Now Edward will marry me'. But father said 'Oh no he won't. I know Edward.'"[1] It was also alleged that he clung to the marriage tie in the hope of laying hands eventually on the remainder of her fortune and, further, that when he left her she was stripped of everything she possessed and without the means to sue for the divorce she wanted.[13]

The truth is slightly different. By the terms of her father's will, Bell inherited a half-share with her sister Emeline Elizabeth of an annual income of £210 5s. derived from freehold properties in Upper Holloway. Insurance and repairs had to be paid for out of this income which came to the daughters on trust without power of anticipation. If Bell died childless — as she did — the property reverted to her sister, her sister's children or, failing these, to the trustees. All this Edward must have known. In the event, Emeline Frank, who had been one of the witnesses at Bell's wedding, never married and outlived her sister. But John Frank also left his daughters £1,000 each on attaining the age of 21 or upon marriage. It was this dowry that Edward could have run through when he married Bell four years after her father had died. He could not have touched the capital of her small income at any time and the derisory sum she left at her death she must have saved from that income or earned by her own efforts.

There was so little to poor Bell's life that the meagre facts are soon told. She lived for 20 years after the marriage and at some stage during her solitary existence joined an Anglican Sisterhood, working as a nurse.* On 12 September 1892, at the age of 43, she died intestate at 36 Brooke Street,† Holborn, in a diabetic coma, with no member of her family present and none but paid attendance. This was a stone's throw from the chambers then occupied by Edward in Chancery Lane. Within three weeks the "lawful husband", having been granted letters of administration, pocketed her estate whose gross value was £126 15s. 4d.

Yet when he married Edward was launched on a successful career that would seem to have made it quite unnecessary for him either to seek a rich wife or to pluck her. In 1874, while regularly employed on Miss Buss's

---

* One of the many Mission Houses of the "Sisters of the Poor", as they were called, was in Baldwin's Gardens, two streets away from where Bell lived. These Sisterhoods, founded by Pusey in 1845, provided the entire nursing staff at one time of, among others, University College Hospital.[14]

† The rather sordid little house still stands.

staff, he was giving a series of evening classes on botany and zoology at the Polytechnic College in Regent Street* and published his first work *Botanical Tables*. In the following year, having been appointed as a Lecturer in comparative anatomy and biology at the Medical School of the London Hospital, he gave his Polytechnic lessons in the mornings and, although it is not known for how long he was connected with this institute, he gave it as his permanent address up to the end of May 1881.[16] His lectureship at the London Hospital lasted until 1882, according to official records,[17] though he was in fact dismissed at the end of the 1881 academic year. In 1876 he obtained his D.Sc. at University College, London, was elected a Fellow of the Linnean Society, his sponsors being two botanists and two zoologists of note,† and in 1877 he published his *Physiological Tables*. In 1878, when still under 30 years of age, he was made a Fellow of University College, and in June 1879 he applied for the vacant Chair of Comparative Anatomy at King's College, London, but on finding that the rules made adherence to the Church of England obligatory, he did not pursue his application and, with a fine gesture, "consigned them to the flames".[19]

The facts about Aveling's life have had to be drawn from sources unpolluted by his own coloured versions and other people's opinions. Thus his claim to be an Irishman – jocularly accepted by Bernard Shaw as a counterweight to the overwhelmingly Scottish influence in literary London[20] and wholly believed by Eleanor Marx – was founded upon no more than his mother's and paternal grandmother's emigrant ancestry. It was widely and erroneously held that he had been at Harrow.[21] A biographical sketch in the 1895 *Labour Annual* published not only that he had been Professor of Chemistry and Physiology at New College, London, on whose teaching staff he never was at any time, but also that he had held the Chair of Comparative Anatomy at the London Hospital where, on his own showing, he was a lecturer who, for a salary of £25 a year, gave two lectures a week.[22]

---

* On its present site it was then the Educational Department of the Royal Polytechnic Institute in association with the Society of Arts, the Science and Art Department in South Kensington and the City of London College. In 1880 this Regent Street Department suffered from lack of support and ceased to function. The building was put up for sale and bought in 1881 by Quintin Hogg, whose statue stands nearby. After extension and alteration, the premises were re-opened in September 1882 and known as the Youth's Christian Institute and subsequently as, quite simply, the Regent Street Polytechnic. It is now called the Polytechnic of Central London.[15]

† George Henshaw, Maxwell T. Masters, James Hurie and St. George Mivart. In November 1881 his name was removed from the list of Fellows for non-payment of subscriptions.[18]

The thundercloud of obloquy and abhorrence which, long gathering about his head, descended on Edward Aveling after the death of Eleanor Marx, never to be dispersed in the brief time that remained to him, has largely hidden from posterity both his early achievements and his solid background. Thus he was said to have come from the gutter, to have fawned upon Marx – whom he never knew – and Engels, worming his way into Eleanor's affections only to exploit and discard her to "marry money", whereafter he vanished again into the shadows from which he had emerged.

The distinction of his scientific career as a young man is beyond question; his origins were no less reputable. Though his father, unlike Eleanor's, did nothing world-shaking, he was the spiritual descendant of Milton's "faithful and freeborn Englishmen" who, hunted, hated and harried since the 17th century, became, as convinced Republicans, the backbone of the Commonwealth, identifying the struggle of conscience with that for liberty, thus earning for themselves on the Restoration the most savagely discriminative legislation ever to reach the Statute Book.[23] Under these crippling measures the Dissenters were driven out of the Church. Ordained ministers who refused to take the Oath adopting the revised Book of Prayer and repudiating the Solemn League and Covenant were forbidden to preach or teach in corporate towns. It was illegal for five or more persons to gather together for Nonconformist religious purposes, a third offence of this nature carrying the penalty of transportation. Constables could break into any house where they suspected that dissenters met. It is estimated that one-fifth of the parochial clergy resigned their livings.

Although the Declaration of Indulgence, granting religious freedom under James II, followed by the Act of Toleration, written into the Revolution Settlement and the Bill of Rights to which William III gave his assent in 1689, lightened the penal code and again allowed dissenters to build their own places of worship, it was possible for Lord Mansfield to protest, almost a century later and after the passing of the Dissenting Ministers Act, that "the City of London, in paltry thieving spirit, nominated Nonconformists to offices they could not fill, so that they might fine them for the non-fulfilment". The repeal of the Test and Corporation Acts did not come into force until 1830, while dissenters were disqualified from holding office under the Crown and were excluded from the Universities of Oxford, Cambridge and Durham until 1871.

In Cromwell's time the idea of a "glorious University" in London had been conceived by the Independents, but it was not until 1828 that the University of London, "open to all creeds", came into being. The "Godless College", as it was called, became University College, founded on its present site in Gower Street in 1831. It gained its Charter as a Constituent College of the newly created University of London in 1836.

Edward Aveling's father thus grew up at a time when his denomination saw new opportunities opening. Throughout his adult life he was a minister of the Congregational Church – the most ancient of the 20 Protestant dissenting bodies in England and Wales – which, as "the Independents", had renounced the authority of "pope, prelate, presbytery, priest and parliament". In the 19th century the Nonconformist minister was looked upon as the only friend to Cobbett's "mass of unregarded humanity in the factories and mines".*

Thomas William Baxter Aveling was born on 11 May 1815 in Castletown, the ancient capital of the Isle of Man, where his father, William, a non-commissioned officer, was stationed. His mother was an Irish girl from Ennistimon, Co. Clare, but the Avelings came of an old Cambridgeshire family centred in Wisbech where, on buying his discharge from the army, William Aveling retired, only to die in 1818. The young widow was left in great poverty but the child, Thomas, was taken into the guardianship of a local burgess who sent him to the best school that Wisbech offered.† The boy showed such aptitude that he not only became an usher at the school but, having voluntarily joined the Independent Church at 16 years of age, he was preaching in the surrounding villages before he was 18. A certain Mr. Byrnes of Wisbech left an account of the youthful lay-preacher: "He looked so young, had such command of language, was so poetical in his conceptions, and possessed such a charming voice, that wherever he went he was followed by crowds anxious to hear ... his marvellous oratory."[25]

Thomas had also published a small volume of devotional poems which met with so singular a success that when, on the recommendation of a minister visiting Wisbech, he was entered at Highbury College in 1834

---

* Greville recorded that on the 1833 petition in the House of Commons to admit dissenters to Cambridge "Old Cobbett made as mischievous a speech as he could to blow the coals between the parties".[24]

† The Wisbech Free Grammar School was founded by a Guild in 1592. The premises are now the Youth Centre of the Unionist and Conservative Club.

he was able to pay for his four years' residence at the theological seminary from the proceeds.

On 11 October 1838, at 23 years of age, he was ordained and immediately offered no fewer than four ministries. An elderly friend, the Rev. William Clayton, persuaded him to accept that of co-pastor to Kingsland Independent Chapel in Stoke Newington.

"My own mind", he wrote, "was strongly disinclined to accept it; my heart was fixed on another people in a different suburb. ... But Mr. Clayton's judgment was entirely opposed to my own; and he most vigorously combatted all my objections. When I observed that there were, among the 150 people assembling in Kingsland chapel, not a dozen young persons with whom a minister was likely to grow up, and from whom he might look for co-operation – that it was literally an 'assembly of elders' – for there were, out of 68 members of the church twelve about 80 years of age – he only replied, 'Go, and call such young people in'. When I said that the place was very small, his answer was, 'Go, and enlarge it'. When I remarked that there was a sparse population among which to work – Kingsland then was a mere hamlet – cornfields and pasture lands lying between it and London – he said. 'Though the beginnings be small, its latter end will greatly increase'."[26]

The young minister's reluctance was understandable. The "mere hamlet" of Kingsland had barely cast off its rude and rustic 18th century character. It was a place of Sunday resort for the nearby City population to indulge in bull- and badger-baiting, cock-fighting and wrestling. Its inhabitants were for the most part unschooled – and godless – brick-makers. The church, such as it was, had been consecrated in 1790 in a disused workshop, originally a leper hospital known as La Loque. The Rev. John Campbell,* a man of high principle and benevolent disposition, whose incumbency Aveling was to share, had held the living since 1804, when nightingales sang in Dalston Fields. He was now 72 and infirm.

Before Campbell died and Aveling, then 25 years old, succeeded to the full pastoral office, he married Mary Ann Goodall. She was of the same age and, though born in Co. Carlow, her father had migrated and become both a farmer and innkeeper in Wisbech where the marriage, according to the rites of the Independents, took place on 3 October 1839 in Castle Square Chapel. Only one member of either family was present at the ceremony: the bride's maternal uncle, Joseph Bishop. More surprisingly,

---

* An Edinburgh man (1766–1840), he had been accustomed to "free prayers" on moors and mountains and, on accepting the Kingsland incumbency, had stipulated that the liturgy and Church prayers should be discontinued, whereupon many of the founder-trustees resigned and the Independent character of the Chapel was established. John Campbell Road, off Kingsland High Street, still commemorates him.

though the bridegroom was a fully ordained minister of the Church, he signed the register as "Gentleman", without profession. The eight children of this marriage were born in the course of the next 17 years, all but the youngest at 6 Nelson Terrace.

When Aveling took over his Kingsland ministry the church seated 400 people. Seven years later it was enlarged to hold 900 and in 1852 the foundation stone was laid for a bran-new Gothic edifice seating 1,350 with a gallery for 800 children. It was so vast a place, furnished with a pulpit of surpassing ugliness bought by the parishioners at the Great Exhibition of 1851, that its flourishing congregation named it with pride the "Cathedral of North London". Ever again enlarged and improved, it remained to ornament, though not embellish, that most depressing area of the metropolis until its demolition in the 1940s.

Another feature of Aveling's ministry was the building and inauguration of schools for the Kingsland children of both sexes, and, indeed, as his patronage of Miss Buss's establishment proved, he was a great believer in the education of females. His own family life, though he presided over a strict Christian household with no fun on Sundays nor frivolity at any time, was not a gloomy one, as it hardly could be with so many youngsters whose father had at heart the welfare – not only spiritual – of all children.

He was a prolific writer of both verse and prose throughout his life, during which he held innumerable honorary positions, including a Doctorate of Divinity at Howard University in the United States, the Chairmanship of the Congregational Board of London in 1873, that of the London Congregational Union in 1874* and, for the year 1876, he was elected to the highest office in his denomination as Chairman of the Congregational Union of England and Wales.[25]

In addition to an outstanding talent for raising funds – £50,000 was subscribed by an overwhelmingly working-class congregation in less than 20 years for the benefit of his Church and the charities he supported – the Rev. Aveling was distinguished by his splendid gifts of voice and delivery as an orator: traits which his son Edward inherited in good measure, though directed to different ends. But the pastor was a comely man, as may be seen both in an engraving and the family photograph taken in 1850. Edward, the "unprincipled windbag" as his brother called him,[4] is seated on his mother's lap here in the centre of the group. It is not easy to identify the infant Aveling, his curls cascading from under an inap-

---

* It is of interest to note that the Rev. Andrew Mearns was Secretary of the London Congregational Union when he wrote his famous pamphlet. *The Bitter Cry of Outcast London: An Inquiry into the Conditions of the Abject Poor*, the first edition of which was published anonymously in October 1883.

propriate hat – everyone else seems to be indoors – with the ill-favoured schoolboy of 1863 shown seated by his handsome younger brother Frederick.

At about the age of 21 Edward went through a phase of vaguely romantic good looks – the curls now trained to cluster at his neck in a poetic sweep – but in maturity there was a disturbing lack of harmony in his features. It is also true that he carried himself in a hunched manner and was not well-grown, but whether his unprepossessing person was a misfortune or a fault, it excited animadversions not usually committed to paper or publicly printed. His "basilisk eye" was more than once referred to as the sign of his awful character. William Morris's daughter called him "a little lizard of a man",[27] and was not the first to do so, Bernard Shaw having used the simile and also said that "he had no physical charm except a voice like a euphonium".[28] Olive Schreiner, in whom Aveling aroused feelings of dread and horror, compared him to an illicit diamond buyer: "the real criminal type",[29] while Hyndman, who found his "forbidding face ... ugly and even repulsive", said that "nobody can be as bad as Aveling looks".[30] One wonders whether, had he been an Adonis, outraged virtue would have been more tolerant of Aveling's conduct. Certainly, in Hyndman's *obiter dictum* that with women "he needed but half an hour's start of the handsomest man in London", it is possible to detect behind some of these strictures on his appearance the unspoken cry: It isn't fair.

When all but their two youngest had left home, the Aveling parents moved to 208 Amhurst Road where on 5 August 1877 Edward's mother died of apoplexy.* Her children were said to have been devoted to her and took it ill that, within a twelve-month of her death, the widower, then 63 years of age, married a much younger lady: Miss Agnes Sarah Joscelyne, the sister of a Congregationalist minister who officiated at the wedding. The first Mrs. Aveling was thought to have known and heartily disliked this member of her husband's flock who was forever sewing exquisite clerical bands and only too plainly "making a set at him". Her offerings were returned and she was sent about her business. Certainly she was not welcomed by her stepchildren, most of whom she outlived, surviving her husband by over 30 years. Edward is not known ever to have communicated with her, while his brother Frederick detested her and would not allow his family to meet her.[1]

The Rev. Thomas Aveling himself died of an attack of gastritis on 3 July 1884 while on a visit to the Reedham Asylum for Fatherless

---

* Family lore has it that, though a lovable woman, Mrs. Aveling drank heavily, suffered from cirrhosis of the liver and expired after falling downstairs when drunk.[1] Her death certificate, signed by her doctor son, Charles, does not bear this out.

Children, near Croydon, of which he had been the honorary secretary for close on 40 years.

By that time Edward was not only an avowed atheist but also an active socialist who had lost much of his standing in and more or less abandoned the academic world, yet he received, without discrimination, his due share of the £8,400 left by his father. It is not known how much he inherited but, with provision for a large family, a youthful widow and his grandchildren by the two sons who had predeceased him,* the Rev. Aveling is unlikely to have endowed Edward with a competence.

---

* Ernest Henry, the youngest son (1856–1884), had died but a few weeks before his father, leaving a widow and daughter. His death on 26 May 1884, notified by Edward who was present, occurred at 12 Fitzroy Street, at which same address Frederick Lessner is known to have lived from 1873 to 1893.

The path leading from Nonconformism to Freethinking and from there to Socialism was neither long nor untrodden. It was more like a public highway along which marched many of the founders of the British working-class movement from the Welsh valleys, the Scottish hills, the rural parishes and industrial centres of England and the London slums.

Edward Aveling's first steps to secularism were taken at a period when high-minded men in Holy Orders wrestled with spiritual doubt, discarded the faith of their fathers and resigned from their comfortable sinecures at the older Universities. Aveling's progress to disbelief was marked by no particular anguish. It was, indeed, almost inevitable that this highly intelligent and scientifically trained young man of Nonconformist background should be drawn towards the dissenting movements of his time.

Nevertheless, viewing his character and career in perspective, it is not immediately obvious why he took this road. Like his father, he had the gift of eloquence and he wanted to preach. In the secularist movement he swiftly rose to prominence and was given a platform for the exercise of his talents. So much is clear. It is also axiomatic that the field of the natural sciences offers few opportunities for self-display. Though he could have continued to make a fair showing had he pursued his scientific career, he was a teacher and populariser rather than an original thinker.

It is unfortunate that, though a Doctor of Science, he considered himself to be a master of all the arts, in particular the art of drama, which offered him the limelight and the plaudits that he craved. He was a playwright of sterling insignificance whom nothing could discourage. Elizabeth Robins* recalls "dingy Dr. Edward Aveling ... appearing at my door with a *suit case* full of plays".[31] She does not remember inviting him in, let alone opening his suitcase. He was an amateur performer of below average stability, bursting into tears at the beauty of his renderings of poetry, and, of course, a poet in his own right. He was also a many-sided

---

* Born in America, Elizabeth Robins (1865–1952) came to London in her twenties making her first stage début in England in 1887. She was chiefly renowned as not only among the first but one of the finest exponents of Ibsen, the English rights of whose plays she owned. She played Martha Bernick in *Pillars of Society* in 1889, Hedda Gabler in 1891 and, one of her finest parts, Hilda Wangel, in *The Master Builder* in 1893.

critic while, in a little over a twelvemonth,* in addition to a long series of articles on Darwin and other matters on which he was qualified to expound, he wrote and spoke on such diverse subjects as Purity, Etymology, Mahomet, the Celts, Shakespeare, Pitt, the Armada, Tennyson, Loyalty, Luther, the Meaning of Life and Death, the National Anthem, Publicans, the Sense of Colour, the Stuarts, Swinburne's literary defects, Courage, Burke and Old Mother Hubbard and all.

In the summer of 1879 he claimed to have held secularist views for two or three years, deterred from making them public because he doubted not the cause but his own worthiness and strength to serve it,[32] but he had not in fact played any active part in the National Secular Society until the beginning of that year, when he began to contribute regularly to its 2d. weekly organ, *The National Reformer*, then edited by Charles Bradlaugh† and Annie Besant.‡

At first Aveling hid his identity by signing his articles "E.D." but used his own initials after his public declaration of faith, by which time he had formed an attachment to Mrs. Besant, whom he shared with Bradlaugh. She hailed the "New Soldier" in the most fulsome terms: "His language is exquisitely chosen and is polished to the highest extent, so that the mere music of speech is pleasant to the ear. Since to this artistic charm are added scholarship and wide knowledge, with a brilliancy of brain I have not seen surpassed ... our friends will not wonder that we ... rejoice that our mistress Liberty has won this new Knight."[33]

From that time forth and for the next few years he wrote for the

---

* 1880–1881.

† 1833–1891. Born in Hoxton, Bradlaugh was in turn errand-boy, coal merchant, enlisted trooper, builder's timekeeper and lawyer's clerk before he became a Freethought lecturer. He was a considerable force for progress and enlightenment in the 'seventies when he enjoyed a large following. A vigorous opponent of socialism, he lost much of his influence with its later revival. With Mrs. Besant he stood trial in 1876 for circulating an American pamphlet that advocated birth control and was sentenced to six months' imprisonment and a fine of £200: a verdict quashed on appeal. He stood successfully as parliamentary candidate for Northampton in the interests of religious Radicalism in 1880, but refused to take the Oath – the indulgence of affirmation being then allowed only to Quakers, Moravians and Separatists, not to atheists – and was re-elected twice more before, following scenes of violence in the House, the setting up of two Select Committees and his own four speeches at the bar, he finally took his seat in 1886, introducing the amendment to the Parliamentary Oaths Bill which received the royal assent on 24 December 1888.

‡ Née Annie Wood (1847–1933). In 1867 she married Frank Besant, a clergyman by whom she had two children, separating from him in 1873. The many causes she espoused veered with her enthusiasm for the men who led them and she ran the whole gamut from established religion, through High Church Anglicanism, the Oxford Movement, Theism, Atheism, Malthusianism, Radicalism, Science, Philanthropy, Fabianism, Feminism and Socialism to Theosophy. She showed not only the courage of her lovers' convictions, but was a bold and energetic campaigner who, like Bradlaugh, did much to broaden men's minds and, unlike him, played an active part in the working-class movement.

secularist press — taking on the editorship of the new monthly magazine, *Progress*, in 1883 when its founder, the militant atheist G. W. Foote, was imprisoned* for the blasphemies published in his *Freethinker* of which Aveling also became interim editor — was elected Vice-President of the National Secularist Society in 1881, showed zeal in Bradlaugh's electoral campaigns and the fight for the amendment to the Parliamentary Oath, lectured throughout the country, inaugurating science classes and giving regular courses on English history and literature at the Hall of Science in Old Street. In addition he published pamphlets, stood for and obtained a seat on the London School Board in 1882, took on the private cramming of medical and science students,† wrote plays, adapted plays, and engaged in amateur theatricals and poetry recitals whenever time permitted.

These activities were not all undertaken in the order given, nor simultaneously. While his public — and some hint of his private — life was excellently advertised, so that it would be possible to render a week-by-week account of where he went and on what he spoke and wrote, there is an ineluctable dreariness about it all. Had he amounted to something in the end, had he become a figure of significance and worth, it might be of interest to record his multifarious doings — for he did so much, buzzing like a fly — but no sooner had he ceased to be a promising young man than he became, so far as posterity is concerned, a thundering bore. Though he was able to move vast audiences — Will Thorne acclaimed him as "one of the greatest orators this country ever heard"[35] — in cold print his speeches, punctuated at the time by prolonged applause and even cheers, appear sorry stuff: pompous, florid, empty and so much hot air. Aveling, in fact, was a gasbag whom time has rudely deflated. The same cruel fate has overtaken his articles which lie today in the files of old newspapers whose pages testify that his contributions to the secularist and socialist press, save in his own field of the natural sciences, are less convincing, less original and far more embarrassing than most of the matter published in these proselytizing journals.

Yet the question remains: why should this self-indulgent, exhibitionistic character have become a socialist at all? Though of an age to do so, Aveling had never heard of the International during its existence, had not read the writings of either Marx or Engels‡ nor yet evinced the smallest interest in the Commune or its victims.§ Not until the late '70s did he turn his attention to social — and then not socialist — questions.

---

* From May 1883 to February 1884.

† H. G. Wells, when he in his turn took to tutoring, said that he and his friends "put all sorts of competing coaches out of business. One of those for whom we made life harder was Dr. Aveling".[34]

‡ Though the first English translation of the *Communist Manifesto* appeared in 1850.

His motives, like those of most people, were exceedingly mixed, and it would be crass to claim that principle played no part in them. "No man is scrupulous all round. He has, according to his faculties and interests, certain points of honour, while in matters that do not interest him he is careless and unscrupulous. One of the several models who sat unconsciously for Dubedat",|| wrote Shaw, referring to Aveling, "was morbidly scrupulous as to his religious and political convictions and would have gone to the gallows sooner than recant a syllable of them. But he had absolutely no conscience about money and women. In contrast with men who were scrupulously correct in their family and business life he seemed a blackguard, and was a blackguard; but there were occasions on which they would cut a poor figure beside him: occasions when loyalty to their convictions called for some risk and sacrifice. ... He had his faith and upheld it."¶[36]

Shaw repeated the same view when he wrote to a friend in 1946 that Aveling had been "quite a pleasant fellow who would have gone to the stake for Socialism or atheism, but with absolutely no conscience in his private life".**[28] Shaw further told his biographer, Hesketh Pearson, that Aveling's case was not unique and that he, Shaw, had been "on pleasant terms with three others, two clergymen and a retired colonel ... with a total lack of conscience in money and sexual relations".[38]

Yet there is in Shaw's characterisations of Aveling something which does not altogether meet the case. One factor omitted is that the Nonconformist tradition never dies; another is that the man – in both his principled and unprincipled conduct – was cold-hearted.

Like his forbears, Aveling set his face against the order of things that stifled men's freedom of conscience and creed – however curiously he interpreted these – and, given his epoch, how better could he express the refusal to conform than by denouncing, first, all organised religion and then the entrenched State – capitalism – itself? Having once made these decisions, he stuck to them, nor can they be regarded as the choice of a vulgar careerist. If, by reason of personal weaknesses, he fell into disrepute, thereby injuring the causes he embraced, it may be conjectured

§ In July 1879, at the time of the amnesty agitation, *The National Reformer* published one letter on the French Communard proscripts exiled in London signed by, among others, Charles Longuet.

|| In *The Doctor's Dilemma* (1911).

¶ Shaw was 91 when he wrote this passage: 38 years after he had created the character of Dubedat and 51 since Aveling's death.

** Shaw's reference to Aveling going to the gallows or the stake for his beliefs is quoted in a slightly different but distinctly Shavian version in Stephen Winsten's *Salt and His Circle*: "If it came to giving one's life for a cause one could rely on Aveling even if he carried all our purses with him to the scaffold."[37]

that he would have been something of a liability in whatever walk of life he had chosen.

The socialist movement, even in its infancy, was bound to attract men of his type, as it has done ever since. They are not so much moved by human misery and injustice as they are rebellious against society, contemptuous of the gullibility, blindness or hypocrisy of those who uphold the *status quo*. This is not Marxism, it is not socialism of any kind, but there was no place, certainly not in Aveling's day, for such nonconformists other than in the only movement pledged to the overthrow of the existing social system.

His anarchic individualism and egotism, never entirely held in check, were to some extent counteracted by his desire to play a prominent part, to which end he sometimes had to subordinate one greed to another, as a child will refrain from taking the largest piece of cake for the greater satisfaction of winning approval. This conflict within Aveling was unequal at best: again and again he forfeited approval, but he snatched a lot of cake on the way.

In background, upbringing, training and experience he was as far removed from Eleanor Marx as he well could be. Their differences of temperament emerge most clearly in their writings. Every line that Eleanor penned, whether in happy or unhappy private letters or for the public – as every recorded word she spoke – is eager, warm, alive, and rings true as a bell. Although his excessive facility enabled Aveling to pour forth lectures, journalism, pamphlets, plays, reviews, reports and a multitude of ephemera that have come down to us, his voice is not merely without character: it is muted, dead. Nothing rings through the words. Nothing at all. There is no means of knowing how he spoke or wrote to his family, friends and lovers, but his perfunctory little postscripts to Eleanor's letters and the occasional notes to colleagues that have been preserved make precisely the same muffled impact. Veiled in facetiousness or dry didacticism his voice is as inexpressive as Eleanor's is revealing of personality.

This was the man with whom she threw in her lot.

REFERENCE NOTES

Abbreviations
Bottigelli Archives Letters in the custody of Dr. Emile Bottigelli, Paris.
Liebknecht   *Wilhelm Liebknecht Briefwechsel mit Karl Marx und Friedrich Engels.*
          Edited by Georg Eckert. Mouton & Co., The Hague, 1963.

(1)   Privately communicated.

(2)   Eleanor to Liebknecht, 2 June 1897. Liebknecht.

(3)   Information kindly provided by Dr. John M. Rae, Ph.D., Headmaster of Taunton School and Mr. Bernard Honess, Manager and Librarian of the Memorial Hall.

(4)   Aveling family papers.

(5)   Information kindly provided by Mr. B. M. Baker, Provost's Secretary, University College, London.

(6)   Aveling to Laura Lafargue, 30 August 1887. Bottigelli Archives.

(7)   Information kindly provided by the Rev. G. F. Nuttall, M.A., D.D., Librarian at New College, London.

(8)   Information kindly supplied by Professor Sir Bryan Matthews, C.B.E., F.R.S., of the Physiology Laboratory, Cambridge.

(9)   Information kindly provided by Miss Madeline McLaughlan, Head Mistress of North London Collegiate School, Edgware.

(10)   Annual Report of Orphan Working School, 1868.

(11)   *Hampstead and Highgate Express* and *Camden & Kentish Towns Gazette*, both of 22 June 1872.

(12)   Edward Aveling. "Charles Darwin and Karl Marx: A Comparison". Part II. *The New Century Review*, April 1897.

(13)   Flysheet issued by Ferdinand Gilles from 6 Everleigh Street, Tollington Park. "Is he the Son-in-Law of Marx?" 10 November 1891. (See Ref. 4).

(14)   Maria Trench in *The Nineteenth Century*, Volume XVI. August 1884.

(15)   Information kindly provided by Mr. Wilfred Ashworth, Chief Librarian of the Polytechnic of Central London.

(16)   *The National Reformer.* 1881.

(17)   Information kindly provided by Dr. H. B. May, M.D., F.R.C.P., Dean of the London Hospital Medical School.

(18)   Information kindly provided by Miss Sandra Raphael, Librarian to the Linnean Society of London, Burlington House.

(19)   *The National Reformer.* 6 July 1879.

(20)   Letter to David O'Donoghue, 9 May 1889. *Bernard Shaw: Collected Letters 1874–1897*. Edited by Dan H. Laurence. Max Reinhardt, 1965.

(21)   Thanks to the Headmaster of Harrow School, Dr. R. L. James, C.B.E. (retired July 1971), the School Registers were examined for the period 1800 to 1895 during which time no Aveling was a pupil.

(22)   In an indignant article on his dismissal in *The National Reformer*, 18 December 1881.

(23)   The Corporation Act 1661, the Act of Uniformity 1662, the Conventicle Acts of 1663 and 1670, the Five-Mile Act 1665 and the Test Act 1673, collectively known as the Clarendon Code.

(24)   *The Greville Diary.* Edited by Philip Whitwell Wilson. Heinemann 1927.

(25)   This quotation and many other details concerning the life of the Rev. Thomas Aveling are from *Memories of Kingsland* by "A.S.A." (Agnes Sarah Aveling, his second wife) published in aid of the Church Restoration in 1887, and from records kindly provided by Mr. Bernard Honess of the Memorial Hall.

(26)   Thomas William Baxter Aveling. *Memorials of the Clayton Family*. Jackson, Walford & Hodder, 1867.

(27)   May Morris. *William Morris, Artist, Writer, Socialist*. Vol. II. Basil Blackwell, 1936.

(28)   Letter to L. Preger, 22 February 1946. Quoted by Warren Sylvester Smith in *The London Heretics 1870–1914* from material in the Berg Collection, N.Y. Constable, 1967.

(29) *Olive Schreiner: Letters* 1876–1920. Edited by S. Cronwright-Schreiner. T. Fisher Unwin 1924.

(30) H. M. Hyndman. *Further Reminiscences*. Macmillan, 1912.

(31) Elizabeth Robins. *Both Sides of the Curtain*. Heinemann, 1940.

(32) "Credo Ergo Laborabo". *The National Reformer*. 27 July 1879.

(33) *The National Reformer*. 17 August 1879.

(34) H. G. Wells. *An Experiment in Autobiography*. Macmillan, New York, 1934.

(35) *My Life's Battles*. George Newnes n.d. *c.* 1925.

(36) "Biographers' Blunders Corrected" in *Sixteen Self-Sketches*. Constable 1949.

(37) Hutchinson 1951.

(38) Hesketh Pearson. *Bernard Shaw. His Life and Personality*. First complete edition, Methuen, 1961.

· PART V ·

TRANSITION

Early in April 1883 Dr. Aveling, editing *Progress* during Foote's trial for blasphemy, asked to buy the block of Marx's portrait which had appeared in *The Republican*,* with a biography, in November 1882. The block was not available, having been sent to the *Sozialdemokrat*, but Aveling had wanted it to accompany Eleanor's two articles on her father which appeared in the May and June issues of *Progress*.

"There is no time perhaps", she wrote, "so little fitted for writing the biography of a great man as that immediately after his death, and the task is doubly difficult when it falls to one who knew and loved him."[1] Her first essay was confined to "strictly historical and biographical details", her second to a clear concise exposition of the theory of surplus value.[2] The two articles taken together reflect Eleanor's grasp of the essentials of Marxism and her power to convey them in the simplest and most telling manner. Without any pretensions to great intellect, she demonstrated here that, by temperament and ability, she was peculiarly fitted to wield in practice with style and vitality the weapons Marx had forged, combining to a rare degree an understanding of theory with deep human feeling, uncommon in the world of politics.

In general, the obituary notices that appeared in English and German were, as Engels wrote to Laura, "inexact and badly informed, but upon the whole decent".†[3]

The lease of 41 Maitland Park Road had still a year to run and there was talk of finding a tenant; but in the meantime it became clear that there would be at least six months' work to do in the house: the reams of manuscript Marx had left, the multitude of letters that came to light – dating back to correspondence with his father in 1837 – and the "garret full of boxes, parcels and books"[4] had to be sorted and examined. The massive material for what had been planned as the second volume of *Capital* – of which only two chapters had been put into order – consisted of endless drafts, with quotations collected from every possible source and

---

* A monthly Radical paper issued from 1880 to 1886. It published an obituary of Marx in April 1883.
† Many of the national newspapers (including *The Times*) received the news of Marx's death from their Paris correspondents; some published that he had died in France. But, as the *Pall Mall Gazette* commented on 16 March, the extraordinary thing was that Karl Marx's death should have been allowed to pass almost unnoticed.

no indication of their intended use, all in Marx's impossible handwriting "which the author himself was sometimes unable to decipher"[5]. It was to occupy Engels for the remainder of his life. "If I had known, I should have left him no peace day or night until it was finished and printed," he wrote to Bebel.[5]

In his preface to the 1893 edition of Volume II of *Capital*,* by which time Volume III, never foreseen by Marx, was in preparation for the press, Engels described the problems he had confronted: "It was no easy task to put the second book of *Capital* in shape. . . . The great number of available, mostly fragmentary, texts worked on added to the difficulties of this task. . . . The bulk of the material was not finally polished in point of language. . . . Thoughts were jotted down as they developed in the brain of the author. Some parts of the argument would be fully treated, others of equal importance only indicated. . . . At conclusions of chapters, in the author's anxiety to get to the next, there would often be only a few disjointed sentences. . . . This is the material for Book II, out of which I was supposed 'to make something', as Marx remarked to his daughter Eleanor shortly before his death. . . ."

At first, as the house was gradually cleared, the papers assembled and dusted by Nim, more and more letters appeared. These, where they touched on incidents in the '40s known to Nim, were read aloud to be greeted by her shouts of appreciative laughter but, as Eleanor later wrote, once the letters had been transferred to his house, Engels, as Nim had told her, "burnt lots of letters referring to himself",[6] while, when after Engels' death she herself tried to order the correspondence for a projected biography of her father, it proved "rather difficult work . . . because I find all the letters are higgledy piggledy. I mean that the parcels the dear old General made up are *quite* unsorted, not merely as to date, but that the letters of various writers are all mixed up, and different portions of a letter are occasionally in different parcels."[7]

Naturally Eleanor did not reproach Engels for the confusion in which she found these letters: she had been unable to cope with the task herself at the time. "This sorting of the papers will be terrible work", she wrote to Laura. "I hardly know how it is to be got through." This was more particularly the case since she had her own work to do and "I am more anxious than ever now to earn my own living". There were "at *least* 500 pages of the second volume", but, while she knew that Engels would take these over, she did go through many of the letters and: "I need not tell you that I have taken the *utmost* care to prevent our good General from seeing anything that is likely to give him pain. Indeed *all* the private

---

* The first German edition appeared in 1885.

letters I shall put aside. They are of interest only to us. . . . Would you like me to send you all your and Lafargue's letters? If so as I find them I will put them together. . . ."[8] Eleanor begged Laura to come to London. Engels added his entreaties, putting his house at her disposal and emphasising that Tussy wanted and needed her there.[4]

Marx had died intestate, but while Laura had been too unwell to attend his funeral or to help now in the disposition of his effects, she was well enough to make an angry fuss at being, as she felt, slighted.

On reading Engels' articles in the *Sozialdemokrat* "On the Death of Marx",[9] the first of which ended: "By word of mouth he appointed his youngest daughter Eleanor and myself as his literary executors", her resentment knew no bounds. "Will you oblige me", she wrote to Engels on 2 June, "by telling me whether Papa told you that he desired Tussy to be, with you, his literary executrix? Not having been with my dear father at the end you will, I know, understand that I am desirous to learn what were his ultimate directions. What his wishes and intentions were at Vevey *I know*."[10] A few weeks later she returned to the attack, repudiating any notion that she was concerned "about the fate of his chairs and tables", but insisting that when she had been with Marx in Switzerland he had "said he would give me all the documents and papers required for a history of the International and with his usual goodness he asked me to undertake a translation of *Kapital*. . . . He invited me to stay at Ventnor, to work with him, and under his direction, there. I accepted his invitation very gladly and but for Jenny's illness and other tribulations should have joined him there."[11] She harked back to old grievances: Tussy's letter asking her to come to London had not reached her until the day after her father's death,* entirely ignoring the letter Engels – who was not nursing Marx – had written to her on 10 March, four days before her father died, to say: "I conclude that in this frosty and snowy weather with east winds you will not be in too great a hurry to come to London. Anyhow, should you make up your mind to come, everything is prepared for you", and then, as gently and tactfully as was his wont, to describe Marx's failing strength.[12] Laura made no move, though it was a letter that should have sped her to her father's side. "When after Jenny's death I expressed a wish to see Papa I was told that my coming would alarm him", she huffed. "I requested you the other day", Laura continued to Engels, "to inform me . . . whether Mohr had told *you* that he wished Tussy to be his literary executrix. You have not answered me. Had you answered in the affirmative I should have simply concluded that long illness had changed my dear father. . . . Papa, in health, would not have made *his eldest and*

---

* But Engels' telegram, on 15 March, had brought Paul to London post-haste.

favourite daughter his sole executrix, to the exclusion of his other daughters – he had too great a love of equality for that – let alone the last of his daughters. Thus much I know...."[11]

Thereupon Engels replied: "When you spoke of your knowledge of what poor Moor's views and wishes had been at Vevey, it was in connection of a more or less testamentary nature.... After poor Mohr's death, on my inquiry, Tussy informed me that he had told her she and I were to take possession of his papers.... If you wish to have Mohr's exact words, Tussy will no doubt give them to you if you ask her to do so.... As to the expression *literary executors*, I am alone responsible for it. I could not find another at the time, and if by it I have in any way offended you, I humbly ask your pardon. How the disposition *itself* can wound you, I cannot see. The work must be done *here on the spot*. The real work, that you know as well as Tussy does, will mostly have to be done by me. But as Mohr had one daughter living in London, I find it but natural that he should associate her to me in such work as she could do. Had you been living here instead of in Paris, all the three of us would have been jointly appointed, no doubt about that.

"But there is another view of the case. According to English law ... the only person living who is the legal representative of Mohr in England is Tussy. Or rather, the only person who can become his legal representative by taking out *letters of administration*. This must be done by the *next of kin living* in England – Tussy.... Of the projects Mohr discussed with you at Vevey I was of course utterly ignorant and only regret you did not come over since 14th March, when we should have known and complied with them as much as possible...."[13]

How bad the relations between the two sisters were at the time of Marx's death is illustrated by the fact that one of the letters of condolence addressed to Laura,* inadvertently opened by Tussy, had to be passed to Lenchen for Engels to forward.

To be sure, Laura's life was not bathed in sunshine: all her children had died, she was 38 years of age and had none of the satisfactions of work to fill her time and mind or to relieve her of the permanent want of money to live in that station of life to which Engels was accustomed. Moreover, her husband – also of no settled occupation – was now, from 21 May, in gaol, where she visited him daily bringing a basketful of the choicest food and wine to take luncheon with him. Certainly she had reason for cheerless reflections. Notwithstanding Paul's valuable contribution to the French socialist movement,† when all is said and done the Lafargues were a trivial

---

* From Rudolph Meyer.
† He is perhaps best known to English readers for his splendid pamphlet *The Right to be Lazy*[14], on which subject he was an expert.

pair. Leaving aside the dedication and majesty of her father's labours, the sacrifices of her mother and the yoke Engels had borne uncomplainingly for the best years of his life, Laura's circumstances have only to be matched against the sufferings of her sister Jenny, so lately dead, and Eleanor's stalwart efforts to become self-supporting, to see her pettishness at this juncture as both indelicate and undignified.

Engels, however, had no wish to interfere between the two sisters and strongly advised Laura to write direct to Eleanor or, better still, to come to London. Nothing could put greater obstacles in the way of the important work to be done, he wrote, and the help she could give "than fresh unpleasantness" between herself and Tussy. "What we are, all of us, desirous of seeing carried out, is a befitting monument to the memory of Mohr, the first portion of which must be the publication of his post-humous works. Let us then contribute what we can towards that end."[13] He had said nothing to Eleanor of Laura's plaints: the only person he had told was Nim.

It was therefore natural for Eleanor to correspond quite freely with her sister, reporting on her efforts to sort the letters and also her concern about her nephew Johnny, whom she felt she could no longer keep with her though quite unable to elicit any reply from Longuet about arrangements for the boy's homecoming. She also worried about Nim, who "after all the terrible work and trouble of these last awful months"[8] sadly needed a little holiday away from "this dreary abode".[15] Thus, killing two birds with one stone, for Eleanor did not know how else to arrange either matter, Lenchen took Johnny back to Paris and, though it had not occurred to Laura to invite her in the first place, she put Nim up at the end of April, Eleanor pleading that she should keep her as long as possible: "Let her have at least two clear weeks", she asked, modestly enough.[15]

Though the major work, as Engels recognised, must fall to his lot, Eleanor played her part and, in June, went to see the publisher Kegan Paul with a view to an English translation of *Capital*, to be undertaken by Sam Moore. "He is by far the best man", said Engels, "slightly heavy, but that can be mended."[16] James Knowles, the editor of *The Nineteenth Century*, had already approached Engels on this question in April and had been told that Moore alone was fitted for the task.*

Although Laura had said no word to Nim of any intention of coming to London, where Engels invited her to make his house her headquarters during Paul's incarceration and share in his holiday plans for a couple of months at least, she did eventually show her "bright face in this dull

---

* Engels had also said: "Allow me to point out that I am no 'Dr.' but a retired cotton manufacturer."

climate" when it was at its least dull, that is, in July, to stay for some ten days.

A week after her departure, on 18 August 1883, letters of administration were granted to Eleanor for Marx's estate valued at £250.

By this time Eleanor had put a few sticks of furniture into rooms she had taken at 32 Great Coram Street* to be nearer the British Museum and also to her friends, Dollie and Ernest Radford, who had married in July and were living round the corner in Brunswick Square. Moreover it was not far from Aveling's quarters in Newman Street, on the other side of the Tottenham Court Road.

Nim had now moved into 122 Regent's Park Road where, for the rest of her life, she was to be Engels' most treasured housekeeper.[41] Maitland Park Road stood untenanted according to the Ratebooks which bear final dusty witness to the end of the Marxes' family life.

Eleanor continued to write for *Progress* – her two articles reviewing Stepniak's† *Sketches and Profiles* appearing as "Underground Russia" in the August and September issues‡ – to teach and, at all times, to work at the Museum. It was here that she had met Miss Potter who noted in her diary on 24 May 1883:

"In afternoon went to British Museum and met Miss Marx in refreshment room. Daughter of Karl Marx, socialist writer and refugee. Gains her livelihood by teaching 'literature' etc., and corresponding for socialist newspapers, now editing 'Progress' in the enforced absence of Mr. Foote. Very wroth about imprisonment of latter.

"'I couldn't see much joke in those particular extracts but there was nothing wrong in them. Ridicule is quite a legitimate weapon. It is the weapon Voltaire used and did more good with it than any amount of serious argument. We think the Christian religion is an immoral illusion and we wish to use any argument to persuade the people we have to deal with. The striking difference of this century and the last is, that free thought was the privilege of the upper classes then and it is becoming the privilege of the working classes now. We want to make them disregard the mythical next world and live for this world and insist on having what will make it pleasant for them.'

"It was useless to argue with her. She refused to recognise the beauty of the Christian religion. She read the gospels as the gospel of damnation.

---

* Renamed Coram Street on 30 January 1900. No. 32 was at that end of the street which no longer exists and is now a building site.
† Pseudonym of Sergei Mikhailovich Kravchinsky (1852–1895) who emigrated to Geneva in 1876 and to London in 1884. His own book with the title *Underground Russia* was published in an English translation in 1883.
‡ See Appendix 5.

Thought Christ, if he had existed, was a weak-minded individual with a good deal of character but quite lacking in heroism. 'Did he not, in the last moment, pray that the cup might pass from him?'

"When I asked what 'socialist progress' was, she very sensibly remarked that I might as well ask her to give me in a short formula the whole theory of mechanics. Socialist progress was a deduction from socialist science which was the most complicated of all sciences. I replied that from the little I knew about political economy (the only social science we English understood) the social philosophers seemed to limit themselves to describing forces that were more or less necessarious. She did not contradict this. I do not know whether it is true or not? In person she is comely, dressed in a slovenly picturesque way with curly black hair, flying about in all directions. Fine eyes full of life and sympathy, otherwise ugly features and expression and complexion showing signs of unhealthy excited life kept up with stimulants and tempered by narcotics. Lives alone, is much connected with the Bradlaugh set, evidently peculiar views on love, etc., and should think has somewhat 'natural' relations with men! Should fear that the chances were against her remaining long within the pale of respectable society."[17]

That Eleanor Marx should fall below the standards of the railway magnate's daughter is not altogether a surprise* – it is conceivable that their papas would not always have seen eye to eye – but the opinion that Eleanor was something of a slut and a drug addict into the bargain does seem a shade bizarre considering her attitude to narcotics – "not much better than dram-drinking and ... almost ... as injurious" – and the innumerable testimonies to her neat if not modish appearance.

When the school term restarted in September, Eleanor went back to teach at Mrs. Bircham's school in Kensington but was looking for other pupils as well. "It is *so* difficult to get work, or at least regular work", she wrote to Laura. "The kind of lessons I give are not like teaching 'all subjects'." She then asked whether Laura and Paul could not send articles to *Progress* which "little magazine is beginning – to the great annoyance of Bradlaugh – to have a really good circulation". Aveling as its acting editor was "not *quite* a free agent", but could do more or less as he pleased. She ended her letter – headed "London", without further address – "Dr. Aveling sends kind messages to you and Lafargue",[19] thus indicating that, on Paul's attendance at Marx's burial and Laura's visit in July, the parties

---

* One is consequently less stunned to find Emma Cons – who founded the Old Vic as a popular Shakespearean theatre on the Surrey Side in the belief that the people of that deprived neighbourhood needed entertainment as much as sanitation – nailed by Miss Potter as "not a lady by birth".[18]

had met, and also that Engels was mistaken in saying to Laura in a letter of the same date that he believed Eleanor to be "out of town".[20]

By October Engels, who knew that he alone could decide on the importance or unimportance of Marx's mass of papers and that Eleanor, with her many undertakings must leave these decisions to him, was far from well. He suffered from rheumatism in the legs and was forced to keep to his bed for eight weeks. While he was laid up Karl Kautsky* came to visit him on his birthday – 28 November – where he met Eleanor again and Aveling for the first time. With Bernstein, Kautsky was later to become Engels' "eyes" in learning to decipher Marx's hand-writing and one of the presumptive heirs to the literary remains of both Marx and Engels on the latter's death.† On this occasion he stayed only briefly in England and, on 4 December, Eleanor dropped him a note at Wedde's Hotel in Greek Street, Soho, to say "... if you have the time, and could come to 13 Newman Street, Oxford Street, at about 11 o'clock, you could meet me there. I am working there with Dr. Aveling."

This relationship, not openly announced as yet, was now obvious enough to make Mrs. Besant scream aloud. In the pages of the *National Reformer*, to which Aveling was still contributing, she attacked an article in *Progress* saying "I do not know who Mr. 'Paul Lafargue' may be"[21] and, on 23 December, vigorously protested at some "gross and scandalous libel on Dr. Edward Aveling" invented by "a Miss Eleanor Marx". The whole matter, except for her uncontrollable rage, is wrapped in mystery. Mrs. Besant, who did not choose to enter into any details, accused this Miss Marx of "hoping ... to cause a break and to hinder and impede the Freethought cause by introducing discord and quarrel among co-workers in the ranks". She warned all London Freethinkers against "any statements made in my name by Miss Eleanor Marx or by any of her friends".[22]

Thus Miss Potter is once again and this time doubly confuted: Eleanor, who is certainly not editing *Progress*, is neither "much connected with the Bradlaugh set" except by hostility, and she no longer, save to keep up appearances, "lives alone".

The facts widely known about Eleanor Marx are that she lived with a man of evil reputation who married someone else and that she killed herself. Of this the stuff of theatre is made: a neurotic woman, a villain, an unhallowed union, betrayal, suicide and, hey presto! the Marx-Aveling

---

* 1854–1938. Writer and journalist, Kautsky was the editor of *Die Neue Zeit*, the theoretical organ of the German Social Democratic Party, from 1883 to 1917. Until 1890 it was a monthly paper and thereafter, until 1923, a weekly. He had been in London from mid-March until early July 1881, when he met the Marxes, including Eleanor, the Lafargues and Engels, of whose household Pumps was then in charge. In 1882 he became engaged to Louise Strasser but, though married at the time, came alone for his brief visit to London at the end of 1883.
† He lost the heritage to Bebel.

melodrama is produced: the Emma Bovary of Sydenham (minus the style). The sub-plot concerns the awful fate and actuarial risks attendant upon being one of Karl Marx's daughters. Laura's death by her own hand in 1911 has been telescoped in time – even made to precede that of Eleanor – in many a vivid account, while there are those who will have it that Jenny participated in this riot of self-destruction.

Eleanor's union with Aveling may have been, was, disastrous in the long run; his character may have been, was, deplorable. Nonetheless, from the time her life was joined with his, it became purposeful. She does not doubt where she is going, she goes. Her manner, unassuming and frank as always, now takes on authority. She has lost none of her humour or humanity – on the contrary, these qualities deepen – but she is a woman complete: responsible, fearless and supremely capable of using her gifts to the full in the service of her fellowmen.

REFERENCE NOTES

Abbreviations

Bottigelli Archives Letters in the custody of Dr. Emile Bottigelli, Paris.
ELC *Frederick Engels Paul and Laura Lafargue: Correspondence*, Volumes I-III. Lawrence & Wishart, 1959–1963.
IISH International Institute of Social History, Amsterdam.
MEW *Marx Engels Werke*. Dietz Verlag, Berlin. 1956–1968. Unless otherwise stated Volumes 27–39.
MIML Institute of Marxism-Leninism, Moscow.

(1)   *Progress*. May 1883.
(2)   *Ibid*. June 1883.
(3)   25 March 1883. ELC, Vol. I.
(4)   22 May 1883. *Ibid*.
(5)   Engels to Bebel, 30 August 1883. MEW.
(6)   Eleanor to Kautsky, 15 March 1898. IISH.
(7)   Eleanor to Laura, 12 November 1896. IISH.
(8)   Eleanor to Laura, 26 March 1883. Bottigelli Archives.
(9)   In Nos. 19 and 20 published on 3 and 21 May 1883.
(10) 2 June 1883. ELC, Vol. I.
(11) 20 June 1883. *Ibid*.
(12) 10 March 1883. *Ibid*.
(13) 24 June 1883. Original in English, MIML. (German MEW.)
(14) *Le Droit à la Paresse* appeared first in *L'Egalité* in 1880 and was reprinted as a pamphlet, with an introduction written in Sainte-Pélagie prison, in 1883. The first English edition was translated and published by Charles H. Kerr in Chicago (n.d.)
(15) Eleanor to Laura, 27 April 1883. Bottigelli Archives.
(16) Engels to Laura, 2 June 1883. ELC, Vol. I.
(17) MS. Diary. By courtesy of the British Library of Political and Economic Science. I

have to thank Mr. Malcolm Muggeridge for drawing my attention to this passage in the manuscript diaries.

(18) Beatrice Webb. Quoted from her diary of 12 August 1885 in *My Apprenticeship*. Vol. II. Pelican Books 1938.

(19) 19 September 1883. Bottigelli Archives.

(20) 19 September 1883. ELC, Vol. I.

(21) *The National Reformer*. 2 December 1883.

(22) *Ibid*. 23 December 1883.

· AUTHOR'S POSTSCRIPT ·

Those who have read thus far will have noted that in the course of this book I have frequently taken refuge in such phrases as "nothing has been traced" and "the reason is obscure".

They do not mean that the matter is untraceable or need remain forever in the dark. They should be regarded not only as admissions of pure ignorance but also as so much bait laid to catch younger and more diligent researchers.

Some of these points may not be worth bothering about – though it has galled me not to bring them to light – but the seeds of this book were curiosity, aroused by tantalising glimpses of Eleanor Marx as she flitted in and out of other people's reminiscences and letters. Should it also bear the fruit of curiosity, it will have served a useful purpose.

Y.K.

· SELECT BIBLIOGRAPHY ·

Adler, Victor. *Briefwechsel mit August Bebel und Karl Kautsky*. (edited Friedrich Adler). Verlag der Wiener Volksbuchhandlung, Vienna, 1954.

Allingham, William. *A Diary*. (edited H. Allingham and D. Radford). Macmillan, 1907.

Anderson, Louisa. *Elizabeth Garrett Anderson*. Faber & Faber, 1939.

Andréas, Bert. *Briefe und Dokumente der Familie Marx aus den Jahren 1862–1873. Archiv für Sozialgeschichte*, II. Band. Verlag für Literatur und Zeitgeschehen. Hanover, 1962.

Ashley, Maurice. *Oliver Cromwell and the Puritan Revolution*. English Universities Press, 1958.

Aveling, Agnes Sarah ("A.S.A."). *Memories of Kingsland*. Published in Aid of Church Renovation Fund, 1887.

Aveling, Thomas William Baxter. *Memories of the Clayton Family*. Jackson, Walford & Hodder, 1867.

Bartel, Horst and others. *August Bebel. Eine Biographie*. Dietz Verlag, Berlin, 1963.

Bax, Ernest Belfort. *Reminiscences and Reflections of a Mid and Late Victorian*. Allen & Unwin, 1918.

Bebel, August. *My Life*. T. Fisher Unwin, 1912. *Briefwechsel mit Friedrich Engels*. (edited Werner Blumenberg). Mouton & Co., The Hague, 1965.

Beer, Max. *A History of British Socialism*, Volume II. G. Bell & Sons, 1920.

Bernal, J. D. *Science in History*. Watts & Co., 1954.

Bernstein, Eduard. *My Years of Exile*. (trans. B. Miall). L. Parsons, 1921.

Bertall. *The Communists of Paris 1871*. Popular English edition Buckingham & Co., Paris and London. J. M. O'Toole & Son, Dublin, 1873. (From the French edition published by Edouard Blot et fils ainé).

Besant, Annie. *An Autobiography*. T. Fisher Unwin, 1893.

Blumenberg, Werner. *Karl Marx in Selbstzeugnissen und Bilddokumenten*. Rowohlt, Hamburg, 1962.

Booth, Charles and others. *Labour and Life of the People*. Volumes 1 and 2, Williams & Norgate, 1889 and 1891. *Life and Labour of the People in London*. Volume 9. Macmillan, 1897.

Bottigelli, Emile. *Lettres et Documents de Karl Marx 1856–1883*. Annali dell'Istituto Giangiacomo Feltrinelli, Anno Primo, Milan, 1958.

La Rupture Marx-Hyndman. Annali dell'Istituto Giangiacomo Feltrinelli, Anno Terzo, Milan, 1960.

Bowley, Arthur L. *Wages in the United Kingdom in the 19th Century*. C.U.P., 1900.

Bradlaugh, Charles. *Speeches*. Freethought Publishing Co., 1890.

Briggs, Asa and Saville, John (editors). *Essays in Labour History*. 2nd edition. Macmillan, 1967.

Brown, E. H. Phelps with Browne, Margaret H. *A Century of Pay*. Macmillan, 1968.

Bruhat, Jean, Dautry, Jean and Tersen, Emile (editors). *La Commune de 1871*. 2nd edition. Editions Sociales, Paris, 1970.

Buchanan-Gould, Vera. *Not Without Honour*. Hutchinson, 1953.

Bunel, Victor (editor and publisher). *Réimpression du Journal Officiel de la République Française sous la Commune du 18 mars au 24 mai 1871*. Paris, 1872.

Burton, Hester. *Barbara Bodichon*. John Murray, 1949.

Cole, G. D. H. and M. I. *The Condition of Britain*. Gollancz, 1937.

Cole, G. D. H. *A Short History of the British Working-Class Movement 1789–1947*. Allen & Unwin, 1948.

Collison, William. *The Apostle of Free Labour*. Hurst & Blackett, 1913.

Craig, E. G. *Index to the Story of My Days 1872–1907*. Hulton, 1957.

Cronwright-Schreiner, S. C. *Olive Schreiner*. T. Fisher Unwin, 1924.

Darwin, Charles. *Autobiography*. (edited Nora Barlow). Collins, 1958.

Documents of the First International. Volumes I–V. (edited Lydia Belyakova). Lawrence & Wishart, 1963–1968.

Dornemann, Luise. *Jenny Marx*. Dietz Verlag, Berlin, 1968.

Durkheim, Emile. *Le Suicide*. Félix Alcan, Paris, 1897.

Dutt, R. P. *The Internationale*. Lawrence & Wishart, 1964.

Ellis, Havelock. *My Life*. Heinemann, 1940.

Engels, Frederick (see also under Marx).

Anti-Dühring. Lawrence & Wishart, 1934.

Friedrich Engels' Briefwechsel mit Karl Kautsky. (edited Benedikt Kautsky). IISH. Danubia-Verlag, Wilhelm Braumüller und Sohn, Vienna, 1955.

The British Labour Movement. (*Labour Standard* articles May–August 1881). Martin Lawrence, 1934.

The Condition of the Working-Class in England in 1844. With 1892 Preface. (trans. Florence Kelley Wischnewetzky). Allen & Unwin, 1936.

Friedrich Engels Paul et Laura Lafargue; Correspondance. Textes recueillis, annotés et présentés par Emile Bottigelli. 3 Tomes. Editions sociales, Paris, 1956–1959.

Frederick Engels Paul and Laura Lafargue: Correspondence. Vol. I–III. (trans. Y. Kapp). Lawrence & Wishart, 1959– 1963.

Introduction to "Class Struggles in France 1858–1850". (1895), *Karl Marx: Selected Works*, Volume II. Lawrence & Wishart, 1942.

History of Ireland (to 1014). (trans. Angela Clifford). Irish Communist Organisation, London. 2nd edition. 1970.

Foner, Philip S. *History of the Labor Movement of the United States* Volume 2. International Publishers, New York, 1955.

Fremantle, Anne. *This Little Band of Prophets.* Allen & Unwin, 1960.

Froude, Henry and others. *Frederick James Furnivall.* O.U.P., 1911.

Frow, Edmund and Katanka, Michael. *1868 Year of the Unions.* Michael Katanka (Books) Ltd., 1968.

Gemkow, Heinrich, and others. *Karl Marx. Eine Biographie.* Dietz Verlag, Berlin, 1967.

Gillespie, Frances Elma. *Labor and Politics in England 1850–1867.* Duke University Press, North Carolina, 1927.

Glynn, Anthony. *High upon the Gallows Tree.* Anvil Books Ltd., Tralee, Co. Kerry, 1967.

Gollin, R. M. *Beerbohm, Wilde, Shaw and Edward Rose.* N.Y. Public Library, 1964.

Harrison, Royden. *Before the Socialists. Studies in Labour and Politics 1861– 1881.* Routledge & Kegan Paul, 1965.

Herzen, Alexander. *My Past and Thoughts.* Volumes I–VI. (trans. Constance Garnett). Chatto & Windus, 1924–7.

Hill, C. and Dell, E. *The Good Old Cause.* Lawrence & Wishart, 1949.

The History of the TUC 1868–1968. (edited Lionel Birch). General Council TUC, 1968.

Hobsbawm, Eric. *Labouring Men.* Weidenfeld & Nicolson, 1964.

Horne, Alistair. *The Fall of Paris.* St. Martin's Press, New York, 1966.

Hutt, G. A. *British Trade Unionism.* (Revised edition). Lawrence & Wishart, 1962.

Hyndman, H. M. *The Record of an Adventurous Life.* Macmillan, 1911. *Further Reminiscences.* Macmillan, 1912.

Jackson, T. A. *Ireland Her Own.* Cobbett Press, 1946.

Jellinek, Frank. *The Paris Commune of 1871.* Gollancz, 1937.

Jenkins, Mick. *Frederick Engels in Manchester.* Lancashire and Cheshire Communist Party, 1951.

Kamm, Josephine. *Hope Deferred: Girls' Education in English History.* Methuen, 1965.

Kisch, Egon Erwin. *Karl Marx in Karlsbad.* Aufbau Verlag, Berlin, 1953.

Kuczynski, Jürgen. *A Short History of Labour Conditions under Industrial Capitalism. Volume I Part I. Great Britain 1750 to the Present Day.* Frederick Muller, 1947.

Lawrence, D. H. *The Collected Letters.* Volume I (edited H. T. Moore). Heinemann, 1962.

Lewis, R. A. *Edwin Chadwick and the Public Health Movement 1832–1854.* Longman, Green & Co., 1952.

Liebknecht, Wilhelm. *Briefwechsel mit Karl Marx und Friedrich Engels.* (edited Georg Eckert). Mouton & Co., The Hague, 1963.

    Karl Marx: Biographical Memoirs. (trans. E. Untermann). H. Kerr & Co. 1901 and *Karl Marx: Selected Works* Volume I (edited C.P. Dutt). Lawrence & Wishart, 1942.

    Karl Marx zum Gedächtnis. Nuremberg, 1896.

Lilley, S. *Men, Machines and History.* Cobbett Press, 1948.

Lissagaray. *Histoire de la Commune.* (précédée par Amédée Dunois). Libraire du Travail, Paris 1929.

    History of the Commune of 1871. (trans. Eleanor Marx Aveling). Reeves & Turner, 1886.

Lozovsky, A. *Marx and the Trade Unions.* Martin Lawrence, 1935.

Mackenzie, Compton. *My Life and Times. Octave 7 1931–1938.* Chatto & Windus, 1968.

Mann, Tom. *Tom Mann's Memoirs.* (First published 1923 by The Labour Publishing Co. Ltd.). MacGibbon & Kee Ltd., 1967.

Marek, K. *Philosophy of World Revolution.* (trans. D. Simon). Lawrence & Wishart, 1969.

Marshall, Calder A. *Havelock Ellis.* Rupert Hart-Davis, 1959.

Marx, Karl. *The Civil War in France.* (1891 preface by Frederick Engels). Martin Lawrence, 1933.

    The Eastern Question. (edited Eleanor Marx Aveling and Edward Aveling). Swan Sonnenschein & Co., 1897.

    The 18th Brumaire of Louis Bonaparte. (trans. Eden and Cedar Paul). Allen & Unwin, 1926.

    On the Jewish Question in *Early Writings* (trans. T. B. Bottomore). Watts & Co., 1963.

Marx, Karl and Engels, Friedrich. *Marx Engels Werke.* Dietz Verlag, Berlin, 1956–68.

    Correspondence of Marx and Engels. (trans. and edited Dona Torr). Martin Lawrence, 1934.

    Selected Correspondence (trans. I. Lasker, edited S. Ryazanskaya). Lawrence & Wishart, 1965.

Mayer, Gustav. *Friedrich Engels.* Chapman & Hall, 1936.

Mayer, Paul. *Die Geschichte des sozialdemokratischen Parteiarchivs und das*

Schicksal des Marx-Engels-Nachlasses. Archiv für Sozialgeschichte. VI./ VII. Band 1966–1967. Verlag für Literatur und Zeitgeschehen, Hanover.

Mayhew, Henry. *London Labour and the London Poor.* Volumes I–III. Charles Griffin & Co. (n.d. probably 1861).

London Labour and the London Poor. Volume IV. Griffin, Bohn & Co., 1862.

Mearns, Andrew. *The Bitter Cry of Outcast London: An Inquiry into the Condition of the Abject Poor.* (edited Anthony S. Wohl). Leicester University Press, 1970. (First edition James Clarke, October 1883).

Mehring, Franz. *Karl Marx.* (trans. Edward Fitzgerald). John Lane, 1936.

Mohr und General. Dietz Verlag, Berlin, 1964.

Moody, T. W. and Martin, F. X. *The Course of Irish History.* The Mercier Press, Cork, 1967.

Morton, A. L. *A People's History of England.* Gollancz, 1938.

Nethercot, Arthur H. *The First Five Lives of Annie Besant.* Rupert Hart-Davis, 1961.

Nicolaievsky, Boris and Maenchen-Helfen, Otto. *Karl Marx Man and Fighter.* (trans. G. David and E. Mosbachér). Methuen, 1936.

"Orme, Michael". *J. T. Grein.* John Murray, 1936.

Payne, Ernest E. *The Free Churches: their History and Witness* (in *Who's Who in the Free Churches*, edited L. G. Pine). Shaw Publishing Co., 1951.

Pearson, Hesketh. *Bernard Shaw, His Life and Personality.* (first complete edition). Methuen, 1961.

Ramelson, Marian. *The Petticoat Rebellion.* Lawrence & Wishart, 1967.

Registrar General's Statistical Review of England and Wales for the Year 1937. H.M.S.O, 1940.

Reminiscences of Marx and Engels. Foreign Languages Publishing House, Moscow (n.d., probably 1956).

Robins, Elizabeth. *Both Sides of the Curtain.* Heinemann, 1940.

Rose, Paul. *The Manchester Martyrs.* Lawrence & Wishart, 1970.

Rossa, Jeremiah O'Donovan. *My Years in English Jails.* (edited Sean Ua Caernaigh). Anvil Books, 1967. (First published 1874 in USA).

Rothstein, Andrew. *A House on Clerkenwell Green.* Lawrence & Wishart, 1966.

Rothstein, Theodore. *From Chartism to Labour.* Martin Lawrence, 1929.

Royal Commission on Population Report. Cmd. 7695, 1949.

Salt, Henry S. *Seventy Years Among Savages.* Allen & Unwin, 1921.

Schreiner, Olive. *Letters 1876–1920.* (edited S. C. Cronwright-Schreiner). T. Fisher Unwin, 1924.

Shaw, G. B. *Collected Letters 1874–1897.* (edited Dan H. Laurence). Max Reinhardt, 1965.

The Perfect Wagnerite. Constable, 1898.

The Quintessence of Ibsenism. Constable, 1913.

Sixteen Self Sketches. Constable, 1949.

Simon, Brian. *Studies in the History of Education 1780–1870*. Lawrence & Wishart, 1960.

Education and the Labour Movement 1870–1918. Lawrence & Wishart, 1965.

Smith, Warren Sylvester. *The London Heretics 1870–1914*. Constable, 1967.

Summerson, John. *Georgian London*. Pleiades Books, 1945.

Survey of London: Volumes 33 and 34. *The Parish of St. Anne, Soho*. (edited F. H. W. Sheppard). The Athlone Press, University of London. Published for the Greater London Council, 1966.

Thompson, E. P. *William Morris*. Lawrence & Wishart, 1955.

The Making of the English Working Class. Penguin Books 1968.

Thorn, George Ernest. *The Story of Kingsland Congregational Church 1789–1936*. Independent Press Ltd., 1936.

Thorne, Will. *My Life's Battles*. George Newnes Ltd. (n.d., probably 1925).

Tillett, Ben. *Memories and Reflections*. John Long Ltd., 1931.

Torr, Dona. *Tom Mann and His Times*. Lawrence & Wishart, 1956.

Tsuzuki, Chushichi. *H. M. Hyndman and British Socialism*. (edited Henry Pelling). O.U.P., 1961.

The Life of Eleanor Marx 1855–1898. Clarendon Press, 1967.

Webb, Beatrice. *My Apprenticeship*. Longman, Green & Co., 1950.

Webb, Sidney and Beatrice. *The History of Trade Unionism 1666–1920*. Printed by the Authors for the Trade Unionists of the United Kingdom, Christmas 1919.

Williams, Gertrude M. *The Passionate Pilgrim*. John Hamilton, 1931.

Winsten, Stephen. *Salt and His Circle*. Hutchinson, 1951.

Woodham-Smith, Cecil. *The Great Hunger*. Hamish Hamilton, 1962.

Worobjowa, O. and Sinelnikova, I. *Die Töchter von Marx*. (trans. Waldemar Dölle). Dietz Verlag, Berlin, 1963.

· APPENDICES ·

APPENDIX I

FREDERICK DEMUTH

Helene Demuth's son, Henry Frederick Demuth, was born on 23 June 1851 at 28 Dean Street in the parish of St. Anne, Soho. There can be no reasonable doubt that he was Marx's son. Engels, however, did not contradict the assumption that he was the father until he lay dying, when he charged his friends to make the truth known if – but not unless – he were to be posthumously defamed for behaving badly to a natural son.

Nothing certain is known of Frederick's childhood and youth, though from his manner of writing – its phrasing and spelling, no less than its simple directness, suggesting that it was much as he must have spoken – it is a fair inference that he was brought up in a London working-class environment and received a limited education.

That he was given into foster care shortly after birth is not surprising. Mrs. Marx's own child, born three months before Freddy, was also put out to nurse for a few months because "the poor little thing" could not be reared at home under the prevailing conditions. Two vivid descriptions of that overcrowded interior at 28 Dean Street have come down to us.

The first relates to Easter 1852, when the year-old Franziska had severe bronchitis. Mrs. Marx records in her reminiscences: "For three days the poor child wrestled with death. She suffered terribly. When she died we left her little body lying in the small back room; all of us went into the front room together and when night came we lay down on the floor, the three living children beside us. . . .". Eleanor, who drew on this passage of her mother's notes for the preface to *Revolution and Counter-Revolution* adds: "In that 'front room' in Dean Street, the children playing about him, Marx worked. I have heard tell how the children would pile up chairs behind him to represent a coach, to which he was harnessed as horse and would 'whip him up' even as he sat at his desk writing."

The second description was written by a Prussian police spy reporting to his masters in 1853: ". . . He [Marx] lives in one of the worst and therefore one of the cheapest quarters in London. He occupies two rooms;

the one looking out on the street is the living room and the bedroom is at the back. There is not a single clean or solid piece of furniture to be seen in the whole place ... in the centre of the living room there is a large old-fashioned table covered with oilcloth on which lie manuscripts, books and newspapers along with children's toys, bits of his wife's sewing things, a few teacups with chipped rims, dirty spoons, knives, forks, candlesticks, an inkpot, tumblers, clay pipes, tobacco ash − in short, everything jumbled together on the same table; a second-hand dealer would shudder at this hotch-potch. ... Sitting down is quite a dangerous affair: here is a chair with but three legs; there another, which by chance is still intact where the children are playing at being cooks. Courteously this is offered to the guest, but the children's cooking is not removed and you sit down at the risk of ruining your trousers. None of this occasions Marx or his wife the slightest embarrassment. You are received in the most friendly manner, cordially offered pipes, tobacco or whatever else is available. In any case the clever, agreeable talk compensates to some extent for the domestic shortcomings and makes the discomfort endurable ..."* The police report mentions the three "really handsome children",† one of whom, the only boy, was to die two years later.

It may well be asked why Marx, longing for a son, did not claim Freddy, who survived to grow up as a total stranger. Since economic considerations did not hinder further legitimate additions to the family it must be conjectured that Mrs. Marx never knew that Freddy was her husband's child.

Existing records show that, as an adult, he was known as Frederick Lewis Demuth, having dropped the name Henry, which is on his birth certificate, and probably incorporated that of his foster-parents. He served an engineering apprenticeship and joined the King's Cross Branch of the Amalgamated Society of Engineers as a skilled fitter in February 1888. He was by then a married man of nearly 37, but both in the Union Report of his Branch and in all subsequent documents he appears as almost two years younger than his true age, which suggests that he was under a misapprehension about his year of birth. Possibly a mild deception had been practised upon him to fit in with the ages of his foster-siblings.

Freddy's life was not a happy one. He was devoted to his son, Harry, but he was a lonely man, dogged by misfortune.

---

* *Akten des kgl. Polizeipräsidiums zu Berlin, betreffend die neuerdings bemerkbar werdenden Bestrebungen der Kommunisten 1853.* (Pr. Br. Rep 30, Berlin C. Pol. Präs. Tit. 94, Geheime Präsidial-Registratur Lit. C. Nr. 286.) Cited by Gustav Mayer in *Neue Beitrage zur Biographie von Karl Marx in Archiv für die Geschichte des Sozialismus und der Arbeiterbewegung* 10 Jg., Hirschfeld, Leipzig, 1922.
† Jenny, Laura and Edgar.

It is not known when Eleanor formed her close friendship with him nor when the other members of the family came to know him. As Helene Demuth's son, whatever his paternity, he would have been a person to cherish as soon as that identity was known. In May 1882 Jenny wrote to Laura: "You cannot imagine what it is to me to think that I still owe poor Freddy his money, and that it is probably my insolvency which prevents our dear Nim* from carrying out her projects of going to Germany."† It is unlikely, however, that much was seen of Freddy in Marx's lifetime, but he is said to have visited his mother regularly after 1883 when she became Engels' housekeeper until she died in 1890, by which time Eleanor evidently knew and liked Freddy well. Clearly under the impression that she was speaking of Engels' son, she wrote to Laura a few weeks after Helene Demuth's death: "Freddy has behaved admirably in all respects and Engels' irritation against him is as unfair as it is comprehensible. We should none of us like to meet our pasts, I guess, in flesh and blood. I know I always meet Freddy with a sense of guilt and wrong done. The life of that man! To hear him tell of it all is a misery and shame to me."‡

Engels, Eleanor and Aveling had witnessed the will drawn up on the day Helene Demuth died by which she left everything she had to "Frederick Lewis Demuth of 25 Gransden Avenue, London Lane, Hackney". Ten days after she had made her mark upon this will – "being too weak bodily to sign my name" – her "monies, effects and other property" were granted to him. The amount in all was £95.

Some eighteen months later it emerged that not only Eleanor but Laura and their brother-in-law Charles Longuet had accepted some financial responsibility for Freddy, though naturally it was Eleanor, as the only one in England, who was in direct touch with him and knew what was going on. "The facts are these," she wrote in July 1892 to Laura who had sent 50 francs, which she could ill afford but had been unable to get from Longuet since he never answered letters, "Freddy's wife some time ago ran away taking with her not only most of Freddy's own things and money, but worst of all, £29 placed in his keeping by his fellow-workmen. This money belongs to a small benefit fund of theirs – and on Saturday he has to account for the money. You will understand now why this is such a bad business. ... It may be that I am very 'sentimental' – but I can't help feeling that Freddy has had great injustice all through his life. Is it not

---

* Marx's grandchildren called Helene Demuth Nim, Nym or Nimmy, nicknames adopted by the whole family.
† 17 May 1882. IISH.
‡ Eleanor to Laura, 19 December 1890. Bottigelli Archives.

wonderful when you come to look things squarely in the face, how rarely we seem to practise all the fine things we preach – to others?..."*

In writing these censorious passages Eleanor plainly did not know to whom they should have been applied. When she did, the shock was fearful. Not until a few days before Engels' death in August 1895 was she confronted with the truth of Freddy's paternity. According to Louise Freyberger† she refused to accept the statement when Sam Moore,‡ in whose presence it had been made, immediately went to see her. She is reported to have said it was a lie and insisted upon hearing it from Engels himself. She visited him the day before he died when, with cancer of the oesophagus, he was no longer able to speak and he wrote down the words for her on a slate.

At the time of this disclosure Eleanor had been living for some eleven years with a man to whom she was not married and it is unlikely that her prudery was outraged. But for most of those years – and possibly even longer – Freddy's sad life had induced in her feelings of misery, guilt and shame whenever she met him. If she broke down and wept, as she is said to have done, it was not because Marx had begotten an illegitimate son but because he had been unkind. That Freddy's wrongs must be laid at her father's door lacerated her heart.

Engels made no provision for Freddy, but the Marx heirs – Eleanor, Laura and Jenny's widower as the trustee for her children – arranged to give him regular support, though the lawyer§ was under the impression that these remittances were a loan to Charles Longuet.

How long this arrangement lasted is not known but, though Eleanor left nothing to Freddy in her own will, her affection for and trust in him grew with the years until he became the only person in whom she confided during the last months of her life. To no one else, neither to her oldest friend, Wilhelm Liebknecht, nor to Karl Kautsky, who had become very close to her, and to both of whom she wrote only a few days before her end, did she reveal anything of her agonies of personal unhappiness.

After her death, Freddy remained in touch with her friends and relatives; his own situation, and something of his character, may be discerned from two letters which he wrote many years later. The first of these, to Laura, written on 7 October 1910 from 54 Reighton Road, Upper Clapton, Stoke Newington, says that he is fortunately in work and now

---

* Eleanor to Laura, 26 July 1892. Bottigelli Archives.
† 1860–1950, née Strasser, married Karl Kautsky 1883, divorced 1889, married Dr. Ludwig Freyberger 1894. Was Engels' housekeeper from December 1890 until his death in August 1895.
‡ See above, fn.*, p. 81.
§ Arthur Willson Crosse.

more pleasantly lodged than formerly, being with a congenial workmate and his wife. His main concern is his son Harry, then working night shifts at a French taxicab company, which Freddy calls "Namier Renaud". The hours were 8 p.m. till 6 a.m., six nights a week, for which he earned 22s., but, a married man with a family, Harry was glad of the work. "His wife and little ones," Freddy writes, "are well although I am sorry to say there has been another little girl born. To me it seems very sad, seeing they have had so much trouble in their young lives, to bring more children into the world appears to one only short of a crime. But I suppose it will go on till the time comes when the birth of children will be hailed with joy instead of sadness. ..." In the same letter he asks whether Laura knows if his mother had any relatives in the engineering trade as he has come across the name Demuth, a Union member "of Austria". His reason for making the enquiry is that, if this were some connection, "they might have a place in England and through them I might be able to get my son a better and more remunerative employment. ... You will realize he and his are the only Beings I have in the world who I can call mine and although I do not see them very often it gives me great Pleasure to help in any way I can do." He ends his letter: "Dear Laura, affectionately your, F. Demuth".*

The following year Laura committed suicide and another friend was lost. But in 1912 Freddy wrote to Bernstein, whom he thanks for great kindness to his son, then recently emigrated to Australia, leaving behind his wife and, by this time, four small children. On arriving in Adelaide Harry was not met by the people who had written to say there was plenty of work to be had and he proceeded to Custon where they lived, only to find there were no openings at all. He then went further up country, prepared to take on anything. Freddy had promised to send out his wife and the children as soon as Harry was settled. "The one great consolation I have," he wrote to Bernstein, "is in knowing that they will not be materially worse off than when he was at home. I am very thankful that I am able to see after them ... at any rate I feel I have done the right thing in sending him to the place he had set his mind on going to, and if things do not turn out as well for him and his family that we all hope for I do not think he can blame me as I have done everything for him that laid in my power."† Harry did not succeed in Australia and came back to England.

In the meantime Freddy himself had become a toolmaker, but no direct documentary evidence of his life during the next 14 years has come to light. He was over 63 when the First World War broke out and he remained at work for another decade when, as a member of the Hackney

---

* 10 October 1910. IISH.
† 29 August 1912. IISH.

Branch of the AEU,* he drew superannuation for the remainder of his life. In his late years he lived at 7 Reighton Road, Upper Clapton, with a Mrs. Laura Payne† who moved with him to his last home at 13 Stoke Newington Common in North Hackney. She was present when he died of cardiac failure on 28 January 1929 at nearly 78 years of age,‡ drew the £12 funeral benefit from the Union and inherited a quarter of his estate.

This gentle, unassuming man has left two puzzles behind: his loving concern for his son and devotion to "the only Beings I have in the world who I can call mine" are strangely disavowed in his last Will and testament, drawn up on 26 July 1926, where the remainder of his personal estate and effects are bequeathed to "Mr. Harry Demuth my nephew known as my son." The second mystery is how an engineering worker drawing superannuation pay of 9s. a week§ could leave, in 1929, the sum of £1,971 12s. 4d. There may be a connection between the two facts. If so, it signifies that these descendants of Karl Marx wished to be left in decent peace and obscurity.

*　　*　　*

That such a wish should be disregarded was inevitable and in recent times there have been many efforts to bring the full Freddy Demuth story to light, some in the interests of truth, others for different reasons. The toilers in this field owe their thanks first and foremost to Louise Freyberger.

In a letter to August Bebel written on 2 and 4 September 1898 she recounted Engels' death-bed statement to herself, her husband and Sam Moore concerning Frederick Demuth's parentage. It is a most extraordinary letter,‖ which, throwing all caution to the winds, forfeits credence on many points. In a vein of high fantasy, Louise Freyberger

---

* By the amalgamation of nine smaller unions with the ASE it became the Amalgamated Engineering Union (AEU) in July 1920. In 1970 with further amalgamations the name was changed to the Amalgamated Union of Engineering Workers (AUEW).

† The widow of Alfred Payne, one of Freddy's friends and a co-founder of the Hackney Labour Party who was the Mayor of Hackney for the years 1919–1920 (an annual office in which he was succeeded by Herbert Morrison). Upon her husband's death Mrs. Payne is thought to have moved in with Freddy as his companion and housekeeper.

‡ The death certificate gives his age as 76, as do the AEU records.

§ Superannuation pay at that date was 8s. a week after 30 years membership, 9s. after 35 years, 10s. after 40 years. Photostats of Branch Records kindly supplied by Mr. George Aitken, formerly Research Officer of the AEU, other information by the present Research Department of the AUEW.

‖ Published, though not in full, in *Karl Marx* by Werner Blumenberg. (Rowohlt, Hamburg, 1962). Grateful acknowledgment is made to Mr. Bert Andréas for providing the passages omitted from that text and to the IISH Amsterdam for permission to see a transcript of the complete letter in the original German.

elaborated the theme of the relationship between Marx and his wife at the time and as a consequence of the Demuth episode. Eleanor, she claimed, was fully apprised of this situation: she "knew very well" that for many years her parents did not sleep together "but it did not suit her to recognise the true reason for it; she idolised her father and concocted the most beautiful myths". Now one thing that Eleanor cannot have known very well, or at all, was the course of her parents' sexual life – unless, of course, they recounted it to her – in the years before her own birth in 1855: itself an event never ascribed to immaculate conception. By the time she had reached an age to make her own observations, they will not have shed much light upon the circumstances surrounding Frederick Demuth's advent in 1851. Further, while Louise Freyberger at the time of writing may not have been conversant with conditions in the Dean Street lodgings of 45 years earlier, where the Marxes lived for seven months before and five-and-half years after Freddy's birth, they were not such as to afford the luxury of separate bedrooms for the parents and, indeed, the painful lack of privacy was the worst feature of family life there. Another matter that Eleanor was said to know perfectly well was that her mother had once deserted her father in London and gone to Germany and that, for Marx, "the fear of a divorce from his wife, who was dreadfully jealous, was ever present".

To be sure, at the end of 1850 Mrs. Marx was distraught owing to the death of her little son Guido. It is equally true that in March 1851, following the birth of the next, her fifth, child she was depressed and not made happier, one may suppose, by her husband's openly expressed disappointment that she had been delivered of a girl.

Marx reported all this to Engels in detail as, in later years, he confessed his lack of patience with his wife's tears and reproaches which bothered him, though he could not find it in his heart to blame her as the money worries piled up. But there is no evidence whatsoever, either before or after Freddy's birth, that the threat of separation, desertion or divorce was in the air. Had it been "ever present" it could not but have received some mention in the letters that passed between Marx and Engels which, however winnowed in after years to eliminate private disclosures, are not without exceedingly frank accounts of Marx's domestic situation and troubles with his wife at all times.

Apart from a brief visit to Marx's uncle in Holland in August 1850, when she herself was pregnant but Frederick Demuth not yet conceived, Mrs. Marx never left her husband in London nor went abroad at all until, in July and August 1854, with Eleanor on the way, she stayed at her old home in Trier on her doctor's orders. That her mother again went to Germany in 1856 Eleanor naturally knew since she herself, aged 18 months, was of the travelling party; but as, shortly after her return to England, Mrs. Marx became pregnant with the child who was born and died in July 1857, the most precocious knowledge on Eleanor's part could have suggested only that her parents' marital relations were fairly normal. It is true that no further children were born, but Mrs. Marx was now 43 years of age and it would be a cause for wonderment if, eight years and two pregnancies after the event, Frederick Demuth's birth should have been the explanation for any abstinence. How, then, was Eleanor to know the "true reason" for all this sleeping apart and wanton desertion had she chosen to do so but for blind idolatry of her father?

The most dubious of all Louise Freyberger's claims is that she had seen the letter Marx had written to Engels in Manchester "at the time". She added, unwisely, that she believed Engels had since destroyed this letter. In the first place, there was no earthly reason why Marx should have written at all: Engels was living in London throughout the whole of 1850 until mid-November. He was there for Christmas, when Helene Demuth was four months pregnant and the fact could hardly be hidden or ignored. At the beginning of March 1851 Marx wrote to Engels to say that he must see him, that letters "confuse, delay and get one nowhere" and Engels accordingly came to London early that month when, in view of Mrs. Marx's approaching confinement, two extra rooms had been temporarily rented in the house where Engels was invited to stay. Marx visited him in Manchester in April for a few days and Engels was in London again from 8 to 14 June that year, when Frederick's birth was imminent, if not overdue. Thus there were no fewer than five occasions during the relevant period with ample opportunity for the two men to discuss the matter and decide upon what was to be done and what was to be said without either of them writing a line to each other about it. In the second place, if Engels ever received a letter on the subject it would have been most irrational of him to keep it for some forty-odd years (including seven after Marx's death) on the off-chance of a Louise Freyberger turning up to read it, and then – concerned as he was at the last to repudiate the fiction of his paternity – inconsequently to destroy the unassailable proof.

Finally, Louise Freyberger states as a fact that Frederick did not use the name Demuth until after his mother's death in November 1890, regardless of documentary evidence to the contrary of which perhaps she was unaware.

These details would be of small consequence but that they give a distorted picture of the Marx family relationships and, in particular, show Eleanor in a false light, while stamping Louise Freyberger as an unreliable and destructive person of coarse mind who waited four years – when Eleanor had been safely dead for six months – to betray Engels' trust. This is not to say that the whole should be dismissed as a fabrication. There is no reason to doubt her contention either that Marx was Frederick Demuth's father or that Engels informed her of the fact, if only because she could not have had the hardihood to invoke Sam Moore's name, which was above suspicion, and run the risk of claiming him as a witness to the scene described when he was alive for another thirteen years to deny it. And if there is any part of her account which emerges credibly it is her twice-repeated assertion that when that scene took place Engels laid it upon the three people present to use the information only if he were accused of treating Frederick Demuth shabbily: he did not, he told them, want to have his name reviled, particularly when it no longer served any purpose. That had not happened. There had been no ugly gossip bringing him – or Marx – into disrepute. So Louise Freyberger, flouting Engels' dying wish, puts pen to paper and kindly provides material for the scavengers of the future.

For those who have gone mad with glee on discovering that Marx had an illegitimate son, as for those who turn pale at the very thought and take to their beds, it is small comfort to reflect that the evidence reposes in so flawed a vessel as Louise Freyberger.* Yet a fact remains a fact even when embedded in vulgar twaddle, and Marx's importance to the history of mankind is not lessened by one jot because he fathered Frederick Demuth. Frederick Demuth, humble and rejected, has made for himself a small place in history, too, as the closest and most loyal friend of Eleanor Marx when her need was greatest.

"... Dear Freddy", she wrote, "you are the only friend with whom I can be quite free ... I tell you what I would tell to no other person. I would have told it to my dear old Nymmy but I have lost her and have only you ..."†

---

* Naturally there has been much hearsay evidence from other sources. Thus it was privately communicated to the present writer by an eye-witness that, in the early years of this century, Laura Lafargue introduced Frederick Demuth to Clara Zetkin in Paris as "my half-brother" (Stiefbruder).

My informant in the 1950s had been, as a young woman, Clara Zetkin's private secretary in which capacity she was responsible for typing the letter Zetkin wrote to Ryazonov in 1929.

It is understanble that after so many years she should have remembered the salient fact in that letter but not the details correctly. The original letter, kept in the secret Moscow archives until 1992, discloses that it was not Laura Lafargue in Paris but Eleanor Marx in London, at the time of the Second International Congress of 1896, who introduced Freddy Demuth to Zetkin as "my half-brother".

† 3 February 1898. *Labour Leader*, 30 July 1898.

APPENDIX 2

LETTER FROM KARL MARX TO PAUL LAFARGUE

LONDON 13 AUGUST 1866

My dear Lafargue,

Allow me to make the following observations:

1. If you wish to continue your relations with my daughter, you will have to discard your manner of "paying court" to her. You are well aware that no engagement has been entered into, that as yet everything is provisional. And even if she were formally your betrothed, you should not forget that this concerns a long-term affair. An all too intimate deportment is the more unbecoming inasmuch as the two lovers will be living in the same place for a necessarily prolonged period of purgatory and of severe tests. I have observed with dismay your change of conduct from day to day over the geological epoch of a single week. To my mind, true love expresses itself in the lover's restraint, modest bearing, even diffidence regarding the adored one, and certainly not in unconstrained passion and manifestations of premature familiarity. Should you plead in defence your Creole temperament, it becomes my duty to interpose my sound sense between your temperament and my daughter. If in her presence you are unable to love her in a manner that conforms with the latitude of London, you will have to resign yourself to loving her from a distance. I am sure you take my meaning.

2. Before definitely settling your relations with Laura I require a clear explanation of your economic position. My daughter believes that I am conversant with your affairs. She is mistaken. I have not raised this matter because, in my view, it was for you to take the initiative. You know that I have sacrificed my whole fortune to the revolutionary struggle. I do not regret it. On the contrary. Had I my career to start again, I should do the same. But I would not marry. As far as lies in my power I intend to save my daughter from the reefs on which her mother's life has been wrecked. Since this matter would never have reached its present stage without my direct intervention (a failing on my part!) and without the influence of my friendship for you on my daughter's attitude, a heavy personal responsibility rests upon me. As regards your present circumstances, the information, which I did not seek out but which has reached me nevertheless, is by no means reassuring. But to proceed. Concerning your position in general, I know that you are still a student, that your career in France has been more or less ruined by the Liège incident, that you still lack the language, the indispensable implement for your acclimatisation in England, and that your

prospects are at best entirely problematic. Observation has convinced me that you are not by nature diligent, despite bouts of feverish activity and good intentions. In these circumstances you will need help from others to set out in life with my daughter. Concerning your family I know nothing. Assuming that they enjoy a certain competence, that does not necessarily give proof that they are willing to make sacrifices for you. I do not even know how they view your plans for marriage. I repeat, I must have definite elucidation on all these matters. Moreover, you, as an avowed realist, will hardly expect that I should treat my daughter's future as an idealist. You, a man so practical that you would abolish poetry altogether, cannot wish to wax poetical at the expense of my child.

3. To forestall any misinterpretation of this letter, I can assure you that were you in a position to contract marriage as from today, it would not happen. My daughter would refuse. I myself should object. You must be a real man before thinking of marriage, and it will mean a long testing time for you and for her.

4. I should like the privacy of this letter to remain between our two selves. I await your answer.

Yours ever,
KARL MARX*

APPENDIX 3

ENGELS' "CONFESSION"†

Your favourite virtue	jollity
" " quality in man	to mind his own business
" " " " woman	not to mislay things
Your chief characteristic	knowing everything by halves
Your idea of happiness	Château Margaux 1848
" " " misery	to go to a dentist
The vice you excuse	excess of any sort
" " " detest	cant
Your aversion	affected stuckup women
The character you most dislike	Spurgeon
Your favourite occupation	chaffing and being chaffed
" " hero	none
" " heroine	too many to name one

---

* MIML. A German version of the French original appears in MEW.
† For Jenny's album. August 1868. MEW.

Your favourite	poet	Reineke de Vos, Shakespeare, Ariosto, etc.
" "	prose writer	Goethe, Lessing, Dr. Samelson
" "	flower	Blue Bell
" "	colour	any one not Aniline
" "	dish	cold: salad, hot: Irish Stew
" "	maxim	not to have any
" "	motto	take it aisy.

F. Engels

APPENDIX 4

LETTERS SENT BY ELEANOR TO 38 LONDON AND PROVINCIAL PAPERS

To the Editor of the ...

Sir,

A Reuter's telegram some days ago announced that a state of siege had been proclaimed in Hamburg, Altona, etc., and some 175 persons expelled from these towns. But the circumstances under which these proceedings have been instituted, the inhumanity with which the expulsions are carried out – these are unknown in England, or assuredly some protest would have been raised. Englishmen have sympathized with Bulgarians and Turks, with Russians and Greeks, will they not give some measure of justice at least if not of sympathy to the Social Democrats of Germany?

The "Socialisten Gesetz" (*sic*) requires that some act or acts "endangering public safety" shall have been committed before the "minor state of siege" can be proclaimed. But in Hamburg and in all the places concerned, positively no excuse of any kind exists for exceptional legislation. There have been no "excesses", no unauthorized meetings, no "seditious" or "incendiary" publications, no conspiracies. Despite the efforts of the police to discover any plot wherewith to justify their own illegalities, they have been unable to find a trace of one; their continual domiciliary visits to the houses of the "suspected" have been absolutely fruitless. The Socialists have abided strictly by the law – even by the exceptional laws which Prince Bismarck framed, and which he – incapable of governing even with these (a state of siege has been declared in his own rural possessions in Lauenburg!) – is the first to break.

Without rhyme or reason, without the shadow of an excuse 175 persons – many of whom had already been driven from Berlin – have been expelled from Hamburg etc; the houses of poor working men have been broken up, their families turned adrift, to find work and a new home elsewhere – or starve, as the case may be. One poor woman, the wife of a printer, seeing her home destroyed and starvation staring her in the face has lost her reason and is now in a madhouse! As to the manner in which the orders of expulsion are executed, let the following case serve as an example. A Social Democrat, confined to his bed for the last six months and in the final stage of consumption, was removed in this cold November weather by railway from Pinneberg in Holstein to Neustadt, where he arrived in a dying condition.

Such eloquent facts need no comment. At a moment when the German press is gagged, and all expression of public opinion impossible, when Prince Bismarck meditates fresh illegalities by proclaiming a state of siege in Leipzig, and uses his utmost efforts to coerce the Swiss government into expelling the Socialists who have taken refuge in Zurich and Geneva, at such a moment it is the duty of the free press of England – the only free press in Europe – to denounce acts as harsh as they are unjust, as merciless as they are illegal.

I am, Sir,

Yours obediently
E.M.

London, November 1880.

41, Maitland Park Road. N.W.

To the Editor of the ...

Sir,

The illegal persecution to which the Socialists of Germany are now being subjected is so opposed to all sense of justice and legality, that I trust I shall not appeal in vain in asking you to give the publicity of your journal to making known the inhumanity with which a section of the German people are being treated. It is no question of sympathy for Social Democracy – but simply one of common justice and fair play.

I am, Sir,

Yours obediently
ELEANOR MARX*

London, Nov. 1880.

---

* Liebknecht.

APPENDIX 5

"UNDERGROUND RUSSIA"

EXTRACTS FROM TWO ARTICLES BY ELEANOR MARX PUBLISHED IN
THE AUGUST AND SEPTEMBER 1883 ISSUES OF *PROGRESS*.

That a book on the Russian revolutionary movement, written by Stepniak, with a preface from the pen of Lawroff, would be of the utmost
interest was to be expected. The little volume which Stepniak modestly
calls a series of "Sketches and Profiles", is in reality a work of the utmost
historical value, for though written by an active Nihilist it is full of just
appreciation and critical insight. It is to be hoped that all the romancing
historians and would-be historical romancers; all the emotional and
tender-hearted old statesmen, and tract-distributing prison-visiting
divines will read it before again expressing their views on Russia and the
condition of the Russian people.

In his excellent "Introduction" Stepniak has, in masterly fashion, traced
the history of the Socialist – or, as it is improperly called – Nihilist
movement from its beginning in 1861 to its latest phase, the "terrorist"
phase of to-day. . . .

The so-called emancipation of the Russian peasants was begun by the
Czar Nicolas. The Czar has always been, and still is, the greatest landed
proprietor of Russia. In 1845 the surveyed State domains in the European
part of the Empire amounted to 261,824,541 *desjatines*, that is rather
more than 50,000 square miles – one *desjatine* being a little over a hectare
– and the State peasants numbered more than half the rural population.
The latter were actually serfs, though legally free men, and though the
commune had been preserved more intact amongst them than the rest of
the peasantry. The ruler was not the landlord but the gendarme, the tax-
gatherer, and the privileged distiller. In this domain, where his sway was
unchecked, Nicolas opened the campaign of autocracy against the landed
nobility. . . .

The emancipation of the serfs had become a moral necessity after the
Crimean failure. Occidentals looked upon the battlefield only; but Russians saw with their own eyes the incomparably greater masses of troops
dragged from all corners of the immense Empire, who, never reaching the
theatre of war, perished miserably by the way, inglorious victims of
administrative incompetency and corruption. The iron-fisted system of
Nicolas had thus broken down before the first serious emergency it had to

cope with. Commotions amongst the peasants, and intellectual revolt in the higher ranks of society, simultaneously signalised serfdom as the corner-stone of the old system, and the true reason of the collapse. The strange condition of the popular mind may be gathered from the rumor widely spread amongst the serfs that their emancipation was one of the clauses of the Treaty of Peace dictated at Paris by Napoleon III, whom they, more or less, confounded with Napoleon I! No Czar, however strong-willed, could have resisted this tide. He would have been only too glad to make his nobles the scapegoats for the accumulated sins of autocracy. . . .

I have spoken of the *moral necessity* of the abolition of serfdom; but if Nicolas already felt that the interest of the crown lay that way, any further doubt on this subject was impossible after the Crimean war. The war left behind it an exhausted exchequer, depreciated paper-money, and rapidly-increasing arrears of the direct taxes, falling only upon the peasants and workmen generally. What was wanted was the power of applying the tax-screw freely, *and making the government the tax-gatherer*. This was impossible with a state of serfdom, where the landowners were liable for the taxes of their serfs. . . .

Still more heavily did military considerations weigh in the eyes of the autocrat. The Crimean war had given the finishing stroke to the clumsy old army organisation, which consisted of a standing army levied from the peasantry – the guards serving twenty-two, all other troops twenty-five years. With such a time of service it was quite out of question to increase its numbers. This was fully understood by the government, which therefore extended more and more, and as an irregular supplement of the standing army, independent of it, Cossack colonies over the whole of the empire. . . . But general compulsory service was not only impossible as long as the peasant remained the property of his landlord; it could not be extended to the other classes while military service – equivalent, in fact, to penal servitude for life – was the stigma of serfdom. The peasant had to become a nominally "free" man before the other nominally "free" Russians could be enrolled at his side. Thus, if Peter the Great, in order to create a standing army had to consolidate serfdom, Alexander II, under quite altered conditions, had to abolish it – in order to introduce general compulsory service.

. . . the Russian people owe no more gratitude to Alexander for his "emancipating" the serf, than English people do to John for signing Magna Charta. Nay, less, for while John's extorted signature conferred some boons upon the English people, Alexander only added to the already terrible misery of the Russian people – only made their chains heavier, their burdens more unbearable.

... the immense debt of gratitude owed by Russia to the Czar Alexander II exists only in the fervid imaginations of certain "West-Europeans". This once admitted, we can not only more thoroughly sympathise with Russian revolutionists, but we can better understand their course of action, and the reason why the first manifestation of the Nihilist movement began in 1860 – i.e. immediately after that huge sham, the Emancipation.

The word "Nihilism" is the invention of the novelist Tourgenieff, "accepted", Stepniak tells us, "from party pride by those against whom it was employed," and now used to designate an entirely different movement from that first denoted by the word. The original Nihilist agitation had no political objects. It was "a philosophical and literary movement ... now absolutely extinct, and only a few traces left of it". Still, it was the germ from which the other and greater movement sprang. ...

The first battle was for religious freedom, and it was easily won. Every cultivated Russian is an atheist, and "when once this band of young writers, armed with the natural sciences and positive philosophy, ... was impelled to the assault, Christianity fell like an old, decaying hovel which remains standing because no one touches it". ...

Religious freedom was not all, however, for which the Nihilists fought. Nihilism recognised the equal rights of women and men. Here the struggle was long and bitter, for the "barbarous and medieval family life" of Russia stood in the way. But again it achieved a victory. In no other country are the women of the "educated classes" so entirely on the same footing as the men.

These victories gained, the Nihilists began to ask themselves what, after all, they had achieved? ... The movement had reached the stage when, to the despairing question, "What are we to do?" the International Working Men's Association gave an answer, and the heroic Commune of Paris showed the way.

... Thus arose the Socialist propagandist movement of '72–'74, a movement that presented an entire contrast to that of '60–'70; and yet, by a strange though not uncommon irony, the later movement came to be known by the name of the earlier one.

... Among the causes that drove the youth of Russia to accept these revolutionary principles, none was more potent than the years of ferocious reaction that had followed the Polish insurrection in '66, a reaction which "swept away everything that still maintained a semblance of Liberalism," and which prepared the way for the Socialist propaganda begun in '72. The young men and women who had been studying at Zurich, and who were recalled by the ukase, equally stupid and brutal, of '73, came to swell the ranks of the revolutionary party. ...

Yet even this was no political movement. The "propagandists" had not yet learnt that political emancipation is a necessary step towards social emancipation, and that a social revolution could no more come about by their preaching than it could have been established by Imperial ukase. . . . For two years it lasted. Thirty-seven provinces were, according to government circulars, "infected". The number of arrests is unknown. In one trial there were 193 prisoners. In 1875 the movement somewhat changed its aspect. . . . The years '77–'78 mark the end of the first revolutionary period. In '77 the trial of the Moscow "Fifty" was, by order of the government, a public trial. . . . But the ability of the prisoners who spoke, their noble heroism and simple, unaffected self-sacrifice, produced the very opposite effect to that expected by the government. . . . these "saints" were of too ideal a type to be fit for the coming struggle, and there appeared in their place a type as noble, but more strong – that of the Terrorist.

In spite of all heroic self-sacrifice and devotion, the Russian Socialists were bound to admit that they had failed, and they began to understand that to grapple with their barbarous enemy, deeds, not words, were needed. . . . "But a revolution, like a popular movement, is of spontaneous growth, and cannot be forced," and the revolutionists soon abandoned the series of "demonstrations" that had been planned, and which, in a country where towns of 10,000 or 15,000 inhabitants form only four or five per cent of the population, were impossible. But if the "demonstrations" ceased the government persecutions increased. Not only were the prisoners subjected to every sort of torture – of the "193", seventy-five "died" or went mad in prison *during the investigations* – but "that which is freely done in every country in Europe was punished among us like murder. Ten, twelve, or fifteen years of hard labor were inflicted for two or three speeches . . . or for a single book read or lent. From time to time, by ways which only prisoners know how to find out, there came from these men buried alive some letters, written on a scrap of paper in which tobacco or a candle had been wrapped up, describing the vile and useless cruelty which their gaolers had inflicted upon them . . . arousing in the most gentle and tender minds thoughts of blood, of hatred, and of vengeance."

The Terrorist movement began on January 24th, 1878, when Vera Sassulitsch shot the governor Trépoff. Vera herself was no Terrorist – she acted to avenge the man whom Trépoff had insulted and tortured, and "to call the attention of Russia and the world" to the condition of the political prisoners. . . . With cynical disregard of public feeling, Alexander ostentatiously visited Trépoff, so that even the "Liberals" – or those among them who were sincere – threw in their lot with the revolutionists. Far from attempting to conciliate, the government, with reckless insolence, sought only to aggravate the people. It forced the Socialist party to transform into a system what had been only an accident; to make an end of what had been a means to an end. Five months after Vera's acquittal and escape into Switzerland, "Terrorism, by putting to death General Mesentzeff,* the head of the police, . . . boldly threw down its glove in the face of autocracy." Since then the avenging arm of the Terrorist has struck often – and its greatest blow on March 13th, 1881.† What the end will be who can tell? But assuredly the coward despot, hiding amid his soldiers and his spies, and trembling every moment for his miserable life, is living a life more terrible than that of his unhappy peasants or of his tortured victims. . . .

This able and valuable book concludes with an interesting "Summary" of the whole movement, in which a most lucid account of the *theories* and *doctrines* of the Socialist Revolutionary Party is given. To this is added a translation of the admirable address to Czar Alexander III by the Executive Committee after March 13th. All those who believe the Russian Terrorists to be either blood-thirsty monsters or mad dreamers and fanatics, would do well to study this document. It is at once a justification of their policy, and an exposition of their moderate demands. In it the Executive offered terms of peace to Alexander. . . . Let the Czar but grant a small measure of reform, let him but give his people "freedom of the press, of public speech, of public meeting, and electoral addresses," and the Terrorists are ready to lay down arms. "And now," they said, "your Majesty, decide. The choice rests with you. We, on our side, can only express the hope that your judgment and your conscience will suggest to you the only decision which can accord with the welfare of Russia, with your own dignity, and with your duties towards the country." The Czar did choose. He replied by hanging Sophie Peroffsky and her fellow prisoners, by exiling and imprisoning thousands. But the end is not yet.

ELEANOR MARX

---

* He was in fact stabbed by Stepniak.
† The assassination of Alexander II.

· VOLUME II ·

THE CROWDED YEARS
(1884–1898)

To the Memory of

ELISABETH HOME WHITMAN (*née* Peel)
d. 11 December 1972

ROBERT STEWART
d. 14 September 1973

· AUTHOR'S NOTE ·

The last fifteen years of Eleanor Marx's life coincided with the revival of socialism in Britain: a subject that has been much explored and well documented.

The Social-Democratic Federation, the Socialist League, the Fabian Society, New Unionism, the Independent Labour Party and the annual May Day demonstration all came into being during that decade-and-a-half which also saw the first election to Parliament of Labour candidates. It was the period when the growth of workers' parties in Europe, North and South America and the Antipodes led to the founding of the Socialist, or Second, International. Thus the labour movement was advancing on all fronts at unprecedented speed.

This is Eleanor Marx's story, a many-sided one, but the movement is always breaking in, for the short life that remained to her was primarily dedicated to those working-class struggles which have been narrated time and time again both by contemporaries recording their own experience and by professional historians.

Since Eleanor was not a major figure in public affairs I have tried to confine myself to those in which she played an outstanding part. In some instances – "Black Monday" and the Match-girls' Strike are cases in point – this has proved impossible: as links in a chain of events they cannot be omitted merely because Eleanor, by chance, did not personally help to forge them.

It is also inevitable that I should dwell upon the last years of Engels who, after Marx's death, was not only Eleanor's mentor but with whom her life and work were closely intertwined.

The first volume of this biography stands complete in itself. Its sequel will have more meaning if read with a knowledge of Eleanor's formative years as child, girl and young woman in a unique family setting.

At the request of foreign translators – who naturally wish to know where to find in the original languages passages I have Englished – this book has an overweight apparatus giving all sources, including the *Marx-Engels Werke*, with page numbers in every case. In that respect it differs from Volume I where I deplored and rejected such elaborate furniture, smacking as it does of social climbing for this class of work. My surrender, for such it is – made largely in deference to Eleanor Marx's own sufferings in connection with the first English edition of Volume I of *Capital* – has the one advantage of obviating any need to expand the Select Bibliography appended to *Family Life*. I draw the line at listing all books relative to my subject read over the last dozen years, while those from which I have drawn appear in the references or footnotes.

For the rest I beg the indulgence of the general reader for this plethora and earnestly advise him to ignore the teeming numerals that deface the pages without providing intelligence he will need or want beyond the assurance that, as nothing is of my invention, neither is anything derived from the work of others without due acknowledgment (save, of course, for the literary borrowings which, by no means ranging from Beowulf to Virginia Woolf, as somebody or other has put it, will be instantaneously recognised).

The footnotes are reserved for explanatory or informative asides, when not mere comments and digressions, inessential to the text.

It may be found that a few quotations attributed to the English translation – my own – of the *Engels-Lafargue Correspondence* are not identical with the published version. This underwent drastic editing after it left my hands and, for reasons of accuracy or style, I have gone back to my original rendering here and there.

Dr. Emile Bottigelli has most generously given me permission to use freely and in full the unpublished Marx family letters in his custody.* This is an immense boon: none but Eleanor's own words, in their entirety, could convey her response to certain situations in her adult life.

In addition to all the benefactors fully acknowledged in the *Author's Note* prefacing Volume I – some no longer among us but many of whom again read the manuscript and offered me their knowledgeable and constructive criticisms – I am also beholden to others who have helped me in the preparation of the present book, for whose content, however, I alone am responsible.

I owe a particular debt of gratitude to Mrs. Gwynydd Gosling, the Librarian of the Highgate Literary and Scientific Institution, for, after the completion of *Family Life*, she winnowed my files and reorganised the source material for *The Crowded Years*, without which I should have been too encumbered to proceed. When the work was done Mr. Nicholas Jacobs with rare kindness volunteered to extract from the text my references, to number and list them in their final form.

To the following individuals who have given me with the utmost goodwill valuable information, access to unpublished material, the benefit of their specialised knowledge or research and technical assistance I now express my warmest appreciation: Professor Paul Avrich, Mr. Peter Bra-

---

* Since this was written the grievous death of Dr. Bottigelli occurred on 12 December 1975.

ham, Mr. David Demuth, Mrs. Julia Dohnal, Mrs. Ann Ebner, Mr. William Fishman, Mr. John Gibbons, Dr. Oakley C. Johnson, Mrs. Margaret Kentfield, Mr. Derek Leask, Mrs. Betty Lewis, Madame Simone Longuet-Marx, Mrs. Hope Malik, Mr. John Peet, Mr. Nenad Petrović, Mrs. Barbara Ruhemann, Mr. Raphael Samuel, Mr. William Sedley, Mrs. Brenda Swann, Miss Angela Tuckett, Mr. Rayner Unwin, Mr. Harry Watson, Mr. Sigurd Zienau; the Librarians and Keepers of historical archives in the London Boroughs of Camden, Lewisham, Newham and Tower Hamlets; and the following institutions for their courteous answers to queries, the loan of rare books, the provision of photostats and other favours: Army Museums Ogilby Trust; British Rail; British Library of Political and Economic Science; Coroners' Society; Greater London Council (Records Department); the Home Office; Labour Research Department; Law Society Services Ltd. (Records and Statistical Department); the London Library; Marx Memorial Library; the Meteorological Office; the National Army Museum; the Post Office; H.M. Stationery Office; the Royal Archives (Windsor Castle), and the Transport Record Library of the Public Record Office.

My sincere thanks go to Mrs. Barbara Cheeseman for her admirable typing of the manuscript throughout its many revisions.

The author acknowledges assistance from the Arts Council of Great Britain.

Y. K.
London, August 1975.

· PART I ·

LABORIOUS DAYS

In the summer of 1884 Eleanor Marx began to live openly with Edward Aveling. She was then at pains to announce the fact to her family and friends that they might be at liberty to accept or reject her. She had no wish either to strike a challenging blow for free love or to be seen as conducting some furtive *liaison*.

To Laura Lafargue, her sister in France, she wrote on 18 June 1884:

> "I must give you some other news – unless Engels has forestalled me – You must have known, I fancy, for some time that I am very fond of Edward Aveling – and he says he is fond of me – so we are going to 'set up' together ... I need not say that this resolution has been no easy one for me to arrive at. But I think it is for the best. I should be *very* anxious to hear from you. Do not misjudge us – He is very good – and you must not think too badly of either of us. – Engels, as always, is all that is good. – We – (such are present plans, but I don't believe in plans, and these may change) – are going in the middle of July to Derbyshire where we shall stay some weeks – then we return to London – and will give our 'friends' a chance of cutting us or not, just as they please. – *Do write soon, Laura, and don't misunderstand him.* If you knew what his position, is,[*] I *know* you would not. ... Mind you write *soon*. I shall await a line from you and Paul[†] very anxiously ... P.S. Will you do me a great favour? – Tell Longuet[‡] of my intentions with regard to Edward. Will you, dear?"[1]

A fortnight later she wrote to her old friend Dollie Radford:[§]

> "My very dear Dollie,
> I had half intended to tell you this morning what my 'plans' I spoke of are – but somehow it is easier to write – and it is perhaps fairer to you, because you can think over what I am going to tell you. Well then this is it – I am going to live with Edward Aveling as his wife. You know he is married, and that I cannot be his wife *legally*, but it will be a *true* marriage to me – just as much as if a dozen registrar's [*sic*] had officiated ... E. had not *seen* his wife for many, many years when I met him, and that he was not unjustified in leaving her you will best understand when I tell you that Mr. Engels, my father's oldest friend, and Helen[‖] who has been as a mother to us, approve of what I am about to do – and are *perfectly* satisfied.
> I do not want you to talk about this *yet*, for the simple reason that I want to be with Edward before we make the matter public. In three weeks we are going away for some

---

[*] Eleanor is referring to the fact that Aveling was a married man separated from his wife.
[†] Laura's husband.
[‡] Her brother-in-law, the widower of her sister Jenny.
[§] *Née* Maitland, married Ernest Radford in July 1883.
[‖] Helene Demuth.

little time – I only need rest – and then, of course, everyone will know – indeed we intend to let everyone we care about know. When we return we shall set up house-keeping together, and if love, a perfect sympathy in taste and work and a striving for the same ends can make people happy, we shall be so. – I have already told a few very dear friends, and so I want you and Ernest to know too, because then you can make up your minds as to what you will do. I shall *quite* understand if you think the position one you cannot accept, and I shall think of you both with no less affection if we do not any longer count you among our immediate friends.

Always, my dear old friend, yours lovingly,

Tussy.

P.S. I did not want to accept your invitation for tonight (though I really *have* another engagement) till you knew, and I don't want to settle about Saturday till I hear from you or see one of you. I do so want you to understand, Dollie, that while I feel I am doing nothing *wrong*, and only what my parents would have thought right, just as Engels does, yet I can understand that people brought up differently, with all the old ideas and prejudices will think me very wrong, and if you do I shall not mind it, but simply 'put myself in your place'. You know I have the power very strongly developed of seeing things from the 'other side'."[2]

On the day after she arrived in Derbyshire, Eleanor wrote to Mrs. Bland:*

"I feel it is only right that before I avail myself of your very kind invitation I should make my present position quite clear to you. The reason why I have not been to see you – and it required a great deal of self-sacrifice to keep away – and why I have not pressed you to come to me was simply that I would not do so till I could tell you frankly and honestly about the step that I have just taken. I am here with Edward Aveling, and henceforth we are going to be together – true husband and true wife, I hope, though I cannot be his wife legally. – He is, you probably know, a married man. I could not bear that one I feel such deep sympathy for as yourself should think ill of, or misunderstand us. I have not come between husband and wife. For many years before I met Dr. Aveling he had been living alone. I may tell you also that my sister and my Father's oldest friends fully approve of the step we have taken. I need not say it was not lightly taken or that I have overlooked the difficulties of the position. But on this question I have always felt very strongly, and I could not now in act shrink from doing what I have always said and what I distinctly feel to be right. I also feel that you and others may think differently, and till you have thought over the matter I dare not yet think of you and Mr. Bland as among those friends whom we hope to see when, four or five weeks hence, we return to London. That we should be delighted to count you amongst our friends I need not tell you.

With kindest regards to Mr. Bland and yourself,

Yours very sincerely,

Eleanor Aveling."[3]

This is almost the only occasion when Eleanor signed herself thus in a

---

* *Née* Edith Nesbit (1858–1924), best known as the writer of children's books. Her first husband, Hubert Bland (1856–1914), a former banker, became a journalist and one of the founding members of the Fabian Society, to which she also belonged. She remarried in 1917.

private letter, though in the pages of *Justice* her contributions appeared over that name from July until November 1884, after which she habitually used "Marx-Aveling" – sometimes hyphenated, sometimes not – being addressed and referred to as "Mrs. Aveling" while retaining her identity.

In other respects her letter to Mrs. Bland was over-scrupulous, for that lady was among the very last to give a fig for such irregularities, her own *ménage* being distinctly lax; while the testimonial to Aveling's many years of celibate life was merely a figure of speech.

Eleanor also wrote on 1 August from Derbyshire to John Lincoln Mahon,* an Edinburgh engineer, almost ten years younger than herself – and thus only 19 at the time – whom she did not even know personally but only by correspondence, yet she held him in such esteem that she felt she could not leave him in ignorance of her situation.

> "It seems only right that I should acquaint you, both – if I may say so – as friend and fellow-worker in the good cause, with the important step I have just taken ...", she wrote. "We are doing no human being the smallest wrong. Dr. Aveling is *morally* as free as if the bond that tied him years ago, and that had been severed for years before I ever met him, had never existed. We have both felt that we were justified in setting aside all the false and really immoral bourgeois conventionalities, and I am happy to say we have received – the only thing we care about – the approbation of our friends and fellow-socialists. May I hope that you will be among those who have not misunderstood our motives? Anyhow, it is only right that as one of our most active and useful Scottish propagandists you should know ..."

This letter is signed Eleanor Marx Aveling (no hyphen) and, in a post-script she refers to "my husband".[5] The tone of this letter differs from that of the other communications, suggesting that Eleanor was aware of the puritanical streak in self-respecting workers and that she must appeal to this young man's socialist outlook to accept her departure from convention.

Engels gave her £50 for her honeymoon, as she reported to Laura on 21 July, adding: "Is it not much too much? I feel quite unhappy about it – tho', as I need not tell you, it was *very* welcome."[6]

It must have come as something of a surprise to Laura that someone should feel quite unhappy about accepting Engels' money. In the course of but the past six weeks her husband had demanded and received well over £50 for running expenses and an outstanding debt: a not unusual rate of

---

* Mahon (1865–1933) was one of the main founders of the Scottish Land and Labour League which, in that same month of August 1884, affiliated to the Social-Democratic Federation, as it then became. He wrote his *Labor Programme* in 1887, in which year he himself married. He held a poor opinion of Aveling because, according to his son, he disapproved of the relationship with Eleanor.[4]

subvention that was taken for granted on both sides. Though Eleanor was often hard pressed for money and even for the means to earn it – "I should be glad to get *any* work I am capable of doing. I need work much and find it difficult to get. 'Respectable' people won't employ me," she wrote in 1887[7] – she never presumed to sponge on Engels.

He now took the trouble to recommend Mr. Aveling as a thoroughly desirable tenant for Mrs. Sarah Allen, the landlady of 55 Great Russell Street,* where the couple proposed to set up house on their return to London. The agreement was signed and, on 18 July, Eleanor moved all her belongings – "save my bed" – from Great Coram Street, though the new tenancy was not to start for some weeks.

To Laura, Engels wrote on 22 July saying that Tussy and Edward were away for the weekend on "honeymoon No. 1", the "grand honeymoon" to begin in a few days' time.

> "Of course," he said, "Nim, Jollymeier† and I have been fully aware of what was going on for a considerable time and had a good laugh at these poor innocents who thought all the time that we had no eyes, and who did not approach the *quart d'heure de Rabelais*‡ without a certain funk. However we soon got them over that. In fact had Tussy asked my advice before she leaped, I might have considered it my duty to expatiate upon the various possible and unavoidable consequences of this step, but when it was all settled, the best thing for them was to have it out at once before other people could take advantage of its being kept in the dark ... I hope they will continue as happy as they seem now; I like Edward very much, and think it will be a good thing for him to come more into contact with other people besides the literary and lecturing circle in which he moved; he has a good foundation of solid studies and felt himself out of place amongst the extremely superficial lot amongst whom fate had thrown him."[8]

It will be seen that Eleanor's repeated assertion that she had Engels' blessing was no empty boast (though whether she would have had her parents', as she also claimed, is another matter). None the less Engels, who had lived most of his happy unmarried life with the daughters of the proletariat, knew how vulnerable a middle-class young woman could be in Eleanor's position and advised her to take the bull by the horns in making it widely known, as she did. "There is," said Macaulay, "no spectacle so ridiculous as the British public in one of its periodical fits of morality,"

---

* Opposite the gates of the British Museum. Now incorporated between Nos. 51 to 58 in the YWCA building, numbered 57, and known as "Helen Graham House".

† Nim, Nym or Nimmy were Helene Demuth's nicknames bestowed upon her by the Longuet children, while Carl Schorlemmer (1834–1892), Professor of Organic Chemistry at Manchester and one of Engels' oldest and closest friends in England, had always been known as "Jollymeier" in the Marx circle. (See above, p. 82.)

‡ The day of reckoning.

and went on to observe that these seizures were entirely unpredictable.* Thus it was wise to err on the side of caution, but this happened to be an era when a great deal of propaganda for Free Love (with capital letters) was in vogue: some of it shrill and rather silly, much of it deeply earnest and directed to storming the citadel of male domination: the home. Eleanor was not involved in this campaign, for she held the view, as she was shortly to expound, that women were among the most oppressed of all the exploited sections of society whose emancipation could come about only by their combined efforts and she did not regard the domestic hearth as the centre of that struggle. She neither rejected marriage as an unholy alliance nor felt that her dignity was impaired, still less that she was doing anyone the slightest harm, by dispensing with it.

Though there were those who might deplore her choice of partner, she never forfeited the least respect. Even among the working men and women who became her colleagues and friends, though they reprobated the licentiousness of their betters, including royal princes, and that of the dregs of society, Eleanor's disarming personality and the probity of her ways overcame any prejudice attaching to her status.

Indeed, all ostracism was reserved for Aveling. Refreshingly, it was not in this case the woman who paid.

"Everyone *almost* has been *far* kinder than I ever expected," Eleanor wrote to her sister.[13] Dollie Radford's friendship had stood the test and, on 2 July, Eleanor wrote to say how glad she felt:

> "You know I care very little for what 'the world' may say or think, but I *do* care, very much, for my friends, and the thought that I might possibly be losing you too has been

---

* Macaulay's dictum, published in 1831,[9] referred to Byron's period but is apt for all time.

In 1953, almost exactly a century after the great writer known as George Eliot entered upon her long and successful union with George Henry Lewes, it was proposed that a new school should have the honour of bearing her name. A letter to the local press, under the heading: "Hardly a Model for Them", criticised the local education authority for showing "no evidence of prudence". What would the children think, asked the correspondent, "when they discover that at an early age" (she was 35) "their Patron revolted at all the restraints of moral and religious teaching and for 25 years (including 13 in the district) lived a life of sustained adultery ... Certainly," he conceded – a temperate man, not given to overstatement – "George Eliot was good at English..."[10]

On the other hand, another moralist, Henry James, had referred to George Eliot's connection with Lewes as "exemplary indeed" and in 1885 (a year, that is, after Eleanor's *début* as an adulteress) James wrote: "To her own sex her memory, her example, will remain of the highest value; those of them for whom the 'development' of women is the hope of the future ought to erect a monument to George Eliot."[11] We are also told, as reported by one of them, that "distinguished ladies, irreproachably married, found themselves dropping curtseys to her when presented."[12] Incidentally, George Eliot lies buried in distinguished company, occupying a corner of Highgate New Cemetery in close proximity to Marx and Spencer. The school, her monument, flourishes in Marlborough Hill, St. John's Wood.

a very sad one . . . I have thought of you very much, and often longed for you. For I am *very* lonely, Dollie, and I never felt lonelier than I do just now . . . I'm being quite lazy, doing nothing. The fact is I have been seriously unwell for the last two weeks, and as I was threatened with an absolute breakdown, I am just resting.

My dear old friend, I am so grateful for your letter.

Yours always,

Tussy."[14]

Although this letter strikes so ominous a note at the very outset of her life with Aveling, Eleanor was not nearing a breakdown but was, in fact, sickening for whooping cough, caught from Pumps Rosher's* little daughter.

---

* Mary Ellen (*née* Burns) who married Percy Rosher in 1881. See above, fn.†, p. 186.

Edward's father, the Rev. Thomas William Baxter Aveling, died on 3 July 1884. Edward came into a little money and on Thursday the 24th – a day later than planned in order to be present at the formation of the Westminster Branch of the Democratic Federation on the 23rd – Eleanor and Aveling set off at five in the morning to stay at the Nelson Arms* in Middleton-by-Wirksworth, a fair-sized village in Derbyshire, "the navel of England", as D. H. Lawrence called it.†

There they were joined for some part of the time by another heterodox couple, Henry Havelock Ellis and Olive Schreiner, then conducting their inconclusive romance‡ in nearby Bole Hill.

After corresponding for a few months, Olive and Ellis had met in May that year, when he persuaded her to join the "Progressive Association" (or "Fellowship of the New Life"); but Eleanor had known Olive since 1882 when she had settled for a while in London, a year after her arrival in England from South Africa. It was as a friend of hers that, in June 1884, Eleanor had sent a little note to Ellis, whom she had met but once, inviting him to join a theatre party. Thus they were by no means intimate, nor can Olive be said to have known Aveling at all until now,

---

* Aveling's pseudonym, Alec Nelson, could as well have been derived from the inn where he spent his honeymoon with Eleanor as from his birthplace, Nelson Terrace in Kingsland.

The fact is that at this time countless Roads, Groves, Gardens, Terraces, Squares and public houses bore "Nelson's peerless name". By 1830 – a quarter of a century after the hero's death – there were no fewer than twelve Nelson Streets in London alone, one of them being in Trafalgar Square, Stepney.

† Lawrence had a "smallish bungalow" there, known as Mountain Cottage, where he stayed on and off for a year from May 1918. He described it as "the darkish Midlands, on the rim of a steep, deep valley" and thought it a beautiful place though it made him feel "queer and lost and exiled".[15] Since these associations are not without interest and George Eliot has already appeared, however irrelevantly, in a footnote to these pages, it may be mentioned that her father's brother, Samuel, managed a tape mill in Wirksworth, living with his wife Elizabeth in a four-roomed cottage opposite his place of work. There Marian Evans, the future George Eliot, stopped with her aunt and uncle as a child, re-visiting it briefly in later life and making it the setting for *Adam Bede*.

‡ Its character and course may be traced, without much relish, in her correspondence.[16] Though she never ceased writing to Ellis, she implored him to return or destroy her letters, several hundred of which – including some dating from this period of 1884 – he most reluctantly burned.[17] In December 1891 Ellis married Edith Lees and in February 1894 Olive, then nearly 40 years of age, married Samuel Cronwright, who was 31.

although he had reviewed her novel *The Story of an African Farm** under the heading "A Notable Book" in the September 1883 issue of *Progress*.

Ellis regarded Eleanor Marx as "probably the nearest of Olive's new women friends in London",[18] which was saying much, for Olive went in for very close, even intense friendships with women. It appears that she identified Eleanor with her sister Ettie,[19] though there is great confusion here, for Ettie–Henrietta Schreiner – who was five years older than Olive lived to be 62, whereas the sister she meant was called Ellie, born when Olive was seven and dying at the age of 3.†[20] It was to this child that Olive attributed her strong emotional feelings for her own sex.

> "The most important event of my childhood," she wrote, "was the birth of my little sister, and my love for her has shaped all my life ... I sometimes think that my great love for women and girls, *not* because they are myself, but because they are *not* myself, comes from my love to her.‡[22]

Remarkable woman and fine writer though she was, Olive Schreiner had certain unamiable traits, the most powerful of which was an egotism so rampant that she insisted upon not only her house but also her husband being known by her name (doing so even before she married him) and begged Ellis, should he have children, to call one of his little girls Olive Schreiner.[24] She believed devoutly in her own gifts – which were far from negligible – but was incapable of sustained effort. In March 1887 Eleanor wrote to Havelock Ellis: "She is not doing the good work she might do. It is terrible to think of the way she seems to be wasting the genius that is in her."[25] Olive's powers of concentration declined with the years: "Her categorical setting down of what was proposed to be done and then not doing it ... she had almost to the last," her husband wrote. "We find her over and over again in later adult life ... lamenting her 'weakness' in failing again and again to carry out her programme."§[26]

---

* Published by Chapman & Hall in 1883 under the pseudonym Ralph Iron. The reader who had recommended it was George Meredith. Not until the 3rd edition of 1887 did it appear under her own name.

† "The little sister I loved so is buried in the garden", Olive wrote from Healdtown in what was then Cape Colony,[21] where the family had lived from 1861 to 1865, but where Henrietta – Ettie – neither was born nor died.

‡ Olive said the child lived only 18 months "but for that 18 my life was entirely in and through her". This contradicts the dates set out for the births and deaths of the Schreiner children by Cronwright-Schreiner, who says that "the errors, if any, are trifling".[23]

§ She had started to write her book known as *From Man to Man* in 1876 and, while she had made many earlier references to it, she had come so far as to speak of revising it in a letter to Ellis dated 28 March 1884.[27] In 1907 she was still at these revisions and, in May of that year, she wrote to Cronwright: "Oh, I wish I could get my book (*From Man to Man*) done before I die."[28] It was published posthumously in 1926.

Yet for the sake of her genius and books that were never to be written at all, she prevailed upon her husband to give up the farming life he enjoyed to become an uneasy if successful businessman. Towards the end of 1913 she went off roaming about Europe for seven years, to see him but once more, briefly, before she died in 1920.

She was, indeed, of a compulsive restlessness. During her first visit to Europe (1881–1889) she never stayed anywhere for longer than six weeks and generally not more than a fortnight. She appears to have been somewhat possessive and domineering in her friendships, venomous in her dislikes and to have put little curb upon her expression of these violent loves and hates. She had a tendency to delusions about her health and also a slight touch of persecution mania, accompanied by its opposite: the conviction that everyone admired and revered if they were not positively in love with her.

There is no doubt, however, that this dumpy little woman – Ellis describes her as "half an inch below 5 feet", measuring "forty inches round the hips"[29] – fascinated those who met her and, while she preferred women, she had a considerable effect upon the many influential men who sought her acquaintance. These included Cecil Rhodes, for whom she felt "the greatest sympathy" in some respects, though "with regard to politics and public life generally . . . absolutely opposed to her".[30] On one occasion she refused to shake hands with him[31] and "always insisted that he had said: 'I prefer land to niggers'."[32]

Her effect upon Eleanor was not bracing. She evidently captivated – one had almost written captured – her; but so great, almost pathological, was her aversion from Aveling that, combined with her affection for Eleanor – the one, perhaps, generated by the other – the double honeymoon cannot have been without its embarrassments. On the very day it started she wrote to Ellis who had not yet joined her: "Dr. Aveling and Miss Marx have just come to see me. She is now to be called Mrs. Aveling. I was glad to see her face. I love her. But she looks so miserable."[33] Some ten days later she wrote again:

"I am beginning to have such a *horror* of Dr. A. To say that I dislike him doesn't express it at all; I have a fear and horror of him when I am near. Every time I see him this shrinking grows stronger. Now, you see, when I am at Bole Hill they come every day to see me . . . and if we are at Wirksworth the Avelings will be always with us. I love her, but *he* makes me so unhappy. He is so selfish, but that doesn't account for the feeling of dread . . . I had it when I first saw him. I fought it down for Eleanor's sake, but here it is, stronger than ever."[34]

She constantly returned to the subject which seemed to obsess her.

"You can't understand," she wrote in July 1889, "that to feel any human creature hopelessly false is more terrible to me than all poverty, all loneliness, all death. The fact of such a nature as Edward Aveling's, for instance, is more terrible to me, does more to cripple my power of life and work, than all the close personal sorrows of my life."[35]

There is no doubt that she meant what she said, but the loathing seems disproportionate to her apparently casual acquaintance with this life-diminishing character. Yet, at that time, she respected Eleanor's feelings for the man and was capable of generosity. In the spring of 1885 when Aveling had a severe attack of renal calculus* Eleanor wrote to Olive, then in Hastings:

"My darling Olive, I always long for you, but now more than ever. Edward is very ill. You will know all that means to me. I need not *tell* you. The real help is that you need no telling – Donkin (blessings on him!)† was here this morning. With care it may be over soon: on the other hand it *may* be serious. You will know all the agony there is in that 'may'. All depends on the 'care' he takes. But how *can* the poor – and we are very poor – take care? . . .

Darling, I can't write though there is much I would fain say to you. You will understand. Write to me my own little Olive.
                              Yours Eleanor."[36]

Olive wrote to Ellis at once: "Please go and see them and tell me just how Aveling is. If he gets dangerously ill, I must go. If the Avelings are very hard up I must try to send them something . . ."[37]

Upon this, Ellis called at 55 Great Russell Street where he found William Morris "sitting in a friendly fashion by the fire; I have little doubt that at this period he was proving financially helpful."[38]

Since Olive was Eleanor's friend and Havelock Ellis hers, his recollections of Eleanor, the earliest of which were set down when he was 77 years of age – more than half a century after his first meeting with both women – followed by yet later reminiscences‡[39] must be treated with reserve.

"I can still see her . . . radiant face and expansive figure," he wrote in 1935. He remembered the pungent smell of her armpits, certain vivid little moments during the days in Derbyshire, and much hearsay conversation retailed to him by Olive. A sensitive and an honest man whose summoning up of the scents, the sights, the anecdotes of times past carries conviction, Ellis nevertheless casts a shadow of doubt by claiming that in

---

* Kidney stone, though Ellis referred to it as gallstones.
† Dr. Horatio Donkin, who had attended the Marx family. See above, pp. 167–8.
‡ His notes on Olive Schreiner, incorporated in Cronwright-Schreiner's *Life* of his wife, were written much earlier – in 1920 or 1921, shortly after her death – and he had always kept in touch with her.

1888, when he was helping her to find literary work, she was "not yet" absorbed in socialist activities.[40] This flagrant error, which shows that he knew little or nothing of her daily life, suspends belief in much of his other good rich gossip, which includes the information, transmitted by Olive, that Eleanor had been deflowered, "when she happened to be lying on a sofa at home", by "a prominent foreign follower of her father's".[41] Ellis had "long since forgotten" who had vouchsafed this "sudden sexual initiation", and with so wide a field it would indeed be risky to lay any odds or try to spot the favourite.

Though Ellis was demonstrably wrong on such facts as time and place, much of what he recorded has gained currency, albeit no corroboration from any other source. However, it is another matter when it comes to letters from which he quotes. These must have been in his possession: he had but to copy them out (even when he assigned questionable dates to them), so their authenticity cannot be doubted and, somehow or other, he had come by an immensely long letter from Eleanor to Olive written on 15 June 1885, which he transcribed in full.

We do not know of others in a similar strain, nor yet Olive's responses. Her published letters include none to Eleanor, though they do reveal that the girls exchanged confidences on their heightened feelings before and during their menstrual periods[42] and compared notes on the lifelong asthma Jenny Longuet had suffered with Olive's symptoms, from the age of 16, of the same complaint, said to be shared by Eleanor.[43]

In her fairly extensive correspondence this letter is unique for Eleanor's overcharged emotional language.

"My Olive," she writes, "I wonder if I bore you with my stupid letters – as I wonder if, one of these days you will get horribly tired of me altogether. This is no figure of speech. I really *do* wonder, or rather fear. I have such a terror of losing your love ... I keep wanting to hear you *say* you love me just a little. You do not know, O, how my whole nature craves for love. And since my parents died I have had so little *real* – i.e. pure, unselfish love. If you had ever been in our home, if you had ever seen my father and mother, known what *he* was to me, you would understand better both my yearning for love, given and received, and my intense need for sympathy ... Edward is dining with Quilter* and went off in the highest of spirits because several ladies are to be there (and it just occurs to me that you may be one! How odd that would be!) and I am alone, and while in some sense relieved to be alone, it is also terrible ... I would give anything just now to be near you ... How natures like Ed.'s (i.e. pure Irish and French ...) are to be envied, who in an hour completely forget anything. If you had seen him, for example, today, going about like a happy child with never a sorrow or sin in his life, you would have marvelled ... and while I feel utterly desperate he is perfectly unconcerned! I do not grow used to it, but always feel equally astounded at his absolute

---

* Art critic on the *Spectator* 1876–1886. He was Whistler's favourite butt, always referred to as "Arry".[44]

incapacity to feel anything – unless he is personally incommoded by it – for 24 consecutive hours ... With all the pain and sorrow (and not even you, my Olive, know quite how unhappy I am), it is better to have these stronger feelings than to have practically no feelings at all ... It is too bad of me to go on scribbling like this. But you would forgive me if you knew the help it is to me. Writing to you I seem to see your dear face before me and that gives me courage and strength. Write me a line ... Just one line – say you love me. That will be such a joy, it will help me get through the long miserable days, and longer, more miserable nights, with less heavy a heart ... There is so little in me to like or interest people ... That *you* care for me is one of those mysteries that remain for ever inexplicable.

  Good night, little girl ..."[45]

A postscript concerns the furthering of Edward's theatrical plans and ends: "Good night again, love."

This melancholy letter suggests, among other things, that though she had known, could not but know of, Aveling's dissolute habits, she had not foreseen that, once "wedded" to her, they would be so little modified, that she would spend quite so many evenings alone. These were her humiliations, or "troubles", as she called them: "No one but you and possibly Dollie should ever hear a word of them if I could help it," she wrote to Olive. Of course she was unhappy. But she had been unhappy before, wretched indeed, without ever losing her restraint. It is possible that something in Olive Schreiner's overpowering personality had reduced her to pulp. One sentence reads: "My mother and I loved each other passionately." This was not quite so: the love between Eleanor and Mrs. Marx had been, on both sides, undemanding, calm and trustful. It almost seems as if Eleanor were pleading for Olive to be as a passionate mother to a slightly hysterical child, stranded and awash with self-pity.

Yet this howl came from a woman of 30 who, endlessly occupied, was coming to terms with herself, her situation and her unworthy partner, learning the love that does not seek itself to please.

However one interprets the letter, of one thing there can be no doubt: after her first year of life with Aveling Eleanor knew that he provided no emotional security.

It is not a case of which to believe: Ellis's remembrance of "her radiant face", or Schreiner's "she looks so miserable"; the Eleanor who penned her sad, infatuated letter to "my Olive", or she who was writing to Laura: "From childhood we have known what it is to devote oneself to the *prolétaire*."[46] There is no necessity to reconcile the varying facets of her personality as they presented themselves to different people, for it is axiomatic that each individual will appear, and react, to others as if reflected in a series of distorting mirrors. But when Havelock Ellis said of Eleanor that: "It seems impossible to find any unfavourable references to her"[47] he was, by and large, speaking no more than the plain truth.

Some of the golden opinions she won – such as Hyndman's tribute to her work* – may have been inspired by the widespread repugnance to Aveling, giving rise to unsolicited sympathy with Eleanor. Thus the Fabian, Henry Salt, wrote:

> "Eleanor Marx was a splendid woman, strong both in brain and in heart and true as steel to the man who was greatly her inferior in both."[48]

There is also the testimony of so unlikely an admirer as William Collison, who, as the founder in 1893 of "Free Labour Exchanges" which undertook to supply "men ... willing to work in the place of ... strikers", bragged that:

> "I was the first man who made that a business. The result is an organization of many thousands of men throughout the United Kingdom banded in a kind of secret service..."

That he was no base mercenary but a man given heart and soul to the exploiters' cause is illustrated by his reference to the policy of Harris the Smithfield sausage king:

> "What could be a happier idea than that of coupling business with philanthropy by employing only deaf and dumb people to peel his potatoes, so that they could not waste their time by talking."

He had known Eleanor, that "strange and beautiful character", in his misspent socialist youth and waxed almost lyrical about her

> "brilliant intellectual gifts, steadfast moral purpose and affectionate woman's heart".

This "faithful and untiring woman", though "the man she loved was a moral wastrel", never flinched:

> "He became unendurable, yet she endured him ... She wrote to her friends, excusing his conduct in letters that, so far as I can read, stand unapproached for clear-eyed stoicism ... I knew the heart and spirit of Eleanor Marx ... her ... laugh and her ... infinite grace..."†[49]

---

* See below, p. 288.

† One hesitates to quote Collison, not because his evidence is suspect – quite the contrary, for when he wrote his autobiography in middle age he can have had no possible wish to curry favour with her surviving friends and associates – but because his offering it at all is so quixotic as possibly to be discounted. When one thinks of all the memoirs written by (or for) ex- (or practising) policemen, criminals, generals, politicians, international spies and even kings, one cannot but reflect how rare it is to come upon any by professional strike-breakers. The *genre* seems never to have had much appeal for them.

There is the further witness of a foreign visitor: the Swedish writer Anne Charlotte Edgren Leffler who spent the three months April to June 1884 in London where she met both Eleanor and Aveling before they had set up house together.

"Eleanor Marx is alone in the world, poor and in difficulties," she wrote in one of her early letters home, "– but so beautiful, talented, enthusiastic and of noble character. She is of the same stuff as martyrs and heroines. She could die for her belief as Sofia Perowski* and I do not doubt she is able to murder an oppressor as Charlotte Corday or fire with enthusiasm a whole people as Jeanne d'Arc."[49a]

---

* See above, p. 173.

Once settled at 55 Great Russell Street Eleanor made the discovery that, contrary to William Morris's belief,* housework was detestable.

"What with scrubbing and cleaning and all sorts of things I know nothing about, my hands are pretty full," she wrote to Laura in September.
"...I'm a born idiot and I swear at myself all day. If Ed. were not very good and kind he'd do the same."
She complained that he was "the very devil of untidiness", adding:
"I'm a good second ... If scrubbing 'is my vexation', cleaning knives is 'twice as bad', joints 'puzzle me' and potatoes 'drive me mad'†... Who is the fiend that invented housekeeping? I hope his invention may plague him in another world."[51]

While Aveling was away on convalescence during April 1885, Eleanor tackled the traditional spring-cleaning, complete with the whitewashing of walls, and wrote:

"How I wish people didn't live in houses and didn't cook, and bake, and wash and clean! I fear I shall never, despite all efforts, develop into a decent 'Hausfrau' "‡[52]

and she declared herself "about as fit as a cat to play the fiddle"[54] when it came to housework.

This is as it may be, but the fact was that she had, literally, no time for it. Moreover, she was the first of the Marx clan – and probably among the rare middle-class women of her day – to dispense entirely with servants for the simple reason that she and Aveling could not afford them.§

In February 1884 when Eleanor had visited her parents' grave in

* " '...perhaps you think housekeeping an unimportant occupation not deserving of respect ... don't you know that it is a great pleasure to a clever woman to manage a house skilfully...' "[50]
† Eleanor's quotations come from an anonymous doggerel dated 1570:
"Multiplication is vexation
Division is as bad;
The Rule of three doth puzzle me,
And Practice drives me mad."
‡ Later, Eleanor, like Mr. Pooter, discovered the wonders of enamel paint. "Though I say it as shouldn't," she wrote to her sister, "I believe I have a genius for house painting. We have a most splendid enamel here now ... which I find invaluable. I enamel chairs, tables, floors, everything. If the climate only permitted, I should enamel myself. ..."[53] At that period a firm called Aspinall's advertised their enamel under the categorical slogan: "Simply perfection". Eleanor would have agreed.

Highgate, "because I want it all nice by the 14th March" – the anniversary of Marx's death – she had taken a few flowers and wrote: "I couldn't take many because I am so hard up."[55] In May she was slogging at the British Museum, writing essays and reviews for a Miss Zimmerman who received 30s. or 35s. for these creative works and paid Eleanor 5s. or 7s. 6d.

> "Cheerful, isn't it?" she commented ruefully to Laura. "I don't half like writing articles for other people to sign, but necessity knows no laws and 5/- is 5/- . . . Indeed, I really work from about 9 in the morning till late at night and often till early into the next day. 'And yet not happy', as Toole used to say – or rather, I am very poor."[56]

A year later, it was still the same story: "I am up to my neck in work of all kinds (not alas! very remunerative)."[57] To Olive Schreiner, in the letter of June 1885 already cited, she said:

> "we have mere money troubles enough to worry an ordinary man and woman into the grave. It is almost impossible for me now to get work that is even decently paid for, and Ed. gets little enough."

At the time of Aveling's illness she wrote frankly to a colleague in the Socialist League: "The prescription of 'no work' is difficult for the poor to follow, and we cannot follow it entirely."[58] To her sister, she expanded on the problems created by Dr. Donkin's decree that rest was "absolutely necessary" for Aveling. ("Doctors are such 'absolute' knaves!" she exclaimed parenthetically.) But though: "you know Donkin never fusses . . . he frankly told me that the matter . . . might be really *very* serious". Aveling was not to move at all or do anything, but there was still "the necessary work of getting a living – *tant bien que mal*". Thanks to help from Paul Lafargue, he was able to take a few days at Ventnor and Eleanor was "doubly grateful", for it made possible both the rest from work and the change of air Aveling "really needed". However, they "could not possibly afford to go away together".[59]

Eleanor wrote to Stepniak‖ on 14 April:

---

§ She did, in point of fact, have "a girl" during 1886 who appears to have kept an eye on the Great Russell Street lodgings in her absence. Whether this girl came daily or lived in is not clear; all that is known of her is that, according to a letter from Eleanor, she was not up to forwarding newspapers.

‖ See above, fn.†, p. 226.

"I hope we shall soon see you. Edward is very seriously ill and has not yet recovered. He has gone away, but will return tomorrow, and I fear no better. I need not tell you how worried I am. You will understand this. I hope if you have time you will call and see him. He will be so glad to have a talk with you ..."*[60]

Never once during their first two years together had she and Aveling managed to visit the Lafargues, not only because of the necessity to get a living, but, as she wrote, regretting that they could not come to France: "You don't know what a chronic state of hard-up-ness we are always in."[61]

To make ends meet Eleanor went on with her teaching in Kensington for a while and gave courses of lectures on Shakespeare,† devilled at the Museum and snatched at any literary hackwork that friends might put in her way. But though money had to be earned it was her – unpaid – political activity that crowded these years.

From January 1884 until the following July she wrote a regular feature for *To-Day*,‡ under the title "Record of the International Popular Movement", as well as translating for its pages an article by Stepniak on "Russian Political Prisons":[62] "the very devil to do, being the translation of a translation"[63] from Russian into French.

Eleanor did not in fact know Stepniak at that time, though he and his wife Fanny were soon to become her friends. She wrote to him – in French – on 11 May 1884:

"I should like to think that my name is not entirely unknown to you ... At all events it is not as a stranger that I write to you. I have just translated your article for 'Today', and I am not quite sure that I have in all respects faithfully rendered your thoughts ... So I should be infinitely obliged if you would tell me where I have made mistakes ... As I shall be seeing the proofs again I could add or change anything that you find requires it ... Very sincerely yours, Eleanor Marx."[64]

This journal had now changed its character, being issued in a new series as *The Monthly Magazine of Scientific Socialism*, under the same editorship until, in July 1884, Hyndman "succeeded in getting poor old Bax turned

---

* In this letter she referred to having seen an advertisement of his book – in all probability *Russia Under the Tsars* (1885) – and was surprised that it was "quite finished and printed" since he had asked her not long before "to help in its translation".
† The advertisement for one such course, on *As You Like It*, given at the Highgate Literary and Scientific Institution, is illustrated overleaf.
‡ A monthly journal, originally started by Ernest Belfort Bax in May 1883 as a "Magazine of Bold Thoughts", published by Champion and Foulger, who ran the Modern Press (which also printed *Justice*), in Paternoster Row.

out" and replacing him by Henry Hyde Champion,* whom Eleanor described as "just a tool of Hyndman's, albeit a talented and I think honest young man".[65]

Her "Record" consisted of news items culled from home and abroad. Thus, in the first issue, she reminded readers of "the heroic old man, Charles Delescluze,"† whose dishonoured grave had been traced after twelve long years. His remains were now to be re-interred with ceremony at Père Lachaise and Eleanor appealed for contributions to raise a monument to his memory. Another paragraph recorded with amusement that the English police were "trying their hand at plots" in an attempt to keep abreast with their opposite numbers in France and Germany, though they were "still such novices in the business that it would be unkind to criticise their first failures".[67]

The next month she called upon her readers to gather outside Holloway gaol on 25 February for "a hearty welcome" to George William Foote‡ on his release.

It was also in the February issue and in March that Eleanor crossed swords with Sedley Taylor§ in the correspondence columns of To-Day, having "no other means of refuting a very serious charge" brought against her father on 26 November 1883 in a letter to The Times which had refused to print her reply, as had also the more liberal Daily News. "Apparently," she wrote, "a dead lion may be kicked with impunity by living professors."‖

This was not the only dispute in which Eleanor was involved. She was well "in the thick of a fight" with a troublesome Austrian anarchist whom

---

* 1859–1928. The son of a Major-General and himself an ex-artillery officer who had served with distinction and won a decoration in the 1879 Afghan war, he resigned his commission in disgust at the Egyptian war of 1882 and joined the Democratic Federation of which he became assistant secretary. He left to join the Labour Electoral Association and started the Labour Elector in 1888. For two years he was the assistant editor of the Nineteenth Century. In 1893 he emigrated to Australia.

† On the evening of 25 May 1871, Delescluze, then aged 62, was in the midst of the Commune street fighting and "had fallen as if thunder-stricken on the Place de Château d'Eau".[66]

‡ (1850–1915) Imprisoned for blasphemy in May 1883. He kept up a correspondence with Aveling, writing in September that year: "... Although I cannot say I am ill, confinement is telling on me generally, and the horrible monotony of this life is very depressing ... I still go to chapel by way of inoculation. After the sermon I often think, 'Heavy tragedy all the week, and high comedy on Sunday' ..."[68] Holloway, known as the City and County of London Prison, built in 1849 by J. B. Bunning, was opened in 1852, a year before the passing of the first Penal Servitude Act under which convicts were no longer sentenced to transportation. It became exclusively a women's gaol in 1903.

§ The author of a book called Profit-sharing between Capital and Labour (1884). In January 1885 he read a paper on the subject before the Industrial Remuneration Conference presided over by Sir Charles Dilke.

‖ See Appendix 4.

she suspected of being a police agent; indeed, she was "beginning to find more and more that it is not all play 'dans le parti'."[69] There was also Mrs. Annie Besant who, with her urge to publicise private grievances, now, in the pages of the *National Reformer*, accused Eleanor of libel.[70] Naturally enough, Eleanor ignored this; but when John Mahon wrote to ask her what it meant, she replied:

"The matter is very simple. I have never taken any public notice of it for two reasons – the first is that I do not think it necessary that *I* should answer such a person as Mrs. Besant, from whom I consider abuse the best compliment; the second, that any explanation of this matter would have placed my informant in an awkward position ... I can assure you that I never 'invented' a word of the so-called libel, but simply repeated what was told me, and what I have every reason to believe was the truth. In calumniating me – and Mrs. Besant is doing this systematically – Mrs. Besant is only trying to imitate Mr. Bradlaugh, who has tried for years to calumniate my father. The reason of this – 'lady's' animosity is not far to seek ... I know enough of this woman to say unhesitatingly that I do not think her honest, and that consequently I can have nothing to do with her..."[71]

Nor could Eleanor be unaffected by Bradlaugh's allegations that Aveling, as Vice-President of the National Secular Society, had borrowed money from the funds, failed to repay it and was guilty of other financial irregularities. This caused some embarrassment in the Social-Democratic Federation.* William Morris was sure Hyndman would use it as a pretext to rid himself of Aveling. "Here is ... a very awkward business," he wrote. "The worst of it is that A. is much disliked," while Morris feared that "Bradlaugh in his character of solicitor's clerk will have been careful not to bring a quite groundless charge."[72] In a letter to *Justice*, published on 27 September 1884, Aveling wrote:

"I shall be glad if I may use your columns for a brief personal explanation, rendered necessary by statements and rumours, more or less vague, that are being made about myself. I am at the present time indebted in many sums to many persons. I am using every endeavour to clear myself of this indebtedness. But I wish to say that to the best of my knowledge and belief all monies received by me as funds in trust for others have been fully accounted for. My monetary difficulties have to do with my poverty and my want of business habits alone."

It is improbable that this paltry waiver inspired much confidence or increased Aveling's popularity; but, since Bradlaugh refused to specify the malversations and Aveling resigned his Vice-Presidency of the Secular Society before the motion to remove him from office was debated, Morris

---

* The name adopted by the Democratic Federation in August 1884. See below, p. 289.

was able to report on 8 October that "the Aveling matter is blown over apparently for the present".[73]

The joint editors – and subsidisers – of *To-Day* were Bax and James Leigh Joynes,* of whom Eleanor wrote:

> "Bax is all that is good. He only wants to be with people who keep him up to the mark. Joynes I am not sure about. Not that I've anything particular against the man but I don't quite like him. He is one of the people who always want to 'avoid shocking' the sensibilities of the British public, and who always end by 'shocking' the public just as much as if they spoke out frankly, and alienate our friends."[74]

For the April issue Eleanor wrote a longer piece than usual on the meeting held in March to commemorate both Marx's death and the Paris Commune. Of this occasion she gave an even more vivid account in a letter to her sister, written on the day after it had taken place.†

> "I never – nor indeed did any of us – for a moment believed that we should have more than a very small gathering, but when I tell you that between 5 and 6,000 people assembled you will see that it was really a splendid affair. The procession – with bands and banners, started in Tottenham Street, and we marched – I going with them – along the Tottenham Court Road, Hampstead Road etc. to Highgate. The Cemetery authorities had had the gates closed, and inside there were drawn up 500 policemen with 6 mounted police! As we were refused admittance – and we asked if I and some ladies bearing crowns could go in alone – we adjourned to the top of the street just by the reservoir.‡ It was a really good sight. From§ the cemetery gate up to the reservoir the streets were one complete mass of human beings. Anyone who had thought the whole thing would be a [fiasco?]|| by this time regretted *he* wasn't to speak. After Aveling *had* spoken I reckon he regretted it still more. A ring was now formed, and after a chorus had sung something – I only caught the one word 'Freiheit' – Aveling mounted on the 2 chairs that had been borrowed and addressed the crowd. He managed to make himself heard at an immense distance (today he is voiceless!) and spoke splendidly, shortly, to the point, full of real enthusiasm and no falutin. The people were deeply impressed. I don't wonder. It was a beautiful speech. Then came the German, Frohme (deputy for Frankfurt) who came over specially and also spoke extremely well. He was followed by a French working man¶ ... who was a failure. He

---

* 1853–1893. Formerly a master at Eton, he had been obliged to resign after his arrest in Ireland as a result of speaking on the same platform as Henry George on the Single Tax question. In 1891 he translated Marx's *Wage-Labour and Capital* (written as an unfinished series of articles for the *Neue Rheinische Zeitung* in 1849), with a new Introduction by Engels.

† Marx died on 14 March 1883, the Commune was born on 18 March 1871. Eleanor's letter of 17 March 1884 refers to "a commemorative meeting of the 18 March at Highgate".[75] This is obviously an error. She also, correctly, refers to "yesterday": that is, Sunday the 16th.

‡ Through Chester Road up to Dartmouth Park Hill.

§ The rest of the holograph in the Bottigelli Archives is missing. An undated fragment (in photostat) found at the IISH continues from the foregoing word "reservoir" to the end.

|| Word illegible.

¶ His name was Lavache.

had actually written a long speech! Then came another chorus and the crowd marched off ... Altogether the demonstration was an immense success. That such thousands should assemble for such a cause! You see we *are* getting on here in this slow old land of yours ..."[76]

Karl Frohme told Eleanor afterwards that he had spoken with the greater ease because "surrounded by police and forbidden to enter the cemetery, he felt he had never left the dear Fatherland".[77]

The demonstration was also briefly reported in *Justice*, the weekly organ of the D.F., started by Hyndman on 19 January that year and edited by Harry Quelch, which journal, though it advertised Aveling's lectures and meetings, went out of its way to carp at Eleanor's contributions in *To-Day*.* Concerning the first of these *Justice* printed an unsigned letter recommending "the illustrious daughter of the International not to condescend to sarcasm in her paragraphs. It is the weapon, or rather the weakness of society-journal editors, Saturday reviewers and very young enthusiasts."[79] Again, on 3 March, it expressed the view that "the dispute between Mr. Sedley Taylor and Miss Marx is ... scarcely suited to such a magazine"; while of the Highgate demonstration it published a short advance notice under the heading "A Sad Anniversary", taking leave to doubt whether Marx would have approved of such a ceremony. "Any renewal of the old pagan and Catholic forms of canonisation of individuals is contrary to the principles of Socialism", but, since the misconceived function was none the less to take place, all socialists should support it.[80]

Behind this ambivalence lay not only Hyndman's deep resentment of any truckling to the Marx clan but also the fact that at one stage he himself had been nominated as the main speaker, which part in the event was assigned to Aveling. This, however, was but one discordant note now heard within the Federation.

In August 1884 until the end of the year Eleanor attended all the sessions of the Executive Council of the SDF, taking the Chair on at least one occasion. Then, from January 1885, save for the weeks of Aveling's illness, she was present at the meetings of the Socialist League's Provisional Council – which became its Central Council after its first Conference, held on 5 July 1885 – until in the following year the number of Council members was reduced from 25 to 15 and Eleanor stood down, though Aveling was re-elected.[81]

She had now also begun to lecture on social and political – as distinct

---

* See fn.‡, p. 283. Later *Justice* was published by the Twentieth Century Press at 44 Gray's Inn Road, to be transferred in 1893 to 37a Clerkenwell Green, now the Marx Memorial Library.[78] Quelch (1858–1913) was a man of outstanding ability, at that time a warehouse packer in a City firm of wallpaper manufacturers, earning 25s a week. He continued for some years at his trade while working in a voluntary capacity on *Justice*.

from literary – subjects, first to her own branch of the SDF and, after resigning from that organisation,* further afield. Early in February 1885 she delivered a speech to the Mile End branch of the Socialist League, writing to Lavrov to say: "Next Sunday I shall be giving a public lecture for the first time in my life (and perhaps the last?). The subject is 'The Factory Acts in England' ...",[82] then to her own – the Bloomsbury – branch at the Eagle and Child coffee-house in Old Compton Street and on 8 March to the Southwark branch. A packed audience listened to her at Neumeyer Hall† at the Commune anniversary meeting held on 22 March, when she earned Morris's praise – "All went off very well," he wrote to his daughter May. "... there was some very good speaking; Eleanor Aveling was the best I think"[83] – and also Hyndman's who in later years wrote:

> "Eleanor Marx made one of the finest speeches I ever heard. The woman seemed inspired ... as she spoke of the eternal life gained by those who fought and fell in the great cause of the uplifting of humanity: an eternal life in the material and intellectual improvement of countless generations of mankind. It was a bitter cold, snow-swept night in the street outside, but in the Hall the warmth of comradeship exceeded that of any Commune celebration I have ever attended. We were one that night."[84]

Earlier on that same snowy day Eleanor had lectured again in Mile End on the Factory Acts and on 18 April at the County Hotel in Croydon to the local branch. She had now become something of an expert on this subject, her first speech on it being anything but the last.

For the English translation of Volume I of *Capital* she had been tracing back to their sources the extracts used by Marx (in German) from the Reports of Factory Inspectors, Medical Officers on Public Health, Select Committees and Commissions enquiring into Children's Employment, the Housing of the Poor, Mines, Railways, Bakeries and the Adulteration of Food. There was probably no one else of her generation in any way connected with the socialist movement who had this historical perspective and wealth of factual information. Thus she was able to speak of the hazards in industry, the loopholes in existing legislation and the conditions in many types of workshop with an authority that added immense weight to her political arguments. Out of these lectures grew the Socialist League "Leaflet No. 3", *The Factory Hell*, published in April 1885, the first work to appear under the joint names of "Edward and Eleanor Marx Aveling".

---

* *Justice* reported on 10 January that "George Bernard Shaw in the absence of Mrs. Aveling delivered an excellent lecture" to the Westminster Branch of the SDF.
† In Hart Street, now Bloomsbury Way, running south from Bloomsbury Square, a stone's throw from where she lived in Great Russell Street.

"Are you going to the Conference?" Eleanor wrote to John Mahon on 1 August 1884 from Middleton. "My husband is, as delegate of the Westminster Branch. I, unfortunately, cannot be there, much as I should like to."[85]

Thus Edward came up to London alone for a couple of days* to attend the annual conference of the Democratic Federation on 4 August, by which time dissensions in the Executive Council of that body had reached an uncomfortably high pitch.

It was at this, its fourth, annual conference that the organisation was renamed the Social-Democratic Federation and resolved to issue a new declaration of aims on Marxist lines. To its Council of 20 members, for which there were 27 nominations, both Eleanor and Aveling were elected,† though she had earlier said: "I've no ambition that way, and want to keep out of it – especially as there's no chance of *both* of us getting elected."[87]

However, elected they both were, which circumstance appears to have interrupted if not curtailed the honeymoon – intended to last from four to five weeks – for on 12 August they were in London for the meeting of the new Executive Council at which, Hyndman having sent a formal apology for absence, William Morris took the Chair and was slightly vexed by Aveling's "ineptitudes" in moving a resolution on Disestablishment and seconding one on the Irish question.[88]

Morris was in every way the noblest and most gifted of Eleanor's English associates;‡ but, while they worked together in harmony and with mutual respect, even admiration at this period, they never became close personal friends. In all probability this was owed less to the difference of age, though Morris (1834–1896) was nearly 21 years senior to Eleanor, than to the wide disparity of background and experience that had brought them to socialism. She, moreover, came to believe that, in his rooted objection to using parliamentary means – and thus compromise with the

---

* By 6 August he was back in Derbyshire, as Engels informed Eduard Bernstein on that date to explain why he had not yet heard what had passed at the conference.
† Among the others were Bax, John Burns, Champion, Joynes, Hyndman, his wife Mrs. Matilda Hyndman, William Morris and Harry Quelch.[86]
‡ Indeed, their biographers cannot but wish to apply to Morris *"Rule Forty-two. All persons more than a mile high to leave the court."*

existing system – for revolutionary ends, Morris leant too much towards the anarchists,* while he, for his part, grew to dislike Aveling heartily, referring to him at one stage as "that disreputable dog".[90]

Morris had joined the D. F. in January 1883; that is, before either Eleanor or Aveling who became members of its London section in the late summer of that year.

There was every good reason why Eleanor should have played no part in the Federation during its early days. Her father's contempt for Hyndman's superficiality; the trials and tragedies visited upon her family in those years and her own craving to train for a career on the stage prevented her from taking an active interest in this new party. Indeed, she had made a glancing reference to it shortly after its foundation in June 1881 only to remark that it would not amount to much. However, its 1883 manifesto, *Socialism Made Plain*, was a great advance on anything so far issued by, as Engels sceptically put it, "some two or three dozen little societies which for at least 20 years under various names (but continually the same members) have again and again, and always with the same lack of success, tried to get themselves taken seriously".[91] But this stage army was now not only attracting an entirely new type of recruit, it was also obliged by force of circumstance to abandon its distinctly amateur performances.

In January 1884 it adopted a clear socialist programme with a new Constitution and Rules, published in the first number of *Justice*. Eleanor and Aveling attended a special meeting of "active supporters" in that month, when a number of resolutions were moved on such matters as the socialisation of the means of production, universal suffrage, the payment of M.P.s† and the reduction of working hours in industry. Aveling's contribution to the discussion was a plea for a scientific approach to socialism.

At this point, on 4 January 1884, the Fabian Society was founded by a number of earnest intellectuals who had belonged to the "Fellowship of the New Life". That body, imported from America in 1852 by Professor Thomas Davidson on one of his frequent visits to Britain, collapsed when

---

* Later Morris himself explicitly repudiated anarchism in these words: "... if freedom from authority means the assertion of the advisability or possibility of an individual man doing what he pleases always and under all circumstances, this is an absolute negation of society, and makes Communism as the highest expression of society impossible..."[89]

† The 3rd Parliamentary Reform Bill of 1884, introduced on 28 February, had its third reading in June, was thrown out by the Lords in July – whereupon some 40,000 people demonstrated in Hyde Park for the abolition of the Upper House – and was finally passed on 6 December. Some 2 million new voters were thereby enfranchised. With this measure more than half the demands in the "People's Charter" of 1837 had been met. The payment of M.P.s had to wait until March 1893, when a private member's Bill was passed with a majority of 47 votes. The remaining demand – for annual parliaments – has never been pressed nor gained much support.

a majority of its exiguous membership resigned in October 1883 on the grounds that "social reform through legislation was at least as important as self reform through ethical contemplation".[92] The new Society shortly drew into its ranks such vigorous minds as the scintillating George Bernard Shaw and the sedate Sidney Webb, then a clerk in the Colonial Office,* the one aged 28, the other 25. By 1885 it had 40 members. Their methods and aims were unrelated to any theory of class struggle or social revolution. By the inevitability of gradualness – a phrase later used by Webb but denoted from the start by the name the Society adopted† – a change of society would be wrought. Edging away from Marx's political and economic theories as totally outdated, the Fabians propounded the need for the public ownership of the means of production and the utility services at municipal and, in some cases, national level, on the grounds that capitalism's most heinous crime was its inefficiency. The evils suffered by the working classes would be removed, gradually, by administrative measures – the Fabians despised the muddleheaded charitable organisations – for which the co-operation of the sufferers was neither required nor desired: if only a bit of sense could be knocked into the heads of competent officials, society might be run on rational lines.

Not long after their formation they publicly dissociated themselves from all other socialist movements and propaganda. Bernard Shaw, in retrospect, defined their position accurately:

> "The Fabian Society of London," he wrote, "... was founded in 1884; and its policy was established by a little group of men who were at that time all under thirty. There was not a single veteran of 1848 in its ranks and not a single person who had ever met Karl Marx ... There were practically no wage-workers: the committee was composed of state officials of the higher division and journalists of the special critical class which produces signed feuilleton, they were exceptionally clever ... They paraded their cleverness ... and they openly spoke of ordinary Socialism as a sort of dentition fever which a man had to pass through before he was intellectually mature enough to become a Fabian. Though at this time the idolatry of Marx by the Socialists was a hundred times worse than the idolatry of Gladstone by the Liberals, the Fabians in restating the economic basis of Socialism, brought it up to date by completely ignoring Marx...[93]

Since Marx had expounded no rigid doctrine but a scientific philosophy to explain the processes by which societies develop, applicable at all times and in all places, indicating the means to analyse the interrelation between men and their mode of livelihood, to diagnose in any given situation the social conditions that are moribund and those still in embryo

---

* He resigned from the Civil Service in 1892, the year he married Beatrice Potter.
† From Quintus Fabius (275–203 BC) known as "Cunctator" – the delayer – who unnerved Hannibal by his cautious tactics, refusing to give open battle.

— "a theory of evolution, not a dogma to be learnt by heart and to be repeated mechanically"[94] — the Fabian Society had no more earthly chance to supersede Marx than to reverse the laws of gravity. However, its tracts and essays undoubtedly exercised an enormous influence on intelligent men and women at the fringes of socialism, even making converts of them, though not necessarily Fabians.

The fact that these sects of various character should come into being at this period reflected an overall change in the political climate, accurately gauged by Engels in an article he wrote for *Commonweal* in March 1885, "England in 1845 and 1885".* He attributed the present veering wind to the "pure delusion" of Britain's Free Trade theory of 1847 which had been based upon the assumption "that England was to be the one great manufacturing centre of an agricultural world". While this had remained "the pivot of the present social system of England", the people of France, Belgium, Germany, America, even Russia

> "did not see the advantage of being turned into Irish pauper farmers merely for the greater wealth and glory of English capitalists. They set resolutely about manufacturing, not only for themselves, but for the rest of the world; and the consequence is that the manufacturing monopoly enjoyed by England for nearly a century is irretrievably broken up ... The truth is this: during the period of England's industrial monopoly the English working class have to a certain extent shared in the benefits of the monopoly. These benefits were very unequally parcelled out amongst them; the privileged minority pocketed most, but even the great mass had at least a temporary share now and then. And that is why since the dying-out of Owenism there has been no Socialism in England. With the breakdown of that monopoly the English working class will lose that privileged position; it will find itself — the privileged and leading minority not excepted — on a level with its fellow workers abroad. And that is the reason why there will be Socialism again in England."

The powerful trade unions, catering for certain sections of adult male skilled workers — such as engineers, carpenters, joiners and bricklayers — had been in so strong a position that they could "even successfully resist the introduction of machinery" where it threatened their craft interests. They had

> "succeeded in enforcing for themselves a relatively comfortable position, and they accept it as final. They are the model working men ... and they are very nice people indeed nowadays to deal with, for any sensible capitalist in particular and for the whole capitalist class in general,"

while the vast majority, both in the East End of London and in other large cities, stagnated in

---

* Later incorporated in the Preface to the 1892 English edition of *The Condition of the Working Class in England in 1844*.

"an ever spreading pool ... of misery and desolation, of starvation when out of work, and degradation, physical and moral, when in work."

Competition from abroad – including countries where, as in Germany, the industrial revolution was not yet completed but was rapidly catching up – had caused the Great Depression lasting, with the usual ups and downs, from 1873 to 1896 and forcing manufacturers to introduce new techniques of mass production. With the carving up of Africa and the expansion of the British Empire, of which the colonial peoples were the primary victims, the workers in the imperial countries had shared, however modestly, in the profits, thus giving rise to the notion that there no longer existed a class struggle at home; even suggesting that, with an "aristocracy of labour" – the craftsmen – there were class divisions within the proletariat tantamount to those between owners and producers. But, however vigorously resisted by the "model" Trade Unions, with their avowed policy of conciliation and the voluntary relinquishment of the strike weapon, the floodgates were inevitably opened now to "machine-minders": semi-skilled and unskilled workers without apprenticeship or organisation behind them, benevolent funds to husband or, indeed, anything at all to lose by rebelling against their lot and claiming a share of the spoils.

Only so keen and highly trained an eye as Engels' could have perceived the emerging pattern with such clarity. To younger men, such as Tom Mann at the age of 28, it seemed that "at this time, 1884 and on ... those who were able to sense the situation recognised that something was buzzing".[95]

Indeed it was. The shrewd and seasoned British ruling class could not fail to hear the buzz and the dangers it portended. Employers allowed concessions to be wrung from them,* ostensibly against their will but clearly in their own long term interests, or, as Eleanor herself put it in another context: "to give a little in order to gain much", recognising, even as had Engels in his *Commonweal* article, that the combustible material now kindling would render the trade unions powerless to serve as "the strongest barrier to social revolution".[97] The stolid officials of those unions might be slow to detect change, but both the employers and the most downtrodden workers were preparing to take up new positions. The conflict between the classes had entered upon a new phase.

Another factor played a small though significant part in this shift of battleground. There might have been little re-orientation in the political thinking of workers – merely an increase of those struggles, frequent enough in earlier decades, for higher wages or improved conditions – had

---

* The national average of earnings by adult males in 1867 was £45 a year. By 1886 it had risen to £57 for 46 weeks: that is, allowing for a national average of 6 weeks' lost time.[96]

not the employers been confronted for the first time by a rather dis-
concerting new type of working man: the awful thing was he could read.

To be sure, that he should learn his letters and do his sums was
essential to the existing stage of technology; but it had other and undesirable side-effects, unknown to earlier generations of masters.

Many of the young workers of the mid-eighties were the product of the
1870 Education Act which had a profound effect upon the entire proletariat. True, there had long been elementary schools before, provided by
various religious and charitable bodies; true that among the Chartists
there had been well-read, even learned, working men; true, also, that the
new Act had as many holes as a sieve. Local authorities were slow to apply
it – the premises had first to be built – education was neither compulsory
nor free; children could leave school at ten years of age and one "reasonable excuse" for not attending at all was if no school existed "within
such distance, not exceeding 3 miles, measured according to the nearest
road from the residence of such child",* thus leaving many rural communities entirely untouched. Meanwhile poorly clad and ill-fed urban
children were herded into overcrowded classrooms where learning by rote
and corporal punishment were alike of a fearful and insensate monotony.
There was also the infamous half-time system by which children went to
school for ten hours out of a working week of, alternately, 57 and 45
hours for a wage of, perhaps, half-a-crown a week (paid fortnightly), from
which school fees were deducted by the employer. It was not, in short, a
measure calculated to inaugurate an age of proletarian *savants*. Nonetheless it meant that many of those who started work in mills and
factories, fields and sweatshops at eight years of age no longer needed the
exceptional will and tenacity of the few among their forefathers who had
mastered the arts of literacy. The incontrovertible facts are that, whereas
in 1857 – two years after Eleanor was born – only 531,000 children in
Great Britain received a primary education, by 1883 the number was
3,560,000, while the free public libraries had increased from 14 in 1868
to 208 in 1890: this in an age when readers who could afford it still
indulged the quaint habit of buying books.

It is not suggested that the majority of young workers in the mid-
eighties now pounced upon the new socialist journals and pamphlets –
their circulation was extremely small – but it had become less easy to
hoodwink them about their own conditions in the richest and most highly
developed industrial country on earth.

What these conditions were, at a time when the employing class was
riding high on the crest of colonial expansion and new inventions, was

---

* Chap. 74 (3). 33 & 34 Vict.

sharply brought home when Hyndman published the statement that one quarter of London's population – then nearly 4 million – was living below the poverty line.

This extravagant claim was challenged by Charles Booth* who, after an interview with Hyndman, decided to conduct his own survey,† only to discover that not a quarter but 35 per cent of the 900,000 Londoners in the East End were living in a state of abject misery, over 100,000 being in acute distress at the time of Queen Victoria's golden jubilee.

This is small cause for wonder when an "ideal" – that is, the most niggardly – budget drawn up in 1884 showed that an average working-class family of 4.61 persons living in England and Wales needed some thing above £74 a year to buy the necessities of life‡ while, to take but one example, the main railway companies, employing some 367,300 males, paid firemen £59, shunters £55, signalmen £52, platelayers £48 and porters £39 a year.[99]

Below the categories of underpaid workers in industry and services there was a yet more starveling group, extending from the self-employed costermonger and the sweated home-worker to the forlorn families of the unemployed, the sick, the drunkards, the incapacitated and the mentally retarded, who merged with the thieves, the pimps, the prostitutes and criminals of the "dangerous classes". To investigate these lower depths

---

* A Liberal Nonconformist (1840–1916) of strong anti-socialist views who, having made a fortune in shipping by the time he was 40 thanks to investing in the most up-to-date steamships, then retired to devote himself to social questions.

† Started in 1886 and published three years later.

‡

£			s.	d.	per annum
Bread	28 lb. p.w. at 6d. per quartern		9.	2.	0
Meat	5 lb. p.w. at 10d. per lb.		10.	16.	0
Butter	1 lb. p.w. at 1/6 per lb.		5.	17.	0
Cheese	½ lb. p.w. at 10d. per lb.		1.	2.	0
Sugar	3 lb. p.w. at 3d. per lb.		1.	19.	0
Tea	½ lb. p.w. at 2/8 per lb.		3.	9.	0
Vegetables and potatoes*			2.	0.	0
Milk*			2.	10.	0
Eggs*			1.	10.	0
Drink 2/-p.w.*			5.	4.	0
Coal and gas*			2.	0.	0
Rent 6/-p.w.*			15.	12.	0
Tobacco 1/-p.w.*			2.	10.	0
Clothing*			4.	0.	0
Furniture*			1.	0.	0
Travel and amusements*			3.	0.	0
Sundries: Church, Doctor, Education			2.	10.	0
			74.	1.	0

No quantities or prices given.

It will be noted that no fish, bacon, fruit (or jam), soap or other cleaning materials for the person or domestic use are included.[98]

had been one of Henry Mayhew's purposes a generation before and the high merit of his work is not invalidated by the fact that he used methods, criteria and, above all, lucid prose quite alien to modern sociology. Booth, who enlisted a band of gifted volunteers, defined the areas for investigation and degrees of poverty, systematically covering in his later surveys the boroughs of inner London and its outlying suburbs, to reveal that an average of 31 per cent came within his classification of poverty.*[100]

Again, no one supposes that the British working man spent his little leisure reading social surveys and statistics to inflame, however unintentionally, his revolutionary ardour. But, while a handful of well-endowed citizens who stood above the battle studied his material circumstances, disclosing the extent of their debasement, specifying its causes and propounding mild remedies, the various socialist sects could use these hard facts to argue a political case by word of mouth and print, to which the worker himself now lent a ready ear and eye.

However, it is clear that these many propagandists did not speak with one voice.† Even among the most dedicated revolutionaries – particularly among the most dedicated revolutionaries – there were conflicting opinions and interminable squabbles. It is a matter of fact that the socialist movement was rent by schisms, heresies and doctrinal differences since its inception.

Obviously enough the anti-Marxist champions of efficiency and the inefficient champions of Marxism had little ground in common, as it is equally clear that a movement powered by such irresistible forces as were present in the mid-eighties could not but be composed of heterogeneous groups and factions: revolutionaries, reformers and rebels of every stripe – parliamentarians, anti-parliamentarians, republicans, anarchists, Christian Socialists, militant atheists, Single Taxers, National Land Leaguers, Left

---

* It comes as no surprise to find the figure for Southwark was 67.9 per cent, for King's Cross 55.4 per cent and for Bethnal Green 58.7 per cent. What does astonish, and must have astonished the investigators, was that in such neighbourhoods as St. John's Wood, the Abbey district of Westminster and Battersea Park the figures were, respectively, 35.4 per cent, 45.9 per cent and 45.6 per cent. Even Mayfair had its 2.7 per cent of "poor" and Kensington its 5.9 per cent. That this was neither a uniquely London nor a contemporary situation may be judged by leaping ahead to 1899, when Seebohm Rowntree began his investigations in York: a city with a population of 75,812 and, in economic and social composition, a fair sample of provincial towns. Rowntree's book, *Poverty. A Study of Town Life* (1901), revealed that 43.4 per cent of wage-earners and 27.84 per cent of the total population did not reach subsistence level of 21s8d. a week.

† As the Great Cham observed in one of his less wayward moods: "Providence has wisely ordained that the more numerous men are, the more difficult it is for them to agree in any thing, and so they are governed. There is no doubt that, if the poor should reason, 'We'll be poor no longer, we'll make the rich take their turn', they could easily do it, were it not that they can't agree."

Radicals, temperance apostles, trade union and anti-trade union agitators – all inspired by the will to bring about changes in a social system so manifestly inequitable, none quite knowing what was to be done. Engels' funeral oration on the First International* of ten years before made it plain that each historical epoch posed its own questions to which ever and again new answers must be found.

Marx in his time had stood almost alone in opposition to a host of empirical revolutionaries, conspiratorial groups and self-styled "Marxists" with whom he disagreed on fundamental principles. It followed that, as his theories began to spread and the pressure of events brought new men into action, his successive interpreters and misinterpreters should claim to be his true heirs, falling out with each other, as heirs will, until sight of the main enemy was often lost in the heat and dust of their hostilities.

"Working men of all countries, unite!" Such are the words with which the *Communist Manifesto* of 1848 ends. Variations of that call – Unity is Strength; United We Stand, Divided We Fall; In Combination Lies Our Strength; Organisation is the Surest Weapon – are emblazoned on many old trade union and socialist banners carried by working-class demonstrators. Yet everywhere the emergent socialist parties found that, as William Morris put it later:

> "There are two main sources of dispute. We cannot quite agree as to what is likely to be the precise social system of the future, and we cannot agree as to the best means of attaining it,"[101]

while, a little earlier, he had written:

> "Men fight and lose the battle, and the thing they fought for comes about in spite of their defeat, and when it comes it turns out not to be what they meant."[102]

At every turn it was found, with some dismay, that the path to a new social order was by no means clearly signposted – indeed, that "the road ... would have to be built before it could be travelled", as a much younger contemporary wrote[103] – and also that, while it may be a better thing to travel hopefully than to arrive, it does buoy hope to have some clue to one's destination.

Naturally no troubles of the kind beset upholders of the *status quo*: they might have their family tiffs, but on the main issue of keeping what they had and adding what they could, they were at one. Not only is money thicker than blood, but nothing is as thick as thieves and so long as

---

* See letter to Sorge. Above, p. 103.

capitalism was viable it would close its ranks in face of the class enemy whenever and wherever the threat of war was in the air.

Thus unity, because it was the most decisive and the most difficult of all things to achieve, became the watchword of the revolutionary left, of those who did not like things as they were and set out on an untrodden path to change them.

Before the *Communist Manifesto* was ever written, Engels had predicted these conflicts within socialism and sounded a warning note on forecasting the exact form of both means and ends.

Almost 40 years had elapsed since Engels had set down his two "Credos" for the Communist League in 1847 in the form of Socratic dialogues,* yet they were still relevant to the rebirth of socialism in the 1880s.

Conflicting views on political tactics were exacerbated by the clash of personalities, as inveterate then as in any previous (or subsequent) period. Indeed, it could be said that the smaller and newer the organisation the more ferocious the quarrels, for there was not the corrective of a mass movement carried forward on its own momentum despite warring factions. However, even at this stage no individual could impede the strong current of socialism into which so many streams already flowed, nor yet divert it according to his will.

Hyndman of the Democratic Federation certainly did his level best. This most improbable socialist (1842–1921), a barrister and company director who had been privately tutored until he went up to Trinity College, Cambridge, had stood, unsuccessfully, as an "Independent" – in effect, Tory – candidate for Marylebone in 1880. While he indulged in the tastes and pursuits of his class, he poured out time and money on the socialist movement from 1881, constantly giving offence to his comrades by the overweening deportment which Marx had found so repelling. Genuinely outraged by "the miserable system of draining India of her wealth to the extent of upwards of £30m. a year for the benefit of the well-to-do classes in the United Kingdom",[105] he nevertheless conserved strongly chauvinist and imperialist views. At the same time his rooted xenophobia – driving him to intrigue against and slander any foreign-born socialist – and his antisemitism† could not but antagonise those to whom socialism and internationalism were synonymous. But so long as

---

* The first of these was not brought to light until 1968 when it was found among the papers of Joachim Martens in a collection of manuscripts he deposited in the University Library of Hamburg, his native city, in 1912. The second was found shortly after Engels' death among his papers.[104]
† Apart from his references to "that damned Jew", "that strange Jew" – who may, for all anyone knows, have been damned or strange – his peculiar use of a noun as an adjective in such terms as "Jew Englishman", "Jew statesman", "Jew officer" and so forth, betrays this prejudice.

Hyndman treated the small Democratic Federation as his personal possession, a private company, as it were, of which he was the managing director and sole shareholder, his own weaknesses were of little moment to the outside world, though a perpetual irritant within the organisation's counsels.

A vain, obstinate and contentious man who could not endure opposition from his colleagues, his mistakes, which were not few, appeared to them gigantic while the value of his contribution, by no means negligible, was dwarfed. Thus, whether right or wrong, Hyndman created strife.* The amazing thing is how often he was right when one considers how weak he was on theory and how strong on egotism. Engels, who regarded him simply as "a pretty unscrupulous careerist",[107] wrote letters at this period deriding Hyndman's pretensions as a Marxist or as any type of socialist at all, fervently thankful that the British workers paid not the slightest heed to his antics.

The antagonism between these two was such that Hyndman, with a newspaper at his command, waged an unedifying public feud against anyone associated with Engels – not excluding Eleanor – venting a petty personal spite that at times resembled the outpouring of a bad-tempered housewife with a grudge against the neighbours.

His disparagement of the trade unions, expressed in reasonably just terms in 1883,† did not yield before the militant New Unionism of a few years later. Indeed, it never yielded; and after half a lifetime as a leader of Social-Democracy, having learned – and taught – a number of valuable lessons, he retained a stubborn lack of faith in the initiative of the proletariat and its mass organisations. As late as 1897 he wrote to Wilhelm Liebknecht:

> "Our working men are so ignorant and depressed by a hundred years of capitalist tyranny that it is hard to rouse them ... Every year that passes brings on more educated lads to take the place of the old hopeless workers; but the process is necessarily slow and meantime the crisis ... may be upon us before we are ready to act ... In fact the Trade Unions ... stand in the way of a genuine organisation of the proletariat..."[108]

That this attitude influenced the course of the British movement cannot be doubted; and here, as in many another of his pronouncements

---

* An additional reason was that he got on everybody's nerves. A contemporary said of him: "'He draweth out the thread of his verbosity finer than the staple of his argument'"; and, having once travelled in a railway compartment with him, found that he "talked and talked till between his oration and the swaying of the train I was actually dizzy. My one hope was that in tunnels ... there would be a temporary lull, but it was not so: he talked underground and overground alike."[106]

† In his *Historical Basis of Socialism*.

over the long years of his active political life, Hyndman exhibited the not unusual contradiction of a sound appraisal of social and economic injustice with a contempt for the working class, unable to credit it with so much as the enlightened self-interest needed to strike off its chains.

His doctrinaire, oversimplified version of Marxism served him well enough in Hyde Park* and at countless meetings up and down the country – indeed, it was from him that tens of thousands of British workers heard about socialism for the first time – but it was a stumbling block when the policies and principles of the Federation were under consideration.

Whatever he might say publicly in *Justice*, at once deploring but inviting support for the Highgate demonstration in March 1884, Hyndman, at the Executive Council's meetings, had employed one of his typical – in this case thwarted – stratagems to prevent it taking place at all. Defeated, he then proposed that the Federation should take no part in it. Eleanor gave a detailed account of these obstructive tactics, describing at the same time how Hyndman had equally objected to the Federation sending a delegate to the Roubaix Congress of the French Workers' Party,† dismissing both projects as a "family manœuvre". He then spread it about that Eleanor and her sister in France had forged a letter to the Council in order to force his hand. The letter of course was never seen by anyone.[109] On this issue he was "opposed by most present", Eleanor wrote to Laura,

> "and I gave him the *coup de grâce* by expressing, so far as I was able, the position of the Roubaix people ... and carried all the Committee with me ... Aveling also spoke, pointing out that Hyndman's exception to the parti ouvrier as being a small section could even better be applied to the Federation, and that we would have to consider the principles at stake, not the persons ... There are *admirable* elements in the Federation, but also endless difficulties, and I foresee not the least of these will be Hyndman."[110]

In the event, Harry Quelch and Belfort Bax (whose nomination Hyndman opposed on the grounds that he was not a working man) attended the Roubaix Congress.

Eleanor, writing to Lavrov from Great Coram Street, introduced Bax as "absolutely 'ours', and more than that he is my personal friend. I am sure

---

* He had at first inveighed against the "foreign and pagan custom" of holding open-air meetings on a Sunday, but when others had paved the way, attracting large audiences, his scruples vanished and he took to the soap-box in his customary garb of top-hat and frock-coat. This, incidentally, was not at Speakers' Corner, but by the "Reformers' Tree", north-east of the Serpentine, inside the park.
† Its 7th National Congress, held from 29 March to 7 April 1884.

that I need say nothing more to you for you to give him a friendly reception..."[111]

In July Eleanor wrote to Laura:

"There has been no end of petty intriguing within that body of late ... besides some very nasty personal affairs ... So far [Hyndman] has things here much his own way, but he is playing his cards very badly, irritating everyone, and his little game will soon be played out. The sooner the better for our movement. It has *every* chance here at this present time if only we had better leaders than Hyndman and his henchmen."*[112]

The mistrust was mutual. In his reminiscences Hyndman referred to Eleanor as "the centre of that curious and capable family clique which carried on the 'Old International' throughout Europe".[114] Not that he was the only one to resent the connection maintained between Marx's circle and the Continental socialists. Bernard Shaw, describing the "highly unfavourable" relations of the Fabian Society with the leaders of the German Party, wrote many years later: "All their sources of information as to the English movement were ultra-Marxite, as they depended for their London news on Friedrich Engels and Eleanor Marx..."[115]

Hyndman believed that any move to link British socialists more closely with workers' parties abroad was a plot hatched by the arch-fiend Engels in the fastness of 122 Regent's Park Road. He was not concerned with the purpose of these diabolical machinations; it was enough for him that they were un-English. In retrospect, he granted that Eleanor's "power of work was inexhaustible" and that "she was extremely valuable to the cause", while not omitting the damaging charge that she "inherited her nose and mouth of the Jewish type from Marx himself";[116] but at the time he would not have assigned to her any but a destructive role. To William Morris he wrote that he and others who had worked for the "front proud position of *Justice*" were not prepared to admit its control to a system which

"has always meant and must always mean ruin; and it is worth notice that the change is specially wanted by the very persons – Dr. and Mrs. Aveling – who ... ruined *To-Day* by their prejudices and advertising puffery of themselves ... people who have never done the paper any good whatever."[117]

It was not, however, a personal feud – indeed, her name was almost invariably coupled with Aveling's whenever he attacked her – nor was Eleanor the only one to subscribe to Engels' view of Hyndman as "a political adventurer" who was trying "to buy up the whole movement"

---

* At about the same time Morris was writing: "I am afraid we are but at the beginning of our troubles."[113]

and causing havoc in the process, so that, before long, the most sincere and disinterested members of the Executive Council formed what Morris himself called "the cabal". This anti-Hyndman faction now made a determined effort to call a halt to the futile rows and disruptions. The ins and outs, the moves and counter-moves of this internecine struggle, lasting for months, have been fully recorded* and might seem to have been a storm in a teacup, so negligible were the numbers involved. However, though matters were brought to a head on a vote of confidence in Hyndman's leadership which ran counter to all democratic methods, a major political concept was at issue, as Eleanor set out in a letter to Wilhelm Liebknecht in January 1885.

> "You will understand without much explanation," she wrote, "... our present position ... One of our chief points of conflict with Hyndman is that whereas *we* wish to make this a really international movement ... Mr. Hyndman, whenever he could do so with impunity, has endeavoured to set English workmen against 'foreigners'. Now it is absolutely necessary we show the enemy a united front – and that we may do this our German friends *must* lend us a helping hand. If you want anything to come of the movement here; if you want to help on the really Socialist, as distinct from the Soz [*sic*] Democrat – jingo – Possibilist – Party – now is the time to do it."[118]

The decisive Executive meeting took place on 16 December 1884. Thereafter the "cabal" met at Eleanor's place on the 18th and a further Executive Council meeting on 23 December was followed by a recalled session lasting four and a half hours on the 27th. Finally a vote was taken on a resolution that, as Morris admitted, was but the *occasion*, not the *cause* of the split[119] which gained a majority of ten to eight, whereupon the secessionists immediately handed in their prepared letter of resignation:

> "Since discord has arisen in this Council owing to the attempt to substitute arbitrary rule therein for fraternal co-operation contrary to the principles of Socialism, and since it seems to us impossible to heal this discord, we the undersigned think it better in the interests of Socialism to cease to belong to this Council and accordingly hand in our resignation."

The ten signatories were Edward Aveling, Eleanor Marx Aveling, Belfort Bax, Robert Banner, J. Cooper, W. J. Clarke, Joseph Lane, John Lincoln Mahon, Samuel Mainwaring and William Morris.[120]

It is natural to ask why, having defeated Hyndman and "his henchmen", the victors should stalk out. The reason is not far to seek: the small

---

* By none better than E. P. Thompson in his *William Morris: Romantic to Revolutionary*, where he remarks that "to the rank and file the whole thing appeared as a mystery" (p. 420). Morris's own letters also trace the course of events in detail.

majority vote represented less than a guarantee that the clashes would now cease and, as Morris wrote to Joynes on Christmas Day 1884:

"*I am sure the split was unavoidable:* Hyndman can accept only one position in such a body as the SDF – that of master: some may think that position on his part desirable; I don't and I cannot stand it. You must not suppose that this is a matter of mere personal likes and dislikes: the causes lie much deeper than that. He has been acting throughout (to my mind) as a politician determined to push his own advantage (if you please along with that of the party) always on the look out for anything which could advance the party he is supposed to lead: his aim has been to make the movement seem big; to frighten the powers that be with a turnip bogie which perhaps he almost believes in himself: hence all that insane talk of immediate forcible revolution, when we know that the workers in England are not even touched by the movement . . . we say let him keep his property with all its 'increments', 'earned' and 'unearned'. But we won't be part of it . . . however small a body we may form, we are at least on a new basis of mutual trust among ourselves . . ."[121]

On Monday, 29 December 1884, the Socialist League was formed and the importance of that fact to politics, as also to the story of Eleanor Marx, is that, at a crucial moment in the early days of the British labour movement, a diminutive band of socialists stood firmly by the Marxist principles of internationalism and the rejection of both autocracy and opportunism.

It cannot be said, however, to have come nearer to realising the dream of unity within that movement nor yet to have put an end to disagreements. It did not inaugurate an era of mutual trust even among its own small brotherhood: a splinter body at best, it was only too soon to be fissured.

Engels wrote to Laura on 1 January 1885:

"I am sorry the crisis in the Social D. Federation could not be retarded a little longer; Hyndman would have got deeper into the mud, and the personal element would have been thrown into the back-ground. However it could not be helped. The reason why the majority, instead of following up their victory, *resigned*, and starts a new organisation was this chiefly, as Morris said to me: the old organisation was not *worth having*. The London branches are about 300 strong in all and those they hope mostly to get, and as to the provinces, it's all bosh and bogus. Well we'll see what they will make. There is this to be said in their favour: that three more unpractical men for a political organisation than Aveling, Bax and Morris are not to be found in all England. But they are sincere."[122]

Eleanor's version of the split and all it implied to an active participant at the time could not be bettered. She wrote to Laura on 31 December 1884 – that is, at the height of the dénouement:

". . . from the disgraceful vilification of everyone to whom he personally objects as not being a 'follower' of himself, Hyndman forced things to such a condition that it was impossible to go on working with him. The personal question – inevitable personal questions will be mixed up in all such movements as these – is after all very secondary to the principal one – that of whether we were to sink into a merely Tory-democratic Party or to go on working on the lines of the German Socialists and the French Parti Ouvrier ... Our majority was too small to make it possible for us to really get rid of the Jingo faction, and so, after due consideration with Engels we decided to go out, and form a new organisation. This is to be called the Socialist League ... The General has promised, now we are rid of the unclean* elements of the Federation, to help us; many others who have till now stood aloof will come to us also we shall of course (through FE) have the Germans with us, and we also count on the Parti ouvrier. A short statement will be drawn up and sent by us to the various Socialist parties, at once to explain our secession, and to ask their support. Hyndman will now no doubt be able to form the alliance he has all along tried to make, and been prevented by us from making, with Brousse† – like will to like ... Oh dear! is not all this wearisome and stupid! But I suppose it must be gone through. I comfort myself by recalling the long Schweitzer-Lassalle-Liebknecht quarrel in Germany and the Brousse-Lafargue split in France. I suppose this kind of thing is inevitable in the beginning of any move-ment...."[123]

On the same day and in much the same terms she wrote to Lavrov, her father's old friend, now over 60, who had lived as an émigré in Paris since 1870. To him she also said how sick she was of the petty intrigues and tiresome disputes. "Still," she went on, "one must not despair – but work for the Cause."[124] She wrote to him again on 20 January, enclosing a copy of the letter sent to all the SDF branches explaining the defection and the Socialist League Manifesto.

"Morris," she said, "who has subsidised *Justice* up to now is not on the terms with Hyndman that you supposed. On the contrary, it was he in particular who insisted that we part company from a man who can only prejudice the success of the party in England. It's not pleasant to be thus forced to mix purely personal questions with important questions of principle. But – as you know, of course, better than anyone else – it is often impossible not to mix them, and very often the personal question becomes a question of principle ... Our friend Engels is entirely with us."

She asked Lavrov to write a word, if only as a letter, for publication in the second number of the new journal:

"We want to bring out the *international* character of the movement ... Liebknecht, and probably Bebel, Lafargue, Stepniak, Engels have already promised to write a few words

---

* Perhaps "unclear".

† Paul-Louis-Marie Brousse (1844–1912), a doctor by profession, who had taken part in the Paris Commune, emigrating after its defeat to Spain and then to Switzerland, taking a leading part in the anarchist movement. On his return to France he was one of the founders of the Workers' Party but broke away from it in 1882 to become the leader of the "Possibilist" – i.e. reformist – Socialist Federation of French Workers (*Fédération des Travaillistes Socialistes de France*).

for us ... and if we could add some Russian names (above all an honoured name such as yours), it would be of immense value..."[125]

The Socialist League's manifesto, *To Socialists*, was issued on 13 January 1885 from its premises at 27 Farringdon Road. It ran:

"We, the members of the Council of the Social-Democratic Federation, who, although a majority, resigned on December 27th, wish to explain our reasons for that retirement, and for our forming a body independent of the Social-Democratic Federation.

It is admitted by those who remain on the Council, as well as by ourselves, that there has been for some time past a want of harmony in the Council; we believe that this has been caused by a real difference in opinion as to what should be the aims and tactics of a Socialist propaganda.

Our view is that such a body in the present state of things has no function but to educate the people in the principles of Socialism, and to organise such as it can get hold of to take their due places, when the crisis shall come which will force action on us. We believe that to hold out as baits hopes of amelioration of the condition of the workers, to be wrung out of the necessities of the rival factions of our privileged rulers is delusive and mischievous. For carrying out our aims of education and organization no over-shadowing and indispensable leader is required, but only a band of instructed men, each of whom can learn to fulfil, as occasion requires it, the simple functions of the leader of a party of principle.

We say, that on the other hand there has been in the ranks of the Social-Democratic Federation a tendency to political opportunism, which if developed would have involved us in alliances, however temporary, with one or other of the political factions, and would have weakened our propagandist force by driving us into electioneering, and possibly would have deprived us of the due services of some of our most energetic men by sending them to our sham parliament, there to become either nonentities, or perhaps our masters, and it may be our betrayers. We say also that among those who favoured these views of political adventure there was a tendency towards national assertion, the persistent foe of Socialism: and it is easy to see how dangerous this might become in times like the present.

Furthermore, these views have led, as they were sure to lead, to attempts at arbitrary rule inside the Federation; for such a policy as the above demands a skilful and shifty leader, to whom all persons and opinions must be subordinated, and who must be supported (if necessary) at the expense of fairness and fraternal openness.

Accordingly, attempts have been made to crush out local freedom in affiliated bodies, and to expel or render unpopular those individual members who have asserted their independence. The organ of the party, also, has been in the hands of an irresponsible editor, who has declared himself determined to resign rather than allow the Federation to have any control over the conduct of the paper.

All this we have found intolerable. It may be asked of us why we did not remain in the body and try to enforce our views by steady opposition in it. We answer, as long as we thought reconciliation possible, we did do so; but the tendencies above mentioned were necessarily aggressive, and at last two distinct attacks on individuals showed us that the rent could not be mended.

We felt that thenceforth there must be two opposed parties in the Social-Democratic Federation. We did not believe that a propagandist body could do useful work so divided, and we thought that it would not be in the interests of Socialism to carry on the contest further in the Federation; because, however it might end, it would leave a discontented minority, ruled by a majority, whose position would have been both precarious and tyrannical.

On the other hand, our view of our duty to the cause of Socialism forbids us to cease spreading its principles or to work as mere individuals. We have therefore set on foot an independent organisation, the Socialist League, with no intention of acting in hostility to the Social-Democratic Federation, but determined to spread the principles of Socialism, by the only means we deem effectual.

13th January, 1885.   (Signed)
       EDWARD AVELING.
       ELEANOR MARX AVELING.
       ROBERT BANNER.
       E. BELFORT BAX.
       J. COOPER.
       W. J. CLARK.
       JOSEPH LANE.
       S. MAINWARING.
       J. L. MAHON.
       WILLIAM MORRIS.

Issued from the offices of
'THE SOCIALIST LEAGUE,' 27, Farringdon Street, London, E.C."[126]

Starting with its first number in February 1885, Eleanor contributed regularly to the Socialist League's paper *Commonweal*.* She resumed her gathering of news items from abroad, now under the title "Record of the Revolutionary International Movement", signed "E. Marx".

The early months of that year were a time of great activity. On 26 January General Gordon had been killed at Khartoum† and the press – in particular *The Times* and the *Pall Mall Gazette* – went almost mad with grief, thus provoking the fury of those opposed to imperial conquest. While Eleanor helped to organise a protest meeting against the war, the Socialist League issued a thousand copies of a four-page leaflet, decorated by Walter Crane,‡ on 2 March.

"Fellow Citizens," it began, "A wicked and unjust war is now being waged by the ruling and propertied classes of this country, with all the resources of civilisation at their back, against an ill-armed and semi-barbarous people whose only crime is that they have risen against a foreign oppression which these classes themselves admit to be infamous. Tens of millions wrung from the labour of workmen of this country are being squandered on Arab slaughtering; and for what: 1) that Eastern Africa may be 'opened up' to the purveyor of 'shoddy' wares, bad spirits, venereal disease, cheap bibles and missionaries; in short that the English trader and contractor may establish his dominion on the ruins of the old, simple and happy life led by the children of the desert; 2) that a fresh supply of sinecure Government posts may be obtained for the occupation of the younger sons of the official classes; 3) as a minor consideration may

---

* A monthly journal whose founders had originally wished it to be a weekly but were dissuaded by Engels. It consisted of eight pages, priced at one penny, and was edited by William Morris, with Aveling as sub-editor until April 1886 when it did become a weekly. Morris "had stipulated that his editorship would chiefly be of a figure-head character, and that the bulk of the technical and drudgery work should be put on the shoulders of the sub-editor, who would be paid for his services".[127]

† At the end of 1883 the British had sent gunboats to put down a general rising in the Sudan. Gordon arrived in the following month but by April 1884 the whole country was in a state of insurrection. Khartoum was invested and a British expeditionary force was sent out to relieve it in August. By 3 September some 14,000 troops were massed in Egypt and, on the 24th, the fleet stood off Alexandria. On the same date several camel corps set out from Woolwich (without camels). The Sudanese were not quickly subdued and, on and off, the fighting continued until 1898, when Kitchener finished it off to great acclaim and an earldom, linking his name forever with this episode in our rough island story.

‡ 1845–1915. One of Morris's close associates, both as artist and socialist. He was the Principal of the Royal College of Art for the year 1898–9.

be added that a new and happy hunting ground be provided for military sportsmen, who ... find life boring at home and are always ready for a little Arab shooting when occasion arises ... Citizens, you are the dupes of a plot."

The manifesto then traced the history of the war in the Sudan and ended:

"... finally, we ask you to consider who it is that have to do the fighting on this and similar occasions. Is it the market-hunting classes themselves? Is it they who form the rank and file of the army? No! But the sons and brothers of the working classes at home. They it is who for a miserable pittance are compelled to serve in these commercial wars. They it is who conquer, for the wealthy middle and upper classes, new lands for exploitation, fresh populations for pillage, as these classes require them, and who have, as their reward, the assurance of their masters that they are nobly fighting for their Queen and country."[128]

This document was signed by the 25 members of the Provisional Council, including Eleanor and Aveling.

They were now working closely with Morris, not only on the paper and in drafting manifestos, but by supporting the meetings he held throughout the country. In February they went with him to Oxford where the well organised opposition proved so ineffectual that the ringleader's windows were broken that night by his angry followers "for not making a better job of it".[129]

Despite the promise and enterprise shown by the newly fledged group, Eleanor was anxious.

"There is the *constant* worry from the 'Socialist League'," she wrote to Laura. "The Anarchists here will be our chief difficulty. Neither Morris, nor Bax, nor any of our people know really what these Anarchists are: till they *do* find out, it is a hard struggle to make head against them – the more that many of our English men taken in by the foreign Anarchists ... are unquestionably the best men we have here."[130]

This hostility to the anarchists stemmed from Marx's bitter quarrels with them as the parodists of revolutionary theory. With their basic faith in conspiracy and violence they were not merely his most implacable adversaries but they provided a happy hunting ground for *agents provocateurs*, so that it became almost impossible to distinguish the true believers from those who incited them to excesses that would land them in police traps. Eleanor had reasons for this fear and hatred, whereas such harmless sects as the Fabians, however wrongheaded she thought their prescriptions for social change, were at least above the suspicion of harbouring spies. She is never known to have attacked them publicly and, on the contrary, they frequently appeared with her upon the same platform while among them she could number many friends. Of the Christian Socialists she was equally tolerant:

"There may be only a dozen of them, but they are truly convinced and very honest people," she wrote to Lavrov in March 1886, "although one must be English to understand this ludicrous mixture of Christianity and Socialism. They are mainly Anglican churchmen, but their religion is as singular as their socialism."

About the anarchists, however – though equally few in number – she was uncompromising since she believed that, unlike the Christians, they exerted a baneful influence:

"...there is a small group of them here, mainly Germans, French, etc. but very few English. Unfortunately in our movement there are many people who do not understand the foundations and the theoretical questions of Socialism, good people who see that the world is out of joint, and who imagine that they know what should be done in order that evil should be turned to good. They do not understand what Communism or Anarchism is, and think that whoever spoke last is right. Among these friends the Anarchists try to carry on propaganda, but you know well enough that when 1½ Anarchists they will claim to be 100. I think that if there are a dozen English Anarchists, that would be the outside figure."[131]

One subject Eleanor reported in her "Record" was the *gendarmes'* unprovoked attack upon the Paris crowd at the unfurling of the red flag during the Père Lachaise meeting on 30 May 1885 to commemorate the dead of the Commune. Though she did not mention it, Lissagaray was present at this ceremony.

"...Without rhyme or reason," she wrote, "without the shadow of a pretext, these absolutely unarmed and quiet persons are suddenly attacked by armed police and soldiers, who, according even to the reactionary press, wildly and indiscriminately charged men, women and children."

Most of her news, indeed, was of the hounding of socialists on the Continent. She was soon to experience such harassments on a smaller scale in the streets of London.

The fight for free speech and the right of assembly had a long and stormy history. In the early 'eighties, the East End Radicals who held regular meetings on Mile End Waste in Stepney were constantly chivvied by the police. They then adjourned to Limehouse where an open air meeting in Piggot Street, off the junction of the Commercial Road and the East India Dock Road, was addressed by a member of the SDF. It was stopped by the police for causing an obstruction. Thereafter both Radical Club and SDF speakers took to nearby Dod Street, mainly occupied by factories and warehouses and thus deserted on summer Sunday mornings.

Nevertheless, towards the end of August *Justice* published a warning that police action was to be expected. From then on, every week, one or other of the speakers was arrested, brought before the magistrate on Monday, bound over not to repeat the offence and fined. On 6 September the arrested man, Jack Williams of the SDF, who was to stand as a socialist candidate in the forthcoming parliamentary elections, refused to be bound over or to pay a fine. He was sentenced to one month's imprisonment in Holloway gaol. In protest, the Radical Clubs and socialist organisations formed a Free Speech Vigilance Committee and called for a mass demonstration to be held on 20 September. Not in vain. Some 7,000 people thronged to Dod Street. There were 27 speakers, including Eleanor who was reported as saying she was "sure that large assembly would show the upper classes an example in the way of orderly conduct"[132], and Aveling, both of whom were "greatly applauded", according to *Justice* which, in the same issue, said that the tightly packed crowd had not noticed "the helmets of the police moving stealthily along the side of the street".[133] As an eye-witness recalled: "On this occasion there was no doubt at all about obstruction! So great was the crowd that the police had to be reinforced before they could charge it."[134] The Socialist League banner was seized and many people were arrested, including William Morris.* The next morning they were brought before Mr. Saunders, the Thames Police Court magistrate, while thousands gathered outside and Eleanor appeared as one of the witnesses for the defence. Asserting the right of free speech, she said she intended to go to future meetings. This was too much for Mr. Saunders. "You need not be continually throwing that into my teeth," he said, "it is an impertinence." Eleanor stated that she had been at many meetings and this was the most quiet and orderly one she had ever attended while the police had acted with great brutality.[135] Thereupon she was roughly handled by the police present in the court, Morris intervened and was himself "violently punched and ill-treated in a most shameful manner".[136]

The determination to protest, this time against the Dod Street arrests, was carried out with a vengeance. On Sunday, 27 September, a crowd estimated at 60,000† marched from Stepney Green, took possession of Dod Street which could not contain it and moved on to the West India Dock Road, undoubtedly causing obstruction. But in view of the forth-

---

* Under an item called "Jottings" in the *East End Gazette* of 26 September, the pseudonymous reporter, Asmodeus, wrote that "the plague of Socialists still afflicts East London on Sunday mornings" and: "a Mr. William Morris, poet, artist and socialist, seems to have dropped from the clouds into the Thames Police Court".

† Even the conservative *Graphic* allowed it 30,000.

coming General Election,* the Home Secretary, Sir William Harcourt, had given orders that there was to be no police interference.

Aveling now got into hot water. After the arrests of 20 September, Engels had written to Laura:

"While you had a fine row in Paris last week, Tussy and Aveling had one here in the East End ... my opinion is that unless they can get the Radicals who are very eager, apparently, on their side, to take the matter up, *le jeu ne vaut pas la chandelle.*† The Socialists are nowhere, the Radicals are a power. If the question can be made one for which a dozen Radicals will have themselves arrested, the government will give way – if only in view of the election. If only Socialists are the victims, they will go to prison without any effect."[137]

The tactics Engels recommended were, in fact, adopted by the Vigilance Committee, if not perhaps for his reasons. Dod Street was primarily the Radicals' pitch; thus, while three people were nominated to speak on the 27th and bear the brunt of probable arrest, it was decided that a Radical should be the first speaker. Ignoring this, Aveling opened the meeting. He was by nature what is called a bad committee man: pushful and undisciplined.

On 3 October *Justice* wrote angrily:

"Social-Democrats have proved that they are on excellent terms with the members of other Socialist bodies, and particularly with those of the Socialist League. It is necessary, however, to state here for the information of our comrades in London and the country, that the breach of faith committed on Sunday last by Edward Aveling will render it impossible for those who are cognisant of the facts ever again to have confidence in any arrangement entered into by him."

A fortnight later, seven SDF representatives wrote a letter to *Justice* to say that:

"We, the undersigned, distinctly remember that an agreement was entered into by all the Socialist speakers at the meeting of the Free Speech Vigilance Committee at the East London United Radical Club ... not to speak at Dod Street or elsewhere until after the Radical speakers appointed by the Committee had addressed the people. This arrangement was never altered by the Committee."‡

---

* In November 1885: the first since the new Reform Bill. Three socialist candidates stood: John Burns for West Nottingham, John Fielding for Kennington and Jack Williams for Hampstead. They polled respectively 598, 32 and 27 votes.
† The game's not worth the candle.
‡ Bernard Shaw's recollection of the matter was slightly different for, according to him: "Three victims had been selected for sacrifice to the police on the day in question; to wit, Dr. Aveling, Mr. George Bateman and myself as a representative of the Fabian Society." Since Aveling represented the Socialist League and Bateman the SDF, there would appear to have been no Radical speaker at all. Shaw's dubious version goes on: "But on the night before the morning of

The argument over the "gross breach of faith" was pursued at great length, the Vigilance Committee dissociating itself from the "false and cowardly personal attack upon Dr. Aveling"[139] and exonerating his action by a vote of 21 to two at a delegate meeting. Possibly the worst sufferer was Eleanor whose natural distress caused her to write to Laura in the hope that the French *Socialiste* would publish the exonerating resolution,* while she denounced "Mr Hyndman's last infamy": the man was a "cowardly cad", many SDF members were "disgusted with Hyndman for this business" which was "all disgraceful", and it was "simply his impotent rage and jealousy that induced him to make such an ass of himself".[140]

Who was the "cad" in this affair hardly matters now; but one's heart goes out to Eleanor. And for more reasons than this.

Though one of the three women on the Executive of the SDF† from August to December 1884, she was the only one on the Council of the Socialist League and shouldered those humdrum little duties so apt to be overlooked. She it was who ensured that the League's journals and pamphlets were on display at meetings; she who found a window cleaner for the premises; who compared estimates for the most economical hire of crockery, cutlery and plate for socialist repasts; who organised the sale of tickets for the various "entertainments" in which – rather more to her taste – she generally played a part.

She also acted as treasurer to the "Tree Committee" for a children's Christmas party.‡ It drove her to distraction. Benevolent people kept on

---

the meeting the police called on Dr. Aveling and announced the welcome news that they had orders to surrender. The news spread; and the next morning, instead of three condemned speakers, the entire oratorical force of the Socialist movement turned up, resolute to assert their right of Free Speech or die on the place. They all wanted to speak first; but Aveling, who had faced the music before the danger was over, claimed first place and got it. A quarrel ensued, in which nothing was agreed on but a general denunciation of Aveling, although the Dod Street incident was perhaps the most creditable incident in his morally somewhat chequered career..."[138]

* It was published in *Commonweal* and Engels promised to get it into the German papers.

† The other two were Mrs. Hyndman and Mrs. Amie Hicks.

‡ The December issue of *Commonweal* issued "An Appeal for Children": "It has been decided by the Council of the Socialist League that the beautiful old Pagan Festival that celebrated the death of darkness and new birth of light, is a very fit one for little Socialists to keep. We, too, want the 'little children to come unto us', and so we are going to give them a 'tree', a good romp, tea and cake on Saturday 26 ... at our Hall, 13 Farringdon Road. Will friends help in the way of simple presents for the tree and money to get the tree and the food." Morris's hand may be traced in this announcement, but helpers and contributors were directed to, among others, Mrs. Wardle, Mrs. Lane, May Morris or E. Marx.

This Mrs Wardle, known as Lena, was Madeleine Smith, born in Glasgow in 1835 and indicted for the murder of her lover in the Edinburgh High Court of Justiciary at the age of 21. She was acquitted on the Scottish verdict of 'Not Proven'. Four years after the trial, in 1861, George Young Wardle, a talented draughtsman born in Leek, Staffordshire, in 1836, married donating toys that they had bought or made which put out the accounts Eleanor so manfully tried to balance; while "in spite of earnest requests to be told the approximate number of children each Branch intended to bring", very few had "the courtesy and good sense to answer ... so that catering became almost an impossibility". It is not fanciful to discern the knitted brow and muddled arithmetic behind these lines. But when it was all over Eleanor said stout-heartedly:

"We have however learnt what to avoid next time, and the fact that some 200 little ones enjoyed themselves is quite enough satisfaction."[141]

At this time she had another, more intimate preoccupation with a "little one", for Johnny Longuet, now 9 years of age, had been in London for the past three months.

Eleanor's concern for her sister Jenny's orphaned brood was heightened by the father's obstinate refusal to communicate. She had long wished to have those issues of *La Justice* in which letters from Jenny had been published,

"but I know asking Longuet for them is useless," she wrote to Laura. "I *did* ask him months ago, but naturally heard no more about it."

Then – just over a year after their mother's death – the three little boys went down with whooping cough. "*Do* let me know how they are," Eleanor wrote in the same letter, "for I am very anxious about them"[142] – an anxiety that was shared by Helene Demuth, their "Nim" – but no news arrived.

For the anniversary of Marx's death Longuet did not come to England, though he sent flowers and, to Eleanor's amazement, a letter, which made her ask Laura: "Is Longuet ill?"[143] In May that year, when she was writing to "my little Johnny" on his 8th birthday, she again enquired about "the amiable brother-in-law", adding: "I need hardly say that *I* never get any news of the children save through you."[144] By the end of the year she was complaining bitterly of Longuet's silence: she yearned to hear about her small nephews and the infant niece. Bitterness rose to anger when the Lafargues stopped sending reports.

---

her in London where he was teaching at the Chelsea School of Art. They had two children: a daughter Mary born in 1862 and a son Thomas Edmund in the following year. In 1870 Wardle became William Morris's business manager, a post he held for 20 years, first at the Queen Square works, later at Merton. From 1885 Lena Wardle was the treasurer and her son the secretary of the Bloomsbury branch of the Socialist League whose council meetings they attended.

"I really *did* swear at you both," she wrote, "– at him* for telling you not to write about the children, and at you for being fool enough not to do it. Can't you understand that I am really anxious to know about the little ones. Remember how I had dear little Johnny and Wolf† with me and you *will* understand."[145]

Certainly the Lafargues were not indifferent to the welfare of the young Longuets – indeed, Paul was to become their legal guardian – and they were also nearer at hand, so that in the early months of 1885 they entertained Marcel‡ for a few days, followed by Edgar, who stayed for the best part of a fortnight, "which was astonishing", said Paul. He reported to Engels that the children were well and so was the father but – and herein lay the explanation – "the grandmother§ who is always on the go, has had an accident, she has a hole in her head and has practically broken her shoulder, which does not stop her from carrying on like an old repaired bridge".[146]

In June Laura ventured to write to Longuet asking about the children.

"At the end of a fortnight he answered me," she told Engels, "inviting me to go down to Argenteuil if I wanted news." She went and found that "Jenny's little girl‖ is growing very charming ... a bright and spirited child with a temper of her own".[147]

At last, in the autumn of 1885, Johnny was allowed to visit Eleanor. On 13 October she wrote to Laura:

"Johnny is still here – and like to be, so far as I can make out, for some time. I want to find out definitely, because, of course, if he stays here, he *must* be sent to school. But to get a letter out of Longuet is, as you know, not to be quickly done."[148]

On the same date Engels was writing to Laura too.

"I am so out of practice in speaking and writing French that positively an hour's chat with Johnny acts upon me as a refresher upon a German Counsel, and really revives my capacity of thinking in French more than ever I could have dreamt."[149]

Engels' pleasure in the company of young children was undimmed at the age of 65. The little boy, in fact, was left with him when Eleanor and Aveling went away shortly before Christmas.

---

* It is not clear whether this refers to Longuet or Lafargue but, written at a time when two of the boys had been staying with Laura and Paul, it could be thought that Paul was the culprit.
† Edgar, now 6 years of age.
‡ Now pushing four.
§ Mme. Félicitas Longuet.
‖ Mémé (Jenny), now two years and nine months old.

"Johnny is with us in the meantime," Engels wrote to Laura on 22 December, "he has picked up his English again, rather quickly, especially since he goes to school. He is a very good boy and reads an awful lot of, to him, unintelligible books."[150]

It seems a little surprising that, having had Johnny in her care and arranged for his education – as she had done three years before – Eleanor should now leave him entirely at Regent's Park Road, not only during the holidays but also when the new term had started, for he was still there in mid-January and, though the length of his stay in England is not certain, Eleanor was in Kingston-on-Thames on and off until almost the end of April 1886, because, as she explained to Laura,

"We get more work done here really than in London, and get some fresh air besides."[151]

It is pure surmise, but since there is not a single reference to Aveling taking the boy about or evincing the smallest interest in him, it may well have been Aveling's wish that Johnny should spend his time in other than Eleanor's charge and even, possibly, that she was hurt by it.

At this point one cannot but ask why Eleanor, with her strong maternal feelings, should have remained childless. It could not have been her wish; it may have been her incapacity. But Aveling's early marriage had been without issue and never in a life of extensive lechery and an era of primitive contraception is a paternity suit ever known to have been brought against him, from which it would not be unfair to draw the conclusion that he was sterile.

This leads to another matter for irrepressible curiosity: how did Aveling, that grey Lothario, acquire his widespread notoriety? He must have been of a singular indiscretion to furnish so much gossip, for, though all his public performances were well advertised, casual fornications do not appear among them. While received opinion – what is scandalous and what acceptable – differs vastly from country to country, between social strata and, above all, in succeeding generations, sexual behaviour does not. A man (or for that matter, a woman) in Aveling's day as now might leap into bed with any willing partner but – unless you were George Moore, who went in for fiction – it was not then as now a matter for table talk as a rule.

As for Eleanor, if her love for the children most dear to her was constantly frustrated, she could at least canalise it into giving pleasure to others quite unknown. Having wrestled with and at last got the better of the obstreperous accounts, she wrote to the Council in May 1886:

"When we found we had a small surplus left over from our Christmas tree fund it was,

I think, decided that we should try to get up a children's picnic. May I suggest that if this is to be done it should be set about at once? We ought not to wait until the weather is unbearably hot ... I shall be glad to give all the help I can (I haven't got any money!) and several friends of mine have also volunteered ... if you decide that we should give the little ones an outing."*[152]

The outing took place on Whit Monday, 7 June 1886.

Because she was away from London at the time Eleanor was not present at a meeting of the workless in Trafalgar Square on Monday, 8 February 1886, called by the Fair Trade League† but to which the SDF leaders flocked, addressing the crowd from the street overlooking the Square – opposite the National Gallery – before the convenors of the meeting, their opponents, turned up.

> "Hyndman and Co. spoke to a mixed audience which was out for fun and, to some extent, had already arrived in a rather merry state," Engels wrote to August Bebel.

When the socialists proposed a march to Hyde Park to hold a further meeting there, the response was

> "largely drawn from those who have no desire whatever to work: idlers, loafers, police spies and rogues".‡[153]

Headed by John Burns carrying a red flag, these "roughs", as Engels called them, marched through the West End, were jeered at by the usually somnolent clubmen in Pall Mall and St. James's Street and, more particularly, by their servants who flung boot and blacking brushes at them, to which provocation they responded all too heartily, lobbing stones and lumps of metal through the windows and then running riot to loot shops in Piccadilly and South Audley Street. "The absence of the police shows that the row was *wanted*," Engels wrote to Laura,[154] and it is a fact that not until the wreckage and plunder had spread as far as Oxford Street did a small number of police intervene, to show, save in the case of a certain

---

* The letter is written in the first person and, unmistakably, Eleanor's handwriting, though it is signed, in pencil by someone else, "Eleanor Marx Aveling, May Morris, Mrs. Wardle".
† A conservative body advocating high customs tariffs to alleviate unemployment.
‡ Engels was not present. His account of the affair came from Karl Kautsky who left the Square before the march set off. What followed is attested by innumerable reports in the contemporary press, by the later memoirs of eye-witnesses, participants and by historians of the labour movement.

Superintendent Cuthbert, remarkable incompetence.* Though not there herself, Eleanor wrote on 9 March to Lavrov:

"As regards 'the riots' everything was ridiculously exaggerated everywhere. In the first place it is clear that a dozen policemen could very easily have put a stop to the small street tumult which took place. Consequently it was not a really serious affair ... Nobody had the least idea that there would be a skirmish, and if it had in fact been the test which the Government was foolish enough to initiate it would already have been completely forgotten. The only comical thing about it all was the shopkeepers' terrible fear. Friends like Morris and Bax tried to see in it a real movement, but they are beginning to agree that it had no great importance. Let us say frankly that, though we have had some successes here, the socialist movement in England is still a literary movement, and to strive to make it seem something different at the present time, would be to strive in vain. It will come, perhaps very soon, but it does not exist yet."[155]

Aveling reported the occasion, which came to be known as "Black Monday", in the March issue of *Commonweal*, under the heading "The Recent Riots", for there had also been rioting by strikers in Leicester, lasting from 11 to 16 February, and demonstrations by the unemployed, not without violence, in other cities. Aveling deprecated these methods, saying that naturally socialists sympathised with the workless and opposed the prosecution of speakers, but it was necessary that socialists themselves should be more disciplined, though it was idle to expect any lasting improvements for the proletariat "apart from a revolutionary change".

"Black Monday" had three resounding sequels: Burns, Hyndman, Champion and Jack Williams were arrested and brought to trial at the Old Bailey on a charge of sedition when all were acquitted on 10 April, but not before Burns had made an impassioned speech from the dock in his mighty voice.† At the same time the existence of the unemployed had been brought rather forcibly to the notice of the rich, so that £75,000 for relief was received by the Lord Mayor of London within 48 hours, while a Mansion House fund was immediately opened, contributions pouring in "not out of pity but fear", as Hyndman remarked.‡[156]

---

* That additional police reinforcements could have been summoned, and clearly signalled to the rioters, is evident from the fact that, in March 1884, 20,000 whistles of novel construction and piercing blast had been issued to the Metropolitan force.
† Later published and widely circulated as a pamphlet: *The Man with the Red Flag*.
‡ The Earl of Meath, then Lord Brabazon, who had founded the Metropolitan Public Gardens Association in 1882, was a member of the Mansion House Fund Committee. He now promised that if this sudden wealth were channelled to the Association, he would find paid work for some of the unemployed. Indeed, within a few weeks hundreds – though not thousands – of men were helping to lay out gardens (mostly in disused burial grounds), receiving not only wages but supplies of food. The following year his lordship proposed a similar operation, but the cupboard was bare.

Newspaperless in Kingston-on-Thames, Eleanor wrote on 21 February to Thomas Wardle, whom she always addressed as "My dear Machine" or "Friend Machine", saying: "I am glad to hear all went off quietly today in the Park."[157] But it had not: the demonstration called by the SDF had been mercilessly charged and batoned by the police.

This was the third resounding sequel to Black Monday; and behind it lay moves with no resonance at all, for something nearly approaching panic had seized the higher echelons of the Metropolitan Police and the Home Office.

The Home Secretary, Hugh Childers,* had at once set up a committee "to inquire into the Origin and Character of the Disturbances that took place in the Metropolis on the 8th day of February, 1886, and as to the conduct of the Police Authorities in relation thereto".[158]

The Committee went swiftly to work so that, understandably, the Commissioner of Police, Colonel – later Sir – Edmund Henderson, made exemplary preparations on Saturday, 20 February, for the next day's SDF meeting in Hyde Park. He issued orders for the disposition of 2,456 police of all ranks – Divisional Superintendents, Inspectors, Sergeants, Officers and Constables, both foot and mounted – with instructions on how the Reserves and Double Patrols were to conduct themselves at the least sign of disorder.

The Committee's recommendation, dated 22 February, made the Secretary of State

"...determined at once to institute an inquiry into the administration and organisation of the Metropolitan Police Force with a view of making such changes ... of the Force in all its Branches as may be necessary to remedy any defects ... The Secretary of State will also consider whether any, and what reforms are desirable in the relations between the Police Authorities and the Home Department."[159]

Immediately, that very day, Colonel Henderson resigned. He need not have worried; nor hurried, for that matter. The ferocious police methods used in the Park on 21 February must have dispelled any suspicion of nonchalance attaching to the Commissioner, thanks to which, it may be, Mr. Childers' enquiries pursued a leisurely course. Not until 30 July were the Home Secretary's directions sent to the Colonel's successor, Sir Charles

---

* 1827–1896. Liberal M.P. for Pontefract (1860–1885) and for South Edinburgh (1886–1892), Childers had held office as First Lord of the Admiralty (1868–1871), Chancellor of the Duchy of Lancaster (1872–1873), Secretary for War (1880–1882), Chancellor of the Exchequer (1882–1885) and, finally, under Gladstone's third, brief administration from January to July 1886, Secretary for Home Affairs. Ironically, the Under-Secretary at that time was Henry Broadhurst, who for the years 1875 to 1884, and again from 1886 to 1889, was Secretary to the Parliamentary Committee of the TUC.

Warren: after five months a memorandum, labelled in all seriousness "Pressing", laid down what hitherto had been "only unwritten law":

> "As soon as the character of the probable extent of a Public Meeting has been fully ascertained by the Police, a report is made to the HO and if necessary the Secretary of State makes further inquiries and usually sees the Chief Commissioner.
>
> "A final report is made on the day before the meeting in which the Commissioner's arrangements, as to the number of police constables to be employed and the name of the officer in charge are set out. This comes at once to the Home Office for the information of the Secretary of State, and on the morning of the meeting the latter may see the Commissioner again if necessary.
>
> From this time the whole arrangements are the responsible charge of the Commissioner and the Home Office does not interfere...
>
> "This general practice should not be interfered with, as it is manifest that the Secretary of State can only rarely intervene with advantage, and it is most undesirable to derogate from the plenary responsibility of the Commissioner. But the Secretary of State should be informed of any abnormal or grave occurrences at the meetings, especially when there is any apprehension that military may be required. Such aid, in cases where very prompt action is necessary may be applied for direct, by the Commissioner; but in all ordinary cases an official application by the Secretary of State should be made and if possible previous warning should be addressed to the War Office.
>
> "After a meeting is over a brief report, and on the following day a full report of the proceedings should be made to the HO."[160]

On 12 August, having mulled this over, the Commissioner declared that he had "no observations to offer as the memorandum ... appears to meet the case".[161]

For the time being, then, everyone – except, of course, those who organised and attended the public meetings – knew where they stood. Later events (for, irrational though it sounds, Black Monday was to be followed by Bloody Sunday) led to some changes in the sweetly reasonable relations between the Home Office and the Metropolitan Police.

Between Black Monday and the Old Bailey trial of the four accused, Eleanor came up to London more than once.

In March 1886 the Commune anniversary meeting was held at the South Place Institute in Moorgate and, though a greater number than ever before addressed the packed audience,* Eleanor's speech was by general consent the best of all.

It is significant that on every occasion commemorating the event of 1871 Eleanor should have surpassed herself. This first, defeated, proletarian revolution had welded her emotional responses to her waking mind at the impressionable age of 16. Many of the Communards were now dead, those who lived on were aging, but Eleanor's ardour seemed to rekindle their heroic past. It was not only that she then showed herself a faithful daughter of the International, but, as other generations which have experienced a total commitment in their youth, she was unshakably loyal to it. Precisely because it had failed, she was rendered proof against the inevitable setbacks and adversities of the revolutionary movement until, like the Commune itself, she was defeated.

This year, Eleanor laid particular stress upon the part women had played in the battle and urged the need for combined and resolute action.

> "When the revolution comes – and it *must* come – it will be by the workers, without distinction of sex or trade or country, standing and fighting shoulder to shoulder," she said.[162]

It was not by chance that, at this moment, she should have raised the question of women. To this subject she had recently devoted much thought and work. In 1879 August Bebel brought out a short book on *Women and Socialism*,† illegally printed in Leipzig but purporting to be published in Switzerland. A second, expanded version, *Woman in the Past, the Present and the Future*,‡ printed in Stuttgart, but again with the

---

* The speakers included Tom Mann of the SDF, Frank Kitz of the Socialist League, representatives from France, Germany and Italy and the Russian geographer and anarchist, Peter Kropotkin (1842–1921), recently released from prison in France, who settled in England from 1886 until 1917.
† *Die Frau und der Sozialismus.*
‡ *Die Frau in der Vergangenheit, Gegenwart und Zukunft.*

imprimatur of Jakob Schabelitz, Zurich, appeared in June 1883. Prohibited in Germany under the Anti-Socialist Law, it nevertheless enjoyed a clandestine circulation wide enough to be venomously attacked in the press.[163] Bebel sent a copy to Engels in January 1884 and Eleanor consulted him about the English translation by Dr. Harriet Adams Walther. This was published during 1885 by the Modern Press in the International Library of Social Science when it also "met in certain quarters with a vituperative reception".*[164]

Eleanor reviewed the English translation in the August 1885 Supplement to *Commonweal*. This formed the essence of a pamphlet, *The Woman Question* – which appeared originally in the *Westminster Review*†[165] – produced jointly with Aveling, the first of her writings to bear the imprint of a recognised commercial publisher.‡

To distinguish the "Edward" from the "Eleanor" in this work it is interesting to compare it with the original review of 1885 and the speeches both authors were making at the time. It could be said that Eleanor's unpretentious article, aimed at the socialist reader, with copious quotations from Bebel's book, stuck to the theme that:

> "We must seek the real cause of woman's enslaved position in her economic dependence upon man, and that her 'emancipation' means nothing but economic freedom."

The pamphlet, on the other hand, was graced with various Latin tags and quotations obviously intended for a public that knew its Shakespeare, Bacon, Tennyson and Shelley if not by heart at least by name.

Despite the substantial improvement in the status of women since her day, Eleanor's main thesis – expounded later by several of her younger contemporaries – remains as true and relevant now as then. Then as now, ladies who became a little over-excited about their wrongs and apt to tip out the baby – most particularly the baby – with the bathwater, paid less attention to economic discrimination as the basis of women's inferiority

---

* Trouble blew up in 1893 when Reeves brought out a new edition under the same title – No. 15 of the "Bellamy Library" – by another translator without consulting the author, Mrs. Walther or her publishers. The copyright laws of the time afforded translators small protection, added to which this second English version, produced by a certain Foulger, was based upon the revised (9th) German edition of 1891, so there was nothing to be done.

† This paper had also published a review of Bebel's book by Eleanor and Aveling in January 1886 which, Eleanor explained in a letter to Lavrov: "we should have had in 'The Nineteenth Century', but the editor took fright!"[156]

‡ From the Swan Sonnenschein letterbooks of the period it is clear that the agreement was concluded in April 1886. The 4th thousand, published in 1887, indicated that it enjoyed some success. Had not Aveling's demands for advance royalties on other – unfulfilled – work put him in debt to Swan Sonnenschein, the pamphlet on *The Woman Question* might have been financially rewarding to Eleanor.[167]

than to the social and civil oligarchy, not to mention the domestic tyranny of men, now called male chauvinism. As Engels wrote:

"The foremost English champions of the formal rights of women* ... are in a large measure directly or indirectly interested in the capitalist exploitation of both sexes."[168]

In Eleanor's time women, as both second-class citizens without civil rights and workers,† represented, according to the 1881 census, almost a third of the total adult labour force aged between 20 and 65. They formed the majority in the textile trades and, including girls under 20 years of age, there were more than 1,750,000 females employed in various industries with another two million in domestic and other services. Their earnings were roughly 50 per cent of the male rate.‡

The protests of articulate women of the governing classes who felt cheated of the privileges and respect accorded to their brothers§ met with some ridicule from male legislators while, as an irrelevant form of warfare between the sexes, leaving the employers of labour totally unmoved. Eleanor, though she would have wished for herself a somewhat higher standard of education, was not caught in that snare: her feminism was inseparable from her socialism. She saw that the most pressing need was for women workers to fight not against but in alliance with their menfolk on a class basis; that only so could they become free and equal human beings, or, indeed, human beings at all in the fullest sense. As the most downtrodden, illiterate and disregarded section of the exploited majority, women must be either consciously involved in the struggle for social change or the unwitting tools of reaction. Denied training and apprenticeship, they would forever be assigned to the most menial work for the longest hours at the lowest wage, while unrelieved of their functions as housewives and mothers. This presented almost limitless problems to which there could be no simple solution, but to the basic question of

---

* A Central Committee of the National Society for Women's Suffrage had existed since 1871.
† With the exception of the few sumptuous whores of that epoch who by a dialectical process turned themselves as use-objects into the most ruthless of exploiters.
‡ In April 1975 when the Equal Pay Act of 1970 was not yet in force women's *hourly earnings* were 65 per cent of men's in manual work (70 per cent if all types of gainful employment are counted). The figures do not allow for the fact that men do more overtime, at higher hourly rates, than women. In 1886 the average wage (*not* earnings) for men (in 38 industries) was 24s. 7d. a week; for women (in 23 industries) 12s. 8d., i.e. 51.5 per cent. Female domestic servants earned an average of £18 a year in London and £16 in other parts of England and Wales.

In this connection the reader is referred to the figures given in Kapp, *op. cit.*, p. 93, fn. 1, with a rider on the official Cost of Living Index: 1968 average = 100, August 1975 = 213.
§ Even today many use distinctive forms of address to denote that educated men are to be respected and their womenfolk cherished. It is quite surprising that circular letters do not start "Dear Sir or Dear".

economic equality there lay an answer in organisation. The kept woman of
the ruling class had not to go out to work, while even her duties in the
home were delegated to servants and nannies. It was the working woman
who took the full brunt of sex discrimination and, as such, she must
spearhead the fight for female equality.

Eleanor was later to come up against the rigid opposition of many male
trade unionists who could not but regard the demand for equal pay as a
threat to their own position. She became extremely familiar with the
argument (still heard today from "heads of families" in the working class)
and the perpetuated objection – entirely in the interests of women, be it
understood – that if female labour power became as expensive as male it
would cease to be employed.

In July 1885 there had been a sensational exposure – not entirely free
from prurience – of child prostitution, published in the *Pall Mall Gazette*
under the title "The Maiden Tribute of Modern Babylon". These articles
had appeared as part of the campaign for the Criminal Law Amendment
Act.* Their writer, William Thomas Stead† had gone so far as to procure a
child for ostensible shipment to a brothel, thus demonstrating how easily
and by what means the thing might be done. For this he was prosecuted,
earning even wider publicity for his campaign and three months'
imprisonment in Holloway.

On 13 July 1885, at the first conference of the Socialist League‡ a
resolution was moved:

> "That this meeting recognises the hideous sexual corruption of the capitalist classes
> and the iniquities practised by them upon the children of the working classes, and is of
> the opinion that these evils are inevitable under a capitalist system and will never be
> removed, or even remedied, until that system is at an end."

Speaking on an amendment to this resolution Eleanor said:

> "You must put the individual into such a position that he can be responsible. How are
> children of ten or 13 to be 'responsible'? Yet they form the largest number of victims.
> But I go further. The men themselves, horrible as their actions are, are not responsible
> ... no more responsible than the children ... The fact is women are driven to pros-
> titution – not only women of the working classes. Governesses are often supposed to

---

* This Act, passed rather hurriedly in 1885, rendered brothel-keepers, procuresses, pimps and
their assorted *aides-de-camp* who kept, managed, or assisted in the management of brothels,
liable to summary conviction, while strengthening the law for the protection of young persons
under 21, with specific reference to girls aged between 13 and 16.
† Stead (1849–1912) replaced John – later first Viscount – Morley in 1883 as editor of the *Pall
Mall Gazette*, creating a precedent by employing women journalists at the same rate of pay as
men.
‡ At Farringdon Hall, 13 Farringdon Road.

teach two or three languages and other 'accomplishments' and dress respectably on six shillings a week* . . . Nearly all women obliged to earn a living have to choose between starvation and prostitution, and this must go on so long as one class can buy the bodies of another, whether in the form of labour power or sexual embraces."[171]

Aveling on the same occasion weighed in more theatrically:

"I . . . wonder at times how you working men can restrain yourselves from seizing the representatives of the capitalist classes and breaking their necks on the nearest curb-stone."

Then, remembering where he was and why he was there, he added:

"Mind, that is not what I, or any Socialist advises you to do, but we do advise you to break the neck of the damnable system that makes these things necessary."[172]

An article written by Eleanor on lines laid down by Morris appeared in the August issue of *Commonweal*, and the League's resolution was sent to the *Pall Mall Gazette*.

"There are some, even among our friends, who will be shocked that a woman should speak of these matters," she said on another occasion, "and who hold that 'womanly custom had better left it unsaid'† . . . If this is no woman's question, what is?"[173]

---

* It is interesting that Eleanor should have used the same example and exactly the same figure a decade earlier. Governesses, as such, were not a classified category of the underpaid and there are no contemporary statistics to support or refute that their earnings had remained stable. However, writing on "Domestic Service" in the August 1890 issue of the *Nineteenth Century*, Ellen W. Darwin said: "Since the birth of the high schools [1872], though the work is infinitely harder, governesses to private families are comparatively hard to find . . . This fact . . . has brought about a considerable change in the position of the private governess. The post is extremely well paid, and care is taken to make it attractive."[169] It was, however, a decade of falling wages and prices. Such information as exists shows that between 1874 and 1886 – the latter a year of severe depression – the wages of manual workers as a whole had gone down by almost 6 per cent, and by as much as 29 per cent in mining, while the purchasing power of the gold sovereign had risen in the decade 1874–84 by over 33 per cent. Booth's enquiries showed that in 1888 the average London labourer with five children earned 25s. a week and spent 24s. 9¼d. on living expenses; the average engineering worker, with four children, earned 27s. and spent 29s. 2d.[170]
† This was, of course, no more than a convention of the times, observed to some extent out of deference to working-class prudishness, itself a by-product of economic conditions. Where whole families, including pubescents of both sexes, share a bed – if they have one – the only moral alternatives are to make a fetish of pudency or break the tabu on incest.
While on the subject of class-determined attitudes to sex, it may be noted that pornography, known as *erotica* or *curiosa*, has been available at all times and in all ages to people in the upper income bracket. What makes them so dreadfully cross is that pretty well anyone can now buy it, quite cheaply and openly.

Certainly it was, and certainly she would not balk it; but Engels' recent book on *The Origin of the Family, Private Property and the State* (1884) had given her a larger view of the "woman question" as a major political issue, and her activity among working women in the years to come owed much both to this classic work on the subject – however controversial its theses in the light of modern anthropology – and to the serious study she had made in the winter and spring of 1885–6 to produce her pamphlet.

It is remarkable – and should be remarked – that Eleanor herself, though labouring under the disadvantages common to all women of her time, with the additional handicap of her extra-marital status, appeared never to suffer from those inhibitions fettering so many of her sex. She treated men as equals, not in the male-mimicry or backslapping fashion, but as fellow creatures; and as an equal she was treated. She felt no need either to exploit the frailty of womanhood or to compensate for it by self-assertiveness. She went her way without fuss, feminism or false constraint and, having no illusions about her own intellectual range, simply did not see herself as in competition with more powerful minds, objectively alive to the social injustices that shackled women's freedom, subjectively free.*

At the end of March 1886, Bismarck, an attempt on whose life had recently been made by a man called Ferdinand Blind,† announced in the Reichstag that his would-be assassin had been schooled by Marx. In the 1 May issue of *Commonweal* – its first weekly number – Eleanor devoted what was to be almost her last "Record" to Germany and the Reichstag session at which the Anti-Socialist Law had been re-enacted. It was a longer item than usual and ended with the paragraph:

> "Among other things Bismarck took occasion to state that he 'did not know whether Marx had bred murderers, but this he had heard, that the man, of whose shots he still bore the scars, was a pupil of Marx'! To this statement my sister Laura Lafargue and I have sent a short reply to Herr Bismarck, in which we point out that the fright our dead father inspired in him was quite unnecessary; that he never saw poor young Ferdinand Blind after he was 12 or 13 years old; that all the objects Blind could have had in courageously braving death by firing at Herr Bismarck were of complete indifference to our father ... Bismarck was to Marx only a comic personage ... the ridiculous idea that a man like Marx could have spent his time 'breeding assassins' only proves how right Marx was to see in Bismarck nothing but a Prussian clodhopper."

The open letter, in more or less the same terms, had been published in the German *Sozial-Demokrat* on 15 April and reprinted in the French *Socialiste* on the 24th. Although it appeared in the name of both sisters,

---

* This was largely a matter of temperament; but to some extent it may have been nourished by the emotional security of her family life from birth.

† The stepson of Karl Blind (1826–1907) who came to England as a refugee after 1848.

Laura, in truth, had not been a signatory nor at all in favour of this move. Engels had recommended it; but

> "for my part," Laura wrote to him, "I should have thought it preferable ... to take no notice at all of Bismarck's 'crazy' assertion ... There seems to me something absurd in defending a man like Marx against such an accusation from such a quarter. Neither bourgeois nor workman, I think, required to be told that Marx never either preached nor practised murder ... But although an open letter to Bismarck may be well enough, I must say that I can see no object in sending a copy of the letter to the fellow himself ... Whatever he says or thinks in his private capacity, whether drunk or sober, I'm sure is of no concern to us and I don't see why we should contribute to M. Bismarck's waste-paper basket."[174]

Eleanor, abashed at having taken her sister's consent for granted, wrote to her on 23 April:

> "I must first ask your pardon for having signed your name the week before last without your permission ... [I] signed with both our names and sent it direct with a little note to Bismarck. The note (merely stating that a copy of the enclosed would be made public) I also signed by your name as well as my own ... I hope you will not mind ..."[175]

The rest of her letter was chatty and affectionate – she bore Laura no ill-will for her reluctance to be publicly associated with rebutting the slander – and a few days later she wrote again referring to the Easter festivities at Engels' house, adding:

> "I wish we could manage to go and be festive with you in Paris for a while."[176]

Now that Morris had his way and *Commonweal* became a weekly paper, Eleanor and Aveling took the opportunity to withdraw.

> "An awful mess they'll make of it 'ere long," Eleanor wrote to Laura. "By dint of much arguing the General and I induced Ed. to give up the sub-editorship. This, I think, was necessary on more grounds than one. First he really has not the time: secondly, and more important, there is no one here really dependable to work with ... we have *no one*. Bax – reasonable on many points is quite mad on others, and both he and Morris are just more or less under the thumb of the Anarchists. We should therefore have been held responsible for a paper that will constantly do things we should be bound to condemn, and yet have no power to prevent from appearing. The position was impossible."[177]

Though Engels was far more critical and less hopeful of the British movement than Eleanor, on this matter she was largely at one with him.

> "Here all is a muddle," he wrote to Laura at about the same time. "Bax and Morris are

getting deeper and deeper into the hands of a few anarchist *phraseurs*, and write nonsense with increasing intensity. The turning of Commonweal into a 'weekly' – absurd in every respect – has given Edward a chance of getting out of his responsibility for this now incalculable organ ... It would be ridiculous to expect the working class to take the slightest notice of these various vagaries of what is by courtesy called English Socialism, and it is very fortunate that it is so: These gentlemen have quite enough to do to set their own brains in order."[178]

Aveling's letter of resignation was made public in the first weekly issue of 1 May 1886. The letter pleaded merely that

"the necessary demands of a weekly on an editor's time can only be met by those in relatively more fortunate positions".

He was replaced by Bax and the "Record" of 8 May was signed by May Morris,* who had not quite the same facilities as Eleanor to gather detailed news from all over Europe, including Russia, as well as both North and South America. Thereafter both Eleanor and Aveling contributed to *Commonweal* from time to time on a freelance basis.

All that early summer the meetings in the East End – and the arrests – continued. Eleven men were taken to court, though let out on bail, for addressing a small gathering on the evening of Saturday, 29 May, in The Grove, Stratford. This had become the "new battleground" and, though Eleanor and Aveling spoke, neither was arrested. Aveling, however, appeared at the West Ham Police Court on the following Monday morning to defend the right of assembly and was reported as saying that the meeting in The Grove had been held "to test the right of public speech".[179] A local paper, *The Eastern Post and City Chronicle*, commiserated with the police who had "a most difficult job to perform":

"If the Socialists were only wise instead of as blind as bats, they would see that the attempt to force Socialism upon the public attention in such an offensive manner is only to fill the public with either contempt or disgust".[180]

Strong words indeed for a meeting which the police themselves, giving evidence in court, estimated at about 100 or 150.

At its first conference in 1885, at which a Constitution and Rules were adopted, the Socialist League had numbered some 230 members. In the following year, by which time it was said to have between 600 and 700,[181] eighteen branches were represented. Eleanor, with W. C. Wade,

---

* Though the following week, 15 May, Eleanor again wrote the major part (on Belgian and French affairs) of this feature. May was William Morris's younger daughter (1862–1948) who married Henry Halliday Sparling in 1890. They were later divorced.

acted as secretary to the conference. On 5 July she sent the Minutes to the Council with apologies for the delay, saying she would

> "be glad if the report could be read over, either by the Council or some members of the Council appointed for the purpose, as, although I took down the speeches almost verbatim ... and not having ever before reported speeches, I may have made mistakes." She had put down nothing that "was *not* said", but "may have overlooked things that were."[182]

This was among the last of her official activities for the League. In August she and Aveling, who had been invited some eight months earlier by the Executive Council of the Socialist Labor Party of North America to tour the United States, resigned from the Executive Council.

The pattern of Eleanor's life during these years – 1884 to 1886 – would not emerge without its inwoven brightest thread: her abiding passion for literature and the drama. Albeit much of this found expression in lectures, recitals and entertainments in aid of the movement, while in other forms it helped her to earn a living, it remained her most pleasurable recreation.

Of physical relaxation there was little enough, unless one counts a boat-race party in 1885 and a Socialist League excursion on a Sunday in June 1886 – for which, naturally, Eleanor organised the sale of tickets – when it rained upon the 196 socialists who invaded Box Hill. Lack of money and pressure of work seldom allowed Eleanor and Aveling to escape from London. The Derbyshire honeymoon, she wrote to Laura, had been for her "the first holiday – except for one week – I have had for some three or four years – and I made the most of it".[183] Early in February 1885 the pair spent eight days by the Thames in Surrey,* where, as Eleanor told Mrs. Stepniak, they were able to work in peace and quiet which was impossible in London.[184] Aveling was preparing his talks on Marx's *Capital*,† and Eleanor was writing "no end of letters" to arrange, with Engels' help, for copies of *Commonweal* to be sent to socialist leaders abroad and to solicit contributions from them.[185]

Back in Great Russell Street, she wrote twice to Stepniak about a translation she had been doing for him:

"I am trying stubbornly and as hard as I can to work at the translation, but I fear that *possibly* I shall not be able to finish it before Monday. It really does involve a great deal of work (you must not be offended by my frank words) because the article is *very* badly written. It takes me twice as much time as it did you," – Stepniak had evidently translated it from Russian into French – "because to set it out in the simplest English terms has proved an extremely difficult task. Often I read a phrase three or four times before I guess and understand what it means, and even so some passages have remained doubtful for me. When I finish it, I shall write to you and ask you to come and advise me about some passages. Some phrases, in the way they are written, could be understood in two opposite senses ... I fear that my translation will not be good enough. As regards the *form*, the material given me to work on was bad. On the other

---

* At 7 Surbiton Terrace, near Hampton Court Park, twelve miles from the City on the old London and South Western line.
† Eight weekly lectures delivered at the South Place Institute on Thursday evenings from 12 February; a further series booked to start on 16 April was interrupted by illness.

hand, the facts were very interesting ..." In a postscript she asked to see the proofs: "The final checking of the printed text produces quite different results."[186]

Three days later she sent Stepniak her manuscript, suggesting the alternative title "Why I Left Russia" to the one originally given which she thought would not attract much interest.

"My dear friend," she wrote,

"I enclose my translation 'as it is'. I have tried, as always in translation, to make it as literary and accurate as possible, although in a number of passages I thought it essential to make small changes for an English reader. In one place I added a footnote ... referring to the Greek and Latin texts ... I hope you will be satisfied. I read my translation to Edward (it took up nearly three hours!) and we think that it will do.

"I shall be very glad to receive other translations," she went on, "(we are so 'demonetised' that we are glad of any work) and would like to know what the payment will be. I will ask about this in the Museum where there are people who know the usual fees for such work..."[187]

That June they went up the river for a few days "with a chap who has a boat and a tent", wrote Engels, "and they both want as much fresh air as they can get. The British Museum is a nice place enough, but not to live opposite to."[188] The only holiday they had was a fortnight at the Star and Garter Hotel in Beach Street, Deal, during August; even then Eleanor kept in touch with the League's affairs. At the end of the year 1885 while, it will be recalled, Johnny Longuet was in London, they went to live at 2 Parade Villas, South Place, Kingston-on-Thames, until the last week of April 1886. For Christmas they came briefly to London to spend the usual festivities with Engels* and attend the children's Boxing Day party. They had kept their rooms in Great Russell Street and came up for a few days every now and again.

The sojourn in Kingston was anything but a vacation. Not only was Aveling still sub-editing *Commonweal* but he had taken on other paid journalism, while Eleanor continued to write her regular monthly "Record". It was now, too, that she resuscitated her earlier work, the English version of Lissagaray's *History of the Commune*, preparing it for publication by Reeves and Turner,† though mainly engaged on the far more ambitious task of translating *Madame Bovary*.

This commissioned work had been put in her way by George Moore,

---

* Eleanor had been invited by Dollie Radford to whom she wrote on 24 December 1884: "Ever since Engels has been in London – i.e. for thirteen years – we have always dined and spent the evening of Christmas with him. It is rather a sad day there now – so many of the dear ones, Father, Mother, Jenny, are gone. But that, as *you* will understand, is only a reason the more why I must be with Father's oldest and dearest friend..."[189]

† The Introduction is dated "June (Whit Week) 1886".

whose *Mummer's Wife** she considered "the strongest and boldest English novel I have read for many a day".[190] The probability is that she had met Moore through Olive Schreiner who had become a close friend of his in 1885. As Moore was about to go to Paris, Eleanor gave him an introduction to the Lafargues, recommending him as

> "a thoroughly kindly and good fellow, though after the manner of his kind he poses as being 'awful bad'. But he isn't! That's the joke ... He has been really kind to us – I mean in the way of helping us to work (you know he got me the order for translating *Mme. Bovary*)..."[191]

When exactly she started the work and how long it took her is not known; but on Good Friday, 23 April 1886, she wrote to Laura from Kingston:

> "I have (the Lord be praised!) finished my translation ... It *has* been work! It will be out ere very long I suppose,[†] and I am now working at an 'Introduction' to it."[192]

This Introduction, dated May 1886, though it raises certain controversial literary points, is a model of good sense. Conscious of the agonies suffered in the gestation and birth of Flaubert's masterpiece, she said:

> "To write anything of such a man as Gustave Flaubert, and of such a work as *Madame Bovary*, must give the boldest pause."

Of the "three possible methods of translation", she did not claim "that of the genius" nor descend to that of the hack, "who, armed with dictionary, rushes in where his betters fear to tread", but followed the path of the "conscientious worker" who

> "cannot if he would belong to the first category of translators. He would not if he could belong to the second. He can but strive to do his best; to be honest, earnest. To this last category I claim to belong. Certainly no critic can be more painfully aware than I am of the weaknesses, the shortcomings, the failures of my work; but at least ... I have neither suppressed nor added a line, a word ... My work ... I know is faulty. It is pale and feeble by the side of the original ... But ... I do not regret having done this work; it is the best I could do."

---

* Moore's second novel, which appeared in 1885 when he was 33. It is regrettable that there is no record of Eleanor's reactions to Moore's later book, denouncing his native country – *Parnell and his Island* – published in the same year and by the same firm as the first English translation of Volume I of *Capital*.

† It was published by Vizetelly in August 1886.

The Athenaeum's anonymous critic[193] was not to be thus easily disarmed. The Introduction he "passed over with no further comment than to remark that it is uncritical in itself" – not in itself a beautiful sentence – and dismissed the whole as done "with more zeal than discretion". He then proceeded to fault Eleanor in the greatest detail, demonstrating, as anonymous critics will, that if there was one thing for which he was better fitted than the person who had done the work it was the work that person had done.

The Academy was more generous. Reviewing it on 25 September 1886[194] William Sharp* wrote:

> "Flaubert is, pre-eminently, an untranslatable writer. He is, as Mrs. Aveling appropriately remarks in her preface, inimitable ... and he is untranslatable, not because he writes perfect French, but because words are to him supremely significant – have a weight, an urgency of revelation so to speak, that is almost of necessity beyond the power of the translator to reproduce in an alien language. It is tolerably certain that no English version of Flaubert's novels will ever adequately reproduce the charm of that master's style.† We must be content with translation that is at once faithful and entirely natural. Mrs. Aveling deserves credit for the way she has accomplished her task; and if again and again we fail to discern Flaubert in the version before us – it is not always her fault."

Sharp then gently drew attention to some "little lapses which more careful revision might have corrected".

Eleanor had used the definitive French edition of 1873,‡ which included an account of the legal action on a charge of immorality brought against Flaubert, "to whose eternal honour," Eleanor wrote in her Introduction, "the book was prosecuted by, of all people in the world, the Government of Napoleon III".

As Sharp pointed out, Flaubert was not, on the face of it, an author to appeal to readers with no French. Eleanor, offering to send Laura a copy of her translation, wrote: "Of course not to read – who would read Flaubert in English if he could help it!"[195] It may be conjectured that her reasons, other than financial, for accepting the commission and working on it so devotedly, sprang in part from her indignation at the crassness of the

---

* A Scottish-born writer (1856–1905) who was something of an authority on contemporary English, French and German poets, writing the first *Life of Robert Browning* in 1890 for the "Great Writers" series edited by E. S. Robertson. From 1894, under the pseudonym Fiona Macleod – never acknowledged in his lifetime but posthumously revealed – he wrote a number of Celtic plays and poems, the best known of which is *The Immortal Hour* as set to music by Rutland Boughton (1878–1960) at whose Glastonbury Festival it was first performed in 1914.
† This is fully borne out by Henry James's version, published in 1902, which, though certainly more stylish than Eleanor's, makes for almost as uneasy reading.
‡ The novel was first published serially 1856–7, in mutilated form, in the *Revue de Paris*.

French authorities in prosecuting the author but, more deeply, as expressed in her introduction, from her view of Emma Bovary straining, like her creator, "after an unattainable heaven". She also perceived that he had put much of himself into the character, whether or not she was familiar with his oft quoted dictum: *Madame Bovary, c'est moi!* She paid little heed – though not oblivious – to the heavy splendour of Flaubert's prose to which, together with his obsessional hunt for the *mot propre*,* she gave short shrift. It is not – she did not claim it was – a good translation and it may be that she relied a little too optimistically upon Paul Lafargue whose English was far from impeccable, for, as late as April 1886, she was sending him queries to which he evidently gave the wrong or no reply. The work is consequently peppered not only with "little lapses" but with almost incomprehensible Gallicisms where, it must be supposed, both she and her brother-in-law had been stumped. On forensic terms, once Paul had explained their precise usage in French law, she consulted Sam Moore. That she took immense pains cannot be doubted and, despite all its failings, her version has remained in print until today,† while, in common with all her translations, then and later, it had the distinction of being the first to be made available to English readers.‡

That Eleanor was no hack translator is clear from the fact that, though her French may have been serviceable rather than elegant, she was fired by her enthusiasm for Ibsen to set about learning an entirely new language and, in due time, though not yet, to produce the first English version from the original Norwegian of *An Enemy of the People, The Lady from the Sea* and a number of short stories by Alexander Kielland.§

None of these works evince great literary or linguistic talents, yet in all Eleanor's translations there is a certain vitality, reflecting her sympathy with the author, his subject matter and her desire to communicate that feeling which does more than a little to compensate for lack of skill. Though Eleanor cannot match present standards, in her own day many more lifeless versions of foreign works were turned out by better qualified translators.

---

* English readers may think the more familiar *"mot juste"* should have been used; but Flaubert himself, infallible in these matters, preferred the term here adopted.

† 1973. Dent's Everyman Library, No. 808, in which edition it has appeared since 1928, when her introduction was dropped and replaced.

‡ Twenty-four years earlier, in 1862, Flaubert himself referred to an English translation which he had supervised and proclaimed a masterpiece. (*"Faite sous mes yeux et qui était un chef-d'œuvre."*)[197] No London publisher could be found and it never appeared.

§ She did not place Kielland (1849–1907) in the same class as Ibsen and it may be that her interest in him was first aroused by the political row that blew up over the Norwegian parliament's refusal to award him a pension for "a literary activity which is held in great measure to conflict with the dominant moral and religious principles of the nation".[198]

The impact of Ibsen upon Eleanor and her immediate circle was violent: as violent as the sense of outrage felt by the majority of English
critics at the first performance of his plays. This new "social drama"
stunned them – though not into silence – by its complete break with the
theatrical conventions of the time, both in manner and content. *A Doll's
House*, under the title *Nora*, had been translated by Henrietta Frances Lord
in 1882;* *Ghosts*† two years later and it was from the unfinished Lord
translation that Aveling read aloud to Eleanor and Olive Schreiner that
summer in Derbyshire. "Yesterday," wrote Olive to Havelock Ellis on 29
July 1884, "I heard part of Ibsen's play *Ghosts*, still in manuscript. It is
one of the most wonderful and great things that has long, long been
written."[200] Another reading took place in November 1885 when Olive
begged Ellis to come. It was not presented on the English stage until
1891 and then only in a technically private performance at the Royalty
Theatre in Dean Street (opposite Eleanor's birthplace). It evoked much the
same response as, in our own time, total nudity on the stage, with the
difference that, whereas practically everyone living will have seen the
adult human body of both sexes in buff without going to the theatre at
all, nobody had ever before come face to face with Ibsen's *exposés*.

The *Evening Standard* stigmatised the audience of *Ghosts* as "lovers of
prurience and dabblers in impropriety who are eager to gratify their illicit
tastes under the pretence of art".[201] In the five years (1889–1893) during
which seven of the plays were produced in England, the abuse showered
upon Ibsen and his admirers – from Clement Scott's virulence in the *Daily
Telegraph* and (anonymous) scurrility in *Truth* through every organ of the
popular press down to the dreadful condemnation of the *Licensed
Victuallers' Gazette* – was assembled by William Archer in an article, "The
Mausoleum of Ibsen", published in the *Fortnightly Review*.[202] These press
comments not only provide tuition in the art of invective but also justify
in more ways than one Harley Granville-Barker's *dictum* that the first
production of *A Doll's House* (1889) "proved to be the most dramatic
event of the decade".[203]

It was, indeed, this play that made the most profound impression upon
its early readers at a time when the number of those who had so much as
heard Ibsen's name was extremely small. For the present generation which
has seen so many new departures in the theatre the effect on the British
public is perhaps difficult to understand.

In 1934 Bertolt Brecht called Ibsen's plays "important historical

---

* The play was written in 1879. An extract from what purported to be an earlier English
version by a Danish schoolmaster was quoted to hilarious effect by Harley Granville-Barker.[199]
† Written in 1881.

documents" which could no longer move anybody,[204] a comment he was bold enough to make in the country – Denmark – where Ibsen was first performed, most admired and still revered. Fifty years earlier – an aeon in the modern drama – he was a force to stir the blood and rouse the passions and, what is more, his audiences did not leave his theatre quite as they had entered it nor sit through his plays in a trance of complacency, but were disturbed, even as Brecht wished to disturb *his* audiences: namely, by an urge to change things as they are in the real world.

It was the era of the great London actor-managers and of the "well-constructed" play that provided any vehicle, however ramshackle, for these star performers. Amidst the melodramas, French farces, Society comedies and similar offerings, where the most promising playwrights were Arthur Wing Pinero and Henry Arthur Jones, Ibsen came as a bombshell. To him is owed the origin of a "fringe theatre": the non-professional productions, independent Clubs and Societies able to give performances without the Lord Chamberlain's licence.*

Olive Schreiner noted in her journal on 9 March 1884: "I love *Nora* by Ibsen"[205] and wrote to Ellis:

"Have you read a little play called *Nora*? by Ibsen, translated from the Swedish [*sic*] by Frances Lord. It is a most wonderful little work..."[206]

She reverted to the subject a few days later:

"With regard to *Nora*, I think Ibsen *does* see the other side of the question, but in a book which is a work of art, and not a mere philosophical dissertation, it is not always possible to show all sides."[207]

The interest of this comment lies in its early recognition of Ibsen the poet, sensed through a text that fell far short of conveying "his choice of words for both their sound and sense and his complexity of meaning".[208] It should be emphasised that the tremendous enthusiasm felt by many socialists among the early Ibsenites† was not a simple-hearted response to the "message" of the plays; it was equally compounded of respect for the novel technique and insight brought to bear upon topics of burning interest to them.

Ibsen's own political position was what we should now call uncommitted. However, when on 13 August 1890 the Berlin correspondent of

---

* Abolished in 1968.

† Notably Bernard Shaw, whose *Quintessence of Ibsenism*, originally published in 1891, was no more than an expanded version of a paper read to the Fabians on 18 July 1890 at St. James's restaurant as one of a series on Socialism and Contemporary Literature and thus politically slanted.[209]

the *Daily Chronicle* published an interview with him which traduced his views, he repudiated it in a letter to H. L. Brackstad, a friend in London, who wrote to the *Daily Chronicle* quoting (in translation) Ibsen's words:

> "'I have not said that I have never studied the Social Democratic question. On the contrary I have with great interest, and as far as I have been able, tried to make myself acquainted with the different aspects of this question. But I did say that I have never had the time to study the large and comprehensive literature which treats of the various socialistic systems.
>
> 'When the correspondent reverts to my expression that I did not belong to the Social-Democratic Party, I wish he had not omitted what I added and which I laid great stress on – that I never had, and probably never was likely to belong to any party whatsoever ... What I really did say, was that I was surprised that I, who principally had made it the object of my life to delineate the characters and fortunes of men, on certain points, without consciously or directly having intended to impute anything of the kind, had come to the same conclusion as the Social Democratic moral philosophers had come to through scientific research. This, my surprise – and I may here add, my satisfaction – I expressed to the correspondent....'"[*210]

In December 1885 Eleanor wrote to tell Havelock Ellis that there was to be a reading of *Nora* at her place in Great Russell Street on the evening of 15 January.

> "I feel I *must* do something to make people understand our Ibsen a little more than they do, and I know by experience that a play read to them often affects people more than when read by themselves."[212]

At this reading Eleanor took the part of Nora, Aveling that of Torvald Helmer, Shaw was Nils Krogstadt and May Morris Kristine Linde.[†] Neither Ellis nor Olive Schreiner – she being in Shanklin on the Isle of Wight – was present.

This was not the only nor the first occasion when Shaw performed with Eleanor and Aveling. On 21 November 1884 there had been an "Art Evening" of music, readings and drama at the Neumeyer Hall to raise funds for the SDF. The programme opened with a piano duet – Mendelssohn – played by Shaw and Kathleen Ina. Aveling was billed to read

---

* Ibsen's latest and exemplary biographer, Michael Meyer, reports him as saying to a friend: "I am a man of the left, in so far as the left fights against what is conservative ... But if they do not also make the workers' cause their own, then the left has shirked its task; I am no longer one of them."[211]

† Nearly half a century later, in 1933, Shaw was to recall the occasion in these words: "At the first performance of *A Doll's House* in England, on a first floor in a Bloomsbury lodging house, Karl Marx's youngest daughter played Nora Helmer and I impersonated Krogstadt at her request with a very vague notion of what it was all about."[213]

Shelley's *Men of England** and there were other items, faithfully described by Helene Demuth, who was there, to Engels who was not – "as I do not ... see my way to sitting three hours consecutively in a stiff chair" – but who passed on the details of her account to Laura. "Mother Wright," he wrote, referring to Mrs. Theodore Wright who had read an extract from *Adam Bede*, "read – very well – Bax played the piano – rather long –" (his rendering of Schumann's *"Carnival"*, as the programme called it, had evidently bored Nim):

> "Morris who was here the other night and quite delighted to find the Old Norse Edda on my table – he is an Icelandic enthusiast – Morris read a piece of his poetry ..." (in fact his own version of *The Passing of Brynhild*) "it went off very well – their art seems rather better than their literature and their poetry better than their prose."[214]

The second half of the evening was devoted to a "dramatic piece", *In Honour Bound*,† Eleanor and Aveling playing the main roles "with great spirit" and "to much applause", according to *Justice*. Nim thought the play more or less related their own story.

On 30 January 1885 Shaw again appeared with Eleanor and Aveling, this time in a Socialist League "Entertainment" at the Ladbroke Hall in Notting Hill, the second part of the programme consisting of a three-act play, *Alone*.‡ At the end of the year, on Saturday, 5 December, "A very successful concert and dramatic entertainment was given by E. Aveling and other friends"[216] at the Farringdon Hall. Ten days later, on Tuesday 15 December, a "Dramatic Entertainment under the Direction of Edward Aveling" was given, again at the Ladbroke Hall. This consisted of two one-act plays in both of which Eleanor and Edward played leading parts. The first, *To Oblige Benson*, was by Tom Taylor,§ the second was *The Test* by "Alec Nelson" and Philip Marston, announced as being "proudly presented for the first time".[217] It is not known ever to have been presented again. To this occasion Shaw was invited in a different capacity. May Morris, who was in the cast – and had also acted in *Alone* – wrote to him:

---

* *Justice* reported on 29 November that he had read "the famous passage from Shelley's *Masque of Anarchy*". There is now no means of knowing what he read, but it is quite possible that *Justice* was right and Aveling did not abide by the advertised programme.

† By Sydney Grundy (1848–1914) of whom William Archer had observed in 1882 that since he was still "not far on the wrong side of thirty ... his opportunity must ultimately arrive".[215] It did not. He continued to write trivial plays in an outworn mode until well into the '90s.

‡ By John Palgrave Simpson (1807–1887) and Herman Charles Merivale (1839–1906) who had written innumerable forgotten plays, several in collaboration. *Alone* was first produced by Vezin at the Court Theatre in October 1873.

§ 1817–1880. One time editor of *Punch* and for some years Professor of English in the University of London, Taylor was in the Health Department of the Civil Service from 1850 to 1871. He wrote over 70 plays, none of great distinction, and was an enthusiastic amateur actor.

"Will you accept the enclosed ticket for the acting the Avelings are shortly giving? We want all the leading critics, and their number would not be complete without you. It is a dismal little play, but clever, and Mrs. Aveling, I am sure, will be very successful in it. I can't do my part a bit."[*218]

May Morris thought highly of Eleanor, calling her in later years

"that gifted and brilliant woman, who worked long and valiantly for Socialism ... I saw a great deal of her at one time," she added, "and had a sincere and rather humble admiration for a woman whose gifts of brain seemed so far above my own!"[219]

Certainly these little amateur theatricals were of no great importance to Eleanor, nor to anyone else, but they gave her keen enjoyment. Her ambitions to act were, in a small way, fulfilled; her training by Mrs. Vezin, so painfully come by, had not after all been in vain. As her sister Jenny had predicted, to acquire perfect elocution was to be "a great gain" to her throughout life,[†] for her naturally melodious voice, professionally schooled, had a quality seldom equalled on the political platform by any woman of her time.

"I have seen," she had written to Jenny, "... that I can *move* an audience,"[‡] and, although at the time she had had in mind a very different type of audience, her "ringing musical voice, full of fire," her "polished English diction" and "thoughtful eloquence" did indeed move her listeners, one of whom described her as "a spellbinder".[220]

Aveling had published occasional pieces on the theatre, as when in November 1884 he wrote an immensely long and detailed review for To-Day of Wilson Barrett's Hamlet, which performance, opening at the Princess's Theatre on 16 October, was marred in the judgment of the most respected critics by the melodramatic style for which Barrett was famed.[§] This, however, was only by the way. Aveling was hoping to persuade Barrett to produce his own work. In this he failed: one-act plays,

---

[*] There is no evidence that Shaw went; but it is known that he appeared as an actor at least once more – this time in wig and costume – on 6 November 1886 in the so-called "copyright performance" of Odd (To Say the Least of It) by his friend Edward ("Baby") Rose at the Novelty Theatre. It was at this theatre that the first professional performance of A Doll's House was presented by the Charringtons on 7 June 1889. An obscure little playhouse, later to be known as the Great Queen Street Theatre, it came under Lena Ashwell's management in 1907, after the building of Kingsway and the Aldwych, when it was renamed the Kingsway Theatre. Damaged by bombing in the Second World War, it was repaired but is now no longer extant.

[†] See above, p. 182.

[‡] See above, p. 176.

[§] Wilson Barrett (1847–1904), the actor-manager of the Princess's Theatre, near Oxford Circus – no longer extant – was the author of The Sign of the Cross and one of the most popular exponents of Denver in that most popular melodrama The Silver King by Henry Arthur Jones and Henry Herman.

he was told, were not acceptable,[221] but he became a regular contributor to the *Dramatic Review*, under the name Alec Nelson, from April 1885.

Swift said: "It is an uncontrovertible truth that no man ever made an ill figure who understood his own talents, nor a good one who mistook them", and it is a sorry thing when a man of parts but no perception is decoyed by vanity into the sphere of the creative arts. Of course, like everyone else, Aveling knew his Shelley who, in the 1880s, though dead, shared with Browning, still alive, the highest public esteem, but there is never a mention of the writers of his own time;* he is not known to have taken the smallest interest in the visual arts – not even in those that formed so large a part of Morris's life and work – of music he was ignorant and in the drama, apart from Shakespeare and Ibsen, his taste, if one may judge by his own plays, adaptations and productions, ran to the gimcrack. How incautious were his pretensions may be judged by the fact that, at roughly the same period, one of his *confrères* on the *Dramatic Review* was Bernard Shaw, who also wrote as an expert on music and, less knowledgeably, on art for *The World*, to which paper William Archer was attached as theatre critic – probably the best of his time – while the *Pall Mall Gazette*, where Aveling's reviews of poetry and fiction occasionally appeared, could claim not only Shaw and Archer but also Oscar Wilde among its contributors: all of them younger men than Aveling, manifesting talents that might have abashed him.

In the first month of his new assignment he was let loose on Tennyson's *Beckett*, by which he was "profoundly unimpressed", calling it "still-born". That was forgivable. By now Tennyson who, aged 75, had been raised to the peerage in 1884 – the year *Beckett* was published – was distinctly out of fashion, while this chilly longwinded verse-drama was considered by so judicious a biographer as Andrew Lang "rather the marble from which the statue may be hewn than the statue itself" and wanting in concentration.†[222] But Aveling, who might well have remarked – as did Lang – upon the "narrow insularities" and "jingoism" of the old Poet Laureate,‡ dwelt rather upon the "pretty phrasings here and there" and chose, most curiously, one passage for quotation:

"*If a man*
Wastes himself among women, how should he love
A woman, as a woman should be loved?"[223]

---

* Among those then being published were Hardy, James, Kipling, Meredith, Stevenson, Swinburne and Trollope.

† For all that, Irving was to give it a long run in 1891 when it proved immensely successful and he scored a personal triumph.

‡ Succeeding Wordsworth and, it must be admitted, the last of any stature.

The following month Aveling had his say on the exhibition mounted by the Royal Institute of Painters in Water Colours.* He remarked upon the "surprising quantity of good pictures" – including Crane's – but what really caught his fancy was Edgar Giberne's "Who is Sylvia?", because it was so "pretty and graceful. Only one artist, however," he added inconsequently, "has hitherto caught Sylvia veritably, and that is Franz Schubert."[224]

On 6 June he devoted himself to a survey of the programmes sold at London's leading theatres, only four of which could be "unhesitatingly called artistic". Twelve, he opined, "can by a large charity be voted not ugly".[225]

In the same month he attended the Handel Festival at the Crystal Palace† giving him a more appropriate occasion to express his musical appreciation. This, however, he did not do. Instead, though he conceded that the oratorio did not leave him entirely unmoved – which could be accounted for by the sheer volume of sound – he censured the programme (for omitting to state the length of the interval) and the audience.‡ The Festival, he informed his readers, was

> "a middle-class affair. The singers and listeners are for the most part of the respectable shopkeeper-cum-dissenting type. The men wear top-hats and badly fitting coats. The women are, as to their dresses and feathers, fearfully and wonderfully coloured. The faces are common-place and generally ugly and there is a tendency to wear wool in the ears."[226]

So much for Handel. These comments are fair samples of Alec Nelson's

---

* Established in 1831 and granted a Royal Charter in 1883 when its new galleries in Piccadilly were opened.

† Joseph Paxton (1801–1865), formerly head gardener and adviser to the Duke of Devonshire whose elegant glasshouses at Chatsworth he designed, had built the Crystal Palace – so named by *Punch* – to house the Great Exhibition of 1851 in Hyde Park, thereby earning a knighthood. At the end of the year it was sold and re-erected – heightened and extended – in Sydenham where it was opened by Queen Victoria in 1854. The first of what were to be triennial Handel Festivals, under the direction of August Manns (1825–1907) – who was also knighted – was held there in 1857, growing ever in scale until, from 1862, no fewer than 4,000 singers and instrumentalists took part. The occasion reported by Aveling was one of the four massed performances given between the 19th and 26th June 1885. Between Festivals, the Crystal Palace was used for bird, cat, fish and flower shows. In 1911 it was purchased for the nation by the Earl of Plymouth and, save for the years of the First World War when it was used as a naval depot, there were firework displays on Thursday evenings throughout the summer until, in the most stupendous of its pyrotechnics, the whole structure went up in flames on the night of 30 November 1936.

‡ His diligent researches into programmes suggest that he spent his time studying them from cover to cover throughout all performances.

work as critic and it is, to use his own words, by a large charity that no more are cited.*

While Aveling, without a blush, was committing this stuff to public print, Eleanor was privately airing her own views on a matter of taste and aesthetic values. She forcefully objected to certain items in a concert given by the Socialist League in February 1886. It appears that a German journalist living in London, Karl Theodor Reuss,† had been responsible for organising the affair, "but," wrote Eleanor to the Council of the League,

> "I really cannot think that he, a musician, could be responsible for the 'comic songs' (save the mark!) sung. I am perfectly certain Comrade Reuss would never dream of having such songs sung at one of his own concerts and I do not think he would say that was 'good enough' for mere Socialists, which he would not judge 'good enough' for a bourgeois audience."

She had heard only one of the songs, but that had been more than enough. It was not, she explained, simply a matter of her personal taste and, even if some members of the audience did not share it,

> "I don't think we, who want our lectures, our paper, all our work to educate people (and surely education to a Socialist means also Art Education) should tolerate them," she wrote. ". . . I know, alas! that we can't pretend to give grand concerts: but let what we *do* give at least be of such a kind that we need not be ashamed of it, and do not let us say 'anything will do' for our audience because it is a poor and working-class one. Of course," she ended, "I speak here only for myself."[228]

It is clear that she was not speaking for Aveling.

However, she, too, had wandered into unfamiliar fields, if only as a "ghost", telling Lavrov in a letter of 7 June that, among other "hack work",

> "I am writing a biography and critical sketch of the artist Alma Tadema for someone who will publish it under his own name, not mine!"[229]

---

* But it must not be overlooked that Aveling was creative too. So, to do him justice without mercy, here are the opening lines of a lengthy poem he published as a ½d. leaflet, "especially adapted for reciting", according to *Justice* of 4 April, 1896:
> "O the clang of the wooden shoon!
> Ah! by God, but it starteth soon."

† He was later denounced in the German *Sozialdemokrat* as one of Bismarck's agents. On 7 January 1888 *Commonweal* published an article, "Police Spies Exposed", upon which Reuss threatened to sue William Morris for libel. Engels was of the opinion that Reuss would not "venture into the witness box" – in which he was proved right – adding: "perjury is only allowed to British police-constables".[227]

This work she did while correcting the last proof sheets of both *Bovary* and *The History of the Commune* while at the same time, on that very day, the first proofs of the English Volume I of *Capital* had come to hand.

The lease of the Marx house at 41 Maitland Park Road had expired on Quarter Day, 25 March 1884, and until the very last moment Engels, aided by Helene Demuth, now his housekeeper, was rummaging among the papers there. By mid-February they had cleared the lumber room and "found a whole lot of things that have to be kept, but about half a ton of old newspapers that it is impossible to sort," Engels told Laura.[230] Among the manuscripts he discovered "the first version of the *Kapital* (1861–63)" and "several hundred pages: *Theorien über den Mehrwerth** partly worked up into the text of the later versions, but there will be quite enough left to swell the 2nd volume into a 2nd and a 3rd."[230]

This came as a not entirely welcome surprise: Engels, who saw it as his primary duty to edit and publish Marx's unfinished work, had up till now envisaged the whole of *Capital* as two volumes. Despite Marx's reference in the Introduction to the original (1867) edition of Volume I, to a second volume ("Books II and III"), with a "third and last volume (Book IV)" to treat of "the history of the theory", neither he nor Engels had realised that the material for the second would expand into Volumes II and III.

However, before the end of February 1884 Engels had mapped out these two volumes and, in December that year, he was able to announce to Sorge that Volume II – some 600 printed pages – was about to go to press while Volume III would be of equal if not greater length.† He then specifically referred for the first time to a fourth volume: *Theories of Surplus Value*, derived from the papers now so unexpectedly brought to light.[232]

It had taken a full year – twice the length of time foreseen – to clear the house, but on 24 March Engels paid the outstanding rent and handed over the keys to the landlord, a Mr. Willis. The last act was the disposal of the remaining furniture, for which Engels had been offered £12. 10s., lock, stock and barrel, but, advised to put it up for sale, he hoped it might fetch £15.

Helene Demuth was thankful.

---

* *Theories of Surplus Value.*
† On 8 March 1885 Engels wrote to Laura: "The 3rd book of *Capital* is getting grander and grander ... It is almost inconceivable how a man who had such tremendous discoveries, such an entire and complete scientific revolution in his head, could keep it there for 20 years."[231]

"There is such a weight off her mind now since the old house is done with that she at last can sleep again; it was a nightmare for her which even an occasional nightcap of 'Irish' could not drive away."[233]

She was at this time 63 years old, roughly a month younger than Engels, and neither of them can have relished the task.

Engels, having rearranged all his furniture and even thrown out some of it in order to accommodate Marx's library, was now ready to start work on Volume II of *Capital*, at which juncture his landlord decided to have the front of 122 Regent's Park Road repainted, with the result that nobody was able to do anything at all as the March winds came tearing through the open windows, whipping up the piles of paper and aggravating Engels' rheumatism.

Throughout January and February 1884 Engels, busy negotiating various translations of Marx – into English, French, German, Polish, Russian – had been sorting out the library, listing those books intended for the German Party archives presently in Zurich; those he hoped would form the nucleus of a Russian revolutionary library to be sent to Lavrov in Paris; others that were to go to Sorge in America; French works that he thought the Lafargues would welcome; and making a variety of generous dispensations on all of which he consulted Eleanor who had selected for herself the best of the French and Italian dictionaries. The Blue Books he gave to Sam Moore for his English translation of the first volume of *Capital*, though in the event it was Eleanor who used them for this purpose.*

As far back as the late 1860s – that is, during Marx's lifetime – Engels had judged Samuel Moore the man best fitted for this work. It was not an obvious choice: a former territorial army officer, a gifted mathematician who was also a brilliant amateur geologist and botanist, Moore was a barrister by profession, living at 60 King's Street, Chorlton-on-Medlock and practising at the Courts of Chancery in Manchester and Liverpool. Born in Bamford, Derbyshire, in December 1838 – so that he was now 46 years of age – he had been educated at Shrewsbury and Trinity College, Cambridge. He was admitted to Lincoln's Inn in 1879 and called to the Bar in January 1882. On 15 June 1889 Moore left England to become Chief Justice to the territories of the Royal Niger Company, residing at its administrative centre, Asaba, on the boundary of the Western Region

---

* A fascinating account of the contents and disposition of both Marx's and Engels' libraries appeared in the 1969 Summer Number of *The Book Collector*, adapted from *Ex Libris Karl Marx und Friedrich Engels, Schicksal und Verzeichnis einer Bibliothek*, edited and introduced by Professor Bruno Kaiser of the Berlin Institute of Marxism-Leninism, published by Dietz, Berlin 1967.

of Nigeria, where he enjoyed the embraces of an African bride.* He held the appointment for eight years, with six months' leave every other year. So far as can be ascertained no biography of this interesting character exists, nor is there any mention of him in the many notable books dealing with this period of the scramble for Africa.†

Moore had been a close friend of both Marx and Engels since before the founding of the First International whose small Manchester section he had joined as a young man. Since entering the law his services to the socialist movement had been confined to giving expert legal advice on such matters as pirated and unauthorised editions of Marx's work and undertaking delicate missions for his revolutionary friends. But, immediately upon the publication of the first German edition of *Capital*, when he was 29, Moore proved to be, in Engels' words, its "most conscientious reader" – with the possible exception of Danielson in Russia – and one, moreover, who took immense pains to grasp its more abstruse theoretical content.‡

"To translate such a book," wrote Engels, "a fair knowledge of literary German is not enough. Marx uses freely expressions of everyday life and idioms of provincial dialects; he coins new words, he takes his illustrations from every branch of science, his allusions from the literature of a dozen languages; to understand him, a man must be a master of German indeed, spoken as well as written, and must know something of German life too ... But there is something more required. Marx is one of the most vigorous and concise writers of the age. To render him adequately, a man must be a master, not only of German, but of English too ... Powerful German requires powerful English to render it; the best resources of the language have to be drawn upon; new-coined German terms require the coining of corresponding new terms in English...[235]

Engels also told Bernstein and Kautsky:

"To be sure, we cannot imitate Marx's style, but the style must not be in direct contradiction to that of Marx."[236]

---

* He would no doubt have had to pay the bride-price and was thus legally married according to the native law he was there to administer, but he did not bring her back to England with him.
† A Royal Charter had been granted to Sir George Dashwood Taubman Goldie's National Africa Co. Ltd., as it became in 1882, though this had been refused the year before owing to the Company's small capital. Its name was now changed again and it became the Royal Niger Company Chartered and Limited, until its Charter was revoked under Lord Salisbury's administration in 1899 whereupon the region, as from 1900, became a British Protectorate, the Company's flag lowered and the Union Jack hoist. In 1920 control of the trading company passed into the hands of Lever Brothers Ltd, until, in 1949, the Government of Nigeria paid £1m. to the United Africa Co. – the successor to the Royal Niger Co. – for the rights to 50 years' royalties. On 1 October 1960 Nigeria became independent.
‡ In June 1868 Engels had written a review of *Capital* for the *Fortnightly Review* which he asked Sam Moore to sign in the hope that this would make it more acceptable. The article was not published.[234]

A few months after Marx's death Eleanor negotiated with Kegan Paul for the publication of an English translation. "S. Moore will translate, and I shall revise," Engels told Laura.[237]

Moore's fitness for the exacting task was beyond question. As translator-elect and to equip himself for the demands, and the privilege, of that position, he went into training for more than a decade, spending his vacations in Germany to perfect his knowledge of the language and submitting to Engels' grooming in both political economy and Marx's idiosyncratic prose.

In September 1883, while in Eastbourne, Engels read through Moore's first rough draft* and found it promising. But progress was slow. Indeed, even had Moore been free to devote his whole time to the work, which he was not, his very excellence, his regard for accuracy, reduced his speed. He was "too conscientious to hurry on with it 'regardless of quality'," Engels wrote to Laura at the end of March 1884[238] and, on 26 May: "Sam, who is doing the first chapter better than I expected, takes such a time over it."[239] Moore, fully aware that he was lagging behind, said that he must have help whereupon, in the spring of 1884, Aveling's services were enlisted.

Not to beat about the bush, this was a case of nepotism – for which Engels paid dearly – since Aveling had none of Moore's preparatory training or address. It was, in fact, his initiation into Marxism: he was being thrown in at the deep end, as it were. To be sure, he had been busily writing and speaking on the subject for some time past. In January 1884 he had published in To-Day an article on "Christianity and Capitalism"; on 2 March he lectured in Islington on Marx's theories; in the same month, under the pseudonym T. R. Ernest, he refuted Bernard Shaw's attack upon Marx's theory of value;[240] on 25 May he introduced a session of "unadulterated socialism" into his course of lessons at the Hall of Science; while up and down the country he lectured on "Socialism and Freethought", challenging George Howell† to a debate on wages, capital, or any other subject on which there were differences of opinion and, by the end of the year, he was discoursing to the Westminster Branch of the SDF on "The Exposition of Economical Terms". Announced in advertisements of his forthcoming public lectures were such subjects as Value, Capital, and Karl Marx. In the spring and summer of 1885 he gave his

---

* This had been done from the second German edition of 1872–3. In the spring of 1884 Moore began to work from the third (1883) edition.
† (1833–1910) A former Chartist, one of the founder members of the First International, Secretary of the London Trades Council 1861–2 and Secretary to the Parliamentary Committee of the TUC from 1872 to 1875.

courses analysing *Capital*, while in May and June various meetings heard him on the subject of "Capital and Surplus Value".

In setting himself up thus early as an exponent of and authority on Marx, Aveling had been living slightly above his intellectual station in life. Certainly Shaw could speak of him later as "saturated with Marx and history and what are supposed by Socialists to be economics";[241] Will Thorne would pay tribute to him as "one of the greatest orators this country has ever heard"[242] and Ben Tillett praise his "exceptionally brilliant intellect",[243] while his tireless activity and mastery of scientific socialism were acknowledged by even the most hostile of his denigrators in the movement. But it took an Engels to discern that in 1884 Aveling came to Marxism "a perfect novice in everything relating to political economy",[244] "a subject entirely foreign to him".[245]

On 20 April 1884 Aveling delivered a speech at the Baskerville Hall in Birmingham claiming that it had required "five years of deep study and close reading" for him to become a socialist, hearing of which Mrs. Annie Besant's fury knew no bounds. She let fly in all directions, nearly scoring a bull's eye when she declared that in all the five years that she had known him intimately, Aveling had shown not the faintest interest in socialism, that he had never studied it nor owned a single book on the subject. Constantly he had discussed politics with her and Bradlaugh and always the trio had been in perfect agreement on principles:

> "though his [Aveling's] political knowledge, like that of most scientific and literary men was very small ... he never touched Socialism in any way or knew anything about it until in 1882 he took to reading at the British Museum, and unfortunately fell into the company of some of the Bohemian Socialists, male and female, who flourish there. Supposing," Mrs. Besant went on, "that his was a 'sudden conversion', Karl Marx acting as a Socialist Moody and Sankey, it could only have taken place two years ago."[246]

In a private letter Eleanor commented on this outburst:

> "The one clear thinker and scientific student whose popularity *in the Secularist Party* almost equals Mr. Bradlaugh's, Dr. Edward Aveling, has joined the ranks of the Socialists and Mrs. Besant does me the honour to make me responsible for this. I am very proud of Dr. Aveling's friendship for myself, but I hope I need not tell you that his conversion to Socialism is due to a study of my Father's book &c not to me. As neither Mr. Bradlaugh nor Mrs. Besant have ever read anything on the subject of Socialism &c are grossly ignorant of it, they cannot understand that Dr. Aveling's 'conversion' can be due to any other than a personal motive."[247]

Only in April 1884 did Aveling for the first time start reading the

German text of *Capital*.* Out of interest, he made a rough translation of a few passages to use in his lectures, which exercise furnished plausible if rather shaky grounds for collaboration with Sam Moore. His preliminary canters were "utterly useless", Engels told Laura.

> "He was however very eager, and so, on his meeting Sam Moore here last week, it was arranged that he should try his hand at the chapter *Der Arbeitstag*,† this being chiefly descriptive and free, comparatively, from difficult theoretical passages for which A is totally unfit *as yet*, that is to say until he has worked himself through the whole book and understands it ... To tell you the truth I have no great faith in Aveling's *present* attempts."[249]

A few weeks later he was writing:

> "I have deuced little confidence in what assistance I may get here. Aveling has the best will, but he is to translate matter from what is for him unfamiliar German into what is for him unfamiliar English;‡ if it was natural science it would be easy enough, but political economy and industrial facts where he is not acquainted even with the commonest terms!"[250]

None the less, Engels, for all his superlative standards, permitted Aveling to continue with this major task. However, he had a particular reason for confiding in Laura the shortcomings of this tyro Marxist: he wanted to coax her to take a hand in the work.

Not a twelvemonth earlier,§ Laura had angrily asserted her rights, claiming that Marx "with his usual goodness" had asked her to undertake a translation of *Capital*.[251] Now Engels told her that, in asking Aveling to help Moore he had

> "made it a condition that you should be asked also ... of which Sam was very glad, and now I come to ask you ..."

He then outlined which chapters had been allocated so far and said:

---

* He had possibly read Deville's abridged French version, published in 1883. This, as Engels explained when the question arose of translating it into German, was totally inadequate: it was well enough for the French and, for that reason, he had held his tongue; but: "I do not see how I can consistently with my duty towards Mohr, let it pass unchallenged as a faithful résumé".[250] Though Marx had personally revised the first and Engels the second part of Deville's text, he now admitted that there had been "absurd hurry at the time" and that their suggested emendations had never been made.

† The Working Day.

‡ "*aus einem ihm unbekannten Deutsch in ein ihm unbekanntes Englisch*": the German phrase is in a letter otherwise in English.

§ June 1883. See above, p. 223.

"All the rest is open for you to choose from ... Any technical terms for which it might be difficult to find the English equivalent in Paris, you might leave room for ... As all parts of the translation pass through my hands, I can easily restore the unity of expression (the application of the same technical terms throughout the book). If you accept our proposal, as I hope you will ... we shall have fulfilled at least partially Mohr's wish and have your name and work associated with this translation."[249]

No less than four times in this letter did Engels bid her select such parts of the book he thought she might prefer. Laura refused.* Engels begged her to

"think it over again. I am afraid we cannot do without help from without ... You might try a few pages and see how you get on..."[250]

This appeal, too, was rejected.

It was now — May 1884 — that, as we know, Eleanor had begun tracing to their original sources all the quotations from English that Marx had used in Volume I of *Capital*. This was not quite as simple as it sounds. Marx had used extracts from 214 English authors (of whom 37 were anonymous), ranging from More's *Utopia* (1516) and Holinshed's *Chronicles* (1577) to works published shortly before the third German edition appeared in 1883, the year of his death. Twenty-four British journals were cited and some 80 Blue Books, Select Committees' and Royal Commissions' Reports, Hansards and Statistical Abstracts. Some of the references given were to editions and page numbers where these passages were not, in fact, to be found. Even a little research of this kind can rapidly lead to despair.† To complicate matters, while still living in Paris Marx had made elaborate preparatory notes, using French translations of English works often without any indication of the English edition from which the French was derived.

Not until she was about to embark for the United States at the end of August 1886 did Eleanor complete these labours, which included listing all the books and authors quoted and it "took me an awful time to get straight," she said.[252]

Small wonder that Engels should tell Laura he was "overwhelmed with proof-sheets, revisions, prefaces to write etc. etc.", so that he had not even "had the time to look seriously at your manifest."[253] For a startling thing had happened: outraged by the botch that Paul Lavigne, a French socialist, had made of translating the *Communist Manifesto* Laura had been galvanised into action.

---

* From internal evidence, in an unpublished letter of 15 May 1884.
† How strange it is that whereas the terrace of the Casino at Monte Carlo has been littered with the corpses of suicides the portico of the British Museum has not.

This change of heart may also have been brought about when, owing to an outbreak of cholera in Paris during the summer of 1884, Paul had insisted upon Laura going to England. She came for a month that autumn, at the moment when not only were Eleanor and Aveling working away at their separate labours for the English version of *Capital* while in the thick of the fight within the SDF – she herself attended a prodigiously unpleasant meeting of the Executive on 14 October when personal insults were freely bandied – but Engels, with whom she stayed, was overworked and feeling the weight of his responsibilities as never before.

"If I'm now to take Marx's place as first fiddle," he wrote to Becker on 15 October, "it won't be without making blunders and no one is more aware of this than I."[254]

Once Laura had begun to play a part he wrote to her:

"I am glad you are at last taking the bushel off your light and helping us get some good things translated into French ... When you are once in it, you will continue by the law of the force of inertia, and gradually begin to like the treadmill."[253]

To give encouragement, he praised her work to the point of flattery making only the most tentative criticisms. "You have hit the nail on the head," he wrote as he returned to her the first few sheets with his notes – "as mere suggestions on the value of which you will have to decide" – adding:

"there are only two passages, where you evidently were interrupted and did not catch the exact meaning. Otherwise the work is excellently done, and for the first time the pamphlet will appear in French in a form we can be proud of and that will give the reader an idea of what the original is.* As you go on ... practice will make you still more perfect, and you will more and more not translate, but reproduce in the other language ... Now we have got you in harness and will do our best to keep you in it. It will be of infinite use to the movement in France ... after the manifest anything you may tackle will appear child's play!"[256]

Laura's translation of the *Manifesto* appeared in France serially in *Le Socialiste* from 29 August to 7 November 1885, thus starting to come out before Engels had been able to go over it. But when he sharply disagreed

---

* A French translation of *The Communist Manifesto* had been brought out in Paris in 1848 and Chapters I and II had appeared in the New York French language paper, *Le Socialiste*, from January to March 1872.[255] This had been taken from Helen Macfarlane's English version, which first appeared in George Julian Harney's *Red Republican* on 9 November 1850, reprinted 21 years later in *Woodhull & Claflin's Weekly*, New York. The English version by Sam Moore, revised by Engels who wrote an Introduction, was published by William Reeves in February 1888.

with a passage in the seventh instalment (of 17 October), Laura took offence, though she consented to make the suggested alteration before the work appeared in pamphlet form.[257]

Just a year before, in October 1884, Engels had been writing in triumph to his old friend Johann Becker to say that three-eighths of the English *Capital* was now ready; at the end of 1884 he was telling Sorge that the first half was done. But by February 1885 it was another story. The book was at a standstill, he wrote to Lavrov in Paris: both translators had "too much other work to set about it with zeal". He still hoped, however, that the summer would see it completed.[258]

Engels himself was laid low with acute rheumatic pain in the legs for months on end; he was unable to walk more than a few steps and each day from ten until five he lay on his sofa dictating Volume II of *Capital* to a secretary, Oskar Eisengarten, whom he had engaged for this purpose. His evenings were passed in revising with the utmost care the many translations of his own and Marx's work now pouring in from abroad, at once thankful that they should be submitted to his scrutiny and loth to give his mind and time to work of the past when that to come was in the throes of delivery.*

It was not, in fact, until March 1886 that Moore and Aveling completed their work on Volume I of *Capital* and then only because they had been sharply spurred by the serial publication in *To-Day* of a rival translation, starting in October 1885,† purporting to be from the original German, by "John Broadhouse": the *nom-de-plume* used by Hyndman who

---

* In the years 1884–5, while completing Volume II and embarking upon Volume III of *Capital*, Engels, now in his mid-sixties, supervised Bernstein's German version of Marx's *The Poverty of Philosophy* (originally published in 1847 in French) and wrote a new preface to it, as well as revising Lafargue's translation of the (German) appendix to a new French edition of that work. He edited the French (by Lafargue) and the Italian (by Pasquale Martignetti) of his own most recent book, completed in May 1884, *The Origin of the Family, Private Property and the State*, published in Zurich in October 1884. He re-wrote *The Peasant War in Germany*, dating back to 1850; corrected Florence Kelley Wischnewetzky's American version of his *Condition of the Working Class in England in 1844*, Danielson's Russian text of Volume II of *Capital*, which was being done from the proofs as they came off the press, Edouard Fortin's French translation of Marx's *18th Brumaire* and Laura Lafargue's *Communist Manifesto*. To this last Engels wrote a new preface, as he did for the German republication of *Revelations about the Cologne Communist Trial of 1853*, and also an introduction to a work by Wilhelm Wolff that was to be reprinted. The manifold activities of these two years were by no means exceptional: any other two years in the following decade, when not interrupted by illness, convalescence or foreign travel, would show an equal if not heavier burden of work which does not, of course, include his wide reading, his voluminous and important political correspondence, his many contributions to the press of various countries or the countless visits from English and foreign socialists for whom he always found time, apart from which he kept open house on Sundays for his personal friends.

† The first chapter ended and the second began in March 1886, the last instalment – without reaching the end of Part I – appearing in the issue of May 1889.

was working from the abridged French edition by Deville, without his consent.

> "'Mr. Broadhouse' has actually had the impudence of having Aveling asked ... whether I would not collaborate with him in the translation of Capital", Engels reported to Laura.[259]

So far as the authorised English text was concerned, Engels admitted that it had been "awful work".

> "First they translate," he wrote, "then I revise and enter suggestions in pencil. Then it goes back to them. Then Conference for settlement of doubtful points. Then I have to go through the whole again, to see that everything is made ready for the press, stylistically and technically, and all the quotations Tussy has looked up in the British originals, fitted in properly ... But then there is another hitch. Edward has missed translating some 50 pages of his share,* and these I hope to get by the end of the week..."[260]

The negotiations with Kegan Paul, initiated by Eleanor, had broken down months before and now Engels was dealing with Swan Sonnenschein, Lowrey & Co. On 22 May 1886 he and Aveling called at their office and, on that day, the agreement was sent to Aveling for signature asking him to fill in

> "Mr. Engels' full names and address (which was accidentally not given us at our interview today)".

The contract was finally sent to Engels on 28 May, having been signed at his request by William Swan Sonnenschein in person, who considered this

> "quite unnecessary as our Mr. Lowrey† had ... signed for the firm".[261]

Mr. Prince, Sonnenschein's reader, began sending proofs to Aveling on 8 June. These were not to be returned without Engels' initials on each sheet, but Engels found them unsatisfactory and would not sign them until Sonnenschein explained that they were only "roughs". On 21 June the printers in Perth were clamouring for more material; by September

---

* Aveling's share consisted of Chapter 10 (The Working Day), Chapter 11 (The Rate and Mass of Surplus Value), Chapters 19 to 22 (Wages), one of the two sections in Chapter 24 and the whole of Chapter 25 (The Division of Labour and Manufacture), Chapters 26 to 32 (The So-called Primitive Accumulation) and Marx's Prefaces to the first and second German editions. This represented roughly a fifth of the whole volume.

† Francis Lowrey was a partner for a relatively short time and left the firm in 1888.

the position was reversed and Engels was complaining bitterly of delays.[261]

In all, Engels spent over eleven months as editor of this text, the first pages of which had gone to press on 23 May, while he was still revising proofs as late as November, but, as he wrote to Sorge: "It was absolutely necessary and I do not regret it."[262]

It was Aveling's part that gave him the most trouble, as he had foretold in a letter of 8 February 1886 to Danielson[263] when Aveling's manuscript first came to hand. In addition to his unfamiliarity with Marxist terms, Aveling had not Moore's "capital eye ... and ... very ready hand"[264] for rendering Marx's style.

Engels' preface was dated 5 November 1886 and in January 1887 the book was published by Swan Sonnenschein in two volumes costing 32s.

Thus nearly two decades after its original publication, the first volume of *Capital* appeared in the language of the country where Marx had written it and where he had spent more than half his lifetime. As Eleanor must have reflected with satisfaction, this, though in all conscience tardy, was less than four years after her father's death and owed not a little to her own and her partner's efforts.

Five hundred copies of this first English edition were printed, 200 going to America and, despite the absence of press notices*, 300 copies were sold in England within two months. In April 1887 a further 500 copies were issued – in stereotype, though called a "second edition" – and in 1889 the first one-volume edition came out, to be reprinted in 1891.†

Between the first and the last of these editions, or impressions, 794 copies were sold in England and 700 in the States.‡ Before Engels' death in 1895 Volume I of *Capital* had appeared in nine languages, eight countries and 17 editions in a total of 50,000 copies.[266] That is later history, but in 1886 that first English edition was still being assiduously revised by Engels when he came up from Eastbourne, where he was recuperating, to see Eleanor and Aveling off to America.

Aveling had given a final lecture – "How to Bring About the Social Revolution" – on 21 August to the Bloomsbury Branch of the Socialist

---

* An anonymous, not unfavourable, review appeared in the 5 March 1887 issue of the *Athenaeum*.

† According to the official historian of the publishers: "After selling steadily for some years ... It was remaindered at Glaisher's. Glaisher's reprinted it and continued to publish the work until the reconstruction of Ruskin House" – the premises in Museum Street, enlarged in 1930 – "when the copyright was re-acquired by Allen & Unwin", with which Sonnenschein had merged in 1911. Allen & Unwin also issued in 1928 the translation by Eden and Cedar Paul and continued to publish both versions.[265]

‡ Aveling, as official co-translator, always received his one-fifth share of the meagre royalties. Eleanor's work, though acknowledged by Engels in his Introduction, was, like his own, unpaid.

League which "wished him good-speed on his journey"; and at the Executive meeting of 20 August he "bade farewell to the assembled comrades ere departing".[267] Then he and Eleanor set sail.

*   *   *

Before they do so, let it be said that Eleanor's relationship with Aveling after two years as his common law wife had found its level. She perceived in him what she called "the weakness, the vanity and the venality"[268] of the Irish to whom all things could be forgiven.* She had discovered that certain shared interests, though she must and did make the most of them, and the irresistible sexual attraction he had for her, as for others at the same time, were not enough to support the plenitude of a true marriage resting on mutual trust. She could not rely upon him; she did not honour him; but she loved him and nothing could shake her loyalty once given. Unlike Emma Bovary, Eleanor, far from seeking solace for the bleakness of her emotional life in a world of false romanticism, escaped into a larger reality: that movement which, from childhood, she had seen as the mainspring of existence.

REFERENCE NOTES

Abbreviations
Adelphi (1) *Adelphi* (2)

    "Eleanor Marx": two articles by Henry Havelock Ellis in *The Adelphi* (1) vol. X, No. 6, September 1935 (pp. 342–52). (2) vol. XI, No. 1, October 1935 (pp. 33–41).

BIML   Institute of Marxism-Leninism, Berlin.

Bottigelli Archives Letters in the custody of Professor Emile Bottigelli.

The Eighteen Eighties Essays by Fellows of the Royal Society of Literature. Edited by Walter de la Mare. C.U.P. 1930.

ELC   *Frederick Engels, Paul and Laura Lafargue: Correspondence.* Volumes I–III. Lawrence & Wishart, 1959–1963.

CMFR   *Perepiska Chlenov Semyi Marksa s Russkimi Politicheskimi Deiateliami.* (Correspondence Between Members of the Marx Family and Russian Political Figures). Political Literature Publishing House. Moscow 1974.

IISH   International Institute of Social History, Amsterdam.

Liebknecht   *Wilhelm Liebknecht. Briefwechsel mit Karl Marx und Friedrich Engels.* Edited by Georg Eckert. Mouton & Co., The Hague, 1963.

MEW   *Marx Engels Werke.* Dietz Verlag, Berlin, 1956–1968.

MIML   Institute of Marxism-Leninism, Moscow.

---

* She persisted in her belief not only that he was Irish, faintly justified by his mother's antecedents, but, as her letter to Olive shows (see above p. 277) that he was also "half-French", intended as an excuse rather than a tribute and without any foundation whatsoever.

OS Letters	*Letters of Olive Schreiner* 1876–1920. Edited by S. C. Cronwright-Schreiner. Fisher Unwin, 1924.
OS Life	S. C. Cronwright-Schreiner. *The Life of Olive Schreiner*. Fisher Unwin, 1924.
Thompson	E. P. Thompson. *William Morris: Romantic to Revolutionary*. Lawrence & Wishart, 1955.
WM Letters	*The Letters of William Morris to his Family and Friends*. Edited by Philip Henderson. Longmans Green, 1950.

(1) MIML.

(2) 30 June 1884. Radford family papers.

(3) 25 July 1884. MIML.

(4) Privately communicated with permission to quote.

(5) MIML. Previously published in Thompson, pp. 859–60.

(6) Bottigelli Archives.

(7) To Havelock Ellis, March 1887. *Adelphi* (2).

(8) ELC I, pp. 218–19.

(9) "Thomas Moore's Life of Lord Byron", *The Edinburgh Review*, June 1831. Later included in *Historical and Critical Essays*.

(10) Letter to the *Hampstead and Highgate Express*, 20 February 1953.

(11) *Partial Portraits*. Macmillan, 1894.

(12) Harley Granville-Barker. *The Eighteen-Eighties*, p. 161.

(13) Eleanor to Laura, 22 September 1884. Bottigelli Archives.

(14) Radford family papers.

(15) *Collected Letters of D. H. Lawrence*, vol. I. Edited by Harry T. Moore. Heinemann, 1962, pp. 552–3.

(16) OS Letters.

(17) *Ibid.*, pp. 212–13.

(18) *Adelphi* (1).

(19) OS Letters, 16 June 1884, p. 22.

(20) OS Life, p. 33.

(21) OS Letters, 19 April 1907, p. 266.

(22) *Ibid.*, 22 October 1907, p. 274.

(23) OS Life, p. 33.

(24) OS Letters, 13 August 1890, p. 195.

(25) *Adelphi* (2).

(26) OS Life, p. 72.

(27) OS Letters, p. 14.

(28) *Ibid.*, pp. 268, 270.

(29) OS Life, p. 162.

(30) *Ibid.*, p. 281.

(31) *Ibid.*, p. 283.

(32) *Ibid.*, p. 315.

(33) OS Letters, 24 July 1884, p. 34.

(34) *Ibid.*, 2 August 1884, pp. 36–7.

(35) *Ibid.*, p. 165.

(36) 5 April 1885. Privately communicated with permission to quote.

(37) OS Letters, 8 April 1885, p. 69.

(38) *Adelphi* (2).

(39) H. Havelock Ellis. *My Life*, Heinemann, 1940.

(40) *Adelphi* (2).

(41) *Adelphi* (1).

(42) OS Letters. 16 July 1884, pp. 31–2.

(43) *Ibid.*, 6 November 1890, p. 199.

(44) James McNeill Whistler. *The Gentle Art of Making Enemies*, 3rd edn., Heinemann, 1904.

(45) *Adelphi* (1).

(46) 12 April 1885. Bottigelli Archives.

(47) *Adelphi* (2).

(48) Henry S. Salt. *Seventy Years Among Savages*, Allen & Unwin, 1921, p. 81.

(49) *The Apostle of Free Labour*, Hurst & Blackett, 1913, pp. vii, 82–3, 85, 99, 109.

(49a) Privately communicated by Mrs. Maj Sylvan of Stockholm.

(50) *News from Nowhere*. First published in *Commonweal* from 11 January to 4 October 1890.

(51) 22 September 1884. Bottigelli Archives.

(52) Eleanor to Laura, 12 April 1885. *Ibid.*

(53) 31 December 1887. *Ibid.*

(54) Eleanor to Laura, 24 June 1888. IISH.

(55) Eleanor to Laura, 13 February 1884. Bottigelli Archives.

(56) 9 May 1884. IISH.

(57) Eleanor to Laura, 12 April 1885. Bottigelli Archives.

(58) The recipient is unidentified, being addressed simply as "Dear Comrade", 6 April 1885. IISH.

(59) 12 April 1885. Bottigelli Archives.

(60) 14 April 1885. CMFR, p. 72 (original in English).

(61) Eleanor to Laura from Liverpool, 31 August 1886. Bottigelli Archives.

(62) June and July 1884.

(63) Eleanor to Laura, 9 May 1884. IISH.

(64) MIML.

(65) Eleanor to Laura, 21 July 1884. Bottigelli Archives.

(66) Lissagaray. *History of the Commune*, translated by Eleanor Marx Aveling, Reeves & Turner, 1886, p. 361.

(67) *To-Day*. January 1884.

(68) Reprinted under the heading 'Ninety Years Ago' in *The Freethinker*, September 1973, p. 135.

(69) Eleanor to Laura, 19 March 1884. Bottigelli Archives.

(70) 4 May 1884.

(71) 8 May 1884. MIML. Previously published in Thompson, pp. 858–9.

(72) Morris to Andreas Scheu, 8 September 1884. IISH.

(73) Morris to Andreas Scheu, IISH. Previously published in WM Letters, pp. 213–14.

(74) Eleanor to Laura, 1 February 1884. Bottigelli Archives.

(75) Bottigelli Archives.

(76) As the footnote explains, Bottigelli Archives and IISH.

(77) *To-Day*. April 1884.

(78) Andrew Rothstein. *A House on Clerkenwell Green*, Lawrence & Wishart, 1966.

(79) *Justice*, 26 January 1884.

(80) *Ibid.*, 15 March 1884.

(81) *Commonweal*. 19 June 1886.

(82) 2 February 1885. CMFR, p. 67 (original in French).

(83) 18 April 1885. BM Add. MSS 45349.

(84) H. M. Hyndman. *The Record of an Adventurous Life*, Macmillan, 1911, pp. 346–7.

(85) MIML. Previously published in Thompson, p. 860.

(86) H. W. Lee and E. Archbold. *Social-Democracy in Britain*, The Social-Democratic Federation, 1935, p. 65.

(87) Eleanor to Laura, 19 March 1884. Bottigelli Archives.

(88) WM Letters, p. 211.

(89) Letter to *Commonweal*, 5 May 1889.

(90) Letter to Dr. John Glasse, 23 September 1887. Quoted by R. Page Arnot in *William Morris, the Man and the Myth*, Lawrence & Wishart, 1964, p. 86.

(91) Engels to August Bebel, 20 August 1883. MEW 36, p. 57. Trans. H. C. Stevens in *Labour Monthly*, September 1933.

(92) Max Beer. *A History of British Socialism*, Vol. II. G. Bell & Sons, 1920, p. 274.

(93) BM Add MSS. 50689. 1964c.

(94) Engels to Florence Kelley Wischnewetzky. 27 January 1887. MIML.

(95) *Tom Mann's Memoirs*, MacGibbon & Kee, 1967, pp. 24–5. Originally issued in 1923 by the Labour Publishing Company.

(96) A. L. Bowley. *Wages in the United Kingdom in the* 19th Century. C.U.P., 1900.

(97) Engels, *Commonweal*, 1 March 1885.

(98) Leone Levi. *Wages and Earnings of the Working Classes*, John Murray, 1885, p. 341.

(99) *Ibid.*, pp. 34, 82. The figures quoted were published officially by the Amalgamated Society of Railway Servants of England, Ireland, Scotland and Wales for the year 1884.

(100) *Labour and Life of the People of London*. Vol. II. Ed. Charles Booth. Williams & Norgate, 1891; and *Charles Booth's London*. Ed. Albert Fried & Richard M. Elman. Hutchinson, 1969.

(101) Quoted from *Cassell's Saturday Journal*, 18 October 1890, by Thompson, fn., p. 661.

(102) *A Dream of John Ball*. First published in *Commonweal*, 1886–7.

(103) William Stephen Sanders. *Early Socialist Days*, Hogarth Press, 1927, p. 23.

(104) *The Birth of the Communist Manifesto*. Ed. Dirk J. Struik. International Publishers, New York, 1971, p. 215; and *Grundsätze des Kommunismus*, MEW 4, pp. 363–80.

(105) Hyndman. *The Record of an Adventurous Life*, pp. 178–9.

(106) Henry S. Salt. *The Company I have kept*, Allen & Unwin, 1930, p. 92.

(107) MEW 36, p. 122.

(108) 31 August 1897. Liebknecht Archives, BIML.

(109) Engels to Bernstein. 29 December 1884. MEW 36, p. 257.

(110) Eleanor to Laura, 17 March 1884. Bottigelli Archives.

(111) CMFR, 26 March 1884 (original in French).

(112) Eleanor to Laura, 21 July 1884. Bottigelli Archives.

(113) Morris to Scheu, 13 August 1884. WM Letters, p. 211.

(114) H. M. Hyndman. *Further Reminiscences*, Macmillan, 1912, p. 138.

(115) BM Add. MSS 50689, 1964c.

(116) Hyndman. *op. cit.*, p. 139.

(117) Hyndman to Morris, 8 December 1884. BM Add. MSS 45345.

(118) Liebknecht, p. 433.

(119) Morris to Robert Thompson, 1 January 1885. WM Letters, p. 228.

(120) *Justice*, 31 January 1865.

(121) BM Add. MSS 45345.

(122) MIML.

(123) Bottigelli Archives.

(124) MIML (original in French).

(125) *Ibid.*

(126) BIML.

(127) J. Bruce Glasier. *William Morris and the Early Days of the Socialist Movement,* Longmans Green, 1921, App. I.

(128) Dona Torr papers.

(129) Morris to Mrs. Burne-Jones, February 1885, quoted from J. W. Mackail's *Life of William Morris* in WM Letters, p. 232.

(130) 12 April 1885. Bottigelli Archives.

(131) To Lavrov, 9 March 1886. CMFR. pp. 82–3 (original in French).

(132) *East End Gazette,* 26 September 1885.

(133) 20 September 1885.

(134) H. W. Lee and E. Archbold. *Social-Democracy in Britain.* The Social-Democratic Federation, 1935, p. 101.

(135) *The Echo,* 21 September 1885.

(136) *Justice,* 20 September 1885.

(137) 22 September 1885. MIML.

(138) Review of J. W. Mackail's *Life of William Morris* in the *Daily Chronicle,* 20 April 1899. Reprinted in *Pen Portraits and Reviews,* Constable, 1932.

(139) *Justice,* 17 October 1885.

(140) 13 October 1885. IISH.

(141) Eleanor to Socialist League, 23 December 1885. IISH.

(142) Eleanor to Laura, 13 February 1884. Bottigelli Archives.

(143) 17 March 1884. IISH.

(144) 9 May 1884. *Ibid.*

(145) 12 April 1885. Bottigelli Archives.

(146) Paul Lafargue to Engels, 27 February 1885. ELC I, p. 269.

(147) Laura to Engels, 11 (?) June 1885. *Ibid.,* p. 293.

(148) IISH.

(149) MIML.

(150) *Ibid.*

(151) 23 April 1886. Bottigelli Archives.

(152) To Socialist League, 10 May 1886. IISH.

(153) 18 March 1886. MEW 36, p. 445.

(154) 9 February 1886. ELC I, p. 334.

(155) 9 March 1886. CMFR. p. 82 (original in French).

(156) Hyndman. *The Record of an Adventurous Life,* p. 402.

(157) IISH.

(158) Public Record Office. Crown Copyright. By permission of the Controller of H.M. Stationery Office.

(159) *Ibid.*

(160) 30 July 1886. *Ibid.*

(161) *Ibid.*

(162) *Commonweal,* April 1886.

(163) *August Bebel, Eine Biographie.* A collective work under the direction of Dr. Horst Bartel issued by the German Academy of Sciences. Dietz, Berlin, 1963. *August Bebels Briefwechsel mit Friedrich Engels.* Ed. Werner Blumenberg. Mouton, The Hague, 1965.

(164) Introduction to *The Woman Question* by Edward and Eleanor Marx Aveling [*sic*]. Swan Sonnenschein, Lowrey & Co., 1886. Price 2d.

(165) 9 May 1886, pp. 207–22.

(166) To Lavrov, 29 January 1886. CMFR, p. 80 (original in French).

(167) The Letterbooks of Swan Sonnenschein, Lowrey & Co. by kind permission of the late Sir Stanley Unwin and the present chairman of Messrs. George Allen & Unwin, Mr. Rayner Unwin.

(168) To Gertrud Guillaume-Scheck, 5 July 1886. MEW 36, p. 341.

(169) *The Nineteenth Century*. Vol. 28. No. CLXII, p. 295.

(170) *Labour and Life of the People*. Vol. I. Ed. Charles Booth. Williams & Norgate, 1889, pp. 136–8.

(171) *Commonweal*, September 1885.

(172) *Ibid*.

(173) *Ibid*. August 1885.

(174) To Engels, 13(?) April 1886. ELC I, p. 348.

(175) Bottigelli Archives.

(176) 27 April 1886. IISH.

(177) 23 April 1886. Bottigelli Archives.

(178) 28 April 1886. MIML.

(179) *East London Observer*, 5 June 1886.

(180) 5 June 1886.

(181) Thompson, fn., p. 489.

(182) To Socialist League, 5 July 1886. IISH.

(183) 22 September 1884. Bottigelli Archives.

(184) 5 February 1885. MIML.

(185) Eleanor to Mahon and Kautsky, 3 February 1885. IISH.

(186) 6 March 1885. CMFR, p. 70 (original in English).

(187) 9 March 1885. *Ibid.*, pp. 70–1.

(188) Engels to Laura, 16 June 1885. MIML.

(189) Radford family papers.

(190) To Laura, 27 April 1886. IISH.

(191) *Ibid*.

(192) Bottigelli Archives.

(193) No. 3075. 2 October 1886.

(194) No. 751.

(195) 25 September 1887. IISH.

(196) Introduction to *Madame Bovary*.

(197) Flaubert to Ernest Duplon, 22 June 1862. #CEuvres complètes de Gustave Flaubert. Correspondance. Nouvelle édition augmentée. Cinquième série (1862–1863). Louis Conard, Paris, 1929, p. 26.

(198) Quoted by William Archer in his Introduction to *Tales of Two Countries*. James R. Osgood, McIlvaine & Co., 1911.

(199) Harley Granville-Barker. *The Eighteen Eighties*, pp. 194–6.

(200) OS Letters, p. 36.

(201) Quoted by William Archer in the *Pall Mall Gazette*, 8 April 1891, in his article " 'Ghosts' and Gibberings".

(202) Edited by Frank Harris. Vol. LIV. New Series. 1 July 1893, pp. 77–91.

(203) *The Eighteen Eighties*, p. 159.

(204) Quoted by John Willett in *Brecht on Theatre*, Methuen, 1965, p. 66.

(205) OS Life, p. 167.

(206) 28 March 1884. OS Letters, p. 14.

(207) 8 April 1884. *Ibid.*, p. 15.

(208) Granville-Barker. *The Eighteen Eighties*, p. 193.

(209) *The Quintessence of Ibsenism. Now Completed to Ibsen's Death*, Constable, 1913, p. xvii.

(210) 28 August 1890.

(211) Michael Meyer. *Henrik Ibsen. The Top of a Cold Mountain* (1883–1906), Rupert Hart-Davis, 1971, p. 152.

(212) Quoted in *Adelphi* (2).

(213) *Shaw on Theatre*. Ed. E. J. West. MacGibbon & Kee, 1958, p. 219.

(214) 23 November 1884. ELC I, pp. 245–6.

(215) *English Dramatists of Today*, 1882.

(216) *Commonweal*, January 1886.

(217) Handbill. IISH.

(218) 6 December 1885. BM Add. MSS 50541.

(219) May Morris. *William Morris. Artist, Writer, Socialist*. Vol. 2. Basil Blackwell, 1936, p. 183.

(220) Aaron Rosebury in an article written *c.* 1927 recording his impressions and quoting Abraham Cahan, the editor of the *American Jewish Daily Forward*. Published in "Eleanor, Daughter of Karl Marx" by Professor Theodor Rosebury in *The Monthly Review*, vol. 24, no. 8. New York. January 1972, pp. 33–4.

(221) Wilson Barrett to Aveling, 29 August 1885. BM Add. MSS 45345.

(222) *Alfred Tennyson*. William Blackwood & Sons, 1901, p. 192.

(223) *Dramatic Review*, 4 April 1885.

(224) *Ibid.*, 2 May 1885.

(225) *Ibid.*, 6 June 1885.

(226) *Ibid.*, 27 June 1885.

(227) To Laura, 25 February 1888, ELC II, p. 97.

(228) To Socialist League, 1 March 1886. IISH.

(229) 7 June 1886. CMFR, pp. 88–9 (original in French).

(230) 16 February 1884. ELC I, pp. 177–8.

(231) 8 March 1885. *Ibid.*, p. 271.

(232) 31 December 1884. MEW 36, pp. 264–5.

(233) Engels to Laura, 31 March 1884. ELC I, p. 186.

(234) F. Engels, *On Marx's Capital*. Progress Publishers, Moscow, 1956. p. 47.

(235) "How Not to Translate Marx", *Commonweal*, November 1885.

(236) 1 January 1884. MEW 36, p. 78.

(237) 2 June 1883. ELC I, p. 137.

(238) 31 March 1884. *Ibid.*, p. 187.

(239) *Ibid.*, p. 206.

(240) *Justice*, 15 March 1884.

(241) To William P. Johnson, Secretary of the National Union of Shop Assistants, 30 January 1893. *Bernard Shaw's Collected Letters 1874–1897*. Ed. Dan H. Laurence. Max Reinhardt, 1965, p. 379.

(242) *My Life's Battles*. George Newnes, n.d. (probably 1925), p. 47.

(243) *Memoirs and Reflections*. John Long, 1931, p. 135.

(244) To Laura, 31 March 1884. ELC I, pp. 187–8.

(245) To Bernstein, 1 January 1884. MEW 36, p. 79.

(246) *National Reformer*, 4 May 1884.

(247) To John Mahon, 8 May 1884. MIML. Previously published in Thompson, p. 859.

(248) To Laura, 17 January 1886. ELC I, pp. 332–3.

(249) 18 April 1884. *Ibid.*, pp. 195–6.

(250) 26 May 1884. *Ibid.*, p. 206.

(251) 20 June 1883. *Ibid.*, p. 142.

(252) To Laura, 31 August 1886. Bottigelli Archives.

(253) 22 September 1885. MIML.

(254) MEW 36, p. 218.

(255) *Manifeste du Parti Communiste (présenté par E. Bottigelli)*. Aubier-Montaigne, Paris, 1971.

(256) 13 October 1885. MIML.

(257) 25 October 1885. ELC I, p. 315.

(258) MEW 36, p. 282.

(259) 7 November 1885. MIML.

(260) To Laura, 28 April 1886. *Ibid.*

(261) Swan Sonnenschein *Letterbooks*.

(262) 16–17 September 1886. MEW 36, p. 534.

(263) MIML.

(264) To Laura. MIML. Quoted in A. Uroyeva, *For All Time and All Men*. Trans. David Fidlon. Progress Publishers, Moscow 1969, p. 225.

(265) F. A. Mumby and Frances H. S. Stallybrass. *From Swan Sonnenschein to George Allen & Unwin Ltd*. George Allen & Unwin, 1955, p. 27.

(266) Uroyeva. *Op. cit.*, pp. 9, 14.

(267) *Commonweal*, 31 August 1886.

(268) Eleanor Marx Aveling, *The Working Class Movement in England*, 1895.

· PART II ·

CONFLICTS

Eleanor and Aveling set sail for America on Tuesday, 31 August 1886, on the Inman liner *City of Chicago*, paying £24 for a two-berth cabin.* Before embarking Eleanor sent a letter to Laura from the Adelphi Hotel in Liverpool:

"In a few hours we are off, but I must send you and Paul a line of goodbye ... I look forward to this journey with no little anxiety. We shall have a difficult time of it in many ways ... we shall be constantly on the move ... *Please* write and tell of yourselves and the children ... Yours affectionately, Tussy." To this Aveling added a note to send his love and the wish that the Lafargues were going with them. "We shall be quite strangers in a strange world. *If'* – he underlined the word six times – "we make millions of dollars we will spend some of the very first of them on a Cook's ticket to 66 Boulevard de Port Royal ..."[2]

The ten-day Atlantic crossing was pleasant, if uneventful, save for the occasional sight of whales and porpoises, though an episode of a very different order broke the monotony: a woman travelling steerage to rejoin her husband in New York died on the voyage and was buried at sea: "in the early morning, at daybreak – the simplest, and most impressive funeral I have ever witnessed", wrote Eleanor.[3]

Landing in New York on 10 September – "the entrance up the bay to the harbour is a marvellous sight"† – the Avelings were met by some "red-ribboned gentlemen", while "reporters were down upon us like wolves on the fold" before they were taken to their quarters "in the German part of the city. I rather regret this, for the *Vaterland* like the poor is always with us here,"[3] said Eleanor, thereby lighting swiftly upon one of the major weaknesses of the American socialist movement.

She gave as her forwarding address W. L. Rosenberg‡ at 261 East 10th Street, New York City: "he will always know whereabouts to send on".[4]

---

* "The *Cunard* is the dearest line of all and no better than many others, and is dear because 'swells' go by it," Eleanor wrote to Liebknecht. "We find after careful investigation that ... on the Cunard in order to be together ... we shd. have to pay £18 each ... The only difficulty is you have to pay (on all lines) a deposit of £5 a berth on securing it ..."[1]

† Auguste Bartholdi's colossal Statue of Liberty, constructed in Paris and shipped to the United States as a gift from the French Republic, was not unveiled until 28 October 1886, so that Eleanor saw it only on her departure.

‡ Wilhelm Ludwig Rosenberg, secretary to the Executive Committee of the Socialist Labor Party of North America.

Poor Rosenberg must have had his work cut out, for the Avelings were swept from city to city and state to state in fulfilment of the arduous programme arranged for their fifteen weeks' stay.* In some places they held as many as four meetings, while in addition both were obliged to keep up a steady flow of journalism. "Edward has about a dozen newspapers to write to," wrote Eleanor to her sister on 14 September and added a sentence that was to become of some importance later: "you know I am bound to 'keep myself' as the Party only pays for Edward".[7]

This letter was written on the day after Wilhelm Liebknecht had joined them. He it was who had suggested that Eleanor and Aveling should be invited when the German Party decided that August Bebel, originally intended as Liebknecht's fellow-propagandist, should not be out of the country at the same time.†

With the arrival of the main guest and elder statesman – Liebknecht had celebrated his 60th birthday in March that year – life, which had been "one whirl these last days", became even more heady:

> "After meeting dozens of people in the morning we were serenaded last evening and then taken off to beer and talk and handshaking with so many delegates from so many organisations that we were fairly tired out ... Every ten minutes someone or other turns up. If I am very incoherent ascribe it to that..."

Nevertheless that same afternoon they left for Bridgeport to make their first public appearance, returning late at night to their lodgings in "this very dirty, shoddy town".[9]

On his way from Germany Liebknecht had broken his journey in England where he met Eleanor and Aveling briefly before they left. Engels had come up from Eastbourne to see them off and then took Liebknecht back to the seaside for a few days before he, too, set out for Liverpool to join the Cunarder *Servia* on Saturday, 4 September, landing in New York on the 13th.

Liebknecht's tour was shorter than that of the Avelings by some five

---

* On 9 September 1886 *Commonweal* published a list of 40 dates and places under the heading "Dr. Aveling's Lecture Tour of the States". Eleanor was not mentioned. In the event the itinerary departed slightly from that advertised and in the book they later wrote Eleanor and Aveling said that, apart from New York and its neighbourhood, they had visited 35 places.[5] However, in an article written by Aveling on the eve of his departure from the States, he claimed they had been to 45 localities.[6] Insofar as it is possible to trace their movements with any precision, they would seem to have spoken in 16 different places.
† There had been an earlier plan in 1883 for Liebknecht and Bebel to visit America in the following spring, Liebknecht proposing that Eleanor – not yet "Mrs. Aveling" – should go with him as his secretary, which she would gladly have done.[8]

weeks.* In the interests of more precise details it is a pity that their engagements did not always coincide with his, for the German government had instructed their *chargé d'affaires* in Washington and their consul in Chicago to render a strict account of Liebknecht's every move and utterance to the Minister of Home Affairs, Puttkamer, for the information of Richthofen, the Police President in Berlin. At first it was thought sufficient to send reports published in the American press but it soon appeared that more painstaking work was required. The demands made upon them were heavier than self-respecting diplomatic and consular officials could meet. They therefore hired Pinkerton's – The Eye That Never Sleeps† – whose employee, one Buddeke, using the code-name Paul – men and women of various nationalities were on the agency's payroll – trailed Liebknecht from place to place, taking down two dozen of his speeches *verbatim*. His expense account, footed by the German embassy in Washington after Liebknecht's departure, amounted to $712.01.[9] The levity of that penny is rather endearing. What could he have spent it on?

Although, from 22 September onwards, Liebknecht was to be the object of these special attentions, there was no lack of publicity for the joint and separate meetings held by the visitors. They were widely advertised and reported at length in the States, while both *Commonweal* in England and the *Sozialdemokrat* – published in Zurich and illegally circulated in Germany – gave regular news of the tour.

Thus on 16 September, the speeches made by Eleanor and Aveling at Loomis' Temple of Music were given generous coverage by the New Haven *Workman's Advocate*.[11] To a mixed assembly Aveling spoke for an hour on Marxist theory. Eleanor, more flexible and quick to sense the feeling of a largely uninitiated and partly middle-class audience, drawn there by curiosity, dealt with some of the more commonly heard objections to socialism. The fear, she said, that with the abolition of all private property no one would be able to say "my coat", "my watch" and so forth, was unfounded. On the contrary, she explained, thousands who today possessed absolutely nothing would, under socialism, be able to say "*my*

---

* He left America on 26 November, though the authorities believed that he was to stay until 19 December.[9]

† This slogan, early adopted as the firm's trademark, is thought to be the origin of the term "Private Eye". Founded by a Scotsman, Allan Pinkerton, who was both an atheist and a fervent Chartist in his youth, the private detective agency was first set up in Chicago during the early 1850s. Its ever-increasing staff and reputation for efficiency led to commissions from police and government authorities in a number of European countries: it could almost be said to have been a forerunner of Interpol. Thus in 1882, at Gladstone's request, Allan Pinkerton was employed to track down two Fenians in America wanted by the British for murder. On his death in 1884 the founder was succeeded by his two sons, one with headquarters in New York, the other in Philadelphia. Their men became extremely effective as strikebreakers, spies and provocateurs whose function it was to act as intelligence agents for employers.[10]

coat", but no individual or body of individuals would be able to speak of "*my* factory" or "*my* land" and, above all, no man should say of his fellowmen "*my* hands". She ended by raising the difficult question of physical force and declared that no socialist wished to use it but, just as Americans had fought to abolish slavery, so, she believed, would socialists have to fight to abolish wage-slavery.

Three days later, on Sunday, 19 September, a mass meeting attended by 10,000 people was held at Cooper Union, followed by an official public reception in Brommer's Union Park to which a crowd of 25,000 flocked.*[12] The meeting was said to have been the largest ever known in New York. On the same day as this tremendous demonstration of welcome took place, *John Swinton's Paper*† gave a full account of the visitors, unfortunately introducing Aveling as a member of the "British Social Democratic Federation", causing *Justice* to accuse him of sailing under false colours and Aveling to retort that he had made no such claim.‡ Swinton also listed the places where both Liebknecht and Aveling could be heard in the forthcoming weeks.[15]

In the next issue of his paper Swinton devoted a leader to the reception given on 19 September under the heading "A Shame for New York". As Aveling was to report to *Commonweal* "the whole went off without the least disturbance although a large body of police were present and did their best to create disorder".[16] Swinton had a deal more to say of what he called this "disgrace" to his city. The police had been "obtrusive" and "insolent" while reserves from several precincts had been held in readiness

---

* It may be mentioned that the report in *Commonweal* of 9 October, by Aveling, from which the figure is taken, differed from that in the *Sozialdemokrat* of 22 September, by Liebknecht, which put the numbers present at 15,000.

† Chief editorial writer of the *New York Times* from 1860 to 1870, John Swinton resigned his position as managing editor of the *New York Sun* in October 1883, launching his own 4-page weekly: "to raise the social question, and to induce the working people to bring their interests into politics". The paper lasted until August 1887.[13]

‡ On 20 September Aveling wrote to *Justice*: "A letter signed by you, addressed John Swinton, has been handed to me. Wherever to my knowledge statement has been made that I am in any way connected with the Social-Democratic Federation, I have at once for my own sake, and yet more, for that of Socialism, done all in my power to contradict a statement, at once so false and so damaging to me. I have taken care not to give the enemy cause to blaspheme me, by saying why the statement is damaging to me, I have only said it was false.' From Boston he wrote again on 15 October: "My attention has been called to the fact that in your paper has appeared a statement to the effect that 'I am posing in this country as a member of the Social-Democratic Federation'. This statement is false and the person who wrote it knew it to be false. I now ask you to print in full my letter dated September 20th ... I had not intended that letter to be published, having no ambition to wash your dirty linen in public. But your double calumny compels its publication. As my letter ... may have been 'lost', I enclose a copy."[14]

for the trouble they had sought to provoke. The three guests had jointly written and sent a letter to the New York press, which Swinton quoted:

" 'We have just returned from a magnificent and orderly meeting in Brommer's Park – a meeting the police did their best to make disorderly. The addresses given in the gigantic hall were listened to in perfect order by an audience of many thousands. The speeches over, we passed out into the open air, followed, not unnaturally, by a considerable number of people anxious to speak with the orators, whom some of them knew personally. The police pushed the people and struck the people; *they pushed and struck two of us*. Nothing but the greatest forbearance on the part of the thousands present prevented an outbreak. We have never seen in Europe such wanton interference on the part of the police with the liberty of the subject* as we saw today in a country proverbially known as 'the land of the free'. What a misfortune," Swinton commented, "that three strangers ... should be forced to publish such a statement. We beg them to understand that at least some of the people of New York feel mortified..."[17]

On both the Monday and the Wednesday – 20 and 22 September – following the reception there were further large and enthusiastic meetings at Cooper Union. The second of these was devoted to the subject of trade unionism as a step towards socialism.

On 27 September May Morris, evidently referring to the 19 September meeting, wrote to Andreas Scheu: "Did you see in the papers Eleanor Aveling's fiery speech on the other side of the water? I was rather amused by it."[18]

The *New York Herald* was not amused. It gave a column to the huge inaugural gathering under the headings: "Socialistic Pleadings. Cooper Union Crowded. Spurred on by a Woman", making much of the fact that not only was seven-eighths of the audience German but that a large delegation of what it called "Socialistische Frauenbund" occupied the platform. Eleanor, introduced under the sub-heading "Carl Marx's Daughter Booms", was described as "a German looking lady with eye-glasses" – a forbidding portrait indeed – while in the report of the meeting of the 22nd stress was again laid on the "thousands of Germans present".[19]

Nevertheless, the *Herald* gave surprisingly full and, quite often, objective news of the visitors. Thus when, on 28 September, Liebknecht and Aveling were thrown out of the Manhattan Club where they were the guests of a respected member, the *Herald* wrote that "the majority of members of the club find great fault with the action of the House Committee", quoting an anonymous Congressman who called the

---

* Should that appear a dubious claim, allowance must be made for a touch of Old World chauvinism. However, the brutality of the American police cannot be questioned.

incident an outrage that must lead to an imminent change in the "entire directory of the Manhattan Club ... with the infusion of new and more liberal blood."[20]

Altogether eleven meetings were held in New York* before, on 2 October, Eleanor and Aveling left for New England, the cities of the Great Lakes and points north, west, south and so back to New York.

* * *

Before the travellers take to the road, it may be useful to sketch in rough outline the situation of the American working-class movement at this period, for 1886 was one of the most eventful and revolutionary years in its history.† It was a time when the number of industrial workers had grown very rapidly; when the powerful corporations, trusts and banks were in control of every major and most minor enterprises; when, America having entered the technological race at an advanced stage, the machine increasingly replaced the craftsman and, as Eleanor judged, the intensity of labour in certain trades was 50 per cent higher than that in England.[6]

The body sponsoring the visitors was the Socialist Labor Party of North America, founded in 1877. It was not, despite its name, a political party in the accepted sense of the word but rather a group of socialists, for the most part of European origin with wide experience of class struggles in their native countries. It owed a great deal to such men as Friedrich Adolph Sorge‡ and, though torn by various factions, the strongest being the Lassalleans, held to a firm if doctrinaire Marxism that encouraged rather than precluded activity in the trade unions to which the majority of

---

* So far as can be determined by comparing a number of reliable sources (including Pinkerton's), the programme seems to have been 14th Bridgeport, 16th New Haven, 17th Meridan, 19th, 20th and 22nd New York City, 23rd Brooklyn, 25th Jersey City, 26th Newark, 28th Philadelphia and 30th Elizabeth (Pa.). It is not certain whether Eleanor spoke on all occasions, but in their own book she and Aveling speak of "large audiences ... addressed in New York, its suburbs, and neighbouring towns to the number of some half-dozen."[21] While this clearly refers to their first, and not their return, visit to New York, it is possible that five of the gatherings were small.

† For a proper understanding of the subject Volume 2 of Professor Philip S. Foner's masterly 4-volume *History of the Labor Movement in the United States* is recommended, together with the *Preface* Engels wrote for the American edition of his *Condition of the Working Class in England in 1844*[22] after discussion with Eleanor and Aveling on their return from the States. These are the main sources for the facts given here, unless otherwise acknowledged.

‡ (1827–1906) A German who, for his part in the 1848 Revolution and under sentence of death, had fled to Switzerland, then to Belgium and later to England. From here, in 1852, at the age of 24, he emigrated to what he hoped was Australia but, having boarded the wrong ship, found himself in New York. A music teacher by profession, he became a leader of the American section of the First International, attended the Hague Congress in 1872 where he met Marx, maintaining a correspondence with him and an even closer one with Engels until their death.

its members belonged, exercising an influence out of all proportion to the size of the parent group.

It was largely dominated by and overwhelmingly composed of Germans (though it had its small English, Russian, Polish, Scandinavian and other national sections), hence the original invitation only to Liebknecht and Bebel. It published German-language papers and made little contact with or impact upon the millions of progressive American-born workers whose language, both in the literal and figurative sense, it did not speak and inflexibly refused to learn. As Pinkerton's men reported and the German officials passed on to Berlin: "The meetings where Liebknecht spoke were attended by ever larger numbers of men and women. Had Liebknecht's English been better, the influence of his speeches would have been even more extensive!"[23]

Thus the Avelings' tour was of especial importance, reaching people who had never before heard the case for scientific socialism put in their own tongue. They hoped thereby to speed the day when, as they wrote in their book, the Germans would "withdraw into the background, and whilst never relaxing in energy or ceasing to inspire from within ... let the forefront of the movement be American."[24]

The SLP's most valuable achievement was the founding in 1882 of the Central Labor Union of New York, primarily to organise foreign workers, though Americans, both black and white, were members and CLU centres were formed in other large cities in the east.

The vast influx of immigrants – five and a half million in the decade 1880–90 – arriving penniless and desperate for work, had been freely exploited to undercut wages and act as blacklegs. Peasants from Ireland, Italy, Scandinavia, Hungary and Bohemia; Germans menaced by the introduction of the Anti-Socialist Law in 1878 – and thus, by definition, the most politically conscious of these national groups – not to mention countless Russian and Polish Jews fleeing from Tsarist pogroms, were now organised by the CLU which, by 1886, had 207 affiliated unions representing over 150,000 members in New York.

An earlier organisation, the Noble Order of the Knights of Labor, originally a clandestine body formed in 1869, came out into the open in 1881 when its local assemblies, as they were called, began recruiting in vast numbers. In three years its membership – which included many of the SLP rank and file – had tripled: in 1884 it stood at 70,000 and could boast of 561 local and a dozen new district assemblies. The following year, as a result of a victorious strike by the workers of Jay Gould, the railway king, the Order grew even more rapidly while, in the single month of October 1886, for reasons which will become apparent, it rose from 110,000 to over 700,000 and was even said to have touched the million mark with its foreign affiliates by the end of that year. As Engels wrote to Laura: "The Knights of Labour, who are a real power, are sure to form the first embodiment of the movement".[25] However, Engels had no illusions about the Order: what he welcomed was that the Americans had started independently of the Germans – "or at least of their leadership" – since these were

> "anything but a fair and adequate sample of the workmen of Germany, but rather of the elements the movement at home has eliminated – Lassalleans, disappointed ambitions, sectarians of all sorts ... As a ferment, the Germans can and will act, and at the same time undergo, themselves, a good deal of useful and necessary fermentation."[25]

The leadership of the K of L held that education should precede if not substitute action, frowning upon strikes for wage increases and shorter hours. In this it was completely out of touch with its rank and file, but opposition to trade union militancy filtered down more easily from the top with the admission in 1878 of non-wage-earners such as shopkeepers, farmers, small businessmen and the like, originally disqualified, but now allowed to comprise up to a quarter of any assembly. With one foot on the lowest rung of the capitalist ladder they represented that "transition class", defined by Marx as long ago as 1852, "in which the interests of two classes are simultaneously mutually blunted".[26] This mistrust of trade union struggle was also shared by the many Lassalleans who were members of both the SLP and the K of L. Thus, while at the peak of its power when Eleanor and Aveling were in America, the Order was even then recognised by Engels as carrying the seeds of its own dissolution; though also of rebirth.

> "Their absurd organisation and very slippery leadership – used to the methods of corrupt American partisanship – will very soon provide a crisis within that body itself," he wrote to Laura, "and then a more adequate and more effective organisation can be developed from it."[25]

He compared this indigenous movement favourably with the German-bred socialism transplanted across the Atlantic.

> "I think the K. of L. a most important factor ... which ought not to be pooh-poohed from without but to be revolutionised from within," he wrote to Mrs Kelley Wischnewetzky* in New York, "and I consider that many of the Germans there have made a grievous mistake when they tried, in face of a mighty and glorious movement

---

* (1859–1932) An American by birth, married to a Polish doctor, both members of the SLP at this time, Mrs. Wischnewetzky was the translator of Engels' *Condition of the Working Class in England in 1844*. In February 1886 he added a new appendix to this American publication, much of which was later incorporated in his 1892 preface to the English edition and in January

not of their creation, to make of their imported and not always understood theory a kind of dogma as the sole means to salvation,[†] and to keep aloof from any movement which did not accept that dogma ... To expect the Americans will start with the full consciousness of the theory worked out in older industrial countries is to expect the impossible ..."[27]

While the K of L, in the same way as the "Model" Unions in Britain, discouraged open conflict with the employers and, by its rules, banned political discussion, another body, first founded in 1881, was now coming to the fore. The Federation of Organized Trades and Labour Unions, under the chairmanship of Samuel Gompers, spent its first three years in rather fruitless pursuit of legislative reforms. This made little appeal to the large national unions and, by 1884, the Federation had an affiliated membership of barely 50,000, was short of funds and appeared altogether ineffectual.

However, it was this body which, at its 1884 convention, passed a resolution – moved by the Brotherhood of Carpenters and Joiners of which Peter McGuire was the leader – that May 1st 1886 should be proclaimed a nationwide workers' strike to enforce the eight-hour working day. The next year's convention ratified the decision with the rider that those unions which did not intend to strike should do all in their power to help their brothers.

Against the advice of the leadership, the K of L assemblies overwhelmingly endorsed the proposal, while in Chicago, on the last Sunday in April 1886, 25,000 workers demonstrated to rally support for the strike.

"The newspapers and industrialists were increasingly declaring that May 1 was in reality the date for a Communist working-class insurrection modeled on the Paris Commune", and on 25 April the *New York Times* pronounced the Eight Hour movement as "un-American".[28]

When 1 May, a Saturday, came, some 350,000 workers from over 11,000 enterprises paraded the streets: 40,000 in Chicago, 11,000 in Detroit, 25,000 workers marching in a torchlight procession – headed by a contingent of bakers – through the centre of New York.

The upshot of this action was to win the eight-hour day for some 200,000 workers – including large numbers whose employers, to prevent them from joining the strike, had granted the concession in advance – while trade union membership and solidarity increased beyond all measure.

1887 he wrote a special preface for the American translation. After a divorce the lady resumed her maiden name and was known as Florence Kelley.

† *"alleinseligmachendes Dogma"* in the original letter, which is otherwise in English.

Thus encouraged, the CLU of New York called a conference of trade union and labour organisations in August which passed a resolution in favour of independent working-class political action. An elected committee, drawn from the K of L, the SLP and the Federation, made its recommendations and, on 19 August 1886, the Independent Labor Party of New York and Vicinity came into being, pledged to stand in the forthcoming mayoral election.

Its nominated candidate was Henry George. Of international repute as the author of *Progress and Poverty* published in 1879* George's fame had spread with his lecturing tours of Europe and the States. He was a celebrated figure, while his progressive views on Ireland and the Irish, no less than on the Negro question, had won him popularity among two of the most oppressed communities. His Single Tax Theory – land rents to be used for public rather than private purposes – was far from a prescription for socialism and totally ignored the production relations of industrial capitalism; nevertheless, the SLP did not oppose his candidature, rising above its sectarian principles in the interests of the new Labor Party. Indeed, the support for the electoral campaign was wonderfully united. Even Terence Powderly, the Grand Master Workman, as the leader of the K was called – albeit at the eleventh hour – and Samuel Gompers, the president of the Federation – both of whom had the strongest reservations on the whole question of a Labor Party – were drawn in, while thousands of foreign workers in New York suddenly became American citizens, entitled to vote, the new party having set up a naturalisation centre to this end. Campaigning clubs were formed both by trade unions, defying the K of L ban on political discussion, and by such separate groups as Negroes, Jews, Italians, Frenchmen, Germans and others.

This surge of activity was met by the employers with attempts at coercion, with slander, a bogus counter-organisation and threats of dismissal, but was not stemmed.

On 2 November, election day, Henry George polled 68,110 votes: a third of the total, beating the Republican, Theodore Roosevelt, by almost 8,000 and wresting from the Democratic victor an overall majority, for he got in with less than 42 per cent of the poll.

Eleanor and Aveling met Henry George before they left New York and devoted a few pages of their book to him, reaching the unhappy conclusion that he was "a ruined man".[30] Yet they were far from immune to

---

* Over half a century later it was acclaimed by Lord Snell (1865–1944), a Labour peer created 1931, who rose from the humblest origin to become a Privy Councillor, Companion of Honour and Deputy Leader of the House of Lords, as "one of the greatest political documents" of his generation.[29]

the excitements of the electoral campaign and the new movement that had given rise to it.

At about the same time as the New York Labor Party was founded in that August of 1886, the Chicago K of L assemblies launched a federation pledged to political action which, in September, took the name of the United Labor Party. With a forceful programme that owed nothing to Henry George's theories, it succeeded in electing to the Illinois state legislature one senator and six members of the lower house.

The New York campaign had electrified the movement: workers' parties sprang up throughout the country and in thirteen states independent labour candidates stood for Congress, while everywhere they ran for state, county and municipal office. Their greatest successes were in Chicago and Milwaukee. In all these electoral contests the K of L members played a leading part; it will now be understood why the Order grew so mightily at this period.

The whole working class was in ferment and even the Federation of Organized Trades and Labor passed a resolution in favour of independent political action. However, it was not only in this respect that the Federation underwent a fundamental change. It became an integral part of a new organisation, brought into being by the initiative of dissident K of L members in revolt against their conservative leadership. On 8 December 1886 the American Federation of Labor was founded at a convention held at Columbus, Ohio.

If there is no smoke without fire, there is certainly no such seething cauldron as that presented by the American workers in 1886 without burning wrongs to keep it on the boil.

It was to be expected that the success of May Day should provoke a swift reaction. The powerful employers, with the press, police and, of course, Pinkerton's at their command, were not going to take so insolent a challenge lying down. The workers might make an ephemeral show of strength, but that it was no more than a flash in the pan and of little avail must be promptly brought home to them, most particularly in Chicago where industry had more or less come to a standstill on 1 May. The opportunity was not slow to present itself. Some 1,400 members of the K of L were then on strike at the McCormick Harvester factory against a hated piecework system, for an increase in wages and the introduction of the eight-hour day, which had not been granted. On Monday evening, 3 May, the strikers were at the gates waiting for the 300 blacklegs who had been escorted into the works that morning by the police.* As they

---

* The Chicago police department, it should be said, had long been "used as if it were a private force in the service of the employers", most of its officers and many of its men drawing "pay from the corporations as well as from the city".[31]

emerged under the protection of Pinkerton's men the crowd surged forward, the armed detectives opened fire as it fled and seven men were killed.

The day after, 4 May, the anarchists hastily convened a meeting of protest against this slaughter, to be held in the Haymarket to which, from early evening, some 3,000 people, including women and children, flocked. This relatively small number did not justify the use of the wide square so the wagon that was to serve as the speakers' platform was drawn into "a narrow blind alley, running down by the side of a large warehouse".[32]

The Mayor of Chicago, Carter Harrison, a fervent anti-socialist, was present in the crowd and stayed until the main speaker, Albert Parsons, had gone home, when the Mayor, too, left to tell the police officials that it was quite a tame affair and that they should withdraw their men mobilised for the occasion. It was then about 10 o'clock, a slight drizzle fell and the audience started to disperse. The last speaker, Sam Fielden, was winding up when, in disregard of the Mayor's advice, an armed posse of 180 police appeared upon the scene and ordered the meeting to stop. Fielden shouted that it was a peaceable assembly. At that moment a bomb exploded, instantly killing one policeman – patrolman Mathias Degan – and mortally wounding six others while 50 more received injuries. There was conflicting evidence "as to whether the police did or did not fire before the bomb was thrown",[32] but at all events they fired, both into the crowd and at those vainly trying to escape from the *cul-de-sac*, whom they also chased and batoned, killing an unknown number of people and leaving some 200 wounded.

On 5 May a panic operation was mounted. Mass arrests were made without warrants – "some ... were kept in prison three or four months and were then released by the police without trial"[32] – suspects were beaten and tortured, their homes ransacked and 31 men indicted. Finally eight of them, of whom only Sam Fielden, on the platform at the time, and August Spies* had been present when the bomb was thrown and none of whom was ever directly or indirectly connected with it according to the evidence produced in court, were charged with the murder of Degan. The grand jury set the trial for 21 June.

This trial was amongst the most venal – and such trials are not few – ever to have disgraced a court of law. Not only were the time and place too nearly associated with the crime for any impartial judgment to be reached, but the jury was hand-picked for its political prejudice against the defendants. Many of the witnesses were suborned and, when the murder could not be pinned upon any individual in the dock, the judge, Joseph

---

* The editor of the anarchist German-language paper *Arbeiter Zeitung*.

Gary, unashamedly shifted his ground, ruling that certain anarchist literature might be produced in evidence regardless of the fact that, being in
German, at least two of the accused could never have read it. In his final
speech to the jury the State Prosecutor plainly stated: "Anarchy is on trial".

The predictable verdict of guilty was pronounced on 20 August: seven
of the men – Albert Parsons, August Spies, Samuel Fielden, Eugene
Schwab, Adolphe Fischer, Louis Lingg and George Engel – were sentenced to be hanged on 3 December. The eighth man, Oscar Neebe, "who
was proved never to have been present at the meeting was condemned to
15 years' penal servitude."[32] The first application for an appeal, made to
Judge Gary, was disallowed; the Supreme Court of the State of Illinois re-
heard the case in March 1887 and confirmed the verdicts on 20 September, when the date of execution was postponed until 11 November
1887, while an appeal for writ of error made to the Supreme Court of the
United States was refused.

In after years Judge Gary was to publish his view that whether the
suspect to whom all the evidence pointed – Rudolph Schnaubelt* – or
someone else had thrown the bomb was "not an important question."

That much had been clear from the start: the object of the indiscriminate manhunt and arrests, the outcry in the press, as of the initial
murders by Pinkerton's and the police, at the McCormick factory and the
Haymarket, had been to terrorise and crush the labour movement.

That the rigged trial and savage sentences would create a stir on an
international scale was not, perhaps, foreseen; but when the Avelings
arrived in the autumn the agitation on behalf of the victims was at its
height. Mass meetings were called by the CLU, the Federation and the
assemblies of the K of L, while leading American citizens from many
walks of life petitioned for a review of the case and the commuting of the
death sentences. This clamour for a re-trial, combined with the unexpected success of the New York Labor Party in the mayoral elections, had
led the authorities to announce a stay of execution on 25 November
(Thanksgiving Day), giving rise to hopes not only that the superior court
would rescind the verdicts but of even greater support for the condemned
men, for ever wider sections of the public now believed them to have been
victims rather than enemies of the State. That this should be so was owed
more to the dishonesty of those appointed to administer justice than to
sympathy with the anarchist movement in America, of which something
should be said.

In 1878 a group of members dissatisfied with the principles and
methods of the New York SLP left it to form what they called a Social

---

* An *agent provocateur*, twice arrested and released by the police before he was smuggled across
the Mexican border never to be heard of again.

Revolutionary Club. Similar clubs sprang up in other cities where there were large numbers of immigrants clinging to the lessons of conspiracy and terrorism imbibed in their countries of origin, although Albert Parsons, the leading figure in the Chicago club – among the most thriving – was a native American. In 1881 a Revolutionary Socialist Party loosely united these clubs, the main plank of whose platform was armed insurrection to overthrow capitalism. A year later – 1882 – Johann Most* arrived in America. With his wide experience, his undoubted ability and his claim to have worked with Marx and Engels, he gave unifying leadership and a strong fillip to the anarchist movement in the States. It was he who formed the International Working People's Association – based on Bakuninist principles – with Parsons and Spies as his ablest lieutenants. They, however, unlike Most himself and their anarchist brethren in the eastern states, were confirmed trade unionists: a form of anarcho-syndicalism which came to be known as the "Chicago Idea".

Many SLP members had been won over to this new anarchist organisation thanks to its influence in the unions, its vigorous leadership of strikes and also – even though it considered it a compromise with the capitalist right to buy labour power – of the campaign for the eight-hour day. Indeed, Parsons was the secretary of the Chicago Eight Hours League.

From the outset, at the great inaugural meeting of 19 September in New York, when Eleanor urged her listeners to "throw three bombs amongst the masses: agitation, education, organisation", she defined with the utmost force and clarity the fundamental difference between anarchism and socialism, stressing that, in highly developed countries, the one could only impede the advance towards the other. At the same time, she pleaded ardently for the retrial of the Chicago Eight, condemned by a corrupt and cynical judicature, neither for deeds of which they were innocent nor for the shade of their political opinions, but simply and solely because they were workers opposed to the social system. It may be said that the anarchists' hostility to the Marxist visitors from Europe was such that, while some of the Chicago papers proposed that they should be hanged on arrival in that city, Most's *Freiheit* was for shooting them on sight before they ever landed in America.

---

* (1846–1906) A former member of the German party, a deputy to the Reichstag and one time editor of the *Berliner Freie Presse*, Most had written a popular summary of *Capital* for the second edition of which he sought the collaboration of Marx and Engels. They found that, without re-writing the book completely, there was little they could do but remove the worst howlers, Marx allowing his revisions to be used only upon the express condition that his name should never be associated with the work. Expelled from Germany after the enactment of the Anti-Socialist Law in 1878, Most emigrated to London where in the following year he brought out a journal of strong anarchist leanings, *Die Freiheit*. After the first number, Marx and Engels neither read the paper nor kept up relations with its editor.[33]

Although not entirely a matter of chance – for the invitation had gone out in May – it so happened that Eleanor and Aveling were in the United States during one of the most stirring and formative periods in the history of its labour movement. As Engels put it:

> "In European countries, it took the working class years and years before they fully realized the fact that they formed a distinct and, under existing conditions, a permanent class of modern society; and it took years again until this class-consciousness led them to form themselves into a distinct political party, independent of, and opposed to, all the old political parties formed by the various sections of the ruling classes. On the more favoured soil of America, where no mediaeval ruins bar the way, where history begins with the elements of modern bourgeois society as evolved in the seventeenth century, the working class passed through these two stages of development within ten months."[34]

During three of those ten months, Eleanor was an eye-witness to that development.

Suddenly, in New York, an almost legendary figure from Eleanor's childhood materialised. Among those most eager to welcome the European socialists and ensure the success of their tour was Serge Shevich,* one of the leaders of the SLP and the editor of its official German-language organ, the *New-Yorker Volkszeitung*. It was natural that he should entertain the new arrivals socially and that they should meet his wife, who turned out to be none other than Helene von Dönniges, the cause of the duel that had cost Lassalle his life in 1864.† Now, 22 years and three marriages later, here was this romantic personage in the flesh.

One would dearly like to know Eleanor's reactions to this character whose interests and temperament were the very antithesis to her own. But, beyond a passing reference to her as "an actress of considerable power" and the heroine not only of the Lassalle affair but also of George Meredith's *Tragic Comedians* (1880), where she appears thinly disguised as Clotilde von Rüdigen, there is, with every good reason, no mention of her in the Avelings' book.[35]

Helene von Dönniges (1843–1911), of mixed Jewish and Baltic-Prussian parentage, was a prodigiously vain and silly though not stupid woman of extravagant beauty who, from the most tender age, was always in love with somebody or other but with none so constantly as herself. Her autobiography, written shortly before her suicide at the age of 68[36], makes clear that, lost in self-admiration, she never had the smallest understanding of politics. She took herself very seriously indeed, as becomes a *femme fatale*, so that what she has to say provides a great deal of the humour she so conspicuously lacked.

On entering upon a stage career, and temporarily marrying someone else, she assumed the name of her first young short-lived husband, Lassalle's killer, Racowitza, and used it for her large variety of less professional activities to the end of her days. On first going to America in 1877 with Shevich, whom she married three years later in New Jersey, she continued to act for a while, gaining, in her own estimation, nation-wide

---

* This and other Russian names are throughout transliterated according to modern English usage. When they appear in contemporary letters or newspapers cited in the text the original 19th century Teutonic form is, of course, retained.
† On which occasion, it may be recalled, the hero's inconstancy in love had elicited a kindly word from the nine-year-old Tussy. (See above, p. 28.)

fame and popularity which she sacrificed for her husband's sake to exercise her gifts, by turns, as an inspired amateur novelist, art and drama critic, theosophist, painter, tailoress and doctor. It is reassuring to know that she neither qualified nor practised professionally in this last capacity and that her tailoring was strictly for home consumption.

Serge Shevich was a self-exiled Russian government official whose property and fortune the Tsar, Alexander II, sequestrated when he left the service without permission and the country without a passport. During his first year in the States he engaged in desultory journalism, working for the New York *World* and contributing to the *Sun* and the *Herald* as an expert on Russian affairs during the Russo-Turkish war (1877–8). This offered no future, because the war ended, but in March 1878 the *New-Yorker Volkszeitung* was launched and he became its editor until, in October 1886, during the Henry George mayoral campaign, he resigned to run an electioneering journal, *The Leader*, which was carried on as a workers' daily paper until November 1887. A brilliant linguist, an eloquent speaker and journalist, he devoted his talents to the socialist cause for twelve years. Then, strangely enough, the reigning Tsar, Alexander III, restored to him his fortune, now vastly augmented by the death of his mother, on condition that he returned to Russia. Thus, in 1890, to regain his material possessions, he and his wife went to Riga, where formerly Shevich's brother had long resided as Governor of Livonia (now Latvia). A year later, however, they joined that enormously wealthy band of expatriate Russians who added colour to cosmopolitan life in western Europe during the late 19th and early 20th centuries. Bebel, whom Shevich called upon in Berlin in 1891, said he "did not make a very sympathetic impression".[37] As Engels summed it up: "A stormy youth and a blasé old age".[38]

This metamorphosis was yet to come: when Eleanor knew the Sheviches they were at the heart and centre of the German SLP colony in New York and he, certainly, one of its most prominent and respected members; though it must be admitted that Engels, who never met him, had earlier been of the opinion that he knew "damned little" and commented ironically: "Dignity becomes him well."*[39]

It is possible that Eleanor, writing home, may have made some revealing comments on the Racowitza, for this encounter must have aroused her lively interest; but these letters – "voluminous" and "worth

---

* These remarks were made in reference to the misuse by the *Volkszeitung* of Engels' telegram to Sorge announcing Marx's death. The paper not only claimed that this had been sent to the editor but published the false information that Marx had died in France. Engels demanded a full public retraction on both counts. Shevich wrote what he called a "dignified" reply, accusing Engels of pettiness, to which he received no answer.

their weight in gold"[40] intended to serve as the basis for her reports and a record of the American tour – albeit Engels kept them safely, have not come down to us.*

"Our travellers appear to be getting on swimmingly," commented Laura on sending back one of the letters Engels had received from New York.[42] To Bebel he wrote on 8 October that the treatment of Liebknecht and the Avelings by the American press had been fairly, indeed, unexpectedly decent. On 23 October Engels passed on two more letters to Laura "from our transatlantic travellers", bidding her to

"keep the lot for me ... They were yesterday in Providence (Rhode Island)† and are now on the road from New England to the Great Lakes, stopping half way tomorrow at Albany and Troy (New York State) on the Hudson. The press in the New England manufacturing districts has been almost cordial in its reception of them," he wrote, "thus showing not only its own dependence upon the working people, but also an evident sympathetic feeling towards socialism on the part of the latter. I am very glad of this and also of the favourable effect they have made on the bourgeois press generally, more particularly on account of their impending arrival in Chicago where the bourgeois, six weeks ago, seemed inclined to get up police rows on their arrival ..."[43]

Chicago, indeed, was the high point of the tour. The Avelings arrived there on Friday, 5 November, and stayed for five days. Their advent

"was naturally looked forward to with more interest, perhaps almost anxiety, than that of any other town in the States. In the first place the town is in a very ferment of excitement; it has for months been more or less in a state of siege: nowhere perhaps at the present time does party feeling on all sides run as high as here,"

wrote the New York *Workman's Advocate*. Moreover, Chicago was recognised as "the stronghold of the anarchists".[44]

The anarchists were, of course, in the forefront of everyone's mind and, speaking at the Young Men's Hall in Detroit the day before leaving for Chicago, Eleanor was reported as emphasising that the working class must never use force: it had no need to. "Perhaps," she went on, "when the political power is in the hands of working men, capitalists may rebel and fight for their ill-gotten gains, but the rebellion must come from them."[45]

Well in advance of the visit the Chicago press, as Engels had noted,

---

* In his book *The Housing Question* Engels quotes from one of Eleanor's letters, written on 28 November from Indianopolis, in which she describes living conditions and rents near Kansas City.[41]

† At the Providence meeting, held on 22 October at Music Hall on Westminster Street where some 1,000 people attended, the speakers were introduced to, among others, James Jefferson, a coloured barber well known as an "advocate of social reform and equality".[42a]

vigorously warned the public against "Dr. Aveling and his vitriolic spouse" who were coming

> "for the purpose of inciting if they can resistance to the execution of the sentence passed upon their co-religionists" – the anarchists – "who now languish in Cork County jail. In order to accomplish this end they will ... seek to inflame the passions of the vicious and the turbulent elements of the community,"

predicted the Chicago *Times*, warning "these incendiaries" that this would prove

> "a dangerous business ... The public sentiment of this community is in no mood to trifle with firebrands of the Aveling-Liebknecht variety."[46]

The Chicago *Tribune* published an equally threatening forecast: if the visitors dared to enter the city, the police would prevent their meetings or, should a meeting be held, they would run the risk of sharing the same fate as the men now held in prison under sentence of death. "If we had not intended to come to Chicago," said Aveling to the third and largest of their Chicago audiences, "those two articles would have made us come."[47]

In the event, the first meeting, held on the day of their arrival, attracted 3,500 people – a figure conceded by the hostile press – and was an unqualified success,

> "the only paper that misrepresented Liebknecht and the Avelings ... in that peculiarly refined and delicate fashion affected by Herr Most and his followers, was the Chicago *Arbeiter Zeitung*."[48]

Two days later the pair were invited by the Liberal League to a Sunday evening *conversazione* where professional people and prominent citizens were able to ask questions after a brief talk by Aveling. An animated discussion followed, at the end of which a resolution was moved:

> "That those present believe the theory of surplus value to be true, and are of opinion that the wage system should be abolished."

So many voices were raised to second this that "it was impossible to say who the seconder really was", and the motion was passed without a dissentient vote, though with some few abstentions.[48]

While sections of the bourgeois – and the anarchist – press continued to fulminate, the Avelings were accorded so many interviews, "profiles", leaders and general publicity that at the next night's meeting on 8 November large numbers had to be turned away from the doors of the Aurora Turner Hall. Even then too many had been admitted: the gallery sagged and threatened to collapse under the weight of "people standing on the forms, between the forms and almost upon each other", while in the body of the hall the crowd was unable to applaud in unison because, as they said:

"We were packed so closely that some of us could not move our arms unless those standing by put theirs down to give us a turn."[48]

Aveling spoke for an hour; but before he entered upon the subject of Marxism he dealt with the trial of the Chicago Eight and their treatment – as of himself and Eleanor – by the press.

"Your newspapers," he said, "have not only called us names, they have misrepresented us. From the outset they have attributed to us views that we have never held ... Now these same newspapers ... have further been doing everything they possibly can to get public opinion so biased against the men that are now in jail ... I am a journalist myself, and I tell you frankly that in all my experience I have never seen anything so wicked, anything so disgraceful as the conduct of your Chicago papers in respect to that trial, and in their attempts to vitiate public opinion since. I tell you that I do not hold the same views as the anarchists, but I should be less than a man if I did not in this huge meeting make it my first business to say that if those men are hanged it is the Chicago *Times* and *Tribune* that will have hanged them."

He went on to say that the *News* informed him that he knew nothing whatever about the case, that he had read only short accounts of it but, on the contrary, he had read

"every line of a verbatim report of everything that occurred at that trial ... not the garbled reports that your newspapers in the English language publish, nor those reports that suppressed everything that told for the defendants, and that printed everything that told against them; but ... a verbatim and literal report, and, therefore, I claim to have some right to speak on the matter of that trial."

He then proceeded to examine, item by item, the perjured evidence and prejudiced conduct of the trial, ending on the note:

"I hold that for the credit of America, for the honor of the American name, for justice's sake, a new trial should be granted ... You have a reputation abroad for courage and for justice. That reputation is smirched by the events of these last few months and by the conduct of your press in this town..."[47]

This was, indeed, spoken like a man and to Aveling's lasting credit, for the reporters were present in force at this meeting. He then gave his formal lecture in which, having learnt fast in the previous few weeks, he drove home many of his theoretical points with examples drawn from American history and experience.

Then Eleanor took the platform.

"If I were speaking anywhere else or at any other time than the present," she said, "I should go straight to my subject, which is to make clear to you what we mean by socialism, but in this town, and at this time, I should feel myself a coward, I should feel I was neglecting a manifest duty, if I did not refer to a matter which I am sure is present in the minds and hearts of all here tonight; which is present in the minds and hearts of all honest men and women. I mean, of course, to the anarchist trial – it is called a trial – and the condemnation to death of seven men. Now I do not hesitate to say most emphatically and explicitly that if that sentence is carried out, it will be one of the most infamous legal murders that has ever been perpetrated. The execution of these men would be neither more nor less than murder. I am no anarchist, but I feel all the more that I am bound to say this. Nor do I make such a statement on socialistic or anarchistic authority alone. Why only this morning, in the Chicago *Tribune*, you will find the statement that 'they hang anarchists in Chicago'. That is they are going to hang these men, not as murderers, but as anarchists. That is the very confession we wanted. Not we, but our opponents, say this – that seven men are to be done to death not for what they have done, but for what they have said and believe. That the cowardly and infamous sentence will *not* be carried out. The votes cast by the working class will put a stop to that, at least so I believe. Should these men be murdered, we may say of the executioners, what my father said of those who massacred the people of Paris 'They are already nailed to that eternal pillory from which all the prayers of their priests will not avail to redeem them'.

"And now I pass to the subject of which I am to speak tonight. That is socialism, and you have, I hope, found by this time that it is not exactly what our enemies and their employers of the press represent it to be. One of the first things you are invariably told is that we socialists want to abolish private property; that we do not admit the 'sacred rights of property'. On the contrary, the capitalistic class today is confiscating your private property, and it is because we believe in your 'sacred right' to your own that we want you to possess what to-day is taken from you. We have seen from Dr. Aveling's speech how all wealth, all we to-day call capital is produced by your labor, how out of the unpaid labor of the people a small class grows rich, and how we want to put an end to this by abolishing all private property in land, machinery, factories, mines, railways, etc.; in a word, in all means of production and distribution. But this is not abolishing private property; it means giving property to the thousands and millions who to-day have none. The capitalists have abolished the 'private property' of the working classes, and we intend that this shall be returned to them, and all men will only then have a right to 'private property', when all men belong to one class – that of producers. And that all men may have 'private' property, no man or body of men must be allowed to own and control what is the property of the whole community. Understand then for the future who it is really that attacks the 'sacred right' of property.

"Then you are told socialists want no law, no order. Truly we don't want what is called order to-day, for the 'order' of to-day is disorder. Anarchy prevails everywhere. You find men who are millionaires and men who starve; women who possess thousand upon thousand and women who have to choose between starvation and prostitution. We do not call that order. We do not think it is 'order' that men should labor 10, 12, 14, aye, and more hours a day, who at the end of their life have nothing before them but the poorhouse. We do not think it is 'order' that women should become prostitutes. We do not think it order when on the one hand you have your factories and warehouses overcrowded, when there is 'over-production', and when thousands upon thousands want those very articles that are rotting in stores. That is all disorder, and we want to do away with it and put true order in its place. Then as to law. We want law; but law that is justice, and is just to all men and women. And those who cry out that we are lawless, do they even respect their own laws? No, they break them, even these bad laws. Laws made by a class in the interest of a class, are broken by the men who make them. Thus there is, I believe, a law which prohibits 'cornering' as a fraudulent practice. Mr. Phillip Armour made his millions by 'cornering' pork. Was he prosecuted for this unlawful and fraudulent practice? Not a bit, and with these very millions made despite the law he to-day employs Pinkertons to shoot down inoffensive citizens.

"Sometimes too, we are asked whether we socialists do not want to 'level down' and make all men equal. How can we make all men equal? But if to give all men and women a chance of developing, of bringing out what is best in them is to 'lower' them, we must plead guilty. But we want to 'call up' and are far from wishing to reduce all men to the condition of the proletariat. To-day we want to do away with this proletariat class, and in doing away with it, and with the idle classes, we do away with all class distinctions, and while we say, all men and women shall perform their share of the necessary labor of the world, we also say that they shall enjoy a fair share of leisure and pleasure. And note that we speak of necessary work – i.e. work useful to the community. Only this afternoon I was asked by a gentleman what socialists would do in the following case: Supposing an architect drew the plan for a house. He would not lay a hand to the work of building it; that would be done by the bricklayers, the carpenters, etc. Yet the architect's work was wanted before the other work could be done, and how would you manage. Would you give him nothing because he did not do manual work? I told that gentleman that in as much as the architect's plans were wanted, their value was unquestionable; that the manual workers could not build without them. But, on the other hand, of what good would his plans be without these workers? Of none. And so the position of architect and bricklayer were equal; one required the other, and so long as each did necessary work each was entitled to the same recognition as an honest laborer; but that the one was no better than the other. Socialists recognize all labor that is needful – as labor is not and cannot be recognized to-day; but mere activity is not labor and is not considered such by us.

"There is one other point I am bound to touch on because it has been put to us many times since we have been here. We are told that 'socialists want to have women in common'. Such an idea is possible only in a state of society that looks upon woman as a commodity. To-day, woman, alas, is only that. She has only too often to sell her womanhood for bread. But to the socialist a woman is a human being, and can no more be 'held' in common than a socialistic society could recognize slavery. And these virtuous men who speak of our wanting to hold women in common, who are they? The very men who debauch your wives and sisters and daughters. Have you ever reflected, you workingmen, that the very wealth you create is used to debauch your own sisters and daughters, even your little children? That is to me the most terrible of all the miseries of our modern society: that poor men should create the very wealth that is used by the man of 'family and order' to ruin the women of your class. We socialists, then, want common property in all means of production and distribution, and as woman is not a machine, but a human being, she will have her profits and her duties like men, but cannot be held by anyone as a piece of property.

"Such, then, is our position.

"We believe in individual responsibility, but believe this can only be asked for and found when all men have collective rights and duties.

"Finally, I have been told that you in America enjoy such freedom that socialism is not needed. Well, all you seem to enjoy is being shot by Pinkertons. I speak not only of what I have seen, but of what I have read in your own labor statistics. I say you, the working-classes of America, have no more freedom than with us. Men who toil from morn to night are not free, women who slave in factories, and then have their household work to do are not free. Above all what freedom can there be for the little children who are forced into mills when they should be at school and at play? You are not free and you have your 'social question' here as elsewhere.

"And now what is to be done? You have to get a strong labor organization. The votes of New York, Chicago and other towns show you how much you can do. But you must hold together as a party, different from, opposed to all others, one with a distinct platform, and pledged only to the cause of labor. And if any of you should feel tempted to work with the Republicans just read a Democratic newspaper, and you'll see that the Republicans are all robbers. If you feel tempted to work with the Democrats, read a Republican paper, and you'll see the Democrats are all thieves. Well, just for once in a way believe both Democrats and Republicans. And, as you believe them, come and work for the one party that is that of neither the thieves nor the robbers, but of honest men and women. Hold together and your victory is assured. That victory has begun. It began with the 68,000 votes for George, and the 25,000 votes given here, and the thousands of votes all over America. And don't forget that to those 68,000 and 25,000 votes, you've got to add 68,000 and 25,000 votes more for the women who couldn't vote. But if the women can't vote they can help all the same, and they do help. And when you men and women have once understood what your rights are, and have once determined to have them, who shall gainsay you? What can the few thousands of the exploiting class do against the millions of the workers, when once these *will* to be free? The battle has begun, and victory has begun too. Help us then in this cause, men and women, work with us, and success must be ours. It must be ours even though we fall here and there by the way, for

> *'Freedom's battle once begun*
> *Bequeath'd from bleeding Sire to Son,*
> *Though baffled oft, is ever won!'* "[*47]

Before they left Chicago on 9 November – though they were to return for another few days after speaking at Bloomington, Sandusky and La Salle – the Avelings were invited to an informal meeting of churchmen (including a bishop), lawyers, writers, doctors of both sexes and ladies of the Chicago *beau monde*. The guests appear to have told this distinguished gathering that their culture was not much to boast of and, in the course of what must have been a slightly embarrassing social event, took the opportunity to explain that women as a means of production in none but the strictly defined function of child-bearing and as a commodity in no sense whatsoever, would follow upon the victory of socialism.

The Chicago visit was undoubtedly the Avelings' greatest triumph, and it is pleasant to record that Eleanor was never quite forgotten in Chicago. During the 1930s one of the clubs affiliated to the Scandinavian Workers

---

* The quotation is from Byron's *The Giaour*.

League – the Scandinavian federation of the Communist Party of the USA – was named the "Eleanor Marx Kvinno-klubb" (women's club).[49]

The tour proceeded as far west as Kansas City, where two days were spent and then, following a detour to the south, the return journey was begun, Eleanor speaking at Davenport and Aveling at Moline on the same night. They reached St. Louis (Illinois), where Eleanor made her speech in German, on the day that Liebknecht, back in the east, was being fêted at meetings in Manhattan and Brooklyn before taking his leave and embarking in the steamship *Aurania* on 27 November, at which time his fellow propagandists had arrived in Indianopolis.

From Pittsburgh, Aveling wrote an article for the *New-Yorker Volkszeitung* published on 12 December, describing, among other things, their stay in Springfield, Ohio, on Tuesday, 7 December, unaware that on the following day, a meeting at Columbus, some 80 miles away in the same state – next door, as it were, in that vast country – the American Federation of Labor was founded. It was a momentous event but, though one of its main architects, Peter McGuire, is referred to by the Avelings as their friend[50] this formidable new structure in the building of the American labour movement is accorded barely a mention in their book;* while neither McGuire, its secretary, nor Gompers, its president, is included in the chapter on "Some Working Class Leaders".

Back in New York on Sunday, 9 December, the pair had still a heavy programme to fulfil. A literary and musical evening, at which they were to speak, was arranged by the American Section of the SLP at the Socialist Free Library for the Monday evening; at the invitation of the Connecticut Valley Economic Association, Aveling spoke on the 22nd in a debate in Springfield (Mass.) where his lecture was described by the *Workmen's Advocate* as "a clincher";[52] and, on the 23rd, there was a further and final SLP meeting at the Florence Building in New York.

This was in the nature of a farewell occasion. Eleanor and Aveling gave a general account of their tour, describing their reception as "enthusiastic and cordial" in all the towns they had visited. They had not, said Aveling, come across a genuine anarchist movement as such, but rather small groups of people here and there who were under the impression that anarchism was more revolutionary than socialism. Were that the case he, as a revolutionary, would also belong to the anarchists. However, their journals – *Freiheit, Der Arme Teufel* and the *Arbeiter Zeitung* – had ceaselessly abused them. He then came to the cardinal and most unwelcome point of his speech: on the basis of what he had seen and experienced

---

* None whatsoever in the first (1887) edition and referred to but briefly in an appendix to the chapter on the anarchists in the second (1891) enlarged edition.[51]

it was his considered opinion that if the socialist movement remained in essence German it would fail.

"If I were a worker settled here," he said, "I would join the Knights of Labor and the Central Labor Union to spread my socialist doctrines in those circles ... If the socialists do not decide to take part in the great general movement, it would be better for them to leave the scene."[53]

Eleanor's speech was less controversial. She stressed that the anarchists were doing exactly what their opponents wanted: the Haymarket bomb, whether or not thrown by the police, had been of the greatest service to them and to all the enemies of the workers. "Any tactic which is of use to the enemy is to be condemned," she said. She went on to speak of American wages and the particular case of working women who, in her view, suffered worse conditions than in England. There was a need for a women's organisation, not as a separate body but as part of the great social movement. Women should attend meetings as men did, and bring their children too; in this the men had a duty to give them a helping hand.

After she had spoken to great applause, the chairman, Hugo Vogt, called for questions. Several were put, Shevich pressing Aveling to say whether he had meant that in America the workers were less intelligent than in England, which Aveling hotly denied. The main discussion, however, centred, not surprisingly, on the role of the German socialists. The questioners were not at all happy about Aveling's remarks, for were not the Germans precisely those who opposed the reactionary Knights of Labor he was recommending them to join. Although he answered each in turn, hammering home the necessity for socialists to be in the ranks of the mass organisations, to win their members, or sections of them, for socialism, he dealt with this vexed question much more fully in an article which appeared after he had left.[53]

On the same day Aveling met members of the National Executive of the SLP to regulate his accounts with them before departing. He and Eleanor then wrote their article – signed by Aveling alone – which appeared in the same issue of the *Wochenblatt* of the *New-Yorker Volkszeitung* as the full report of their final meeting.

It gave a complete account of their tour, the places visited, and their general impressions in the east and west, the north and south.

"I must remark," he said at the start, "that I shall deal only with general principles and questions relating to the Party. I have, of course, nothing to do with differences of opinion which may exist between sections or individual party members."

They had found everywhere that:

"the movement has already penetrated deeply into English speaking people; unconscious socialism is widespread. Again and again people came to our meetings and said: 'Yes, if that is socialism, we are socialists too.' One of the greatest benefits of our journey was that this unconscious undefined socialism was turned into conscious socialism for hundreds, nay, for thousands."[53]

The article then turned to the position of the Germans, and quoted from the *Communist Manifesto*:

"They [the socialists] fight for the attainment of the immediate aims, for the enforcement of the momentary interests of the working class; but in the movement of the present, they also represent and take care of the future of that movement ... In short, the Communists everywhere support every revolutionary movement against the existing social and political order of things."

Engels had sent a letter received but two days before in which he had said:

"You see, the best theory is not worth anything when it is transformed into a 'credo' to be learnt by rote and repeated. And this is generally the case with our theory. The tactic which follows from our theory is very simple ... to join every national working class movement and carry it forward. We have always taken the workers as we found them and tried to advance them ... The same must be done in America ... Without doubt, the Germans believe that the present movement is their work alone. This, however, is not the case, or it would have issued from their own platform, which it did not do. On the contrary, it arose from the healthy, instinctive ingenuity ... of the uneducated masses, who realised their miserable condition and saw that they were the 'mass', and therefore the power. Here is material of rare malleability, found in circumstances which favour its moulding to a degree never before witnessed: a society with an unprecedented rate of development, a society modern through and through, without any feudal traditions or appendages ... and, in its midst, a community of German workers with relatively the most advanced ideas..."

The Avelings' article went on to deal with the new workers' party founded as a result of the Henry George campaign which socialists had been perfectly right to support though, as every socialist knew, this party would have to pass through many a test before its principles were clearly defined, as at present they were not. Here again, whatever mistakes it made – in particular by putting the agrarian question in the forefront – it was the task of socialists to do their propaganda inside that party and lead it to an understanding that capital rests upon unpaid wages and therefore the whole system must be fought.

Then, turning to the matter which had ruffled the feelings of those who had heard Aveling's speech the article went on:

"The same thing" (as with the Workers' Party) "can be said of the relations of the socialists to the other working class organisations of America. The socialists should join these organisations, particularly the Knights of Labor. Many socialists I met here learnt their first lessons in socialism from the Knights of Labor, and these can only make progress in the socialist school when the socialists are in touch with them and open their eyes. I believe that very soon a split will occur in the organisation of the Knights of Labor. Those of them who want to remain 'conservative' will lean towards the reactionary mass, while the progressives among them will declare themselves openly as socialist. This is quite inevitable and therefore we must be prepared for it."

The attitude of the press was referred to and the hostile papers pilloried – among them the *Holyoke Transcript*, the *Wilmington News* and in particular the Chicago *Tribune* and its "chief liar", Joe Medill –

"a model of stupidity, vicious mendacity, brutality, sordid mentality and inability to speak the truth", who "towered above all his accomplices" –

but on the whole the reporters had treated them with fairness.

The article concluded with an appeal to the generosity of spirit and the devotion to principle that had inspired the author of the *Rights of Man*; the former tenacity and energy of a great people would re-emerge,

"but yet again, and for the last time: the hopes of the movement rest on the working class, here and everywhere".

This article – and the speeches made at the final meeting – showed that Eleanor and Aveling felt that they had learnt more than they had taught in those few months. They had arrived in America but three weeks after sentence had been passed on the Chicago Eight – those human sacrifices to that first of all May Days, itself the culmination of a long struggle for the human right to leisure – they had witnessed the formation of independent workers' parties in one city after another and their triumphal entry into the political arena; they were, even if oblivious to it, in the country when the A.F. of L. was born: in short they were present during one of the most vital periods of growth in the American working-class movement. Small wonder that they should have drawn not only large and unusually receptive audiences but that, in conversation and debate with their listeners, they themselves drew new and inspiring lessons to take back when, on the morning of Christmas Day, they embarked for England.

While Eleanor and Aveling were on the high seas an ugly storm was brewing. It broke with full force on 30 December. Primed with inside information from a member of the National Executive of the SLP, the *New York Herald* printed a banner headline: "Aveling's Unpaid Labor", with sub-headings: "The Socialists are Disgusted and Say so about his Exorbitant Bill. Cigarettes and Corsage Bouquets. Some of the Items which he calls 'Legitimate Expenses'." This defamatory article, discreditable both to the Avelings and to the American SLP Executive, was but the opening gambit in a sorry game:

"The socialists will nevermore import a professional agitator from the effete monarchies of Europe.

The recent experiment with Dr. Edward Aveling and Mrs. Eleanor Marx Aveling has had a most disastrous effect upon the exchequer of the National Executive Board, and a scene in which the much lauded elements of fraternity and equality were sadly missing occurred just prior to the departure of the 'distinguished foreigners' on Christmas morn. The upshot of that scene is now agitating different sections of the socialistic labor party, but strenuous efforts are made among more prudent members of the tribe to avoid publicity of the scandal as they claim it would hurt the 'cause'.

Aveling's Idea of 'Unpaid Labor'

'Unpaid labor is the greatest curse of modern civilization – that's the whole problem in a nutshell', proclaimed Dr. Aveling, as the axiom of his system of politico-economy, on all the platforms through his lecturing tour. With that phrase as a keynote he could grind out any number of melodies or, as he called them, 'discourses' on scientific socialism. The unwary socialistic audiences applauded the revamping of the doctrines of Karl Marx. With the enthusiasm of a proselyte they never paused to inquire for details on the 'unpaid labor' chestnut until the doctor and his fair spouse got to the end of their tether.

Then they did get specifications, and more of it than agreed with their constitution as well as that of their treasury. The scientific Dr. Aveling demonstrated his eminent ability to raise a bill, and remarked, dryly, when the socialists denounced it as exorbitant, 'Well, it's English, quite English, you know!' The Executive Committee honored his drafts, amounting to $1,300 for thirteen weeks' work, without demurring, though the price was considered rather stiff for a socialist who professed to have only the welfare of the poor and disinherited at heart.

But the patience of the Board, with Herr Herman Walter* as spokesman, broke

---

* Though spelt thus by the *Herald* throughout, the name was in fact Walther.

down when the couple returned last week to the city from their Western tour and presented a supplementary bill of $600.

Corsage Bouquets and Theatre Tickets

'Do you consider these items legitimate expenses?' queried Herr Walter, in a rage, as he pointed to a charge of $25 for corsage bouquets, required to enhance the beauty of Mrs. Aveling.

The husband wished to give the irate Executive Committee a philosophical explanation of the value of floral embellishments in 'catching an audience', but Herr Rosenberg, editor of the party organ *Der Sozialist*, cut his oratory short with the remark, 'We want none of that'.

Other objectionable items were overhauled in the same fashion. The extraordinary bill had a round sum of $50 for cigars to the doctor and cigarettes to his emancipated lady. Their official correspondence during a period of three months had involved an expense of $26 for postage stamps. Theatre tickets were summarized at $100, though it is a notorious fact that the great disciple of Karl Marx showed himself an expert at deadheading it* at all theatres on the plea of being a dramatic critic for the *Saturday Review* and other English publications.

A Deadhead at the Hotels

The enterprising socialist lecturers went to study poverty at a first class hotel in Baltimore, and patronized the wine cellar so liberally that their bill for two days amounted to $42. Wherever the Avelings stopped they always managed to select the very best hotel accommodation, and reports have reached the Executive Committee alleging that they played the same trick on hotel proprietors out West as they did on theatre managers in this city, and by puffing, or promising to puff, the various hostelries, lived almost free of expenses. This mode of economy did, however, not deter the apostles of unpaid labor to ring it in on their bill of expenses all the same.

Crisp Bills Flung in his Face

Besides the $1,300 Dr. Aveling has received a considerable sum for special correspondence to the *Volkszeitung, Leader* and New Haven *Workingmen's Advocate*. The Committee refused flatly to pay the additional $600, and, finally, after many harsh words, Herr Walter flung $100 at the Avelings, saying 'Here is enough to pay your passage back to England. We are glad to get rid of you.'

Dr. Aveling looked thoroughly mad, but took the crisp bills as a last souvenir of his visit to America. Before embarking on the *Nevada*† he lodged a protest against 'the brutal treatment he and his wife had received at the hands of the Executive Committee'. This curious document is now retained as a memento by Mr. Julius Bordello, secretary of the socialist party."

On 1 January 1887 the London *Daily Telegraph* picked up the story, cabled by the *Herald,* and printed an abridged version.

When they landed on 4 January, Eleanor and Aveling were shown the

---

* American colloquialism for obtaining free admission.
† According to Engels, writing to his brother on 9 August 1888, they had returned in the *City of Berlin*.[54]

Herald article, which was rehashed in the *Evening Standard* on the 13th with its own comment: "Altogether, delivering lectures on socialism seems a lucrative business."

Before that, however, Aveling had at once sent a cable to New York and, on 10 January, the *Herald* published "A denial from Dr. Aveling".

"He describes his cordial and delightful meeting with the New York Socialists."
                                                              "London, January 9, 1887
The Central News Agency sends to every paper the following statement: – 'Dr. Edward Aveling writes us that on his arrival in England he was shown a newspaper paragraph indicating that the agency had quoted the N.Y. *Tribune* for the statement that the New York socialists were disgusted with Dr. Aveling's charges. To this he gives a most explicit denial. No charges were made and the last meeting was of a most cordial and delightful kind, abounding in expressions and hopes for another visit next year from him.'

Great Commotion over the Official Report
of Dr. Aveling's Bills

Dr. Aveling, the recently departed apostle of 'underpaid labour', has evidently left the socialist party in a state of internal strife.

A secret conference was held yesterday* at Clarendon Hall, when the Executive Board of the party rendered an account of the expenses incurred by Dr. Aveling's tour of agitation throughout the country during the last three months of 1886. Herr Herman Walter presented the report ... showing that Mr. and Mrs. Aveling had drawn about $1,600 for more or less illegitimate expenses.

The reading of the report created a perfect storm of indignation. The members learned now officially that the exclusive publication in the *Herald* of Dr. Aveling's exorbitant bill, with its extravagant details was substantially correct ... a dozen prominent socialists jumped to their feet and denounced it as an outrage that the Executive Board had allowed such items to be honored ... Within five minutes the scene resembled a perfect pandemonium. Herr Walter in vain tried to drown the noise by his gavel. Finally he explained that the Board had only paid the bills under protest, and to avoid a public scandal.

'The relations between the Avelings and the Executive Board,' declared Herr Walter, 'have certainly not been of a friendly character. We had a scene with the fellow just previous to his departure, and I understand that he has lodged a complaint against us with Mr. Bordello, secretary to the party.'

Several delegates declared freely that the scientific Mr. Aveling had wrought more harm than good by his lectures. A resolution denouncing a part of Dr. Aveling's agitation, and particularly refuting his advice that all socialists should join the Knights of Labor was carried with an overwhelming majority. The meeting then adjourned ..."

The sting was in the tail.

Bordello admitted that he had a statement signed by both the Avelings, but would not disclose it to the *Herald*. "It is an affair that I am in honor bound to keep strictly private," he was quoted as saying to its reporter; and though he did not deny that such a document existed: "No

---

* Sunday, 9 January 1887.

one outside our circle will be allowed a copy!" In no time at all the *Herald* had of course obtained one, vouched for by a member of the Executive, while two other members, Rosenberg and Herbert Eaton, "reluctantly admitted" that it was genuine.[55]

This document was duly published on 15 January:

> "To the Members of the Socialistic Party of America: — Pending the forwarding to the various sections of the party of a more formal protest against our treatment by Mr. Walter, we desire to state that from the National Executive Committee we have received no single word of sympathy or thanks, and that from Mr. Walter in the presence of the Executive Board on Thursday night,* we received the most brutal and foul-mouthed abuse.
>
> Dr. Edward Aveling
Eleanor Marx Aveling."

On the same day the *Evening Standard* published a letter from the Avelings, explicitly repudiating item by item the frivolous and unjustified expenses he was said to have incurred, ending with the words:

> "...But it is true that we were invited to America by the socialistic labor party; that they made all the arrangements as to the tour; that those arrangements were accepted and adhered to by us; that, according to the final statement of accounts $176 were due to us as money advanced towards the expenses, and that we handed that $176 back to the party.
>
> Edward Aveling
Eleanor Marx Aveling."

The *Herald* reprinted this with an editorial comment making the most of the SLP's discomfiture: "The socialists here are evidently not in love with the Avelings or the Avelings with them." It then recapitulated the story of the Executive meeting at which the report on Aveling's expenses had been given and the vote of censure passed. Two days before that meeting, on 7 January, the Executive had issued its circular setting out the accusations which, however, was not sent to Aveling himself until 3 February,

> "so that it had a whole month's unhampered start for its slander before we even learned of what A. was really accused,"

wrote Engels to Sorge.[56]

On 21 January the *Volkszeitung* came out with its own version:

> "In the last few days the capitalist press has received capital pleasure from the fact that

---

* 23 December 1886.

Edward Aveling from London, who – as our readers know – with his wife has travelled for about three months through the United States, doing propaganda for socialism with great success, on his return submitted a bill which was $500 to $600 more than the sum originally estimated by the National Executive of the Socialist Labor Party, and in addition contained items which a working propagandist, who should know that the money to cover the propaganda expenses came almost entirely out of the pockets of hard-working men, ought not to have been listed. The National Executive gave Mr. Aveling a plain hint to this effect by crossing off the bill these particular items, reducing the excess to something a little over $100, which was paid. The sensational capitalist press, of course, makes a major scandal out of this simple fact ... We want only to emphasize that it is precisely the indignation in socialist circles at Aveling's conduct, precisely the voracity with which the capitalist press seizes upon the affair to exploit it against the socialists that *bear the most striking testimony to the integrity and high-mindedness* of the socialist movement. This indignation proves that socialists, including their propagandists, are accustomed to such self-sacrificing work that even a single instance of no more than a slight deviation arouses their just anger.

The merest approach to what is taken for granted by the corrupt rabble of the capitalist parties and is practised by them to the top of their bent, namely, making money at the expense of the party, creates an outcry among socialists. And the eagerness of the capitalist press in a solitary, personal case of un-socialist conduct, only goes to prove that it is impossible to damage the socialist cause and its many representatives by any well-founded aspersions."[53]

This was the first time the SLP had publicly denounced Aveling, accusing him of "un-socialist conduct". In all he issued no fewer than five *démentis*, the second being a formal protest sent on 26 February both to the National Executive of the SLP and every one of its sections. In this he cited examples of Walther's abuse: he had called the Avelings "aristocrats living on the money of the workers" and "not worthy to belong to the party." Aveling further set out the details of the arrangements agreed upon with the Executive both for himself and for Eleanor: she, as was recognised from the start, not being paid for her living expenses while on tour but only the railway fares.

Engels' first reaction to the *Herald's* "filthy article", which he read on 11 January – a week after the Avelings' return – was recorded in a letter to Sorge.

"It is most valuable to us," he wrote, "or the Avelings might not have known what a pack of lies the bourgeois press concocts."[57]

This was not quite the point. The Avelings needed no lessons on that particular subject and, indeed, Engels' roseate view swiftly faded as he found himself involved in a lengthy argument with Mrs. Kelley Wischnewetzky which had nothing whatsoever to do with the salutatory effects of a hostile press. She had written him a prolix letter:

"from which it appears that the idiots of the Executive Committee of the Socialist Labour Party want to bring some kind of action against Aveling, accusing him of having robbed the party over his touring expenses, want the sections to pass resolutions against him and then denounce him in a circular to the European workers' parties as a *swindler*. She even had the impudence to suggest that I should tell Kautsky* that he would be well advised not to print anything by Aveling in future. And all this without the slightest suggestion that at least the accused has the right to be heard."[58]

Mrs. Wischnewetzky, the preface to whose translation of *The Condition of the Working Class in England in 1844* Engels had deliberately held up to await the travellers' return for the latest account of the American scene, had also expressed the fear that Engels might be "unduly influenced" by Aveling's views. This, he told her in his reply of 9 February, was groundless.

"As soon as there was a national American working-class movement," he wrote, "independent of the Germans, my standpoint was clearly indicated by the facts of the case. That great national movement, no matter what its first form, is the real starting point of American working class development; if the Germans join it in order to help it, or to hasten its development in the right direction, they may do a deal of good and play a decisive part in it; if they stand aloof, they will dwindle into a dogmatic sect, and be brushed aside as people who do not understand their own principles. Mrs. Aveling who has seen her father at work, understood this quite as well from the beginning, and if Aveling saw it too, all the better. And all my letters to America, to Sorge, to yourself, to the Avelings, from the very beginning have repeated this view over and over again. Still, I was glad to see the Avelings before writing my preface, because they gave me some new facts about the inner mysteries of the German party in New York."

He then turned to the charges against Aveling which his correspondent had blindly accepted and Engels now stoutly rebutted:

"You appear to take it for granted that Aveling has behaved in America simply as a swindler; and not only that; you call upon me, upon the strength of the assertions and allusions contained in your letter, to treat him as such and to do all in my power to have him excluded from the literary organs of the party. Now for all these assertions you *cannot* have any proof because you have not been able to hear any defence. Still you are better off than we here; you have at least heard *one* side, while we do not even know what the distinct charge is!"

Engels then vindicated Aveling in a handsome tribute:

"I have known [him] for four years; I know that he has twice sacrificed his social and economical position to his convictions, and might be, had he refrained from doing so, a professor in an English university and a distinguished physiologist instead of an

---

* (1854–1938) Editor of the *Neue Zeit* (1883–1917) the German party's theoretical organ.

overworked journalist with a very uncertain income. I have had occasion to observe his capacities by working with him, and his character by seeing him pass through rather trying circumstances more than once, and it will take a good deal more than mere assertions and innuendos before I believe what some people tell about him now in New York.

"But then," he went on, "had he tried to swindle the party, how could he do that during his tour without his wife being cognisant of it? And in that case the charge includes her too. And then it becomes utterly absurd, in my eyes at least. Her I have known from a child, and for the last seventeen years she has been constantly about me. And more than that, I have inherited from Marx the obligation to stand by his children as he would have done himself, and to see, as far as lies in my power, that they are not wronged. And that I shall do, in spite of fifty Executives. The daughter of Marx swindling the working class – too rich indeed!

"Then you say: 'No one here imagines that Dr. Aveling put the money in his pocket, *or spent it as the bills indicate*. They believe that he merely tried to cover his wife's expenses'. That is a distinct charge of forgery, and this you give as an extenuating, charitable supposition. What then, if this be the attenuated charge, what is the full charge?"

It was all very well for the Executive to rant about "ridiculous bills"; the fact was that for 15 weeks Aveling had sent in his accounts every Sunday to the Executive which had never questioned them, nor had it expressed any misgivings when the pair returned to New York on 19 December.

"It was only on the 23rd, when they were on the point of leaving, when they could no longer defend themselves against charges real or trumped-up, that the Executive discovered these bills, to which *singly* they had never objected, were ridiculous when *added up*! That is to say they object, not to the bills, but to the rules of addition. Why, then, did the Executive, instead of shortening the tour, try to extend it, and just at the close of it plan a second visit to Chicago, which fortunately did not come off?"

Engels then denounced the odious rumours and reports spread by the Executive, for

"...having, as it appears, succeeded in their N. York circle to slander Aveling not as a man who has spent their money extravagantly (for such, rightly or wrongly, might be their honest conviction), but as a swindler and forger of accounts. They rise to the level of the occasion created by their own inventive genius, and promise a circular proclaiming Aveling a swindler and forger to the working class of the whole world! And all this, mind you, behind the back of, and unknown to, the man whom they charge, and who can, not only not defend himself, but not even make out the precise facts on which the charge is based! If this is the way people are to be judged in our party, then give me the Leipzig Reichsgericht* and the Chicago jury."

At least Bismarck and the American bourgeoisie, Engels pointed out,

---

* The German Supreme Court.

respected the forms of justice and allowed a hearing to the prisoner at the bar.

> "Fortunately," he went on, "we have passed that stage in the older parties in Europe. We have seen Executives rise and fall by the dozen, we know they are as fallible as any pope, and have known more than one that lived sumptuously on the pence of the working men, and had swindlers and forgers of accounts in its midst ... And as I cannot allow the Avelings to be accused of infamies ... it was my duty to communicate your letter to Mrs. Aveling ... and to read her my reply. And if at any time circumstances should require the publication of this my letter, you are at liberty to publish it *in full*, while I reserve to myself the same right..."[59]

Three days later Engels wrote to Sorge, furious at the "abominable behaviour" of the SLP Executive which had allowed the *Herald* article to be published "through their indiscretion, if not inspiration" and then followed it up with its own "infamous" piece in the *Volkszeitung*. He referred, though not by name, to Mrs. Wischnewetzky's letter which assumed, "out of Christian charity", that Aveling had merely put in false accounts to cover Tussy's hotel expenses, knowing full well that these were not being paid by the party. That he was owed $176 the Executive passed over in silence, quietly pocketing the money. If there had been any swindling, it was not on Aveling's part. What Engels really wanted to know from Sorge was how such people as Shevich stood in the matter: whether or not they "have already let themselves be duped by the Executive's lies".[60]

The wretched affair dragged on. The *Volkszeitung* deferred the publication of Aveling's first circular for a month; the threat to brand him in the eyes of the European parties as a cheat and a swindler was carried out; and Engels was ever more reduced to pettifogging.

Not until the middle of March did it emerge that Aveling had paid some of Liebknecht's minor expenses but failed to mention them. There had been a plan for Gertrud, Liebknecht's 21-year-old daughter by his first wife, Ernestine,* to travel with her father to America.[61] In the event Gertrud followed him a month later, sailing direct from Bremerhaven early in October.[62] Once there, father and daughter naturally spent some leisure time together and, as naturally, when their lecturing engagements accorded, the Avelings joined them. Thus this friendly foursome had met in Boston, where they stayed for two days, on which occasion:

> "L. let all the wine, etc. be brought to A.'s room and thus charged to A.'s account".

---

* See above, fn.*, p. 51.

Such things had occurred throughout the trip, for Liebknecht did not submit any bills at all.

> "He said ... that the party must stand all my expenses, and so I shall not put anything down. And they were content with this."[56]

The SLP's circular, with its "absurd accusations", was to be put before all the sections, whose votes were to reach New York by 15 March. The delay in sending the circular to Aveling made it impossible for him to prepare a reasoned reply in time; the more so since, in early February, he was laid low with quinsy,[63] which he immediately took to be diphtheria. He was a most intractable patient: for three or four nights, wrote Engels, Tussy had had no sleep and, "with all this going on, you can imagine that (she) has her hands full".[58] Aveling had suffered

> "an awful shock about these ridiculous accusations ... He is not over-endowed with power of resistance to malady, and so this threw him back very much. He has been off and on at Hastings," Engels wrote to Laura.[64]

There seemed nothing for it but that, while Aveling was convalescing, Engels should draft a circular to announce that a full statement in his defence would be sent and to ask that the SLP sections postpone taking a vote until this had been received.[58]

Meanwhile the American Executive's accusations had a mixed reception abroad. Paul Singer* in Germany dismissed them with the remark:

> "It's the old story; but it's a pity that the Avelings, too, have to smart for it."[65]

Justice, on the other hand, took a running dive into the quagmire. Under the item "Critical Chronicle" it published an article on 30 April: "A Costly Apostle."

> "... A good deal was written in the capitalist press at the time about [the Avelings'] expensive charges. The circular fully bears out all that was stated. Resolutions have been passed by the Executive Committee of the SLP pointing out that Dr. Aveling, after his return to New York, recommended that all Socialists should become members of the Knights of Labor instead of urging them to join the SLP for which he was engaged; that he denounced all those who protested against his action as 'God-damned fools, acting out of stupid egotism'; and that the 'brutal abuse' which the Avelings allege was used against them by H. Walther, a member of the Executive, was simply a denunciation of the luxurious and expensive manner of living adopted by Dr. Aveling as unworthy of a labour agitator, which the Executive consider fully justified. We

---

* (1844–1911) Member of the German party's Executive from 1877 onwards and deputy to the Reichstag from 1884.

gladly give publicity to this, 'for our own sakes and yet more for that of Socialism' (*vide* Dr. Aveling's letter ...) and our American comrades will see that the SDF has had every reason for repudiating any connection with Dr. Aveling, when a statement appeared in the press that he was a member of that organisation."

Another black mark against Aveling in the eyes of *Justice* – that is, Hyndman – was that his circulars and denials had been issued from Engels' home address. On their return from the States he and Eleanor had stayed at 122 Regent's Park Road, moving briefly to lodgings in 32 St. George's Square, Pimlico, which they vacated on 22 March to spend a few days with Engels again until they took up their quarters in New Stone Buildings, 65 Chancery Lane* where they were to live for the next six years.

Aveling replied to *Justice* in a letter published on 14 May:

"Sir, the paragraph on the front page of your last issue ... is a sad proof of the fact that even Socialists may be willing to condemn a man unheard. You refer to 'a circular' in reference to the dispute between the Executive of the Socialist Labour Party of America and myself. There have been four circulars, and a fifth is in course of preparation. The one you refer to is antagonistic to me. No mention is made by you of the following facts, all but the last of which are public property.

(1) That in my circulars I have dealt with and disproved *seriatim* every one of the false charges made by the Executive. (2) That the Executive and I appealed to the sections, and thus far all the results communicated to me are in my favour, with the one exception of New York, where the Executive sits. (3) That, probably because the verdict of the sections was adverse to them, the Executive appealed to the Board of Supervisors. (4) That this Board have written to me a most friendly letter, stating that the question is not within their jurisdiction, and appealing to me to allow the matter to drop.

The first circular of the Executive quoted by you was sent by them to every Socialist paper in Europe. *Justice* is the only one that in any country has taken any notice of it. Of the capitalist press in England, only the *Evening Standard* attacked me, but that journal in its next issue inserted my reply ...

As to the three chief points in your attack on me ... (1) I never 'recommended that all Socialists should become members of the Knights of Labour instead of urging them to join the Socialist Labour Party.' (2) I never denounced anyone whatever as 'God damned fools.' ... When on the showing of the Executive themselves, there was an actual balance to me of 176 dollars for expenses paid out of my own pocket, I, in the face of the insults of Herr Walther, a member of the Executive, returned that sum to the party in America.

I enclose you copies of my 2 circulars, where you will find the lengthy details summarised above.

Faithfully yours, Edward Aveling."

---

* Destroyed by bombs in 1940. The only building in Chancery Lane never to have been replaced. It remains a gap, the number incorporated in a new block.

This could not be allowed to go unchallenged and a parenthetical note of almost equal length, was appended:

"(We greatly regret that Dr. Aveling should only have sent us two circulars of his own in support of the above letter, both dated from 122 Regent's Park Road, the address of Mr. Frederick Engels. Mr. Engels has held for upwards of 40 years so distinguished a place in the Socialist party that he, more than any other man, must be able to appreciate the gravity of the misunderstanding between Dr. Aveling and the most active men of the Socialist Labour Party in America. Messrs. Walther and Rosenberg, to speak only of two of them, certainly began with a strong feeling in favour of Dr. Aveling, and it was in great part owing to their energy that the expenses of his trip to the United States were raised at all. Now they, in common with the whole of the New York Executive, accuse him of gross extravagance and his behaviour, giving details of their charges in a circular to all Socialist bodies. We ourselves studiously avoided any reference whatever to this matter until it was forced upon our attention. Dr. Aveling's defence seems unsatisfactory; and we know that there is a strong opinion among Socialists of all shades of thought that this scandal has deeply injured the cause. We would therefore suggest to the Socialist League, of which body Dr. Aveling is an original member, and to Mr. Frederick Engels, his close friend, that something more is required than a mere personal denial by Dr. Aveling himself of charges which affect his personal character, and are certainly harmful, indirectly, to all English Socialists. There must be Socialists, or sympathisers with Socialism in New York and its neighbourhood who could be trusted by Dr. Aveling, as well as by the authors of the circular on which our note was based, to examine into the whole of the facts and report upon them. Until some such 'Court of Honour' has sat upon the question and cleared Dr. Aveling his position must necessarily be a very unpleasant one – Editor. *Justice*.)"[66]

Justice, however, was too late; altogether and knew it. It extricated itself the following week with as little squelch as possible, in a modest paragraph under "Tell Tale Straws":

"We have received another long letter from Dr. Aveling, for which we are unable to find space. The gist of it is that the Board of Supervisors in America exonerate him from all blame, and that Mr. Frederick Engels, Mr. F. A. Sorge, and Mr. Wilhelm Liebknecht (who writes a letter to that effect) are ready to answer for Dr. Aveling's correct behaviour in the matter of his expenditure on his American trip."[67]

Almost a month earlier Engels had told Laura:

"The NY Executive have launched in their despair another circular against Aveling saying that his statements are lies, yet making very important admissions in our favour ... the affair is practically ended, the Ex. are themselves accused in NY as swindlers and liars in another affair and on their trial before the NY sections; so that whatever they have said, say, or may say, loses all importance. In the meantime the Control Commission* of the American party appeals to them (to Edward and Tussy) to let the

---

* *Aufsichtsbehörde* in the original letter, otherwise in English.

matter drop, and from very many places they receive very nice letters both from Americans and Germans. So that matter is virtually settled."[68]

Engels then told Mrs. Wischnewetzky he had heard from Sorge that she and her husband deeply regretted the dissimulations and suppressions of the Executive which had so unhappily misled them and that they were now making every effort to obtain justice for Aveling in the New York section. If that was the case, wrote Engels, "then I am perfectly satisfied, and have no desire to return to that subject in a spirit of controversy".[69]

The last word – almost a postscript – came from *To-Day** in an editorial dated August 1887:

"We have received from Dr. Aveling certain *pièces justicatives*. concerning his recent lecturing tour in the United States. It will be remembered that Dr. Aveling, at the end of his trip, was accused by the Socialist Labour Party of America, which paid – or was to have paid – his expenses, of unbecoming extravagance in his style of living. Some publicity was given to the matter by the capitalist press here; but it was a Socialist paper – *Justice* – which made the most and worst of it. Hence the *pièces justicatives*! We are bound to say that the impression they leave is that Dr. Aveling has his own unbusinesslike arrangements to thank for the opportunity which his enemies have seized. He travelled partly as a missionary from the Socialist Labour Party, and partly as a correspondent of various London newspapers. But he sent in to the Labour Party an account of *all* his expenses, and said virtually, 'Here is what I have spent: now pay me whatever you think was fairly incurred on your account.' This was frank, brotherly, and free from all taint of *bourgeoisisme*. And it ended, as most brotherly affairs do, in a quarrel. The Socialist Labour Party found the task of deciding whether this or that particular cigar or bottle of soda water was 'a means of production' of lecturing or of dramatic criticism, invidious and impossible. Dr. Aveling took a high tone, and told them, in effect, to pay what their conscience told them they ought to pay. They then lost their tempers; accused him of 'trying it on'; and expressed their belief that if they paid the account in full without remonstrance he would have pocketed the total without a word. Obviously they could neither be proved nor disproved; and Dr. Aveling, declining to pursue the transaction, returned to Europe, leaving the Labour Party in his debt.

*   *   *

"In short, the upshot of the unbourgeoislike arrangements was just what any person of common sense might have predicted from the moment the parties fell out. But why did they fall out? Because Dr. Aveling urged from the platform the importance of gaining over to the Socialist cause the existing organisation of the Knights of Labour, just as he is now most sensibly urging the necessity of gaining over the Radical party here. Instantly the ill-conditioned and Impossibilist sections, with the natural dread of incompetent or supersensitive persons for practical work, became his bitter enemies, and brought forward his washing bill as proof positive that the Knights of Labour should be treated as lepers by every true Socialist. We have exactly the same spirit

---

* Hubert Bland took over the editorship in 1886.

shown here by that absurd body the anarchist voting majority (anarchists voting!!!) of the Socialist League ... These gentlemen vilify the advocates of political activity in England just as heartily as their transatlantic brethren vilified Dr. Aveling. The parallel alone gives the incident any significance. Until Socialist bodies fix a standard of comfort for their members, personal extravagance will remain a matter of private opinion; and people who make silly arrangements with regard to expenses must do so at their own risk."

So, at long last, the storm blew itself out; not, however, before Engels had been driven to the verge of frenzy by taking up the cudgels for Aveling and the repercussions affecting his own affairs.

The American edition of his book, *The Condition of the Working Class in England*, though the translation was completed, had not been published because his new preface to it, sent off on 27 January 1887, had displeased the SLP.

"That party," he wrote to Sorge, "may appropriate to itself the successes of its predecessors as much as it pleases, but insofar as it is the only workers' organisation existing in America that stands wholly on our basis with more than 70 sections throughout the North and West, it is a platform and as such, but only as such, do I recognise it ... they themselves belong to the wing which I say will ruin the party if it gains the upper hand. And on that they seem bent."[70]

While still the book did not appear, the New York *Volkszeitung*, adding insult to injury, printed a German version of the new preface in April without consulting Engels:

"a double effrontery; first because I can have nothing to do with the paper as long as it behaves so basely towards Aveling. But secondly, because I cannot put up with having my English writings turned into outlandish German which, moreover, teems with howlers and misinterprets the most important points."[71]

He told Mrs. Wischnewetzky categorically that this translation could not "pass under any circumstances".[69] He held her responsible in that, as he wrote to Sorge, "this creature has had my preface since the beginning of February" and was now seeking his consent to a German version, knowing that he had no copy of his English original.[71]

Her letter about Aveling, he said, could be characterised by only one word: shit.[71] It had gravely affronted him and, as time wore on, he also grew exasperated by her conduct of their working relations.

Ever one to look upon the bright side, Engels saw in this new offence an excellent pretext to be rid of her once and for all.

"I welcome it as I hope it will now relieve me of Mrs. W's pressures about translations.* Firstly, she translates like a machine, leaving the real work to me, secondly, she
has hopelessly bungled the publication,† by letting it fall into the hands of those oafs
... and now, after I had written an additional preface for her, there is obviously a hitch
for no better reason than that this preface does not suit the taste of the Executive!"[74]

By May he had had enough:

"Up to now the Wisch. has made a hash of everything she has touched. I shall never
again give her anything. She can do what she pleases ... but ... in future let her leave
me in peace."[75]

Eventually this matter was cleared up too; and, after extracting his
English preface from Mrs. Wischnewetzky, Engels translated it into
German himself.[76]

His *Condition of the Working Class in England in 1844* eventually came
out in America, complete with his preface, in May 1887 and remains to
this day the authorised English translation.

Exactly what happened in the New York office of the SLP on 23
December 1886 will never now be known. That a row took place is
beyond all doubt for both parties admitted as much in public. But, as
To-Day cogently asked – and answered – what was it about?

If after barely eight months the political differences underlying the
quarrel could be discerned, how much more evident they are when seen
from this distance of time.

They were partly obscured by the fact that Aveling was known to be
careless, not to say unscrupulous, in money matters. It was not the first,
nor was it to be the last charge of this nature to be brought against him.
None was ever pressed or substantiated, but each time a little mud stuck.
To that Engels would have replied, as he did in a letter to Sorge, that
Aveling, though talented, competent and honest, was as raw as a boy,
always liable to commit some folly or other and that he could remember a
time when he himself had been "just such an ass".‡[77]

---

* Earlier, Mrs. Wischnewetzky had pestered him about translating his *Origin of the Family*,
which he said he had offered – "though not absolutely promised" – to Aveling;[72] then she had
tried to persuade him to let her undertake the *Communist Manifesto* which, as Engels told Sorge,
only Sam Moore could do and was in fact doing.[73]
† Of *The Condition of the Working Class*.
‡ It should perhaps be remarked that, whether an ass or not, at the same age – 37 – Engels was
employed on an uncongenial job in his family's firm of cotton manufacturers, supporting not
only himself and Mary Burns but also the entire Marx family, while behind him were such
major works as *The Condition of the Working Class in England*, his collaborations with Marx on
The Holy Family, German Ideology, the Manifesto of the Communist Party, the *Address of the Central
Committee to the Communist League* and an impressive body of political and scientific material,
produced as ephemera but to become of lasting value.

It was only after Aveling's speech of 23 December, when he had urged that the SLP should be an integral part of the American trade union movement, that trouble was made about his own and Eleanor's expenses and their name brought into disrepute.

Yet on the political issue Aveling was essentially in the right and he had been misrepresented: even by *To-Day*. While it was said that he had rudely enjoined the SLP members to make common cause with the Knights of Labor – against whose reactionary leadership they considered themselves the foremost combatants – he had in fact equally recommended joining the Central Labor Unions, fathered by the SLP itself. This was the organisation, he had claimed, in which, as a socialist, he would be most active were he settled in America. Speaking before he was aware of the newly formed A. F. of L., he had advised working within *both* these bodies which represented, as the SLP did not, the rank and file of American workers: black and white, male and female, immigrant and native.

To be sure, it is slightly galling to engage a propagandist to tour the country on behalf of your party only to be told that you would do better to merge into some other organisation. The Avelings' assignment had been to propagate the gospel according to the Socialist Labor Party of North America and, while they had faithfully done so, they had travelled through the States when a number of other working-class bodies were initiating bold and effective action. They had reached the conclusion that, though its principles might be sound, the SLP was missing golden opportunities to apply those tenets in the most effective quarters by reason of its narrow outlook, Germanic traits and virtual isolation from the mass movements that had come into being.

Even had Aveling not been a sitting target for the loaded charge of extravagance and improbity – which he was – dangers always lurked, as Engels pointed out, for any man of middle-class origin and higher education rash enough to enter into cash transactions with the working-class movement in its "early hole-and-corner stages".

> "This I have constantly seen for more than forty years," he said. "The worst of all were the Germans; in Germany, the growth of the movement has long since swept that failing away, but it has not died out with the Germans out of Germany. For that reason Marx and I have always tried to avoid having any money dealings with the party, no matter in what country."

He had felt serious misgivings on this score when the Avelings went to America but was reassured by the knowledge that Liebknecht would be with them, for if anyone knew how to deal with such matters it was this "old hand" and "because any charges brought against him ... would merely make the complaints ridiculous in Germany and in Europe everywhere."

However, Liebknecht had not stayed to the end of the Avelings' tour and "here is the result".[59]

That this rumpus benefited nobody but anti-socialists in Europe and America goes without saying. Whether or not the Executive of the SLP were fond of the Avelings, whether or not they squabbled with each other, is perfectly immaterial. What mattered was that yet again discord was sown among socialists. That was the harm done.

One curious omission from the voluminous correspondence on the affair, lasting from January until May 1887, is that nobody – not even Engels, despite his passing reference to the first *Herald* article as possibly "inspired" by the SLP – remarked upon the fact that publicity to the private quarrel, to the secret party meeting and to the Avelings' statement which the secretary was under a solemn oath not to reveal, was first given in the columns of the capitalist press. It is not an unimportant factor: however improper Aveling's expenses, they were not claimed from the class enemy for services rendered; and if the SLP, that seagreen incorruptible, felt itself threatened by the unwelcome proposition that it should play a part in the mass movement or bow itself out altogether, it was also most certainly, obviously, deliberately and treacherously, if not venally, undermined from within.

One could have thought that nothing else at all was happening in these months, but that would be far from true. In the first place, the English edition of the first volume of *Capital* came out early in January 1887: quite an event, one might say, and celebrated not only by the Avelings but also the Lafargues, who had come from Paris to spend Christmas with Engels and stayed on. Eleanor found, too, that during her absence her translation of Lissagaray's *Commune* had been handsomely reviewed by Bax in *Commonweal* of 4 December.

> "This important work," he wrote, "has at last appeared in English and we do not hesitate to say that it ought to be in the hands of every Socialist. The history of the Commune ... bears a profound moral with it ... But the moral to be drawn is of more immediate application than to the next popular rising. To compare small matters with great, there are Socialist organisations (save the mark!) in existence to-day which are literally qualifying for disaster when the time comes ... The cause was wrecked in 1871, in great part at least, not because of spies and traitors, for there were marvellously few of those ... who can fairly be accused of sinister motives, or of attempts to make personal gain out of it – but because of well-meaning, conceited, faddy cantankerous persons, who wasted time in long-winded speeches about personal matters, etc., and who would neither do any work themselves nor let any one else do it ... The translation of the book, we should say, is excellent."

These tangible results of work done in the past were gratifying; but more important was the fresh activity into which Eleanor and Aveling plunged as soon as they arrived back in England: lecturing here, there and everywhere on the political situation in the United States. They also wrote the articles which appeared in *Time** from March to May 1887 – to be enlarged and issued as a shilling pamphlet by Swan Sonnenschein on 18 October that year as *The Working-Class Movement in America*. The Swan Sonnenschein *Letterbooks* reveal that Aveling's demand for an advance on this joint effort was twice rejected – in August and September – on the grounds that he had an outstanding debt of £22 "for goods supplied", in addition to the £25 paid in April 1886 on signing an agreement to translate Tikhomirov's *Russia, Political and Social*, not fulfilled until almost two years later. At the second time of asking, Aveling was also reminded that, thanks to these transactions, there was still a debit balance on *The Woman Question* despite its excellent sale.

In the event, before the Avelings' pamphlet was even published, the high promise of 1886 had been betrayed: the American labour movement was split and confused, the workers' parties were in retreat, their challenge to the Democrats and Republicans an empty gesture. Yet the after-glow of that fiery year was never entirely to fade but, in different settings at different seasons, was to be the common light of day for generations of American socialists.

On 19 January, having been home a fortnight, Aveling lectured to the Clerkenwell Branch of the Socialist League at the Farringdon Hall on "Socialism in America", while on the 26th Eleanor spoke on "The relative Position of English and American Workmen".

"Edward was to lecture again tonight at Farringdon Hall," wrote Engels to Laura on 2 February, ". . . He and Tussy have had two crowded nights on Wednesdays. But he has got a sore throat, and may be Tussy will have to replace him."[78]

Aveling was now invited to address one of the Radical Clubs in the East End. From that time on these Clubs were to become the centre of both his own and Eleanor's propaganda work, though they did not drop their regular lectures to branches of the Socialist League.

This was the period – late February or early March 1887 – as indicated by Havelock Ellis's reference to "a temporary stay at St. George's Square", when Eleanor was said to have attempted* suicide "by deliberately taking a large over-dose of opium".[†79] Had she been minded to do away with herself at this period, it would have been as good a time as any: plagued by the vexatious American affair and without a settled abode, she might well have succumbed to despair. However, it so happens that not only was she busily writing her account of the transatlantic tour but there exists a complete record of her lecturing engagements during those same weeks – as for all others throughout her public life – and documentary proof that she fulfilled them. Further, as Engels' letters reveal, she had to deputise for Aveling on occasion, and also to nurse him, during his attack of quinsy. To be sure, she could have slipped in many a suicidal gesture between these various activities, but it is a rather flighty supposition.

The Commune meeting of 1887 was held in South Place on 17 April – a date when Eleanor also spoke at the Hoxton branch of the League on "The Working Classes of America" – and Morris signalised this, the 16th

---

* Run by Lowrey of Swan Sonnenschein.

† The very term "over-dose" suggests – as did Beatrice Potter see above, p. 227 – that Eleanor was a drug addict. The vital energy she applied to all her undertakings rules this out. It may well be that at times of stress she resorted to narcotics which, in some form or other, most often the tincture known as laudanum, were used in much the same way, if not so habitually, as today's tranquillisers to which no odium whatsoever attaches (unless it be to the manufacturers' exorbitant profits).

anniversary, by writing a front page article for *Commonweal* on "Why we Celebrate the Commune". He had

> "heard it said, and by good Socialists too, that it is a mistake to commemorate a defeat; but it seems to me that this means looking not at the event only, but at all history in too narrow a way ..."

He concluded with the words:

> "Who can doubt that the nameless multitude who died so heroically had sacrificed day by day other things than life, before it came to that?"[80]

On 20 March, his first lecture after recovering his health, Aveling addressed another of the Radical Clubs and Engels noted with approval:

> "He is making a very useful and probably successful campaign amongst the East End Radicals to engage them to cut loose from the Great Liberal Party and form a working men's party after the American fashion. If he succeeds, he will get both Socialist Associations into his wake; for here he gets hold of the real spontaneous working men's organisations and gets at the heart of the working class."[81]

Eleanor, when she spoke at Hoxton, urged the branch

> "not to stand aloof from the Radical Clubs and other organisations, but to join them and fraternise with the members, and by these means induce them to enquire into Socialism".[82]

On 19 May Aveling addressed a large audience at the Communist Club, 49 Tottenham Street, and a fortnight later, talked to his own, the Bloomsbury, branch of the League on "Radicalism and Socialism", defining the areas of common ground. This was followed by questions and a keen debate in which Bernard Shaw took part.[83]

Naturally the propaganda was mutual and in October 1886, before the Avelings had begun theirs, the *Radical* had published an article saying: "Come over then, O ye Socialists, and work with us."

The campaign to induce the Radicals to "enquire into Socialism" gathered momentum that following spring.*

> "The Avelings have started doing very effective agitation in the Radical Clubs," Engels wrote to Sorge, "and in particular holding up the American example of an independent workers' party ... It's going well and could cost the Liberals ... the whole of the East End of London in a year's time."[84]

---

* On 5 April, in the midst of an already over full programme, Eleanor and Aveling took part in one of the "Musical and Dramatic Entertainments" given by the Bloomsbury branch of the SL at the Athenaeum Hall, 73 Tottenham Court Road.

He enlarged upon this some ten days later:

"The Radical Clubs – to whom the Liberals owe twelve of their 69 London seats – have approached Aveling to lecture on the American movement, and he and Tussy are busily working at this ... if all goes well, it will push the Social Democratic Federation as well as the Socialist League into the background, which would be the best solution to the prevailing brawls ... At present the Avelings are doing more than anyone else here, and being more effective..."[85]

In all this Eleanor and Aveling were drawing upon the American experience which, oddly enough, made a far deeper impression upon British workers than the example of the more advanced socialist parties in Germany and France. It may be that they thought of the Continent as infested with foreigners, whereas America, no matter that its working population might be largely composed of European emigrants, was somehow or other kin, in the way that our ex-colonies – if inhabited by white settlers – quite often seem to Britons.

The importance of these East End Radical Clubs – which covered the boroughs from Poplar and Hackney, Bermondsey and Stepney as far west as Islington and Finsbury, with their local Federations* – lay in that they drew together politically conscious working men who voted Liberal for want of an alternative to the Tories. Thus they were fertile soil for implanting the notion of an independent workers' party. Week in, week out, Eleanor propagated that aim and the means by which it could be achieved, pursuing this work "quietly and steadily", as Engels wrote to Laura.[86]

Things had not stood still in the English socialist movement during the Avelings' absence. Ill-feeling between the SDF and the SL had grown and, although they had joined forces in October 1886 – together with 32 Liberal and Radical Clubs – for a meeting in Trafalgar Square to protest against the London School Board's fee-paying policy, the League's approach to the Federation to hold a combined demonstration on the Irish question in January 1887 was rebuffed and, as Morris explained at the time, any attempt to

"get up an Irish meeting of the Radicals led by the Socialists will fail; we are not big enough for the job: the radical Clubs are civil to us but afraid of us and not yet prepared to break with the Liberals".[87]

He had not Eleanor's intuitive perception of the dormant buds of socialism. Within the SL itself differences had also widened, above all on the

---

* There was also a Metropolitan Radical Federation with headquarters in Battersea. The Secretary was James Tims.

parliamentary issue, bringing in its train a sharp division between "collectivist" and "anarchist" factions. Morris put the matter clearly in a letter of 1 December 1886:

"...I do not mean that at some time or other it might not be necessary for Socialists to go into Parliament in order to break it up; but again, that could only be when we are very much more advanced than we are now; in short, on the verge of a revolution ... At present it is not worth while even thinking of that, and our sole business is to make Socialists. I really feel sickened at the idea of all the intrigue and degradation of concession which would be necessary to us as a parliamentary party, nor do I see any necessity for a revolutionary party doing any 'dirty work' at all, or soiling ourselves with anything that would unfit us for being due citizens of the new order of things. As for the SDF ... their present successes are won at the expense of withdrawing real Socialism from view in favour of mere palliation and 'reform'. "[88]

This was hardly the voice of anarchy, but certain other of the League members, concerned only to "make socialists" and not soil their hands, extended this policy to dismissing the eight-hour day agitation, all immediate demands by trade unionists and to the trade unions themselves as utterly futile:

"...the day for this unequal and losing battle between the bloated capitalist and the starving workman for a mere increase or to prevent a decrease of wages is past",

wrote one of them.[89]

However, on Easter Monday, 11 April 1887, there was a gigantic demonstration in Hyde Park protesting against the Irish Perpetual Coercion – or Crimes – Bill, introduced in March.* Engels said that "it was without exception the largest meeting we have ever had here."[91] It was estimated that between 100 and 150,000 people were present. The

---

* Gladstone's Home Rule Bill of April 1885, conceding the principle of self-government for Ireland, had been defeated on the second reading, as a result of which Gladstone himself was brought down by a narrow majority in 1886, to be succeeded by Lord Salisbury. Under the Coercion Bill, the Irish National League, founded in 1882, was declared illegal, its journals suppressed and its meeting prohibited, while any manifestation of Irish nationalism, however trivial, was designated an "outrage" and punishable as such. To whip up feeling in support of the Bill, *The Times* ran a series of articles, starting in 1886, on "Parnellism and Crime", but overreached itself by publishing the facsimile of a letter, purporting to have been written by Parnell, condoning the Phoenix Park murders of 1882. This appeared on the very day in April 1887 when the Coercion Bill was to receive its second reading. The forgery, as it turned out to be, was traced to Richard Piggott (see above, fn.†, p. 61) who broke down under cross-examination in court and then absconded, leaving a confession. It emerged that there was a gang in Paris busy manufacturing and selling false information on Fenian activities. The upshot of the exposure of Piggott and *The Times* was that Parnell won unprecedented popularity. Nevertheless, the Coercion Bill was rushed through the House on 17 June 1887. Engels called it "a worthy counterpart to the Anti-Socialist Law".[90]

speakers from the 15 platforms included Gladstone for the Liberal Party, Bernard Shaw for the Fabians, John Burns for the SDF, as well as Michael Davitt – who refused to meet Aveling because he was an atheist – with Aveling on two and Eleanor on one of the SL platforms. Morris, to his regret, was not present as he was that day in Newcastle where the miners were on strike.

The *Daily Telegraph* reported that

"... The Socialists had sub-divided their platform into two divisions, at one of which Mr. Mainwaring and Dr. and Mrs. Marx Aveling were the chief attractions ... Considerable interest was naturally taken in the speech delivered with excellent fluency and clear intonation by Mrs. Marx Aveling, who wore beneath her brown cape a dress of green plush with a broad hat trimmed to match. The lady has a winning and rather pretty way of putting forth revolutionary and Socialistic ideas as though they were quite the gentlest thoughts on earth. Her speech was chiefly confined to impressing on her Socialist friends the necessity for helping poor Ireland, as in so doing they would be helping their own poor selves and the cause to which they were attached. She was enthusiastically applauded for a speech delivered with perfect self-possession."

Aveling, according to the *Telegraph*,

"in fierce vein inveighed against ... 'Aristocracy and Capitalism'" – which does not seem to have been quite what the demonstration was about – "but the bugle sounding the voting time cut short the learned gentleman's peroration."[92]

This description of Eleanor's wearing of the green and her plea for "the necessity of helping poor Ireland" takes one back to her childhood and is but one example of that continuity of thought and feeling which in maturity enabled her to respond so fully and with such ease to the demands of each new situation as it arose.

The Radical Clubs were staunchly on the side of the Irish peasants. In December 1886 they had sent 16 working-class delegates to Ireland to express their solidarity and, in January 1887, they held a mass meeting on Clerkenwell Green – opposite the premises of the Patriotic Club,* one of the most militant of their units – to protest against the landowners' rack-renting and evictions.[93] Indeed, every shade of humane opinion was united on the Irish question and represented at this Hyde Park rally.

At its (third) Annual Conference, held on 29 May 1887, the SL adopted a resolution "endorsing the policy of abstention from Parliamentary action", passed by 17 to 11 votes, which diverted it from the main current of political thinking. *Justice* said that it had now become the "Anarchist League"[94] but, though this was meant as a jibe, for only a handful of

---

* Now those of the Marx Memorial Library.

members favoured anarchist tactics, the wrangle over whether to stand workers' candidates for Parliament – as against inculcating socialist principles for some undefined means of taking power in some unforeseeable future – came dangerously near to rendering the SL impotent. Neither Eleanor nor Aveling allowed their names to go forward for election to the Central Council.

Among those who had voted for the anti-parliamentary resolution was a Mrs. Gertrud Guillaume-Schack, a lady in her early forties who had been active in the middle-class and, later, in the working-class women's movement in Germany. She was strongly opposed to the introduction of State licensed and supervised brothels and very keen on what Engels designated "Free Trade in whores".[95] In 1886 her paper, *Die Staatsbürgerin*, was closed down by the police in Berlin and she was expelled. She came to London in July that year, briefly enjoying Engels' hospitality, and returned in mid-September with her close friends from America, the Wischnewetzkys ("male Russian, female Yankee".[96])

Now, in 1887, she was back and temporarily settled in London, tending more and more towards the "bogus anarchist" wing, as Engels called it, of the SL. Early in May he wrote to Bernstein in Zurich to say that, should she come to Switzerland, it would be as well not to entrust her with any responsible work as she appeared to consort with a very mixed crew: on the one hand her former middle-class Liberal acquaintances, on the other, workers with anarchist leanings. Engels had nothing against her moving in whatever circles she pleased and she was really quite a nice woman, lively and intelligent, but one had to be a little on one's guard against someone who had earned herself the sobriquet "the anarchist Countess".*

Although, at that stage, Engels rather liked her, she got on old Helene Demuth's nerves while staying at Regent's Park Road by waxing sentimental over the Avelings: how deeply in love they seemed to be; if only it could last forever, and so on and so forth.

> "'Well, what of it?' Lenchen spluttered, 'if it doesn't last then they'll just part again and that's all there is to it.' Whereupon Madam tittle-tattle was struck dumb, not having expected so practical a view from Lenchen."[97]

Out of the blue, on the day after the SL Annual Conference, Mrs. Schack wrote to Engels, one of whose regular Sunday guests she had been, saying she could no longer frequent his house – to his great relief, as it

---

* According to the German custom of assuming paternal titles, she was born Countess Schack. Her husband, who does not appear upon the scene, was a Swiss schoolmaster, James Guillaume, the editor of various Bakuninist papers and a member of the Jura section of the First International until 1878. This accounted for Mrs. Schack's circle of anarchist friends.

happened – for fear of meeting Aveling. She declined to give her reasons and, when challenged, fell back upon insinuations and hints of "discreditable acts", including the eccentric charge that Aveling was slandering, of all people, Eleanor. This turned out to be nothing more than that he was reported to have said that she was extremely jealous: of whom was not revealed. However, as Mrs. Schack had been hobnobbing with Annie Besant it does not leave too much to the imagination. "Mother Schack", as Engels called her,

> "invited me to inquire into Edward's character and antecedents generally, in which case she would assist me."

Since he ignored this invitation, she issued the awful caveat that "the credit of his house" was at stake, to which he replied that this required of those who met there "the courage to stand by what they said of one another". Amused, if slightly put out of patience by this correspondence, he reported it to Laura, adding:

> "I am happily rid of this Madame who has a foot in every camp, religious cranks, anarchists, etc. and is a thoroughgoing scandalmonger*."

He was also of the opinion that, the two gossips having got together, "Mother Besant" thought she could count upon Aveling

> "doing the virtuous hero of melodrama who is slandered right and left and rather glories in it because it belongs to the part and the eternal justice will end in bringing out the truth and show him resplendent in all the glory of his virtue..."[98]

At this time "Mother Schack" was staying with the Kautskys. Karl and his wife Louise – whom Engels pronounced "a nice little body"[99] – had come to England in February 1885 to remain until June 1888. For a while they had lived at 50 Maitland Park Villas, near to the old Marx home, but in December 1886 they agreed to share a house in the Archway Road with Andreas Scheu and his 18-year-old daughter. The Kautskys were on the friendliest terms with Engels and his immediate circle, so it was quite natural that the Avelings should call upon them. When they did so on 10 June 1887, Mrs. Schack refused to see Aveling and the three ladies retired to her bedroom where there was a royal row. Eleanor demanded to know what she had against Edward; Mrs. Schack refused to tell her; Eleanor called her vile; Mrs. Schack said no one could be allowed to insult her thus; if that was so, Eleanor retorted,

---

* *Klatschschwester* in the original letter, otherwise in English.

"you will now let me repeat it in Louise Kautsky's presence: it is vile to make such accusations and not to substantiate them."

Mrs. Schack then "bolted from the room", leaving Eleanor in possession.[100] Engels told Laura that one day when Mrs. Schack had "Mother Besant" for tea she had said that all the German socialist deputies to the Reichstag were corrupt,

"upon which Kautsky jumped up and put his fist under her nose, he was in such a rage..."*[100]

A few days after this painful incident, Mrs. Schack went back to Germany. Had she not been staying with the Kautskys "we should have shaken her off long ago," said Engels:[101] and, possibly using the unpleasantness as an excuse – for it was not an entirely happy arrangement – the Kautskys shortly moved from Scheu's house to take a flat of their own in Lady Somerset Road, Kentish Town. But Engels was pretty sure they had not heard the last of Mother Schack who, determined to play a role in the English movement, was bound to reappear.† He also wished Sorge to be fully informed about her, inasmuch as her intimacy with the Wischnewetzkys – expelled by the American Socialist Party in July 1887, to be re-admitted in April 1888 – must have had some bearing upon her attitude to Aveling. In the meantime she was blazoning abroad the great news that Aveling's wife was neither divorced nor dead and that he was living in sin with Tussy. She had also informed Mrs. Liebknecht of her rupture with Engels because of her refusal to associate with Aveling, but again withheld her reasons. Mrs. Liebknecht, one of those mild and innocent persons who so often hit the nail, apologetically, on the head, was much surprised and thought this lack of frankness very wrong.

"I should never have thought Mrs. Schack unprincipled," she wrote to Engels, "what I really believe is that she is perhaps not quite clear yet about the principles of the party."[104]

The day after the SL Conference had declared its policy, the

---

* Kautsky was later to write that Mrs. Schack was "a woman as cultivated as she was courageous, with a warm heart for all the oppressed, for women and for the proletariat." He professed to know nothing of the reasons for her falling out with Engels until long after he had left London.[102] These passages do not quite tally with Engels' contemporary account of Kautsky's fury at her slandering Bebel, Liebknecht, Singer and their fellow M.P.s; nor with the fact that his wife Louise, not one to hold her tongue, had been present at the scene between Eleanor and Mrs. Schack.
† Her desire to play a prominent part was not satisfied but she certainly came back to London and was to be seen in February 1888 rushing about at meetings in a slightly demented state, hawking copies of the anarchist paper, *Freedom*.[103]

"parliamentary" faction met in a room in Fetter Lane where it was proposed, largely upon John Mahon's initiative, to set up a committee – in effect, a splinter party – to concentrate activity mainly in the provinces. The only trouble was that any such committee – or party – would have Aveling as its chairman in London and to this objections were raised from more than one quarter. Ernest Radford, Eleanor's old friend, wrote to Mahon on 11 June to say that the "general idea as sketched is very good" and that if a new party were formed he would certainly wish to join it; but Aveling had maligned Radford in some way and "would make it crooked if he could. What he says about my having obtained, or having caused to obtain any special information from him is the merest bunkum and blather..."[105]

Then Mahon himself took exception to Aveling, on whom he called in July, writing to Engels on his return to Edinburgh:

> "...from my conversation with you ... I understand that your financial help to the provincial propaganda will only be given on the conditions that I treat Aveling with the fullest confidence, consult him on all party matters and regard him as an essential person in the movement. You insist upon a clear understanding in this matter and therefore I am compelled to say bluntly that I *do not* accept these conditions..."[106]

Engels replied that

> "of all the Socialist groups in England, what is now the 'opposition' in the League, was the only one with which so far I could thoroughly sympathize".

If Mahon's letter meant anything, it was that he intended, as far as he could, to

> "shove Aveling entirely out of the movement. If you decline to work along with Aveling on *public* grounds, you are bound to come out with them, so as either to enable Aveling to clear himself or to free the movement from a dangerous and false cooperator...'.[107]

Once more it was a case of unspoken imputations: a mistrust based on personal or political grounds which no one was willing to state openly. If Engels felt an obligation to stand up for Marx's children in all circumstances, extending this to his beloved Tussy's partner, it is no less certain that the respect in which Eleanor was held silenced many a tongue (except that of Annie Besant, but there the heart had its reasons). Nevertheless it was hard upon her that, time and time again, first this friend and then that should be lost to her; that Edward should excite such general loathing.

Both publicly and privately she always defended him. Accustomed from her earliest youth to the defamation of those she loved, this no doubt came to her quite naturally. Yet she cannot but have felt humiliated by the contrast between championing her father's principles and refuting accusations of fraudulent or shabby conduct. Nevertheless, in addition to her emotional ties, she owed allegiance to the same principles as Engels: in Aveling's calumniators she saw the enemy; the nature of the charges mattered not one whit so be it they were politically motivated. The trouble was that far too often they were not; nor were they even charges. Comrades in whom she had the greatest confidence simply declined to work with him.

Some years later, when this situation had come into the open, Eleanor was alleged by a young friend to have admitted that she knew the slurs on Aveling to be true.

> "One alternative," she is reported to have said, "is to leave Edward and live by myself. I can't do that; it would drive him to ruin and wouldn't really help me ... My father used to say that I was more like a boy than a girl. It was Edward who really brought out the feminine in me. I was irresistibly drawn to him ... Our tastes were much the same ... We agreed on Socialism. We both loved the theatre ... We could work together effectively ..."[108]

She also looked up to him as her intellectual superior, a man with a university education and honours degrees which she both envied and admired. But more than that, though this she did not say: for all his greater knowledge and all his insufferable faults, he did not exact subservience from her as his housekeeper and bedfellow but gave her encouragement and self-confidence to become a writer, a notable speaker and a brilliant organiser in her own right. Of how many clever, vain and selfish men could this be said?

Whether or not she believed – as Engels did – that he was as unpractical in money matters as a three-year-old cannot be known. The truth is that in moral terms Aveling presented something akin to an optical illusion: looked at in one light, he could be seen as feckless, happy-go-lucky but fundamentally sound; in another, as an unmitigated scoundrel. What, however, could not escape notice from any angle was his infinite propensity to borrow money, which age could not wither nor – more surprisingly – custom stale. He might be cheated – he had been cheated – by Bradlaugh, who had not only made him sign all the printer's bills but had leased the Science School premises jointly while drawing up an agreement by which Aveling alone was legally responsible for the rent, so that on resigning from the Secular Society he was loaded with debt. Yet this hardly accounts for his habit of borrowing from the rich, the poor and the positively indigent for trifling amounts – though sometimes cleaning them out – since he never at any time – and this in an age of ostentatious spenders, if not the bucks and rakes of pre-Victorian days – lived in a style above that of any other middle-class socialist who had neither business interests nor inherited wealth.

A Russian visitor to Chancery Lane spoke of "the dim gaslight of the endless staircase" which had "entirely preserved the Dickens spirit of commercial slums", describing the flat, "almost at the very top", as "grey, unattractive and thoroughly poverty-stricken."*[109] Aveling's indulgences were, indeed, paltry: cabs and drinks and the occasional dinner in a fashionable restaurant to impress a foreign guest, for all of which in any case he generally saw to it that somebody else paid.

It is not uncommon to come across individuals from whose company and a small sum of money one simultaneously parts. This compulsion to borrow is not easy to explain in those who are neither on their beam ends nor aspire to high living. Similarly, the compulsive lecher is no rare bird, though he may sometimes create awkward situations in a society called, for convenience, monogamous. It is not that such persons have taken "vows of unchastity"† and the amateur psychologist might claim that both these traits in Aveling argue a desperate need for reassurance. They also argue a great many easy touches and promiscuous women.

One curious little sidelight on Aveling's relations with Eleanor is that apparently he did not call her Tussy. For example, in the same letter to which she signs a postscript "Tussy", Aveling refers to her as "Eleanor".[111] It also emerges from an episode recounted by Aaron Rosebury, the young man in whom she confided. He had left some committee meeting with the pair and was invited by Aveling to go to a pub where, to

---

* This Russian picture of England as essentially "Dickensian" persists to this day, and is in some ways similar to the English *idée fixe* that the Russian temperament is essentially "Dostoyevskyan". It would seem that at some period the intelligentsia of each country developed a passion for these foreign authors – who died, respectively, in 1870 and 1888 – which was not only arrested but passed down as a cultural heritage.

In this particular case it may be that the visitor was misled by a preconceived notion of Dickensian London, for 65 Chancery Lane was built in 1883, that is, 13 years after Dickens' death, and had been standing for no more than a decade at the time of which she wrote. It may also be said that Eleanor herself was proud of "our new London quarters", and the up-to-date advantages of flat life, writing to Laura: "We have three large rooms, a kitchen, a smaller room, and little boxroom on one floor – and that the fourth! But really the going up and down once or twice in the day is not nearly so tiring as the constant running up and down in the usual houses and apartments. It is a good deal less trouble for me, anyhow, especially as I have given up having a servant and do my own work..."[110]

† The phrase was coined by Dame Rebecca West in the late 1920s and, it may shock the innovators of today's permissiveness to learn, was applied to the devouter members of that generation.

Eleanor's "visible distress", he asked Rosebury to lend him half-a-sovereign, promising to repay it in a week's time and adding that, if he did not, "Tussy" would. Rosebury had never heard this nickname and

> "Aveling grinned as he pronounced it – somewhat maliciously, I thought; and Eleanor herself, flushed and trying to smile, explained that it was the name her parents had used for her ... She had evidently been hurt..."[112]

Yet "Tussy" she had always been to the friends of her childhood and so she was known to a host of intimates both old and new in later life. Why not, then, to Aveling? It is a trivial point; none the less it indicates a certain alienation, a little token, as it were, that he never constituted nor replaced her family life.

The last thing Eleanor would have done was to analyse this personal relationship: she made the best of it, displaying that same "generosity and self-devotion" which the young Shelley had discerned in unions made irksome by the despotism of indissoluble ties. And she made the best of Aveling too; for there can be no question but that he played a valuable role as lecturer and populariser in the cause of Marxism while, despite the antipathy felt by so many of his fellows, he was always to be found on the correct side of the political fence.

With open-air meetings to assert the rights of free speech and a heavy programme of lectures, broken only by the United Socialist Societies of London taking their annual outing on 10 July – this time to Epping Forest and "for the benefit of the condemned comrades in Chicago" – the Avelings were kept hard at work that summer. Eleanor made her last speech to the Clerkenwell branch of the SL on "The Woman Question" on 27 July; on 4 August Aveling, whose choice of subject tended to be capricious, addressed the Bloomsbury Branch on "The Value of Brain-work".

The year 1887 was Queen Victoria's golden jubilee, celebrated on 21 June with a deal of pageantry and pomp. This world of less than 90 years ago – still within the memory, it may be, of some few of the 26,000 elementary schoolchildren entertained in Hyde Park where a Miss Florence Dunn, aged twelve, was presented with a memorial cup by the Sovereign in person – is evoked by the list of foreign guests who graced the official celebrations. There were the Kings, with their Queens, of Denmark, the Belgians, the Hellenes and Saxony; the Queen of Hawaii; the Crown Princes and Princesses of Spain, Germany, Austria-Hungary, Portugal, Sweden and Schleswig-Holstein; the Grand Dukes and Duchesses of Russia, Saxe-Weimar, Mecklenburg-Strelitz, Hesse and Leiningen; Amadeus, Duke of Aosta; the Royal, Imperial and Serene Highnesses of Prussia, Siam, Persia, Japan, Teck, Baden, Battenberg, Bavaria* and every other minor German principality; the Nawab Ali-Khan with other native chiefs from an India of which the Queen had been proclaimed Empress the year before; envoys from the Pope, the Sultan of the Ottoman Empire, the Kings of the Netherlands, Servia, Roumania, the Emperor of Brazil, the Presidents of the Republics of France, the Argentine, the United States of Mexico, Ecuador and Peru,[114] and representatives of an empire on which the sun never – or hardly ever – set.

It was also the occasion for a heady display of republicanism. Several town councils refused to pay for the local celebrations, some exceedingly rude things were printed and the Socialist League circulated a leaflet drawing attention to the real achievements of the 50-year span and its impressive technological advances to which the "mean old woman" who held sway had contributed absolutely nothing. The Metropolitan Radical Federation issued an appeal for a special "Anti-Jubilee Service" to be held on Sunday, 19 June. But it was left to Morris, in *Commonweal* of 25 June, to point the moral of what he called these vulgar royal "antics" designed to hide the commercial realities of the "respectable robbery" and "Privilege of Capital" represented by the Crown.

At last, in August, Eleanor and Aveling retired to the country for over a month. This was something new for them. They had taken a labourer's cottage in the sparsely inhabited hamlet of Dodwell – "pronounced Dad'll by the 'natives' "[115] – which, combined with neighbouring Luddington, mustered a population of 109 in 1891: an increase of five persons in a decade. It consisted of some half-dozen farmsteads set in "some of the richest soil in the kingdom ... very pleasant to the eye", as old Cobbett wrote, two miles south-west of Straford off the ancient road from Evesham to Warwick. †

Engels, with the townsman's contempt for self-inflicted rural life, referred to it as "their country house" or "castle" and, when they went

---

* Not he of the infatuation with Wagner and passion for building castles who, a year before, was not only certified as insane but had ended his life by taking a jump – and his doctor – into the Starnberger lake. In the ordinary course of events he would have been succeeded by his brother Otto, but he, alas, had been mad for years and years, so this was Ludwig's nephew, Otto's son, then Prince – not King – Ludwig. He did not come to the throne until 1913, the last of the Wittelsbachs to do so, and enjoyed but a short reign, being deposed in 1918 when the enormous family fortune was confiscated, though obligingly restored in 1923 by the Weimar Republic. This recently made news when the Wittelsbach ladies sued for their cut of an annual income estimated at £4m, published in the "Berlin Notebook" of the *German Democratic Report*, with the comment that "the Women's Liberation Movement is having repercussions in very unexpected places".[113]

† Dodwell today is much as it must have been in Eleanor's time. The tumbledown remains of cottages are to be seen; but in all likelihood the place where the Avelings lived was the small dwelling, still extant, attached to a substantial, lonely farm, then owned by a Mr. J. Wilkin.

back there in March the following year, taking the Kautskys with them, he wrote to Lafargue: "It must be nice ... in the recurrent cold and wind and snow that we are having."[116]

But Eleanor was in ecstasies, writing to Kautsky:

> "We are in a little place of three houses ... we are well and happy. ...". "Such a garden ... potatoes, lettuces, cabbages, etc. etc."[117]

To Laura she gave a fuller description of its delights.

> "Have you heard from the General of our Kastle?" she wrote.
>
> "If not – and I assume not – I must tell you how we happen to be here, in Warwickshire, the heart of England, Shakespeare's country. A few weeks ago the North Western started a cheap excursion from the Friday to Tuesday to Stratford. Ed., for one of his papers, got two 'passes'. We came down here, saw and were conquered. One day, walking from Stratford to Bidford, (one of Shakespeare's well known walks) we saw a farm – near the farm two cottages, one unlet. We inquired, found the rent was 2/- a week and ... decided to rent this lovely little place. It is two miles from Stratford and Dodwell consists of this farm and its two cottages. The farmer at first tried to explain these were only for ... labourers – he could not understand our wanting to come. You would. Downstairs we have a large kitchen – stone-flagged of course, a back kitchen and wash-house in one and a pantry. Upstairs three rooms – two, of course, very small. Besides this we have ¼ of an acre of garden ... Ed. goes out and digs up our potatoes as we need them and we have been sowing all sorts of things. Next spring our garden will be not only ornamental but useful ... Our furnishing has not cost more than two or three weeks at the sea-side would have done (and our railway journey costs nothing), and I have already two or three people to whom I am going to sub-let when we are not here. The living is very cheap, and next summer when we have all sorts of vegetables will be cheaper still. We *do* so wish you and Paul would come over some time. There's plenty of room ... I can't tell you how charming this country life is after the hurry and worry and tear of London ... Think of it Laura, Shakespeare's home! We work two or three times a week at his 'birthplace' (by permission of the Librarian of the place) and we have been over his home, and seen the old guild Chapel that stands opposite 'New Place', and the old grammar school – unchanged – whither he went 'unwillingly to school'; and his grave in Trinity Church, and Ann Hathaway's cottage, still just as it was when Master Will went a-courting, and Mary Arden's cottage at Wilmecote – the prettiest place of all. Now that I have been in this sleepy little Stratford and met the Stratfordians I know where all the Dogberries and Bottoms and Snugs come from. You'll meet them here today. Just near our 'Kastle' is a bank – many think it Titania's for it is covered with wild thyme and oxlips and violets (in the season). I never knew before how Stratfordian Shakespeare was. All the flowers are Stratford ones and Charlecote I would wager is Rosalind's Arden ... we are settled here till our lessons and other work call us back to London ... We shall, I think, be here till about September 10th. Then we get back to Chancery Lane to our teaching and usual dreary round of work..."[110]

The "dreary round" referred to hackwork at the British Museum and a particularly stupid private pupil. To her political activities, apart from committee meetings which bored her to death, Eleanor brought the utmost vivacity.

In Dodwell they did "a good deal of walking and 'lazing' (as the Yankees say)",[110] "went about in rags", dug up hundredweights of potatoes, triumphantly bringing to London for

> "Nym and the General a hamper and even the critical Nym pronounced our country eggs and ducks and chickens and butter and fruit excellent",[118]

but they also pursued the revision and expansion of the *Time* articles on America. This was to be issued in the form of a pamphlet of which they now also corrected the proofs; they planned to write a series on Shakespeare's Stratford* – their reason for working in the library there – and Eleanor translated Kielland's "wonderful short stories" from the Norwegian,[110] having now taught herself that language.

Aveling may have spent some of his time catching up with his long overdue translation of Tikhomirov's book, but he was much preoccupied by his theatrical ventures which began to look more promising. A short one-act play called *Dregs* had been accepted by "a very popular and 'rising' young actress" whom Eleanor named as Rose Norreys;† and two other plays were on the stocks,[110] one of which – an adaptation of Hawthorne's *Scarlet Letter* – was indeed to be produced by Charles Charrington in June 1888 at the Olympic Theatre, his wife, Janet Achurch,‡ taking the leading part, a performance which led Shaw to say that he would remember it "out of dozens of forgotten matinées ... as I remember the Bayreuth performance of Tristan and Isolde".[119]

Something certainly was needed to brighten their financial prospects; but it so happened that at this point Havelock Ellis, then in medical practice, was invited by the publisher Vizetelly to become the general editor of the Mermaid Series of unexpurgated plays by Elizabethan dramatists.§ He invited Eleanor to review the Marlowe and later put

> "a congenial little job in her hands ... a single play, little known but of considerable interest, *A Warning to Fair Women* ..."‖ [120]

---

* Not traced.

† She cannot have risen very high for there is no mention of her in letters between those interested in the contemporary theatre nor in standard works of reference.

‡ She was to create the great Ibsen roles, scoring a major success as the first Nora in 1889. Charrington was her second husband. In 1916 she committed suicide at the age of 52.

§ Henry Richard Vizetelly (1820–94) was later to bring out Zola's novels in English (Ellis translating *Germinal* in 1894) which involved him in two actions for obscene libel. See below p. 252.

‖ Of unknown authorship, it is thought to have been first performed in 1599 at the Curtain Theatre in Finsbury Fields, opened in 1577, which is said by some to be "the wooden O"

The Lafargues had suggested that Eleanor and Aveling should join them that summer in Jersey, but they were too contented with Dodwell. The only thing that tugged at Eleanor was that the Longuet children would be with Paul and Laura.

"It must be pleasant to have them about," she wrote with yearning and a little envy. "We have nothing but our dogs and cats (whom we brought with us) and I long to see the little ones. I haven't seen Mémé since she was a wee baby three months old.* Have you all four with you?"†

she asked and came back to the subject after Laura had written in reply.

"It must have been charming to have the children with you. I was *very* glad to hear so much about them. I often long to see them and especially Mémé. Is she like Jenny? I wish I could have one with me. A house is so different that rings with a child's laughter. But I suppose *le père* would not give me one..."[118]

She was right. For some reason Longuet kept his children estranged from their English aunt, even "correcting and amending" the rare letters her beloved Johnny wrote, so that they gave her "no pleasure",[110] though she came to regard even this as better than nothing, for she complained to Laura in November that now she never heard either of or from the children "and I do think Johnny might write now and then".[122]

That she suffered under this estrangement and her own lack of family were also made plain when she wrote affectionately at the end of the year to her old friend Dollie Radford, asking about her two babies – Maitland, born in 1884 and Hester, a newcomer – and to say that she was

"sending off a few toys to the little ones in Paris, whom I should very much like to have over here. Especially just now, Christmas without children is a mistake..."[123]

As soon as they were back in London the Avelings restarted their lectures to Radical Clubs and took part in the now massive agitation on the Irish question.

---

referred to in *Henry V*, originally produced there. The play was certainly printed – by Valentine Sims for William Aspley – in 1599 as *A Warning to Faire Woman. Containing, the most tragicall and lamentable murther of Master George Sanders of London, Merchant, nigh Shooters hill. Consented unto by his own wife, etc. (A tragedy).* It was not published again until 1878 when it appeared in Vol. 2 of Richard Simpson's *Shakespearean Scholar*.

* Presumably referring to the time of Jenny's death in January 1883 when, in fact, Mémé was four months old. She was now almost five years of age.

† Only Marcel, aged six, and Mémé went to Jersey with the Lafargues. Edgar, now eight, was with his grandmother while Johnny, having reached the ripe age of eleven, was being "coached by his father for college"[121] by which was meant, no doubt, the *lycée*.

"Everywhere large meetings are being held," Eleanor wrote, "and for the first time the English working class is supporting Ireland."

On 21 September she and Aveling had spoken

"at a splendid meeting in the East End, in supporting the Irish Home Rule movement and to condemn the Coercion policy of the government."

She also went to Engels' house "for the usual Sunday debauch".[118] These regular dinner parties, held punctually at 2.30 p.m., were not Engels' only form of hospitality: he continually invited friends to stay. Sam Moore had spent some part of his leave there that June; on the day after he left, Schorlemmer took his place, having come up from Manchester to discuss arrangements with the British Association* of whose chemistry section he was the Vice-President; while the Roshers – Pumps, her husband Percy and their surviving children, a girl of five and a boy of four – seemed to be almost perpetually at Regent's Park Road though they had their own house in Kilburn. Now, on coming back from the country, Eleanor found old Lina Schoeler in residence. She was as deaf as a post and had already stayed for ten days but remained on, wanting Tussy to "tell her all about our Mohr and Möhmchen",[118] for if anyone harked back to the old days, of which she never tired talking, it was this aged friend of the family, the discarded *fiancée* of Mrs. Marx's brother, who had known Eleanor since birth.

There were also less familiar faces at the Sunday dinner-table. August Bebel, who had spent ten months in Zwickau prison, to be released in mid-August 1887, was invited in a letter of great charm and tact to recuperate his strength in London at Engels' house and at his expense. After attending the German Party Congress in St. Gallen, Bebel arrived on 26 October to stay some ten days during which time both Paul Singer and Eduard Bernstein turned up. On 27 October Bebel went to one of the meetings of the unemployed in Trafalgar Square and told his wife that

"the police were out in full force, both on foot and mounted, but were careful not to intervene in any way".

On the Sunday morning, 30 October, the Avelings arranged a Regent's Park meeting in honour of the German socialists.[124]

Eleanor was again seeing much of Olive Schreiner, recently back from

---

* The British Association for the Advancement of Science whose first meeting took place at York on 27 September 1831 under the Presidency of its founder, Sir David Brewster. This, its 57th and most successful meeting, was held in Manchester in August 1887, with Sir Henry Roscoe in the Chair.

Paris, where she had met Laura – writing to say: "Mrs. Lafargue is like Eleanor, not half so nice, but very kind, she says Lafargue is a fine fellow"[125] – and she was now planning to rent rooms in Chancery Lane next door to the Avelings.*

The main issue engaging Eleanor's attention at this time was the reprieve of the Chicago anarchists, due to be executed on 11 November. She and Aveling jointly signed a letter to the press, headed "Chicago 1886", in the following terms:

"We are all so anxiously concerned, and so rightly, in the question of Home Rule for Ireland, that we run the risk of neglecting no less weighty matters. The decision of the Supreme Court of Illinois in the case of the Chicago Anarchists has thus far been passed by in England with an indifference only possible because of the absorption of men's minds in the burning question of Ireland. Let us remind your readers of the following facts:

In May 1886 a perfectly peaceful and orderly meeting, as orderly and peaceful as that at Mitchelstown,† was being held in Chicago. The police attempted to break it up. A bomb was thrown. Certain policemen were killed. A reign of terror broke out in Chicago.

Eight of the men arrested without warrant were tried by a jury more than one of whom had declared their minds to be made up as to the guilt of the accused; before a judge whose every word and deed during the trial was that of an advocate for the prosecution; at a time when most of the American newspapers were clammering [sic] for the blood of these men at all costs; upon evidence insufficient to convict a man of picking pockets.

The evidence of Seliger, Waller, Gillmer and McThompson the witnesses of the police, of Shea and Jansen, policemen, of Dr. Taylor and of the Mayor of Chicago, independent witnesses, not only failed to connect the accused with the throwing of the bomb, but proved positively that it could not have been thrown by any one of them.

The eight Chicago Anarchists were found guilty. Seven were sentenced to death; one to 15 years penal servitude. The Working Class of America as a whole protested against such a travesty of justice. A stay of execution was obtained in November last, as one result of the Working Class successes at the elections. The appeal for a new trial came before the Supreme Court of Illinois in March. They had given their verdict in September. It is adverse to the prisoners.

The working class of America is up in arms about this crime in the name of the law. On absolutely no evidence whatever seven men after being kept in prison and in suspense for 19 months, are to be murdered. Cannot the Working Class of England take the matter up? They have no more sympathy with Anarchism than we as Socialists have. If only every working man's club will pass resolutions protesting against this murder and send them to the Supreme Court of the United States, to the President of the United States and to the New York "Leader", their voice joined with the working men of America may yet prevent the execution of men against whom no crime has been proved.

---

* Whether she did so is uncertain, but it could not have been for long, as by mid-November she was in Alassio.
† County Cork, on 9 August 1887.

Yours faithfully,
Edward Aveling
Eleanor Marx Aveling."[126]

On 14 October a crowded meeting held at South Place Institute, addressed by Morris, Stepniak, Annie Besant and many others, unanimously passed a resolution which included the words:

"That the fate of the seven men now under sentence of death ... is of deep concern to us as English workers, because their case is the case of our comrades in Ireland today, and is likely to be ours tomorrow unless the workers from both sides of the Atlantic declare with one voice that all who interfere with the rights of Public Meeting and Free Speech act unlawfully and at their own peril..."[127]

The November issue of the *Radical* gave an account of this

"very remarkable meeting ... convened for the purpose of protesting against the death sentence passed upon the seven men known as the Chicago Anarchists..."

and *Commonweal* reported that the Radical Clubs themselves were organising similar protests.

"Edward and I managed to work the Radical Clubs into something like sympathy," wrote Eleanor to her sister, "and ... we got – on the one day – 16,405 votes for the petition we cabled over."

On 19 October the Radicals sent a second petition,

"signed by a few well known names ... One funny thing was that the very people who are always inveighing against Edward and myself had to come to us and beg our help and without us they could not get at the Clubs."[122]

Money was collected to send the cable to the Governor of Illinois, Oglesby. Some years later – in 1891 – Aveling was accused of having pocketed the money for quite other purposes: namely, to pay the printer's bill for the pamphlet he and Eleanor were writing on the Chicago anarchists. They had not, as it happens, written a pamphlet at all but an article for the November issue of *To-Day* which Reeves reprinted as a penny leaflet.

On 8 November the *Pall Mall Gazette* published a lengthy interview with Eleanor on the subject, which vexed her when it appeared.

"The published version," she wrote, "was all Stead and precious little of what I really said. However, it is so important to get things into so immensely read a paper as the Pall Mall that one can't quarrel with its queer editor."[122]

An article, "From the Prison Cell", by Albert Parsons, the condemned man who had voluntarily surrendered to the police when his equally innocent comrades were indicted, was published in *Commonweal* on 29 October and, on the day before that fixed for the execution Governor Oglesby, flooded with messages, petitions, letters and resolutions from all over the States and many parts of Europe, commuted the death sentences on Samuel Fielden and Eugene Schwab to hard labour for life, while a third man, Louis Lingg, in whose cell bombs had been planted, committed suicide or was done to death by the police. Parsons, Spies, Fischer and Engel were hanged on 11 November 1887 and have gone down to history as the Chicago Martyrs.

Some of the events leading up to Bloody Sunday – 13 November 1887 – were decidedly rum.

Not the least of these was a struggle for power in high places. It was clear that during the riots in February 1886 the police had not been on their toes. It was not, however, intended that they should tread too heavily on other people's. Yet that is what they did.

The civil exchanges between the Liberal Home Secretary, Hugh Childers, and Colonel Henderson, the Commissioner of Police, gave way to a distinctly acrimonious correspondence after Sir Charles Warren,* a staunch Freemason, stepped into Henderson's shoes on 3 April 1887 and Henry Matthews, a devout Roman Catholic, became Home Secretary† under the Salisbury administration. There was little love lost between these two.

Naturally the Metropolitan Police had been responsible for security arrangements during the Queen's jubilee, attended by so many exalted foreigners not all of whom perhaps were wildly popular with the British public or even with their own nationals who had found asylum in this country.

Sir Charles Warren had shown himself equal to the task; indeed, the police chief was decorated by the Queen; but he had tasted blood, so to speak, and, when vigilance in controlling crowds of a quite different order came within his province, he decided to assert himself.

"You ... say," he wrote to the Minister, "that the C[ommissioner] of P[olice] is in the same position in relation to S[ecretary] of S[tate] as the head of any other H[ome] O[ffice] Dept. I beg your attention to the fact that I am in no way whatever under the

---

* (1840–1927) Special Commissioner of Bechuanaland in October 1884, Warren met and came to an agreement with Kruger in January 1885 by which he established military government in February. He was recalled in August and, in January 1886, became Governor of Sudan after the defeat of the rebels at Suakin. Before he was translated to these higher spheres he had been a moderately distinguished archaeologist and an expert on ancient weights and measures. As Commissioner of Police his ferocious attitude to the unemployed led to a certain uneasiness in his subordinates and to some disaffection among the rank and file of the constabulary. When, in addition to his bad relations with the Home Secretary, unpopularity with the force, execration at public meetings followed by petitions for his dismissal, he proved helpless to solve the "Jack the Ripper" murders terrorising Whitechapel he was driven from office and resigned in November 1888.

† (1823–1913) In office until 1892.

direction of the H.O. In some matters I am directly under the authority of the S. of S. in other matters I have my duties and responsibilities defined ... by Act of Parliament just as a Constable or Magistrate or a Judge has and I know of no power by which I can be deprived of these duties and responsibilities as long as I remain Commissioner of Police and the Act continues in force ... but it is to be noted that it is impossible at any moment to say what small matter may develop into a great question, and to tell me to refer to S. of S. all matters which may be or may hereafter be of great public interest would oblige me to bring many matters before S. of S. which at present I delegate to my subordinates. Truly Yours."[128]

"I entirely concur," said the Home Secretary, delegating the matter to a subordinate, one I. Monro of the Secret Service, "as to the responsibility for Police action in London resting with you, and I should be sorry if I have said anything to make you think otherwise.

"All that I wanted is to secure the safety of informants which might be compromising if the reports went into the office.

"I shall send you the reports in a book like those sent into the H.O. The book to remain with you, and to be sent to me every Tuesday. This will save copying."[128]

To this the Commissioner replied to Mr. Monro:

"I find that the time has arrived when it is absolutely necessary that we should have some organised staff for collecting and collating information concerning the agitators' movements connected with the present riotous proceedings.

"Recently I have had little or no info. except from the newspapers.

"The S. of S. has instructed me to prosecute persons who advise the crowd to resort to violence and loot shops and terrorize and alarm the public and for this purpose we must have some more satisfactory information than from newspaper reports.

"Again it is of great consequence that we should have the antecedents of the agitators who turn up from time to time and some account of their present mode of life: so that we may have some idea of the line they may be inclined to take.

"It is also of consequence that we should have the various newspaper reports collated in such a manner as to show at short notice what is said and done at various places ... I should like to be able to get the information from someone in the office at any time, say an Inspector.

"This is work that appears part of the Duties of the C.I.D. and I shall be glad of your observations as to how you would propose to carry this out."[128]

One of the "small matters" which had become "a great question" was the conduct of the unemployed. Some of them had hit upon novel ways of drawing attention to their plight, such as holding church parades in various parts of the country, marching into places of worship to swell the congregation which they treated as a public meeting, objecting loudly and strongly whenever they did not agree with the sentiments of the speaker in the pulpit. Now if there is one thing to which the clergy are unaccustomed it is heckling and they did not take to it kindly, so that some of the parishioners landed up in the police courts.

These pilgrimages of the unemployed reached their climax on 23

October 1887, at a time when seasonal unemployment was at its worst in one of the years of deepest economic depression. Many of those who had been demonstrating in Trafalgar Square,* as had become their daily practice, made their way down Whitehall to Westminster Abbey. Despite a strong police guard on the spot with large reserves – as well as three companies of Grenadier Guards – held in readiness, some two or three hundred men managed to enter the Abbey by the north door while an equal number sneaked in through the opening at Poets' Corner. Here Canon Rowsell took them aside, counselling brotherly love, Christian fellowship and charity as altogether more desirable than shouting and creating disturbances in the streets, whereupon the rude fellows cried: "We don't want charity", but otherwise "maintained a respectful demeanour"[129] and did not interrupt the afternoon service about to begin, the verger tipping off those unversed in etiquette to remove their hats.

Sir Charles Warren, however, was not to be trifled with and on the following Saturday, 29 October, Police Orders were issued under the heading: "Indecent Behaviour – Brawling at Westminster Abbey", with instructions to "apprehend any person who misconducts himself under the Act".†[130] There were several arrests made under this Order leading to fines of £5 or imprisonment.

How the authorities thought such fines could be paid by unemployed men defeats the imagination‡ but for the single man, at least, prison was preferable to most doss-houses: at least you were not turned out first thing in the morning, which is of some comfort in an inclement season. It so happened that the weather, for the most part fine and dry, despite a good deal of fog in the middle of October, turned to snow and hail, high gales and heavy rain and was colder than average for the time of year as the month wore out.[131]

The suffering had been terrible enough the autumn before; now it was worse.

"Of the misery here in London I do not think even you ... can form a faint conception," Eleanor wrote to Laura. "To walk through the streets is heartrending. I know the

---

* Built between 1829 and 1841, the Square was designed by Charles Barry whose original more grandiose plan had been rejected as too costly. Nelson's column, by William Railton, was completed in 1849 and Landseer's quadruplet lions took up their couchant positions in 1867. Trafalgar Square was declared Crown Property by an Act of 1844 when, though far from sylvan, it was placed under the charge of the Commissioners for Woods and Forests for six years, after which it was transferred, more suitably, to the Commissioner of Works. The right to prohibit public meetings in the Square was affirmed in the House of Commons by a majority (316 to 224) in March 1888.

† Sect. 3 of 22 & 23 Vict. cap. 32.

‡ In fact, an *ad hoc* Socialist Defence Committee approached ratepayers willing to pay fines and to go bail for men taken into custody during collisions with the police.

East End well, and I know people who have lived there for years, both working men and people like Maggie Harkness,* interested in the conditions of life in the East End, and all agree that they had *never* known anything approaching the distress this year. Thousands who usually can just keep going at any rate during the first months of the winter are this year starving. Tomorrow I am going to some people in Lisson Grove (the *west* end). A father, most 'respectable' man, with 'excellent character', willing to do any work, and who is overjoyed at the prospect of earning 2/6 a week cleaning the streets for the vestry; eight children, who for days have tasted nothing but bread, and who have not even that now; the mother lying on some straw, naked, covered with a few rags, her clothes pawned days ago to buy bread. The children are little skeletons. They are all in a tiny cellar. It is pitiable but all round them people are in the same state, and in the East it is just the same. One feels almost desperate at the sight of it all ... How these starving thousands are to live through the coming months is a mystery. Is it not extraordinary that these people will lie down and die of hunger rather than join together and *take* what they need, and what there is abundance of. – Of course one of the main reasons for putting down meetings is the fear of the middle class. They know how things are, and they are in mortal dread..."[122]

As the months advanced, with extreme cold, Eleanor wrote to Dollie Radford:

---

* Under the pen-name John Law, Margaret Harkness wrote a number of novels on working-class life, including *A City Girl* (1887), *Out of Work* (1888), *In Darkest London* (1889) and *A Manchester Shirtmaker* (1890). Vizetelly, who published the first of these, sent Engels a copy at the author's request upon which he wrote to her: "...I have read it with the greatest pleasure and avidity ... What strikes me most in your tale besides its realistic truth is that it exhibits the courage of the true artist ... If I have anything to criticise it would be that perhaps after all, the tale is not quite realistic enough. Realism, to my mind, implies, besides the truth in detail the truthful reproduction of typical characters under typical circumstances ... In *The City Girl* the working class figures as a passive mass, unable to help itself and not even making an effort at striving to help itself ... All attempts to drag it out of its torpid misery come from without, from above ... it cannot appear so in 1887 to a man who for nearly 50 years has had the honour of sharing in most of the fights of the militant proletariat ... The rebellious reaction of the working class against the oppressive medium which surrounds them, their attempts – convulsive, half-conscious or conscious – at recovering their status as human beings belong to history and must therefore lay claim to a place in the domain of realism. I am far from finding fault with your not having written a point-blank socialist novel, a 'Tendenz-roman', as we Germans call it, to glorify the social and political views of the author ... The more the opinions of the author remain hidden, the better the work of art ... Let me refer to an example. Balzac whom I consider a far greater master of realism than all the Zolas *passés, présents et à venir*, in *La Comédie humaine* gives a wonderfully realistic history of French 'Society' from 1816 to 1848 ... from which ... I have learned more than from all the professional historians, economists and statisticians of the period together. Well, Balzac was politically a legitimist ... his sympathies are all with the class doomed to extinction ... And the only men of whom he always speaks with undisguised admiration are his bitterest political antagonists ... the men who at that time ... were indeed the representatives of the popular masses. That Balzac thus was compelled to go against his own class sympathies and political prejudices ... that I consider one of the greatest triumphs of Realism and one of the grandest features of old Balzac..."[132]

"...in the streets here one sees so many starving people – people with hunger in every line of their faces that one cannot but be wretched..."[123]

With the bleak prospect of the winter before them the unemployed held meetings every day in Hyde Park and, in particular, on 18, 19 and 20 October, there had been what the *Illustrated London News* called "riots and severe conflicts". These were largely brought about by the refusal of the police to allow the 2,000 or 3,000 demonstrators to march out of the park in procession at the end of their quite orderly meetings. A deputation went on Thursday, 20 October, to the Home Office to protest against the severity of the police, to ask that an Eight-Hours Bill be enacted and that the Government and local authorities provide outdoor relief and employment on public works for 10,000 men. A crowd accompanied the deputation as far as Piccadilly where it was joined by others whom "the police ... sought to disperse ... and ... sent flying".[129]

On the morning of the 23rd – the same day as that of the unusually well-attended service at the Abbey – the Patriotic Club held an open air meeting on Clerkenwell Green, addressed by both Eleanor and Aveling,

"to protest against the conduct of the police in connection with the recent gatherings of the unemployed and the violent suppression of public meetings and to demand the immediate dismissal of Sir Charles Warren and the appointment of a civilian in his place."

This resolution was taken to the Home Office on the 24th where the deputation was received by the Permanent Under-Secretary (Lushington) who behaved rather well, promising to look into the complaints. On the other hand the deputation to Scotland Yard on the following Friday (28 October) was not received at all either by the Commissioner or anyone else.

While the clashes in Hyde Park had caused some anxiety and the uproar in Piccadilly great alarm, neither was allayed when Trafalgar Square became the venue for regular daily meetings of the workless who were as regularly moved on by the police, not without violence. On 4 November Sir Charles Warren answered an indignant letter from a Dr. Duckworth:

"...I cleared Trafalgar Square on the previous occasion on my own responsibility. I quite agree that you have just cause of complaint, but the S. of S. has restricted me from clearing the Square unless the meeting is disorderly: this view of what is disorderly is not yet defined. I will forward your letter to him. I am glad to get it to support the action I would wish to take."[128]

"That locality" said the *Illustrated London News* of 29 October, "contains shops and hotels rented at high prices the owners of which must lose a great part of their custom by such occurrences frightening away their visitors at the best time of the day ... it cannot be doubted that many families from the country who would spend money in London would be deterred from coming up at the season by fear of annoyance."

It pressed home this irresistible argument with the question:

"Who would bring a party of ladies and children to a hotel at Charing Cross with the chance of their exit being blockaded all the afternoon?"

Indeed it did seem that the owners of luxury hotels and shops, no less than their patrons, might suffer most frightfully. Sir Charles Warren could not remain unmoved.

On Tuesday, 8 November 1887, an advertisement appeared in the public press and was displayed at all police stations in the Metropolitan and City police districts:

"NOTICE
Meetings in Trafalgar Square
In consequence of the disorderly scenes which have recently occurred in Trafalgar Square and of the danger to the peace of the Metropolis from Meetings held there: –
And in view to prevent such disorderly proceedings, and to preserve the public peace: –
I, Charles Warren, the Commissioner of Police of the Metropolis do hereby give notice, with the sanction of the Secretary of State and the concurrence of the Commissioner of Her Majesty's Works and Public Buildings that until further instruction, no public meetings will be allowed to assemble in Trafalgar-Square, nor will speeches be allowed to be delivered therein; and all well disposed persons are to be cautioned and requested to abstain from joining or attending such assembly; and notice is further given that all necessary measures will be adopted to prevent any such meetings and assemblage, or of the delivery of any speech and effectively to preserve the public peace, and to suppress any attempt at the disturbance thereof..."

The scene was now set; and since such coincidences are never quite irrelevant, it may be recalled that thousands of miles away across the Atlantic, it was but three days after this proclamation was issued in London that four men were wrongfully hanged to preserve the public peace.

Times without number the tale of Bloody Sunday has been told. It bears the repetition.*

---

* The description given here is derived mainly from the public prints of the day. Where these contradict each other on particular incidents or minor matters of fact – though a fully detailed account is not to the purpose – some check is provided by contemporary letters and comments by those who were present as participants or witnesses. The many accounts set down in after years are chiefly useful in proving yet again how unreliable are ancient memories.

From nine in the morning Sir Charles Warren picketed the Square with police. By eleven o'clock they were at their stations: a hundred constables in single file lined the back and front of the surrounding parapets – north, west and east – reinforced by 120 in double rank. At the head of the two flights of steps on the north side 100 were posted in columns of four. Fifty more, standing two deep, manned the south corners between which, across the open face to the street, were 750 also in fours. Mounted police patrolled the Square two abreast. In all 4,000 constables, 300 mounted police, 300 foot soldiers of the Grenadier Guards and 350 Life Guards of the Household Brigade were on duty.

The meeting – announced before the ban on Trafalgar Square – was called for four o'clock by the Metropolitan Radical Federation and the Irish National League to protest against repression in Ireland, the imprisonment of Irish M.P.s and to assert the right of free speech. It was not a cold day, but a bitter east wind blew and from midday onwards a drizzling rain fell throughout the afternoon.

At two o'clock the members of the Patriotic Club crossed the road from their premises to the open space in Clerkenwell Green where Morris, Aveling and other Socialist Leaguers spoke from a cart. Within an hour large numbers of the Irish National League, of Radicals from the East Finsbury Club and members of the Clerkenwell branch of the SDF had turned up and shortly after three o'clock a procession, including several waggonettes, was formed, estimated at some 6,000 strong, headed by two bands and a woman carrying a red flag. Other red flags tied with black crepe were borne aloft and one enormous red banner was surmounted by a cap of liberty. The column marched down Theobalds Road, along Hart Street, crossing Oxford Street and Shaftesbury Avenue, making for St. Martin's Lane by way of Seven Dials. At that point the attack came, the police charging into the midst of the procession, seizing the band instruments, tearing the flags and scattering the marchers into the adjoining streets despite a fierce resistance.

The large contingent from Rotherhithe, Bermondsey and the south-east was attacked as it approached the Strand; foot police fought them off, chasing them into Wellington Street and through Tavistock Street into Covent Garden. At four o'clock other columns from Peckham, Battersea and Deptford, some 8,000 in all, met and crossed over Westminster Bridge where, the foremost line linking arms, they rushed Parliament Square, using pokers, lengths of gas-pipe, iron bars and oyster knives to defend themselves against the horse and foot police who laid about them with their staves and truncheons. The battles raged in Bridge Street and Parliament Street; banners were snatched and their poles broken.

The marchers from Notting Hill and the west were ambushed in the

Haymarket. As they came level with the Haymarket Theatre, police poured out from the side streets on the left and right, dispersing the crowd in a matter of minutes.

All the mêlées, other than this in the Haymarket, took place at strategic points where the junction of many roads afforded the easiest means for the crowds to escape. Had they been caught in blind alleys or lanes there must have been a massacre. That was not the intention. Mayhem, yes; murder, no. Not that day.

Trafalgar Square itself was ideally suited to the purpose of the authorities, as Engels pointed out:

"easy to defend, approachable from the east only by marching in narrow file, far from working class districts, in the centre of a shopping area, with barracks a stone's throw away and St. James Park [sic] – to form up the military reserves – at three paces from the battlefield..."[133]

But if no single column managed to reach the Square in marching order, large numbers of the 20,000 scattered demonstrators formed up again in the Strand, pressing forward, pouring into Northumberland Avenue and St. Martin's Lane, to be charged again and again by mounted police.

At about the time when the meeting was supposed to have started, 400 people who had filtered into the east side of the Square, standing in front of Morley's Hotel,* crossed the road, headed by John Burns and Cunninghame Graham, a colourful figure, M.P. for North-West Lanark (1886–1892) whom Engels called "an enlightened Marxist".[134] Graham lunged out at the posse of police on the south-east corner where he was savagely cut and beaten about the head, still using his fists though almost blinded by blood, while Burns flailed his way into the Square to test, as he said, the legality of the Warren proclamation. Both men were arrested.

Fifteen minutes later 200 troopers of the first regiment of Life Guards arrived upon the scene. Riding at the side of the colonel in command was one of the Metropolitan police magistrates who, as they reached the corner opposite St. Martin's Church, faced the Square and read the Riot Act.

The troopers, by fours, with swaying plumes and dazzling uniforms, trotted slowly past the police cordons several times; then, in pairs, pranced round the square, crossing each other at points north and south in the most captivating style, as in a circus ring, to jeers and yells of derision. While these gyrations were being performed another squadron of 150 Life Guards came riding up Whitehall and thirty-five minutes later 300

---

* Where South Africa House now stands.

Grenadier Guards, from nearby St. George's barracks,* wheeled into the square with fixed bayonets, rifles and twenty rounds of ammunition.† They were drawn up in front of the National Gallery, a "thin red line", faced about, and then advanced, forcing everyone off the road into the waiting ranks of police on the parapet, smartly banging down their rifles – which weighed $8\frac{3}{4}$ lb – on the feet of those foolhardy enough to turn round; but neither bayonet nor shot was used for it was quite unnecessary.

At the same time the mounted police staged a continuous series of baton charges to clear the south of the Square and by six o'clock all resistance was at an end.

The police did not go entirely scot-free: 112 were wounded, more or less severely, in the mêlées.

Some 200 of the demonstrators were taken to hospital, 150 of them in need of surgical treatment; at least two men – John Dimmock, a young Socialist, and William Curner, a Deptford Radical – died, directly or indirectly as a result of their injuries; while a young poet, John Barlas, was said to have "had the pleasure of being batoned and floored"[135] with serious consequences; 300 were arrested; 126 summarily charged at Bow Street, of whom 27 were discharged, the remainder being sentenced to anything from a fortnight to six months' hard labour. There were appeals in 22 of these cases, but only two of the convictions were quashed. Seven men were brought before the Surrey or Middlesex Assizes early in December; none was acquitted and one was sentenced to a year's imprisonment. Two were sent for trial to the Central Criminal Court, one of them being condemned to five years' penal servitude. In all 160 people were sent to gaol.

The case against Cunninghame Graham and John Burns was adjourned. They were allowed bail until their trial at the Old Bailey on 10 January 1887, when Burns, who was defended by William Marcus Thompson,‡ spoke – vociferously – from the dock, while Graham was represented by

---

* Built in the reign of George III at the back of and adjoining the National Gallery. Robert Blatchford enlisted there in 1871.

† The Grenadier Guards – the First Foot Guards regiment – so named for their part in the defeat of the French Grenadiers of the Guard at Waterloo, carried Elcho heavy short-sword bayonets attached to breech-loading Martini rifles. Their normal equipment was seventy rounds of ball cartridges.

‡ (1857–1907). An advanced Radical who had earned the title of "the People's Attorney-General" by taking up the cases of those arrested on Black Monday and appearing as counsel for the defence in many actions against trade unions and individual socialists. Called to the bar at the early age of 23, he combined with his profession of barrister-at-law that of journalist on the *Standard* until, in 1880, he transferred to *The Radical* until it ceased publication in 1882, when he joined *Reynolds's Newspaper*, a penny weekly, for which he wrote most of the leaders under the pseudonym "Dodo", becoming its editor in 1894 until his death.

another young barrister, Henry Herbert Asquith, M.P. for East Fife from 1886 to 1918, who became Home Secretary in 1892 and Prime Minister in 1908. On 18 January both the accused were sentenced to six weeks' gaol, to be served in Pentonville, but were released on 19 February.

The Monday issue of the *Pall Mall Gazette* was devoted almost entirely to the events of Bloody Sunday. The paper had received a "mass of letters" and in one of its columns headed: "Who Were the Peace Breakers Yesterday?" they recounted "Personal Experiences of the Crowd". Under the sub-heading "A Woman's Experience" they said:

> "Karl Marx's daughter writes to us as follows:
> 'I have never seen anything like the brutality of the police, and Germans and Austrians who know what police brutality can be, have said the same to me. I need not tell you that I was in the thick of the fight at Parliament Street'" –

this indicated that when her own contingent from Clerkenwell was routed at the top of St. Martin's Lane, she had somehow made her way through back streets to the Victoria Embankment* to join the battle of those arriving over Westminster Bridge from the south –

> "'and afterwards in Northumberland Avenue. I got pretty roughly used myself. My cloak and hat (which I'll show you) are torn to shreds; I have a bad blow across the arm from a policeman's baton, and a blow on the head knocked me down – but for a sturdy old Irishman (a perfect stranger to me), whose face was streaming with blood, I must have been trampled on by the mounted police. But this is *nothing* to what I saw done to others.'"†

Engels described the condition in which she had arrived at his house:

> "...her coat in rags, her hat battered and slashed by a 'staff‡ blow. ... Edward," he added, "saved his skin, the contingent with which he found himself having hopped it at the outset..."[133]

Eleanor wrote to Laura at some length on 16 November:

> "... I daresay the General will tell you in what a condition 'tattered and torn' I reached Regent's Park on Sunday evening. You know it really is no joke to get knocked about, and knocked down by a brute of a policeman. Edward – from whom I got separated before the skirmish began – turned up later. Not so tattered but looking pretty well

---

* From Blackfriars to Westminster Bridge. Opened to the public in 1870.
† Eleanor told Laura: "...I am very much annoyed ... that Stead published a private letter of mine. Torn from its context, it is absurd, and I was very angry. But you can't argue with Stead."[122]
‡ English word in the original letter, otherwise in French.

battered and worn out. *Entre nous* the people behaved in most cowardly fashion. They fled in panic before the police. Edward was left quite alone; so was I, and only after I had shouted myself hoarse calling on the men to stand and show fight, did a few Irishmen close round. These attracted others, as you will see from the papers we on Westminster Bridge made a fair sight. But it was sickening to see the men run. As to the police, no words could express their brutality. They kicked men and women when they had fallen, delightedly tried to force people under the horses' hoofs, struck right and left with their staves. . . . The *môt d'ordre* on Sunday was *not* to arrest well known people, and till after the fighting was over, not to arrest at all. Two bobbies wanted to run me in, but the superintendent ordered them to let me off, and they wouldn't take Edward at any price. To-night there is a delegate meeting of all the clubs where they will decide what is to be done next Sunday. We shall urge going to the Square, but I fear many will funk . . . If we can induce them to go next Sunday, it will mean very warm work. Last Sunday the troops had ammunition ready and stood with fixed bayonets. Next Sunday I think it very possible they will actually fire. That would be *very* useful to the whole movement here. It would complete the work some of us have been doing this long while past, of winning over the better Radical element to Socialism. I hear that our fire-eating Anarchists here as usual are getting frightened now that there really is a little danger and that Morris on Monday declared a demonstration useless, and that the revolution won't be made till the people are armed! I did not hear this myself, but from all I know of our friend Morris I can quite believe it. He doesn't seem capable of understanding that by the time all the people are armed, there will be no need for the Revolution (– with a very big R). . ."[122]

What Morris said – at least, in print – was slightly different. In *Commonweal* of 19 November he described the attack on the Clerkenwell contingent – the capture of the band instruments, the destruction of the banners and flags –

"there was no rallying point and no possibility of rallying and all that the people . . . could do was to straggle into the Square as helpless units . . . I could see that numbers were of no avail unless led by a band of men acting in concert and each knowing his own part . . .

"Sir Charles Warren has thus given us a lesson in street fighting, the first part of which is that mere numbers without organisation or drill are useless; the second, which ought also to be noted, is the proper way to defend a position in a large town by a due system of scouts, outposts and supports . . . The mask is off now, and the real meaning of all the petty persecution of our open-air meetings is as clear as may be. No more humbug need be talked about obstruction and the convenience of the public: it is obvious that those meetings were attacked because we displeased the dominant class and were weak . . ."

Morris, it will be seen, was less scornful than Eleanor of those who had fled,* but what he read into that day's events might have been put into

---

* Not so Bernard Shaw who had been with the Clerkenwell contingent. In a letter to Morris of 22 November he said: ". . . you should have seen that high hearted host run. Running hardly expresses our collective action. We *skedaddled*. and never drew rein until we were safe on

Burke's words: "We must not attempt to fly when we can scarcely pretend to creep." That is not to say he gave up hope, but he found little to encourage it. In Eleanor's view only those who tried their wings would ever learn to fly. Revolution for her did not have "a very big R": it was a process inherent in the small act of standing your ground, asserting and extending your rights, defending your dignity as a human being in every situation and in all the circumstances of daily life. In that way, and in that way alone, would men and woman change their conditions, their circumstances and, in doing so, themselves. This is where her strength lay. Not for nothing had she mastered the lessons of the Commune, the continual defeats of the Irish Fenians, the harsh conflicts in America, leading from massacre in the streets to judicial murder. In short, while Eleanor learnt from Bloody Sunday that the working class had not yet enough experience of struggle, Morris drew the conclusion that it had not yet enough education or organisation to engage in struggle.

Certainly for many of those who took part in it Bloody Sunday was a traumatic experience, literally and psychologically.

They who in our own days have met with police violence for the first time (there is always a first time) will recognise the shock felt by the crowd on 13 November 1887. Although it was an era when the horse was a more familiar feature of the urban scene than it is now, police mounts in those days were less well – or it may be better – trained; they could and did wilfully ride down and trample upon bodies in their path.* Be that as it may, it was the naked display of State power in action that constituted the shock: the sudden realisation, possibly known in theory but not in the flesh or, as is lightly said, in your bones, that behind the civilised usages of bourgeois democracy lay brute force.

But how did the Radicals react? Were they prepared for the "very warm work" of setting Sir Charles Warren at defiance again? Engels was of the opinion that the workers' anger was so great that a fresh collision with the police was more than likely on the following Sunday,

---

Hampstead Heath or thereabouts. Tarleton" [a member of the SL] "found me paralysed with terror and brought me on to the Square, the police kindly letting me through in consideration of my genteel appearance. On the whole, I think it was the most abjectly disgraceful defeat ever suffered by a band of heroes outnumbering their foes a thousand to one."[136] Shaw's respect for facts and figures was erratic: they meant just what he chose them to mean. The "foe" is known to have numbered something under 5,000 and nobody supposes that five million Londoners were out in the streets demonstrating that day nor that formations of five, six or eight thousand determined marchers were overpowered by some half-dozen policemen.

* In a letter to *Commonweal* a year later Cunninghame Graham, an expert on such matters, described the police horses as "clumsy and badly bitted".

"... in which case." he wrote to Lafargue, "... there will be a fresh defeat ... The philistine, both bourgeois and worker, being in favour of constitutional action, one can expect the next demonstration to be too weak to attempt anything serious. And it would be a pity to see the best elements sacrifice themselves to save the honour of the cowards who draw back now..."[133]

On the same date as Engels wrote that letter, Wednesday, 16 November, a meeting was held at the Patriotic Club in Clerkenwell Green. The editor of the *Radical*,* George Standring, who was also the printer to the Fabian Society which he joined in 1893, reported it fully in the December issue of the paper, under the heading "A Fateful Meeting":

"... It would not be too much to say (metaphorically) that the eyes of Europe were turned towards the room in which delegates from all the London Radical Clubs had assembled to decide whether or no a second attempt should be made on the following Sunday to hold a demonstration in Trafalgar Square despite the prohibition issued by Sir Charles Warren and endorsed by the Home Secretary. On Sunday, Nov. 13th., as all the world knows, the Radicals of London assembled to take part in a meeting decided upon and announced several days before Warren issued his ukase against it ... The people were beaten by brutality and batons. They did not and could not hold the meeting they gallantly but fruitlessly endeavoured to hold; and Victory perched with outstretched wings upon the banners of the gallant police and lion-hearted soldiery. But the people who went home with broken heads and bruised limbs; the people who had been charged and bludgeoned by foot-police, charged and ridden down by horse-police; astonished and overawed by a display of military force – these people went home with rage in their hearts and revenge in their minds."

The writer went on to explain that the meeting, called to decide upon the course of action on the following Sunday, was composed of two delegates from every Radical and Working Men's Club in London, with representatives of the socialist organisations. After some debate, it was agreed that the press should be admitted. A resolution was then moved by Mrs. Ashton Dilke, the owner of the *Weekly Dispatch*, that a demonstration should take place in Hyde Park on 20 November.

"This ... raised the question ... Shall we again offer our heads to the bludgeons of the police; or shall we hold our demonstration in an undisputed spot, and rely upon legal action for the maintenance of the right of meeting in Trafalgar Square? The latter course was the one favoured by the M[etropolitan] R[adical] F[ederation]; the former was that preferred by the Socialist element, and also by some earnest and active members of the Federation. The discussion was protracted, the speeches on both sides brief, and of marked ability. Mrs. Besant moved an amendment to the effect that a second effort should be made to hold a meeting in Trafalgar Square ... a verbal duel took place ... The spirit throughout was admirable ... In front of the platform sat Lady Macbeth Aveling and the redoubtable Edward, D.Sc. They were, of course, in

---

* (1886–1889). Formerly (1880–1886) *The Republican*.

favour of a spirited dash at Trafalgar Square; and very fine it was to see the lofty scorn of Lady Macbeth when any speaker on the pacific side rose to address the meeting. When the resolution proposing the Hyde Park meeting was read Lady Macbeth turned to Edward, D.Sc., and hissed 'C-o-w-a-r-d-s!' between her teeth. It was very fine indeed: something of the 'Infirm of purpose! give *me* the daggers!' school of acting. The heroine of the 'corsage bouquets' looked as if she were ready to fight single-handed any number of policemen, or, at any rate, to look on whilst others fought them ... The great majority of delegates present were convinced of the utter uselessness" – Morris's word – "of a second attempt to dislodge a mass of armed and disciplined men ... They saw that Trafalgar Square could be preserved to the people without paying the penalty of cracked heads, and they were content to leave the legal question to be settled in a legal manner ... after a debate lasting two hours and a half ... the result was no longer doubtful ... Soon afterwards the meeting dispersed ... and probably every one (always excepting Lady Macbeth) was very glad that there would be no immediate repetition of the Trafalgar Square scene."

That, however, is where Standring was wrong. All that he and his supporters had done was to fulfil Engels' prediction. It seemed as though Eleanor's and Aveling's months of effort to wean the Radicals from the pure milk of constitutionalism had been in vain since the editor of their official journal could permit himself to fling that now rank and withered "bouquet" in the Avelings' face and reserve his noblest prose to deride Eleanor. It should be borne in mind that the Radicals were by no means of one stamp or class, nor was their journal the mouthpiece of them all. Indeed, the very facetiousness of Standring's article betrays the dichotomy within Radical circles and the fear that these formidable propagandists, the Avelings, were effectively winning over to socialism those with no stake in the system of private property.

The article on the "Fateful Meeting" of 16 November was to be overtaken, even before it appeared in print, by a matter more fateful.

Sir Charles Warren, with his wide experience of putting down rebellious natives, was probably under the impression that on Bloody Sunday he had saved the British Isles from red revolution since he had not the foggiest notion of the pre-conditions for such an event. He called for volunteers to enrol as special constables; not, it must be thought, because he needed any help from the citizenry but rather to put heart into those who shared his delusion.

On 18 November he issued a further proclamation to announce that the Trafalgar Square Police Regulations and Directions, "pursuant to the powers vested in me" would continue in force until further notice.[130] This, in effect, declared the Square, though a public thoroughfare, the property of the Crown and anyone setting foot in it without leave a trespasser.

On that day a remarkable meeting took place at the Memorial Hall in Farringdon Street. It was attended by Eleanor and Aveling, Morris, Stead of the *Pall Mall Gazette*, Hyndman, Sidney Webb, John Burns, a great many Radicals and a representative of the Salvation Army. It brought into being the Law and Liberty League, with J. A. Seddon as the secretary, to protect the right of free speech, of assembly in Trafalgar Square and against police violence. It also took over the functions of the earlier Socialist Defence Committee to go bail and pay police court fines. The SDF, the SL, the Fabian Society and the Metropolitan Radical Federation affiliated and it appeared that a genuinely united front organisation had been formed, though as a federated body it lasted but four months.*

The authorities intimated to the Radicals that if they held their meeting in Hyde Park there would be no interference. Accordingly a somewhat ragged procession with a strong escort of police obediently followed an agreed route, making but "a poor show", according to the *Illustrated London News*, "having failed to join in combined bodies as they did on the Sunday before."[137] It was a particularly cold and gloomy day and, although 40,000 people are estimated to have assembled in the Park, most of them were idlers who melted away when the speeches began. A resolution was passed by acclaim:

> "That this meeting regards the imprisonment of Mr. O'Brien, MP, and other Irish patriots as an act of tyranny and an insult to the people of the United Kingdom, and demands their immediate release.
>
> "That this meeting condemns the conduct of the Government in allowing the Commissioner of Police to proclaim away the hitherto undisputed right of the people to hold bona-fide meetings in Trafalgar Square, and desires to record its indignation and disgust at the wanton brutality of the police last Sunday – a brutality which has excited the surprise of the civilised world."[137]

While this meeting was going on in the Park, the 1,000 newly sworn-in special constables were patrolling Trafalgar Square. Not alone, however. The foot and mounted police were out in force again; for, despite good resolutions taken by others, a very large crowd had gathered to challenge the validity of the Warren proclamation. It was ceaselessly

---

* What happened was that in March 1888, the Executive of the MRF passed a formal resolution denying its affiliation to the LLL or any other body. The League formed independent "circles" of members on a constituency basis. There were 20 of these in London by the end of March 1888, while one in Manchester and one in Edinburgh were formed in the following month. These circles were composed of 240 people in 20 groups of twelve members. The secretaries included Morris's son-in-law, Sparling, in Holborn; Mrs. Wardle, Eleanor's SL colleague, in St. Pancras; her son – "Machine" – in East Marylebone; Graham Wallas in Chelsea and various members of the Patriotic Club, the Liberal Club and the Fabian Society in other boroughs, not as representatives of their own organisations but as individual members of their circle. A delegate meeting of the circles was held at the premises of the Patriotic Club on 12 May 1888.

charged and batoned. One eye-witness, the Secretary of the Bow Branch of
the Amalgamated Society of Carpenters and Joiners, wrote that he saw

> "the patrols make wild charges on the people, both in the road and on the pavement. I
> thought they were trying to imitate the heroes of Balaclava, six mounted police
> rushing backwards and forwards to and from Trafalgar-square to a line of foot police
> drawn across the bottom of [Northumberland] Avenue ... people were being knocked
> about recklessly, and those that ran in front or were compelled to run in front ... were
> met by this line of policemen ... (who) struck out right and left and hit the people
> wickedly. I saw one knocked down insensible from a full butt punch in the face ... I
> assisted him into a cab. I wanted to go to the hospital with him, but was prevented by
> the preservers of order, saying at the same time, ' 'Tis a pity it hasn't killed the b –.' ...
> I was politely told, 'You'll damned soon get served the same if you are not off' ... I was
> set upon by half-a-dozen police ... I swear that this is the plain unvarnished truth. W.
> Green. 17, Fairfield Row, Bow.
>   P.S. I ought to add that these wild charges were enthusiastically applauded by the
> occupants of the verandahs of one of the hotels."

This letter was written to the sister of a 41-year-old Law-writer named
Alfred Linnell who had strolled up Northumberland Avenue that afternoon to see what was going on in the Square. He was caught up in the
press of people, fell and

> "in a moment the cavalry were upon him, and the charger of one of the constables
> trampled him as he lay, smashing his thigh bone beneath the horse's hoof. Then they
> rode on, leaving Linnell writhing on the ground ... no attempt was made to succour
> the poor wretch whom they had done to death at the base of Charles Stuart's
> statue..."*[138]

Alfred Linnell was simply a man in the street of no political affiliation.
In all probability he would not have been wandering about the town on
that cold and foggy Sunday afternoon but that he had nothing better to
do. He was a lonely, rather unhappy fellow, earning a poor salary in a far
from secure job since he was said to be given to bouts of intemperance. He
was a widower who, on the death of his wife, had sent his three children –

---

* That was a figure of speech, for the equestrian statue of Charles I on its Grinling Gibbons
pedestal – the one wholly admirable piece of sculpture in the centre of London among all the
rubbish – stands now, at the top and slightly to the west of Whitehall, where it has always
stood since it was first erected in 1675 (cast by Hubert Le Sueur in 1633 but rather a lot of
things had happened in between). It was and is on the spot where the 13th and last of Edward
I's "Eleanor" crosses had been set up in 1291: "Charing Cross", removed in 1647, of which a
reminder, not a replica but a Gothic cross, was placed in the station yard two centuries later.
Charles I never was and could not have been where the incident occurred in Northumberland
Avenue, a relatively new thoroughfare completed two years after the demolition of Northumberland House in 1874, upon the site of which the Grand Hotel, on the south-east corner of
the Square, was built and formally opened by the Lord Mayor in 1880.

two girls and a boy – to live with relatives. They, having too large a family of their own to accept the responsibility, placed the young Linnells in the workhouse school at Mitcham.*

Now Linnell lay on the ground in fearful pain, his thigh-bone pro-truding through the skin, until some of the bystanders lifted him as gently as possible and carried him to Charing Cross hospital. There, owing to a tangle of misunderstandings, his nearest kin did not trace him for a week, during which time the fracture was set, but unsatisfactorily, and he had to undergo an operation for part of the femur to be removed. When finally his sister, who lived nearby, came to visit him, he was in agony and despair. She saw him for the last time on Wednesday, 30 November.

On that day the Home Office wrote to the Commissioner of Police

"desiring a consecutive statement of the occurrences in Trafalgar Square ... which led to the successive Orders issued by the Come. and copies of the most important reports.† S. of S. is anxious to learn that this has been put in hand".[128]

Linnell died at four o'clock on the afternoon of Friday, 2 December. Neither his children nor any other members of his family – two sisters, a brother-in-law, three nieces and a nephew – were notified. Further con-fusion followed. Seddon, the secretary of the newly formed Law and Liberty League, swore on oath at the inquest that the house surgeon at Charing Cross Hospital, one Smith, had told him that the dead man had been trampled upon by a police horse. Smith, equally on oath, denied it in court stating that there had been no bruises on the body.

The Law and Liberty League had made arrangements two days after the death to give Linnell a public funeral on 11 December. This had now to be postponed since the coroner, faced with the conflicting evidence, ordered a fresh *post mortem* examination and adjourned the case for a week. At the resumed inquest the jury – having heard, on the one hand, medical evidence that the body showed severe bruising and, on the other, police witnesses swear that they had seen nobody ridden down in Trafalgar Square that day – returned an open verdict. The body was then handed over for burial and arrangements were made for the funeral to take place on Sunday, 18 December.

But on these arrangements the Commissioner had the last word. The hearse was to have set off from the spot where Linnell had fallen at the top

---

* There are some discrepancies in accounts of the number, the ages and the fate of the children. However, all are agreed that at the time of their father's death one girl aged ten was under the care of the Mitcham Guardians while an older boy was in Harwich.

† These Orders and reports are not on the files for 1887 at the PRO, nor is the reply to the Home Secretary's request.

of Northumberland Avenue. On Friday, 16 December, after the route had been published, bills printed and circulars distributed, Sir Charles Warren – the Dictator, as the *Pall Mall Gazette* now called him – issued a new decree forbidding the hearse, the mourning coaches or any part of the funeral procession to enter Trafalgar Square or its adjacent streets.

"The Square is a place where the police may kill a man with impunity. It is no longer a place from which we may bury our dead," wrote the Law and Liberty League.[138]

Sir Charles would not even " 'stand back and let the coffin pass'."[139]

The body had lain at the undertaker, Dawes, in Lexington Street, Golden Square, from where at one o'clock the relatives of the dead man and the committee of the Law and Liberty League escorted the funeral carriage, drawn by four horses, to the assembly point in Great Windmill Street. An enormous throng had gathered and the procession, headed by a scarlet banner borne aloft, with a brass band playing Handel's *Dead March* from *Saul* wound its way through Coventry Street and Cranbourne Street making for Garrick Street, only to find the road cordoned off by police who diverted it into Long Acre and through Bow Street, Covent Garden, into the Strand. Here a multitude from south London fell in carrying banners and then the march proceeded eastwards, through Fleet Street, Cheapside, Cornhill, Aldgate, Whitechapel Road, Mile End Road and Bow Road to the City of London and Tower Hamlets cemetery.[*]

In death Alfred Linnell emerged from obscurity. A vast concourse of people followed the open hearse from whose roof the red flag of the socialists, the green flag of the Irish and the red-yellow-green flag of the Radicals fluttered above a shield bearing his name and the words: "Killed in Trafalgar Square". The coffin itself, black draped with a red pall, carried a brass plate with the inscription:

"Alfred Linnell, aged forty-one. Died December 2 of injuries inflicted by the police in Trafalgar Square, November 20, 1887."

Morris walked on one side of the hearse, Stead on the other. The pall-bearers included Cunninghame Graham, John Burns, Annie Besant, Seddon of the Law and Liberty League, and Tims of the Metropolitan Radical Federation.[†] At a quarter to three the cortège reached St. Paul's Cathedral where groups of people had assembled both at the west and the

---

[*] In Southern Grove, E3, and locally known as "Bow cemetery", its 33 acres first used in 1841. Over 240,000 bodies had been interred there by 1887, many of them in common graves.
[†] Hyndman watched the procession from a front seat on the upper deck of a tram.

east side to bare their heads as the coffin passed. With the crowd continually swelling

> "the throng became so vast as to defy computation ... by the immensity of its numbers,"

wrote the *Pall Mall Gazette* on the following day. Some journalists estimated that altogether 120,000 people took part in the procession, which, had it been an orderly column, would have stretched further than the distance of the whole route; but in fact it was joined at various points – first at Cranbourne Street, where the choir's brake fell in, then, in turn, at Wellington Street, Fetter Lane, Ludgate Circus, the Mansion House, throughout the City and at every quarter mile east of Aldgate – by more and more onlookers who attached themselves loosely to the march. A friend walking behind Morris told his daughter May that he had not seen such a public funeral since that of the Iron Duke in 1852. Other impressive occasions were recalled – the Chartist funerals of 1848, Victor Hugo's interment in 1884 – by those who had witnessed them but none, it was said, could compare with this massive parade of anonymous Londoners.

It was "very fine," wrote Eleanor, who had been in one of the wagons in the cortège.

> "... The streets were a wonderful sight especially as we neared the East End. There was one very curious scene – we saw it because the horses of our dray had fallen, and we were rather behind. In the Mile End Road (right out East) a large number of people stood ready to fall in behind the procession, when some omnibuses tried to drive through and break up the procession. They were called on to desist, but one man lashed his horses to a gallop, while a passenger outside had a long stick and lashed and struck out at the people. Then one man threw himself in front of the horses, clung to them and actually stopped them. In one second the traces had been cut, the passengers taken down, and the beast who had lashed the people thrown down in fine style. He was howling to be 'let alone'. He will think twice another time before he strikes the people. Then, the 'bus turned out of the procession, the people quietly fell in and marched on in order as if nothing had happened. It really was fine to see. If only the Radicals were not so many of them cowards, we could carry the Square. As it is they are all 'funking' more or less."[140]

The day had started clear, even mild for the season but now clouds gathered and the small rain came down, growing heavier. When at the end of the long and solemn journey the main gates of the cemetery were found closed and guarded by 100 policemen, many, wet, chilled and discouraged, drifted off home. It was none the less an enormous press of people that was forced through a narrow turning to a side entrance. At five o'clock in the darkness of the short December afternoon, under a steady downpour, the Rev. Stewart Headlam read the burial service. Then Morris spoke at the graveside for the Socialist League, Quelch for the Social-Democratic Federation, Tims for the Metropolitan Radical Federation and Dowling as the London organiser of the Irish National League. By matchlight, under umbrellas, the choir now sang *A Death Song*, written by Morris and set to music by Malcolm Lawson, copies of which had been sold all along the route, and that dense crowd, drenched and black against the blackness of the graveyard took up the refrain.

An eight-page penny pamphlet, with a cover design by Walter Crane, was sold for the benefit of Linnell's orphans. It published the story of the hapless man with the words and music of his requiem:

> *What cometh here from west to east a-wending?*
> *And who are these, the marchers stern and slow?*
> *We bear the message that the rich are sending*
> *Aback to those who bade them wake and know.*
> *Not one, not one, nor thousands must they slay,*
> *But one and all if they would dusk the day.*
>
> *We asked them for a life of toilsome earning,*
> *They bade us bide their leisure for our bread,*
> *We craved to speak to tell our woeful learning,*
> *We come back speechless, bearing back our dead.*
> *Not one, not one, nor thousands must they slay,*
> *But one and all if they would dusk the day.*
>
> *They will not learn; they have no ears to hearken.*
> *They turn their faces from the eyes of fate;*
> *Their gay-lit halls shut out the skies that darken.*
> *But, lo! this dead man knocking at the gate.*
> *Not one, not one, nor thousands must they slay,*
> *But one and all if they would dusk the day.*
>
> *Here lies the sign that we shall break our prison;*
> *Amidst the storm he won a prisoner's rest;*
> *But in the cloudy dawn the sun arisen*
> *Brings us our day of work to win the best.*
> *Not one, not one, nor thousands must they slay,*
> *But one and all if they would dusk the day.*

While 1888 saw the final split within the Socialist League and the exclusion of their own branch, which became the Bloomsbury Socialist Society, the Avelings were increasingly occupied with their literary work during that year.

Much of the time, on and off from early spring until after midsummer, they spent at the Dodwell cottage. This was made possible partly because, although Eleanor went on with

"teaching, literary hackwork ... and ... also still sweating for Miss Zimmerman",[141]

four of the "Anglo-Indian" pupils the Avelings were coaching had elected to come and live at Shottery, less than two miles from Dodwell, to continue their lessons. Eleanor's means of earning her daily bread had always been humble and tedious, but by now she had shown herself worthy of more interesting assignments. It was here, in the country, that she translated her first Ibsen play, *An Enemy of Society* as it was called at the time,* for which she received £5. She finished the work at the end of June and it was published in August 1888 with, as well as an *Introduction*, a foreword by Ellis:

"Of the three dramas presented to the reader in this volume, two have not previously been translated into English; a translation of the third has only appeared in a magazine. Mr. William Archer has presented to us the translation of 'The Pillars of Society'† ... which he has revised for this volume. ... To Mr. Archer also we are indebted for a most careful revision of 'Ghosts'. The translation is to some extent founded on that of Miss Lord ... which appeared in *To-Day* a few years ago ... To Mrs. Eleanor Marx is owing

---

* In a footnote Eleanor explained: "For the title of this play – *En Folkefiende* literally 'a folk enemy' or 'an enemy of the people' – no exact idiomatic equivalent can be found in English. 'An Enemy of Society' has seemed the most satisfactory rendering available."[142] In Archer's revised version of her translation, published in 1890, it was given the title by which it has ever since been known: *An Enemy of the People*. Under this name the Heinemann "William Archer Edition" of Ibsen's plays continued to publish it until 1952, attributing the translation to Eleanor Marx Aveling.

† Archer's earlier version had been given a single performance at the Gaiety Theatre at the end of 1880: the first Ibsen play ever to be produced on the English stage.

the skilful version of 'An Enemy of Society', perhaps the most difficult of Ibsen's social dramas to translate."[143]

The three plays chosen were

"a very unwise selection for a *first* volume in English it seems to me",

Eleanor wrote to Laura when sending her a copy of the book.* She also complained:

"Unfortunately I did not see the proofs ... and had no opportunity of revising..."[145]

Whether she would have made a better job of it had she revised the proofs is questionable: the language was naturally and perfectly of the period – which cannot be said of all the excellent modern versions – but it was too literary, not "of the theatre", and many of the lines would have been awkward if not impossible to deliver on the stage. This is no doubt what Shaw meant when he pronounced the translation "not a success", while praising and even recommending an actress to use Eleanor's version of *The Lady from the Sea*,†[146] published by T. Fisher Unwin as a separate graceful little volume in 1890 with an introduction by Edmund Gosse. Between tackling these two Ibsen plays, Eleanor had learnt something about the drama, though of a very different period.

Before this, however, she and Aveling wrote the first of two speeches to be made to the Shelley Society, of which they were members from 1885‡ when it was first founded by Furnivall for whom she had done endless hackwork in the past. He, too, now recognised that she was capable of better things. The first lecture was published in *To-Day* under the title "Shelley and Socialism",[149] later issued as a pamphlet, presumably by the Shelley Society, in 25 copies, bearing both Eleanor's and Aveling's names and the title *Shelley's Socialism*.

Though never printed, the second lecture may yet have been delivered. This conjecture is supported by the fact that Harry Buxton Forman – whose four-volume edition of Shelley's poetry Reeves and Turner brought out in 1876–77, followed by a two-volume unannotated edition in 1882

---

* To Ellis, congratulating him on the *Introduction*, she wrote more explicitly: "But I am sorry 'Nora' was not included in the volume. It should have been, I think, in any *first* volume of Ibsen."[144]
† The title-page states: "Translated, with the Author's Permission, by Eleanor Marx-Aveling."
‡ "There was sad trouble ... when Dr. Aveling applied for membership, for the majority decided to refuse it – his marriage relations being similar to Shelley's – and it was only by the determined action of the Chairman, Mr. W. M. Rosetti, who threatened to resign ... that the difficulty was surmounted," wrote Henry Salt[147] who thereupon proposed that the name be changed to the "Respectable Society".[148]

– had compiled a Shelley bibliography "of which the Shelley Society printed the first part – volume one – in 1886 ... Volume two, which was to have contained collected editions, was apparently never published."[150] Engels translated it into German and it appeared at the end of the year in *Die Neue Zeit*.[151]

In 1879 Aveling had given a lecture on Shelley to the Secular Society,* described by Annie Besant as a "simple, loving, and personal account of the life and poetry of the hero of the freethinkers".[152] Eleanor could cite earlier examples of Shelley's popularity in progressive circles and is reported to have said:

> "I have heard my father and Engels again and again speak of this; and I have heard the same from many Chartists it has been my good fortune to know as a child and a young girl – Ernest Jones, Richard Moore, the Watsons, George Julian Harney and others. Only a few months ago, I heard Harney and Engels talking of the Chartist times, and of the Byron and especially Shelley-worship of the Chartists; and on Sunday last Engels said: 'Oh, we all knew Shelley by heart then'."[153]

There can be no doubt that this lecture, though delivered by Aveling, was a true collaboration between two people who had long and devotedly studied the poet with equal enthusiasm, Aveling primarily as an atheist, Eleanor as a revolutionary, though no one at that time had read Shelley's most telling political work, *A Philosophical View of Reform*, for, written exactly a hundred years before, it was not published until 1920.

It was towards the end of the year 1888 that Eleanor set about editing the Elizabethan play – *A Warning to Fair Women* – promised her by Havelock Ellis for his Mermaid series. It was this, which she found enthralling, that taught her to think in terms of theatre. She wrote to Ellis begging him to ask the publisher, Vizetelly, whether he would pay her return fare – ten shillings – to Oxford

> "in order to look up the original there ... I fancy certain passages that seem corruptions may be simply due to the transcriber's mistakes. I would gladly go on my own account but really can't afford it. Of course, the text if compared with the original would be far more valuable..."[154]

The fare was paid, she went to Oxford and then reported to Ellis:

> "...I am dividing the *Warning* into five Acts. Not only is this more consistent with the Elizabethan manner, but the play really so divides itself ... Of course, I give the locality of the Scenes. Why. The *social* interest is the only real one in these plays. And happily the text (in well nigh every case) identifies the scene. Might I suggest that Norden's map (1593) should be printed along with the play? ... It makes it all so

---

* *Modern Thought* published it in 1880.

much more interesting and amusing. I suppose you issue the 'murder plays' in the same volume. If you have not yet disposed of them could you give me another? I have become much more interested in the subject *as a whole*. I used to know the individual plays well enough. I don't think I before realised their value as 'documents': they are, for the most part, so poor as plays..."[154]

As Vizetelly was shortly to be prosecuted for publishing Zola in English, whereby he was not only ruined but the Mermaid Series was taken over by T. Fisher Unwin and out of Ellis's hands, nothing further came of this; it is almost certain that Eleanor's text was never published.*

However, Eleanor was now definitely enrolled in the "other ranks" of literature. At the same time Aveling was at last enjoying a minor success in the theatre that augured a bright future. Towards the end of 1887 one of his adaptations from the French had been performed at the Ladbroke Hall and, although an amateur production, earned a notice in the *Dramatic Review*. The critic spoke well of the play, *By the Sea*,† but was more than disobliging about the players.

"Miss Eleanor Marx," he observed, "... is said to be a pupil of Mr. Hermann Vezin, and it must be admitted that some of her elocution was worthy of her distinguished tutor. But small though the theatre was, she was frequently inaudible, even close to the stage, and never for a moment seemed to understand that she ought to be heard by anybody more than a few feet off. Some of her lines were prettily spoken," the critic conceded, but he did not think she had risen to the height required of the part.‡[155]

"Alec Nelson's" acting was dismissed as too inferior to his clever adaptation for "the two efforts to be compared". On the other hand, in his third role, that of stage manager of a farce put on by the Welbeck Amateurs at the same hall, he was highly commended for the "cleanness and smoothness" of a well-rehearsed production.[155]

---

* No such publication exists either in the British Museum or the London Library. However, there is a copy of the play, *A Warning to Fair Women*, edited by A. F. Hopkinson, published in 1893 and again in 1904 by E. M. Sims and Co. of Delancey Street, Camden Town, "For Private Circulation". The *Introduction* to the 1904 edition states that the play "was entered on the Stationers' register Nov. 17, 1599 ... nor was there another edition issued until 1878, when Mr. R. Simpson published a verbatim reprint of the old quarto ... Mr. Simpson did not divide the play into acts or scenes ... *In 1893 I made an 8vo. reprint of the play, and divided it into acts and scenes, and also marked the location of the latter* ..." (My itals. YK) This is precisely what Eleanor had done five years earlier.

† From the novel *Jean-Marie* by André Theuriet (1833–1907) who, though he became a member of the Académie Française in 1897, left no deathless works.

‡ Vezin immediately wrote a letter of repudiation to the paper: "Please contradict the report that Miss Eleanor Marx is or ever has been a pupil of mine. I have never had a pupil of that name..."[156] He did not say that his wife had.

It will be seen that Aveling was thus working his way to become an all-round man of the theatre with prospects of graduating from the amateur *via* the provincial to the West End stage.

As the year 1887 came to an end Eleanor wrote to Dollie Radford, to whom she still felt very close, thanking her for a Christmas greeting.

> "It is pleasant to know you have thought of me," she said, "it is *so* hard to give up old friends. And you are a very old friend, Dollie, one of the few who knew my Father and Mother well and therefore doubly dear to me."

On that day, 28 December, Edward had left for Torquay, she told Dollie, where he would stay until after the New Year,

> "to superintend the production of a little play of his":

an actor manager named Outram having taken the theatre there for six months.*[157]

On 3 April 1888 Eleanor wrote to John Burns to remind him of the three "Entertainments" to be given for the benefit of the Law and Liberty League during that month and asking him to follow up his suggestions for press publicity.[158] Aveling went further: he insisted that Burns should act in one of his pieces, to be produced at the Athenaeum Hall on 18 April.

> "...It is only ¼ of an hour part and about 4 short speeches," he told Burns. "You'll learn the part in ½ an hour and you must give about ½ an hour a day from Wed^y. to Wed^y. to rehearse it. Can you? Tis a strong character part..."†[159]

For these functions the Avelings came up to London "bringing eggs, butter, pork pie, sausages from the truly rural retreat" for Engels[160] who took a lively interest and even some pride in Aveling's new career.

> "Of Edward's remarkable *preliminary* successes in the dramatic line you will have heard," he wrote to Laura. "He has sold about half a dozen or more pieces which he had quietly manufactured; some have been played in the provinces with success, some he has brought out here himself with Tussy at small entertainments, and they have taken

---

* Outram had acted with Vezin in Shelley's *The Cenci* on 7 May 1886: a private performance given under the auspices of the Shelley Society at the Grand Theatre, Islington.

The theatre in Torquay had been opened in 1880. It was customary at the time for provincial theatres to put on a main play and an "afterpiece", producing each item in the repertory two or three times in the season.

† This function yielded a profit of £5.5s. 8d. which sum, together with a detailed account of expenditure and takings, Aveling presented to the Law and Liberty League.

very much with the people that are most interested in them, viz. with such actors and impresarios as will bring them out. If he has now one marked success in London, he is a made man in this line and will soon be out of all difficulties. And I don't see why he should not, he seems to have a remarkable knack of giving London what London requires...[161]

Engels was not much interested in the plays themselves but he hoped and believed that they would release Aveling from the drudgery of journalism.

The one "marked success", of course, was the matinée performance on 5 June of *The Scarlet Letter* which, Eleanor told Laura, was to go into the evening bill at the Olympic Theatre in the following season.[162] At the end of that month she came up to London, staying with Engels, to see a one-act play at the Strand Theatre both written and produced by Aveling. He seemed, indeed, to be in a fair way to success and worked at it consistently.

"Ed. has just gone out on a long walk to finish a little comedy he is to have (? performed*) next Saturday," wrote Eleanor on 24 June. "That's the fourth play in as many months! It's awful..."[162]

Engels, too, was elated by these mounting triumphs. This fourth play was produced on 30 June, a fifth and sixth were probably to be given the week after and:

"no mistake about it," he wrote to Lafargue, "in dedicating himself to the drama 'he has struck oil'† as the Yankees say."[163]

Aveling himself added one of his rare postscripts to a letter from Eleanor to Laura, saying:

"I've been very lucky to get rid of five plays certain and three may be."[164]

In July he was

"again brought to London by his dramatic industry," Engels reported. "He is going to read two plays to-day to speculative actors (Alma Murray is one) ‡ who intend to invest in a bit of novelty."[165]

---

* Word illegible.

† English phrase in the original letter, otherwise in French.

‡ Alma Murray (1854–1945), married to Alfred Forman – the translator of the libretti of Wagner's *Ring, Parsifal* and *Tristan and Isolde* – had played Beatrice opposite Vezin's Cenci in the 1886 performance and was a noted actress of the day, though in a long and successful career she rarely played leading parts.

What was more, he had been invited to produce a few of his plays in America and was to go there in August.

Some of his pieces were written in collaboration with more talented authors. At the end of July Eleanor wrote to Stepniak, more or less in the capacity of Aveling's literary agent and, one suspects, at his dictation:

"Since Edward saw you he has seen Alma Murray ... who is looked upon as one of the best – and certainly is one of the best of our actresses. She is about to open a theatre and has not yet decided on her first piece, but she is willing if you and Edward can give her a sketch of a Russian drama of which she approves to pay you down £10 per act on commission (i.e. £50 for a 5 act play). This payment to secure her the right of the piece for 3 years and to cover the first twenty performances. After the first twenty, you to receive (i.e. you and Edward) 10/- per act, £23. 10s. for a 5 act play, per performance. Miss Murray to have the option within one week after the first performance of buying the play right out at £100 per act. From this sum the original £10 per act to be deducted ... It is very important and if you can hit on a good story there is money to be made and good work to be done..."[166]

and a few days later:

"Edward has seen Miss Murray and says that you *must* let her have a sketch of the play (even if still rough and unfinished) on Tuesday morning, and you *must* send him a copy at the same time. He needs this copy because Miss Murray, if she accepts it, will telegraph to Queenstown, and Edward wants to think about the play during our journey..."

adding in a postscript:

"Have you promised any English author to collaborate in any form on another play? We should like to know this because Miss Murray told Edward today that there were rumours about your wanting to help another playwright. This would damage our chances of a bigger success in our joint work. To ensure this success there should not be even a shadow of any connection on your part with anyone but Miss Murray and Edward..."[167]

In the late autumn Eleanor wrote to say that Edward was to meet the Formans (Alma Murray and her husband) during the next week "and then I hope the fate of the play will be decided".[168] There was some difficulty, it appeared, about a shocking young girl in the play who was not seduced but the seducer. Whether, indeed, any such five-act "Russian drama" ever saw the footlights is not known, but one thing is quite certain: the tone of these letters – and in particular that postscript warning Stepniak that he must not dare to work with anyone but Aveling – is not Eleanor's. Nevertheless, that she pinned one of her most cherished hopes on

Aveling's thriving new industry is made clear in a passage she wrote to
Laura as she embarked once again for America:

"If only Edward goes well with his plays," she said, "we want to try and have Johnny
with us for good..."[169]

They were off, as Engels explained, for Aveling

"to superintend the *mise en scène* of three of his pieces to be played simultaneously in N.
York, Chicago and God knows where besides. If his dramatic success goes on at this
rate, maybe he will have to go next year to Australia at the expense of some theatrical
impresario."[170]

"Alec Nelson" undoubtedly made some money out of these ventures,
but no mark upon the English drama. Had not his little one-act plays and
adaptations of other writers' work been given as benefit performances for
the movement, transforming so many well-known socialists into enter-
tainers, it is doubtful whether any but students of the most recondite
theatrical history would ever come upon his name. He was "one of the
many who have made themselves *public* without making themselves
known".

In that year of 1888 Macmillan published not the first but the most
successful novel by a writer named Amy Levy, then 27 years of age. This is
the only book, not a long one, that Eleanor is known to have translated
not into but out of her native tongue. She must have done so immediately
upon its publication, for her German version appeared in 1889. Later that
year, at the very moment when she had begun to make a name for herself,
Amy Levy committed suicide, having corrected the proofs of her last book
a week before she died.*

This young woman had been a very close friend of Olive Schreiner's,
with whom she had gone to the seaside at the end of August 1889.[171]
There may be no connection between the facts, but it so happens that
Olive Schreiner left England for South Africa a few weeks later,† by which
time Amy Levy was dead.

On 1 April 1892 the *Pall Mall Gazette* published the following paragraph:

"Not many years ago two literary ladies – one of whom is widely famous – were
spending a holiday at the seaside together, and both were indulging in very gloomy
views of life. After discussing the question, they both agreed to commit suicide and the

---

* Her little book of verse, *A London Plane-Tree*, was published posthumously in the T. Fisher
Unwin Cameo Series edition in which Eleanor's *Lady from the Sea* appeared.
† On 9 October 1889.

younger hurried home and but too effectively carried out her purpose. The other happily thought better of the matter, and refused to fulfil her terms of the contract. The only pity is that she did not let the other party to the agreement know in time."

Upon reading this in Matjiesfontein (Cape Province), Olive wrote rather disingenuously to Ellis on 23 April:

"A funny idea has struck me about the enclosed cutting, that perhaps *I* am meant! So many lies have been told about me already that now I wonder at nothing ... What makes it likely that I am meant is that it is exactly *opposite* to the truth; I was always trying to cheer up Amy Levy (if it be intended for her) and professing that *I* found life so delightful and worth living. I've often felt since that, if I'd been more sympathetic to her melancholy mood, I might have done more for her. In her last note to me she said 'You care for science and art and helping your fellow-men, therefore life is worth living for you: to me it is worth nothing', and the last thing I sent her was Edward Carpenter's 'Do not hurry, have faith', which she sent back to me the night before her death with the words, 'It might have helped me once; it is too late now; philosophy cannot help me'..."[171]

Max Beer, a German socialist, read Eleanor's translation of Amy Levy's *Reuben Sachs* while he was in prison from 1892 to '94 and was enormously impressed by it. On his release he emigrated to London where he resolved to call as soon as possible upon Eleanor to learn something more about the author.[172] Eleanor told him that Amy had been of a melancholic disposition and they discussed her book at some length, for it seems to have meant much to both of them. Indeed, there must have been stronger reasons than personal friendship with the tragic young Amy Levy for Eleanor to take the unusual step of writing in a foreign language – she was never particularly proud of her German – but, while the novel deals entirely with upper-middle-class Anglo-Jewry, it contains certain passages which provide a significant motive.

"Ah, look at us," cries one of the characters, "where else do you see such eagerness to take advantage; such sickening, hideous greed; such cruel, remorseless striving for power and importance; such ever-active, ever-hungry vanity, that must be fed at any cost? Steeped to the lips in sordidness, as we have all been from the cradle, how is it possible that any one among us, by any effort of his own, can wipe off from his soul the hereditary stain?"

The reply is of equal force and fairly represents a viewpoint Eleanor was coming more and more to share:

"...Have you forgotten for how long, and at what a cruel disadvantage, the Jewish people has gone its way, until at last it has shamed the nations into respect? Our self-restraint, our self-respect, our industry, our power of endurance, our love of race, home and kindred, and our respect for their ties – are none of these things to be set down to our account?"

To which the sceptic replies:

"Oh, our instincts of self-preservation are remarkably strong; I grant you that."[173]

The argument goes on and, in essence, resolves the conflict that must have tormented Eleanor in reconciling her father's anti-Semitic fleers with her own awakening pride in her Jewish antecedents, roused not by the milieu portrayed in *Reuben Sachs*, of which she knew next to nothing, but by the poverty-stricken and persecuted working-class Jews – from all lands – to whom Marx had never given much thought.

"I am the only one of my family," Eleanor said to Max Beer, "who felt drawn to the Jewish people."[174]

While Aveling pursued his theatrical ambitions with Eleanor's full support they were not of primary importance to her. A development of lasting significance, whose onset she could not have dated, was taking place.

1888 was a year of trade recovery and the great wave of demonstrations subsided. But it was something beyond the ill-usage of the unemployed that now produced a shift in her attitude to the working class. She had begin to explore the East End, sometimes alone, occasionally with Margaret Harkness,* not as a speaker nor a demonstrator but more as an explorer, and what she discovered left her deeply and personally involved with the lives of the people. They were not any less the downtrodden and exploited "masses" for whose freedom her father had charted the course and to whom she could carry that message, but they were no longer featureless crowds which suffered silently, repined or struggled. They were sad and sentient individuals – such as those she had visited in Lisson Grove – however great their number.

It may seem extraordinary, but it is the truth that not until now – she was 33 years of age – did Eleanor cross the line between serving a cause and identifying herself with the men and women that cause was intended to serve: the anger and the pity she had always felt were crystallised. From now on the seal was set upon her friendship with working men and women; from now on her recognition of the cardinal difference between the hand-to-mouth existence she had lived all her days and that of people whose empty hands did not reach the mouth. Eleanor had never known real hunger: debts and duns and short commons, yes, and sometimes "doing without", but not the ravening need of those clinging to the brink of survival who asked bread and were given a stone.

In letter after letter written at that time, whether from London or the

---

* Another friend Eleanor was to lose. Some 18 months after Engels had sent her his amiable letter (see fn. p. 432) he was writing to Laura: "We have got hold of another Mother Schack in Miss Harkness. But this time we have nailed her, and she will find out whom she has to deal with."[175] If this meant, as it implies, that she had turned against Aveling, it may be that Olive Schreiner's influence had been at work. In May 1888 Margaret Harkness had spent a little time house-hunting in Surrey with Schreiner who entertained a passing fancy that she might settle there.

country, this preoccupation with personal suffering is reflected; her painful steps as she bridged the way from political commitment to the human heart of the matter can be followed.

"The people are starving," she wrote from Dodwell. "... and poor wretches lie in the ditches and drenching rain..."[176]

"The last three weeks we have had only about three fine days ... Till I lived here I never realised what an amount of misery such weather entails. The small farmers hereabouts – and there are many – are ruined: the hay is all spoilt and they will have to get rid of their few cattle for want of fodder ... the first crop – what remained of it after the caterpillar pest – is lost, and now the potatoes are beginning to rot. All the roads are full of poor tramps: men, women and children who have trudged weary miles to come for the hay making, and who have to therefore trudge back again, starving."[177]

"Our half-acre and cottage are glorious. Or would be glorious but for the militia, 700 of whom camp a mile from here, and the tramps. The militia are beasts – ne'er a one will live to be drowned – but the tramps! It is heart-rending. And yet, horrible as it is, it is better than London ... It is a nightmare to me. I can't get rid of it. I see it by day despite our green fields and trees and all the flowers, and I dream of it o' nights. Sometimes I am inclined to wonder how one *can* go on living with all this suffering around one. One room especially haunts me. Room! – cellar, dark, underground – In it a woman lying on some sacking and a little straw, her breast half eaten away with cancer. She is naked but for an old red handkerchief over her breast and a bit of old sail over her legs. By her side a baby of three and other children – four of them. The oldest just nine years old. The husband tries to 'pick up' a few pence at the docks – that last refuge of the desperate – and the children are howling for bread ... that poor woman who in all her agony tries to tend her little ones – We got her to the hospital – for a long time she would not go because of the 'little 'uns' and now she's dead. What has become of those children heaven knows. – But that's only one out of thousands and thousands..."[176]

The early stages of this involvement, stemming from her closer acquaintance with the unemployed, were clear enough in letters to both Laura and to Dollie Radford towards the end of 1887, but a new note of distress crept into the words she sent to Dollie in February 1888, lamenting the death of a young woman they had both known.

"...At a time like this," she wrote, "the sense of the hardness of life comes upon us almost too painfully for endurance. I fear I am incoherent, but indeed Dollie I am sore at heart."[178]

As the months went by Eleanor realised that there was but a hair's breadth between the misery of the down-and-out and those who still thought of themselves as workers.

"To go to the docks," she wrote, "is enough to drive one mad. The men fight and push and hustle like beasts – not men – and all to earn at best 3d. or 4d. an hour! So serious has the struggle become that the 'authorities' have had to replace certain iron palings with wooden ones – the weaker men got impaled in the crush! ... You can't help thinking of all this when you've seen it and been in the midst of it..."[176]

Nothing had so moved her since the days of the Commune; and then she had known only the refugees, the flotsam of humanity washed up by that storm, stranded, stripped and pitiable enough in all conscience; but these dispossessed "thousands and thousands" were her countrymen, degraded and unwanted in the land that gave them birth: not living but staying on earth.

The distress of which she now became so agonisingly aware at every turn was far from new; to alleviate it had been the motive power of all her political activity and her compassion had ever been quick. The subtle, the pervasive thing, as her letters of the time disclose – when they could have been full of her advancement in the literary world – was that she became

> ... of those to whom the miseries of the world
> Are misery, and will not let them rest.

Now, if ever in these years, would have been the time when she might have attempted to commit suicide. Caught up in the swiftly moving events of the period she must either have abandoned hope – as, at moments, she came near to doing – or else become, as she did, one of those rare characters who transmute into positive action the unhappiness that comes of identifying themselves, finally, totally, in heart, with the victims of society.

To break the fetters binding these, her brothers and her sisters, to a system that condemned them to squalor, indignity and beastliness became so urgent and impassioned that she could well have been led into political blind-alleys but for her disciplined training, her guide to action; yet now she knew that whatever and however well one may be taught, no lessons are truly learnt by the human heart without pain. In practice, this meant that first things must come first; there could be no leap-frogging to some chimerical future; no side-stepping the immediate pedestrian task if those thousands and thousands were ever to acquire dignity and, in their own name, claim their rights. The nature of her consistent work did not alter; it was she who had undergone a change. As in a kaleidoscope, the parts had always been there but, suddenly shaken, a new pattern was formed. It is an experience sometimes called gaining insight; and it hurts.

It also meant, however, that Eleanor felt out of tune – and out of patience – with the ceaseless factionalism of the Socialist League. John Mahon, discouraged by the lack of support for his agitation in the provinces, joined the SDF in Northumberland in January 1888. Others, too, felt they could be more effective in local branches of the Federation without resigning from the League. But, in truth, it was the futility of both organisations that sickened Eleanor. As Engels had noted at the time, their lack of contact with the people and their needs had been thrown into sharp relief by the spontaneous actions of the workless. *Commonweal* in particular, he said, had shown itself "totally at sea and helpless",[179] while the SDF, though making representations to Boards of Guardians and to the government for outdoor relief and public works to be provided, had thrown up the sponge. Even its most faithful historians record that, after a parade to St. Paul's Cathedral, organised by the SDF in February 1887 – some eight months before the real battles were joined – the

"phase of spectacular agitation by the SDF among and on behalf of the unemployed may be said to pass".[180]

As a matter of course Eleanor went on with her propaganda work: there are records of her speaking at South Place on 18 February 1888; at Store Street Hall on the occasion of the Commune anniversary meeting held on 19 March, with Hyndman in the Chair and Morris, Annie Besant, John Burns and Kropotkin among the speakers; and, on 14 April, to the Junior Socialist Education Society, where she spoke on the woman question, while she continued to lecture to the left-wing Radical Clubs whenever invited.

At the 4th Annual Conference of the Socialist League, on 20 May, the Bloomsbury branch – partly because the Law and Liberty League had failed of its promise as a political federation since the defection of the Radical Clubs – moved that a meeting of all socialist bodies should be called to discuss the forming of a united organisation. This resolution was heavily outvoted, as was another from the Avelings' branch in support of contesting seats in both local and parliamentary elections.

The anti-parliamentary faction which carried the day was now made up of two separate strands: the one, Morris's aversion from the compromises and corruption which he saw as inseparable from electioneering; the other, those objections raised by the anarchists who, under Kropotkin's tutelage, had become a force to be reckoned with, strong in numbers and determined to capture the League. It troubled Morris sorely to find himself ranged on the side of a faction whose political philosophy he rejected, but on the parliamentary issue he was adamant.

Neither Eleanor nor Aveling stood for the Council nor, had they done so, would they have stood any chance of election. Indeed, their branch of some 80 members was suspended on the grounds that it had put up candidates jointly with the SDF for the local Board of Guardians and, in general, supported dual membership. Thereupon, as an independent splinter group, the Bloomsbury Socialist Society came into being and with this began the decline and fall of the Socialist League. In the autumn of 1889 the Edinburgh branch amalgamated with the SDF and Mahon formed the Scottish Socialist Federation; within two years *Commonweal* had become an anarchist organ from which Morris himself withdrew, forming the Hammersmith Socialist Society in November 1890, and what was left of the Socialist League – possibly some 100 members – ceased to be a viable body.

It has sometimes been supposed that Eleanor played a leading part in the celebrated match-girls' strike of 1888. In fact she had nothing whatsoever to do with it. The credit – no mean one – goes to Annie Besant, ably supported by her current admirer, Herbert Burrows.*

At the end of January 1888, during the short heyday of the Law and Liberty League as a federated body, Mrs. Besant had launched a little halfpenny paper, *The Link*, subtitled "A Journal for the Servants of Man", † which was in effect the LLL's official weekly organ. It ran a fierce and well-informed campaign against Sir Charles Warren and his "bludgeon men",[181] the ban on Trafalgar Square and police violence before, during and after Bloody Sunday. It gave detailed reports of the savage prison sentences and the serious injuries suffered by Warren's victims, whom it named. Nor did it leave the Home Secretary's position in any doubt but exposed Matthews' shifty attitude to the Commissioner's ukase, printing side by side his contradictory statements on the subject. It called upon its readers to canvass M.P.s to vote for Sir Charles Russell's‡ motion in the House on 8 March for the appointment of a Select Committee and Bradlaugh's amendment for a Public Enquiry into the conduct of the police. Both were defeated. *The Link* at once published the names of eleven Liberal M.P.s representing London constituencies who had voted "For Liberty", 45 Tories "Against Liberty", and five – three Tories and two Liberal Unionists – who had "Stayed Away".[182]

In April Bradlaugh moved for the reduction of the police estimates by £1,500 – Warren's salary – but the motion was lost.

---

* (1845–1921). At that time a member of the SDF, Burrows followed Mrs. Besant's conversion to Theosophy which caused her to resign from the Fabian Society in November 1891.

Some might say that a live theosophist is better than a dead socialist and Annie Besant, who survived Eleanor by 65 years – dying at the age of 86 – remains one of our splendid English eccentrics flitting from one movement to another with *panache*. Perhaps her greatest importance to succeeding generations was her bold advocacy of birth control (in reality, neo-Malthusianism): one of her earliest causes, championed together with Bradlaugh against whom legal proceedings were taken in 1877.

† Published at 34 Bouverie Street. Exactly what the sub-title means is hard to fathom.

‡ Born and educated in Ireland, Russell (1832–1900) was a Liberal M.P., knighted in 1886, who became Attorney-General in 1892 and, in 1894, Lord Chief Justice and a peer for life as Lord Russell of Killowen (the term "life peerage" was not then in use). As a QC he was Parnell's leading Counsel at the Special Commission (1888–9) which eventually cleared his client of the charges of condoning criminal outrages in Ireland. (See note on Piggott forgeries, fn., pp.)

Ceaselessly *The Link* challenged the legality of declaring "Our Square" Crown property and banning it as a place of public assembly:* but once Mrs. Besant had replaced Seddon as the secretary of the LLL, towards the end of May 1888, the paper took a new turn, embracing wider issues. On 23 June Mrs. Besant wrote an article "White Slavery in London":[183] a forthright attack upon the Bryant & May Company, whereupon Mr. Theodore Bryant† threatened her with a libel action. Three days later, on Tuesday, 26 June, she and Burrows, with another helper, stood outside the match factory in Bow at six o'clock in the evening distributing the article as a leaflet to the girls – of 13 years upwards – and women – many of whom were the mothers of large families – as they came pouring out at the end of their eleven-and-a-half-hour working day.‡

The subject had first come to Mrs. Besant's notice at a meeting of the Fabian Society on 15 June 1888 when Clementina Black – that friend of Eleanor's earlier days who had often read aloud to Mrs. Marx during her last illness – gave "a capital lecture on female labour". In the discussion that followed Henry Hyde Champion "drew attention to the wages paid by Bryant & May, while paying enormous dividends to the share-holders."§[185] At once Mrs. Besant and Burrows interviewed some of the workers, compiling a list of earnings and other factual information upon which she based her article. She kept up the barrage week after week in *The Link*, exposing not only the conditions, pay and hazards of the work,‖ the iniquitous system of fines imposed for the slightest mishap or error –

---

* Not until 31 October 1892, under Gladstone's fourth administration when Asquith became Home Secretary, was the ban lifted and the Square, from 1 December that year, open again as a public meeting place.

† Not a director but the holder of 1,400 £5 shares in the company. Between them the seven members of the Bryant family, two of whom were directors, held more than 10,000 shares in 1888.[184]

‡ In winter, work started at 8 a.m. instead of 6.30. In both seasons half an hour was allowed for breakfast and an hour for the midday meal.

One of the long-standing and ineradicable grievances of the women was that the boss had been moved by his veneration for the GOM to erect a statue to Gladstone, docking a shilling from every one of his employees' wages towards the cost and granting them the loss of half a day's pay by closing the factory for the unveiling.

§ Champion may well have done so on this occasion, but two years earlier Tom Mann had drawn attention to Bryant & May's huge profits and the vile conditions of their employees in his pamphlet *What the Compulsory 8 Hour Working Day Means to the Workers*.[186]

‖ The use of white phosphorus in the making of lucifer matches, from which the women eating their bread in the workrooms contracted caries of the jaw-bone (known by them as "phossy-jaw"), was not prohibited until 1908. However, the Factory Acts of October 1901 laid down certain rules for "Lucifer Match Factories in which White or Yellow Phosphorus is used" of which the most important were the provision of dining rooms; a prohibition on leaving, let alone preparing or consuming any food or drink in a room where phosphorus processes were carried out; washing facilities; the compulsory wearing of overalls provided by the employers and regular examinations by a certifying surgeon and appointed dentist.[187]

often due to sheer fatigue – but also details of the shareholders enjoying their 22½ per cent dividend.[188] On 5 July, despite their fear of dismissal and lack of funds, 672 of the women came out on strike * and, in less than a fortnight, thanks to a publicity campaign that brought in donations amounting to £400 for the strikers and to the arbitration of the London Trades Council, major concessions were won. Fines and deductions were abolished, wages were raised and, most important of all for their continued self-protection, this notoriously difficult section of workers to organise – unskilled females – formed the Matchmakers' Union. For the first year Annie Besant acted as its secretary – one of the two delegates who represented the Union at the International Trades Union Congress held in London from 6 to 10 November 1888 – while Burrows was the treasurer.

It was "the largest Union composed entirely of women and girls in England";[189] and so it remained for many years, with a membership of 800 of whom 650, against all odds, had kept up their weekly contributions at the time when Booth's investigator, Clara E. Collet,† made her survey of women's work in the East End. It is worth quoting from her table[189] of the earnings of matchmakers since it demonstrates better than words can do the effects of the strike.

Weekly Earnings

Percentages of Women and Girls Employed

1888	4s.–6s.	6s.–8s.	8s.–10s.	10s.–12s.	12s.–15s.	Over 15s.
11 May	21.59	29.73	29.63	14.86	3.96	0.23
14 Sept.	11.48	17.97	27.16	30.00	12.03	1.36

This was a triumph which, as the Webbs wrote:

"turned a new leaf in Trade Union annals. Hitherto success had been in almost exact proportion to the workers' strength."[190]

It is remarkable that it elicited no traceable comment from any member of Eleanor's immediate circle, not even Engels; an indifference that must have been owed to Annie Besant's undying hostility to Eleanor, which forbade either party to salute even the most laudable deeds of the other, though Eleanor was to redress this omission handsomely a few years later.

---

* In her autobiography Annie Besant claims that it was 1,400. This is not borne out by any other source and, since it is known from official contemporary records that there were other match factories in the East End, where the total of all women and girls employed was not much above 1,000, the higher figure is implausible.

† A friend of Eleanor's (1860–1948) whose father, Collet Dobson Collet (1813–1898), had been in frequent correspondence with Marx, publishing some of his articles in the *Free Press*.

That the lessons of the Bryant & May strike were not lost upon her is
clear, for it was the small spark that ignited the blaze of revolt and the
wildfire spread of trade unionism among the unskilled in which Eleanor
was to play so outstanding a part.

She was in fact at Dodwell during the matchgirls' strike, had just
finished her Ibsen translation when the campaign started and was now
making ready for the voyage to America where Aveling was to produce his
plays.

On her brief visits to London that summer she found various changes at
Regent's Park Road. Engels had engaged a new maid, Ellen, so that

> "Nim will at last be able to do no more than she really likes and have her sleep out in
> the morning",

which was a veritable "revolution in our household", Engels wrote to
Laura.[191] What was more, Nim herself was to have a proper holiday,
setting out with Schorlemmer and Pumps on 24 July to visit friends in
her native town, St. Wendel, from where the other two travellers would
pick her up, returning by way of Paris to stop with the Lafargues from 31
July to 4 August.*

In late December 1887 Paul and Laura had moved from the boulevard
de Port-Royal to 60 Avenue des Champs-Elysées (an address that led to
great confusion) at Le Perreux (Seine), some ten miles outside Paris near
Nogent-sur-Marne. Here they had taken a large house, with

> "plenty of fresh country air, pretty scenery and a kitchen and flower garden into the
> bargain".[192]

The move had a capital effect upon Laura or it may be that, now in her
forties, she had mellowed. In the spring of 1888 she wrote happily of Paris
friends "trooping to our place" and a "house full of people"; she had given
Schorlemmer hospitality earlier in the year and was "cherishing a
sneaking hope, against hope" that Engels might visit them that summer.
Moreover, when he on his side pressed her to come to London – he and
Nim had just been to Highgate cemetery on Marx's birthday (5 May) –
she, for the first time, expressed a sentiment long overdue.

> "Your letter" she wrote, "adds one other to the numberless acts of kindness you have
> showered on us during the last quarter of a century."[193]

---

* Pumps was in the meantime to visit the Paulis: the Rheinau family which had shown her so
much kindness during her schooldays in Heidelberg. (See above, p. 140.)

Throughout the long years of sponging on Engels this phrase is so singular that the reader can hardly believe his eyes. Laura's reason for being
unable to leave Le Perreux at the time also wins respect: Longuet's "little
ones", in whom she took an ever-growing interest and pleasure, often
having them to stay for long periods, were due to arrive. She now wrote to
Eleanor about them more fully than ever before, reporting with tenderness
and understanding on the progress, character and temperament, difficulties and talents of the pretty creatures.

Though she described Le Perreux as "the refuge of all the riff-raff of
Paris"[194] – surly characters on the run who did not care to hobnob with
their neighbours – the Lafargues were now most agreeably settled, 20
minutes' train journey from the city yet with all the advantages of country
life. Nim was deeply impressed and

> "has told us so much of your lovely house and garden that Edward is frightfully
> jealous," Eleanor wrote to her sister. "You beat our Castle hollow. But then I comfort
> him by reminding him that our rent is only £5 a year, and we this year have sold £3
> worth of potatoes..."[195]

It is not known what rent the Lafargues paid for their stately home but,
having for once acknowledged their debt of gratitude to Engels, they
must have considered it discharged, for their demands were now considerably stepped up and sometimes couched in quite unseemly terms.
Thus Paul is found writing to Engels shortly after having received an
extra £25:

> "I forgot to tell you to send me a cheque for £15 to fill the gap left by the wine",[196]

for they had treated themselves to a cask of 226 litres for bottling.

These exactions became so relentless that, in June, Engels felt obliged
to put a stop to them. Enclosing £100 – which Paul said "I gladly accept
at the moment" – he wrote a letter which has not come down to us for the
simple reason that Paul burnt it "as soon as read". "I wanted to hide it
from Laura," he explained. But his reply makes the nature of that letter
abundantly clear and, though Engels had given a cast-iron reason (as well
as the £100) to soften the blow, it must have been a firm refusal to be held
to ransom in this way. Paul was shattered.

> "The situation described in your letter is so serious," he wrote, "that I was over-
> whelmed by it ... Our settling in cost us more than we had expected; that is what
> obliged me to make such heavy demands upon your purse."

This 46-year-old man even went so far as to say that:

"I had, however, hoped to be able to announce that soon I should be fending for myself; and it was indeed that hope which carried me away and led me into spending more than I should have done."

Any idea of concealing the matter from Laura was plainly absurd, but it might be conveyed to her, Paul thought, in terms less mortifying:

"I beg of you to write and tell her the lamentable state of Percy's affairs* and she will understand that you, who have been truly providential for us, must extricate them from their difficulties."[198]

He knew full well that Engels would spare Laura's feelings, whatever he might say to her husband and, with the wormwood safely destroyed, he could rely upon the news reaching her in some innocuous form. There is no record of Engels writing any such letter to Laura.†

While Engels had used Percy Rosher's troubles as the pretext to fend off Paul's demands, there were also other claims upon him that summer, for a newly-arrived and needy group of Germans was now constantly at Regent's Park Road. With only one of these – Eduard Bernstein – was Eleanor at all acquainted.

As early as April 1887 there had been rumours in the English Tory press that the German socialists, running their party paper from Zurich, might be forced to leave Switzerland. It was no more than he expected, Engels wrote to Sorge: the threat of a Franco-German war was quite enough to make the Swiss feel their neutrality endangered by harbouring these undesirable aliens.

How exceedingly undesirable they were was no longer in doubt when, towards the end of that year, they published in full the names of Bismarck's police spies in the German Social-Democratic Party.‡ Thus, in April 1888 the German government put pressure upon the Swiss authorities to expel the staff of the *Sozialdemokrat*, though it continued to appear under Swiss management until September, by which time

---

* Percy Rosher, Pumps' husband.
† Before going away Engels naturally sent the Lafargues £25 "to go on with during my absence."[199] And equally of course he went on sending Laura cheques, while Paul's importunities were shortly, and regularly, renewed.
‡ As Heine had always said: "Prussian police-spies are the most dangerous because they are not paid: they are always hoping to be, and this makes them energetic and intelligent."[200]

arrangements had been made for its transfer to London,* together with the archives of the German Party.

Eduard Bernstein, Julius Motteler and Hermann Schlüter† – a quarrelsome crew – arrived in England at the end of May – or possibly the first days of June – rather bewildered and unable to find their feet or anywhere to live, let alone an editorial office, in the great city. With Engels' help they solved these problems, but it took time. On 6 July Engels was writing to Laura:

> "Our Zurich friends are not settled yet – but on the way towards it. It is most astonishing, the bother, delay and kicking about of heels that is caused by the London system of monopolist landlords who prescribe their own terms to their leaseholders so that when you want to take a business place from one of these latter – and that you have to do – you have to wait the great landlord's pleasure ... And the Londoners have stood this for centuries..."[201]

However, by the end of the month the Zurichers had found premises for the German Co-operative Publishing Company which printed the *Sozialdemokrat* in the imposing edifice of 114 Kentish Town Road‡ where Bernstein also lived, and private accommodation for the others in Holloway, joined there by their wives.

Engels, who gave them lavish hospitality, did not think much of "the female part". Regina Bernstein "seems the pleasantest", he confided to Laura, "a sharp little Jewess, but she squints awfully". Mrs. Schlüter was "an exceedingly good-natured and retiring little Dresden article, but uncommon soft"; while Emilie Motteler – *Tante* (Auntie) as he called her behind her back – was "a dignified juvenile of fifty (so they say)" of Swabian origin and extreme parochialism who gave herself the airs of a *femme du monde*. This did not preclude her from telling Engels at his table

---

* The first number issued in London was dated 1 October 1888.

† Bernstein (1850–1932) (see fn. † above, p. 157) had announced to Engels in September 1886 that in the following year he intended marrying Regina Schattner, a widow with a young son, Ernst, born 1879, and daughter, Kate, born 1881. Schlüter had been the manager of the *Sozialdemokrat*. He emigrated with his wife to America in 1889 and therefore played little part in London. Engels corresponded with him from time to time and remained on friendly terms. He died in 1919.

Motteler (1838–1907), the oldest and most experienced of the three, had been a member of the IWMA, a founder of the German Party in 1869 and a deputy to the Reichstag from 1874 to 1878. He stayed in London from 1888 until 1901.

‡ The number unchanged since 1863, it is still there: the corner house forming the junction with Royal – formerly Great – College Street. The site and architectural style proclaim its origin as a noble public house – The Nag's Head – as it remained until 1881 after which it was put to various dispirited uses, or left empty. From 1888 until 1890 Bernstein was the tenant at a rateable value of £59 p.a.

that the custard was burnt* nor from greeting Pumps Rosher with the exclamation: "My word, how fat you are!". Engels anticipated "some pleasant little sparring when Tussy and she do meet." He hoped that, as they were all housed near the Junction Road in Holloway, distance would "lend enchantment to the view – of considerably reduced visits from the lot": he was not going to have "the German element swamping everything at No. 122".[202]

Notwithstanding, when *Tante* was out of the way, he quite enjoyed receiving the other two couples who, on a Sunday afternoon in July, met Eleanor and Aveling at his house, when "we were very jolly", he wrote.[203]

But if Engels were not entranced by these foreign ladies who were, it seemed, to be firmly saddled upon him, there was another to whom he felt warmly attached. This was Kautsky's wife, Louise, and now, to everyone's surprise, on 14 June, almost immediately after the arrival of the Zurich contingent, she and her husband left England. It emerged that not only was Kautsky in love with someone else but that all had not been well with his marriage for the past twelve months. The news came as a bolt from the blue. Engels could scarcely believe it: when the couple had stayed at Dodwell in March that year, surely Eleanor would have noticed had anything been wrong. However, though Kautsky's love affair was short-lived – the new lady of his choice discovering in no time at all that she far preferred his younger and unmarried brother, to whom she transferred her affections and became engaged in a matter of five days – there was no question of patching it up with Louise. They were divorced in 1890, when Kautsky married another Luise† – spelt differently – by whom he had three sons.

Since the consequences of the Kautsky divorce were to be of some moment to Eleanor in the years to come, the rough outlines of the tale may as well be told.

From the first when apprised of the situation, Engels had no doubt where his sympathies lay. Everyone in England had taken to Louise – that "nice little body" – and everyone, he now assured her, thought her heroic in adversity. In his opinion Kautsky was not only behaving atrociously but was an utter fool who would live to regret to the end of his days the spurning of such a treasure. As so often happens when married couples separate, their friends seemed better able to judge the rights and wrongs of the matter than either of the partners. In this case, Engels declared, Tussy and Edward, Nim, Bernstein and his wife, Schorlemmer, the Lafargues and those of Tussy's women friends who knew the Kautskys –

* One of the early confections of the new maid – not yet fully broken in by Nim – who, however, "prided herself on cooking for company" and was not, in Engels' view, to be criticised by impertinent outsiders.
† *Née* Ronsperger (1864–1944), an Austrian socialist.

in short, everyone who had been let into the "secret" – sided with Louise. "How it will all end, I do not know, but I guess K. wishes it was all a dream," Engels wrote to Laura.[204] With uncharacteristic heat he inveighed against Kautsky: it was all very large and fine for a man to be free of marital ties; it was not he who suffered in the prevailing moral climate. But what of the invidious, the humiliating position of the deserted wife, the *feme sole*? While castigating the black-guard, Engels wrote letters of fulsome admiration to Louise. In the first, of which he made and kept a draft,* addressed to "My dear, dear Louise," he confessed that the news had dumbfounded him.

> "You realise that the longer I have known you has my respect for you risen and the fonder I have grown of you ... that anyone could give up such a noble-minded woman is beyond me ... Your heroism will carry you triumphantly through all difficulties and struggles ... We are wholly at your service and should fate ever bring you here again, you must without fail look upon our house as your own."[205]

Smiling through tears, she refused to attach any blame to her faithless husband and even went so far as to protest that it was she who had been impossible to live with. Though meant to invite contradiction, it is not an unconvincing claim. She gently chided Engels for being so indignant on her behalf and, heroine that she was, took up the study of midwifery in Vienna. Had she but stayed there to practise this productive trade she must have merited the praise Engels showered upon her. But she did not. In less than six months after the divorce she threw up her work – after much hesitation and at great sacrifice, be it understood – to become Engels' secretary-housekeeper for the last five years of his life, in the course of which she earned Eleanor's implacable hatred.

Engels had first learnt of the breakdown of the Kautsky *ménage* from Percy Rosher in a letter that reached him in New York. After making plans "constantly being crossed by all sorts of obstacles,"[206] he had finally decided to go to America with Schorlemmer when Tussy and Edward went. His leave-taking was not made easy:

> "There was such a scene when [he] at last plucked up courage to tell Pumps, but she went too far and the General got cross and bullied her and then she somewhat recovered. Why she should be so wild ... that the General is coming with us I don't know..."

---

* Engels' correspondence with Louise Kautsky – or Freyberger, as she became on remarriage in 1894 – is rumoured to have been sold, either during her lifetime or after her death at the age of 90 on 31 March 1950, to an American institute with a non-answering device. Her will, drawn up on 2 July 1924, left all her property to her daughter, Louise Frederica, who died at East Sheen on 20 December 1977 at the age of 93.

more particularly since Pumps herself had just returned from "her pleasant continental trip".[207]

Despite her growing tendency to put on more weight, put down more drink and assume more flirtatious airs than she could gracefully carry, Pumps knew all too well that she could count upon Engels' indulgence, for he was as true to her – and for their sake – as he had been to her aunts, Mary and Lizzie Burns, so that she had become something of a despot, above the law of even that easygoing household. This was the second time that Engels put his foot down – the first had been when Helene Demuth took over as the rival queen at Regent's Park Road in 1883 – though it was not to be the last.

In the belief that the Avelings' movements and the length of their stay would be determined by Edward's theatrical triumphs, Engels mapped out for Schorlemmer and himself an independent and purely private sightseeing tour, which he strictly enjoined Sorge "to keep absolutely secret."*[208] There were to be no politics or publicity: he wanted "to see and not to preach", to avoid reporters and, above all else, "the delicate attentions of the German Socialist Executive etc. of N. York", which would "spoil all the pleasure of the trip..."[206]

Eleanor wrote to Laura on 9 August from Queenstown, on board the *City of Berlin* – in which she and Aveling had made their return journey in 1886 – to say that she had not dared to tell her beforehand that "the General and Jollymeier" were going with them, because Engels had been

"so anxious to keep it dark ... I thought if it leaked out we should get the blame. I can hardly realise that we are actually off to America again and that the General is actually coming too. I believe this sea voyage and the perfect change, and perfect air will do him a world of good ... Both our old men seem to be enjoying themselves and eat, drink and all as merry as possible..."[207]

Despite his 68 years, Engels brought enormous zest to his travels in the New World.

"Everything in America has to be new, everything has to be rational, everything has to be practical, consequently everything is different from the way it is with us", he noted.[209]

It was a wonderful journey from which he learnt much, he wrote to Liebknecht from Boston.[210] Eleanor had never known him "to be so well

---

* He planned to stay with Sorge in New York for a week and then his itinerary took him to Concord, Boston, the Niagara Falls, over Lake Ontario to Toronto, down the St. Lawrence to Montreal, then back to the States: Plattsburg, Lake Champlain, the Adirondacks and Lake George, returning to New York by way of the Hudson.

– or so lazy! – for years." On the other hand Schorlemmer who, on the way
to Germany that summer had stumbled and fallen as he disembarked at
Flushing, had suddenly aged.* Though 14 years younger than Engels he
walked, talked and looked "like an old grandfather", said Eleanor, writing
from St. Nicholas Hotel on Broadway, to which she and Aveling had
removed from an uncomfortable boarding house.[211] Later, back in
Chancery Lane, she reported to Laura that Engels had benefited enormously by the American trip and was in excellent health.

> "I wish the journey had been of equal use to Jollymeier," she went on. "He is only a sad
> meyer now. He is terribly broken down, and I doubt if he will ever be the same again.
> He never seemed to enjoy anything at all while we were away, but used to sit there
> dumb and brooding. I say dumb – that is not accurate. He was embarrassingly
> eloquent – at the wrong end, and called blushes even into the cheeks of the Gen'l,
> when he persistently thundered this not v. pleasant music into the ears of American
> ladies. That so modest a man of science as Schorlemmer shd. thus become his own
> trumpeter!"†[212]

Eleanor gave as her forwarding address the publisher, Lovell, who had
brought out Aveling's account of the propaganda tour – *American Journey*
– in the States and was now handling his plays. The Avelings' trip, too,
was to be entirely non-political and, as it turned out, non-theatrical as
well: the grandiose projects seem to have evaporated. How seriously
Engels had taken these plans – even boasting of them – is evident from a
letter written to him by the old Chartist, George Julian Harney, then in
Macclesfield,‡ on 7 September:

> "And so Aveling has evoluted into a successful dramatist author, and with the
> Avelings you and the Manchester Professor have crossed the briny to carry Yankeedom
> by storm and carry off, I hope, sundry bags of dollars. But are you all going to perform
> as well as dramatise? If so, good luck to you. I am amused by your first impression of
> Yankeeland: '*a beautiful country to live – out of.*' I thoroughly agree. Cannot Aveling get
> up a new piece 'The Teuton in N. York', with you for the hero?"[213]

Although Eleanor shortly after their arrival spoke of Edward being
unable to leave New York and having to spend "the next few days seeing
after rehearsals", there were no further references to his plays or
productions, either there or elsewhere.

---

* He had received medical treatment when he reached Bonn but, though he travelled on, he
had not been well enough to carry out the plan of rejoining Lenchen and Pumps to stay with the
Lafargues.
† He was to die in 1892 at the age of 58, during most of which last four years he was unable to
enjoy anything, being physically and mentally ill from premature senile decay.
‡ (1817–1897). He emigrated to America in 1863 where he stayed until 1888. His wife was
still in the States during Engels' visit.

"This city of iniquities," as Eleanor called New York, was "more hideous than ever – and yet it might be so beautiful. I don't believe there is any large town in the world so exquisitely situated as N.Y. – and commerce has made it a very hell."[211]

In the event, from 31 August, when all Edward's work in America was at an end and as the fragment of a letter dated 11 September makes clear, the Avelings simply tagged along with the General – and, it may be assumed, at his expense – for Eleanor wrote a somewhat conventional description of the Niagara Falls, Montreal and the St. Lawrence river, entirely in accordance with Engels' planned itinerary. They passed through many American townships "which are all of them unpaved and would be considered disgraceful in a European village,"[214] she wrote from Paul Smith's Fouquet House, Plattsburg.

Engels succeeded so well in avoiding all political contacts – apart from Sorge, Mrs. Harney and Willie Burns, a young married man with three children, the nephew of Lizzie Burns, who had emigrated from Manchester, worked for a railway company and was, as Engels wrote to Sorge from Boston, "heart and soul in the movement"*[215] – that he mortally offended Florence Kelley Wischnewetzky. Naturally she had got wind of his visit and he felt obliged to write her a letter of exquisite diplomacy explaining that he had embarked on 18 September, immediately on his return to New York. He did not say that he had spent eight days there upon his arrival in August. Before leaving he wrote formal letters to the editors of the *New Yorker Volkszeitung* and the *Chicagoer Arbeiter Zeitung* regretting that the time and range of his tour had been too limited to allow him to call at their offices.†

Contrary to Engels' assumption that the Avelings would be in the States "for more than eight to ten weeks"[217] and, later, that

"Edward and Tussy will not come back with us ... They are sure to be kept there at least a fortnight longer",[206]

they had not only spent all their time with him and Schorlemmer but sailed home with them on 19 September in the *City of New York*,‡ arriving in London on the 29th.

It is clear that the American trip did not advance the fortunes of "Alec

---

* Later Eleanor was to describe him as "the one really decent and able member of the Burns family" – meaning of that generation and amongst the living – "a really excellent fellow".[216]
† He did not go to Chicago at all; and neither did Aveling who was supposed to have had theatre engagements there.
‡ The newest and largest passenger steamer in service (10,500 tons). This was but its fourth voyage and, though supposed to do 500 nautical miles a day, never in fact did more than 370 – once only 313 – an engine having packed up. Engels called it a "humbug".

Nelson" nor make his name in the States. Equally there can be no doubt that this carefree holiday of four weeks – seven if one counts the leisured sea voyages – recharged Eleanor's forces for the strenuous time that lay ahead. It may also be surmised that it gave her a welcome breathing space to shake off her obsession with the abominable distress she had witnessed and to put it in perspective. Certainly she no longer felt haunted day and night.

REFERENCE NOTES

Abbreviations
Adelphi (1) *Adelphi* (2)

    "Eleanor Marx": two articles by Henry Havelock Ellis in *The Adelphi* (1) Vol. X, No. 6 September 1935 (pp. 342–52). (2) Vol. XI, No. 1, October 1935 (pp. 33–41).

BIML   Institute of Marxism-Leninism, Berlin.

Bottigelli Archives   Letters in the custody of Professor Emile Bottigelli.

CMFR   *Perepiska Chlenov Semyi Marksa s Russkimi Politicheskimi Deiateliami* (Correspondence Between Members of the Marx Family and Russian Political Figures). Political Literature Publishing House. Moscow 1974.

ELC   *Frederick Engels, Paul and Laura Lafargue: Correspondence.* Volumes I– III. Lawrence and Wishart, 1959–1963.

Liebknecht   Wilhelm Liebknecht. *Briefwechsel mit Karl Marx und Friedrich Engels.* Edited by Georg Eckert. Mouton & Co., The Hague 1963.

IISH   International Institute of Social History, Amsterdam.

MEW   *Marx Engels Werke.* Dietz Verlag, Berlin, 1956–1968.

MIML   Institute of Marxism-Leninism, Moscow.

OS Letters   Letters of Olive Schreiner 1876–1920. Edited by S. C. Cronwright-Schreiner. Fisher Unwin, 1924.

Thompson   E. P. Thompson, *William Morris: Romantic to Revolutionary.* Lawrence and Wishart, 1955.

(1)   17 July 1886. Liebknecht, p. 436.

(2)   31 August 1886. Bottigelli Archives.

(3)   To Laura. From internal evidence 14 September 1886. Undated fragment. Bottigelli Archives.

(4)   To Laura, 31 August 1886. *Ibid.*

(5)   Edward and Eleanor Marx Aveling. *The Working-Class Movement in America.* On the cover of the 1888 paperback shilling reprint, though not on the title-page, the book was called *The Labour Movement in America.* The second, 2s. 6d. hardback edition gave it only the title by which it is generally known. Swan Sonnenschein, 1889 and 1890, p. 8.

(6)   "*Das Recit der Aveling'schen Agitations-Tour*" in the *Wochenblatt der New Yorker Volkszeitung,* 1 January 1887. BIML.

(7)   Bottigelli Archives.

(8)   Engels to Sorge, 24 April 1883. MEW 36, pp. 16, 17.

(9)   Gerhard Becker. *"Die Agitationsreise Wilhelm Liebknechts durch die USA 1886"* in *Zeitschrift für Geschichtswissenschaft* XV – Jg. No. 5, 1967, pp. 842–62.

(10) James D. Horan. *The Pinkertons: The Detective Dynasty that Made History*. Robert Hale, 1970.

(11) 19 September 1886.

(12) *Commonweal*, 25 September and 9 October 1886.

(13) Philip S. Foner. *History of the Labour Movement in the United States*. Vol. 2. International Publishers, New York, 1955, p. 30.

(14) *Justice*. 13 November 1886.

(15) *John Swinton's Paper*. 19 September 1886.

(16) 9 October 1886.

(17) *John Swinton's Paper*. 26 September 1886.

(18) IISH.

(19) 21 and 23 September 1886.

(20) 1 October 1886.

(21) Edward and Eleanor Marx Aveling, *op. cit.*, p. 8.

(22) Published by John W. Lovell. New York, 1887.

(23) Becker, *op. cit.*, p. 855.

(24) Edward and Eleanor Marx Aveling, *op. cit.*, p. 148.

(25) To Laura, 24 November 1886. ELC I, pp. 395–6.

(26) Marx. *Eighteenth Brumaire of Louis Bonaparte. Selected Works*. Vol. II. Lawrence & Wishart 1966, p. 123.

(27) 28 December 1886. MIML.

(28) Richard O. Boyer and Herbert M. Morais. *A History of the American Labour Movement*. John Calder, 1956. pp. 88 and 90. Originally published by Cameron Associates in the USA under the title *Labor's Untold History*.

(29) Lord Snell, CBE, LID. *Men, Movements and Myself*. Dent, 1936, p. 58.

(30) Edward and Eleanor Marx Aveling, *op. cit.*, pp. 183–90.

(31) Boyer and Morais. *op. cit.*, p. 91. The first quotation is taken by the authors from Henry's David's *The Haymarket Affair*, New York, 1936.

(32) Edward Aveling and Eleanor Marx Aveling. "The Chicago Anarchists". *To-Day*. November 1887.

(33) Engels to Phillip von Patten in New York, 18 April 1883. Published in the *Sozialdemokrat*. 17 May 1883. MEW 36, p. 12.

(34) Engels. Preface to the American edition of *The Condition of the Working Class in England*, p. ii.

(35) Edward and Eleanor Marx Aveling, *op. cit.*, pp. 199, 200.

(36) *Princess Helene von Racowitza. An Autobiography*. Authorised trans. Cecil Mar. Constable, 1910.

(37) To Engels, 29 September 1891. *Briefwechsel mit Friedrich Engels*, ed. Werner Blumenberg. Mouton, The Hague, 1965, p. 437.

(38) To Sorge, 27 September 1890. MEW 37, p. 467. The French word is used in the original German letter.

(39) To Sorge, 24 April and 29 June 1883. MEW 36, pp. 16 and 46.

(40) Laura to Engels, 5 October and 15 December 1886. ELC I, pp. 380 and 404.

(41) Note to 2nd German edition, 1887. English version, Martin Lawrence, n.d., p. 35.

(42) 5 October 1886. ELC I, p. 380.

(42a) Quoted from *The People*, 30 October 1886, by Professor Carl Gersuny in an article, "Eleanor Marx in Providence", in *Rhode Island History* Vol. 37 No. 3 August 1978.

(43) 23 October 1886. MIML.

(44) 30 November 1886.

(45) *Advance and Labor Leaf,* 10 November 1886, a weekly paper published in Detroit from 1885 to 1889, edited by John Rich Burton. Its first three numbers appeared under the title *Labor Leaf.* Details kindly provided by Professor Philip Foner of Lincoln University, Pennsylvania, and Professor Paul Avrich of Queen's College in the State University of New York.

(46) Quoted in the *New York Herald,* under the heading "Beware the Noose", 30 September, from the Chicago *Times* of 29 September 1886.

(47) *Knights of Labor,* 4 December 1886, a paper published in Chicago from 1886 to 1889 under the editorship of G. E. Detweiler and Bert Stewart. See acknowledgments Note 45.

(48) *Workman's Advocate,* 30 November 1886.

(49) *Ny Tid,* 11 July and 26 September 1935. This paper was published in Chicago by the Scandinavian Socialist Federation from 1905 to 1931 with a new series from 1931 to 1936. My attention was drawn to it by Mr. Michael Brook, Reference Librarian of the Minnesota Historial Society, St. Paul, Minnesota and I am indebted for further details to Dr. Oakley Johnson and Mr. Evert Volkersz, Curator of Special Collections in the State University of New York at Stony Brook.

(50) Edward and Eleanor Marx Aveling. *op. cit.,* p. 76.

(51) *Ibid.,* p. 237.

(52) 26 December 1886.

(53) For the decipherment of *Volkszeitung* articles (see Note 6), in almost illegible photostat, I am indebted to Mrs. Barbara Ruhemann.

(54) MEW 37, p. 85.

(55) *New York Herald,* 10 January 1887.

(56) 16 March 1887. MEW 36, p. 629.

(57) 11 January 1887. *Ibid.,* p. 591.

(58) To Lafargue, 16 February 1887. MIML. (Original in French.)

(59) Engels to F. K. Wischnewetzky 9 February 1887. MIML.

(60) 12 February 1887. MEW 36, pp. 611–12.

(61) Eleanor to Liebknecht, 17 July 1886. Liebknecht, p. 436.

(62) Natalie Liebknecht to Engels, 29 September 1886. *Ibid.,* p. 298.

(63) Engels to Laura, 2 February 1887. MIML.

(64) 24 February 1887. ELC II, pp. 26–7.

(65) Quoted by Engels to Sorge from Singer's letter of 7 March, 10 March 1887. MEW 36, p. 624.

(66) 14 May 1887.

(67) 21 May 1887.

(68) 26 April 1887. ELC II, p. 38.

(69) 7 May 1887. MIML.

(70) 10 March 1887. MEW 36, p. 625.

(71) To Sorge, 23 April 1887. *Ibid.,* p. 642.

(72) Engels to Florence Kelley Wischnewetzky, 13 August 1886. MIML.

(73) 10 March 1887. MEW 36, p. 624.

(74) Engels to Sorge, 9 April 1887. *Ibid.,* p. 637.

(75) Engels to Sorge, 4 May 1887. *Ibid.,* p. 648.

(76) Engels to Florence Kelley Wischnewetzky, 7 May 1887. MIML; Engels to Kautsky, 27 May 1887. MEW 36, p. 661.

(77) 8 August 1887. MEW 36, p. 689.

(78) 2 February 1887. MIML.

(79) *Adelphi* (2).

(80) 19 March 1887.

(81) To Laura, 21 March 1887. ELC II, pp. 31–2.

(82) *Commonweal*, 23 April 1887.

(83) *Ibid.*, 21 and 28 May 1887.

(84) 23 April 1887. MEW 36, p. 643.

(85) To Sorge, 4 May 1887. *Ibid.*, p. 649.

(86) 21 May 1887. ELC II, p. 44.

(87) J. W. Mackail, *The Life of William Morris*. Vol. II. Longmans Green, 1901, p. 180.

(88) To Bruce Glasier, 1 December 1886. *William Morris Letters*. Ed. Philip Henderson, p. 263.

(89) Quoted from Joseph Lane's *Anti-Statist, Communist Manifesto* of April 1887 in Thompson, p. 257.

(90) To Sorge, 13 June 1887. MEW 36, p. 675.

(91) To Lafargue, 13 April 1887. ELC II, p. 33.

(92) 12 April 1887.

(93) Andrew Rothstein. *A House on Clerkenwell Green*, pp. 49, 50.

(94) 11 June 1887.

(95) To Sorge, 4 June 1887. MEW 36, p. 667.

(96) Engels to Laura, 24 August 1886. ELC I, p. 367.

(97) Engels to Sorge, 30 June 1887. MEW 36, p. 681.

(98) To Laura, 7 June 1887. ELC II, pp. 45, 6.

(99) To Laura, 8 March 1885. ELC I, p. 272.

(100) Engels to Laura, 11 June 1887. ELC II, p. 47.

(101) *Ibid.*, p. 48.

(102) *Friedrich Engels' Briefwechsel mit Karl Kautsky*. Ed. Benedikt Kautsky, Danubia-Verlag, Vienna, 1955, p. 168.

(103) Engels to Liebknecht, 23 February 1888. Liebknecht, p. 304.

(104) 3 August 1887. *Ibid.*, p. 299.

(105) 11 June 1887. Fragment. Dona Torr papers.

(106) 21 July 1887. MIML. Previously published Thompson, p. 866.

(107) 26 July 1887. MIML. *Ibid.*, p. 867.

(108) Aaron Rosebury. "Eleanor, Daughter of Karl Marx", *c.* 1927. *Monthly Review*, New York, January 1973, pp. 45–6.

(109) Zinaida Vengerova. "On the Daughter of Karl Marx". Unpublished MS n.d. MIML.

(110) 30 August 1887. Bottigelli Archives.

(111) Aveling to Kautsky. 9 August 1887. IISH.

(112) Rosebury *loc. cit.*, pp. 36–7.

(113) John Peet, *German Democratic Report*. 2 June 1971, p. 88.

(114) Royal Archives, Windsor.

(115) Eleanor to Laura, 24 June 1888. IISH.

(116) 19 March 1888. ELC II, p. 108.

(117) 16 and 9 August 1887. IISH.

(118) Eleanor to Laura, 25 September 1887. MIML.

(119) *Bernard Shaw. Collected Letters* 1874–1897. Ed. Dan H. Laurence. Max Reinhardt, 1965, p. 240.

(120) *Adelphi* (2).

(121) Laura to Engels, 10 August 1887. ELC II, p. 59.

(122) 16 November 1887. MIML.

(123) 28 December 1887. Radford family papers.

(124) Bebel to his wife Julie 29 October 1887. BIML.

(125) OS Letters, 24 May 1887, p. 118.

(126) British Library of Political and Economic Science.

(127) *Commonweal*, 22 October 1887.

(128) Public Record Office. Crown Copyright. By permission of the Controller of HM Stationery Office.

(129) *Illustrated London News*, 29 October 1887.

(130) By permission of the Controller of HM Stationery Office. Public Record Office. Crown Copyright.

(131) Meteorological Office, to which this and all subsequent weather reports are acknowledged.

(132) Draft of unfinished letter, April 1888. MIML.

(133) To Lafargue, 16 November 1887. MIML. (Original in French.)

(134) To Niewwenhuis, 23 February 1888. MEW 37, p. 31.

(135) Henry S. Salt. *The Company I have Kept.* Allen & Unwin, 1930, p. 76.

(136) *Bernard Shaw Letters, op. cit.*, p. 177.

(137) 26 November 1887.

(138) *Alfred Linnell.* Pamphlet printed and published by Richard Lambert for the Law & Liberty League from the address of the *Pall Mall Gazette*, 2 Northumberland Street, Strand. December 1887.

(139) *Pall Mall Gazette*, 17 December 1887. Quotation from *Richard III*.

(140) To Laura, 31 December 1887. BIML.

(141) Eleanor to Laura, 24 June 1888. IISH.

(142) *The Pillars of Society and Other Plays* by Henrik Ibsen. Edited with an introduction by Havelock Ellis. The Camelot Series. Walter Scott, 1888, p. 199.

(143) *Ibid.*, p. xxxi.

(144) *Adelphi* (2).

(145) 10 October 1888. IISH.

(146) To Alma Murray, 25 November 1890. *Bernard Shaw Letters, op. cit.*, p. 272.

(147) Henry S. Salt. *Seventy Years Among Savages.* Allen & Unwin, 1921, p. 95.

(148) Stephen Winster. *Salt and His Circle.* Hutchinson, 1951, p. 84.

(149) April 1888, pp. 103–16.

(150) Frederick A. Pottle. *Shelley and Browning.* The Pembroke Press. Chicago, 1923 (limited edition of 125 copies). Appendix A, p. 65.

(151) *Revue des geistigen und öffentlichen Lebens. Die Neue Zeit.* 6ter. Jg. Dietz, Stuttgart, December 1888. The original English pamphlet was reprinted, with a foreword by Frank Allaun, by Leslie Preger, Oxford Bookshop, Manchester, in 1947.

(152) Quoted by Arthur H. Nethercot in *The First Five Lives of Annie Besant.* Rupert Hart-Davis, 1961, p. 163.

(153) Quoted by Henry S. Salt. *The Company I have kept.* George Allen & Unwin, 1930, pp. 50, 51.

(154) December 1888. *Adelphi* (2).

(155) *Dramatic Review*, 3 December 1887.

(156) *Ibid.*, 10 December.

(157) 28 December 1887. Radford family papers.

(158) Author's archives.

(159) 7 April 1888. BM Add. MSS 46288.

(160) Engels to Laura, 11 April 1888. MIML.

(161) Engels to Laura, 9 May 1888. ELC II, pp. 121–2.

(162) 24 June 1888. IISH.

(163) 30 June 1888. MIML.

(164) July 1888. IISH.

(165) To Laura, 15 July 1888. ELC II, p. 141.

(166) 30 July 1888. MIML.

(167) 5 August 1888. CMFR, p. 95. (Original in English.)

(168) 3 November 1888. *Ibid.*, p. 97. (Original in English.)

(169) 9 August 1888. Bottigelli Archives.

(170) To Laura, 6 July 1888. ELC II, p. 140.

(171) OS Letters, p. 207.

(172) Max Beer. *Fifty Years of International Socialism*. Allen & Unwin, 1935, pp. 69–72.

(173) Amy Levy. *Reuben Sachs*. Macmillan, 1888, pp. 117–19.

(174) Max Beer, *op. cit.*, p. 72.

(175) 16 November 1889. ELC II, p. 344.

(176) To Laura, 24 June 1888. IISH.

(177) To Laura, (fragment) July 1888. *Ibid.*

(178) 23 February 1888. Radford family papers.

(179) To Sorge. 29 October 1887. MEW 36, p. 711.

(180) H. W. Lee and E. Archbold. *Social Democracy in Britain*, Social-Democratic Federation, 1935, p. 119.

(181) *The Link*, No. 6. 10 March 1888.

(182) *Ibid.*, No. 7. 17 March 1888.

(183) *Ibid.*, No. 21.

(184) Companies Register.

(185) Annie Besant. *An Autobiography*. T. Fisher Unwin, 1893.

(186) Modern Press 1886. Reprinted, with an introduction by Richard Hyman. Pluto Press Ltd., 1972.

(187) Alexander Redgrave. *The Factory Acts*. 9th edn. by H. C. Scrivener and C. F. Lloyd. *Statutory Orders, Special Rules & Forms* revised by W. Peacock of the Home Office. Shaw & Sons & Butterworth, 1902.

(188) *Stock Exchange Year Book,* 1888, p. 584.

(189) *Labour and Life of the People.* Ed. Charles Booth. Vol. I, *East London*, 1889, pp. 435–8.

(190) Sidney and Beatrice Webb. *The History of Trade Unionism* 1660–1920. TU edition, Christmas 1919, p. 402.

(191) 3 June 1888. ELC II, p. 132.

(192) Laura to Engels, November 1887. *Ibid.*, p. 66.

(193) 12 May 1888. *Ibid.*, p. 123.

(194) To Engels, 16 January 1888. *Ibid.*, p. 86.

(195) 9 August 1888. Bottigelli Archives.

(196) 5 February 1888. ELC II, p. 91.

(197) *Ibid.*, p. 190.

(198) 26 June 1888. *Ibid.*, p. 138.

(199) To Laura, 6 August 1888. *Ibid.*, p. 152.

(200) Quoted by Engels to Lafargue, 29 December 1887. *Ibid.*, p. 84.

(201) 6 July 1888. *Ibid.*, p. 140.

(202) 23 July 1888. *Ibid.*, pp. 145–6.

(203) To Laura, 30 July 1888. *Ibid.*, p. 149.

(204) 13 October 1888. *Ibid.*, p. 158.

(205) 11 October 1888. MEW 37, pp. 106, 7.

(206) To Laura, 6 August 1888. ELC II, p. 151.

(207) Eleanor to Laura, 9 August 1888. Bottigelli Archives.

(208) 11 July 1888. MEW 37, p. 73.

(209) Quoted by Oakley C. Johnson in *Marxism in United States History Before the Russian Revolution*. Humanities Press, New York, 1974, p. 13.

(210) 31 August 1888. Liebknecht, pp. 319–20.

(211) Eleanor to Laura, 21 August 1888. Bottigelli Archives.

(212) 30 October 1888. IISH.

(213) *The Harney Papers*. Ed. Frank Gees Black and Renée Métivier Black. Van Goreum & Co., Assen, Holland, 1969, p. 324.

(214) To Laura, (fragment) 11 September 1888. IISH.

(215) 31 August 1888. MEW 37, p. 87.

(216) To Laura, 24 October 1895. Bottigelli Archives.

(217) To Laura, 6 July 1888. ELC II, p. 140.

· PART III ·

THE CROWNING YEARS

Utter confusion preceded the Congress at which the foundations of the Second International were laid in 1889.

The atmosphere coruscated. Volumes have been filled with the stormy exchanges between and within the various factions of the Congress's well-wishers before it ever took place, with many a forked shaft after the event, so that, were this a history of the international socialist movement, no chapter would be more thunderous or, for that matter, enlightening.

If the First International took an unconscionable time dying – fortunately for us, in America – the Second was born in great travail. Conceived in November 1888, after a far from normal gestation, it was nevertheless, at the end of the usual term, safely delivered in July 1889. Its birthplace was Paris. Though of fragile constitution, it was the perfectly legitimate child of the healthiest bodies in the working-class movement – the most progressive trade unionists and socialists of the time – yet everybody seems to have done their best to bring about a miscarriage. That they failed was almost entirely owed to the specialist advice of Engels who was in constant attendance, so to say, which consultations were bought at the price of his work on Volume III of *Capital*. Eleanor was one of its most efficient midwives, providing antenatal care from the earliest stage and present, of course, at the birth.

Indeed, had that not been so, this would hardly be the place to relate, however sketchily, the pathological course of that pregnancy; but it falls within the limits of Eleanor's life story in so far as it was of the uttermost concern to her. It will be recalled that Hyndman's jingoism, his personal antipathy to foreigners and resulting blindness to the need for the workers of the world to unite had been among Eleanor's strongest reasons for leaving the SDF.

From 28 October to 4 November 1888 the French National Federation of Trades Unions, in which the French Workers' Party under the leadership of Lafargue and Guesde* exercised much influence, held its congress at Bordeaux. It passed a resolution to convene an International Congress in 1889 to mark the centenary of the Revolution. This was endorsed at the National Congress of the Workers' Party at Troyes on 23 December.

---

* See above, fn.*, p. 119.

In between these two events an International Trades Union Congress was held from 6 to 10 November in London, at St. Andrew's Hall, Newman Street, under the auspices of the Parliamentary Committee of the British TUC,* the first such meeting in England.†

There were 19 French, ten Belgian and ten Dutch delegates with two from Denmark and one from Italy who were mandated by their respective Federations of Trades Unions.‡ No Germans, Austrians or Russians were present because the political regulations obtaining in their own countries made them unable to comply with the Standing Orders to produce credentials from *bona fide* trade union bodies.§ Among the large French contingent there was but one member of the French Workers' Party: Gabriel Farjat‖ of Lyons, who represented the 10,000-strong French Federation of Trades Unions and was mandated by 250 separate Union bodies opposed to Brousse and his party.¶

This international congress of trade unionists decided to hold annual meetings, the next one to be in Paris during the summer of 1889 when, to celebrate the centenary, a Universal Exhibition was to be open from 6 May to 6 November,** as a world-wide tourist attraction.††

Thus two Paris international congresses were now proposed for 1889: that of the International Trades Unionists and that of the French trades unionists and Workers' Party, or, to give them the full titles they adopted, "The International Workers' Congress" (supported by the Possibilists) and "The International Socialist Labour Congress" (supported by the Marxists).

---

* This became the General Council in 1921.

† There had been two earlier International Trades Union Congresses – 1883 and 1886 – both in Paris, the first attended by nine, the second by seven British delegates. Before that, in 1878, under a law of March 1873 prohibiting any form of international organisation in France, British trade unionists had gone to a Paris Congress only to be expelled while the French delegates were arrested.

‡ Although the names listed in the official *Report* add up to 42 foreigners and 81 British delegates, the text states that there were 44 foreigners and 79 "English". No one will ever know, or care, which is correct.

§ In the case of the Germans, the Anti-Socialist Law, debated in February 1888, was re-enacted in October for another two years despite Bismarck's efforts to extend it to five: that is, until 1893. It was repealed in 1890, having been in force for twelve years, while certain restrictions on socialist activity were not finally removed until 1900.

‖ In the *Report* he appears as "Fourgat".

¶ See above, fn.†, p. 304.

** The Eiffel Tower was inaugurated on 31 March 1889 as the showpiece of the Exhibition which occupied the whole site of the Champ de Mars.

†† Whose "most certain result ... will be the propagation of syphilis", commented Paul Lafargue.[2] It was really a Trade Fair, or Commodity Olympics, at which *grand prix* and *médailles d'or* were awarded to and commemorated upon the wrappings of the most surprising contestants, causing children of later generations to wonder whether individual sardines, biscuits and chocolates, or whole boxes, had lined up for small medals to be pinned upon them.

In passing it may be said that at the (illegal) St. Gallen congress of the German Social-Democratic Party in 1887, Bebel had moved for an international congress to be held in Geneva at the end of October 1888. This plan was abandoned when Engels pointed out that it was doomed to failure since not only would it clash with the British International TUC, already announced for the first week of November, but he foresaw that the French socialists would wish to commemorate the Revolution – and, he presumed, in their own country, not Switzerland – with some form of international workers' assembly.

From the start the two Paris congresses were seen to be in opposition, with more to sunder than unite their adherents, whereupon the splits and divisions, the libels and intrigues, the lies, denunciations, muddles and manœuvres went beyond all reason. It is exceedingly difficult to keep in mind when wading through the public prints and private letters of the time that what they were about was the international brotherhood of the working class.

At the heart of this turbulence lay the political situation in France itself. General Boulanger, a powerful demagogue, had won high regard as War Minister (1886–7) among the non-commissioned ranks of the army whose conditions he had vastly improved, while his bellicose anti-Prussianism was shared by large sections of the population, including workers who had either forgotten or were too young to know that he had been one of the butchers of the Commune. Heavily backed by the monarchists, he sought to establish a military dictatorship, but failed.*

The real trouble, however, was that Lafargue, the leader of the Marxist party in France, saw Boulangism as "a popular movement with many claims to justification".[3] He wrote to Engels:

> "Boulanger may be scum, and he is; but the Boulangist movement is the expression of the general uneasiness and discontent. Boulanger stands for the revolution in the eyes of a great many workers and petty bourgeois; there is no denying the fact. We should not seek to destroy this sentiment by abuse, as the Possibilist traitors do."[4]

Engels looked upon this as dangerous folly. Advising Lafargue to

---

* Boulanger's popularity was reflected in the Paris parliamentary by-election of 27 January 1889 when he polled 244,000 votes, but he was prosecuted by the government for an attempt upon the security of the State and was to be tried by the High Court on 12 April. Warned by the Minister of the Interior and aided by the police, he fled to Belgium on 1 April and, to avoid an expulsion order, to England three weeks later. Though his popularity was temporarily diminished it was restored and even heightened by the incompetence of the French government so that in the *canton* (district) elections of July 1889 he was returned with an overwhelming majority in the first ballot by no fewer than 16 *cantons*. On 30 September 1891 he shot himself in Brussels upon the grave of his lately deceased mistress

withdraw an article he had submitted to the *Sozialdemokrat*, he told him that its preamble, covering past history, contained nothing that was not generally known and agreed.

"But," he went on, "when you come to the Possibilists you simply state that they have sold themselves to the government, without an iota of proof or a single fact. If you can't say anything other than that about them, better say nothing ... the bare assertion ... has no effect whatsoever. Don't forget that those gentlemen will reply that you have sold yourself to the Boulangists. There's no denying that your attitude to Boulangism has damaged you enormously in the eyes of socialists outside France. You have coquetted, flirted with the Boulangists out of hatred for the Radicals, whereas you could have easily attacked both the one and the other without leaving a shadow of doubt to hover about your independent position in relation to either party. You were not obliged to choose between these two idiocies, you could have derided them equally. Instead of which you showed indulgence to the Boulangists, even talked of having a joint list with them at the next elections: with people in alliance with the Bonapartists and royalists who are certainly no better than M. Brousse's Radical allies! ... You say that the people needs to personify its aspirations – if that were so, the French would really be congenital Bonapartists, and we might as well shut up shop in Paris. But even if you believe that, is it any reason for giving such Bonapartism your support? You say that Boulanger does not want war. As though it mattered what the wretch wants! He must willy-nilly do what the situation ordains. Once in power, he is the slave of his chauvinist platform, the only platform he has, apart from that of achieving power ... If it's Boulanger, then it's war, that's as good as certain. And what war? France allied to Russia and in consequence the impossibility of revolution; at the faintest stirring in Paris, the Tsar would connive with Bismarck to destroy the seat of revolution once and for all ... So to throw yourself in Boulanger's arms out of hatred for the Radicals is as good as throwing yourself into the arms of the Tsar out of hatred for Bismarck. Is it really so difficult to say that both of them stink?"[5]

Engels returned to this theme a little later, to impress upon Lafargue that he was playing with fire.

"On the question of war," he wrote, "it is the most terrible contingency to my mind. But for that, I should not care a straw for the whims of Mme. la France. But a war that would involve 10 to 15 million combatants, unparalleled devastation ... obligatory and universal suppression of our movement, the recrudescence of chauvinism in every country and, at the end, a debility ten times worse than after 1815, a period of reaction based upon the inertia of all the peoples bled white ... this is what horrifies me."[6]

It was this compromising – what we should call opportunist – dalliance with Boulangism, regardless of where it might lead, that lent such ferocity to the internal strife in France over the two congresses: a situation imperfectly understood abroad where dissensions of a different but equally embittered nature were nourished by the inflammatory allegations issued from Paris by both sides. Elevated to the international plane, the effect upon the socialist parties – each with its own revolutionary, reformist, anarchist and other irreconcilable factions – can be imagined. Generalship was, indeed, required; and, but for Engels, "the General", there would certainly have been no Marxist congress in Paris that year, for never was Lafargue's ineptitude displayed to greater advantage than in the course of its preliminaries.

He excelled himself at the organising committee's conference, held at The Hague on 28 February, by being absent when a resolution to call the congress for September was moved by the Belgian and Swiss representatives, voted upon and adopted. Determined that it should take place at the same time as the Possibilists' "counter-congress" – "the key thing," he wrote to Engels, "is the date July 14"[7] – and at the risk of losing foreign support, Lafargue not merely ignored the Hague decision but asserted that it had been taken "surreptitiously" and, further, that he had never been informed of it, both of which disclaimers had not even plausibility to recommend them.

Dismissing this nonsense, Engels admonished him to withdraw his demand for a change of date.

> "You act the spoilt child, you haggle, you ask for more ... The point for you is that *there should be a congress* – and in Paris – where you will be acknowledged by one and all as the only internationally recognised French Socialist Party; and that, on the other hand, the Poss.'s congress should be a *'bogus congress'*,* despite the prestige which July 14th and secret funds may lend it. Everything else is secondary and less than secondary ... I have already said that, for the effect *in France*, I believe your date to be the better one. But then this should have been raised at The Hague. No one else is to blame if, at the decisive moment, you went into the next room and it all took place in your absence."[8]

Nevertheless, by dint of interminable rumpuses and delays, Lafargue had his way – beside which the storming of the Bastille upon that memorable date appears a puny triumph – but at the cost of allowing the Possibilists to outstrip the Marxists by over a month. The circular announcing the "International Workers' Congress of 1889 for the latter end of July" appeared in *Justice* on 13 April; the "International Socialist Labour Congress 14th to 21st July" was heralded in the *Labour Elector* on 18 May and in *Commonweal* on the 25th.

It was Liebknecht, however, who was held responsible for the delays in summoning the congress and issuing the invitations. Blessed – and cursed – with unbounded optimism, he believed that if nothing were done in a hurry all would turn out for the best. By mid-April he was still declaring that to hold two congresses simultaneously was out of the question unless the Marxists reached agreement with the Possibilists, or at least talked it

---

* English in the original letter, otherwise in French.

out with them. Naturally he was not suggesting that they should offer their backsides to be kicked by the Possibilists, but surely everyone was in favour of a combined assembly, to achieve which he could be counted upon to do all in his power.

Liebknecht, in fact, was suspected of having backstairs dealings here, there and everywhere with Possibilist sympathisers and of holding up arrangements until these parleys were concluded when, to universal applause, he would announce a single, united congress.* In Engels' view, Liebknecht did not care what political complexion the congress had "so long as he himself is there".[5] He fancied himself,

> "or would like to figure as the centre of the international movement . . . being cocksure of bringing about a union . . ."[10]

While Lafargue was too busy finding excuses for himself – and too thick-skinned – to take offence at Engels' reprimands, it was otherwise with Liebknecht and the stage was reached in the correspondence between these two friends of more than 40 years' standing, when Liebknecht wrote:

> "I let your discourtesy pass, the more willingly as it indicates that you yourself see that you have made a bloomer . . . It is not likely to come to *oral* disagreements in the future, since your suggestion that, in this matter of the congress, I 'as usual', 'owing to unforeseen circumstances' was prevented from fulfilling my duty goes beyond discourtesy – it is a gross insult which makes it impossible ever again to accept your hospitality."†[11]

Of greater relevance than Liebknecht's role in the bungled preparations for the congress was Lafargue's handling of relations with the British movement. He had invited the Socialist League to the organising

---

* In this connection it is interesting to note Hyndman's comments on Liebknecht in his reminiscences: "Of all the socialist leaders . . . he most fully deserved the title of 'statesman'." Such failings as he may have had Hyndman attributed to his unfortunate intimacy with Engels, Eleanor and Aveling: "He took what I may call the Engels view of our movement . . . and steadily supported our worst enemies", but "afterwards admitted it was a great mistake".[9]

† Engels did not answer this letter for four months. When he did, on 17 August, he used the occasion to rub in Liebknecht's failure to redeem his word – which was all that had been needed – to clear Aveling's name on the charge of having fiddled his accounts in America and various other sins of omission. However, early in September Liebknecht came to London with his son and daughter and naturally accepted Engels' hospitality. During his visit Engels wrote to Laura "he is personally the opposite of what he is in correspondence – he is the old jovial, hail-fellow-well-met Liebknecht."[12]

conference at The Hague in February, but not the Social-Democratic Federation: "a blunder", in Engels' view.

> "You should have ignored both or invited both. In the first place the Federation is unquestionably more important than the League; and secondly, it will give them an excuse for saying that the whole conference has been arranged without their knowledge. Hyndman would not have harmed any of you."[13]

Though the Possibilists had been invited – at the eleventh hour, it must be admitted – and had declined on the grounds that they alone were authorised to convene an international congress, Hyndman, as foreseen, now spread it about that the Hague conference had been organised in a deliberately underhand manner in order to exclude the Possibilists, he himself being on excellent terms with Brousse.

Lafargue had added to his folly by writing to William Morris personally, first on 3 January to announce the congress and again on 14 March to invite the SL to attend,[14] in which second letter – a fortnight after the Hague resolution to hold it in September – he gave the date as 14 July.

Eleanor had something to say about this.

> "Of course a mistake was made about the Hague meeting," she wrote. "The English *should* have been invited, and Paul's writing to Morris was a great mistake. His army is one that wd. have put even Falstaff to the blush. He himself blushes at it. Morris is personally liked, but you would not get a $\frac{1}{2}$ dozen workmen to take him seriously..."[15]

Lafargue had stirred up more of a wasps' nest than he knew. To be sure, there was nobody comparable with Boulanger to bedevil the socialists in Britain, but there was no lack of small fry bent upon making trouble. Had Lafargue paid a little more attention to a letter Eleanor had written to his wife in October 1888 – at the very time when the French Federation of Trades Unions was in session at Bordeaux and the British International TUC was about to meet – he might, just possibly, have been more on his guard.

> "For some time past," wrote Eleanor to Laura, "there has been a deadly feud between Hyndman and Champion. Each wants to be boss of the show. This has now broken out into an open row ... and now the Council of the Fed. by 7 votes to 2 have decided in favor [*sic*] of C."

Champion then sought an interview with Engels:

> "this, of course, solely for the purpose of using the General's name. I need hardly say that the Gen. is too old a bird to be caught by such chaff and so 'politely but firmly'

declines to receive the great H.H.C. Then I get a letter in which C. says he wants to see me because of the calumnies of Adolphe Smythe-Headingly against Mohr whom he has been accusing of dishonesty and of having been a spy!*[5] I saw C. last night and I am bound to say he at once dropped the tack of 'defending' Mohr and frankly explained that he wants all the information he can get about Headingly for his own purposes. He stayed talking some time, but neither party so much the wiser. – The position now is this. Any stick will do to beat a dog with and C. will use anyone now to help him against Head-Hynd. For my part I don't see any harm in telling him anything one knows about Smythe and as one thief is always best at detecting another, so I think C. (who is v. able but utterly unscrupulous) might be used in this matter – only we must not let him use us. The immediate cause of this squabble is the coming 'Int. T.U.C'. In a correspondence in the 'Times' – Headingly after a long (and C. says imaginary) list of countries to be represented, contrasts this 'genuine' Congress with the bogus ones of the 'old' International. The Broadhurst-Brousse lot want to work up the affair to try to palm it off as a really representative Congress. Smythe – on the strength of his supposed great influence in England, has managed to get some influence (all this according to C.) in France, just as here he is supposed to be a power among the Fr. workers. C. wants to show him up (for purposes of his own) and to this end wants to see you, Longuet, Hirsch, Vaillant and as many of the Commune people as he can. Of course Mr. C. was hand in glove with both Head and Brousse so long as he thought he could use either. Now he finds them in the way and wants to kick them out of the 'movement'. Both J. Burns and T. Mann are delegates to the Congress, others intend to stand out against Broadhurst & Co.[†] and show that not all the English workers are /not/ at the tail of these gentlemen. I am not at all sure that C. is not still on good terms with *Brousse* – so be careful. On the other hand I don't see that we need care what C. does and any information ... given about what Head. calls his own 'heroic conduct' during the Commune, might, I fancy, be given him ... C. is not a man to be too far trusted ..."[16]

Much of this lengthy screed – apart from revealing the petty intrigues rife within the British movement before ever an international congress was set in train – would be beside the point were it not that in June 1888 Champion, the former Secretary of the SDF, expelled in November that year, had launched a little anti-Hyndmanite weekly, *The Labour Elector*, sub-titled *The Organ of Practical Socialism*.[‡] Thanks largely to Eleanor's

---

* Adolphe Smith (1846–1924), a negligible but self-important member of the SDF, had indeed devoted some of his journalism to attacks upon Marx. He frequently acted as official interpreter – some said misinterpreter – at international meetings, appointing himself as "mahout" – Engels' word – to English visitors in Paris and to foreigners in London where their ignorance of the language gave him ample opportunities to hoodwink them. Once, shortly after this letter was written, he turned up at Regent's Park Road with two Dutch socialists on a Sunday – sacred to Engels' intimate circle – where he was shown the door: "Can you imagine such impudence," Engels exclaimed.

† At the 1888 International TUC, Burns had represented the 225 members of the West London Branch, Mann the 1,176 Bolton District members of the ASE. Henry Broadhurst (1840–1911), a Liberal M.P., was Secretary to the Parliamentary Committee 1875 to 1884 and again from 1886 to 1889. (See also above, fn.*, p. 318.)

‡ Issued until 1894.

pleasant if not wholly disinterested chat with him, which took some of the sting out of Engels' snub, Champion placed his journal unreservedly at the service of the Marxist congress, albeit to discomfit Hyndman.

The only other paper the Marxists could count upon was the *Star*.* In April 1889 its assistant editor, Massingham, went to Paris and it so happened that Adolphe Smith went with him, never to let him out of his sight, "monopolised him, would not let go of him, made him tipsy with absinthe and vermouth",[17] and, as his interpreter, craftily tried to enlist him – and his paper – in support of the Broussists.

On 3 May a peculiarly vicious unsigned article, datelined Paris, appeared in the *Star*. Since Massingham was abroad, Engels charitably assumed that it had been "smuggled in, probably by Hyndman and Smith".[17] Eleanor was not so sure. Aware that Massingham had been, as she put it, "nobbled" by Smith in Paris, she wrote to Laura urgently on 8 May† "of course this does not excuse Massingham, whose *duty* it was to hear both sides ... We shall try to force the insertion of a *leader* putting our side of the case" as soon as Massingham returned.

Should this move fail, as it well might, protests must be sent to the *Star*. Bax had promised to write to the paper, but that was not enough: there must be letters from the French themselves, translated by Laura. Eleanor personally could do nothing in view of the phrase used in the offending article that the Congress was "only 'one of the Marx family-affairs'".

"*Entre nous*," she went on, "our good friend Liebknecht is responsible for the whole affair. Had we got out our own invitations *at once* we should have had all the English. Now I much fear it is too late. And we must be fair. They know nothing here of the real movement and the dissensions between you and the Possibilists. They think it only a replica of the Socialist League and Federation differences. The deuce of it is that the League is Anarchist, and Champion's *Labour Elector* very 'shady (and held, not unjustly, in great contempt by most of the working members) and we have no one else to be sure of. I *did* think Massingham quite safe ... I fear we shall not do much more here now. We are too late in the field. But all that can yet be done shall be. You meanwhile see the *Star* is bombarded with letters ... *A la guerre comme à la guerre* ... You see Hyndman, and Smith, and a whole lot of these fellows having nothing on earth to do but loaf about, and wait till they catch a man like Massingham ... We, poor devils, who have to work for our living *can't* loaf on an off chance of netting someone. Here we are at a great disadvantage..."[18]

---

* A halfpenny evening paper, started in January 1888 – as "the paper-for-the-people, all classes, creeds and occupations" – by T. P. O'Connor. The editorship passed in July 1890 to his assistant, Henry William Massingham (1869–1924), who adopted a radical line, espousing the cause of the working class. It had a circulation of some 130,000 at this time.
† The holograph is misdated April.

Lafargue did write a letter of protest and submitted it to Engels who passed it on to Eleanor. She returned it, explaining

"(1) it is *much* too long and deals too much with generalisations. What we think or don't think of the Possibilists is of no interest here. We are doing all we can to get the facts about our Congress into the press (no easy matter). Your cue is to show up the *lies* of the other side ... but *don't* enter into any long account of the constitution of the Congress and so forth. *That* won't go in as a letter ... (2) The letters *must* go direct to the *Star*. It is no good sending through us ... (3) Be sure *all* your statements are quite reliable. Don't be surprised to hear the Socialist League disclaims us. They have not (I hear) sent any official acceptance, and Paul's including them is a mistake. At best they don't count as they are Anarchists: but if they disclaim us we are doubly discredited. It's all a damned nuisance. What makes me so angry is that but for the long delay, due to Liebknecht, we shd. have carried the English. But when ... I had to tell the working men that I had no definite news, and this, week after week, they lost heart and faith, and the Hyndman-Broussists with their cut and dried arrangements ousted us ... Now all we can do is to get *our* Congress talked of. Send letter after letter (but the letters must be *short* and *crisp*) to the *Star*. Some will go in..."*[19]

Meanwhile *Justice* had been running so malevolent a campaign against the "Marxist clique" that eventually Engels drafted a 16-page pamphlet – *The International Working Men's Congress of 1889. A Reply to 'Justice'* – signed by Bernstein. Two thousand copies were distributed in London with a further 1,000 in the provinces "and thanks to Tussy, in the right quarters".[20] It came as a bombshell and had, in Eleanor's view, an excellent effect which could not be followed up to advantage owing to the lack of congress material. However, it produced a long and somewhat devious but more conciliatory article by Hyndman wherein he referred to

"a difference of opinion which we hope will eventually prove to be only a friendly difference of opinion between a section of the German Social-Democracy and *Justice*", ending with the words:

"We are confident that our comrades in every country, so soon as they understand the situation, will decide by an overwhelming majority that all minor points must be sunk in the general endeavour to hold in this year 1889 an International Congress of the Workers of the World worthy of the great cause we are striving for."[21]

Striking while the iron was hot, Eleanor and Bernstein called upon Hyndman two days after this article appeared, because "after all," she said, as "a single Congress is desirable, we must do our best for that". Hyndman was far from pleased to see her. He

"looked green ... and knowing what an awful temper I have did his best to irritate me,

---

* This holograph is also misdated April: an error beyond all doubt, since Eleanor refers to it as being Johnny Longuet's birthday which was on 10 May.

but tho' I've a bad temper I'm not a fool. I saw his game and would not play up to it. I remained quite polite and amiable, even when he began with the usual calumnies against us and Paul," she wrote to Laura. "I only remarked (I couldn't for the life of me resist that) that if Lafargue was accused of all manner of sins to the party, he, Hyndman, too was so accused. 'You say Lafargue has ruined the movement and is etc. etc. etc. Well, Champion and Mann and others innumerable say *you* have ruined the movement here. They may be right or wrong. But what's that to do with the Congress?' Then came up the old sore of our *family*. You and I should feel proud. *We're* supposed to be doing it all! About 20 times Hyndman informed Bernstein and me that I was a 'bitter partisan'. I am and I'm not ashamed of it. However the upshot of it all is (you cd. trust me and Bernstein, Jews that we are, to drive a bargain) that Hyndman will, we think, do all he can to bring about some sort of 'conciliation'. He evidently was staggered when he heard that all Socialist Europe is practically with us ... the Broussists are, I am convinced, lying to Hyndman and taking *him* in. It would all be very funny if it weren't very sad. Meantime the *real* movement – as distinct from all the small Socialist sects – is going on well here..."[15]

Despite all these efforts, made by different people with differing motives, it was perfectly clear by the end of April – even before the circular convening the Marxist congress was drafted, in French,* translated into English by Laura and revised by Engels, who produced the German version himself – that there would be two international congresses held simultaneously in Paris. Engels was now reconciled to the date of 14 July and told Lafargue to go ahead with it. The mere fact of the rival meetings taking place side by side, he said, would "be enough to create a current of opinion, particularly among the foreign delegates, to force the two to merge".[22] To this end he advised Lafargue to adopt a moderate tone in the manifesto announcing the congress.

On 11 May Engels told Lafargue:

"For the last three months Tussy and I have done practically nothing but work in your interest",[23]

and a fortnight later:

"Now, my dear Lafargue, buck up ... Liebknecht with his waverings and procrastinations lost us a great many positions; don't follow his example, for I can assure you, if you cause us to lose yet another battle owing to delays that no one can understand, we here will justifiably lose patience and let you shift for yourselves.† There is no way of helping people unless they are willing to help themselves a little ... Don't spoil your own congress; don't be more German than the Germans."[24]

---

* By 6 May 1889. Edited by Engels on 16 May in its final form.
† Last three words English in the original letter, otherwise in French.

Nonetheless, there was still a deal of work to be done and Engels had more patience with than faith in Lafargue's unaided efforts.

No sooner was it obvious to others that the "current of opinion" at the two congresses would force them to unite than the SDF issued a manifesto in the name of its International Committee and General Council, "ordered to be translated into several European languages and distributed to all countries", setting out under 13 heads and couched in the most provocative terms its now familiar attack upon "The Hague Caucus" whose "chief promoters" were

"Lafargue, Guesde, Mrs. Eleanor Marx Aveling (whose sister, a daughter of Karl Marx, Lafargue married), Bernstein (editor of the *Sozialdemokrat*), Bebel and Liebknecht. Friedrich Engels is in full accord with the proceedings."

(Little did they know.)

"Comrades and Fellow-Citizens," exhorted the SDF, "It is for you to see to it that your cause, the cause of the workers of the world, is not deliberately injured by those who should be the first to suppress their personal jealousies for the sake of Socialism."[25]

Once more Engels set to and wrote a reply, signed by Bernstein, which was published as a pamphlet on 1 June. Eleanor, without so much as waiting for the SDF manifesto to appear, had been canvassing those delegates to the Possibilist congress who were known to be sympathetic to the Marxists. On 23 May Tom Mann wrote to John Burns from the offices of the *Labour Elector:*

"Dear Jack, Seeing Mrs. Aveling I was asked by her if we could have a talk ... as to the actual position of the Int. Congress. I have asked Cunninghame Graham and he is willing to meet at 65 Chancery Lane at 11 a.m. Saturday. I hope you will try and be present too if only for half an hour..."[26]

Thus on the day that *Justice* spat its venom Eleanor had

"Burns, Cunninghame Graham, Mann, Banner, Davis, Bernstein and Bonnier (W. Parnell cd. not come but wrote up here) to talk over matters. Burns *promised* (but he's a rather uncertain quantity) to put the following suggestion (suggested by us) before the Council of the Engineers Trades Union, of whom he is a delegate. He is to point out that *the International* Congress is ours, and that therefore he be empowered to ask the other Congress to send delegates requesting the co-operation of our Congress. If refused he to resign and come to us. – If only we'd had our circular a week earlier! I've seen three or four Trades Unionists who would all have come to us but for Liebknecht's blundering – I'm very glad we have Keir Hardy [*sic*]. I took him up to see the General

last November (at the time of the Congress here*) and Engels has written him frequently since. We then explained matters to him, and Hardy, who is a splendid fellow,
had helped us immensely in Scotland. I hope he may get money to be at the Congress.
He wd. interest you. Till recently he worked in the mines (now he gets £80 a year as
sec. of his Union – not much for a man with a wife and four children!) and is quite self-
educated. – To Stepniak I wrote, and you need not notice any letter of his saying his
name shd. be withdrawn. He only withdrew under the impression that signers of the
Convocation must represent Societies. I've explained that he cd. sign in his individual
capacity. Kropotkin and the Anarchists as well as the Lavroff people are against
Stepniak, and he was afraid of getting us into trouble. – He has written to Vera
Sazoulitch and other Russians for us.† I've sent off 500 copies of the last invitation, and
some 100 letters and postcards, and am dead tired – for I've also 'typed' a play! ... I've
to see half a dozen Trade Unionists tonight about the Congress – so goodbye for the
present. We've lectured at Radical Clubs steadily, and now I hope to turn our work to
some account..."

Eleanor had also to think of her own arrangements for going to Paris and,
in this letter to Laura of 1 June, she inserted:

"One thing more. I daresay you'll have your place full, for the Congress week. Can you
get me and Edward any room *cheap* (we're very poor!) in Le Perreux for about 3 to 4
weeks – from say – the first to the end of July? I don't want to bother *you* – and I don't
want to trust to luck just now in getting rooms."[27]

In the meantime she had a few other things to do, one of which was to
go with her friends to the first performance of Ibsen's *Doll's House* on 7
June,‡ while another, of a different order, was to write a letter to the
Labour Elector – published on 22 June – in reply to Karl Blind§ on the
question of Irish Home Rule, calling him "an out-and-out Bismarckian
and a well known contributor to the German 'reptile press'".

Incidentally, as her reference to typing a play demonstrates, she had
now launched out in other directions. On 10 May she announced to Laura:

---

* The International TUC in London.
† Unlike its rival, the Marxists' congress accepted delegates in an individual capacity, as well as
those sponsored by recognised workers' organisations, thus enabling the exiled and proscribed
socialists of various nationalities to be represented.
  Stepniak did not in the event go to the congress. Nor did Zasulich. The four Russians present
were Lavrov (resident in Paris), Plekhanov (recently expelled, with Axelrod and Zasulich, from
Switzerland), Beck, Kranz (the last from London), and three delegates from the United Hebrew
Trades of New York who were listed as Russians.
‡ See above, p. 334.
§ Karl Blind (1826–1907), the stepfather of the young man who had made an attempt on
Bismarck's life, had emigrated to London after 1848 and became a leader of the German
Liberals in exile.

"I'm going in for a new business – typewriting. I'm buying a machine, and as soon as I've learnt the work – which is very easy, I shall set up and issue a prospectus."[19]

From that time forth many of her own – and Aveling's – business letters (never those to family or friends, which would have been thought unmannerly) appeared in not quite faultless typescript. She seems to have had some little trouble about living in "Cancery Lane".

As the time drew nearer and the hope of a single congress receded, Engels took the commonsense view that if, despite all efforts, amalgamation failed

"it will be no disgrace. For it is a known fact that socialism does not yet unite the whole working class of Europe under its banner, and the existence of the two congresses side by side would do no more than give recognition to the fact."

He went further: should there be an amalgamation it would

"not be a merger, but rather an *alliance*, and it is a matter of carefully considering the terms of that alliance."[28]

He foresaw that the Possibilists, who would have

"a pretty fair show of French and English (which two nations, as you know, make up, in their own opinion, the whole civilised world)",

might set a trap for the socialists by proposing a perfidious merger and that Liebknecht, with his "mania for unity", would fall into it. "In that case," he wrote to Laura, "I reckon upon you especially, upon Tussy and D. Nieuwenhuis* to prevent it."[29]

But the thing he feared above all was that the Possibilists and SDF would use their congress as a means to resuscitate the International at a time when any such move would call down "prosecutions innumerable" upon the Germans. They, and the Austrians, were the only socialists engaged in a genuine struggle, entailing bitter sacrifices with never less than 100 or more of their number in prison: "They cannot afford to play at international organisations," he wrote.[30]

---

* Ferdinand Domela Nieuwenhuis (1846–1919), one of the most strikingly beautiful men ever to grace the socialist movement, had been a Protestant pastor turned Freethinker. He was one of the founders and became the leader of the Dutch Socialist movement in 1882 and was the editor of its weekly journal, *Recht voor Allen* (Justice for All) which he himself had founded in 1879. Elected to the Lower House in 1888, where he held a seat for three years, he later adopted the anti-parliamentary policy of the anarchists, to whom he adhered. Until 1890 his paper played an outstanding part in propagating socialism in Holland. There is a museum in Amsterdam devoted to the memory of his life and work.

Eleanor had been insistent that their own congress should be open to the press and public: a view opposed by Lafargue who was in favour of closed sessions. Indeed, he gave this as the reason for having taken a small meeting place, the Salle Pétrelle off the rue Rochechouart in the 9th *arrondissement*, for he thought it more desirable that people should be turned away than that the hall should be half-empty. "The press will have to take notice of it [the Congress] whether it likes or not,"[31] he argued. Engels gently broke the news to him that a congress "held for the benefit of the whole world" to discuss such items on the agenda as the eight-hour day, legislation on women's and children's labour and the abolition of standing armies was not a private assembly, adding that publicity was, for the German delegates, the "sole safeguard against fresh accusations of secret societies".[32]

Eleanor and Aveling crossed to France on Saturday, 6 July, to put up at Le Perreux, though not with the Lafargues. However, they spent the next day with them, lunched at their house the day after and, on the 10th, went to Paris together to visit the Exhibition. During this time Eleanor saw as much of the Longuet children as she could. Aveling's equipment appears to have been inadequate for what was to be a three weeks' stay: almost at once Laura was sent bustling to the Grands Magasins du Louvre to buy him braces, a sponge and some underpants. She also tried, in vain, to get him a sleeping draught for which he had omitted to bring the prescription.*

Naturally Engels had been invited to come to Paris too and attend the congress, but he declared that "if this weather lasts ... the only congress I care for is one with Nim over a bottle of beer from the cool cellar".[30]

It was indeed a sweltering July – in Paris as in London – so it is no wonder that, when Liebknecht turned up on the 9th, he was appalled to find that Lafargue, who was responsible as "foreign secretary", had failed to provide lodgings for the hot and tired Germans on their arrival. Also that the hall booked was so totally inadequate as barely to hold the 391 delegates present at the inaugural session – opened at 9 a.m. on 14 July by Lafargue in the name of the Paris Organisation Committee – with more arriving hourly and daily, a few laggards trickling in even as late as the 19th. The aging Liebknecht had to chase all over Paris seeking accommodation for his compatriots – he himself was staying with Edouard Vaillant – and a more suitable venue: the nearby Salle des Fantaisies Parisiennes at 42 rue Rochechouart, to which the congress transferred on the second day.

By Saturday, the 13th, the majority of the delegates from every country

---

* It is interesting in the light of later events that, despite his "doctorate", Aveling did not attempt to write a medical prescription for himself.

had arrived, including most of the 20 British. There were seven from branches of the Socialist League (including our old friend Mrs. Schack for the East London branch); Kitz and Morris represented the General Council of the League; the Radicals' three delegates included Aveling for the East Finsbury Club; Cunninghame Graham, who did not arrive until the 16th, represented the Electoral Labour Association; Keir Hardie the Ayrshire Miners; four came from Workers' Clubs and Socialist Societies in Bloomsbury, Walsall, Hoxton and Sheffield (the last sending Edward Carpenter), one from the Scottish Workers Party and one from the International Workers' Club.*[33]

The British delegates to the Possibilists' Congress, held at 10 rue de Lancry, had been recommended to reach Paris not later than the evening of Saturday, 13 July, so that

> "they may have a good night's rest before facing the fatigues of the 14th July fêtes ... So exhausting are they, that the Congress will not meet until one o'clock on the following day, Monday 15th."†[34]

Fifteen SDF branches were represented – some jointly by one nominee – fifteen Trades Councils, five Radical Clubs, the Fabian Society, the Dublin Socialist Club and various trade unions, with a large delegation from the TUC Parliamentary Committee.

There have been many – and conflicting – accounts of both congresses, including those in the contemporary press of various countries, all of which, as also the official *Reports* with the resolutions and speeches in full, may be read elsewhere.

Two matters only are pertinent here: the vexed question of amalgamation and the outcome of that congress for which Eleanor had worked so steadfastly and where she herself played the modest but indispensable role of interpreter for the French, the Germans and the English.

On the first of these matters John Burns provides useful evidence, for he was present at both congresses, being delegated by his Union, the ASE, to that of the Possibilists but allowed, by acclaim, to take the tribune in the rue Rochechouart on the last day but one (Saturday, 20 July).

> "I went to Paris," he wrote, "with high hopes of bringing about a fusion of the two Congresses and presenting to the world a united workmen's Congress ... The English

---

* Among the small number of women at the Congress – there were but three in the British delegation – was Clara Zetkin (1857–1933), recently widowed, her husband, Ossip, having died at the end of January 1889 after a long and painful illness leaving her with two young sons to bring up.

† Though of no moment to anyone, the Congress, to its credit, opened in fact at 9 a.m. that day.

delegates went ... morally pledged to amalgamation, but did not vote either way ... The most amusing, nay villainous part of this business was that the objections to fusion came not from men ... who represented vast organisations, but from men like Hyndman, sent by 28 persons, and by Burrows, who was so doubtful of the *bona fides* of the Clerkenwell Branch of the SDF as to get a double-barrelled mandate from some other people who knew nothing of Socialism and if they did would have sent someone else."*35

On the second day (15 July) Nieuwenhuis had moved a resolution to merge the congresses, reminding his listeners that Marx had not said "*Socialists* of all lands" but "*Workers* of all lands, unite". It was a good point; but since Nieuwenhuis recommended amalgamation "in that the agenda of the two Congresses are the same", which they were not, nobody could very well vote for his motion. On the third day, Liebknecht spoke, sensibly and effectively, expressed his regret that nothing had come of the preceding moves to reach agreement with all other socialist and workers' organisations and now proposed that efforts should be renewed with the aim of uniting, on condition that the Possibilists passed an acceptable resolution to the same effect. The inevitable lunatic (in this instance French, it is sad to say) moved that any negotiations with the "dissident" congress should be rejected out of hand and that nobody should have anything to do with these enemies of the working class.

Liebknecht's proposal was endorsed by an overwhelming majority. However, this discussion had taken up almost two days, everyone speaking at inordinate length and, when in a language other than French, "the Parisian delegates chatted together so that Eleanor Marx Aveling and the other translators could not make their voices heard".36

On the following day – 17 July – the Possibilists sent a message to the rue Rochechouart declaring their willingness, on the basis of a resolution they had passed, to merge the two congresses provided that the credentials of all delegates were submitted for inspection.

Thus the negotiations broke down on an ostensibly technical point, as a result of which the Dutch and Italian delegates – but not John Burns, because he did not arrive until the day after – withdrew from the Possibilist congress. The stipulation was, as the Broussists well knew, impossible of fulfilment, since the largest foreign delegations – and some of the smallest – were clandestinely present. It was, in truth, the "trap" against which Engels had warned: those from banned parties and illegal groups would have laid themselves open to prosecution while enabling Hyndman, among others, to start up the hare of "faked" credentials and "sham" delegates to discredit the Marxist congress in British eyes.

---

* Burns himself was there, in his own words, "as the chosen spokesman of 57,000 skilled artisans combined in the strongest trade union in the world".

On the same day as these moves were made, Engels was writing to Sorge to say that their own congress now in session was

"a brilliant success. 358 delegates up to the day before yesterday and more arriving all the time.* Over half of them are foreigners, of whom 81 are Germans ... The Possibilists have 80 foreigners,† almost all trade unionists. Also 477 Frenchmen, representing only 136 Trade Union and 77 socialist bodies, as every little clique is entitled to send three delegates, whereas each of *our* 180 French people represents a separate organisation. The amalgamation eyewash is naturally very strong at both congresses; the foreigners want to merge, the French hold back in both cases ... If the two parallel congresses have fulfilled no other purpose than to allow the forces to take up their positions – the Possibilists and London sectarians on one side, the European socialists (who, thanks to the former, now figure as "Marxists") on the other – thus showing the world where the genuine movement is concentrated and where the bogus, that is good enough. Naturally, a real amalgamation, if it comes about ... will mean ... an impressive demonstration to the great bourgeois public – a workers' congress of more than 900 – from the tamest Trade Unions to the most revolutionary Communists."[37]

Since this was not to be, the Marxists got on with their own congress, resolving to set up in Switzerland a permanent International Executive Committee of five members, to which Morris was elected as the British representative. It was to issue a journal on the Eight-Hour Working Day. This, the most immediately urgent item on the agenda, was the subject of the main resolution passed:

"A great manifestation will be organised on a fixed date, in such a way that simultaneously in all countries and in all towns on the same agreed day the workers will call upon the public authorities to reduce the working day by law to eight hours and to put the other resolutions of the Paris Congress into effect.

In view of the fact that a similar manifestation has already been decided for May 1, 1890, by the American Federation of Labour at its Congress held at St. Louis in December 1888, this date is adopted for the international manifestation.

The workers of the various countries will have to accomplish the manifestation under the conditions imposed on them by the particular situation in each country."

In effect, it was a call for a general strike in every country on May Day, following the trail blazed by the Americans in 1886 and, in the discussion that followed, a general strike was recommended as the most effective weapon to achieve the social revolution. The last paragraph had been tacked on when Liebknecht, speaking against this view, made it clear that any such action would imperil the German Social Democrats if May 1st

---

* Engels' information was slightly out of date: since he had heard from Paris another 33 delegates had arrived in time to attend the opening session. The final count was well over 400, of whom 221, including members of the organising committees, were French. Twenty-two countries were represented.
† From fourteen countries.

were inaugurated in 1890, when it would fall on a working day (Thursday), thus furnishing a pretext for the renewal of the Anti-Socialist Law, due to expire in October that year. Nonetheless, the resolution as framed was passed with one dissentient vote.

The other resolutions, debated during the previous days, were also passed on Saturday, 20 July, when the final session closed at 8.30 p.m. On the last day, the entire congress went to the Père Lachaise cemetery and laid a wreath at the base of the *mur des Fédérés*, with the words: "The Commune is Dead, Long Live the Commune!" The Germans also placed a wreath on Heine's grave in the Montmartre cemetery and, in the evening, a banquet was held to toast the "New International" and the unbreakable solidarity of the proletariat. The *Marseillaise* was sung and then everybody, having brought their partners, danced.

Thus out of this fearful jumble of events, of goodwill and ill-will, of striving and strife, of personal quarrels and organisational bungling, the Second International – though not so christened at the time – came into being.*

And what of Eleanor? She wrote her own account of the week's events to Engels on 23 July, but unfortunately that letter has not come down to us.

Cunninghame Graham, who spoke on the last day, made special reference to her as "an able and untiring translator" in his report on the Congress written for the *Labour Elector*.[38] Her work was later described by Bernstein who was there as a member of the German delegation.

"She officiated as interpreter," he wrote. "Some few of us were struck by the superhuman effort she put into this task. She was ceaselessly busy, from morning till evening, generally interpreting in three languages. She gave herself no respite, missed no session. Despite the oppressive heat in the hall she stayed the course of the whole Congress doing this thankless, gruelling work: in the truest sense of the word the 'proletarian' of the Congress."[39]

What this meant can be appreciated when it is known that many of the morning sessions were adjourned for no more than half-an-hour, to reassemble until 9.30 p.m., or to last uninterruptedly from an early start until three in the afternoon.

Bernstein's were not the only recollections Eleanor left behind. Nearly 60 years later, approaching his 70th year, Dr. Edgar Longuet wrote in a private letter to say that he had retained

---

* This collapsed in 1914 and was reconstituted after the First World War as the Labour and Socialist International, which is still in being. The Third (Communist) International was founded in March 1919.

"the moved memory of my loved Ant [*sic*] Tussy, who was so good to her nephews, my late brother Jean* and me and often I recall to myself . . . a trip she made to Paris and the pleasant walks made then with her. And true to the old fame of greediness given to me by my grandfather (K. Marx) when he called me 'The Wolf', I keep still the taste in my mouth of a remarkable strawberry sirup she presented to me in a call to the 1889 exhibition in Paris." In this letter of 1948 he added:

"I wept the premature death of my beloved ant a long time."[40]

---

* Jean – Johnny – died following a motor accident in 1938 at the age of 62, his brother Edgar in 1950 at the age of 71.

While the International Congress was in session a singular victory was being celebrated by a small section of London workers who, without a strike or a forfeit of wages, had won the eight-hour day.

The first move, with far-reaching consequences, had been made on 31 March 1889 when Will Thorne* and a few of his fellows employed at the Beckton gasworks, the property of the Gas, Light & Coke Co. in East Ham, called a meeting at Canning Town. Thorne described the occasion vividly:

> "a sunny morning ... a big enthusiastic crowd ... a contingent from Barking ... with a band ... The atmosphere was electric."[41]

The purpose of the meeting was to form a union with the single aim of demanding that working hours should be reduced from twelve to eight. It was received with such acclaim that 800 men joined this nascent union on the spot, tossing their 1s. entrance fee into a bucket.

Within a fortnight, though no subscription cards, none but the most rudimentary constitution and no elected executive were yet in being, there were 3,000 members. A Provisional Committee, so far self-appointed, full of energy but "ignorant of Trade Union methods",[42] met every Sunday at its headquarters – a temperance bar in the Barking Road – and then set out in brake-loads to recruit gasworkers in other areas, always stressing the objective of the eight-hour day.

These activities received fairly wide publicity, if for no other reason than that they were somewhat unconventional and in no time at all help came from such experienced trade unionists as Tom Mann, John Burns, Ben Tillett† and Herbert Burrows, fresh from his success in organising the match girls.

Many have written of their part in the campaign; but Thorne, as the only gasworker among them, then aged 32 and doing his 12-hour shifts in the retort-houses at Beckton, has left the most telling account.

---

* (1857–1946). Born in Birmingham, Thorne settled in London in 1882, joining the Canning Town branch of the SDF in 1884. For later career see fn.†, p. 515.
† In the summer of 1887 Tillett (1860–1943) formed and was the secretary of the small Tea Coopers and General Labourers' Association "after 12 years service on the wharves".[43]

As undertakings chartered and protected by government legislation, the gas companies had but little incentive to technological progress – they managed quite well without – and were, indeed, extremely backward by the industrial standards of the time, relying upon the heavy labour of underpaid men. Thus the recent introduction at Beckton of what was called the "iron man" – compressed-air machines which were always going wrong – came as a most unwelcome innovation: not only did it throw men out of work, but those who remained found themselves obliged to tend the new monsters for as long as 18 hours at a stretch, including Sundays. Since the gasworks drew its labour force from as far afield as Poplar and Canning Town, these immoderate hours were often preceded and followed by a walk of as much as four miles.

Gasworkers were not "tradesmen" in the sense that they had served an apprenticeship: the work depended largely upon navvying and Thorne spoke of himself as "a common labourer"; yet it required considerable skill, particularly for the carbonisers, to survive the hazards, the heat and the abominable conditions in the retort-houses, during twelve hours, by day or by night, for 52 unbroken weeks of the year. Nevertheless, they certainly did not come into the category of those industries which had formed trade unions to protect their craft interests. There were many practical deterrents to combination, not the least of which was that, in a gas-lit era,* the work was seasonal, men being laid off from February onwards to look for other jobs, since demand fell by half during the summer, though assuredly the labour of those kept on was not thereby lightened.

---

* Electric light was first supplied in January 1887 to 2,324 customers in Kensington and Knightsbridge; next came 2,137 in St. James's and Pall Mall in April 1889; then 5,572 in Westminster in November 1890 and so on down the social scale to Southwark's 179 in July 1899, Poplar's 176 in October 1900 and Fulham's 170 in 1901.

At the end of December 1899 the London gas companies – who had provided the first street lighting in Pall Mall in 1807, on Westminster Bridge in 1813 and to the parish of St. Margaret's, Westminster, in 1814 – served 666,204 consumers north and south of the Thames, making a profit of £1,904,450, of which the lion's share of £1$\frac{1}{4}$m. went to the Gas, Light & Coke Co. (which had a paid-up capital of something over £22$\frac{1}{2}$m.) and another £400,000 to the other main companies: the South Metropolitan and the Commercial (with a combined paid-up capital of some £7m.). By an Act of 1876 half the profits, after the payment of a 10 per cent dividend, was enjoyed by the shareholders; the other half was to serve the purpose of reducing the price of gas to the consumer. It is self-evident that with 666,000 public and private users – street lighting in the main, but also places of entertainment, pubs, clubs and other such establishments as distinct from domestic purposes – the population of roughly four million Londoners, inhabiting some half million houses, must still have been largely dependent upon oil lamps and candles at the turn of the century.

Lord Kelvin, giving evidence to a Select Committee, said in May 1896: "I call it terrible that 25 per cent of all the deaths by fire in London during the year were due to paraffin lamp accidents."[44]

Nevertheless the union grew apace and when it was but a few weeks old the committee named it the National Union of Gas Workers and General Labourers of Great Britain and Ireland.*

"We took as our motto 'Love, Union and Fidelity'," wrote Thorne. "our slogan was 'One Man, One Ticket, and Every Man with a Ticket'."[42]

Now that the "ticket" was printed, it was agreed that weekly dues should be 2d. The union sent a petition to the four gas companies† demanding an eight-hour shift and no Sunday work unless paid at double time rates. After waiting for what seemed ages, though it was in fact merely a matter of a few weeks, the Gas Light & Coke Co. conceded the demands. The Chief Engineer, A. A. McMinn, had been authorised by the company's "Court of Directors", whose Governor was Sir William Makins, Bart.,‡ to negotiate and his report on the justice of the claim was accepted. The eight-hour shift was adopted on 31 May, the new scale of payment for Sunday work coming into force a month later.

The South Metropolitan was less amenable. It proposed a joint committee of the directors of all the companies to decide upon a common policy, but Sir William Makins would have none of this: his company had reached agreement with its employees and the subject was no longer open to discussion.§

At a delegate meeting held on 20 May 1889 the provisional rules of the union were endorsed and, whereas the committee proposed that a General Secretary be elected at a salary of £2 10s. the delegates reduced this to £2 5s. There was also strong pressure to put forward a wage claim for an extra 1s a day, but the men were persuaded to put their whole drive behind the demand for shorter hours and no Sunday work without overtime pay.

On 26 June the ballot was held for the election of a General Secretary. Ben Tillett was nominated on the strength of his trojan service and trade union experience, but Will Thorne won by an overwhelming majority,‖ taking up his duties at the agreed salary – no lavish one for a man with a wife and five children – on 1 July, by which time 90 per cent of all London gasworkers were organised.

Before that month was out there were over 60 branches – 44 in London

---

* It was registered as such on 7 June 1889.
† As a result of various amalgamations and Gas Acts in the previous decades, the companies were the Gas, Light & Coke which had obtained its charter in 1810; the City of London Gas Co. founded in 1817, the South Metropolitan and the Commercial. In 1899 the City of London was absorbed into the remaining three.
‡ From 1883 until his death in 1906.
§ The South Metropolitan men came out on strike in December 1889 and were defeated for, although the company accepted the eight-hour day, it refused to take back the strikers after agreement had been reached in February 1890.
‖ The figures were Thorne, 2,296; Tillett, 69.

– and a membership of 20,000. To celebrate the victory a mass meeting was held in Battersea on 17 July, followed by a concert at which Thorne was presented with an address of thanks and a silver watch and chain by the workers of the newly inaugurated "Third Shift" at Beckton. John Burns was at this meeting and that is why he arrived late in Paris where, on the 20th, the resolution was passed calling for an international demonstration on 1 May 1890 to legalise the eight-hour day.

*   *   *

This was not the first time that gasworkers had formed a union.

It has the charm of coincidence – better expressed in the famous epigraph "Only connect ..." – that, in the same year as the demise in Europe of the First International, the gasworkers' organisation was defeated, while in the year that saw the birth of the Second International, they triumphed. During the 17 years between every effort to combine had ended in failure.

In December 1872 the gas stokers, who had formed the Amalgamated Gasmen's Association two months earlier, staged a strike in protest against the dismissal of one of their members at Beckton, his replacement by a non-union man, the lockout of two gangs of organised workers, the use of blacklegs and similar incidents at one gasmaking plant after another. Nearly 2,000 men had come out – at Beckton, Stepney, Bow, Hackney, Fulham and Bermondsey – representing in some cases, though not in all, the entire labour force. On 8 December at a demonstration in Trafalgar Square attended by 4,000 gasworkers, these cases of victimisation were reported in detail and a resolution was passed to the effect that the men be reinstated and the demand for improved conditions and the abolition of Sunday work – or to be paid at time-and-a-half – go to arbitration. The directors of the Chartered Gas Companies met and refused both reinstatement and arbitration, instructing their managers to prosecute the strikers and to import blacklegs from the provinces. It was clear that they were resolved to crush the union and indeed one director was heard to declare that he would do so if it cost a million. Five hundred summonses were taken out and held in reserve, while five Beckton stokers were charged with conspiracy to intimidate. In December they came before Mr. Justice Brett at the Old Bailey where they were found guilty of breaking the Masters and Servants Act (1867) by breach of contract – under which the maximum penalty was three months' imprisonment – and also the Criminal Law Amendment Act of 1871: an exceedingly confused measure which made unlawful almost any action taken by a legal Trade Society. The jury recommended the men to mercy "on account of their great ignorance and being misled", but they were sentenced to twelve months' hard labour. "Nothing," said Lloyd Jones, the union leader, "so atrocious as this sentence has occurred since the evil days of Judge Jeffreys."

A Defence Committee was formed, protest meetings were held and a Memorial was sent to the Home Secretary who ignored it and refused to meet a deputation. On a petition from the prisoners themselves the year-long sentence was commuted to four months in February 1873; but this was not enough. It settled no principle upon which working men might or might not be convicted and the demand for the laws to be repealed gathered strength.* A combined deputation representing the gasmen, a number of other trade unions, the Labour League and the London Trades Council was received by the Prime Minister (Gladstone).

Upon the release of the five stokers from Maidstone County Gaol on 15 April 1873 there was a vast demonstration, with representatives from many organisations, a speaker on Trade Union law, a procession through the town and a resolution passed on the necessity for labour to be directly represented in Parliament.[45]

Yet the stokers' union was crushed, as were later attempts – in 1884 and 1885 – to organise gasworkers. But in 1889 the National Union of Gasworkers and General Labourers was firmly established. Within six months it had thousands of adherents in every part of the country and the membership rose with ever-increasing speed. To be sure, there were breakers ahead, but the "New Unionism" of the unskilled had been launched once and for all. It was, as Thorne said,

> "the culmination of long years of socialist propaganda amongst the underpaid and oppressed workers. Politics had been preached to them, vague indefinite appeals to revolution, but we offered them something tangible, a definite, clearly-lighted road out of their misery...[46]

He also made the point that

> "It was this spirit of the 'New Unionism' that made international working-class solidarity a reality, and," he added, "strange to say, the historians hardly notice the revolution we created...."†[47]

---

* In 1875 the Conspiracy and Protection of Property Act and the Employers and Workmen's Act replaced both the former laws as a result of this agitation which had led to the setting up of a Royal Commission in 1874.

† Thorne meant no offence to historians. His point, a valid one, was that the coming Dock Strike was to overshadow the gasworkers' achievement in having formed the first substantial organisation of the unskilled: an example to those who followed in its wake.

At the time Thorne was not the stout and solid figure familiar in the House of Commons to later generations. He was described as

"slight and fine-drawn through the heavy labour of his arduous calling. He came to the platform straight from the retort house with the mark of that fiery place burnt into his features. Round his eyes were dark rims of coal-grime, and his hands were, and are still, gnarled and knotted by the handling of the charging tools."[48]

It is not known whether Eleanor, "that very brave and intelligent woman", as he called her,[49] had ever met him before he emerged as the gasmen's leader in 1889.* It is possible that she had come across him in her explorations of the East End and certain that he had heard her speak there, if not at the Commune meeting held that year on 16 March under the joint auspices of the SDF and SL at the South Place Institute. The fact is that, although his autobiography stresses again and again his lack of education – at the time of his marriage in 1879, when he was 22, he could not sign his name – Thorne had been a prominent member of the Canning Town branch of the SDF for a number of years and, while never much of a speaker himself, had ably chaired many a meeting in the Dod Street days. There he had listened not only to Eleanor but also Aveling, whose oratory he praised above all others, remarking upon his splendid voice, stronger even that that of Burns, and his talents as a teacher. He recalled to the end of his days "the Doctor's" courses on physiology at the Barking Road evening institute, and said that education officials had told them they had the best man in the country.[51] Bernard Shaw did not go down so well because his "keen flashes of wit" were largely "lost on his hearers": "the East End of London has never taken kindly to 'highbrows'," he remarked.[52]

Eleanor did not come into this category, and shortly she and Thorne were to become not only fellow-trade unionists but fast friends.

On her return from Paris on 29 July 1889 Eleanor had brought back with her the two elder Longuet boys. Johnny, now 13, who was growing "taller and taller ... a good-looking lad with very taking ways", and Edgar, pushing ten, who had recently "gone in for a spell of idleness,

---

* The only indication that he might have known her and other members of the Marx family is a sentence in his memoirs where he claims to have seen Johnny Longuet as a baby "and often played with him".[50] This does not, however, quite accord with his movements and circumstances during the years of Johnny's infancy, for Thorne first came briefly to London in November 1881 while Johnny, at four years of age, had left for France in March that year. It is of interest that he named one of his children Karl, after Marx.

Late in life, when he was interviewed at the age of 82, he said he thought he had first met Eleanor when she organised the Silvertown rubber workers,[51] but there is ample evidence to show that they had worked together for many months before, both with the gasworkers and the dockers.

having been the *student* of the family".[53] For a month or so they stayed at
65 Chancery Lane, where Edgar fell in love with Eleanor's black cats and
remembered long years afterwards being taken to a "scenic performance in
which Edward Aveling was playing a part".[40]

At the beginning of September they joined Engels, Nim and the
Rosher family in Eastbourne* for a short time and stayed at Regent's Park
Road for another ten days, enjoying such London treats as going to the
nearby Zoo. Engels, now in his 69th year, had not lost his touch with the
young. He took immense pleasure in the boys, was not in the least
troubled by their noisy presence and even courteously ceded his desk that
they might write letters to their papa. Then they went back to Chancery
Lane where Eleanor, not foreseeing what was in store for her and that she
was to become "quite an East Ender",[54] gave them all her affection and as
much of her time as she could. It was during these weeks that Thorne met
"the very young Jean Longuet",[55] for it was at this time that he visited
Eleanor who, as he recalled,

"helped me more than anyone else to improve my very bad handwriting, my reading
and my general knowledge",[50]

the need for which he had begun to feel acutely now that he was struggling with the perplexities of paperwork as General Secretary of his
thriving union.

The Longuet boys went to stay with Engels while Eleanor and Aveling
were in Dundee as visitors to the TUC, held at the Gilfillan Memorial
Hall in Whitehall Street from 2 to 7 September, where Keir Hardie was
to move the Paris Congress resolution. Before he did so, however, there
was a great debate on the Eight Hour Day, in the course of which much
heat was generated. Alexander Bissett, the Joiners' delegate from
Aberdeen, expressed the view that since, as he understood, Broadhurst
"was not in favour of the eight hours' day ... it would be necessary for the
Aberdeen delegates to find some man to occupy the position of secretary
to the Parliamentary Committee who would favour the carrying out of the
reform." To this Broadhurst replied: "I insist upon political freedom, and
that politics have nothing to do with trade-unionism."[56]

The year before, the TUC, held in Bradford, had decided to ballot the
affiliated organisations on the Eight Hour Day and, as James Mawdsley,†
the secretary of the 17,000 strong Amalgamated Cotton Spinners, now
said, this should finally resolve the question and be "simplicity itself".
Unfortunately, only 33 societies, representing a membership of 169,540 –

---

* Engels was there from 3 August to 6 September.
† Chairman of the TUC Parliamentary Committee in 1886.

less than 50 per cent of the total – had returned ballot papers, recording 62,883 votes against and 39,629 for the measure. Those who were in favour had been asked whether they thought it should be introduced by Act of Parliament, to which 28,489 said yes, while some 12,000 held that it was a matter for action by the organised trades. The number of votes recorded was stated to be 102,512 with a majority of 23,254 opposed to the reform. There were found to be so many errors and irregularities in these returns that in the end the Congress unanimously agreed to set them aside altogether.

While the debate went on in Dundee, it had already been overtaken by events elsewhere. Nevertheless, the arguments advanced were of considerable interest in that they reflected the temper of the last TUC to be dominated by the aristocrats of labour. Only in the case of the miners was legislation for the eight-hour day approved at the 1889 TUC* and the fatuity of looking to Parliament was brought home to the delegates by J. Toyn of the Cleveland (Yorkshire) miners who reported that when it had been raised in the House an M.P. had asked Cunninghame Graham: "'Graham, what is all this noise about the Eight Hours Bill? If these miners cannot finish their work in eight hours, why cannot they take it home and finish it there?'"

At last, on Thursday, 5 September, Keir Hardie put before the TUC the International Resolution in its entirety which provoked the familiar attacks upon the character of the Paris Congress, ignored by Hardie, who pressed the point that the maximum legal working day for all trades and in all countries should be eight hours. A direct negative was moved by W. Mosses of Glasgow, the Secretary of the Patternmakers. The Nine Hours battle had been won, he said, without any aid from Parliament and they had no need of outside interference now

> "to further restrict their hours of labour. If trade unionists were proud of anything it was the immense progress that they had made during the past seventeen years."

Mosses was unconscious of harking back, precisely, to 1872 and thus to the growth in political maturity which had brought into being the Second International, the Gasworkers' Union and, even as he spoke, the Dockers' Union. It was pointed out that in 1887 Britain had imported £80m. of goods manufactured by foreigners "who worked very much longer hours than the workers of this country did". By limiting themselves to eight hours they would simply increase the consumption of such foreign goods. Then, again, most of the skilled trades – which meant those represented

---

* The Miners' Eight-Hour Act did not become law until December 1908. The 48-hour week for other sections of workers was introduced in 1919 and 1920.

here – were on hourly pay: a reduction of hours would mean a decrease in wages. By all means let the government regulate the conditions of labour for "defenceless women and children",* but leave adult men to conduct their own fight provided they had "a fair field and no favour". What he can have meant by this is obscure. Another delegate pointed out that factories working round the clock would have to employ three shifts instead of two, reducing each man's earnings in proportion. He had evidently not heard a whisper of Beckton's "Third Shift", so resoundingly inaugurated three months earlier. To Robert Knight of the Boilermakers the real danger of allowing Parliament to legislate on such matters was that if it could reduce hours it could equally increase them and, moreover, was an admission that it had the power to regulate wages: "going back to the old days", he said, from which they were struggling to free themselves. Knight went on to tell the Congress that he had been reading a history of England and had found that 300 years ago an M.P. had asked how the people of Britain who were paid "the enormous wage of 1s. a day" could expect to compete against the Indians, yet the cry against foreign competition was still loud and even growing in volume. The debate continued. Hardie won considerable support from many speakers, but on the vote he was defeated by 88 to 63. He might have done worse.

On the day before she went to Dundee, Sunday, 1 September, Eleanor spoke in Hyde Park to a meeting of 100,000 people.

"It is not a little matter," wrote Cunninghame Graham in the *Labour Elector*, "that can make hungry men walk 12 miles on such a day as this." The hungry men were the dockers who had come from the East End in their thousands to the Park.

> "And so speaker succeeds speaker," Graham went on. "To Mann and Burns succeed Mrs. Aveling, Tillett and MacDonald. Curious to see Mrs. Aveling addressing the enormous crowd, curious to see the eyes of the women fixed upon her as she spoke of the miseries of the Dockers' homes, pleasant to see her point her black-gloved finger at the oppression, and pleasant to hear the hearty cheer with which her eloquent speech was greeted."[58]

This demonstration was held in the third week of the great Dock Strike which had started in earnest on 14 August: the only industrial action – until the General Strike of 1926 – which, as Ben Tillett put it, "has the dignity of capital letters".[59]

---

* It is interesting to note that in her day Emma Paterson (1843–1886), a pioneer in the field of organising female workers, had been adamantly opposed to special legislation to protect them. Indeed, when a Home Office enquiry in 1873 "recommended a reduction of women's hours from 60 to 54 and a Bill to this effect came before the House, the opposition of the 'feminists' killed it."[57]

Now if there is one chapter in the annals of the British working-class movement that does not need to be retold it is that of the Dock Strike. Its immortalisation rests too secure, and in better hands, to justify an account here of this triumphant action by the most desperate, dehumanised and defenceless of all workers,

"who shivered with hunger and cold, bullied and intimidated by the petty tyrants who took a delight in the brutalities of the 'call-on' ";[60]

men for whom

"no abasement was too abject ... who battled against hunger and exhaustion, dying as their greedy fingers clutched at the few shillings which a day's labour had exacted, dropping dead at the pay-box. Others, and in multiplicity of martyrdom, dying after reaching home ... Strong men weep, and so the curse of living is accepted wolf-like, and so our fellow-creatures die without courage enough to wail a protest against social murder."[61]

Without any funds behind them, these men to all intents and purposes brought the commerce of London to a standstill. The Chairman of the Conciliation Committee of the London Chamber of Commerce was later to complain that the strike had interfered with the business interests of 3,000 firms and that "the paralysis of trade in general ... could hardly have been much greater ... if a hostile fleet had held triumphant possession of the mouth of the Thames."[62]

Although they did not win their full demand of 6d. – instead of 5d. – an hour, the dockers achieved the enormous benefits of fixed times and places for the "call-on" and access to the accounts regulating an enigmatic system of "plus" payments.*

From workers in the ten docks on the north and one on the south – the Surrey Commercial – of the London river, as the men called it, the Dock, Wharf, Riverside and Labourers' Union of Great Britain, Ireland and the Netherlands was formed with an initial membership of 800 rising, with the inclusion of other transport workers, to 154,000 in 1892.†

Ben Tillett was the elected General Secretary, an office he retained until 1921 when, as a result of amalgamations, it became the Transport and

---

* "The basis of calculation is not only unknown to the men, but apparently is unknown to the officials themselves, since they are never able to give an explanation of how the calculation is arrived at."[63]

† The Strike had had the support of the United Stevedores, the Amalgamated Stevedores' Protection League, the National Amalgamated Seamen and Firemen's Union, the Amalgamated Society of Watermen and Lightermen, the United Ship Scrapers' Protection League, the Riggers' Association, the Shipwrights' Provident Union, the Coal Porters and a number of other small riverside organisations.

General Workers' Union. In like manner, Will Thorne, the first General Secretary of the National Union of Gasworkers and General Labourers, continued to hold that position throughout the First World War (during which it changed its name to the General Workers' Union) and after, when it became, also by a series of amalgamations, the National Union of General and Municipal Workers in 1924 (now known as the General and Municipal Workers' Union). Indeed, he remained its General Secretary until 1933: a period of 42 years, retiring at the age of 76.*

Thus, from the ranks of the most ill-used and the least educated – Tillett had started to work in the brickyards at the age of eight, Thorne at little over six years old had earned his 2s. 6d. a week turning a wheel for twelve hours a day in a rope-spinning factory – these two men,† by virtue of their "tact, pluck and energy",[65] in the year 1889, fathered two of the largest trade union organisations in the Britain of our own time.‡

To anyone writing of this period it is tempting to recite the mounting drama of the Dock Strike – in which 10,000 men participated within three days of the start, to reach ten times that number at its peak – not excluding the last act when such incongruous figures as Cardinal Manning, the Bishop of London (Dr. Temple)§ and the Lord Mayor (Sir James Whitehead) took the centre of the stage as mediators.‖

Yet it is a temptation to be resisted here, for Eleanor was on the scene – as at the Paris Congress, in whose staging, however, she had played a major part – only in a supporting role, entirely without the limelight. Not that she was overlooked or underestimated by the principal actors in the Dock Strike. Thorne records that

> "John Burns' wife and Eleanor Marx-Aveling acted as correspondents for the committee; they worked long hours and walked bravely late at night or in the early

---

* Since this chapter was written an excellent little book on Will Thorne has come out which expresses the view that: "It would have been better if Thorne had retired in 1924."[64]

† Tillett became a member of the General Council of the TUC when it replaced the Parliamentary Committee in 1921; an alderman of the London County Council and a Labour M.P. from 1917 to 1924 and again from 1929 to 1931.

In 1891 Thorne became the first SDF member of the West Ham Town Council on which he remained for 40 years. He was a member of the Parliamentary Committee of the TUC from 1894, its Chairman in 1896 and in 1911. He became Deputy Mayor of West Ham in 1898 and Mayor for the year 1917–18. He was the Labour M.P. for West Ham South – Keir Hardie's former constituency (1892–5) – from 1906 until 1945.

‡ In 1973 the Transport and General Workers' Union had 1,746,554 members; the National Union of General and Municipal Workers 848,481, of whom 255,240 were women.

§ Translated in 1885. Could he, perhaps, have been the "old Bishop T." referred to by "Aggie" in her letter to Eleanor of 1871, at which time Dr. Temple was Bishop of Exeter? (See above, p. 102.) In 1896 he became Primate of all England.

‖ Not, alas, wearing the fancy dress and funny hats appropriate to their high office.

morning, to their distant homes. Sacrifices unnoticed and numberless were made ...
but all distinction was lost in this great inspiring phase of the class struggle."[66]

Tom Mann recorded that

"offers of clerical help were numerous during the strike. One of these volunteers who
rendered valuable service was Eleanor Marx Aveling ... a most capable woman. Possessing a complete mastery of economics, she was able alike in conversation and on a
public platform to hold her own with the best. Furthermore, she was ever ready, as in
this case, to give close attention to detailed work, when by so doing she could help the
movement."[67]

The third and most prominent leader of the strike equally paid his
tribute. Tillett wrote:

"Another of our helpers at headquarters, doing the drudgery of clerical work as well as
more responsible duties, was Karl Marx's daughter, Eleanor ... Brilliant, devoted and
beautiful ... a Londoner by birth ... she ... had lived all her life in the atmosphere of
the Social Revolution. She lived with Aveling under very unhappy conditions, which
did not, however, break her spirit, or cause her to waver in her devotion to the
working-class cause ... she was also active in support of the efforts we were making to
organise unskilled labour in the East End of London. She gave active help in the
formation of the Gas Workers' Union, and, as I say, during our great strike, she worked
unceasingly, literally day and night ... Among those who live in my memory ...
Eleanor Marx remains a vivid and vital personality, with great force of character,
courage and ability."[68]

Three minor facts which perhaps have not been dulled by repetition
may be mentioned here as reflecting, each in its way, the response evoked
by the Dock Strike. John Burns recorded that

"Five pawnbrokers out of six in the East End issued notices to the effect that they
would charge no interest on articles pledged with them during the Strike; and
lodging-house keepers remitted their rent during the same period."[69]

The second small incident concerns Tom Mann who, though employed
south of the river, was on the strike committee with headquarters at the
Wade's Arms in Jeremiah Street, Poplar, where he often stayed to work as
late as 1 a.m., having taken part in the daily marches which were a regular
feature of the strike. When this had gone on for three weeks his boots
were worn out. Passing a bootshop on the route, he dropped out of the
column, hastily bought a new pair and caught up with his fellows. A few
days later, passing the shop, there were his dilapidated boots on proud
display in the window – as might be the Van Gogh* – with a placard

---

* But that they were not for two left feet.

bearing the words: "The boots worn by Tom Mann during the long marches of the Dock Strike."[70]

The third and as eloquent an item, arid though it may sound, is the *Statement of Accounts from 14 August to 16 November 1889* issued by the members of the newly founded Dockers' Union Council.[71] The general public had contributed £11,732 12s. 5d., of which all but a fraction – from street collecting-boxes and a benefit performance at the Queen's Palace of Varieties in Poplar – was donated by individuals and sent either direct to the strike committee or through such newspapers as *Reynolds's Newspaper*, the *Star*, the *Evening News & Post* (a Liberal paper founded in 1889), the *Labour Elector* and others. The British trade unions added £4,234 10s. 2d. to the funds, according to their size and means, while from France, Belgium, Germany and America came £108 14s. 7d. But from what was entered as "The Colonies" came £30,423 15s., of which £30,000 was from Australia, making a total of £48,736 3s. 1d. This money did not flow in overnight and, indeed, at one stage towards the end of the second week, there was serious alarm that the "250,000 stomachs to feed"[72] would go empty and that the men would be forced to their knees. The daily allowance of 1s. 6d. was reduced to 1s. and then relief tickets were issued.* Of the entire sum contributed £35,510 12s. 8d. – that is, well over 70 per cent – was given in relief to the strikers who, however meagre the amount seems for the father of a family, had depended upon earnings of 5d. an hour with sometimes no more than an hour's work a day and seldom as much as four,† making an average wage of 6s. or 7s. a week.

The only other two items not absolutely negligible were some £1,250 for "Pickets and Banner Bearers" and £936 for bands. There is, however, another outlay that tells its own story: "Payments to Blacklegs and

---

* Over the five weeks 14 August to 18 September 440,000 such tickets were distributed.
† "At the London and St. Katherine's Docks ... Payment by the hour, with the uncertainty as to whether a job will last two or twenty-four hours, and the consequently incalculable nature of even the daily income, encourages the wasteful habits of expenditure which are characteristic of this class ... as a class they are quixotically generous ... Socially they have their own peculiar attractiveness; economically they are worthless, and morally worse than worthless ... They are parasites eating the life out of the working class, demoralising and discrediting it ..." Thus Miss Beatrice Potter, writing in 1887.[73] In the course of her researches, which produced, despite their censoriousness, the most scrupulous account of the life, wages and conditions of dockers before the strike, she had attended some meetings in the docks and Tillett commented: "Neither I nor any of the other people ... appeared to have made a very satisfactory impression upon our rather aristocratically prejudiced visitor; she was young, clever, much petted by the intellectuals of the older generation; undoubtedly sincere, anxious to help, but somewhat condescending," after shooting which bolt he added: "But I would not write a word in criticism of this brilliant and devoted woman."[74]

Expenses incurred in sending men back to Liverpool, Glasgow and else-where" amounted to £1,107; while another tale must lie behind the sum of £52 odd incurred for "Rent of Halls for Meetings, Hire of Rooms and Compensation for damage of same." It is droll to note that in this situation, which drew thousands of pounds out of the pockets of workers and the general public, the legal profession did not hesitate to take fees of £350 5s. for counsel and solicitors to defend pickets and others charged with intimidation. Against this – probably heroic – sacrifice should be set the £107 claimed by Ben Tillett to cover his outlay over a period of more than twelve weeks on fares, telegrams and postage; John Burns' £65 11s. for five-and-a-half weeks' expenses and Tom Mann's £28 for the same period. They were not paid for their services.

The last word on the Dock Strike, as on so many events of his time, may be left with Engels. From Eastbourne he wrote to Laura on 27 August when the dock labourers had been out for 13 days:

> "They are, as you know, the most miserable of all the *miserable* of the East End, the broken down ones of all trades, the lowest stratum above the Lumpenproletariat.* That these poor famished broken down creatures who bodily fight amongst each other every morning for admission to work, should organise for resistance, turn out 40–50,000 strong, draw after them into the strike all and every trade of the East End in any way connected with shipping, hold out above a week, and terrify the wealthy and powerful dock companies – that is a revival I am proud to have lived to see." He added: "And all this strike is worked and led by *our* people ... the Hyndmanites are nowhere in it."[75]

Nowhere indeed. On 5 August 1889, close upon the victory of the gasworkers and but a few days before the Dock Strike was to shake the country, the SDF had held its Annual Conference in Birmingham where the Programme and Rules were revised. This document might have been drawn up by God in his Heaven, or on another planet, so remote was it from the actual struggles of the working class led though they were by members of this supernal body. Its nine-point Programme does not so much as mention trade unionism. Only in an addendum of "measures called for to palliate the evils of our existing society" does it stoop to refer in a single line to: "Eight hours or less to be the normal working day in all trades." Among the 27 revised Rules the General Council was to appoint six Executive Committees responsible for every aspect of the SDF's activities, omitting industry altogether.[76] It is a pitiful comment upon the character of the most important of the socialist organisations in existence at this juncture.

* * *

---

* This is best translated here as down-and-outs, or dregs.

No sooner was the Dock Strike at an end than Eleanor was faced by other imperative claims. First, there were her nephews who remained at 65 Chancery Lane from mid-September until their father came from France to take them home on 11 October. The boys made demands upon her time to which she responded with all her heart; but she was not to be allowed to indulge herself. She and Aveling now helped Thorne to draw up the formal Rules of the Gasworkers' Union and his first half-yearly Report and balance sheet – March to September 1889 – to be submitted to the 30,000 members.

At this point a fresh strike broke out in West Ham, lasting for twelve weeks. It failed to gain its objects, but not before Eleanor had found herself involved in it heart and soul, speaking daily at the factory and forming the first women's branch of the National Union of Gasworkers and General Labourers of Great Britain and Ireland, of which, at its Annual Conference, held on 19 May 1890 at the Gye Street Workmen's Club, she was the only nominee to be unanimously elected to the Executive Council, a position she was to hold until she retired in June 1895.[77]

This new struggle in the East End, unlike that of the gasworkers and the dockers upon whose heels it closely followed, did not make history but, in a particular sense, is of historical interest.

The gas companies, it is clear, were great monopolies, their areas of operation, their allocation of profits governed by Acts of Parliament. At the time the gasworkers formed their union and met the representatives of faceless Boards or Courts of Governors, the four companies had a paid up capital of some £10m., a very large sum for those days.

The dock employers, though they might combine to form a joint committee and appoint a spokesman to negotiate with recalcitrant labour, were, in reality, a mixed crew of wharfingers, granary keepers, shipowners, freighters, import merchants, rivercraft proprietors and an assortment of contracting companies.*

Messrs. Silver's India Rubber, Gutta Percha and Telegraph Works Ltd. was of a different order. In 1852 S. W. Silver & Co., "the well-known outfitter of Cornhill", bought one acre of land between Bow Road and Barking Creek to which it removed its small waterproofing works from Greenwich. It was the oldest factory on the river front. Seven more acres were added in the next few years and, by 1860, the premises were so extensive "that the name of Silvertown was given to the district of which they formed the centre".†[78] In 1864 there was an amalgamation with another small firm; a trusted employee who had risen from the bench, Matthew Gray, was made managing director and Silver's Rubber Works and Telegraph Cable Co. Ltd. was registered. In 1878 it was reorganised and by 1889 it had six main departments in Silvertown – rubber, ebonite, gutta percha, electrical, submarine and chemical – offices throughout the United Kingdom and a second factory in France. It was a typical private enterprise of its time; what might be called the extended-family business: no longer paternalist, not yet a monopoly – there were many competitors in the field – and thus more representative of a flourishing late 19th

---

* Brought under the Port of London Authority in 1909, though the wharves and jetties remained in private hands.

† It came to occupy 17 acres with a river frontage of 860 feet. Severely damaged by bombs in September 1940 it carried on for some years, but now (1975), one part of Silver's former premises has been taken over by Tate & Lyle, much of the site is an empty yard and the remainder is occupied by new factories whose products have no need of a waterfront.

century industrial establishment than such amorphous undertakings as the docks or such public utilities as gas. It had a paid up capital of £416,000 and 72 shareholders – a high proportion of whom were the directors and their relatives – drawing for many years past an annual dividend of 15 per cent.* In 1889 the factory employed some 2,000 manual workers, most of them labourers with a majority of men and boys, though there were well over 100 women and girls. Some of the workers were semi-skilled and there was a small proportion of fitters and turners, maintenance engineers and carpenters. These last, of course, were in their appropriate trade unions; the labourers were not organised at all.

It is a matter worth more than passing comment that the cradle of "New Unionism", though it grew sturdily throughout the country, was this district not five miles east of Aldgate pump, where a starveling population – the matchgirls of Bow, the gasmen of Beckton, the casual workers of Dockland – lived and laboured on the doorstep, as it were, of the august City of London; its sanitary conditions so unwholesome that in the last cholera outbreak of 1866 in the metropolis the overwhelming majority of deaths occurred in West Ham. It was not what is called a pleasant residential district, yet for a variety of reasons it was more densely inhabited than any other on the outskirts of London.

According to the first report of an Outer London Inquiry Committee, published in 1907:† "The growth and needs of the district, such as roads, drainage, and lighting were not adequately recognised until 1888."[79]

By 1891 there were over 43 persons to the acre,‡ which included docks, wharves, railway yards, whole factory areas and other large uninhabitable tracts, with an average of almost 6.4 persons to a house (as against 5.32 for the whole of England and Wales) and over 1,000 people living from five to twelve persons in one room.

*　　*　　*

In the mid-18th century, on the main road between Stratford and

---

* For the year 1882 it had risen as high as 25 per cent.
† Under the presidency of Canon Barnett, the founder of Toynbee Hall in 1884. The 24 members of the Committee included A. L. Bowley, W. H. Beveridge, J. A. Hobson, L. T. Hobhouse, C. F. G. Masterman and Mrs. Sidney Webb.
‡ Before the Second World War the population had risen to 56 persons to the acre. Bombing and evacuation reduced it by one-third, when it fell below the London average to only 36 persons to the acre.[80] In West Ham South – Thorne's old constituency – 19,000 of its 51,000 dwelling houses were destroyed. On the other hand, industrial premises within the Factory Inspectorate's District of West Ham rose in absolute numbers by over 36 per cent between 1939 and 1951.[81]

Plaistow* there had been a village of 700 houses: 455 "noble mansions" where "men of rank and wealth or opulent City merchants" resided, 245 cottages housing their "industrious artists" (artisans).[82] The agricultural parish of Bromley St. Leonard was built over during the first decade of the 19th century to become the domain of certain trades so unsavoury as to be driven out of London. Originally for

> "reasons of isolation ... on wide tenantless tracts ... remote from the habitations of man, chemical manufacturers first chose this neighbourhood for their secret operations, and noxious effluvia; and when the Trustees of the River Lea Navigation had excavated the new canal from Bromley to Limehouse, the Bridge they created here was called *Stink House Bridge*" – an appellation it retained for many a long year – owing to "the numerous factories erected on the Cut or Canal for the manufacture of various drugs, viz. – vitriol, pitch, varnish, grease, naphtha, manure, animal charcoal, etc. etc. which fill the air with the most noisome vapours and repulsive smells."[83]

The easterly part of the parish was transformed by the opening of the East India Dock in 1806.† Even greater changes came with the Royal Victoria Dock, constructed in 1855 on the Plaistow marshes, to be enlarged and renamed the Victoria and Albert in 1880.‡ In this one parish of Bromley St. Leonard the population rose from 4,000 in 1830 to 24,000 in 1860 while that of West Ham as a whole was 18,817 in 1851, 99,142 in 1871 and 204,903 in 1891.[84]

The first volume of the *Survey of London* (1900) was devoted to this parish, then called St. Leonard-by-Bow, on the accompanying map of which were shown, in addition to the disgusting substances cited by the historian of a generation earlier, works producing soap, tallow, candles, matches, patent leather, oakum, coconut fibre, felt, jute, rope, paint, nitrates, phosphates and distilleries of tar, benzine and resin.§

Manufactories whose raw materials came by sea were built in ever increasing numbers on the quaysides. In 1878 the cube sugar factory of

---

* Both these, together with East Ham, North Woolwich and some part of Barking were incorporated in West Ham when, with the advent of the London County Council in 1886, it became a municipal borough of Essex and two years later was raised to the status of a County Borough with twelve wards. Under the London Government Act of 1899 it became a Metropolitan Borough. With certain boundary changes this has been known as Newham since April 1964.

† Closed in 1966.

‡ At a cost of £2m. In 1921 the King George V was added to the Royal Docks.

§ The 1907 Report by the Commission of Inquiry (see above, p. 521) explained that "As West Ham was extra-Metropolitan ... the bye-laws about ... the emission of fumes and smells were less stringent than in London. Moreover there was and is less danger of actions for nuisance at common law ... 'Offensive trades', which are now altogether prohibited in the Metropolitan area, are still admissible."[85]

Henry Tate – to whose profits we owe our second National Gallery* – was started, later to amalgamate with Abram Lyle's sugar and golden syrup manufactory, built in 1881 on the river front; while the Grain Elevator Company added its towering hoists and silos to the cranes, the masts, the derricks that, mile upon mile, pointed to the skyscapes of the unaccidented Essex fens and marshlands of an obliterated past. In Silvertown, too, John Tomlinson Brunner, the chemist, and Ludwig Mond, his partner, who had come from Kassel to England in 1864 – the founding fathers of ICI – set up in due course a modest chemical plant.†

Further north were "the Great Central Gasworks", a public company formed in 1810 on the initiative of F. A. Winser, who had experimentally illuminated the Lyceum Theatre by gas in 1803. This became the Gas, Light & Coke Co. by Act of Parliament and started operations with a capital of £20,000 in 1812, deriving its name Beckton, later extended to the whole area, from its first chairman, Simon Adam Beck. The gasworks were built upon the six-acre site of a field which, too coarse for cultivation, had been turned into gravel pits. It was rated at £34; in 1860 at £3,000. The new works, constructed in 1869, covered 150 acres and went into production in 1870, giving "employment to no less than 3,000 hands".[86] The *Illustrated London News* went into raptures:

> "Vast piles of building, with a stately monumental clock on the spacious front lawn; and with seven or eight immense gasholders – cylindrical iron structures painted bright red, supported by lofty iron pillars – rise near the water's edge."

Twelve hundred men, the writer marvelled, worked in the retort-houses alone; on the beauty of their working environment he had, however, nothing to say.

Still further to the north-west, on the fringes of Stratford-by-Bow, where formerly there had been a locomotive factory, the vast complex of the Great Eastern Railway marshalling yards were laid out in 1880 on what had been known as Fulton Fields. This intricate junction covered an enormous tract of land; in its great repair sheds steam engines rested on their turntables like to so many Gargantuan toys round which scurried tiny men.

Despite the appalling damage inflicted upon Dockland during the Second World War, its essential character remained intact. Physically, in the early post-war years, it presented a scene of desolation: acres of derelict

---

* On the site of the Millbank Prison, demolished in 1890. The Tate Gallery was formally opened in July 1897 and enlarged two years later.
† Silvertown might never have been heard of by the rest of London had it not been brought to its ears by an explosion of such loud report in the munition works there on 19 January 1917 that no one then living has ever forgotten it.

wasteland came to be dotted with prefabricated boxes and troglodytic tunnels of corrugated iron, called homes, with here and there a stark building – pub or shop – left standing, a footpath trodden to it through rank fields of weed and rubble.

The northern area was still a warren of dilapidated backstreet hovels bearing witness to their 19th-century origins, speculative jerry building and the negligence of landlords. Although its 1,374 factories – with and without mechanical power – represented but 7 per cent of those falling within the Central Metropolitan Division of the Factory Inspectorate's Districts, over 80 per cent of these establishments employed fewer than 100 people, not to mention the countless workshops, some little more than sheds, which, with under eleven men, did not figure on the Inspector's register.* It is noteworthy that in 1946 these seven or so square miles showed so high a concentration of industry that, of the nearly 19,000 factories in the Division, West Ham suffered 10 per cent of all its notified accidents and 42 per cent of those that proved fatal.[87] Furthermore, the area had retained its ancient tradition as the habitat of the "offensive trades" and workers were uncommonly exposed to the hazards of every toxic substance recognised by the Factory and Workshop Acts, to which were added year by year ever larger quantities of new and more sophisticated industrial chemicals whose deleterious effects only time – or some peculiarly hideous death – would bring to light.

To the south, in the Custom House and Silvertown Ward, there still huddled dingy rows of little terraced houses whose dead-ends were overshadowed in gigantic disproportion by the spick and span gunwales, bulwarks, superstructure, masts and funnels of great ships in dock. On the riverside, across the two railway tracks – the freight line now disused – moored lighters rocked on the tide at the base of forbidding factory walls.

That horrendous and fascinating district, its very name, has now been transformed, its delicate skyline defaced by tower blocks (whether to the greater happiness of former prefab. and cave dwellers, expert opinion seems in doubt); its topography ravaged by roundabouts and overpasses; there are still tumbledown houses and acres of soiled wilderness, including those of the long abandoned famous old Thames Ironworks; time-honoured landmarks have been wiped out by agents almost as effective as war itself; yet even today it needs little imagination to conjure up the Silvertown of 1889.

*   *   *

In the third week of September in that year, fired by the success of the

---

* This applied also to railway depots, docks, shops, offices and catering premises.

Dock Strike, the general labourers in the telegraph and cable shops at Silver's, earning $3\frac{1}{2}$d. to $4\frac{1}{2}$d. an hour, agitated for their own "tanner". They had other grievances: the working day was from 6 a.m. to 6 p.m., but it was common for men and women to put in as much as 80 hours a week for which – emulating the gasworkers – they now demanded overtime pay. There were even isolated cases of men having done 115 and 120 hours in the ebonite department. Food was eaten in the workshops amidst filth and stench. The discipline was such that those who arrived half an hour late twice in one week were sent home on the second occasion to forfeit that day's pay. Though they knew the penalty, they must nevertheless suffer the humiliation of presenting themselves on pain of losing their employment so that the punishment might be meted out with due severity. A "pass ticket" had to be shown by every worker; should anyone forget to apply for a ticket, though this might not be discovered until eight or nine hours later, those hours went unpaid.

The first response of the management to the demands was to post notices throughout the factory announcing that any employee who was dissatisfied would be taken off the payroll, whereupon 280 yardmen walked out. Slightly taken aback, since these were not the men who had been making all the fuss, the management offered reinstatement on the basis of an additional three farthings an hour. This was accepted, the men went back; at which point the labourers in the electrical shop struck for an extra halfpenny. The employers withdrew then offer of three farthings to the yardmen and on Tuesday, 17 September, 1,200 men and women downed tools.

Eleanor played no part in the early weeks of the strike because she had Johnny and Edgar with her. Notwithstanding, four days before they left for France, having heard that there had been complaints about the lack of speakers, she went to Silvertown. From that time forth she traipsed daily to the East End,* where, using anything that would serve as a platform, she addressed the strikers outside the works each morning, often speaking again at afternoon and evening meetings.†

By the time Eleanor appears upon the scene it is the 22nd day of the

---

* For anyone curious to know how she got there it may be of interest to learn that Metropolitan and Inner Circle trains ran from 6 a.m. to midnight. There was a station at Farringdon Street and, from Aldgate, connections by the Great Eastern and Blackwall Railways to Silvertown Station (which, in a dilapidated condition, still stands opposite Silver's original site). In addition there were the North Metropolitan Company's tramcars starting from Aldgate every few minutes to Bow, Stratford and Dockland. There was also a Blue Bus from Fleet Street or Ludgate Hill and a Green Bus from Holborn every ten minutes to the docks. No difficulty there; and probably no more tiresome a journey than that made twice daily by tens of thousands of modern Londoners who would not, however, claim it as one of the pleasures of life.

† Later Clara Zetkin, visiting London with her boys, went to Silvertown and, as Engels told Laura, "gave me news of Tussy whose agitation she is very enthusiastic about, especially her getting on tables and chairs to harangue the Silvertown women strikers".[88]

strike and much has happened.* A Strike Committee of some 30 odd men, with headquarters at the Railway Tavern, known as Cundy's, on the corner of Constance Street, facing Silvertown Station, has been set up under the elected leadership of a semi-skilled worker named Ling who, earning 4¾d. an hour, is among the better paid. He has organised regular meetings in front of the factory every morning, mobilised local brass bands and led processions with collecting boxes through the streets. More important, he has gained the support not only of the Gasworkers' Union but that of the Dockers, the Stevedores, the Sailors and Firemen and the Coal Porters, all of whom contribute to a Strike Fund and send speakers who urge the men to stand firm but, above all, to organise. The great stumbling block is that the skilled engineers and carpenters refuse to strike in solidarity. There are also 400 labourers still at work. They say, however, that they will come out as soon as the piecework they are doing is finished. A great meeting is held in Hyde Park by the Gasworkers on Sunday, 29 September, the 13th day of the strike, when Thorne announces that his Union has voted £250 to the Silvertown fund. Relief money is distributed at the end of the second week: 5s. to each man and 2s. 6d. to every woman, boy and girl. Day by day ever larger crowds assemble outside the factory. The strikers are joined by other workers in the neighbourhood attracted by the street parades with their bands and banners. The next Sunday, 6 October, despite the bitter cold and damp, 10,000 people assemble in Victoria Park, Hackney, where among other speakers Burns castigates his own ASE members for failing to come out and he exposes the huge profits of the company and the large dividends plundered by the most respectable members of society from Silver's sweated labour.†

In the meantime the management has not been idle. The engineers have been instructed to dismantle some of the machines for transfer, with raw material, to the French branch at Persan-Beaumont near Nogent-sur-Marne. A few Manchester girls are brought in as blacklegs; when they learn the facts, they refuse to go into the factory. The next day the strikers

---

* The account that follows is derived almost entirely from the contemporary local press and records, for which mine of information I am indebted to the archivists of the Stratford Reference Library and to Mr. Peter Braham for working the seam.
† Profits in 1888 were £163,000. Although Burns claimed that the Marquess of Salisbury, "the head of Her Majesty's Government" (his second administration: July 1886 to August 1892), was at the top of the list of shareholders, this particular Cecil was not, in fact, in the 1889 file of the Company's Register. It did include such respected persons as the Hon. Reginald Capel, Lord Eustace Cecil, Mr. Andrew Grant, M.P., the Rev. Henry Latham, Mr. Sebag Montefiore, Viscount Monck, the Hon. Henry Marsham (a director), the Rev. Robert Rackham, Sir Philip Rose, Bart., Lady Eliza Stainer, Mr. Mark Stewart, M.P., and Lieut-Colonel Sir William Wallace.[89]

pay their return fares and see them off at the station. The managing director, Gray, behaves, according to a trade union speaker, "as though he were the Emperor of all the Russias"; he has told the workers to get out until they come to their proper senses. The sympathy and enthusiasm drummed up for the strike, which has now lasted 18 days, call for counter measures. The company's Secretary writes a letter to the press:

"As misleading statements are being circulated with reference to a strike at our Silvertown factory, we ask you to give publicity to the following particulars of wages paid by us up to September last, which will be found to compare favourably with those paid for similar works in other parts of England:

	Hours	Pay	
Labourers (including yardmen and stokers)	63	26s.	1d.
India Rubber departments	$63\frac{1}{2}$	33s	7d.
Cable, wire covering, battery, gutta percha, electric light and general departments	60	28s.	1d.*

No able bodied labourer employed by us receives less than $4\frac{3}{4}$d. per hour. The above payments do not include those made to foremen, clerks and skilled mechanics of various classes, who, of course, draw much higher wages.

We employ a considerable number of women and boys, who are not included in the above statement, but who are paid on a scale proportionate to that of the men.

The workpeople were practically in permanent employment, their weekly number not varying much during the years; and our workshops are large and well ventilated, and our appliances of the best.

Our factory is in the neighbourhood of the docks, and the recent strike there appears to have unsettled the minds of some of the workpeople. The majority of them, however, have been intimidated into leaving their work, having when going to their meals to pass through a crowd who hissed at and groaned at them, and used violent language. In some cases they have been hurt, but will not give evidence lest worse shall befall them. Yesterday about 115 women who were satisfied with their pay left the work under intimidation, and there are now about 1,600 workpeople thrown out of employment, leaving only 250 still at work."

Though the figures given are demonstrably untrue, this letter receives wide publicity which is hardly surprising, as Eleanor points out, since in the main the press is under capitalist control and, until Labour has an organ of its own, its voice will not be heard nor its case fairly represented. Nevertheless, the local paper, the *Stratford Express*,† publishes an editorial on 12 October (the 26th day of the strike) saying that the Silvertown workers are gaining public sympathy,

"partly through their own admirable behaviour, and partly by the fact that their statements remain practically unanswered ... 'We pay as high as any firm for similar

---

* These rates represent, respectively, just under 5d., over 6d. and something above $5\frac{1}{2}$d. per hour.
† A weekly launched in 1854 as the *Stratford Times*, the name being changed in 1855.

work in England', says the Secretary of the Company. That may be perfectly true, but if it be, it is no answer. If wages are too low everywhere, that may be a reason for keeping them down at Messrs. Silver's. 'The majority of our workpeople ... were satisfied, but have been intimidated into leaving their work'. If that were so it would be as well if the secretary explained how a majority can be intimidated by a minority. We understand that the manager of the company has stated that the works are open and the hands can return, if they wish, 'at the old rate of pay'. If we had not been told this upon the very best authority we should have declined to believe it. How can Mr. Gray expect the workpeople to go in at the old rate of pay, when he himself gave them, in the first instance, nearly all they now ask for? If the demand was unreasonable he should have said so at first. Instead of that he granted an increase, which is surely a confession that he was able to give it."

"The very best authority" is that of the vicar of St. Mark's Church, Hackney, who has approached Gray in person, to be snubbed for his pains. On the same day, the strikers march through the City, where Eleanor watches them, having just read the Secretary's letter in the press. She can hardly believe that satisfied people tramp 20 miles for the fun of it. This is on 10 October, the 24th day of the strike and the third time Eleanor has addressed the meeting at the works. If only one of their number is getting $3\frac{1}{2}$d. or $4\frac{1}{2}$d. an hour, she says, the thousand are justified in coming out. A wrong done to one is a wrong done to all. This is what the engineers have still to learn. She warns, however, that even should an increase of wages be won it will be no lasting victory unless the strike teaches them to organise. That, she points out, was the real triumph of the Dock Strike and will be the real triumph in Silvertown. On the day before she has appealed directly to the women, telling them that they must form a union and work in harmony with the men's organisations. The great lesson of the Dock Strike is that the skilled and unskilled must combine; the lesson here is that men and women have to work in unison. Women are used by the employer to keep men's wages down and not until women refuse to undercut their husbands and brothers will this situation change.

Another speaker remarks that while there is much objection to workmen combining there has never been anything to equal the combination of capitalists in London.

The Mayor of West Ham, Robert Curtis, J. P., has taken a hand and offered to mediate. He writes to the company and is as roundly rebuffed as the vicar, receiving a reply from the Secretary on 10 October:

"Dear Sir, I am directed to thank you for your kind note of yesterday, offering to mediate between ourselves and our workpeople ... We have found from inquiry that we have been paying higher wages than any other firm in our trade; and the directors have decided not to pay more.

Our workpeople have always been well paid and kindly treated; but they have been too easily misled by unscrupulous agitators, who try to cause dissension between employers and their men.

The directors regret that they cannot see the advantage of the mediation suggested. Our men know that they can return to their work when they wish to do so. They have made a mistake; and the directors are very sorry that the wives and children are suffering through the folly of the men.

Again thanking you for your kind offer, and regretting that we cannot avail ourselves of it."

On the evening of that same day, Eleanor forms the first women's branch of the National Union of Gasworkers and General Labourers.

The Strike Committee now approaches the directors in the hope of a settlement. On Saturday, the 26th day of the strike, the company announces that the factory gates will be opened on Monday. Any worker is free to go in, but at the old rate of pay.

That Sunday the Executive Council of the Gasworkers formally admits the Silvertown Women's Branch and its secretary, Mrs. Eleanor Marx Aveling, to the Union.

The Finsbury Radical Club convenes a meeting on Clerkenwell Green at which Eleanor, Ben Tillett and a representative of the Patriotic Club speak to an audience of 3,000 in support of the Silvertown strike. Eleanor says that the next few days are critical, for if funds are not forthcoming the workers will be starved into submission. Already the relief given at the end of the last week has been reduced to 4s. for each man, 2s. 6d. for the women and 2s. for the boys.[*]

In the afternoon Eleanor speaks again at a large demonstration in Victoria Park. A procession is formed at Silvertown, others joining its ranks on the route until some 10,000 people march into the Park. At the head of the parade come Silver's workers, men and women, with union tickets stuck in their hats. They are followed by contingents of stevedores, coal porters, dockers, lightermen, painters, sailors and workers from other Silvertown factories, with bands and banners all the way. Amongst the crowd Eleanor encounters a sympathetic onlooker who turns out to be one of Silver's shareholders. She extracts £5 from him towards the strike fund.

The next day the factory gates stand open. Not a single striker goes in. The Committee, having met with a flat refusal to negotiate a settlement, writes again to the directors. Eleanor tells the morning meeting that the women from the local jam factory – Keiller's, first started in 1879 – have asked to meet the newly-formed branch of Silver's workers to learn more about the union.

On 16 October, the 30th day of the strike, Aveling goes to France with

---

[*] Relief had also been distributed on the Wednesday, making the total for this, the third, week of the strike, 7s. a man, 4s. a woman and 3s. a boy.

the mission of persuading the men at the Persan-Beaumont works 36 miles outside Paris, to support their English fellow-workers. He stays at the Lafargues' and discusses the matter with them and with Longuet who think that as the French workers are well paid they will not risk their jobs. Aveling meets representatives at the works and finds that this is so. A letter is drafted to the Paris press publicising the Silvertown strike and appealing for French support.

As arranged, Eleanor and members of her branch meet the women from the jam factory who decide to join the union. An hour later, she talks to the women still at work in Silver's.

The directors peremptorily refuse to meet a deputation. They say they will not "treat with their workpeople whilst led by agitators". On 19 October the *Stratford Express* publishes another leader on the matter:

> "Of course the directors know their own business best, but ... if 'agitators' are present, why need the company trouble? If the 'agitators' are in the wrong, a plain statement of the facts, in the presence of the workpeople and of an arbitrator, would soon knock the bottom out of their case. On the other hand, if the company refuse to meet them, the public will conclude, rightly or wrongly, that the 'agitators' are in the right."

The following Sunday sees yet another demonstration in Victoria Park, reinforced this time by various unions and clubs whose members fall in with the march at the East India Docks, while a second contingent joins the crowd in Hackney. Tom Mann expresses the view that if the strikers are to blame for anything it is that their demands are too moderate.

On the 36th day of the strike, 22 October, another letter goes to the directors asking them to meet the strikers' spokesmen without a mediator. To this they agree, saying they will receive ten or twelve workpeople. The interview is to take place on Thursday, 24 October. Before setting off Ling, the secretary of the Strike Committee, calls for and receives a vote of confidence. Eleanor says that two or three women will go on the deputation and, all told, 18 workers present themselves at the Cannon Street offices of the company. The confrontation is not a success. The figures so widely publicised in the press are challenged, the workers giving chapter and verse on their weekly pay. The matter of a dining room is raised. The directors say they will give this their consideration and are also prepared to rectify certain other minor grievances. On the question of wages they remain adamant: nothing will be conceded; the workers can go back at the old rate or not at all.

Ling reports to the strikers the next morning and they endorse his refusal to accept these terms.

That Sunday some of the housewives have asked the advice of a local parson who tells them to go back home and put pressure on their men to return to work. Staying out is wrong. This is reported on the Monday morning – the 44th day of the strike – and is denounced as an injury: it is not the business of any clergyman to dictate what the men and their families shall do.

Aveling, back from France, reports to the Strike Committee. He reads out the letter sent to the Paris press.* The delegates think it too mealy-mouthed and recommend that a stronger letter be written. Aveling agrees to this and then addresses the outdoor meeting. He expresses the optimistic view that, since the directors have shown themselves willing to meet the workers on certain small points, it is a sign that sooner or later they will cave in.

By now the girls who have been tramping about with collecting boxes are in need of new boots and they are given vouchers for this purpose.

Eleanor tells the next morning's meeting that, because the girls are the most active collectors in the streets, it is being spread abroad that, unable to subsist on relief, they are resorting to prostitution. This is a slander, put about to antagonise public opinion. She says she has never met more self-respecting factory girls than those now on strike in Silvertown.

A procession goes to Cannon Street to stand silently outside the company's offices where the men bare their heads. In the following week this derisive gesture is repeated, now accompanied by a brass band blaring out the *Dead March* from *Saul*, which helps to cause obstruction and create disturbance, advertising to every company director, city clerk and office boy within sight and sound of that staid quarter that all is not well at Silver's.

On the 50th day, 5 November, it is clear that some of the strikers are wavering and may go back to work. The steadfast majority turn out at 5.30 a.m. and assemble at the factory gates to be ready for their arrival at 6 o'clock. Gray has mobilised his own sons in case of trouble, but also a large force of police. The scabs go into the factory. Later, the band parades in front of the works playing the *Dead March* as loudly and slowly as possible. A short meeting takes place at which Eleanor calls for a collection to enable the girls on strike to pay their union dues. She has organised a fund for their entrance fees: the sum of £2 11s. 6d. is needed; so far there is only £1 14s. 3½d. The meeting donates 5s.

On Sunday, 10 November, there is a great demonstration in Hyde Park in support of both an impending bakers' strike and the Silvertown workers.

The strike pay, despite the funds voted by unions and generously given to the marchers on their parades, is again reduced: 4s. a man, 3s. a woman

---

* Published in *L'Intransigeant* on 31 October.

and 2s. a boy, which includes 1s. to all who have taken part in the two processions that week: 6d. for each occasion.

Two of the three men who go into the factory on 14 November do so because they are living in houses owned by Silver's and Gray has threatened to evict them. The factory is forcibly kept clear of pickets throughout the week because a number of men from Sevenoaks are being brought to Silvertown by steam tug from London Bridge. Told by the strikers how matters stand, the Kentish men refuse to enter the works.

The Mayor now makes a fresh effort to intervene. He suggests that two or three of the workers meet the directors accompanied by himself, Mr. Sydney Buxton* and a Mr. Hume Webster. The directors refuse to meet such a deputation. Buxton gets in touch with them and is told that no concessions will be made and potential mediators are wasting their time.

On the 60th day of the strike Thorne addresses the meeting and proposes that the Gasworkers should vote £500 to the Strike Fund and make a weekly grant until the strike is over. His is a fighting organisation, not interested in hoarding money. If the old unions, such as the ASE which takes £1,000 a week in contributions, were as liberal as the new, the whole strike might have been brought to a successful conclusion. At the same time he points out that trade is slack, that the public has been digging into its pockets a good few times of late and if a compromise can be reached, he recommends acceptance. Organise, he exhorts the strikers, and await a favourable opportunity to press your just claims.

There is another meeting in Victoria Park on the Sunday, addressed by both Eleanor and Aveling. It is announced that Gray will not receive a deputation with the Mayor; great bitterness is expressed: the strike is a matter of life and death to the workpeople; their children are being condemned to starvation but the managing director, who is the more vindictive and tyrannous because he has risen from their own ranks, will not so much as listen, is bent upon trampling them into the gutter and counts upon the snows of winter to drive them back to work.

This proves only too true. On Monday, the 63rd day of the strike, a number of men, heedful, perhaps, of the covert warning in Thorne's advice, start drifting into the factory. For the most part they are not among the lowest paid and have come out as a matter of principle rather than in their own interest. There is great anger and excitement among the

---

* (1853–1934). Buxton had acted as one of the mediators in the Dock Strike. Radical M.P. for Poplar (1886–1914); Under-Secretary of State for the Colonies (1892–5); Postmaster General and a member of the Cabinet (1905–10); President of the Board of Trade (1910–14); responsible for the Copyright Act and the Unemployment Insurance Act of 1911; High Commissioner and Governor-General of South Africa (1914–20). Created Viscount 1914 and 1st Earl 1920.

more determined strikers who try to prevent them entering the gates. At 7 a.m. a local alderman, who has given both active and financial support, appears on the scene and advises them to remain united but not in any circumstances to resort to violence which will only harm their cause. He proposes that delegates should go to every india rubber works in the country, find out what help, if any, they will give and then hold a general meeting to vote on whether the strike should continue. He also suggests that another approach to Gray be made. His words have a pacifying effect and none of the men go into the factory.

There is a rumour that 70 French workers are being imported as blacklegs. Eleanor telegraphs at once to Lafargue and Vaillant asking them to do what they can to prevent this. Engels follows up her appeal by writing to Guesde on 20 November. The workers, both men and women, have landed in England, though whether they will be taken to Silvertown is not yet known. In all probability they have been brought over on false pretences, unaware of the strike.

A few men have been recruited from Colchester, but two of them decide to return home. On the platform at Silvertown Station they are approached by a police inspector who talks them round and escorts them back to the factory, now surrounded by police. The day after, between one and two o'clock, as the band stops playing, another police inspector strikes one of the men and then gives orders for truncheons to be drawn. The police, who allege that they have been pelted with stones, charge into the crowd, laying about them and seriously injuring several people, including women and children. Two men are taken into custody though one of them turns out to be merely a bystander, unconnected with Silver's. The strikers stay outside the works and conduct a meeting which goes on throughout the whole afternoon; the speakers include two strangers who come forward from the audience, having witnessed the affray. The police are not blamed for obeying orders, though they might have done so less savagely, but the inspectors – Parsons and Vady – are reviled. That evening a further meeting is held in a field behind the Tate Institute.* The well-disposed alderman advises the men and women to lie low for a day or two and then to hold their mass meeting indoors to take the ballot he has recommended.

At last the ASE sends a deputation to meet the Strike Committee. It is made clear that, but for the action of the engineers, the strike might have been won and that, while labourers elsewhere are counted upon to back up the skilled men, here at Silvertown the skilled men have left the labourers

---

* In the North Woolwich Road. Another of the public benefactions of the sugar king.

in the lurch. As a result of this conference, hopes rise that the ASE will call out their members officially.

On 21 November (66th day), Gray receives a deputation of strikers. It is an informal interview, but he says he has nothing to add to his former uncompromising answer. That evening members of the Strike Committee put their case to a full delegate meeting of the London Trades Council. Tom Mann, as a member of the ASE, is convinced that if his members are withdrawn the works will come to a stop and that this demand should be put to his executive. He moves a resolution of support for Silvertown with a strong recommendation on the ASE position. This is amended and all reference to the engineers deleted. The resolution is then carried unanimously.

Mr. Hume Webster, who was to have accompanied the Mayor and Sidney Buxton on the deputation that Gray declined to meet, approaches him directly and urges him to yield so that the forthcoming mass meeting will vote to end the strike. He is rudely brushed aside.

On 26 November 150 men return to work. The police are present in large numbers, but there is no need for them: the defectors are not molested. Some 1,000 strikers declare that they will stand firm. The next day more workers go back, though a few decide to come out again.

The London Trades Council issues a circular dated 27 November 1889 to the "Trades of the Metropolis":

"Fellow Workers,
    At a general delegate meeting of the societies connected with the London Trades Council which represented 27,000 organised workmen, the dispute of the Silvertown workers with their employers was fully investigated, and found to be worthy of your prompt and generous pecuniary and moral support. It is of the utmost importance not only to the workers engaged in this struggle, but also to the whole industrial population of the metropolis, that the contest should be honourably terminated on a basis of mutual justice to all interests involved. To accomplish this it is imperative that the workers should be placed in a position of dignified independence by your immediate financial assistance. Whilst making this appeal to you the Trades Council is also making an earnest effort to effect a just and satisfactory settlement by a conciliatory approach to the employers to secure this object at the earliest possible moment."

On the 28th the stampede back to the factory ceases: many of those who went in two days before are now resolved to stay out. Eleanor tells the meeting that others, too, will think better of it and change their minds. She is indignant at the seizure of a banner, forcibly confiscated by the police during an injudicious visit to Silvertown by Princess Beatrice of Battenberg.* Eleanor reports that several Radical and Liberal M.P.s have written to the Home Office complaining of the conduct of the police in

---

* Queen Victoria's youngest daughter (1857–1944); married Henry, Prince of Battenberg, on 23 July 1885. On 30 July he was naturalised.

Silvertown and that other representations will be made. The Strike Committee issues a manifesto to those who have gone back to work acknowledging the generous sacrifices they have made in the interests of their lower-paid brothers and sisters but reminding them that the strikers' case is unchanged. It assures them that if they will rejoin their fellows, no unkind word on their temporary desertion will be spoken.

On the 74th day of the strike, 29 November, there is a biting wind, yet the morning meeting in the open air, with many of the female workers in the crowd, is as well attended as ever and two other women besides Eleanor are among the speakers.*

The London Trades Council has fulfilled its promise to intercede with Gray, who replies:

"As you seem to hope that the strikers at Silvertown will resume work, you will be pleased to learn that the total number we now have at work amounts to 961. Many of those still out have agreed to return, and we are now getting the work prepared for them as quickly as we can. Some doubts have arisen in our minds as to the sincerity of your desire to see them all at work, from the efforts that have been made within the last few days to induce the men, who are now at work, to go out again. We understand our business, and our men perfectly understand the pay they have been receiving, and you do not, and therefore cannot help us or them. The agitators are entirely responsible for the loss of £20,000 in wages to our workpeople and we are very sorry that they were led away by the misstatements and misleading promises of these agitators."

---

* One of these was Honor Brooke – the eldest of the Rev. Stopford Augustus Brooke's six daughters – who was among the first to organise country holidays for children from the London slums. Her father, a brilliant divine appointed Chaplain to Queen Victoria in 1867 and Royal Chaplain in Ordinary in 1872, was refused the Canonry of Westminster, despite the Sovereign's displeasure, by both Disraeli and Gladstone owing to his unorthodox principles. From his early days in Holy Orders Brooke had held the most eccentric views on Eternal Punishment, which he decried as "that intolerable doctrine", and when he ceased to believe in both the Incarnation and the Resurrection, coming also "to regard the Church ... as on the side of the rich", his position was untenable and he resigned from the Church of England in 1880: "Others may stay in her fold and deny the miraculous – I cannot", he wrote to his sister.[90] On Sunday, 1 December 1889, he preached a sermon on the Silvertown strike in his own church, Bedford Chapel, New Oxford Street, where, since 1884, he had instituted a fortnightly Debating Society attended by such notable heretics as Herbert Burrows, Bernard Shaw and Sidney Webb, while William Morris was not only a close personal friend but responsible for many of the furnishing in Brooke's own house. He died at the age of 84 in 1916.

The second lady, referred to as "Miss Lees", was undoubtedly Edith, whom Havelock Ellis was to marry in December 1891. In his reminiscences Ellis says that both he and she were "in relations of friendship – quite independently – with Karl Marx's brilliant and attractive daughter Eleanor".[91] In her own publication, *Stories and Essays* (1921), Edith Lees wrote: "Thirty years ago ... how well I remember how after the first performance of Ibsen's drama in London ..." (she is referring to *A Doll's House* at the Novelty on 7 June 1889) "a few of us collected outside the theatre breathless with excitement. Olive Schreiner was there and Dolly Radford, the poetess ... Honor Brooke (Stopford Brooke's eldest daughter) ... and Eleanor Marx. We were restive and impetuous and almost savage in our arguments...."[92]

Gray has already threatened to close the factory if those who have gone back rejoin the strikers; and, in case the letter to the LTC is not widely enough publicised, he writes to the press giving the number of those who are at work, adding that the amount of the wages bill that week:

> "will go to alleviate the distress in the neighbourhood – distress which has been caused by the action of the strikers, and prolonged by the misstatements and misleading promises of the agitators."

Tom Mann and four other members of the LTC go to Silvertown to investigate the situation. They ask the Strike Committee what is the lowest rate the workers will accept and are told not less than $5\frac{1}{2}$d. an hour.

The President of the East Finsbury Radical Association addresses the Victoria Park meeting on Sunday, 1 December, praising the manful battle, the suffering and struggle, of the past many weeks as an example to all labour. While the Gasworkers' Union has voted another £200 to the funds and passed a resolution levying their members 3d. a week, it is frankly recognised that it will become increasingly difficult to stop the men who came out in solidarity from returning to work.

Gray now tells those who apply to go back that he will take on those he needs and no others.

When relief is distributed on 4 December – 5s. a man, 3s. a women and 2s. a boy – the total paid is less than on any previous occasion. The number of strikers is down to 640.

On the 83rd day, Sunday, 8 December, Tom Mann advises them to give up the fight. They should stipulate that the miserable three farthings originally offered and then withdrawn should be granted and then call off the strike.

At a mass meeting on Monday in the Hack Road Lecture Hall, attended by those still out and some few of those who have gone back, a resolution is passed with one dissentient vote:

> "That it is the opinion of this meeting that the strike must be closed without dishonour on account of the action of the men and women who came out on principle, and after twelve weeks deserted the actual strikers, leaving 450 workers practically locked out, and dependent on the public for support, until such time as they can get work elsewhere."

The strikers are advised to negotiate individually for the best terms they can get. On Tuesday, 10 December, they do so, but those whose demands are above the old rate are refused work.

The last manifesto is issued on this, the 85th day of the strike:

"The Strike Committee after twelve weeks of conflict, after careful consideration and a prolonged discussion by the men and women still out, decided to declare the strike at an end. Nearly 1,000 hands have returned to work, and the committee feel that, in justice to the public generally, and to those strikers who are honourably awaiting the instructions of the committee as to returning to work, they should publicly announce that the Silvertown strike is at an end.

Any subscriptions that may henceforth be sent, will be devoted only to the help of the 450 men and women who are still out of employment in consequence of the lock-out by Messrs. Silvers...

The Committee look upon their defeat as a victory, and upon the struggle of the last twelve weeks as an earnest of future demands on the part of the underpaid labourers and the granting of them by overpaid capital. The Committee state publicly that they look upon the action of the Executive Council of the Amalgamated Engineers Society in a large measure the cause of the present failure of the Silvertown Strike, and they further desire to thank publicly those Associations that have helped them, among others the Gas Workers' and General Labourers' Union, the Coal Porters' Union, the East London Painters' Society, the Cigar Workers' Union and more especially the East Finsbury Radical Club and the Salvation Army..."

So the strike ended. On Saturday, 14 December, the last relief funds were distributed among the 450 locked out workers: 8s. to the men, 5s. to the women and 3s. to the boys.

*   *   *

Naturally, some people are not much interested in strikes – their cause, their course or their outcome – unless they are either a blazing success or an ignominious failure. The reason why this particular strike, which was neither, has been followed in detail is threefold. Firstly, it is a classic example of private industry in the late 19th century prospering on the sweated labour of unorganised men and women in an area where, until the gasworkers and the dockers rebelled against their conditions, this was accepted as in the natural order of things. It also shows the emergence of the new managerial type. Matthew Gray, though a director and the holder of 1,000 shares, was neither the founder nor the owner of the firm: he was as much its slave, though a pampered one, as any other employee. The *Companies Register* might designate him as "Gentleman"; that is precisely what he was not. Of the humblest origins, he had been vested with almost unlimited power over the workers; his loyalty to the interests of his masters was absolute, but he had not their self-confidence. His intransigence, his asperity, and his terror of agitators were characteristic of the man who had clambered out of his own class and despised it accordingly. Gray was a portent and a symbol, without which contemporary "labour relations", as they are now one-sidedly called, cannot be fully appreciated.*

---

* To be sure, the Grays of this world have come a long way since then and vastly changed their tune. They became those genial Works Managers who welcomed into the factory psychologists,

Secondly, and more to the point, it was the first down-to-earth struggle in which Eleanor played a leading part and an organising role, to become a trade unionist herself. In Silvertown, day by day, she expressed in practical form her identification with working-class men and women which was as unshakable as Gray's allegiance to the employers.

Lastly, and of even greater relevance to Eleanor's story, it was in Silvertown that she had discerned one of those growing points – Shelley's "seeds ... sleeping in the soil" – which were, for her, "the real movement". The SDF might mumble over its lofty programme; the TUC weigh up the pros and cons of the eight-hour day; the anarchists of the SL breathe revolutionary fire: here, in an ambit so near and yet such worlds away from the centres of capitalist pomp, were people deprived, overworked, underpaid and on the borderline of starvation. Nobody whose sensibilities – if they had any – were not blunted by self-absorption, greed or arrogance could remain indifferent to that state of affairs.

Certainly the rubber workers had been stimulated by the example of the dockers among whom they lived, but they were in no position to bring industry to a standstill nor to undermine British capitalism, however essential to our clime the waterproof coat may be. To whom could it matter, indeed, if Silver's little company went out of business?†

The strikers and their families had, as the company's secretary put it, brought their sufferings upon themselves; and it was they themselves who were thereby changed. As was Eleanor.

That this small group of men and women, against all odds, should suddenly awaken to the need to fight, should stand their ground week after week and defy their exploiters had nothing ignoble about it and, in Eleanor's eyes, it was the very essence of socialist action. True, they were beaten, but not to their knees, and in the process they had grasped and learnt to handle the only weapon of those who are weak in all but numbers. Eleanor no longer stood upon the sidelines, the politically educated lady who could make rousing speeches, write revolutionary articles and exhort others to action. Her voice, that of Marx's daughter, had reached the masses many a time before; now she spoke as a member and representative of a mass organisation she had helped to bring into

---

sociologists and research specialists in every field (bar industrial medicine); but however many superfluous investigations into the self-evident they encouraged; however many winsome statistical tables on such nebulous subjects as "job satisfaction" were produced as a result, they knew every bit as well as any Matthew Gray – which is to say as much as their job was worth – that what was at stake was the satisfaction of shareholders.

† Some charitable readers may mutter: "the 72 shareholders". It is reassuring to know that most of these had such large, well-balanced portfolios and so many cross-directorships that the question is purely rhetorical.

being. As she warmed to the work, she grew in stature, assuming personal responsibilities as a living part of the working class in action.

From 11 October 1889, as the secretary of the Silvertown Women's Branch of the Gasworkers' Union she

"sat as a delegate from this branch at all our delegate meetings," wrote Thorne, "and was elected to the committee of the union when the rules were altered to permit women to be seated on the committee".[93]

Had she lived, he said,

"Eleanor ... would have been a greater women's leader than the greatest of contemporary women."[93]

When he was over 80 Thorne referred to her in an interview as

"the most intelligent woman he had ever known".[94]

On Christmas Day she wrote to Laura:

"You want to know what we're doing ... hard at it, as usual. Ed. writes plays, and newspaper articles and books on Botany, and essays and 'pomes'. He goes to the theatres to criticise other folks' plays; he occasionally travels for a Railway Paper; he keeps Bax in order, teaches and sometimes lectures. He harbours, I believe, a private ambition to train as an 'homme fort'. He seems well and happy withal. For my own poor part, look you, life seems to be becoming one long strike. First there was the Dock Strike. No sooner was that over than I was summoned to Silvertown, and for 10 mortal weeks I travelled daily to that out-of-the-world place; speaking every day – often twice a day, in all weathers in the open air. I began to hope for peace – when lo! the Gas Strike begins.* For this, I have, so far, not had much to do (we both spouted in Hyde Park o' Sunday) but I go down now and again to the Committee and I may be called at any moment to 'help' with the Committee work. I am a member of the 'Gas Workers and General Labourers Union', and secretary of a Woman's Branch wh. I started at Silvertown, and that takes up no end of time. How this strike will go it is difficult to say. I am doubtful of victory, though, I need hardly tell you, you must not take what the newspapers say for gospel. The Blacklegs in the works are getting v. unmanageable. 132 were seriously burnt (through lack of skill) in one week; they had had a fight y'terday and one Blackleg had stabbed another. Moreover out of 45 men brought from Brighton 42 had had enough of it, and had not only 'given notice' but have promised to put 'a shilling a man' in our collection boxes. In many ways this fight is the most interesting we have had. It is distinctly on a question of principle. It is v. useful too, for us, that the public and the police are not so 'enthusiastic' as they were for the Dockers ... The great danger here in England is the spirit of compromise. I am glad the Gas Workers are saved from the 'patronage' of the bourgeois ... Picketting – wh. is

---

* At the South Metropolitan Gas Co., starting 5 December 1889 and lasting until early February 1890. See fn.§, above, p. 507.

perfectly legal, they refuse to allow us; blacklegs are dragged by main force into the works by policemen; government vans have driven food into the works (where all the blacklegs sleep) which shop-keepers wd. not or dared not supply. The irritation is naturally intense. All this 'makes' for us. The other night I was up at the Cttee. Rooms talking to the men, and one and all declared themselves Socialists ... Things *are* moving here at last, and tho' the methods differ from those on the Continent, the movement is none the less certain. When there is another Congress England will not again be represented by the Socialist League, I promise you.

Presently we shall set out for the General's to join in the annual 'festivity'..."[95]

It was indeed a "festivity": Engels had invited as many friends as he could seat at his table: the Avelings, Pumps and her family, the Bernsteins, the Mottelers, Richard Fischer – the compositor on the *Sozialdemokrat* – and his wife, with Schorlemmer who was staying in the house. On the day before he had written to Mrs. Liebknecht to say that Nim was at her cooking and baking, the plum puddings made ready a week ago:

"It's a fearful effort, and all for the sake of incurring indigestion. But that's what custom dictates and so one goes through with it; after all, it will be jolly, even if the second festive day is followed by crapula."

He went on to give a glowing account of Tussy's activities in Silvertown and, only two days ago, on Sunday, she had spoken to a mass meeting in Hyde Park on behalf of the South Metropolitan gasworkers, but that, said Engels, "is certainly less arduous and leaves her time".[96] In the New Year she and Aveling were to be assistant editors to Bax, who had bought the paper *Time*.

The truth was that Eleanor had been plunged in this work almost from the moment that Silver's strike ended: as she said to Laura she had "not ... too little but ... too much *Time*".[95] On 20 December she wrote to her "dearest Dollie" (Radford) about the "terrible rush" of the past week: Bax had taken over the shilling monthly journal only a fortnight ago

"and we then found there was nothing in hand of any sort – no serial, 'no stories, no articles, nothing'. And we had to try to get all this ready to be 'out' next week. We've been writing letters, reading proofs, and sending telegrams (to add to our difficulties the printers live in Perth!) all day long."

Eleanor was yearning to see her "dear little Dollie", to have "a long, long talk" with her – "there are so few left who knew my parents and our home" – she longed to meet the three babies (to Maitland and Hester, Margaret had now been added), to "talk of old times" and to keep up this cherished connection with the past, but she felt unable to accept an invitation to dinner because

"Edward feels that our intercourse was broken off by Ernest [Radford] ... I wanted to tell you this quite frankly and not merely invent excuses..."[97]

Admittedly Eleanor's life was less strenuous than when she had travelled to Silvertown early each morning – though she continued to go once a week to collect the union dues of her branch – but helping to launch a journal with nothing on the stocks and speaking at a monster meeting in Hyde Park on a particularly nasty mid-December day* is not every woman's notion of a good rest.

---

* The colloquialism "parky" (*Shorter OED*: "nippingly cold") was undoubtedly coined for just such occasions.

Eleanor's "typewriting business", as might have been anticipated, did not make her fortune.* It did, however, change her status to that of a manual worker: one who earned a living by operating a machine (writing by hand is not manual labour, as everyone knows).

In January 1980 she received a commission from Olive Schreiner, who sent her *Prelude*† to Havelock Ellis from South Africa with a letter saying: "Please give it to Eleanor Marx to typewrite, paying her the full rate." Later that year, in May, Aveling tried to sell her services to Swan Sonnenschein who sent him a paper of which they wanted twelve copies made. The accounts show that, two months later, she received 2s.[98]

The full rate was such that quite soon Eleanor sent an article to the press on "Sweating in Type-Writing Offices" proposing that a union should be formed both by those who typed at home and in business houses where, she claimed, "if you want to live by your labour you must work at high pressure and a good many more hours than eight a day".‡[99]

Eight hours a day: that was the main theme of the year 1890 though, as always, Eleanor had other preoccupations too. First, Aveling went down with 'flu in January and she fulfilled his speaking engagements. Then there was a slight to-do about buggery in exalted circles which changed the course of Eleanor's journalistic career.

Ernest Parke, an assistant editor of the *Star*, wrote a couple of articles for the little *North London Press*§ objecting that, while certain members of the nobility and gentry were in the habit of frequenting a male brothel in Cleveland Street, Fitzroy Square, not they but a number of messenger boys and other small fry eking out their wages had been arrested and sentenced to imprisonment following a police raid. Parke named in

---

* Typewriters had been mass produced in America since 1878. The various models available in Eleanor's day in England cost up to £20, though a "Simplex" machine was marketed in London for 10s. 6d. in 1887.

† The opening chapter of *From Man to Man*, the novel never completed and published posthumously (see fn.§, p. 274).

‡ As it happens female typists were among those who had formed a "society" under the auspices of Emma Paterson's Women's Protective and Provident League in the late '70s though, like many of these small fragile organisations existing "to promote an *entente cordiale* between labourer, employer and consumers",[100] it had but a short life and no part in the established trade union movement of the day.

§ 28 September and 16 November 1889.

particular the Earl of Euston* who brought a charge of criminal libel against the paper.

The *Star* castigated Parke, as it was bound to do in so far as he was a member of its staff. Everybody else, no matter what – or if – they thought about Lord Euston, immediately penned impassioned letters to the press defending Parke. Champion's *Labour Elector*, however, leapt gratuitously into the fray to condemn the journalist in a high-minded paragraph followed by a vehement leader on "the terrible accusation", with "no evidence to support it", and so on and so forth.[101] Thereupon John Burns, whose opinion was equally unsolicited, took it upon himself to write to the *Star* denouncing Champion's attitude, while a number of people sent letters to the *Labour Elector* itself in the same vein. Among these was Tom Mann who wrote:

> "It is with extreme regret that I find myself compelled to protest against the paragraph in the current issue of the paper re Mr. Parke. In my opinion, it is not only wrong in judgment but heartless in the extreme. I must ask you to publish this statement, as I cannot have it thought that I could be party to such statements",

to which Champion appended the editorial comment:

> "We are very sorry that our friend Tom Mann differs from us in our judgment on this matter. Mr. Parke's accusation against Lord Euston was indeed atrocious, and if Lord Euston had gone to the *Star* office and there and then physically twisted the little wretch's neck nobody would have blamed him..."[101]

Even those who did not for one moment disbelieve Parke's story admitted that he had "displayed a marvellous incapacity for weighing the value of evidence and an almost inexcusable rashness in a responsible journalist", but were outraged by Champion's "cowardly attack" and "regretted that the *Labour Elector*, of all papers in the world" should have made so bitter an onslaught upon him.

This little pother† – this storm in a teacup, as Engels described it – had only one consequence that concerns us here: Eleanor, without troubling to write any letters at all, parted company from Champion and withdrew from the *Labour Elector* to which she had been contributing international notes on France, Germany, Belgium, Holland and Scandinavia.‡ She

---

* The eldest son of the Duke of Grafton who was a Fitzroy descendant of Charles II by the Duchess of Cleveland, so he was really on home ground.

† In case anyone wishes to know its outcome: Parke was swiftly sentenced at the Old Bailey to a year's imprisonment for libel. On health grounds and as a result of a Memorial to the Home Secretary – "a proof to Mr. Parke of the sympathy of his fellow-journalists" – he was released after 25 weeks to be welcomed at the offices of the *Star* "by the members of [his] profession and the public generally".[102]

‡ Cunninghame Graham wrote those on Portugal, Spain, Mexico and other Latin American countries from then on.

continued in an editorial capacity on *Time*, "a perfectly ordinary bourgeois affair", according to Engels, Bax being in deadly fear of making it a socialist journal,[103] until, in March 1890, the *North London Press* was incorporated into the *People's Press* ("A Weekly Paper Devoted to the Interests of the People") as the official organ of the New Trade Unions, under the editorship of Robert Dell,* to which for the first six months Eleanor now contributed.

Somehow or other during her Silvertown autumn – or it may have been earlier and together with her young nephews – she had planted her parents' grave with crocus, hyacinth and primrose. Now, on 14 March, the anniversary of Marx's death, she and Engels went to Highgate cemetery together, gladdened to see the flowers in bloom. A few days later she spoke at that other commemoration – so closely connected both in date and feeling – celebrating the Commune, held again at South Place Institute under the auspices of the Socialist League.

On that same day, 19 March 1890, William Morris was writing:

> "... Socialism is spreading, I suppose on the only lines on which it could spread, and the League is moribund simply because we are outside those lines, as I for one must always be ... The main cause of the failure (which was obvious at least two years ago) is that you cannot keep a body together without giving it something to do in the present, and now, since people will willingly listen to Socialist doctrine, our rank and file have nothing to do..."†[104]

Earlier that month Eleanor had found herself involved with trade unionists of a different calibre from the labourers, though with similar aims and problems. On Sunday, 2 March, she had attended a meeting of the local branch of the Shop Assistants' Union at the Hammersmith Palace of Varieties – ironically, Morris's own neighbourhood where he thought the rank and file of the Socialist League had "nothing to do" – and found that they had boldly issued a handbill calling for a boycott of the shops which refused to introduce shorter working hours.‡

---

* (1865–1940). A young journalist who had joined the Fabian Society in 1889 and was elected to its Executive Committee the following year but who was in ardent sympathy with the movement of the unskilled workers. The journal, whose offices were at 10 Red Lion Court, Fleet Street, lasted only until February 1891.

† The Sixth Annual Conference of the Socialist League was attended by only 14 delegates.

‡ "Shop assistants under eighteen were granted a 74-hour week by the Shop Hours Regulation Act of 1887, which, for lack of inspectors, was never operated."[105]

According to Tom Mann, London shop assistants' weekly hours were, on an average, 86, "while thousands work 96 to 100. The effect upon young men is most baneful, but upon the young women it is scarcely less than murder..." He claimed that at least 40,000 were employed in the distributive trades in London.[106]

Cunninghame Graham took the Chair and several clergymen were on the platform. Eleanor, who "was received with loud cheering"[107] seconded the resolution urging shop assistants to join their union and support the eight-hour day in all trades. She admired the audacity of naming the shopkeepers to be blacklisted but suggested that, while perfectly willing to sign the petition herself and take the consequences, it might perhaps be wiser to avoid the word "boycott" – an indictable offence – and substitute the parliamentary expression: "We will go in for exclusive dealing."* The following Sunday a procession with bands and banners marched from Hammersmith Broadway to Turnham Green where the Allied Trade Unions of Hammersmith held a mass meeting and heard Eleanor and representatives of the organised shop assistants put the case against those employers who had not only refused to limit the hours of work but had now threatened to take legal action against the branch secretary for boycott. On 3 April there was a further meeting at the West End Chapel, King Street, Hammersmith where Eleanor again spoke, but this time to celebrate the victory over the shopkeepers, all of whom had capitulated.

It was in this small section of the full orchestra that Eleanor sounded the eight-hour motif. A fortnight later she was bidden by the Gasworkers' Union to go to Northampton at the weekend where, on Saturday, she attended a closed session of the local branch and, on Sunday, spoke at two "magnificent meetings" – one in the morning, the other at 6.30 – in the market square. On this experience she wrote an article in the 19 April issue of the *People's Press*, reporting that her

"attack upon Mr. Bradlaugh's attitude† with regard to the working class called forth no opposition whatever ... What roused more enthusiasm than anything else was the *legal eight-hour* working day, and there were loud expressions of hearty approval when, quoting Mr. Bradlaugh's statement that the well-organised unions could enforce an eight-hour day if they chose, I referred him to the Miners' Union which is demanding a legal limitation of the working day, and which has just declared, like the Labour Electoral Association, that Mr. Chas. Bradlaugh does *not* represent the workers either on the question of the working-day or the liability of employers.

As is well-known, the greater part of the Northampton operatives are 'small masters'. They work 'at home', and employ (i.e. sweat) boys. I referred to this system and denounced it, and was pleased to find the men agreed that the whole thing was iniquitous.

Up to the present time the Trades Council and old Trades Unions have been not merely indifferent, but actually hostile to the union of the unskilled workers. But there

---

* There was a slight flurry at this point, for it emerged that one of the clergymen had not studied the handbill with sufficient care and clearly did not wish to render himself liable to prosecution.

† Bradlaugh had been elected M.P. for Northampton in 1880 but did not take his seat until 1886. (See below, fn.†, p. 212.)

are hopes that ... this suicidal opposition will cease and the skilled and 'unskilled' will row together. The latter sorely need organising. They work terribly long hours for wretched wages. Our Union, however, has started work and is being cordially helped by the Socialists..."[108]

Both mass meetings unanimously approved the eight-hour day and the May Day demonstration, towards which they contributed the sum of £1 13s. 4½d.

Up to the very last Eleanor was rallying support for May Day. On the Sunday before – 27 April – she was engaged to lecture at the Prince of Denmark public house in Portland Road to the South Norwood Labour Union on "A Labour Programme". While such a programme was an excellent subject for discussion, its realisation, she said, depended upon the immediate step of supporting the International Congress resolution on eight hours of work and the May Day demonstration, for which she collected 8s. 1d. She also spoke in Bristol from the No. 1 Platform at the Ropewalk on Saturday, 3 May, when an eight-hour demonstration was held. The date had been changed in fact so that Cunninghame Graham and Eleanor could be present.

"Mrs Aveling (a daughter of Karl Marx) wrote she 'would gladly come and speak, but was so poor that only if her railway fare was sent in advance was it possible.' The Committee sent thirty shillings, and after the meeting she handed ten back to the treasurer, a beautiful expression of enthusiasm and comradeship ... Mrs. Aveling, a charming personality, made a stirring appeal."[109]

In the meantime the plans to organise the great London event had been gathering momentum; and also running into difficulties.

Always the objective had been May First: a day of international action to be simultaneously observed wherever workers were not under any prohibitive law.

While the Americans had inaugurated May Day to demand eight hours of work in 1886, Tom Mann in England had in that year published a pamphlet – his first – on the subject[110] making out a well-documented case in lucid, even masterly language. He also formed small agitational "Eight Hours Committees". But this made little impact at the time. The question had been debated for years and, as already described, at the TUC of 1889 – three months after Mann's second pamphlet, *The Eight Hours Movement*, had appeared – the craftsmen rejected any form of legislation for all but the miners,* and with precisely the arguments Mann had contested.

Not only the craftsmen: an unskilled worker wrote:

---

* The case for and against the Legal Eight Hour Day were fairly well expounded by Champion

"It is a common occurrence for the labourer to be out of work two, three, four and even five months during the year, and during that period he gets behind with the rent. He gets credit where he can from the shopkeepers, everything that is pawnable is pawned, and in many instances the home or what constitutes the home is sold through no fault of his own, for the labourer gets no out-of-work pay from his union, and it is impossible for him while in work to put anything by for a rainy day. Then, when he gets work, where there is an extra shilling or two to be earned by working a little overtime, the law is to step in and prevent him earning it. I am speaking on authority when I tell you that the unskilled labourer depends entirely on a little overtime ... to pay debts etc ... and to get a little clothing for himself, wife and children ... The maximum wage of the unskilled labourer is 4s. per day, and should he have a family of five or six children to support, and even in constant employment, he will have to live a bare hand-to-mouth existence, and no chance whatever of earning a little extra for any little comforts or necessaries he may require, but he will have plenty of time to sit at home and bemoan his fate, and condemn the cruel law that prevents him from earning ... It seems to me that the legal eight hours day has emanated from the mechanical class. It will, I think, suit them well. Their wages average from 38s. to £2. 10s. per week. They would save in one week as much as some unskilled labourers earn, our expenses are as great as theirs, the same amount of food and clothing are required for us. There are hundreds of very intelligent men among the unskilled labourers who would not be slow to avail themselves of anything that would tend to better their condition, and it would not be necessary to be continually trying to knock the legal eight hours into their heads. I have not heard one advocate it yet, and until I do, I have not much faith in it. First of all let us, through our organisations, get a sufficient wage to live without working overtime, and then we can see about the legal eight hours.

Yours truly,

George Elleston.

105 Vanburgh Hill, East Greenwich.
December 2nd. 1890."[112]

This letter naturally drew a number of replies. Among them one from Eleanor:

"There is one statement in the letter of my friend George Elleston ... which I feel bound to answer. Into his arguments against a legal eight hours' day for the 'unskilled' I have no need to enter. Thousands of 'unskilled' can answer better than I, especially now that Bro. Elleston has confirmed our contention that a number of workers can only get 'the bare necessaries of life' by working overtime ... The statement ... that I must answer is that he 'has never heard one (i.e. unskilled worker) advocate it (i.e. the legal eight hours' day) yet'. How George Elleston, who is a member of the G.W. and G.L.U., and the secretary of one of our branches, can say this passes comprehension. Has Brother Elleston never heard our past and actual presidents, Mark Hutchins and Will Watkinson? Has he never heard our organisers? Has he never heard the members of our executive? Has he never attended our delegate meetings and our other meetings? Why, to a man the officials of our Union – and they are elected by the whole Union – are what Cunninghame Graham calls eight hour blokes. (Please, Mr. Editor, note that according to the rules of our Union, 'wherever the word "man" occurs it shall be taken to mean "man and woman".')

---

in the form of a dialogue between seven characters representing the various attitudes of legislators, employers and a supporter of such a Bill.[111]

If I am not mistaken Bro. Elleston was present at the delegate meeting held (I believe) in January at which a vote in favour of the universal May demonstration was unanimously passed. Anyhow he must know that our Union, together with the Bloomsbury Socialist Society, organised and carried out the great Hyde Park *legal* demonstration − a demonstration that not merely impressed our opponents but actually converted to the 'legal eight hours' men, like Tom Mann* and Ben Tillett, not to speak of smaller Unionist fry.

In the name of the Union to which I, as a more or less unskilled worker, am proud to belong, on whose Executive I am proud to serve, for which I have had the pleasure to work hard almost since its foundation, it is my duty to protest against the statement of Bro. Elleston that the 'unskilled' do not demand a legal eight hour working day. The Union to which Bro. Elleston belongs demonstrated for this legal eight hour day on May 4th; voted for it at its Conference in May last; has never ceased to work for it; I think I may say will never cease to work for it until the Eight Hours Bill has passed into law.

Yours faithfully,
Eleanor Marx Aveling

(Member Executive G.W. and G.L.U.)"[113]

This drew some criticism from other members of the Union:

"Surely Mrs. Aveling must know from her intimate acquaintance with the unskilled labourer," wrote one, "that there is no sane man who would object to an eight hour working day, providing he could earn sufficient wage to secure even the moderate comforts of life ... I will show Mrs. Aveling that the legal eight hours would inflict a great hardship on many that work at a factory where the work is uncertain..."[114]

Another found it very wrong that Eleanor had "thought fit to attack Brother Elleston's letter". She was no unskilled labourer; he was given to understand that she was

"a type-writer of the very highest degree. I should hardly think she works only eight hours per day and subsists on 3s. 6d. per day, as many of her fellow unionists are doing..."

Most of the letters that had been written on the matter were from people

"who have their bread well buttered and might be doing better by trying to get for those who are working 12 and 13 hours a day what we have, viz. nine hours per day."[115]

---

* This reference to "converting" Mann is somewhat mystifying, for his 1886 pamphlet had called explicitly for "the immediate passing of an Eight Hours Bill", while that of 1889 stated that "the new unionists look to Governments and legislation", not as an alternative but as an accompaniment to Union pressure on the employers.

For his part, Elleston, who had initiated the correspondence, wrote to say he was grateful that his letter had been published: it had produced exactly the result he had hoped for, namely, stimulated discussion. He wanted to explain that the unskilled were eager for an eight-hour day, even a six-hour day, if it could be made clear to them that they would not be worse off than at present:

> "Sister Aveling," he went on, "a lady whom I respect very much and has done excellent work for the workers,"

had asked whether he had never heard Thorne and other leaders of their union advocate the legal eight hours:

> "I distinctly say I have given them great credit for their good intention – but how Sister Aveling can class them as unskilled labourers passes my comprehension ... Sister Aveling ... also says that to a man the officials of our Union are ... eight hour blokes. Well they may be eight hour blokes, but not Legal Eight Hour blokes, that is, not all of them ..."[115]

Thus, even within the ranks of the labourers there were reservations about a parliamentary enactment and it is small wonder that this divided opinion should have been reflected in every debate.

Basically it came down to the role of the trade unions: where to draw the line between industrial and political action. In this campaign Eleanor refused to admit that any such line could or should be drawn. Certainly the organised workers must wring from individual employers the best wages and conditions they could; that was no hindrance to combining on a far broader basis to change the law of the land in their favour and, by making their voice heard in the very citadels of power, challenge the right to unlimited exploitation by capitalism itself. In expressing this view on every occasion Eleanor became, almost against her will, one of the most prominent figures in the movement, renowned far beyond the circles of her own union.*

On 28 March 1890 the Labour Electoral Association† had called a meeting at Aldersgate School to which 50 trade unions sent delegates. The Chairman explained that members of the Bloomsbury Socialist Society, of whom some four or five were present,

---

* A very bad picture of her, done from a photograph, appeared in the 3 May 1890 issue of the *People's Press* as one of "Six Portraits of Well-known Labour Leaders".
† Formed by the TUC in 1886.

"in conjunction with the Gasworkers' Union had begun to take steps to organise a demonstration at about the same time as the Association, and had, in fact, got out its first circular earlier".

For a moment it looked as though there were to be a repetition of the rival International Congress situation – each faction claiming priority in the field – but Aveling cut through this knot by moving at once that the meeting should approve the plan of holding "a general public demonstration in favour of the legislative enactment of an Eight Hours Day". George Barnes of the ASE seconded this and Thorne vigorously supported it on the grounds that, though his union had won the concession, he thought it unlikely to be maintained without the backing of the law. A great argument then raged about the merits and demerits of a statutory measure, until some sensible gasworker said it seemed very odd to him that at a meeting expressly called for those in favour of legislation there should be people who did not seem to know whether they were or not. This rational view prevailed, a vote was taken and passed unanimously.

A dockers' delegate then moved that the demonstration should take place on 13 April, a proposition so inconsequential that it found no seconder; neither did an amendment that it should be on 24 May, because that was the Queen's birthday and an enforced holiday anyway for all docks and Customs Houses (without pay). Finally a cabinet-maker moved for 1 May, the date to be observed in America and on the continent. This was seconded by Mrs. Amie Hicks, of the SDF, here speaking as a member of the East London Ropemakers. Eleanor, representing the women trade unionists of Keiller's and other Silvertown factories, told the delegates that in Germany – where the Anti-Socialist Law had been debated in January, was repealed, but would not lapse until 30 September 1890 – it had been resolved that

"where the workmen's organisations were strong enough, all men should leave work, except such as were certain of being dismissed altogether if they did so; and that where they were not strong enough, there should be a meeting in the evening and a petition should be signed".[116]

Tailors', dockers', joiners' and carpenters' delegates spoke in favour of 1 May; the motion was put and carried.

That, however, was not the end of the affair.

On 6 April the Bloomsbury Socialist Society organised three open-air meetings – in Hyde Park, Regent's Park and on Clerkenwell Green – to appeal for funds towards the great May First demonstration.

"Mrs. Aveling met – as she always does – with a hearty reception, prolonged cheering following the announcement of her name."[117]

It was all a huge success. But it then emerged that the Labour Electoral Association, the big trade unions and the Radical Clubs, having been approached by the May Day organisers, had convened their own delegate meeting on 16 March when only a small majority voted for the May First proposal, many of those present declaring that they had no mandate.

Thus a recalled meeting at the Working Men's Club,* in Gye Street, Vauxhall, on the evening of that tremendously lively day of outdoor rallies, reversed the decision taken nine days earlier and 94 delegates – a large majority this time – voted for the first Sunday in May, namely, 4 May, the demonstration to take place in Hyde Park at 3.30.

There was no going against this clear expression of opinion. A representative Central Committee was formed, with Aveling from the Bloomsbury Socialist Society as chairman and Will Thorne as organising secretary, with a sub-committee of seven – including Aveling and Thorne – "told off to do the detail work".[118] Thus, while it remained in the hands of those who had most staunchly campaigned for May First, they were in honour bound to carry out arrangement for "the nearest Sunday". The *People's Press* expressed the editorial view:

> "It is unfortunate that this year the English workers could not see their way clearly to falling in line with their continental brethren on 1st May, for which the 'apathy and abstention' of the older and richer unions were held responsible."[117]

The London Trades Council had still to be approached and a delegation of eight members from the May Day Central Committee was elected to meet the Council, to emphasise that nothing less than the *legal* eight-hour day was at issue.

With some condescension – after having left all the work to others, as the *People's Press* commented – the LTC agreed in writing to admit two representatives to its delegate meeting on 23 April and hear their case. The Committee replied that there would have to be three, since it represented the Radical Clubs, the trades unions and the Socialist Societies. It proposed that Pete Curran, Harwood† and Eleanor should go. To this the secretary, George Shipton,‡ replied that the first two would be accepted, but Mrs. Aveling, not being a manual worker, would not. His

---

* Of which the Rev. W. A. Morris, Robert Dell's colleague, was President.

† The first, employed at Woolwich Arsenal, was a member of the Woolwich Radical Club though also on the Executive of the Gasworkers' Union; the second was in the event replaced by A. Evans as the official trade union representative.

‡ (1839–1911). A Front Bencher of the Trade Union "Junta" and Secretary of the TUC Parliamentary Committee in 1885, he was secretary of the LTC from 1872 to 1896. He wrote *A Reply to Messrs. Tom Mann and Ben Tillett* on the publication of their pamphlet *The New Trade Unionism*.

objection was that "the person referred to never has been and never can be a manual worker". (Curran complimented him upon "his powers of negative prophecy".) The Committee retorted that it

> "did not know by what authority admission was to be denied to Mrs. Aveling, who did earn her living as a manual worker, i.e. as a typewriter:* that she would attend with the other Committee members and the question of her admission would be referred to the delegate meeting itself".[119]

Eleanor went along of course; the delegates – possibly because they did not wish to have an invidious argument about someone who was held in general respect – moved "the previous question", whereby she was excluded. The LTC, which favoured neither legal enactment for the eight-hour day nor May First – they were not having any truck with these Marxist ploys, no matter how 400 delegates from 22 countries and the representatives of 75 British workers' organisations had voted – then discussed arrangements for participating on 4 May, insisted upon having their own seven platforms – one for the SDF – and a separate route to the Park. Thus, then and there, the pattern was set for the disunited May Day which, with a few exceptions, has become an integral part of our great British tradition.

By 27 April the number of organisations which had formally agreed to support the "legal enactment" demonstration had risen to 80, including three branches of the SDF.† Fourteen head marshals were appointed and over 100 auxiliaries, whose orders everyone was urged strictly to obey.

Since there was hardly a contemporary newspaper that did not describe the occasion, the superabundance of sources, this mighty torrent of *reportage*, might present an embarrassment. However, the purest spring is Engels who had not, by and large, much good to say of the British movement – albeit he approved and was proud of Tussy's activities among both the Radicals and the unskilled labourers – and who was not only one of the keenest observers present – his first public appearance since Marx's death – but in whom there bubbled up an enthusiasm as fresh and sparkling as though he had been approaching his 20th rather than his 70th year.

"This epoch-making event", he called it in an article he wrote for the Vienna *Arbeiter-Zeitung*,[120] stressing the role of the gasworkers, the importance of their struggle for the eight-hour day in 1889 and the

---

* Although this sounds peculiar to us it is really no different from calling a man a typesetter or a machinist.
† Battersea, Wandsworth and Greenwich.

excellence of their organisation. He gave it, indeed, its full due as the true begetter of the New Unionism and the legitimate father of May Day in England. It is sad that Will Thorne, who ruefully said in his memoirs that contemporary historians had overlooked the significance of the stokers' action, which "made international solidarity a reality", could not read German and that nobody, apparently, made this handsome tribute known to him, for surely Engels' insight would have compensated him for the fact that the Dock Strike had "overshadowed, and even blinded, men like Sidney Webb".[121]

In a letter to Laura of 10 May, Engels ran over the preliminaries to the demonstration:

> "... it was a great victory for *us*, specially for Tussy and Aveling who with the help of the Gas Workers (by far the best Union out amongst the new ones) have done it all. In their naïveté they had called in the Trades Council without ensuring to themselves the possession of the Park first.
>
> The Trades Council allying itself with Hyndman and Co., stole a march on them and applied for platforms for Sunday at the Office of Works and got them, thus hoping to shut us out and being able to command; they attempted at once to bully us down, but Edward went to the Office of Works and got us too seven platforms ... That brought the other side down at once, and they became as amiable as you please..."[122]

Writing to Sorge before the event Engels summed up the situation:

> "If next Sunday," he wrote on 30 April, "brings together a gigantic demonstration for the Eight-Hour Day we have only Tussy and Aveling to thank for it. Tussy is on the Council of the Gasworkers' and General Labourers' Union as a delegate from her Silvertown women workers and is so popular on that Council that she is simply called 'our mother'. .... Thus the Gasworkers and the Bloomsbury Socialist Society (those, the best section, including Lessner, Tussy and Aveling, who left the Socialist League two years ago) initiated the matter and gained strong support from the smaller Trades Unions and Radical Clubs who are more and more separating into socialist Workers' Clubs and bourgeois Gladstonians. .... This is *our first great victory in London* and proves that here, too, *we* have the masses behind us. From the Social Democratic Federation, which has two platforms of its own, *four strong branches will march with us* and are represented on our committee. That goes for many of the skilled trades – the out-dated leaders will go with Shipton and the Trades Council, the masses with us. The whole East End is with us. The masses here are not yet socialist, but on the way towards it, and are already so far that they will not have *any but socialist leaders*...."[123]

Then, on 9 May, he wrote to Bebel:

> "The demonstration here on 4 May was nothing short of *overwhelming*, and even the entire bourgeois press had to admit it. I was on Platform 4 (a huge dray cart) and could catch sight of only a part – a fifth or an eighth – of the throng, but it was head upon head, as far as the eye could reach. 250 to 300,000 people, of whom over three-quarters were workers demonstrating. Aveling, Lafargue and Stepniak spoke from my platform

– I was but an onlooker ... Stepniak, and also Ede [Bernstein] on the platform where Tussy was, had a brilliant reception. The seven platforms were 150 yards apart, the last some 150 yards from the end of the Park, thus over 1,200 yards long and *our* meeting (that for the introduction of the 8-Hour Day by international legislation) was at least 4 to 500 yards wide and all tightly packed, and on each side the 6 platforms of the Trades Council and the two of the Social Democratic Federation, though not even half as well attended by the public as ours. All in all, the most gigantic meeting that has ever been held here...."[124]

This almost breathless account reflects better than anything else Engels' excitement and joy. To Laura he wrote:

"I can assure you I looked a couple of inches taller when I got down from that old lumbering waggon that served as a platform – after having heard again, for the first time since 40 years, the unmistakable voice of the English Proletariat."[122]*

---

* Of that remarkable occasion, it may be recorded that the "legal enactment" organisations assembled on the Embankment and marched to Hyde Park *via* Bridge Street, Holborn and Oxford Street to Marble Arch; the Trades Council and its associates (including, alas, Ben Tillett and the Dockers' Union) up Grosvenor Place to Hyde Park Corner where, from the Achilles statue, its platforms spread out. From the north, starting near the Reformers' Tree, the speakers of particular interest were: *Platform* 1. Miss Robertson for the Women's Trade Union League (originally formed in 1874 by Emma Paterson as the Women's Protective and Provident League, of which she remained the honorary secretary until her death in 1886 when she was succeeded by Clementina Black); W. M. Thompson, Radical candidate for Deptford; Wardle of the Bloomsbury Socialist Society and Turner of the Shop Assistants. *Platform* 2. Chaired by a member of the North Camberwell Progressive Club; Cunninghame Graham, Michael Davitt and George Lansbury (then aged 31), who represented the Radical Clubs. *Platform* 3. Chaired by the treasurer of the Gasworkers' Union, William Byford; Eleanor; Robert Dell; his right-hand man, the Rev. W. A. Morris; Bernstein; Graham Wallas of the Fabians and several Gasworkers' members. *Platform* 4 on which Engels sat, though he did not speak, was chaired by Aveling and included Stepniak, Lafargue, members of Radical Clubs, School Boards and the West Ham Councillor on the LCC. *Platform* 5. Will Thorne, John Burns and Mrs. Taylor of the Women's Trade Unions. *Platform* 6. Chaired by a member of the East Finsbury Radical Club; Pete Curran of the Gasworkers; Bernard Shaw of the Fabians and a representative of the West Newington Reform Club. *Platform* 7. A Gasworkers' Union member presiding, had mainly a number of speakers from that Union and from the Street Masons' and Paviers' Union and the Coach, 'Bus and Van Trades Union.

In her May Day speech* Eleanor had said that this was not the end but the beginning of the struggle. So it proved.

On the following day she was invited to take her brother-in-law, Paul Lafargue, to a meeting of the Canning Town No. 1 Branch of the Gas-workers' Union, where, at the chairman's request, she gave a short address to such effect that a spontaneous vote of thanks was moved to Dr. and Mrs. Aveling for having been the prime movers of the successful Sunday demonstration.

On the Wednesday she took part in a fund-raising entertainment at the Athenaeum Hall in Tottenham Court Road on behalf of the May Day Central Committee.†

The next Sunday, 11 May, saw another demonstration in Hyde Park, called this time by the railway workers who were demanding a maximum of 54-hours on day duty and 48 on nights, with time-and-a-half rates paid for all hours above ten on any one day, double time for Sunday work, 5 per cent, 10 per cent and 19 per cent wage increases, according to grade, and one week's paid holiday in the year. It was a pouring wet afternoon – indeed, Eleanor, speaking from Platform 3, said that the railway directors must have "nobbled the clerk of the weather" – nevertheless, 15,000 marched to the park where another 5,000 joined them to stand in the rain listening to the speeches. Eleanor, seconding a resolution moved by Cunninghame Graham, expressed the view that, of all sections, railway servants were the hardest worked and the worst paid. Yet none held more potential power: if they but realised that power by combining it would be utterly impossible for the railway companies to resist their claims. They could paralyse the industry of the whole country and men who could do that could surely achieve so small a boon as they were demanding that day. Robert Dell, presiding, asked for a show of hands in favour of the eight-hour day, to which there was an impressive response.

---

* See Appendix II.
† It is not known what she recited, but she played the part of the thrifty landlady in J. M. Morton's *Box and Cox* with Aveling and Percy Rosher. What brought the house down, it seems, was a rendering of *The Charge of the Light Brigade* in a variety of dialects. It is surprising to find that these popular verses, composed in tribute to the doomed heroes of Balaclava, should have been treated with levity during the Poet Laureate's lifetime.

As the workers of one trade after another began to agitate for the reduced working week, the Central Committee, formed for the demonstration on May Day, met and decided to remain in being on a wider basis as an Eight Hour Day Committee. Aveling, who had been a brisk and efficient chairman throughout, was against admitting those who had done no work in the preparations for May Day. A sub-committee of five – including Aveling, though not Eleanor – was elected to draft a new Constitution. Fresh credentials were to be furnished to the members of what had been a purely *ad hoc* body.

In May, when the first Annual Conference of the National Union of Gasworkers and General Labourers took place* and the Union was one year old, it had some 40,000 members in 89 branches, including two composed entirely of women. Will Thorne and Eleanor were elected as the conference secretaries under the chairmanship of the president, Mark Hutchins. The address, delivered by Thorne, was written by Eleanor and the conference then proceeded to consider the new rules – also drafted by Eleanor† – and to elect the officers of the Executive.

One of the striking features of this first conference was that the majority of the delegates were from the provinces, showing how far and wide this cockney-bred organisation had taken root.‡ The *People's Press* commented on "the soft, pretty 'burr' of the south and west, the broad, hard dialect of Yorkshire and Lancashire, the curious slow sing-song of Wales, the broadest of broad Scotch ... and every variety of Irish brogue."§ Hutchins was said to have been a bad chairman in so far as he allowed many of these accents to mingle in a confused chorus but, on the whole, it was a businesslike affair. Thorne, however, had to admit that he had been unable to get out his financial report despite his best efforts and sitting up for three nights: the branches, for lack of experience, had

---

* The first half-yearly Report and Balance Sheet were presented to a conference held at the Cannon Street Hotel from 4 to 11 November 1889, at the height of the Silvertown strike.

† Writing to Kautsky to suggest an article for *Neue Zeit*, she said: "... So much is being said just now about the 'new' organisations of the 'unskilled workers' that perhaps some account of the starting, organisation, and work done during the eighteen months of its existence by the first, the largest, and most advanced of these Unions – i.e. that of the Gas Workers and General Labourers might be of interest. As I am on the Executive of this Union and drew up their address, and the Rules for the most part, I could give a thorough description of our 'Objects', organisation and work. We have nearly 100,000 members and over 60 different Trades and Industries...."[125]

‡ Four months later the membership had risen to 60,000 – not yet 100,000 as Eleanor claimed – represented at the TUC by nine delegates, only three of whom were from London. The other six came from Birkenhead, Bristol, Dublin, Leeds, Manchester and Uxbridge.

§ There were 33 London delegates (apart from the Executive), 45 from the provinces, eight from Ireland and one from Wales. Scotland was not as yet represented in the union but, as is well known, the broadest Scotch may be heard throughout the land since "the noblest prospect a Scotchman ever sees, is the high road that leads him to England!"

presented their accounts in somewhat baffling form and to have made a correct audit in time for the conference required more mathematical skill than he possessed.*

The Rules were then debated and it was agreed that there should be no age limit for membership, since a union catering for the unskilled must recognise that boys from 14 to 16 were employed by their thousands as sweated labour in brickfields and factories. On a motion from the floor, moved by a male delegate, Nicol, from Bristol and a Mrs. Burgess from Norwich, the objects of the union included the demand that, wherever possible, women should receive the same wages for doing the same work as men.

Thorne was unanimously re-elected as General Secretary, Watkinson of Barking as the new President; Byford, the Treasurer, did not wish to stand again but was persuaded by the cordial entreaties of one delegate after another to remain in office for another year. Of the 15 Executive members, on Thorne's recommendation, seven were to be from south of the river, eight from the north. Eleanor was elected by general acclaim without a vote being taken, so unanimous was the welcome, so full-throated the response to her nomination.

The conference then pledged itself "to use every effort to place upon the statutes of the country a legal eight hours day" and that "the workers should do their utmost to obtain direct representation on all governing bodies, Parliamentary and local."[127] Eleanor was included among those elected to represent the union at the forthcoming TUC.

The day after the conference closed, the Bloomsbury Socialist Society held its usual weekly meeting at the Communist Club with Lessner in the chair. Aveling reported on the decision of the May Day Central Committee to perpetuate itself with the primary aim of achieving the legal eight-hour day, which made it in effect a new Labour Party. The Bloomsbury Society which, he said, had had the honour of initiating the most successful demonstration of all time in any place, should elect delegates to the Committee, thus carrying forward the work it had started. It was agreed that a manifesto should be drafted setting out the past activities and the aims of the Bloomsbury Socialist Society, with an invitation to all Social-Democrats to join in working for the same end. This was issued in the following terms:

---

* The following year auditors were appointed, including, of all people, Aveling. However, an auditor is not a treasurer – he does not so much as catch sight of the money – it is purely paperwork, though of an exacting nature. That he proved to be uncommonly good at it throws a strange light on the shadier side of Aveling's character.

"Comrades, – The organisation which bears the above title dates its existence as a distinct and separate body from August, 1888. Its aims were set forth in the following words –

'We aim at realising Socialism – i.e., a condition of society in which wealth will be enjoyed by those who produce it; also, at removing all conditions whatever that render it possible for an idle class to exist. The economic change that would bring about this condition we believe to be the Nationalisation of Land and Industrial Capital. We will work along any lines that tend in this direction, and will devote ourselves to the education of the people in Social and Political matters: also to the getting of all political power into the hands of the whole people.'

The work of the society, therefore, has been principally of an educational and political character. So far as educational work is concerned, the Society can boast of having provided one of the most complete series of lectures on economic subjects of any Society in the metropolis. In its meeting-place at the Communist Club, 49, Tottenham St., W., almost every accepted leader of advanced thought has lectured before its members. In its political work much has been accomplished. The registration of its members as voters has been regularly carried out, many of them having been also placed upon the Liberal Associations of Holborn, South St. Pancras, East Marylebone, and West Islington, where they keep the Social Question well to the front. At the London County Council election the Society put forward its Secretary as a Socialist candidate for South St. Pancras, who, despite the determined opposition of both the Tory and Whig parties, made a very good fight.

Later on the Bloomsbury Socialist Society earned the distinction of being the first to make any subscription towards supporting the London Dock Labourers in their historic struggle against the capitalists.

Last January the Society set to work to organize for the Demonstration in favour of an Eight-Hour Legal Working Day, in accordance with the resolution passed by the International Socialist Working Men's Congress, held in Paris last July. The Demonstration was held on the 4th inst., and was a complete success. The work of the organisation was shared in towards the last by others, though the members of the Society which commenced the work continued their efforts to the end.

Having, therefore, as we think, established some claim upon the workers, we now ask them to join our ranks and work with us towards the bettering of the conditions of our fellow men and women, and to the ultimate establishment of Socialism. Our cause, in a word, is the cause of all those who labour. We, in conclusion, repeat the words of the old Communist Manifesto –
'WORKERS OF THE WORLD – UNITE!'
W. W. Bartlett
Hon. Sec. Bloomsbury Socialist Society."[127]

It was also proposed that, if the directors of the paper agreed, regular reports of the Society should be sent to the *People's Press* which the members would undertake to sell and would look upon as their official organ.

From that time forward until 1895 Eleanor was perpetually involved in organising, speaking, writing for and representing her union. On 7 June she contributed an article to the *People's Press* on the Beckton Gas Works where, it had been widely reported, there was a strike impending because machinery had been introduced.* Eleanor called this a "persistent, mis-representation ... It is time," she wrote, "that the workers, at least, should know the actual facts." It had gone the rounds that the men were opposed to the use of machines and were demanding "compensation" pay for working them.

> "Both statements are absolutely incorrect. ... As to a 'strike', there is none, nor does any member of the Union wish for one."

Though the matter had been put quite clearly in Thorne's address to the Conference, Eleanor now publicly explained that machinery had been introduced in November 1889 and that all had gone well, a wage of 5s. 9d. a day having been agreed. Then, suddenly, a Mr. West turned up, the patentee of a machine not unlike that already in use but which, he guaranteed, as he had done at other gas-making stations, would do more work at less expense. The Gas, Light and Coke Co. welcomed him with open arms, gave him *carte blanche* to take on or discharge men "at his own sweet will" and run his celebrated machine as he pleased.† But to fulfil his promise of savings to the company and ensure his own profits, Mr. West naturally reduced the men's wages to 5s. 4d. a day, to which they as naturally objected. So much for the Luddite attitude to machinery and a "compensation" wage.

The second difficulty concerned a new agreement,

---

* Obviously more mechanical appliances were being introduced in every branch of industry at this period. Indeed, the advances in technology furnished two important arguments in favour of the compulsory eight-hour day: first, from the workers' point of view, the shorter day meant the employment of more men; second, from the employers', "the strain ... consequent upon the increased complexity of the machinery was so great that the power of attention was exhausted before the day was over. The work done during the last hour was less satisfactory and less profitable than the work done during the earlier part. It was therefore a serious question ... whether it would not be more profitable to shorten the day...."[128] The great leap forward, however, had taken place in the earlier period of 1851 to 1881, the great railway era, as the census figures reflect. The wealth of the United Kingdom had almost trebled in those 30 years with an increased population of some nine million (roughly 43 per cent), only 153,000 more persons (3 per cent) being engaged or connected with agriculture, textile fabrics, minerals, transport service and the making of machinery and tools.

† According to the *Stratford Express*: "Retort house no. 12 has been fitted with a number of labour-saving machines called steam stokers. As they dispense with much of the skill formerly requisite for charging the retorts, and as unskilled labourers and untried men are now available, the directors sought to make some slight reduction in the wage paid for this work ... but even if all the men should leave their fires, the company entertain no apprehension, they believe it would not be difficult to fill their places very speedily with non-union men."[129]

"so preposterous that the men are convinced it is the work of some youngster with a little too much zeal".

The old agreement had laid down that 28 days' notice must be given on either side. It was now proposed to introduce a clause whereby the company could dismiss any workman "forthwith and without any notice" if he did, or failed to do, a number of things so ill-defined and all-embracing that it only needed a foreman to bear a personal grudge against an individual worker for him to be sacked on the spot and, what was more, to forfeit the whole of the wages he had earned during the week. This Eleanor claimed to be on good authority "an infringement of the Truck Act and absolutely illegal". The men refused to sign this agreement and drew up another which, among other changes, inserted: "that a shift shall be understood to be one of eight hours."*

This article not only elucidated a complicated situation, clearly separating its several strands and thus showing why it had been open to misinterpretation, but also Eleanor's firm grasp of the minutiae of industrial problems and how seriously she took her union responsibilities.

Throughout that month of June she was involved with the Gasworkers, the Bloomsbury Socialist Society and the Central Committee for the Eight Hours, which last, totting up its accounts for the May Day demonstration, found listed among the donations £1 from F. Engels and 2s. 6d. from H. Demuth.

Eleanor spoke on Clapham Common to the Labour League, to Gas-workers' branches in Northampton and to women workers in Kent. She successfully organised a branch in Chatham where, having at her first meeting on 8 June expounded the Union's aims and purposes, 30 women joined at once and recruited twelve others in the following week.

Indeed, her invitations to speak, and the announcements that she would do so – with the certainty of drawing record attendances – were so numerous that she was compelled to write a letter to the editor of the *People's Press*, published on 21 June under the heading "Hard on Mrs. Aveling":

"Dear Comrade, – Will you please allow me through your columns to ask the branches of the G.W. & G.L.U. not to announce me to speak anywhere without first asking for, and, second, receiving my assent? I am willing and anxious to go anywhere where there

---

* The new agreement granted coal porters six days' holiday – the demand had been for seven – in place of their one day in the year, and they were guaranteed work in the yards, so that their wages, which had often fallen as low as 8s. 10d. a week, would reach a minimum of 24s. Notice was increased to 28 days, the power of dismissal confined to the chief engineer, or any person vested with the right to enter into agreements with the workers, and no pay earned while under dismissal was to be forfeited.

is work to be done. But it is neither fair to the audience nor to myself to publish my name as a speaker unless it is certain that I can be present. The difficulty is not lessened when one is announced to speak at two or three different places at the same time without having been consulted in respect to any of them. Let me, therefore, ask, through the medium of the People's Press, the organisers of meetings who may want my services to be good enough to communicate with me before making any public announcement,

Yours fraternally,
Eleanor Marx Aveling."

The day after this letter appeared in the press, a demonstration planned by the Northampton gasworkers was prohibited by the authorities, causing deep resentment and some stir, in consequence of which, despite her plea that arrangements should be agreed beforehand, Eleanor – and also Aveling – went to Northampton the following Sunday (29 June) where their presence added zest to an enormous meeting.

Such prohibitions were not rare and a special "Open-Air Meetings Committee" was formed to organise a procession from Clerkenwell Green to Hyde Park on 6 July, Cunninghame Graham saying that he would carry any "rag of a banner" and did not care if his head were broken again. They would march along Theobald's Road, Holborn and Oxford Street to Marble Arch where those who had not been arrested, disabled or killed *en route* would hold a meeting in the Park. This demonstration was, as usual, frowned upon by the elements and at 4 o'clock in appalling weather, the leaders, including Hyndman, William Sanders,* Graham Wallas and the Avelings, left the shelter of the Patriotic Club to deliver speeches on Clerkenwell Green to an undaunted crowd. The procession then formed up to reach Marble Arch, soaked to the skin, singing the *Marseillaise*. The police did not attempt to interfere and two platforms were set up for the speakers at a large, though short and exceedingly wet meeting.

A "Grand Concert" was announced for the evening of 15 July, under the auspices of the Nine Elms Branch of the Gasworkers and the Vauxhall Working Men's Club in aid of that institution, whose President, the Rev. W. A. Morris, had so generously and often given his services and lent his premises. It was indeed a grand and very prolonged affair, with speeches galore, telegrams from those unable to be present, songs of every variety, sketches and recitations, to which last Eleanor contributed Hood's *Song of the Shirt* and Aveling Shelley's *Address to the Men of England*, moving the audience deeply and reducing Aveling himself to tears. During the interval the Gasworkers' Union banner was ceremoniously unfurled on the stage by Keir Hardie and Cunninghame Graham. It was a splendid sight:

---

* (1871–1941). A member of the Battersea Branch of the SDF who acted as chairman of the "Open-Air Meetings Committee".

"a real work of art, beautifully painted on silk. It shows on either side two groups, one representing the old or twelve hours' system – viz. a gas-stoker going home in the middle of the night, tired and poorly dressed; the second, representing the new or eight hours' system – a man, decently dressed, walking home in broad daylight with elastic step. On the reverse side four working-men of different branches of labour – viz. a gasworker, a seaman, a fireman, and a coal-porter, shaking hands as Union men and brothers."[130]

On the Sunday before an event of more lasting importance had taken place. On 13 July, on the anniversary of the Paris International Congress, the Legal Eight Hours' League was formally brought into existence. The conference was attended by over 70 delegates and, having been called by the former May Day Committee, Aveling was voted into the chair. The Metropolitan Liberal and Radical Federation, the Fulham Liberal Club, the Radical Clubs of Herne Hill, Mildmay, Chiswick, Woolwich and East Finsbury, the London Patriotic Club and the Scottish Labour Party* were represented, side by side with the trade unions of gasworkers, railwaymen, women, clerks, farriers, cement makers, photographic cabinet makers and the National Federation of all Trades and Industries.

This was not intended to be a debating session – the issues were supposed to have been settled at a meeting on 22 June jointly convened by the May Day Committee and the International Labour League – and delegates were advised to come ready to cast their votes, as mandated by their organisations, upon a Draft Constitution.

It was beyond all hope that any such injunction would be observed. Wide-ranging and irrelevant discussion lasted from 11 a.m. until 2 in the afternoon, at the end of which the formal proposals were at last considered and, in principle, agreed. The new body was to be called The Legal Eight Hours and International Labour League; its object was to obtain the eight hours' working day and other legislative measures tending towards the ultimate emancipation of the working classes. All *bona fide* workers' organisations who agreed with this aim were to be asked to affiliate. A Central Committee would be elected to organise the work and an Executive to carry out the resolutions of the Committee and of delegate meetings. As individual members men should pay 1s. and women 6d. a year, in two instalments; affiliated societies the same amounts for every 100 men and 100 women. The management of the League was to be vested in the Central Committee and its Executive, which would grant charters to provincial and district committees and lodges. Finally it was proposed that all societies and branches paying an affiliation fee should be

---

* Formed in 1888 on the basis of the Scottish Land and Labour League by John Mahon and represented here by James Shaw Maxwell who replaced Robert Dell as editor of the *People's Press* in August 1890.

entitled to send delegates to meetings: one for every 500 members. The means to attain the ends of the League were defined as education, agitating and organising for an Eight-Hour Bill, the resolutions passed at the Paris Congress,* and the foundation of an independent Labour Party.

It was further agreed that lectures should be given to clubs and organisations; social and political literature was to be distributed; labour bureaux, run by workers, should be established in London and the provinces; a congress should be held at an early date in London, and Labour candidates, pledged to the League's programme, should stand in Parliamentary, Municipal, School Board, County Council and other elections; where this was not possible, all influence should be brought to bear upon candidates to support, at the very least, the legal eight-hours' working day.

A Provisional Executive was then appointed – pending the election of the Central Committee at a future delegate meeting – on which the Finsbury Federation of Radical Clubs, the National Federation of All Trades and Industries, the Woolwich, the Mildmay and the *Star* Radical Clubs, the Gasworkers' Union, the Scottish Labour Party and the Greenwich Cement Workers were represented, with Eleanor, Aveling and a gasworker named McCopley as acting honorary secretaries *pro tem*.

In the 19 July number of the *People's Press* Eleanor's name appeared for the first time in the "Labour Directory" and in all subsequent issues under that heading. The entry, listing the Gas Workers and General Labourers' Union read: "Branch 54. Silvertown (women). Secretary, Eleanor Marx Aveling, 65 Chancery Lane." She hardly needed the publicity – announcing her private address can only have multiplied the invitations to speak – yet she was not perhaps displeased by this advertising of the humblest office she presently held and the one in which she took the greatest pride.

A demonstration was organised by the Gasworkers on 27 July to celebrate the inauguration of the eight-hour day a year ago.† Other unions

---

* To recapitulate the ten points in brief: (1) limitation of working day to a maximum of eight hours for adults; (2) prohibition of labour for all under 14 years of age and reduction of the working day to six hours for all between 14 and 18; (3) prohibition of night work except where continuous processes were necessary in certain branches of industry; (4) prohibition of women's labour in all branches of industry injurious to the female organism; (5) prohibition of night work for women and all under 18; (6) a minimum of 36 hours uninterrupted rest a week for all workers; (7) suppression of the sweating system; (8) suppression of the truck system and of rings and trusts; (9) suppression of employment agencies (i.e. the French *bureaux de placement* which were used, particularly in the case of waiters, for robbing workers); (10) inspection of all workshops and industrial establishments, including domestic industries, by State-paid inspectors, half of whom to be elected by workers.

† Not that in those twelve months all had gone smoothly nor that the agreement had been honoured everywhere without bitter strikes and struggles, if at all.

were invited to join in and there were five platforms, well attended, with Aveling presiding on Platform 2 and Eleanor, introduced as speaking for the Executive, on Platform 5.

On 2 August she was the signatory to a letter concerning the women employed at Crosse & Blackwell's factory in East Ham as onion skinners, 400 of whom had struck for an increase of wages. They were getting from 6d. to $8\frac{1}{2}$d. for a peck of white onions – at best earning 2s. 3d. for a day of 15 hours – $3\frac{1}{2}$d. to $4\frac{1}{2}$d. for green onions: in some cases no more than 1s. a day. They now demanded, respectively, 1s. and 6d. a peck. The management had offered a small increase, but they were resolved to stand out for the full claim.

"The work is particularly arduous," the letter went on, "and even dangerous, as it leads to affections of the eyes. Further, the work is casual in a sense, as it can only be carried on during a certain portion of the year."[131]

It ended with an appeal for donations, as the women had no funds behind them but were stubbornly resolved not to give in.

Whether Eleanor's attention had been drawn to the plight and action of these women during her weekly meetings with the Silvertown branch* is not known, but largely thanks to her efforts, the onion skinners won their strike.

On Sunday, 3 August, the Ponders End Gasworkers, near the River Lea, held a mass meeting in the Railway Field. Eleanor, greeted as enthusiastically as always, made a powerful appeal on behalf of the Crosse & Blackwell workers, who were then near the end of their tether and unlikely to hold out for more than another two days without aid. She also stressed the need to sink all petty jealousies between different sections of labouring workers, none of whom should be satisfied with the paltry wage of between 15s. and 20s. a week, condemning their children to die of starvation. Young women, she urged, should insist upon their lovers showing them a fully paid-up union card and, if they could not, show *them* the door. Earlier the point had been made by Keir Hardie at the "Grand Concert" that men who could not be true to their fellows would make but poor husbands.

*   *   *

One learns with something of the relief Eleanor and Aveling must have felt that they now took a holiday. Indeed, save for a week or so in Cornwall during the uninviting month of January 1889, Eleanor had

---

* On Thursday evenings at 8 p.m. in Mecklenburgh Terrace, Gray's Inn Road (a street no longer extant) and, later, at 161 Barking Road.

breathed no country air at all. On 6 August 1890 they set off for Norway, where Engels with his travelling companion Schorlemmer had recently spent some weeks.*

"I'm amazed that such zealous Ibsenites could bear to wait so long before setting eyes on the new Promised Land,"

wrote Engels.[132] He hoped they would not feel as disappointed as in America.

Events had moved so rapidly – the movement now advancing on a united political and industrial front – that Eleanor had scarcely time to stand back and take stock. She was not physically or mentally exhausted but, with the demands made upon her even before the strenuous autumn in Silvertown and unremittingly since, she needed a breathing space. Aveling, too, had shouldered no light burden as the Chairman of the May Day Committee and its scion, the Eight Hours League, while he had also taken part in an ugly strike of gasworkers at the Wortley Works in Leeds during July, when there had been pitched battles with the police and troops protecting scabs who, for their part, wisely took to their heels.

Yet in this year 1890, Eleanor's praiseworthy translation of the *Lady from the Sea*† had come out and both she and Aveling had written additional material and revised *The Working Class Movement in America* for a second edition. Moreover, during this year of 1890 they were each contributing "Dramatic Notes" to *Time*, while, at Engels' request, Eleanor typed out copies of all Marx's letters to Danielson which he had sent back on loan from Russia for this purpose.

Although Eleanor must have written letters from Norway, these have not been traced and all that can be known is that the holiday lasted a bare three weeks, for on 31 August she was back in London, ready to attend the TUC at the Hope Hall in Liverpool from 1 to 6 September. On that day she wrote a letter to the *People's Press* under the heading: "The Trades Congress and Mrs. Aveling".

"Sir, – May I ask space for a line or two on my exclusion from the Congress? I was, as you perhaps know, elected to represent the Gas Workers and General Labourers' Union at the conference of the union last May. Although Miss [Clementina] Black and Lady Dilke are admitted, my mandate – conferred upon me by representatives of the whole union – is rejected on the ground that I am not a working woman!

Now, to begin with, I am a working woman – I work a type-writer; and secondly it

---

* 1–26 July 1890.
† It is not impossible to understand why Eleanor should have chosen this play with its undertow of implications that a woman can be almost irresistibly drawn to the wild seas of the unattainable but settle for inland, home and duty.

is surely preposterous for anyone except the Congress itself to declare who shall sit and who shall not. As the friends who elected me may not know why I am not at Liverpool as their delegate, they may think I am shirking the work. Miss Black, who has never done a day's manual labour, is admitted. I am boycotted! Thorne did all he could, but to no good. The other delegates have been instructed to bring the matter before the Congress.

Yours faithfully,

Eleanor Marx Aveling.

65 Chancery Lane, W.C. August 31st. 1890."[133]

None the less, in Liverpool she was and on 1 September she wrote to Kautsky – who by now had divorced Louise I and married Luise II – on *Time* letter-headed paper from "Trades Union Congress. Liverpool".

"Dear Karl,

As you will see ... we are at Liverpool for the Trades Union Congress which, as you no doubt know, is the largest, and will be one of the most important yet held in England. Would you like an article for the *Neue Zeit* about it? Of course the great struggle will be upon the 8 hour question; but the whole of the Congress will practically resolve itself into a struggle between the 'Old' and 'New' Unionists.

I was elected at the Annual Conference of the Gas Workers and General Labourers' Union – i.e. by the whole Union, to be one of the nine delegates to the Congress. But Shipton & Co. have refused to accept my mandate, on the ground I am not a working woman. ... We are here chiefly to push the Legal Eight Hours League, and because many very important meetings are to be held and much important work has to be done. ... My only chance of securing a seat was as 'press' – and so I figure as correspondent of the *Soz. Dem., Neue Zeit, Time,* and *Volksblatt*! Of course I asked Ede's* permission. There was no time to write to you. ... Yours, Tussy."[134]

Clementina Black replied to Eleanor's letter in the *People's Press* explaining that she was not and had not asked to be a delegate.

"I do not at the present time hold any position that would entitle me to have done so. Coming late to the meeting and finding literally no space at the Press table, I was allowed by the special kindness of the president and vice president to sit in a vacant place at one of the delegate's tables....†[135]

---

* It was he, Bernstein, not Eleanor, who reported the TUC for *Neue Zeit*. Her article appeared in *Time*.

† Lady Dilke was not a delegate either. In fact, apart from a Miss Taylor, who was one of the two representatives of the Glasgow Trades Council, there were 447 men and but nine women present. These represented eight separate Unions with a total of 2,610 members, 1,300 of whom were in the Matchmakers' Union. Of the other eight, one was delegated by the 40 members of the (London) Shirt and Collar Makers' Trade Union Society, two by the 70 in the Bristol Association of Working Women, and one each by the 120 in the Liverpool Tailoresses' Trade Society, the 200 in the (London) Society of Women Employed in Bookbinding, an equal number in the Liverpool Bookfolders, the 286 in the Liverpool Coat Making Union and the 400 in the (London) Amalgamated Society of Laundresses and General Working Women. Had Eleanor been admitted, she would have represented an additional 60,000 workers.

Eleanor was not having that.

"I find," she wrote, "that the newspapers were in error in announcing that Miss Black and Lady Dilke were to be present as delegates at the Liverpool Congress. But this fact in no way affects the principle of labour representation at the Labour Parliament. Passing over the fact that I am a worker, the important points are: – (1) That according to the standing orders any legal member of a trade union duly elected is eligible, this condition I fulfilled, having been elected not even (as most of the delegates) by a small Executive, but by a conference representing the whole Union. (2) A Union of men and women has a right to decide by whom it shall be represented, a principle recognised in Parliamentary representation. (3) And this principle was recognised at the London Trades Union Congress of 1888, when the old Unionists were for keeping out Mrs. Besant and Miss Simcox,* and the progressive Unionists, like John Burns and Tom Mann, together with the 'foreigners' outvoted them on the question. Lastly, the refusal of any delegate or any society should be vested in the Congress alone, and not in any permanent official or officials."[135]

There, at the press table, Cunninghame Graham espied "Mrs. Marx Aveling, thoughtful, shortsighted, eloquent of speech and pen", listening to one of the most tremendous debates ever to take place at a TUC.

There had been a significant change in the composition of Congress. The affiliated organisations had risen from 171 to 211, representing some $1\frac{1}{2}$ million trade unionists: an increase of more than 585,000 workers, the majority from the ranks of the unskilled.† However, it must not be supposed that they had it all their own way nor yet that the embattled forces of the "Old" and the "New" Unions dominated the Congress. Certainly that conflict was reflected to some extent in the votes cast; but it has to be remembered that the "Labour Parliament", the TUC, was as rigidly governed by its own rules and as narrowly preoccupied with sectional interests, when not with personalities, as Westminster. To the advent of the newcomers with a wholly different view of its functions it attached so little importance that it could not even spell Thorne's name correctly.‡ He himself had to appeal for a hearing to protest that the

---

* There is an error here, for the 1888 TUC was held in Bradford. Eleanor must have meant the *International* TUC, to which Edith Simcox as the president and Annie Besant as the secretary of the Matchmakers' Union were delegated.

† The figures for these years are:

		Organisations	No. members represented	Delegates
(Hull)	1886	122	635,580	143
(Swansea)	1887	131	674,034	156
(Bradford)	1888	138	816,944	165
(Dundee)	1889	171	885,055	211

‡ This may have been what is called a Freudian error, for as "Thorn" in the flesh he no doubt seemed.

representatives of unskilled labour were not receiving any consideration; when Tom Mann moved the suspension of standing orders that the most important debate should be adjourned and renewed the next morning, he was heavily outvoted. "John Burns was given a very poor hearing by the old school of trade unionists," being obliged to mount a table and finally delivering his speech "amidst howling and cat calls".[136]

The Congress became in the main a clash over the Parliamentary Committee's failure to carry out the previous year's decision on the miners' legal eight-hour day. It was argued that no action had been taken because William Crawford* was personally opposed to the measure; that, had he approved, the Committee would have worked for it; that this individual's views in no way relieved the Committee of its responsibility; that Congress was its own master and its decisions inviolable; that if the Parliamentary Committee imagined it was above and could override Congress, its members should resign. It came to a vote of confidence and Broadhurst, speaking for the Parliamentary Committee,† the secretaryship of which he resigned at this Congress, won the day being upheld by 258 votes to 92.

The Address of the President – William Matkin of the Carpenters and Joiners – and the speeches of several members of the Parliamentary Committee were in favour of the legal eight-hour working day for all trades, but they might never have heard of the May Day demonstration or the Eight Hours League and opinion was as hotly divided as ever. The battle swayed to and fro. Some of those who supported legislation, such as the delegate from Manchester and Salford Trades Council, defended it on the grounds that it was in no way "a reflection of Socialism". Others denounced it as a pernicious measure; had been mandated to vote against it; held the view – as in 1889 – that nobody should be asked to do for the organised workers what they could well do for themselves; that it was an admission of weakness to apply to parliament; that any Bill was a double-edged weapon which could equally be used against them; that it tied their hands and one delegate even went so far as to claim that not half-a-dozen trades were demanding an eight-hour day.

Against this it was contended that the question was one of the workers' health and well-being; that it came down to the alternatives of a legal enactment or widespread strikes; that there was practical unanimity in favour of the measure and that while the trade unions could do much,

---

* (1833–1890). Secretary of the Durham Miners' Association from 1867 and of the Miners' National Union 1877–1890, M.P. for Mid-Durham from 1885 until his death in the spring of 1890.

† In the course of which he broke his spectacles and was kindly handed a pair by one of the pressmen who, he said, had "never been more personally useful to him" than in this crisis.

were the one-and-a-half million represented at the Congress expected to wait until the seven million workers in the country were organised and then call a universal strike?

The amendment which, in its roundabout way, rejected the legal eight hours was lost by 173 votes to 181 – a very near thing – and the substantive motion was won by 193 to 155: not a landslide victory either. Studying these recorded votes, one cannot but ask what were all the 246 new boys up to. Their proportionate numbers are not reflected in any of these results.[137]

One important resolution was passed, and this at the instance of the New Unionists: the acceptance of the Belgian Workers' Party invitation to send delegates to an international Congress in Brussels in 1891.

This produced an exceedingly awkward situation. In 1889 the Belgians had been officially delegated to the Possibilists' Congress in Paris but had also attended that of the Marxists where it was decided to hold the next International meeting in Switzerland. Now they had jumped the gun.

Engels, much put out by the TUC's response, wrote to Lafargue:

"Naturally, we were not there to invite them instead. Why are we always so conspicuous by our absence whenever there is something decisive to be done? ... Tussy and Aveling tell me that the English will certainly go to the Belgians' Congress, that is, the Possibilists', and that there is not the slightest hope of making them understand that there is another congress which will be of greater importance ... The English will go *en masse*, and with the fervour of neophytes, to the first international congress which has invited them."

He proposed that, this time, there should be an agreed merger beforehand and added:

"If the French approve this in principle I would suggest taking advantage of the Halle Congress* ... to settle the preliminaries. ... Tussy would come to explain the position in England to you. ... It's a case of the decisive opportunity, possibly the last for five or ten years, for the French, Germans and English to form an alliance. If we let it slip, don't be surprised if the movement here sinks once and for all into the rut of the SDF and the Possibilists. Our rivals are active and astute. They have always been superior to you in this respect; we have indulged in the Right to be Lazy† too freely in our international affairs. Let's put an end to that, let's be up and doing...."[140]

---

* Of the German Social Democratic Party.

† This was not the first nor the last time Engels twitted Lafargue with the title of his celebrated pamphlet (see above, fn †, p. 224). Anxiously awaiting the list of votes cast for the Workers' Party candidates in the French elections of September 1889, he had written to Laura: "Surely Paul will not push the Right to be Lazy far enough to refuse me that little bit of work ...",[138] while in 1895, praising the "brilliant style" of Paul's contribution to a book on the origin and evolution of property, Engels remarked that it did not suffer from the defects of a work by a certain German professor in which "what was true was not original and what was original was

First, however, Eleanor, Aveling and Cunninghame Graham were invited in the name of the Executive of the French Workers' Party to attend their Congress in Lille on 11 and 12 October. The invitation was issued by Louis de Lavigerie, an enigmatic figure since he was described in the press as "Secretary of the French Trade Labour Intelligence Office in London", a body of which nobody had ever heard, while he was characterised by Lafargue as a self-appointed busybody, an intriguer with no official mandate from the French Party and of whom "no account should be taken".[141] Lavigerie claimed to be fully furnished with documents from Guesde and other Executive members but these were alleged to be forgeries. Aveling was asked to find out precisely what they were and how they had been obtained but nothing came of his efforts. However, Lafargue eventually sent an official invitation to the Avelings on 29 September which gave them very short notice, so perhaps it was just as well that, whether by fair means or foul, they had been alerted in advance.

In the event Aveling must have been invited as a visitor or a press reporter, for Eleanor was the only recognised delegate from a foreign country* and the sole woman – *citoyenne* – officially listed together with the 67 delegates representing 98 *communes* and 231 French Workers' Groups and Trade Unions. She was described as mandated by the International Eight Hours League, but more probably represented the Eight Hours League and International Labour League.[142]

The German Social Democratic Congress was to take place from 12 to 18 October at Halle – the first to be held in Germany since May 1877† – and to this Eleanor was also invited as one of 17 foreign guests. Engels hoped that her presence would prevent things going wrong over the preparations for the 1891 International Congress which, it was now generally agreed and endorsed at Lille, should be held in Brussels since the British TUC, too important a body to be ignored, had already received and accepted the invitation. At this stage of political and industrial development, the danger was not that reformists, amongst whom were numbered many of the most active trade unionists, should combine with revolutionary socialists to debate issues of concern to the working class in all countries but, precisely, that they should fail to do so.‡

---

not true" but, on the other hand, it showed signs of too hasty writing: "especially for a Paris public ... the Parisian, too, claims his right to be lazy."[139]

* There was one from Bruges, but not as a representative of Belgium.

† The Anti-Socialist Law had come into force in October 1878. During the intervening twelve years there had been three illegal German Party Congresses abroad: in Wyden, Switzerland (1880), in Copenhagen (1883) and in St. Gallen (1887).

‡ It may be said that this question of reformism and revolutionary socialism was never resolved throughout the whole course of the Second International's existence (until 1914) as a combined body.

Meanwhile, Eleanor's regular work went on. One day – 14 September – it was to address a mass meeting of some 5,000 in the Tottenham area where 250 of the 600 girls employed at Barratt's sweet-making factory had struck in protest against the fines imposed. Some 800 marched from South Tottenham and Woodberry Down to the Jolly Butcher's Hill,* where Eleanor plainly told the crowd that the girls should have joined the union before the fining system had driven them to it, that they had done nothing to support the union and would have to put that right if they hoped to win their struggle. It appeared that the firm, to placate their angry employees, had offered them what Eleanor called "a beanfeast" and she hoped they would give Messrs. Barratt's "beans". She cited the example of the onion skinners whose employers had resorted to every form of bribery – from increased wages for the few to beer all round – but had failed to move the strikers because not a single one had betrayed her workmates by accepting.

At a meeting in the same place during the next week Aveling gravely sermonised, taking as his text "Thou shalt not steal" and drawing the lesson that the masters could not exist without thieving morning, noon and night. He said it was necessary to preach the gospel of the union or another kind of Union – that is, the workhouse – would be their fate. Eleanor, in less doom-laden terms, explained to an attentive public the iniquitous system of fines operated at Barratt's and that the girls had been told by the factory owner in person that they would get neither better wages nor shorter hours but if they were not satisfied, they could get out, whereupon they had struck. Thus another active women's branch of the Gasworkers' Union was formed.

Next it was the turn of the brickmakers of West Drayton† who, unfurling their own branch banner of silk, marched to the Green. It was a special occasion, not only in that the ceremony was attended by Executive members of the Union, including the President, the General Secretary and Eleanor, but it was also the first time a woman had ever spoken on West Drayton Green, a wide open space, used from time immemorial for local meetings. She was therefore greeted with exceptional interest and enthusiasm. This was at the end of September and on 10 October Eleanor set out on her travels, to return on the 19th.

---

* So named after the Three Jolly Butchers public house in what is now Wood Green High Street.
† In the vicinity of today's Heathrow airport where Middlesex borders on Buckinghamshire.

Two of the very few letters from Eleanor to Engels that have come down to us were written from Halle.*

The first letter, begun on Tuesday, 14 October 1890, the day after Eleanor's arrival in Halle, was addressed from the Hotel Goldene Kugel.

"My dear General,

I have just got back from the afternoon sitting, and have had what I may fairly call the first really quiet moment since we left London on Friday night. What with the travelling, the Congresses, and the private talks I am quite bewildered.

We left London as you know on Friday, and reached Lille at 3 o'clock in the morning. At 9 we were at the Hall of the Congress. Our attending was, I think, good in many ways. It made – so all of them said – an excellent impression, and in private I fancy, we were of some use too. As to the Congress, I am bound to say it was really admirable, and never would I have believed, unless I had been present, that 64 Frenchmen cd. be so quiet, talk so very well, whenever they did talk, talk strictly to the point, in the most business-like fashion without even a hint of high falutin' (though such talking as there was, was excellent from even the rhetorical point of view), that they cd. be so absolutely unanimous and on the whole so very clear-headed and theoretically, so free from anything like muddle. But I saw, and so I believed. In those two days an immense amount of work was got through, and that without a single hitch. The feeling was evidently one of perfect confidence all round. What a contrast to the Brousse-Allemane Congresses! – The two questions that I had rather dreaded were the one as to the Brussels Congress, and the 'Universal Strike'. – On the first question there was less difficulty than I fancied there'd be. Of course the bitterness against the Possibilists is immense, but the facts were very well put by Guesde and Lafargue so then, the decision to go to Brussels (with such provisos as you yourself suggested) was unanimously agreed to. – The 'Universal Strike' business called forth more discussion than any other question. Happily the 'Revolution' was not decreed – only 5 out of the

---

* Although from the time Eleanor could write until the end of Engels' life there are frequent references to the correspondence between them, diligent search has failed to trace any but a fraction of it. Here it is surmised, rightly or wrongly, that whereas, after Engels' death, the bulk of his private letters (other than those to and from Marx) were returned to their writers, Laura preserved all those she and her husband had written and received (since these we have in an almost complete series), Eleanor did not. To be sure, since she lived in the same country and, from the age of 15 until the end of his life, in the same town as Engels, seeing him regularly, correspondence will not have figured so largely as in the case of the Lafargues abroad: political no less than personal matters will have been discussed orally rather than set down on paper. Yet it is significant that far more letters survive from Tussy to Laura than from Laura to Tussy; none from Dollie Radford, Olive Schreiner or from Aveling himself. As against the supposition that Eleanor simply did not keep private correspondence there is the greater likelihood that, upon her death, Aveling destroyed it.

64 delegates voting for the Resolution. – But think of my horror, General, when huge placards on the Lille walls calling a meeting with a large white slip pasted across stared me in the face with the following announcement 'Sous la présidence de Eleanor Marx Aveling'! I felt mightily inclined to clear out – but couldn't very well, and the meeting went off all right under my 'présidence'. But it was a mean trick to play on me. – After the meeting, where Edward spoke a few words in English, and where I saw once again what born speakers the Frenchmen are, we adjourned to a very charming and very jolly 'banquet' at 1 franc a head! We tried to get off as early as we could, but it was past twelve before we were back at the Hotel. As I was to leave at 3.5 I only lay down on the bed for a little rest. Then at 3.5 I met Guesde, Ferroul,[*] and a young man, rather a lad (whose name neither I nor Guesde who is looking after him know) and whom Guesde has brought here to find a situation! – and after getting out our various belongings together started on our long journey.

My dear General, the Frenchies were very nice and very charming on the whole, but if I ever travel in 'foreign parts' with one – let alone three – again, may I be damned. I would rather travel with two babies in arms and half a dozen others. They couldn't be more helpless and they wouldn't be nearly so troublesome. We were very jolly though, and laughed not a little – especially at our absolute inability to keep awake in Belgium. We all tried. Impossible. Not till we were out of Belgium did we manage to wake up. Of the details of our long journey I will tell you more when I get back. At about 12.30[†] we got to Cologne. I sat my three Frenchmen down to their déjeuner – wh. they had been clamouring for, and wh. I think they wd. have cried for if they had not got soon – and went off to get their luggage – I only, of course, carried my small bag and your portmanteau – to have it re-registered for Halle, and to get our tickets for Halle. Of course, this took some time – but there was plenty of time to catch the 12 train by wh. we had arranged to go on, I wd. have been quite content to forego a big déjeuner and take a 'snack' with me in the train. But my charges weren't nearly 'through', and the waiter had persuaded them that a 12.50 train wd. be far better. We still had 3 minutes after all this explaining – but I saw it was no good, and as a train really *was* to leave at 12.50 I resigned myself to my fate and my déjeuner. But lo! when we went to the train we were told that it was not the one and that our tickets were for another route! So after much running about – by me – neither of the other three dreamt of even going with me – I got the tickets changed and we started. For a time all was very jolly. – We talked and laughed – and about every 5 minutes one of my three companions disappeared into the little lavatory attached to our carriage (they also got out at each station – and had the cheek to ask me to get out and show them where to go!!!) till I wondered how on earth they managed it. But presently they began to get hungry. Now at one station where we stopped (at about 5.30) for 20 minutes all three were fast asleep, and I hadn't the heart to wake them. I regretted that later. They wanted something to eat. They nearly cried – or rather Guesde did, but Ferroul was much better – because they didn't stop long enough for me to get out and fetch 'des provisions' for them. I comforted them and a conversation on hypnotism – wh. Ferroul

---

[*] Joseph-Antoine-Jean-Frédéric-Ernest Ferroul (1853–1921), a doctor and a Socialist deputy since 1888. He had attended the Paris (Marxist) International Congress in 1889. At the Lille Congress it was resolved to send these two delegates to Halle. Undoubtedly Lafargue would have been elected, rather than Ferroul, had he not arranged to go as a reporter, all expenses paid, to the French Trades Union Congress held in Calais from 11 to 18 October.

[†] From what follows this is a mistake made either by Eleanor or the transcriber of her holograph.

uses largely in his practice – distracted them for a time. Then at Cassel – at least I believe it was Cassel – we stayed and a boy appeared with 'Brötchen' and beer. I got all I could, but had to send a friendly guard for more and I felt relieved. But Guesde's protégé wasn't satisfied – railed at all and sundry and refused to eat. So the poor lad had to starve! But I couldn't help it. Well, on we went, and on, and as the three had smoked all day and had shivered even when the sun was broiling hot if I kept open a window, and as, when the sun went down, they closed the ventilators, you can imagine what the air was like. I had a splitting headache and felt thankful when at 10 or 12 we reached Halle. I got my three out, and see their belongings out, and got their boxes (these had come by the 12 train) and then held council as to what shd. be done. I had telegraphed to Grothe* from Cologne that we shd. arrive at 11 (thinking we shd. leave by the 12 train), and now it was midnight, and no Grothe and no Genosse† of any sort visible.

Thinking rooms had probably been secured for us I suggested taking a cab and going to Jacobstrasse 2 – the address sent me by Fischer. We did get the cab and we started, but before very long our cabby – who was as drunk as Billy, turned round and requested me to tell him where the Jacobstrasse was. This was too much! I asked him how on earth I, who had just arrived, was to tell a Hallenser where the streets in his own town were. Thereupon the cabby swore by all his gods there *was* no such street. Another more or less interested person in the street was appealed to; then another. Same answer from all. No such street in Halle. 'Take us to the first hotel you come to then' quoth I in despair. And presently we were deposited at the 'Goldne Kugel' [*sic*]. Think of our astonishment when this morning at the Congress we heard that Bebel, Liebknecht, Adler, and some dozen others are all here too! But to return to my tale. – By this time my companions were famished – and no wonder, they'd only had a small 'Brötchen' and then nothing since 12 in the morning. (I had supped full of the horror of the air in our railway carriage!). So I asked if we cd. get something to eat. No! It was too late. 'Can't we have *anything*, bread, cheese?' 'Nothing'. 'Not even a little bread?' 'Impossible'! This struck me as so comic I roared with laughter and laughed so that even my three hungry ones joined in – although they thought civilisation a failure in Germany at least. But the *comble* was when appearing with a Directory (I had casually asked the Kellner‡ if *he* knew the Jacobstrasse, he didn't) he showed me that there *was* a Jacobstrasse but it contained only 2 houses – and so how could any one know it? he asked. – Well, we drank a glass of beer and got to bed. (Bebel just fetches me to go to supper and a 'jollification' got up by the local folk.)

Wednesday morning. So to resume. Yesterday morning then we got up and after finding out where the Congress sat, and having some coffee, we set out for it.§ There, of course, we found everybody. The Hall is a large one, but it is very inadequate, and the people are packed so close we all feel and look like sardines. I mention that because in spite of the very uncomfortable over-crowding the people are so quiet and attentive. There are 413 delegates‖ (Bebel tells me he expected 250) and there are Anseele,

---

* One of the Halle delegates on the credentials committee.
† Comrade.
‡ Waiter.
§ An establishment called *Zum Hofjäger*.
‖ Only four of whom were women. They took little part in the political debates, save for a few interventions, and when they jointly moved a clause to be inserted in the Party Programme concerning female and child labour, it failed to win enough support to be taken. However, one of them expressed thanks to the Congress for admitting women at all. To this the Report adds a

Nieuwenhuis, Branting (Sweden), some one from Copenhagen, and from Switzerland, the Frenchmen and myself.* Duc Quercy is also here for the 'Temps'. – Bebel at once told me that the opposition was practically squashed. Werner had tried to get up a row the day before – i.e. the Monday, and 2 or 3 Berliners had supported him, but they were quite alone, and he believed Werner wd. now be deserted even by his remaining 2 or 3. And this was so. Not a hand was held up against Fischer's Resolutn. (the actual Resolution you will of course see in the 'Volksblatt') and only Werner said he refrained from voting either way. – Yesterday on the main question really – the Report on the Parliamentary Fraction – Werner alone spoke against, and such awful nonsense that I cd. hardly believe my own ears. Vollmar in a way tried also to support (not avowedly) Werner. But they are *hopelessly* beaten. Indeed there seemed practically nothing to beat. It is quite disappointing! I did think there'd be something of a fight. But how *can* 400 fight one? – And that's about what it comes to. – In the afternoon Guesde and Ferroul spoke admirably and produced a great effect. – Last night to our relief the Entertainment was so crowded, thousands – Bebel, Adler, Singer among them – couldn't get in. So we had a quiet and most interesting talk. Tomorrow we have our International Conference. – More, shd. anything important happen, later on. Now I must off to Congress.

Love to you both.† (If I sent you all the Grüsse‡ I'm told to, I shd. fill a dozen pages with names.)

Your Tussy.

Wednesday.

I am adding a line to say that the SDF has sent over a Resolution which is really an insult – full of good advice and hopes that the 'differences' will not 'dim the glory' of the 'spectacle of solidarity' the Germans have given, or check the movement etc. But probably you will see the thing in 'Justice'. Adler is translating it, and felt its insolence so much he was modifying it, but I said *no*: translate it as it is. I am certain the people will not be very pleased at this really cool assumptn of superior wisdom. – Werner is evidently done, but a man who in my opinion is infinitely more dangerous is Vollmar. He is cleverer than Werner, and carefully avoids going too far, so saving his position and retaining a certain influence. – Liebknecht spent the whole of yesterday evening with Guesde and Ferroul, and as far as I can gather from Guesde, lied hard. We were *all* to have met, but without letting any of us know, Liebknecht sent word to the Frenchmen to meet him – not at the Hotel where we are all living, but at another. He evidently didn't want to have us present. However, I don't think anything special can have been done. – This is immensely interesting – but *entre nous* I can't deny that the Germans are too much like the Liverpoolers – i.e. painfully respectable and middle-class looking. There *must* be a strong sprinkling of philistines among them. In this respect the Frenchmen seemed far better. Though, of course, there there were 64, and

---

footnote stating that women had never been excluded from any Congress either before or since the passing of the Anti-Socialist Law, but regrettably hardly any had ever come forward.[143]

* Of the 17 foreigners present, including Eleanor from London, four (of whom two were journalists) came from Paris, three from Vienna, one – the only other woman – from Amsterdam and one each from Basel, Copenhagen, Ghent, The Hague, St. Gallen, Stockholm, Warsaw and Zurich.[144]

† That is, including Nim.

‡ Greetings.

here there are 417. – I have just been having a long talk with Adler – both about party matters and about the Kautskys. He says Louise is looking ten years younger, and is getting on very well. Adler is as witty as ever – and to hear him and Auer chaff one another is really delicious – for Auer is one of the most humourous people I have ever met. I have also had a long talk with Nieuwenhuis. He is still as mild as milk. Anseele, as I told you, I talked with yesterday. I may be quite wrong, but I always fancy – I fancied the same at Paris last year – he rather fights shy of us, and he always looks like a man who hasn't a very good conscience about something or other.

Good-bye again, dear General,

Your

Tussy.

Nieuwenhuis and Adler (who know I'm just sending this off) send all sorts of messages."

Written across the top of the letter:

"Neither Hyndman nor Gilles nor Schack are here. Hyndman I expect did not care to come, when he heard from Bax we should be here. As to Schack, she evidently intended to come, as Fischer says letters are here addressed to her. What a blow to that lot! They who had hoped for a split, at least a serious quarrel – lo, nothing now comes of it!"*[145]

Left out of her account is her own part in the proceedings at Lille.

"Tussy had a great success," wrote Lafargue to Engels, "her speech at the Lille Hippodrome was very well conceived and very well delivered. She is very self-assured."

He then made clear why it had been sprung upon her – by catching sight of a poster – that she was to preside over one of the sessions: Lafargue had forgotten to tell her.

"It was I who got her elected to the chair," he wrote with some pride. "Fearing that she might feel embarrassed by that position" (had she known of it), he had appointed two old hands "to assist her; they know how to chair stormy meetings. But she acquitted herself to everyone's satisfaction. . . ."[146]

Aveling reported the Lille congress – he was not at Halle – for the *Daily Chronicle* on 14 October:

"a good brief account," according to Lafargue, ". . . but he did not have the time, nor the freedom of expression to convey the real character of the congress, the most important one that we have had in France – with the exception of the International

---

* From a typescript of the holograph. Eleanor's spelling, known to be faulty, has not been altered, but her handwriting has been imperfectly deciphered in a few obvious cases, including personal names. These have been corrected and certain, though few changes made in cases of punctuation – whether Eleanor's or the typist's – which obscure the sense.

Congress and the Marseilles congress* – at which for the first time the aristocracy of the French proletariat lisped communist phrases, without quite understanding their import."†147

While Lafargue told Engels about Lille, Eleanor wrote him her second . letter from Halle, dated 16 October:

"My dear General,
   The actual details of the Congress no doubt you see in the daily reports of the 'Volksblatt'. Everything seems to be going very well indeed. I am bound to say, however, that the more I see of the people the more I see what a very strong current of philistinism there is. No doubt it is easy to understand how and why this is, but it is a blessing for the Party that behind these men are the mass of the people to keep them up to the mark. – The so-called opposition from the Werner clique certainly seems quite done – and Bebel and all to whom I speak say the same. But where I think our people are making a mistake is in not sufficiently realizing the danger of Vollmar. He is certainly no remarkable intellect or anything of that sort, but he is a very clever intriguer, in my opinion a thousand times more really dangerous to the movement than a dozen Werners.‡ – As to Bebel, it is clear to me both from what has been said publicly and from what I hear privately, that the Party owes everything – so far of course, as it does not owe it to the strong good sense of the people – to him and to his really incredible work. I don't think even you, General, know *what* this man has done and is doing. Practically everything is left on his shoulders. As you know, there are two Commissions, one (apart from the purely business one) busy working at the Amended Organizat'n. plan, and the other enquiring into the Werner accusations. Bamberger (Ede's brother-in-law) was the chief witness and tells me privately that the Commission is all right, and that Werner will be quite done for.
   The Programme is adopted with almost no changes at present, but with the understanding that an 'Entwurf'§ will be drawn up, discussed everywhere and decided upon at the next Congress. Liebknecht was the 'Berichterstatter'‖ on the Programme, and talked an awful lot of nonsense – with some excellent passages and very effective. – We were to have had the International Conference last night, but as Singer, Auer and Bebel were on two Committees, it was impossible, and now an arrangement is made wh. I think quite wrong, but there is such a pressure of work, and so little time, I cd. do nothing to prevent it. Adler agrees with me, but also sees no help for it. This is the present arrangement. At 9 to-night the whole Fraktion – or as many of them as are here, give a 'banquet'¶ to all of us foreigners, and after it we are to consider the

---

* Of 1879, regarded as the foundation Congress of the French Workers' Party.
† One touching incident at the Congress was that, amongst the messages received – from the German Social Democrats, the British Gasworkers' Union, the Dutch and the Belgians – was one sent from Switzerland by four old Communards in exile, still proscribed after nearly twenty years.142
‡ Werner was the relatively insignificant spokesman for an opposition group known as "The Young". Georg Heinrich Vollmar (1850–1922) as the leader of a right-wing "gradualist" faction held – as Lassalle had done before him – that social change might be brought about by personal and prudent negotiations with the heads of State.
§ Draft document.
‖ He who gives the official Report. Liebknecht spoke for the best part of two-and-a-half hours.
¶ At the "Prinz Karl" restaurant.

question of the Congress and so forth.* I think this is a pity, d'autant plus,† that I find Liebknecht has also asked Duc Quercy (reporting here for the 'Temps'). Now Duc I know is intimate with Guesde and on good terms with our Party in France, but I did *not* think he was really *in* the Party, and if we are to discuss Party matters I don't see why we shd. have such a person as Duc Quercy in it. Then too – unless I can induce Bebel to ask him on the ground that he is here from *London* – Fischer can, under the present arrangement, not be present – a decided loss. The difficulty, of course, is that I hardly see Bebel, who is hard at work all day, and that very naturally, all of these men are worried about their own home affairs, and are hardly in the humour to realise the importance of external questions. – Yesterday I had long and very interesting talks with several people – especially Adler. Like Bebel he also feels that it is a blessing for the movement that, for a time at any rate, the movement can be carried on openly, and that more pressure can be brought to bear on the Reichstag members – many of whom, according to Bebel, are nothing more nor less than small middle-class men, and are, in a sense, almost a danger.

Tonight the Organizat'n. Committee finishes its work, and therefore all the most important questions will be settled tomorrow, although the Congress will sit *at least* till Sunday, and possibly longer. But as I said, all the really big questions will probably be settled to-morrow and Sat'y. I am glad of this as my return-ticket to Cöln must be used on Sat'y. My leaving before the actual end, however, will not matter, as we have the International Conference to-night, and after to-morrow morning Bebel will be comparatively free, he tells me, to talk to me. Of course everybody is asking me everywhere, especially the Berliners, but as my ticket is only good for 6 days I must refuse. In a way I am glad. Here I have seen all the friends (I wd. only have liked to see Uncle Edgar‡ – tho' I don't know how I shd. have found him,) and Friede Bebel§ and if I went to one at Berlin I shd. offend another, and so the much simpler not to go at all. Besides I hope by this to escape my Frenchmen, who did not take return tickets. The one journey was enough. – I shall have much to tell you when I get back. – Fancy that three big Paris papers are represented by three men who neither understand nor read one solitary word of German! – You shd. see those people at table! First one gets really angry, but at last Adler and I nearly got fits of laughter last night. For *at least* $\frac{1}{2}$ an hour they discussed what they should eat; then they nearly cried because they didn't get all they wanted; all the time they discussed food and their digestions; in fact Longuet isn't in it with Guesde and Duc Quercy.

Good-bye, dear General, I shall see you soon. – Lots of messages from all and sundry.
Love to Nymmy
Your
Tussy.
Among the telegrams and greetings received to-day is one from London from the Salvation Army!! – Did I tell you how funny it is – to me, anyhow – to see the Police Commissary on the Platform, and the two official short-hand writers?"[148]

Engels sent this letter on to Bernstein, with a few comments of his own, on the day after Eleanor's return to London.

---

* This refers to the Brussels 1891 International Congress.
† The more so.
‡ Her mother's brother, Edgar von Westphalen.
§ August Bebel's daughter (1869–1948).

A resolution, among all the others not recorded in Eleanor's letters because they were fully reported in the press, was the Germans' decision to observe May First, rather than the first Sunday in May, as a workers' general demonstration.

One of the details Eleanor is unlikely to have mentioned was that when she and her two French colleagues appeared at the Congress, the new arrivals being formally welcomed at the opening of the afternoon session, the announcement of her name was the signal for loud applause even before the speaker was able to introduce her as "the daughter of Karl Marx, the representative of the London Gasworkers and the General Labourers of Great Britain and Ireland".[149]

She wasted no time in acquainting the English public with the Halle Congress, comparing its conduct favourably with that of the Liverpool TUC, in an article for the *People's Press*, published on 1 November. It lacked, of course, the comments – both on inner Party matters and personalities – contained in her letters to Engels, and she referred to herself as "a born Cockney", but what emerged most clearly was that, as a bred-in-the-bone internationalist, she understood better than any contemporary British socialist the character and problems of the movement on the Continent.

Thus it was fitting that, when the Brussels Congress of July 1891 took place, Eleanor should reach the apogee of her public career and, giving the Report on Great Britain as the delegate of the National Union of Gasworkers and General Labourers, the Legal Eight Hours League, the Bloomsbury Socialist Society and the Battersea Labour League, she should make the most important speech in her life.

In our day, when it is a commonplace for women to take their seats on political and trade union platforms, in local government and, however negligible their number, in Parliament and the highest councils of the State – let alone in the jockeys' saddle – while their voices are heard piping on every wave-length and microphone in the land, it may seem extravagant to have dwelt in such detail upon Eleanor's activities. Yet during her time – even after it, had she lived a full span – the women who made an impact upon any substantial section of the people could just about be counted on the fingers. Of course, we have had at least a couple of Queens whose reigns have been more glorious than those of any Kings of England, but that is History, with a capital letter; and as Marx and Engels said:

"*history*" (with a small h) "does *nothing* ... 'history' is not as it were a person apart, using man as a means for *its own* aims; history is *nothing but* the activity of man pursuing his aims."[150]

To be sure, there were among Eleanor's contemporaries the brave and often brilliant pioneers for women's rights but their crusade led away from rather than towards labouring men and women combining harmoniously for the defence and advancement of their class.

Further, though this need hardly be said, Eleanor was not a woman who sought public attention: to her message, yes; not to herself. Her *amour-propre* was vested in her service, not in her ego. That was what Lafargue meant when he called her "self-assured"; perhaps it would have been nearer the mark to say "self-forgetful". She did not suffer from stage fright because she knew she spoke well and her urgency to convince lent fire to eloquence. Indeed, the respect and affection in which she was held were such that, had she desired it, she could have become one of the foremost figures in the annals of British socialism. But this implies an urge to be in the fore; and that she never had. She was not trying to make a name for herself. Indeed, she would have wished to be counted among the ranks of that great army of anonymous men and women who, over the generations, without recognition or reward, have given their volunteer service to end the exploitation of man by man and, in doing so, helped to make history. The lives of any one of them might be worth the telling. We happen to know Eleanor's name because it was Marx.

REFERENCE NOTES

Abbreviations

BIML   Institute of Marxism-Leninism, Berlin.
Bottigelli Archives   Letters in the custody of Dr. Emile Bottigelli.
ELC   *Frederick Engels, Paul and Laura Lafargue: Correspondence.* Volumes I–III. Lawrence & Wishart, 1959–1963.
IISH   International Institute of Social History, Amsterdam.
Liebknecht   *Wilhelm Liebknecht. Briefwechsel mit Karl Marx und Friedrich Engels.* Edited by Georg Eckert. Mouton & Co., The Hague, 1963.
MEW   *Marx Engels Werke.* Dietz Verlag, Berlin, 1956–1968.
MIML   Institute of Marxism-Leninism, Moscow.
Thompson   E. P. Thompson, *William Morris: Romantic to Revolutionary.* Lawrence & Wishart, 1955.
WM Letters   *The Letters of William Morris to his Family and Friends*, Edited by Philip Henderson. Longmans Green, 1950.

(1) Printed by C. F. Roworth and "Published by the Authority of the Congress and Parliamentary Committee", 1888. Library of Political and Economic Science.
(2) To Engels, 25 July 1888. ELC II, p. 148.
(3) To Engels, 29 July 1889. *Ibid.*, p. 296.
(4) 3 January 1889. *Ibid.*, p. 186.
(5) 4 December 1888. MIML. (Original in French.)

(6)   25 March 1889. ELC II, p. 210.

(7)   14 April 1889. *Ibid.*, p. 221.

(8)   27 March 1889. *Ibid.*, p. 212.

(9)   Hyndman. *Record of an Adventurous Life*, pp. 423–4.

(10)   Engels to Laura, 7 May 1889. ELC II, p. 236.

(11)   19 April 1889. Liebknecht, pp. 336 and 338.

(12)   9 September 1889. ELC II, p. 312.

(13)   12 March 1889. *Ibid.*, pp. 201–2.

(14)   William Morris Papers. BM Add. MSS 45345 (145).

(15)   To Laura, 11 April 1889. Bottigelli Archives.

(16)   30 October 1888. IISH.

(17)   Engels to Lafargue, 11 May 1889. ELC II, p. 240.

(18)   Bottigelli Archives.

(19)   Eleanor to Laura, 10 May 1889. *Ibid.*

(20)   Engels to Liebknecht, 5 April 1889. Liebknecht, p. 329.

(21)   *Justice*, 6 April 1889.

(22)   30 April 1889. MIML. (Original in French.)

(23)   ELC II, p. 241.

(24)   24 May 1889. *Ibid.*, p. 261.

(25)   *Justice.* 25 May 1889.

(26)   John Burns Papers. BM Add. MSS 46285 (15).

(27)   Bottigelli Archives.

(28)   To Lafargue, 15 June 1889. ELC II, p. 279.

(29)   To Laura, 28 June 1889. *Ibid.*, p. 283.

(30)   *Ibid.*, p. 282.

(31)   To Engels, 2 July 1889. *Ibid.*, p. 285.

(32)   5 July 1889. *Ibid.*, p. 286.

(33)   All references to the Congress delegates and proceedings, unless otherwise stated, are from the official German Report, *Protokoll des Internationalen Arbeiter Congresses zu Paris*, Nürnberg, 1890. IISH. The copy used is stamped as having originally belonged to the library of the *Communistische Arbeiter Bildungs Verein* (Communist Workers Educational Association), 55 Grafton Street, London, W.

(34)   *Justice.* 25 May 1889.

(35)   "The Paris International Congress", *Labour Elector*, 3 August 1889.

(36)   Thompson, p. 625.

(37)   17 July 1889. MEW 37, pp. 250–1.

(38)   27 July 1889.

(39)   *Eleanor Marx. Erinnerungen von Eduard Bernstein. Die Neue Zeit. XVI Jg. Band II*, No. 30. 1897–8, pp. 120–1.

(40)   Letter in English, 28 January 1948, written from 48 rue des Acacias, Alfortville (Ivry). Privately communicated with permission to quote.

(41)   Will Thorne. *My Life's Battles*. George Newnes, n.d. (probably *c.* 1925), p. 67.

(42)   *Ibid.*, p. 71.

(43)   Ben Tillett. "The Dockers' Story". *English Illustrated Magazine*, 1889–90, p. 98.

(44)   Quoted in *The Deadly* 738, 2nd (revised and enlarged) edition. Simpkin, Marshall, Hamilton, Kent & Co. 1898, p. 35. Subtitled "A Business Tragedy in Two Hemispheres", the pamphlet was a well-documented attack upon Rockefeller's Standard Oil Trust for selling to Europe what it called "refuse oil" with a low flash-point. Originally it appeared as a series of unsigned articles in the *Star*.

(45) *The Bee-Hive.* 2 November, 7, 14, 21 and 28 December 1872; 4, 18 and 25 January; 1 and 8 February and 19 April 1873.

(46) Thorne, *op. cit.*, p. 76.

(47) *Ibid.*, p. 77.

(48) William Stephen Sanders. *Early Socialist Days.* Hogarth Press, 1927, p. 52.

(49) Thorne, *op. cit.*, p. 125.

(50) *Ibid.*, p. 117.

(51) G. Allen Hutt. Unpublished interview at the House of Commons, 5 December 1939. Privately communicated with permission to quote.

(52) Thorne, *op. cit.*, p. 56.

(53) Laura to Eleanor, 17 April 1889. IISH.

(54) Engels to Laura, 17 October 1889. ELC II, p. 330.

(55) Thorne, *op. cit.*, p. 118.

(56) *Report of the* 22nd Annual Trades Union Congress. Co-operative Printing Society Ltd., Manchester. British Library of Political and Economic Science. All subsequent quotations from this source.

(57) Harold Goldman. *Emma Paterson.* Lawrence & Wishart, 1974, p. 73.

(58) 7 September 1889.

(59) Ben Tillett. *Memoirs and Reflections.* John Long, 1931, p. 116.

(60) *Ibid.*, p. 119.

(61) Quoted by Thorne, *op. cit.*, p. 82, from Tillett's *Brief History of the Dockers' Union, Commemorating the 1889 Dockers' Strike.*

(62) S. B. Boulton. "Labour Disputes". *The Nineteenth Century.* Vol. XXVII. June 1890, p. 988.

(63) Tillett. *Illustrated London Magazine,* 1889–90, p. 99.

(64) E. A. and G. H. Radice. *Will Thorne. Constructive Militant.* George Allen & Unwin, 1974, p. 17.

(65) *The Dockers' Record* No. 7, October 1890. A penny journal, started in April 1890 as *The Monthly Record* of the Union. This was the first issue to appear under the new title when it had a circulation of 22,500.

(66) Thorne, *op. cit.*, p. 86.

(67) Tom Mann. *Memoirs* (1967 edn.), pp. 68–9.

(68) Tillett. *Memoirs and Reflections,* p. 135.

(69) John Burns. "The Great Strike". *New Review,* October 1889, p. 420.

(70) Mann, *op. cit.*, p. 67.

(71) Printed by Green & M'Allen, 1889.

(72) Burns, *loc. cit.*, p. 417.

(73) "The Docks", originally published in *The Nineteenth Century,* Vol. XXII, October 1887, pp. 483–99 and later incorporated in *Labour and Life of the People,* Vol. I, *East London.* 1889, pp. 197–9.

(74) Tillett, *op. cit.*, p. 109.

(75) ELC II, p. 304.

(76) *Programme and Rules of the Social-Democratic Federation.* (*As revised at the Annual Conference held at Birmingham, April 5th, 1889.*) British Library of Political and Economic Science.

(77) Research Department of GMWU. For this and all subsequent references to the elections, speeches and proceedings at the Union's Conferences and Congresses, 1890–6, I am indebted to the Research Officer of the General and Municipal Workers Union for access to his department's archives, unless otherwise stated.

(78) *Silvertown: An Account of the Works and Products of the India Rubber, Gutta Percha and Telegraph Works Co.* 1920. Stratford Library Special Archives.

(79) *West Ham: A Study in Social and Industrial Problems.* Compiled by Edward G. Howarth and Mona Wilson. Dent, 1907, p. 408.

(80) Reports on census returns.

(81) *Annual Report of the Chief Inspector of Factories for the Year* 1939. Cmd. 6251, 1941; *Ibid.*, for the year 1951, Cmd. 8772, 1953.

(82) Morant. *History of Essex*, 1768; R. Goadby and J. Towers. *A New Display of the Beauties of England, West Ham.* Vol. I (3rd edition), 1776, p. 56; James Dunstan. *The History of the Parish of Bromley St. Leonard.* Hunt & Son, High Street, Bow, 1862, p. 238.

(83) Dunstan, *op. cit.*, pp. 239–40.

(84) *Ibid.*, p. 242 and Census returns.

(85) *West Ham: A Study in Social and Industrial Problems.* Compiled by Edward G. Howarth and Mona Wilson. Dent, 1907, p. 145.

(86) Katherine Fry. *History of the Parishes of East and West Ham.* Printed for private circulation by E. Siegle. Revised and edited by G. Payenstecker, 1888.

(87) *Annual Report of the Chief Inspector of Factories for the year* 1946. Cmd. 7299, 1948, p. 111.

(88) 14 November 1889. ELC II, p. 338.

(89) Companies Register, 25 March 1889.

(90) Lawrence Pearsall Jacks. *Life and Letters of Stopford Brooke*, Vol. I. Murray, 1917, pp. 319, 325.

(91) Ellis. *My Life.* Heinemann, 1940, p. 229.

(92) Quoted by Vera Buchanan-Gould in *Not Without Honour.* Hutchinson, 1953, p. 221.

(93) Thorne, *op. cit.*, pp. 96 and 149.

(94) G. Allen Hutt. Unpublished MS of an interview at the House of Commons, 5 December 1939. (See 51 above)

(95) 25 December 1889. IISH.

(96) 24 December 1889. Liebknecht, pp. 355–6.

(97) Radford family papers.

(98) Swan Sonnenschein *Letterbooks.*

(99) *People's Press.* 5 June 1890.

(100) Quoted by Goldman, *op cit.*, p. 67.

(101) *Labour Elector.* 1 February 1890.

(102) *People's Press.* 12 July 1890.

(103) To Sorge, 8 February 1890. MEW 37, p. 354.

(104) To Bruce Glasier, WM Letters, pp. 321–2.

(105) Dona Torr. *Tom Mann and His Times.* Lawrence & Wishart, 1956, p. 211.

(106) *The Nineteenth Century*, Vol. XXVII, May 1890, p. 718.

(107) *People's Press.* 15 March 1890.

(108) "Northampton" by Eleanor Marx Aveling.

(109) *An Account of the Labour and Socialist Movement in Bristol* recorded by Samson Bryher (the pseudonym of Samuel Bale), Part II. July 1931, p. 24. Reprinted as a pamphlet from a series of articles in the *Bristol Labour Weekly.* I am indebted to Miss Angela Tuckett for a copy of the pamphlet and the identification of the author.

(110) *What a Compulsory 8 Hour Working Day Means to the Workers.* The Modern Press, 1886.

(111) "A Multitude of Counsellers". *The Nineteenth Century*, Vol. XXVIII, October 1890, pp. 501–16.

(112) *People's Press*. 6 December 1890.

(113) *Ibid.* 13 December 1890.

(114) *Ibid.* 20 December 1890.

(115) *Ibid.* 27 December 1890.

(116) *Labour Elector.* 5 April 1890.

(117) *People's Press.* 12 April 1890.

(118) *Ibid.* 3 May 1890.

(119) *Ibid.* 26 April 1890.

(120) "*Der* 4. Mai in London", No. 21. 23 May 1890.

(121) Thorne, *op. cit.*, p. 77.

(122) ELC II, pp. 375–6.

(123) MEW 37, p. 398.

(124) *Ibid.*, pp. 400–1.

(125) 22 September 1890. IISH.

(126) 31 May 1890.

(127) British Library of Political and Economic Science.

(128) Quoted as the opinion of one of the largest cotton manufacturers by J. A. Murray Macdonald in "The Case for an Eight Hours Day". *The Nineteenth Century*, Vol. XXVII, April 1890, p. 564.

(129) 24 May, 1890.

(130) *People's Press.* 19 July 1890.

(131) *Ibid.* 9 August 1890.

(132) To Sorge, 9 August 1890, MEW 37, p. 439.

(133) 6 September 1890. Also published in *Le Socialiste*, 21 September 1890, for drawing my attention to which I am indebted to Mr. Bert Andréas.

(134) IISH.

(135) *People's Press.* 13 September 1890.

(136) Thorne, *op cit.*, p. 133.

(137) Details (not *verbatim*) from *Report of the Twenty-Third Annual Trades Union Congress held in the Hope Hall, Hope Street, Liverpool, on September* 1, 2, 3, 4, 5 and 6, 1890. British Library of Political and Economic Science.

(138) 8 October 1889. ELC II, p. 325.

(139) 3 April 1895. ELC III, pp. 370–1.

(140) 15 September 1890. ELC II, pp. 391–2.

(141) To Engels, 4 August 1890. *Ibid.*, p. 381.

(142) *Huitième Congrès National du Parti Ouvrier. Tenu à Lille. Le Samedi* 11 et Dimanche 12 Octobre, 1890. IISH.

(143) *Protokoll über die Verhandlungen des Parteitags der Sozial-demokratischen Partei Deutschlands. Abgehalten zu Halle a S vom* 12 bis 18 Oktober 1890. Berlin, 1890. IISH, pp. 114–15, 184, 196, 236, 240.

(144) *Ibid.*, p. 10.

(145) Transcription dated 17.5.65 from the archives: MS. 64/142 (8233a). BIML.

(146) To Engels, 16 October 1890. ELC II, pp. 408–9.

(147) *Ibid.*, p. 406.

(148) MIML.

(149) Halle *Protokoll* (as 143), p. 109.

(150) *The Holy Family or a Critique of Critical Criticism* (1845). Lawrence & Wishart, 1956, p. 125.

· PART IV ·

LAST LUSTRE OF THE GENERAL

On Friday 28 November 1890 Engels celebrated his 70th birthday. In honour of the occasion Eleanor was invited by the Vienna *Sozialdemokratische Monatsschrift* "to write a short essay ... on the acknowledged head of the present Party". This she did, saying: "Of all the various qualities necessary for such a difficult task, I can claim only one: that I have known Engels all my life." After giving a concise biographical sketch up to the time of her father's death, Eleanor referred to the great body of work Engels had since produced – though "it would be pretentious of me to try and give any analysis" of it – not only in bringing out Marx's unfinished manuscripts as his major contribution, but, thanks to his facility in eight languages,* supervising the innumerable translations of his own and Marx's works, to which he wrote many a new preface. She then spoke with loving admiration of his unimpaired vigour of body and spirit. He had no grey hairs; "he carries his six-foot-odd so lightly ... and although Engels looks young he is even younger than he looks. He is really the youngest man I know. As far as I can remember he has not grown any older in the last twenty hard years ..." She recalled accompanying him to Ireland – "the Niobe of the nations" – when she was a girl of 14 and to America almost two decades later: "In 1869 and in 1888 he was the life and soul of every party and every group in which he found himself."†[1]

Earlier, Engels himself had written to his brother boasting of his fitness: he had regained his full maximum weight of twelve stone – "all healthy firm muscular brawn, no flabby fat" – his eyes which had troubled him for so long were better.

"Even the doctors won't believe me when I tell them I'm in my 70th year, saying I look ten to fifteen years younger. Admittedly that's only on the surface, deceptive even in my case, for beneath it lurk all manner of little infirmities and in the long run many a mickle makes a muckle. But on the whole I can't complain and when I see the way so many others fash themselves to death about nothing and less than nothing, without the slightest reason or earthly use, I count myself lucky to have kept my serenity of spirit and can laugh at all such bunkum."[3]

---

* In fact he was conversant with nine modern languages, for Eleanor did not include Russian.
† Engels pronounced this article "ghastly, nauseous adulation".[2]

One sign of his resilience was Engels' capacity to move with the times. This is perfectly reflected in his vernacular style. Whether writing letters in English, French or German he used, at every stage, the most up-to-date colloquialisms.*

Early in September 1890, before he would agree to renew the lease of 122 Regent's Park Road for a further three years, at the annual rent of £60 that he had always paid, and threatening to give up the house on the following Lady Day, he demanded of his landlord and the estate agents† "the replacing of the present useless bath with appliances for hot and cold water", a water-closet and – a request Jakins had previously refused – "an efficient kitchen range to replace the present one which is 20 years old and quite worn out".[5] This despite the new gas cooker against the perils of which Paul Lafargue had issued fearful warnings.

On her birthday, 26 September, Laura was promised that "next time you come here you will be able to have a hot bath in the house", for Engels had "carried his point".[6]

Less than eighteen months later, in May 1892, Engels appears to have been negotiating for a telephone to be installed, which would have put him among the most *avant-garde* of private householders.‡

---

* In several cases where his English idioms appear startlingly modern it has been found that the *Shorter Oxford English Dictionary* attributes their earliest appearance in the language to the year, if not to a year or two after, they occur in Engels' letters. In this – not, after all, his native tongue – his correspondence is of peculiar interest for its flexibility and ever-changing usage, ranging over the years – despite vestiges of a Teutonic turn of phrase never wholly eradicated – from an English that would have been acceptable in the 18th century to that of the 20th.

† A Mr. Jakins became the owner of the house following the death, at the age of 81, of the original landlord in March 1890. This elusive character, Richard Rainshaw de Rothwell, whose occupation was entered on his death certificate as "a marquis", had taken an active interest in the Italian struggle for liberty, contributing to its patriotic funds, for which he was made a Count by Victor Emmanuel in 1860, the title of Marquis de Rothwell being conferred on him by Charles III, prince of Monaco, in the following year. The agents were Messrs. Strutt & Parker, an Essex firm founded in 1855 which moved to Russell Square five years later and is still, though elsewhere, going strong. They had not acted for Rothwell and, indeed, when Engels first leased the house in 1870, he had experienced the greatest difficulty in concluding the agreement with his landlord who never answered letters and was always away shooting something or another in Lancashire where he owned large estates. Rothwell lived at Sharples Hall, Bolton-le-Moor, a few miles north-west of Manchester. It has disappeared from modern gazetteers, no doubt swallowed up, but in the early decades of the 19th century it was a thriving town, with a population that rose to over 50,000 in the 1830s, engaged in the manufacture of fustians, dimities and muslins. Rothwell died at 118 Regent's Park Road, next door but one to Engels – which became a lodging house – on the corner of Rothwell Street, for he also owned property in the neighbourhood.[4]

‡ The first usable telephones were brought to England from America in 1877; the first private subscriber was in Coleman Street, in the City, where the Edison Telephone Co. supplied an instrument in 1879. By 1889 the various companies, some of whom, such as Edison and Bell, had already amalgamated into the United Telephone Co., were absorbed by the National Telephone Co. Ltd. and some ten years later the Post Office established a competitive service

The 70th birthday fête went with a swing. Engels was showered with letters and telegrams from the socialists of every country and gifts poured in; among them one which touched him deeply, for a comrade in Barmen, under the guidance of an old inhabitant, had taken a series of photographs of the country house and gardens of his childhood days. "In short, I was overwhelmed," he wrote to Laura[7] who had spent a few days in London earlier that month but had not stayed for the celebrations.

In the evening there was an animated party at the house where, though some of the guests arrived having already toasted their host too heartily, they were all regaled with claret and champagne until half-past three in the morning, when twelve dozen oysters were consumed. "So you see," Engels wrote to Laura, "I did my best to show that I was still alive and kicking."[7] Among the foreigners present were Liebkneckt, Bebel and Singer who, despite the opening of the Reichstag session on 2 December, were persuaded to stay on for a few days to meet John Burns, Will Thorne and other English working-class leaders at Eleanor's flat.

Cunninghame Graham has left a description of this gathering at 65 Chancery Lane, published on 6 December in the *People's Press* under the heading "Eight Hour 'Blokes' in Council". After several speakers – including Liebknecht "in a torrent of well chosen English" (*pace* Pinkerton's man) – had had their say,

> "Freidrich Engels, who all the time as solid as a Chinese Joss, has listened to our talk, gets up. Talk of 70 years of age! Why he seems more to be seventeen. Yet he has reached the three score years and ten the Bible speaks of, yet his mental force is not abated (for his eyesight, all Germans I think are born with little spectacles which grow with them as they grow), his spirits more buoyant than a youth's. He gives the credit to 'K-Ka-Karl, to my friend Marx' – the voice just trembling for a moment as he thinks of him. Still, he has seen the Chartists, remembers the stagnation period, rejoices at the great 4th of May meeting of this year, gently chides me for my overcaution and argues that in ten years' time, if he lives (and there seems no adequate reason why at this rate he should not live for ever), that crowns, principalities, priests and powers will lie howling, and that the proletarians will rule the roast and eat it.
>
> Speaker Aveling, after his wife has put reciprocally the speeches into Deutsch and English, bids us charge our glasses. We do so, and after Burns has, in a few well chosen phrases, proposed the toast we drink it (Burns in the cheerless but not innocuous water), light our cigarettes. Shake hands and so dissolve.
>
> So the eight hours blokes in Council met and talked and then Bebel, Singer and

---

with the National in the Metropolitan area. In 1891 a cable had been laid across the Straits of Dover and land lines connecting Paris to London, with direct extensions to the GPO, the West Strand Post Office and, of course, the Stock Exchange. (A three-minute call cost 8s.) The Post Office, which though at that time it took its 10 per cent royalty on the gross receipts of the private companies, would not have been responsible for furnishing Engels with this modern device and has been unable to trace his number in contemporary records. It may be that, in self-defence, he was "ex-directory". What a boon to posterity that he did not have a telephone in Marx's lifetime nor, if at all, during any but the last three years of his own.

Liebknecht, in their broadbrimmed, floppy hats, looking like pictures by Franz Hals, fare forth into the fog. The Avelings, to whom the English workers owe much of the international character the movement is assuming, are left alone..."

In Thorne's *Address* to the Second Annual Meeting of the Gasworkers' Union in March 1891 he reported that:

"Early in last December the following letter was addressed by your Executive Committee to all genuine Working Men's Organisations:

'Dear Comrade,

'During the recent visit of Comrades Bebel, Liebknecht and Singer, on the occasion of Frederic Engel's 70th birthday, they met representatives of the Gas Workers and General Labourers' Union (comprising about 70,000 men and women belonging to over 70 different trades), and of several other organisations, besides John Burns, Cunninghame Graham, M.P., and others. At this meeting the feeling was very strong that the time had come to bring about close and organised relations between the Labour Parties of the different countries. The most immediate question is that of preventing the introduction from one country to another of unfair labour – i.e. of workers, who not knowing the conditions of the labour struggle in a particular country, are imported into that country by the capitalists, in order to reduce wages, lengthen the hours of labour, or both. The most practical way of carrying this out appears to be the appointing in each country of an International Labour Secretary, who shall be in communication with all the other International Secretaries. Thus the moment any difficulty between capitalists and labourers occurs in any country, the International Labour Secretaries of all the other countries should be at once communicated with, and will make it their business to try to prevent the exportation from their particular country of any labourers to take the place, on unfair terms, of those locked out or on strike in the country where the difficulty has occurred. Whilst this is the most immediate and most obvious matter to be dealt with, it is hoped that an arrangement of the kind proposed, will in every way facilitate the interchange of ideas on all questions between the workers of every nation that is becoming every day and every hour the most pressing necessity of the working class movement. If your Organisation agrees with the views of the Gas Workers and General Labourers' Union, will you at once communicate with us, and give us the name of the Secretary appointed by it to take part in this important movement.

Yours fraternally,

William Thorne, *General Secretary*

Eleanor Marx Aveling, (*On behalf of the Executive Committee of the G. W. and G.L.U.*)'."[8]

It was natural enough that Eleanor should be the co-signatory to this invitation which "reprinted in dozens of working-class papers all over Europe and America",*[8] met with a good response, being accepted by 13 organisations in ten different countries. In his report, Thorne spoke of the steps taken, even before the December meeting with the German socialists, to form an International Federation.

---

* It was addressed on 25 January 1891 to Samuel Gompers, the elected President of the AF of L from the end of 1886.

"This work," he said, "has been carried on by one of our Executive Committees (Mrs. E. M. Aveling), whose knowledge of foreign languages has been the means of our Union receiving hearty congratulations from all parts of the continent of Europe and America."[9]

He was also happy to announce that the new International Organisation brought about by the circular letter had been put to the test successfully:

"When the Manningham delegates* attended at our Executive Committee, Mrs. Aveling was instructed to make the matter known abroad. The result of this was, that the Calais workers, mindful of the generous help sent from Nottingham, at once voted a sum of £50 ... Then Mrs. Aveling was sent a letter from the Glass-blowers of Lyons, which was translated and sent to the Glass-blowers Association in Lancashire, which at once sent out appeals..."[10]

That his anniversary – itself an international occasion – should have served to forge these new links between the workers of the world gave Engels unqualified pleasure.

He himself came through the ordeal of that overwhelming day and rather boisterous night without any ill-effects and set to almost at once acknowledging the salutations from abroad. He accepted the laurels bestowed upon him with his usual dignity and grace, in no sense concealing pride in his work or faith in its value, yet disclaiming all but the role of adjutant to Marx's genius. His letters of thanks, to parties and individuals alike, are a very pattern of personal modesty, coupled with stout-hearted affirmation and joy at having helped to win and lived to see "victories which should suffice to rejuvenate a man older and more spent than I".[11] To his old friend Lavrov he wrote:

"The major part of the honours heaped upon me last Friday are not owed to me and nobody knows it better than I. Allow me therefore to lay them on Marx's grave ... As for the minor part which, without presumption, I may claim for myself, I shall do my best to prove worthy of it..."[12]

Replying to Vaillant he said:

"Destiny has willed it that I, in my capacity of survivor, should reap the honours due to the labours of my deceased contemporaries, and above all to those of Marx. Believe me, I do not cherish any illusions on that score nor on the very small part of all these tributes which is owed to me personally,"[13]

while to the French Party he wrote:

---

* Weavers who were in what Thorne called "a new, a poor organisation"[10] which had recently emerged from a long and bitter strike.

"You may rest assured that what remains to me of life and strength shall be devoted to the fight for the proletarian cause. When I am no longer capable of fighting, may it be granted that I die."[14]

Engels had not looked forward to these festivities. On the contrary, he had dreaded them, writing to Sorge when congratulations and guests from abroad were already arriving:

"I wish the whole thing were over, I'm in no birthday mood and, on top of it, all this unnecessary fuss which I can't stand anyway."[15]

The reason why he was in "no birthday mood" was that close behind lay a great personal sorrow: on Tuesday, 4 November – little more than three weeks before – Helene Demuth had died.

On the following day he had written to Sorge, referring to her by the old familiar name and even qualifying her in the very words which the Baroness von Westphalen had used 45 years earlier:

"My dear good faithful Lenchen died yesterday afternoon ... We spent seven happy years together in this house. We were the last two of the pre-1848 Old Guard. Now I am alone again. It was essentially her doing that over the long years Marx was able to work in peace and I myself in the last seven. I don't know what will become of me now. I shall also sadly miss her wonderfully tactful advice on party matters..."[16]

At Lenchen's funeral he spoke of the honour she had done him by coming to live in his house, while Eleanor's article in the Vienna *Monatsschrift* concluded with a quotation from that speech and her own tribute:

"We alone can measure what she was to Marx and his family, and even we cannot express it in words. From 1837 to 1890 she was the true friend and helper of every one of us."[17]

In her "Stray Notes on Karl Marx", written at the request of Austrian comrades, she referred to "Nym" as "the lifelong friend of my parents", who had stood by them through all their

"years of storm and stress, of exile, bitter poverty, calumny, stern struggle and strenuous battle ... and those who knew Marx in his home remember also the name of as noble a woman as ever lived, the honoured name of Helene Demuth."[18]

Marx had always said, Eleanor wrote to Liebknecht in after years, "that under reasonable conditions of Society she wd. have been as invaluable to Society as she was in a small way to us. She had a real genius for organising and managing, and he said that his 'Demuth, Wehmuth, Hochmuth' (an old family joke)* could have managed the universe."[19]

On 22 November an unsigned obituary appeared in the *People's Press* under the heading: "An Old Friend of Labour". From internal evidence it was not written by Eleanor — it differs in several respects from the biographical details she later sent to Liebknecht for his *Reminiscences of Karl Marx* — though she undoubtedly had a hand in it and it may have been Aveling's work. The article opened with the words: "By the death of Helena Demuth the Socialist Party has lost a remarkable member". Then followed an outline of her history and her connection with the Marx family — always on the assumption that she had been born in 1823 and not, as now established, in 1820 — stressing that from her early youth

> "to the death of Mrs. Marx in 1881, with the exception of the first few months of the married life, the two women were constant companions ... The leaders of the socialist movement bore testimony to 'her strong common sense, her absolute rectitude of character, her ceaseless thoughtfulness for others, her reliability, and the essential truthfulness of her nature'. Engels at her funeral declared that Marx took counsel of Helena Demuth not only on difficult and intricate party matters, but even in respect of his economical writings.[†] 'As for me,' he said, 'what work I have been able to do since the death of Marx has been largely due to the sunshine and support of her presence in the house.' Helena is buried at Highgate in the same grave as Marx and his wife."

So the grave was opened once more to receive the body of Helene Demuth and in that earth, as in life, they "together were folded away there exposed to one weather".[21]

For Engels it was indeed as though the sun had gone out. That is not an uncommon sentiment and has been expressed on occasions more illustrious than the demise of an elderly servant,[‡] yet there is a special poignancy in the old man's grief at the loss of this last contemporary tie with Marx's own family life: the companion who had shared with him the smaller pleasures and the greater nastiness of aging and the remembrances of close on half a century.

* * *

---

* The pun on Lenchen's name is untranslatable, but the words (from which nowadays the final 'h' is dropped) mean modesty, melancholy, pride: the last in the sense of coming before a fall.
† If this sounds extravagant it should be recorded that, in addition to her practical outlook, forthright manner and long commerce with the Marxes, she was by no means illiterate. There are many references to her reading. Sorge always sent her the German-language Socialist Annual, *Pionier* (published in the United States from 1883), while in the last month of her life Engels quoted with glee her unfavourable comparison of the *Berliner Volksblatt* (published from April 1889) with a certain German parish magazine.[20]
‡ As, for example, by Sir Walter Scott on Byron's death.

Lenchen's last years had been among the happiest in her life. Unencumbered by financial cares and surrounded by creature comforts unknown to the Marxes, her domestic duties, which she would have scorned to relinquish, were lightened by a constant supply of auxiliaries,* while added to her sovereign status in the kitchen was that of presiding hostess on many social occasions. When Engels went to the seaside Nym went too; during the time he toured Norway she spent two weeks in France with the Lafargues, planting beans – which did well – and delighting in the company of little Mémé Longuet – "the sweetest, prettiest child imaginable"[23] – now almost eight years of age, who was much at Le Perreux during holidays. Nym's stay had been proposed by Laura herself and warmly approved by Engels, who thought it would "do the old girl good",[24] writing afterwards to her hosts:

> "she never enjoyed herself so much, and if I am not mistaken and you do not take care, you will have her an annual customer".[25]

In a letter of condolence written to Eleanor, Vaillant said how shocked he was by the news of her death, recalling that it was but a few months ago, on 14 July, that he had seen "Madame Helene so well and strong". From the whole tone of this letter – its sincere sympathy with "*Madame votre soeur*" and "*le citoyen Engels*", who must indeed be hard hit by this blow – it is clear that on all sides and wherever she went Lenchen in these latter years had come to be regarded as a friend of the family rather than a servant.[26]

Shortly after her return from France, while the maid was put on board wages and workmen moved in to renovate the house, though not yet in accordance with the major improvements demanded of the landlord, off Nym went again with Engels and the Roshers to stop at a little pub in Folkestone during August and part of September. Back in London and no doubt pleasurably anticipating Engels' birthday celebrations, she was suddenly "quite out of sorts ... went to bed of her own accord ... and actually sent for the doctor": an unheard-of proceeding. However, the doctor, Read,

> "told her there was no need to stick in bed ... He cannot as yet exactly make out what it is, there are symptoms (jaundice) of liver complaint, she has no appetite and is weak..."[27]

---

* One of whom was instantly dismissed, with reluctance but as a matter of course, when she was found to be six months pregnant. It would be of interest to know whether Nym took it equally for granted that the girl, being in this condition, "had consequently to leave".[22] It was not self-understood: one of Carlyle's servants gave birth in the back drawing-room the while he entertained a lady for tea in the front.

A fortnight later, on 2 November, Engels wrote a long and detailed account of her condition to Lafargue, for she was now critically ill. Dr. Read was of the view that "in the cachectic condition of her blood ... the coagulated blood is decomposing and poisoning the healthy blood', though it had also crossed his mind that she might have a tumour in the uterus. The consultant called in from University College Hospital, a Mr. Passard, held the opinion that

> "there is a spreading suppuration of the foot causing septicaemia ... The uterus has been examined after a fashion but so far nothing has been found except a small slightly suspect spot at the orifice, to which, however, '*so far*' no importance is attached ... the fellow sees the case in a more 'hopeful' light than Read" and prescribed quinine.[28]

In two days she was dead, the cause being registered on 5 November as "cancer of bowel perforative peritonitis" which, though certified by Read, had not been suspected, let alone diagnosed, by the physicians.

So ended this humble life of service to others. But if those last years were made pleasant to her it was beyond all things by visits from her son Freddy and the little grandson, Harry, born in 1882. Thus the child was but eight years old when she died, but he recalls her as "a motherly sort of person" whom he remembers being taken to see "in a basement".*

Although the Marx girls were well aware of Freddy's existence and concerned for his welfare before this period,† it was probably now that Eleanor's close friendship with him ripened. He had never crossed the Marxes' threshold, save to make his exit as a new-born infant. Certainly Mrs. Marx had not set eyes upon him, either as boy or man, nor is there any evidence that her husband had done so. Now, however, he came regularly to the quarters where his mother reigned in Regent's Park Road‡ and, since he was a working man – a skilled engineer – his visits

---

* All subsequent quotations and recollections are derived from conversation with Mr. Harry Demuth to whom I owe an immense debt of gratitude and respect. (On 19 February 1975 *The Times* diarist carried the news, with other misinformation, that he was dead. As in Mark Twain's case, the report was an exaggeration. He died on 22 January 1980 at the age of 98.) Although I have had the good fortune to talk to and hear from many people whose parents were Eleanor's friends and who, from their own early childhood, were able to recall affectionate and admiring accounts of her, Mr. Demuth is the only living person I have met who knew both Eleanor and Lenchen personally. Thanks to his vivid memory and lively mind at an advanced age, he conjured up these figures from the distant past in a most moving way. I also wish to express my thanks to his eldest daughter for receiving me and, above all, to his grandson, my good friend Mr. David Demuth, who has been kindness itself.

† Witnessed by a letter from Jenny Longuet to her sister in May 1882. (See above, p.241)

‡ One of the more absurd fabrications in Louise Freyberger's letter to August Bebel of September 1898 (see above, p. 244) is her self-congratulatory claim that, before her time, Freddy came to see Nym every week but "oddly enough" never by the front door, always through the kitchen entrance:

"Only after I came to the General and his visits continued, I saw to it that he was accorded all will have been paid on a Sunday: the day on which Eleanor habitually dined at the house.

Engels never appeared on the scene when Harry and his father were at Regent's Park Road; and that Freddy's presence irked him is made clear in Eleanor's letter describing the General's tetchiness with him at the time of Lenchen's death.§ Equally it is known that he left him no money and, in short, gave every sign of rejecting him.

This is in striking contrast to Engels' indulgent, even fatherly tenderness towards Pumps and the trouble he took, going out of his way in America, to meet Willie Burns: in both cases for no other reason than that they were related to Mary and Lizzie Burns. But if these old attachments meant so much to him, his affection and solicitude for Helene Demuth were no less and of even longer standing. In the seven years that she had ordered his *ménage* he continually referred in letters to her doings, her health and her views. She might have been his own flesh and blood so deeply concerned was he during her last illness, so heartsick at her death. Moreover, it was he who ordained that she should be buried with the Marxes – taking pains to consult Eleanor and Laura, but not Freddy, on the inscription for the gravestone – which indicates as nothing else could do his recognition that she truly belonged to those he had most esteemed in life, for it was not customary to inter the servant with the masters.

How, then, to explain his attitude to her only child? Why did Freddy exasperate him? Eleanor, still believing him to be Engels' natural son, thought it was owing to a sense of guilt. But since this cannot, in fact, account for his reactions, they seem totally out of keeping with his inexhaustible charity of mind and spirit, not to mention his devotion to Freddy's mother.

It remains an insoluble mystery which only two conjectures, of little

---

the rights due to a guest."[29] The authenticity of this letter has been questioned recently on the alleged authority of a present member of the Central European Department of the International Institute of Social History in Amsterdam.[30] While it is true that in late years the letter has been available for inspection only in typescript (corrected by hand, presumably on a revised decipherment of the holograph), it is inconceivable that so eminent a scholar as the late Werner Blumenberg (1900–1964), until his death the Director of the German Section of that Institute, should have jeopardised his reputation by publishing – *verbatim*, almost in its entirety – a document spurious. (See Werner Blumenberg: *Karl Marx in Selbstzeugnissen und Dokumenten*. Rowohlt, Hamburg, 1st 15,000 published 1962, pp. 115 *et seq*. English translation Douglas Scott. *Karl Marx*. New Left Books 1972, pp. 123, 124.) In view of the fact that Louise Kautsky – as she then was – took up her residence at Regent's Park Road after, and precisely because, Freddy's mother was dead and since Engels could not bear the sight of him, Freddy is unlikely to have visited the house very often in her day. There is but a single occasion when he can be known for certain to have been there: on 1 July 1894 he was one of 13 signatories to a postcard sent from Engels' address to Mrs. Liebknecht saying they were all drinking German beer while they awaited the telegram announcing the Reichstag election results.[31]

§ See above, p. 241.

worth, can penetrate at all: it is just possible that he had harboured a deep-seated and lasting grievance at having had Freddy's paternity foisted upon him; a resentment unjustly visited upon the most innocent of all those involved; but who in such matters is perfectly rational or just? The other, perhaps more probable explanation, is the sense of guilt that Eleanor attributed to him, albeit for the wrong reasons. Precisely because of his generous nature, Engels may have felt to blame for Freddy's neglectful upbringing which ran counter to all his principles and instincts. The uncouth young Pumps had enjoyed not only all the advantages of being reared in the benevolent, jovial atmosphere of Engels' household, where books and the talk of brilliant men abounded, but she had also been sent abroad to acquire polish; all to no great effect, it must be said. But what might not Freddy have become – Freddy with his earnest mind and love of learning – had he been granted similar benefits? Even more: Lenchen's deprivation, she of the motherly heart, robbed of her child, may have made Engels conscious of a wrongdoing which he had connived at or acquiesced to, and against this there could be no defence but to turn his back upon it and try to blot it out. Thus every reminder, particularly Freddy in the flesh, caused him that remorse which pricks to anger. Further than this speculation should not go.

Had Harry ever seen Engels "in the basement", he thinks he would have remembered it, for his father, a good socialist and one of the founders of the Hackney Labour Party, adorned his walls with large photographs of both Marx and Engels. These were always before Harry's youthful eyes and later bequeathed to him, though unhappily destroyed, with many other of Freddy's former possessions, during the Second World War. Not only in this way was the boy familiar with the appearance of people whom he never met. Freddy had inherited and passed on to Harry a stout little leather album of family photographs – which treasure survived the bombing in Southwark – given and inscribed by her "affectionate friend Jenny" (Longuet) to "dear Helene Demuth". She herself appears among them: a sweet-faced, bonneted old lady in whose charming features the young Lenchen can still be traced.

But if Harry knew other members of the Marx circle only from their portraits, with Eleanor he was well acquainted. He was sixteen years of age when she died; as a child he saw her in his grandmother's kitchen and visited her later "in a country house",* where his young mind was indelibly impressed by the magnificent teas served, moreover by a maid. "Eleanor was always very nice, but I didn't like Aveling. He was very educated and that, but he wasn't nice," says Harry. He also speaks of him

---

* He believes it was in Sevenoaks, but it must have been in Green Street Green – not far away – and in the year 1895 when he was 13.

as "arrogant and ignorant", by which he meant discourteous in manner: an observation fully in accord with what is known of Aveling's lack of response to young people. Eleanor, on the other hand, is recalled as exceptionally kind and friendly to the lad.

Harry's mother, it is known, finally left her husband but, although this was not until after Lenchen's death,* it is possible that she never met her daughter-in-law. At all events she was not present on any of the occasions when Harry went to see his grandmother and there is unimpeachable evidence that Freddy brought up his boy singlehanded. All Harry's recollections – which do not of course stretch back to early infancy – are of living alone with his father, though in quiet contentment for they were the best of friends.

> "There were just the two of us," says Harry. "Of an evening we used to sit on either side of the table with an oil lamp and read to each other – Shakespeare it was – and I helped him with his pronunciation. He couldn't pronounce all the words as well as I could."

It was, he admits, a somewhat lonely and a "rough childhood", but his father

> "was the best; none better. He hadn't had much schooling but he taught himself everything. Wonderful what he knew."

Freddy himself is believed to have had a "rough childhood"; a surmise based upon the fact that, once old enough to fend for himself, he never again saw his foster parents, the Lewises, of whom Harry knows purely by hearsay; while only after the age of 30 was Freddy in close touch with his own mother. But so strong was the bond between father and son that had Harry's Australian venture in 1912 succeeded, it was planned that Freddy, then over 60, should join him there for good.

It is heartening to know that this solitary small boy, Harry, whose father had been an even more forlorn one, grew up to enjoy a loving and lasting married life and, as if in compensation, to found a close-knit family of nine children, all but one of whom reached man- or woman-hood though a beloved son, the youngest, was killed in the Second World War at the age of nineteen, and that, until Freddy's death in 1929, those of proper age went every fortnight with him to the local pub: a ritual observed to this day by Harry, his six remaining children and their spouses; while one and all, including grand and great-grandchildren, foregather at Harry's on Boxing Day each year.

---

* See above, p. 241.

Leaving him thus, a happy man, surrounded by his kin, takes one sharply back to the dark hours through which Engels passed when Harry's grandmother died. What, indeed, was to become of him? It was not merely a question of the management of his house: he could not bear to be alone. There was always Pumps of course – she and her family had lived with him for months on end when her husband, facing bankruptcy, was "completely smashed up" and "in a precious mess"[32] – but, from the time that Lenchen first took charge at Regent's Park Road, Pumps had never ceased to look down upon her, treat her abominably and contest her rights. For all his toleration of her coarse and unlovely ways, not to speak of the mint of money she had cost him since her marriage to the nugatory Percy Rosher – perhaps not the most satisfactory of his parents' 19 children – Engels knew it would not do: at his age he needed a more tranquil domesticity than any a Pumps could provide.

In no time at all he hit upon the solution: Louise Kautsky, young, energetic, to all intents and purposes unattached, should come from Vienna. A special favourite with Engels, she had enjoyed much popularity before her divorce and would feel at home in London. On the Sunday, but five days after Lenchen's death, he wrote to her. He did not plead for compassion nor dwell too heavily upon his woe but told her that, day and night, one vision of life-restoring solace had ever appeared before his eyes: "and it was you". He dared not hope that she would realise this chimera but he would "never know peace of mind if I did not put this question to you first and at once". Whoever took charge, it was assumed in England that "no lady undertakes manual services": she would merely supervise, the rest of her time being free to do whatever she pleased. "We can discuss the whole matter," he wrote, "and either remain together on the old footing or, on the old footing, apart." She must decide, think it over and take counsel with Adler. If she felt that the disadvantages and burdens would outweigh the benefits and pleasures, she must say so with no beating about the bush. "I am far too fond of you to wish you to make a sacrifice for me"; were any such thing involved in the plan then Adler should advise her against it.

> "You are young and have a splendid future before you. In three weeks I shall be 70 and, when all is said and done, have but a short time to live. No young life, full of hope, should be sacrificed for the sake of those few years. After all, I still have the strength to manage."[33]

The answer was prompt. On 18 November, exactly a fortnight after Lenchen died, Louise Kautsky was in Engels' house to remain there for the rest of his life.

Her arrival was not attended by the most favourable auspices. First she telegraphed for money to pay the fare: Aveling immediately sent her a cheque for £10 and it bounced.* Then another telegram came with the curt announcement transmitted as: "Thusday morning Victoria", which could have meant Tuesday – as it did – or Thursday. To add to the confusion, Louise failed to say whether she was crossing the Channel from Calais, Flushing or Ostend, so nobody could tell whether she would reach London at 5 or 8 o'clock in the morning, according to the route. Eager as Engels was to meet her, in company with Eleanor, neither of them can have relished the prospect of hanging about Victoria Station for three hours on the wrong day in a mid-November dawn.

However, this little matter was cleared up and so was Engels' gloom. A week later he was writing to Sorge to say there was sunshine in his house again; Louise was an admirable woman and Kautsky must have been out of his mind when he separated from her.

The length of her stay was still uncertain. Bebel, in London and stopping with the Bernsteins for Engels' birthday, did his best to find out how the land lay. But, as he wrote to Adler, he had little opportunity to talk to Louise because

> "Engels has the habit of accompanying his female *alter egos* at every step they take out of the house and of going to look for them indoors if he hasn't seen them for a little while. It was the same with Nimmy and now with L., who naturally doesn't wish for these attentions."

Bebel also remarked that her relations with the Roshers were most unpleasant, adding: "and, between ourselves, I had the impression that Tussy, too, would not be too well pleased if L. stayed on."[34]

Before that letter was written the die was cast. On 17 December Engels gave Laura the glad news:

> "Louise Kautsky stays here for good. So my troubles are settled. She seems to like it better after all than setting other people's children into this world. And we get on capitally. She superintends the house and does my secretary's work which saves my eyes and enables me to make it worth her while to give up her profession..."[35]

But let Eleanor speak of all this. She wrote to Laura, too, "for the pleasure of a gossip", on 19 December: two days after Engels had sent the tidings of Louise's decision.

---

* Whether with Eleanor's knowledge or not, Aveling had borrowed £15 from Engels in the summer of 1889. This, however, was quite a new and ingenious form of borrowing, for naturally Engels had to send a second cheque himself.

"I wish you were here to gossip," Eleanor wrote. " ... I shd. like to *tell* you the history of the last weeks. I'm incapable of writing the Epic that alone cd. do justice to the facts of the case. The Sat. – to Sunday after your departure* I spent with the General, and 'pumped' till 2.30. I was so sleepy that I hardly remember what we pumped. I have only a general impression of valiant defiance breathed against the redoubtable Pumps. Well, that Sunday passed over in comparative quiet, but Pumps retired early & the General began to quake. Then things grew more exciting. There were telegrams from Austria. Louise was coming. There were many 'alarums and excursions'. Finally Louise arrived. Meantime the General had screwed his courage to the sticking point & Pumps had been informed that on *my* (!!) invitation Louise was coming over, & must be properly treated – on pain of a New Testament being substituted for the Old. Louise came. She was – as you may suppose – dead tired: the journey straight from Vienna, coming on top of weeks of hard work is no slight affair. That very day Engels wd. have dragged her off to Pumps, but as (we had met Louise in the morning) I had said I wd. call in the afternoon, the visit was postponed till the next day. Then they called, & the first day Pumps deigned to return the visit she had champagne galore. Of course the 'head of the table' question cropped up. At first the General insisted, in spite of Louise's protests that she cd. not & wd. not 'carve', on the head of the table being occupied by her, but at the last moment he funked, & so as usual Pumps presides. – To tell you all the ups and downs wd. be to write a volume ... Only one thing is too charming to omit. On the General's birthday Pumps getting more drunk than usual confided to *Louise* that she 'knew she had to behave to her, or she'd get cut out of the Will'! I am sorry for Louise. Bebel and all the others have told her it is her *duty* to the Party to stop. It hardly seems fair to her. She was getting on so well at Vienna, and to sacrifice her whole career is no trivial matter. No one wd. ask a *man* to do that. She is still so young – only just 30. It seems not right to shut her up, & keep her from every chance of a fuller and happier life. And *you* know what her life here will be. Why, our poor Nymmie cdnt. get out – unless she took Pumps. *Then* it was all right. Moreover, entre nous I don't think it will or can last. But I can, naturally, do nothing. But I see well that it will end in unpleasantness ... Well, all we can do is to look on & wait. Meantime there has been any amount of comedy and farce – and the Gen. is more afraid of Pumps – or is it of her eye? – than ever, and more abject. On one or two Sundays when Pumps has gone home he has sent her half the food in the house – not to mention the drinkables...

News beyond the Pumpsiad there is little. We go our usual round – wh. means a good deal of 'sweating' for damned little pay. Edward's 'Madcap' is still running at the Comedy, & he has hopes of other things. The devil of it is hopes won't pay bills. I am doing hack translations (very bad) for a new Magazine. We are both doing Drama Notes, no longer for 'Time' wh departed this life in the December Number, but henceforth for Tinsley's Magazine.† I do typing, & Edward writes all sorts of things – good, bad & indifferent. We both have meetings & work of that sort in every spare hour. There's really no time to consider whether Life is worth living or is a most unmitigated nuisance ... I dread the coming 'Festivities'. It is horrible. The only good thing is that the dear old General is as jolly as a sandboy (what a sandboy is, or why he shd. be jolly *I* don't know) & seems to get younger and younger ..."[36]

---

* Laura had come to London at the time of Lenchen's death and burial, leaving on Friday, 7 November. The weekend referred to was thus 8–9 November.

† A shilling monthly, started in 1867, specialising in fiction and light articles.

A further instalment of the "Epic" was sent to Laura on New Year's Eve when the dreaded season of good cheer was all but over.

"Here's another year gone, and here we are wishing one another a happy 'new' one. Well, wishes do no harm anyway. We have got over the Christmas festivity. But for some excellent fooling by Bernstein & Edward we shd. not have got over it so easily. Pumps – ever since she knows Louise is to stay – is spoiling for a fight, & on Christmas day being – well, being elevated – scenes seemed unavoidable. Fortunately she fell asleep, and awoke in a less bellicose mood. But we all constantly feel as if we were executing Mignon's dance, & that we are about to tread upon eggs – & corns. Poor old Jollymeier* cd. not come over. We miss him much ... I *did* intend writing you a long letter: but I've now to go & get ready for Pumpeian festivity (I almost wish I'd broken a leg or arm & cdn't go!)...."[37]

From these despondent letters, slightly reminiscent of the doom-laden winter solstices that had dogged her parents throughout her own blithe years of childhood, Eleanor can be seen as in no way ill-disposed towards Louise, merely sorry for her, and fearful that Pumps would make her life a torment.

It is also apparent that, though Engels regained his high spirits, no newcomer could at one stroke break the spell old intimacy weaves, binding him to Pumps. "The General is happiest with his drunken enchanter ..." wrote Eleanor in August 1891.

"'Tis a Prospero in love with a lower kind of Caliban; for Pumps hasn't Caliban's redeeming qualities...";[38]

and again, a few days later:

"He *does* love the tipsy Pumps, but for all that distance lends enchantment even to the tipsyness ... He rages against Pumps – & loves her. Louise had to tell him to stop his talk against her, or she could not possibly be polite to her. 'How can I be friends with her when you say she is only counting upon your death?' asked Louise. The General had no answer handy. And so things are much as they were – except that the General has to be a little more guarded in his denunciations wh. *we* know mean nothing."[39]

This love-hate relationship was acted out against Engels' increasing attachment to Louise. He lectured Pumps severely and warned her that, unless she mended her manners she would not be welcome in his house: a threat never put into effect of course. She had insisted upon going on a tour of Scotland and Ireland with Engels "and *once* having a holiday 'as she had never had one'!" wrote Eleanor,

---

* Schorlemmer.

"They have returned & Pumps is as discontented as ever. On Sunday Edward & I met Louise & the General on their return (Pumps had gone on to Manchester) and he, of course, swore hard at her (Pumps). But he is just as fascinated as ever, & however much he may upbraid, she prevails."[40]

The old, like beggars, cannot be choosers and, what is sadder – in the eyes of the beholder – they are protected from this knowledge by becoming less "choosey" – less fastidious and discerning – so be it their immediate needs are satisfied. In Louise Engels had found a competent and lively young woman to shoulder his household cares and, at his time of life, was more dependent than ever before upon these ministrations, while, as Eleanor was to say: "the General is always under the thumb of 'the lady of the house'."[41] But now he was not dealing with a daughter of the people – a working-class Mary or Lizzie Burns, a roaring Pumps, a Nym of peasant stock – but with a gentlewoman* who had moved in political circles as Kautsky's wife and was not without pretensions of her own. These were nourished by Engels who took her advice, quoted her opinions, encouraged her to write articles and pulled strings for her to go as a delegate to the 1891 International Congress in Brussels.

He came to dote upon her and, in time, she gained a greater influence over him than any former "lady of the house", and of a more ruthless nature, until Pumps had grounds for her anxiety concerning his "New Testament". So, too, had Eleanor, though of a very different order. But that was yet to come.

---

* At the time of his betrothal Kautsky had written to Engels: "A fine family I'm marrying into! The grandfather was a former Gentleman-in-Waiting to Count Chambord, one of her uncles a Public Prosecutor, her late father Master of the Horse in the Emperor's Household Cavalry ..."[42] This is possibly the reason why both Eleanor and Engels almost invariably wrote to Kautsky as "Dear Baron".

When Engels' eyesight troubled him so sorely that he was forbidden to read for more than two or three hours at a time, never on foggy days or by artificial light, he realised that if the work were ever to be done, younger eyes must learn to decipher Marx's hand.

In the last five years of his life Engels had some 135 works of greater or less importance to his credit. These ranged from Volume 3 of *Capital* – which, to all intents and purposes, he may be said to have written from Marx's very rough first draft – and revisions of the English translation of Volume I for the (4th) 1891 edition,* to lengthy interviews, weighty articles, including the complete redaction of *The Peasant War in Germany*; new prefaces to explain in the light of later political and economic theories his own, Marx's and their joint early works, both for new editions and for innumerable translations, many of which he supervised, published in countries as far afield as America, and Armenia: an output that he himself at the age of 74 thought "work enough for two men of 40".

"I have to follow the movement in five large and a lot of small European countries and the U.S. America. For that purpose I receive 3 German, 2 English, 1 Italian *dailies* and from Jan. 1, the Vienna daily, 7 in all. Of *weeklies* I receive 2 from Germany, 7 Austria, 1 France, 3 America (2 Engl., 1 Germ.), 2 Italian and one each in Polish, Bulgarian, Spanish and Bohemian, three of which languages I am still gradually acquiring. Besides that, calls of the most varied sorts of people (just now, a few minutes ago, Polak from Amsterdam sent me a German sculptor penniless and in want of employment) and an ever-increasing crowd of correspondents, more than at the time of the International! many of whom expect long explanations and all of them taking away time ... Now the next thing is the publication of Lassalle's letters to Mohr. Tussy has typed them ... That means notes, references to facts long gone by as well as to my own old correspondence to Mohr – and a preface to be written diplomatically ... Then – not to speak of other *little* jobs hanging over me – I want to write at least the chief chapters out of Mohr's political life: 1842–1852, and the International. The latter is the most important and urgent, I intend to do it first. But that requires freedom from interruption, and when shall I get that?"[43]

---

* Of what precisely these consisted lies in the province of the scholar and no doubt work on the variants has been done, but even I know that Engels verified yet again every one of the original English quotations on which Eleanor had laboured so long and faithfully for the first edition, in which connection it is interesting to note that never in his life did Engels hold a British Museum Reader's Ticket.

For years he had been grumbling about distractions, of complete strangers who

> "conspired to overwhelm me with letters, visits, inquiries, requests of all sorts ... Austrian student-clubs, a Viennese inquirer after 'truth' who wishes to know had he not better devour Hegel (better not, I replied), a Roumanian Socialist in *propria persona*, an unknown man from Berlin, etc. etc.",

all demanding "to be attended to at once".[44]

Although by mid-1891 he had abandoned the design to issue Marx's collected works,* for which he had gone to great lengths and every possible source to recover the early writings and letters scattered about the globe,† he still hoped as late as April 1895 to complete *Theories of Surplus Value*, as Volume IV of *Capital*.‡ He had

> "intended to remove from the text of this manuscript 'numerous passages covered by Books II and III' ... Only Engels, the great companion and comrade-in-arms of Marx, and in a certain sense, the co-author of *Capital* ... had the right to work over Marx's text in such a way."[45]

With sober foresight he cast about for potential successors and, at the end of 1888, put the proposition to Bernstein whom he held to be "a capital fellow, both in character and intellect"[46] and who, moreover, lived close at hand in Kentish Town. He consulted both Eleanor and Bernstein on the matter and, with their agreement, wrote to Kautsky in January 1889 inviting him to become his second pupil. Once Kautsky had mastered the art of reading the hieroglyphs, he would have enough free time – and the help of his wife – to carry on the task in Vienna. Engels assured him that he would always be able to count upon Eleanor if the cherished plan to publish his own and Marx's complete works should not be realised before his death, for which contingency he must now start making provision.

Then came the news of the Kautskys' separation and divorce. Outraged though he was by Kautsky's behaviour Engels wrote to him in September

---

* Little could he have foreseen that, with the vicissitudes of war, revolution, the rise of German fascism, not to mention the misadventures of the original manuscripts, involving such hazards as shipwreck, theft and illicit sale, the first complete edition, including his own works, would not appear in any language for over six decades: first in Russian (1955 to 1974), and then in German (1956 to 1968), while the first volumes of the English version are being issued as these words are written in 1975.

† Nikolai Danielson, the Russian translator of the first three volumes of *Capital* (Volume I in collaboration with Herman Lopatin) sent Engels all the letters Marx had written to him. These had been typed by Eleanor and the originals returned to St. Petersburg in June 1890.

‡ Edited by Kautsky it first appeared, in three parts, between 1905 and 1910.

1889 to say that none the less their working arrangement held good: the man might have taken leave of his senses in parting from Louise; in other respects Engels considered him mentally sound and politically reliable.

> "The work must be done, and you and Ede are the only ones to whom I can entrust it,"[47]

he wrote and was not to live long enough to know whether that trust was fully justified. Accordingly, Kautsky, between marriages, as it were, came to London from November 1889 until March 1890* and under Engels' tutelage became adept at breaking the code. Before he left, Engels offered him £100 to make a fair copy of Marx's scribbled notes, but at the end of 1892, when nothing had been heard and Engels wanted to compare it with certain passages in Volume III of *Capital*, he asked Kautsky to send back the manuscripts and whatever he had transcribed, which turned out to be roughly an eighth part of the whole.†

There were other responsibilities that Engels knew he alone could and must discharge before it was too late. In the same letter as he had informed Laura of the onset of Lenchen's last illness he had written to say that he had

> "sorted out about four cubic feet of old letters of Mohr's ... of the period 1836–64. All higgledy-piggledy, in a big basket which perhaps you may remember. Dusting, straightening, sorting – it took me more than a week to put them in rough order. During all that time my room was upset ... so that I could neither go out nor do any other kind of work. Then ... loss of time for me by callers, etc."[49]

Thus time and again, while training his heirs-apparent and engrossed in Volume III of *Capital*, he complained of interruptions. Yet he himself initiated the most far-reaching of them all early in 1891. The truth was that, however pressing his formidable task, there seemed little point in labouring intensively to make Marx's theories known in days ahead if, here and now, the movement was being led astray by grave theoretical errors for lack of such knowledge actually available.‡

At the Halle Congress of the German party, as Eleanor had described, a new programme was outlined, the first since that adopted on 25 May

---

* On his return to Vienna he announced his official engagement to Luise Ronsperger (1864–1944) whom he married later that year, their first son being born in January 1891.
† Early in 1893 Kautsky must have offered his services again, for Engels wrote to him: "Had I known you would go on with it, I should have left it with you."[48]
‡ To many readers what follows will be so familiar that they are advised to skip.

1875 by the so-called Unity Congress, held at Gotha* by the two wings of the German socialists: the Marxist Social-Democrats, or Eisenachers as they were called,† led by Liebknecht and Bebel, and the General Association of German Workers, founded by Lassalle. This programme, the result of conciliatory discussions between Liebknecht for the Eisenachers and Hasselmann for the Lassalleans in February 1875, was published on 7 March and immediately came under the most rigorous criticism from both Marx and Engels.

Little more than a week after it had appeared in print, having heard nothing about it before, Engels wrote an immensely long letter to Bebel underscoring its mistakes and weaknesses. Among these he stressed that only in very exceptional circumstances – such as the Paris Commune – would it be true to call all other classes "one reactionary mass" in relation to the proletariat.‡ He also deplored that there was not one word about the trade union movement:

> "a very essential point," he wrote, "for this is the real class organisation of the proletariat, in which it fights out its daily struggles with capital, in which it trains itself, and which nowadays, even despite the worst reaction ... it is utterly impossible any longer to destroy."[51]

Over the weeks Marx carefully studied the programme, clause by clause, making elaborate marginal notes on every postulate. On 5 May he sent these notes to Wilhelm Bracke, one of the founders of the German Social-Democratic Party, with the request that they be shown before the Congress met on 22 May, to Liebknecht, Bebel, Geib, the treasurer, and Auer,§ the Secretary of the party, subsequently to be returned to him. A few days later he wrote to his wife, then in Shanklin on the Isle of Wight:

---

* The name is associated in most people's minds, depending upon their class interests, either with a socialist programme or with an Almanach. As a matter of fact it was a town, near the Thuringian forest in Saxe-Coburg-Gotha, of some 30,000 inhabitants in the 1870s, which produced sausages, toys, shoes and, in 1819, our own Albert the Good.

† After the founding Congress held at Eisenach in Upper Saxony from 7 to 9 August 1869.

‡ Long after the events here described, in October 1891, Kautsky used the same words – "one reactionary mass" – in an article for Liebknecht's paper *Vorwärts* (known as the *Berliner Volksblatt* from 1884 until it became the organ of the Social-Democratic Party in 1891). Engels reproved him sharply, saying it was "a demagogic phrase of the utmost sectarianism and therefore ... totally false." "So long as we are not strong enough to seize the helm ourselves ... there can be no talk of *one* reactionary mass as *against us*. If it were so the whole nation would be divided into a reactionary majority and a powerless minority ... The English of both official parties – who have extended the franchise enormously, increased the electorate fivefold, equalised the Borough constituencies, introduced compulsory education and better teaching, who in every session vote not only for bourgeois reforms but also time and again for new concessions to the workers – make slow and sluggish progress, but no one can simply convict them of being 'one reactionary mass'."[50]

§ He whom Eleanor had found so vastly entertaining at Halle. See above, p. 576.

"I have sent off the circular (by now it will be in Bracke's hands) on the Liebknecht-Hasselmann hodge-podge; it is a little brochure..."[52]

That Liebknecht read the "little brochure", now known as *The Critique of the Gotha Programme*, there can be no doubt. It is equally certain that he did not pass it on to Bebel. The Congress ratified the programme as originally drafted with but a few slight amendments, drawn from Marx's points though put forward by Liebknecht as his own. The 56 Social-Democratic delegates, and most of their leaders, were left totally unaware that in criticism of that programme Marx had produced a major theoretical work, comparable in importance for its own time with the *Communist Manifesto*.

For over 15 years – during which the Gotha writ ran – this document had lain gathering dust, unknown alike to the rank and file and the rising leadership of the German and every other Marxist party. Only after a desperate search through Marx's papers did Engels succeed in laying hands on it.* Had he been able to find it earlier, he wrote to Kautsky in February 1891, he would have insisted upon bringing it to light before the Halle Congress was held in October 1890: the first legal Congress since Gotha and thus the first opportunity to draw up a new programme.

Liebknecht's lengthy speech introducing the draft on that occasion made no reference whatsoever to Marx's *Critique*, nor did he recommend the incorporation of its main tenets. He merely said that the principles laid down in 1875 should be brought into line with present conditions; that the Party had always recognised that changes must be made but there had been no time before the Anti-Socialist Law of 1878 rendered useless any such revision. Though perfectly acquainted with Marx's view that the Gotha programme was unprincipled, its formulations slipshod and misleading, its theoretical premises false; equally aware of the effect that this authoritative voice – albeit from the grave – would have upon the delegates, Liebknecht declared that the Gotha programme had been as a battle standard borne aloft by the Party in its inexorable forward march, a guide and a compass to show the way, a lodestar by which they had steered their course[53] and so on and so forth, giving it the stamp of unalloyed approval.

Precisely because the *Critique* had been ignored at Halle, Engels was now determined to publish it in full, convinced that "the party was quite strong enough to bear it"[54] and it appeared in the *Neue Zeit* at the end of January 1891,[55] to be reprinted in the Saxony Workers' Paper in four instalments between 6 and 12 February. Leading articles were written about it in organs of the Swiss, Austrian and German press immediately

---

* Not the original manuscript but a copy in an unidentified hand.

after its publication which gave ample time and opportunity for it to be widely discussed before the Erfurt Congress of the German Party in October that year when, to Engels' satisfaction and Liebknecht's discomfiture – for it was he who had to swallow the "bitter pill"[56] of introducing the main report – it adopted a programme substantially in accord with Marx's *Critique*.

The resurrection of this old but by no means outdated document did more than flutter the dovecotes; it put the cat among the pigeons, for it challenged not simply the Lassalleans of sixteen years before but every present organisation, in Britain as on the Continent, which professed itself Marxist and claimed to represent the ultimate interests of the working class.

It also brought to light that Liebknecht had deliberately suppressed the "little brochure" in order to push through a "thoroughly objectionable programme" at a "Congress of Compromise", as Marx had called it in his covering letter to Bracke and which, once it had been adopted, Engels denounced as "in the highest degree disorderly, confused, disconnected, illogical and discreditable."[57]

In self-defence Liebknecht claimed that it had been impossible to show the "Marginal Notes" to Bebel because he had been in prison at the time, but Kautsky reminded Engels that Marx's document was dated 5 May and Bebel had been released on 1 April 1875. Thus Liebknecht stood exposed as a liar. It should be said, however, that neither Kautsky himself nor Bebel was at all eager to see the *Critique* published in 1891 and had not Engels threatened that if the *Neue Zeit* refused to print it, he would unhesitatingly send it elsewhere, they might not have given their consent, for it:

> "excited great anger in the Central Committee of the Party and much praise in the Party itself ..." Engels wrote. "When they calm down, they will thank me for having prevented them from having another equally outrageous programme drawn up by Liebk ... In the meantime I am not receiving news of them directly, they boycott me a bit."[58]

This respite will not have been unwelcome; but Engels was inundated with letters from younger people, thanking him for publishing the *Critique* and the lessons they had learnt from it. There were also repercussions in many other quarters where it had come as an eye-opener, for it was the first, one might say the only one, of Marx's theoretical writings which outlined the form that socialist society would take in the hands of those who, of necessity, would themselves be the products of capitalism and by no means a new breed of mankind without a national history or social traditions.

It is exceedingly doubtful whether Eleanor had read or even knew of the existence of the "Marginal Notes". They were penned when she was 20 years of age, much taken up with Lissagaray and his affairs and greatly influenced by his political thinking.* Now, in 1891, the day-to-day questions facing her – hours of work, free education, women's and children's labour, relations with the Radicals and, above all, trade union activity – were seen in a fresh light; or, to put it more justly, had received, so to speak, her father's imprimatur, for her own intuition had served her fairly well: she had never lost sight of the goal as she took each small step on her path.

As predicted, the German leaders shortly calmed down and by April, Singer and Bebel had come out of their sulks and were again corresponding amiably with Engels, while Kautsky, after overcoming his initial reluctance to publish the *Critique*, had never been party to the boycott.

But the slow-burning fire of Engels' contempt for Liebknecht burst into flame. He had criticised him in the past for repeated instances of foolish, injudicious, even mischievous conduct; now in letter after letter he dismissed him as of no account to the movement whatsoever: a prematurely aged and obsolete phrasemonger, an incubus to the Party, a figurehead who ought to be retired, gradually perhaps and with honour of course, but once and for all. Engels attributed Liebknecht's arrested political development to the long years he had spent idling in banishment† and, when finally he moved to Berlin in September 1890, he attended the Reichstag sessions‡ and dealt with his own correspondence as the titular head of a regenerated party with which he was totally out of touch. He had failed to keep his ear to the ground or his finger on the pulse of the movement while the Anti-Socialist Law was in force, during which time the party had grown and matured in a hard school. Its ranks were now formed by members of a new type: militant socialists alert to the constant threat from the law no less than from the spies and provocateurs to which all persecuted factions play involuntary host. These younger Marxists were extremely wideawake, active, far from naïf and closely involved with the daily problems of the working class – from which they themselves were largely drawn – whereas Liebknecht, in Engels' view, had confined himself for twelve years to executing such formal – and censored – activities as the authorities allowed (which included standing for election) as though the entire movement were in a

---

* See above pp. 126–130.
† Expelled from Leipzig at the end of June 1881, he had withdrawn to a small village, Borsdorf, in Saxony.
‡ A Deputy from 1874 to 1900, Berlin re-elected him with 14,159 votes in February 1890.

state of suspended animation, waiting, as inert as he, for happier times to dawn.

In her letters from Halle Eleanor had remarked upon the "philistinism" of the leading – Reichstag – crew and, by contrast, the freshness and vigour of the rank and file delegates; but she did not think, or did not say, that Liebknecht should be shuffled off the scene. He was, it may be, too dear and old a friend, too closely associated with days that were no more: with her parents' home, her early family life which, as we know, remained the centre of her deepest feelings.

Naturally, for all his ire, Engels did not address his most cutting condemnations to Liebknecht himself. Indeed, their correspondence lapsed between December 1890 and January 1893, save for friendly New Year's greetings. Then Liebknecht came to London for a fortnight at the end of June that year and visited Engels frequently, re-establishing good relations.

In July Liebknecht and his second wife celebrated their twenty-fifth wedding anniversary. With effortless magnanimity Engels wrote:

> "The day after tomorrow, i.e. on the 30th, you and your wife will have your silver wedding, on which joyful occasion I send you both my most affectionate congratulations. May you both greet it in perfect wellbeing and unclouded happiness and may you live in joy and health for the next 25 years to your golden wedding.
>
> When such a festive event occurs for any of us old comrades-in-arms, one thinks back to old times, to the old storms and strife, the defeats at the start, the triumphs at the end, which one has experienced together, and rejoices that it has been granted to us in our old age no longer to stand in the same breach – indeed, we long ago went over from the defence to all-out attack – but rather to be marching ahead in the same line of battle. Yes, old chap, we've been through a good few assaults together and shall do so again more than once I hope, and if all goes well, that one which, even if it does not achieve final victory, will yet finally assure it. Happily we can both still hold our heads high, also we are both hale and hearty for our age,* so why shouldn't we bring it off?"[59]

Thereafter Engels wrote infrequently and more often to Natalie Liebknecht† than to her husband who, for his part, did his best to prevent the correspondence petering out but received short practical answers, if any, until, in the year 1894, there came but a single response and then silence.

---

* Engels was then almost 73, Liebknecht 65. The first was to live another two years, the second another nine.

† In 1888 she had translated Disraeli's *Sybil*, in 1890 Kingsley's *Alton Locke* and, two years later, Morris's *News from Nowhere*, so, while she never showed off nor gave the least hint of it, she must have known English pretty well, though Eleanor did not think much of her translations.

Although the last person on earth to be shaken by the *Critique of the Gotha Programme*, for he was not partial to theory, Hyndman chose this moment to launch a public attack upon Engels. On 21 February 1891 an article appeared in *Justice* under the heading "A Disruptive Personality". Engels, it allowed, was brilliant, but he had "a perfect genius for overthrowing good understanding" and, so long as he remained alive, there was no hope of international comity among Social-Democrats. A further instalment appeared in the next issue, this time with the familiar title "The Marxist Clique".

> "Engels," wrote Hyndman – for the authorship is unmistakable – "has been resident in England for nearly 50 years, and, since the foundation of the 'International' in 1864, his personal influence has been more baneful than his literary work has been useful to the Socialist movement. He has been head of the Marxist clique – far more Marxist than Marx himself* – which has never ceased to intrigue against and vilify any Social-Democratic organisation not under its direct control ... It may be necessary, though we hope it will not, to give a full account of the proceedings of Engels and the Marxists of all countries before the International Congress meets at Brussels.† Meantime it may explain a good deal to our readers if we give a list of the present members of the little Marxist clique and mutual admiration society in London. They are or were:– Friedrich Engels, H. H. Champion, Edward Aveling, Eleanor Marx, Maltman Barry, John Burns, Tom Mann, Keir Hardie, W. Parnell, Margaret Harkness ('John Law'); with them has been closely associated, though happily he is opposed to their methods in some particulars, Cunninghame Graham."

Hyndman's rogues' gallery reads something like a roll of honour today.

It is interesting to note that, shortly before, Eleanor's name – but as "Mrs Aveling" – had been coupled with that of Bax (and Smith Headingley for good measure) as among the "two or three exceptions" to Hyndman's dictum that

---

* It will be recalled that Hyndman could not rid himself of the delusion that he had been one of Marx's dearest friends, offering a wholesome alternative to Engels, hence this kindly word of exoneration. Nor was he in the least troubled by the fact that until two years before the International was wound up in Europe (1872), Engels had been a cotton manufacturer in Manchester and, to his regret, unable to play as full a part in its counsels as he would have wished. Equally false is the implied suggestion that Hyndman had engaged or was interested in socialist activity during the period of the International.

† From 16 to 23 August 1891.

"every prominent Social-Democrat or Socialist in Great Britain has been directly or indirectly educated by the Social-Democratic Federation."[60]

The reprise of the "Marxist Clique" theme was inspired by Hyndman's fury upon learning that Aveling had been asked to stand as a Socialist candidate following the death of Bradlaugh,* the Radical M.P. for one of the two constituencies in Northampton Borough. At first Hyndman was not merely outraged, he was incredulous and flatly denied that so preposterous a notion could have entered anyone's head.

Even after the by-election had come and gone on 12 February,† *Justice* declared:

> "Dr. Aveling is reported to have said that he was invited to stand by the Northampton Branch of the S.D.F. This, so far as we can learn, is not true."[61]

Beforehand, showing unnecessary concern for the eternal rest of the departed atheist, *Justice* had written:

> "Bearing in mind the relations between Dr. Aveling and the late Mr. Bradlaugh, the mere suggestion that he should fill his place in parliament is enough to make Bradlaugh turn in his grave,"

enquiring in another paragraph: "By the way, who are the 'socialists' who want Dr. Aveling to stand?"[62]

The answer was that on 3 February Aveling had received two letters asking whether he would be willing to accept nomination: one from the secretary of the Northampton branch of the SDF, the other from that of the Gasworkers' Union. Though as "unsolicited as they were unexpected"[63] by Aveling, he and Eleanor had gone down on the following day to talk things over with some twenty representatives of these local organisations. It will be recalled that, the year before, Eleanor had held two tremendously successful meetings in the town — at the second of which Aveling had also spoken — after which she had written her article on Northampton. Since she — being a she — could hardly stand as a parliamentary candidate, Aveling had been invited to do so. "The difficulty," he wrote, "was the £100 necessary for the Returning Officer's fees."[63] It seemed insuperable, but, since his supporters were convinced

---

* On 30 January 1891 at the age of 58.
† In a straight fight with the Tory, Alderman Moses Manfield was returned with a majority of almost 1,700 votes as a Gladstone Liberal: a classification adopted to distinguish the Home Rulers from the Liberal Unionists "in consequence of the disruption of the Liberal Party", as Whitaker's (1892) has it, thus demonstrating that Socialist parties had no monopoly of splits and divisions.

that he would poll at least 1,000 votes, he was asked to come down again on the following Sunday, spoke in the market square both in the morning and the evening, while the afternoon was spent discussing the financial problem. It appeared that twenty working men had pledged themselves to put up £5 each, but as they could not raise it overnight, a friend would advance the money. Aveling's nomination and the £100 were handed in to the Returning Officer the next morning, but upon investigation it was found that the "friend" was a Tory agent and Aveling withdrew.

> "The Labour Party cannot afford to take anything either from the Tory or the Liberal Party. We are fighting both, and can have no peace, no truce, no monetary dealings with either,"

he wrote and added:

> "the enforced deposit of large sums of money to guarantee the payment of fees ... presses unduly on workers, on their representatives, and on their cause."[63]

This was not calculated to mollify Hyndman, who had accepted £340 from the Tory Party in 1885 to put up socialist candidates. Indeed, it exacerbated his rage.

> "Dr. Aveling's past record is not of a kind to recommend him as a representative of Socialists either in the House of Commons or elsewhere,"

wrote *Justice*, commenting in the same issue:

> "Dr. Aveling is, we understand, a member of the Gas Workers and General Labourers' Union. It would be interesting to know how much gasworking and general labouring he has done. He certainly belongs to no Socialist organisation in Great Britain" – the Bloomsbury Society was nothing but "a little local clique" – "and it is a mere piece of impertinence to run down to Northampton and make himself ridiculous as 'the Socialist candidate'."[61]

When the official letter from the Northampton Branch of the SDF was sent to *Justice* and published on 21 February, Hyndman had to admit that he had been wrong, in which case the Northampton members had "broken the rules of the Constitution". That, however, was another question and one that would be taken up in no uncertain manner, but, in the meantime, Aveling remained the target and, dipping his pen in venom, Hyndman set about dredging up every incident from the past that had brought him into disrepute. Specifically he posed five questions, which "if he ever comes forward again as a Socialist candidate ... should be put straight to him to begin with.

(1) Why was he forced to leave the National Secular Society?

(2) What were the proceedings as regard to his classes in Newman Street, Oxford Street, which occasioned so much talk?

(3) What sort of bills did he run up for Mrs Eleanor Marx Aveling and himself when the Socialist workers of the United States (all poor men) paid the expenses of his tour? What was the effect of his conduct on the movement in America?

(4) What did he do in relation to money collected to send a cable despatch with signatures of well-known Englishmen to the Governor of Illinois, when the fate of the Chicago Anarchists was trembling in the balance?

(5) What was his action in regard to a certain family whose children he undertook to educate?"[64]

Two of these matters were well documented: that of the Secular Society – which Aveling was not "forced to leave", having resigned beforehand, and where the charges were never pressed because highly intricate personal and financial irregularities (not all one-sided) lay behind – and the American affair, long since a dead horse not worth the flogging. On the face of it those, if any there were, who had followed Aveling's career with close attention would tend to suppose that the other more obscure matters were equally invidious.* But the point, not lost upon Hyndman, was that it would have required a dissertation of ineffable length and tedium, quite unprintable in *Justice*, for Aveling to render an account of himself under the five heads. To that extent it was a faultless exercise in mud-slinging.

The paper announced in the following issue that it had received, though it did not publish, a letter from Aveling in which

"he says he wishes to meet any charges against his personal character. We understand it is the intention of the SDF, should he ever stand anywhere as a representative of Socialism, to send down a delegate to inform the electors fully as to what manner of man he is. This course would have been adopted and had indeed been arranged for, if he had continued his ridiculous candidature at Northampton."[66]

Now it was that Hyndman made his onslaught upon Engels who, though in no way responsible for the whims of the Northampton socialists, would naturally favour the nomination of any Marxist candidate to replace Bradlaugh since it indicated not only a marked political advance among some sections of the local electorate but also, by implication, approved the developing internationalist character of the British movement: in itself an affront to Hyndman's xenophobia.

---

* Question No. 2, which hints at some fascinating sexual episode, turns out upon investigation to concern a simple sordid case of Aveling striking up a friendship with a young biology student, borrowing her microscope and selling it.[65]

This was, in truth, the heart of the matter, but not one that could be suitably worn on the sleeve of the most important and self-proclaimed Marxist party leader in the land. Thus, though he fired his two shots at Engels – a rather dangerous game, similar to lion-baiting, which will have won the admiration of those abroad who considered the publication of the *Critique* little short of treachery – Hyndman could not miss his mark by aiming at a man so constantly in scrapes as Aveling who was by no means short of personal enemies and could be vilified on other than political grounds without the need to express the private opinion that, with a few exceptions, foreigners are beastly and the less you have to do with them the better.

One way and another *Justice* devoted a quite inordinate amount of space to Aveling in those early months of 1891, starting in January when (Adolphe) Headingley Smith accused him of having claimed to represent *The Times* rather than *Time* at the TUC, and ending with a last dig on 11 April, when it published a review* of the revised edition of *The Working-Class Movement in America*, commenting self-righteously on another page:

> "Dr. and Mrs. Aveling did a great deal of harm to the Socialist cause in America in more ways than one – harm that it will take years to undo. But we can always separate personal conduct from useful information given by the persons..."

The end of the vendetta appeared to have come when, in May, the paper published a letter from Bax dissociating himself from the "personal polemics" of the recent past and "from any attack on certain individuals who have been for years personal friends of my own and still remain so", on which grounds he declined the invitation to co-operate with the Twentieth Century Press.[67]

Although Hyndman could not stifle his feelings about the ridiculous and impertinent candidate – who had not stood – for Northampton Borough, he had to uphold a certain political dignity in public; but there were others with nothing at stake whom he could use as his mouthpiece.

One such was Ferdinand Gilles, a German émigré journalist who, at a committee meeting of the Tottenham Street Communist Workers' Club on 27 February, leapt to his feet to direct the members' attention to the five questions put to Aveling by Hyndman. The object of the meeting was to arrange for the celebration of the anniversary of the socialist victories in the 1890 Reichstag elections, an occasion when Aveling was billed to speak, and Gilles declared that he

---

* By A. P. Hazell

"would not allow Dr. Aveling ... to address the Communist Club before those questions were properly answered",

adding that "undoubtedly most of the members detested" the fellow anyway.[66]

This was but the overture to a relentless campaign of defamation.

Gilles had come to England in 1886. The reason is unclear. According to his own account

"it was proved that in November 1885 the confidential men of the Social Democratic Party in Elberfeld and Barmen had elected me as editor for their daily paper, *Freie Presse*, at that time the only organ of the party in Rhineland and Westphalia, that I worked hard and suffered much in the service of the party, and that on July 15th 1886, I had officially and formally joined the party ..."[68]

This reversal of the formalities usually observed in appointing the editors of political party organs may have been owed to the innate frivolity of the Germans. Be that as it may, having joined the party, Gilles left for London where he immediately became active in the Communist Workers' Club

"which belongs and has always belonged to the German Social Democratic Party."[68]

His devotion to the cause did not prevent him, however, from quarrelling with the party's paper in London, Bernstein's *Sozialdemokrat*, as early as 1887. This he frankly admitted a few years later and attached no importance to it, not knowing that Bebel took occasion to tell Engels that a progressive member of the Reichstag, not a socialist, had warned him against Gilles as a thoroughly unsavoury character to be shunned and that Bernstein should be on his guard: his benevolent disposition having more than once led him into such traps, he might easily be taken in by so slippery a customer.

Following the performance at the Communist Club, when Gilles's outburst against Aveling cast him in the role of Hyndman's agent, enquiries were made and, in March 1891, the German party officially denied that Gilles was or ever had been one of its members and, moreover, was suspected of being a police spy: information which Bebel communicated to Engels saying that it might be freely published.

At the Brussels International Congress in August 1891 Gilles brought out a handbill with Hyndman's five questions, printed in English and German, "to explain Dr. Aveling's position in the British Labour movement to my German friends".[69]

As ill luck would have it, one of the leaflets fell into Will Thorne's hands. He confronted Gilles and was told that they had been printed on the instructions of the British delegation. The following day, Eleanor rushed into the fray to challenge this and accused Gilles of lying. Since Thorne was not present – it will be understood that all these odious encounters took place at snatched moments, in the *coulisses*, when two or three were gathered together – Gilles simply denied having said anything of the kind. The handbill was never intended for general distribution; very few copies had been printed and those only at the request of two German delegates, not previously known to him, who wished to use them as an "agenda paper" should the question of Aveling's position arise at the Congress. Paul Singer now joined in and asked for the names of those delegates. They turned out to be two Reichstag deputies, one representing Hamburg the other Bremen, and Gilles had handed the leaflets over on the understanding that they would not be broadcast. Why then did they appear in English as well as German? Were these two gentlemen acquainted with the English language? And how came it that the leaflet, of which so few copies existed, was published by the German press in Hamburg, Frankfurt and the Rhineland? Gilles could not account for this at all: he had no connection with any of these newspapers. Gilles who, after all, was merely acting as Hyndman's errand boy without compromising his master too far, was now in what is called *un joli pétrin*, or fine old pickle. It must have come as something of a relief to him when the Germans ruled that the matter was not to be raised in the Congress nor the handbills used by their delegation since it was a purely English affair.

In a later interview Gilles explained that

> "having been told by English Socialists that the position of Dr. Aveling was only based on the support he got from German party leaders, and that the Germans had always tried to force him as the leader on the English Socialists,"[70]

who repudiated him, he was thus the sole hindrance to "close international union between the two parties", which obstacle Gilles had considered it "my very unpleasant but compelling duty to try what I could in removing." He did not name either the English Socialists or the German party leaders involved.*

---

* Over a quarter of a century later, in 1918, by which time Belfort Bax had assumed many of Hyndman's prejudices and enthusiasms – including jingoistic support for the First World War – he revived some of Gilles's charges, but accused Engels, rather than unspecified Germans, of "trying to foist [Aveling] as a leader upon the English Socialist and Labour movement". While repeating Hyndman's waspish opinions of Engels in general and his "utter incapacity to judge men" in particular, Bax showed a certain want of judgment himself in venturing the prediction that Engels' writings were such as to suggest "a danger of their more or less falling into oblivion within a generation or two from the time of his death." If further proof were needed of

This strong sense of duty did not fail him when, back in London, on 8 September to be precise, Aveling literally took matters into his own hands by calling upon Gilles at 6 Eversleigh Street, Tollington Park, in Islington, accompanied by Louise Kautsky as a witness, and boxed his ears, for which assault he was brought up before the North London magistrate and fined 40s.

The case was eagerly seized upon by the press, the *Daily Chronicle* according it as much space as if it had been a sensational murder trial, to which, indeed, it was compared by Aveling's counsel, W. M. Thompson, when at one stage he tried to cite a legal precedent on provocation as related to the law of homicide. Charles Young, the lawyer for the prosecution, mildly remarked: "But this is not homicide," to which Thompson replied:

"The case is strongly analogous – in one a man murders another, in this a man murders another's reputation by circulating broadcast the vilest insinuations."[72]

The *Workman's Times** published a zestful report of the case "Gilles v. Aveling",

"done by the Editor of the paper," Eleanor wrote. "This man was till 29 years old a mill hand; is now anxious to get into 'the' movement of wh. he knows about as much as a new-born babe. But he seems honest & the paper may be useful. Theoretically it is valueless, but for more practical news as to what is being done it is reliable."[73]

The police court report was followed up by front-page interviews with Aveling and with Gilles, letters from both were published and the pot was kept merrily boiling from the time of the hearing, on 17 September, for another month.

Hyndman's inspiration it would be found in Bax's eulogy on that "excellent Socialist, Adolphe Smith" (Headingley).[71]

* Started first in Huddersfield in August 1890 and then moving to London, this penny weekly was edited by Joseph Burgess, a Lancashire textile worker, who wrote under the name "Autolycus". It amalgamated with Tom Mann's *Trade Unionist* in 1892 and lasted for another two years. One of its early contributors was Robert Blatchford (writing regularly as "Nunquam" for Hulton's *Sunday Chronicle*) until he became one of the co-founders of *The Clarion* in December 1891. In the 6 February 1891 issue of the *Workman's Times* there was some criticism of Eleanor and another speaker who, in the course of a meeting on the Scottish railway strike held at Clerkenwell Green the Sunday before, had "condemned the old Unionism for looking down with scorn upon the new, thereby showing their own foolishness and want of knowledge". Another paragraph by Autolycus on the same date said: "Speaking about labour leaders and leaders of labour who have not been artisan workers, I think many unions would be better without the domination of people like Mrs. Aveling and a score of others", this being entirely in accord with the reason given by the most rigid of the "old" craft unionists for having excluded Eleanor from meeting the London Trades Council or attending the TUC.

Justice did not lag behind; and nor did Gilles. An article curiously entitled, "Aveling v. Gilles", published on 26 September, reported the court proceedings, in the course of which reference had been made to certain questions "quoted from this little journal", and then went back to the vital issue:

> "Whatever our opinion of Aveling may be we should probably have left him severely alone but for his impudent attempt to foist himself upon us as the candidate of the S.D.F. for the representation of Northampton in Parliament ... a wholly unfit and improper person to represent the S.D.F. (of which he is not a member)."

Gilles had no direct personal quarrel with him, so far as *Justice* knew, but

> "he had learned that certain passages in Aveling's career had cost him the confidence of English Social Democrats,"

and had very properly opposed the Communist Working Men's Club joining the Legal Eight Hours League

> "on the ground that Aveling was simply attempting to form a labour party of his own; and that by doing so he would split up the English labour movement still more, as he was an absolutely discredited man."

Challenged to substantiate his charges, Gilles had done so, according to the article, whereupon Aveling called him a spy.

> "This, naturally enough, gave rise to some ill feeling on Gilles' part. Gilles is an active, able, and, as we have every reason to think, honest Social Democrat ... we have yet to learn that it is our duty, or the duty of Gilles, or of any Social Democrat, to hold his peace when the good repute of the cause is endangered by a Socialist who has done much by his conduct in the past to harm the Socialist movement in England and elsewhere."

Hyndman's rancour was tenacious, as were his efforts to come to the rescue of his cat's-paw whom he might well have thrown over now to heal his wounds as best he could with 40 pieces of silver. But Gilles had not yet outlived his usefulness. He reprinted the article from *Justice* in German (where it was more correctly entitled "*Gilles contra Aveling*") and, encouraged by his triumph in court, set about fresh enterprises on his own account.

On 25 September Eleanor wrote to Laura:

> "At present Gilles is said to be preparing a pamphlet. Let him! The only difficulty here is that one never knows where one may be landed in a libel case, & every word of what we may say wd. be in a sense libellous. And you know what that means here in the way

of money. As Bebel writes, 20s. per 'Ohrfeige'* is temptingly cheap. Paul writes that Deville regrets Edward did not bring up the thing at the Congress. That was impossible. We *could* not introduce the matter into the work done there."[73]

An even more obvious consideration, one would have thought, though it seems to have escaped Eleanor, was that, leaving aside the cost of being sued, the Avelings could never have afforded to take legal action against anybody. It was Gilles's trump card and, prudently avoiding any mention of Engels, he may be said to have played it well.

At the end of September he produced a flysheet, the first of two issued from his home address, entitled "Dr. E. B. Aveling: Have I Slandered Him?". This was printed in English and in German, side by side. It provided some answers to three of Hyndman's questions, using in one instance correspondence from the old files of the National Secular Society (in which one may detect Mrs Besant's hand) and a fresh insinuation that the author could, if he would,

"throw a little more light on the astonishing deficit in the accounts of last year's May Day demonstration."

Though writing in his own name, Gilles was clearly still taking instruction from Hyndman, which caused Engels to tell Laura on 2 October:

"We are trying to bring the slanders home to Hyndman who is using Gilles as his tool – and who, we hope, will not be able to wash off the dirt which the dirty Gilles has spattered involuntarily on the man who uses such a tool."[74]

A few months later he wrote that Hyndman, who was "getting more foolish every day", was keeping

"as his German chief of staff that outrageous scamp Gilles, who is evidently in the pay of the German Embassy."[75]

It had, indeed, been observed that Gilles was more flush than his common avocations would explain; apart from several gestures of unwonted charity, how, it was asked, could he afford the printing and world-wide distribution of flysheets?

The second one, dated 10 November, was more besmirching. Headed "Is He the Son-in-Law of Karl Marx?" it gave a detailed account of Aveling's wife, Bell Frank – when and where they had been married, the exact amount of her inheritance, her present whereabouts, occupation and

---

* Box on the ears.

tragic poverty – citing an unnamed authority for these facts and quoting *verbatim* Aveling's own false account of the marriage and its failure.*

But the facts, whether distorted or not and however damaging, were not so deadly as Gilles's opinions – derived from no source but his own vindictiveness – on the nature of Aveling's relationship with Eleanor. It was a loveless union, no "socialistic marriage", but a mere device for exploiting the name of Karl Marx. The article concluded with the words:

> "Is this disgraceful blackguard, who has traded so long on the reputation of the father of the woman he is cohabiting with, the son-in-law of Karl Marx? ... He is not ... and his prominent position amongst the Continental and American Socialists was an infamous fraud. I say *was*, because I trust that is over now, once and for ever."

This masterstroke, as insulting to Eleanor as to Aveling, was beyond challenge in a court of law: the tissue of scandal, half-truths and calumny was such that no lawyer could have unravelled it to the satisfaction of a British judge or jury, let alone to that of his client.

Initially, of course, Gilles had taken on the quarrel with Aveling at second hand on Hyndman's behalf: he scarcely knew the man personally. While only too many of Eleanor's friends fought shy of Aveling and could not abide him, they had – in contrast with Gilles – preferred to withhold their reasons in public, if not in private; partly, it may be, out of consideration for Eleanor, partly, it is certain, because Aveling's character, however objectionable, could not be said to detract from the value of his work. It is also significant that Olive Schreiner, the most articulate as also the most vehement of his abhorrers, never could formulate the reason for her feelings. But Gilles went far beyond his brief and, while he served Hyndman's purpose well enough in branding the Northampton nonstarter as a thief, a cheat, a liar, a mercenary, deceiver and fraud, it may be doubted that this German journalist, who was not a member of the SDF,

---

* By a chain of happy chances the source of this information and of Aveling's words can be identified. In the German – though not in the original English – version of the *Justice* article ("Gilles contra Aveling") of 26 September, Gilles could not forbear to append a footnote to the effect that even Aveling's own brother, a highly respected man, had not a good word to say for him, and had commended Gilles who "could have done nothing better in the interests of the working class" than to expose Edward's true character. At that time Aveling had three brothers living, but it so happens that under the footnote on the copy of this German reprint among the Aveling family papers there is a note in a hand familiar to the author from much personal correspondence with the late Mrs. Gwendoline Redhead (1885–1973): "Written by Father (F. W. Aveling) of course. G.R." Thus it is proved beyond all question that Gilles had garnered the facts from the Rev. Frederick Wilkins Aveling, known to be a stern critic of Edward and partisan of Bell, the deserted wife. It must be remarked that, reliable witness though the Rev. F. W. Aveling undoubtedly was, there are some highly questionable details in this version which must have been owed to Gilles's malicious embroidery, probably never seen by his informant at all.

cared two pins whether its fair name were fouled if Aveling stood for parliament.

Thus Gilles's campaign must have had some ulterior motive, and the one that comes most readily to mind is that to discredit two of the very few English Marxists who had close relations with those on the Continent would be of service to the functionaries employed to counter the spread of Marxism, particularly where it had the strongest hold and, under the Prussian police state, they abounded.

With his expulsion from the Communist Workers' Club in January 1892* Gilles lost his only political foothold in England and his usefulness as a *liaison* man was spent. Since it is utterly out of the question that Hyndman was in the pay of the police, either here or abroad, it cannot but be asked who had used whom: whether Hyndman or Gilles was the tool.

Gilles's campaign was not primarily directed to the British movement at all: a fact which, had he not been blinded by his own anger, Hyndman would have perceived and, in so far as he did not, was certainly the dupe. The whole thing fell rather flat in England. Good journalistic sport could be made of one socialist slapping another, but murky political waters are not the English working man's natural element nor does he rise easily to poisoned bait. Thus, while Aveling and Gilles continued their recriminations in *Vorwärts* and letters flew to and from the Continent, where they order these matters better, the majority of those in the British socialist and trade union movement continued to hold Aveling in esteem as an impressive orator, the capable organiser of May Day and the Legal Eight Hours League and the author, not only of popular articles on Marxism but of innumerable books for students on such subjects as Darwinism, Geology, Botany, Biology, Physiology and the other natural sciences, not to mention his joint works with Eleanor on Women, Shelley and America: a brilliant man and an ornament to their cause.

Nevertheless, many a later characterisation of Aveling has been based upon Gilles's adulterated evidence, to become part of our folklore. One of his contemporaries described Aveling as "Quite the strangest personality among the socialists of that time ... It is easy to set him down as a scoundrel, but in truth he was an odd mixture of fine qualities and bad ... there was something rather uncanny and impish in his nature."[77] His complex personality with its redeeming features – most clearly discerned by Bernard Shaw† – defies analysis and does not lend itself to simplification.

---

* By 48 votes to 21, according to Julius Motteler who was present. *Justice* reported "the Marxists counted 47 votes, a number of the wives of the social members and the intoxicated waiter included".[76]
† See above, pp. 214–5.

This ugly squall would scarcely be worth the logging were it not that Engels, yet again, sprang to Aveling's defence, involved Louise Kautsky by drafting a letter for her to sign as a witness to the physical assault on Gilles and was furious with Bebel who declined to publish it or Aveling's own refutation of the slanders on the grounds that this would merely pour oil on the flames.

"Inside every German," wrote Engels scornfully, "there lurks a bureaucrat who pops out the moment he occupies any petty office."[78]

Bebel was setting himself up as a censor: it was irreconcilable with honour to allow Gilles's filth to go unanswered and he, Engels, did not have such reservations in matters of honour. Once more he recited Bradlaugh's bygone charges and their true explanation, proving Aveling's innocence in every particular: he had been a greenhorn, a poet, quite monstrously swindled but one who should never have been allowed to meddle with money matters in the first place.

A few months later, early in 1892, Engels' championship of Aveling was put to its most severe test. Despite the explicit agreement to submit the manuscript of his translation of *Socialism: Utopian and Scientific** to Engels for revision, Aveling sent it off to Swan Sonnenschein who set it up in paginated proof before Engels ever saw it. While he could brush aside disdainfully or stoutly challenge slurs on Aveling's reputation, here was no matter of loose conduct where women or money was concerned, not the vagary of a dreamer caught in the snares of more worldly persons, but a patent failure to keep his pledge or meet the one uncompromising demand Engels made upon his working associates: a respect for the political and literary decencies.

To Laura and to Adler he wrote blaming the publishers who "by some blunder", due to "malice, stupidity or both",[79] had printed the rough draft. As soon as it came into his hands in this form he realised that it was not a question of correcting a word here and there: fundamental changes were needed entailing a vast amount of work and the expense of re-setting. Yet, to the last – even when he had to pad out the "awfully meagre" and heavily leaded type by writing a lengthy preface, "about half as long as the whole book"[80] to make it worth the price of 2s. 6d. – he maintained that the fault lay entirely with Swan Sonnenschein.

It so happens that the draft of a letter he wrote to Aveling at the time is on record, though whether it was ever licked into shape and sent cannot be known.†

---

* Based upon the historical chapter in Part III of *Anti-Dühring*.

† In what follows the words between square brackets appear in the original English, though not in the German version of the draft.[81]

"My dear Edward,

It was a perfectly understood thing that I was to revise your translation of the MS and that, having done so, I should give it the character of an authorised translation by writing a new preface to it.

After the [independent] action taken by Messrs. S.S. & Co. [in direct] without consultation with either of us, and in direct contravention of the above understanding, I am bound to reconsider my position.

[A revision of proof-sheets – not even in] [but in pages is quite a different thing from writing a MS.] Your translation being made with the knowledge that I would revise it, is necessarily a rough draft, moreover, you, as translator, would feel bound to stick to the letter of the original, when I, as the author, might deviate more or less from it and then make the [work] book read not as translation but as an original work. To revise not the MS. but paged [the] proofs in this spirit, would [require] imply, more or less, the upsetting of the paging [which has been carried to the word of the book].

Now, as far as I can see at present, there are but two courses open to me:

Either I revise the proofs in full liberty, exactly as I would have revised your MS., regardless of the expense this may [mean] occasion [which expense is to be borne, of course, by Messrs. S.S. & Co.]. In that case our original understanding holds good, the translation is authorised by me, and I write a preface. In that case we must have [many] four more copies of proofs at least and [read] revise afterwards.

Or, I am to respect the proof-sheets, as far as the paging is concerned, and merely make verbal changes within the limits of each page. In that case I will do my best to make the translation as good as I can, but I [am] must decline to being in any way connected with it before the public, and reserve to me the right of publicly declining any responsibility for it if such would be imputed to me.

As a matter of course the expense caused in either case would have to be borne by Messrs. S.S. & Co. who alone have brought it about.

And on all these points I must ask for this decision in writing before I stir in the matter."[82]

Whatever undertaking Aveling gave, he and Engels were closeted for days on end, rewriting the whole translation* and when the book finally appeared in April 1892, it was a fully authorised version containing one of Engels' finest introductions.

It will not go unremarked that in Engels' letter to Aveling, by a subtle elision, the betrayal of the understanding between them is attributed to the publishers in printing the manuscript that was sent to them and thus it is they who will be made to pay for the breach of faith.†

---

* It differs in many details from the *Anti-Dühring* chapter from which it derives.

† Far be it from any author to spring to the defence of publishers, but the Swan Sonnenschein *Letterbooks* of this period reveal that Aveling had given them bitter cause for grievance. They had agreed with him to publish Bax's *Time* and, unwisely, that he should collect the payments due to the contributors who, of course, never saw their money. In March, April, May and June 1891, the firm was driven almost mad by these wronged men of letters whose work had long since appeared and not been rewarded. Both they and the firm finally threatened proceedings against Aveling if he did not meet his obligations. His unremitting demands over the years for advances led them to write on December 1891 that he had been paid "for several books not yet

Engels' unswerving loyalty to anyone connected with Marx's kin, even when touched upon his most sensitive spot, is thereby proved to the hilt. But it gives one, as they say, furiously to think.

---

ready", to refuse a further advance and finally, on 18 January 1892, to reject altogether his translation of *The Origin of the Family* (an English version of which eventually first appeared in America in 1902,[83] and in England not until 1940[84]). In May 1890 Swan Sonnenschein had paid £10 in advance for Aveling's *Student's Marx*, due for delivery that June, and another £10 in the following July before they received it for publication in October 1891 and now, on 1 January 1892, he was grudgingly given another £10 for the translation of Marx's *The Eighteenth Brumaire* on condition that it was delivered within a month. It was not. (The first complete English translation, by Eden and Cedar Paul, was issued by Allen & Unwin in 1926.) On 8 January 1892 Swan Sonnenschein wrote to Aveling somewhat tartly: "You already have a book on hand for us ..." – this could have referred to either *The Eighteenth Brumaire* or *Socialism: Utopian and Scientific* – "we say nothing about the geology." This was his promised *Introduction to the Study of Geology*, finally delivered a year later (1893) when he failed to return the proofs for over a month, to the printers' extreme vexation since in those technologically backward days it took but a matter of weeks to print and publish a book.

The second May Day in London was celebrated under the auspices of a Joint Committee on the first Sunday of the month – 3 May 1891 – in Hyde Park. The Legal Eight Hours and International Labour League, which had formed a special Demonstration Committee under Aveling's chairmanship, and the London Trades Council led by Shipton, though they had their own processions and platforms, had amalgamated and agreed upon a single resolution proposing an international eight-hour day for all workers, put to the crowd at every platform and carried by acclaim.

Engels, accompanied by Louise Kautsky and Sam Moore – home on leave from Nigeria – went to the park and declared both the weather and the demonstration "glorious . . . the platforms extended in an immense arc across the park",[85] "stretching from near Hyde Park Corner to close upon Marble Arch", according to the *Daily Chronicle* on the following day. Engels was convinced that the crowd was even larger than the year before: "all of 500,000 people", he claimed.*[86] Engels and Moore sat on the platform chaired by Aveling and supported by Morris, Shaw and Quelch, while Louise Kautsky joined Eleanor on another waggon over which a gasworkers' representative presided.

The whole thing, Engels wrote, had been

"almost exclusively Edward's and Tussy's work, and they had to fight it through from beginning to end."[85]

Nevertheless, a majority at the Liverpool TUC having voted in favour of an eight-hour day regulated by law "had considerably smoothed their way" and Shipton was "awfully polite" to Aveling. In the light of this combination, the London Trades Council was not prepared to make special concessions to the SDF or grant it any platforms, which was rather hard, since its three delegates, sent to attend the first meetings of the Demonstration Committee, had then ostentatiously withdrawn, so that it was not welcome in either fold. "The SDF arranged an auxiliary meeting," reported the *Daily Chronicle*. Although the "auxiliaries" had marched with the Aveling contingent from the Embankment – part of the procession that, when assembled, stretched from Blackfriars Bridge to Big Ben – "in

---

* Equally reliable counts halved that number – none the less an impressive gathering – for Engels' sunny optimism was apt to run away with him.

order to get into the park in an orderly and showy manner", as Engels put it, once there they held their private demonstration at an uncontaminating distance from the main throng, the speakers being obliged to mount on chairs to address their followers. The number of these was slightly depleted, for many of the SDF branches had ignored the ukase and stayed in the ranks of the Joint Committee, pointedly illustrating, Engels observed, the real position of the SDF as "that of a sect".

> "It is very characteristic of the Anglo-Saxon race and their peculiar development," he went on, "that both here and in America the people who, more or less have the correct theory *as to the dogmatic side of it*, become a mere sect because they cannot conceive that living theory of action, of working with the working class at every possible stage of its development, otherwise than as a collection of dogmas ... recited like a conjurer's formula or a Catholic prayer."[87]

Eleanor was the last speaker from her platform. She was greeted, as always, with cheers and, if Bernstein and Bax are to be believed, "with shouts of 'good old stoker!'" whenever she addressed the gasworkers.[88] These composed the majority of her listeners, though there were members of other trade unions and a large sprinkling of Jewish immigrants, one of whom, Stanislas Mendelson,* addressed the meeting in Polish.

The burden of Eleanor's speech was that everyone would have to put in a deal of hard work during the next twelve months so that on the next May Day they would come to the park not to demand but to celebrate the eight-hour day. Then, noting the many women who had flocked to her platform, she said that her "great object" was to see the women's unions as strong as the men's whose support and help were essential to this end.

That evening she and Aveling, together with the Bernsteins, repaired to Engels' house, all in the highest spirits, to drink the cold punch of Moselle, claret and champagne with woodruff: a rather grand version of the traditional German *Maibowle* of an older May Day festival.

In April Eleanor had written two letters to her "dear, dear Dollie" (Radford). They showed the importance she attached to that continuity of affection which so often binds people whose lives have taken divergent ways, as also a significant glimpse of the personal philosophy underlying her manifold responsibilities: matters which, unlike her other interests, she could not share with this companion of her youth. In the first letter she repudiated Dollie's notion that

> "by the time your life is finished you will have learned just enough to begin it well. No, Dollie, we must just live our lives, and what we have missed, who knows? we may

---

* He and his wife, Maria, whom he married in 1889, were founders of the Polish Socialist Party in 1892, long active in the émigré revolutionary movement and friends of Engels'.

help others to realize ... But at least what life has taught you, will make more easy and more beautiful their" – her children's – "lives and tho' each one must work out his own salvation we can make the work* perhaps a little less hard for those that shall come after..."[89]

Some ten days later she wrote again to thank for a copy of Dollie's first little volume of poems† which, she said, "will always be a very precious thing". She then referred to Elizabeth Robins as "simply magnificent" in that "wonderful play", *Hedda Gabler*.‡ "We have in her a really great artist," she declared: an opinion held by many others who attended the opening performance, among whom were Henry James, Thomas Hardy, George Meredith and Bernard Shaw, according to the last of whom there was "a large and intelligent contingent of Fabians" and also "John Burns ... in the gallery."[90]

On a more personal note in this second letter to Dollie, Eleanor said:

"Yes. An old friendship is something very beautiful and very sacred and the longer one lives the surer one grows that nothing can ever take the place of an old friend."[91]

Without reading too much into it, one cannot but feel that this sentiment was a true – and sad – reflection of her barren love for Aveling.

At Whitsun both she and he went to Dublin to attend the Second Annual Conference of the Gasworkers' Union, held in the Antient Concert Rooms from 18 to 20 May. Eleanor was again elected as Minute Secretary – but would accept no payment – and Aveling to the chair. There were the usual objections that he was not "a *bona fide* workman", and some rather less expected opposition from Michael Davitt – who, it will be recalled, could not abide an atheist – but Aveling's unflagging work on behalf of both Ireland and the union were strongly pressed and won the day. Eleanor again came top of the poll in the elections for the ten-man Executive Council and she was nominated for the Presidency, a position she had no mind to hold and thought inappropriate; but she was pleased that she and Thorne were voted to go as the two Executive members to represent the Gasworkers' Union at the forthcoming International Congress, to which Aveling was mandated by the Dublin and Belfast Districts and two London branches.

A short article in *Justice* reporting the conference managed to get in a few digs at Eleanor – "Miss Marx" on this occasion – and described Aveling's concluding address as "a masterpiece of the 'kissy-kissy' kind", with a helpful interpretation of what he really meant in case anyone

---

* Possibly "world".
† *A Light Load*, E. Matthews, 1891.
‡ Produced for a week of matinées from 20 April 1891 at the Vaudeville Theatre.

should believe a word he had said.[92] Even allowing for the inexhaustible choler certain individuals excited in Hyndman – nor were Eleanor and Aveling the only ones to inflame him – it does strike one, at this distance of time, as rather disquieting that he should mount his hobby-horse to tilt against a young trade union, then organising some 70,000 workers under the leadership of Will Thorne, a faithful member of the SDF.

This unbalanced attitude was also apparent in the leading articles preceding the Brussels Congress, *Justice* reminding its readers of the wicked Marxist manoeuvres in Paris two years ago and paying little heed either to the forthcoming event itself or to the fact that so respectable a body as the TUC had forced everyone else's hand by welcoming it, quite against the decisions and wishes of these Marxist evildoers.

It would be absurd to suppose that the preliminaries to the Congress went off without a hitch. Indeed, the official sponsors were so dilatory and inept that unauthorised persons began sending out invitations, sometimes to the wrong people; the right people received no information – let alone invitations – until far too late; at the last moment the date was brought forward by a few days so that some of those who were both informed and invited were unable to arrive in time, while delegates from the Parliamentary Committee and many of the unions which had set the ball rolling by their vote of acceptance at the Liverpool TUC never went at all.

Nevertheless, despite the bickerings, the telegrams and anger, a single if not united Congress of 363 delegates – with a larger proportion of women than had come to Paris – foregathered at the Maison du Peuple in the Place de Bavière for the inaugural session on Sunday, 16 August 1891. On the following day they adjourned to a larger hall in the rue d'Or.

The *Pall Mall Gazette* feared the influence of the Congress would "not be as great as it might and should be";[93] the *Daily Chronicle* remarked upon the "vacant places" and "the gaps in the ranks",[94] referring to no physical vacancies or gaps – for by the time the full complement of some 400 delegates had turned up, the place was packed to the doors, while its public gallery was daily crammed with Belgian workers – but to the absence of precisely those representatives of labour who had willed the whole affair.

The twenty-three British delegates, representing some 200,000 workers, included such old stalwarts as Frederick Lessner, now 66 years of age, and such novices as the 22-year-old William Stephen Sanders,* the

---

* This good young member of the Fabian Society, later to become its secretary, was not a Marxist and made the idiosyncratic diagnosis that the whole trouble in England stemmed from a mistranslation of Marx's word *Klassenkampf* as "class war" instead of "class struggle". None the less, he never lost his admiration for Eleanor of whom he wrote in later years as "an attractive woman who had inherited a good portion of her father's brain-power and combative qualities

one from the Bloomsbury Socialist Society, the other from the Eight Hours and International Labour League, both of which bodies had also mandated Eleanor. To Thorne's disappointment, only one of the Gasworkers' branches – Tottenham – other than those who had nominated Aveling, sent a delegate.

Some of the "gaps in the ranks" were owed to causes other than that people had either been left "in a state of ignorance", as the *Pall Mall Gazette* complained, or because "Socialism is still in the cauldron of the sectaries", according to the *Daily Chronicle*. Tom Mann and Ben Tillett, for example, were at the (4th) Co-operative Festival, held at the Crystal Palace on that Sunday,* while Paul Lafargue – who viewed it as of

"exceedingly small importance, a purely ornamental Congress; its only job is to recognise May Day and to lay the foundations for a few international trade organisations"[96]

– happened to be in gaol at the time.

Engels, too, held that there was "but little real work for it to do";[97] nevertheless, Eleanor laboured earnestly for its success during many weeks. Ill-judged, badly organised and rather pointless it might be, but no international congress was going to miscarry for lack of efficient preparation if she could help it. She translated the various *Reports* into English, adding a few explanatory footnotes to the German one, which Engels agreed were needed,† but refused, though asked, to put them into French, saying "I'm sure I should make a mess of them,"[99] eventually finding an old émigré Communard to undertake the work.

The *Report* on Britain she had written herself, sending it to Laura on 6 August with the words:

"Please don't judge it too critically. I had to write it while I was terribly worried,‡ & not very well, & constantly interrupted. It had to be so long because we have not one Party here to Report for – but a dozen."[98]

In the same letter she said:

---

which she placed unreservedly at the service of the masses. Highly educated, mistress of three languages, widely read, deeply interested in literature and the drama, witty and infinitely good-natured..."[95]

* Attended by some 30,000 co-operators.

† She pointed out, for example, that: "English people cd. not know what the 'Gesinde Ordnung' is – though we have something rather analogous with regard to Farm Servants."[98]

‡ Worried, because in July Aveling had a recurrence of his kidney trouble. He was recuperating at St. Margaret's Bay in Kent at the time she wrote her *Report*.

> "*What* a muddle the Belgians are making! I shall write & tell you all about how they mismanaged things here...",

and again, shortly before the Congress:

> "Your compatriots* are muddling most splendidly!"[100]

Yet when it was all over she had to admit that

> "the Brussels Congress was really a big success: far bigger than I ever expected it would be ... Wise in their generation the Brussels people saw that it was a case of no Marxists no Congress, and so pitched their Possibilists overboard..."[101]

There had been over 100 messages of greeting from those unable to be present, many of them from Russians, including the letter Lavrov had sent for Eleanor to read to the Congress.

The agenda posed few questions of substance that had not been raised in Paris and, as the *Star* reporter noted:

> "the old differences between Socialists and trade unionists of course arose, but it was exceedingly friendly."[102]

One fresh, not entirely welcome item was raised by the New York delegate, Abraham Cahan, of the American Union of Hebrew Labor Organisations, who wished a resolution to be passed on the position of Jewish workers. *Justice* observed:

> "We happen to know that the object with which the question had been placed on the Orders of the Day was simply to evoke a declaration from the Congress that in its eyes there was no distinction between Jew and Gentile workers,"[103]

and pronounced that:

> "There appears to be strong feeling against the Jews in the Congress. This is a pity. Even on the ground of tactics, apart from general humanity, we need the poor Jews to beat the rich Jews. When Greek meets Greek, etc."[104]

The last thing the Standing Orders Committee desired was a full debate or formal resolution on the Jewish question in an assembly where such antisemitism was known to exist. The Congress compromised by adopting a report to the effect that the only way to achieve the emancipation of Jewish workers was to bring about their amalgamation with the

---

* Laura was born in Brussels.

socialist and labour parties of their respective countries: socialists, it declared, could recognise no distinction of race or nationality but only the struggle of all workers against all capitalists.

For the first two days the programme was held up by the concerted efforts of "Autonomie" – the London Anarchist Club – whose exclusion, as an "unfortunate necessity", was put to the vote and carried but axiomatically ignored by the autonomists themselves, until finally, on the second day, Herbert Burrows moved and Eleanor seconded that the Congress proceed at once to business. This motion was passed unanimously, the most vociferous filibusters having been persuaded by moral force to leave the body of the hall and take to the gallery. Unfortunately one of them was then arrested by the Belgian police for illegal entry and his deportation was announced, whereupon the Congress went wild with indignation at such methods of removing its unwelcome guest.

Ironically enough, Engels and Hyndman were – unknowingly – agreed upon the main potential danger at Brussels.

Thus to Laura Engels wrote on the first working day of the Congress – 17 August – that he saw few difficulties ahead

"... unless the various velleities of a restoration of the 'International' venture to come out, I hope they will not for that would cause new splits and throw us back, here in England at least, for years to come. The thing is an absurdity in every respect, especially so long as neither in France nor in England there is one strong and united party. If that were the case, and both united heart and soul with the Germans, then the end would be obtained without any formal union; the moral effect of the three great western nations acting together would suffice ... The fact is, the movement is too great, too vast to be confined by such hampering bonds. Still, there is a hankering after this restoration and Bonnier* was full of it last time I saw him. Certainly he looked rather perplexed when I told him my objections and had not a word to say – but will that stop him and his friends at Brussels?"[105]

Here comes Hyndman's *Justice* in the person of J. Hunter Watts, writing the leading article on the Congress which he had attended as one of the eight SDF delegates:

"We are glad to say that the proposal to establish an International Committee was not acted upon. The pages of the history of the International movement have been sufficiently blurred and disfigured by the intrigues of individuals who, in the desire to assert their personality, availed themselves of the position they held in the old International (of necessity an irresponsible one in the sense that no effective control over them could be exercised) to strangle any independent action, any independent organisation of the workers. To this day we suffer from the intrigues of some of them,

---

* A French socialist and member of the Workers' Party, for a long while domiciled in England, who was one of the active organisers of the International Congresses in 1889 and 1891.

or of some of the people who imagine that the cloak of the old prophets of the International has fallen upon their shoulders..."[106]

Thus, for vastly differing reasons, everyone was satisfied that the threat had been averted; and *Justice* had amply confirmed Engels' view that there was no basis for a *political* international structure that could accommodate workers' organisations of such diverse trends and unequal stages of development as those represented at Brussels.* Instead, it was agreed that national Correspondence Committees – a Bureau – should be set up to exchange information, collect statistics and so forth. Since labour conditions varied widely not only from country to country but from industry to industry, the Marxists thought and Aveling moved that these committees should operate on a union basis to be of practical value to workers engaged in struggles with their employers or enticed to act as strike-breakers abroad.

Mr. Hunter Watts quickly picked up the scent:

> "If Dr. Aveling's proposal that this work should be left to separate labour organisations had been accepted, the door would have been left open for any intriguer to organise a Trade Union – say, of shrimp catchers – to establish himself as its secretary or president, and then open relations with foreign labour organisations which hitherto have had no sufficient means of knowing the character and position of individuals who have entered into correspondence with them in the self-assumed role of Labour leaders."[106]

To compare Engels' approach and Hyndman's to the question of what was best for the international relations of socialists is to know their respective weight and measure to a nicety: the one with his sweeping embrace of a movement "too great, too vast to be confined", the other with his stultified vision of intrigues and conspirators bent upon the strangulation of that movement.

Certainly the Brussels Congress was no world-shaking occasion, even though Thorne declared it "admittedly – even by the middle-class press – one of the most remarkable gatherings the workers have ever held".[107] Perhaps the greatest innovation was that one of the main national reports was not only written but delivered by a woman: namely, Eleanor.

Her *Report from Great Britain and Ireland* was a long and comprehensive document, presented in the name of the Gas Workers and General Labourers' Union, the Legal Eight Hours and International Labour League, the Bloomsbury Socialist Society and the Battersea Labour League.† Thorne claimed that it was "generally admitted to be one of the best and

---

* With no General Council or formal constitution, the Second International was generally referred to as the "International" until the Communist, or Third International, came into being.
† Subsequently published as a penny pamphlet.[108]

most valuable presented to the Congress"[107] but she stated at the outset that it did "not pretend to be complete or exhaustive". Nor could it speak for a British Labour Party, for:

"Unhappily, there is as yet no such party in existence ... There are a great many Socialist parties all doing good work in their way; they each have, if not a little Hell, at least a little coterie of their own ... the largest and the one that has done more, perhaps, than any ... to spread the teachings of scientific Socialism among the workers, is the Social Democratic Federation."

Eleanor went on to characterise the Fabians –

"middle-class folk too honest to be contented with the present conditions of society; too educated to throw in their lot with the Salvation Army; too superior to identify themselves wholly with the profane vulgar"–

but she stressed, above all, the importance of the Socialist-inspired New Unionism, quoting from (her own) *Address* to the Gasworkers' Rules wherein the Union:

" 'clearly recognises that to-day there are only two classes, the producing working class, and the possessing master class. The interests of these two classes are opposed to each other. The masters have known this a long time; the workers are beginning to see it ... They are beginning to understand that their only hope lies in themselves, and that from the masters, *as a class*, they can expect no help ...'."

She made special reference to the 25,000 members in Ireland, north and south, reporting that:

"no words were more enthusiastically cheered ... at a huge demonstration in Pheonix Park ... than ... 'Let Ireland be free, but let it be an Ireland of free workers; it matters little to the men and women of Ireland if they are exploited by Nationalist or Orangemen; the agricultural labourer sees his enemy in the landlord, as the industrial worker sees his in the capitalist'."

The movement following upon the great Dock Strike – itself a consequence of the lead given by the Gasworkers – had resulted in making trade unionists of some quarter-of-a-million hitherto unorganised workers, and had

"helped to awaken the old Unions from the lethargy into which they had fallen. If not quite 'Sleeping Beauties', these were certainly sleeping partners in the labour movement",

which, for 20 years had been sick and benefit societies and were now "recognising that shorter hours of labour are, after all, the highest benefit a Union can bestow upon its members."

The Legal Eight Hours Demonstration of May Day 1890 had been up against not only the opposition of the Social-Democratic Federation, but it

"was new, and like Snug, the Joiner, the British workman being somewhat slow of study, it took some time and work to make the idea ... popular."

However, many of those who had been least willing to demonstrate at all on that first occasion had been amongst

"the most enthusiastic 'Legal' demonstrators of the present year, 1891."

Eleanor spoke of the "unspeakable poverty and wretchedness" of the agricultural labourers, to which was added

"the ignorance of these men and women, their isolation, their terrible dependence upon parson and landlord",

but they, too, were beginning to realise

"their fraternity of poverty and suffering with the town worker",

so that, although the campaign was still in its infancy, it promised well:

"in one county, in eight weeks, some 2,000 workers were enrolled into a Union."

But the organisation of women was even

"perhaps more difficult ... especially in London ... Even the working man for the most part still looks upon the women of the household as domestic animals, more or less his personal property ... And the woman herself ... earning a wage that – even in the more skilled kinds of labour – generally means starvation ... or where she is a widow, or unmarried mother with children dependent upon her, or even when she is alone in the world ... what time could she have – even if she had the desire – for attending meetings or for organising?"

Eleanor then paid her tribute to

"the admirably conducted strike of Bryant & May's match girls; the efforts of many notable women to organise their sister workers", although the results were, she admitted, "as compared with the efforts, disappointingly small".

She referred to the tremendous number of strikes witnessed in the past two years and – obviously with Silvertown in mind, though she mentioned only the South Metropolitan Gasworkers and the Scottish railwaymen – said:

> "a strike won is not always a pure gain, nor an unsuccessful strike of necessity a pure loss. Sometimes ... 'it is better to have fought and lost than never to have fought at all'," and that "all the hundreds of large and small strikes ... point the same moral and adorn the same tale – that Trade Unionism and Strikes alone will not emancipate the working class," whose "economic freedom can only be attained through the taking hold of political power in the interests of their own class."

She explained to her foreign friends the obstacles presented to independent labour candidates by the electoral system in the United Kingdom:

> "the enormous cost of elections, the non-payment of these expenses by the State, and the non-payment of Members, the want of a second ballot, the systematically complicated condition of the franchise and of the registration laws ... difficulties of an almost insurmountable character to the return of working-class representatives. But the greatest difficulty is the want ... of a national working-class party."

In local and municipal government, she said, labour had been successful

> "and always with the happiest results for the constituents".

She cited Battersea which, through the good offices of the Labour League, had returned and maintained a Social-Democrat on the London County Council,* as a result of which it had

> "declined to give contracts for any work which can be done by workmen employed directly, without the intervention of a contractor," or to "employers who do not pay the recognised standard of wages, or comply with the conditions of labour laid down by the trade unions..."

Summing up, Eleanor said:

> "What has been done in Great Britain and Ireland within the last two years may seem little when compared with what has been done abroad."

While Germany had its one-and-a-half million Social-Democratic voters

---

* John Burns.

and 35 Reichstag deputies and France was also far ahead, the United Kingdom could show but one Socialist in the House of Commons* and one on the LCC. It had no working-class press, no

"organs belonging to a definitely constituted working-class party. Such papers as we have are either private property, run more or less as a speculation ... or ... newspapers, giving very valuable information, no doubt, but absolutely no theoretical teaching; or, as in the case of the Social-Democratic Federation organ, *Justice*, they belong to sects, and do not reach the mass of the workers...

But still there is, at last, a genuine working class movement in England, and its success since 1889 augurs well for the formation of a Labour Party, distinct from all other political parties. Above all, the feeling of working-class consciousness and the understanding of the class struggle have grown beyond all expectation, and with them the knowledge of the solidarity of labour the world over. Each nation has, and must have, its own special means and methods of work. But whatever those means and methods, the end is one all the world over – the emancipation of the working class, the abolition of all class rule."

*   *   *

Eleanor added a small footnote to the Brussels Congress by writing a front-page article for the Vienna women's paper†[109] which was Louise Kautsky's special nursling.

Citing the resolution passed on equal rights for both sexes, she said that at its first session this socialist Congress had made abundantly clear that it had absolutely nothing to do with the middle-class movement for women's rights, in the same way as its approach to the question of war differed completely from the bourgeois peace organisations which cried "Peace, Peace", where no peace existed. As the men and women of the ruling class went hand in hand, so must those of the working class combine to fight the common enemy.

The Brussels decision was splendid in principle but how, Eleanor asked, was it to be put into practice? So long as no sober and matter-of-fact consideration was given to what was to be done, nothing could come of any theoretical proclamation however well-intentioned. It was not enough to acknowledge the fact of the class struggle. Workers must learn which weapons to use and how to use them; the positions to attack and how to consolidate the gains already won. That was why they were now finding out when and where to conduct strikes and boycotts, how to achieve protective measures, what had to be done in order that such legislation already extorted did not remain a dead letter. And what, she asked, must they, as women, do? Of one thing there was no doubt: they must organise,

---

* Cunninghame-Graham.
† The *Arbeiterinnen-Zeitung*. A fortnightly edited by Adler.

not as "women" but as proletarians, not as female competitors to their working menfolk but as their fellow-fighters.

The most serious question of all was how to organise? To her it seemed that organisation had to start with women as trade unionists, using their combination as a means to reach the final aim: the emancipation of their class. The work would not be easy. Indeed, the conditions of women's labour were such that it was often heartbreakingly difficult to make progress. But the work would grow easier day by day and seem less hard as time went on and in the measure to which women, and more especially men, grasped the fact that their strength lay in the unity of all workers.

She then cited the three things from which to draw conclusions: first, wherever women had organised, their situation had improved in the form of higher wages, reduced hours of work and better conditions; second, it was a positive advantage at least as much to men as to women that the earnings of the latter should be treated as genuine working wages and not as a paltry contribution to the general household kitty; third, it was essential, save in certain specialised trades, but particularly in the case of unskilled workers, that men and women should belong to the same trade union, just as they were members of the same workers' party.

The year 1891 witnessed Paul Lafargue's finest hour. With his eyes open he stood trial on a charge of incitement to murder and went to prison for a speech he had not made, refusing to allow the real culprit* to come forward, either in court or by sending the self-incriminating letter he had drafted to the Minister of Justice. For Lafargue the outcome – in both senses, for it led to his release before he had served his full sentence – was that he became a member of parliament.

Le Temps of 5 May cited such inflammatory words as:

> "All the bosses are rotten. When an animal dies, it serves some purpose, but you can't make a glove out of a boss's hide,"

and a direct appeal to young conscripts to lay down their arms if called upon to defend the "strongboxes of that bloated crew". On 14 May the same paper quoted Lafargue as saying:

> " '. . . though it is unfortunate, French workers, that you are inferior to the British in the matter of labour organisation, you have this vast superiority over them that you have all been soldiers, and know how to handle rifles. And I have no need to tell you against whom you should use those rifles: the employers, they are the enemy . . . if ever you are ordered to fire in no matter what circumstances, you will turn about and fire the other way'."

"Garbled passages from my speeches", Lafargue claimed, had appeared in both the local and national press.[111]

During the weeks before 1 May, which was celebrated by the French workers throughout the country, Lafargue and leading socialists in the region had toured the department of the Nord, to mobilise support for the event. When the day came troops fired upon the demonstrators at Fourmies – a textile manufacturing town – wounding thirty-six people and killing ten, including a child and a young girl. On 10 May a protest meeting was held in Calais, addressed among others by Cunninghame Graham, who was arrested and deported that same evening.

---

* This was a socialist named Renard, from St. Quentin, and Lafargue later wrote: "It must not be said that I allowed Renard to run any danger in order to clear myself."[110]

Naturally enough, feeling ran high in the region but, as Lafargue pointed out, the repercussions were widespread:

"This massacre has made a tremendous impression in France: the government has provided us with May Day martyrs. Fourmies was a quiet place where they had never even heard of socialism before the series of lectures I gave there with Renard ... At one moment I was afraid I should be had up for my speeches ... but fortunately for me the government is interested only in hushing up the incident and no more is heard of Fourmies..."[112]

By a Cabinet decision of 8 May the regional organiser of the *Parti ouvrier*, Culine, was swiftly prosecuted and later sentenced to six years' hard labour and ten years' banishment from the area.* Lafargue, however, had been lulled into a false sense of security. The authorities held their hand until the storm over the Fourmies outrage had died down and on 20 June he was summoned to appear before the Assize Court of the Nord, charged with having used the offending words. At the

"preliminary investigation and before the jury I confined myself to saying that I had never said them; several of my witnesses remembered the fact perfectly well, but I forbade them to breathe a word about Renard."[113]

Eleanor was horrified when she read in the *Daily News* that he had been sentenced to twelve months' imprisonment.

"But I suppose he can appeal against this iniquitous sentence," she wrote to Laura.

"Here, of course, he could not, but in France, I fancy, it is possible. Surely if he can appeal he will get off altogether, or with a month or so at the outside ... It wd. be most unfortunate if he cd. not be present at Brussels..."[114]

But, as we know, he was not. On the morning of 30 July, while the case came before the Court of Cassation, he was taken into custody and lodged in the Concièrgerie. The appeal was dismissed and, after a few days, he was transferred to Ste. Pélagie where, Laura wrote, she was "happy to say [he] is safely installed, for to get quartered there had come to be 'le comble de tous ses voeux' †..." He was

'settled and comfortable. Ste. Pélagie is a very mitigated prison ... Paul is in high health and spirits. He has plenty of books and newspapers; takes a hot and cold

---

* Thanks to the delays inseparable from the processes of law, he was able to petition for the verdict to be quashed since misdemeanours committed at public meetings or in the press became void after three months: a legal loophole of which Lafargue declined to avail himself.
† The summit of his whole desire.

showerbath every morning, drinks milk on the top of wine and scribbles away with a will. I go every other day and take him letters, books and garden produce; cucumbers, strawberries and new-laid eggs and what not. He sees all the people he cares to see and saves boot-leather..."*[115]

Eleanor could not imagine a more enchanting way of life. "... Ste. Pélagie is making a splendid correspondent of Paul," she wrote.

> "The more I hear of that Saint's hotel the more I wish Constans† would fall in with the plan I suggested to Guesde ... It was that whenever a man is condemned to Ste. Pélagie that his friends and relations shd. be allowed to take 'des abonnements'‡ for a term of not less than 6 weeks of his sentence. Thus Paul being condemned to 12 months I wd (& I'd pay for the chance!) take say 3 months; Edward wd do the same; you might like a retreat of 6 weeks, & so forth. In this way the government cd indulge in heavy sentences & even profit commercially – because on s'abonnerait à prix fixe..."§[117]

A few days before this letter was written, Werquin, the Radical deputy for the First Lille constituency died and Lafargue was nominated as the Workers' Party candidate. Vain efforts were made early in October to obtain his release for the campaign – which was "not legally possible since my sentence is definitive", wrote Paul[118] – but Guesde deputised for him at the hustings to such good purpose that in the first ballot Lafargue topped the poll with 5,005 votes – a majority of more than 2,000 over the runner-up – and in the second he romped home with 6,470 votes.

On 31 October – in the fortnight between the two ballots – the Socialists in the Chamber initiated a debate on Lafargue's continued imprisonment which had no result beyond airing the question; but on 9 November a motion to suspend the sentence on the convicted candidate was tabled and passed on a show of hands. The Ministers of Justice and the Interior gave the order of release for the remainder of the parliamentary

---

* By some chance an undated letter from Lafargue written to tell his wife of his transfer to this pleasure dome and inform her of his immediate needs has landed among the William Morris papers in the British Museum. It runs:

"*Ma chére amie,*

    I am at St. Pélagie – come and see me.

    Bring me the little lamp with some paraffin in a litre [? bottle] – some candles –

    My manuscript notebooks which you will find on my table – Some paper, some pens.

                I embrace you,

                  P. Lafargue.

Bring a pencil

Some envelopes and writing paper, soap, comb – table-napkins."[116]

† The Minister of the Interior.

‡ Subscriptions.

§ One would subscribe at a fixed price.

session: thereafter he would have to go back to gaol with no remission for the ticket-of-leave period.

He left the tranquil delights of Ste. Pélagie in the second week of November and was immediately plunged into a wild orgy of celebrations. On the 17th a dance was given by the Paris regional party at the Tivoli Vauxhall. He and Laura returned from this festivity at 2 a.m. to depart at midday for Lille, where they were to stay but 24 hours that he might be back in Paris to take his seat. Small wonder that he wrote:

"I am beginning to feel worn out by the rush in which I am living."[119]

Laura's letter describing the reception at Lille is among the best she ever wrote and, in the circumstances of her husband's months of incarceration and her new-found reunion with him, extremely moving.

It was addressed to Engels on 22 November 1891 and began by conceding that the Lille papers had reported the occasion well and accurately, but

"they did not give the faintest idea of the extraordinary reception of the new deputy.

We reached Lille (myself suffering from cold and incipient influenza and Paul from extreme fatigue, and no wonder) at half past five p.m. No sooner had his electors caught sight of Paul than they took possession of him, crowding round him and carrying him off in triumph...

We then dined ... At 8 o'clock we started for la Scala where the meeting was to take place. We managed to get in by a side-door, and once inside the hall I saw a sight such as I had never seen before. The body of the hall was crowded to suffocation, the gallery was stuffed and hundreds of men and women were making superhuman efforts to get in. The doors which had been closed were forced open and a second gallery (closed for repairs) was taken by storm and in a few seconds was as chokefull as the other. And still the people outside clamoured for admittance. 'Serrez les rangs', shouted Delory, and instantly there was a move forward effected with a precision and rapidity that would have caused your general's heart to beat. A few benches broke down under the weight of the masses. A couple of windows were smashed. Nearly all the people were on their feet throughout the evening and packed so closely that, as one of the reporters said, if we had wanted to turn anybody out, it couldn't have been done.

The tenor of Paul's speech you know. But at the end of his speech the meeting was by no means at an end. The people would not leave the hall before their deputy had left, so that we had to make our way through the crowd and I thought we should never get through. The perspiration ran down Paul's face, he had an enormous bouquet on one arm and gave his other arm to his wife. I rather think he thought we should be crushed for he looked intensely unhappy as we moved on jammed and wedged in by his too enthusiastic electors. We got out however safe enough and once in the streets of Lille it was all smooth sailing. I don't know how many hundreds or thousands brought up the rear, but we were escorted right and left and in front by a body-guard of friends and citizens who cleared the way for us. Men and boys and girls and women shouted Vive Lafargue and sang a variety of popular and revolutionary songs:

> *C'est bien vrai ce qu'on dit;*
> *Au sortir de Ste-Pélagie*
> *Il va siéger à Paris.**

On reaching our destination, Paul had again to address the people before they would consent to go home and it was to the cry of 'A bas Constans' that they finally dispersed. A large number of men, Delory informed us, would inevitably be fined on the morrow for having abandoned their workshops too early in the day ... It is impossible to see a more ardent population than these Lillois, but these men who smash windows and break open doors ... took off their hats and caps to me when I shook hands with them. It was a grand sight and I wish you had been there to see it..."[120]

*   *   *

It was as well, perhaps, that Lafargue had not conducted his own electoral campaign but only reaped its fruits, for no sooner was he at liberty than he committed the worst blunder in his public career. Naturally enough the capitalist press had been hostile to his candidature, first by preserving silence and then by going into the attack. The weapon was handed to the reporters by one of the opposing candidates who wrote to the Election Disqualifications Committee claiming that Lafargue was not a French citizen.† Thereupon he was of course obliged publicly to aver his nationality and also his patriotism, for it was asked why had he not fought for his country – if it was his country – in the Franco-Prussian war.

On 22 November, Lafargue spoke in Bordeaux, his home town, and was reported by Reuter's in a message, datelined "Bordeaux, Nov 23rd", containing this passage:

"Mr. Paul Lafargue, the socialist deputy recently elected in Lille, spoke here yesterday at a meeting of 200 Socialists. He was at pains to prove to his audience that he was a French subject and explained that he had not fought in the French army in 1870 because he was at that time serving France in his own way by communicating to the members of the National Defence Government the plans he had obtained from colleagues of the International living in Germany and among whom were several German officers..."

As though this were not enough to cause a sensation in the press, Lafargue had previously given an interview to *Le Matin* on similar lines. The French papers pounced upon Reuter's report which was also published in the *Evening Standard* – "The Lille Election" – on 23 November.

Anti-German and revanchist feeling in France was still, after 20 years, both strong and vocal,‡ thus for a socialist M.P. to claim that he had

---

* What they say is very true;/On coming out of Sainte-Pélagie/He will take his seat in Paris.
† It was stated not only that he had been born in Santiago de Cuba but that his real name was Pablo Fonseca.
‡ At the first performance of *Lohengrin* at the Paris opera on 16 September 1891 pandemonium broke out and there was an organised demonstration.

engaged in a form of espionage by virtue of his First International connections with members of the German military caste was little short of insanity.

It was a most unlikely story at best for, as Engels pointed out, nobody on the General Council of the IWMA had ever been in touch with any German officers* and if Paul had made such contacts during the three years he had spent in France (1869–71) before he was forced to flee, he had certainly kept it a dark secret from everyone, not only until the amnesty of 1880 but ever since. The extraordinary thing was less that, under fire from reporters, Lafargue should have lost his head than that he did not realise the implications.

Engels was appalled. As the newspaper cuttings from France reached him, sent by Laura without a word of comment, his perturbation grew: he could not even grasp at the straw that Lafargue might have been misreported. In a letter that has not been traced, he wrote to Laura evidently expressing his alarm and displeasure. Laura, temperamentally given to resentment rather than reason, answered on the day it arrived:

"Your letter to hand I have sent off so hastily to Paul after running over the contents of it that you must forgive me if I reply in the spirit rather than the letter of it. And forgive me for saying that I consider the spirit of it most unjustifiable...

I think Paul and I have *done* and *suffered* enough ever since we came over here to further and indeed to *invent* the cause of internationalism ... to be quit of charges of this kind.

If Paul were not the soul of honour in all things public and political, I should not now be here and living with him, for he has faults enough and to spare of his own!

Forgive me for saying that your letter has spoilt the short-lived pleasure I have had in Paul's election."[121]

Paul was less touchy and more lighthearted about the matter. He wrote to Engels from Lyons, where the 9th National Congress of the French Workers' Party was held from 26 to 29 November, that he was "hurrying from town to town", to make the most of his "parliamentary" freedom.

"I cannot be held responsible for everything the papers have put into my mouth for weeks past ... But this is what I said at Bordeaux and elsewhere. I did not take up arms in 1870–71 because I had to re-form the International, decapitated by the siege of Paris; and that the Internationalists of France no less than of Germany and of other countries regarded it as their duty to prevent the crushing of the French Republic by

---

* But see Ershard Kiehbaum: *War Engels mit einem Offizier in preussich-deutscher Generalstab befreundet?* and *Anmerkungen zur Briefen von L. Gumpert and Engels* in *Beiträge zur Marx-Engels-Forschung* No. 10 1981, pp. 99–113.

Bismarck's troops; and that ... the German Internationalists protested against the continuation of the war..."[122]

The matter of his nationality had still to be decided and the validity of his election confirmed, so that he cannot have been quite as easy in his mind as this hastily written explanation suggests.

Engels now sent a lengthy letter to Bebel, full of his disquiet. Though he had earlier referred to Lafargue as "something of a spoilt child"[123] he was in no mood now to be indulgent. He reported what Paul was "supposed to have said" at the Bordeaux meeting and went on:

> "now Laf. *cannot* have said this, yet I cannot for the life of me think what he *did* say...
>
> You yourselves" (that is, the German socialists) "can have sent neither military information, either directly or indirectly, to the French Government in Bordeaux, nor German officers' plans, since, so far as I know, you had absolutely no connection with officers at the time...
>
> What L can have said and what came into his head is utterly incomprehensible to me. Because even here, in the General Council of the International, we had absolutely no contact with German officers and were thus never once in a position to pass on the 'plans' of such gentry...
>
> In any event, he has made a quite inexcusable blunder: either lied or told tales out of school, he alone knows which..."[124]

Engels did what he could to smooth Laura's ruffled feelings but he would not dissemble.

> "You need not be afraid that it ever entered my mind to think Paul capable of a wilfully mean and dishonourable action," he wrote on 27 November. "That is entirely out of the question. But a man may be the very soul of honour and yet commit a folly, the consequences of which may be incalculable...
>
> Now you yourself admit that it is just possible he *may* have been led to commit such a blunder..."

She had sent him cuttings from *Le Temps* and *l'Intransigeant** from which

> "I was forced to conclude that *you knew* the contents of these two reports, and that the very fact of your sending them to me *without a word of comment*, implied a tacit acknowledgement that they were in substance correct ... Now of course I see that you had never read a report of Paul's speech, and that my letters to you and Paul gave you the first intimation of what had been put into his mouth. But now you will also see that this is a matter which must be attended to; that the statement about the action of some German Socialists during the war of 1870–71 – whether substantially true or

---

* Whether he had seen the interview in *Le Matin*, some part of which was quoted in an article in *Paris* published on 17 November – that is, some days before the Bordeaux speech – is more than doubtful, for he later insisted upon seeing the *Paris* article in full.

substantially false – ought never in any circumstances to have been made, *if it was made*, and ought to be clearly and unmistakably disavowed, *at once*, if it was not made; that so long as this report is not completely and absolutely disposed of, it will be absurd to expect our German friends to place any confidence in our French friends; and that the government and bourgeois in Germany will at once exploit this report against our German party in a way which is absolutely incalculable; if it leads to nothing more than a renewal of the old socialist law, *it will be lucky!*

So if Paul has been slandered, if he is prepared to declare publicly that he never said a word implying in any way the asssertion that German Socialists, *either in or out of Germany*, provided him with military statements, plans, news or anything of the kind for the use of the French Government during the war 1870–71 – then let him send me that declaration *at once* and in a registered letter. But it must be plain, without reservation or qualification of any kind, or it will be useless and may turn out worse than useless.

If that plain declaration cannot, for one reason or another, be made, then I see no other way out of the mess but that you and Paul come over here at once and discuss by word of mouth such matters as will evidently be fitted for that mode of settlement alone. Your presence will be almost as necessary as his, to moderate our hot heads and to give us the views of your cool head on the situation in France; and also to help us in finding 'the way out' by your feminine sagacity and *souplesse*, in cases where we male clumsy stick-in-the-muds are left in the dark. You see I am anxious, as anxious can be, to help Paul out of the difficulty if he has got himself into one; but the very first thing is to prevent the commission of fresh mistakes in case *one* has already been committed. To-morrow his election will be settled,* on Monday at latest I shall have the first reports from Germany on the effect of this thunderbolt from a clear sky ... A telegram 'coming to-night' would be agreeable, as we receive no letters on Sunday. And under all and any circumstances I do hope Paul will not take any public steps in a matter deeply concerning other people without first consulting these people; the slightest blunder might be fatal to himself, and he will see, I hope too, that this is no joking matter..."[125]

Of course the Lafargues did not come to London. Nor did Paul issue a *dementi*. But he mandated Laura to write stating that (1) he had said no more than was contained in his letter of 26 November:† namely, the need to prevent the French Republic from being annihilated by Bismarck's troops; (2) the Bordeaux meeting was private, closed to all but members of the *Parti ouvrier*, no reporters were admitted nor official minutes taken; (3) the incriminating expressions were the fabrications of a reporter, embroidering on an article written by Ranc;‡ the words used were: "I insisted on the continuation of the war because, according to information

---

* That is, by the Disqualifications Committee.

† See p. 645.

‡ Republican M.P. and former Communard to whom, when he was head of the Bordeaux local security organisation under Gambetta in 1871, Lafargue was alleged to have communicated military secrets. He was the author of the article in *Paris* already mentioned which included the words that during the Franco-Prussian war Lafargue "behaved and spoke like a patriot, a Frenchman".

at my disposal, Germany was not in a position to hold out much longer
... and there was no question of plans provided by or through the
mediation of Germans", explicitly denying that he had any communication whatsoever with Germany throughout the whole war.

Sending on to Bebel Laura's statement, Engels commented:

> "Well, we're over *that* hurdle ... But I don't mind telling you that all of us were in an
> almighty sweat here whilst this uncertainty lasted ... But what donkeys! As Tussy said
> only last Sunday: If such news about our opponents came *our* way, how we should have
> made use of it."[126]

Engels now apologised handsomely to Lafargue:

> "Following your formal repudiation of all the passages in the Bordeaux report of which
> I had a right to complain, it only remains for me to retract all the wounding words I
> used towards you, and formally to ask your pardon."[127]

He then explained once again that, receiving without comment a number
of newspaper reports in which all versions agreed, he could do no other
than accept them as true. With the greatest good luck trouble had been
avoided – "the opportunity for scandal trickled out and ran into the
sand,"[128] – albeit the consequences for the German party could have been,
and might yet be, serious indeed.

> "at best ... the re-introduction of the anti-Socialist Law ... the banning of our papers
> and meetings, and all our literature; and, in the event of war, the arrest of all leaders, at
> the very hour when we should have the greatest need of them ... Besides that, it was a
> matter of an element of mistrust being sown between the French and German workers
> just when their union was more essential than ever. Thanks to the stupidity of our
> enemies, these articles have not so far been taken up by the German press. But it is
> certain that the Embassy will have used them in its reports. And, although your
> disavowal, immediately transmitted to Berlin, has taken a tremendous load off my
> mind, there is always the danger that the German government will hold this charge in
> reserve, in order, when there is a war, to imprison our best people and smash them with
> an accusation doubly frightful at a time of chauvinist passions let loose..."[129]

On 7 December Lafargue's election was ratified, the Committee's
findings declared him eligible and were passed in the Chamber by 255
votes to 27. On the following day he made his maiden speech, which
included tabling a motion for a complete amnesty. This, too, was carried
and then he was off to lecture in Lille, Roubaix and Armentières and, in
the following week, to Givors, Lyons, Thizy and Tarare in the Rhône
department and Roanne in the Loire.

> "As I am a bit tired," he wrote, "I shall spend two days in Bordeaux and in Calais to

breathe some sea air and eat fish. If the weather were not so wet and if, above all, I could devote a few more days to resting, Laura would have come with me, for she, too, needs to rest after the period of excitement we have been through."[130]

In this mild understatement Lafargue's character is typified. He was no more in an "almighty sweat" over the possible results of his indiscretion than he was ever heard to murmur against his quite unjustified imprisonment. His nationwide speaking tours were part and parcel of his single-minded work for the *Parti ouvrier* of which he had been one of the main founders. He produced a number of pamphlets and articles which helped to educate a whole generation of French Marxists, and though in no way abashed by being dependent upon Engels for the best part of his life,* he tried to make a living by writing for journals outside the movement scholarly articles which sometimes earned Engels' praise and sometimes the far greater compliment of his detailed criticisms and revisions. In many ways Lafargue had not matured. Passionately zealous and sincere, but rather silly, he was honest to a fault with a vein of youthful naïvety that could land him in abysms of ineptitude. His high and serious intelligence lacked inbuilt warning signals: he simply had no means of knowing when he was off the rails. There was an endearing clownishness about Lafargue. As Marx had admitted, reluctantly, one could not but like him.

*   *   *

Lafargue was not Eleanor's only brother-in-law whose triumphs and misdeeds caused a stir just now.

Charles Longuet had not been an altogether satisfactory husband and his shortcomings as a father had wrung from poor Jenny in her last years the most forceful plaints that gentle creature ever uttered.† After her death he had largely cut loose from the English connection, there being no particular reason why he should have any dealings with a deceased wife's sister living abroad and some very good reasons why he should not. Eleanor's constant grievance that he never answered letters about the children, his reluctance to let them visit her, had caused her pain and anger for years. Yet the explanation was not far to seek. Longuet had thrown in his lot with Clemenceau and the Radicals; he had stood in their interest, successfully, as a Councillor for the Municipality of Paris and was thus politically out of sympathy with Eleanor. He could have had little

---

* Countless letters he wrote to Engels have never been published because they contain nothing but monotonous demands for money.
† See above, pp. 188–192.

wish to foster relations or advertise his family ties with his Marxist sister-in-law nor yet to expose his children to her influence.

Laura was another matter: she lived near Paris and, thanks to Engels, in sufficient ease to offer a holiday home to the boys and more prolonged hospitality to their little sister, Mémé. She could even take them to the seaside. Nor was she actively involved in politics. That is to say, once broken in, as Engels had predicted, she was now in harness and pulling her full weight as a translator, but her role was essentially that of a wife and *ménagère*, participating wholeheartedly in her husband's interests but not – as was Eleanor – in her own right. For the three children she had lost – who would now have been nearing their twenties – the Longuet youngsters, ranging from 14 to 8, were a compensation and a solace. Though a gulf divided them politically, Longuet and Lafargue avoided any open breach; indeed, they seem hardly ever to have mentioned each other* save in the most casual fashion or concerning family affairs.

Never having been a very serious *père de famille* Longuet's relationship with his motherless children appears to have been of that charming, affectionate and irresponsible nature which often produces the best results. A letter he wrote to his little daughter on Christmas Eve 1890 also suggests that he did not spend much time or celebrate festive occasions with his offspring, relying rather upon such communications.

"My dear little mouse," it runs,
  "You wrote me a very sweet letter about your cats ... I had hoped that you would also tell me about your little brothers who must remind you a bit of your cats to judge by their handwriting.
            Your papa,
              Charles."[131]

Now, at the age of 52, a widower for some eight years, he had found some consolation. This aroused what, on the face of things, was vastly exaggerated disapproval. It seems out of all reason for Engels to have spoken ill of the lady on the grounds that (a) she was not a virgin and (b) she lived in Caen, neither of which circumstance quite warrants his coarse and unmannerly comments.†

At the end of June Laura sent an account of the Longuet situation to Engels which he passed on to Eleanor. She was in a great taking as is clear from a letter of 6 July when she exploded:

---

* Paul did remark in November 1890, but without rancour, that he thought Longuet must be out of his mind not to stand down in the second ballot for a certain by-election.
† On 13 June 1891, he wrote to Laura: "If Longuet has regained his youth with Marie, has Marie also managed to regain her maidenhead?"[132]

"I haven't the heart to write about the children. It is so unspeakably disgusting."[133]

There was much talk about a "family council", suggesting that Longuet's new-found happiness was in some way so detrimental to the children's welfare that he could no longer be permitted to exercise paternal rights. Yet there was no hint that he proposed depriving them of a settled home, placing them in an orphanage, foisting upon them on undesirable step-mother or otherwise disturbing their young lives which, on any count, cannot have been the happiest on earth, in particular for the small girl who had never known a mother. Yet Engels found Longuet's conduct "worse than incomprehensible":

"It's a good job for poor Mémé that she is with you again," he wrote to Laura,

"For the rest you leave us in the dark ... And how are the boys getting on? What's to become of them while he is gallivanting at Caen? How about the Family Council? etc.? etc.?[134]

But

"after reading the legal clauses, we doubt whether the family council can do very much apart from appointing a tutor".[135]

Despite this, Eleanor was still anxious that some such *Conseil de famille*, should be set up as she wrote, in September, much troubled about the children.

"Where is poor little Mémé? Of course I know nothing of them all."[136]

Thus all that summer she worried away and one cannot but ask why. As it is generally a mistake when more solid evidence is wanting* to ignore the obvious, it could be surmised that Longuet, at no time popular with what in this context may properly be called "the Marxist family clique", fell into yet deeper disfavour by regularising his personal affairs, living more openly and more often away from home than before without adversely affecting his children at all.

One of Aveling's rare letters show that he and Eleanor went to France that winter, on their own business, it appears, but to stay with the Lafargues.

---

* Laura's letter with the "important tidings" concerning Longuet, written late in June, is known to have been in Eleanor's hands. Either it went the way of most of the correspondence she received (see above, fn.*, p. 572) or it was returned to the writer on Engels' death and destroyed in order not to cause pain to the young Longuets.

"Best of Lauras," he wrote on 29 December 1891,

"After all, we only want *one* room, with two beds. Only for a week or less. We hope to come on Monday next. It would have been jolly if we could have been days as well as nights with you, but never mind!

Ever so much love,

yours, Edward."[137]

No doubt, when they arrived on 4 January 1892, the Longuet affair was discussed up hill and down dale to reach some conclusion, for little more was heard of it beyond a comment from Eleanor when, a year later, she had received "a delightful letter from Jean":

"Poor lad! It does not need much reading between the lines to see what he really thinks of his father, nor what a miserable position he is in. At 17 one feels things so acutely!..."[*137a]

* * *

A rueful aspect of the relations between Engels and the Lafargues was that, while they lived upon his charity, they declined again and again his warm invitations to visit him. These were often extended as a means of

---

* Since writing the above, I have had the inestimable benefit of consulting Johnny Longuet's daughter-in-law, Madame Karl-Jean Longuet-Marx who so largely corroborates what was already written – on the basis of contemporary letters and commonsense interpretation – that no revision has been found necessary. However, though unable to give any more precise information, Madame Longuet-Marx has made some valuable comments which she has most kindly given me permission to quote.

She states that the children never had the slightest feeling of having been abandoned by their father and continues (I translate):

"Charles Longuet no doubt had the faults generally misprised by in-laws, however broad-minded: he was Bohemian, careless and unstable in practical matters (though not in his political convictions!). But he loved his children tenderly and they reciprocated the feeling. And my husband affirms that he always heard his father – Jean – and his uncles Edgar and Marcel, as also his aunt Jenny [Mémé] – speak with much gratitude and affection of this father, eternally harassed by financial cares, of course (but that is now a time-honoured family tradition!) though often misunderstood by his kin.

Charles Longuet never remarried ... Jean, Edgar and probably also Marcel were boarders at the Caen *lycée* and spent their Sundays with a Longuet cousin...

The children appear to have known nothing or to have forgotten about the Caen *liaison* and apparently did not suffer as a result of it ... The political differences of opinion between Longuet and Lafargue do not seem to have put their family relations in jeopardy...

In short, poor Charles Longuet, doubtlessly volatile in practical ways, cumbered by family and worries, seems to have lived from day to day, without involving his children in the rather unpleasant family troubles ... the fact that his own children and grandchildren were never drawn into these quarrels speaks ... in favour of Charles Longuet who managed to keep them out of this disagreeable family matter.

Jean had a real veneration for his aunt Eleanor who was of great importance to him and, in a small way, replaced his mother..."

help – offering Laura indefinite hospitality during Paul's imprisonment – or for practical reasons, as when he proposed a face-to-face discussion to sort out the Bordeaux muddle. But there were also occasions when, though he would not have deigned to confess it, Engels felt lonely and longed for the company of these closest reminders of Marx and the cherished past. On 20 December 1891 he wrote to Laura:

"Schorlemmer cannot come this Christmas, and Pumps and family ... are in the same position. So then it struck me: would it not be a bit of a change and rest for you and Paul to come over and take possession of the top front bedroom for a week or so? Surely you must want some interruption of that restless sort of life which Paul's election and its consequences have thrown you both into ... So I do hope you will make up your minds, and if Paul should have engagements up to Christmas you might come first, and he follow next week to spend at least the passage from '91 to '92 with us..."

He enclosed a cheque, "which I hope you will do me the kindness to accept", coupled with the hope "of soon learning that you are getting ready for the road..."[138]

This tacit appeal to those who knew, as did Laura and Paul, how greatly Engels loved a hearty Christmas and how dearly he prized, as old people do, the narrowing circle of his intimates, must have evoked a response. It did. Paul, to whom the letter had been addressed, wrote to say that his

"friends in France do not want to let me go, they feel that I belong to them and that I ought to devote all my Saturdays, Sundays and eve of holidays to giving lectures";

since his release he had been to eighteen towns and held twenty-three meetings.

Some dim awareness of its lack of grace and the disappointment this answer might cause seems to have penetrated Paul's consciousness for he ended with the words:

"A merry Christmas and a happy New year is what we wish you who have been so kind and so generous to us, to you who have been our good angel for so long."[139]

Laura for her part wrote on 28 December without so much as a reference to the invitation, the festive season or a New Year's greeting: she was "eternally packing and unpacking" for the itinerant M.P., "so great a favourite ... with the people", that "men and women ... everywhere welcome him with songs and flowers and kisses".*[140]

It struck neither of them apparently that at 71 Engels would perhaps be asking himself how many more merry Christmases he would see, nor that

---

* Engels later predicted that by making what he called the *tour de France* instead of attending to his parliamentary duties by speaking in the Chamber of Deputies, Paul was nursing constituencies for others. He was proved right: in the August 1893 elections Lafargue lost his seat.

they, of all people, could have revived for a brief moment, albeit at the sacrifice of the songs, the flowers and the kisses of ebullient strangers, the embers of his hearth.

It so happened that, within a few weeks, Engels was forced in his turn to reject an appeal from the Lafargues.

"Last night I had a letter from Paul," he wrote to Laura on 20 January 1892, "... in which he writes me to send you a cheque to pay the *propriétaire*. Now I should be only too glad to help you over this *mauvais quart d'heure*,* but the fact is, January and February are my worst months of the year, Christmas pumps one out almost completely, and I have next to nothing to come in before 1–5th March. In fact I do not yet see my way how to get over this awkward time myself, as besides the usual Christmas expenses, I had some considerable extra advance to make ... Tussy and Edward have mortgaged me with the proceeds of four agreements with Sonnenschein, on which I advanced them a pretty round sum which comes in from Sonnenschein only gradually and at rather uncertain times – certainly not now when I want it most. In fact I am hard up myself..."

Laura forwarded this letter to Paul, who was in Bordeaux, with the postscript:

"I shall not answer this until I hear from you. I should have thought you might have had 100 francs from your mother to keep things going till the 1st of next month. The landlady can wait till then..."[141]

That Engels' failure to stump up at this juncture was no form of rebuff nor unconscious retaliation is proved by a letter sent to his brother in Barmen a few days later asking whether some of his German stocks could be sold and another, written on the morrow, explaining that he would have none but paltry dividends coming in until March and could Hermann, his brother, send him £30 against his securities. The depleted state of his finances is therefore proved to have been absolutely genuine; nevertheless, that it coincided with the Lafargues' refusal to visit him does afford a little wry satisfaction.

In the following year Engels pressed Laura once again to come to London. It is easy to understand – though evidently not by the Lafargues – that he hoped his 72nd birthday would be celebrated among his oldest friends. The death of Schorlemmer, who had almost always been present at these anniversaries, had occurred in June and Engels himself had been incapacitated by rheumatism throughout the summer. On 3 November he wrote to Paul:

"I am beginning to go out again a bit ... And about time, as I feel that the lack of

---

* Bad patch.

exercise in the open air must come to an end. And when I am completely restored, we can, I hope, arrange things so that you and Laura give us the pleasure of spending a few weeks with us. We have so many things to discuss, and it is time Laura saw London again."[142]

The next day he was writing to Laura:

"...Now you ought to take seriously into consideration your impending visit to London; we have talked so much about it that at last it ought to be put into execution. We all should be glad to see you here again once more..."[142]

Sam Moore, though

"going to spend the greater part of his leave in the country with his parents and will be back in January,"[143]

was present for Engels' birthday, celebrated the day before, that being a Sunday, to prevent him tippling two days running, as he put it.

On 28 November Laura wrote a chatty long letter to Engels without a word of birthday greeting or congratulations.

"I had put off writing to you from day to day, in the hope of being able, at last to say something definite about crossing the Channel. But I don't yet know *when* and *whether* ... Paul will be able to get away. For my part, I have a new servant coming tomorrow ... and I could not possibly leave the house and my livestock in charge of a new comer ... Anyhow, if we cannot manage to run over for a week or ten days this year, we shall certainly do so next April and celebrate our *silver wedding* with you and yours *at home* ... Good-bye, my dearest General, and I wish I were giving you a warm kiss or two instead of sending you this cold black and white stuff..."[144]

Her consideration for the smaller livestock – the hens and dogs and rabbits – does credit to her feelings, and the advent of a new servant had naturally obliterated all memory of Engels' birthday, though not of her wedding anniversary five months ahead.

"It's a long time yet till April," wrote Engels on 5 December, "but if it cannot be managed otherwise, well then we must submit ... And maybe you could manage a few days with us in the meantime..."[145]

This hope was not fulfilled and he "submitted".

To pity Engels for these small unkindnesses would be to diminish him; but they do not add one cubit to the stature of the Lafargues.

"I am a Jewess," announced Eleanor Marx at the time of the Dreyfus affair,[146] undoing in four words her paternal grandfather's years of cogitation and eventual baptism.* It is already known that she told Max Beer she was the only member of her family to be "drawn to the Jewish people" and also that at the 1891 May Day demonstration her audience in Hyde Park had included many Jewish immigrants.

On 21 October 1890, shortly after her return from Halle, she had replied to an invitation:

> "Dear Comrade,
> I shall be very glad to speak at the meeting of Novbr. 1st, the more glad, that my Father was a Jew."[147]

That, too, rather neatly disposed of some controversial questions.

The tone of this letter suggests that this was Eleanor's first public appearance as a speaker among the Jewish socialists in the East End: a supposition to which their stage of development at this period lends colour.

The Great Assembly Hall in Mile End Road had been booked for this meeting, called to protest against the latest persecution of the Jews in Russia which had driven out thousands of terrorised victims, some of whom had newly reached these shores. Under pressure from the Chief Rabbi† and Samuel Montagu, M.P. for Whitechapel, the owner was coerced into refusing the use of his hall. The meeting was therefore held out of doors, on Mile End Waste, where

> "a strong resolution censuring the heads of the Anglo-Jewish community for procuring the boycott of the meeting was carried unanimously",

---

* There is no certainty but much circumstantial evidence that grandfather Marx formally adopted the Lutheran faith in the year of, or following, the birth of his son Karl who, on 26 August 1824, at the age of six, was baptised together with the one brother and five sisters then living.

† Dr. Hermann Adler, who had succeeded his father in June 1890.

according to the *Arbeter Fraint**[148] which said the motion had been inspired by Aveling and was supported in a speech by Eleanor.

It may seem astonishing that the powerful leaders of the Jewish community should have "intrigued" – as the *Arbeter Fraint* put it – to prevent a meeting which concerned the fate of their tormented brethren; yet, held under socialist auspices and on a Saturday, the Sabbath, it served to unite them as nothing else could.

It is generally accepted that the Montagues and Capulets were not on good terms but that is nothing to the feud between the Montagus and Rothschilds. While everyone knows that those old Veronese families behaved execrably when it came to intermarriage, some people have never quite got to the bottom of what it was they had against each other. But why the millionaire chiefs of Anglo-Jewry were at daggers drawn in the late 19th century is in no doubt at all: they were vying for the patronage of their needy co-religionists in the East End among whom there existed differences of opinion on how their faith should be practised in their new environment.

There were those who saw in an Anglicised form of Judaism a means to equip themselves – and even more their sons – for a prosperous life. They were catered for by Lord Rothschild,[†] the banker, with his United Synagogue and the blessing of the Chief Rabbi. But there were also many, lately emerged from the Pales of Settlement in Eastern Europe where their age-old Talmudic traditions alone had sustained them, who held that Anglicised Judaism as a form of worship was a deal more English than Jewish, lacking the fervour and piety of their accustomed rituals to which they obstinately clung. For them Mr. Samuel Montagu,[‡] the bullion broker, established the independent Federation of Minor Synagogues in 1888, the diminutive being dropped a couple of years later to indicate parity with the house of Rothschild.[§]

The rival patrons, however, were at one in upholding orthodoxy and abhorring apostasy. In their own circles, and for very good reasons, it had

---

* *The Worker's Friend*, a weekly Yiddish-language socialist paper started in 1888. Yiddish – derived from a High German dialect with an admixture of Hebrew, Russian, Polish and a smattering of words from the languages of the dispersal – is fairly comprehensible to some German speakers (and *vice versa*) though not readable since it is written in Hebrew characters. For the translation of items from published Yiddish sources I am indebted to Mr. William Fishman, Senior Research Fellow and Tutor in Labour Studies in the Department of Economics at Queen Mary College in the University of London.

† Raised to the peerage in 1885.

‡ Created baronet in 1894 and first Lord Swaythling 1907.

§ Only the charm of the absurd can justify noting here that Wilhelm ("Friedolin") Pieper, at one time Marx's unpaid secretary, incompetent coach to his young daughters and Eleanor's outclassed chess opponent (see above, pp. 12, 34) later became house tutor to a branch of the Rothschild family.

never done them a scrap of harm to be known as good Jews – whatever might be said behind their backs – and, conceivably, they may have been unaware that from Whitechapel to Stepney Green insuperable social barriers existed between the native Gentiles and the alien Jews, reinforced by an antisemitism that served only to make the immigrants huddle more closely together in self-sufficient communities.

That they should learn the English language and unlearn the customs of the ghetto was one thing and in their own best interests; that their religion itself should be held up to ridicule, mocked in Yiddish papers and flouted on the streets by slumdwelling Jews was quite another.

Mr. Samuel Montagu may possibly have chuckled to himself when, on the Sabbath of 16 March 1889, cohorts of these emancipated Israelites, headed by a German band, marched to Rothschild's Great Synagogue in Aldgate; but he must have laughed on the other side of his face when dinners and dances were organised for the Day of Atonement.

These offensive gestures were but the outward signs of a far more insidious pollution: that of socialism among the poorest Jews, to counteract which the powerful benefactors subsidised trade unions, one of which went so far as to make a modest proposal to limit the working day to twelve hours. Nonetheless, in August 1889 – coincident with the Dock Strike, though it may be remarked that at this period the Jewish immigrants had moved away from their point of arrival and settled in enclaves no nearer to the river than Cable Street* – 10,000 London tailoring workers in the East End came out for six weeks, causing 120 workshops to be closed by September, and then went back only under the misapprehension that they had won their demand for a 72-hour week.

On 4 January 1890 *Commonweal* reported that 4,000 Jewish workers had attended a meeting on Saturday, 28 December – this time in the Great Assembly Hall –

"under the auspices of the Hebrew Cabinetmakers' Society; Stick and Cane Dressers' Union; International Furriers' Society; Tailors' Machinists' Union; Tailors and Pressers' Union; Amalgamated Lasters' Society; United Cap-Makers' Society and International Journeymen Boot-finishers' Society",

which passed a resolution

"that this mass meeting of East London workers, recognising the great benefits that can be derived from a combination of all existing Unions, hereby inaugurates the

---

* The scene of the great clash between demonstrators, estimated at close upon 300,000, and the police – 6,000 on foot and the entire mounted force – mobilised to protect Oswald Mosley's Blackshirts on 4 October 1936.

'Federation of East London Labour Unions', and pledges itself to do its utmost to support and strengthen it."

Addressed by W. Wess* in Yiddish and by Tom Mann among other English speakers, the meeting, by its very nature, declared itself not only in favour of amalgamation with Gentile fellow-workers but also for assimilation with them.

On 19 April that year, under the heading "Strikes in Progress", the *People's Press* published an item on another mass meeting of Jewish workers, in the course of which it was stated that "some English workmen . . . refused to work in certain shops with Jewish workmen". An English speaker gave an assurance that "steps would be taken to stop such ill-natured action" and that, as trade unionists, "the Jews have acted most loyally". It was resolved to call a joint meeting of all trade unionists to combine in refusing to work for any masters who did not accede to the demand for improved conditions.

These two meetings took place at the period when the militancy of the Jewish workers was reaching its peak. To organise them was not easy. While the Jews had exceptionally strong family and community feeling, the concept of trade unionism was wholly extraneous: an attitude fortified by the example ever before their eyes of earlier Jewish immigrants who had become the very pillars of British capitalism, among the richest in the land as financiers, merchants and industrialists, glittering ornaments of the higher paid professions and those who had risen from dealing in rags to riches.

The majority of newly arrived immigrants had not even the experience of factory work, let alone the traditions of class struggle, to link them to the British movement with its history of Combination Laws, Tolpuddle Martyrs and Chartists. Jewish Marxists, few in number, were the disciples of Lavrov, the Russian, who was Eleanor's old friend, as he had been Marx's, and it was they who in 1885 founded the International Working Men's Club at 40 Berner Street† off the Commercial Road, to become known as the "Berner-Streeters". It was they, too, who recognised that in segregated communities and organisations they would remain helpless and who, defecting from the Synagogue, became aggressively anti-religious and anti-Zionist while retaining that intense consciousness of being Jewish – of having weathered all trials and all ages – which antisemitism everywhere perpetuates. They ran classes in Yiddish for adults to learn not only English but also politics and economics. Yet it must be admitted that they were planting the seeds of Marxism in virgin and somewhat

---

* Who had attended the Paris International Congress in 1889.
† Now Henriques Street.

stony soil inasmuch as the students were cut off from their own class in England not only by language, social customs and prejudice but, above all, by their means of livelihood. In the nature of things the Jewish immigrants, when not pedlars and individual traders as they had been in their countries of origin, became sweated labour: often outworkers in the clothing industry – sub-contracted by Savile Row tailors – employed for limitless hours either in their own cramped dwellings or on the fetid premises of some "master" who earned little if any more than they, which, in 1890, was rarely as much as £1 a week. The "masters" were thus as much victims as exploiters, a fact which the Chief Rabbi was not slow to point out when trouble was brewing, while he dismissed the very idea of a legal eight-hour day as beyond the dreams of Jewish dreamers.

Indeed, the history and conditions of the East End Jews of that period* make it clear that it needed enormous efforts and a quite exceptional capacity for adaptation to persuade them to combine at all as workers, most particularly in the East End itself where they had nothing in common with their neighbours except poverty. The most important advance was made when they began to call upon individual members of the British trade union and socialist movement for support. That is where Eleanor came in. Nor was she the only one to show that there were sympathisers and friends in organisations to which, the Jews as such, were unacceptable. The Fabians ignored them, they could have no truck with the antisemitic leaders of the SDF and found a footing only in the Socialist League, for the most part forging ties with its anarchist wing since there was a strong tendency towards anarchism among the Jewish socialists.

In June 1890 William Morris took the chair at the fifth anniversary meeting of the Berner Street Club, Henry Sparling and Cunninghame Graham being among the speakers who included only two foreigners: Stepniak and Kropotkin. The occasion was celebrated in song by the Hammersmith socialist choir.[149]

Eleanor's practical work in the East End during the most active years of the Jewish socialists was of relatively short duration for the two good reasons that, as shown, it was not until fairly late in the day that they fully recognised their need for outside help and because the best of them left England for America in the first half of the '90s. Those who remained, with certain exceptions, fell into the usual non-Marxist factions, while many individuals were absorbed into the general British trade union and labour movement to play an intelligent and valuable part.

However, in May 1891, when the anarchists had swallowed up the

---

* A splendid introduction is provided by Lloyd P. Gartner's *The Jewish Immigrant in England 1870–1914* (Allen & Unwin, 1960), upon which this chapter has leant heavily and gratefully.

Berner Street Club, its journal and its premises, so that its original membership had to forgather in each other's homes – a little socialist diaspora in the East End of London – a new paper was started, *Fraye Velt* (Free World) which, though it lasted but little more than eighteen months, had a more revolutionary policy than any of the earlier Yiddish papers and reflected the new approach to British Marxists.

One of the friends Eleanor made at this period was the young Israel Zangwill, nine years her junior, who had been educated from the age of 8 at the Spitalfields Free Jews' School where, when he was 16, he became a pupil teacher. He was to publish his first book of stories, *Children of the Ghetto*, in 1892 but before that he and Eleanor collaborated in a little *jeu d'esprit*.

Sir Walter Besant* had published an alternative ending to *A Doll's House* and, in January 1891, "Alec Nelson" had contributed one of his less lobbish essays in criticism on "The Ibsen Influence" in the *Playgoer's Review*, either or both of which may have put it into Eleanor's and Zangwill's heads to write *A Doll's House Repaired*, first printed in the March 1891 issue of *Time* and later issued by the authors as a 2d. 16-page pamphlet. They had "perfected the drainage of the 'Doll's House' ", they wrote in the preface, though "not found it necessary to seriously alter the building in order to carry out these sanitary repairs" that it might be "hospitably thrown open to the English public and . . . the most modest woman may enter its portals without bringing a blush to the cheek of the *Daily Telegraph*." With their aim of satisfying "clean, wholesome ideas" in keeping with "the English sense of morality and decency", they re-wrote the end of the third Act, restoring "what was evidently Ibsen's original idea": namely, that Nora, far from walking out, submitted to her re-education as a sweet and proper wife by being denied her husband's bed and access to her children. The parody is a little heavy-handed – more of Zangwill, it may be, than of Eleanor – but they obviously had huge fun writing it.

While there were many other occasions when Eleanor worked away quietly among the Jewish women in the East End, there were two on succeeding Saturdays (after she had returned at the end of August from her holiday in Norway) which were reported in the English socialist press. She was the main speaker at a meeting held in the Christ Church Hall, Hanbury Street, Spitalfields, under the auspices of the United Ladies Tailors' Association. In the same way as the German-American socialists had been urged to enter the ranks of the indigenous workers' movement and as Eleanor over and again emphasised that women must combine with

---

* (1836–1901), Annie's brother-in-law, who was responsible for organising the first volumes of the *Survey of London*, published after his death.

their organised menfolk, so here she appealed for unity between English and Jewish workers in the fight against the single enemy, capitalism.[150]

At about the same time *Justice*, now being edited by Quelch,* reported another meeting at the International Social Democratic Association's Hall, opened that January at 77 Christian Street, parallel with Berner Street off the Commercial Road† where

> "about 200 of our Jewish comrades gathered to partake of a substantial repast ... The company had gathered to celebrate the re-union in one society of two sections of Jewish workers and to welcome our friend Abraham Cahan, of New York."

Aveling took the chair and, despite the "babel of tongues", there was complete harmony

> "for the spirit of Socialism, which heals all divisions of nationalities, animated every man and woman present."[151]

Stepniak spoke in Russian, Cahan in Yiddish, others in English, but Lessner here and Eleanor at both her meetings made their speeches in German, though she was well aware that Yiddish was the common language of her audience. However, it is known that she now took steps to make good her deficiency.

At about this time – though from internal evidence it must have been in the late autumn or winter of whichever year – Eleanor was visited by a Russian lady, Zinaida Vengerova, who was in London to study early English literature. Introduced by Stepniak, she was invited to take tea at 65 Chancery Lane and, many years later, she set down her impressions "On the Daughter of Karl Marx".[152]

She described Eleanor's "intelligent, somewhat masculine features, with a big nose of the Jewish type"‡ and found her "rather plain though attractive," with the careworn lines that suffering had etched upon her countenance but "gentle and warm-hearted". Stepniak had told this lady a great deal about Eleanor who was on the friendliest terms with him and his wife, but he had not so much as mentioned Aveling – despite their known collaboration as playwrights – for whose presence the guest was not at all prepared. He appeared to her as

---

* Bax had taken over the editorship in June 1892 for a couple of months.

† It is pure chance that both these meeting-places should have invoked Christianity.

‡ Eleanor herself wrote: "I unfortunately only inherited my Father's nose (I used to tell him I could sue him for damages as his nose has distinctly entailed a loss upon me) and not his genius."[153]

"a typical Irishman ... His face was clever but one felt immediately in him the self-absorption of the Irish and there was something repulsive about it..."*

This, and some other comments, must be attributed to information which Vengerova later gleaned, for there was nothing typically Irish about Aveling — nor indeed about the characteristics she described — that a citizen of these islands would have detected and the writer admits that she

"did not know at the time when I went to see them that this outstanding and talented Irishman ... did not enjoy any respect in his own circle and that his private life was very murky," nor that "Eleanor's marriage was very unhappy".

Nevertheless, it would be doing Vengerova a wrong to suggest that she was influenced by subsequent knowledge when she wrote that she had found "the atmosphere in their house oppressive", for she added that it made a "painful impression" upon her, "even though I could not explain to myself at the time why that should be so".

In view of Aveling's notorious borrowing, which has given rise to the notion that he indulged an extravagant way of life,† it is interesting that Vengerova recalled that domestic interior as drab and seedy, the small parlour into which she was shown furnished in "the usual boringly philistine" taste of the period and she certainly could not have derived from any but her own feelings the sense that this "commonplace setting" was in marked contrast to the life and personality of her hostess "who seemed to be here by accident".

They talked of Eleanor's labours at the British Museum where Vengerova had frequently seen her surrounded by piles of books and had assumed she was engaged upon some major work. Eleanor explained that her occupation was far less exalted: she was merely plundering published material for use by other writers, a modest if not debased activity without so much as original research to recommend it though, for her own pleasure, she was studying and writing on Chaucer, fascinated by "the as yet unfused Anglo-Saxon and Norman elements" of his language. She had "a special interest in philology ... in transition periods, and also in folk dialects".

---

* As Aveling is chiefly remembered for his bad character, could this be racial prejudice? Even today there are those Russians who persist in calling him an Irishman (e.g. see *Die Töchter von Marx* by Olga Vorobyova and Irma Sinelnikova, translated by Waldemar Dölle. Dietz, Berlin 1963, p. 145), as also in misdating his birth and that of his adherence to the socialist movement (e.g. see *For All Time and All Men* by A. Uroyeva, translated by David Fidlon. Progress Publishers, Moscow, 1969, p. 221).

† "utterly unscrupulous about the way in which he satisfied his desires, which were of none too frugal a nature. The best was good enough for him — at no matter whose expense", wrote H. W. Lee.[154]

The reminiscence then goes into direct quotation:

" 'My latest linguistic acquisition is Yiddish,' she said. 'I even deliver lectures in Yiddish and easily distort German grammar so that my audience should understand me better.' "

The Russian lady was surprised that

"in enlightened England there still existed the language of the Jewish ghetto. But Eleanor explained to me that she was active among the Jewish working women in Whitechapel, and that in the interests of socialist propaganda it was more sensible for her to learn Yiddish than to wait for the ignorant masses of immigrants from Eastern Europe to become Anglicised.

'Besides, the Jewish language is akin to my blood,' she said. 'In our family it is thought that I am like my paternal grandmother, who was the wife of a learned Rabbi.' "*

The Russian writer continues:

"One somehow felt from these words that Eleanor Marx set greater store on the heritage of the spiritual life of her forefathers, the Jewish Rabbis, than on the pure class arrogance of the aristocratic family to which her mother belonged."†

One small touch in Vengerova's recollections brings Eleanor to life in a vivid and familiar way:

"her two black cats with smooth shining fur, bright eyes and crimson ribbons round their necks ... were creatures of a special kind ... and they seemed, so to speak, the guardians of her home."

Eleanor, as she might have done when a little girl, introduced them as "my friends":

"and the smile that lit up her eyes gave a glimpse into a tender interior world under the mask of care that life had imposed on her face".

Even allowing for the passage of years and the distortion of hindsight,

---

* There was obviously a misunderstanding here. Eleanor's paternal grandmother, *née* Henriette Pressburg, was the *daughter* of a rabbi – out of respect for whose feelings she postponed her baptism until the year 1825 – but she was, of course, married to Karl's father, Heinrich Marx, the lawyer.

† This unkind cut at humble Mrs. Marx may be explained by the vogue for such phraseology at the time – the 1920s – when Vengerova was writing (though it cannot be said that the notion of a spiritual heritage was much *à la mode*). While among the Argyll-Westphalen forbears there may have been individuals given to "pure class arrogance", it left not the faintest trace upon Eleanor's mother nor yet upon her uncle Edgar: the only members of that family she ever knew.

this account presents not only a picture of Eleanor in her later thirties through the eyes of an observant stranger but also direct evidence of her having learnt Yiddish and her involvement with the East End Jews.

Another aspect is shown by one of their outstanding leaders of the time: Morris Vinchevsky (*né* Benzion Novochovits), who emigrated to London in 1879 at the age of 23, expelled from Germany under the Anti-Socialist Law. In 1918 he wrote a study of Eleanor for the New York journal *Tzukunft* (The Future) incorporated later (1927) in his *Collected Works*.

Vinchevsky was a journalist and poet as well as a devoted socialist who, in 1884, brought out the first Yiddish socialist journal in London, *Der Poilisher Yidel* (The Little Polish Jew) whose name was shortly changed to *Die Tsukunft*.* When that paper, under the influence of his partner, turned towards Zionism, Vinchevsky started the *Arbeter Fraint*, published from the Berner Street premises.

Whilst others left for America too soon to be considered little more than transmigrants, Vinchevsky spent 16 years in England. During the last few of these he often found himself on the same platforms and demonstrations as Eleanor though they had no close personal acquaintance until, in August 1893, he was one of the sixty-five British delegates to the International Congress in Zurich. Then, whether by chance or Eleanor's contrivance, he travelled in the same railway compartment with her and Aveling and they "became more intimately befriended than ever before". Aveling, who, he believed, was present as the *Daily Chronicle* reporter,† joined in their discussions and Vinchevsky, unlike anyone before or since, described him as "joyous and lively". But it was Eleanor, "always laughing and joking" on the journey, who took special trouble to ensure that this rather self-consciously Jewish delegate – though there were at least a dozen other Jews at the Congress – was not neglected. Immediately upon arrival in Zurich she was so surrounded by her German friends that, characteristically, Vinchevsky felt "she had little time for me". This proved quite untrue. She sought him out and gave him the opportunity to tell her that he was there to represent eight trade unions with some 600 Jewish members. He thought that many good socialists were unaware that there existed any such being as a Jewish worker: "that is, a Jew engaged in manual labour, let alone organised Jewish workers". He saw little hope of giving this information to the Congress since the large British delegation at its regular morning sessions assigned the speakers for the day and, being largely composed of what he called "moderates", was unlikely to select him who was among "the most extreme radicals".

---

* As *Tzukunft*. The difference in spelling is that between the English and the American transliteration of Yiddish at that time.
† He was in fact also a delegate from the Gasworkers' Union.

" 'You know what, Winchevsky'," he reported Eleanor as saying, " 'you write down what you have just told me, the names of your unions and the number of workers and as translator I will somehow smuggle this into the Congress.' An hour later, at the Congress session she announced in three languages (German, French and English) that real Jewish workers organised in eight unions had their representative present ... This information was received in each language with tumultuous applause. Eleanor's face was radiant with pride."

On the afternoon of the inaugural session of the Congress there was an impressive parade through the streets of Zurich.* Vinchevsky watched it assemble, unsure, as might have been expected, where, if at all, he belonged in the ranks now lining up four abreast.

"Eleanor ran up to me in great haste," he wrote. "She placed me next to herself with Will Thorne on one side and Edward on the other.

'We Jews must stick together,' she said.

And together we remained and we made plans. I was to tell the Jewish workers who her father was and she would give me material no one else has."†

Nothing came of these plans, for in 1894 he left England for good and never saw Eleanor again.

There is little in common between Vinchevsky's merry, chattering, radiant Eleanor and the sombre figure who received Vengerova in Chancery Lane. Both descriptions were recollected in tranquillity and based upon a single encounter; yet each in its way has the afterglow of that warmth Eleanor never failed to kindle.

With the departure of such men as Vinchevsky, socialist activity

---

* Will Thorne described it as "one of the most extraordinary demonstrations that I have ever seen ... Thousands of young children, in snow-white dresses, marched with men and women through the town. The procession was led by excellent brass bands, and the line was made gay with gaily coloured banners on which were inscribed various mottoes."[135]

† Earlier, in 1908 – and thus 15 rather than 25 years after the event – Vinchevsky described the occasion in "A Persevering Woman" (not Eleanor), one of his short tales published as *Stories of Struggle*[156] in the preface to which he vouches for the truth of every incident. There the passage reads: "...I am to join those others, but I do not seem to realize the fact. I feel more lost than Alice ever felt in Wonderland. I stand there and dream.

Presently there is a gentle tap at my shoulder. I am startled at first, but the surprise turns out to be a very pleasant one. There is a familiar sound in the words:

'Say, Edward and Will Thorne are to bring up the rear as marshals. Let us two march between them. We Jews ought to stick together.

It was poor Eleanor Marx who spoke...

We got into line. She was talking all the time, now and then taking notice of a jest on the part of her husband, sometimes answering a question put to her by Thorne, but allotting to me most of her attention, as I had touched upon a topic always near to her heart: the life of her father – of Karl Marx, whose daughter she not only was, but deserved to be..." In this version, Aveling is not "joyous and lively" at all but, more in keeping with received opinion, "the cause of her [Eleanor's] untimely death".

among the Jews declined, but when the Cardiff TUC of 1895 approved a resolution to control immigration, a mass protest meeting was called on 7 December by ten London Jewish unions at which Aveling took the chair. Among the speakers were Burrows, Wess, Stepniak, Kropotkin, trade union leaders both Gentile and Jewish, and "Mrs. Eleanor Marx", billed thus with the simple description "Karl Marx's daughter". Speeches would be in English and Yiddish, announced the leaflet* calling the meeting:

"Jews!
   The English anti-Semites have come to the point where the English workers' organisation calls on the government to close England's doors to the poor alien, that is, in the main, to the Jew. You must no longer keep silent. You must come in your thousands to the meeting in the Great Assembly Hall..."

A few weeks before, she and Aveling had found their last home and Eleanor wrote to Laura;

"The house we are about to buy ... (Edward swears this is my only reason for wanting it) is in JEWS Walk, Sydenham..."[157]

They moved in mid-December and, as she made her preparations, Eleanor told her sister:

"I am Jewishly proud of my house in Jew's Walk."[158]

Poor Eleanor. Her pride was touching but, alas, ill-founded. Local archivists and historians have established that, though many picturesque theories have been advanced for the derivation of the street name – the most popular attributing it to its proximity to the Crystal Palace many of whose visiting musicians were Jewish – Jew's Walk appears as an open road crossing Sydenham Common on a map of 1833 – long before the advent of the Crystal Palace – and in all probability it was a local, South London corruption of "Doo's Wharf". Doo is an ancient place-name in Kent – formerly the county in which that part of Lewisham was – and such a wharf existed on the short-lived canal cut through Sydenham where now the railway runs.[159] But whether or not she was to live – and die – in a street whose name was owed purely to mispronunciation, Eleanor's own pronouncement was clear and uncompromising: "I am a Jewess".

---

* Printed in Yiddish.

Without question the most important development in the British working-class movement in the years 1892–3 was the founding of the Independent Labour Party. Not that it played a vital part in Eleanor's affairs. For too long she had charted her own course, attending – in both those years – every Executive meeting of the Gasworkers without fail and responding, whenever physically possible to every invitation to speak, from no matter what quarter. Her reputation as an expositor of Marxism with its application to the specific character and needs of her audience was now firmly established and, while still a member of the Bloomsbury Socialist Society, she knew that her real effectiveness, and thereby her deepest satisfaction, lay in addressing any group of men and women who spontaneously called for her.

However, she was present at the opening Conference of the ILP, held at Bradford on 13 and 14 January 1893. She was merely a visitor, but Aveling went as the delegate from both the Bloomsbury Socialists and the Legal Eight Hours and International Labour League. He was elected to the Executive, to the committee of six assigned to draft the new Party's programme and it was he who presented its Report to the Conference.

At the start Aveling, together with Bernard Shaw and a second Fabian were asked to retire while the Standing Orders Committee considered their position. The vote went in their favour, Aveling's credentials being unanimously accepted, those of the two Fabians by a narrow majority. It was known that Aveling would pledge the unqualified co-operation of the bodies he represented, while Shaw on behalf of the Fabian Society declined to sink its identity in any federated party: a course, he correctly predicted, that the SDF would also take.*

Another important loss was that of Robert Blatchford, the most popular of all socialist propagandists, 750,000 copies of whose pamphlet *Merrie England* had been sold upon its first appearance in 1892. He dissociated himself and his Clarion groups from a party which rejected the wildly unrealistic proposition that its members should abstain from voting for any candidate nominated by the Liberals – however radical the

---

* At the SDF Annual Conference an emergency resolution to support the new party – not yet formally constituted – was defeated by an amendment "to preserve an attitude of benevolent neutrality towards the Independent Labour Party".[160]

individual – or the Conservatives: a policy which, at that stage, would have meant disfranchising adherents to the ILP in most constituencies.

This, known as the "Fourth Clause", which was to be debated again and again, elicited one of Aveling's most telling political articles, published in the *Clarion* of 18 March 1892.*

"... Unlike Hardie," he wrote, "I had not reserved my opinion ... until I came to Bradford. My mind was made up on the subject, which is by no manner of means the same thing as saying that one is cocksure. That making up of my mind and of the minds of those that instructed me was due largely to the fact that we had learnt lessons from the Communist Manifesto of 1848 ... Now the last section of the Manifesto is headed 'Position of the Communists in relation to the various opposition parties ... whilst in the different countries the actual political relations have changed since 1848, the general principle of taking part in political struggles, and throwing weight to this side or to that in the interests of the working class only, still holds.' "†

Aveling then cited the passages which referred to fighting for the immediate aims while taking care of the future interests of the working class and the examples of tactics suited to each country in the circumstances of the time.

"... The chief spokesman for the Fourth Clause – Blatchford ... regards any voting by us for candidates other than our very own people as a danger to the independence of the Party. It would be unjust to deny that there is that possibility of a danger ... An individual can be bought. An independent party if it can be bought as a whole, is clearly unworthy of its name, is not worth buying, and had better perform for itself a happy despatch ...

If Blatchford can't get a candidate of his own choice, he desires not to vote at all ... This seems to me individualism run rampant ... in this country at present the choice of the party might have to be made between two men, neither of whom was whole and sole independent labour. But if one of them was, e.g. three-quarters or even half or even a smaller fraction independent labour surely the party would do wisely and well in advising its members of the two evils to choose the less ... if the 'bad candidate' were, before election, in favour of the good bill, or was even pledged himself to introduce it, and if the other man was not, and no ILP candidate was on hand, where is the rhyme or reason of cutting off your nose to spite your face, and sulking in your tents because you can't get absolute victory out and out? ...

Blatchford does well to be angry at the idea of the ILP men selling their votes, being nobbled, attempting to intrigue, or to ally themselves with either of the old parties ... If a man is base enough to sell himself to either of the old parties, is it likely that any amount of Congress resolutions or party ties will check him in his vile career? ... We must proclaim openly and in the light of day, and most clearly of all to the particular party with whom for the time being we may vote, our real reasons for doing this. We can afford to wear our political hearts on our sleeves ... This makes it imperative that, in season and out of season, with a most damnable iteration, every speaker, writer,

---

* As one of a series under the general title "The Fourth Clause".
† The last sentence was a quotation from the preface to the 1872 edition.

debater, arguer in private, of the ILP, should insist upon the fact that this party is equally antagonistic to Tory and Radical . . .

Education by all manner of means. But organisation also, with, for its special immediate end, the formation of an Independent Labour Party pledged, wherever it is possible to make the best use of its voting power, even the use of abstention, in the interests alone of the party. We can do all this without any compromise, without any fear, without any lack of resolution. But to throw over the principle and practice recommended . . . of leaving the local party to decide . . . where no ILP candidate runs whether the labour vote should be cast on this particular man, or on that, or on none at all, would be, I think, wrong in principle, wrong in tactics, and impossible in execution."

If Joseph Burgess of the *Workmen's Times* was the John the Baptist of the ILP, Keir Hardie was certainly its Messiah. As Margaret Cole has said: "it was his creation and his darling till the day of his death".[161]

Some of the resolutions passed at its first conference have a remarkably modern ring, such as that there should be provision for the sick, disabled, aged, widows and orphans, the funds for which were to be raised by a tax upon unearned increment and that there should be free, secular education up to and including the universities. Unlike the SDF, the new party attributed the greatest importance to the trade unions as the mass organisations of the working class; unlike the Fabians, it was led by and largely composed of workers and, moreover, those from the north and the large industrial regions rather than London; unlike Morris and his followers among the old Socialist Leaguers, it was pledged to contest parliamentary and local government elections wherever possible; and, unlike the Parliamentary Committee of the TUC, it was sworn to an out-and-out collectivist programme.

This, indeed, was a breakthrough. Yet, from the start, the ILP had inherent weaknesses, not the least of which lay in Keir Hardie himself, whose socialism was inspired by a Methodist fervour but had absolutely no basis of scientific theory and some contempt for it.*

With the defects of its virtues, the ILP could neither supplant nor unify the existing socialist bodies in Britain: it added yet another, though by no means the most negligible. A more fortuitous circumstance was that it had failed to take the tide of New Unionism at the flood. It came into being at the end of the great economic depression, at a time when not only were the employers counter-attacking in strength but the "Old"

---

* He was reported as saying from the Chair at this first conference: "it was neither a programme nor a constitution, but the expression of a great principle – the determination of the workers to be the arbiters of their own destiny. There were not at that meeting any of the great ones nor the learned ones amongst the sons of men, and therein lies the hope of the Labour movement."[162] It sounds very good. Hardie was, in a small way, standing Hyndman on his head, as Marx had stood Hegel, with this difference: no new philosophy resulted from the capsizal.

Unions, taking advantage of the ebb, vigorously reasserted themselves. The Parliamentary Committee decided at the 1892 (Glasgow) TUC to recognise *"only bona fide working men,* and then only those who are organised in unions".*[163]

It was, in short, an unpropitious moment to launch a new Party of this type and the *Report from Great Britain and Ireland,* almost certainly of Eleanor's drafting, presented to the Zurich Congress in the name of the Gasworkers, the Legal Eight Hours and International Labour League, the Bloomsbury Socialist Society and the Battersea Labour League, gave a sober assessment of the position:

> "We are still not able to speak in the name of a British Labour Party. Such a party, in the sense of an absolute unity of programme and method, does not yet exist here ... But it has also to be noted that a new organisation, the Independent Labour Party, has been formed ... and is evidence that the class-consciousness of the workers is passing from the dim to the clear stage."

Of the 115 delegates who had come together at Bradford,

> "91 ... represented branches which had already been formed provisionally of the Independent Labour Party. The other 24 came from various organisations pledged to political independence in the interests of labour ... it was decided by the Conference that its object 'shall be to secure the collective ownership of all the means of production, distribution and exchange'. The party has already a large number of adherents and branches, especially in the north and midlands of England, and is endeavouring, by education and organisation, to prepare for the running and supporting, at all kinds of elections, candidates pledged to the objects of the Independent Labour Party, and entirely apart from either of the old political parties ... there is more than one organisation in this country working along the same lines but not necessarily affiliated to the new organisation ... all of which have always recognised the necessity of a distinct Party ... It is hoped that ultimately all the bodies having the common end in view may be united into one great, powerful, irresistible British Labour Party."[164]

Before the embryo ILP had quickened, in May 1892, Eleanor had gone at the request of the German Party† to talk to German miners working in Ayrshire. Unaccustomed to British ways, and in particular those of infinitely more astute managers than in their own pits; not speaking English, let alone Scots, these Germans had earned an unenviable reputation for undercutting wages and as scabs. This had caused an ugly

---

* Three years later, at the Cardiff TUC of 1895, new Standing Orders were arbitrarily decreed whereby Trades Councils were excluded as also unionists not actually working at their trade – making even Keir Hardie ineligible – and the "block vote" was introduced, favouring the officials of large unions with their "benevolent society" Bourbonism and ingrained caution.

† Bebel and Singer, in London for a fortnight at the end of that month, had given her this mission.

situation and, as Eleanor now explained, was harming not only the local Ayrshire Federal Union but, more gravely, the whole international miners' movement. She was willing to act as an intermediary if they cared to write to her in German, but the main things were for them to learn the language and to be on their guard against being exploited as foreign labour. Above all, they should keep in regular, daily, hourly touch with their stalwart Scottish fellow workers to avoid any further misunderstandings.

> "...it wasn't a holiday by any means," Eleanor wrote to Laura. "I left ... on the Thursday evening at 9.15; reached Cumnock about 9 a.m., was hard at work all day, caught the 9.15 on the Friday evening and was back in London considerably the worse for wear, at 8 on Saturday morning."[165]

Ten days later, at the beginning of June 1892, she was off to the (3rd) Annual Conference of the Gasworkers in Plymouth, where it was decided that the union should stand its own candidates in parliamentary and local elections, while she and Thorne were delegated to attend the Zurich Congress in the following year.

In the meantime she had written a letter published in the Berlin *Sozialpolitische Centralblatt*.

> "The details I give them about the Engineers' strike ..." she wrote to Laura, "are a piece of 'inside' history, & have not been published anywhere else. I know the facts from a delegate of the Tyneside engineers* to the Executive of my Union. He complained that these facts were carefully suppressed in all papers. You see, our 'unskilled men' being employed as 'labourers' in every trade, we get to hear all the facts about *all* the skilled trades. And very interesting some of them are!"[165]

Engels wrote to tell Kautsky that the Gasworkers had given a lead and the best possible example to the "Old" Unions by refusing to admit a Liberal – albeit one who had contributed in a small way to their funds – since neither he nor any other representative of his party was welcome as an "honorary guest" to their councils. Back in London on 9 June, Eleanor was just in time to attend the last and most important day of the (3rd) International Miners' Congress where delegates from five countries, representing close upon a million workers, were in session.

> "It was real bad luck that Tussy wasn't there to translate and advise",

wrote Engels. These functions had been taken on by Julius Motteler,

---

* 5,000 engineers had been locked out on the Tyne over a demarcation dispute. "The employers had been quick to take advantage of the rivalry between skilled workers."[166]

"who misunderstood all the English and French, who has no relations with these people and knows nobody, but had to make out that he knew and understood everything."[167]

The General Election of early July 1892, in which nine working men won seats, was "a tremendous victory for the Socialist movement". Thus wrote Eleanor and Aveling in an article, dated 17 July, for the *Neue Zeit*. For the first time, they said, it had become as clear as daylight and more or less recognised that the political interests of the workers as a class differed intrinsically from those of both the old political parties: that they expected as little from the one as from the other. This was the direct result of the "New Unionism" which was in essence, if sometimes not consciously, a socialist movement. Since no Workers' Party as such existed, the genuine workers' candidates had not stood on a clearly defined or common programme, each differing on matters of detail though agreeing on certain cardinal points. By "genuine" workers' candidates, they explained, they did not mean the hangers-on of the Liberals who, working-class though they might be, were no better than the political jobbers with whom they had thrown in their lot. They then analysed the position of all those who had stood and won – or lost – seats.*[168]

Of the "genuine" workers' candidates, Keir Hardie was elected with a 1,200 majority in South West Ham – a seat he held until 1895 – John Burns in Battersea with a majority of 1,600 – in both of which constituencies the Liberal had stood down – while in Middlesbrough J. Havelock Wilson – the Secretary of the Sailors and Firemen's Union who was also the Chairman of the Parliamentary Committee at the 1892 TUC – had beaten both his Liberal and Tory opponents by a narrow margin.

Wilson, though something of a careerist, said Engels, was "deeply engaged and mortaged to *New* Unionism"; thus, in the most hazardous of the three contests, his was no hollow victory. "The *new* working-class movement enters Parliament triumphantly," Engels wrote to Laura on 7 July when these results had been announced.

"The election has done already what I maintained was all we had a right to expect from it: give fair and unmistakable warning to the Liberals that the *Independent Working Men's Party* was approaching, that it cast its shadow before it, and that this was to be the last general election carried on between two parties only, the Ins and the Outs."[170]

---

* To Engels' annoyance, the article was cut, omitting the appraisal of the SDF and the Fabians which, in his view, was absolutely essential to a comprehensive view. He sent the deleted passages to Bebel.[169]

It was, indeed these triumphs small in number but significant in portent, that heralded Burgess's campaign in the *Workmen's Times* to form the ILP.

Eleanor, too, wrote to Laura about the elections:

> "Some of the internal history of this campaign has been very funny. What could be made public at present Edward and I . . . have sent to the *Neue Zeit*. One of the funniest things though we could not mention there, but here it is for you. Champion – of all people! – wrote and offered to get Edward all the money necessary if he cared to 'run' anywhere!!! Of course Edward replied that first of all he had no desire to run, and secondly that he cd. only take money through a Committee – shd. he ever stand – of his constituents, but nothing privately. Of course everyone has not been so scrupulous. Other offers – direct or indirect – were made Edward from other quarters too."[171]

In the same letter, Eleanor referred to the Glassworkers' Congress which, she said,

> "Kept me at it all one week translating and keeping a verbatim report, and that Report I am now copying from the shorthand on to the machine."*

At this juncture it was revealed how close she had grown to Freddy Demuth who confided in her all his troubles: things he did not "want anyone to know – particularly not Engels". The Marx heirs, including Longuet as one of the trustees for Jenny's children, had assumed some financial responsibility for Freddy who was now in difficulties which could not be resolved without the consent of all parties, in particular that of Longuet under cover of whose trusteeship the subventions to Freddy were made. He and Eleanor wrote

> "again and again to Longuet. But he does not even *answer* the letters and so Freddy begged me to try if Paul could not in some way put the matter before the trustees."

The situation was urgent and desperate. On deserting him Freddy's wife had taken not only most of his possessions but all his money, some of which he held in custody as a benefit fund for his fellow-workers to whom he had to account on 30 July.† With but four days to go, Eleanor wrote that Aveling hoped "to get something for a little operetta (don't be

---

* This is Eleanor's first reference to having learnt shorthand. It may be recalled that as Minute Secretary at the Socialist League Conference seven years earlier she had been a complete novice, fearful of missing out anything said. That she now combined the roles of interpreter, shorthand-writer and typist is rather impressive even today.

† See above, pp. 241.

alarmed – he was only responsible for the words) today or tomorrow"* and that "with what Freddy has it will be all right".

Laura had generously sent a money order for £50 but, with time running out, Eleanor wrote an anxious postscript:

> "My dear. You do not say to whom the Order is made out. I thought it would probably be to me so as to save Freddy the trouble: but they say not. Will you write & say in whose name it is made out" –

adding, in pencil, underlined: *"exactly"*.[172]

Hard upon the heels of this personal preoccupation, with its irresistible claims upon her, both out of loving concern for Freddy and a fellow-feeling for those who never have the ready cash when it is most needed for honourable purposes, came a request from the organising committee of the Zurich Congress for a rush of work.

This hampered her preparations for going to Norway on a much needed holiday. Even while there she found herself obliged to answer a letter from one of her Italian friends – "Carissima Dott. Anna" (Kulishov), the wife of Filippo Turati – about Zurich Congress matters which, she thought, should have been communicated to Engels in her absence since she was now unable to consult him. Her letter was dated 21 August 1892 from Faleide† and, in one short sentence, testified that the respite, however brief, held enchantment for her:

> "We are in Norway," she said, "– and your beautiful Italy can hardly be more beautiful!"[173]

---

* "A Hundred Years Ago", with music by Henry Wood; a one-act piece produced together with another, "Faithful James" – both written by Alec Nelson in collaboration with B. C. Stephenson – at the Royalty Theatre on 16 July 1892.
† Eleanor wrote "Faleyde". This was the small place on the Nordfjord, served by a steamer route to Visnes and less frequented in her day than it became a decade later.

The fifth anniversary of Bloody Sunday – also a Sunday, 13 November 1892 – was marked by a vast demonstration in Trafalgar Square.* There were six separate platforms: three on the plinths of the Column, with Hyndman presiding over that which faced the Square, and three on the balustrades. Eleanor spoke from the west plinth – platform two – together with John Burns and members of both the London Trades Council and the LCC.

As the *Clarion* reporter found as he mingled with the crowd "in the outer circle amongst the curious and indifferent spectators" round Eleanor's platform, there was some derision and hostility.

> "The masculine oratory of Mrs. Eleanor Marx Aveling, however, commanded attention," he went on, "although two gentlemen (?) who throughout had indulged in a running commentary of contemptuous sneers did not cease their remarks. And when Mrs. Aveling remarked that the starving children of poorly-paid factory workers were crying for bread, one of these persons observed contemptuously, 'And always will be'."†174

But for those who had not come – or remained – to scoff, it was a tremendous success; the demonstrators no fewer and from even more varied organisations than those who, in pitched battles, had vainly tried to capture the Square in 1887. This time the police were

> "acting as the guardians instead of as breakers of the public peace, a most convincing proof that rioting, disorders and disturbances at public meetings are, in the great majority of cases, caused by the tyrannical and absurd misuse of police and military

---

* Variously estimated at anything from 30,000 to 150,000, though the latter explicitly included onlookers as well as participants and it is notoriously difficult to count heads – even for the police, let alone journalists – in an open space with surrounding areas loosely or closely packed.
† When Vengerova, the Russian visitor, described Eleanor's features and her oratory as "masculine" this indicated surprise rather than dispraise: it did not mean mannish. As males were not expected to look charming so females were not supposed to excel in rational discourse. Eleanor was handsome, even beautiful in a touching way – though certainly not pretty – with, in womanhood, the honest eyes and wide, good-humoured mouth of the little girl seen in the very first photograph of her that exists.

forces by the classes who fear more than anything else the growing organised power of the workers."[175]

Two days before the Trafalgar Square demonstration Eleanor had at last answered after some delay an invitation from William Diack, the Secretary of the Aberdeen Socialist Society.*

"...I have been trying to see how I am fixed for the next weeks and months," she wrote. "It will be a great delight to me to speak at Aberdeen – I have never addressed a Scotch audience, and save for a flying visit to Cumnock have never been in Scotland. If your Glasgow and Edinburgh comrades want me also I should be glad to go – only it would all have to be done in as short a time as possible, as I can't be away long from my work here. And, of course, you must think if you can manage the expense – for I am too poor to afford my expenses." (Small wonder she had sympathised with Freddy Demuth.) "I could come on the 27th November, if you can fit in the Edinburgh and Glasgow dates within a day or so either side of this. I do not wish – if I can possibly help it – to miss the Executive of my Union which meets on Wednesdays. If the 27th will not do, I fear it will have to be after Christmas..."[176]

After Christmas it was to be. Indeed, she did not fulfil this engagement until 22 January 1893 when, following the ILP Conference in Bradford, she and Aveling spent four days on a speaking tour of the Black Country before Eleanor went on alone to Edinburgh, addressed the Fabian Society at the Iron Hall on the Working Class Movement Abroad† and arrived in Aberdeen on the next day, a Sunday, to give two lectures.

Diack has left an account of her visit.

"Eleanor Marx, when I first met her, was still in the heyday of life; and I have vivid recollections, not so much of her lectures (though I doubt not these were admirable in their way, and as sound in the 'fundamentals' as the rocks of Rubislaw themselves) as of the jolly gathering of our little band when the work of the day was over. And that, curiously enough, seems to be the impression of Aberdeen that was carried away by the daughter of Karl Marx ... glancing over some of the letters which I received from her at the time, I can see again in my mind's eye her slightly Jewish cast of features, and her fine dark eyes glowing with the enthusiasm of perfervid faith...

At the close of her lecture, a Communist critic – for there were 'Reds' of a kind in the Labour movement even forty and more years ago – greatly daring, ventured to take Mrs. Aveling to task, and endeavoured to explain to her what Karl Marx really meant by Social-Democracy. Eleanor Marx listened patiently to the luridly red exposition,

---

* A precursor of the local branch of the SDF.

† *Freedom*, the anarchist paper, reported in April 1893, under "Scotch Notes": "... Mrs Aveling at Edinburgh lecturing the Fabians of that town ... warns those innocents against the Anarchists, who were, she said, evilly disposed persons that made the propaganda of Socialism almost impossible wherever they gained a footing. (The Anarchists were defended ... but Eleanor proceeded with the denunciation, declaring us to be always hand in hand with the police...)"

then, rising from her seat, she said in tones of caustic solemnity: 'Heaven save Karl Marx from his friends!'

After the Sunday evening lecture was over, a little band of comrades took the opportunity of showing their distinguished visitor some of the beauty spots and places of historic interest..."[177]

From Chancery Lane Eleanor sent a letter to Diack, some part of which he quoted in his recollections of her, with the comment that it "glows with pleasure over the memory of her visit".[177]

"Dear Comrades," she wrote,

"I am back again in our murky London, but even our London fog – and we have a very fair one at the present moment – seems quite bright and pleasant when I think of the happy time I spent with you in Aberdeen. It is such a delight – and help – to find people *alive* – as you are, when most of us are so dead – and eager, and hardworking for the Cause. Assuredly whenever I feel despondent (and there are times when one cant help desponding) I shall think of Aberdeen and take heart again.

You said you were afraid of me. I didn't know I had such a formidable reputation. (Friend Leatham said he expected an 'intellectual iceberg' – and seemed relieved to find I wasn't an iceberg or intellectual.) And let me say I was not a little afraid of you. In spite of all Edward's enthusiasm about his visit to Aberdeen* I pictured you as a very cold, hard, stand-offish, critical fold. I can't tell you my relief when I found you were nothing of the sort. Excuse my implying that you are not critical. But really your kindness about my talks makes me think you are not so hard headed as I feared.

I only wish now that London weren't so far from Aberdeen, or that we weren't all so damnably poor. If the distance were shorter, or our purse longer, you wd. soon see us again.

Meantime, quite seriously let me thank you with all my heart for all your kindness. The sunset of Monday with its golden glory will always live in my memory – but I shall think of your work as promise of no sunset but of an ever more glorious sunrise.

Yours fraternally,
Eleanor Marx Aveling."[178]

At the end of December 1892 Eleanor had sent Dollie Radford a letter of aching compassion. Ernest, her husband, had been afflicted for the first time with the malady that was to dog him for the rest of his life,† while one of the children was slightly ailing.

"My dearest Dollie," she wrote,

"The year is coming to an end and I know what a very, very terrible year it has been for you. I need not tell you that with all my heart I am hoping that this new year may bring you happiness, and that before long Ernest will be as strong and well as ever. How much I think of you, dear, how I have grieved for you, I am sure you understand

---

* Aveling had been there in June 1892, immediately after the Plymouth Gasworkers' Annual Conference.
† He died in September 1919, Dollie in January 1920. Both are buried in Hampstead Parish churchyard.

without any words from me. Indeed, Dollie, I don't seem to have any words. Only I feel that you will understand without them.

With all my heart, dear, I wish you a really good New Year – to you, & Ernest, & the children.

Always your
Tussy."[179]

Now, the day after her return from Aberdeen, she found to her dismay that Dollie, turning to her in her trouble, had called at Chancery Lane only to find Eleanor out. It was almost more than she could bear and she wrote at once:

"My dear, dear, Dollie,

I was out only for a *very* little while this afternoon – & yet during that little while you came. I can't tell you how I feel about it – your coming up all those stairs, your coming to see me for nothing. And I have been longing to see you! ... I think of you constantly. I didn't write because I know how tired you must be – tired with that tiredness of body and soul that is so hard to bear – & I did not want to worry you even with a letter. Dollie, don't think me *very* stupid – but when I got back & found that little slip of paper & realized I had missed seeing you, I just sat down & cried as if I had been 16 – or 6 – and had had one of those overwhelming sorrows that only come to us when we are young. Your coming is comfort only one way. It means that your dear wee girlie is getting quite well.

Ada Radford* wrote me Ernest was going on well, tho' slowly. I know *how* slowly it must be to you. Oh! Dollie, why can't we do anything to help those we wd. so gladly give anything to be of service to?† I can do nothing for you, dear old friend, but perhaps just to know I *do* care is some little good to you...‡

She then explained that she had just come back from Scotland after touring the Black Country which she described as *"too* horrible."

"They talk of 'Christian faith'. I don't know how anyone with only *Christian* faith can

---

* Ernest's sister, who married Graham Wallas in 1897.

† Later, that summer when Ernest was recovered, Eleanor twice did him the service of typing, which she sent to him with the words: "...Dear Ernest, you ask me 'not to hurt you by withholding the bill'. I ask you to remember that one of my greatest pleasures is to be able to serve a friend however slightly. I am, & shall always be only too happy to do anything for you and Dollie. But you recommend me to any of *your* friends & see what a bill I'll send!"[180] On the second occasion she wrote: "...I have been v. careful of the *commas*. & I have carefully copied the capitals whenever you used them, because you (like most of us) use them as the spirit moves you. 'Tis no trouble to do any little thing like this for you."[181] Yet this was at a time when she admitted "The 'movement' has a rapacious maw & swallows more work & time than most people wd. believe. The 'show' work of lectures and meetings is the least part of it. And then you know we are poor as the proverbial church mice, & find earning a living no such easy matter. Ah well, I suppose the work will result in something someday",[180] and also shortly after Aveling had been ill and she obliged to take over many of his commitments.

‡ Eleanor's dots.

bear to see & feel all this misery & not go mad. If I had not faith in Man in *this* life, I cd. not bear to live ...*

"Goodnight, dear, dear Dollie. When do you go to Ernest? ... Only feel v. sure that my thoughts are always with you and yours.

Your old
Tussy."[182]

On New Year's Day 1893, a Sunday, the unemployed from every part of London had paraded to St. Paul's Cathedral.† The first detachment to arrive had assembled in Trafalgar Square marshalled by Eleanor and Aveling. Then, on Easter Sunday, 2 April, the Gasworkers' Union cele- brated its fourth anniversary *Justice*, in diametrical opposition to Eleanor's view of this, the first of the New Unions, claimed that, though it owed its existence to Social-Democrats, it was "no more a socialist organisation than any other union". Hyndman was therefore piqued and wished to know why Bebel and Lafargue had been

"brought over here to speak at the Gas Workers' Union meeting whilst among Socialists little or nothing is known of their visit? Is this because the Avelings are prominent members of the G.W.U.? Is this another of the petty intrigues hatched at Regent's Park Road, and if so when are they going to end and give place to an open and aboveboard understanding? ..."[183]

Lafargue was in London with Laura, as promised, for their silver wedding which fell on that very day: 2 April. They had arrived the Tuesday before, while Bebel, having attended the Brussels preliminary conference of the International Congress on 26 March, had been invited by Engels earlier in the month to travel on to London for a discussion of the Zurich prospects. To that extent the presence of these foreigners at this moment was certainly owed to the diabolical powers of the "Socialist Mahatma"[184] of Regent's Park Road; but it was Eleanor, of course, who had engaged her brother-in-law and her good friend Bebel to be present at this landmark in the annals of a trade union which was, in a special sense, her own.

There came a splendid moment on Good Friday, 31 March 1893, when the advance of the movement could be measured in Engels' long experience by the meeting at his house of John Burns, August Bebel and Paul Lafargue, socialist members of the three foremost parliaments in Europe. He wished that Marx had lived to witness this unique occasion: "a landmark in world history."[185]

---

* *ditto.*
† Under the auspices of the Unemployed Organisation Committee, set up in November 1892 with Hyndman as chairman.

In the meantime, by the middle of March, Eleanor and Aveling had moved just across High Holborn to the tranquil oasis of Gray's Inn Square, occupying for some two-and-a-half years the top floor – or "third pair" – of No. 7 on the north side, their last home in Central London.*

This coincided with the tenth anniversary of Marx's death which Engels commemorated in two ways: he announced – "in strict confidence" – to Laura that "the 3rd volume† is as good as ready" and, a few days later, assisted at the

> "joint Commune Celebration of the Verein‡ and Bloomsbury Society – a *joint* festival, though I'd rather have a good butcher's joint."[186]

It seems ironical that in its issue of 1 April *Justice* should complain that Engels did not make more public appearances, that he "carefully secludes himself" – quite as though preparing Volume III of *Capital* were the spare time occupation of a professional entertainer – and, in the same issue, carp at his having spoken at the "little Paris Commune meeting in the supper-room of the Tottenham Street Communist Club". However, this new spate of grievances against the ringleader of "international family intrigues",[187] whom Hyndman had now been arraigning "personally and politically for ten years whenever he could", as Engels wrote to Sorge, was precipitated, it may be, by Eleanor's refusal to write for *Justice*. The startling proposition was that she should contribute a regular feature on the international labour movement. "So long as the endless, infamous libels on her and Aveling ... have not been publicly retracted"[188] she could hardly accede.§

No doubt the request had been made in good faith and because Eleanor, though a member of the nefarious cabal, was unquestionably better informed on the continental movement than anyone else in England. On 12 February she had addressed the Central Finsbury Radical Club on the subject with what the *Weekly News & Chronicle*‖ called her

> "peculiar talent, full resonance, readiness for repartee, and forcibly argumentative periods."[189]

In the course of this speech she had remarked that such a term as

---

* It is possible that the little lump sum that came to Aveling upon the death of his estranged wife in September 1892 facilitated the move. (See above, p. 203.)
† Of *Capital*.
‡ The German Communist Workers' Club.
§ In April 1894 Engels was invited by H(enry) W(illiam) Lee, the Secretary, to address the members of the SDF. He declined on the same grounds.
‖ Formerly the *Weekly News & Clerkenwell Chronicle*.

"independent" labour party would be quite incomprehensible to workers on the Continent: "a labour party there meant something that was a fact". Here in England, she pointed out, where there was but one socialist paper, barely keeping its head above water, the working class had to depend upon the capitalist press and it was small wonder that it was completely ignorant of and out of touch with the aspirations of its continental brothers. She was reported as saying that

> "It was a sorry reflection ... to see the country that was freest to the working class not to make use of the privileges it possessed."[189]

If Eleanor could lecture to the Radicals of Finsbury and the Fabians of Edinburgh, why should she not give the SDF the benefit of her specialised knowledge? It did not seem to occur to Hyndman that neither of these bodies, though at variance with her political views, had indulged in the obsessional practice of using their publications to insult her and her partner.*

May Day 1893 – with two separate demonstrations – had lost not only its novelty but with it a little of its zest. Eleanor marked the occasion by writing her only historical work – *Der Böse Maitag*† – an account of the night of 1 May 1517, with the background and conditions prevailing at the time, when London mobs attacked the dwellings of the hated foreigners living in the city. Carefully annotated, with all sources given and an estimate of their reliability, this was the most scholarly of her writings. Only in the concluding paragraph did she explicitly suggest that

> "in better, happier times to come, it may be that the bygone May Day of 1890, when the people came together for the first time to herald the new gospel of international brotherhood, will be known as the Good May Day..."

The time and research this must have taken could have provided yet another reason – though she needed none – for not contributing to *Justice*; but once it was behind her, she had no hesitation in approaching a government department with a view to an official exchange of information on British and German trade union and labour conditions. On 5 June she wrote to the Board of Trade enclosing

---

* Though not the most recent of his almost maniacal outbursts, Hyndman had devoted a leader in *Justice* on 23 January 1892 to the Free Speech Demonstration Committee wherein "Miss Eleanor Marx" and Dr. Aveling – jointly with Shaw and Burns – were shown up as "envious detractors", actuated "by the desire to do something which they thought would injure the SDF" which, for years past, "they have been doing their utmost to cripple".

† "The Ill May Day". Published in *Die Neue Zeit*, Nos. 30 and 31 of 1893–4.

"...(1) a list of strikes for 1890 & 1891, from the 'Hamburger Echo' (a Socialist daily) & (2) the list of the German Trades Union organs. This wd. have been sent sooner, only the Secretary, C. Legien, of the German Trades Union Federation is one of the 380 Socialist candidates at the General election. He writes me that he has sent you the Halberstadt Report, & that he will send you every week the 'Correspondenzblatt'; he also asks if a copy of the Labour Gazette cd. be sent him in exchange, as it wd. be of great value to him & the German Trades Unions.

Yours faithfully
Eleanor Marx Aveling.

P.S.C. Legien's address is Osterstrasse 76, I Hamburg."

The draft reply (illegibly signed and officially initialled for a "Mr. Coppinger to copy") courteously thanked for the lists, the writer saying he was

"obliged for the trouble you have taken to procure these for the Labour Dept. from Herr Legien, to whom I have forwarded a copy of the current issue of the Labour Gazette.

I have also given instructions that a copy of the Gazette shall be regularly forwarded to him as published; and shall be glad to receive the Correspondenzblatt in exchange as you suggest Madam."[190]

The International Socialist Workers' Congress, held in the Zurich *Tonhalle* – a concert hall on the Alpen Quai – from 6 to 12 August 1893 took much the same course as its predecessors, save that the Swiss proved to be admirable organisers. As early as January 1892 their preparatory committee of 15 was set up; on 1 February circulars and invitations went out to the Socialist Parties and Trade Unions of England, France and Germany.* During August, Eleanor was asked to translate additional material and also a second, special invitation to the TUC,† opening in Glasgow on 5 September, since the Parliamentary Committee had ignored the first. After some delay the Committee replied that it was intending to convene an International Congress in London on the Eight-Hour Day: a pretext written off by Eleanor as

"sheer nonsense. And not just out of stupidity, but with malice. Because the Union gentry would be only too delighted to play a dirty trick on the Zurich Congress (and thereby the English socialists). They believe that if the great English Unions show themselves so gracious as to call an 8-Hour Congress the whole world will be enchanted, that all workers will take part in that Congress – and then no longer have the means to go to Zurich, to the 'rabid' Socialists!..."[191]

---

* Followed by a second in November 1892 and a third in June 1893.
† Dated 25 August 1892 and, only under pressure from Will Thorne, read out to the Congress by Fenwick, the secretary to the Parliamentary Committee.

Undeterred by the British manœuvre, the Swiss reminded the Parliamentary Committee that – whatever notions might have occurred to it since – it had agreed to the Zurich Congress a full year ago at Brussels.

The organising committee held their preliminary conference, attended by representatives of eight countries, in March 1893. In July they turned down the *Parti ouvrier's* plea – backed by the Germans – to postpone the whole thing in view of the forthcoming French elections. They were standing no nonsense, but they courteously telegraphed the Parliamentary Committee to enquire whether the Congress dates would conflict with the 1893 (Belfast) TUC. However, the answer was so dilatory that the Australian and, it was supposed, the American delegates were already on their way to Europe; so, despite obstructions, resentments and the certainty of some absentees, the Swiss went ahead according to plan.

As usual, Eleanor, aided by Engels, had worked hard to ensure agreement with the continental socialists. Equally as usual, when it met the Congress was unable to broach its agenda for days, the first four sessions being taken up by opposition from the anarchists who, to almost everyone's relief, were eventually excluded together with all those whose credentials were not accepted* by their fellow nationals.

Twenty-two countries were represented (the Czechs separately listed under the Austrians) by 435 delegates, of whom a few were jointly mandated by more than one nation. The British delegation, with a majority from the trade unions – 45 out of a total of 65 – included four members of, respectively, the ILP, the Fabians, the Parliamentary Committee of the TUC and five women.†

There was, indeed, a higher proportion of women here than at any previous International Congress – twenty-one in all‡ – of whom seven

---

* Among these was Rosa Luxemburg.

† The ILPers were Champion, Arthur Fields of the Executive* (Leicester), L. A. Glynn (Leeds) and Shaw Maxwell (the general secretary)*. The Fabians were J. W. Martin (Wolverhampton), Sydney (later Lord) Olivier, Bernard Shaw* and H. Russell Smart* (Cheshire). (Those marked* had been present at the First Conference of the ILP.) The women, apart from Eleanor representing the Gasworkers' Executive, were Margaret Irwin of the Glasgow Women's Provident Protective League, May Morris of the Hammersmith Socialist Society, Miss Ogilvy of the Scottish Labour Party and "Ad." (?Ada, Adeline) Smith of the Women's Trades Union League.[192]

‡ It is not always possible to distinguish them in the list of delegates and there may have been more. Engels, the gallant, wrote: "The women were splendidly represented. Besides Louise, Austria sent little Dvorzak, a charming little girl in every respect; I fell quite in love with her and whenever Labriola gave me a chance, eloped with her from the entanglements of his ponderous conversation. These Viennese women are Parisiennes by nature, but the Parisiennes of 50 years ago. Regular grisettes. Then the Russian women! There were four or five with wonderfully beautiful luminous eyes, and there were besides Vera Zasulitch and Anna Kulischoff. Then Clara Zetkin with her enormous capacity for work and her slightly hysterical enthusiasm, but I like her very much..."[193]

spoke in the debate on the protection of women workers. Louise Kautsky gave the opening report in the unconvincing *persona* of delegate for the regional organisation of Lower Austria.* The motion, in the name of four national delegations, including the British, amended to embody the principle of equal pay for equal work, was adopted by acclaim in disregard of Louise Kautsky's reply to the discussion.†

The official languages of the Congress were English, French and German, in all of which Eleanor alone of the five interpreters appointed was equally fluent. She acquitted herself so brilliantly that at the end of the day the British delegation presented her with a gold watch. All the interpreters were made members of the Presiding Committee which needed their skills and thus Eleanor was present at the inner councils of the Congress.

One of the outstanding women delegates, representing the Milan Working Girls' Union, was Eleanor's friend, Anna Kulishov, whose husband, Filippo Turati, was the delegate for the socialist organisations of Palermo, Moffeta (Apulia) and his own district of Milan. It was Anna Kulishov who presided over the eleventh and last session on Saturday, 12 August. The Secretaries, from eight countries, who were to constitute the International Commission had been elected; it was decided to hold the next Congress in London – not, as first proposed, in 1895 but the year after – and this completed the formal proceedings.

Anna Kulishov announced:

"Herewith the business of the Congress would be concluded, but I have one thing more to tell you. At this moment we have in our midst the most renowned champion of the proletariat, the intellectual pioneer of International Social Democracy, Frederick Engels. The Presiding Committee has unanimously agreed to invite him to take the Honorary Chair to close the Congress."

Engels' appearance was greeted with such prolonged and ever-renewed applause from those in the hall and public galleries that silence was not soon restored. Then Engels spoke:

"Citizens and Citizenesses, let me make my speech – as the last speakers made theirs in English and French – in my beloved German. The unexpectedly magnificent welcome you have given me and which I could not but receive with deep emotion, I accept not in my personal capacity but as the collaborator of the great man whose portrait you

---

* She was not the only one to appear in a perplexing guise: the irrepressible Gilles was there representing the "Workers' Productive Society". He caused acute embarrassment to the presiding committee when the Swiss delegation lodged a formal complaint that he had ridiculed Clara Zetkin at a public meeting.

† In justice to her it should be said that she disagreed with the principle in so far as, since there was no law on wages for men, it was impracticable.

have here.* It is just 50 years ago that Marx and I came into the movement, when we wrote the first socialist articles for the *Deutsch-Französische Jahrbücher*.† From the small sects of that time, Socialism has since developed into a powerful Party making the officials of the whole world tremble. Marx has died, but were he still alive there would be no one in Europe and America who could look back upon his life's work with such justifiable pride. It is also another anniversary. In 1873 the last Congress of the International was held. It did two things. The first was to dissociate itself finally from the anarchists. Was that a superfluous decision or not? The Paris, the Brussels and this present Congress have had to do the same thing. The second was to put an end to the activities of the International in their old form. That was the time when the violence of reaction, intoxicated with the blood of the glorious Commune, was at its height. To continue the old International would have led to martyrdoms out of all proportion to their effect; it transferred its headquarters to America, that is, it withdrew from the theatre of war. It was left to the proletariat of each country to organise in its own way. That is what happened and today the International is stronger than ever before. In this spirit we must go forward, working on common ground. We must allow discussion to avoid turning into a sect. But our common standpoint must be preserved. This free union, this voluntary cohesion, sustained by Congresses, suffices for us to achieve victory, a victory which no power on earth can ever wrest from us. It gave me a sense of special pleasure that the English were represented here in such numbers, for they, after all, have been our teachers in organising workers; but however much we may have learnt from them, they will nevertheless have discovered various new things here from which they, too, can still learn.‡ I have been travelling through Germany and heard regrets in some ways that the Anti-Socialist Law was ended. It was far more fun fighting the police. No police, no government in the world will ever get the better of such fighters.

At the request of the presiding committee I declare the Congress closed.

Long live the International Proletariat."[195]

As he ended, tumultuous and ringing cheers broke out. Everyone rose to their feet and, when the ovation subsided, sang the *Marseillaise*.

This was on the occasion of Engels' last visit to the Continent – when he also addressed the Social Democrats in Vienna and Berlin – and these were the last words spoken to the assembled representatives of the workers of the world by that great international socialist.

---

* Engels turned towards the large picture of Marx, painted by Margaret Greulich, which, surrounded by red flags, hung above the platform.

† Written in German, published in Paris 1844.

‡ This was an oblique reference to the fact that while there were only some 200,000 trade unionists in Germany, as against nearly 1,220,000 in Britain, the German Social Democratic Party had 36 M.P.s and no less than 70 official organs, including 32 daily newspapers. It also reminded some of the ILP delegates of Ben Tillett's words at their Party's opening Conference that "he was glad to say that if there were 50 such red revolutionary parties as there were in Germany, he would sooner have the solid, progressive, matter-of-fact fighting Trades' Unionism of England than all the hare-brained chatterers and magpies of Continental revolutionists". It may be added that Chisholm Roberts, the delegate from the Scottish United Trades Council, had asked whether Tillett meant that Karl Marx was a chatterer and a blatherer.[194]

Back in England at the end of September, he wrote to Laura:

"...You may have seen in the papers how I was drawn out of my reserve – first at Zurich, then at Vienna, and finally at Berlin. I fought as hard as I could but it was no use, they must have me out. Well it will be the last time. I have informed them I will not go there again except as a private individual. Anyhow they everywhere received me more than splendidly, far more so than I did, or had a right to, expect...

At Vienna I was at a meeting of some 6,000 and at the beano in Berlin they honoured me with, there were 4,000 present – only the representative men and women of the party – and I can assure you it was a pleasure to see and hear these people. When you come from England with this distracted and disgruntled working class we have here, when you have heard for years nothing but bickering and squabbles, from France, from Italy, from America, and then go amongst these people – the German-speaking ones – and see the unity of purpose, the splendid organization, the enthusiasm, the unquenchable humour that springs from the certainty of victory, you cannot help being carried away and saying: this is the centre of gravity of the working class movement ... I like the people very much, and the Viennese women remind me very much of the French working women of 40 years ago; of course they are over-sanguine of success just like the French, but I think they are a deal clearer headed than those Parisians who fell in love with Boulanger..."[196]

Louise Kautsky must have owed her rather grand position at the Zurich Congress to the favour she enjoyed as Engels' protégée, for she had never played a prominent part in the Austrian movement in her own right and was not now even living in the country she officially represented. For the same reason and under Engels' tutelage she had also become a contributor to the socialist press in Vienna, generally writing signed articles for the working women's paper, though she also sent a report to the *Arbeiter Zeitung* about the British elections* on which subject she cannot have been among the foremost authorities.

Her journalistic enterprise had already led to a spat. The trouble was that, while Engels was encouraging his *Louise* to deploy her talents in this field, Kautsky was doing the same for his equally qualified *Luise*. It so happened that his mother, Minna, was a novelist of some repute and, to his mind, four scribbling Kautskys were altogether too many, the more so since two of them bore the same initial and almost indistinguishable first names. He therefore wrote to Engels, who was asked to consult Tussy, suggesting that his former wife should sign her articles "Strasser-Kautsky" so that "there could be no doubt as to her identity".[197]

Engels was roused to hot indignation. He thought Kautsky's attitude despicable: the wife he had deserted and who had lived with him through his – and her – most formative years was perfectly entitled to use, if she chose, a name that now carried some weight in political circles.

> "That she bears your name is the result of your own free action. That you are no longer together is equally the result of your own initiative. That confusion may now be possible is again entirely your own fault ... I will be quite frank with you ... If you were to propose to her what you now write to me and she were to ask my advice, I should unhesitatingly say: No!"[198]

Kautsky, slightly cowed, was ready to drop the matter, though he put up a show of fight, arguing that for a woman to appear publicly under her own name, far from being a surrender of her personality, betokened that she had fully regained her independence. Engels answered with redoubled vehemence, quoting the relevant sub-sections of the legal code, brushing

---

* Published 5 August 1892.

aside the two precedents Kautsky had cited* and contending that the social position of a divorced woman was quite bad enough without her having to prove to the whole world that she was not the "guilty party". Was every Kautsky who came before the public necessarily his wife? Ought his mother to adopt a different name to show that she was not? While Kautsky might now dismiss the whole thing as dead and buried Engels feared that this was far from the case for Louise.

> "By raising this matter you have awakened memories that cannot be thus lightly laid to rest. By your unreasonable demand you have hurt her feelings deeply, more deeply, I'm afraid, than you can make amends for. It weighs her down all the time..."[199]

Engels' special brand of feminism posited that, in a man's world, women's rights were paramount. Also, it should not be overlooked, he was still a highly susceptible old gentleman and Louise still a not unattractive young lady. However, he need not have expended quite so much energy, for by remarriage Louise was soon to change her name anyway.†

Dr. Ludwig Freyberger (1865–1934), Louise's second husband, five years her junior, first appears upon the scene at the beginning of November 1892 as "a young Viennese doctor who has just arrived here".[202] Louise had spent that summer, from the end of July until mid-September‡ in Vienna and her beguilements may have drawn him to England. He is next heard of when Louise is receiving treatment at his hands for some minor ailment late one evening in January 1893, on which occasion she was supposed to go with Engels to a concert and ball in aid of

---

* That of Gertrud Guillaume-Schack – who, Engels pointed out, had simply conformed to the aristocrat's habit of proclaiming titled birth though married to a commoner – and Florence Kelley Wischnewetzky, who had never discarded her maiden name but only that of her husband after they parted.

† It was unfortunate, however, that Kautsky should have stirred up trouble shortly before Engels was forced to the conclusion that his other heir-apparent, Bernstein, was a "neurasthenic". Nobody could tell whether this was the cause or the effect of his infatuation with the Fabians but, either way, he suffered a nervous breakdown and repaired to Zurich for a rest cure. Both Bebel and Kautsky were bidden to handle him with the utmost tact, on no account ever to mention the Fabians or anything that might impede his recovery. Engels followed his own prescription by writing to him on 14 July only about his health, his diet and the general election.[200] By December 1894 Engels was still chary of exacerbating his nerves by asking him to do extra work and suggested that Eleanor should approach him instead, while as late as March 1895 he found Bernstein's review articles on Volume III of *Capital*, written for *Neue Zeit*, very "confused",[201] for the "neurasthenia" turned out to be of the long-lasting variety.

‡ During the best part of which time Engels went to stay with Pumps and her family, then living in Ryde on the Isle of Wight.

the Communist Club. In March that year Messrs. Thomas Cook & Son*
applied to Engels for a reference and were informed that Freyberger would
be "a very desirable client":

> "a young physician and member of the University of Vienna, Austria, where he
> graduated and practised with distinction,"†

and was, moreover, "highly recommended for me by a prominent member
of the Austrian Parliament."[203]

A year later, by which time he was a member of Engels' household,
Freyberger was described as the young physician who had resigned his
university appointment because the authorities had not allowed him to
disclose to workers the social causes of their ills. Engels told Sorge that he
had

> "already shown the English that more medicine is learnt on the Continent than
> here".[204]

From that time forth Engels' encomiums of Freyberger became ever
more fulsome: he had a "splendid scientific career" before him;[205] he
could knock spots off the English in any branch of medicine one cared to
name – "the clumsy people here cannot come up to the Vienna standard"
in such "delicate matters" as anatomical dissection;[206] these benighted
practitioners were made to realise "how much better their continental
colleagues are in ... physiology, pathology, etc."[207] – and he was certainly
assured of outstanding success.

That such a paragon should be at hand – a doctor about, if not in, the
house – was most timely, as Louise did not fail to point out to "Dearest
Laura" saying: "The G(eneral) has not been his old self since my
return..."‡[208]

In effect, Engels had been obliged to cancel his well-laid plans to visit
Germany that summer owing to a recurrent attack of the

> "old complaint which from 1883 to 1887 laid me up lame from time to time",[209]

---

* Whose founder (1808–1892), an Australian by birth, a printer by trade, a missionary by zeal
and the publisher of the *Children's Temperance Magazine*, later, in 1841, ran the first excursion
train in England and, by dint of organising special transport for official occasions and tourist
services for the public at large on an ever expanding scale, became the first and most famous of
world travel agencies, joined by his son in 1872.
† He qualified in 1889 and for a few years held the position of Demonstrator of Anatomy under
Professor Nothnagel at the university. From University College, London, he qualified for his
MRCS (Eng.) in 1893 and his MRCP (Lond.) in 1894.
‡ From Vienna on 14 September 1892.

whose origin he put down to a fall in the hunting field 25 years ago, aggravated by what he called "excesses" over the past decade.*[210] He had consulted innumerable doctors but all except Gumpert, he claimed, had been totally at sea in treating his condition.

In early June, before he was thus incapacitated, he had hastened to Manchester where Schorlemmer, that dear companion of so many years, lay mortally ill. Though Engels went to see him six times in the few days he was there, the dying man was unable to bear visits of more than five or ten minutes and then could not take in what was said. Engels could "only hope ... for a painless end".[212] On the day he died, 26 June,† Engels at once returned to Manchester to stay for the burial on 1 July. He was grievously affected by this loss and, as Eleanor wrote to Laura:

> "The death of our poor old Jollymeier has been a very great blow to him, as you can imagine."[213]

In the following spring he was back again on a similar sad errand to be present at the cremation of Gumpert who had died on 20 April 1893.

Engels had spent some part of March convalescing at his favourite resort, Eastbourne – "the pleasantest seaside place I know"[214] – going there again with Louise for another week towards the end of July for he was now quite resolved to visit the Continent and felt

> "the want of a little recruiting of strength before undertaking my trip to Germany. Last year's disappointment has made me careful..."

he told Laura.[215]

The death of these two old friends – both far younger than himself‡ – preceded by grave disorders which had robbed them of their mental and physical powers long before the end, was not only a *memento mori* but

---

* Intemperance there may have been, for he loved a carousal, but it had not been continuous. In the spring of 1890 he told Sorge that his conjunctivitis and insomnia had forced him to abjure cigars and alcohol at least until the autumn. "What bitter irony it would be if at my time of life I had to become a teetotaller," he commented, with the exclamation "*Quelle horreur!*"[211] Since Louise's arrival she had kept a watchful if not particularly effective eye upon his drinking; but again in January 1892 he was lamenting to his brother Hermann that he must cut down his smoking while the good wine that was his pleasure – and even Pilsner beer – seemed to affect the muscles of his heart and disturb his sleep. These abstinences, he hoped, would be unnecessary in the spring. They may have been, yet that August he told Bebel that for a whole fortnight he had observed the strictest moderation which he had stood up to so well that he felt free to indulge.

† The immediate cause was lung cancer.

‡ Schorlemmer was 58; Gumpert, who qualified at Würtzburg in 1855, must have been in his sixties and left a young widow whom he had married *en deuxième noces* in 1887.

Gumpert had been named as one of his executors. Thus three days before he set out on his travels, he drew up a new will. On 29 July 1893 he appointed

> "my friends Samuel Moore of Lincoln's Inn Barrister at Law Edward Bernstein of 50 Highgate Road London Journalist and Louise Kautsky who now resides with me at 122 Regents Park Road as EXECUTORS..."[216]

In this testament, witnessed by Frederick Lessner of 12 Fitzroy Street* and Ludwig Freyberger of 11 Gower Street, he directed:

> "that all manuscripts of a literary nature in the handwriting of my deceased friend Karl Marx and all family letters written by or addressed to him which shall be in my possession or control at the time of my death shall be given by my executors to Eleanor Marx Aveling of 7 Grays Inn Square W.C. the younger daughter of the said Karl Marx..."[216]

Engels had not been to Germany since 1876[†] nor in Berlin for over half a century. He now mapped out a strenuous tour, lasting from 1 August, when he left England with Louise and Freyberger, until 29 September, to return with health and spirits improved beyond measure.[‡] Travelling *via* the Hook, the trio met Bebel and his wife Julie in Cologne, spent a night in Mainz, another in Strasbourg and a third in Zurich. From there he went to Thusis in the Alps – at the foot of the Heinzenberg – to spend a week with his brother Hermann's family, coming back to Zurich on 12 August – the day he addressed the International Congress – to stay with a cousin, Mrs. Friedrich von Beust, for a fortnight. He went into the Bernese Oberland with Bebel and together they journeyed on to Munich, Salzburg and Vienna by way of Prague and Carlsbad, finally reaching Berlin on 16 September where he remained until his departure for London *via* Rotterdam. He had stopped six days in Vienna and, while in Berlin, had called upon the Liebknechts in Charlottenburg. Apart from the fatigues of travel it was a heavy programme, large social demands being made upon him everywhere, not to mention the three public addresses he had given. Nor was he an apathetic tourist. He observed everything with the keenest interest and excitement, describing to Laura his impressions of a "completely metamorphosed Germany". In Mainz and Cologne factory

---

* The house where Ernest Aveling, Edward's youngest brother, had died in 1884. (See above, p. 210.)

† When, with Lizzie Burns, he had visited Pumps in Heidelberg. (See above, p. 140.)

‡ On 11 November, less than three weeks before his 73rd birthday, Eleanor wrote: "The Gen'l, as you no doubt gather from his letters, is wonderfully well. His trip has done him an immense amount of good, & the reaction after all the excitement was not as bad as I feared it might be. Louise has him splendidly in hand, & he is happy as a schoolboy...".[217]

chimneys and "splendid buildings" had sprung up; there were amazing developments in Strasbourg and Mühlhausen. In short, "the Continent has undergone a complete revolution since I was last here", while he was entranced by the scenery in Switzerland where "the Jungfrau had put on an extra clean white night-dress for us".[218]

Naturally at Zurich there had been a general reunion with Eleanor, Aveling, Bernstein, Liebknecht, Adler, and a host of Engels' other intimates and acquaintances. Kautsky had brought his wife as a visitor to the Congress – "to the astonishment of everybody", according to Eleanor – where Louise the First was much in evidence and the two ladies met.

> "...but things went very smoothly," Eleanor reported, "& Karl seemed to be feeling he cd be happy with either were t'other dear charmer away..."

This was written after Eleanor's return to England when Johnny Longuet was staying with her again and she added:

> "If my letter is disjointed & wandering put it down to the fact that Johnny is holding forth on the virtues of his beloved Clemenceau, and is reading out passages from the various French papers he daily sallies out to buy."[219]

She also referred to her nephew in the letter she wrote to Ernest Radford on 16 September. After enquiring about Dollie, she said:

> "Tell her her old admirer Johnny is stopping with us. When he was 4 he was desperately in love with her. Now he is a great laughing lad of 17! Ah me! How the time goes..."

It was clear that for her, too, the trip to Zurich had not been all work, for she asked Radford:

> "Do you know, that in Switzerland on the top of Mount Pilatus we met your brother Charles & Bessie, & had some v. pleasant talk with them?"[*220]

However, the Avelings had not lingered abroad, for on 7 September Eleanor wrote from Gray's Inn Square to tell Laura that Edward had gone to the TUC in Belfast, which opened on the 4th of the month and where, though it was agreed that Congress should support candidates for parliamentary election, Hardie's resolution that, if successful, they should form an independent party in the House was outvoted.

On 29 September the Avelings went to the station to welcome Engels

---

* It was quite the usual thing for English travellers in the 19th century to run into their friends and acquaintances upon some Alpine peak.

on his return and thereafter, throughout October, Eleanor was busy typing out Lassalle's letters to Marx, work which Engels paid for, checked and hoped to publish.*

Early in November she had the unusual experience of addressing suffragists in St. James's Hall. "Like the fine gentlemen Fabians," *Justice* remarked, they had "carefully held aloof from the Adult Suffrage Demonstration of the SDF", adding

> "Fine-lady suffragists of the Mrs. Henry Fawcett type are quite of the opinion that the poor should keep their place, and if common women as well as common men were to get votes there's no knowing what use they might make of them..."[221]

An amendment, seconded by Eleanor, to enfranchise adult women was overwhelmingly defeated.

At the time she was far from well, feeling

> "so thoroughly ill without being ill ... that I fancy I must be enjoying a little bout of influenza. I can hardly see out of my eyes; my head & back ache like mad; I've an ulcerated throat, & I'm constantly sick."

Aveling on the other hand was "a good deal better" than he had been recently, though disappointed that his latest play had failed, as Eleanor had

> "fully expected because it was *not* a good play. He knew that too, but thought *that* might save it," she added.[222]

Engels celebrated his 73rd birthday in the usual high-spirited manner, interrupting momentarily his preparation for the press of a large part of Volume III of *Capital*; he was determined to send it off to Meissner, the publisher, immediately after Christmas.

At the beginning of February, to the astonishment of everyone but Engels, who had not breathed a word of warning, Louise Kautsky married the brilliant young Viennese doctor with the enlarged social conscience. She was then 34 and he 29. The wedding was rather sudden and quite in secret, a formal card being sent out only after the event.

A couple of weeks later Eleanor received a letter from Eastbourne where a honeymoon *à trois* was in progress.

"My dear old Tussy," wrote Louise on 22 February in her haphazard English,

---

* This hope was not fulfilled. Lassalle's letters both to Marx and Engels were brought out in 1902 by Franz Mehring who used Eleanor's typescripts as far as they went.

"I am so glad that you have been frank to me and perhaps more glad that you grumbled with me although you are mistaken. That I would marry, was only decided that Monday, you went to the North, then I had to inform G[eneral] and did not know when the marriage would take place as G. wanted consideration. G. wanted me to stay, and I had no reason whatever to leave him, in fact I would not have left him and settled my private affairs in a way the most convenient to him. Monday night came a letter to G. from P[umps] and P[ercy] announcing that the whole family is in town* and wants to come and stay with us to enjoy London life after all the trouble, and make all preparations here, to send the children with all they wanted to school. This letter settled the question for G. at once. He asked me to go the next morning to Eastbourne and settle there for at least a fortnight and asked me further to make our intended marriage public that L[udwig] and I could stop with him as soon as he comes back to London. He offered me the spare room and I told our girls that when I come back from Eastbourne that I am married; that was all. Up to Monday Ludwig and I have been the very best comrades but nothing more, with an unspoken intention of both side to settle down in life together latter on. What you wrote about Zurich made me smile. I know best, how very amiable most of my friends tried to settle me in life. You write 'marriage is a lottery in whatever society', may I add of my experience that *no* society would tolerate a friendship between man and woman, without sneers and comments. It was overflowing friendship again that I heard again and again everything, what was spoken about me and some more startling news of their own intention† into the bargain. All this 'Klatsch'‡ showed me that I have to step in, so that I would not be considered as the source of this spreading and therefore I told Ludwig in Vienna everything, what was said about him and everything concerning my former life. He went back to Salzburg to meet G. and August [Bebel]. That dear girl is the simple story.

* * *

I am happy now and hope that we still will be happy. I am as Independent as I was before I married and hope to be so allways. I have a lot to care for my mother and sister and would not like to give anyone trouble...".§[224]

Before this letter arrived Eleanor had written to her sister whose curiosity was very naturally piqued by the bare announcement of the marriage.

"I can understand you asking the questions you do – only I cant answer them! I know absolutely nothing, & the whole affair has been 'wrop in mistry'. As to the Freyberger match being a foregone conclusion, I suppose it was. Only I did rather doubt. For certain private reasons, & because I *cant* see how anyone can stand Freyberger. It's all

---

* Pumps had given birth to her fourth child – one of whom had died – in November 1892, heralded by Eleanor in July that year with the rather unpleasing remark: "the beloved is going to bring another monster into the world. Isn't it awful?"[223]
† Possibly "invention".
‡ Gossip.
§ Here the holograph breaks off, incomplete.

very well to say that all tastes are in nature. This taste seems to me a very abnormal one.

Well, we'd all our opinions one way or the other, though no hint was ever dropped to us, & and though in public the 'du' into wh. they slipped in unguarded moments – (& but for the pretence of 'Sie', as you know the 'du'* in German means very little) – was carefully avoided. Last week I was away in the north lecturing for a week,† & Edward wrote me that the General & Louise had gone to Eastbourne. Louise had told me the General meant going there to get rid of what we all politely term his 'lameness',‡ so I took no special notice of this. Judge of my surprise when I get a card – like the one sent you. Not another line, not another word! But it *does* seem queer to take the General a-Honeymooning with them. You can imagine the delicacy of his jokes on such an occasion. You ask me how he takes it. I don't know, any more than I know what arrangements they are making. I've not seen or spoken to the General alone for many months§ & whatever he may think he cd hardly express his opinion before those concerned ... When Pumps was with him, lo, she was good in his sight; now Pumps is dethroned and Louise is the queen who can do no wrong. But I *am* anxious to know what the household arrangements are to be, for frankly it will be intolerable if Freyberger permanently installs himself at Regent's Park Road. It was unpleasant enough to constantly meet him there, but to know him always there!

As to Pumps' opinions I am also in the dark. If it (i.e. the marriage, not Pumps' opinion) means – wh. I am well-nigh sure it does not – Louise's leaving, of course she will rejoice greatly.‖ If it means the General's house being turned into a Freyberger ménage she will swear, & feel herself more aggrieved than ever.

You see now why nothing was said to Paul when he was here.¶ Nothing was said to anyone. Isn't it all odd? Louise's saying no word to me is as strange almost as the General's silence. I say almost because she had 'confided' in me before so may have felt uncomfortable in doing so again. Has the General not written to you about it? I fancy I've rather put my foot into it because I'm such a poor hand at pretending, & I never could pretend to admire the profound sagacity & brilliant wit of the new bridegroom. Well, on the whole I'm glad Louise is married. She was too young for the rather dreary

---

* The familiar as opposed to the formal "you".

† A speaking tour of seven days organised by the SDF during which she gave eight lectures in Lancashire, all but one to SDF branches.

‡ There is no explanation for this innuendo: he *was* lamed by rheumatism every spring.

§ On 3 November 1893 Engels told Kautsky "I've seen hardly anything of Tussy at all and only for brief moments since my return ... and practically never on Sunday,"[225] attributing this break with old-established custom to her constant meetings and colossal amount of work; but there was also the reason of her antipathy to Freyberger who was invariably present. Her repeated pleas that Laura should write more often – "You don't know how glad I shd be to get a letter now & then, for though I am always busy I am also very lonely"[226] – were surely not unconnected with this estrangement from Engels.

‖ Before the Freyberger marriage, in November 1893, Eleanor had told Laura that "Pumpsia's nose is hopelessly (at present) out of joint. She came up to town & had to stop with Charlie!" – i.e. her brother-in-law – "She tried to remain at least for the Sunday, but was ruthlessly bundled off! When I remember how she treated our poor Nimmy, I can't help feeling a certain malicious pleasure in her discomfiture..."[226] The Roshers had also come to London for the previous Christmas and New Year – shortly after the birth of the baby – when Louise had neatly arranged to put them up in nearby lodgings.

¶ There is no traceable record of Lafargue coming to London since the spring of 1893, but from internal evidence it could be inferred that he paid a flying visit in January 1894.

life at the General's, & no doubt Karl* will be delighted. I've not seen the Bernsteins, so I dont know their view of this epoch-making event..."†[227]

A week later, with Louise's explanation to hand, namely –

"that she had only decided upon the grand step of marriage on the very day I left London for my lecturing tour ... So, of course, she cd. tell me nothing"–

Eleanor was able to report

"the latest news from the ménage of Regents Park Road. (Oh! for a Balzac to paint it!) ... She informed me that she – & he – were to remain with the General!!! I enclose a note received yesterday wh. will tell you more eloquently than I can what the present situation is. That Freyberger shd hold 'at homes' at the General's is certainly coming it strong.

To complicate matters still more it wd seem that the Pumpses were in London (& may be still are for all I know) & that their advent was the signal for the flight to Eastbourne. How it will all work out the Lord knows. But personally I confess that invitations to the General's from a man like Freyberger are a little queer, &, in my opinion bode no good for the future. In this sense, that the General, after all, *is* getting old. You wd realize how old if you saw him more often, & I question much if the Freyberger influence is likely to be a good one for the party. Anyone who has the slightest knowledge of human nature must know that this gentleman is playing his own game alone. So I say again, how it will end goodness knows. The family were to return yesterday, & as we have always been to see the General directly he came back after any absence from town I suppose we must do so now. But frankly I don't look forward to the visit. And poor Louise! She *has* dropped from the frying pan into the fire. But then with us women it is generally a question of the frying pan or the fire & it is hard to say wh. is the worse. At the best our state is parlous ... After our state visit I will report again..."[228]

A few days after his return from Eastbourne, Engels wrote to Lafargue:

"... So you were surprised by Louise's marriage? It has been brewing for some months ... Freyberger ... has found very good openings in the hospitals here. Once that was settled, there was no further reason for delaying the wedding. While waiting for his expectations to materialise he came to join his wife here. You can see it is an entirely matriarchal marriage, the husband is his wife's boarder!"[229]

In truth, both husband and wife were Engels' boarders. While Lafargue confessed that the "great news received from Eastbourne" had come as a thunderbolt – though it was hardly surprising that Engels had foreseen it since he had the protagonists under his nose day by day and could detect them sickening for this ailment – he was relieved. He had

---

* Kautsky.
† Although the letter continues on other matters for a few lines the holograph is incomplete.

"feared that the turtle-doves would take wing from Regent's Park Road ... but since, on the contrary, they are settling down in a matriarchal nest, as you say, so much the better. This is a case of saying all's well that ends well, if ever there were one. Give the lovers our best compliments: we wish them prosperity, much pleasure and few children...".[230]

But all was not well; nor was it the end. The Lafargues, at a comfortable distance, might regard the arrangement as a happy outcome and Laura even profess to think Freyberger "good-natured", but Eleanor, with the situation "under her nose" grew more and more uneasy.

"I wd not trust a fly to his tender mercies," she wrote on 22 March. "He is an adventurer pure and simple, & I am heartily sorry for Louise."

Then she came to the main cause for her disquiet:

"I confess I am also anxious on another matter – & that is all the papers, letters, MSS etc. wh. are at the General's. That I am not alone capable of the thought is shown by the fact that the Bernsteins have been here & after some hawing and ha'ing admitted that they felt anxious 'about the MSS'. Shd anything happen to the General, they said, F. is quite capable of getting hold of anything he can & selling it. For you must remember F. is simply an anti-Semite (tho' I wd wager my Jewish head that he's a Jew) & has nothing to do with the movement ... you know very well that anyone living with the General can manipulate him to any extent. Sam Moore (who is over again) also seemed doubtful, & he came up here & I had a talk with him. He was (& I believe is) a trustee under the General's Will, & if he were here always it wd be all right, as he wd immediately have all papers 'sealed'. But he is half his time in Africa! However he told me he wd try & get an opportunity of speaking to the General (who is sure to consult him as the other trustee under the Will, Gumpert, is since dead) & of making sure about all papers ... it is really a serious question. Mohr's MSS etc are things we cant be too careful about. And that F. is just an adventurer playing for what he can get, you wd know also if you saw him as often as I have done. It is *very* difficult because, of course, I cant well say anything to the General (it is all very well for the Bernsteins to say I *should*!) & I must just wait & see what Sam Moore says...".[231]

Evidently Engels was not altogether well that spring, or else Freyberger was proving his worth, for the old man wrote to Sorge:

"Never in all my life have I been so medically bullied as in the past 4 weeks and can only console myself that it's all done for my own good...".[232]

Notwithstanding, on the day before this letter was sent the last manuscripts of Volume III of *Capital* went off to the publisher and, in no time at all, he was faced by two stubborn problems. Louise was pregnant and, as he wrote to Laura in July:

"...I am not sure of remaining much longer in 122; I ought to have settled that business last year, but was enjoying myself on the Continent, and now have to face the dilemma: either to get the whole house thoroughly overhauled or to look for another. I have attended to both eventualities, and maybe in a few weeks may know where I am, or at least where I am to be in future...".[233]

Later he told Sorge:

"After Louise's marriage the old house was a bit cramped for us and since the results of the marriage shortly made their appearance, it simply wouldn't do any longer...".[234]

Behind this laconism lay a vast upheaval. Engels could not accept an invitation to stay with the Lafargues, replying:

"...Where do I go this summer? alas all hope of going to Le Perreux is knocked on the head by that beautiful new law!* ... My impression is that the government will not lose much time before it sees that a precedent is established of the application of that law to Socialism, and to the inclusion of Socialism under the heading of anarchism ... The German Socialist law kept me from Germany for thirteen years, let us hope this new law will not last long enough to prevent me from coming to France once more in my life...".[233]

Nor, though pressed, could he go elsewhere abroad: he must remain within reach of London to deal with the housing question. In the event he went to Eastbourne with the Freybergers from 14 August until 18 September.

While there Louise picked an ugly quarrel with Eleanor who, for her part, had gone to the Lafargues with Aveling in July. That the two couples, and in particular the two sisters, should have been together may have had some bearing, as later events suggest, upon Louise's action in writing a letter that brought out the worst in her character and syntax.†

"I herewith send you as I have heard from very credible sources news of the breach of confidence in regard to me of which you have been guilty. Liebk. passed on your outpourings at once to Singer and he naturally told the matter to Bebel, whose friend

---

* Promulgated after an anarchist, Auguste Vaillant, had exploded a bomb in the Chamber of Deputies on 9 December 1893 and made more stringent in July 1894 following the assassination of the President, Carnot, who was stabbed to death at Lyons on 24 June by Santo Caserio, also an anarchist.
† The letter, in German, is here rendered as faithfully as possible into English, neither employing the unfair device of a too literal translation nor going to the extreme of setting the original to rights.

you also were. On the matter itself I wish to waste no word yet one I should like to say, since I have lost all trust in our intimate association.

> With greetings,
> Louise Kautsky."*235

Eleanor was so exasperated that she answered in a home-made short-hand, designed to baffle the semi-literate, saying she had received letters from both Liebknecht and Singer, both of which she would show Louise, and demanding a retraction of the charge that she had gossiped for which there was no foundation. A more explicit though illegible pencilled note, dictated by Aveling, was enclosed.

Eleanor wrote:

> "(As you will not be able to make out Ed's scrawl, I translate)
> Dear Louise,
> I never mentioned your name to Liebknecht, let alone Bebel's. Bebel himself had – as you wrote to me – told Singer.† That L. *did* say something (tho' I do not know exactly what) to the Tante‡ I have heard in a roundabout way. I can only repeat that *absolutely* no mention of you or your relations to Bebel was made by me to Liebknecht, or by Lieb. to me.
>> Yours
>> E M A."236

The holiday in Eastbourne was marked by two other disasters: Engels suffered a slight stroke and arrangements were concluded for moving, on 9 October 1894, into 41 Regent's Park Road on the other side of the street, nearer the entrance to the Park. This was a far larger house, taken on a renewable seven-year lease at £85 a year.§ For its size and position Engels thought it exceedingly cheap.

> "The secret," he wrote to his brother, "is that the landlord lives in Lancashire and is interested only in collecting and not laying out any money. So I had to advance about £200 for repairs",237

in consideration of which the rent was remitted for two-and-a-half years. When Engels was having

> "no end of trouble with lawyers, house-agents, contractors etc. before I got the house into tenantable condition...".238

---

* It should be said that Louise did not as a rule – nor in this instance – enter the year when dating her correspondence. Although she signed herself Kautsky when she was supposed to be Freyberger there can be no shadow of doubt that the letter was written in 1894. A postscript says: "The General will be back on Tuesday", which would have been 18 September, on which date he did, indeed, return to London, and does not accord with his movements or fit the day in any other year.

† About his affair with Louise.

‡ Mrs. Emilie Motteler.

§ No. 122 had always been £60, but the previous tenant of 41 had rented it at £130 a year, showing, as Engels remarked, the fluctuations in the value of house property.

he was nearing 74 and, in the event, had less than a year to live. Nor were these the end of his exertions. The coal-cellar was flooded, the walls of the wine-cellar were sweating with condensation, a new kitchen range had to be installed but, above all, there were the contents of eight enormous crates of books to unpack so that only by 11 November did he put

"the last heaps of books from my study floor into the book-cases, where they await sorting...".238

He could hardly look to Louise for assistance, for on 6 November – less than a month after the move – she was delivered of her only child, Louise Frederica, nicknamed Lulu.

Nevertheless, though

"more than once I felt inclined to throw all my books into the fire, and house and all, such a bother it was",

he was back at work, rummaging among "my higgledy piggledy" to find the original of Laura's latest French translation of the *Manifesto*, which he read with "real and unbroken pleasure", while

"at the same time I had to hurry off the very badly printed proofs of the last 5 or 6 sheets of Capital"238

which, somehow, he had managed to go through and revise.

This uprooting of an old man in a precarious state of health after nearly a quarter of a century's settled residence ordered to suit his needs may not have hastened his end but will have done little to give him a new lease of life. Beyond recounting some of the horrors of the removal to Laura, he did not repine but, on the contrary, gave his brother the rosiest picture of the Freyberger marriage and its sequel.

"My house companion had been engaged to an outstandingly fine Viennese doctor ... for over a year* and soon wished to put an end to the betrothal by marriage. Since at the same time I had no wish to surrender myself to the hands of strangers, things were so arranged that all three should stay together, which necessitated a larger house ... and we ... soon found a very pleasant big ... house in a far better part of the same street and took it. We have been there since October and, at the beginning of November, Louise with rare punctuality presented her consort with a little girl..."

He went on to describe in detail the arrangements in the new house:

---

* No such engagement was ever announced or so much as hinted to anyone during that period and, since the marriage came as a complete surprise to all who were closely associated with Engels, his version must be seen as the kindly construction he always put upon the conduct of those he cherished.

"...a basement downstairs with, as well as the kitchen etc., a comfortable breakfast room, on the ground floor a drawing room and a dining room where 24 people can be comfortably seated at table ... on the second floor four rooms occupied by the Freyberger family, third floor ditto four rooms for servants, guests, lumber room etc..."[239]

He himself had two rooms on the first floor: a commodious study in the front and bedroom at the back. Three servants were now found necessary, including a nursemaid, to ensure the wellbeing of Dr. Freyberger and his ménage. He, indeed, put up his plate on the front door and these dependants, upon whom Engels had become utterly dependent, ruled the roost.

On the day before the Freyberger child was born Eleanor wrote a frantic letter to Laura about "the very serious state of affairs at Regents Park". She said she had not had the heart to write before

"but apart from everything else I feel I must not delay any longer, as ... things have reached a pass beyond joking ... I say to you most earnestly that your presence here is *urgent*. Believe me I am not exaggerating, & shd not say what I am saying except on the best grounds. You may say how can you come over now. You must *make* a reason. There are two spare rooms in the new house; while Louise is 'lying-in' the General will be left alone; it is a very good time to come & 'keep him company'. With three servants there can be no question of your being too much trouble ... It is high time you came. Paul's coming wd be comparatively useless – without counting that the General has been and is being very much set against Paul, whose influence wd therefore be nil. *You* alone have some influence left, & if you came you might prevent most serious wrong. This is not my opinion only. The Bernsteins who are very true friends, & who know exactly what the position is, have been begging of me for weeks to write and urge you to come. Alone I can do nothing. Together we might do something. When I tell you that Freyberger thro' Bax and others, is spreading all through the S.D.F. & through the S.D.F. all over London (so far as our acquaintances or political relations extend) that 'the Avelings have been turned out by the General, and that *now*, that things are in the hands of the Freybergers all will be different'; that Louise is spreading the same report all over Germany (with personal calumnies about myself that I am ashamed to write) you will see to what a pass things have come. The Bernsteins and the Mendelsons (whom the F.s hate worse than poison, I suppose because they are very friendly to us & always speak so charmingly of you & Paul) *are* practically turned out, & though I dont think the poor old General even fully realises what he is made to do, he has come to the condition where he is a mere child in the hands of the monstrous pair. To give you but one example of the General's change to me. Last Tuesday I went to see him & in passing asked if he had heard or seen anything of Bax. I saw he looked very confused, but supposed this was because he thought I knew that F. had dined with Bax on Saturday. I added I shd like to know what he (Bax) wd say to the General of the latest attacks in 'Justice'. The General said he had no news of Bax ... Yet, as I have since heard, that very afternoon Bax had been invited & had had a grand luncheon at the General's & cd not have left the house $\frac{1}{2}$ an hour after* I arrived! You will say 'why this secrecy?' If you knew all the wire-pulling of the F.s you wd understand. Bax, the

* "before" is obviously meant.

greatest gossip in London, is told *I* am turned out; he in turn is asked to tell the General any lies he may have heard against us, & so it works round. This is only a *small* matter, but can you imagine the General coming to this? For a long time things have been going from bad to worse, & it is a positive pain to go to the General's. When he sees me alone – wh. is only for a moment, he seems glad enough – & then when the two other appear, he becomes like them, & in all but words I am told I am de trop. And except when they bear anyone with the General the poor old man (who so hates to be alone) is left quite to himself. The two are *always* in their own 'flat' – you can imagine how depressed and miserable this is for him. But I fancy things may come to a crisis, & in this wise. When the General returned from Eastbourne I told you we did not think him at all well – but as you know I said nothing definite as to his illness. This was because the poor old man had told me *in strict confidence* of his illness – he *had had* a stroke, but that *no one* except the F.s & myself were to know, & said he trusted to my honour not to mention it. As I did not breathe a word of it even to you, you may be sure I did not to anyone else. But on Thursday last Ede Bernstein came to me with a post card from Kautsky in wh. the latter wrote: 'do you know anything of the stroke wh. Adler (who had been to the Congress)* says the General has had. Is it true or an invention of the F.s.' Ede thought it *was* an invention but when I found this matter wh. the General was so anxious to keep quiet was being talked about & knowing the sort of things Louise is constantly writing about him, I felt that in self-defence I must let know that the painful matter *was* known & not through me. I wrote therefore, & told him of Karl's post-card, telling him quite straight *why* I wished him to know – i.e. that shd the rumour come back to him he might look for its origin anywhere but in my direction.† I have not heard in reply, but have reason to know ... that he is very angry – probably with me! But I go to see him Wedy & then no doubt there'll be the devil to pay. But it was necessary to stop this matter. I have only too often let things go. I cant enter into all the miserable details – it is sickening to think of them – but the broad general fact is there. Pumps *is* got rid of, & even tho' the General will not treat me quite like Pumps, the result may come to the same. For despite all one owes the General, we cannot submit to everything. *You* are the one person Louise dreads, & you alone could help now. The position is too serious for remaining quite passive. If you dont want to see the F.s *sole literary* executors you must act, & that promptly. You will remember that Bebel wrote the papers wd be in the right hands. I think you & I shd know *whose* hands. If outsiders know we shd, for when all is said & done this is *our* business & no one else's. The papers – especially all the private papers – are *our* concern; they belong to us – not even to Engels.

If I cd tell you everything, if you cd only faintly realise how matters stand, if you cd see the General looking like a child at Louise before he dares even ask a friend to come & see him, if you knew how they bully & frighten him by constantly reminding him he is too old for this and too old for that, & that when one has had the 'warnings' he has had a man must etc. etc. etc.; if you understood how they are making the old man believe his very life depends on them – & saw how utterly depressed, & lonely, & miserable he is, you wd see that I am not exaggerating when I say that every delay now is a danger, & that for all sakes your presence is essential ... You could still do much. How much is proved by Louise's hatred of you, & the fact that she has not *yet* dared to set the General against you. Think very seriously of what I have written, & be assured I

---

* Of the German Party from 22 to 28 October at Cologne.
† For confirmation that these rumours had reached Germany see *Victor Adler: Briefwechsel mit August Bebel und Karl Kautsky.* Ed. Friedrich Adler. Vienna 1954, fn., p. 165.

shd not be so foolish as to urge your coming over like this unless there were very good cause . . .

I wish, dear, I had better & pleasanter news to give. It is all so painful (when you hear all the petty treacheries & meannesses you will be like myself & wonder if it is not some horrible nightmare) I have put off writing in very cowardice. But you *ought* to know. I can only say to you again, with all the earnestness I can, if we – you & I – are to make a final effort it must be made soon, & your presence here is urgently needed . . .".[240]

On 22 November Eleanor wrote an even more agonised appeal to Laura who had not responded to the first in any way. Eleanor could only suppose that the letter had not reached her, so there was much repetition of the same anxieties though by now she feared that the Freybergers had already taken possession of the Marx papers. Also the German party press had published a statement

"that the 4th volume of 'Capital' will *not* be issued. Now the General has again & again said, – not merely to me & Edward, but to the Bernsteins, Mendelsons etc. – that the 4th vol. wd give him comparatively very little trouble, it being in a far more complete state than the 3rd vol. & so on . . . Now we are suddenly told – through a public announcement, & no *private* communication with you & myself, whom, after all, it most deeply concerns – that the data are insufficient & that Engels will not issue it. Of course we are convinced that Freyberger has persuaded the General that he is not well enough to do it; the MS will pass into the Freybergers' hands, & *they* as literary executors will issue it . . ."

This "utterly unscrupulous" couple were frightening Engels about his health and

". . . 'Ludwig's' influence grows greater the more he persuades the General he is indispensable, & now that a baby is there the General will be still more enslaved . . .

Now, once more, dear Laura, will you not consider my suggestion and come over? There are *two furnished* rooms at the General's. He cant refuse or find a pretext (not that I believe *he* wd wish to do either) for putting you off. And if he *did* try to put you off it would only show that greater need for your coming. Could you not come for the 28th (his birthday)? Anyhow, if you feel as I do, that it would be an absolute wrong to allow these MSS, papers and documents (including the practically complete 4th volume!) that are not only *ours*, but that we have a very distinct duty with regard to, to fall into the . . . hands of the Freybergers, you will not delay . . .

It is a miserable business. The Sunday before last the General had asked me to go to dinner as usual, but *had not dared* tell Freyberger he had done so! wh. will show you how little he is now master of his own house."

To this second lengthy letter Aveling added a postscript reinforcing Eleanor's plea:

"Dear Laura, Come, *come*, COME. You have no idea of the immediate importance of it. The General is in this mood. He will brook no interference from *any* but you two women, whose right to demand account of your father's papers he must admit. You have to make that demand and declare point-blank your reason, that you do not trust the Fs. Believe me – this is the only way to save the M.S....."[241]

Between the writing of those two letters to Laura, Engels himself had set down directives of some importance. He had drawn up a document, signed but not witnessed, expressing his wishes in the event of his death and he had written a letter to Eleanor and Laura jointly. Both were in English, dated 14 November 1894.

The first, addressed to his executors, was evidently taken down at his dictation, the first paragraph in Bernstein's handwriting, the rest in Louise Freyberger's. It was found in a drawer of his writing table after his death.*

"(1) The following lines are supplementary and explanatory to my will. They express merely what are my wishes and are in no way *legally* binding upon my Executors. On the contrary, wherever they should be found to clash with the legal meaning of my will, they are to be disregarded.

(2) My distinct wish is that my body be cremated and my ashes thrown into the sea at the first opportunity.

(3) Immediately after my death I desire a copy of my will to be forwarded to my brother Hermann Engels, Barmen, or in case of his death to Hermann Engels junior, Engelskirchen, near Cologne.

(4) Unless Sam Moore is in England at the time of my death, and can attend at once to his executorship, Bernstein and Louise will have to act without his assistance. In that case and even if Sam Moore should not be in London but somewhere else in England, I recommend to make a copy of my will for their own use and hand the original to Crosse & Sons solicitors 7 Lancaster Place Strand, to get it proved and to legally assist my executors. These latter will have to attend at once to the following points:

(a) To ascertain from Mess. Crosse what steps they must take to obtain as soon as possible the full control of my balance at the Union Bank of London Limited Regent st Branch and the right to dispose of such parts of my investments as may have to be sold to defray current expenses,

(b) To ascertain the value of my estate. My furniture, books etc. will have to be valued. Mess. Crosse will attend to that. The value of my investments in stocks, shares etc. at the time of my death can be calculated from the official Stock and Share List with which my Stockbrokers Mess. Clayton & Aston 4 Tokenhouse buildings Tokenhouse Yard E.C.† will supply my executors.

(c) As Messrs. Crosse will tell my executors, the various legacies in money made in my will are not to be paid in the full nominal amount but are subject to deduction of the share of death duties appertaining to each of them.

(5) There will be found in my books various sums of money, paid for a good many

---

* Certified (in German) by, it is thought, Bebel.

† Tokenhouse Yard, Lothbury, in which ancient City precinct Defoe's *Journal of the Plague Year* places the incident of "a casement violently opened ... and a woman gave three frightful screeches, and then cried, 'Oh, death, death, death!' "

years back by me to Laura and Paul Lafargue, Percy and Ellen Rosher, Edward and Eleanor Marx-Aveling. These sums, as I wish to state expressly, do not represent loans owing to me, but are *and always were free gifts on my part*. They are therefore not to be claimed in any shape or form.

(6) In part-payment of the legacy left by me to Ellen Rosher, there is to be used by my executors the Reversion of certain funds payable to Percy Rosher after the death of his father and mother and which I bought from the said Percy Rosher. I desire it to be charged to Ellen Rosher at what it cost me, namely £250 – paid to Percy Rosher – and £30 solicitors expenses incurred on account of this transaction...

(7) I desire to supplement my will by the following details as to the disposal of papers left by me, viz:

(a) All papers in Karl Marx's handwriting except his letters to me and all letters addressed to him except those written by me to him are to be restored to Eleanor Marx-Aveling as the legal representative of Karl Marx's heirs.

(b) All letters written to me by Percy and Ellen Rosher, Laura and Paul Lafargue, Edward and Eleanor Marx-Aveling, or by my relations in Barmen and Engelskirchen, or by the Beust family in Zurich are to be restored to the writers thereof.

That is all I believe I have to say.

London 14 November 1894.
Frederick Engels.

P.S. It is understood that the honorarium or royalties paid by Sonnenschein for *Capital* and for my *Condition of the Working Class* are to be paid as heretofore, the first to the heirs of Marx and the translators (1/5th to Laura, 1/5th to Tussy, 1/5th to Jenny's children, 6/25ths to Sam Moore, 4/25ths to Ed. Aveling) and the second in full to Florence Kelley."[242]

To Eleanor and Laura he wrote:

"My dear girls,

I have to address to you a few words with regard to my will.

First you will find that I have taken the liberty of disposing of all my books, including those received from you after Mohr's death, in favour of the German Party. The whole of these books constitute a library so unique, and so complete at the same time, for the history and study of Modern Socialism and all the sciences on which it is dependent, that it would be a pity to disperse it again. To keep it together, and to place it at the same time at the disposal of those desirous to use it, has been a wish expressed to me long ago by Bebel and other leaders of the German Socialist Party, as they do indeed seem to be the best people for that purpose. I have consented. I hope that under the circumstances you will pardon my action and give your consent too.

Second. I have had many a discussion with Sam Moore as to the possibility of providing, in my will, in some way for our dear Jenny's children. Unfortunately, English law stands in the way. It could only be done under almost impossible conditions, where the expense would more than eat up the funds to be taken care of. I therefore had to give it up. Instead, I have left each of you *three*-eighths of the residue of my estate after defraying legacies etc. Of these, *two*-eighths are intended for yourselves, and the third eighth is meant to be held by each of you in trust for Jenny's children, to be used as you and the children's guardian, Paul Lafargue, may think best. In this way you are freed from all responsibility with regard to English law and can act as your own moral sense and love for the children may dictate.

The money I owe to the children for shares of profits on Mohr's writings are put down in my ledger, and will be paid by my executors to the party who, according to English law, will be the children's legal representative.

And now good-bye, my dear, dear girls. May you live long and healthily in body and soul and enjoy it!

London, 14 November 1894.

Frederick Engels.

Tussy will have to inform Meissner, Dietz, and the *Vorwärts Buchhandlung* of Berlin that they will henceforth have to pay to her direct any sum due to the heirs of Karl Marx for honorarium etc. As to Sonnenschein, that will have to be settled in some other manner, the agreement about *Capital* being between him and me.

F.E."[243]

A third letter, written in German on the same day and similarly left to be found among his papers, was directed to August Bebel and Paul Singer:

"The £1,000 that I have left you for 'Election purposes' – less death duty – had to be made in this manner because I could not leave money to the Party in any other way that would be legal in this country. Make sure you get the money and, when you have it, that it does not fall into the clutches of the Prussians. And when all is satisfactorily settled, crack a bottle of good wine to my memory."[243a]

Presage of imminent death need not be read into these missives nor more than the wish any prudent man of his years and disposition might entertain to amplify with friendly, human words the formal terms of his will. Indeed, in the same month he wrote an article on "The Peasant Question in France and Germany"* and kept up a world-wide correspondence not only then but for months to come, as involved as ever in political life, while in March 1895 he produced a completely new introduction to a German re-issue of Marx's *Class Struggles in France 1848 to 1850*. The documents intended for his executors and heirs were by no means his "last words", nor were they penned as such.

In her desperate letter of 22 November Eleanor had referred to "the practically complete 4th volume" of *Capital* Volume III, despite continuous interruptions and Engels' solemn, reiterated declaration – generally in the lengthiest of his letters – that he would engage in no more correspondence, was completed and came out at the end of 1894: some nine years after the publication of Volume II. On 17 December he wrote to Laura:

"You say, after finishing the 3rd. vol. and before beginning with the 4th, I must long for a little rest ... Now the thing is the publication of Lassalle's letters to Mohr. Tussy has typed them, they are in my desk but – thanks to the removal – I have not been able

---

* Published in *Neue Zeit* 13 Jg. 1894/5 1 Band. No. 10.

to touch them ... And then Vol. 4. Now of that there is a *very* rough manuscript, of which up to now it is impossible to say how much can be used. I myself cannot again undertake to unravel it and dictate the whole as I did Vol. 2 and 3. My eyesight would break down completely before I was half way through...".[244]

Thus Eleanor's notion of a "practically completed 4th volume" was quite erroneous and it may be that on other points her judgment faltered. Indeed, the fury and forebodings contained in these old hand-written letters still exhale a breath of panic. She had underestimated Engels' capacity to manage his own affairs judiciously, however besotted with Louise, and her belief that he could be cozened into betraying his trust to Marx's daughters was a pure delusion, while her hatred of the vulgar scheming Freybergers was so intense that she may have exaggerated the menace.

To be sure, she was under great stress at the time. Not only was she trying to finish an article for the *Neue Zeit* castigating Brentano's distortions* but, shortly before her second heart's cry to Laura, "poor Edward" had arrived home from St. Mary's in the Scilly Islands†

"looking very ill and complaining of a fearful pain in his side that he had been suffering from some 10 days or a fortnight. When I looked I found he had an enormous abscess – twice the size of my fist! I at once sent for the doctor ... he said it must be opened there and then. It was no joke, I can tell you, for the abscess was a very bad one, & of course, in his already weak state, such an operation was very trying...".‡[247]

It was "an immense cut" and he was "suffering not a little from the drainage tube" that had been inserted.

"However it seems getting on all right, although ... it has been a bad and anxious week, I can tell you, and Edward is still very ill and weak, but I hope on the mend now. I don't think we shall be able to stop here, however. He will need further rest and change so soon as he can get about again. The General has written most kindly and nicely – but he says he is not allowed out as he has a cold. I know he will not be allowed to come here if the Freybergers can prevent it..."

---

* *"Wie Lujo Brentano zitiert".*[245]

† From where he wrote to Laura asking 54 questions about French terms for his translation of Eugène Pottier's songs[246]. Several of these had appeared in *Commonweal* throughout 1889 and in April 1890, done into English by Laura who had promised the author of the *Internationale* when he was dying in 1887 to make his work known abroad. She was now too involved in other work and was doing Aveling a good turn by giving him the commission.

‡ Aveling had been ailing for some time past and had written to *Justice*, which published his letter on 10 October, to say that he had been and still was very ill and, "under medical injunction" could accept no engagements until the New Year. This was the onset of the malignant kidney disease from which he never recovered.

How far it was true that

"the General has been convinced that, like Pumps, I am only speculating on him, and am only *jealous of Louise being in his house etc*...".[247]

it would be hard to say; but that Eleanor had grounds for uneasiness is clear. Freyberger, a comparative stranger, with no socialist affiliations – he was a member of the National Liberal Club – had burrowed his way into Engels' life and established himself in well-appointed premises on the strength of being a medical practitioner beyond compare. For such a man not merely to sanction but determine that his elderly patient should undergo the rigours of a move; that he should constitute himself Engels' bodyguard, controlling whom he might and might not receive, denying access to those with stronger ties, would seem to call his competence in question. So peerless a physician should have diagnosed that the ambience of conviviality was as necessary to Engels as the air he breathed and to leave him much in solitude – "with a bell fitted up ... so that should he 'suddenly need help' "[247] he could summon the doctor – could not but give rise to anxiety, if not in Engels himself, then certainly in Eleanor who had known and understood him all her life.

With Louise the matter went deeper. In Eleanor's view this somewhat pretentious woman who had climbed into political circles first on Kautsky's, then on Bebel's and now on Engels' back, was the soul of indiscretion. Eleanor was not personally jealous of her: she might as well have felt jealousy of every former "reigning queen" – and certainly of Louise during the few years when she had held single sway – had she been disposed to regard Engels' idolising of the women who cared for him as other than an accepted pattern of behaviour. But Louise was no longer in a position to care for him: she was neither housekeeper nor secretary since she had become a wife and mother. What she could do, and what she did, was to tattle: to communicate regularly with the socialist leaders in Austria and Germany, using her position in the household to garner scraps of information about Engels' plans and work and health to scatter them abroad. Eleanor did not simply hold her in contempt and suspicion as she did the husband, she positively loathed her.

It will have been noticed that this feeling did not mount until the pair had dislodged Engels from his accustomed surroundings for their own convenience. At first the marriage, because of her aversion from Freyberger, had excited nothing but Eleanor's compassion for Louise. This attitude did not change – despite that lady's unprovoked dig at her in referring to the "sneers and comments" invited by any relationship other than marriage between a man and a woman – until Louise took the offensive by writing her rubbishy letter to Eleanor. In the light of the removal to the new house, then pending, this could be seen as a deliberate means of causing friction, to create a breach, to put an end to "intimate association" and thus debar any exchange of views on plans afoot.

Eleanor's bitterness now stemmed on the one hand from genuine alarm – if these two people could so manipulate Engels as to devastate his home life their self-interest would stop at nothing – and, on the other, from profound emotional disturbance. Engels – her "second father" – was being alienated from her and thereby she might be alienated from Marx's precious heritage. That he, her Mohr, had never ceased to be the fixed centre of her universe, the inexhaustible spring and fount of her existence, hardly needs to be stated. Her love for Engels had been but deepened when Marx's mantle descended upon him. The papers in his safe keeping were Marx's outward, palpable and immortal remains. They were hers, as he who had said "Tussy *is* me" was an integral part of her being.

Early in December she became aware that, after all, Volume IV of *Capital* was not as far advanced as she had thought: there was much copying out of manuscripts still to be done. Though Engels did not seem overjoyed by the proposal that Bernstein should undertake the work, he agreed to ask him, but did not. Thereupon Eleanor approached him herself and he, Bernstein, "said, of course, he wd accept, if there was no one else", but was strongly of the opinion that Eleanor and Laura "were the proper persons" to do it.

> "It wd, moreover, be a means of getting at the MSS. What do you think?"

Eleanor asked her sister in a letter written a few days later.

> "The General *may* refuse me on the ground that I am very busy & wd delay the work, & he *might* urge against you that you are away and the danger of the post ... You cd offer to fetch the MSS you wd copy, & Bonnier, who so often goes across cd take them back. We cd *both* work at it, & so, at least establish some claim. I shall not say anything till I hear from you, so please answer as soon as possible...".[248]

Upon this Laura was at last stirred up to write; and Laura, roused, could be distinctly forceful in defence of her rights. This letter was passed on to Engels and then, in Eleanor's words, "the fat was in the fire".[249]

On Saturday, 22 December, Eleanor left for Salford where, on the next day, she gave three lectures* to the SDF. Because of Aveling's operation – the wound was not yet healed and needed dressing – she had postponed this engagement until the last possible date. Before catching her train she called briefly at Regent's Park Road where she found everyone out and Engels left to "shift for himself". Aveling was to deliver Laura's "fateful letter", as he called it, on the following day when, though Eleanor could not be there, he would attend the usual Sunday dinner.

It was on Christmas Day, in a style too fanciful to transcribe here, Aveling wrote "To my well-beloved Laura and Paul ... This despatch from the seat of war." To put the matter simply: he had handed over Laura's letter to Engels who immediately agreed that Eleanor should copy out the manuscripts of Volume IV. Engels then read aloud, in Freyberger's presence, Laura's question concerning the disposal of Marx's literary remains. To this he replied in

"a quiet, dignified statement that, *of course* Marx' M.S. & papers were held safe in charge for his daughters & could have no other destination. This was all clear and definite..."

"But now," the despatch went on in Avelingese, "'gather and surmise.' Likewise perpend." Aveling had taken his Sunday after-dinner nap, during which interval the Freybergers had evidently had their say, for the lady was brought downstairs in tears. When Aveling awoke he was ordered by the General "in his most military manner" to show him the letter again. "Then the storm broke out": Engels said there was a conspiracy, there had been conspiracies ever since he had taken the new house; he knew all about it and who was in it; Laura had been "put up" to writing this letter; the whole thing had been concocted when the Avelings and Lafargues had been together in France; Laura and Eleanor mistrusted him. Did they perhaps want a legal assignment?

"All this in the spluttering vein & under the workings of a yeasty conscience, and with much marching up & down and more or less effective dodging of furniture. I said it

* On "The International Socialist Movement", "Socialism, Scientific and Otherwise" and "Women and the Socialist Movement".

was no good bullying me. I was only a messenger and he must have it out with you two women..."[250]

Aveling's regrettable fondness for the pompous and facetious tends to cloud the picture. However, he reported everything to Eleanor on her return whereupon she wrote at once to Engels asking why he should take amiss a simple question about the fate of her father's papers unless he had a bad conscience. Had she thought he could so wildly misinterpret Laura's letter she would never have let him see it. She quoted to Laura what she had written to Engels:

> "... 'As to the general MSS of Mohr, you surely must know that Laura and I are sure *you* wd. deal with them as Mohr himself wd have done. But you can surely understand that we shd not like the letters & papers (many of a purely personal nature) to fall into other hands than yours or ours ... Edward says you seemed to believe in some deep-laid scheme. I can quite believe you do, for I shd be blind indeed if I had not seen the efforts to set you against us, & I can hardly wonder if you think what could never have occurred to you had our Nymmy been with you ... It seems impossible you cd *really* believe Laura and I mistrust you. Whom on earth cd we trust but you? ... After this (Xmas) is over I shall speak to you of it all, & I wish Laura cd be here to speak for herself. I shall say no more now, except that if you had not been very much poisoned against us you cd never have thought so meanly of Mohr's children as to think they cd mistrust *you*'.
>
> There! C'est la guerre," she continued. "– but it *had* to come, & we'd better have it out. Of course what I shall say is that we do *not* trust the F.s – & I shall tell him *my* reasons: that Louise is asking me to sign & get you to sign a paper making *her* the responsible owner of the papers (for fear Pumps shd get hold of them first suggested the matter) & that all we ask – surely no harm in that – is to know, *what apparently an outsider like Bebel does know*, what he has decided to do with the Nachlass. I shall then show him the whole Louise-Bebel-Lieb.-Singer correspondence and have *that* out too. In a word, my dear, it's war, & we've got to fight...".[249]

All this Eleanor wrote in haste before getting ready for the "humbug" of "a merry Xmas with our dear friends the F.s".*

It turned out to be a "Bad Christmas Day", as Eleanor reported to her sister early in the New Year. But in the meantime Engels himself wrote to Laura.

> "... Last Sunday, Tussy being in Manchester sent me your letter to her about Vol. IV. I am quite willing and shall be glad to assist her if she will undertake the work of writing out the original MS.
>
> As to what you say about Mohr's papers and their treatment in case of my death, the matter is simple enough. All these things I hold *in trust for you*, that you know; and consequently on my death they revert to you. In the last will I made (when Sam Moore

---

* The omission marks in citing her letter to Engels are Eleanor's. The punctuation of her own words to Laura has been slightly amended to make the sense clear.

was here last time but one) there is no special provision, but in the instructions to my executors accompanying it, there is a distinct direction to them, to hand over to Tussy, as the administrator of the will, the whole of Mohr's Mss. that are in his own hand-writing, also all letters addressed to him with the sole exception of my correspondence with him. And as Tussy seems to have some doubt about the matter, I shall as soon as Sam M comes back in Summer ask him to draw up a new will in which this is distinctly and unmistakably declared. If you have any other wish please let me know…"[*][251]

On 2 January Eleanor told Laura that she was really "so sick of the sorry business" that she had put off sending "the latest war bulletins"; but, since her sister must know how to answer Engels' letter:

"here are the facts up to date.
     To begin at the beginning. On Xmas Day – as an appetiser for the festive meal – the General took me off to his 'droring-room' & we proceeded to our first round. He had been very angry, he said, at my 'want of tact' in sending him your letter. Against the letter – as from you to me – he had nothing to say, but he thought my sending it to him was etc. etc. etc. Of course I did not tell him you had told me to send the letter. I simply pointed out that my sending it was the best proof that I did not think he wd be offended at it. After a certain amount of sparring – during wh. I told him he had not been angry until others had made him so, to wh. he replied indignantly 'No! I only was with Louise $\frac{1}{2}$ an hour while Edward slept!' – we came to the point: the MSS. He said these were ours & wd, of course, come to us. I said if I had his assurance of that I was quite satisfied & knew you wd be. I added that I *had* been uneasy as I had no confidence in the F.'s & that perfect outsiders had spoken of knowing all about his intentions while we did not. This was the main result of the Xmas day round – but I declared we must have it out, & as this was what the General wished, he came up here to lunch on Friday last. Then we had our second – & so far as the General is concerned, our final round. We then went over much of the same ground again. I told him some of the things L. has been saying & writing of us, & told him too that naturally the people to whom she had said these things wd deny it; that we shd ourselves have the greatest contempt for August[†] if he shd round on L. The General really *knows* pretty well, but naturally *must* make the best of things. I never for a second have believed that he wd or cd make a stand against the 'energetic' mother of the 'energetic' baby. But it was *essential* he shd understand that *we* know also, & that we do not consider Louise a second 'himself'. He again said he *wd see* all papers of Mohr came to us, but said nothing of his will. Of course I said I was quite satisfied & that for the rest, I shd say nothing more about it & so on. I think you should say too that you are satisfied as to

---

[*] This was not strictly accurate: the "last will", drawn up in July 1893 – when Sam Moore was not in England, his leave having expired on 28 January that year – laid down explicitly that Tussy was to have "all papers of a literary nature in the handwriting of … Karl Marx". Moore's "last time but one" in England had been from March to November 1891, when Gumpert was still alive though a sick man. It may be that a will was then made appointing Tussy as an executor in his stead. If so, it was destroyed, and it is not at all clear what was meant by Engels now calling her "the administrator of the will", Gumpert having been replaced by Louise Kautsky as the third executor in 1893.
[†] Bebel.

the MSS. Of course the question of the F.s getting hold of the papers has to be faced, but that we can say & do nothing about. My reason for showing the General Bebel's letter (he had had L's version of the Bebel-Louise 'affaire') was that he shd see Bebel's cool assurance to me that you & I need not trouble about Mohr's papers as *he* knew it was all right. The General was very vexed, because he knows Bebel cd only [have] repeated what L told him, & I saw that his tone altered very considerably after this. However at present the upshot is that the General *will* (I hope!) take definite steps to make sure about the papers, & that he declares two such 'famose Frauenzimmer'* as L. & I – tho' I am *not* so 'noble' as she is – must agree. Well, we – i.e. the noble one & I, will no doubt have a stormy interview – & then all will be peace – on the surface! I *wish* you cd come over soon. It wd be *very* good if you cd ... Thank Heaven the ghastly festivities are over ... I wish you & Paul all good in this year. For myself I have one comfort. It *cant* be worse than the last one!

Love & kisses
Your
Tussy."[252]

Laura's reply to Engels' letter must have been written in her most aggrieved manner. Despite his familiarity with the mode, Engels was "startled" by it and wrote back on 19 January 1895:

"...I have tried, not very successfully, to recollect the terms used in my letter to you of Dec. 29th; still, in what I do remember there is not a word which ought to offend you. And indeed, if there is anything in the tone of that letter which you think strange, it is then entirely against my will and intention.

It never could occur, nor has it ever occurred to me for a moment to doubt the right or the propriety, on your part, of inquiring at any time what steps I had taken or intended to take in order to secure the return, at the time of my death, to you, the rightful owners, of those papers of Mohr's which you have entrusted to me. Nor have I ever found anything to object to in the terms in which you spoke of that subject to Tussy. It seems, therefore, so exceedingly strange to me that I should have written to you in a tone that ought to give you reason to complain.

I did indeed feel nettled at the *way* Tussy caused the question to be submitted to me, and, under the circumstances, thought I was bound to speak to her about it. When I did, I told her *not once but three or four times over*, that I had not a word to say against your letter, neither as to the subject-matter, nor as to the terms used. Anyhow, Tussy and I had an explanation, which, as far as I know, settled everything connected with the subject and left us as good friends as before; and I should regret very much if, through any unguarded words of mine or through some other circumstance, that little incident had thrown its shadow as far as Le Perreux..."†[253]

A few days earlier he had given his brother Hermann the "pleasant news" that he had at last become an old man. If he looked younger than

---

* splendid females.

† "Oh! for a Balzac ...!" Eleanor had exclaimed. This all too human comedy does indeed call for the pen of the inspired novelist rather than that of the plodding biographer earthbound by facts and documents.

his years it was because, though with only 17 teeth left, there were no
gaps in the front, but he had "to accept Freyberger's word for it that I
can't afford to get up to my old tricks any more".[254] His appetite for food
and drink had dwindled; colds that in the past he had been able to shake
off now lingered and turned into bronchitis: there was no getting away
from it, 74 was a very different thing from 47, but at least his sense of
humour had not deserted him.

In February Aveling wrote a card to Kautsky announcing that he was
now "responsible for the editing" of the *Clarion* and issuing the command: "Kindly send me a few lines at once ..."[255] but, while having
assumed this new responsibility, Aveling was not at all fit and, in March,
he and Eleanor went to Hastings from where she wrote twice to
Liebknecht to say that they were there

"for Edward's health, and even these few hours of fresh air – though it is bitterly cold,
have done him good. Still, he is not very strong yet."[256]

Her second letter was written on 14 March:

"... Today it is twelve years since Mohr died – and I think I miss him and my mother
and Jenny more to-day even than when we lost them."

Her letter that day was mainly in support of Thorne's request for Liebknecht to address a West Ham meeting of the Gasworkers' Union.[257]
It was an unusually severe March. As a result of the hard frost

"London was thrown back to barbarism ... four weeks without water ... A fine mess it
was..."[258]

wrote Engels but claimed that

"the cold weather suited me down to the ground, like a strong tonic, I felt 20 years
younger while it lasted..."[259]

Nonetheless, if Engels' death certificate – signed by Freyberger – is to
be taken at its face value, then cancer of the oesophagus and larynx was
diagnosed in the first fortnight of that March. There are no indications
that he knew and many that he did not, for his correspondence then and
thereafter was as cheerful, as full of political interest and as alert as ever,
while even to Sorge, in whom he confided many personal matters, no word
was said of any but his usual "spring ailment" – the rheumatism of his
legs – and the unaccustomed difficulty in ridding himself of colds and

stomach troubles. Only in a letter of 3 April did he betray a glimpse of waning concentration when he wrote to Lafargue:

"...I intended to say a lot of other things ... as well, but I cannot bring them to mind at the moment when I need them. I am gradually aging..."[260]

The fact remains that on 26 March 1895 he drew up a codicil to his will. Witnessed by the cook and nurse employed in his house it made certain vital changes. He now bequeathed

"...to Doctor Ludwig Freyberger of 41 Regents Park Road London as an acknowl-edgment and in consideration of the unremitting care with which he has for years professionally attended me without ever accepting any remuneration the sum of eighty pounds for every complete year elapsed from the first day of July one thousand eight hundred and ninety three down to the date of my death and also the sum of fifty pounds for the fraction of a year however small which may have elapsed from the first day of July preceding my death down to the day of my death And I make this bequest conditional on his making no claim against me or my estate for his professional services I empower and direct my executors before they dispose in open market of the lease of my house No 41 Regents Park Road aforesaid to give to Louise Freyberger referred to in my said will as Louise Kautsky and who is now the wife of the said Doctor Freyberger the option of taking an assignment of the said lease subject to the payment of the rent and the performance of the covenants therein she indemnifying my estate and executors against all claims by the Lessor under the said lease The said option to be exercised by Notice in writing to any of my executors other than the said Louise Freyberger within one month of my death Whereas by my said will I have directed that all family letters written by or addressed to Karl Marx which shall be in my possession or control at the time of my death shall be given by my executors to Eleanor Marx Aveling now I hereby revoke the said direction as to family letters and in lieu thereof I direct that all letters written by or addressed to the said Karl Marx (except my letters to him and his letters to me) which shall be in my possession or control at the time of my death shall be given by my executors to the said Eleanor Marx Aveling who is the legal personal representative of the said Karl Marx and I further direct by this codicil that all letters in my possession at the time of my death written by my relatives in Barmen and Engelskirchen by Percy W. Rosher or Ellen his wife by Paul Lafargue or Laura his wife by Doctor Edward Aveling or Eleanor Marx his wife by Doctor Ludwig Freyberger or Louise his wife and by the Beust family in Zurich be returned by my executors to the respective writers thereof And accordingly I hereby revoke the bequest in my said will to Auguste Bebel and Edward Bernstein of 'all letters (except the said family letters of Karl Marx)' and in lieu thereof I bequeath to the said Auguste Bebel and Edward Bernstein all letters (except those directed to be given by this codicil to the said Eleanor Marx Aveling) and except those otherwise disposed of by this codi-cil..."[260A]

This rigmarole meant, in short, that Eleanor inherited not only Marx's *family* letters but, except for those between Marx and Engels, *all* letters written by or to Marx. Her position as the heir to his manuscripts was unchanged, as was Bernstein's and Bebel's inheritance of Engels' manuscripts – including his correspondence with Marx – and that of Bebel and Singer of his copyrights and books. The residue of his estate, after bequests, was to be divided between Eleanor and Laura, as set out in his letter to them: that is, they were each to receive three-eighths – one part of which was to be regarded as on trust for the Longuet children – the remaining two-eighths going to Louise who, in addition to the furniture and effects "in or about or appropriated" for the house, now had an option on the lease of the house itself – rent free for some 18 months in the event* – and in common with the other two executors, Moore and Bernstein, £250. Bebel and Singer were jointly bequeathed on trust the sum of £1,000 for the purpose of supporting elections to the Reichstag at their discretion. There was one minor change: the £3,000 to Pumps under the will was now reduced to £2,230 taking some complicated transaction with her husband into account.

Thus Louise had the lion's share, casting a shadow of doubt on Engels' perfect sense of justice since, on his own showing, her husband was embarked upon a well-paid profession with brilliant prospects, which could scarcely be said of either Eleanor's or Laura's partners. Equally, however, Engels could be credited with the fine discernment that, whereas Louise was greedy for material possessions, Marx's daughters were not. While providing them with financial security for the first time in their lives, he paid them the supreme compliment of assuming that what mattered to them – their father's legacy – could not be assessed in terms of cash or chattels. Certainly they never felt anything but gratitude to him.

That he had lost none of his gumption is proved by the fight he put up to prevent the mutilation of his new introduction to Marx's *Class Struggles in France* as published in *Neue Zeit*,[262] of which extracts, torn from their context, appeared in *Vorwärts* without his consent, giving, in both cases, a totally false impression of his views. He lost that battle and explained to Laura that the original text

> "had suffered somewhat from the, as I think, exaggerated desires of our Berlin friends not to say anything which might be used as a means to assist in passing the Coercion Bill† in the Reichstag. Under the circumstances I had to give way."‡[263]

---

* Although the Freybergers continued to live at 41 Regent's Park Road for another ten years – until 1905 – their little daughter, born there, never heard any mention of the previous householder who died when she was nine months old. Nor did she learn that there was a "Mr. Engels" until she was grown up and then not from her parents.[261]

† *Umsturzvorlage.* Engels himself referred to it in English as here translated.

‡ After his death, Bernstein, by suppressing the passages whose omission had been reluctantly accepted at the time, used this *Introduction* to insinuate that, in his last days, Engels had switched from revolutionary to reformist principles.

He was still full of plans. For years, he told Kautsky, he had looked forward with enormous pleasure to writing Marx's biography for which he had assembled all the material covering the early years. Now, at his age, he must hasten to record the most important period, that of the First International, which none but he could do.

But by May it was a different story. He wrote to Richard Fischer on the 9th to say that, after a short bout of influenza, he was suffering from terrible head pains which he put down to rheumatism of the scalp. He could neither sleep nor work. He invited the Lafargues to come to England and, to his great delight, they agreed. He wrote to Laura on the 14th saying that the "confounded pains" had driven him nearly mad "and even now have not left me". He felt

> "extremely stupid and unfit for anything. The fact is this. Some time ago I got a swelling on the right side of the neck, which after some time resolved itself into a bunch of deep-seated glands ... The pains arose from direct pressure of that lump on the nerve and will of course only give way when that pressure disappears ... a couple of these glands are suppurating and will have to be cut ... the time for the operation cannot be exactly fixed, but, it is hoped, will come off this week. That once performed, I am ordered to the sea-side ... Now as things are situated, would it not be the best thing for you to come over, say, in the course of next week, and then as soon as possible you and I could bundle off to Eastbourne ... Louise ... might come and join us for a week or so; after that Tussy and Edward might come ...
>
> This is such a sort of rough prospectus as a man with neuralgic pains in the head after a series of sleepless nights has been able to excogitate ..."

To this he added a postscript:

> "There is another reason to avoid unnecessary delay; to get to E *before Whitsun* week* on account of cheap trippers, etc."[264]

In fact he was not operated on at all, nor did he get to Eastbourne until June.†

In the meantime he had suffered one of the cruellest blows to his pride. Kautsky, Bernstein, Mehring, Lafargue and others were preparing a history of socialism and had not so much as informed him. Now Kautsky, on 6 May, sent him the first part, for which he was responsible, and said would it not be a splendid idea if the material Engels had in hand for writing Marx's life during the period of the First International were used as an introduction to the fourth volume which was to deal with modern socialism in every country. Indeed, for anybody else to do this – though they had someone in view – would be an absurdity if Engels were willing.

---

* Whit Sunday fell on 26 May that year.
† The date is uncertain, but it was during the second week.

The only thing was it would have to be ready by the autumn of 1896, which was rather short notice, but no more than 20 or 30 pages were needed, and so on and so forth.

In a letter of dignified rebuke Engels replied:

"...Of all those alive today – I think I may venture to say – there was only one whose collaboration appeared absolutely necessary, and that one was I. I dare go so far as to say that without my help a work of this nature today cannot be anything but incomplete and inadequate. And you know this as well as I do. Of all possibly useful people I am precisely the only one who was *not* invited to collaborate. You must have had very cogent reasons for excluding, precisely, me. I am not complaining about this, far from it. You had every right to do so. I merely state the fact.

What did vex me, though only for a moment, was the peculiar secretiveness with which you shrouded the matter from me while the entire world was talking about it. I first learnt of the whole undertaking only through third parties, first of the general outline of the plan from the printed prospectus. Not a word from either you or Ede, as though you had a bad conscience. But at the same time whispered enquiries about my position from all manner of people, whether I had declined to collaborate etc. And then finally, when silence was no longer possible, the good Ede brought himself to speak of the matter with a sheepishness and embarrassment worthy of a worse cause – since no offence had been committed other than the farcical play-acting which in the meantime, as Louise can testify, gave me some hours of hearty laughter.

Well and good. You have confronted me with a *fait accompli*. 'A History of Socialism' without my collaboration ... But this is a situation of your own making which you cannot obliterate, cannot ignore, when the occasion suits you. And I can obliterate it just as little. If, after due consideration, you shut the entrance gates in my face at a time when my advice and help could have been of appreciable use to you, please don't ask me now to slink in through some little back door in order to get you out of an embarrassment. I must say that, were the roles reversed I should have meditated for a long, long time before coming to you with a request such as you now make. Is it really so difficult to realise that everyone must take upon themselves the consequences of their own actions? As you made your bed so you must lie on it. If there's no room for me in it, that's simply because you willed it so.

Well, that's over and done with. And now do me the favour of accepting my reply as irrevocable. Let this whole episode be dead and buried for us both. Nor will I mention it to Ede if he doesn't raise it...".[265]

He then went on at some length and quite typically to make constructive criticisms of Kautsky's part, giving freely of his knowledge and suggesting improvements to the style.

The inescapable conclusion is that, while Engels was not aware of the terminal nature of his illness, everyone else was and that the information had been put about in such a way that it was thought to be not merely indiscreet but almost indecent to approach him on the subject of this long-term project for a history of socialism, to which self-evidently in other circumstances he must have been the chief consultant and guide. His friends were made to feel shamefaced and ill at ease in even mentioning it to him. Their plans were made behind his back and he was totally excluded. It was the most atrocious injury the grand old man could suffer. Whoever was responsible for inflicting it had done a vile thing.

Laura came to England without Paul and had been in Eastbourne with Engels for a little while when both Eleanor and Aveling came at the end of June.

They had vacated. Gray's Inn Square and left London for good to live in Green Street Green, near Orpington in Kent* from 1 July.

Louise, with husband and child, came only at the weekend and, on 1 July, Engels wrote asking her to bring a certain bottle of medicine and the newspaper cutting about Aveling's nomination as a parliamentary candidate by the ILP.† For the rest, he was concerned that Louise and the baby should be warmly clothed on their next visit as the weather in Eastbourne had turned chilly. She arrived on 3 July and then stayed on, for Laura was to leave the next morning.

On the day after, he wrote to Eleanor at Green Street Green teasing her for having accepted the translation of Plekhanov's *Anarchism and Socialism*:‡

> "... there indeed I do pity you," he said. "Where is the poor girl to have picked up the necessary knowledge for such work?
>
> Here," he went on, "everything 'as you were', as the military command says. I am much as usual, that is to say subject to all sorts of variations of temper and spirits. That will last for some time yet to come.
>
> Either Louise or myself will keep you informed of how I go on.
>
> Love to you both..."[266]

He wrote to her once more, in a letter dated 9 July from 4 Royal Parade:

> 'My dear Tussy,
>
> Thanks for Johnnie's letter returned herewith. Of course the boy is right in sticking to the house. Edgar seems a downright Normand, looking after momentary§ advantage. More's the pity.
>
> Edward's reply to Glasgow is allright. The solution is to be found Labour Leader 6

---

* Now so entirely built up that although a few anachronistic dwellings still stand remote from the new housing estates and there are vestiges of what may have been the ancient Green, the topography of this rural area as it was in Eleanor's day is no longer traceable.

† The Glasgow Central Division branch had asked him to stand in the forthcoming election (12 August 1895). He refused on the grounds of health, but Engels thought "the Glasgow affair might be a trap...".[266]

‡ This was from the German and the first of Plekhanov's works to appear in English. Eleanor's version was published "with the permission of the author" in the *Weekly Times and Echo* to be re-issued as a pamphlet by the Twentieth Century Press in October 1895.

§ Perhaps "monetary".

July page 2 K[eir] H[ardie] against E A in the Jeunesse Socialiste. Now the noble nature of K.H. shines out brilliantly. While E.A. attacks him, K.H. generously finds him a candidature, which if E.A. accepted, K.H. could on general grounds get cancelled by the Executive Council.

I was pretty fairly going on till Sunday night, since then had two bad nights and days, maybe partly from the acceleration, by the sea air, of the processus of elimination going on in my neck, but chiefly from the decreasing effects of the anaesthetics which I now have been using daily and in increasing quantities for about eight weeks. On the other hand I have found out several weak sides of my capricious appetite and take lait de poule* with brandy, custard with stewed fruits, oysters up to nine a day etc.

> Love to you both
> F.E."[267]

Sam Moore wrote to Eleanor on 21 July from 2 Stone Buildings, Lincoln's Inn:

"My dear Tussy,

I felt very anxious to know how the General was getting on, so went down to Victoria to meet the 7.15 p.m. from Eastbourne this evening by which train Dr. Freyberger generally returns.†

I met him and I am sorry to say that his report is anything but cheering; he says that the disease has attained such a hold that, considering the General's age, his state is precarious. Apart from the diseased glands of the neck there is danger either from weakness of the heart or from pneumonia – and in either of these two cases the end would be sudden. He may go on for some weeks if pneumonia does not intervene, but if it does then it will be a question of a few hours. In spite of all, however, the General is quite hopeful and is certain that he will recover – he intends, and has arranged with the 2 doctors to return to London on Wednesday evening – so that if you want to see him you had better go to 41 R.P.R. on Thursday.

This is sad news and I trust the doctors may be mistaken. There is so much work to be done which the General alone is capable of doing, that his loss will be irreparable from a public point of view – to his friends it will be a calamity.

I have just time to write this – in haste–

> Yours very sincerely,
> S. Moore."[267]

Engels told Laura on 23 July that they were returning to London the next day.

"There seems to be at last a crisis approaching in my potato field in my neck, so that the swellings may be opened and relief secured. At last! . . .

The elections here have come off as I said: a large Tory majority, the Liberals hopelessly beaten . . . The brag of the ILP and SDF face to face with a reality of some 82,000 votes for Labour candidates up to now (hardly any yet to come) and the loss of K. Hardie's seat. Still that was more than they had a right to expect.

---

* Egg-nog.
† On a Sunday evening.

Victor Adler is here.* Have you or Paul any questions to ask him about Paul's arrangement with the *Arbeiter Zeitung* or can I be of any use in any way to you with him?

I am not in strength to write long letters, so good-bye. Here's your good health in a bumper of egg-nog fortified by a dose of old brandy.

Cordial greetings to Paul,

     Ever yours,

      F. Engels."[268]

This is the last letter he is known to have written.

Eleanor followed Moore's advice and went to see Engels that week. She had more than one reason, for, since writing to her, Moore had been much at Engels' bedside and had come to Green Street Green to tell her as gently as he could of Engels' revelation concerning Freddy Demuth's paternity.† Shattered but disbelieving, Eleanor was determined to hear it from Engels' own lips. This she was not to do. When she arrived at Regent's Park Road Engels was beyond the power of speech.

This, their last meeting, was in more ways than one the unhappiest in all the long years. The beloved old friend from whom hostile forces had estranged her in the recent past, mute and near to death, was still able to write down the words that destroyed her faith in the consistent loving-kindness of her father. Thus bitter gall was added to bitter grief and her sombre feelings as she travelled back to Kent can be imagined.

On 3 August Engels became unconscious and two days later at 10.15 in the evening he died, alone. The immediate cause, certified by Freyberger, was "broncho-pneumonia for 1 day and 16 hours". Louise wrote to Eleanor (in German) that she had

"... gone out of the room to change for night-duty, was not away for 5 minutes and when I came back, all was over."[269]

Five days later at eleven o'clock on the morning of Saturday 10 August some eighty people assembled at Waterloo Station for his obsequies. Eleanor wrote to John Burns that:

"By his own express wish our dear General is to be cremated, & equally by his definite instruction the funeral is to be strictly private, only his personal friends being invited or such political representatives as were also his personal friends ... we should be glad if you will attend ... we shall be grateful if you wd mention time & place to *no one*..."[270]

---

* He had been imprisoned from 8 May to 18 June in Vienna. On his release Freyberger told him of Engels' condition and, having raised the money for his fare, Adler came to England in July, remaining until 3 August.

† See pp. 239–247.

To the last *Justice*, reporting the occasion with due solemnity, bore a grudge:

"... It was a matter of regret to the few English Socialists who were present that among these floral tributes to the memory of our departed comrade, and of the esteem in which he was held by the Socialists of all countries, there was nothing from the Socialists of Great Britain ... This, however, was due to the complete secrecy ... with which the whole arrangements had been carried out. Even the few who were invited had but twenty-four hours' notice and were strictly enjoined to secrecy ... As it was there was an entire absence of ceremony..."[*271]

Such ceremony as there was had to be postponed for three hours owing to a last-minute official intervention, the coroner not being satisfied until an informal inquest had been held[†] while the mourners waited.

Short speeches were made by Gustav Schlechtendahl of Barmen on behalf of the German relatives - among whom Hermann Engels, another nephew, was present - Sam Moore, Aveling, Liebknecht, Lafargue, Bebel, Anseele of Belgium and Van der Goës of Holland. Though speaking officially in the name of the French Workers' Party, Lafargue's voice was stifled with emotion as he said:

"Farewell, dear friend, I shall never again know so lovable, so good and so indulgent a friend..."[272]

Apart from the members of Marx's family — the Avelings, Lafargues and Johnny Longuet — those who came included the Roshers, the Freybergers, Lessner, Stepniak, Mendelson, Vera Zasulich and Frederick Demuth.

Such secular valedictions took place in the small edifice at the head of the private single track of the London & South Western Railway from which hearse trains departed three times each day for Brookwood and thence on a spur line to the Woking Necropolis:[‡] that bourne from which all travellers but one returned.

Engels was cremated shortly after quarter past four that afternoon.

On a blustery morning, Friday, 27 September,[§] Eleanor, Aveling,

---

* *Justice* did, however publish two respectful though not uncritical obituary notices: a short front-page one on the day of the funeral (10 August) and a second of two columns on 24 August written by Bax, in the course of which he said: "Of all the present English working class leaders personally known to him, I think ... Will Thorne was the greatest favourite with Engels."

† Cremation could not be sanctioned without the certificate of a second, independent medical practitioner who had examined the facts and established that death was due to natural causes, failing which there had to be an autopsy. (See Appendix 3.)

‡ Discontinued since the First World War.

§ See H. Gemkow. *Beiträge zur Marx-Engels-Forschung* No. 13 1982, pp. 41–45.

Lessner and Bernstein went to Eastbourne – "the pleasantest seaside place" Engels had known – hired a small rowing boat and, "six miles out to sea, almost straight from Beachy Head",[273] consigned his ashes to the waves.

Engels' remains lay fathoms deep. He had no monument, no tomb, nor any shrine at which homage could be paid. This man of "Genius, Learning, strong Comprehension, Quickness of Conception, Magnanimity, Generosity, Sagacity",[274] in death as in life spurned the veneration* he had always felt was owed to Marx alone.

Only two more summers were to come and go before Eleanor's body followed Engels' into the furnace.

REFERENCE NOTES

Abbreviations

Bebel	*August Bebel. Briefwechsel mit Friedrich Engels*. Edited by Werner Blumenberg. Mouton & Co., The Hague, 1965.
BIML	Institute of Marxism-Leninism, Berlin.
BLPES	British Library of Political and Economic Science, London School of Economics.
Bottigelli Archives	Letters in the custody of Professor Emile Bottigelli.
ELC	*Frederick Engels, Paul and Laura Lafargue: Correspondence*. Volumes I–III. Lawrence & Wishart, 1959–63.
IISH	International Institute of Social History, Amsterdam.
Liebknecht	*Wilhelm Liebknecht. Briefwechsel mit Karl Marx und Friedrich Engels*. Edited by Georg Eckert. Mouton & Co., The Hague, 1963.
MEW	*Marx Engels Werke*. Dietz Verlag. Berlin, 1956–68.
MIML	Institute of Marxism-Leninism, Moscow.

(1) *Sozialdemokratische Monatsschrift. Nr.* 10–11 II Jg. 30 November 1890. Vienna. pp. 1–8.
   The original German has been translated into English in *Reminiscences of Marx and Engels*. Foreign Languages Publishing House, Moscow, n.d. pp. 182–90.
(2) To Adler, 12 December 1890. MEW 37, p. 519.
(3) To Hermann Engels, 9 January 1890. *Ibid.*, p. 338.
(4) *The Times*, 13 March 1890. J. F. Smith. Admissions Register, Manchester School, Vol. II, 1898, pp. 49 & 298, published in *Modern English Biography*. Vol. III Boase. 1901, for tracing which I am indebted to Mrs. Gwynydd Gosling.
(5) Draft letters to Jakyns and to Strutt & Parker, 23 September 1890. MIML.
(6) 26 September 1890. ELC II, p. 403.
(7) 1 December 1890. *Ibid.*, p. 422.

---

* Interestingly enough, the Quakers held the same view, saying that it "consorted not" with their principles "unduly to exalt the honoured dead; their names we canonise not, and o'er their graves we raise no costly monuments".[275] It also comes to mind that the exact spot where such immortals as Mozart and Laurence Sterne lie buried is unknown. Naturally, portraits and statues of Engels abound today and he has not escaped iconolatry.

(8) 2nd Yearly Report of the Gas Workers and General Labourers' Union of Great Britain & Ireland, to March 31, 1890–1891. General Secretary's *Address*, pp. 12, 13. From their archives by kind permission of the General and Municipal Workers' Union.

(9) *Ibid.*, pp. 9, 10.

(10) *Ibid.*, p. 16.

(11) To the National Council of the French Workers' Party. 2 December 1890. ELC II, p. 424.

(12) 5 December 1890. MEW 37, p. 515.

(13) 5 December 1890. ELC II, p. 424.

(14) 2 December 1890. *Ibid.*, pp. 423, 424.

(15) 26 November 1890. MEW 37, p. 505.

(16) 5 November 1890. *Ibid.*, p. 498. Gustav Mayer. *Friedrich Engels*. Tr. Gilbert and Helen Highet. Ed. R. H. S. Crossman. Chapman & Hall 1936, p. 272.

(17) *Reminiscences of Marx and Engels*, p. 191. (See (1).)

(18) *Ibid.*, pp. 254, 255. n.d. No provenance given. (Original in English.)

(19) 12 March 1896. Liebknecht, p. 445.

(20) Engels to Liebknecht, 7 October 1890. MEW 37, p. 481.

(21) Thomas Hardy. *Rain on a Grave*.

(22) Engels to Laura, 27 August 1889. ELC II, p. 302.

(23) Lafargue to Engels, 14 April 1889. *Ibid.*, p. 222.

(24) To Liebknecht, 19 June 1890. MEW 37, p. 417.

(25) To Laura, 30 July 1890. ELC II, p. 379.

(26) 7 November 1890. IISH.

(27) Engels to Laura, 19 October 1890. ELC II, p. 409.

(28) *Ibid.*, 2 November 1890, pp. 417, 418,

(29) IISH.

(30) Heinz Monz. *Karl Marx. Grundlagen der Entwicklung zu Leben und Werk.* NCO Verlag. Trier, 1973, p. 360, fn. 39.

(31) MEW 39, p. 539.

(32) Engels to Laura, 29 October 1889. ELC II, p. 334.

(33) 9 November 1890. MEW 37, p. 500.

(34) 20 December 1890. Victor Adler. *Briefwechsel mit August Bebel und Karl Kautsky.* Ed. Friedrich Adler. Verlag der Wiener Volksbuch-handlung. Vienna 1954, p. 66.

(35) 17 December 1890. ELC II, p. 426.

(36) Bottigelli Archives.

(37) *Ibid.*

(38) To Laura, 6 August 1891. *Ibid.*

(39) To Laura, 12 August 1891. *Ibid.*

(40) To Laura, 25 September 1891. *Ibid.*

(41) To Laura, 22 February 1894. *Ibid.*

(42) 23 November 1882. *Friedrich Engels' Briefwechsel mit Karl Kautsky.* Ed. Benedikt Kautsky. Danubia-Verlag. Vienna, 1955, p. 70.

(43) To Laura, 17 December 1894. ELC III, pp. 347, 348.

(44) To Laura, 27 August 1889. ELC II, p. 301.

(45) Preface to *Karl Marx: Theories of Surplus Value, Part I* (Volume IV of *Capital*). Tr. Emile Burns. Lawrence & Wishart 1963, pp. 18, 19.

(46) Engels to Vera Zasulich, 17 April 1890. MEW 37, p. 392.

(47) To Kautsky, 15 September 1889. *Ibid.* p. 273.

(48) 20 March 1893. MEW 39, p. 56. *Friedrich Engels Briefwechsel mit Karl Kautsky, op. cit.*, p. 380.

(49) 19 October 1890. ELC II, p. 409.

(50) To Kautsky, 14 October 1891. MEW 38, pp. 179, 180.

(51) 18–28 March 1875. *August Bebel, op. cit.*, pp. 28–31. This letter was first published in Vol. II of Bebel's memoirs *Aus meinem Leben*, Stuttgart, 1911, pp. 318 *et seq.*

(52) 10 May 1875. Emile Bottigelli, *Lettres et documents de Karl Mark 1856–1883*. Annali dell' Istituto Giangiacomo Feltrinnelli. Anno Primo. Milan 1958.

(53) *Protokoll über die Verhandlungen des Parteitags der Sozialdemokratischen Partei Deutschlands. Abgehalten zu Halle a S vom 12. bis 18. Oktober 1890.* Berlin 1890. IISH, p. 179.

(54) To Kautsky, 23 February 1891. MEW 38, p. 39.

(55) 9 Jg. Band I. Nr. 21. 1890/91.

(56) Engels to Bebel, 24 October 1891. MEW 38, p. 185.

(57) To Bebel, 12 October 1875. MEW 34, p. 159.

(58) To Lafargue, 10 February 1891. ELC III, pp. 29, 30.

(59) 27 July 1893. Liebknecht, pp. 388, 389.

(60) Editorial, "Ten Years of the S.D.F." *Justice*, 10 January 1891.

(61) *Justice*, 14 February 1891.

(62) *Ibid.*, 7 February 1891.

(63) *People's Press*, 14 February 1891.

(64) *Justice*, 21 February 1891.

(65) Aveling family papers by permission of Dr. Paul Redhead.

(66) *Justice*, 28 February 1891.

(67) *Ibid.*, 9 May 1891.

(68) *Ibid.*, 17 October 1891.

(69) *Ibid.*, 12 September 1891.

(70) *Workman's Times*, 2 October 1891.

(71) Ernest Belfort Bax. *Reminiscences and Reflections of a Mid and Late Victorian.* Allen & Unwin. 1918, pp. 55, 56; 52, 53; 108.

(72) *Daily Chronicle*, 18 September 1891.

(73) To Laura, 25 September 1891. Bottigelli Archives.

(74) ELC III p. 109.

(75) To Laura, 14 March 1892. ELC III, pp. 163, 164.

(76) 30 January 1892.

(77) Henry S. Salt. *Seventy Years Among Savages.* Allen & Unwin, 1921, pp. 81, 82.

(78) 29 September, 1 October 1891. *August Bebel, op. cit.*, p. 442.

(79) 5 March 1892. ELC III, p. 160. 19 February 1892. MEW 39, p. 278.

(80) To Laura, 19 April 1892. ELC III, pp. 166, 167.

(81) MEW 38, pp. 275, 276.

(82) First half of February 1892. MIML.

(83) Translated by Ernest Untermann and published by Charles Kerr & Co. of Chicago.

(84) Translated by Alick West and published by Lawrence & Wishart.

(85) To Laura, 4 May 1891. ELC III, p. 56.

(86) To Lafargue, 19 May 1891. *Ibid.*, p. 65.

(87) To Laura, 4 May 1891. *Ibid.*, pp. 56–8.

(88) *"Eleanor Marx: Erinnerungen von Eduard Bernstein"*, *Die Neue Zeit. XVI Jg. II Band Nr.* 30, 1897/9. Ernest Belfort Bax. *op. cit.*, p. 108.

(89) 14 April 1891. Radford family papers.

(90) To Elizabeth Robins, 20 April 1891. *Bernard Shaw. Collected Letters, 1874–1897.* Ed. by Dan H. Laurence. Max Reinhardt, 1965, p. 291.

(91) 25 April 1891. Radford family papers.

(92) 11 July 1891.

(93) 15 August 1891.

(94) 17 August 1891.

(95) *Early Socialist Days,* Hogarth Press 1929, pp. 83–5.

(96) To Engels, 17 July 1891. ELC III, p. 94.

(97) To Laura, 17 August 1891. *Ibid.*, p. 98.

(98) To Laura, 6 August 1891. Bottigelli Archives.

(99) To Laura, 6 July 1891. *Ibid.*

(100) 12 August 1891. *Ibid.*

(101) To Laura, 25 September 1891. *Ibid.*

(102) 20 August 1891.

(103) 29 August 1891.

(104) 22 August 1891.

(105) 17 August 1891. ELC III, pp. 98, 99.

(106) 29 August 1891.

(107) *Report to the Third Annual Conference of the Gasworkers Union,* 1892, pp. 5, 6. GMWU.

(108) BLPES.

(109) 1. Jg. No 3, 3 February 1892. BIML.

(110) To Engels, 10 July 1891. ELC III, p. 89.

(111) To Engels, 18 May 1891. *Ibid.*, p. 63.

(112) To Engels, 7 May 1891. *Ibid.*, p. 61.

(113) To Engels, 10 July 1891. *Ibid.*, p. 89.

(114) 6 July 1891. Bottigelli Archives

(115) To Engels, 20 August 1891. ELC III, pp. 99–101.

(116) William Morris papers. BM. Add. MSS. 45345 (278). (Original in French.)

(117) To Laura, 25 September 1891. Bottigelli Archives.

(118) To Engels, 10 October 1891. ELC III, p. 113.

(119) To Engels, 18 November 1891. *Ibid.*, p. 133.

(120) 22 November 1891. *Ibid.*, pp. 134–6.

(121) 25 November 1891. *Ibid.*, p. 137.

(122) 26 November 1891. *Ibid.*, p. 138.

(123) To Kautsky, 30 April 1891. MEW 38, p. 88.

(124) 25 November 1891. *Ibid.*, p. 219.

(125) 27 November 1891. ELC III, pp. 139–42.

(126) 1 December 1891. MEW 38, pp. 225, 226.

(127) 3 December 1891. ELC III, p. 144.

(128) Engels to Bebel, 1 December 1891. MEW 38, p. 226.

(129) To Lafargue, 3 December 1891. ELC III, pp. 144, 145.

(130) To Engels, 9 December 1891. *Ibid.*, p. 146.

(131) BIML. (Original in French.)

(132) ELC III, p. 78.

(133) To Laura. Bottigelli Archives.

(134) 13 June 1891. ELC III, p. 78.

(135) 28 June 1891. ELC III, p. 83.

(136) To Laura, 7 January 1893. Bottigelli Archives.

(137) BIML.

(137a)
    To Laura, 7 January 1893. Bottigelli Archives.
(138) ELC III, pp. 147, 148.
(139) *Ibid.*, pp. 148–50.
(140) *Ibid.*, p. 152.
(141) 20 January 1892. MIML.
(142) ELC III, p. 209.
(143) 22 November 1892. *Ibid.*, p. 213.
(144) 28 November 1892. *Ibid.*, pp. 215, 216.
(145) *Ibid.*, p. 220.
(146) Quoted in *Eleanor Marx: Erinnerungen von Eduard Bernstein. Die Neue Zeit. XVI Jg.* II Band. No. 30 1897/8, p. 122.
(147) Holograph by kind permission of Mr. William Fishman.
(148) 7 November 1890.
(149) *Commonweal.* 7 June 1890.
(150) *Reynolds's Newspaper.* 4 September 1892.
(151) *Justice.* 10 September 1892.
(152) Unpublished and undated MS., probably of the mid-1920s. MIML.
(153) To Kautsky, 28 December 1896. IISH.
(154) W. H. Lee and E. Archbold. *Social-Democracy in Britain.* Social-Democractic Federation, 1935, p. 87.
(155) Thorne, *My Life's Battles.* George Newnes. n.d. probably 1925, p. 152.
(156) Charles Kerr, Chicago, 1908.
(157) 17 November 1895. IISH.
(158) 10 December 1895. Bottigelli Archives.
(159) Information kindly provided by Mr. Roy D. Rates. Borough Librarian, Lewisham.
(160) *Justice,* 13 August 1892.
(161) *Makers of the Labour Movement,* Longmans Green. 1948, p. 214.
(162) *Report of the First Conference of the Independent Labour Party.* BLPES, p. 6.
(163) Engels to Lafargue, 17 September 1892. ELC III, p. 194.
(164) *Report from Great Britain and Ireland to the Delegates of the Zurich Socialist Workers' Congress,* 1893. BLPES. pp. 2, 7.
(165) 30 May 1892. Bottigelli Archives.
(166) James B. Jefferys. *The Story of the Engineers.* Lawrence & Wishart for the AEU on the 25th anniversary of the foundation of the Union, 1920–1945, p. 104.
(167) To Kautsky, 11 June 1892. MEW 38, p. 361.
(168) *"Die Wahlen in Grossbritannien"* – *Die Neue Zeit.* No. 45. X-Jg. II Band. 1891–92.
(169) To Kaustsky, 12 August 1892. MEW 38, p. 422.
(170) ELC III, pp. 183–4.
(171) 26 July 1892. Bottigelli Archives.
(172) *Ibid.*
(173) To Dr. Anna Kulishov. IISH. (Original in German.)
(174) 19 November 1892.
(175) *Justice.* 19 November 1892.
(176) 12 November 1892. Original typescript lent by W. Diack to the late G. Allen Hutt in 1939 and kindly passed on in photostat.
(177) William Diack. *History of the Trades Council and the Trade Union Movement in Aberdeen.* Printed for the Aberdeen Trades Council. 1939, pp. 62–63.
(178) 27 January 1893. Holograph letter lent by W. Diack to the late G. Allen Hutt.
(179) 28 December 1892. Radford family papers.

(180) 15 July 1893. *Ibid.*

(181) 13 September 1893. *Ibid.*

(182) 25 January 1893. *Ibid.*

(183) *Justice*, 15 April 1893.

(184) *Ibid.* 1 April 1893.

(185) To Ludwig Schorlemmer (brother of Carl who had died in 1892), 29 April 1893. MEW 39, p. 70.

(186) 14 March 1893. ELC III, pp. 249, 250.

(187) *Justice*, 15 April 1893.

(188) Engels to Sorge, 18 March 1893. MEW 39, p. 53.

(189) 18 February 1893.

(190) Public Record Office. Unpublished. Crown Copyright material by permission of H.M. Stationery Office.

(191) To Anna Kulishov, 15 September 1892. IISH. (Original in German.)

(192) Delegates' names – not always correctly spelt – organisations and all other details of the Congress are from the *Protokoll des Internationalen Sozialistischen Arbeiterkongresses in der Tonhalle, Zürich.* Published Zurich 1894. IISH.

(193) To Laura, 21 August 1893. ELC III, p. 286.

(194) *Report of the First General Conference of the Independent Labour Party*, BLPES, p. 3.

(195) *Protokoll., op. cit.*, pp. 52–3.

(196) 30 September 1892. MIML.

(197) 13 May 1892. *Friedrich Engels Briefwechsel mit Karl Kautsky. op. cit.* p. 340.

(198) 17 May 1892. MEW 38, pp. 339–40.

(199) 25 June 1892. *Ibid.*, 375–6.

(200) MIML.

(201) To Adler, 16 March 1895. MEW 39, p. 436.

(202) Engels to Lafargue, ELC III, p. 208.

(203) 6 March 1893. MIML.

(204) 23 February 1894. MEW 39, p. 212.

(205) To Sorge, 21 March 1894. *Ibid.*, p. 225.

(206) Engels to Laura, 11 April 1894. ELC III, p. 331.

(207) Engels to Lafargue, 2 June 1894. *Ibid.*, p. 334.

(208) 20 December 1892. *Ibid.*, p. 224.

(209) To Laura, 22 August 1892. *Ibid.*, p. 189.

(210) To Adler, 25 September 1892. MEW 38, p. 473.

(211) 8 February; 12, 17 April 1890. MEW 37, pp. 355, 382, 395.

(212) To Ludwig Schorlemmer, Carl's brother, 5 June 1892. MEW 38, p. 356.

(213) 26 July 1892. Bottigelli Archives.

(214) To Hermann Engels, 12 January 1895. MEW 39, p. 380.

(215) 20 July 1893. ELC III, p. 279.

(216) Somerset House.

(217) To Laura. Bottigelli Archives.

(218) 21, 31 August; 18 September, 1893. ELC III, pp. 282–5, 287–8; 292.

(219) To Laura, 7 September 1893. IISH.

(220) Radford family papers.

(221) 19 November 1893.

(222) To Laura, 11 November 1893. Bottigelli Archives.

(223) To Laura, 26 July 1892. *Ibid.*

(224) Bottigelli Archives.

(225) MEW 39, p. 162.

(226) 11 November 1893. Bottigelli Archives.

(227) 22 February 1894. *Ibid.*

(228) To Laura, 2 March 1894. *Ibid.*

(229) 6 March 1894. ELC III, p. 326.

(230) 8 March 1894. *Ibid.*, p. 327.

(231) Bottigelli Archives.

(232) 12 May 1894. MEW 39, p. 244.

(233) 26 July 1894. MIML.

(234) 10 November 1894. MEW 39, p. 307.

(235) 15 September 1894. Bottigelli Archives.

(236) 21 September 1894. *Ibid.*

(237) 12 January 1895. MEW 39, p. 380.

(238) To Laura, 12 November 1894. MIML.

(239) 12 January 1895. MEW 39, p. 380.

(240) 5 November 1894. Bottigelli Archives.

(241) 22 November 1894. *Ibid.*

(242) BIML.

(243) ELC III, pp. 341–3.

(243a) MEW 39, p. 316.

(244) ELC III, p. 348.

(245) *Neue Zeit XIII Jg. I Bd. Nr. 9.* 1894/5.

(246) 21 October 1894. Bottigelli Archives.

(247) 22 November 1894. *Ibid.*

(248) 15 December 1894. *Ibid.*

(249) To Laura, 25 December 1894. *Ibid.*

(250) 25 December 1894. *Ibid.*

(251) 29 December 1894. ELC III, pp. 352–3.

(252) 2 January 1895. Bottigelli Archives.

(253) ELC III, pp. 360–61.

(254) 12 January 1895. MEW 39, p. 381.

(255) 26 February 1895. IISH.

(256) 7 March 1895. Liebknecht, p. 439.

(257) *Ibid.*, pp. 439–40.

(258) Engels to Laura, 28 March 1895. ELC III, p. 366.

(259) To Kugelmann, 19 March 1895. MEW 39, p. 442.

(260) ELC III, p. 373.

(261) Privately communicated by Miss Freyberger.

(262) *XIII Jg.* 2 Bd. Nos. 27 and 28. 1894/5.

(263) 28 March 1895. ELC III, p. 368.

(264) 14 May 1895. *Ibid.*, pp. 379–81.

(265) MEW 39, pp. 481–2.

(266) To Eleanor, card postmarked 5 July 1895. Bottigelli Archives.

(267) MIML.

(268) ELC III, p. 381.

(269) 5 August 1895. Bottigelli Archives.

(270) 8 August 1895. IISH.

(271) 17 August 1895.

(272) *Justice. Ibid.*

(273) Eleanor to Kautsky, 29 September 1895. IISH.

(274) Swift. *Intelligencer Papers*, No. V. Dublin 1728.

(275) W. Beck and T. F. Ball. 1869. Quoted by Mrs. Basil Holmes. *The London Burial Grounds*. T. Fisher Unwin 1896, pp. 259, 260.

· PART V ·

THE CLOUDED YEARS

At the age of 40 Eleanor Marx became a lady of independent means. Engels' will, first proved on 28 August 1895, was subject to a corrective affidavit and double probate was granted in January 1896 when his estate was valued at £25,265 os. 11d.* The residue, after death duties† and bequests had been paid, was roughly £20,378. Eleanor and Laura each received some £7,642, one-third of which was on trust for Jenny's children, leaving for themselves something over £5,000.‡

Foremost in Eleanor's mind was her responsibility for Marx's literary remains, but she found she had to deal with such matters as investments – hitherto encountered only as one of the more disgusting things capitalists had§ – deeds of trusteeship, publishers' royalties, formerly parcelled out by Engels, and Louise Freyberger.

On 27 August Laura wrote to say that she agreed with the advice of Crosse, the solicitor,‖ and was

> "...distinctly in favour of selling the stocks and securities because a transfer of them would involve difficulties and, possibly, disputes...".[1]

---

* The first probate was on a valuation of £25,115 os.3d. but granted to only two of the executors: Louise Freyberger and Bernstein. Moore is known to have been in London from the third week in July and to have stayed until after the will was read, but he then went, as usual, to stay with his parents in the country from where he wrote to Laura on 28 August and to Eleanor early in September. It must be presumed that he came back to London towards the end of his leave and that double probate – that is, the inclusion of the third executor – was on the basis of the corrective affidavit.

† Estate Duty, first introduced by the Finance Act of July 1894, was 4 per cent on this amount. Duty would also have been paid by those who received bequests, but not by the residual legatees.

‡ In today's terms (1975) it could be reckoned equivalent to investment capital of roughly £40,000.

§ Engels' fortune in stocks and shares, indeed his whole life in commerce, was rightly seen as the outcome of his dedication to Marx's interests.

‖ Arthur Willson Crosse, who practised at 7 Lancaster Place, Strand, died on 21 October 1929. The firm of Crosse & Sons, of which he was the senior partner, had by then moved to Bedford Square and, in 1950, was amalgamated into Messrs. Capron & Crosse of 24 Queen Anne Street. In the course of these removals documents relating to long-deceased clients were necessarily discarded and, though Crosse drew up Engels', Eleanor's and Aveling's wills, none of the papers now remain, as Messrs. Capron & Crosse were good enough to inform me by letter dated 6 April 1967.

Johnny Longuet had come to England for Engels' funeral and stayed on with Eleanor at Green Street Green until the end of September, but she is unlikely to have discussed finances with her nephew, even though he was now a young man of 19, and she instructed Crosse that she and her sister were

"quite sure the wish of the General was that all the children should share equally."[2]

Laura's forebodings of "difficulties and, possibly, disputes" were not so much concerned with the transfer of holdings for the young Longuets and herself in France as with Louise Freyberger whom she had told that Pumps' legacy must be

"paid out in money as soon as possible. She flared up when I said so, but Moore told her authoritatively that that must be so, and happily Moore's word is *law*. I do not understand the objections, seeing that she can please herself about reinvesting at once..."[3]

Bernstein had gone away on holiday and, rid of the tiresome interference of her co-executors, Louise took matters firmly in hand. From Ventnor she wrote to Eleanor on 3 September decreeing that the solicitor would not be satisfied with "your new receipt" for the Marx papers.[4] She was in busy correspondence and on the 9th she wrote again, in German,[5] that Eleanor's acquittance simply was not good enough, as she had foretold; that the formality of signing for the manuscripts which she, Louise, had passed over to Eleanor must be completed forthwith and, three days later, back at 41 Regent's Park Road, she repeated: "Your receipt is not the proper thing". She also made much of the fact – almost an accusation – that, whereas she possessed Eleanor's receipt for typing Lassalle's letters, these were nowhere to be found. What, she further enquired, was she to do about Eleanor's third of Engels' wine: was it to be stored in the wine merchant's cellars at Eleanor's expense – or sold?[6] The next day she was at it again:

"Dear Tussy,
You make a mistake. You have forgotten that Bernstein has already gone to the seaside when you came for the boxes and that all papers and letters on Gener. and my list have been signed in Laura's presence by Mr. Moore. You must know that the letters of Lassalle have been during the last time in your hands for typing ... In no case therefore they could have been among the manuscripts and letters already put in order about 1892.*
You know further that nothing could be given away bequeathed to persons in G.

---

* Typed in October 1893, the Lassalle letters, as Engels had told Laura in December 1894, were in his desk drawer. (See above, pp. 707–8.)

will, not even the letters to his family etc. before this will was proofed. Your things have been excepted as they have not been considered as G. property but manuscript being under his care at the time of his death. Your letters Laura's Lafargue's and Aveling's I gave you back directly with the comment* of Mr. Moore as I had not the slightest intention to take care of these things longer than absolutely necessary ... I alone for my part would not look after G. things till the Will has been proofed..."[7]

Four days later, reverting to German, she blandly informed Eleanor that her things had been put in a depository in Albany Street.[8] On 4 October Dr. Freyberger sent a formal letter to "Mrs Aveling" to say that the books bequeathed to the German Party would be "taken away from our house"† and sent to Berlin.

"You would greatly oblige us," the doctor went on, "by taking away as soon as possible ... those articles which belong to you, viz. one armchair, three bookshelves, one bookcase, one newspaper shelf and 7 – seven – framed photos and drawings.
If you should not find it convenient to have the above mentioned articles in your present house, we shall be glad at your request to deposit same in your name at the Regents Park depository, Albany Street at your expense.
Yours faithfully,
L. Freyberger."[10]

Eleanor reported to Laura that she had

"heard from that unmitigated cad ... that they wish to remove our 'articles' – & he was ill-bred enough to add 'at our expense'! As I cd not (even if I were in London) get them into our Green St. Gn. place, I'm having them stored until we find a house..."[11]

The Freybergers' haste to shake off any connection with members of the Marx family and to be rid of everything that so much as reminded them of Engels – provided they did not have to pay – roused Eleanor, upon her return from a speaking tour with Aveling in Scotland,‡ to send one of her coded letters to Louise:

"what h u d abt the bk cases etc. Are they with u? Or h u, as WA suggested transferred Ø to country In former case I'll get Ø moved at once; v. latter, let me know & wht 2 pay & who 2 = Cr or who. I want Øm..."[12]

The hateful business dragged on: Engels' wine, kept in the cellars of Mr Briggs, wine merchant, of Dublin, was sold and, upon Eleanor's insis-

---

* Perhaps "consent".
† As regards "our house", it transpired that Engels' estate owed Crosse £57 for negotiating the lease of 41 Regent's Park Road. "So," as Eleanor commented, "we pay the piper to wh. the two thieves dance."[9]
‡ From 7 to 14 October when they lectured in Edinburgh, Dundee, Glasgow, Blantyre and Greenock to SDF and ILP branches.

tence, the proceeds divided into four parts, since she saw no reason why the Longuet children's share should not be put directly to their account: an eminently fair arrangement with the added satisfaction of depriving the Freybergers of a fraction.

Percy Rosher now made trouble – there is nothing to compare with a legacy for scenting out the skunk beneath the skin – since Engels, out of personal concern for Pumps, had assumed responsibility for her husband's life insurance policy and, egged on by their client, the company now threatened to sue the executors if they did not continue to pay up, thus mulcting the estate of £87.

The worst of it was that not until late in October were transactions far enough advanced for Crosse to forecast

> "a probability that everything will be sold out … in about 4 weeks – so there is a chance things will be arranged by Christmas!"[13]

"The Duchess", as Eleanor now called Louise, had written a stupid letter to Hermann Engels and was prevented only by Bernstein from offering him the "gratuitous and unwarranted insult" of permitting him to keep his late brother's money in Germany: a matter of some £300.

> "She told Crosse that she wished the money retained by the Engels family because Engels and his family were not at one on political matters! … Of course I told Ede [Bernstein] I did not see any reason for being rude to people who have behaved admirably…"[14]

For months to come the Duchess led

> "Bernstein an awful life. I can assure you," said Eleanor to Laura, "we owe him a famous candle – for I don't know where we should be without him…"[15]

Meanwhile:

> "The Duke and Duchess are 'launching out' in grand style. They have – or *say* they have spent £300 on new furniture, and speak only with contempt of what they made the poor old General pay…"[*14]

On Crosse's advice it was decided that the Longuet children's share should be put into Consols which, Eleanor pointed out to Laura, who agreed, had

---

* Presumably for the complete furnishing of their apartments when they first moved into 41 Regent's Park Road.

"the advantage of *perfect* security and no trouble or responsibility for us..."[14]

But, as late as January 1896, there was not yet enough money available to invest in anything. Nor was this the end of the financial problems for, though provision for the Longuet children was a paramount responsibility and Eleanor chafed at the delay, there was some little complication about the hidden subsidy to Freddy Demuth.

"Crosse has asked me to give him a statement as to this debt & its repayment to keep along with the other papers referring to the children," she told Laura. "As soon as I get Freddy's receipt I will do so. Of course I shall simply say Loan to Longuet, such and such a date, etc..."[16]

In short, Eleanor tasted the galling consequences even before she savoured the sweets of coming into money.

The Freybergers had sent off the books to Germany and Eleanor was rather hurt that this gift was announced in *Vorwärts* in a *"very* cool and unfair way".* She was

"more than surprised that Bebel & Singer did not so much as mention Mohr ... it wd be only decent to say that a good half of the 27 cases contained the admirable library of Marx, presented to the German Party (in order that the General's wish that the libraries shd remain together might be carried out) by Marx's children. The Party itself wd like to know, and *should* know this ... I feel it very strongly, & moreover, before long, unless we see to this at once, it will be said that Louise graciously *gave* all the books to the Party. Though she refused to give even the bookcases!"[14]

This misstatement about the books was apparently set right, though not before it had appeared in the English press; but Louise's meanness about the bookcases rankled. Eleanor had written to Liebknecht:

"...By the way, I hear that when Mohr's and General's books are sent over ... the *bookcases* in which they have stood all these years, and that I think should go too, will *not* be sent. Laura and I had, of course, at once expressed our willingness, since the General wished the books given to the German Party, to give also Mohr's large bookcase – that has been at the General's since 1883, provided Mrs. Freyberger gave the General's bookcases (not mentioned in the will) as the one case without the others

---

* Engels' fears that there might be difficulties in Germany were fully justified. On 20 October under the heading "Friedrich Engels' Legacy to German Social Democracy" *Vorwärts* wrote: "As our readers know, Friedrich Engels left his library and a considerable sum of money to the Party. Comrades Bebel and Singer have received the legacies from the Executors. The important library was dispatched to the Party offices and arrived at the Customs in 27 cases a few days ago. There the cases were opened and as a result of a report to the criminal police the handing over was stopped. (The legal grounds for this action are unknown and an inquiry has been addressed to the Customs authorities.) On the following day it must have become evident that the seizure could not be justified and the consignment was released..."[17]

would have no value. I believe – though I am not yet certain, that Mrs. Feyberger does not wish to make any present to the Party of the bookcases, which, of course, are *legally* hers. I merely mention this so that you, at least, dear Library, may know that if the bookcases are not sent it is no fault of Laura's or mine..."*[18]

On 16 October 1895, though still far from being in full possession of her inheritance, Eleanor drew up her will, witnessed by Crosse and his clerk. She described herself as "Eleanor Marx Aveling (wife of Edward Aveling) of Green Street Green Orpington in the County of Kent" and the short document ran:

"I appoint my said husband sole EXECUTOR of this my Will and bequeath all my interest of whatever nature the same may be in the works of my late father Karl Marx and all sums payable as royalties or otherwise unto and equally between the children of my late sister Jenny Longuet Subject to the payment of my debts and funeral and testamentary expenses I give and bequeath the residue of my estate and effects to my said husband but in the event of my said husband dying in my lifetime then I give and bequeath the same (subject to the bequest hereinafter mentioned) unto and equally between the children of my said late sister. In the event of the death of my husband in my lifetime then I appoint my friend Edward Bernstein EXECUTOR of this my Will and I bequeath to him all my books and the sum of twenty five pounds for the trouble he shall have in carrying out the trusts of this my WILL IN WITNESS whereof I have hereto set my hand..."[19]

A little over a year later, on 28 November 1896, she added a codicil, witnessed by her "excellent but rather stupid" servant, Gertrude Gentry,[20] and an unidentified John Smith, whereby she bequeathed:

"all my interests of whatever nature the same may be in the works of my late father Karl Marx and all sums payable as royalties or otherwise ... unto my husband the said Edward Aveling during his life and upon his death the said sums to be paid to the children of my said sister..."[19]

It has often been suggested that Aveling exerted undue influence on her to revise her will in this manner; but when all is said and done, he had by this time collaborated in translating and editing Marx's writings, while during all their years together he had worked manfully in his own way to spread a knowledge of Marxism, so it does not seem unnatural that she

---

* While one knows that it is impossible to make provision for every contingency and tie up all the loose ends in a last will and testament, Engels might have foreseen that Louise would not lightly let go of any "furniture and other effects" unless legally bound to do so. He may well have considered the bookcases inalienable from his bequest of the library to the Germans, but he did not lay this down in so many words and the Freybergers were hardly the people to make free gifts to socialist parties from whom, upon Engels' death, they dissociated themselves.

should wish him while he lived – rather than the non-Marxist Longuets – to enjoy this patrimony.*

Moreover, as it later transpired, these young people were not even grateful for what they had received.

> "...I think we have done the best we cd for the 'children'," Eleanor wrote to Laura, "although *all* of them (except Mémé) seem dissatisfied. Edward says (please excuse the language) they all want their bottoms smacked. – They *are* a trial to one's patience, I must admit..."[21]

In 1897, after Eleanor, stopping with Laura in France, had had a short, unpleasant interview with her brother-in-law Charles Longuet at his Paris flat in the rue Berthollet, that celebrated non-correspondent wrote her a letter of inordinate length setting out the expenses of his children's education. Jean, now 21, was studying law; Edgar, 18, intended to take up medicine in due course; Marcel, 16, had still to get his *baccalauréat* in classics, while Mémé, 15, required 25 francs a month for her somewhat inferior education and 20 francs for piano lessons. No detail was spared, down to the very books and instruments needed for these vocations and the whole dissertation – of some 1,500 words – though signed *"votre bien dévoué"* was that of a bitterly wronged man.[22] It might have been thought that Engels, whom he had never known well, had expressed the generous wish to provide for Marx's grandchildren and that his sisters-in-law, whom he did not even like, had respected that wish with the sole object of relieving Monsieur Charles Longuet of his paternal responsibilities.

Marx's literary remains were so much her primary concern that, within twelve days of Engels' funeral, Eleanor asked Kautsky whether he would take on the most urgent and important task of copying out the manuscript and taking charge of Volume IV of *Capital*. When he agreed she wrote back:

> "...Your letter has been such a delight & such a relief to me ... I feel so deeply the awful responsibility placed upon me – apart from being *legally* responsible to Laura and Jenny's children..."[23]

a sentiment she frequently repeated.

While she had offered to decipher the manuscript as a means of ensuring that it would not fall into the Freybergers' hands, she knew full well that it was beyond her powers to order, edit and revise so difficult a

---

* It may also be noted that, at the date of this codicil, Eleanor was laid low with so violent an attack of influenza and its attendant depression, bringing to a standstill her work with Aveling to issue a huge volume of Marx's articles on the Crimean War, that she may well have thought she would not live to see it through and must leave him to complete this formidable task alone.

work. Kautsky did not tell her that, in the past, he had broken his promise to come to England and work with Engels for a few weeks every year, nor that he had been so dilatory over his copying that in the end Engels, needing the material, had demanded the return of the MSS. and such parts as Kautsky had completed.* On the contrary, he gave Eleanor the impression that "... the General had stopped your going on with the work", and she was amazed that "he never said a word about it to me!" She went on:

"of *course* the original plan must be carried out, & your proposal to spend some 2 months here in each year, meets every difficulty there might have been..."†[24]

She pressed him again and again to come to London and he as constantly postponed the visit until the spring of 1896, when he met her briefly and announced his intention to settle there, which he did not do.

It is understandable that Kautsky should have felt chagrin at not being so much as mentioned in Engels' will. To be sure, there is the possibility that, in leaving Marx's papers to Eleanor, he had taken it for granted that she would entrust to Kautsky such major work as Engels himself had trained him to do. But Kautsky attributed his exclusion to Engels' personal feelings about his divorce and the tiff over Louise's subsequent use of his name.‡ Eleanor shared this view to some extent and now drew very close to Kautsky partly, it may be, because of her hatred for Louise who, she must have felt sure, had persuaded Engels to deny his former pupil any share of the literary remains.

In after years Kautsky gave his own version of the matter, but he did put his finger on one disastrous flaw in Engels' dispositions: by separating everything in Marx's handwriting from his own manuscripts – the one going to Eleanor and thus remaining until her death in England, after which they went to Laura in France, the other being left to the leaders of the German Party in Berlin – endless confusion was caused. Posterity suffered for an unconscionable time from this arbitrary division of the Marx–Engels *Nachlass*, while the correspondence going to Bebel and Bernstein, the first living in Germany, the second in England, thwarted Eleanor's every effort to assemble Marx's letters for publication.

In point of fact, the Bebel–Bernstein legacy did not leave England for five years. The old German Anti-Socialist Law was not entirely extinct –

---

* See above, p. 606.

† Although Engels had explicitly designated *Theories of Surplus Value* as Volume IV and an integral part of *Capital*, Kautsky eventually put it out as a separate work unconnected with the whole grand design.

‡ See Appendix to *Friedrich Engels' Briefwechsel mit Karl Kautsky*, pp. 445–7, from *Aus der Frühzeit des Marxismus* (1934).

indeed, in less draconian form, it was to be revived in 1897 – and until 1900 Engels' papers lay, unsorted, in two wooden chests in the cellar of Julius Motteler's house at No. 30 Hugo Road, Tufnell Park. To the one, with a double lock, containing the Marx–Engels correspondence, only Bernstein and "the female Freebooter"[25] – that is, Louise – as Bebel's representative, had keys and, at this stage, Bernstein was not willing to approach her.*

In September 1895 Eleanor similarly stowed away Marx's papers in two boxes with special locks, and, no doubt to the Duchess's relief, took them from Regent's Park Road by cab to the Chancery Lane Safe Deposit – almost next door to her former dwelling – to be held in a strong room for three months. Her hope was that Laura would come over to help sort out the papers before this term expired.

> "I believe if we 'weeded' them we cd get the *really* valuable things into a £1.1.0 or £2.2 safe..."

she wrote.[27] But that was not to be: Eleanor paid a year's rent and on 14 January 1896 ruefully reported to Laura that the whole enterprise had cost £7. 8s. 6d. to date, so it is small wonder that she felt no compunction in helping herself generously to the Safe Deposit's writing paper on which henceforth she wrote most of her private letters.

Henceforth, also, she was forever running to and from Chancery Lane, sorting out letters, bundled up by Engels many years before in haphazard fashion, and sending them in batches – at the "ruinous" cost of 3s. 6d. for postage –[28] to Laura for return. She also came upon remarkable finds, taking them away to make fair copies and then replacing them to pounce on others. But

> "... the arranging, sorting, careful reading of unsigned articles & so forth takes more time, & is far more complex work than I first thought..."[29]

she confessed and told Laura that it was impossible for her to do all the copying single-handed. Since she no longer needed to type for a living but

---

* He later not only did so but obtained access to the letters for a proposed biography of Engels, to be published by Fisher Unwin. He had said nothing of this to Eleanor but, as she commented to Laura when she got wind of it in January 1898: "Of course we cant prevent the *use* of the letters, but by English law not a single letter of Mohr's can be published without *our consent*. The Courts have again declared that a letter is the property of the *writer* of the letter & his heirs or executors! *not* of the person to whom the letter is written..."[26]

could, at a pinch, employ a typist, she engaged Edith Lanchester* who was
out of work

> "at the usual rate of 1/- an hour. This will eventually come out of what Moore calls the
> 'Marx estate', & be equally divided between the three 'heirs' ... If you agree ... will
> you advance the money required to pay for the immediate work? I can't, I fear, quite
> manage it by myself alone. Last week I paid Miss Lanchester £1. 12 (32 hours work) &
> shall probably have to pay about the same this week. If we have another copyist we
> must reckon about £3 a week. If you approve of this plan I can also get the children's
> share out of the interest (I don't know how much that is but it certainly must be
> enough) of their 'Marx' Consols..."[29]

In a box that had belonged to her grandfather, long ago passed on to
her by Marx, Eleanor came across a few "odds and ends of lupus"† and
letters from Darwin and Herbert Spencer to which she now added the
many expressions of sympathy from distinguished men written to the
family at the time of Marx's death. And on one occasion she was driven to
exclaim: "Glory to God in the Highest!"[31] for, against all hope, she had
found the contract with Lachâtre‡ which, dispatched to Laura, would
enable her to deal with the French royalties.

Nikolai Danielson had long ago sent Engels all the letters he had
received from Marx and now, little by little, she unearthed those from
Joseph Weydemeyer, Ernest Jones, Charles Dana, Friedrich Sorge and
German members of the old Communist League and First International.
Laura did not consider them for the most part "of great interest", though
she thought "some ... worth reading", if only "Mohr's letters in answer"
were available.[32]

While on her Scottish lecture tour Eleanor wrote to her sister from
Edinburgh enclosing the draft of a letter she proposed sending to the
world press in both their names. It was

---

* Known by the nickname "Biddy", Edith Lanchester (1871–1966) had joined the SDF in
1892, was a member of its Executive and sprang into public prominence when, in 1895, she
began to live openly with an Irish railway clerk, James ("Shamus") Sullivan. Her outraged
family had her certified insane by a Dr. George Fielding Blandford and she was more or less
kidnapped, struggling, to be confined in a private asylum. Sullivan immediately applied for
habeas corpus and talked to the press which gave the scandal dramatic publicity. Thanks also to
her colleagues in the movement swiftly organising "Lanchester Meetings", at which there were
such speakers as Lansbury, Burrows and her landlady, Mrs. Mary Grey – a member of the
Battersea SDF and, in 1892, the founder of the first Socialist Sunday School in London – she was
released after three days. *Justice*, while welcoming her escape from captivity and deploring that
"a respectable physician ... should have lent himself to what was in effect a family conspiracy",
published a highly censorious leader on "Socialism and 'Free Love'". Edith Lanchester's
unmarried union lasted until Sullivan's death and she bore him two children.[30]
† Wilhelm Wolff.
‡ The publisher of the French edition of Volume I of *Capital*, translated by Joseph Roy and
edited by Marx over the years 1872 to 1875.

"...the form adopted by Darwin's and Ernest Jones's sons, & is the best for England. Of course for Germany we need only send to the Vorwärts with a request that the Party Press shd re-copy. As to France you know best. Let me hear what you think or if you have any suggestions to make. If you agree I will send to all the London papers and through the Press Ass. to the provincial. Unfortunately here unless you *do* send to each one the letter will only go to one or two papers. Of course I will send to America – but Schlüter and Sanial* will suffice there..."[33]

The letter ran:

"May we appeal through your columns to all those who may have any correspondence of Karl Marx, to be good enough to forward them to one of us? We are anxious to get as complete a collection of our father's letters as possible with a view to publication. Any letters or documents that may be sent will, of course, be taken the utmost care of, and if the senders wish it, returned as soon as they have been copied. We should carry out any instruction that the possessors and senders of the letters might give us as to the omission of any passage they might desire not to have published.
        Laura Lafargue, Le Perreux, Seine, France.
        Eleanor Marx Aveling, Green Street Green,
        Orpington, Kent."

It appeared in almost every country and many languages, copies having also been sent to Liebknecht, Kautsky and Adler, who could "practically cover the German, Austro-Hungarian-Bohemian press".[34] On the whole, the response was disappointing and Eleanor later decided that, to obtain the most vital letters – those to Engels – she and Laura should write officially to the legal heirs, Bernstein and Bebel, besides making a personal approach to Sorge, Kugelmann and Liebknecht to ask for the Marx letters they must have had and might have kept.

In the meantime, however, a very rare fish had swum into their net bringing with it after many years news of Marx's relatives scattered about the world.

Lina (Caroline) Smith of Maastricht, a cousin then living at The Hague with Harriet Schill – another cousin – had read the appeal in the Dutch press. She, the daughter of Marx's elder sister Sophie who had married a lawyer, Wilhelm Schmalhausen, had visited England in 1865.† It is doubtful whether Eleanor had ever seen her since. Lina now wrote to tell her that their aunt in South Africa, Mrs. Louise Juta, had died in 1893; that Willa, one of the Juta girls, was living in Scotland with her husband and children, while another, Louise, was settled in Manitoba. "Harry" – Henry Juta –

---

* The first was now the editor of the *New Yorker Volkszeitung*, the second, until 1892, of the English-language weekly, *The People* and, from 1894, of *The Journal of the Knights of Labor*.
† See above pp. 36, 37. For details of other relatives here mentioned, see above, p. 148 and 174.

"...has been 'attorney general' at the Cape, but as the post did not 'bring in' enough he has returned to his private practice...".[35]

Jettchen Conradi, the daughter of Marx's sister Emilie, was mad – Eleanor recalled that she had always thought so ever since, as a girl, Jettchen had claimed to be the author of *Little Women* – and she had retreated into a Yorkshire convent. Other cousins were "getting on fairly well", but Lina's only child, Sophy, had died that March and, a widow, she was now entirely alone.

But all this family gossip was as nothing compared with the occasion for it: among her late mother's* papers Lina had found a letter from Marx, the only one his sister had kept, and this she now sent to Eleanor. It was

"...several pages long and written by Mohr to his father while he was a student in Berlin. It is simply invaluable from the biographical point of view...".[35]

Eleanor showed it to Bernstein who, in great excitement, wanted it published at once in *Neue Zeit*; however, Aveling advised and Eleanor agreed that letters should not be put out singly but form part of a collected edition. She asked for Laura's views on this.

Nevertheless, Eleanor herself had second thoughts on the matter and, in July 1897, she wrote to Kautsky about "the very remarkable letter of Mohr to his father": she had just read it over again and was

"somewhat in doubt as to whether, after all, the letter shd not go forth at once. So I am sending it (tho' I'm half afraid of trusting it to the post!) to you, & I shall be glad if you will, as soon as may be, let me know what you think..."

Lina was grumbling because this valuable document had been kept for so long and she ought to return it to her:

"But I have full powers to deal with it & if you think it shd be at once published I shd re-consider my earlier decision...".[36]

Naturally, if it were to be published, Marx's age at the time of its writing must be mentioned and she begged Kautsky to take good care of the manuscript for which Lina might whistle until it went into print.

But second thoughts tend to put people in two minds and Eleanor vacillated. She had thought very carefully and anxiously about it. Certainly they had no right to wait and it was

"a real duty to Mohr to show him to the world in 'his habit as he lived'. At the same

---

* Mrs. Schmalhausen, widowed in 1862, had died in 1886 aged 70.

time" – and that was why she had not dared to copy the letter – "it is very painful to me – because I know – no one knows as well as I – how Mohr *hated* to have his private life dragged into public ... So while I *do* feel this letter shd be published, I at the same time feel half a traitor in giving it to the world..."[37]

She wavered on other more trivial decisions. At one moment she was convinced that she had identified the date as 1836 – by reference to his album of poems – when Marx was 18: "What a letter for a lad of that age!" she exclaimed to Kautsky.[38] A few weeks later she was "almost sure"[39] it must have been a year later.* She had definitely given permission for its publication in the October issue of the *Neue Zeit*, but there were still some problems. For a start, there was one "impossible word": even Bernstein was beaten by it.

"I suppose," she wrote to Kautsky, "you must leave it a blank and admit we can't decipher it". In so long a letter – it was later re-issued as a pamphlet – "to miss only *one* word, is not under the circumstances so bad!"[40]

Then there was the vexed question of an introduction. On the one hand Eleanor wanted it to be

"read by itself – free from all interpretation & explanation. It is (or seems to me) so immensely valuable as a perfectly unconscious picture of the young Marx drawn by himself"; on the other, she wished to consult Laura "as the elder", and perhaps there ought to be a prefatory word by both daughters. In any case, Laura must see the proofs and decide. Eventually, of course, Eleanor produced a brief accompanying essay,† the writing of which had been "worse than having a tooth out".[39]

It appeared early in October, when Eleanor asked for extra copies to send to her cousins – "especially for Lina to whom we owe the letter" –[41] and told Kautsky it should also go to Louise von Westphalen, the daughter of Mrs. Marx's half-brother, Ferdinand.‡

---

* It was: 10 November 1837.
† See Appendix 4.
‡ Prussian Minister of the Interior, 1850–1858: "the worst of all bigots", in Eleanor's estimation.[42]

One great good thing came out of these interminable exchanges and the sharing of responsibilities and problems: Eleanor and Laura drew together with a lovingness unknown since they had lived under their parents' roof. This renewed affection was expressed in letter after letter and although, as always, Eleanor shouldered the greater burden that was mainly because, by virtue of her British domicile, only she had physical access to the Marx papers and could deal with practical and legal affairs. Certainly Laura might have come to England – as Eleanor implored her again and again – to help sort out the papers; also she might well have initiated the request for letters throughout the world; but such efforts remained foreign to her nature. She did, however, observe Tussy's birthday – often overlooked in the past – in a "princely fashion" enabling her to buy

> "all sorts of things I have long hankered after – especially the 'Paston Letters' and other historical works I've much wanted..."

and also one of Hachette's dictionaries: that "most marvellous of books".[43] Laura, too, now that they could both afford it, received handsome presents; but the real change was manifested in such details as that Eleanor addressed her sister by the old, half-forgotten nickname "dear Hottentot" and when ill in the winter of 1896 wrote:

> "...do you know, my dear Laura, while I am sorry you shd have worried I'm glad too. It *is* rather pleasant to feel that there is anyone in the world who cares enough for you to worry on your account..."

adding

> "I am writing to you on Christmas Eve. I remember times when you & Jenny dressed dolls for me, & times when there were Xmas trees," adding: "... Anyhow, it is good to know one has a sister",[44]

while Laura sent "kisses for your kisses"[45] and, in many a dulcet phrase, showed the close harmony which now existed. The truth was that Eleanor consulted Laura and deferred to her opinion on every detail and Laura responded with grace, knowing full well that her concurrence was not strictly necessary. It was almost as though Marx – who had so clearly identified himself with Tussy and loved "our Jenny" best of all his daughters – and then Engels, who had stepped into their father's shoes, had stood between them. The cause for Laura's jealousy, if such it had been, or feelings of rejection, was now finally removed. She stood upon an equal footing with Eleanor, thanks to whose courtesy and scrupulous honesty her rights as Marx's daughter were fully recognised and respected.

Another to whom Eleanor drew much nearer in these last years was Liebknecht. He, too, was *very* sore at the General ignoring him absolutely in his will",[46] not that he was a legacy-hunter but it made him feel he was amongst the unloved.* To be sure, Engels had been vehemently critical of Liebknecht, as of Kautsky; but for that matter he had also deprecated Bernstein's crotchets, yet had appointed him to be one of his executors. The simple fact, not appreciated by those who now felt hurt, was that Bernstein, living in England, was the only member of the German Party fitted to carry out that function, while no individual in Germany could receive so much as a token bequest without creating complications; for which reason the £1,000 to Bebel and Singer had been expressly assigned "for Election purposes". Indeed, Engels must have been in something of a quandary: it may be doubted whether, his first loyalty being, after the Marx descendants, to the German Party and his old comrades-in-arms, he would have elected Bernstein or even Louise Kautsky – Sam Moore was an utterly reliable and inevitable choice – to control his affairs had his home been where his heart lay.

As early as July 1895 – even before Engels' death – Eleanor had pacified Liebknecht's feelings.

> "I have a bone to pick with you," she wrote to her "dear old Library", "and if you were here I should give you the scolding you certainly deserve. How *dare* you say you are glad we are not estranged from you? Who could estrange us? ... I am very cross with you for saying such a thing ... Unless you make a handsome apology, and then *perhaps* I may forgive you..."[47]

Now, in 1896 and '97, he came to England three times and saw a great deal of Eleanor when not actually staying with her. Here again, in a curious way, it was as though the past reasserted itself, overleaping the years between, to establish the old intimacies of her childhood. He had asked her to write a 34-page article on "The Working Class Movement in England" for the second volume of the *Volks-Lexikon*.†

> "They have thought it good enough to issue as a pamphlet with an introduction by Library. It is not worth anything because I had to cram an immense amount of material into a very small space..."[48]

---

* *"nicht mitgeliebt"*.
† *The People's Encyclopaedia*. Published by Wörlein & Co., Nuremberg.

Eleanor told Laura, to whom she promised to send a copy when it appeared.* Liebknecht's six-page preface, dated September 1895, said in its opening paragraph:

> "...the writer not only knows the history and the present condition of the English workers' movement – not only knows it, I may say, almost by heredity; but, ever since she was able to think and act, she has been heart and soul in that movement, her feelings and emotions one with those of the English workers. So that the historical sketch she has promised will be written, not simply with the head, but from the heart..."

He now planned to write his reminiscences of Marx and, plied with a certain amount of misinformation by Tussy† – most of which he quoted – he remembered with especial vividness occasions that, in themselves so rare as never to have figured at all in the correspondence of the time, had illuminated the darkness of his twelve-year exile when he had known Marx best. He made much of the picnics on Hampstead Heath and of tramping all the way from Kentish Town to Sadler's Wells, for in his old age – he was now 70 – these glowing experiences shone with a magnified brilliance that has coloured many a later picture.

But it was not only in recollection that he visited the past. While staying with Eleanor in late May and early June 1896, during which time he made a speaking tour of the whole country – ending with a meeting in his honour called by the Socialist Societies, Trade Unions and Jewish Workers' Organisations of the East End in the Great Assembly Hall in Mile End on 6 June, at which Eleanor, Lessner, Motteler and Burrows also spoke under the chairmanship of Aveling – he also made another tour of a different order.

On 8 June, a Monday, he set out with Tussy on what could have been termed an archaeological expedition – "like Schliemann intending to excavate Troy" –[49] in search of the London he had known almost half a century ago. Back and back they went trying to recognise the lodgings he had occupied, though the street names and numbers had been changed and the buildings put to other uses. After some hesitation he identified the house in Dean Street where the Marxes had lodged – his sheet anchor in those days – and Eleanor had been born. Those upper rooms they now found closed and could not visit. But when they reached the wilds of Kentish Town there was no mistaking the old haunts: Roxburgh Terrace – though that, too, had been renamed‡ – such familiar pubs as the Mother

---

* Translated by Aveling, it was published by the Twentieth Century Press as a 2d. pamphlet in 1896, when it was reviewed in *Justice* on 25 July.

† See above, fn. ‡, p. 29.

‡ Demolished in 1969.

Shipton and Mother Redcap and the well-trodden way up Malden Road to
the little house in Grafton Terrace where Tussy had lived until the age of
nine. It must have seemed, as houses will, much smaller than she had
remembered it and she may well have asked herself with wonderment how
six people ever managed to squeeze themselves into that modest dwelling
not only comfortably but with pride in what Mrs. Marx had pronounced a
veritable palace compared with the hovels she had known.

For Eleanor, far more even than for Liebknecht, this excursion must
have evoked profound emotions. People tend to look upon the scenes of
their childhood with nostalgia of a largely narcissistic nature – there is
nobody so adorable as oneself when young – but, as she gazed upon No.
46 Grafton Terrace,* she probably had fewer thoughts for the lively little
Tussy who had grown up there in an atmosphere of unbounded love than
aching recollections of the dead it had once sheltered. Even now she was
about to give the world work Marx had done in that very abode in those
very years; his posthumous fame rested upon her and it is not fanciful to
suppose that, knowing at the age of 41 the grim realities hidden from her
in those far-off days, she conjured up the magisterial figure of her father,
grinding away in his cramped little study at the back; the loyal, tender
mother uttering sharp cries of pain at the stings of poverty; Helene
Demuth, at once despot and slave, ruling the household whose members
she kept fed and clothed, warmed and clean by unremitting toil; and
sweet Jenny, the sister whose life was to be so short and full of tears.

When Liebknecht's book appeared in December 1896, Eleanor was not
entirely happy about it.

"...He has muddled finely," she wrote to Laura. "But all the same I think Kautsky
wrong when he says ... that it will do Mohr infinite harm and so on. After all, Marx
the 'Politiker' & 'Denker'† can take his chance, while Marx the *man* – the 'mere' man,
as K.K. says, is less likely to fare well. Tell me what *you* think...";[50]

while to Kautsky she said:

"As to Liebknecht. His book is disappointing in many ways, but I do not think it will
do any harm ... The *man* is least known, most misunderstood. And Marx as a *whole* ...
was so very many sided that many sides of him will have to be considered ... Not only
Science appealed to him – but Art and Literature. Mohr's sympathy with *every* form of
work was so perfect that it will take many men to deal with him from their own point
of view. I only despair when I think of the task of gathering together all these loose
threads and weaving them into a whole. Yet it must be done, though it is work to give
the boldest pause..."[51]

---

* No. 9 in her day.
† Thinker.

In these last years Eleanor's closest friends, apart from Laura, were Freddy Demuth, Kautsky and Liebknecht, all three, for differing reasons, having known certain embarrassments in their relations with Engels. She still saw much of Will Thorne for, although she had resigned from the Executive of the Gasworkers' Union in June 1895 when she was about to leave London, he and his family often visited her in Green Street Green, while Aveling continued to be one of the Union's auditors. She also formed a new friendship, both in personal and working relations, with Benno Karpeles.

This opened inauspiciously. An Austrian Social-Democrat, Karpeles had introduced himself to Eleanor in May 1896 as a busybody who wrote offering to pay for the tending of Marx's grave which he had visited while in England and found in a neglected state. In a note to Aveling while he was on tour with Liebknecht she enclosed this

> "most impudent (tho' I daresay well meant) letter . . ." adding: "I now understand Mrs. Mendelson's speaking of his being so very mal élevé . . . You know that for years I've paid (even while the General lived) to have the grave seen to, & that our Socialist gardener said all wd have to be renewed, but better not till summer . . .".[52]

To Karpeles himself she replied with freezing courtesy that the roses she had put in six or seven years ago were to be replaced but this was not the season for it; that naturally she did not wish to disturb the ivy Engels had planted and, while thanking him for his unsolicited kindness, could assure him that she and her sister were quite able to care for their parents' grave.

However, he came to London again in October that year, she met him at The Horseshoe in Tottenham Court Road and took a liking to him which grew warmer when she came to know his wife and enchanting babies and he undertook in 1897 the translation of her edition of Marx's English writings.

On the other hand, her relations with Bernstein deteriorated. At first he had been a tower of strength, standing firmly between herself and Louise Freyberger; but as time went on and he encroached upon her preserves by using the Marx-Engels letters without her consent, even allowing his projected biography of Engels to be advertised,* she was worried about him, though, unlike Engels, she thought he was suffering not from any nervous disorder but from political disorientation. In January 1898 she was writing to Laura that *Vorwärts* was

> "falling more & more under Bernstein's influence, & his wet-blanket articles . . .

---

* It never appeared.

Assuredly the critical attitude is necessary & useful. But there are times when a little enthusiasm – even if 'uncritical' – is of greater value. Bernstein's position is a most unfortunate one for the movement, & one that makes *our* position very difficult. It is impossible to defend his attitude ... Unhappily there is no one, now we have not the General, to influence Bernstein, & pull him together...".[53]

In the very last letter she wrote to Kautsky, she went much further:

"...I have more than once been on the point of writing to you about him, but refrained, partly from a fear of paining you – for I know how deeply you are attached to him – partly from a fear that you might misunderstand me. His attitude has for some time been a matter of great pain to us: he was harming his own position, & was doing his best to set everyone against him. And *you* can form no idea of how *his* position is being exploited by the Fabians against the Marxists. 'Marx *must* be played out', said one (this I heard in Portsmouth!) 'when Bernstein has come over to us.' ... No doubt the Fabians are 'nichts schlimmes'* as such – but they *are* a danger in England ... If the English Socialists were a really strong party all this would not be of importance. But as things are it *is* important, & that the man whom, with yourself, we have most counted on should make it possible for people to jeer at 'Marxism' is not a very happy condition of things ... He is *terribly* irritable ... If you had seen the state of almost frantic rage into which he worked himself when Liebknecht on his visit here quite harmlessly & casually spoke of Hyndman as an authority on India (wh. he really is), you would know that it is not an easy matter to speak to Ede. Still I *do* think he will come right again ... *you* should be near him, if only for a little time ... You alone can make Ede our old Ede again. It hurts me more than I can say to write this, &, of course, I speak only to you. Ede is so dear a friend that it is horrible to see things as they are just now ... We think of the good old days at the General's – especially the early Nymmy days – and then this all seems unbearably sad...".[54]

Other older companions vanished before their time: Leo Frankel, who had aspired to the hand of the 17-year-old Eleanor, died at the age of 52 on 29 March 1896; William Morris, not yet 63, on 3 October of that year.† But with neither of these had Eleanor been involved during the recent past. The sudden and appalling death of Stepniak, whose valued friendship dated back to her early translation of his work, was a bereavement that touched her deeply, for she was devoted to him and his wife.

---

* Not a bad thing.
† Morris's executor or lawyer wrote to Aveling on 4 November and received the following reply, dated 13 December: "Dear Sir, ... The position of affairs was this. The late William Morris at different times advanced me different sums of money. About a year ago, I wrote to him – he never at any time made any application to me for any repayment – asking him how we stood. He wrote back saying he thought he had let me have £50, but was not sure. I sent him £5 and have not been able to send more. And I regret to say that I am not in a position to repay now. Long arrears of difficulties are still slowly being cleared off, and the end of them is not yet. Faithfully, Edward Aveling." A note attached to this says: "Wrote again Dec 13, 1897 asking whether now prepared to pay."[55]

On the morning of Monday, 23 December 1895, Sergei Kravchinsky –
Stepniak – then 44 years of age, living in Chiswick, was on his way to see
his compatriot and greatest friend, Felix Volkhovsky, in Hammersmith –
a most familiar walk – when, crossing the railway line near Acton,* he was
so engrossed in his reading that he failed to hear an oncoming train, was
struck by the engine's buffers, dragged a few yards and almost instantly
killed.† An inquest was held on Boxing Day and the funeral took place on
28 December. Eleanor was so unnerved by the horror of this accident that
she could not at first bring herself to write to his wife‡ or any member of
the tight-knit group of Russian émigrés in London with whom she was on
close terms. However, on Christmas Day she sent a letter to Vera
Zasulich:

"...We have learned from the newspapers of the frightful misfortune which has
overtaken you and all of us. I wanted to write to you and to Fanny, but I could not, I
had not the courage. I am thinking about our poor Fanny the whole time. For her this
death is terrible, yes, but perhaps such sudden death is better than death after prolonged agony and such torture as our dear General suffered. But for her it is terrible. I
very much want to come and embrace her, but I am afraid of being a nuisance. Tell her,
dear Vera, that my husband and I are thinking of her constantly, and if we could do
anything for her it would give us happiness.
  And we think of you too, dear friend. He was your old friend, and friends are so rare.
Of course we shall come to Woking on Saturday..."[56]

She also brought herself to write to Fanny that same day.

"...I could not write to you yesterday... When we learned the news, it seemed to us
impossible to believe or really to imagine what had happened. I realise that no words or
anything can help; the saddest thing in life is that we are unable to help each other
really and each has to bear their grief alone. The only consolation, not a great one, for
you is the thought that all who knew you and him grieve together with you now. We
feel intolerable pain, not only because of the loss which we have all suffered, but even
more because of the loss which has befallen you...
  All my heart is with you, dear Fanny..."[57]

It was, indeed, the unhappy end to a most sorrowful year.

Eleanor not only went to the funeral – to which Lansbury and Lee
brought a wreath from the SDF – but spoke at it: a most unusual thing for
a woman. The cortège following the hearse to Waterloo was accompanied
by a Russian band playing a funeral march and so great was the assembly

---

* Now closed, of course, though the deserted railway land may still be seen.
† For many of the details I am indebted to Mr. Nenad Petrović who has written a recent paper
on Kravchinsky's life and death (in Serbo-Croat, so I cannot read it).
‡ Fanny Markovna Kravchinsky, who outlived her husband by 50 years, dying at the age of 92
in 1945.

that John Burns was asked to act as chairman for the speakers who included Volkhovsky, Kropotkin, William Morris, Herbert Burrows, Keir Hardie, an Italian, an Armenian and a Pole.

It must have seemed to Eleanor that not only the older generation which had meant so much to her but her contemporaries, too, were slipping away.

Ever since 1894, when Plekhanov had asked her to translate his pamphlet,* Eleanor had enjoyed a growing intimacy with the Russians. The Stepniaks were, of course, friends of long standing and she had never lost touch with Lavrov in Paris, but it was in all likelihood through Vera Zasulich, on whom Aveling had written an immensely long article – almost a biography – for the *Clarion* of 23 February 1895, Plekhanov and their circle that she was invited in 1895 to contribute a series of articles to the Liberal journal *Russkoye Bogatstvo*,† in the form of reports on Britain, covering, as the first instalment announced, political parties, the social life of the people and new developments in literature, the arts and science.

This was not the first time Eleanor had written for non-socialist papers, but in such cases her subjects had generally been of a literary nature. These "Letters" – or *reportages* – were unique in her work in that they gave a detailed account of such matters as the constitution of the School Boards in their historical setting; the first elections to parish and rural councils;‡ Mrs. Annie Besant, unkindly listing her train of lovers with their variety of creeds which she had equally embraced, ending up with theosophy; current statistics on alcoholism; Clementina Black's novel *The Agitator*;§ the Oscar Wilde case; education in England; the LCC; poverty in London; remedies for unemployment; prohibition; the Tories and the Liberal Unionists; the Factory Acts; the aged poor; the May Day demonstration of 1895 and a multitude of other topics on which she was extremely well informed giving, in every case, a lucid and simple exposition of the background to British institutions and personalities such as foreigners would require and which thus still provides information of exceptional interest today.‖

---

* See above, p. 720.

† *Russian Wealth*, a monthly edited by N. K. Mikhailovsky, published from 1876 to 1918 in St. Petersburg. It was supported by the Liberal wing of the *Narodniks* (The Friends of the People).

‡ With such engaging asides as that: "a parish was deserted by reason of its inhabitants going to work on the construction of the Manchester-Liverpool canal, leaving but a single resident who, since he belonged to the parish, exercised his right to hold a meeting and elect himself, thus constituting the entire council..."

§ Said to have been based on an amalgam of John Burns and H. H. Champion.

‖ Regrettably it has proved impossible to trace the original English articles. Retranslation from the Russian is an unsatisfactory substitute. For Eleanor's attitude to the Oscar Wilde trial see above, fn. ‡, p. 184.

This was by no means her only activity during the autumn of 1895: in October there was her Scottish lecturing tour and from 24 November to 1 December she spoke in Burnley, Blackburn, Darwin and other Lancashire towns, while the local papers reported and old people recall from their early childhood her visits to Crewe and Lincoln, Wigan, Aberdeen and Bristol, not to mention the savage public and private correspondence with Bax on the "Sex Question", when she challenged him in *Justice* to an open debate which he funked.

Threaded through all these activities, incredible as it may seem, Eleanor had been looking for a new home. Green Street Green, she wrote to Kautsky in September, was

"very pleasant – but too far away from everyone and everything. I have a grand scheme for you and the Bernsteins & ourselves to get to some *convenient* suburb – & live near one another..."[58]

This was in the days when she hoped that Kautsky would settle in England to work on Volume IV of *Capital*, when Bernstein was her ally against the Freybergers and when she first realised she could afford better quarters.

Let no one suppose that in those bygone days house-hunting was an easy or pleasurable pursuit. She and Aveling

"trudged mile upon mile; ... spent a small fortune in train, tram, bus and cab fares. Whenever a small house *seemed* suitable it was jerry built ... Or else a railway train ran through the garden; or it was practically inaccessible from London...".[59]

She wrote of the "agonies" of finding a place and, by October was crying out to Laura:

"Lord send we soon may! The searching for one is misery...".[60]

The prospect of remaining at Green Street Green appalled her; it was "not pleasant for winter weather that is setting in with a vengeance", she moaned as October advanced[61] and, less than a week later:

"We are still house hunting ... We find that all the nice houses are either let or too dear and the 'noble residences' we go to see are more often than not in some unspeakable slum. Rents here are something fearful ... Sometimes I feel like investing in a caravan...".[62]

Crosse had advised her that if she could find a "really nice place" she should buy rather than rent; but

"All the *nice* houses are too dear, & all the cheap ones are shoddy in shoddy neighbourhoods. How are you faring?"[63]

she asked, because at the same time Laura was "'doing' the suburbs of Paris in search of a house on sale".[64]

Eleanor thought that

"getting a house near this monster of London is more difficult than getting one within reasonable distance of Paris..."[59]

and certainly Laura was quicker off the mark, for towards the end of September a place that had caught her fancy was coming up for auction and she intended to bid for it. The house was

"so-so and requires repairing but the garden is splendid and stretches right into the forêt de Sénart..."[64]

But the repairs must have been extensive for the Lafargues did not take up residence for another six months, whereas Eleanor, who had found a house in November, told Laura:

"Crosse thinks it a bargain. It is big for us (but I *do* hate small rooms) and Paul will turn up his nose at our little garden, wh. however, will be quite big enough for us..."[59]

and within a few weeks she had moved.

It is not without social interest that, even before they had received their inheritance in negotiable form, both sisters should have set about immediately looking for a house in some respectable suburb, just as Marx had done – though without the means to pay rent and rates – the instant he came into a little money. Now, in 1895, neither Eleanor nor Laura was prepared to settle for some rented dwelling in an under-developed area, such as Grafton Terrace had been in 1856. To be sure, they were richer and, what is more, their income was an assured one. But the fact remains that they became owner-occupiers, which was distinctly unusual in their day for all but the grander families and, though Eleanor had to be advised to take this step, nothing less than outright purchase even occurred to Laura.

Laura moved to 20 Grande Rue, Draveil, Seine-et-Oise, in March 1896 to become the châtelaine of "... a wonderful place – really a 'propriété'" wrote Eleanor[65] who pronounced it "magnificent" and "very fine":

"The house has about 30 rooms, not counting out-buildings like the large billiard room ... & studio ... a large house where the gardener lives, endless greenhouses, & houses of every sort of winged (& unwinged) beast; a huge 'orangerie'..."

As for the grounds:

"It is more a park than a garden and there is, apart from the flowers, every vegetable & fruit you cd possibly think of. As to the livestock there are 100 fowls, dozens of pigeons, rabbits, pheasants, partridges, ducks, a lamb – & they're going to get a cow!..."[66]

The countryside surrounding this demesne was "exquisite", with the forest of Sénart and the banks of the Seine at its very gates.

Eleanor did wonder how Lafargue would fare if re-elected to parliament, Paris being then somewhat inaccessible from Draveil and she warned Kautsky that, though Lafargue

"...has two articles 'in his head' ... I should not advise you to expect them too soon, for Paul is very much absorbed by his garden & his livestock..."[66]

She did not suppose that he would undertake to bring out Marx's valuable series of articles on the *Crédit Mobilier*, while she was later to say that "as Paul (so far as I know) is only cultivating his cabbages and his livestock"[67] she saw no good reason why he should not do a little research on 1848 in the contemporary French newspapers unavailable at the British Museum, but pinned little hope on it.

Eleanor's choice was of a different order: a semi-detached, half-hearted neo-Gothic affair built in the mid-1870s, hideous enough to quicken the pulses of present-day conservationists had it been more imposing and on a more conspicuous site. But it was merely of two storeys tucked away in that quiet suburban part of Lewisham then in West Kent. Crosse thought it was "a bargain" and was responsible for the conveyancing.*

Early in December 1895 Eleanor was able to announce triumphantly that she had bought it – "but who or what is bought and sold remains to be seen"[68] – and described it in detail to Laura:

---

* Jew's Walk, the name of the street, was officially adopted on 15 March 1878 indicating that it was fully built up by then. It is not and cannot be known what Eleanor paid for it, from whom it was bought nor yet whether on a lease or as a freehold. Although compulsory registration did not become operative in that district until 1900, the property was not in fact notified to HM Land Registry until 1974, while the Lewisham Borough Ratebooks of the period no longer exist having perished either by bombing during the Second World War or, according to some local residents, in a fire at the Town Hall shortly afterwards. The house is now converted into two flats, the lower rated at £250 p.a., the upper at £240. Both are presently (1975) unoccupied.

Ground floor: large room (Edward's study & general room combined); dining room (opens on back garden) kitchen, scullery, pantry, coal & wine cellars, cupboards, large entrance hall. One flight of stairs (easy) – Bedroom – spare bed-room (*yours*), servants' room, bath room (large enough to be another spare room on special occasions) my STUDY! Everywhere we have electric light – wh. is far cheaper, as we are near the Palace,* than gas, the gas is laid on too, & I have a gas cooking stove & gas fires in most of the upper rooms..."[68]

At this late date it comes as something of a revelation that Aveling was the part-owner of property in Austin Friars, possibly left him by his father or even, it may be, an investment of the legacy from old Miss Elizabeth Bibbins, after whom he was named.† Its value had

"... gone up so much that he has been able to get a very good mortgage (without, of course, losing his rights in the property) on it & he is buying all the furniture that unluckily we can't do without. I want you to know this as it wd not be fair to think *I* was paying for it all..."

she told Laura.[68]

On 14 December she and Aveling took possession of No. 7 Jew's Walk and christened it "The Den". It gave Eleanor enormous pleasure: as a "married" woman she had never before lived in any but chambers or lodgings and now her home-making instincts were aroused. She was eager for Laura to see the lovely place herself.

"Seriously," she wrote, "you *ought* to come over, – and why not for the New Year? ... I ought to say that my invitation is not quite as amiable as it looks. I want Paul badly to help me with the garden! There! The cat's out of the bag. If Paul has any little affection left for me he'll come & teach us to garden..."[68]

She also wanted to get "a small pigeon cote and a pair or so of pigeons" who could at once be let free. What pigeons would Paul recommend? "I want them for pleasure, not food," she explained. She also seemed to think it something of a miracle that the common or suburban garden blackbird, thrush and robin were her daily visitors. "So you see, this is almost the country," she exclaimed with the sweet innocence of one who has been long in city pent.‡ She did her best to persuade Paul to give her the benefit of his *expertise* – "there is no end of garden work for him to do. He shall get 'fair' wages (6d. an hour) & his 'keep'. Won't that tempt him?"

---

* The Crystal Palace, to which "we have free passes & like the Classical Concerts – not to mention the fine grounds & excellent reading room...".[69]
† See above, pp. 199, 200.
‡ The few agitated months – from July to December 1895 – in Green Street Green had not been conducive to bird-watching, while horticulture in the Dodwell days had been of a sporadic and severely practical nature to produce – and sell – food.

–[70] but the Lafargues were too preoccupied with their own housing problems to come to England and Eleanor asked in mid-winter:

> "Will Paul kindly tell me *when & how* I should sow sweet Peas and Beans (French and scarlet runners)..."

which dreams were possibly owed to her being at the time

> "a victim of the Influenza Demon, & now I understand why so many people have committed suicide in the Demon's clutches."[70]

One other thing that seems to have been much in her thoughts at this period was that she was now over 40 years old, the owner of a settled and, by her standards, roomy house, which would never "ring with a child's laughter". She had written to Kautsky in September 1895 when she was looking forward to his coming over with his wife and three little boys to say:

> "As to the young men Aunt Tussy hopes they will approve of her. Like Mohr I wd rather have the good opinion of a child than of all the grown ups..."[71]

Spending her second Christmas in The Den she wrote to Laura:

> "This is a stupid & a sad time where there are no children. I sometimes wonder if it is worse to have had & lost little ones or never to have had them?..."[72]

When stopping with the Lafargues and describing their gorgeous mansion to Kautsky, she said not only that, if it were hers – though she would not exchange her little Den for this "palace" – she would turn its vast orangery "into a lecture & meeting hall', but also

> "...I keep wishing your boys cd be here, for it wd be a paradise for children..."*[73]

More explicitly, when the Kautskys gave her news of the family she said:

> "...how I really *enjoyed* what you both wrote about the boys. I envy you those delightful little men, & the more you tell me of them the better I shall be pleased. If you knew how I love children you wd know that every little detail about them is a joy to me..."[74]

---

* It should be said that Laura did, in fact, fill the place with young people: not only her nephews and niece but almost whenever she wrote she spoke of children staying, their birthday parties and their arrival or departure.

She entertained often and generously at The Den while, released from her need to scrape a livelihood sweating away in the British Museum, she took an increasing interest in such affairs as teaching at the Battersea Socialist Sunday School and singing in the local Socialist choir with what she called her "dear Lewishamers".[75]

Considering the short time that she lived there, no more than two years and a quarter, it is surprising how many Lewisham residents have come forward to recount their elders' memories of Eleanor – down to such details as her favourite dress of dark blue velvet – not one of whom spoke of her death but only with admiration and affection for the vital personality they had known.

Nikolai Danielson, Marx's faithful Russian translator, sent Eleanor a copy of his Volume III of *Capital* at the end of November 1897. He had never corresponded with her before and now wrote very civilly:

> "Dear Madam,
> ...I cannot find words to express with sufficient accuracy my regret that the author was unable himself to finish (or complete) his classical (or great) work, to publish it and so see the impression which it is creating. Permit me, Madam, to ask you to send me the proof sheets of the 4th volume as they are printed. I shall be very grateful to you for doing what I ask.
> With deep respect..."[76]

Within a few days of settling into her new house, Eleanor replied:

> "Dear Sir,
> I cannot express the pleasure I had in receiving your letter. It reminded me of how happy my dear father always was to have news of you.
> The translation has not yet arrived, but when it comes I shall treasure it greatly, even though it be in Russian!
> Of course I shall see to it that you get the sheets of Volume 4. But I fear it will be a long time before they are ready. The work on it is *very* difficult. I have entrusted it to Kautsky. Both of us – my sister and I – think he is the only person who can cope with this task properly. I know that Engels thought so too.
> Meanwhile I want to send you the recently published edition of 'The Poverty of Philosophy',* and also the volume which I have just published containing a series of articles by my father in the 'New York Tribune'. The book, 'Revolution and Counter-Revolution in Germany', represents a most valuable pendant to 'The Eighteenth Brumaire'...
> With sincere greetings and all good wishes..."[77]

In one of her early raids on the Chancery Lane strongboxes Eleanor had found, as she told Kautsky in September 1895, a series of "18 articles on Germany"[78] of which she at once made three copies. The print was "trying", she wrote to Laura in October, and it was slow going, but "a wonderfully interesting history of 48".[79]

The articles were not in fact by Marx at all: his English at the time was still very imperfect – he had been but 18 months in London – and Engels

---

* A French edition. There was no English one until, translated by Harry Quelch, it was published by the Twentieth Century Press in 1900.

wrote them in Manchester, sending them to Marx for approval, signature and dispatch to the *New York Daily Tribune*. By January 1896 Eleanor had edited and arranged them under chapter heads and was negotiating with Sonnenschein for their first publication in book form under the title *Revolution and Counter-Revolution, or Germany in 1848*,* of which 400 copies were sold in the first three months.

The "Note by the Editor", dated April 1896, is of abiding interest for, under the impression that her father had written the articles in the years 1851–2, Eleanor drew upon her memory of family anecdotes and her mother's autobiographical sketch to describe life in Dean Street before her own birth, quoting Liebknecht as saying: "It was a terrible time but it was grand nevertheless". The "Note" also presaged work that was to engage her for many a long day: the letters and articles – originally published in the *New York Daily Tribune*, Ernest Jones's *People's Press* and Collet Dobson Collet's *Free Press* – which she here referred to as "the Kars papers".

A year later Sonnenschein brought out the bulk of these as *The Eastern Question*, edited by Eleanor and Aveling. Bulk indeed it was: a volume of some 650 pages, containing 113 letters written between 1853 and 1856 on the Crimean war. It attracted a good deal of attention, being reviewed in *Justice*, the *Daily Chronicle*, the *Liverpool Post* and the *Westminster Gazette*, which last wrote:

> "... With all Marx's faults and his extravagant abuse of high political personages, one cannot but admire the man's strength of mind, the courage of his opinions, and his scorn and contempt for everything small, petty and mean. Although many and great changes have taken place since these papers appeared, they are still valuable not only for the elucidation of the past, but also for throwing a clearer light upon the present as also upon the future."[80]

Liebknecht, while staying at The Den in August 1896 – his second visit that year – suggested that these articles should be brought together and published in Germany. In September Eleanor asked Kautsky whether he would do the translation, to which he agreed though in the event it was Benno Karpeles who undertook it.

To assemble the letters and articles was far from easy, as she soon realised. In the first place there were "*far* more of them than we supposed",[81] while of some there were four variants and Eleanor wished to use only a text which "seems to have been more carefully revised."

---

* She asked Laura to translate it into French and sent Kautsky the proofs for a German edition. Even before they reached him, he made this work his latest excuse for not responding to Eleanor's urgent appeals that he should come to London to discuss Volume IV of *Capital*.

Secondly, not all were among Marx's papers. Those missing would have to be copied at the British Museum where, to her dismay, she found that one version had been "mislaid".[82] Last but not least, there were no files of Ernest Jones's *People's Paper** at the Museum at all. Eleanor wrote to Jones's son, Atherley – who did not reply for many weeks – to the Manchester Free Library and to Edward Truelove.†

While of "immense historical interest",[81] Marx had included enormously long press reports and extracts from Hansard which, where not in full essential to the text, should, in Aveling's view, be summarised. Eleanor solicited Laura's opinion but at the same time insisted:

> "...they must be boiled down. Else it will make a volume or volumes *no one* will take. And much *can* be boiled down... Anyhow, we've *got* to..."[83]

By the beginning of the year 1897 the "boiling down", collating and editing was done and the work almost ready for publication; but still there was "no end of trouble" as Eleanor explained:

> "...I tried – Sonnenschein is *such* a thief – to get another publisher. I have tried Methuen, Macmillan, Unwin (the only *likely* ones) & failed. I will make a last effort with Longman. If he fails too, we must go to Sonnenschein. I want the work out. It is so very brilliant..."[83]

Then came the problem of an introduction.

> "...It would not be fair to preface such a volume with any 'views'. – His work must stand as it is, & we must all try to learn from it. And we can all 'walk under his huge legs' – & find ourselves not *dis*honourable but honourable graves..."[84]

At the time of Queen Victoria's Diamond Jubilee – June 1897 – Eleanor had "a devil of a job" to press her way once more to the British Museum through the

> "idiots of sightseers – seeing 'sights' that don't exist, for anything shabbier or meaner than the London 'decorations' you cd not dream in a nightmare..."[85]

but by the end of the first week in July the introduction was written ending with a graceful tribute to Collet, to Seddon of the Free Reference Library in Manchester and:

---

* "...to which, as Mohr says in Herr Vogt, – he gave a revised edition of the celebrated 'Kars' articles (Tribune)..."[83]

† A small publisher and bookseller of 256 High Holborn, persecuted in 1858 for putting out a pamphlet on Orsini's attempted assassination of Napoleon III, he printed and published Marx's *Civil War in France* in 1871.

"We are especially glad of this opportunity of thanking the British Museum officers, as it had been the intention of Marx, who read there for some thirty years, to make public acknowledgment of the ready assistance always given, and especially of the invaluable services rendered to him in his work for so many years by Dr. Richard Garnett..."[86]

Work on *The Eastern Question* had been seriously interrupted when, in November 1896, Eleanor for the second winter running found herself in "the grip of the demon influenza".[87] She told Kautsky: "I *could* not do anything for quite four weeks",[88] though it did not stop her from making a propaganda tour of Lancashire from 6 to 13 December. – "... the doctor swears I *can't* go: but where there's a will there's a way, & I think I shall risk it!"[89] – which "cure", as she called it, did wonders. It was most successful, she told Laura "and I'm glad I went"[90] for

"...If I had followed the doctor's advice I should be quite a confirmed invalid by now!..."[88]

However, once *The Eastern Question* was out by the end of August, she turned back to the splendid material she had been forced to omit if the book were to be kept within reasonable limits. She began to edit the series of articles on *The Story of the Life of Lord Palmerston* and *The Secret Diplomatic History of the Eighteenth Century* and, by September 1897, was correcting the proofs. She wanted

"to add some admirable sketches of Lord John Russell, Napoleon III, & Wellington..."[91]

combining all in one small volume.

A find she had made in April that year, causing her greater excitement, was

"...a *magnificent* paper of Mohr's read by him (Oh! the work that man did!) to the Council of the I.W.M.A. An admirable *economic exposition*..."[92]

"Written for workingmen ... and therefore very simple & clear."[93] Of some 23 or 24,000 words, it would "make a *very* popular pamphlet", she wrote to Kautsky when she was correcting the proofs and trying to trace the circumstances that had led to the "reading and writing of this long essay".[94]

Marx's *Secret Diplomatic History of the Eighteenth Century* and his *Story of the Life of Lord Palmerston*, "edited by his daughter, Eleanor Marx Aveling", were brought out separately by Sonnenschein in 1899, the first with a short Publisher's Preface:

"...Mrs Aveling did not live long enough to see these papers through the press, but she left them in such a forward state, and we have had so many inquiries about them since, that we venture to issue them without Mrs Aveling's final revision in two shilling pamphlets."

The "magnificent paper" Marx had read to the Council of the First International in September 1865 also came out in 1899 with a preface by Aveling, some of which was devoted to claiming credit for his share of the work. And who could argue with him? He was dead. He did, however, state the incontestable fact that

"...The paper was never published during the lifetime of Marx. It was found amongst his papers after the death of Engels..."

The title-page read: *"Value, Price and Profit: Addressed to Working Men* by Karl Marx. Edited by His Daughter Eleanor Marx Aveling",* and it was never published during the lifetime of its editor either.

*   *   *

The darkening of Eleanor's skies may be said to have begun with her estrangement from Engels. At first a little cloud like a man's hand had appeared upon the horizon to spread in a gathering gloom of suspicion and alarm until her sunny relations with this best of lifelong friends were blotted out for at least a year before his death, which event, surrounded by grievous circumstance, was a loss so immeasurable as to contribute to her own end.

Thereafter came her stormy dealings with Louise Freyberger; the legal and financial obfuscations from which she struggled to emerge into the light of common day by reasserting her familiar way of life: organising, lecturing, interpreting and writing, while also carrying the precious but heavy burden of Marx's posthuma.

The vexations of house-hunting took additional toll of her natural buoyancy, while no sooner had she come to rest, gratefully, in Jew's Walk than she was stunned by Stepniak's death, whereafter she fell ill: a victim not only of the "demon" but of utter exhaustion and suicidal depression.

She put a brave face on it, but the clouds did not lift and her days were troubled: too many business transactions – which she called "a damned nuisance" – too much work, too little time to enjoy the thrushes and the blackbirds: Though after her death, her maid Gertrude Gentay wrote to Edith Lancaster on 1 May 1890, saying: "oh how we do miss her, and it nearly breaks our hearts when we go out into the garden and see all the

---

* It is now known as *Wages, Price and Profit.*

flowers coming out that she was so fond of ..." [952] after that first winter she never again mentioned her garden. And there was no "General" to turn to: that last link with the cherished past, her sure guide in the present that held futurity for them both.

Her Russian visitor in the early '90s had found her appearance woebegone and her surroundings dingy. The lady did not observe, or did not record the observation, that Eleanor had *style*: that indefinable but unmistakable quality inherent no less in human beings than in artefacts. Those outward blemishes were the signs that Eleanor had spent years of her life being overworked and underpaid, while she would have scorned, could she have afforded, cosmetic adjuncts beyond the reach of working women with whom she chose to identify herself. They might skin onions and she sit at a typewriter; they might slave at a factory bench while she slaved at a desk in the Reading Room; they might make raincoats while she made outdoor speeches in the rain without one; her work was clean where theirs was dirty and injurious to health, but she had little more leisure than they and the main difference in that respect was that she had not to meet the demands of a growing family as well: a deprivation that she felt above all else. Now she could have indulged a little ease, a little comfort, even a degree of elegance about her house and person, but for such things she had small or no taste.

In a letter to *Justice* published on 26 June 1897 she said she had "given 41 lectures and spoken or taken the chair at ten meetings" in the past eight months, not counting a week's lecturing in Holland at the end of February that year.

> "in order to save time and trouble, *and* postage stamps, will you let me tell the many S.D.F. branches that are so kindly asking me to lecture for them that I am obliged to decline, for the present at any rate, all open-air work? My throat unfortunately will not stand the strain. Those who know me will not suspect me of shirking work ... When the indoor propaganda begins again I shall, as always, be at the service of my comrades and of the cause..."

This was printed under the heading "Branches Take Note". And whose Branches? Those of the SDF. A reconciliation had been effected and Eleanor was not only speaking throughout London and the provinces under the auspices of – with her expenses paid by – the SDF, but, from September 1896 until 8 January 1898, with but few weeks' intermission, she contributed a regular feature, "International Notes", to *Justice* and, from October 1896, gave a class each Wednesday in French and German for SDF members, while Aveling ran courses on mathematics, chemistry and other sciences.

Not that the personal insults and unmannerly public squabbles had ceased,* but the Federation and its journal had become Eleanor's formal platform, because it was "useful to the movement".[96]

In a letter to Hermann Schlüter in America on 1 January 1895, Engels had written:

> "... It goes here much the same as with you. The socialist instinct grows stronger and stronger among the *masses*, but as soon as it comes to translating the instinctive urge into clear demands and thoughts, everyone falls apart, some go into the Social Democratic Federation, some into the Independent Labour Party, others stay within their Trade Union organisations etc. etc. In short, a lot of sects and no Party ..."[97]

By now there is no need to labour the point that Eleanor, as a genuine Marxist and thus the least dogmatic of any for her time and place, did not really give a fig for these sects as such even when she worked with them in a disciplined fashion. Always she had homed her way unerringly to such groups in which she sensed this "instinctive urge" to socialism: to any zone where her words would fall on fertile ground. By the late '90s, the SDF appeared to her more "socialist" – and to have more influence – than any other existing organisation, so she rejoined it.

Keir Hardie's position, in her view, was "becoming very precarious" and "his power here is growing less and less", she wrote to Van der Goës, a Dutch socialist with whom she had been corresponding since the end of 1895. Hardie had recently come back from an "American journey – no one knows who paid his very heavy expenses –" which had "been a fiasco" and he was now trying to make common cause with the reformist and anarchist wings of the continental parties "and any other stragglers he can pick up" in order to "rehabilitate" himself.[98] (It may have given Eleanor a little *Schadenfreude* to report the "heavy expenses" of Hardie's unsuccessful tour of the United States.)

Although the SDF leadership, unlike that of the ILP, was *for* rather than *with* the working class, Eleanor – and also Aveling – had

> "... for years ... (to the General's distress) been on good terms with S.D.F. *members*. Now we are *officially* to work together. You know what such 'official' friendships mean – Edward & Hyndman no more love one another than Paul & Brousse ..."†[96]

---

* In passing it may be said that Ferdinand Gilles had died on 5 December 1895. "The circumstances attending his death were extremely painful ... his nervous system became completely shattered, and eventually he lost his reason ... from overwork and insufficient rest ... One trouble followed another, accentuated by an intrigue by persons with whom Gilles was at variance ... [He] possessed too excitable a temperament for public work, and it was a most unfortunate circumstance that he took up any responsible position in a public movement ..." Thus his obituary in *Justice*,[95] his foremost champion and open forum when his "too excitable a temperament" had served a public purpose.

† The leader of the French "Possibilists".

As is often the case, the first move towards this truce went almost unnoticed. On 23 March 1895 *Justice* published a letter from Aveling on the changed position of the Eight Hours League and International Labour League consequent upon the London Trades Council ballot in favour of the annual demonstration being held on the first Sunday rather than the first day of May. The joint Demonstration Committee was bound by this decision and any delegate who did not agree with it was free to resign. This Aveling did – "Naturally with considerable regret, as for five years I have served on the committee" – and he further thought the time had come for him to resign from the Legal Eight Hours Demonstration Committee, at whose meeting, "after repeated appeals to Dr. Aveling to reconsider his position, a vote of 'thanks to him for his invaluable services' ... was unanimously adopted."[99] In effect, the May First cause was lost in Britain and with the resignation of its Chairman the only body still advocating it collapsed. Thus an obstacle to joining what with some hyperbole might be called the "big battalions" was quietly removed.

The final rapprochement was not without a hitch as, indeed, nothing that involved Aveling ever was. The Executive of the SDF had passed a resolution on 17 December 1895, issued as a circular:

"In view of reliable information concerning Dr. Aveling's recent relations with the Social Democratic movement both at home and abroad, the Executive Council after most careful consideration of the whole matter request that he be no longer invited by the branches of the S.D.F. to lecture for them".[100]

In February 1896 Aveling wrote to Kautsky complaining about the latest of

"...the Freybergers' tricks ... They want to stir up discord between us and the S.D.F...."[101]

On the same date he sent letters to all the most influential socialist leaders on the Continent asking them to write confuting the statement published aboard that he had

"been using his influence to prevent the establishment of cordial relations between the Social-Democratic Federation and the German Social-Democratic Party..."[*102]

He protested that he had done no such thing; had, indeed, made "attempts with the General of late to make him less bitter against them";[102] had spoken no word against the SDF which, but for this

---

* This particular phrase was used in writing to Van der Goës on 8 February 1896, but there is no doubt that all the letters were on the same lines.

groundless rumour, was prepared "to let bygones be bygones".[102] The response was conclusive:

> "... we had such replies that Hyndman *could* not hold out," Eleanor told Laura. "As a matter of fact he was really taken in (this time) by the Freebooters* who made him believe the poor old General was *longing* to meet him – Hyndman – & that we prevented it. In the face of the excellent letters from *all* the Continental people ... written before consultation with the Freebooters ... the Executive of the SDF on Tuesday *unanimously* withdrew their statement; everyone shook hands & the Free-booters have thus *unwillingly* helped to bring about a very useful 'reconciliation' between us and the SDF..."†[103]

A couple of months later *Justice* published a letter from a member of the ILP, Arthur Field:

> "Dear Comrade,
>   In last week's *Labour Leader* appears the following note:– 'Dr. Aveling has joined the S.D.F. the I.L.P. having expelled him and the Eight Hours League being defunct, he had to get a footing somewhere for the coming International'.‡ I write as a friend of the SDF and of Dr. Aveling, and as a member of the ILP, to say that members of the SDF ought to be informed that the paragraph is untrue in substance and in fact. Dr. Aveling has not been expelled by the ILP and is in no danger of lacking a credential from a branch of that organisation. The London E.C. of that party is *not* 'the ILP', nor is the *Labour Leader*, by the way, the organ of 'the ILP'. I say this so that they may take at its true value this latest example of the lying venom which is, strange to say, unfortunately characteristic of Mr. Hardie's organ towards Dr. Aveling.
>   I am, yours fraternally..."[104]

It was always the same story. With monotonous regularity slurs and slanders followed Aveling as its slime a slug; yet, as regularly, he acquired new prestige. *Justice* announced his meetings and reported his lectures without fail. It advertised his penny pamphlets, *Wilhelm Liebknecht* and *Socialism and Anarchism*, even his bathetic verses *The Tramp of the Workers* – but at ½d. – published by the Twentieth Century Press; it printed his long reports on the 1895 TUC and a whole series recording Liebknecht's speaking tour in May and June 1896. His name was given prominence in extra large type if he so much as chaired a demonstration in some provincial town, while the joint proposal made by him and Eleanor to inaugurate the science and language classes, with faithful reports on their progress, were given ample space.

---

* Freybergers.
† The circular was withdrawn and, on 3 March, the Executive absolved Aveling from "any recent intrigues such as its information led it to believe he was guilty of".[100]
‡ The London International Congress 27 July to 1 August 1896, at which Field was a delegate from the Chatham Branch of the ILP.

On 26 July 1896 an International Peace Demonstration was held in Hyde Park, Aveling, representing the Gasworkers, presiding over one of the platforms. In anticipation of this event, Eleanor wrote to *Justice* to recall that at the Zurich Congress

> "...the most beautiful and impressive part ... arranged by the Swiss was the children. I know it is far more difficult to arrange anything of the kind here. Still, I think we might manage something, though we do take our pleasures so sadly...
> Could not, e.g. all the S.D.F. children (and all others we could get) be brought to 337 Strand* and thence marshalled to the Embankment and the Park? The smaller ones would have to go in brakes, the bigger ones could walk..."[105]

As it happened, it poured that day and although an impressive programme of speakers was announced and "a magnificent processional display"[106] was mounted, the occasion was utterly ruined, few speeches were delivered and it is to be hoped that the children stayed at home.

Aveling went from strength to strength and, at the 17th Annual Conference of the SDF,† held at the Co-operative Hall in, of all places, Northampton on 1 August 1897, he was elected to the Executive Council. (Hyndman must have suffered a twinge or two at the rise to position within his very own organisation of the impudent upstart who had once dared to accept nomination for that parliamentary constituency.)

Meanwhile Eleanor's "International Notes" enjoyed a keen readership, as was shown, to take but one example, when, in 1910, Alfred Greenwood, the Secretary of the International Glassworkers' Union, wrote an article recalling her work as a translator at its Congresses and the passage she had written on 10 July 1897.

> "...The highest compliment and tribute that can be paid to her memory is now to reprint in the Quarterly Report her last International Notes on the Glass Bottle Trade. In doing this her words will be preserved let us hope for some years at least from oblivion and will revive the recollection, and we are sure be greatly appreciated by everyone, of the British glass bottle workers' delegates who had the pleasure of listening to her interpretations of the speeches made by the foreign delegates..."

Greenwood had been no stranger to her and wrote:

> "...the last visit I paid her at her new home 'The Den' at Sydenham, several months before she died, we sketched together the prospective arrangements for the next International Glass Workers' Congress, to be held in Berlin, in September 1898..."[107]

---

* The SDF Hall, where her own and Aveling's classes were held.
† Attended by 56 delegates from 47 branches.

It is not common for such ephemera to be reprinted 13 years later as a "compliment and tribute" to the writer.

Engels, who had never ceased to feel contemptuous of the SDF – its sectarian tactics, self-styled Marxism and total inability to maintain a solid organisation* – had foreseen monstrous difficulties over the 1896 London International Congress, with, on the one hand, the SDF believing the moment was ripe for Simon Pure socialists to detach themselves completely from the trade union movement and, on the other, the TUC Parliamentary Committee bent upon admitting none but delegates organised in and working at their trades, each party out to "boss the Congress".[108] However, as he conceded:

> "Much water will flow down the Thames before then, the quantity and quality of which no one can foretell..."[109]

That stream had borne Engels away and carried Eleanor and Aveling into the SDF.

To be sure, there were the usual preliminary manœuvres on all sides to gain advantage, but the preparations for the Congress went ahead in a tolerably businesslike manner. From April Eleanor, after fulfilling her weekend engagements in the provinces – which entailed being out of London from Saturday mornings until Tuesday evenings many a time – became wholly involved in this work. The Zurich Bureau met a deputation from the British Parliamentary Committee in February, decided that the name should be the "International Socialist Workers' and Trade Union Congress" and set up a conjoint executive of six members from each side. The Zurich Committee included Aveling, Quelch, Thorne and Sydney Olivier; the Parliamentary Committee Tillett, Broadhurst and Mawdsley. Thorne was appointed Secretary to this joint body, while he was also on the Organisation Committee in London with Aveling, Quelch and Tom Mann among others. Eleanor was elected Secretary to the committee responsible for the reception and accommodation of foreign and provincial delegates and also Minute Secretary to the Conjoint Committee.

On 20 May she wrote to Kautsky that this letter was the 18th – underlined three times – she was sending out that day; and it was probably the only one not directed to finding rooms in London. She

---

* At the time of its 14th Annual Conference (5 and 6 August 1894 in London), he had written to Lafargue: "...It has 4,500 members. Last year there were 7,000 names on its membership list, so it has lost 2,500. But what of it? asks Hyndman. In the 14 years of its existence the SDF has seen a *million people* pass through its ranks ... Out of one million 995,500 have hopped it but – 4,500 have stayed!..."[108]

compiled a list of 175 hotels, lodgings and boarding houses with their charges* and a note indicating which foreign languages were spoken at each. This was distributed as a pamphlet in three languages, giving the programme of extra-Congress events, the meeting places for each of the national delegations and the badges by which the members of various committees and the interpreters could be identified, together with a map of London.

As the time drew near Eleanor wrote to Liebknecht from the Hotel and Reception Committee's headquarters at 19 Buckingham Street, Strand, to tell him that within the last few days she had received.

> "...letters from German comrades saying they will arrive on such or such a day and wd like to be met. I think our German comrades hardly realise what London is, and that there are no end of stations at wh they may arrive..."[110]

It would be impossible to meet them if they did not let her know their route, station and hour of arrival, and the sooner she heard what rooms they required the better.

The Congress was to have been held in St. Martin's Town Hall[†] but it was too small and from the start the venue was changed to the Queen's Hall in Langham Place.[‡] Preceded by the wet Peace Demonstration in Hyde Park and an evening reception at The Horseshoe to welcome the delegates that Sunday evening, the Congress opened on Monday morning at 11 o'clock.

Eleanor was not only one of the translators,[§] she was also a delegate from the London Gasworkers' Union, as was Aveling who was mandated too by the Maidstone branch of the ILP and the Social-Democratic Federation of New South Wales.

There were 120 SDF delegates, 115 from the ILP, while the Fabian Society came a very limp third with 22. But the trade unions were represented in strength with 185 delegates, including 26 from Trades and Labour Councils. Thus Great Britain mustered, with such small bodies as

---

* It will entertain modern Londoners to learn that at the Horseshoe in Tottenham Court Road, where French and German were spoken, bed and breakfast cost 4s.; the Tour Eiffel in Percy Street (French only) charged 1s. for a bed and from 6s. 6d. to 7s. 6d. for bed, breakfast, lunch and dinner (wine and coffee included); the Bedford in Southampton Row was 4s. 6d. for bed and breakfast, but the average price in the nineteen hotels – where at least one foreign language was spoken – was 2s. 2d. and dinner 1s. 6d. Eight Temperance Hotels competed for custom, though more expensive than any others, and in the Bloomsbury area there were no fewer than 111 boarding houses and lodgings, 17 of which were in Torrington Square.

† At the lower end of Charing Cross Road, facing Trafalgar Square.

‡ Promenade concerts were first given there in 1895.

§ The others were Bernstein, Liebknecht, J. Sigg (of Geneva), the inevitable Adolphe Smith and Clara Zetkin.

the Hammersmith, Bristol, Oxford and Berkshire Socialist Societies and
the Labour Church Union, a total of 459 delegates.* It was only natural
that representatives of the host country should far outnumber the foreigners, but the 21 other nations made, on the whole, a poor showing,
only the French sending a substantial delegation of 127, the remaining 20
no more than a combined 164 some of whom held credentials from more
than one country. A striking feature was the vastly increased number of
women present: in all there were 55, of whom 42 were British: close on 10
per cent of the native contingent.

The list of those present is as a bridge from the 19th to the 20th
century: here were John Robert Clynes (Oldham Trades Council); Mrs.
Charlotte Despard (Ilkeston SDF); Jean Jaurès; George Lansbury (Bow and
Bromley SDF); Rosa Luxemburg; James Ramsay MacDonald (Fabians);[†]
Alexandre Millerand; Albert Arthur Purcell (London French Polishers);
Bernard Shaw; Vandervelde; the Webbs and Clara Zetkin.

A fortnight earlier Eleanor had written to Liebknecht:

> "The Congress promises to do well – if only the Anarchists – whether outspoken or
> cowardly – dont spoil it, as they mean to do if possible. You are quite mistaken if you
> fancy that you have made the slightest impression upon Hardie. Not only – that is the
> least thing – does his paper[‡] week by week bring Anarchist letters etc. but privately he
> and his henchman – Mann – are doing all they can to get the Anarchists in on the usual
> grounds of 'fair play'. And on the 25th July[§] Messrs. Mann and Hardie *hold a large
> demonstration at the Holborn Town Hall in favour* of the 'Anti-Parliamentarians' – in
> favour, i.e. of the Anarchists! This is announced on big placards..."[111]

Her prediction was accurate. The first session, on Monday 27 July,
dissolved into "a scene of confusion, many delegates speaking at once"[||] on
the question of admitting the anarchists. So great was the uproar that the
President for the day – Cowey, the Chairman of the TUC Parliamentary
Committee – threatened to call the police. The next day Paul Singer,
presiding, said the police would not be called but that stewards had been
posted in all parts of the Hall to maintain order and he appealed to the
Congress not to waste precious time in quarrelling. Idle words. Keir

---

* A few represented more than one organisation.
† MacDonald had formally joined the ILP in 1894 and was on its National Council from 1896,
but he did not resign from the Fabian Society until 1900, having been and remained a member
of the New Life Fellowship and its honorary secretary for the year 1892–3.
‡ The *Labour Leader*.
§ That is, the day before the Congress when most of the delegates would have arrived.
|| This and all subsequent direct quotations are from the official *Report of Proceedings of the
International Socialist Workers and Trade Union Congress, London 1896*, published by the Twentieth Century press, as corrected and approved by the "various representatives of the different
nationalities serving on the Standing Orders Committee".[112]

Hardie, as vice-president, spoke of "toleration" – what Eleanor had called "fair play" – for those who disagreed with the Zurich resolution of 1893 on the exclusion of anarchists and those who opposed parliamentary action. Jaurès, while quite in favour of tolerance, was determined to abide by the Zurich decision, but Tom Mann thought this extremely intolerant: he himself was not an anarchist but was willing to learn from others "as good, and better than I" and opposed the exclusion of such people. Hyndman, who had not been at Zurich and was in no way bound by its resolutions, supported the motion from "an independent point of view".

> "What is the title of the Congress, and on what basis has it been called?" he asked. "I see no word in its title referring to Anarchism or Anarchist-Communism.* And of what use is it to invite these people to Congresses when they themselves have admitted over and over again that they do not believe in Congresses?"

A personal friend of his for whom he entertained "a most kindly feeling" had

> "declared at Paris that they had come here with the intention of upsetting a lot of fools like ourselves. There was order, there was tolerance, there was fraternity!"

He was vociferously interrupted at every mention of anarchism and, as he continued "great disorder" broke out.

> "I yield to no one in toleration ..." he declared amidst the hubbub, "but I denounce Anarchy ... and I stand up for the order and organisation of International Social-Democracy."

Nieuwenhuis of Holland hotly denied that they – the anarchists – had come to the Congress to create a disturbance. It was not an Anarchist Congress admittedly, but neither was it a Social-Democratic Congress.

> "I dare anyone to say that Anarchist-Communists† are not Socialists",

if they were not, he could "bring forward documentary evidence" that Liebknecht was not a socialist.

> "Had we understood," he said, "that the Dutch delegates would be unwelcome, we would have absented ourselves..."

---

* It is sometimes hard to tell whether such contradictions in terms are owed to political ignorance or sophistry. In Hyndman's case there can be little doubt.

† This, too, was not pure ignorance; it was sheer naïveté: Niuewenhuis sincerely believed there were such people and, what is more, he was one of them.

and, indeed, eight of the 13 Dutch delegates – including Nieuwenhuis – withdrew after the Congress had decided in favour of socialists standing for parliament.

A vote was taken by nationalities, but Keir Hardie was reminded that the British had already endorsed and were committed in favour of the Zurich resolution. This led to a violent argument: for all anybody knew the delegates might have changed their minds since then; but the President ruled that they could not vote again, whereupon Tom Mann shouted:

"I wish to protest and I shall continue to protest."

Seventeen nationalities supported the exclusion of the anarchists, two were against (France 57 to 56 and Holland 9 to 5)* while Italy abstained.

But did this dispose of the plaguy question? Not a bit of it. At the third session, two having been misspent, Clara Zetkin rose to give her report on the credentials of the German delegation, to be followed in turn by each nationality's spokesman.†

The proposal to exclude six German anarchists led to an alarming demonstration, one speaker being threatened by the Chair that he would be turned out of the Hall if he did not sit down. This "credentials" procedure turned into nothing more nor less than a renewal of the entire debate on the anarchists and went on interminably. Various "Debating Clubs" and mystifying trade unions whose very existence was in doubt were found to be small groups of anarchists and in every case those whose mandates would not bear too close a scrutiny raised their voices high.

At this point of the proceedings poor Eleanor complained that the speakers on the floor were inaudible owing to the ceaseless din. "If the delegates will keep quiet the interpreters will be able to hear," she announced from the platform, but it is doubtful whether she herself was heard: it was not the age of microphones.

Plekhanov spoke for the eight Russian delegates, "almost all of whom hold many credentials from actual workers' organisations in Russia", one

---

* It is impossible to reconcile the figures given in the *Report* with the list of delegates, where Holland is shown to have had 13 – not 14 – present (though perhaps one voted both ways); nor is it clear why the British, who were supposed to be out of the count, were recorded as voting 223 in favour to 104 against.

† So far as the British were concerned, one of the two delegates from the Berkshire Socialist Society was excluded on the grounds of being one too many to represent a total membership of four. Aveling's mandate for Australia was accepted, as was Bernard Shaw's for the Irish Fabian Society. The Americans ran into a little bother over two delegates from the New York "Hackowners Union", said to be an association of employers, not workers, but they were eventually admitted.

of which had recently led and conducted a great strike in St. Petersburg. This was the first International Congress at which such a claim could be made.

"At last the Russian proletariat is entering into the ranks of the class-conscious Socialists of the whole world,"

he declared. The trouble here arose over the Revolutionary Socialist Union. Upon being challenged by one of its members, Plekhanov denied that he held it against them that they were university graduates but he did not regard this in itself as

"a reason for speaking on behalf of the Russian working class. In justice to that class, and to those who are its direct representatives, who hold credentials from Russia and not from a few students in Switzerland,"

he did not wish them foisted upon this first genuine Russian delegation and won his point. A singular difficulty arose when it came to the French: three delegates – Jaurès, Millerand and Viviani – were Deputies to the Chamber and, as such, were said to have no credentials whatsoever though "as a matter of goodwill and tolerance" they might be accepted. Jaurès was having none of that. French anarchists had wormed their way into the Congress with fictitious mandates and "it would be the height of absurdity" to admit them while excluding men elected to parliament by thousands of organised workers and who could, moreover, also speak for the peasantry. "Great confusion followed", according to the *Report* and was not stilled by Lansbury's proposal to delete the phrase granting the M.P.s admission as an act of grace which, in effect, excluded them. Keir Hardie wished to know why M.P.s should be favoured above other men – "it might lead to mischief" – but was overruled.* Millerand tried to speak, was shouted down and "the excitement was so great that it was impossible to take a vote", though eventually they were admitted. But on the following afternoon – by which time half the Congress week had elapsed without a single item on the agenda having been reached – Millerand was able to get in his word that the French, having rejected the Zurich resolution by 57 votes to 56, 47 members of the minority had withdrawn.

"Those Anarchists present at the Congress had in many cases admitted that they used the mantle of trade unionism only for the purpose of getting into the Congress. The minority, therefore, ask to be allowed to vote separately ... Will you force us Socialists to accept the responsibility of a collaboration with the French Anarchists?"

* Hardie had lost his West Ham seat in 1895 and was not again an M.P. until he won Merthyr Tydfil in 1900, a constituency he represented until his death in 1915.

A formal separation was absolutely necessary to make the position clear in the eyes of public opinion. If this were not done, the Socialists would "be compelled, reluctantly", to leave the Congress since they refused to be identified with "all kinds of double dealing machinations". The question was put to the vote and the French divided into two sections.*

At some point in these debates – if such they can be called while the Queen's Hall resounded with unaccustomed discord – Sydney Olivier with true Fabian mildness suggested that Congress should forgo these reports. But no: the Poles, the Austrians, the Czechs (Bohemians), Hungarians, Danes, Swedes, Italians, Spanish, Portuguese and Dutch – in all, ten other national delegations – still had to have their say and, in every case where credentials were not acceptable, those in question rose to make long speeches, with constant interruptions, to justify themselves. Some exasperated fellow from the Amalgamated Society of Carpenters and Joiners objected to this "farce" and, amidst the pandemonium, Bernard Shaw and the carpenter tried again and again to move "next business" and stop this pointless waste of time. They might have saved their breath.

Yet it was not altogether as pointless as it appeared, for the underlying political issue at stake was that of parliamentarians *versus* anti-parliamentarians and it emerged only too clearly that, despite the vote on their exclusion, the anarchists had remained in force and were still exercising considerable influence. At one stage that heroic, passionate and slightly mad lady, Louise Michel,† who wished to sit with the Italian delegation, addressed the Congress from the platform and then swept out.

At 7.30 on the evening of that Wednesday, the delegates, weak with fatigue and more than a little hoarse, adjourned. Not until the fifth session was well under way on Thursday were they able to turn their attention to the first of the five Commissions' reports on the Agrarian Question, Political Action (introduced by Lansbury), Education and Physical Development (Sidney Webb), Organisation, War and, finally, the Economic and Industrial Report. To each there was, of course, a Minority Report, followed by heated discussion. There were also miscellaneous resolutions, squeezed in on the last day – Saturday, 1 August – on such matters as liberty of conscience, speech, the press and the right of public assembly; amnesty for political prisoners and condemnation of police provocation; the establishing of labour exchanges under the jurisdiction of local authorities or trade unions to replace profit-making agencies; and the question, in the absence of an international language,‡

---

* Fifteen nationalities were for the motion and five – including Britain (114 to 110) – against.
† Owing to whose presence as a speaker Eleanor refused to preside over the International Platform on May Day 1897.
‡ Volapuk, invented by a German priest, Johann Schleyer in 1879, was much in favour at the

whether English, French or German should be officially adopted at future Congresses. It was resolved that the next Congress should be held in Germany in 1899 and if the laws of that country rendered this impossible, then in Paris in 1900. Liebknecht, moving the report, said:

> "... The next International Congress must take place without the unpleasant scenes of the last two Congresses ... Up till now we have not succeeded in bringing together, without disturbance, the representatives of revolutionary Social-Democracy and of the trade unions that stand upon the same basis. As democrats we have many difficulties when uninvited and undesirable people come; we cannot call in the police ... Thus we were obliged to have days of fruitless discussion which were forced upon us with a view to discrediting the Congress, and causing disgust at its proceedings so that our enemies might say in triumph, 'behold the men who want to create a new world cannot even keep order at their own Congress'. We must therefore, once for all, put an end to this ... The Bureau upon which were represented all shades of opinion and tendencies, has been quite unanimous ... and plainly declares that Anarchists have no right to admission to the Congress ..."

At the eleventh hour two British voices were raised. Dan Irving of Burnley moved an amendment on behalf of the SDF:

> "That the mandate for the next International Congress shall be confined to delegates from genuine Social-Democratic organisations (as well as Trade Unions) whose object is the socialisation of the means and instruments of production, transport, distribution and exchange under the ownership and control of the democracy in the interests of the whole people; who strive to attain this end by parliamentary and other general political methods; who are in favour of the establishment in each country of a parliamentary and political party independent of and apart from all other political parties; and who are ready in existing circumstances to accept and abide by the rule of the majority."

Thereupon one of the two delegates from the United Builders Labourers' Union, W. Stevenson, burst forth:

> "I claim the right to represent the opinions of trade unionists who have sent me here. I am not surprised at the intolerance shown. It is only of a piece with the treatment which the English trade unionists, who do happen to represent somebody, have received during the week of this so-called International Congress. The British section has all along swamped the trade unionists in it. I am prepared to say this, so far as the industrial questions and matters affecting the life of the workers are concerned, very little practical good has been done. The amendment is only a little sop to drag a few trade unions into another Congress. I protest against the waste of time which has been going on. Questions that do affect the industrial welfare of the people have been shunted, and you have spent your time in hearing brilliant disquisitions on an ideal state of society which is as far off from you as the millennium."

---

time. Esperanto, the invention in 1887 of Dr. Lazarus Zamenhof, a Warsaw oculist, had not yet caught on.

So significant were the viewpoints – and their divergence – implicit in these last-minute interventions that it is small wonder they received no attention whatsoever.

Then *Auld Lang Syne* "was played on the organ and sung after the British fashion",* after which came the *Marseillaise* and the *Carmagnole*.

That afternoon the delegates were entertained at the Crystal Palace – near home for Eleanor, thank heavens – followed by a banquet at which Aveling presided, a concert and, in a final burst of glory, "the celebrated fireworks".

---

* That is, with crossed hands clasped.

Originally Liebknecht had been invited, as before, to stay at The Den during the Congress, but Eleanor thought this

> "... perhaps a little – or indeed very selfish and inconsiderate. Yesterday returning late and tired from a Committee meeting it struck me that after all Sydenham is a good way from St. Martin's Hall* ... it wd of necessity mean very early morning trains, and often enough late night ones..."

She therefore thought it wise that he should live nearer to the meeting place and his co-delegates during that week.

> "Of course afterwards is another matter. *Then* you BELONG to us and you and your wife may as well make up your minds to the fact that from *Saturday, August* 1st 10 p.m. ... you are our prisoners. From the Palace fête ... you will both be brought (by *force* if need be – we have a strong gasworkers Branch here!!) to the Den..."[113]

So Liebknecht – it is not clear whether Natalie was with him† – was Eleanor's guest again, while she had no doubt put up Johnny Longuet during the Congress to which, aged 20, he came as a full-blown delegate representing the Lower Normandy Federation of the Workers' Party. He was thus in good company and in the same section, when it split off, as Jules Guesde, his uncle Paul Lafargue and the three controversial Deputies.

International Congresses were not, nor were they intended to be, a proving-ground for national policies. Nevertheless, in 1896 far more than at any previous Congress, the opposing tendencies within each country's approach to what all called Socialism were sharply defined. With both Irving's amendment and Stevenson's criticism Eleanor could not but feel sympathy. She did not consider shorter hours, higher wages or any other amelioration of workers' conditions under capitalism either trivial or ends in themselves: for her they had precisely that degree of importance the workers attached to them. In that lay her distinctive contribution. She was zealous to work for any and every practical reform without for a

---

* The *Town* Hall, not that at which the IWMA had been inaugurated in 1864. See above, fn. *, p. 35. The Queen's Hall was even further from Sydenham.
† During his earlier visit that year he had written to William Morris to say she was not there at present but "will come with me to the Congress".[114]

moment losing sight of the revolutionary aim; to agitate for the total overthrow of the system without brushing aside a single immediate demand for which the working class was prepared to fight. This was her interpretation of Marxism. It was unlike that of the SDF whose policy and propaganda were Marxist but whose practice was not. Indeed, the two were divorced; hence, perhaps, the turnover of membership so ironically mocked by Engels. People came in and went out of the SDF as through a revolving door. Personally insufferable to her, Hyndman's thorough knowledge and decrial of Britain's role in India won her respect; she stood four-square with him in abominating anarchism and she believed with him – and Dan Irving – in using parliamentary as well as extra-parliamentary means to further the interests of the working class. But his scorn for the trade unions – his apparent inability to recognise that the key to the capitalist system was to be found at the point of production and that only the producers, by combining, could defeat the owners who produced nothing – was an insuperable barrier between them. Where she saw organised men and women as possessed of the strength of a sleeping giant, he saw in them only the inertia of befuddled pygmies. There were, of course, fervent socialists in the trade unions, as there were active trade unionists in all the socialist organisations – except the Fabians – but they were only now beginning to speak a common language.

Eleanor had not the gift of prophecy. She could not foretell that the word "socialism", still a beacon to millions of working men and women, would – unlike that "spectre haunting Europe" – be misappropriated to make capitalism more viable, for which service feudal honours, lordships and knighthoods, would be conferred upon the low-born; nor that "Marxism" would become one of the most popular games to be played at the universities, without the smallest application to the life of the people and, though no cups might actually be presented by royalty, there would nonetheless be prizes for the winning in the academic field. But it needed no powers of divination in 1898 for anyone with an ear so close to the ground as Eleanor's to recognise that the stage was rapidly approaching when the two wings of Labour – the non-political trade unions and the empirical socialists – would merge to form a peculiarly British type of federated body, unlike any continental Workers' Party.

Within two years of her death, the Labour Representation Committee,* to be renamed the Labour Party in 1906, came into being to form a single political party opposed alike to Liberals and Conservatives. This marked a most significant advance but a year later, at the first LRC conference in

---

* Meeting at the Memorial Hall in Farringdon Road on 27 February 1900.

1901, the SDF withdrew from this new Party because it would not accept in its constitution the ultimate aim of achieving socialism.

The growing militancy of the employing class certainly helped to bring about the climate for this growth. As early as 1893 the Free Labour Association, organised by William Collison to supply blacklegs and strike-breakers, had been founded; and in 1896 – when the Edinburgh TUC, with Thorne as that year's chairman of the Parliamentary Committee, represented well over a million members* – the Engineering Employers' Associations formed a Federation "to protect and defend the interests of employers against combinations of workmen".† The Employers' Federation covered only the North of England, Scotland and Northern Ireland at first and its affiliated firms were expected to refer to it all disputes however unimportant.

Eleanor had little notion that its operations would shortly engross all her time and energy. Following Liebknecht's departure and a brief holiday in the Scillies, she threw herself into work with a vengeance, writing her weekly articles, holding her weekly classes and speaking at meetings all over London and the provinces. Indeed, by November 1896 she felt "sick of lecturing" and told Kautsky she was looking forward to "a week's holiday at Xmas".[115] One of the happiest occasions in the following spring was the celebration of the 8th anniversary of the Gasworkers' Union in Battersea Park where, in April 1897, a resolution was passed calling upon the assembled crowd to join their unions and take part in political activity

"with a view to combining in our great international army to fight against and break down the organised forces of capitalism".[116]

The *Labour Leader* reported

"...a cutting east wind ... a dull sky, a fringe of dark trees ... under the platform a shock of upturned, anxious, toilscarred faces. Around are the trade union banners gay with silk and paint. On the platform stands Marx's daughter, as youthful and strenuous as ever...".[117]

It was indeed appropriate that Eleanor's last major involvement should have been in an industrial struggle.

That July Liebknecht came once more to stay at The Den, Eleanor having written to him:

---

* Out of a working population of over 22 million.
† Seventy-two years after the repeal of the Combination Acts and at a time when the ASE alone had a membership of over 87,000.

"...You *must* come ... and have your three weeks rest (as it cant be more) and *then* come for a good long holiday – (then perhaps you could both come) – in March or April ... So we shall expect you in July *and* in the spring of next year, and, as our good East-enders say 'don't you forget it'..."

He was not likely to; and when the spring of 1898 came he may well have re-read that letter with its note of appeal:

"...we are looking forward to your *visits* (plural, please,) with more pleasure than I have words for or time to write them in. Dear, dear old Library, do you think there are so many of the *old* friends left that I can *afford* not to want *you*?..."[118]

Before his arrival on 11 July 1897 a London branch of the Engineering Employers' Federation was set up with Siemens as President. The ASE refused to recognise this central body and an Eight-Hour Joint Committee of twelve engineering unions, formed in May that year, advised its combined membership to down tools on 3 July in all firms which had refused to introduce the shorter working week. The Federation hit back by threatening to lock out one-quarter of all union men each week the strike lasted in every federated firm throughout the country from 13 July. Upon this 17,000 ASE members and several thousands of other unionists struck. Siemens told the press frankly that the object was to "get rid of trade unionism altogether".

On 15 September the ASE issued a circular to the public in the name of its Executive Council signed by George Barnes, the General Secretary.*

"The Federation of Engineering Employers' Associations started out a couple of months ago on the mad project of crippling the A.S.E. and have succeeded only in crippling the Engineering Trade of the country. Notwithstanding many denials, the purpose of the Federation has been made pretty clear, partly by the blundering statements of its own officials and partly by the unkindly light thrown upon the facts of these officials being found in close alliance with the freaks of the 'Free Labour Association'..."

It gave in full the Employers' statement on the 48-hours demand, dated 8 September, which analysed, with figures, the "drain on A.S.E. funds".

"This interesting document was not intended for publication, but was addressed from the Federation office to those employers who have been deluded into locking out, the intention obviously having been to keep their courage up to the sticking point by representing the A.S.E. as in a bankrupt condition. It begins, continues, and ends in lies and misrepresentations..."

---

* From 1896 to 1908.

of which the union gave a detailed refutation, added that the funds had not "appreciably diminished" and that

"the cost of the lock out has been met by special efforts of the 65,000 members still at work and by the help sent from outside sources, of which we have had intimation of some £1,500 today and yesterday..."[119]

At the end of September the Eight Hours Joint Committee of engineers put out a circular from its rooms at the Lord Nelson in Nelson Square, Blackfriars, listing the London firms "who are working or have conceded the Eight Hours Day". Headed "Concessions up to Tuesday, Sept. 28th 1897" it named 202 establishments "and four other firms who decline to have their names published".*

By the beginning of October almost 600 firms had locked out some 45,000 ASE members and the Free Labour Association was in heavy demand to supply non-union labour. On 3 November Barnes issued a circular "To the Workmen of Great Britain and Ireland and Other Countries". For 17 weeks, it said, the engineering unions had

"sustained a battle raised against them by the greatest combination of capital the world has ever known.

Only a small part of the fight is due to our action.

The Eight-hours day was being peaceably negotiated in the London engineering works. Two-thirds of the shops had accepted the shorter day...

The Federation then began a pitiless war against Trade Unions, and locked out at least 50,000 men in the country who had no part in the London dispute or negotiations..."

Twice the Government had intervened; the unions had accepted its terms unconditionally in the first case, in the second with "certain amendments in strict accord with the letter and the spirit of the Conciliation Act", but the employers had refused.

"They ask us to meet, not in order to discuss or to conclude the terms of peace, but, with every circumstance of shame, to surrender our arms, like the soldiers of a conquered city, while they hold theirs over our heads and crush us with the combined menace of an unreal Conference and an only too real lock-out."

---

* The list included all the Royal Ordnance Factories (as one), Trinity House Corporation, numerous private gun and ammunition factories, the Post Office, most of the dock engineering works and twenty other shipbuilding, ship repair and shipping firms; the engineering departments in thirteen of the Gas, Light and Coke Company's works (as one); six of the largest breweries and two distillers; the *Daily Telegraph, Daily Chronicle, Standard* and *Strand Magazine* engineering shops; six cycle and two motor car factories; the Co-operative Wholesale Society and its Printing Works; Brunner Mond; and the vestry of the Parish of St. Mary, Battersea.[120]

They were "overwhelmed with false charges", of having crippled the work of the machines, of "domineering interference in the workshops" and so forth, while the law could do little to "break the force of these great and secret associations of capital that exist in virtual defiance of it." They had "but two weapons left": their citizenship and their right to combination. The Federation sought to strike the second from their hands. No unionist was safe from its stratagems. Its agents had

"run from factory to factory – intimidating, cajoling, and bribing. Your turn may come next. The moderation of your leaders, the prudence of your tactics, will be no protection ... We have spared no effort to secure an honourable compromise ... It has been interpreted as signs of weakness or fear; and the only inference we can draw is that the Federation want us to come cap in hand, and on bended knee, to confess our faults and sue for a dishonourable peace...

Federated capital is bent on a determined fight, in which there has been and will be brought to bear against you all the force of wealth and resources of civilisation...".[121]

At last, on 3 December, an Allied Trade Conference, arranged by the Board of Trade, met at the Westminster Palace Hotel; high-handed proposals for settlement were put forward by the employers and sent out, with ballot papers, to the union branches which rejected them by an overwhelming majority. A second Conference, lasting four days, was concluded by 17 December when the unions admitted that the terms "on the whole ... do, to some extent, risk your interests", but did represent at least "a return to work and some degree of certainty of lasting peace and return to good will". The demand for a 48-hour week had been modified to 51 hours and the branches of the ASE, the Steam Engine Makers' Society and the United Machine Workers' Association were asked to convene a special meeting if necessary and to issue each man with a voting paper.[122] Again the terms were refused, though by now the employers' claim that union funds were being exhausted was somewhere near the truth.

The "outside sources" – continental and colonial contributions which amounted to £28,000, of which half came from Germany – were largely tapped by Eleanor who acted as Barnes's "foreign correspondent", working with him at the Head Office of the ASE at 89 Stamford Street, Blackfriars, issuing circulars to the Continent and translating the letters pouring in from abroad.

"I find it pretty heavy work," she wrote to Karpeles on 1 January 1898, "but this movement is worth the work! ... Though I fear some of our Socialists here do not understand it..."[123]

The circular, in Barnes's name, put out by Eleanor on 31 December 1897 read:

"Comrades,

After six months Lock-out, the Engineering Employers have issued an appeal to their workmen to return to work on terms which the men have twice rejected by overwhelming majorities. In the Employers' 'Manifesto' occur the remarkable words: 'The Federation hope that the time is not far distant when the workmen will appreciate the goodwill of their Employers'.

The men are not likely to be misled by this most specious appeal, nor are they likely to soon forget the harsh treatment they and their families have endured at the hands of those who have endeavoured to starve them into a surrender of all the principles and rights of Manhood.

We are convinced that a very short period longer will see a complete and solid victory for Labour.

Meanwhile we have to acknowledge our indebtedness to our Continental Brethren for their magnificent support, which has largely contributed to placing us in our present favourable position.

Trusting soon to announce a lasting triumph for the workers, and wishing all our fellow labourers in all lands a happier and brighter New Year than they have ever known.

Yours, with fraternal greetings,
G. N. Barnes."

The men held out until the end of January and, though Aveling was seriously ill and Eleanor obliged "to do the nursing and look after things generally",[124] she continued to help Barnes.

"... Apart from Edward's illness which has made most work out of the question – my time is a good deal taken up by the great Lock-out ..." she wrote to Kautsky on 1 January. "I am writing and answering letters right and left on the great fight. It is, in my opinion, the biggest movement we have had here since '53 & '59 – excepting the Dockers Strike. And in some respects this movement is even more important than the 1889 one. It is doing more for socialism here than 20 years of our 'propaganda'. Of course some of the out-&-out SDF people (by no means all of them) pooh-pooh it all as 'mere' Trade Unionism. If they cd. see a little further than their own noses they would know better. And I am bound to say that they are *beginning* to grasp the facts of the case. It is a *grand* struggle. The men are simply admirable, though the suffering is very great. How some of the families live is a mystery. If only we could now spread our Socialist nets properly we should get a splendid haul – but I fear our fishes slip away. *You* want to be in London – but sometimes I wish I could be, like you,* in a country where there *is* a live movement. I suppose we shall move here one of these days – & this lock-out is helping to give what football players call a fine 'kick-off' ..."[125]

To Natalie Liebknecht she wrote on 14 January 1898:

---

* Kautsky had now moved from Stuttgart to Berlin.

"...Unhappily the SDF are pretty stupid in this matter, & fail to grasp the *real* importance of this movement. Unless much help is forthcoming (this of course entre nous) we are hopelessly beaten. It is true – this again entre nous – the beating may, in the long run be as useful to our cause, more useful perhaps, than a half-hearted 'victory', and a *complete* victory is out of the question ... Meantime the Socialist feeling is rapidly growing, and though we are so abominably slow, we are *sure*, and once we do move, we move with a will..."[126]

The demand for the eight-hour day being withdrawn, the employers proposed fresh though scarcely less exacting terms of settlement and by over 28,000 to nearly 14,000 the unions voted to accept. In short, they were beaten. Nor did they turn towards socialism. Unlike the dockers, they had not won the day nor yet – as even the Silvertown workers had done – the sympathy of the public and the sustained backing of trade unionists in other industries.* They were perhaps paying the price of having reigned too long as the haughty mechanics, the aristocrats of labour, the most highly-skilled and highly-paid workers organised in the most craft-conscious union which, until the lock-out, had funds of over £300,000.

In believing that this battle was of greater importance than the Dock Strike Eleanor was misled. While her eyes were opened to the dismal fact that the SDF members "could see no further than their own noses" – that she was wedded to a political body that, despite its professions, held aloof from the real struggles waged by the working class – she could not face the equally bitter truth that the engineers' battle against the lock-out, despite the courage and tenacity of the men, had miserably failed to do more than wring a few minor concessions from the entrenched employers while exhibiting not a trace of political awareness. But who, in the midst of the fray, can admit defeat? Eleanor, the happy warrior, for whom the homely beauty of the good old cause was an almost literal truth, could see only that the engineers, that most conservative body of men, had not feared to meet the challenge when it came.

Her foreign correspondence on behalf of the ASE was her last work as a translator but earlier that year of 1897 she had acted as official interpreter, not only for the Glassworkers, but also at the 8th Miners' International Congress, held in St. Martin's Town Hall, which, as she told Kautsky, "took a whole week".†[127]

It opened on 7 June 1897. On 8 June Aveling, under the *alias* Alec Nelson, reducing his age by three years, falsifying his father's name and

---

* The ASE was not represented at the London International Congress, held just before Barnes was elected General Secretary in August 1896.

† The Congress lasted only five days, but she looked after the foreigners on their arrival and departure.

giving a spurious address,* was married by special licence at the Chelsea Register Office to the daughter of a music teacher, a young woman of 22 named Eva Frye.

---

* 410 Strand. There was at that time no such private residence, Nos. 410/411 being the Adelphi Theatre, Nos. 409/410 Gatti's restaurant. However, the two buildings nominally housed the Playgoers' Club, founded in 1884, of which Aveling was a member. There exists a letter from him, dated 12 March 1897, saying he was to open a discussion at St. James's Hall, Regent Street: "... As it is my first appearance at the Playgoers' Club for some two years, owing to my illness, I shall be glad to have the support of as many of my own friends as possible."[128]

Aveling's furtive marriage is to be explained only by the supposition that the young lady refused to go to bed with him unless he married her, alternatively that she was pregnant, or said she was.*

If Eleanor suspected that there was an Eva Frye skulking behind the scene it would have caused her no more – and no less – unhappiness than Aveling's other casual infidelities; indeed, she knew that such a person existed,† but the notion of a little Mrs. Nelson cannot have crossed her mind which, in any case, was preoccupied by other matters.

Johnny Longuet was staying with her and on 2 June she wrote to Liebknecht saying this young man was "a very great anxiety" to her because, although "undoubtedly gifted" he was "hopelessly (I fear) lazy; incapable of real work or any sustained effort" and "at 21 no more minded to work seriously than if he were 10". But, she added,

> "I am very much worried too about Edward. The abscess in his side (open now for over $2\frac{1}{2}$ years) *may* necessitate an operation (though we hope not), which would be a serious one. He yesterday saw one of our best surgeons and sees him again tomorrow..."[129]

In a long letter to Kautsky of 19 June she repeated her uneasiness about Aveling's condition and reported that she had her hands full, not only because of this anxiety but the strenuous work she had done at the Miners' Congress while Johnny was in the house and Edith Lanchester

---

* The number of Fryes and Nelsons in the United Kingdom who gave birth at any time during the relevant – as at any other – period is legion. Without a clue to the mother's whereabouts, which might even have been beyond these shores, not to mention the hazards of miscarriage or stillbirth, which were not registered, it is humanly impossible to verify or deny this conception.
† On 30 January 1897 *Justice* mentioned her as taking part in a Dramatic Entertainment, directed by "Alec Nelson" at the Social Hall in Wandsworth in aid of the SDF Science classes. She was said to have played in one of his small comedies, *The Landlady*, and to have rendered "'Love's Old Sweet Song' in fine style", while distinguishing herself by her "spirited acting" in the play by Sydney Grundy – *In Honour Bound* – which, 14 years earlier, Helene Demuth had described as telling Eleanor's and Aveling's own story (see above, p. 337). This play was repeated in a triple bill on 17 February at the Public Baths between Forest Hill and Sydenham, when Alec Nelson's own *Judith Shakespeare* was also performed. However, Eva Frye was not – though this was often said in later days as if to emphasise Aveling's low tastes – a professional actress.

"who is very ill after her confinement* is coming to me for a few weeks' nursing..."[130]

On the same day Aveling was "by doctors' orders off to the sea". He went to St. Margaret's Bay for ten or twelve days – if this were his honeymoon it cannot have been much fun – and was back with Eleanor early in July, as she announced to Liebknecht who was expected on the 11th. The Introduction to *The Eastern Question* was dated "Sydenham, 8 July 1897" – bearing both their names – and, when Liebknecht arrived, Aveling shepherded him about and was present when Hyndman and his wife honoured The Den with a visit on the following Saturday.†

It is known that Eleanor and Aveling attended the (17th) Annual Congress of the SDF held on Sunday, 1 August and – though it does not rule out that he was accompanied by his bride – Aveling lectured to the new Aberdare branch of the SDF and at Barry later in the month, while continuing to hold his science classes every week.‡

These details of Aveling's activities and whereabouts are mentioned to show that his life was unchanged to all outward appearances and in every respect until, towards the end of August – it may be after a quarrel – he walked out of The Den, would not say where he was going and, so far as one can read between the lines, must have broadly and brutally hinted, if not actually announced, that he was leaving Eleanor.

The lines in question were written to Freddy Demuth with whom she must have been in close touch at this period. He was nearly the only

---

* She had given birth to a son.

† Hyndman, under the mistaken impression that Liebknecht had brought Natalie, wrote to him on 15th July: "My Dear Comrade, I am very sorry I missed you on Tuesday night at the S.D.F... Present my compliments to Mrs Aveling and say we will come down, if convenient to her, to call on Saturday afternoon about four o'clock when we shall hope to see Mrs. Liebknecht and yourself... I am glad you think well of what I am doing about India. That has always been the weak joint in the harness of English capitalism but I couldn't get people to see this until now. A genuine impost in India means – well, what does it not mean? Forty millions sterling or therabouts yearly brought in here without return renders the upper middle and retired professional class almost independent of the ups and downs of trade. Let this external tribute be withdrawn suddenly – & it will be – and some of our worthy countrymen and countrywomen, many of them in fact, will be going short of food. They won't starve quietly as the workers do. You may safely bet your life on that. Besides the economic shake will stir things a good deal all round. There are one or two mistakes in my article in the *Petit République* though on the whole young Jean Longuet translated it very well. I have not the article by me but I remember that it was stated that the purchasing power of the gold had 'diminué'. This of course is the exact contrary of the truth. It was 'augmenté' by fully 80%. India forms an excellent lesson on the effect of capitalistic loan-mongering and absenteeism, as well as of alien administration on a large scale. The professor of economics of 1997 will have some fine illustrations to put before his pupils! With very kind regards yours sincerely, H. M. Hyndman."[131]

‡ The premises at 337 Strand had to be given up for lack of funds in October, when he and Eleanor gave a "farewell course", after which he took to giving "Elocution and Dramatic" lessons at Mrs. Charlotte Despard's hall in the Wandsworth Road.

person in whom she confided, and the letter, the first of a series,* leaves no doubt that he was already fully aware of all the circumstances.

He had apparently written to Aveling on Eleanor's behalf and was now asked to find and intercept him if possible.

The letter was headed "The Den, 30th August, 1897".

"My dear Freddy,

Of course not a line this morning! I have at once sent on your letter. How can I thank you for all your goodness and kindness to me? But, indeed, I do thank you from the bottom of my heart. I wrote once more to Edward this morning. No doubt it is weak, but one *can't* wipe out 14 years of one's life as if they had not been. I think anyone with the least sense of honour, not to mention any feeling of kindness and gratitude, would answer that letter. Will he? I almost fear he will not.

Meantime, I see that M – plays to-night at the G – Theatre.† If Edward is in London, I think he is sure to be there; but you can't get there, and I really feel I cannot go.

I have had a letter from C – ,‡ in which he says – but I enclose the letter to save the bother of writing. (Please return it.) I am now writing to C – to say I shall be there, but should like to see him before Edward – in the *very improbable* event of Edward turning up.

To-morrow evening is the Executive of the S**.§ I *can't* go – because if he is not there I can't explain. I hate to give you all this trouble; but could you go? They meet at 8 o'clock and sit till 10, so that if you went about 9 or 9.30 you could find out. You could ask if he had been. You would then know, at any rate. If *he is* there you can get at him – before others he can't get away – and wait for him till the sitting is over. Then you can *assume* he is coming here; if you find he simply lies – *go with him to London Bridge*. Then go with him, and *say* (you can tell him *that* from the outset) that you had told me you were coming, and must come late because of your work, but that I had replied I would put you up for the night. Then he either must tell you he is *not* coming – and you can get your chance of speaking to him – or he will come. I don't know that it is very probable; but in any case I hope you will go to *** and find out if he is there.

Ever your
Tussy."

---

* This and all subsequent letters from Eleanor to Freddy were, naturally, written in English. They were published for the first time, however, in German, Freddy having allowed Bernstein to use them for an article which was clumsily retranslated into English and, with many changes and omissions, appeared in *Justice* on 30 July 1898. On the same date Keir Hardie wrote a separate article on the same subject for the *Labour Leader* which, while drawing upon Bernstein to some extent, used the letters to Freddy from the original English, though not in full. By a careful comparison of all three versions – since the originals have not been seen – it is possible to arrive at a reasonably complete and accurate transcription.

† It was possibly Freddy's express wish that names should not be published. In no version of the letters do they appear save as initials and, though some efforts have been made to ascertain who was playing where on that night, the only – and improbable – thing that fits the bill was *The Circus Girl* at the Gaiety Theatre, a musical comedy by James Tanner and W. Palings, with music by Ivan Caryll and Lionel Monckton, in which Harry Monkhouse, not known to be a friend of Aveling's, played the part of "Sir Titus Wemyss".

‡ There is no difficulty in identifying this as Crosse, her solicitor and, indeed, both the *Neue Zeit* and *Justice* did so.

§ No doubt the SDF.

Two days later – 1 September – she wrote to Freddy again:

> "My dear Freddy,
>   This morning I got a note saying, 'Have returned. Shall be home early to-morrow' (that is to-day). Then a telegram 'Home for good, 1.30'
>   I was working – for even with all the heartbreak one has to work – in my room – and Edward seemed surprised and quite 'offended' I did not rush into his arms. He has so far made no apology and offered no explanation. I – after waiting for him to begin – therefore said one *must* consider the business position – and that I should never forget the treatment I had been subjected to. He said nothing. Meantime I said you *might* be down, and if you can come to-morrow or any evening this week, I trust you will. It is right he should have to face you in my presence, and me in yours. So, if you can, come tomorrow – if not, let me know when you can come.
>   Dear Freddy, how can I ever thank you! I am *very*, very grateful. When I see you I will tell you what C – said.
>   Always, dear Freddy,
>   Your Tussy."

Whatever passed between Eleanor and Aveling that night, she sent a distraught letter to Freddy on the following day:

> "My dear Freddy,
>   Come, if you possibly can, this evening. It is a shame to trouble you; but I am so alone, and I am face to face with a most horrible position: *utter* ruin – everything, *to the last penny*, or utter, open disgrace. It is awful; worse than even I fancied it was. And I want someone to consult with. I know I must finally decide and be responsible; but a little counsel and friendly help would be invaluable. So, dear, dear Freddy, come. I am heartbroken.
>   Your Tussy."

There was no hint of the frantic state that she was in when, on 31 August, between these distressful cries to Freddy, she wrote with the utmost composure to Kautsky on matters connected with the young Marx's letter to his father: how many pulls of the proofs she wanted, whether Laura would undertake the introduction and a variety of practical details, discussed with Liebknecht during his visit, on the form and price of a separate publication of what she now called "the Essay" after its first appearance in *Neue Zeit*. It is true that the bottom of the page has been cut off this letter,[132] but if Eleanor had added under her signature a reference to her personal troubles, she must have thought better of it, for there is a perfectly self-contained PS on the (incorrect) dating of the Marx letter.

Indeed, throughout the first half of September there is correspondence of a similar nature, which did not cease when she and Aveling went to stay with the Lafargues in Draveil for a fortnight. From there they wrote jointly to Kautsky on the 21st and two days later she sent a note to Lavrov:

"Dear Citizen and old friend,

We, my husband and I, are staying a few days with the Lafargues, and of course we should like to come and shake you by the hand. We expect to be in Paris tomorrow, Friday, and to have the pleasure of seeing you.

> Yours,
>
> Eleanor Marx-Aveling."[133]

The Lafargues had not an inkling that anything was amiss nor that, save for worrying about Aveling's health and fatigue from overwork, Eleanor was other than her usual self. The sisters had not met for two years. So much had happened in the time between that – given the renewed intimacy their frequent correspondence had engendered and the many problems arising from their joint responsibilities, not to mention the new house and grounds to be admired – they had more than enough to discuss without entering into or seeming to avoid more personal affairs.

The nature of the crisis that had occurred but a couple of weeks before, why Eleanor saw herself faced with "utter ruin ... to the last penny" or "utter open disgrace", will never be known. The gap can be filled only by pure guesswork; but, as such, one may hazard that the situation which brought her to her knees, described with such pain to Freddy, was that Aveling divulged his marriage and, exploiting her distress and humiliation, used some form of blackmail: possibly proposing that if she made over to him the remainder of Engels' legacy he would not openly desert her to set up a Nelson *ménage*.

Certainly there is a distinction between the social status of a publicly acknowledged common law wife and a discarded mistress. Nonetheless, Eleanor's phrase: "it is awful; worse than even I fancied it was" would be more understandable if Aveling had dipped his fingers into political or trade union funds. That, indeed, would have represented the alternatives of "utter ruin" or "utter disgrace" to her, though there is not a shred of evidence to support this conjecture nor was it ever adduced by Aveling's most intemperate critics.

Whatever odious bargain was then struck, he was certainly in Sydenham during some part of October when, in a letter to Kautsky, with whom she was in regular correspondence, Aveling added a postscript and negotiated the publication of an article he had written for *Neue Zeit*. It may even be that the pact allowed him freedom to carry on his affair with his wife, provided nobody knew she was; but Aveling's hopes of having his cake and eating it were rudely dashed by his falling ill. With the same obstinacy of purpose as drove his Dissenting forefathers to preach on moors and mountains at all seasons, he set out in November with Eleanor, though suffering from an attack of influenza, to make a propaganda tour of Lancashire. She had begged him to stay behind but to no avail and, at

Burnley, which they made their headquarters for the School Board election campaign at the end of the month – helping to score a signal victory for the SDF candidate, Dan Irving – Aveling was in a pitiable state.

"... we had 'real' Lancashire weather," Eleanor told Kautsky. "What *that* is only those who have experienced it can say. But certainly if Dante cd have dreamed a Lancashire factory town in bad weather he wd have added circles to his hell, & to his 'lowest depth a lower deep'. Getting wet through daily was not calculated to cure an invalid..."[134]

Small wonder that from Sydenham Eleanor wrote to Mrs. Liebknecht:

"by the time we got back here, his neglected influenza developed into congestion of the lungs and a touch of pneumonia..."[135]

Throughout December he was gravely ill. Eleanor reported to Laura:

"the doctor told me Edward might at any moment (his temperature was up to 103 at times) 'take a turn for the worse' and that I 'ought' at once to communicate with his relations. Of couse I did not, because (except perhaps his sister, now living in Devonshire) there is not a relation he wd want to see at any time.* I only wished *you* had been a little nearer, & during the anxious hours, I did think Draveil was terribly far from Sydenham..."[136]

Eleanor, then involved with the engineers' lock-out, sent a Christmas letter to Liebknecht who had been sentenced to four months' imprisonment under the "Little Anti-Socialist Law" of 1897 and in Charlottenburg gaol since 14 November. She wrote triumphantly about the Burnley campaign and was optimistic about the engineers: she had no wish to dwell at any length on the subject of Aveling's health when Liebknecht's own situation was so cheerless and said little more than that she was

"busy looking after Edward and after Barnes' correspondence. In both cases it is a labour of love. And now, my dear old Library, goodnight."

She went on:

---

* This is in direct contradiction to the claim made by the Rev. F. W. Aveling's children that he had remained in friendly contact with Edward to the end, despite his poor opinion of his brother. How such myths are fostered is partly explained by his grandson, Dr. Paul Redhead, who wrote to me in December 1973: "I believe that my mother, in common with most of her family, derived a certain vicarious pleasure from contemplating the wickedness of my Great-uncle Edward. His photograph hung above our mantelpiece for all my youth. My brother and I were never allowed to know who was the subject of the photograph. It was not until I was over twenty-one that I was considered old enough to survive the shock of knowing of the *existence* of Edward." The sister Eleanor meant must have been Mary (1842–1936) who had married Robert Wilkins in 1863. The only other, a younger sister – Alice – was in Canada.

"I am writing on Christmas Eve – and I remember (or think I do) a Christmas Eve at Grafton Terrace when you were there – and others who have now finished their work. Or rather their share of the work, for that itself is immortal, and lives more vigorously today than then. *You* are still at work and your magnificent courage, invincible good humour, and splendid cheerfulness are an example and a lesson to us all.

> '*Stone walls do not a prison make*
> *Nor iron bars a cage*'*

and the prison has not been built, nor the iron forged that could hold *your* spirit captive. I do not even feel it incongruous to wish to a 'Merry' Xmas!

A happy New Year I know awaits you, because work for others awaits you.

Our dear love to you, dear Library, my kind, dear friend and friend of Mohr and Möhme and Helen and Jenny.
                         Your
                              Tussy."[137]

On New Year's Day she wrote to both the Kautskys explaining that her deadly fears for Aveling were because

"any illness is doubly serious since his abscess is still open ... & it will be long before he is fairly strong again..."[138]

Laura sent Eleanor a birthday greeting for 16 January and a sum of money well in advance of the day.

"...It was very welcome," she replied on 8 January, "for, as I hardly need tell you, illness means immense expense in every way. Doctors' visit at 5/- a time, & sometimes twice a day – are no joke.

Edward *is* better. Indeed, he is working again, though I wish he wouldn't. But I did not exaggerate the danger ... he is still terribly weak and terribly emaciated. He is a very skeleton – mere skin and bones. And so he is not yet out of the wood, & I am still very anxious. The slightest chill wd, the doctors say, be absolutely fatal – & Edward is a most unmanageable person. I write freely because he is in bed asleep (thank goodness he *does* sleep well!) & except in a letter to *me alone* you must not let him know there is still such cause for anxiety.

If I can I shall get him off to Hastings away from the awful fogs we are having here..."[139]

With careful nursing he recovered sufficiently and, on 13 January,

"...on the doctor's orders left for Hastings, where I hope the warm air and bright sunshine may do him good. I am anxious at having to let him go alone, though the people he is with – we have lodged there before – will, I know, look after him..."[140]

---

* Lovelace's lines may seem banal to us but we do not know whether they were equally hackneyed in 1897.

On the day Aveling went away Eleanor answered a letter from Freddy, who had also been ill, unable to come to Sydenham and had evidently bemoaned the ill-luck that seemed to dog both Tussy and himself.

"The Den, 13th January, 1898

My dearest Freddy,

We were so sorry not to see you, and doubly so thinking you were ill. Yes – I sometimes feel like you, Freddy, that *nothing* ever goes well with us. I mean you and me. Of course, poor Jenny had her full share of sorrow and of trouble, and Laura lost her children. But Jenny was fortunate enough to die, and sad as that was for her children, there are times when I think it fortunate. I would not have wished Jenny to have lived through what I have done. I don't think you and I have been very wicked people – and yet, dear Freddy, it does seem as if we get all the punishment. When can you come? *Not this* Sunday, but next? Or during the week? I *do* want to see you. Edward is better, but very, very weak.

Your Tussy."

But Freddy was not well enough to come to Sydenham and, during Aveling's absence, Eleanor told Kautsky that, while the lung trouble was clearing up

"... the side (the abscess) is very bad, & again it seems likely that after all a *very* serious operation may be necessary..."[141]

Upon his return to The Den at the end of the month, Aveling's condition fully justified this prognosis. But it was not only his kidney disease that was aggravated: his relations with Eleanor had also worsened and to Freddy she wrote on 3 February:

"My dearest Freddy,

I am glad you are even a little better. I *do* wish you were well enough to come, say from Saturday to Monday, or at least Sunday night. It is brutally selfish, I know; but, dear Freddy, you are the *only* friend I can be quite frank with, and so I do love to see you.

I have to face such great trouble, and *quite* without help (for Edward does not help *even now*), and I hardly know what to do. I am daily getting demands for money, and how to meet them, AND the operation and all else, I don't know. I feel I am a brute to trouble you, but, dear Freddy, you *know* the situation; and I say to you what I would not say to anyone now. I would have told my dear old Nymmy, but as I have not her, I have only you. So forgive my being selfish, and *do* come if you can.

Your Tussy.

Edward has gone to London to-day. He is to see doctors, and so on. *He would not let me go with him!* That is sheer *cruelty, and* there are things he does not want to tell me. Dear Freddy, you have your boy – I have nothing; and I see nothing worth living for."

That Freddy was unwilling to see Aveling is quite clear. He told Eleanor he would not, upon which she wrote two days later:

"Sydenham, 5th February, 1898

My dear Freddy,

I *am* sorry you are not coming to-morrow. In common justice, let me say that Edward had *no idea* of asking you again for money. You don't know how ill he is. He wanted to see you because he believes he will not see you again after the operation.

Dear Freddy, I know how kindly your feeling to me is, and how truly you care for me. But I don't think you quite understand – I am only *beginning* to. But I do see more and more that wrongdoing is just a moral disease, and the morally healthy (like yourself) are not fit to judge of the condition of the morally diseased; just as the physically healthy person can hardly realise the condition of the physically diseased.

In some a certain *moral* sense is wanting, just as some are deaf, or have bad sight, or are otherwise unhealthy. And I begin to understand that one has no more right to blame the one disease than the other. We must try and cure, and, if no cure is possible, do our best. I have learnt this through long suffering – suffering in ways I would not tell even you; but I have learnt, and so I am trying to bear all this trouble as best I can.

Dear, dear Freddy, don't think I have forgotten what Edward owes you (I mean in money: in loving-kindness it is beyond calculation), and you will, of course, get what is owing to you. For that you may take *my* word. I expect Edward to go into hospital early next week. I hope soon, for this waiting is trying him terribly. I will let you know anything definite, and I do hope with all my heart *you* will soon be better.

Your Tussy."

He was evidently sceptical of her diagnosis. Indeed, though we have only one side of this correspondence, it is fairly plain that all along Freddy had thought Eleanor should have cast off this scoundrel and saw her elaborate exculpation now as but another sign of weakness rather than of the strength of her love. She replied to him on 7 February:

"My dear, dear Freddy,

I daresay I am so worried I did not make myself clear. But you have not understood me at all, and I am too troubled to explain. Edward goes to the hospital to-morrow for the operation on Wednesday. There is a French saying that to *understand* is to *forgive*. Much suffering has taught me to understand – and so I have no need even to forgive. I can only love.

Dear Freddy, I shall be quite near the hospital, at 135 Gower Street, and I will let you know how things go on.

Your old Tussy."

Aveling went into University College Hospital* on Tuesday, 8 February, and was operated on the next day. Eleanor wrote to Liebknecht on the morrow from her lodgings in Gower Street. She had felt obliged to let him know of Aveling's condition, though she said it "made me feel cruel to have worried you". But it was, she explained, only natural that as "the *only* old friend left, the old comrade of Mohr and Möhme and Helen – the dear Library of us younger ones" she should turn to him:

> "I thought I ought to let you know, as any *sudden* bad news might have been even worse for you. – So far Edward seems to be progressing: but he is *very* ill, and it will be many days before we can say he is out of danger. The operation itself was very serious, but that he has got over without any great 'shock'. The four year old abscess was due to a disease of the kidneys, and whether much can be done remains to be seen ..."

As a Fellow of University College, holding "several gold and silver medals", Aveling was receiving privileged treatment: "the great surgeon Heath"† who had known him in his student days put him in a private ward – "i.e. he has his own room and so I am with him the whole day, only leaving when he goes to sleep at night" – while Eleanor herself was almost next door and could be called at any moment.

> "As he is under the *special* care of Heath *everyone*, from the House Surgeon (who is said to be *very* able) down to the Hall porters, is aux petits soins,‡ and he thus has care I *could* not have secured him elsewhere ..."

Eleanor then described the nightmare of waiting for the operation – she felt that the patient ought not to be told beforehand when it was to be done, "because then every second of delay becomes an eternity" – said it was "horrible ... but I wd gladly have changed places with Edward and have counted myself happy"; the gruesome preparations:

> "It was like the 'toilette' of the condemned prisoner to me – except perhaps worse, because certainty is less terrible than uncertainty";

and then the anguish of what seemed hours – "though really only little over half an hour" – for his return from the theatre.

It was, in fact, merely an exploratory operation, with the strong like-lihood that another and more serious one would follow, but that she did not know until the next day and, at the time, believed he might not come through the ordeal. Such was her relief when he did that she was able to write:

---

* The hospital, founded in 1833 with 154 beds, is not the present building which was opened by the Prince of Wales, later Edward VII, in June 1898, shortly after Eleanor's death.
† Christopher Heath (1835–1905), MRCS (1856), FRCS (1860) of 36 Cavendish Square, Holme Professor of Clinical Surgery at University College, London; President of the Royal College of Surgeons, 1895.
‡ most attentive.

"...There has been one help in all this trouble (and the *material* trouble of meeting these awful expenses is no small one) and that is the great sympathy and kindness I have found on all sides..."

and then turn to quite other matters, such as the Zola case,* the engineers' lock-out, Henry Irving and all manner of things, as much, it may be, to distract her own thoughts as those of Liebknecht in gaol. She ended her long letter, written during the night, by saying that she was

"too anxious to sleep much and so it has been a pleasure more than ever to talk to you – even though it has to be so cold a talk as that of pen and ink. Not to mention that it must pass through prison bars.

I know you are thinking of us, dear, dear old Library. Whatever turn things take I will let you know. But one matter is certain: all that *can* be done.
                    Your Tussy."[142]

Eleanor also kept Kautsky informed, writing to him from Gower Street on Thursday, 10 February,

"...nothing certain can be said *yet*. He is *very* weak, & we do not yet know what the real mischief (the operation was chiefly to find that out) is",

adding: "If you see any friends let them know."[143]

Eight days after the operation Aveling was allowed to go home. Eleanor took him back to Sydenham on 17 February in a carriage as she felt she could not risk his travelling by cab and train for, although he had not suffered too severely from surgical shock, his wound was still open. As she wrote to Kautsky three days after her return,

"...There is just a possibility (remote) of the abscess healing. If – as is likely – it does not, it will mean doing nothing and just waiting, or the terrible operation of removing one kidney..."[144]

On the same day she wrote to Freddy:

"20th February, 1898

My dear, dear Freddy,
    I brought Edward home on Thursday, as the doctors thought he would have a better chance here than at the hospital (oh! how *awful* a hospital is), and they want him taken to Margate. It is all so surely *going to the one thing* that I am giving up all the little I have left. You will understand – *I* can get on anyway, and I must now see to *him*. Dear Freddy, do not blame me. But I think you will not. You are so good and so true.
                    Your Tussy."

---

* His famous *J'Accuse!* on the Dreyfus affair had appeared on 13 January 1898.

Eleanor did not believe that Aveling would survive: she wanted Freddy to realise that, however despicable the man, she could not but devote herself to him until the end which she feared was only too near.

On Saturday, 19 February, she left Aveling briefly in the care of Gertrude Gentry and went to Margate to book rooms at 6 Ethelbert Crescent – "recommended by Hyndman", as she told Kautsky with two points of exclamation[144] – and on the 22nd they went there for over a month.

Eleanor wrote once more to Freddy:

"6 Ethelbert Crescent
Margate, 1st March, 1898

My dear, dear Freddy,

Don't think my not writing neglect. It is just that I am tired, and often have not the heart to write. I can't tell you how glad it makes me that *you* do not blame me too much, because I think you one of the grandest and best men I have ever known.

It is a bad time for me. I fear there is little hope, and there is much pain and suffering. Why we go on is the mystery to me. I am ready to go, and would gladly. But while he *wants* help I am bound to stay.

The beautiful thing, and the one thing that helps me, is the kindness of everyone. I can't tell you how good to me all sorts of people are, I am sure I don't know why.

And I am quite proud of it, the Miners' Federation and Miners' Union, as I would not be paid for my work of the translating at the International Miners' Congress (it *was* work!) last June, have sent me a beautiful little writing case and stylographic pen. I am ashamed to accept such a gift, but I can't help doing so. And it *does* please me!

Dear Freddy, how I wish I could see you! But I suppose that can't be just now. Your Tussy."

She also sent a letter to Natalie Liebknecht, apologising for not doing so before

"... But while Edward is up (i.e. lying on his chair-bed) I cant write freely, and then I am often too disheartened to write at all ... The air of Margate is wonderful ... I was here once with Mohr, after his serious illness, and Jenny in the spring of 1868.* And I am here again now with Edward. For a week I looked after him alone – but the responsibility became too great, and now I have a good surgeon ... who ... does the morning 'dressing' of the wound – I did it alone before – while I do the evening one. It is a terrible business ... It means forcing a syringe into the open wound ... and then ... a 'plug' into the wound. You can think what pain this is to Edward, and how awful it is to have to do this. If *I* cd bear the pain how gladly I would! –

After the morning 'dressing' as soon as he feels strong enough, I get Edward into a 'bath chair'. Then back here, and after eating (he eats, alas! nothing) and resting, weather permitting again the bath chair.

One of the things that helps us both is that the time for our dear old Library's release is drawing near: Tell Library that in all his pain and suffering Edward never misses a

---

* It was in fact 1866. See above, p. 42.

day without saying 'only —— days now for Library!' – I think Library will be glad to know that.

You wd not know my poor Edward if you saw him now. He is a very skeleton and can hardly walk a few yards. He is – after the evening dressing – in bed now and asleep . . .

Sometimes I hardly know how I shall hold on! It is not only the awful anxiety, but the actual material difficulties. Our joint income is (for London) very small and my present expenses are enormous. – Doctors, chemists' bills, 'chairs' for going out, and so forth, added to the home that must be kept up – all this means a great deal. – I speak so frankly, because I know you will understand.

Meantime we both look forward to March 18th,* and Edward wants Library to know that – if he is living still – he will drink Library's health in a glass of the General's port."[145]

On 4 March Eleanor wrote to the secretary of the Irish Socialist Republican Party, founded in Dublin by Connolly in 1896, sending Aveling's subscription of ten shillings.[195a] On the 15th, after being three weeks in Margate, she wrote to tell Kautsky that Aveling was not gaining much strength and

"I fear there is *very* little hope of ultimate recovery. Today he did – leaning on my arm & a stick – walk a little . . . It is, as you may suppose, a terribly anxious time in all ways . . ."[146]

Eleanor sent almost her last, as she had written her very first letter to Liebknecht. It was to greet him on his release from gaol, sent from Margate on 16 March:

"Dear, dear old Library,

In a very few hours now you will be free, and it is good to know that this letter will find you in your home. We shall be with you all on Friday, and with all our heart we wish we could be with you in the flesh as well as the spirit.

Our love to you, dear old Library, and
Welcome home!
Your
Tussy
Edward."[147]

Old "Library" replied on 23 March:

"My dear, dear Tussy!

I am well, but how are *you*? I got your letter as soon as I came home last Friday, but I had no time yet, to send you a single line, although a thousand times I thought of you.

---

* The day of Liebknecht's release, which happened to coincide with the anniversary of the Paris Commune.

I have been so overwhelmed with love, and sympathy – étouffé sous des roses* – that I feel still as if it all was a dream. And think of the work I found on my return to liberty! Many hundred *weights* of *papers* (& hundreds of letters and telegrams) to read . . .

Yet I should have written before; only you had promised me some notes about the Engineers' Struggle.

But now I cannot wait any longer. How are you? How is Edward? Write only a few lines – I don't expect a long letter.

We all send our love! And we all wait anxiously for *good* news.

Your
Library."

Underneath Natalie had written: *"Meine liebe, liebe* Tussy."[148]

In none of these letters – to the Liebknechts, the Kautskys or Laura – was there a word of Eleanor's fearful despair; to no one but Freddy Demuth was it so much as hinted that she was suffering from other than the misery caused by Aveling's illness, its drain upon her financial resources and her dismal forebodings on both counts. Quite enough, her friends must have thought, to account for such black thoughts as she expressed which, in every case, were counterbalanced by comments on her objective interests, and theirs, signifying that her troubles were no more than an unhappy interruption of her usual active life.

---

* Smothered with roses.

Aveling, still infirm, and Eleanor, still gravely anxious, returned to Sydenham on Sunday, 27 March. On the 29th she wrote to Edith Lanchester who had worked for her during the past two years and whose little boy, Waldo, born in 1897 she adored. "It is an awful responsibility to bring a child into the world," she had written at the time of his birth, "but it must also be the greatest joy woman can know. Forgive a childless woman if she feels a little envious."

In this last letter to her friend she said: "I am so worried in *all* ways (material as well as others) that I hardly have the heart to write. Edward is *very* ill. I fear hopelessly. You will understand. How is your dear little man? ... And how are you yourself? Let me know when you come this way ... I am *absolutely* tied and cannot get out. Not that I want to ... I often wonder why one goes on at all with all this fearful suffering. Of course I could not say so to my poor Edward but I often think it would be easier to make an end of it. You see I have no little one as you have. Yours always Eleanor." [148a]

Two days later, at about 10 o'clock on the cool, bright morning of Thursday, 31 March 1898, Eleanor sent the maid, Gertrude Gentry, to the chemist George Dale of 92 Kirkdale – the main street at the lower end of Jew's Walk – with a note saying: "Please give bearer chloroform and small quantity of prussic acid for dog." This was initialled "E.A." and Aveling's card enclosed.* The girl returned with a packet containing two ounces of chloroform and a drachm (one-eighth of an ounce) of prussic acid. She also brought the poison-book. This Eleanor signed with her initials – E.M.A. – in the large living-room on the ground floor of The Den whereafter Gertrude took the book back to the chemist. When she came home again – it was now about 10.45 a.m. – she went upstairs and found Eleanor lying in bed, undressed, and scarcely breathing. She asked

---

* The account of events leading up to and surrounding Eleanor's death is drawn entirely from contemporary newspaper reports in which there are many discrepancies and, without doubt, some inaccuracies. It is therefore confined to a bare record of facts elicited at the inquest on which there is general agreement, while attention is paid to matters of substance on which there is not. It is most unfortunate that the official transcript of the proceedings, kept in the LCC Records, was destroyed by bombing during the Second World War, of which fact the Clerk to HM Coroner was good enough to inform me in a letter dated 31 March 1967: by chance, the anniversary of Eleanor's death 69 years before.

what was wrong and getting no reply rushed next door to fetch the neighbour, Mrs. Kell,* who came at once, and to the doctor. By the time Mrs. Kell reached Eleanor's bedroom the poison had done its work. When Dr. Henry Shackleton† finally arrived, he was of the opinion that she had been dead for two hours. He later conducted a *post mortem* examination, concluding that the cause of death was poisoning by prussic acid.‡

Eleanor was said to have left behind two suicide notes, the authenticity of which cannot be confirmed although, according to *Justice*, the first, to Aveling, was "read at the inquest, but ... not published".[149] It ran:

"DEAR. It will soon be all over now. My last word to you is the same that I have said during all these long, sad years – love."[150]

The second was to her nephew, Jean Longuet:

"My dear, dear Johnny,
    My last word is addressed to you. Try to be worthy of your grandfather.
            Your Aunt Tussy."[151]

The inquest was conducted on the evening of Saturday, 2 April, at Park Hall, Sydenham, by the Deputy Coroner for West Kent and South East London, Mr. E. N. Wood, who was exasperated by Aveling as a witness and called him "a most difficult man to deal with".[152] He quibbled over whether or not he was married to the deceased woman; could not say precisely what her age was – "I believe about 40, but I am not quite sure"[152] – and seemed unable to give a straightforward answer to anything. The one point upon which the only two possible witnesses – and all the subsequent press reports – seem to have been agreed was that Aveling had announced his intention of going to London that morning to which

---

* The wife of Frederick Kell, the Head of the local Art School, who lived in the twin semi-detached house, No. 5 Jew's Walk.

† The father of Sir Ernest Shackleton, the great Antarctic explorer, then a young man of 24 who had not yet made his first notable expedition. Of Irish origin, the doctor had qualified in Dublin somewhat late in life after which he removed his large family to South London, settling in 1885 at Aberdeen House, No. 12 West – now Westwood – Hill at the top end of Jew's Walk where he practised successfully for some 32 years. He had seen Eleanor from time to time though not attended her professionally.

‡ There can have been little difficulty in establishing the fact: the peculiar odour of the poison – that of bitter almonds – remains in the atmosphere round the body for some time. The action of prussic – or hydrocyanic – acid is horrible, agonising but swift. The symptoms, which appear in seconds rather than minutes, are difficult breathing, convulsive spasms, the face turns blue and, after a brief stage of muscular paralysis, death occurs. It was, not surprisingly, unpopular as a means of self-destruction, particularly with women, who represented roughly a quarter of all suicides in the late 19th century and whose most-favoured method was drowning. Men, in statistically significant numbers, preferred to hang themselves.

Eleanor had strongly objected on the grounds of his health. According both to the *Daily Chronicle*[153] and *Justice*[149] the maid was sent to the chemist after Aveling's departure. But Gertrude Gentry testified that Mrs. Aveling had sent her to Dale's just before 10 a.m., Aveling that he had last seen her alive at 10.10 a.m.

These statements raise a number of questions that were not, apparently, asked at the time and cannot now be answered. How did the two wit-nesses know the time so precisely? Aveling, with a train to catch, may well have consulted the clock, but why should Gertrude Gentry have done so? Did Eleanor's objections to his going to London lead to a violent quarrel? What was to prevent her from waiting until he had left the house, writing the prescription herself, using his initials and enclosing his card? In short, had he or had she ordered the poison? Why should Aveling incriminate himself by claiming to be present when the maid was sent to the chemist? Given the uncontroverted evidence that he was going out against Eleanor's wishes, he could have denied all knowledge of her subsequent actions. However, none of these points engaged the attention of the coroner whose statutory duty was no more than to establish the name of the deceased, the time, place and circumstances of the death and its cause as certified by a qualified doctor. Under the heading of "cir-cumstances" it might have been possible to indict Aveling as an accessory to the act, but the evidence he gave appeared to exonerate him of complicity.

The chemist had the worst of it. It came out that he had always thought that "Dr Aveling", a fairly well-known customer, was a medical man even though not in practice, and he believed the note was in the doctor's handwriting.* He had not at the time noted that the prescription was initialled "E.A." and the poison-book "E.M.A.". The coroner said Dale ought to have ascertained that Aveling was not a qualified and registered doctor and, in any case, when selling a deadly poison he should have gone to the house with it himself and not entrusted it to a mes-senger. He, the coroner, would have the duty of reporting Dale's conduct to the Public Prosecutor since it contravened the Parliamentary Acts.†

The jury returned a verdict of "Suicide by swallowing prussic acid at the time labouring under mental derangement" and the death was

---

* Hyndman claimed that the handwriting of Eleanor and Aveling was almost indistinguish-able.[154] That was not so: hers was fine and rather small, his large and bold. In particular their use of initials differed markedly.

† 31 & 32 Vic. Cap. 121 (The Pharmacy Act of 1869, which was amended in July 1898: 61 & 62 Vic.). Dale was evidently not prosecuted. The Secretary of the Coroners' Society – whose mother by a strange coincidence had lived in Jew's Walk – was good enough to inform me that, had there been such a case, it would have been reported in the Society's *Journal* whose files for that period he searched but found nothing.

registered in the sub-district of Sydenham in Lewisham on 4 April 1898 as that of Eleanor Marx, aged 40, a single woman.[155]

After the verdict, Aveling told the coroner that the reason Eleanor was not his wife was that "he had been married before":[156] a succinct but somewhat misleading description of his past and present marital status.

There is nothing to indicate that the deed was long premeditated. On the contrary, the day they came back from Margate, a letter signed by Eleanor and Aveling was sent to the editor of *Reynolds's Newspaper*, published on 10 April, which read:

> "Dear Mr. Thompson,
>   Please put our names down in connection with the proposed dinner to Mr. H. M. Hyndman",

an occasion planned for May. Moreover, Eleanor was not only "seeing through the press an epitome of ... *Capital*"*[157] and editing two other of Marx's works, but, while in Margate, she had been reading Georg Brandes' vast tome on Shakespeare† in order to review it for *Neue Zeit*. On the face of it, to complete the tasks she had set herself needed time and, if she had already taken the decision to kill herself, she had evidently no intention of forewarning it. Nor does her despairing letter to Edith Lanchester presage the imminence of a desperate act: merely the thought of it.

The obituary notices are too numerous and too similar to cite. Some twenty-six articles on her death have been traced in the English press, several in German and French papers, a Polish, an Italian and a Spanish one, from which it may be assumed that in other countries, too, where Eleanor was well known to the party leaders, the socialist papers would have paid their tributes. A message of sympathy was sent to Liebknecht by Enrico Ferri of Florence who wrote

> "we are still grieving over the sudden death of Eleanor who won all our hearts at the London Congress...",[159]

while letters flew about the world from her friends commiserating with each other in their sorrow.

---

* *Value, Price and Profit.*
† Published 1895–6. An English translation by William Archer and M. Morrison was published later in 1898. Eleanor of course was reading it in the original and did not think much of it. She wrote to Kautsky on 15 March: "...I am toiling steadily through the 1,000 pages (!!!) ... and am bitterly disappointed in the book. So I fear I shall not be able to send a very favourable review. It is a re-hash – and not a good one – of all others have done and he cribs all his ideas – or at least the best of them and naturally does not say whence he has stolen."[158]

Resolutions lamenting her death were passed by continental parties, at local branches of the SDF, the ILP, and the Gasworkers' Union, as also at the ILP Annual Conference in Birmingham and by the May Day Committee, while the May Day Supplement of *Justice* published an *In Memoriam* drawing by Walter Crane, dedicated to "E.M.A.". Many of the obituaries expressed condolence with Aveling in his bereavement.

One discordant and appalling note was struck, though not in public. In June 1898, Olive Schreiner, who had heard the news from Dollie Radford, wrote from Kimberley eager to learn further details:

"I have felt that if I was in England I would find the servant who was the last person with her and get her to tell me all she knew . . ."

She then indulged her hatred of Aveling by recounting with gloating prurience some of his more *outré* sexual escapades, ending her letter with a sentiment not untypical of her destructive personality:

"*I am so glad Eleanor is dead.* It is such a mercy she has escaped from him . . ." (My italics. Y.K.)[160]

On Easter Sunday, 10 April, preaching at St. Nicholas Cole Abbey,* the Rev. Thomas Hancock must have startled his congregation out of its wits by delivering himself of the opinion that:

"Probably the most significant event which has happened in these last few days, in the midst of the hurly-burly and bluster, has been the quiet tragedy of one poor corpse. I mean the deliberate self-destruction of the daughter of one of the most powerful and productive leaders of men in our generation; it may be the most influential of them all, for good or evil, or both. Karl Marx, the Social-Democrat, has more international subjects at this moment, among men belonging to that estate of life out of which the Redeemer chose his Apostles, than any emperor, king, or president, army or navy, of any nation on the globe",[161]

after which extraordinary piece of propaganda his pious listeners must have been relieved to learn that the death of this Messiah's daughter was brought about by falling into a state of agnosticism and losing faith. But it is not absolutely clear in what the Rev. Hancock thought her faith had been lost.

The funeral took place on Tuesday, 5 April, and a very large throng assembled at the necropolis building in Waterloo Station, where speeches

---

* In Queen Victoria Street, the site of an ancient place of worship going back to before the dissolution of the monasteries, the origin of whose name is obscure. Rebuilt by Wren in 1677, it was restored in 1876.

were made by Aveling, Robert Banner, Bernstein, Pete Curran, Hyndman and Will Thorne. The last was almost too overcome with grief to speak and openly wept. Later, in his autobiography written in 1925, he said:

> "But for this tragedy, I believe Eleanor would have still been living, and would have been a greater women's leader than the greatest of contemporary women."[162]

He would certainly have endorsed the words published in the *Labour Annual* of 1899 where, referring to Eleanor's work for the Gasworkers' Union, it said:

> "When that, the only completely successful union of unskilled labourers, has its history written, her name will, like Abou Ben Adhem, 'Lead all the rest'."

Both the articles published and the speeches at the funeral dwelt upon her steadfast service in the cause of socialism, her outstanding gifts as a speaker and a linguist, her wide literary culture and, above all, the lovable, heart-warming personality of this woman who had given her best to the working-class movement.

There were wreaths on the coffin from the SDF, the Gasworkers' Union, the Hammersmith Socialist Society, the French workers' Party, the German Social-Democratic Party, many branches of the SDF and the union, the directors and staffs of *Justice*, the Twentieth Century Press, the *Hamburger Echo*, *Vorwärts* and her own relatives, Paul Lafargue and Johnny Longuet.* Those two were among the many, including Hyndman and his wife, who accompanied the hearse by train to Woking where her body was incinerated.†

Aveling did not claim the ashes. The small cinerary urn provided by the crematorium‡ was received by Lessner who laid within it a card, signed and dated, with the words: "These are the ashes of Eleanor Marx". He took it to the Maiden Lane premises of the SDF where the Assistant Secretary,§ Albert Inkpin, placed it upon a shelf in the upper, glass-fronted part of a cupboard where it remained for 23 years. In 1912 the offices became those of the newly founded British Socialist Party and, after its foundation in July 1920, of the Communist Party. A year later that party moved to headquarters at 16 King Street, Covent Garden – a stone's throw from Maiden Lane – and the urn with Eleanor's ashes moved with

---

* Laura, said to be prostrated by the blow, Charles Longuet and his other children did not come to the funeral.
† She had left no such instruction in her will but, after an autopsy and inquest, there was no hindrance to cremation.
‡ See Appendix III.
§ The General Secretary was H. W. Lee.

it, to be placed again upon the same shelf of the same cupboard which now stood in the office of the Communist Party's General Secretary, Albert Inkpin.

On 7 May 1921, not long after the move, the premises were raided and ransacked by the police who arrested Inkpin, Robert Stewart, the National Organiser, and subsequently other members of the Central Committee in various parts of the country, including William Gallacher in Scotland, none of whom was allowed bail. *The Communist* of 21 May reported that:

> "...The Editorial office was sacked. The scene ... was one of complete devastation ...
> The only article left in the room was an old suit of Comrade [Francis] Meynell's flung
> indiscriminately over the reading desk ... A tragic note was sounded when the
> detectives were begged not to disturb the ashes of Eleanor Marx Aveling, reposing in
> an urn ready to be conveyed to Moscow. They were left in peace..."

(No one can now recall why or by whom it was decreed that the ashes should go to Moscow, nor is it of any moment since nothing came of this ill-conceived plan.)

In 1928 the Acting General Secretary in office during Inkpin's absence opened the lid and, for the first time after 30 years, the words written by Lessner, who had died in 1910, were found. For a short period after the Marx Memorial Library on Clerkenwell Green was opened in 1933 – on the 50th anniversary of Marx's death – the urn is thought to have been housed there – nobody quite knows why – and to have stood in a place of honour on the bookshelf in what is known as the Lenin Room.* With the advent of war in 1939 the fate of Eleanor's ashes is somewhat uncertain. According to several people's recollections, the casket was stored in the basements of 16 King Street; but there is no shadow of doubt that it was later reinstated on its original shelf in the original cupboard standing in the General Secretary's room, where it was always to be seen decorated with a red ribbon. In 1956 it was again opened, Lessner's certification still intact, and then it was closed forever, to be buried with the remains of Marx, his wife, his grandson and Helene Demuth, exhumed from their simple grave in New Highgate Cemetery, under the ugliest and best-known monument in London, to which thousands of pilgrims from all lands flock each year to pay homage to Karl Marx and thus, perhaps unwittingly, to Eleanor.†

---

* Between April 1902 and May 1903 Lenin edited seventeen issues of *Iskra* in a small partitioned corner of the Twentieth Century Press.[163] With the restoration and reconstruction of the 18th-century building in 1966, this corner, with its little writing table, chair and bookshelf, was preserved and may be seen today as it was when Lenin worked there.

† The committee responsible for planning this monument decided that "the ashes of Eleanor Marx which are in a casket and which are still awaiting their final resting place will be buried in

Though not concerned about Eleanor's ashes, "Edward Aveling, gentleman" was granted probate of her will on 16 April 1898, eleven days after her cremation. The gross estate was valued at £1,909 3s. 10d.*[164]

On 24 May Crosse, the solicitor, wrote to Laura as the next of kin asking her to sign the papers giving him Power of Attorney to transfer the fund for the Longuet children to an unnamed trustee newly appointed to replace Eleanor. Who this was is not known. It had to be someone domiciled in England and it is safe to guess that it was not Aveling since Eleanor would have left such an instruction in her will. There is the possibility that it was Crosse himself.

It is not unnatural that myths surrounding Eleanor's suicide should have accrued, nor that many people sincerely believed they had been present at her macabre and solitary deathbed for her to expire in their arms.[†] The interesting thing about these fantasies is that the wish to have been the last to look upon Eleanor should be so persistent; that she should have become the subject of such legends in her lifetime, that to have been thus intimately associated with her agony was accounted a merit to claim with pride and hand down from one generation to another.

*　　*　　*

That everyone in their later references to Eleanor should lay her death quite simply at Aveling's door, while rightly dismissing the notion that her mind was deranged,[‡] is no cause for surprise. Unfortunately, the articles drawing this inescapable conclusion and most of the memoirs written by her contemporaries contain such flagrant inaccuracies that they are not to be trusted, while none, so far as can be traced, thought to look at the manner of her death in the context of her life as a whole.

Eleanor's was a robust nature. To be sure, a girlhood friend recalled her as "the gayest creature in the world – when not the most miserable", as "white, tragic, despairing", even "sick of life" and ready to do away with

---

the grave or otherwise uncorporated and the design must provide for it ..." The casket's dimensions were given as $14\frac{3}{8}$" $\times$ $8\frac{1}{4}$ $\times$ $7\frac{1}{4}$", not unlike the size and shape of a shoe-box.[163a]

* While the will is on record under the name Aveling, the death certificate is registered under Marx.

† Astonishing number have told me or written to say that such was the case of their mothers, fathers, grandmothers, great uncles, aunts or other close relatives.

‡ This formula was a survival from the days when suicides could have their property confiscated and were refused decent burial. Although the law had long been changed (in 1870 and 1882), removing both penalties, some form of words to indicate that the deceased had not been responsible for his actions continued in use until recent times when the Departmental Committee on Coroners[165] pointed out that while such verdicts were seldom based upon medical evidence they left surviving relatives with the stigma of insanity in the family. Attempted – that is, bungled – suicide was an indictable offence in common law until 1961 (9 & 10 Eliz. II, Cap. 60).

herself upon being told that she would never succeed as an actress of the first rank, but such moods could be dispelled by so simple an expedient as a 'bus ride through London.[166] True, and more significant, is it that Aaron Rosebury wrote:

> "She admitted to being sometimes tired of life, especially when it seemed that the movement no longer needed her",[167]

yet both these recollections were penned long years after her death.* There are, indeed, dozens of writers who, wise after the event, recorded her suicidal tendencies.

At the inquest Aveling was reported to have said that she had several times threatened to destroy herself. Asked whether he had taken these threats seriously, he replied: "I regarded them as idle, because they were so frequently repeated";[168] while the *Daily Chronicle* reporter put into the mouth of a juryman the statement: "Deceased had often suggested that they should commit suicide together, and thus end their difficulties." The Coroner asked: "Do you mean pecuniary difficulties?" to which the unnamed witness† answered: "Yes, sir, there were some, but not recently."[169] Though it does not diminish Eleanor's tragedy, one is irresistibly reminded of Mrs. Marx who, when more harassed than usual, declared that she wished she and her children were in the grave.

There were but three occasions when Eleanor manifested symptoms of what could be termed the neurotic personality. The first was her *anorexia nervosa* during her mother's terminal illness in 1881, followed, after that mother's death, by acute depression and threatened breakdown as she tried to arrive at some decision on her future course in life which, up till then, had differed little from that of the familiar 19th-century anti-heroine: the unmarried daughter who stays at home. Then came her incontinent love-letter to Olive Schreiner when she was under the stress of her first disillusionment with Aveling and, last, after an interval of some thirteen years, the desperate letters to Freddy Demuth.

Yet, in all but this final tribulation – real enough and, it cannot be too strongly emphasised, kept secret from all but Freddy while she maintained a level-headed correspondence with her other close friends – she had shown herself able to cast off those short-lived attacks of instability the moment demands were made upon her. She nursed her mother – and her father at the same time – with unflagging steadiness and compassion.

---

* The first in 1922, the second in 1927.
† It is hardly credible that a member of the jury, or its foreman – as was also published – should have given any such evidence. The likelihood is that it was a police witness who had questioned Aveling before the court proceedings.

Within a few weeks of what she herself had called a mental disorder, she was the delighted and delightful companion of her little nephews in Paris, whereafter she flung herself into the hard discipline of training for a stage career and also into a social life of great exuberance. With Aveling she reached a *modus vivendi* that endured for over 14 years, during which she knew herself necessary not only to him but to great numbers of people whose responses gave her whatever strength and warmth her partner was unfitted to provide. Long after she had lost her illusions about Aveling and despite his final treachery, she devoted herself to him so long as he needed her.

Sane people, unless threatened by death in some even more terrible form, do not commit suicide for any but extremely complex reasons: the culmination of many despairs no one of which will drive a human being to self-annihilation while a gleam of hope remains. Alas, they do not live to tell – even supposing that they themselves fully understood – so it is for those who are left to make their own deductions.

Aveling alone could not have destroyed Eleanor, though his cold heart, incapable of love, undoubtedly froze her eager hold on life. He was simply the last straw. The dire resolve to kill herself must surely have been taken because she believed she was no longer needed by anyone or anything.

The two strongest motive powers in Eleanor's life had been her deep love for her father, with whom Engels was closely identified, and her zeal for the cause that had been theirs. Magnificently she had carried into action their theoretical guidance and, with its loss, it may be surmised that she felt herself inadequate. Added to this, but a few weeks before Engels died she had resigned from the executive of the Gasworkers and Labourers Union, thereby severing an organic connection with masses of working people: another vital source of strength. Thus her resistance to the blows that subsequently fell upon her was weakened. She will have had more than ample time during the dejected weeks of isolation in Margate to contemplate a situation in which the mainstream of the British working-class movement – her native element – was flowing ever more swiftly, broadly and deeply into channels far removed from Marxism, to leave her in a rivulet whose current would not be strong enough to bear her forward. The sense that she was ineffectual – that deadliest of poisons – would have undermined her will to struggle. This, in its turn, could well have made her feel guilty of failing the two great men who had believed in her: if she did not justify their faith then her whole life had been futile. Futility and guilt: such feelings are among the common causes for self-destruction. Everything that is known of Eleanor – she whom her mother had described as political from top to toe at the age of seventeen – betokens that her final despairs were compounded of such factors.

Of course her voluntary death was an admission of defeat; yet by none but her own subjective standards can she be seen to have failed. She took the tirelessness, the dignity and the dedication of her father, the capacity for self-sacrifice and womanly *caritas* of her mother into the streets and to the assemblies of working people; she was modest, well-tempered and gentle but she carried a fiery message imparted in the diction of common life to reach the hearts and minds of multitudes.

Some may think that throughout Eleanor's years with Aveling she had been sublimating an unsatisfactory relationship in compulsive political activity,* but that is to misinterpret the story of a life moulded and directed from earliest youth to that end. As a mature woman she followed through with quite remarkable consistency – thus proving a fundamentally steadfast character – the work into which she had been initiated since childhood.

Nor was her life with Aveling all sadness and suffering: as late as May 1896 – while he was briefly away on his tour with Liebknecht – she forwarded his letters and enclosed a note addressed to "My dearest", ending with the words: "Goodnight, my love, Your Eleanor",[170] which are those of a woman who feels happily and securely united.

Balzac, who knew a thing or two about the human condition, wrote:

> "Work and love have the virtue of making a man more or less indifferent to external matters."†

Eleanor had reached the point when her work and her love seemed hopeless; and it broke her brave spirit. Her other troubles were then magnified out of all proportion, as in her frantic anxiety about money during those last few months, freely mentioned to one and all, for it obsessed her. Yet she, who had known nothing but the pinch of poverty for all but the last years of her life, died possessed of a sum of money eight times greater than her father had left. She might even have conquered her fatal attachment to Aveling and let the man go had she still seen a purpose in life, an effective mission to which she could cling.

If there was one thing Marx did not inculcate in his followers it was patience. Not that it was absent from his teaching: indeed, it is the lesson lying at the very heart of his major discovery that the laws of development and change in society are amenable to scientific analysis. But those who

---

* I once had the pleasure of meeting Thurber who told me that a psychoanalyst had written to say he could cure him of his drawings.

† *"L'amour et le travail ont la vertu de rendre un homme assez indifferent aux choses extérieures."*[171]

were fired with enthusiasm for his message of social revolution – based on the experiences of 1848 and 1871 – were convinced that "the day is drawing nigh":[172] were inspired with a tremendous sense of urgency, the will to act *now* and the faith that action would bear fruit *tomorrow*. Eleanor had thought to see the dawn of a new world. For her the light receded and she would not stay.

At her death Jenny Julia Eleanor Marx was 43 years of age: but 13 months older than her mother had been on the day of her birth. She should have died hereafter.

REFERENCE NOTES

Abbreviations

BIML	Institute of Marxism-Leninism, Berlin.
BLPES	British Library of Political and Economic Science.
Bottigelli Archives	Letters in the custody of Dr. Emile Bottigelli, Paris.
CMFR	*Perepiska Chlenov Semyi Marxa s Russkimi Politicheskimi Deiateliami.* Correspondence between members of the Marx family and Russian political figures. Political Literature Publishing House, Moscow 1974.
ELC	*Frederick Engels, Paul and Laura Lafargue: Correspondence.* Volumes I–III. Lawrence & Wishart, 1959–63.
IISH	International Institute of Social History, Amsterdam.
Liebknecht	*Wilhelm Liebknecht. Briefwechsel mit Karl Marx und Friedrich Engels.* Edited by Georg Eckert. Mouton & Co., The Hague, 1963.

(1) Bottigelli Archives.
(2) To Laura, 4 September 1895. *Ibid.*
(3) Laura to Eleanor, 27 August 1895. *Ibid.*
(4) Louise Freyberger, 3 September 1895. *Ibid.*
(5) Louise Freyberger, 9 September 1895. *Ibid.*
(6) Louise Freyberger, 12 September 1895. *Ibid.*
(7) Louise Freyberger, 13 September 1895. *Ibid.*
(8) Louise Freyberger, 17 September 1895. *Ibid.*
(9) To Laura, 24 October 1895. *Ibid.*
(10) Ludwig Freyberger, 4 October 1895. *Ibid.*
(11) 24 October 1895. *Ibid.*
(12) 15 October 1895. *Ibid.*
(13) Eleanor to Laura, 19 October 1895. *Ibid.*
(14) Eleanor to Laura, 24 October 1895. *Ibid.*
(15) Eleanor to Laura, 17 November 1895. IISH.
(16) Eleanor to Laura, 14 January 1896. *Ibid.*
(17) 20 October 1895. From the Introduction to *Ex. Libris Karl Marx und Friedrich Engels* by Dr. Bruno Kaiser. Dietz, Berlin 1967. Adapted in the 1969 Summer Number of *The Book Collector* ("Portrait of a Bibliophile XIV") from which the above passage is

taken, p. 193. See also Heinz Stern and Dieter Wolf. *Das grosse Erbe* (The Great Heritage) Dietz Verlag, Berlin 1972.

(18) Eleanor to Liebknecht, 25 September 1895. Liebknecht, pp. 443, 444.

(19) Somerset House.

(20) Eleanor to Laura, 24 December 1896. IISH.

(21) 8 January 1898. Bottigelli Archives.

(22) Of uncertain date in 1897. BIML.

(23) 28 August 1895. IISH.

(24) To Kautsky, 27 December 1895. IISH.

(25) Eleanor to Laura, 2 January 1897. Bottigelli Archives.

(26) Eleanor to Laura, 8 January 1898. *Ibid.*

(27) 24 October 1895. *Ibid.*

(28) Laura to Eleanor, 16 December 1896. *Ibid.*

(29) To Laura, 12 November 1896. IISH.

(30) *Justice*, 2 November 1895; *Labour Annual*, 1896, pp. 59, 60; communicated by Edith Lanchester's niece, Miss Blanche Ward, in an interview with the author in February 1967.

(31) To Laura, 7 September 1895. Bottigelli Archives.

(32) Laura to Eleanor, 16 December 1896. *Ibid.* (Incomplete letter.)

(33) 8 October 1895. *Ibid.*

(34) To Laura, 19 October 1895. *Ibid.*

(35) Eleanor to Laura, 17 November 1895. IISH.

(36) 3 July 1897. *Ibid.*

(37) To Kautsky, 19 July 1897. *Ibid.*

(38) 31 August 1897. *Ibid.*

(39) 21 September 1897. *Ibid.*

(40) 7 September 1897. *Ibid.*

(41) To Kautsky, 14 October 1897. *Ibid.*

(42) To Liebknecht, 15 April 1896. Liebknecht, p. 448.

(43) Eleanor to Laura, 17 January 1896. Bottigelli Archives.

(44) 24 December 1896. IISH.

(45) 30 September 1896. *Ibid.*

(46) Eleanor to Laura, 3 March 1896. Bottigelli Archives.

(47) Liebknecht, pp. 440, 441.

(48) Eleanor to Laura, 24 October 1895. Bottigelli Archives.

(49) *Karl Marx. Biographical Memoirs* by Wilhelm Liebknecht. Trans. Ernest Untermann. Charles H. Kerr, Chicago 1901, p. 165.

(50) 24 December 1896. IISH.

(51) 28 December 1896. *Ibid.*

(52) 27 May 1896. *Ibid.*

(53) 8 January 1898. Bottigelli Archives.

(54) 15 March 1898. IISH.

(55) William Morris Papers. BM Add. MSS. 45346.

(56) 25 December 1895. CMFR, pp. 129, 130. (Original in French.)

(57) *Ibid.* (Original in English.)

(58) 17 September 1895. IISH.

(59) To Laura, 17 November 1895. *Ibid.*

(60) 8 October 1895. Bottigelli Archives.

(61) To Laura, 19 October 1895. *Ibid.*

(62) 24 October 1895. *Ibid.*

(63) 19 October 1895. *Ibid.*

(64) Laura to Eleanor, 23 September 1895. *Ibid.*

(65) To Kautsky, 21 September 1897. IISH.

(66) To Kautsky, 28 September 1897. *Ibid.*

(67) Eleanor to Kautsky, 15 March 1898. *Ibid.*

(68) 10 December 1895. Bottigelli Archives.

(69) To Laura, 17 November 1895. IISH.

(70) 14 January 1896. *Ibid.*

(71) 29 September 1895. *Ibid.*

(72) 24 December 1896. *Ibid.*

(73) 28 September 1897. *Ibid.*

(74) 20 February 1898. *Ibid.*

(75) To Kautsky, 10 November 1896. *Ibid.*

(76) 30 November 1897. CMFR, p. 136. (Original in English (draft).)

(77) 17 December 1897. *Ibid.* pp. 136, 137. (Original in English.)

(78) 18 September 1895. IISH.

(79) 9 October 1895. Bottigelli Archives.

(80) Quoted in first edition of *Secret Diplomatic History of the Eighteenth Century.* Swan Sonnenschein, 1899.

(81) To Laura, 12 November 1896. IISH.

(82) To Laura, 24 December 1896. *Ibid.*

(83) To Laura, 2 January 1897. *Ibid.*

(84) To Kautsky, 3 June 1897. *Ibid.*

(85) To Kautsky, 19 June 1897. *Ibid.*

(86) *The Eastern Question* by Karl Marx. Edited by Eleanor Marx Aveling and Edward Aveling, D.Sc. (Lond.) Swan Sonnenschein, 1897, p. x.

(87) To Kautsky, 16 November 1896. IISH.

(88) 28 December 1896. *Ibid.*

(89) To Kautsky, 3 December 1896. *Ibid.*

(90) 24 December 1896. *Ibid.*

(91) To Kautsky, 28 September 1897. *Ibid.*

(92) To Kautsky, 27 April 1897. *Ibid.*

(93) To Kautsky, 3 June 1897. *Ibid.*

(94) To Kautsky, 19 June 1897. *Ibid.*

(95) *Justice,* 14 December 1895.

(96) To Laura, 3 March 1896. Bottigelli Archives.

(97) MEW 39, p. 361.

(98) To Van der Goes, 25 January 1896. IISH.

(99) *Justice,* 23 March 1895.

(100) Quoted by Aveling to Van der Goes. 14 March 1896. IISH.

(101) 8 February 1896. *Ibid.*

(102) To Van der Goes, 8 February 1896. *Ibid.*

(103) 3 March 1896. Bottigelli Archives.

(104) *Justice,* 23 May 1896.

(105) *Justice,* 11 July 1896.

(106) *Justice,* 1 August 1896.

(107) 18 September 1910. BLPES.

(108) 22 August 1894: ELC III, p. 339.

(109) To Bernstein, 14 August 1894. MEW 39, p. 286.

(110) 16 July 1896. Liebknecht, pp. 451, 452.

(111) 11 July 1896. *Ibid.*, p. 450.

(112) Author's collection.

(113) 11 July 1896. Liebknecht, pp. 449, 450.

(114) William Morris Papers. 5 June 1896. BM Add. MSS. 45345.

(115) 10 November 1896. IISH.

(116) *Justice.* 10 April 1897.

(117) 10 April 1897.

(118) 2 June 1897. Liebknecht, p. 453.

(119) ASE Circular. Author's collection.

(120) Eight Hours Committee Circular. *Ibid.*

(121) ASE Circular. *Ibid.*

(122) Allied Trades Conference Circular. *Ibid.*

(123) IISH.

(124) To Natalie Liebknecht, 24 December 1897. Liebknecht, p. 458.

(125) 1 January 1898. IISH.

(126) Liebknecht, pp. 459, 460.

(127) 19 June 1897. IISH.

(128) Author's collection.

(129) Liebknecht, p. 453.

(130) IISH.

(131) Liebknecht Archives. BIML.

(132) IISH.

(133) 23 September 1897. CMFR, p. 138. (Original in French.)

(134) To Kautsky and Luise Kautsky, 1 January 1898. IISH.

(135) 24 December 1897. Liebknecht, pp. 457, 458.

(136) 8 January. Bottigelli Archives.

(137) 24 December 1897. Liebknecht, p. 457.

(138) IISH.

(139) Bottigelli Archives.

(140) Eleanor to Natalie Liebknecht, 14 January 1898. Liebknecht, p. 458.

(141) 21 January 1898. IISH.

(142) Undated (probably 10 February) 1898. Liebknecht, pp. 461–3.

(143) 10 February 1898. IISH.

(144) 20 February 1898. *Ibid.*

(145) 1 March 1898. Liebknecht, pp. 463, 464.

(145a) National Library of Ireland

(146) 15 March 1898. IISH.

(147) Liebknecht, p. 465.

(148) Bottigelli Archives.

(148a) Photocopy of letters the property of Mr Peter Sinclair.

(149) 9 April 1898.

(150) *Reynolds's Newspaper.* 10 April 1898.

(151) *"Eleanor Marx: Erinnerungen von Eduard Bernstein". Die Neue Zeit. XVIJg. II Band. Nr.*
30, 1897–98 (April 1898). (Translated from the German.)

(152) *Forest Hill & Sydenham Examiner and Crystal Palace District Intelligencer.* 8 April 1898.

(153) 4 April 1898.

(154) *Further Reminiscences*, p. 146.

(155) Somerset House.

(156) *Forest Hill & Sydenham Examiner*, etc. 8 April 1898.

(157) *Daily Chronicle*, 6 April 1898.

(158) IISH.

(159) 12 April 1898. Liebknecht Archives. BIML. (Original in French.)

(160) Radford family papers.

(161) *Justice*, 16 April 1898.

(162) Thorne, *My Life's Battles*, p. 149.

(163) Andrew Rothstein. *A House on Clerkenwell Green*. Lawrence & Wishart 1966, pp. 68, 69.

(163a) Minutes of committee. Privately communicated Mr Jack Gaster, a member of that committee, has kindly confirmed that the ashes were contained in the caskets, a photograph of which is in the author's collection.

(164) Somerset House.

(165) Cmd. 5070, 1936.

(166) Marian Comyn. "My Recollections of Karl Marx". *The Nineteenth Century and After*. Vol. 91, No. 539. January 1922.

(167) *Monthly Review*. New York. January 1973, p. 45.

(168) *Forest Hill & Sydenham Examiner*, etc. 8 April 1898.

(169) 4 April 1898.

(170) 27 May 1896. IISH.

(171) *Une Double Famille. (Scènes de la Vie privée. Livre I)* Houssiaux, Paris 1870, p. 293.

(172) William Morris. *Chants for Socialists*. "All for the Cause". *Selected Writings*. Nonesuch Press 1934, p. 459.

· EPILOGUE ·

Aveling had four months more to live.

There are conflicting accounts of his conduct on the day that Eleanor died. According to Aveling family lore, he paced up and down the street until he judged the poison to have taken effect and then re-entered the house. He is said, on the one hand, to have left for London before the maid was sent to the chemist, on the other, to have been present in the room when Eleanor signed ·the poison-book. Some have it that he was distraught with grief and flung himself weeping into the arms of Mrs. Despard; others that he was unmoved to the point of total and shocking indifference.

Be that as it may, he certainly caught the Brighton line train at Sydenham station to London Bridge that morning and reached the offices of the SDF in Maiden Lane at about 11.15 not to return to Jew's Walk until 5 o'clock when he was met by a tear-stained Gertrude Gentry with the news. The only remarkable thing about this is that, in his wretched state of health, he should have spent so long a day abroad.

Despite the many expressions of sympathy published in the socialist press during his months of illness, the opinion that he was responsible for Eleanor's death – had connived at or contrived it, if not guilty of manslaughter – rapidly gained ground. Matters that had not come out at the inquest were reported to the Director of Public Prosecutions and communicated to the Deputy Coroner but the case was not reopened.

However, though he is known to have kept possession of the Jew's Walk house for at least two months, Aveling immediately resigned his auditorship of the Gasworkers' Union and from the SDF, to settle down – after, it was said, taking a short holiday in foreign parts – at 2 Stafford Mansions in Albert Bridge Road, Battersea, with Mrs. Nelson.

It could be thought that hers was not a happy married life. Of the ten months since the wedding her husband had spent by far the greater part with Eleanor. The young woman, who must have looked to a livelier future, now found she had an incurable invalid on her hands.

On 30 April the lurking suspicions, ignored by the authorities, were brought out into the open. Robert Banner* wrote a letter to the *Labour*

---

* (1855–1910) An Edinburgh bookbinder who had joined the Democratic Federation before it became the SDF, came to London, was a member of the "cabal" which split off to form the

820

Leader in the role of Eleanor's avenger. Never an intimate friend, he had known her since 1884 and he now went into the attack on the grounds that Aveling had run through the fortune bequeathed by Engels, emphasising Eleanor's own "extremely modest requirements ... known to all her friends". That was merely a preliminary shot. On the basis of "facts and letters put at my disposal", he wrote,

"I ASSERT POSITIVELY

(1) that the determined resolution to end her life by self destruction cannot have been taken earlier than the morning of the fatal day, 31st March, 1898.

(2) That on that morning Eleanor Marx received a letter of which someone who had read it says 'It throws a very discreditable light on a certain person'.

(3) That Dr. Aveling, who lived as the husband of Eleanor Marx, has stated at the inquest under oath that deceased had repeatedly threatened to commit suicide, or suggested to commit suicide together.

(4) That Eleanor Marx ordered the poison on the 31st of March while Dr. Aveling was still in the house.

(5) That Eleanor Marx received the poison whilst Dr. Aveling was still in the house.

(6) That Eleanor Marx took the poison and the poison-book into the room where Dr. Aveling was and signed the poison-book there whilst he was present.

(7) That Dr. Aveling then left the house to go to London.

(8) That facts 4, 5, 6 and 7 were not brought out at the inquest.

(9) That Eleanor Marx, as Dr. Aveling admitted at the inquest, did object to his going out that day.

(10) That Eleanor Marx, before taking the poison, herself wrote a letter to her solicitor containing the names of several persons; that Eleanor Marx put into that letter the aforesaid letter received that same morning, and wrote on the envelope the name and address of her solicitor.

(11) That both these above mentioned letters were, after the inquest, handed by the Coroner to Dr. Edward Aveling.

Socialist League in 1885 and one of the signatories to its first manifesto (see above, p. 306), though he did not thereafter play a significant public part. He became a founder member of the Fabian society and was among the first to start a branch of the ILP in Woolwich which had always been his main centre of activity.

(12) That the letter destined for her solicitor by Eleanor Marx has not been delivered to the assignee..."

A barrister, Alexander Karley Donald* had been consulted to find out whether, though no official action had been taken, Aveling could be prosecuted. Donald advised that there was not sufficient evidence to bring a criminal charge, though it would be possible to overturn Eleanor's will so that Aveling should not benefit materially by her death, but nobody was interested in that.

Banner's assertions contained some highly curious points. How, for example, could he know that Eleanor had received a letter on that morning which threw "a very discreditable light on a certain person" unless, to be sure, he had written it himself? Who else could have been privy to its contents? Only Gertrude Gentry. Was it then read aloud while she eavesdropped at the door? And did she thereupon report it to Banner? This mysterious letter was said to have been enclosed in another that she wrote to her solicitor, Crosse, which never reached its destination but was handed back to Aveling after the inquest. But who could possibly have informed Banner that Eleanor named "several persons" to the solicitor? Only the Coroner and Aveling are positively known to have read these two letters: did either of them put those letters at Banner's "disposal"? There is only one – an extremely remote – alternative: namely, that the police, who must have been called in by Dr. Shackleton, had taken possession of this and all other letters written in Eleanor's hand – including the alleged "suicide notes" – in order to produce them in court and, violating their usual discretion in such matters, had shown them to Banner before the inquest.

It should be remembered that three-quarters of an hour, at most, elapsed between the delivery of the poison and Eleanor's demise, during some part of which time the servant was out of the house returning the poison-book to the chemist, to find her mistress beyond help when she came back. Thus the letter "naming several persons" to her solicitor can have been written only in the brief interval when Eleanor was quite alone. It is inconceivable that she should have given instructions to her legal adviser running counter to Aveling's interests while he was present and that he did nothing to prevent or destroy them before leaving the house

---

* A member of the Socialist League from 1885 – also originally from Edinburgh – for some years an assiduous and effective speaker who became one of the leaders of the "parliamentary" faction of the League, joined the Bloomsbury Branch and, later, the ILP. By this time – 1898 – he had withdrawn from active politics though he remained on good terms with his former colleagues.

for seven hours, knowing full well, according to this account, that Eleanor was about to kill herself.

It is hardly surprising that Aveling did not react in any way to the charges. They simply did not hold water.

On 21 July a will was drawn up by "Edward Aveling professionally known as Alec Nelson" appointing Arthur Willson Crosse as sole executor and bequeathing to Eva Nelson

> "all my household effects books plate china glass pictures prints and all other articles and effects belonging to me at No 2 Stafford Mansions absolutely All the residue and remainder of my estate and effects whether real or personal and whether in possession or remainder I give and bequeath to my said executor Upon trust that he shall sell the same in such way as he shall think fit and at such time as he may deem desirable and stand possessed thereof Upon trust thereout to pay himself a legacy of fifty pounds free of duty and as to the residue after payment of all my debts funeral and testamentary expenses to pay the same to the said Eva Nelson for her own use and benefit absolutely..."

At precisely this date in July Bernstein's fictionalised version of Banner's letter to the *Labour Leader*, publishing for the first time nine of Eleanor's letters to Freddy Demuth, appeared under the title "What Drove Eleanor Marx to her Death".*

This article, carelessly translated and badly cut, appeared in *Justice* on 30 July, on which day Keir Hardie, also using the letters to Freddy, wrote an article in the *Labour Leader* on much the same lines.†

All three articles went much further than Banner while taking his version of events as if proven beyond all doubt.

Bernstein – who was mainly responsible, the others merely following his lead – stated not only that a mysterious letter to Eleanor had arrived on the morning of 31 March but that "as soon as it was received by Dr. Aveling he destroyed it", adding:

> "Anyone who would so immediately destroy a document that leads to the suicide of a person closely connected must be suspected of having grounds for fearing its disclosure. It must have dealt with ... an action which left only one course open to Eleanor, since she could not face Aveling's public exposure: escape from life..."

For German readers that may have been good enough: the hypothetical letter has now become an established fact and the direct cause of Eleanor's suicide, and it is *immediately* destroyed by Aveling, not handed back to him by the Coroner after the inquest.

---

* "*Was Eleanor Marx in den Tod trieb*". Neue Zeit. XVI Jg. II Band. Nr. 42, 1897–8.
† See fn. *, p. 792.

"Dr. Aveling by his own confession," said Bernstein, also destroyed the letter to the solicitor, thus withholding "the last expression of her wishes". At no time did Aveling make any such confession but Bernstein professed to be fully informed that Eleanor had instructed her solicitor to alter her will and claimed "strong grounds for believing" that Freddy Demuth occupied "a prominent place" in these revised dispositions. It did not occur to him that, in the particular circumstances, any such last-minute "expression of her wishes" would have been unwitnessed and legally invalid, nor that it would have been more convincing had he explained how he knew the contents of a letter so swiftly destroyed. It may also be remarked that from all that is known of Frederick Demuth's exceedingly modest character, he was the last person in the world to expect, or suggest to Bernstein, that he was intended to inherit any of Eleanor's money.

Bernstein further over-reached himself by stating, without any substantiation, that Aveling "gave no single glance at the corpse". How on earth could he know? Even had Gertrude Gentry and the police been his bosom friends, they are unlikely to have given him this piece of information and yet suppress it when examined by the Coroner. Equally without foundation was the statement that Aveling had destroyed the last letter "his lifelong comrade" had left for him. There is nothing to corroborate the existence of that letter but press reports, according to which, however, it was read out at the inquest and at least one paper published it. If Aveling subsequently destroyed it he must have taken Bernstein into his confidence and told him so. Nevertheless, by a more vigorous use of imagination than a respect for facts or the elementary rules of evidence, Bernstein built up a chilling picture of this monster, beside which such minor misstatements as that his first wife had been dead for three – instead of seven – years are of little significance.

The *Labour Leader* had its own brand of fabrications. According to Hardie, Aveling, who had been "early expelled from the I.L.P.", was one of those rare beings who had read *Capital* so diligently that he was "thus thrown a good deal into the society of the Marx family". The result was that, following Marx's death, when at "about the same time Eleanor lost her mother and one of her sisters", she, being "lonely and young" fell an easy prey to Aveling, that "consummate actor", upon the death of whose wife he had come into an annuity of £150. This *canard* was also served up by Bernstein and *Justice*.

Freddy Demuth was introduced as having been "brought up together" with Eleanor. Their relations were much those of brother and sister "and as children they knew each other by their pet names 'Tussy' and 'Freddy'." He had been her "lifelong companion" and, it was added for good measure, he was a "working labourer, and married." That he was a skilled engineer – a toolmaker – long ago deserted by his wife was not more worth ascertaining than that his very existence was unknown to Eleanor until she was grown up.

Inaccuracy is admittedly the occupational hazard of journalism, but it ill became a Bernstein and a Keir Hardie to concoct such farragos when the heartbreaking letters to Freddy Demuth – in their hands – were sufficiently damning and told all that and more than was needed to throw "a very discreditable light on a certain person" without this melodrama about a death-dealing revelation, a purloined will and a sinister reluctance to gaze upon the corpse.

Only *The Critic*, commenting on the same date – 30 July – on the allegations in *Neue Zeit* adopted a more judicious attitude:

"...a case wherein a woman has lived for 14 years with a man and commits suicide with poison bought to his knowledge, after a series of sordid domestic developments, leaving a number of letters which throw a disagreeable light upon that man and one epistle he is alleged to have destroyed for his own purposes, seems ... a fit subject for police investigation. Either Dr. Aveling is being grievously wronged, or he is a thorough-paced scoundrel. If the authorities do not take the matter up, the accused scientist owes it to himself to personally insist on searching enquiry..."

Whatever Aveling may have owed to himself, all these articles appeared three days before he died on Wednesday, 2 August 1898. W. Long, a neighbour living in the same block of flats, was present at the death caused, the certificate stated, by four years' malignant kidney disease, a last month of "lardaceous disease"* of the kidney and the after-effects of the operation in February. His age was given as 47: he was in fact approaching his 49th birthday but at least he had aged two years during his marriage of 14 months. His effects were valued at £852 7s. 3d. He had thus spent over £1,000 of Eleanor's legacy in less than 16 weeks. Perhaps he had paid off some of his debts, or they had been claimed from his estate before probate.

He was cremated on 5 August. Some half-dozen people were said to have attended the coffin at Waterloo and Woking. No member of the dead man's own family nor a single representative of the socialist movement was present.

But locally Edward Bibbins Aveling was not so soon forgotten. At the General Election of 1906 his brother, the Rev. Frederick Wilkins Aveling, stood for Lewisham in the Liberal interest to be assailed, despite his cloth and exemplary marriage, with cries of "Atheist!" and "Wife-murderer!"

---

* Fatty degeneration.

· APPENDICES ·

APPENDIX I

MARX AND SEDLEY TAYLOR

A

COMMUNICATION FROM ELEANOR MARX PUBLISHED IN "TODAY", FEBRUARY 1884

There is so much to record concerning this Socialist movement in England that I rather hesitate to take up these columns for speaking of a personal matter. As, however, I have no other means of refuting a very serious charge brought against my father, I hope the readers of TO-DAY will forgive my touching on the matter here. On the 29th of last November a letter from Mr. Sedley Taylor appeared in the *Times*, which repeated the old calumny that my father had knowingly misquoted a passage from one of Mr. Gladstone's speeches to suit his own purpose.

There has never been a better calumniated man than my father, but his calumniators were, as a rule, too contemptible to be worth answering. In this particular case my father did answer his anonymous accuser, because the alleged misquotation appeared in the inaugural address of the International Workingmen's Association.

On reading Mr. Taylor's letter, which is only a *rechauffé* of the old story, I at once wrote to the *Times*. So often had I read in English papers of the "fairness" of the English press that I never doubted my answer would be given the same publicity as that accorded to Mr. Taylor's accusation. Days passed, and my letter did not appear. Still impressed with the idea that even the *Times* might be honest in a personal matter, I again wrote to the editor. With no result. Then I addressed myself to the *Daily News*, which I had so far found very fair. But apparently a dead lion may be kicked with impunity by living professors, and the

Liberal *Daily News* could not stretch its liberality to the length of publishing my letter. I therefore publish both Mr. Taylor's letter and my own reply:–

TO THE EDITOR OF THE "TIMES."

Sir,–I ask leave to point out in the *Times* that the origin of the misleading quotation from Mr. Gladstone's Budget speech of April 16, 1863, which so eminent a publicist as Professor Emile de Laveleye has been led to reproduce through reliance on German sources, and with respect to which he inserts a correction in the *Times* of this day, is to be found as far back as 1864 in an address issued by the council of the famous International Working Men's Association.

What appears extremely singular is that it was reserved for Professor Brentano (then of the University of Breslau, now of that of Strasbourg) to expose, eight years later in a German newspaper, the bad faith which had manifestly dictated the citation made from Mr. Gladstone's speech in the address. Herr Karl Marx, who as the acknowledged author of the address attempted to defend the citation, had the hardihood, in the deadly shifts to which Brentano's masterly conduct of the attack speedily reduced him, to assert that Mr. Gladstone had 'manipulated' (*zurechtgestumpert*) the report of his speech in the *Times* of April 17, 1863, before it appeared in 'Hansard,' in order 'to obliterate' (*wegzupfuschen*) a passage which 'was certainly compromising for an English Chancellor of the Exchequer.' On Brentano's showing, by a detailed comparison of texts, that the reports of the *Times* and of 'Hansard' agreed in utterly excluding the meaning which craftily-isolated quotation had put upon Mr. Gladstone's words, Marx withdrew from further controversy under the plea of 'want of time!'

The whole of the Brentano-Marx correspondence is eminently worthy of being unearthed from the files of newspapers under which it lies buried, and republished in an English form, as it throws upon the latter disputant's standard of literary honesty a light which can be ill spared at a time when his principal work is presented to us as nothing less than a fresh gospel of social renovation.

I am, Sir, your obedient servant,
Trinity College, Cambridge, November 26th. SEDLEY TAYLOR

TO THE EDITOR OF THE "TIMES."

Sir,–In the *Times* of November 29th Mr. Sedley Taylor refers to a certain quotation of a speech by Mr. Gladstone, 'to be found as far back as 1864, in an address issued by the council of the famous International Working Men's Association.' He continues: (I here quote Mr. Taylor's letter from "What appears" to "want of time").

The facts are briefly these. The quotation referred to consists of a few sentences from Mr. Gladstone's Budget speech of April 16th, 1863. After describing the immense increase of wealth that took place in this country between 1853 and 1861 Mr. Gladstone is made to say: 'This intoxicating augmentation of wealth and power is entirely confined to classes of property.' An anonymous writer, who turns out to be Professor Brentano, published in a German paper, *Concordia*, of the 7th March, 1872 a reply in which it was stated: 'This sentence does not exist in Mr. Gladstone's speech. Marx has added it lyingly, both as to form and contents' (*formel und materiel hinzugelogen*).

This was the only point at issue between my father and his anonymous opponent.

In his replies in the Leipzig *Volkstaat*, June 1st and August 7th, 1872, Dr. Marx quotes the reports of Mr. Gladstone's speech as follows: 'The *Times*, April 17th–The augmentation I have described, and which is founded, I think, on accurate returns, is an augmentation entirely confined to classes of property. *Morning Star*, 17th April–This augmentation is an augmentation confined entirely to the classes possessed of property, *Morning Advertiser*, April 17th–The augmentation stated is altogether limited to classes possessed of property.'

The anonymous Brentano, in the 'deadly shifts to which his own masterly conduct of the attack had reduced him,' now took refuge under the assertion usual in such circumstances, that if the quotation was not a forgery it was, at all events, 'misleading,' in 'bad faith,' 'craftily isolated,' and so forth. I am afraid you would not allow me space to reply to this accusation of Herr Brentano, repeated now, after eleven years, by Mr. Taylor. Perhaps it will not be required as Mr. Taylor says; 'The whole of this Brentano-Marx correspondence is eminently worthy of being unearthed from the file of newspapers in which it lies buried and republished in an English form.' I quite agree with this. The memory of my father could only gain by it. As to the discrepancies between the newspaper reports of the speech in question and the report in 'Hansard' I must leave this to be settled by those most interested in it.

Out of thousands and thousands of quotations to be found in my father's writings this is the only one the correctness of which has ever been disputed. The fact that this single and not very lucky instance is brought up again and again by the professorial economists is very characteristic. In the words of Mr. Taylor, 'it throws upon the latter disputant's [Dr. Marx] standard of literary honesty a light which can ill be spared at a time when his principal work is presented to us as nothing less than a fresh gospel of social renovation.'

I am, Sir, yours faithfully,

London, November 30, 1883. ELEANOR MARX

Having spoken of the bourgeois press which, after giving publicity to a libel on a dead man refuses to insert the reply, I must also refer to a paper that pretends to represent the working class. In the *Labour Standard* of Dec. 8th appeared an article, a *leader* (I emphasize the word leader, because some of Mr. Shipton's friends have tried to make Continental workmen believe the article in question was a mere "unofficial" contribution from an outsider), positively begging Sir William Harcourt to hang O'Donnell. Said the trades-union oracle; "We most earnestly hope the Home Secretary will listen to none of those appeals for mercy which are certain now to flow in; that, upon the contrary, he will insist upon justice"! To appeal to our virtuous Home Secretary *not* to show mercy is worthy of Mr. W. S. Gilbert at his wildest.

B

LETTER FROM DR. SEDLEY TAYLOR, IN "TODAY", MARCH 1884

No one can regret more than I do that Miss Marx should have been refused the public hearing to which she was so manifestly entitled. I am, however, far from thinking with her that the question whether a particular sentence did, or did not, occur in Mr. Gladstone's speech

"was the only point at issue between" Dr. Marx and Professor Brentano. I regard that question as having been of very subordinate
importance compared to the issue whether the quotation in dispute was
made with the intention of conveying, or of perverting, Mr. Gladstone's meaning.

It would obviously be impossible to discuss in this letter the contents of the voluminous Brentano-Marx controversy without making
an inadmissible demand on your space. As, however, Miss Marx has in
your columns characterised as a "calumny" and "libel" an opinion
publicly expressed by me, I feel bound to ask your insertion, side by
side, of the two following extracts, which will enable your readers to
judge for themselves whether Dr. Marx has quoted fairly or unfairly
from the Budget Speech of 1863 in his great work, "Das Kapital." My
reason for using the "Times" report in preference to that of Hansard
will be obvious to readers of Dr. Marx' letters in his correspondence
with Brentano.

"Times," April 17, 1863.
"In ten years, from 1842 to 1852
inclusive, the taxable income of
the country, as nearly as we can
make out, increased by 6 per
cent.; but in eight years, from
1853 to 1861, the income of the
country again increased from the
basis taken by 20 per cent. That is
a fact so strange as to be almost
incredible. . . . *I must say for one, I
should look almost with apprehension
and with pain upon this intoxicating
augmentation of wealth and power if
it were my belief that it was confined
to the classes who are in easy circumstances. This takes no cognisance
at all of the condition of the labouring
population.* The augmentation I
have described, and which is
continued overleaf

"Das Kapital," 2nd edition,
1872, page 678, note 103.
"From 1842 to 1852 the taxable
income of the country
increased by 6 per cent . . . In the
eight years from 1853 to 1861, it
had increased from the basis taken
in 1853, 20 per cent! The fact is
so astonishing as to be almost
incredible . . . . . . this intoxicating
augmentation of wealth and
power. . . .

. . . entirely confined to classes of
property . . . . . . must be of indirect benefit to the labouring
population because it cheapens
the commodities of general consumption—
while the rich have been growing
richer the poor have been growing
continued overleaf

founded, I think, upon accurate returns, is an augmentation entirely confined to classes possessed of property. Now, the augmentation of capital is of indirect benefit to the labourer, because it cheapens the commodity which in the business of production comes into direct competition with labour. But we have this profound, and I must say, inestimable consolation, that, while the rich have been growing richer, the poor have been growing less poor. Whether the extremes of poverty are less extreme than they were I do not presume to say, *but the average condition of the British labourer, we have the happiness to know, has improved during the last 20 years in a degree which we know to be extraordinary, and which we may almost pronounce to be unexampled in the history of any country and of any age.*"

less poor! At any rate, whether the extremes of poverty are less I do not presume to say."

MR, GLADSTONE, *in House of Commons, 16th April,* 1863.

I invite especial attention to the hearing on Mr. Gladstone's meaning of the passages in the "Times'" report which I have thrown into italics. The sentence, *"I must say ... easy circumstances,"* conveys the speaker's belief that the intoxicating augmentation of wealth and power previously described was *not* confined to those in easy circumstances. There is, it is true, a verbal contrariety with the later sentence, "The augmentation ... property," but the intervening words; *"This takes no cognisance ... population,"* unmistakably show what Mr. Gladstone meant, viz., that the figures which he had been given, being based on the income-tax returns, included only incomes above the exemption limit,* and therefore afforded no indication to what extent the total earnings of the labouring population had increased during the period under consideration. The closing passage, from *"but the average"* to the end, announces in the most emphatic language that, on evidence independent of that obtained from the income-tax returns, Mr. Gladstone recognised as indubitable an extraordinary and almost unexampled improvement in the average condition of the British labourer.

Now, with what object were these essential passages almost wholly struck out in the process by which the newspaper report was reduced to the remarkable form in which it appears in Dr. Marx' work? Clearly, I think, in order that the arbitrarily-constructed mosaic, pieced together out of such of Mr. Gladstone's words as were allowed to remain, might be understood as asserting that the earnings of the labouring population had made but insignificant progress, while the incomes of the possessing classes had increased enormously–a view which the omitted passages explicitly repudiate in favour of a very different opinion.

I must not pass over unnoticed the fact that the German translation of this docked citation in the text of "Das Kapital" is immediately followed there by the expression of Dr. Marx' contemptuous astonishment at the "lame anti-climax" presented by the sentence made to figure as the conclusion of Mr. Gladstone's paragraph, when compared with his previous description of the growth of wealth among the possessing classes.–I am, Gentlemen, yours truly,

Trinity College, Cambridge. SEDLEY TAYLOR
February 8th, 1884.

C

REPLY BY ELEANOR MARX TO DR. SEDLEY TAYLOR, IN "TODAY", MARCH 1884

Mr. Sedley Taylor disputes my statement, that, when the anonymous slanderer fell foul of Dr. Marx, the only point at issue was whether Mr. Gladstone had used certain words or not. According to him, the real

---

* This stood at £150 from 1842 to 1853, and was then lowered to £100.

question was, "whether the quotation in dispute was made with the intention of conveying or of perverting Mr. Gladstone's meaning."

I have before me the *Concordia* article (No. 10, 7th March, 1872,) "How Karl Marx quotes." Here the anonymous author first quotes the "Inaugural Address" of the International; then the passage of Mr. Gladstone's speech, in full, from Hansard; then he condenses the passage in his own way, and to his own satisfaction; and lastly, he concludes, "Marx takes advantage of this to make Gladstone say, 'This intoxicating augmentation of wealth and power is entirely confined to classes possessed of property.' *This sentence, however, is nowhere to be found in Gladstone's speech. The very contrary is said in it. Marx has lyingly added this sentence, both as to form and contents.*"

That is the charge, and the only charge, made against Dr. Marx. He is indeed accused of perverting Mr. Gladstone's meaning by "lyingly adding" a whole sentence. Not a word about "misleading," or "craftily isolated" quotations. The question simply is, whether a particular sentence did, or did not, occur in Mr. Gladstone's speech.

Of two things, one. Either Mr. Taylor has read Brentano's attacks and my father's replies, and then his assertion is in direct contradiction of what he cannot help knowing to be the truth. Or else he has not. And then? Here is a man who dates his letters from Trinity College, Cambridge, who goes out of his way to assail my dead father's literary honesty in a way which must needs turn out to be a "calumny" unless he proves his case; who makes this charge upon the strength of a literary controversy dating as far back as 1872, between an anonymous writer (whom Mr. Taylor now asserts to be Professor Brentano) and my father; who describes in glowing terms the "masterly conduct" in which Saint George Brentano led his attack, and the "deadly shifts" to which he speedily reduced the dragon Marx; who can give us all particulars of the crushing results obtained by the said St. George "by a detailed comparison of texts;" and who after all, puts me into this delicate position that I am in charity bound to assume that he has never read a line of what he is speaking about.

Had Mr. Taylor seen the "masterly" articles of his anonymous friend, he would have found therein the following: "Now we ask; does anyone tell a lie only then when he himself invents an untruth, or does he not tell a lie quite as much when he repeats it contrary to what he knows, *or is bound to know better?*" Thus saith the "masterly" Brentano, as virtuous as he is anonymous, in his rejoinder to my father's first reply (Concordia, No. 27, 4th July, 1872, p. 210). And on the same page he still maintains against all comers: "According to the *Times* report, too, Mr. Gladstone said he believed this intoxicating augmentation of wealth and power *not* to be confined to classes of property."

If Brentano thus appears utterly ignorant of what was the real point at issue, is Mr. Sedley Taylor better off? In his letter to the *Times* it was a quotation made in the "Inaugural Address" of the International. In his letter to TO-DAY it is a quotation in "Das Kapital". The ground is shifted again, but I need not object. Mr. Taylor now gives us the Gladstonian passage as quoted on pages 678 and 679 of "Das Kapital," side by side with the same passage as reported–not by Hansard, but by the *Times*. "My reason for using the *Times* report instead of that of Hansard, will be obvious to readers of Dr. Marx' letters and his correspondence with Brentano." Mr. Taylor, as we have seen, is not of these "readers." His reason for his proceeding may therefore be obvious to others, but upon his own showing at least, it can hardly be so to himself.

Anyhow, from Hansard the Infallible we are brought down to that very report, for using which the anonymous Brentano (Concordia, same page, 210), assails my father as quoting "necessarily bungling (*stümperhafte*) newspaper reports." At any rate, Mr. Taylor's "reason" must be very "obvious" to his friend Brentano.

To me that reason is obvious indeed. The words which my father was accused of having lyingly added ("an augmentation," etc.,) these words are contained in the *Times* as well as in the other dailies' reports, while in Hansard they are not only "manipulated," but entirely "obliterated." Marx established this fact. Mr. Taylor, in his letter to the *Times*, still awfully shocked at such unpardonable "hardihood," is now himself compelled to drop the impeachable Hansard, and to take refuge under what Brentano calls the "necessarily bungling" report of the *Times*.

Now for the quotation itself. Mr. Taylor invites especial attention to two passages thrown by him into italics. In the first he owns: "*there is, it is true, a verbal contrariety* with the latter sentence; the augmentation ... property; but the intervening words: this takes ... population, unmistakably show what Mr. Gladstone meant," etc., etc. Here we are plainly on theological ground. It is the well-known style of orthodox interpretation of the Bible. The passage, it is true, is in itself contradictory, but if interpreted according to the true faith of a believer, you will find that it will bear out a meaning not in contradiction with that true faith. If Mr. Taylor interprets Mr. Gladstone as Mr. Gladstone interprets the Bible, he must not expect any but the orthodox to follow him.

Now Mr. Gladstone on that particular occasion, either did speak English or he did not. If he did not, no manner of quotation or interpretation will avail. If he did, he said that he should be very sorry if that intoxicating augmentation of wealth and power was confined to classes in easy circumstances, but that it was confined entirely to classes of property. And that is what Marx quoted. The second passage is one of those stock phrases which are repeated, with slight variations, in every British budget speech, seasons of bad trade alone excepted. What Marx thought of it, and of the whole speech is shown in the following extract from his second reply to his anonymous slanderer; "Gladstone, having poured forth his panegyric on the increase of capitalist wealth, turns towards the working class. He takes good care not to say that they had shared in the intoxicating augmentation of wealth and power. On the contrary, he continues (according to the *Times*): "Now, the augmentation of capital is of indirect benefit to the labourers," etc. He *consoles* himself with the fact that while the rich have been growing richer, the poor have been growing less poor. He asserts, finally, he and his enriched parliamentary friends "have the happiness to know" the contrary of what official enquiries and statistical data prove to be the fact, viz., "that the average condition of the British labourer has improved during the last 20 years in a degree which we know to be extraordinary, and which we may almost pronounce to be unexampled in the history of any country and of any age." *Before* Mr. Gladstone, all his predecessors "had the happiness" to complete in their budget speeches the picture of the augmentation of capitalist wealth by self-complacent phrases about the improvement in the condition of the working class. Yet he gives the lie to them all; for the millennium dates only from the passing of the Free Trade legislation. But the correctness or incorrectness of Gladstone's reasons for consolation and congratulation is a matter of indifference here. What alone concerns us is this, that from his stand-point the pretended "extraordinary" improvement in the condition of the working-class is not at all in contradiction with the augmentation of wealth and power which is entirely confined to classes possessed of property. "It is the orthodox doctrine of the mouth-pieces of capital–one of the best paid of whom is Gladstone–that the most infallible means for working men to benefit themselves is–to enrich their exploiters." (Volkstaat, No. 63, Aug. 7, 1872).

Moreover, to please Mr. Taylor, the said passage of Mr. Gladstone's speech *is quoted in full* in the Inaugural Address, page 5, immediately before the quotation in dispute. And what else but this address did Mr. Taylor originally impute? Is it as impossible to get a reference to original sources out of him, as it was to get reasons out of Dogberry?

"The continuous crying contradictions in Gladstone's budget speeches" form the subject of Note 105 on the same page (679) of "Das Kapital" to which Mr. Taylor refers us. Very likely indeed, that Marx should have taken the trouble to suppress "in bad faith" one of the contradictions! Quite the contrary. He has not suppressed anything worth quoting, neither has he "lyingly" added anything. But he has restored, rescued from oblivion, a particular sentence of one of Mr. Gladstone's speeches, a sentence which had indubitably been pronounced, but which some how or other had found its way–out of Hansard.

ELEANOR MARX

APPENDIX 2

AN ABRIDGED REPORT OF ELEANOR MARX'S SPEECH ON THE FIRST MAY DAY. HYDE PARK, 4 MAY 1890

We have not come to do the work of political parties, but we have come here in the cause of labour, in its own defence, to demand its own rights. I can remember when we came in handfuls of a few dozen to Hyde Park to demand an Eight Hours' Bill, but the dozens have grown to hundreds, and the hundreds to thousands, until we have this magnificent demonstration that fills the park today. We are standing face to face with another demonstration, but I am glad to see that the great masses of the people are on our side. Those of us who have gone through all the worry of the Dock Strike, and especially the Gasworkers' Strike, and have seen the men, women and children stand round us, have had enough of strikes, and we are determined to secure an eight hours' day by legal enactment; unless we do so, it will be taken from us at the first opportunity. We will only have ourselves to blame if we do not achieve the victory which this great day could so easily give us. There is in the park this afternoon a man whom Mr. Gladstone once imprisoned–Michael Davitt; but Mr. Gladstone is now on the best of terms with him. What do you suppose is the reason for the change? Why has the Liberal Party been so suddenly converted to Home Rule? Simply because the Irish people sent 80 members to the House of Commons to support the Conservatives; in the same way we must kick these Liberal and Radical members out if they refuse to support our programme. I am speaking this afternoon not only as a Trade Unionist, but as a Socialist. Socialists believe that the eight hours' day is the first and most immediate step to be taken, and we aim at a time when there will no longer be one class supporting two others, but the unemployed both at the top and at the bottom of society will be got rid of. This is not the end but only the beginning of the struggle; it is not enough to come here to demonstrate in favour of an eight hours' day. We must not be like some Christians who sin for six days and go to church on the seventh, but we must speak for the cause daily, and make the men, and especially the women that we meet, come into the ranks to help us.

"Rise like Lions after slumber
In unvanquishable number,
Shake your chains to earth like dew
Which in sleep had fallen on you –
Ye are many – they are few."

APPENDIX 3

CREMATION

Incineration usually took some 90 minutes after which the colourless ash, weighing between three and four lbs., was gathered up by a crematorium official and placed in a simple reliquary with a screw lid "modelled after an ancient Roman cinerary urn ... provided for the purpose without charge"* – designed and made by Messrs. Doulton,

---

* Sir Henry Thompson in *Modern Cremation*. 4th edition. Smith Elder 1901.

who also produced a variety of more elaborate urns and caskets which could be bought–and then put at the disposal of relatives and friends.

Although no Act of Parliament reached the Statute Book until 1900, nor came into force until 1903, cremation was not illegal. The Cremation Society of England, founded in 1874, had been restricted for a whole decade to propagating its aims in the face of public prejudice and the powerful disapproval of Church and State which regarded any literal interpretation of "ashes to ashes" as in pretty poor taste. Then, in February 1884, a Dr. William Price stood trial in Wales for incinerating the body of his dead child. The judge, Mr. Justice Stephen, ruled that the act was not illegal. As one writer later put it:

> "So completely did burial take the place of burning that the latter expedient has never been formally forbidden, or, until 1884, even referred to in English law ... "*

In the same year a Bill to authorise cremation by Act of Parliament was defeated on the second reading. Nevertheless, the Cremation Society was now legally able to inaugurate the Woking crematorium, built six years earlier on an acre of land bought from the London Necropolis Co., to which another half-acre was added in 1888 for a chapel and ante-rooms. In its first year of operation – 1885 – three bodies were cremated there. The procedure was hedged about with safeguards, the Society being as much concerned to reform the laxity of medical certification and the registration of deaths as to introduce a healthy alternative to earth burial as a source of pestilence in urban areas: an argument advanced as early as 1843 by Edwin Chadwick. Without benefit of legislation, the number of those who wished to be cremated rose steadily and within a decade, in the year of Engels' death, 150 bodies were incinerated at Woking. By 1900 – that is, in a period of 15 years – there had been a total of 1,824 cremations at Woking.

APPENDIX 4

ELEANOR MARX ON HER FATHER

(Written by Eleanor in German for the *Neue Zeit*, Vol. I, 1897–8, on the publication of the young Marx's letter to his father.)

---

* Mrs. Basil Holmes *The London Burial Grounds*. T. Fisher Unwin 1896, p. 263.

Karl was a young man of seventeen when he became engaged to Jenny. For them, too, the path of true love was not a smooth one. It is easy to understand that Karl's parents opposed the "engagement" of a young man of his age ... The earnestness with which Karl assures his father of his love in spite of certain contradictions is explained by the rather stormy scenes his engagement had caused in the home. My father used to say that at that time he had been a really ferocious Roland. But the question was soon settled and shortly before or after his eighteenth birthday the betrothal was formally recognised. Seven years Karl waited for his beautiful Jenny, but "they seemed but so many days to him, because he loved her so much".

On 19 June 1843 they were wedded. Having played together as children and become engaged as a young man and girl, the couple went hand in hand through the battle of life.

And what a battle! Years of bitter pressing need and, still worse, years of brutal suspicion, infamous calumny and icy indifference. But through all that, in unhappiness and happiness, the two lifelong friends and lovers never faltered, never doubted: they were faithful unto death. And death has not separated them.

His whole life long Marx not only loved his wife, he was in love with her. Before me is a love letter the passionate, youthful ardour of which would suggest it was written by an eighteen-year-old. Marx wrote it in 1856, after Jenny had borne him six children. Called to Trier by the death of his mother in 1863, he wrote from there saying he had made "daily pilgrimages to the old house of the Westphalens (in Römerstrasse) that interests me more than the whole of Roman antiquity because it reminds me of my happy youth and once held my dearest treasure. Besides, I am asked daily on all sides about the former 'most beautiful girl in Trier' and 'Queen of the ball'. It is damned pleasing for a man to find his wife lives on in the imagination of a whole city as a delightful princess ... "

Marx was deeply attached to his father. He never tired of talking about him and always carried an old daguerrotype photograph of him. But he would never show it to strangers because, he said, it was so unlike the original. I thought the face very handsome, the eyes and brow were like those of his son but the features were softer about the mouth and chin. The type was in general definitely Jewish, but beautifully so. When, after the death of his wife, Marx undertook a long, sad journey to recover his health – for he wanted to complete his work – he always had with him the photograph of his father, an old photograph of my mother on glass (in a case) and one of my sister Jenny. We found them after his death in his breast pocket. Engels laid them in his coffin.

· INDEX ·

843